Chapter 11

http://www.law.cornell.edu/uniform/vol7.html#comin
http://www.cnyc.com/index.html
http://www.libofmich.lib.mi.us/law/publicacts/
   condominium.html
http://orlink.oldrepnatl.com/

Chapter 12

http://www.Realtor.com/
http://www.hud.gov/fha/res/sc2secta.html
http://mktg.sba.uconn.edu/fin/realest/other/other.
   htm#FederalGovernmentLinks
http://www.highprobsell.com

Chapter 13

http://www.willhall.com/geninfopg4.html#tyitletakingtitle
http://www.murdoch.edu.au/elaw/indices/subject/4.
   html
http://trevilians.com/deedinde.htm
http://tdi.state.tx.us/consumer/cbo58.html

Chapter 14

http://www.hud.gov/
http://www.hud.gov:80/fha/sfh/ils/ilsstat.html
http://www.freddiemac.com/community/homebuy.htm
http://www.willhall.com/geninfopg13.html#
   conditionsofrealpropertytransferdiscstat

Chapter 15

http://www.law.cornell.edu/topics/mortgages.html
http://www.hud.gov/
http://www.homeowners.com/
http://www.va.gov/vas/loan/

Chapter 16

http://www.hud.gov/fha/sfh/res/respa_hm.html
http://www.hud.gov/fha/sfh/res/resappa.html
http://www.valleybrokers.com/ag0/escrow.shtml

Chapter 17

http://www.law.cornell.edu/uniform/probate.html
http://www.law.cornell.edu/uniform/vol9.html#teril

http://www.itslegal.com/infonet/wills/Estate1.htm
http://www.uslivingwillregistry.com/
http://www.mindspring.com/~scottr/will.html
http://www.ca-probate.com
http://www.law.cornell.edu/topics/estate_gift_tax.html
Canada: http://www.sentex.net/~lwr/
U.K.: http://www.euthanasia.org/lwpdf.html

Chapter 18

http://www.capitol.state.tx.us/statutes/statutes.html
http://www.grandoffice.com/location/property.asp
http://www.cityofalhambra.org

Chapter 19

http://www.co.rockingham.va.us/variance.htm
http://www.revisor.leg.state.mn.us/slaws/1997/c082.html
http://leg.state.mt.us/Services/Lepo/subcommittees/
   edsub.htm
http://www.geocities.com/CapitolHill/Congress/6444

Chapter 20

http://www.lib.lsu.edu/gov/fedgov.html
http://eelink.umich.edu/why.html
http://www.bergen.org/AAST/Projects/ES/WL/
http://endangered.fws.gov/esa.html
http://www.fs.fed.us

Chapter 21

http://www.irs.ustreas.gov/prod/search/index.html
http://www.taxweb.com/index.html
http://www.cnyc.com/index.html

Chapter 22

http://www.greatlakesreit.com/
http://edgar.stern.nyu.edu/EDGAR/SC13d.html
http://www.irs.ustreas.gov/
http://www.gao.gov/AIndexFY98/abstracts/he98028.htm
http://www.co.rockingham.va.us/subagland.htm
http://www.bbrc.com/lib00033.htm
http://www.1st-ap-mortgage.com/webconst.htm

Real Estate Law

SIXTH EDITION

Marianne M. Jennings

Professor of Legal and Ethical Studies
Member of the Arizona State Bar

WEST
™
THOMSON LEARNING

Australia · Canada · Mexico · Singapore · Spain · United Kingdom · United States

Real Estate Law, 6e by Marianne M. Jennings

Senior Acquisitions Editor: Rob Dewey
Senior Developmental Editor: Susanna C. Smart
Marketing Manager: Nicole C. Moore
Production Editor: Elizabeth A. Shipp
Media Developmental Editor: Peggy Buskey
Media Production Editor: John Barans
Manufacturing Coordinator: Sandee Milewski
Internal Design: Ramsdell Design/Craig Ramsdell, Cincinnati
Cover Design: Michael H. Stratton
Cover Images: ©PhotoDisc, Inc.
Production House: The Left Coast Group
Printer: West Group

Printed in the United States of America
1 2 3 4 5 04 03 02 01

For more information contact West Legal Studies in Business, South-Western College Publishing, 5101 Madison Road, Cincinnati, Ohio, 45227 or find us on the Internet at http://www.westbuslaw.com.

For permission to use material from this text or product, contact us by
• **telephone:** 1-800-730-2214
• **fax:** 1-800-730-2215
• **web:** **http://www.thomsonrights.com**

Library of Congress Cataloging-in-Publication Data

Jennings, Marianne.
    Real estate law / Marianne M. Jennings.—6th ed.
        p. cm.
    Includes indexes.
    ISBN 0-324-06198-6
    1. Vendors and purchasers—United States. 2. Real estate business—Law and legislation—United States. 3. Real estate development—Law and legislation—United States. 4. Real property—United States. I. Title.
    KF665 .J4 2001
    346.7304'3—dc21   2001023750

Brief Contents

Contents

Part 2: Real Estate Ownership and Interests 124

Part 3: Transferring Title to Real Estate 254

12: THE BROKER'S ROLE IN THE TRANSFER OF REAL ESTATE 254

Part 4: Real Estate Development 464

Preface

Real estate law was once regarded by attorneys and scholars as a lay term for the law of real property. However, with the phenomenal growth of the real estate market in the past twenty years, the term *real estate law* more accurately reflects—and is more often used to describe—the legal issues in the ownership, transfer, and development of land or real property. Those involved in the real estate market require a better grasp of the legal issues involved in their day-to-day transactions. Since the fifth edition, dramatic changes in the economy, resulting changes in land values, and the impact on mortgage holders have made knowledge of the law even more critical. The Internet has heightened the need for hands-on knowledge in fast-moving transactions.

Legal issues no longer revolve around how the law of real property developed in England, but on how real estate law can help to streamline transactions. Real estate professionals need a clear set of rules that will enable them to recognize, solve, and prevent legal problems. These rules and the ability to analyze them should be taught in a three-step approach:

1. What law is applicable to this area of real estate and this particular transaction?
2. What issues exist in the circumstances?
3. Can a legal problem be prevented or solved?

In spite of this strong need for clear and quick reviews of legal issues and solutions, the need has not been met by existing books on real estate law. This dynamic field is still treated by many books as a history course, in which the students are required to memorize the structure of feudal land systems in fifteenth-century England. Such learning is of no use to a broker faced with a dual-representation issue or the rights of multiple lenders in a foreclosure.

Further, many of the new developments in real estate financing and marketing remain untreated by many books. For example, significant issues of taxation in land ownership and transfer are lightly considered or ignored; the complications of real estate development through limited partnerships or syndications are overlooked; and the problems of disclosure issues on property conditions and nature and due diligence in the investigation of environmental hazards are largely ignored.

In addition to the omission of many topics, most real estate law books have chosen a straight, black-letter law approach. In those texts, the rules and terms are given, but there are few or no cases or examples to help students with their application.

This book has been developed with these problems and needs in mind. The problems and cases have been used by my students for 24 years with remarkable results—the students really understand and learn the material, and they are able to use their knowledge and problem-solving skills in personal and professional real estate transactions. If there were ever a remark that I dreaded to hear from a student, it was, "I'll never use this!" Since using this book, that phrase has slipped from my students' vocabularies.

Real estate law has too long been labeled a boring subject that was acknowledged as existing but not worth the effort of authors and publishers in the development of a helpful book. This book will put to rest any such labels—real estate law is anything but boring. There are cases on selling homes that were the sites of murders, dueling relatives on inheritance, and fighting neighbors. There are problems with high-rise hotels casting shadows on neighboring hotels' swimming areas and eccentric people with eccentric wills. This book shows the life and color of real estate law in day-to-day settings.

This book cannot make real estate lawyers of readers, but it can help them recognize problems related to real estate law. When the reading of this book is complete, the law will stick in the minds of readers because of the ghosts, the hotels, and the eccentric neighbors.

THE REVISED EDITION

As the saying goes, "If it ain't broke, don't fix it." The first through fifth editions of *Real Estate Law* were well received by students and instructors. Indeed, many brokers, agents, developers, and lawyers have found it to be a useful handbook. It has proved to be a successful textbook as well as a practical guide for those who work in the industry, and so the sixth edition continues the successful and unique features of the previous edition.

Nevertheless, the complexion of the real estate industry has changed since the earlier editions. Therefore, the primary focus of the sixth edition has been to update the materials in light of the changes in the tax laws, the financial markets, environmental issues, and the judicial imposition of liability on brokers, agents, and developers. Critical social issues such as all-adult covenants, group homes, and the unavailability of low-cost housing have created new legal issues. The environmental concerns about toxic waste have also raised new legal questions and resulted in additional environmental regulation. Issues related to lender liability for Superfund properties are updated in this edition. The new issues facing brokers and agents are covered at length with all the latest in statutory and judicial change. Because of all these changes, the past few years have witnessed significant partnerships and alliances in real estate ownership and development.

The real estate industry, particularly in the area of agent/broker relationships, has continued its rapid pace of activity, and a new body of case law has developed over the past few years. These new cases have been added or substituted in the sixth edition in order to provide cutting-edge information for the classroom as well as for practical use.

Real Estate Law, Sixth Edition, has some reorganization within several of the chapters, as well as across the text, to provide better coverage of the law in this field's changing complexion. But the color, excitement, and interest levels of the first five editions have been increased. Real life is still present.

ORGANIZATION

The book remains divided into four parts, but has been reorganized so that materials are grouped together according to particular transactions and the application of the law to those transactions. Part 1 covers the basics of real estate law: the nature of real estate, and real estate interests.

Part 2 covers legal issues related to the types of land ownership. New to this edition is the combination of Chapters 7 and 8 (present and future interests) into a single Chapter 7, Land Interests: Present and Future. Part 3 covers all aspects of the law involved in transferring title to real estate, from adverse possession and deeds to the roles of brokers and the intricacies of real estate financing mechanisms.

Part 4 covers real estate development and related issues such as environmental law, zoning, and constitutional issues. Also new to this edition is the updating and integration of all aspects of real estate development into one chapter (on construction, subdivision, and syndication), Chapter 22, Legal Issues in Land Acquisition, Finance, and Development.

The coverage can be as detailed as the reader or instructor desires. For example, the chapter on land descriptions (Chapter 6) could be eliminated if the students had sufficient exposure to descriptions in a principles class. Likewise, the details on future interests (Chapter 7) could be eliminated so that there is just the basic coverage of these forms of potential ownership.

TEXT FEATURES

Cases

Very few real estate law books have the benefit of reported cases. This book includes reported cases to illustrate major points of law. I have rewritten the case facts to help simplify the sometimes complex real estate issues. After the judge's name, the remainder of the case appears in actual case language. I have also edited the language to zero in on the particular point of law. Included in the cases are United States Supreme Court decisions on such controversial topics as red lining, environmental issues, and eminent domain. A Case Index is provided so that the better-known cases can be easily found by the curious reader. The sixth edition contains new cases to provide the most recent legal theories and offer insight into social issues affecting the real estate market.

Case Questions

In addition to fact summaries and careful editing, "Case Questions" follow each case to assist readers who may find it difficult to wade through the judicial language and reasoning of the case. These questions help readers sort out the facts and reach conclusions about the courts' decisions.

Practical Tips

Highlighted suggestions for avoiding legal problems and litigation in real estate, called "Practical Tip," have been expanded and updated in each chapter. These tips include lists, questions, and ways to avoid the problems that caused litigation in the chapter cases and questions. The tips provide yet another practical component to the text and increase its value as a handbook.

Consider Questions

Numbered "Consider" questions, appearing immediately after their applicable text material, help readers grasp the segments of each chapter as they read along. These questions refine reading habits as well as improve comprehension.

Ethical Issues

Continuing the popular feature from the fifth edition, this edition includes updated "Ethical Issues" for each chapter. These real and hypothetical problems allow students to discuss and debate real world dilemmas that real estate professional face regularly.

Web Exhibits

In a new feature in this edition, a number of forms have been omitted from the text and replaced with "Web Exhibit" designations. These exhibits are found on the text Web site as links; this enables students and instructors to see the most up-to-date sample forms illustrating the text discussions. Simply go to the Website at **http://jennings.westbuslaw.com**, click on this book, then on Internet Applications to select the correct chapter and exhibit.

Internet Features

At the beginning of each chapter is an Internet screen from a Website relevant to the chapter—its Internet address is repeated in the margin at a section corresponding to the topic highlighted in the screen. In addition, numerous Internet margin notes are interspersed throughout the text. Students and instructors are encouraged to visit these sites for additional information, updates, and examples relevant to text discussions.

As in the previous edition, end-of-chapter Internet activities are also provided, many of them new or updated, for students to gain proficiency in moving about the Web for research in real estate topics.

Charts, Diagrams, and Illustrations

Throughout the book, charts, diagrams, and illustrations aid readers' under-standing of lengthy and complex topics. For example, there are charts and dia-grams depicting the relationships of land interests, sample leases, and easements. New charts on development and property rights and interests have been added.

Cautions and Conclusions

Each chapter concludes with "Cautions and Conclusions," a feature that wraps up the issues addressed in the chapter. In some chapters, these are precautions, rec-ommendations, or points of which to be aware when dealing in the real world with the chapter issues. In other chapters, these are conclusions to be drawn from the material covered.

Chapter Problems

Most of the end-of-chapter problems are actual cases, with the case cites noted. Answers are provided in the *Instructor's Resource Manual*. The cases are short enough to spark interest and yet detailed enough to allow discussion and review of chapter concepts. They have been revised to include more recent develop-ments. Many chapter problems were once cases in the first through fifth editions and have become end-of-chapter review problems as newer cases replaced them. Some of the previous edition cases can be found in the *Instructor's Resource Manual* and can be assigned as in-class exercises.

Glossary

The glossary of key terms appears at the end of the text and provides short def-initions of the terms that are bold–faced in the text.

SUPPLEMENTAL ITEMS

Instructor's Resource Manual

The *Instructor's Resource Manual* was designed to help in lecture preparation. Each chapter is outlined in detail, with examples and illustrations of each of the chap-ter points. The cases are briefed within the outline as they appear in the text. Answers to all of the Case Questions, Consider questions, and Chapter Problems are provided in the *Instructor's Resource Manual*. Also included are discussion sug-gestions and their resolution for the Ethical Issues. The manual has been updated for this edition to include coverage of the *new* cases, Consider questions, Case Questions, and Chapter Problems.

Each chapter has a list of books and law review articles called "Resource Materials." These materials can be used to enhance the instructor's understand-ing of a topic. They have been increased and updated for this edition.

Some cases that were eliminated from the first through fifth editions to make way for new ones have been added to the *Instructor's Resource Manual* to provide supplemental readings for the instructor or for class use. Interactive learning exercises for each chapter, called "In-Class Exercises," are again provided in this edition.

Also included in the manual are sample examination questions. There are true/false, multiple-choice, and essay questions for each of the chapters. The true/false questions are easier and can be used for a quick quiz. The multiple-choice and essay questions test the ability of students to apply real estate law principles. This edition offers additional questions to provide a larger menu for the instructor.

The *Instructor's Resource Manual* is available in electronic format to instructors only at the text Website.

Real Estate Law *Website*

The Website for *Real Estate Law,* at **http://jennings.westbuslaw.com**, contains supplements, Internet materials from the text, Web Exhibits, case updates, and links to other useful West Legal Studies sites, including West's Legal Resources Center. The Resources Center provides course support for students and instructors. Other West products available to qualified adopters include Westlaw, West Legal Studies Video Library, monthly Court Case Updates, and a Handbook of Basic Law Terms from the Black's Dictionary Series. Instructors should contact their sales representative for details.

DEBTS OF GRATITUDE

Although only my name appears on this book, I cannot claim it as *my* book alone. As with all achievements in my life, my finished work is the result of the cooperation, work, and sacrifice of many. I cannot name everyone who has helped, but there are those who labored long hours to bring this book to its present state:

- Dick Crews, my original editor, who had the educational foresight to see the need for this book and who has been proven correct through the success of five editions. In 1983 Dick said, "Your book will be around for a long time." Eighteen years and counting!
- James Moody, my dad, a never-ending source of stories, fodder, and the right thing to do in real estate.
- Susan Smart, my Developmental Editor
- Libby Shipp, my Production Editor
- The students of *Real Estate Law,* who provided feedback on each edition, have my gratitude for their responsiveness and encouragement.
- Kris Tabor, for the unenviable typing tasks.
- The instructors who used *Real Estate Law* and have provided feedback on how to improve the book. Their feedback is a labor of love and evidence of their dedication to seeing higher education at its best.
- All of the realtors, insurers, lawyers, publishers, lenders, contractors, and real estate professionals who consented to have their forms and works reproduced in this text. Their names cannot be listed here, but their works are acknowledged throughout the book. Their dedication to education is evidenced by their complete cooperation in granting permission for these items to be used.

- My thanks to the anonymous reviewers of this and the previous editions who provided helpful comments, suggestions, and encouragement. Their efforts reflect a love of students and respect for quality education.
- Last, but certainly not least, I am grateful to both my immediate and extended family for their support of me, my work, and this project. My husband (Terry), my two daughters (Sarah and Claire), and my two sons (Sam and John) not only provided great mental support but also sacrificed some of their "quality" time for the law library, page proofs, and my sleep. They are grateful not to have to ask, "How many chapters do you have to go?"

A WORD FOR STUDENTS

In using the book, read the narrative material that describes the law first. Follow that by reading the cases that appear after each section. Answer the Case Questions after each case to make sure you understood the case and that you grasped the issues and principles of law. Try to solve the Consider questions and Chapter Problems on your own before your instructor gives you the answers. If you can solve all of the Consider questions and Chapter Problems, you understand the chapter material. The figures in chart form are designed to streamline ideas and summarize lengthy topics so that you can commit the concepts to memory. The charts are an excellent form of review for examinations or quizzes. Be sure to explore the Internet sites and research problems—this hands-on experience can teach you as well. Also visit the text's Website for important case updates and other useful links.

Finally, remember to apply what you have learned when your course is over. Application is the true test of learning. Good luck with the book and its application. Enjoy the color and the flavor of real estate law—it is abundant in this book.

Marianne M. Jennings

Chapter 1
Introduction and Sources of Real Estate Law

Possession is nine points of the law.

  Source unknown

The above quote is but one example of a principle of law relating to ownership of property. The source of this principle may be unknown, but there are a significant number of sources of real estate law, and this chapter answers the question, Where can real estate law be found? One distinguishing feature of real estate law is that problems are not solved by turning to a single statute or ordinance. A problem with a zoning issue cannot be resolved by examining only city ordinances, and a question on adverse possession is not always answered by turning to a statute.

Real estate law is not one simple body of law, as its name implies. Rather, it is made up of many different types of laws that have been passed by many different bodies at varying levels of government. No single governmental body possesses laws that are complete or exclusive sources of real estate law. To engage in real estate transactions, the parties should at least be familiar with the laws affecting the transactions and the sources from which those laws come. A familiarity with who and what are involved in the making of real estate law is helpful to those

1

engaged in the real estate business or anyone involved in some type of real estate transaction. Knowing which sources to check to determine applicable legal boundaries for a real estate transaction enables parties to the transaction to complete their business in a manner that will avoid major problems, dissatisfaction, and perhaps even litigation.

SOURCES OF REAL ESTATE LAW

If all the sources of real estate law were diagrammed in a scheme depicting their relationships, such a scheme would probably take the pyramidal form depicted in Figure 1.1.

The discussion of these sources of law will begin at the bottom of the pyramid with the United States Constitution. All other sources of real estate law must be consistent with the rights set forth in this foundation of the pyramid. Court decisions will be the final topic of discussion, and their position in the pyramid as well as in the discussion is based on the fact that they can deal with laws in any of the listed pyramid sources.

The United States Constitution

The **United States Constitution** has several provisions that apply to transfers and ownership of real estate. The Fourth Amendment affords property owners the

FIGURE 1.1   *Sources of Real Estate Law*

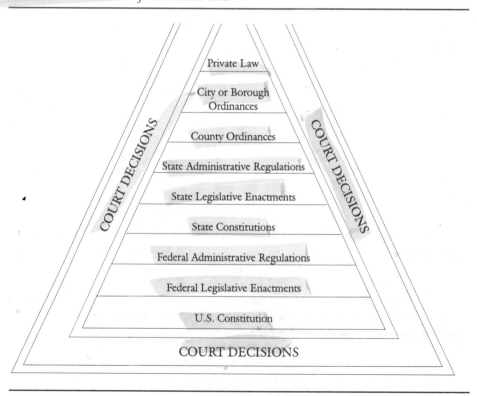

right to be secure in their "houses," and from this language has sprung a long series of cases providing rights that pertain to searches and seizures and the issuance of search warrants for real property.

The provisions of the Constitution most relevant to real estate law are two similar clauses found in the Fifth and Fourteenth Amendments. The **Fifth Amendment** prohibits the federal government from depriving any person of "property without due process of law" and from taking private property for public use "without just compensation." The due process provisions have resulted in many cases that contain legal discussions on obtaining judgments against a person's property and foreclosing on a security interest in real property. (See Chapters 4, 15, and 19.) The just-compensation provision offers protection for landowners when their property is to be taken by the government. This practice, referred to as **eminent domain,** has resulted in a long series of litigated cases (Chapter 19) involving questions such as, When is the government actually taking property? and What constitutes just compensation? For example, one issue related to the taking of property by the government might be whether landowners are entitled to compensation when noisy Air Force jets use the airspace above their property.

The **Fourteenth Amendment** has wording almost identical to the language of the Fifth Amendment, but it is applicable instead to state governments. The Fourteenth Amendment provides that no state may "deprive any person of . . . property, without due process of law." The amendment puts further restrictions on laws passed by the states by declaring any state law that denies or interferes with any rights given to citizens in the Constitution unconstitutional and invalid. The Fourteenth Amendment also requires the states to apply the law equally to all citizens so that all are afforded the same protections, entitled to the same forms of relief, and provided with equal opportunities for land ownership. Many of the racial discrimination cases on land purchases and sales have been based on this portion of the Fourteenth Amendment, which is referred to as the **Equal Protection Clause.**

These constitutional provisions set the parameters or establish the minimum rights that cannot be violated by the other governmental bodies involved in making the laws in the pyramid. Although these constitutional provisions seem very broad and general, they protect fundamental rights that cannot be infringed by the remaining sources of real estate law.

Federal Legislative Enactments

The Constitution establishes a legislative branch of the federal government, which is authorized to enact laws to carry out the objectives of the Constitution and the operation of the federal government. On the basis of authority given, Congress passes legislation to carry out its responsibilities, and regulation of real estate transactions is one of the responsibilities it may properly exercise. All enactments of Congress are printed in a series of volumes called the **United States Code (U.S.C.).** Each of the major enactments of Congress relating to real estate transactions will be discussed in great detail in subsequent chapters, but the following examples serve to illustrate the types of laws passed by Congress and found in the United States Code:

- The **Interstate Land Sales Full Disclosure Act (ILSFDA)** deals with the sale of undeveloped land to out-of-state residents. 15 U.S.C. § 1701 *et seq.* (discussed in Chapter 14).

- The **Real Estate Settlement Procedures Act (RESPA)** deals with maximum closing costs and good-faith estimates of closing costs. 12 U.S.C. § 2601 *et seq.* (discussed in Chapter 16).
- The **Internal Revenue Code (IRC)** deals with the income tax and depreciation aspects of real estate transactions. 26 U.S.C. § 1 *et seq.* (discussed in Chapter 22).
- The **Comprehensive Environmental Response, Compensation and Liability Act (CERCLA)** is a federal act that authorizes the cleanup of disposal sites for hazardous waste and permits the government to collect cleanup costs from current and former property owners. 42 U.S.C. § 9601 *et seq.* (discussed in Chapter 20).

http://
Visit the United States Code at: **http://www4.law.cornell.edu/uscode/**.

With each of the above-mentioned statutes, an abbreviation such as 26 U.S.C. § 1 appears after the name. This abbreviation is referred to as a **citation** or **cite** and represents the location of the statute in the series of volumes that make up the United States Code. The number preceding U.S.C. is the title or volume number of the United States Code where the statute may be found. The symbol § after U.S.C. means "section"; it is followed by the section number, which represents the location of the statute within the particular volume. For example, 26 U.S.C. § 305 would be a cite for a statute that could be found in the 26th volume of the United States Code where Section 305 appears. This particular section describes the proper methods for depreciating property for purposes of determining income. When a cite is furnished, the applicable law can be found by looking in the United States Code according to the citation system described.

Federal Administrative Regulations

http://
Visit the Code of Federal Regulations at: **http://www.access.gpo.gov/nara/cfr/cfr-table-search.html**.

For each federal legislative enactment passed by Congress, a new agency is created to enforce the particular enactment or an existing agency is assigned the task of enforcing it. For example, the Interstate Land Sales Full Disclosure Act (ILSFDA) is enforced by a federal agency, the Department of Housing and Urban Development (HUD). The Department of Housing and Urban Development has been delegated the responsibility of carrying out the general provisions of the act and will be required to develop procedures for compliance with and enforcement of the law. It is the responsibility of the agency designated in the act to fill in the details by passing regulations on procedures, compliance, and enforcement.

For example, the ILSFDA was passed by Congress in a general form and was intended to protect those who purchased undeveloped property without first having the opportunity to visually inspect it. The general provision established in the statute was for each buyer to be furnished with a full report disclosing critical information about the property, such as whether water is available and whether the property is accessible by road (see Chapter 14).

http://
Visit the HUD Website at: **http://www.hud.gov/fhe/index.html**.

Given the responsibility of enforcement under the act, HUD then passed regulations establishing the details for disclosing the information Congress had required. HUD has since passed regulations that establish how such information is to be disclosed, what information must be on file, what form the disclosures are to take, and how disclosures are to be organized. The regulations of an administrative agency fill in the details on the skeletal purpose outline given in the congressional enactment.

Another example of a federal regulatory scheme is that set of regulations adopted by the Environmental Protection Agency (EPA) under authority granted by Congress in CERCLA. CERCLA authorized the EPA to clean up sites contaminated by toxic wastes (42 U.S.C. § 9601 *et seq.;* see Chapter 20). The federal regulations for this environmental cleanup statute list 700 substances classified as toxic wastes covered under the required cleanup and liability provisions (40 C.F.R. § 302). Congress established the statutory authority for cleaning up "toxic wastes," and the regulations define what is included in that broad statutory authority.

All federal regulations appear in a series of volumes referred to as the **Code of Federal Regulations (CFR).** When an abbreviation, citation, or cite such as 12 C.F.R. § 226 appears in a book or a real estate document, it is possible to find the particular regulation referred to from the given cite. In the example, 12 is the volume number within the Code of Federal Regulations, and 226 is the section number of the regulation within that particular volume.

The Code of Federal Regulations is a series of paperback volumes that is reprinted every year because of the many changes in administrative agency regulations. In addition, a daily update to the Code of Federal Regulations, called the Federal Register, is published each working day and includes changes and proposed changes in existing regulations.

State Constitutions

State constitutions use methods similar to those in the United States Constitution to provide a framework within which state legislative bodies and agencies must act. However, most state constitutions tend to be more detailed than the basic structure and language of the United States Constitution, which emphasizes government structure and powers. For example, California's state constitution has a provision covering *usury,* or charging in excess of a certain maximum interest rate in a credit transaction (Cal. Const. Art. 15, § 1). Three additional examples of provisions from state constitutions are as follows:

- California—several sections that provide exemption of certain types of property from taxation including property used for religious worship or higher education (Cal. Const. Art. 13, § 3).
- Arizona—allows any person who holds a real estate broker's or salesman's license to draft and fill out any forms related to the sale or leasing of real property including earnest money receipts, purchase agreements, deeds, mortgages, leases, bills of sale, and other necessary documents (Ariz. Const. Art. 26, §§ 1–3).
- New Jersey—exempts the real property used exclusively for religious, educational, charitable, or cemetery purposes from taxation (N.J. Const. Article VIII, Section 1 Paragraph 2)
- New York—several sections creating preserves, recreational areas, reservoirs, and wildlife conservation policies (N.Y. Const. Art. XIV, §§ 1–3).
- Texas—covers the requirements for homestead exemptions (Tex. Const. Art. 16, § 51).

As these examples illustrate, state constitutions tend to be more specific than the United States Constitution and are viable sources for relevant real estate law.

State Legislative Enactments

Just as at the federal level, the legislative bodies in each state enact various provisions governing property rights and transactions. In most states, statutes provide procedures for obtaining licenses for selling real estate, methods of financing real estate purchases, time periods for adverse possession, and provisions for creating a will or probating an estate. A great amount of the detail of real estate law is found within the state legislative enactments.

State legislative enactments contain the so-called uniform laws, a great many of which apply in real estate transactions. Uniform laws are drafted by representatives of industry, academe, and the legal professions after comments and input by members of all three groups. Examples of uniform laws adopted by states that affect real estate transactions include the Uniform Marital Property Act, the Uniform Probate Code, the Uniform Commercial Code, the Uniform Partnership Act, and the Model Residential Landlord/Tenant Act.

These state legislative enactments are found in varying volumes and sources. In Texas, the legislative enactments are found in *Vernon's Texas Codes, Annotated* (for example, *V.T.C.A.: Water Code* § 1.001). In Illinois, the state statutes are found in *Smith-Hurd's Annotated Illinois Statutes* (for example, S.H.A. Ch. 96 § 4601). Oregon's Statutes are called *Oregon Revised Statutes* (for example, O.R.S. § 79.1090).

http://

For a look at both state and federal law, visit **http://www.loislaw.com**.

State Administrative Regulations

Again, as at the federal level, state legislative bodies also create administrative agencies to enforce their enacted legislation. These state agencies perform the same functions as the federal agencies in that they provide details, forms, and procedures necessary for compliance with state laws. For example, all states have laws regarding the licensing of real estate agents and brokers. In each state an agency is responsible for the collection of licensing fees, administration of exams, enforcement of state laws, and passage of regulations related to the state statutes.

County, City, and Borough Ordinances

A great amount of real estate law can be found in the smallest and most local entity, such as a county, city, or borough. For example, most of the laws relating to zoning can be found in the laws passed by local entities and are referred to as **ordinances.** Other topics covered by ordinances on a local level include building permits, building inspections, fire codes, building height restrictions, noise regulations, and curfews. All of these topics affect the transfer and use of real estate. (A complete discussion of zoning is found in Chapter 18.)

Private Law

In addition to the law of governmental bodies, one other type of law comes from individuals and landowners: **private law.** Private law consists of those rules and regulations created by landowners for their protection in the use of their land by others. For example, landlords are permitted to pass and post regulations pertaining to the use of common facilities such as pools, laundry areas, parking lots, and walkways. (A complete discussion of residential landlord-tenant relationships is found in Chapter 8.) In some instances private developers have placed added restrictions and covenants on the use of property sold or transferred to others. Some residential developments permit only those above the age of 18 years to live as residents in the area. (See Chapter 19 for a complete discussion.) Many private laws are necessary to keep townhouses and condominiums operating smoothly (see Chapter 11).

Private law also consists of the rights and obligations parties choose to impose on themselves through a contract for the purchase, sale, lease, or mortgage of real estate. The parties who validly and voluntarily enter into contractual obligations are bound by the terms of the contract as a form of private law, and such obligations can be enforced, like public laws, through the courts.

Private transactions in real estate have unique standing in that substantial public records and filings are maintained on private transactions in parcels of land. For example, the typical recorder's office will contain all the filings on the transfer and pledge of a parcel as well as information about methods of financing and any back-due taxes. The information in public records controls the rights of the parties, both present and future, with regard to that land. These recorded documents (see Chapters 13–15) of private transactions provide public notice with respect to that land, and rights of parties are determined by the presence or absence of these documented private transactions.

All private law is still subject to the boundaries and rights established in the previously discussed constitutional and statutory sources. A private law related to real estate may not abridge constitutional rights and freedoms. (A complete discussion of constitutional restrictions on real estate law is found in Chapter 19.)

Practical Tip

Know how and where to find your state statutes and regulations along with your city and county ordinances. Learn the names of your statutes, regulations, and ordinances, and how they are organized. Request to be placed on mailing lists of state administrative agencies so that you will know of enforcement actions, proposed rule changes, and compliance information. Check the agendas for the meetings of city councils. When they will consider zoning issues, you can attend and provide input. Follow legislative sessions and proposed laws through the media or through professional organizations such as the National Association of Realtors.

Court Decisions

The prior discussions of the various sources of law seem complete, and it would be difficult to imagine that much more detail could exist in real estate law. However, the constitutions, statutes, and ordinances are only general statements of the law that leave many terms undefined and also result in questions of application and interpretation. To whom does the law apply? When does the law apply and how is it to be applied? Finding the answers to these questions requires interpretation of law from all levels, a process that is carried out by the various courts in the state and federal judicial systems. The role of the courts is to answer the questions of application and to clarify ambiguities in statutes, ordinances, and contracts.

For example, suppose that a state statute requires "good faith" by all parties in performing their contract obligations. The meaning of "good faith" will be established through court cases and judicial interpretation. Is a party acting in good faith when she is unable to obtain financing from one lender and refuses to apply with another lender? Is a broker acting in good faith when he lists a property and then does not advertise or promote its sale? Without case examples and judicial opinions on the definition of "good faith," the statute would be meaningless.

Permanent records of courts' decisions are found in opinions published in books that far exceed in number the volumes devoted to statutes. These opinions must be consulted in discerning the complete meaning of a statute or ordinance. Further, an opinion can be used as a precedent when a later, factually similar set of circumstances again results in the need for the court's interpretive function.

In addition to their interpretive function, the courts also have the responsibility of making, applying, and analyzing the **common law.** Common law is law that is recognized as being law but is not in any code or statute.

Common law originated in England and continues to exist within case law, changing and growing on a case-by-case basis. Because most American real-property concepts can be traced to the English rules on real estate ownership and transfer, common law is a source to be checked regardless of whether a statute is involved.

The concept of nuisance (see Chapter 2) was developed by the courts to prevent others from interfering with your use and enjoyment of your property. Nuisance examples and the requirements for establishing a nuisance as well as appropriate remedies are found in case law. The law on nuisance comes largely from the courts, not from statutes.

Reliance on common law or prior court opinions in developing resolutions to factually similar problems is also called following **case precedent.** Precedent can be used as a guideline for contracts and transactions that occur after the judicial decision. Once a court has interpreted a particular statute or contract, other parties can use the court's interpretation to assist them in carrying out their transactions and intentions in those transactions.

For example, a statute from the state of New York (see box below) gives tenants the right to habitable premises when they lease residential property. Notice that the statute uses very general terms in defining what is required for premises to be habitable. Specific application of these general terms to landlord/tenant disputes will require litigation and court interpretation.

While the rights of landlords and tenants are discussed at length in Chapters 8 and 9, the purpose of the following cases is to illustrate the role of the judiciary in applying the general standards of the statute on habitability to different sets of facts.

Real Property Law § 235-b Warranty of Habitability

In every written or oral lease or rental agreement for residential premises the landlord or lessor shall be deemed to covenant and warrant that the premises so leased or rented and all areas used in connection therewith in common with other tenants or residents are fit for human habitation and for the uses reasonably intended by the parties and that the occupants of such premises shall not be subjected to any conditions which would be dangerous, hazardous or detrimental to their life, health or safety. When any such condition has been caused by the misconduct of the tenant or lessee or persons under his direction or control, it shall not constitute a breach of such covenants and warranties.

Any agreement by a lessee or tenant of a dwelling waiving or modifying his rights as set forth in this section shall be void as contrary to public policy. In determining the amount of damages sustained by a tenant as a result of a breach of warranty set forth in the section, the court; [*sic*]

(a) need not require any expert testimony; and

(b) shall, to the extent the warranty is breached or cannot be cured by reason of a strike or other labor dispute which is not caused primarily by the individual landlord or lessor and such damages are attributable to such strike, exclude recovery to such extent, except to the extent of the net savings, if any, to the landlord or lessor by reason of such strike or labor dispute allocable to the tenant's premises, provided, however, that the landlord or lesser [*sic*] has made a good faith attempt, where practicable, to cure the breach.

Solow v. Wellner

658 N.E.2d 1005 (N.Y. 1995)

Facts

Sheldon Solow (landlord/petitioner) is the manager of a 300-unit luxury apartment building on the Upper East Side of Manhattan. Rents in the building ranged from $1,064.89 per month for a studio apartment on the fourth floor to $5,379.92 per month for a two-bedroom apartment on the 44th floor. Prior to signing a lease, each tenant was given a brochure that contained the following descriptions of the building and its amenities:

> Panoramic views of New York City, its rivers and bridges; Long Island Sound and the Palisades. Solar glass thermopane windows. Private membership, rooftop, year-round Pool Club. 24-hour attended lobby.

> Video-monitored service and garage entrances. Four pipe central air-conditioning system providing a choice of cooling and/or heating during transitional seasons. Air-conditioned lobby and corridors.

> Kitchens:
> Ceramic tile floors
> Formica counter tops and cabinet areas
> G.E. 4-cycle dishwasher
> G.E. 2-door frost-free refrigerator and
> Automatic Icemaker
> Tappan range with 2 continuous cleaning
> ovens, digital clock and automatic timer
> Charcoal filtered range hood
> Stainless steel sink

> Bathrooms with Dupont "Corian" molded sinks and counter tops; quarry tile floors

> Sprinkler and smoke alarm systems in all public corridors

> Oak parquet floors

> 4 high speed Otis elevators equipped with intercom phone

> Master T.V. antenna system; Cable T.V. available

> Direct access to underground garage

> 46th floor laundry room with spectacular city views

> Smoke alarms in each apartment

Many other amenities were listed in the brochure. However, despite the promises and brochures, the tenants endured a building with many problems. The elevator system did not function and tenants waited interminable lengths of time for elevators, particularly during the morning and evening rush hours. The result was frequent lateness to work and other appointments and using the stairs to and from their apartments. In addition, the elevators skipped floors and opened on the wrong floors. Although there were four cars serving the building, one is a service car used primarily by building staff. When one of the regular cars was out, only two were left to service a 301-apartment, 46-story building.

Tenants complained about the stench emanating from garbage stored between the package room and the garage. Tenants spotted mice in that area. The door separating the garage from the building was always unlocked, creating a security problem. Fixtures were removed in the public areas, leaving exposed wiring for extended periods of time. In February and March of 1988, there were two floods at the front entrance that turned egress and entry into the negotiation of an obstacle course. In October 1988 water cascaded down the front of the building, barring entrance and seeping into the mailboxes and their contents. The package-room service began deteriorating in 1985 and 1986 and remained at a low level thereafter, resulting in delivery delays of one to two weeks.

The air conditioning in the lobby was frequently inoperative. The lobby carpets were often left dirty. The hallway fire alarms did not function on several occasions. The laundry room on the 46th floor was dirty, had overflowing sinks, had sections of acoustical tile missing, and suffered from roach infestation. The tiles were not replaced, but another sink was connected to one-half of the washing machines in late winter or early spring of 1988 and this stemmed the overflow. There were often 60 to 70 bags of garbage piled inside the main entrance inside the building. The compactor room on the ground floor had garbage all over the floor and was heavily infested with mice and roaches. The electronically operated security door at the valet station had an inoperative lock, thereby allowing anyone to walk into the building. The boiler room in the sub-basement had four to five inches of standing water.

There were no sign-up sheets for tenants to request an exterminator. To get extermination services, they had to leave a note with the concierge. An exterminator did not come to the building on a regular basis.

The air conditioners for the public area never functioned. The chilled water cooling coil, which provides conditioned air from the outside, was cracked in about 20 places.

The air conditioner that serviced the individual apartments leaked. The galvanized pipes that provided the runoff of drainage were placed at an angle that prevented them from carrying the water into the building's drainage system and ultimately into the city sewer system. Apartments where such leaking occurred were observed to have buckling floors at the same time. Approximately, between 10,000 and 11,000 square feet of parquet floors were replaced between January 1, 1988, and May 31, 1988.

There were soiled carpets in the public hallways, trash in the rear stairwells, unemptied ashtrays, and graffiti on some walls caused by a lack of cleaning supplies or equipment (one operable vacuum cleaner for the entire building!).

From October 1987 through May 1988, many of the tenants in the building stopped paying rent on the grounds that the landlord had breached the implied warranty of habitability as provided under Section 235-b of Real Property Law. Solow brought suit seeking payment of rent. The tenants counterclaimed for breach of the implied warranty of habitability. Following a 21-month trial, 12,000 pages of transcript, and frequent acrimony, the trial court held that the landlord had breached the warranty of habitability and awarded attorney fees. The appellate court modified the finding by limiting the breach of warranty of habitability only to the lack of elevator service, reversed and remanded, and the tenants then appealed.

Judicial Opinion

Levine, Judge. Pursuant to Real Property Law Section 235-b, every residential lease contains an implied warranty of habitability which is limited by its terms to three covenants: (1) that the premises are "fit for human habitation", (2) that the premises are fit for "the uses reasonably intended by the parties", and (3) that the occupants will not be subjected to conditions that are "dangerous, hazardous or detrimental to their life, health or safety". In *Park W. Mgt. Corp. v. Mitchell*, 391 N.E. 2d 1288, *cert. denied* 444 U.S. 992, this Court described the statutory warranty as creating an implied promise by the landlord that the demised premises are fit for human occupancy. We specifically rejected the contention that the warranty was intended to make the landlord "a guarantor of every amenity customarily rendered in the landlord-tenant relationship" and held that the implied warranty protects only against conditions that materially affect the health and safety of tenants or deficiencies that "in the eyes of a *reasonable person* . . . deprive the tenant of the *essential functions* which a residence is expected to provide."

While Civil Court based its finding of a breach of warranty of habitability in part on conditions reasonably related to health and safety and essential functions, it did not limit the implied warranty to such matters. Instead, the court interpreted the second prong of the statutory covenant—that the premises are fit "for the uses

reasonably intended by the parties"—as encompassing the level of services and amenities that tenants reasonably expect to be provided under the financial and other terms of their individual leases.

We reject Civil Court's interpretation of the statute. As discussed, the implied warranty of habitability sets forth a minimum standard to protect tenants against conditions that render residential premises uninhabitable or unusable. Thus, the statutory references to "uses reasonably intended by the parties", rather than referring to a broad spectrum of expectations arising out of the parties' specific contractual arrangement, reflects the Legislature's concern that tenants be provided with premises suitable for residential habitation, in other words, living quarters having "those essential functions which a resident is expected to provide". This prong of the warranty therefore protects against conditions that, while they do not render an apartment unsafe or uninhabitable, constitute deficiencies that prevent the premises from serving their intended function of residential occupation. Thus, for example, Appellate Term correctly concluded that operable elevator service is an essential attribute of a high-rise residential apartment building because a reasonable person could find that it is indispensable to the use of the demised premises.

The trial court's contrary interpretation based on expectations arising from the terms of the lease, would make the statutory implied warranty of habitability coextensive with the parties' lease agreement. However, the statute's nonwaiver clause indicates a legislative intent to insure the independence of the warranty of habitability from the specific terms of a lease. Moreover, section 235-b was intended to provide an objective, uniform standard for essential functions, while the trial court's standard creates an individualized subjective standard dependent on the specific terms of each lease. Furthermore, grafting the tenant's contractual rights onto the implied warranty would unnecessarily duplicate other legal and equitable remedies of the tenant.

Affirmed.

Case Questions

1. Describe the type of building and apartments the tenants were led to expect.

2. Describe the problems in the building.

3. Did the problems reach the level of threats to life, health, and safety?

4. Is the warranty of habitability one that varies according to lease agreements and the nature of property?

5. Is the information in the brochure relevant for the case?

6. If you had been a tenant, would you have withheld your rent?

Ethical Issue

In a case related to *Solow v. Wellner*, a motion for sanctions against the attorney for the tenants was heard by the civil and supreme courts of New York. As a result, the attorney for the plaintiffs/tenants was sanctioned $1,000 for each plaintiff for a total of $62,000 for "frivolous conduct." The courts held that Ray L. LeFlore had engaged in that conduct "primarily to delay or prolong the resolution of litigation, or to harass or maliciously injure another."

Was it ethical of the lawyer to prolong the litigation? Should the landlord have settled the case? Why do you think the landlord's case was in litigation for so many years? Do you think the tenants should have been permitted to rely on the brochure? *Solow v. Wellner*, 618 N.Y.S.2d 845 (1994)

Palais Partners v. Vollenweider

640 N.Y.S.2d 272 (City Civ. Ct. 1997)

Facts

Jean Vollenweider (defendant) is a tenant in a condominium apartment owned by Palais Partners (plaintiff). Vollenweider refused to pay rent during the months of March and April, 1995 (the rent is $3,870 per month) because Palais did nothing in response to Vollenweider's complaints about the conduct of a neighbor. The neighbor, who did not have coverings on his windows, would walk about nude in his apartment and occasionally engage in behavior related to his nudity. Vollenweider's apartment faces the nude neighbor's and the scenes were unavoidable when Vollenweider was at home. Palais brought suit for nonpayment for rent and Vollenweider defended on the grounds of constructive eviction and breach of the warranty of habitability.

Judicial Opinion

Stallman, Judge. Defendant's second affirmative defense asserts that he was constructively evicted from the premises because plaintiff allowed another tenant in the building to engage in illegal and immoral conduct.

Defendant has not met his burden of proving that the plaintiff deprived him of the beneficial use of a substantial portion of the premises, thereby forcing him to vacate. Defendant has not proven that he actually moved out because of the condition, within a reasonable time of the condition's occurrence. Indeed, because the neighbor moved out five months before defendant vacated, defendant cannot assert that his own move resulted from the neighbor's continued offensive conduct. Neither can defendant claim that he did not have use of the premises. Defendant continued to live there and is obligated to pay the agreed upon rent. Accordingly, the second affirmative defense is hereby dismissed. It is not necessary to consider the validity or effect of the lease clause that

appears to exculpate the unit owner from the acts of other building occupants.

Defendant's third affirmative defense asserts that as a result of the alleged constructive eviction, plaintiff was able to rent the apartment, commencing May 1, 1995 at a higher monthly rate than the amount set forth in the parties' lease, and that plaintiff thereby benefited. This does not state a cognizable defense to plaintiff's claim. Defendant's voluntary decision to vacate during the lease term does not create a constructive partnership or an equitable trust or give rise to an unjust enrichment claim. Defendant is not entitled to claim a share of the increased rent paid by the new tenant as an offset against unpaid rent. Accordingly, this defense is hereby dismissed.

Defendant's counterclaim seeks $25,000.00 in damages for the alleged resulting "uninhabitability" and constructive eviction. Whether analyzed in a light most favorable to the pleader as the court must on a motion to dismiss, or as a motion for summary judgment as urged by defendant himself, the counterclaim does not plead, and defendant's accompanying affidavits do not set forth, a valid claim. Defendant's allegations about the neighbor's acts, even if true, are insufficient as a matter of law. Neither the pleading nor the proof demonstrates that the neighbor's acts rendered the leased premises unfit for human habitation, or that they created conditions that were dangerous to life, health or safety or that they denied defendant any essential functions. See, *Solow v. Wellner*, 86 N.Y.2d 582, 635 N.Y.S.2d 132, 658 N.E.2d 1005. By definition, the warranty of habitability does not extend to aesthetics or inconveniences which do not render premises dangerous or unsafe (*Park West Mgt., supra*, at 328, 418 N.Y.S.2d 310, 391 N.E.2d 1288) even if unexpected in a luxury building. Disinclination to catch an occasional glimpse of a neighbor under the circumstances set forth here does not constitute breach of the warranty of habitability. Moreover, the lease clearly prohibited the interposition of counterclaims in any action between the parties related directly or indirectly to the lease. Accordingly, the counterclaim is dismissed.

Dismissed.

Case Questions

1. Why did Vollenweider withhold rent?
2. Does the warranty of habitability cover issues of aesthetics?
3. Will the landlord be entitled to the rent that was withheld?

Consider 1.1

Applying both the law and the case precedent on a landlord's warranty of habitability, discuss the following issues and questions.

a. Suppose a landlord included the following clause in a lease.

> *Landlord . . . shall not be liable for any damages to . . . property resulting from falling . . . water which may leak from any part of said building or from the pipes, appliances or plumbing works unless caused by or due to the negligence of Landlord . . . nor shall Landlord be liable for any such damage caused by other tenants.*

Is the clause enforceable? Does it eliminate the warranty of habitability? *Spatz v. Axelrod Management Co., Inc.,* 630 N.Y.S.2d 461 (City Civ. Ct. 1995)

b. Several tenants complain to their landlord that the doorbells and buzzers for their apartments don't work and that there are no mailboxes. Has the landlord breached the warranty of habitability? *Kachian v. Aronson,* 475 N.Y.S.2d 215 (1984)

c. Would the warranty of habitability apply to a restaurant tenant experiencing water leaks onto its grill? *Manhattan Mansions v. Moe's Pizza,* 561 N.Y.S.2d 331 (1990)

d. Would the warranty of habitability protect a condominium owner who experiences defects in the common areas? *Matter of Abbady,* 629 N.Y.S.2d 6 (1995)

e. Janet L. Benitez is a tenant in a basement apartment in Yonkers, New York. Sebastino Restifo is the landlord. On August 10, 1995, a large quantity of water cascaded from the ceiling of the Benitez apartment, causing severe water damage to a carpet, bed, bureau, clothing, phone, and compact disc player. Benitez replaced the carpet, bureau, mattress, and some clothing.

    The water had come from the third floor apartment of Mrs. Alamar. The Benitez apartment had been flooded previously by Mrs. Alamar because she was a problem tenant who filled her kitchen sink so that the water would overflow onto the kitchen floor and eventually down to the apartments below, including Benitez's. Benitez filed suit seeking to recover the cost of replacing her property on the grounds of breach of the implied warranty of habitability as provided in Section 235-b. *Benitez v. Restifo,* 641 N.Y.S.2d 523 (City Civ. Ct. 1996). Should she recover for her property damage under 235-b?

JUSTIFICATION FOR STUDYING REAL ESTATE LAW: SOME CAUTIONS AND CONCLUSIONS

Real estate is an industry in which small investments can yield high returns; property appreciation alone exemplifies this profitability. However, investment profits can be absorbed easily if legal difficulties arise with the property or the transaction providing the return. A piece of property that doubles in value in two years is not worth much if there is a defect in the title that prevents the owner from selling the property to realize that profit. A new home purchased at a bargain price is a comfort and achievement for a young couple until the announcement that a feed lot is to be constructed only 200 feet from their front door. The purchase of an apartment complex by an overextended corporation is a good tax write-off and cash producer until the discovery is made that the furniture, refrigerators, and stoves did not transfer with the property.

All of the errors made in these transactions involve legal issues that could have been avoided if the parties had a basic knowledge of some fundamental aspects of real estate law. The remainder of this book is devoted to providing such knowledge.

As you proceed through the book, think about the following excerpt developed by the author to introduce the notion of "real estate law." Pay close attention to the Cautions and Conclusions in each chapter as you look for answers.

The Most Frequently Asked Real Estate Questions

1. If I move out of my apartment before the lease expires, do I still owe the rent? What if the landlord re-rents the apartment? Will I still owe rent?
2. If a seller backs out of the sale of property, does she still owe the broker the commission?
3. If a buyer backs out of the purchase of property, does the broker still get his commission? What happens to the earnest money deposit?
4. Do all real estate contracts have to be in writing?
5. What if I buy a home and the general contractor hasn't paid all the subcontractors? Will I have to pay them?
6. If I die without a will, does my property go to the state?
7. If I own a house before I am married, does my spouse own it after we are married?
8. Who is the mortgagor? Who is the mortgagee?
9. How long does it take to foreclose on a property mortgage?
10. If people cut across my property for a path, am I liable if they are hurt? Can they claim any interest in my property?
11. If the fence on my property is in the wrong place, do I own the property that was accidentally included?
12. Can the Environmental Protection Agency require me to clean up or pay for the cleanup of toxic waste on land that I just bought?
13. Is my broker working for me or for the buyer?
14. What happens if my property deed is not recorded?
15. If a property has two mortgages, which mortgage has priority?

For each of the frequently asked questions, list the sources of law from the pyramid shown in Figure 1.1 on page 2 that would be consulted for answers.

Consider 1.2

Key Terms

United States Constitution, 2
Fifth Amendment, 3
eminent domain, 3
Fourteenth Amendment, 3
Equal Protection Clause, 3
United States Code (U.S.C.), 3
Interstate Land Sales Full Disclosure
    Act (ILSFDA), 3

Real Estate Settlement Procedures
    Act (RESPA), 4
Internal Revenue Code (IRC), 4
Comprehensive Environmental
    Response, Compensation, and
    Liability Act (CERCLA), 4
citation, 4
cite, 4

Code of Federal Regulations
    (CFR), 5
ordinances, 6
private law, 6
common law, 7
case precedent, 8

Chapter Problems

1. A farmer's southwest corner acre of his 40-acre parcel is to be taken by the state for the construction of a superhighway. Name at least two sources of real estate law involved in determining the farmer's rights.

2. Mr. and Mrs. Ralph Williams of Montana purchased an acre of land in a new Florida development called Sunnydale. When the Williamses arrived at Sunnydale they did not find the green, lush parcels they were told of, but instead found property resembling the moon's surface. In determining their rights, to which sources of law should Mr. and Mrs. Williams turn?

3. The Internal Revenue Service is challenging Iva Case's depreciation deduction for her law office building. What sources of law will govern the issue?

4. When Tom Buttom purchased his home, he was promised by the builder that the neighborhood would consist of single-family dwellings. Tom has just learned that because of economic conditions, the builder will be constructing duplex houses on Tom's street. What sources of law will be helpful to Tom in determining his rights?

5. Jane Jenkins, a licensed real estate agent in New York, will be moving to California. To what sources of law can Jane turn to find the requirements for becoming licensed in California?

6. A deed restriction requires every house in a subdivision to have a "minimum of 2,000 square feet of living space." Although the restriction seems clear, consider the following interpretive problems:

    a. Is a garage part of the 2,000 square feet?

    b. Are porches part of the 2,000 square feet?

What sources of law would be helpful in determining what is considered to be included in the term "living space"?

7. Ralph and Lillian Palmer owned a dump site in a wooded area in the northern part of Arizona. Cabin owners in the area used the dump site for their trash, and commercial trucks often would bring their loads of trash to the site for a fee. The site has had old batteries, medical refuse, and oil discarded from auto repair shops. The Environmental Protection Agency (EPA) maintains that substances from the site are leaking into the surrounding soil and water supply. What sources of law provide the EPA with its authority?

8. Some isolated parcels within national forests are privately owned. Often, the United States Forest Service will try to arrange exchanges with landowners. With an exchange, the Forest Service will then have a clean parcel and the landowner is given property in an area with development potential near a city or small town. Discuss the types of laws and government agencies that would be involved in such an exchange.

9. Susan Hewitt is a licensed broker in Arizona. She is confused and concerned about her role as an agent for sellers when she lists properties. For example, often prospective buyers will ask her questions about the sellers, their cash needs, their reasons for selling their property, and whether their circumstances require them to sell quickly. What sources of law would help Susan clarify her role with both sellers and buyers?

10. Mr. Fred Saddy leased the premises known as 61 George Street, Manhasset, New York, from John and Helen Kekllas for the period from September 6, 1976, to May 7, 1977, for a monthly rent of $575.00.

    The Kekllases had just purchased the premises, which were in disrepair. There were strong odors of cats and cat urine in the garage, the basement of the premises, and in and about a dinette area in the kitchen. During the summer of 1976, the Kekllases had made substantial repairs to the premises including painting and wallpapering. This work was done after the Kekllases had contracted with Checkmate Exterminators to treat the premises for the odor of cat urine. Checkmate gave a three-month guarantee on its odor treatment.

    Mr. and Mrs. Saddy moved in on September 8, and by September 10, Mrs. Saddy was complaining of nausea and watery eyes due to the smell of cat urine. The house had been previously occupied by a mother, age 75, and her daughter, who was in her mid-50s, who housed two to four cats during their residency there. One was kept in the basement, one in the garage, and the others in the house. Mr. Saddy refused to pay rent on the grounds that the odor breached the warranty of habitability, and Mr. Kekllas filed suit to have the Saddys evicted. Has the warranty of habitability been breached? Refer to the cases and problems in the text to determine your answer. *Kekllas v. Saddy*, 389 N.Y.S.2d 756 (Dist. Ct. 1976)

Internet Activities

1. RESPA (The Real Estate Settlement Procedures Act) is a HUD consumer protection statute designed to help consumers during the home-buying process. RESPA requires that consumers receive disclosures at various times in the transaction. It also outlaws kickbacks that increase the cost of settlement services. RESPA is enforced by HUD. Visit HUD's Website **http://www.hud.gov** to find pamphlets and information on RESPA.

2. CERCLA (Comprehensive Environmental Response, Compensation and Liability Act) data is available from CPI; CERCLA services provided by CPI; link to CERCLA Mini-Site at **http://www.citation.com/hpages/cercla.html**.

3. ILSFDA (Interstate Land Sales Full Disclosure Act) lists the most commonly asked questions from purchasers at: **http://www.hud.gov/fha/sfh/ils/ilspurqa.html**.

4. Look for court decisions in your state: **http://www.fastsearch.com/law/**.

State of Nevada
Commission on Mineral Resources
Division of Minerals

Regulation

Nevada Revised Statutes	Nevada Administrative Code
The Revised Statutes (NRS) are the actual Laws.	The Administrative Code (NAC) are Rules and Regulations.
Chapter 513 - Commission on Mineral Resources; Division of Minerals	NAC 513 - Commission on Mineral Resources; Division of Minerals, Jul-94
Chapter 517 - "Mining Claims, Mill Sites and Tunnel Rights"	NAC 517 - Maps of Mining Claims, Jul-94
Chapter 519A - Reclamation of Land Subject to Mining Operations or Exploration Projects	NAC 519A - Reclamation of Land Subject to Mining Operations or Exploration Projects, Apr-98
Chapter 522 - Oil and Gas	NAC 522 - Oil and Gas, Jul-94
Chapter 534A - Geothermal Resources	NAC 534A - Geothermal Resources, Jan-96

This page was last updated on October 12, 2000 15:03

[Home] [Up] [About Our Division] [Administrator's Page] [Forms and Publications] [Regulation]

Chapter 2
Extent of Real Estate Interests

Broad acres are a patent of nobility; and no man but feels more of a man in the world if he have a bit of ground that he can call his own. However small it is on the surface, it is four thousand miles deep; and that is a very handsome property.

My Summer Is a Garden
Charles Dudley Warner (1871)

An old maxim in property law is "The owner of the soil owns also to the sky and to the depths." Land ownership involves so much more than surface rights. For example, the Trump Tower in New York City is built in the air rights once owned by Tiffany's. Tiffany's retained its surface rights but conveyed its air rights in its land to Donald Trump. This chapter answers the following questions: What do I own when I hold title to land? Where does my ownership interest start? Where does it end? Land ownership has been depicted as a wedge that runs from the core of the earth to the "heavens," as shown in Figure 2.1. Land interests include the surface, that which is below the surface, and the air that extends above the surface parcel.

LAND INTERESTS ABOVE THE SURFACE

Air Rights

The discussion of **air rights,** or the land interest above the surface, can be divided into two topics: (1) a determination of who can use the air and to what extent, and (2) a determination of what air interests can be transferred.

FIGURE 2.1   *Extent of Land Ownership*

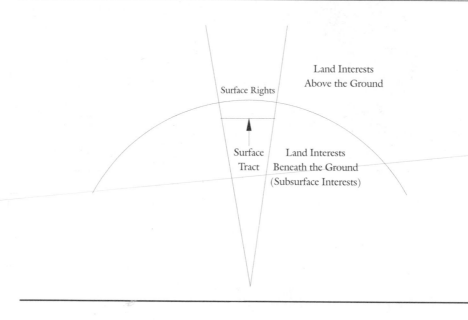

WHO CAN USE THE AIR?

In dealing with topic 1, it must first be noted that the airspace of all property owners is used by others. In addition to constant air traffic in the airspace above property, manufacturers, processors, and auto drivers use the airspace in that their gases, smokes, and fumes invade the airspace in many pieces of property. Land owners enjoy limited protections in these types of uses through environmental regulation (see Chapter 20), but specific relief for individual landowners often requires them to bring suits in nuisance or trespass. (The concepts of nuisance and trespass are discussed later in this chapter.) The following case is an example of how much the airspace of another can be used and deals with the rights of landowners in preventing and controlling the use of their airspace.

United States v. Causby

328 U.S. 256 (1946)

Facts

Mr. and Mrs. Causby (referred to as respondents) owned 2.8 acres of land near an airport outside of Greensboro, North Carolina. On the property were a house where the Causbys resided and various outbuildings used for raising chickens. The end of the airport's northwest–southwest runway was 2,220 feet from the Causbys' barn and 2,275 feet from their house. The path of glide to the runway passed directly over their property at 67 feet above the house, 63 feet above the barn, and 18 feet above the highest tree. The United States government leased the airstrip in 1942, with the lease carrying renewal provisions until 1967. Bombers, transports, and fighters all used the airfield. At times the airplanes came close enough to blow old leaves off trees, and the noise of the airplanes was startling. As a result of the noise, six to 10 of the Causbys' chickens were killed each day by "flying into the walls from fright." After losing 150 chickens, the Causbys gave up their business. They could no longer sleep well and became nervous and frightened.

The Causbys sued the United States government on the grounds that the United States was taking their airspace by eminent domain without compensating them. The lower court found for the Causbys, and the United States government appealed.

Judicial Opinion

Douglas, Justice. The United States relies on the Air Commerce Act of 1926. Under those statutes the United States has "complete and exclusive national sovereignty in the air space" over this country. They grant any citizen of the United States "a public right of freedom of transit in air commerce through the navigable air space of the United States."

And "navigable air space" is defined as "airspace above the minimum safe altitudes of flight prescribed by the Civil Aeronautics Authority." And it is provided that "such navigable airspace shall be subject to a public right of freedom of interstate and foreign air navigation." It is, therefore, argued that since these flights were within the minimum safe altitudes of flight which had been prescribed, they were an exercise of the declared right of travel through the airspace. The United States concludes that when flights are made within the navigable airspace without any physical invasion of the property of the landowners, there has been no taking of property. It is ancient doctrine that at common law ownership of the land extended to the periphery of the universe—*Cujus est solum ejus est usque ad coelum.* But that doctrine has no place in the modern world. The air is a public highway, as Congress has declared. Were that not true, every transcontinental flight would subject the operator to countless trespass suits. Common sense revolts at the idea. To recognize such private claims to the airspace would clog these highways, seriously interfere with their control and development in the public interest, and transfer into private ownership that to which only the public has a just claim.

But the general principle does not control the present case. For the United States conceded on oral argument that if the flights over respondents' property rendered it uninhabitable, there would be a taking compensable under the Fifth Amendment. It is the owner's loss, not the taker's gain, which is the measure of the value of the property taken. Market value fairly determined is the normal measure of the recovery. And that value may reflect the use to which the land could readily be converted, as well as existing use. If, by reason of the frequency and altitude of the flights, respondents could not use this land for any purpose, their loss would be complete. It would be as complete as if the United States had entered upon the surface of the land and taken exclusive possession of it.

The path of glide for airplanes might reduce a valuable factory site to grazing land, an orchard to a vegetable patch, a residential section to a wheat field. Some value would remain. But the use of the airspace immediately above the land would limit the utility of the land and cause a diminution in its value.

We have said that the airspace is a public highway. Yet it is obvious that if the landowner is to have full enjoyment of the land, he must have exclusive control of the immediate reaches of the enveloping atmosphere. Otherwise buildings could not be erected, trees could not be planted, and even fences could not be run. The principle is recognized when the law gives a remedy in case overhanging structures are erected on adjoining lands. The landowner owns at least as much of the space above the ground as he can occupy or use in connection with the land. The fact that he does not occupy it in a physical sense—by the erection of buildings and the like—is not material. As we have said, the flight of airplanes, which skim the surface but do not touch it, is as much an appropriation of the use of the land as a more conventional entry upon it. We would not doubt that if the United States erected an elevated railway over respondents' land at the precise altitude where its planes now fly, there would be a partial taking even though none of the supports of the structure rested on the land. The reason is that there would be an intrusion so immediate and direct as to subtract from the owner's full enjoyment of the property and to limit his exploitation of it. While the owner does not in any physical manner occupy that stratum of airspace or make use of it in the conventional sense, he does use it in somewhat the same sense that space left between buildings for the purpose of light and air is used. The superadjacent airspace at this low altitude is so close to the land that continuous invasions of it affect the use of the surface of the land itself. We think that the landowner, as an incident to his ownership, has a claim to it and that invasions of it are in the same category as invasions of the surface.

The airplane is part of the modern environment of life, and the inconveniences which it causes are normally not compensable under the Fifth Amendment. The airspace, apart from the immediate reaches above the land, is part of the public domain. We need not determine at this time what those precise limits are. Flights over private land are not a taking, unless they are so low and so frequent as to be a direct and immediate interference with the enjoyment and use of the land. We need not speculate on that phase of the present case. For the findings of the Court of Claims plainly establish that there was a diminution in value of the property and that the frequent, low-level flights were the direct and immediate cause. We agree with the Court of Claims that a servitude has been imposed upon the land.

Affirmed.

Case Questions

1. What type of business did the Causbys operate?
2. How close was the airstrip to the Causbys' home?
3. How close to the Causbys' land were the airplanes (in altitude) upon their runway approach?
4. What happened to the Causbys' chickens as a result of the airplanes?
5. What happened to the Causbys as a result of the airplanes?
6. Are the Causbys suing for nuisance?
7. What statute does the government say is controlling?
8. Can the use of airspace diminish the value of the surface of the land?
9. Do the Causbys win?

The *Causby* case illustrates the limitations on the use of airspace. The landowner is subject to use of the airspace by air traffic but is entitled to compensation in the event that the airspace is used in such a manner as to prevent use of the surface property. Other uses of airspace can interfere with the land of another. For example, when the eaves of a building or branches from a tree located on one parcel of land hang over onto another landowner's parcel of land, there is a taking of airspace. In the *Causby* case, the court mentioned that a remedy is available for overhang. The property owner affected by the overhang can bring suit for a court order requiring the removal of the eaves or branches, and in some states is even permitted to unilaterally end the invasion by clipping the tree branches.

WHAT AIR RIGHTS CAN BE TRANSFERRED?

The second aspect of landowners' rights in the air covers the ability of landowners to transfer interests in the air located above their property. The air above property is divided into two areas, the **column lot** and the **air lot**. The column lot comprises everything between the earth's surface and an imaginary plane 23 feet above the surface, and the air lot comprises everything above the 23-foot plane. It is possible for landowners to transfer some interest in their column or air lot.

For example, both the column lot and the air lot could be sold for the construction of a large building. Those constructing the building need only have title to or an easement (see Chapter 3) for small segments of the land surface for the placement of beams or the steel girder foundations of the building. In these types of transfers of column and air lots, landowners retain title to the surface but have conveyed their air rights or a portion thereof.

The construction and sale of condominiums is an example of the use and transfer of airspace. When buyers purchase condominiums, they are actually purchasing the airspace located between the walls of their particular units. Ground or surface ownership is not conveyed as part of the title, but the condominium owners do hold real property interests. (See Chapter 11 for a complete discussion of condominiums.)

In addition to the previously mentioned Trump Tower, there are several other examples of large buildings constructed through the use of airspace. In Chicago, the Prudential Mid-America building is built in both the air and column lots above

Practical Tip

Check property for noise, air activity, and overhangs. Determine flight paths and plans for construction of airports, runways, and possible expansion of airport capacity and facilities.

http://

Visit a Website targeting commercial lease space in multistory buildings at **http://www.comro.com**.

the Illinois Central Terminal. The 52-story Prudential Tower is built in the column and air lots above Boston. In New York, the 59-story Met Life building is built in the column and air lots above Grand Central Station. These examples illustrate that dividing air and surface ownership enables maximum use of real property. Transfers of air rights have become so common that many states are reviewing the Model Airspace Act for possible adoption to govern these transfers.

Practical Tip

The sale of air rights has become more popular in areas where upward construction is the only means for growth and expansion of existing facilities. Building height limitations in some areas, such as San Francisco, increase the value of limited air space. Creative solutions to the space problems businesses face include contacting current surface holders to determine their interest in the transfer of air rights.

The Right to Light

Corresponding to the ownership of air as part of a real property interest is the ownership of light. In this era of energy-technology development, the issue of who owns the light is becoming a critical one. Suppose the following hypothetical situation has occurred:

> Anna and Beverly are neighbors. Anna has installed a series of solar collectors on the roof of her home. The collectors are positioned so that Anna obtains maximum efficiency in the use of the sun. However, Beverly has decided to plant several trees for backyard shade and within three years of planting, the now tall trees are interfering with the collection of sunlight by Anna's collectors.

In the absence of any statutory right and under common law, Anna has no legal rights against Beverly unless Anna can establish that Beverly's conduct was malicious and done with the intent of obstructing light from the collectors. Many states have passed statutory protections for the right to light, and New Mexico (N.M.S.A. §§ 47-3-1 *et seq.*) and Wyoming (W.S.A. §§ 34-22-101 *et seq.*) both grant a statutory right to sunlight. Under the statutes, the first user of light for solar energy purposes acquires the right to unobstructed continued use. Other states have passed **solar easement laws** that permit the execution and recognition of easements for the protection of solar access.[1] These easement laws do not, however, create or protect solar rights. Some states have encouraged zoning as a tool to be used to incorporate solar access considerations.[2] Other states have enacted statutes that permit solar energy users to petition administrative review boards when adjoining landowners refuse to negotiate solar access easements.[3] Finally, California applies the law of easements to solar easements that meet the requirements of the statute (Cal. Civ. Code 801.5).

In California, deed restrictions or covenants that prohibit or restrict the installation of solar energy systems are void and unenforceable (Cal. Civ. Code § 714). Presently, proposed uniform laws on solar rights and solar energy systems are being developed for use by state legislators in regulating this area of land ownership.

The courts have undertaken some protection for solar rights through the use of property theories. In *Prah v. Maretti*, 321 N.W.2d 182 (Wis. 1982), the court held, "The law of private nuisance is better suited to resolve landowners' disputes

---

1.   California, Colorado, Florida, Georgia, Idaho, Illinois (although *O'Neill v. Brown*, 609 N.E.2d § 55 Ill 1995 held that Illinois was not a solar easement state despite its comprehensive solar energy Act), Kansas, Kentucky, Maine, Maryland, Minnesota, New Jersey, North Dakota, and Virginia.
2.   Connecticut, Minnesota, Oregon, and Utah. Note: Oregon affords considerable authority to planning commissions in treating rights for solar systems.
3.   Iowa and Wisconsin.

about property development in the 1980s than is a rigid rule which does not recognize a landowner's interest in access to sunlight."

At common law, the **Doctrine of Ancient Lights** provided protection for the use of light. Under the doctrine, anyone who used the light for an uninterrupted period of 20 years was entitled to protection for use of that light, and obstruction was prohibited. However, this doctrine has been rejected by the American courts, with most of them following the ruling set forth in the following landmark light-obstruction case.

Fontainebleau Hotel Corp. v. Forty-Five Twenty-Five, Inc.

114 So.2d 357 (Fla. 1959)

Facts

The Fontainebleau, a luxury hotel, was constructed in Miami facing the Atlantic Ocean in 1954. In 1955, the Eden Roc, another luxury hotel, was constructed adjoining the Fontainebleau and also facing the Atlantic Ocean. Shortly after the construction of the Eden Roc in 1955, the Fontainebleau undertook the construction of a 14-story addition to extend 160 feet in height and 416 feet in length running from east to west. During the winter months from about two in the afternoon and for the remainder of the day, the shadow of the addition would extend over the cabana, swimming pool, and sunbathing areas of the Eden Roc.

The Eden Roc (Forty-Five Twenty-Five Corp., plaintiff/appellee) brought suit against the Fontainebleau Hotel Corp. (defendant/appellant) to stop construction of the addition after eight stories had been built. The Eden Roc alleged the construction would interfere with its sunlight, cast a shadow, and interfere with the guests' use and enjoyment of the property. The Eden Roc further alleged the construction of the addition was done with malice. The trial court found for Eden Roc. Fontainebleau appealed.

Judicial Opinion

Per Curiam. It is well settled that a property owner may put his own property to any reasonable and lawful use, so long as he does not thereby deprive the adjoining landowner of any right of enjoyment of his property which is recognized and protected by law, and so long as his use is not such a one as the law will pronounce a nuisance.

No American decision has been cited, and independent research has revealed none, in which it has been held

that—in the absence of some contractual or statutory obligation—a landowner has a legal right to the free flow of light and air across the adjoining land of his neighbor. Even at common law, the landowner had no legal right, in the absence of an easement or uninterrupted use and enjoyment for a period of 20 years, to unobstructed light and air from the adjoining land.

There being, then, no legal right to the free flow of light and air from the adjoining land, it is universally held that where a structure serves a useful and beneficial purpose, it does not give rise to a cause of action, either for damages or for an injunction even though it causes injury to another by cutting off the light and air and interfering with the view that would otherwise be available over adjoining land in its natural state, regardless of the fact that the structure may have been erected partly for spite.

We see no reason for departing from this universal rule. If, as contended on behalf of plaintiff, public policy demands that a landowner in the Miami Beach area are [*sic*] to refrain from constructing buildings on his premises that will cast a shadow on the adjoining premises, an amendment of its comprehensive planning and zoning ordinance, applicable to the public as a whole, is the means by which such purpose should be achieved.

The record affirmatively shows that no statutory basis for the right sought to be enforced by plaintiff exists. The so-called Shadow Ordinance enacted by the City of Miami Beach at plaintiff's behest was held invalid in *City of Miami Beach v. State ex rel. Fontainebleau Hotel Corp.* It also affirmatively appears that there is no possible basis for holding that plaintiff has an easement for light and air, either express or implied, across defendant's property, nor any prescriptive right thereto—even if it be assumed, *arguendo*, that the common-law right of prescription as to "ancient lights" is in effect in this state. And from what we have said heretofore in this opinion, it is perhaps superfluous to add that we have no desire to dissent from the unanimous holding in this country repudiating the English doctrine of ancient lights.

Reversed.

Case Questions

1. Who owns the Eden Roc?
2. Who brought the original suit?
3. Why was the suit brought?
4. Will the court recognize the Doctrine of Ancient Lights?
5. Will the court recognize an easement?
6. What remedy does the court suggest?
7. Who wins on appeal?

Today, some courts have begun to use a theory of prescriptive easements (see Chapter 3) or one of nuisance (discussed later in this chapter) to afford some protection for a landowner's light.

However, there are still only limited statutory and judicial protections afforded for solar access, so it is easy to conclude that parties desiring to maintain rights to light should do so through the execution of private agreements with adjoining landowners who will give them easements for such rights. Some mortgage lenders that are lending for property with solar panels will require such easements to be obtained before the mortgage money will be advanced to the borrower. However, in spite of the need for such easements, many parties do not take the time to protect their rights. Recent surveys reveal that 95 percent of all owners of solar energy systems have not obtained easements for the protection of sunlight.

If an easement for light is executed, the document should carefully specify the extent of the easement. Stating the purpose (for solar panels, windows, or a swimming pool) of the easement in the document helps indicate the intent of the parties as to the extent and scope of the easement. Including the times of day when the sun is to be unobstructed will make the rights of the parties clear and can limit the burden on the adjoining land. An easement may be needed from more than just the adjoining landowners because light obstructions can come from larger structures located some distance away. Establishing rights and remedies for obstruction in the parties' agreement can prevent litigation later. The agreement should set forth in detail the types of structures (height, width, and so on) that cannot be constructed. Finally, every agreement and easement should comply with any statutory restrictions.

Homeowners' associations and the conditions, covenants, and restrictions (CC&Rs) for subdivisions should address the issues of type, attachment, and aesthetics of solar units. The following language is an example of CC&R restrictions on solar devices upheld in California (*Palos Verdes Homes Ass'n. v. Rodman,* 182 Cal. App.3d 324, 227 Cal. Rptr. 81 [1986]):

1. Solar Units not on the roof should be maintained a minimum of 5 ft from the property line and concealed from the neighboring view, and a fence or wall of sufficient height to accomplish same may be appropriate.
2. Solar Units on a roof should be within the wall line of the structure.

Practical Tip

Before buying, selling, or listing property, ask the following questions and find answers:

1. Does the home have solar reliance, passive or active?
2. Are the solar components in compliance with the CC&Rs?
3. Do the CC&Rs permit installation of solar devices?
4. Are there restrictions in the CC&Rs on expansion of solar units?
5. Are there obstructions or potential obstructions for the solar units (growing trees; possible construction)?
6. Does an easement for light exist?
7. Can I get an easement for light?
8. Are there statutory protections for light access?
9. Is there backup power for the solar panels and system?

http://

Visit the Florida Solar
Energy Center at: **http://
www.fsec.ucf.edu/**.

However, the Art Jury may require more roof area between solar unit and roof edge if the roof overhang is minimal. . . . 4. Solar Units should be in or below the plane or roofing material. 5. Solar Units should be constructed of rigid materials . . . The Art Jury may ask for alternative combinations in smaller groupings when large areas of grouped solar panels are found not to be aesthetically satisfactory.

Ethical Issue

While case law makes it clear that in the absence of any private agreement or statutory protection there is no right to light, individuals and their property values are affected greatly when an adjoining landowner obstructs light. While the obstruction may not interfere with solar access, the obstruction nonetheless affects the character of the property and perhaps its value. What are the ethical issues in a situation in which a new landowner or current owner of a neighboring property undertakes a construction project that interferes with the light of surrounding property owners? How should the conflict between the right to use their property and the rights of adjoining landowners be resolved? Are the issues different when, as in the *Eden Roc* case, the effect will be a loss of business and strength for the competitor/adjoining landowner? How do you feel about the statement, "All landowners assume the risk of changes in the use of surrounding property?"

Practical Tip

There is no right to a view. If property is purchased or carries additional value because of location and view, the owner's only protection from obstruction is an easement, height restrictions, or other covenants placed on the adjoining properties. There are no legal guarantees that a view will always be preserved.

Right to a View

Several recent cases have raised the issue not of the right to light, but the right to a view. Many resort homes and homes in high-rises or located near mountains, oceans, or other scenic vistas carry a premium price because of the view from the home's interior. Do landowners in these premium properties have any rights when construction on adjoining properties results in obstruction of their view? In the following case, the court discusses the new issue of "right to a view."

Pierce v. Northeast Lake Washington Sewer and Water District

870 P.2d 305 (Wash. 1994)

Facts

Arthur and Patricia Pierce (petitioners) own property on a hillside near Seattle. The Northeast Lake Washington Sewer and Water District (District), a municipal corporation providing water and sewer services to 50,000 people, acquired 5.4 acres of residential property adjacent to the Pierces' land. The District applied for a permit to construct a 4.3-million-gallon water storage facility on the site. The District chose the location because the sloping hillside would enable it to obscure the sight of the tank from neighboring residences. The permit was granted with modifications in the tank's location.

However, the final position of the constructed tank blocked the panoramic view the Pierces had enjoyed of wooded terrain, Lake Washington, Mount Rainier, and the Cascades. The tank was visible from any window in the house.

After an appraiser issued his opinion that the construction of the tank resulted in a $30,000 reduction in value of the Pierces' property, the Pierces filed suit against the District for nuisance, trespass, negligence, and inverse condemnation. The trial court dismissed the suit for the failure to demonstrate compensable damages and the court of appeals affirmed. The Pierces appealed.

Judicial Opinion

Smith, Justice. This is an action in inverse condemnation brought by Petitioners against Northeast Lake Washington Sewer and Water District, a municipal corporation. Inverse condemnation is an action to "recover the value of property which has been appropriated in fact, but with no exercise of the [condemnation] power." "Our constitution requires that just compensation be paid a landowner in the event of either a governmental 'taking' or 'damaging' of property."

Under a general takings analysis, the elements of an inverse condemnation action are not in dispute. However, the only Washington case which considered a property owner's right to a view is *State v. Calkins*. In that case the court stated

> Clearly, there has been no specific declaration by our legislature of an intention to pay compensation for nonexistent property rights; i.e., access, air, view, and light; furthermore, absent such rights, the condemnation proceedings herein do not violate Art. I, Section 16, of our state constitution, which requires the payment of just compensation for the taking or damaging of property rights.

Although *Calkins* was not an action for inverse condemnation based upon interference with a property owner's right to a view, it is nevertheless somewhat indicative of this court's position on the matter. Because our own decisions have not squarely addressed this issue, we may look to decisions from other jurisdictions . . .

In *Pacifica Homeowners' Ass'n v. Wesley Palms Retirement Comm'ty*, 224 Cal. Rptr. 380 (1986), the California Court of Appeal concluded that "[a]s a general rule, a landowner has no natural right to air, light or an unobstructed view and the law is reluctant to imply such a right." However, "[s]uch a right may be created by private parties through the granting of an easement or through the adoption of conditions, covenants and restrictions by the Legislature."

In *Pacifica*, the Homeowners' Association (Association) attempted to enjoin the Wesley Palma Retirement Community from allowing trees on its property to grow higher than the Association's five-story building. The Association claimed a conditional use permit placed a limitation on tree height, which was "imposed particularly for the benefit of the uphill landowners including the Association." However, the court rejected the Association's arguments and stated that "[i]n the absence of any agreement, statute or governmentally imposed conditions on development creating a right to an unobstructed view, it cannot be said Wesley Palms . . . interfered with any right."

In *Gervasi v. Board of Comm'rs of Hicksville Water Dist.*, 256 N.Y.S.2d 910 (1965), the facts closely parallel those in this case. The plaintiffs in that case sought to enjoin the water district from completing construction of a water tank or to recover damages measured by the reduced value of their homes caused by construction of the water tank. In that case, the water district constructed a storage tank on its own property. The plaintiffs claimed construction and maintenance of the tank reduced the market value of their properties. The Court concluded that the plaintiffs had failed to state a cause of action because they had not been deprived of "property within the meaning of that provision as it ha[d] been construed by the courts." The court determined that the plaintiffs had no cause of action because the water district constructed the water tank on its own property. The court found no deprivation of property under the takings clause of the New York Constitution.

Similarly, in the case now before us, the District constructed a water tank on its own property. We conclude that Petitioners have not been deprived of any property rights because the District is acting only upon its property.

The court in *Gervasi* further concluded that "[d]amages cannot be recovered because of the unsightly character of a structure and aesthetic considerations are not compensable in the absence of a legislative provision." . . . we conclude that Petitioners are not entitled to compensation for damages solely because of the unsightly character and the unaesthetic appearance of the water tank.

Following the reasoning of . . . *Pacifica* . . . and *Gervasi*, we conclude that Petitioners do not have a cause of action for inverse condemnation based on their claimed "right to a view." The water tank was a permissible use constructed and maintained solely upon the property of the District.

Property value, or landowners' economic interest in their property, may be considered an essential element of ownership. In *Highline Sch. Dist. 401 v. Port of Seattle*, 548 P.2d 1085 (1976) this court concluded that "an inverse condemnation action for interference with the use and enjoyment of property *accrues when the landowner sustains any measurable loss of market value* . . . " Although *Highline* involved inverse condemnation based on aircraft noise and vibration, the premise that a measurable loss in a market constitutes interference with a landowner's use and enjoyment of property would be applicable in this case only if the decline in market value was caused by unlawful government interference.

In this case, based upon appraisal of Petitioners' property, there is no dispute that there was in fact a measurable loss in market value after construction of the water tank. David E. Hunnicutt conducted an appraisal and concluded that construction of the tank had caused an actual loss in value to Petitioners' property of at least $30,000.00. However, our prior decisions do not lead to the conclusion that loss in market value of Petitioners' property is of itself evidence of governmental interference with the use and enjoyment of property entitling them to compensation. If property, or a substantial portion of that property, is destroyed by the government for a public purpose, the landowner would unquestionably be entitled to compensation. . . . That section, however, does not "authorize compensation merely for a depreciation in market value of property when caused by a legal act."

Petitioners claim they are entitled to compensation because the unaesthetic appearance of the unsightly water tank and the proximity of the tank to their property has caused a loss in market value. This court has not allowed compensation based merely upon proximity of a building or structure.

Petitioners further claim the overbearing presence of the water tank interferes with their use and enjoyment of their property and that they should therefore be compensated for damages. "Damages for which compensation is to be made is a damage to the property itself, and *does not include a mere infringement of the owner's personal*

pleasure or enjoyment. Merely rendering private property less desirable for certain purposes, or even causing personal annoyance or discomfort in it use, will not constitute the damage contemplated . . . but the property itself must suffer some diminution in substance, or be rendered intrinsically less valuable by reason of the public use."

Petitioners are not entitled in this case to just compensation under the takings clause of the Washington Constitution. They cannot establish a property right or interest in their right to a view.[4]

Affirmed.

Case Questions

1. Describe the problem with the placement of the tank and the impact on the Pierces' property.
2. What are the grounds the Pierces use for their claim?
3. Is there a right to a view for which the Pierces are entitled to compensation?
4. Is the right to a view a property interest?

Ethical Issue

In 1997, Donald Trump began construction of his Riverside South project in New York City on a railroad yard located between Lincoln Towers and the Hudson River. The first two towers (of 16 planned) blocked the views of the Lincoln Towers residences. One resident noted, "Can you imagine what this man is taking away? Can you imagine somebody taking away the moon?" Another said, "All of a sudden, here was this thing looming up against the sky. You couldn't see the sky. I felt anger—that someone could be allowed to take away your beauty for money." Those in the Lincoln Towers apartments with views of the Trump project have trouble selling their units and overall have fewer prospects view their units. The price difference between a Trump-facing apartment and one facing the river is $50,000. Evaluate the ethical issues in development projects like Trump's.

SURFACE AND SUBSURFACE RIGHTS

The preceding discussion covered ownership of rights above the land. This section deals with the second part of Blackstone's famous quote, which is the ownership of subsurface rights. Ordinarily, landowners own to the center of the earth, so that mineral rights are included in fee simple absolute ownership. However, landowners are free to convey their subsurface rights as liberally as the air rights can be conveyed. When subsurface rights are conveyed independently of surface rights, there are two different landowners. The owner of the surface rights

---

4.   Some states have begun to classify interference with a view as a nuisance (see infra at page 36). There are also municipalities passing ordinances that prevent interference with views. *Kucera v. Lizza,* 69 Cal. Rptr. 2d 582 (1997). However, the statutes are only for prospective actions and do not grant an easement for, or property rights in, a view.

cannot affect the ownership rights of the subsurface owner. Likewise, the subsurface owner cannot destroy the surface and thereby destroy the surface owner's interest.

Mineral Rights: Oil and Gas Ownership

NATURE OF OIL AND GAS

Oil and gas are petroleum found in liquid and gaseous forms, respectively, beneath the earth's surface. Because oil and gas are not solid like other minerals and will flow from one location to another very readily, this type of property interest presents legal issues not encountered in connection with other subsurface mineral rights.

When oil was first discovered in 1859 at Titusville, Pennsylvania, the courts applied the standard Blackstone adage of he who owns the surface owns what is beneath the surface as well. However, when a well is drilled and oil and gas are brought to the surface, it is impossible to tell whether they came from directly beneath the landowner's surface or were drawn from another pool under adjoining land. Figure 2.2 illustrates the possible conflicting claims of oil and gas ownership between adjoining landowners.

Under Blackstone's rule of subsurface ownership, a landowner pumping oil and gas would be liable to other nearby landowners in the event the well drew oil from reservoirs that extended beneath property owned by others. Such a taking would constitute trespass and would discourage development of the resource. As a result, the courts developed a different rule of ownership for oil and gas rights called the **Rule of Capture.** Simply stated, the rule gives the owner of a tract of land title to all the oil and gas produced by wells located on his or her land even though some of the oil and gas may have migrated from adjoining lands or the well is actually taking oil and gas from a reservoir that stretches across a boundary line onto another's property. This form of ownership protects the driller from liability for trespass so long as the drilling is conducted from his or her property.

http://

Regulations on Nevada mineral rights are at: **http://minerals.state. nv.us**.

FIGURE 2.2   *Oil and Gas Ownership Issues*

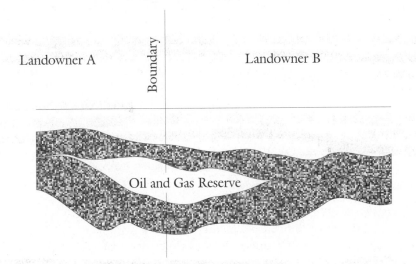

Landowner A   Boundary   Landowner B

Oil and Gas Reserve

However, drilling at an angle would be a physical trespass and is not protected under the Rule of Capture.

Two theories are followed under the Rule of Capture. So-called **ownership states** follow the Rule of Capture but provide that the landowner is the owner of the mineral rights that can be lost only if someone else first captures the oil and gas through drilling. The **nonownership states**—which include California, Louisiana, Oklahoma, and Wyoming—provide that no one owns the oil and gas until it has been captured. The difference between these two theories is simply the status of the rights prior to capture. Once capture has occurred, the rights are identical and vest at the same time under either theory.

The Rule of Capture has limits. For example, the rule does not apply after the gas is first captured by someone and stored in a subsurface or surface area. In other words, once the gas or oil has been captured, someone else cannot tap into the storage area and claim ownership under the Rule of Capture. The rule applies to drilling of oil and gas in their natural as opposed to stored states. Also, the Rule of Capture does not apply to what are referred to as "enhanced recovery operations," or sweeping. These types of processes involve, for example, using high-pressure water systems to drive oil reservoirs from beneath another's property to sweep them into reservoirs on your property so as to capture this oil and gas once it is beneath your land. Again, the Rule of Capture applies to oil and gas located naturally beneath your land or acquired through drilling from your land and not to recovery initiated by artificial shifting of the minerals. Some states permit recovery for trespass against those who use these "sweeping" techniques to recover oil and gas. Others will not permit a trespass action for "sweeping" if it can be shown that the adjoining landowner would not respond to a reasonable and fair proposal for recovery of the oil and gas. The idea behind this immunity for trespass is to encourage the development of the resource.

The **Doctrine of Correlative Rights** is another limitation on the Rule of Capture that imposes a good-faith requirement that no action will be taken that will cause the destruction of the oil and gas beneath the surface to prevent recovery by adjoining landowners. In other words, landowners cannot use the Rule of Capture to take action that prevents others from capturing the resources beneath their property. This type of action could occur if one landowner allowed a well to burn and drain the oil and gas from an adjoining landowner's subsurface reservoir.

A final limitation on the Rule of Capture is government regulation. Both state and federal governments have oil and gas conservation laws to both prevent waste of these resources and control the extent of drilling. For example, well-spacing regulations limit the number of wells that can be erected according to either a per-acre basis or the amount of space between wells. Also, particularly at the federal level, production limitations control the amount of drilling that can be done. Often referred to as **prorationing rules,** they establish limits on daily, weekly, or monthly production. Prorationing rules can be established either to prevent the early exhaustion of a well or to meet fluctuations in the price of oil and gas in the international markets.

CLASSIFICATION OF OIL AND GAS INTERESTS

States vary in their positions as to whether oil and gas rights are real or personal property and what type of property interests they are. For example, some states treat oil and gas rights as a *profit a prendre*, or simply the right to enter the land of another and take a part or product of that land (see page 61). Other states have characterized these interests as fee simple determinables that end upon the Rule of Capture ownership by another. Other states have established a separate set of rules for oil and gas rights and the determination of issues such as trespass and suits to resolve title issues. The classification of oil and gas rights as real or personal property also varies and may largely be determined by taxation statutes that control whether the rights would be taxed as real or personal property under the state's revenue system.

TYPES OF OIL AND GAS INTERESTS

Acquiring the right to drill for oil and gas can take several different forms. For example, many oil firms will refer to the fact that they own a **fee interest.** This form of ownership simply means that the company owns both the surface and subsurface rights. In other words, the firm has a fee simple absolute in the property where it is drilling.

Other firms will state that they own the **mineral rights** or a **mineral interest.** This form of ownership simply means that the subsurface rights have been severed from the surface and air rights, and the company has the right to use the surface to capture the minerals but does not own the surface. This form of ownership affords the owner an easement on the surface to bring in the equipment necessary for drilling. In Louisiana, this form of ownership is called a **mineral servitude.**

A commonly used term, the **oil and gas lease,** is a form of ownership in which a portion of the mineral interest is assigned, usually in exchange for a royalty or share of the profits. A lease is the right to use the surface *and* remove the oil and gas. The lease could be an interest in perpetuity or one that ends when oil and gas are no longer produced. For example, suppose that farmer Adam has fee simple title to his farm and the subsurface rights. Farmer Adam could sell a mineral interest to Exxon. Exxon could then lease the interest to Xavier Oil Company in exchange for a share of the profits. Farmer Adam could also simply lease his mineral interest to Exxon and Exxon could use the surface to recover the oil and gas.

The oil and gas lease may also be used to create a **royalty interest,** which is a share of the oil produced from the land without any payment for the costs of its production. Royalty interests are usually stated in fraction form, such as one-eighth of production. Different amounts and names for royalty interests are used according to whether a landowner, lessee, or mineral interest is involved. Royalty interests are not real property interests. They are very similar to the personal property interest in the form of book royalties.

The various forms of ownership of oil and gas rights have many combinations, and the only limitations seem to be the creativity of those involved in the proposals. Any agreement for oil and gas rights should cover the issues of rights and responsibilities when land ownership is divided in this way between surface and subsurface interests. The issue of liability for damage to the surface caused by the subsurface owner should also be covered.

CREATION OF OIL AND GAS INTERESTS

For purposes of the **Statute of Frauds,** oil and gas interests are treated as real property, and the documents creating these interests, regardless of type, must be in writing. The documents should specify the types of minerals that are to be included if more than oil and gas are covered. For example, in *Western Nuclear, Inc. v. Andrus,* 664 F.2d 234 (10th Cir. 1981), the parties were in a dispute about who owned the right to gravel on a piece of property, because it was unclear whether gravel was a mineral and the mineral rights had been severed from the surface rights.[5]

The agreement should list all forms of consideration to be paid under the agreement whether in the form of full payment for subsurface rights or as a royalty interest or some combination of the various interests.

Geothermal Energy

Another difficulty in the classification of subsurface rights arises in connection with geothermal resources, because of the difficulty of classifying these resources. Because **geothermal energy** consists of steam in rock-surrounded pockets, some states classify it as a water resource and use their water laws to determine ownership and other rights. Other states classify it as an energy resource similar to oil or coal and treat it as a mineral. Some states (such as Idaho) have declared that geothermal resources are neither minerals nor a water resource and have developed a specialized scheme of regulation for this interest in real estate. Parties transferring land with geothermal resources should specify whether title to those areas is conveyed or reserved in the transferor.

The federal government has passed two acts relating to geothermal resources. The Geothermal Steam Act of 1970 (30 U.S.C. §§ 1001 *et seq.*) regulates permits and use, and Geothermal Energy Research, Development, and Demonstration Act (30 U.S.C. §§ 122 *et seq.*), encourage the development of this resource. Much of this resource is found on federal lands.

> ## Practical Tip
>
> Mineral rights are complex and require special details in the sale or lease agreement. The questions to be answered: Who owns the mineral rights? Will ownership be exclusive? Can the surface be used? What is included in the mineral rights? oil? gas? How and when is payment made? How much will the payments be? What happens upon default?

Water Rights

The rights to take water and use water on land are considered to be a real property interest. The rules of law that establish the nature and the extent of a landowner's right to use water vary depending on both the type of water source and the geographic region. The rules of law that developed in the Eastern jurisdictions where water is plentiful are quite different from the rules of law in the West, where water is scarce.

Water rights also vary according to the type of water body involved. The first type is surface or navigable waters, or those that flow. Ownership is considered to be in the states as trustees for the public, subject to any federal rights and programs such as dams and water conservation systems built by the Army Corps of Engineers. Navigable water is defined as water that could be used for navigation regardless of whether it is so used, including natural and artificial lakes, rivers, and streams. Two theories of water rights are applicable to these bodies of waters: the **Riparian Doctrine** and **Prior Appropriation Doctrine.** Most states east of the Mississippi follow the Riparian Doctrine, and the arid Western states follow the Prior Appropriation Doctrine.[6] Some states employ a combination of the two theories.[7]

---

5. In a subsequent case, *Watt v. Western Nuclear, Inc.*, 462 U.S. 36 (1983), the U.S. Supreme court reversed all prior gravel cases (pertaining to federal lands) and held that gravel is indeed a mineral.
6. Alaska, Arizona, Montana, Nevada, Utah, and Wyoming.
7. California, Kansas, Mississippi, Nebraska, North Dakota, Oklahoma, Oregon, South Dakota, Texas, and Washington.

The Riparian Doctrine is based on sharing, and the Prior Appropriation Doctrine is based on "first in time is first in right," or the first to use the water has first claim to it. Figure 2.3 summarizes and compares the two doctrines. (The figure deals only with water use rights and not with the actual ownership of the land [riverbed] beneath the water.)

The title to the riverbeds or land beneath surface water is different from the water rights and may be with the state. Or the state may follow what is known as the **centerline rule,** which provides that the streambed is owned to the center by the abutting landowners.

http://

Look at the history of water rights in New Mexico at: **http://nm.water.usgs.gov/public/publications/biblio75-93.html**.

FIGURE 2.3   *Water Rights*

The Common Law Rules of Riparian Water Rights Compared with and Distinguished from the Doctrine of Prior Appropriation

Common Law Riparian Rules	Prior Appropriation Doctrine
1. THE DISTINGUISHING FEATURES OF THE COMMON LAW RIPARIAN RULES ARE EQUALITY OF RIGHTS AND REASONABLE USE—There is no priority of rights; the reasonable or permitted use by each is limited by a similar use in every other riparian.	1. THE DISTINGUISHING FEATURE OF THE PRIOR APPROPRIATION DOCTRINE IS FIRST IN TIME IS FIRST IN RIGHT—There is no equality of rights and no reasonable use limited by the rights of others.
2. To be a riparian, one needs only to be an owner of riparian land. Riparian land is land that abuts or touches the water of a lake or stream.	2. To be a prior appropriator, one must do four things: (a) have an intent to appropriate water, (b) divert the water from the source of supply, (c) put such water to a beneficial use, and (d) when applicable, follow the necessary administrative procedures.
3. No one can be a riparian who does not own riparian land.	3. One need not own land to be a prior appropriator. There is one exception—in some jurisdictions such as Arizona, if the appropriation is for irrigation purposes then the appropriator must own arable and irrigable land to which that water right is attached.
4. Riparian lands are lands bordering the stream and within the watershed. Under the natural flow theory, a riparian cannot use water on nonriparian lands. Under the reasonable use theory, a riparian may use water on nonriparian lands if such use is reasonable.	4. The prior appropriator may use the appropriated water on riparian and nonriparian lands alike. The character of the land is quite immaterial.
5. Under the common law riparian rules, the use of water for natural purposes is paramount and takes precedence over the use of water for artificial purposes. Natural uses include domestic purposes for the household and drinking, stock watering, and irrigating the garden. Artificial purposes include use for irrigation, power, mining, manufacturing, and industry.	5. The prior appropriation doctrine makes no distinction between uses of water for natural wants and for artificial and industrial purposes.
6. The riparian owner, simply because he owns riparian land, has the right to have the stream of water flow to, by, through, or over his land under the riparian rights doctrine.	6. An owner of land, simply as such owner, has no right to have a stream of water flow to, by, through, or over his land under the prior appropriation doctrine.

continued

FIGURE 2.3   *Water Rights, continued*

The Common Law Rules of Riparian Water Rights Compared with and Distinguished from the Doctrine of Prior Appropriation

Common Law Riparian Rules	Prior Appropriation Doctrine
7. The riparian has the right to have the water in its natural state free from unreasonable diminution in quantity and free from unreasonable pollution in quality.	7. The prior appropriator has the right to the exclusive use of the water free from interference by anyone, reasonable or unreasonable.
8. The rights of the riparians are equal.	8. The rights of the appropriators are never equal.
9. The basis, measure, and limit of the riparian's water right is that of reasonable use (unless natural flow states: limit use to not interrupting the natural flow)	9. The basis, measure, and limit of the water right of the prior appropriator is the beneficial use to which he has put the water. He has no right to waste water. If his needs are smaller than his means of diversion, usually a ditch, then his needs determine his right. If his ditch is smaller than his needs, then the capacity of his ditch determines his right.
10. The doctrine of riparian rights came to this country from the common law of England, although it seems to have had its origin in French law.	10. The doctrine of prior appropriation is statutory in our western states, although its origin seems lost in antiquity.

Reprinted from *Survey of the Law of Real Property*, Ralph E. Boyer, third edition © 1981 with permission of the West Group.

Many landowners have private ponds that are contained solely within the boundaries of their properties. These ponds are considered part of their real estate, and they have all rights in them with the exception of any waters passing through them from upper to lower lands.

Still another type of water is *percolating* or *groundwater*. This type of water is defined to include all subsurface water other than water that flows in underground streams. The waters included in this group are Artesian waters, aquifers, underground lakes or pools, and waters that seep, ooze, or filter from an unknown source. These waters are subject to both the Riparian Doctrine and the Prior Appropriation Doctrine; however, the application of the rules differs because of the nature of the water source.

In the following case, the court discusses the rights of Riparian landowners with respect to government regulation of the use of bodies of water.

Stupak-Thrall v. U.S.

70 F.3d 881 (6th Cir. 1995)

Facts

Kathy Stupak-Thrall and others (plaintiffs) own land on the northern shore of Crooked Lake in Michigan's Upper Peninsula near the Wisconsin border. Under Michigan law, these property owners are riparians and as such are given the right to use the surface of the lake including those uses "absolutely necessary for the existence of the riparian proprietor and his family, such as to quench thirst and for household purposes." Additional permissible riparian uses include "those which merely increase one's comfort and prosperity/ . . . such as commercial profit and recreation."

The United States is also a riparian owner along Crooked Lake because about 95 percent of the lake's shoreline lies within the Sylvania Wilderness Area, a national wilderness administered by the Forest Service.

In 1992, the Forest Service adopted regulations (Amendment 1) that prohibit "sail-powered watercraft," "watercraft designed for or used as floating living quarters," and "nonburnable disposable food and beverage containers" on the lake. The regulations also discouraged use of electronic fish-finders, boom boxes, and any other mechanical or battery-operated devices.

Stupak-Thrall and other property owners filed suit challenging the authority of the federal government to regulate lake use on several grounds including their rights as riparians. The federal district court found for the Forest Service and the landowners appealed.

Judicial Opinion

Moore, Circuit Judge. . . . riparian rights are not absolute. Michigan law divides riparian uses into uses for "natural purposes," which are "those absolutely necessary for the existence of the riparian proprietor," and uses related to "artificial purposes," which are "those which merely increase one's comfort and prosperity." Each use for an artificial purpose must be for the benefit of the underlying land and reasonable in light of the correlative rights of the other proprietors. In other words, riparian uses such as sailing, waterskiing, and swimming are subject to "reasonable use" limitations and may not interfere materially with other riparian owners' similar rights. In *Thompson v. Enz*, 154 N.W.2d 473 (Mich. 1967), the court stated that a finding of reasonableness should center on three factors: (1) the "watercourse and its attributes," (2) the "use itself" and its effect on the water, and (3) the "consequential effects" on other riparian proprietors and the state.

We do not agree that the "reasonable use" doctrine governs the federal government's actions in this case. Although the *Thompson* decision is important here because it shows that the riparian rights of private citizens are not absolute under Michigan law, the "reasonable use" doctrine itself only makes sense when one riparian owner challenges another's use as unreasonable and the court makes a subsequent determination of reasonableness. It is inapplicable when one riparian proprietor unilaterally decides to ban certain uses of others, whether or not the uses themselves are unreasonable, and whether or not the banning proprietor actually has the power to do so. Indeed, the federal government's ability to impose restrictions does not stem from its status as a fellow riparian proprietor; it stems from its status as a sovereign. Its authority to regulate cannot come from a state law doctrine that merely balances the property rights of private owners vis-a-vis one another.

. . . the Forest Service possesses a power delegated to it by Congress that is "analogous to the police power," and its exercise of this federal power does not violate Congress's express limitation deferring to "existing" state law rights in wilderness act, so long as it does not exceed the bounds of permissible police power regulation under state law.

Amendment 1's purpose of preserving wilderness character is undoubtedly a proper aim under the Property Clause's police power and under Congress's delegation to the Forest Service, and the prohibition of certain forms of mechanical transport and certain types of food containers on Crooked Lake is certainly rationally related to achieving this goal.

Given the "minimal impact on plaintiffs' riparian uses of Crooked Lake," we conclude that the Forest Service's restrictions here are a valid exercise of the police power under state law, and they are therefore a valid exercise of the police power conferred on the Forest Service by the Property Clause and limited by Congress's express reservation for state law rights in the wilderness acts.

Affirmed.

Case Questions

1. What regulations were considered objectionable?
2. What rights did riparians have under Michigan law?
3. Are riparian rights subject to government regulation?
4. What advice could you offer those who purchase property near government-controlled wilderness areas?

Shanty Hollow Corporation was issued a permit by the New York State Department of Environmental Conservation to withdraw water from Schoharie Creek for purposes of its snowmaking equipment. Shanty Hollow operates a winter sport recreational area. The Catskill Center for Conservation and Development, property owners along the creek, and anglers brought suit against both the state and Shanty Hollow for excessive withdrawal of water from the creek. What is the result under the Riparian Doctrine? In contrast, what would be the result under the Prior Appropriation Doctrine? Like the *Stupak-Thrall* case, could there be a justification on the grounds that water use needs to be regulated? *Catskill Center v. NY Dept. of Environ.*, 642 N.Y.S.2d 986 (1996)

Consider 2.1

Water Rights at the Crossroads

The discussion of water rights presented here is the longstanding law. However, this area of real estate law has proven to be a dynamic one over the past few years because of the role of environmental regulation (see Chapter 20 for more information on environmental regulations on water user). Some scholars have written that the prior appropriation doctrine is often at odds with environmental goals and have encouraged government intervention regardless of water rights. For example, many state and local authorities have intervened in water-use and water-level issues because of public safety or issues surrounding the flora and fauna in or around the water. For example, in *Wortelboer v. Benzie County*, 537 N.W.2d 603 (Mich. App. 1995), the court upheld the right of the state to maintain lake levels to avoid the death of fish and the resulting smell.

Development projects that involve water (see Chapter 22 for more information on development) have been subjected to municipal and county reviews for project approval. California courts have noted that the traditional lines of legal reasoning on water rights and use have been changed to broader ones that are based primarily on whether the water use is "reasonable or wasteful." *Imperial Irrigation District v. State Water Resources Control Board*, 225 Cal. App.3d 548 (1990).

Thompson on Real Property summarizes the changes in water rights and their relationship to real property as follows: "Although the general rule is that water rights are a species of real property, that designation refers to the right of access to the water while it is in its natural state. Once the right is exercised and water is reduced to possession, it may be considered personal property of the water-right holder. As such, it may become an article of commerce." So the distinction between the traditional laws of real property and the new trends is that the proposed commercial use of water once it is captured pursuant to the legal rights can be regulated by various government entities. These entities now grapple with those who sell their riparian rights, for example, to nonriparians. The issue becomes one of deciding whether to honor the real property origins of water rights and the reliance land owners have placed on that system or to intervene for the sake of allocation of a scarce resource, protection of the environment, and easier commercial transfers. In resolving the issue, states, local governments and courts have asked whether cities should have higher priorities than the countryside, whether government can intervene for protection of water quality, whether water can be moved to address shortages and allocation proposals and who will do the moving, and what the legal status of water rights should be. Perhaps at the heart of evolving changes in water rights is the classic economic issue of supply and demand. Water shortages were not a uniform issue at the time the traditional water rights were de eloped. Intervention may be necessary, and the law is adjusting to permit intervention with private property rights.

PROTECTION OF PROPERTY RIGHTS

Trespass

Trespass is defined as the intentional interference with landowners' reasonable use and enjoyment of their property. General examples of trespass include parties' walking across another property owner's land or placing objects on another's land, although trespass can also arise from indirect objects intentionally set in motion by the trespasser. For example, if one landowner were to dam water so that it flooded an adjoining landowner's property, trespass has occurred. Even the simple act of opening shutters so that they extend across a boundary line to an adjoining property owner's land is an act of trespass. Bullets fired across the land of another also constitute trespass. In one unique trespass case, a child hurled a brick at a neighbor. When the neighbor reached across the boundary line and grabbed the child, he committed not only the torts of assault and battery but also that of trespass.

Practical Tip

Landowners faced with periodic trespassers should take precautions in protecting themselves from liability. Signs and barriers should be erected so that trespassers do not gradually become classified as guests because of the owners' implied acquiescence through inaction. Furthermore, if physical action does not stop the trespass, a court injunction or damages may be appropriate so that the landowners have judicial records of their positions on and relationships to trespassers.

Brian Barton, Craig Barton, and Timothy Barton are brothers who acquired 53.5 acres of wooded property in Gray, Maine, from their grandmother. The property was bordered on the east by land belonging to Gordon Fraser. In 1987, the Barton brothers hired a contractor to harvest timber from their land. Because of several errors the Barton brothers' father had made in laying out the boundary lines, the contractor cut and removed trees valued at $9,742.84 from Fraser's property. Fraser brought suit against the Bartons for trespass. Was there a trespass? Who is liable for the trespass? *Fraser v. Barton,* 628 A.2d 146 (Me. 1993)

Consider 2.2

Nuisance

"Use your own property in such a manner as not to injure that of another [*Sic vere tuo et alienum non laedas*]." **Nuisance** is the unreasonable interference with others' use and enjoyment of their property. Nuisances are generally thought of as bad odors and excessive noise. Pollutants from a factory causing property damage and medical problems can constitute a nuisance. "A nuisance may be merely a right thing in the wrong place, like a pig in the parlor instead of the barnyard."[8]

Nuisances can be classified as private, public, or frequently a cross between the two. A nuisance affecting one property owner or a small group of property owners is a private nuisance. For example, a restaurant's storage of garbage bins behind a store is a private nuisance affecting the immediate neighbors.

However, the burning of used car materials to salvage metal can create smoke and smells affecting an entire community and would thus be labeled a public nuisance.

The remedies for nuisance usually fall into one of two categories: monetary or equitable relief. **Monetary relief** is compensation for illness and medical expenses or compensation for the reduction in property values because of the nuisance. For example, destruction of plants or paint caused by pollutants would be compensable. **Equitable relief** is injunctive relief where the nuisance-creating party is ordered by a court to cease the nuisance-creating activity. This injunctive relief is used sparingly since in some circumstances the result will be the closing of a business. In determining whether injunctive relief will be afforded, courts

Practical Tip

Verify property boundaries prior to sale, lease, purchase, listing, construction, landscaping, or excavation of that property.

8.   *Village of Euclid, Ohio v. Amber Realty Co.,* 272 U.S. 365 (1926).

balance the extent of the property owner's harm against the beneficial aspects of the wrongdoer's conduct. The following case deals with both a trespass issue and a nuisance issue, particularly in balancing landowners' interests against the economic interests of others as well as the interests of the public in a suit where the landowners have requested injunctive relief.

Jordan v. Georgia Power Co.

466 S.E.2d 601 (Ga. App. 1995)

Facts

Larry Jordan purchased property in Douglas County, Georgia, in 1972. At the time of the purchase, Jordan was aware of an easement Georgia Power held in the property. Power lines were built on the property in 1973. Mr. Jordan married Nancy in 1983 and she then moved into his home. In 1985, Nancy Jordan was diagnosed with breast cancer, and in 1989, she was diagnosed with non-Hodgkin's lymphoma. In 1990, the Jordans moved from the property but had a difficult time selling the house. The bank foreclosed on the property because it did not sell, and Larry Jordan could no longer continue to make double payments on their new house and the old one.

The Jordans filed suit in 1991 against Georgia Power Company and Olgethrope Power Corporation, alleging that electromagnetic radiation from the electromagnetic fields (EMFs) created by the presence of the power lines on their property caused Mrs. Jordan's breast cancer and lymphoma. Their suit alleged both trespass and nuisance. The trial court found for the power company and the Jordans appealed.

Judicial Opinion

Pope, Presiding Judge. The Jordans claim that the court erred in granting summary judgment on their trespass claim. They argue that the court invaded the province of the jury.

In their motion for summary judgment, Oglethorpe and Georgia Power argued that EMFs are not tangible matter and that their alleged presence on the Jordans' property could not constitute a trespass. In response, the Jordans filed the affidavit of Roy Martin, a licensed professional electrical engineer, in which he stated that electromagnetic radiation from high power lines is tangible. Martin further stated that a magnetic field could be detected and measured by appropriate measuring devices and that such fields obeyed physical laws.

In its order granting the motion, the court concluded that although the Jordans claimed that there was a detectable entry on their property by the EMF's, these fields were not tangible as defined by law for purpose of

trespass determinations. The court stated: "in Georgia a physical invasion of some kind is required in order to state a cause of action for trespass. There has been no physical injury to the real estate alleged. There has been no physical entry alleged. The plaintiffs allege there is a detectable entry by non-tangible, magnetic fields. However, such fields are not tangible as that term is defined by law for purpose of trespass determination."

OCGA Section 1-3-3(20) provides: "This '[t]respass' means any misfeasance, transgression, or offense which damages another's health, reputation or property." With respect to injuries to real estate, OCGA Section 51-9-1 defines the cause of action for interference with enjoyment of property, stating: "[t]he right of enjoyment of private property being an absolute right of every citizen, every act of another which unlawfully interferes with such enjoyment is a tort for which an action shall lie."

Although arguably the Jordans' trespass action could present a jury question, we conclude that for policy reasons, the trial court's grant of summary judgment was proper. The scientific evidence regarding whether EMF's cause harm of any kind is inconclusive; the invasive quality of these electric fields cannot generally constitute a trespass. In reaching this conclusion, we do not close the door on the possibility that science may advance to a point at which damage from EMF's is legally cognizable and a trespass action may lie.

The Jordans claim that the court erred by granting a directed verdict on the nuisance and property damage claims. In directing the verdict, the court concluded that there were no measurable damages or injury and that there was no nuisance.

Here, the Jordans argue that the court's conclusion that there was no evidence of property damage ignored the fact that the trial was bifurcated as to damages and causation. They contend that because of the bifurcation, evidence of nominal damages was sufficient to prove this claim.

OCGA Section 41-1-1 defines a nuisance as "anything that causes hurt, inconvenience, or damage to another and the fact that the act done may otherwise be lawful shall not keep it from being a nuisance. The inconvenience complained of shall not be fanciful, or such as would affect only one of fastidious taste, but it shall be such as would affect an ordinary, reasonable man." Moreover, "while a physical invasion is generally necessary, noise, odors and smoke which impair the landowners' enjoyment of his [*sic*] property are also actionable nuisances, if, and only if, a partial condemnation of the property results."

Here, the trial court properly directed a verdict on the nuisance claim. . . . the present state of science does not authorize recovery based on these facts.

While the court found there was no cause of action for trespass or nuisance, it did reverse the case for error

on evidence admissibility and for retrial on the other grounds the Jordans alleged for liability including negligence.

Reversed on other grounds.

Case Questions

1. What do the Jordans allege occurred as a result of the power lines being located on their property?
2. Is it important that the Jordans could not sell their house?
3. What is missing that is needed to establish nuisance?
4. What is missing that is needed to establish a trespass?

Spur Industries operates a cattle feedlot near Youngtown and Sun City (communities 14 to 15 miles west of Phoenix). Spur had been operating the feedlot since 1956, and the area had been agricultural since 1911.

In 1959 Del E. Webb began development of the Sun City area, a retirement community. Webb purchased the 20,000 acres of land for about $750 per acre.

In 1960 Spur began an expansion program in which it grew from an operation of five acres to 115 acres. Webb began to experience sales resistance on the lots nearest Spur's business because of strong odors. Nearly 1,300 lots could not be sold. Webb then filed suit alleging Spur's operation was a nuisance because of flies and odors constantly drifting over Sun City.

At the time of the suit, Spur was feeding between 20,000 and 30,000 head of cattle, which produced 35 to 40 pounds of wet manure per head per day, or over one million pounds per day. How should the court rule? Should it make any difference that Spur was there first? How does the court balance retirement communities and beef production being two of Arizona's biggest industries? *Spur Industries, Inc. v. Del E. Webb Development Co.*, 494 P.2d 700 (Az. 1972)

> **Consider 2.3**

In each of the following circumstances, determine whether a nuisance is involved, whether it is public or private, and what remedy would be appropriate. Determine any additional facts that would aid in the decision.

> **Consider 2.4**

a. Damage and annoyance caused by blasting in a nearby quarry (the town developed because of the quarry)
b. Operation of a dog kennel
c. Construction of a proposed nuclear power plant
d. A neighbor with 55 cats residing in her three-bedroom/1200 square-feet home

DUTIES OF LANDOWNERS

In addition to avoiding the problems of trespass and nuisance, landowners owe certain responsibilities to those entering their property. Those parties entering property are classified into one of three categories: trespassers, licensees, and invitees. Traditionally, each category has a different status when on another's property, and landowners owe different degrees of responsibility to those in each category. While these differing categories and duties are discussed here, states are blending together the responsibilities and degree of care more and more so that the standard becomes one of reasonable care.

Trespassers

Trespassers are persons on the property of another without permission. Landowners may take the appropriate actions to seek removal of the trespassers, but while trespassers are on their property, landowners have only the responsibility of not intentionally injuring them—that is, landowners may not intentionally injure trespassers or erect mantraps to injure or kill trespassers.

Licensees

Licensees are persons on the property of another who have some form of permission to be there. For example, in most states, fire protectors, police officers, and medical personnel would be classified as licensees. These groups have an implied invitation to a landowner's property so that their services are available to the landowner when needed. It is possible that meter readers would be classified as licensees because the implied invitation arises from the use of the utility or service. In some states, social guests are classified as licensees because although there may not be an express invitation to all social guests, an implied invitation arises from friendship.

To the licensees, landowners owe a greater duty of care. In addition to the duty not to injure intentionally is the responsibility of warning licensees of any defects of which landowners have knowledge. Thus, landowners must warn of broken steps, cracked concrete, or dangerous animals.

Practical Tip

Many malls and shopping centers are providing additional security guards. Grocery stores often mandate that customers be accompanied by an employee when they return to their cars in the parking lot. The issue of potential liability to their invitees has taken new prominence in security procedures for commercial areas.

Invitees

Invitees are persons on the property of another by express invitation. Every public place offers an express invitation to all members of the public. Customers are always invitees in places of business. A repair person on the premises to fix a washer or refrigerator is there at the landowner's express request. Invitees are afforded the greatest degree of protection by landowners. Landowners must exercise reasonable care to protect invitees from injury. This generally includes the duty not only to warn invitees of any defects of which they have knowledge but also to inspect their property for defects and take reasonable steps to correct them. For example, a leaf of lettuce on the floor in the produce section of a grocery store is a hazard for invitees. Grocery store owners are required to periodically check and sweep aisle areas to protect invitees. Figure 2.4 provides a summary view of landowner liability and duty.

Consider 2.5   Classify each of the following parties in terms of landowners' responsibilities. Describe the landowner's duty to each.

a. Paramedic
b. Customer in a department store
c. Marketing researcher doing a door-to-door survey
d. Burglar

FIGURE 2.4   *Landowner Duties and Liabilities*

Type of Person Entering Property	Landowner Duty	Liability*
Trespasser	Not to intentionally injure	Liable for intentional injury; mantraps, automatic traps, etc.
Licensee	Not to intentionally injure	Correct defects aware of; Liability for intentional injury; injury caused by known defects
Invitee	Not to intentionally injure; Correct defects aware of or should be aware exist	Above, plus liability for should-have-known-defects

*   There are variations from state-to-state. For example some states classify social guests as licensees whereas, others classify them as invitees, hence changing the duties and liability of the landowners.

Breach of Duty

A landowner's breach of any of the above responsibilities can result in the imposition of tremendous liability, especially if the trespasser, licensee, or invitee is seriously injured. Landowners must be cautious in exercising their responsibilities and can be further protected through maintenance of adequate insurance.

The following case deals with an evolving and important area of the liability of landowners. The case involves an issue of the landowner's liability to invitees when the invitee is injured by the criminal activity of a third party.

Delta Tau Delta v. Johnson

712 N.E.2d 968 (Ind. 1999)

Facts

Delta Tau Delta (DTD) is a fraternity located on the campus of Indiana University at Bloomington and is the local chapter for the national DTD. On October 13, 1990, Tracey D. Johnson, an undergraduate student at Indiana University, attended a party at the DTD fraternity house, at the invitation of a DTD member.

When Johnson arrived at the DTD house at about 10:00 P.M., the beer was flowing and the atmosphere was rather chaotic. At about midnight, as Johnson and her friends prepared to leave the party, they encountered Joseph Motz, an alumnus of DTD who had driven into Bloomington that day for the football game. Motz brought along his own case of beer, which he kept in room C17 of the DTD house. At the time of this encounter, Motz had already quaffed four to five beers.

While Johnson and Motz spoke, Johnson's friends left and she was without a ride to her home. Motz offered to drive her home and she agreed, but only after he had

sobered up some. The two went to C17, where they had some hard liquor and listened to music with other guests.

Sometime between 3:30 and 4:00 A.M., Johnson searched for a ride again and Motz offered again, whereupon Johnson again required that he become sober. Motz then locked himself and Johnson alone into C17 and Motz sexually assaulted her there.

Johnson field suit against Motz and DTD, both the local and the national fraternities. The trial court denied motions by DTD for summary judgment, the Court of Appeals reversed all the denials and the parties appealed to the Indiana Supreme Court. (Note: Motz pled guilty to sexual battery.)

Judicial Opinion

Selby, Justice. The question of whether and to what extent landowners owe any duty to protect their invitees from the criminal acts of third parties has been the subject of substantial debate among the courts and legal scholars in the past decade. See, e.g., *McClung v. Delta Square Ltd. Partnership*, 937 S.W.2d 891, 897 (*Tenn.* 1996) (noting that the debate caused the court to reconsider its law in this area). The majority of courts that have addressed this issue agree that, while landowners are not to be made the insurers of their invitees' safety, landowners do have a duty to take reasonable precautions to protect their invitees from foreseeable criminal attacks. Indiana courts have not held otherwise.

A further question arises, however, in that courts employ different approaches to determine whether a criminal act was foreseeable such that a landowner owed a duty to take reasonable care to protect an invitee from the criminal act. There are four basic approaches that courts use to determine foreseeability in this context: (1) The specific harm test, (2) the prior similar incidents test (PSI) (3) the totality of the circumstances test, and (4) the balancing test.

Under the specific harm test, a landowner owes no duty unless the owner knew or should have known that the specific harm was occurring or was about to occur. Most courts are unwilling to hold that a criminal act is foreseeable only in these situations.

Under the prior similar incidents test, a landowner may owe a duty of reasonable care if evidence of prior similar incidents of crime on or near the landowner's property shows that the crime in question was foreseeable. Although courts differ in the application of this rule, all agree that the important factors to consider are the number of prior incidents, their proximity in time and location to the present crime, and the similarity of the crimes. Courts differ in terms of how proximate and similar the prior crimes are required to be as compared to the current crime.

The public policy considerations are that under the PSI test the first victim in all instances is not entitled to recover, landowners have no incentive to implement even nominal security measures, the test incorrectly focuses on the specific crime and not the general risk of foreseeable harm, and the lack of prior similar incidents relieves a defendant of liability when the criminal act was, in fact, foreseeable.

Under the totality of the circumstances test, a court considers all of the circumstances surrounding an event, including the nature, condition, and location of the land, as well as prior similar incidents, to determine whether a criminal act was foreseeable.

Courts that employ this test usually do so out of dissatisfaction with the limitations of the prior similar incidents test. The most frequently cited limitation of this test is that it tends to make the foreseeability question too broad and unpredictable, effectively requiring that landowners anticipate crime.

Under the final approach, the balancing test, a court balances "the degree of foreseeability of harm against the burden of the duty to be imposed." In other words, as the foreseeability and degree of potential harm increase, so, too, does the duty to prevent against it. This test still relies largely on prior similar incidents in order to ensure that an undue burden is not placed upon landowners.

We agree with those courts that decline to employ the specific harm test and prior similar incidents test. We find that the specific harm test is too limited in its determination of when a criminal act is foreseeable. While the prior similar incidents test has certain appeal, we find that this test has the potential to unfairly relieve landowners of liability in some circumstances when the criminal act was reasonably foreseeable.

As between the totality of the circumstances and balancing tests, we find that the totality of the circumstances test is the more appropriate. The balancing test seems to require that the court ask whether the precautions which plaintiff asserts should have been taken were unreasonably withheld given the foreseeability of the criminal attack. In other words, the question is whether defendant took reasonable precautions given the circumstances. We believe that this is basically a breach of duty evaluation and is best left for the jury to decide.

On the other hand, the totality of the circumstances test permits courts to consider all of the circumstances to determine duty. In our view and the view of other state supreme courts, the totality of the circumstances test does not impose on landowners the duty to ensure an invitee's safety, but requires landowners to take reasonable precautions to prevent foreseeable criminal acts against invitees.

Applying the totality of the circumstances test to the facts of this case, we hold that DTD owed Johnson a duty of reasonable care. Within two years of this case, two specific incidents occurred which warrant consideration. First, in March 1988, a student was assaulted by a fraternity member during an alcohol party at DTD. Second, in April 1989 at DTD, a blindfolded female was made, against her will, to drink alcohol until she was sick and was pulled up out of the chair and spanked when she refused to drink. In addition, the month before this sexual assault occurred, DTD was provided with information from National concerning rape and sexual assault of college campuses. Amongst other information, DTD was made aware that "1 in 4 college women have either been raped or suffered attempted rape," that "75% of male students and 55% of female students involved in date rape had been drinking or using drugs," that "the group most likely to commit gang rape on the college campus was the fraternity," and that fraternities at seven universities had "recently experienced legal action taken against them for rape and/or sexual assault." We believe that to hold that a sexual assault in this situation was not foreseeable, as a matter of law, would ignore the facts and allow DTD to flaunt the warning signs at the risk of all of its guests.

As a landowner under these facts, DTD owed Johnson a duty to take reasonable care to protect her from a foreseeable sexual assault. It is now for the jury to decide whether DTD breached this duty, and, if so, whether the breach proximately caused Johnson's injury. While this may be the exceptional case wherein a landowner in a social host situation is held to have a duty to take reasonable care to protect an invitee from the criminal acts of another, when the landowner is in a position to take reasonable precautions to protect his guest from a foreseeable criminal act, courts should not hesitate to hold that a duty exists.

The final issue which Johnson raises is whether National owed her a duty of care. Johnson contends that genuine issues of material fact exist concerning whether National assumed such a duty. Specifically, Johnson argues that National undertook actions which raise the inference that it assumed a duty to protect against date rape and alcohol abuse. Thus, she concludes, the trial court was correct to deny National's motion for summary judgment.

In the present case, the most compelling evidence which Johnson presents in support of her claim refers to a series of posters which National sent DTD to hang for the public to see. These posters professed that the Delta Tau Delta Fraternity was a leading fighter against date rape and alcohol abuse, and they were placed, by DTD, in places where they could be seen by the public. These posters do not create an inference that National gratuitously assumed a duty. For example, one poster stated that, "It may come as a surprise, but one of the most active organizations in the fight against alcohol abuse, date rape and hazing is a fraternity." Another stated that, "while date rape may be all too commonplace an occurrence, there's absolutely no place for it at Delta Tau Delta." The posters did not profess to have security available as did the pamphlet in *Ember*, nor did they state that one could call National for help with problems such as date rape or alcohol abuse. This Court, therefore, while it expresses no review with regard to any other theory of liability, reverses the trial court's denial of summary judgement [*sic*] on the gratuitous assumption of duty theory.

We vacate the Court of Appeals decision and affirm the trial court in part and reverse the trial court in part.

Affirmed in part and reversed in part.

Case Questions

1. What duty does a landowner owe to invitees for protection against criminal activity by third parties?
2. What evidence existed that DTD knew there was a risk of date rape?
3. List the differences between the "totality of circumstances" test, the "prior similar incidents" test, the "specific harm" test, and the "balancing" test.
4. Will the case eventually be decided by a jury?

Jane Doe, a 16-year-old runaway, using a pass obtained by another person, entered the Brainerd International Raceway (BIR) to watch the Quaker State Northstar National race. Doe indulged in alcohol and drugs, which were supplied to her by other patrons at the race.

An annual tradition at the race was a wet T-shirt contest. Flyers had been printed advertising the contest, and they were posted at the raceway at the time of the race. Doe participated in the contest, which began with sopping of the contestants' clothes and ended with Doe completely naked and subjected to crowd (consisting of 2,000 to 3,000 men) fondling for 45 minutes, all of which was captured on a videotape by one of the spectators.

Doe filed suit contending that BIR had breached its duty to her as an invitee in its failure to warn her about the contest and by not providing adequate security at the event. BIR maintains that Doe was a trespasser who did not have a valid pass for the event, which required that pass holders be age 18 or above.

Doe has requested damages for BIR's breach of duty as the property owner. Was Doe a trespasser or an invitee? Should BIR be held liable? *Doe v. Brainerd International Raceway*, 514 N.W.2d 811 (Ct. App. Minn. 1994)

Consider 2.6

CAUTIONS AND CONCLUSIONS

The discussion in this chapter has centered on ownership of land and what is included as part of that land. To avoid problems in this area, there are several circumstances in which the parties should take precautions. In the first circumstance, a buyer is purchasing property, and all parties (seller, buyer, agents, and financiers) should analyze the sale with the following questions:

1. What water is available? Are the water rights protected?
2. Are mineral rights being transferred? What minerals are included? If minerals are not being transferred, who owns them and what do they own? What land use rights do they have? What are the royalties or payments and who is entitled to receive them?
3. Is light available to the buildings, landscaping, and solar panels? If not, is an easement possible? Will future structures block the light?
4. Are the column and air lots included or have they been transferred? Who owns them?
5. Is air traffic unusually burdensome, close, or noisy?
6. Do any nuisances such as pollution, smell, or insects exist? Can they be remedied?
7. Are there any persons using the property? Do they hold any rights or are they trespassers?

Failure to check on these seven factors can result in losses to the buyer and the possible imposition of liability on the seller or the broker or agent for failing to disclose relevant information.

In the second circumstance, a property owner wishes to convey mineral rights and may be faced with a complex and lengthy document. The situation may be clarified by answering the following questions:

1. What interest is being conveyed? What minerals? Subsurface only? Fee simple interest? Lease? Right of removal?
2. What rights are given on surface use? Will the lessee pay for restoration?
3. How much is the royalty? Are there any other fees to be paid? If no minerals are drawn, is there any payment?
4. Can the land be sold to someone else? Who gets the royalties?
5. Can they transfer the mineral rights to someone else? Will the same restrictions apply?

In the third and final circumstance, property owners are responsible for the way they use their property and may want to answer these questions in assessing potential liability:

1. Are there significant noises, smells, or other emissions from the property? Do they interfere with others' use and enjoyment of their own property?
2. Are there individuals using the property in an unauthorized manner? Are there trespassers? Are there any mantraps to injure them? Have steps been taken to prevent trespass?
3. Are there licensees on the property or potentially on the property? Are there appropriate signs and methods of warning them of dangers?

4. Do invitees enter the property? Are there any dangerous conditions? Have they been remedied? Are periodic inspections done to find and eliminate dangerous conditions?

5. Are nuisances from others affecting the property? Can action be taken to stop the conduct or recover damages?

The topics in this chapter have significant impact on landowners in various circumstances. The preceding questions integrate the topics and serve as a checklist to prevent or minimize legal problems

Key Terms

air rights, 17
column lot, 20
air lot, 20
solar easement laws, 21
Doctrine of Ancient Lights, 22
Rule of Capture, 27
ownership states, 28
nonownership states, 28
Doctrine of Correlative Rights, 28
prorationing rules, 28

profit a prendre, 28
fee interest, 29
mineral rights, 29
mineral interest, 29
mineral servitude, 29
oil and gas lease, 29
royalty interest, 29
Statute of Frauds, 29
geothermal energy, 30
water rights, 30

Riparian Doctrine, 30
Prior Appropriation Doctrine, 30
centerline rule, 31
trespass, 34
nuisance, 35
monetary relief, 35
equitable relief, 35
trespassers, 38
licensees, 38
invitees, 38

Chapter Problems

1. In 1962, Rudolph and Bonnie Sher entered into a long-term lease agreement with Stanford University. The lot they leased was in a residential subdivision on the campus known as Pine Hill 2. Design approval by Stanford was required prior to construction of any homes on the lots. Herbert and Gloria Leiderman leased their lot located next to the Shers shortly after the Shers had signed their lease agreement.

The Shers' home was designed and built to take advantage of the winter sun for heat and light. Their home was placed on the lot so that its length faced the south. The windows on the south of their home are larger than the other windows in the house. The south side of the house is serrated to expose the maximum area to the sun. Roof overhangs were designed and constructed to block sun in the summer and permit winter sunlight to enter the home. Deciduous trees and shrubs on the south side of the house aid in shading and cooling in the summer, yet allow winter sunlight to reach the house. The Sher home is known as a "passive" solar home because it does not make use of any active solar collectors or panels.

The Leidermans undertook a landscaping scheme designed to attract birds and other small creatures and provide shade and privacy. By 1972, the Leiderman trees were casting shadows on the Sher house in the winter. The offending trees were removed at the Shers' expense. By 1979, the Shers had spent $4,000 on tree maintenance and removal in the Leidermans' yard. In 1979, the Leidermans refused to allow any further trimming at anyone's expense.

As a result of the ever-expanding trees, the Sher's house was cast in shadow between 10:00 A.M. and 2:00 P.M. A skylight was added in the kitchen but had little impact. Heat loss from the shadows amounted to 60 therms of natural gas. The Shers brought suit on the grounds of private nuisance, violation of the California Solar Shade Control Act, and negligent infliction of emotional distress. Is the Leidermans' landscaping a nuisance? Does it violate the Shade Control Act? Is it significant that the case involves passive solar devices and not solar panel access? *Sher v. Leiderman*, 226 Cal. Rptr. 698 (Cal. App. 1986)

2. Barclay and Marjorie Sloan own property directly north of and higher than the property of Robert, Joe, and Myrtle Wallbaum. Water drained from the Sloans' property through the Wallbaums' property through a grassy drainage ditch. In 1985, the Sloans tiled their land and had the ditch sloped and somewhat straightened.

The result was erosion on the Wallbaums' property. The Wallbaums then blocked the ditch with a piece of tin and later fill dirt. The result was that the Sloans' property became flooded. The Sloans filed suit for an injunction ordering the removal of the blockage the Wallbaums had installed. Are the Sloans entitled to the injunction? Discuss the water rights issues (*Sloan v. Wallbaum,* 447 N.W.2d 148 [Iowa 1989]).

3. Glen Prah constructed a residence during 1978 and 1979. He installed solar collectors on the roof for purposes of supplying energy for heat and hot water. Richard Maretti purchased the lot adjacent to Prah's and submitted proposed home plans that would result in a substantial obstruction of Prah's solar collectors and a corresponding reduction in the system's output and efficiency. Prah brought suit claiming that the construction of the home would be a private nuisance. If Maretti simply repositioned the layout of his home, the impact on Prah's system would be reduced, but Maretti has refused because his plans are in compliance with all zoning ordinances and other regulations. What factors should the court examine in balancing the parties' interests (*Prah v. Maretti,* 321 N.W.2d 182 [Wis. 1982])?

4. Bruce Rankin occupies real estate in rural Platt County, Illinois, that is zoned for agricultural use. He has lived there since 1959 and, along with a partner, operates a business from his house known as Williams Trigger Specialties. In this business, Rankin, a federally registered gunsmith, works on firearm firing mechanisms.

Also located on the property, which has also been there since 1959, is a firing range. Rankin allows his friends to use the firing range in addition to using it himself. He does not permit strangers to use it. In the last several years, he has also permitted various law-enforcement agencies to use the range for training, practice, and qualification, including the Champaign Police Department, the Urbana Police Department, and the Ludlow Police Department. The Champaign Police Department Strategic Weapons and Tactics (SWAT) team, consisting of 12 people, has used the range 10 to 15 times in the last year.

Rankin has never charged a fee for use of the range. He has, however, considered putting his range to commercial use at some time in the future. Rankin is almost always present when the range is used by private individuals other than law-enforcement agencies. There has never been an injury or near injury or complaint to Rankin about the range or its use.

Charles Kolstad owns the property immediately west of Rankin's parcel. Mary Heath Hays and Mary Lucille Hays reside on another parcel of land to the west of Rankin's parcel. Kolstad and Mary Lucille Hays have children who play together.

The Kolstads and Hays lived with the noise from the gunshots but on October 4, 1988, they became alarmed when the new noise of rapid short bursts of gunfire

sounded. Kolstad recognized the noise as the firing of automatic weapons. Both neighbors became concerned about their safety and filed suit for an injunction to halt the use of the property as a firing range. Should the court issue an injunction? Should it be an absolute prohibition on operation of the range or something less (*Kolstad v. Rankin,* 534 N.E.2d 1373 [Ill. 1989])?

5. The Great Cove Boat Club had a wharf on the Piscataqua River in Maine. The Bureau of Public Lands, in its work for the preservation of public waterways, entered into lease agreements with private parties so that they could create and operate wharfs, floats, and moorings for public enjoyment. One such 30-year lease resulted in construction of public access wharfs that flooded the area of the Great Cove's wharf cutting off access by the owners. Great Cove claimed, as a riparian, that its rights had been violated through the use of the water in such a fashion that its water access rights were destroyed. The Bureau of Public Lands claims that it has the right, as a state agency, to regulate land use and that leasing to parties is part of that regulation that Great Cove is subject to. Is the Bureau correct or have Great Cove's riparian rights been violated (*Great Cove Boat Club v. Bureau of Public Lands,* 672 A.2d 91 [Me. 1996])?

6. Consider whether the following types of conduct would constitute a nuisance, and discuss the type of remedy available. Be sure to use the doctrine of balancing interests.

   a. The operation of a dump causing smoke, odors, flies, rodents, and wild dogs to enter neighboring properties.

   b. Stadium lights on at night that disturb a neighbor's sleep.

   c. The operation of a 24-hour car wash next to a home when the car wash employees play loud music, curse, sell illegal drugs, urinate in plain view, and throw trash onto the grass surrounding the home. Would it matter if the customers were responsible for these activities (*Packett v. Herbert,* 377 S.E.2d 438 [Va. 1989])?

7. Alan C. Bir owned Lot 20 in the Meadows Subdivision located in Allegheny County, North Carolina. Michael Kent Lee and his wife, Anne P. Lee (plaintiffs), owned Lot 21 in that same subdivision.

In May or June, 1990, Bir contacted Kenneth Miles and asked Miles to cut down trees in an area he showed Miles from the deck of his home. Miles proceeded to cut trees down for two to three weeks. After the trees were cut, Miles began to chop up the trees and burn them. Bir appeared and told Miles, "hurry up," because "they were cutting on someone else's property." Bir also told Miles to keep quiet about the cutting. Miles later learned that he had been clearing trees from the Lees' property believing them to be located on Bir's property, with the removal needed for Bir's view.

When the Lees discovered that a significant amount of their property had been cleared, they filed suit against Bir. Two days before Miles was scheduled to give his deposition, Bir told Miles to say that the trees were cut because of damage from Hurricane Huge. What would be the basis of their suit (*Lee v. Bir,* 449 S.E.2d 34 [N.C. App. 1994])?

8. Douglas Margreiter was severely injured in New Orleans on the night of April 6, 1976. Margreiter was the chief of the pharmacy section of the Colorado Department of Social Services and was in New Orleans to attend the annual meeting of the American Pharmaceutical Association.

On Tuesday evening, April 6, Margreiter had dinner in the Royal Sonesta Hotel with two associates from Colorado who were attending the meeting and were staying in rooms adjacent to Margreiter's in the New Hotel Monteleone. Margreiter returned to his room between 10:30 P.M. and 11 P.M.; one of his friends, Peebles, returned to his adjoining room at the same time. Bogan, another friend, was to come by Margreiter's room later to discuss what meetings of the association each would attend the next day.

About three hours later, Margreiter was found severely beaten and unconscious in a parking lot three blocks from the Monteleone. The police who found him said they thought he was highly intoxicated; they took him to Charity Hospital. His friends later had him moved to the Hotel Dieu.

Margreiter said two men had unlocked his hotel room door and entered his room. He was beaten about the head and shoulders and had only the recollection of being carried to a dark alley. He required a craniotomy and other medical treatment and suffered permanent effects from the incident.

Margreiter sued the hotel on the grounds that it was negligent in not controlling access to elevators and hence to the guests' rooms. The hotel says Margreiter was intoxicated and met his fate outside the hotel. Should the hotel be held liable (*Margreiter v. New Hotel Monteleone, Inc.,* 640 F.2d 508 [5th Cir. 1981])?

9. Jane Doe was confronted by Billy Jo Hampton on February 23, 1994, as she was preparing to leave the Beckley Crossings Shopping Center in Raleigh County, West Virginia. She had been shopping at the Center's Wal-Mart store (defendants), which was managed by Belcher. The actual property itself was owned by B. C. Associates Ltd. Hampton placed a knife in her side, forced her into her car, drove the car out of the parking lot to a remote area, sexually assaulted her and then abandoned her and the car. Mr. Hampton was apprehended several days later in Greensboro, North Carolina, where he had abducted another woman. He was charged with attempted murder of Ms. Doe.

Ms. Doe filed suit against Wal-Mart and the limited partnership that owned and operated Beckley Crossings, alleging that they had failed to take reasonable precautions to prevent this kind of injury to customers invited to the shopping center. Is either Wal-Mart or the limited partnership liable (*Doe v. Wal-Mart Stores, Inc.,* 479 S.E.2d 610 [W.Va. 1996])?

10. A private foundation has proposed the construction of a 72-bed facility for the mentally disabled persons in a residential neighborhood. Two neighbors have filed suit to halt construction as a nuisance on the basis of evidence that residents of existing facilities tend to roam the neighborhoods going through trash cans and approaching neighbors for money and food. Will the facility be enjoined (*Miniat v. McGinnis,* 762 S.W.2d 390 [Ark. 1988])?

Internet Activities

For more information on state sponsorship of solar developments go to: **http://www. ncsc.ncsu.edu/**, which is The North Carolina Solar Center, located in the College of Engineering at North Carolina State University. It provides programs and resources that help people throughout North Carolina take advantage of solar energy. To view homes with solar energy go to: **http://www.ases.org**. List the new developments in solar energy.

DIVISION OF MINING, LAND & WATER

Division of Mining, Land & Water
Public Easements:
Update on Proposed Regulations

On December 18, 2000, Pat Pourchot, Commissioner of the Department of Natural Resources, officially signed some of the department's proposed public easement regulations. Those proposed regulations are now being reviewed by the Department of Law. Thanks to everyone who commented on the full proposal during its public review period from November 1999 to March 2000. Your comments helped the department improve the draft and decide which parts should become DNR's official policy and which parts need further review.

Public comments were very extensive. They came from private landowners (especially agricultural landowners), individual access users, utility companies, Native organizations, municipalities, other government agencies, and special-interest groups.

Comments showed a wide range of opinions. Some Alaskans opposed public access. Others wanted no restrictions on access at all. Still others supported most public access easements, but made an exception for one type, RS 2477 rights-of-way. There was even substantial disagreement over what a public easement is, although that is primarily a legal matter rather than a policy choice.

In response to these public comments, Commissioner Pourchot divided the proposal into two parts. He adopted some of the regulations (Phase 1), but set the rest aside (Phase 2) for a new round of public review after the Department of Law approves the first set.

Chapter 3
Nonpossessory Interests
in Real Estate

Good fences make good neighbors.
  Robert Frost

Nonpossessory land interests are those that give their holders certain definite and clear-cut rights that always fall short of possession of the land. These nonpossessory interests might be labeled privileges, liberties, or advantages. Nonpossessory interests give their holders some right of entry or use of the land of another. This chapter explains the creation and extent of these nonpossessory interests.

EASEMENTS

An **easement** is a liberty, privilege, or advantage in another's property. It is nonpossessory but may be valid for perpetuity. There are many different types of easements and methods for their creation, as covered in the sections that follow.

FIGURE 3.1   *Easement Appurtenant*

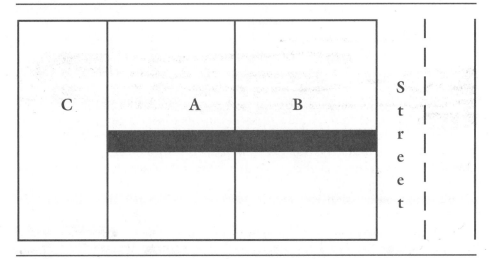

Types of Easements: Appurtenant v. Easements in Gross

An **easement appurtenant** is one attaching to or benefiting a particular tract of land. The purpose of an easement appurtenant is to benefit a landowner.

For example, refer to Figure 3.1 and suppose both landowners C and A need access to the street that runs parallel to B's property. The dark strip represents the appurtenant easements held by C and A in B's land and C in A's land that give them access and benefit them in the use and possession of their land.

In contrast, an **easement in gross** is not created to benefit any landowner with respect to a particular tract of land; rather, it belongs to the holders regardless of whether any adjacent property is owned. Generally, public utilities hold easements in gross through residential property (in the back six or eight feet of the lots, for example) so that telephone, electrical, and water lines can be connected to all parcels of the property. At common law, easements in gross were not transferable, but in most states they are now transferable if they are commercial in nature.

Types of Easements: Affirmative v. Negative Easements

The situation diagrammed in Figure 3.1 is an example of an **affirmative easement,** which means that the owner of the easement right can use another's land (the land subject to the easement). In Figure 3.1, A and C have an affirmative easement in B's property. Likewise, C has an affirmative easement in A's property.

A **negative easement** is one in which the holders of the easements prevent other property owners from use of their property in a particular way or prevent particular acts by other landowners; for example, an easement restricting the building heights on adjoining property. These negative easements, often called *scenic easements,* can have a possible twofold tax advantage. First, the tax-payer/landowner can perhaps take a charitable contribution deduction. For example, a business might grant a neighboring church a negative easement that prevents the blockage of sunlight from the church's stained glass windows. The business can take the value reduction this easement causes in its property as a charitable contribution deduction. Second, the taxpayer/landowner's property taxes can be reduced by the decrease in value brought about by the easement restrictions. An easement that prevents the shading of solar panels (as discussed in Chapter 2) is an example of a negative easement.

Another type of negative easement that has been used extensively over the past few years is the **conservation easement.** This is an easement granted by a landowner who owns land that possesses historical, cultural, or architectural significance. These landowners grant negative easements that will prevent them from tearing down buildings on the property so as to preserve their significance for the community. In many cases, again, these easements can be treated as charitable donations. These forms of easements are being used more and more as governments lack funds to buy or condemn the property. Private landowners are thus able to accomplish the goal of conservation without the costs being borne by governments and taxpayers.

Recently, conservation easements have been used to preserve farmlands in those areas where development would otherwise force farmers, due to increased property taxes, to abandon their land to further development. The farmers grant to their communities negative conservation easements, often referred to as *purchase and development rights (PDR) contracts,* in which they agree to limit their land uses. In exchange, the communities give the farmers reduced taxes for the promise to preserve their land as natural farmland. The result is a solution to encroaching development as well as to the high taxes faced in agricultural production.

The Parties: Dominant v. Servient Estates

In an easement relationship, the property owned by the easement holder is called the **dominant tenement** or **dominant estate,** and the property through which the easement runs is called the **servient tenement** or **servient estate.** In Figure 3.1, B holds the servient estate for dominant tenants A and C. Since C also has an easement through A's property, A is also a servient estate to C's dominant estate.

| Consider 3.1 |

For each of the following, determine what type of easement (affirmative, negative, appurtenant, gross) is being created and who will hold the dominant and servient estates:

a. Angela holds an easement that prevents Bill from planting willow trees. (Angela and Bill are adjoining landowners, and Angela obtained the easement because she felt the roots of willow trees would harm her in-ground swimming pool.)

b. Community Cable has just placed television wires along the back wall lines of several neighbors' lots in a new subdivision. The landowners object—they allege a trespass has occurred.

c. Oscar owns a passive-solar home (dependent upon window sunlight for heat), and Oscar's neighbor has agreed not to plant trees or shrubs or construct walls on the boundary he shares with Oscar to prevent obstruction.

d. Nordstrom, the retail store, has its name placed on the top of the public parking garage (owned by the city of Scottsdale, Az) located next to its store.

Creation of Easements

EASEMENTS BY EXPRESS GRANT OR EXPRESS RESERVATION

An **easement by express grant** or **express reservation** is one in which the parties actually draw up papers as if transferring an interest in land. Since an easement is a land interest, creation of express easements must comply with all requirements in the state for the conveyance of land interests.

Most states require the conveyance of a land interest to be in writing. Whether an easement is created by express grant or express reservation depends on the physical layout of the land transferred: The two contrasting physical setups for easements are illustrated in Figure 3.2. In both situations, A was the original owner of the full parcel that contained an access route to the street that runs parallel to the tract. In the express grant situation, A retains that portion of the parcel with the access route and must therefore convey to B an easement by express grant. In the express reservation situation, A conveys that portion of the parcel with the access route and must therefore grant himself an easement by express reservation.

The same easement is involved in both circumstances, but the method of acquisition is different. In the deed transferring title to the property conveyed, A would either grant or convey the portion of the parcel B has purchased and would also include a grant to B of the easement for ingress or egress or, in the second circumstances, would reserve that ingress and egress for himself when B is granted title to the land with that access.

An express easement need not arise solely in the circumstances of land partition. It may be executed alone without the division or transfer of title to property. For example, a solar easement may be drafted and executed between two neighbors who already own their adjoining parcels of land.

Practical Tip

In creating easements, the parties should be cautious in wording the easement language. The following suggestions should be kept in mind:
1. Accurately describe the location, length, and width of the easement.
2. Describe the intended use of the easement. Is it for a right-of-way? Is it for ingress and egress?
3. Are there limitations on the use of the easement? Is it residential or commercial?
4. Who is responsible for maintenance of the easement?
5. Describe any limitations. For example, "Until the construction of the highway along the southern boundary of the property is completed."

FIGURE 3.2   *Express Grant and Express Reservation Easement*

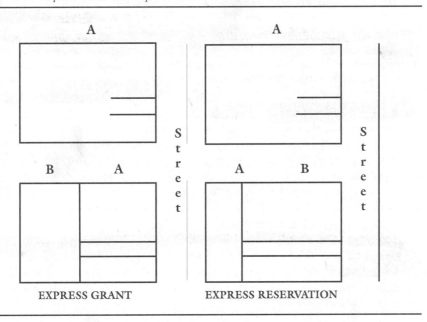

EXPRESS GRANT   EXPRESS RESERVATION

Consider 3.2

In 1960, the Martins, who owned a large tract of land with some waterfront portions near the Gulf of Mexico, sold to James and Doris Baynes a portion of that tract. The Baynes told the Martins that they could not afford waterfront property, so the Martins sold them a portion of their land that did not front the water and agreed to provide them with an easement. The deed for the transfer contained the following language:

> *An easement not to exceed 25 feet in width and extending 260 feet east of lot herein conveyed to a roadway leading to the Gulf of Mexico.*

The Martins then sold the remaining portions of their land to Richard Haston and Tannin, Inc. Haston's deed contained language nearly identical to that in the Baynes' deed. Tannin, Inc., owned the portion of the original tract through which both Haston and the Baynes walked for beach access. Tannin claimed the easement through his property was for access to a road and not the beach.

What should the parties have done to clarify the grant? Do you feel the language indicates an intent for access to the Gulf of Mexico? What impact do the easements held by Haston and the Bayneses have on Tannin's plans for development of the waterfront property? *Tannin, Inc. v. Haston,* 690 So.2d 398 (Ct. Civ. App. Ala. 1997)

EASEMENTS BY IMPLICATION

An **easement by implication** is one arising from necessity. Suppose, for example, that in the express grant of Figure 3.2, B's property is landlocked and that crossing A's parcel is B's only method of ingress and egress. Suppose further that in the conveyance from A to B, no provision or express grant was made in the deed to provide B with an easement. To prevent B from having to hold title to a worthless piece of inaccessible property, the doctrine of easement by implication was developed and may be used to assist B in the landlocked predicament.

In order to establish that an easement exists by implication, several factors must be present. First, there must have been unity of ownership between the two tracts prior to the partition and sale. In this case there was unity of ownership, since A owned the entire parcel prior to the division. Second, there must have been a **quasi easement** at the time of the sole ownership of the parcel. A quasi easement is an access route used by the landowner when the land was not yet divided. Figure 3.2 indicates that A used the road as a means of access, and so a quasi easement existed. The term *quasi* is used because landowners cannot hold an easement in their own property. Third, the prior quasi easement must have been apparent and used continuously. This requirement is satisfied in the figure and is easily satisfied in most access cases because the road or path is visible. However, visibility is not required to meet the apparent standard in most jurisdictions. For example, sewer-line accesses, although not visible, have been held to be apparent because of their need in property use. Although not shown in the figure, continuous use can probably be assumed in most access cases where, as here, the roadway is the only means of access. Continuous use is normal use and does not require use every day.

The final requirement for an easement by implication is to establish that requiring the dominant estate to obtain access any other way would require unreasonable expense. In Figure 3.2, B's landlocked circumstances would indicate that the access through just one parcel is the least expensive and least troublesome method of obtaining access.

Easements by implication can arise in either grant or reservation cases so that there are both easements by grant implication and easements by reservation implication. The following case involves a factual question of whether an easement by implication exists.

shopping dev to war time [handwritten]

Granite Properties Limited Partnership v. Manns

512 N.E.2d 1230 (Ill. 1987)

Trucks to use Apt lot to load trucks - grocery didnt have enough room (50 ft) [handwritten]

Facts

Granite Properties Limited Partnership (Granite/plaintiff) owned all of the parcels shown in the diagram below. Between 1963 and 1982, Granite conveyed certain of the parcels, and, in 1982, parcel B was conveyed to Larry Manns and others (defendants). The present status of the parcels is as follows:

- Parcel A contains a shopping center (built in 1967 and currently owned by Granite). To the north of the shopping center is an asphalt parking lot with 191 feet of frontage on Bethalto Drive.
- Parcel B is undeveloped and is owned by the defendants.
- Parcel C contains five four-family apartment buildings (owned by a third party).
- Parcel D contains a health club (owned by a third party).
- Parcel E contains the Chateau des Fleurs Apartments (owned by Granite).

The rear of the shopping center is used for deliveries, trash storage and removal, and utilities repair. To gain access to the rear of the shopping center for these purposes, trucks use a gravel driveway that runs along the lot line between parcel A and parcel B. A second driveway (noted in diagram), located to the east of the shopping center on

parcel D, enables the trucks to circle the shopping center and deliver to the stores, including Save-a-Lot Grocery, without having to turn around in the limited space behind the stores. The trucks can thus make a convenient entrance, delivery stop, and exit.

The two pictured driveways existed before Manns purchased the property, and he saw them during an inspection of the land prior to his purchase. There are no references to the driveways in any of the deeds relating to the parcels.

Robert Mehann, owner of the Save-a-Lot grocery store located in the shopping center, testified on direct examination that groceries, which are delivered to the rear of the store, are loaded by forklift on a concrete pad poured for that purpose. Mehann indicated that there are large, double-steel doors in the back of the store to accommodate items that will not fit through the front door. Mehann testified that semitrailer trucks make deliveries to the rear of the grocery store four days a week, with as many as two or three such trucks arriving daily. An average of 10 to 12 trucks a day, including semitrailer trucks, make deliveries to the grocery store. Mehann further explained that because the area behind the Save-a-Lot building extends only 50 feet to the rear property line, it would be difficult, if not impossible, for a semitrailer truck to turn around in the back and exit the same way it came in. In response to a question as to whether it would be feasible to have trucks make front-door deliveries, Mehann suggested that such deliveries would be very disruptive; pallets that would not fit through the front door would have to be broken down into parts, requiring extra work, and there would not be adequate space in the front of the store to do such work during business hours. Mehann admitted that he had not investigated the cost of installing a front door that would be big enough for pallets of groceries to be brought in by forklift. There would not be enough space to manipulate the forklift around the front of the store, although it could be run between the shelves of food to the back of the store.

Darrell Layman, a partner for Granite, testified that, although it was very difficult, he had seen semitrailer trucks exit the same way they came in. Layman also

NORTH

BETHALTO DRIVE

PARCEL A

SHOPPING CENTER

PARCEL D

PARCEL E

PARKING LOT

PARCEL B

PARCEL C

PRAIRIE STREET

WEST

EAST

ROU DES CHATEAUX STREET

SOUTH

acknowledged that he had not investigated the cost of expanding the size of the front doors of the building. He also claimed it "would seem impossible" for him to put in any kind of a hallway or passageway that would allow equipment to bring supplies into the store from the front. Layman explained that the delivery trucks follow no set schedule and, therefore, their presence may overlap at times. He stated that he had seen as many as four or five delivery trucks backed up. Layman opined that there was "no way" the trucks could back up and turn around when there were multiple trucks present.

Granite claimed an easement by implication for the shopping center and the parcel E apartment complex. The trial court found an easement by implication for the apartment complex but denied such for the shopping center. Granite appealed. The appellate court affirmed the apartment complex easement and also reversed the trial court's ruling on the shopping center easement and found that one also existed by implication there. Manns appealed.

Judicial Opinion

Ryan, Justice. The plaintiff contends in this court that it acquired, by implied reservation, easements over the driveways which provide access to the rear of the shopping center located on parcel A and to the parking lot of the apartment complex situated on parcel E. Plaintiff alleges that parcels A, B and E were held in common ownership by the plaintiff and its predecessors in title until 1982, at which time the defendants received a warranty deed to parcel B; that the driveways in question were apparent and obvious, permanent, and subject to continuous, uninterrupted, and actual use by the plaintiff and its predecessors in title until the time of severance of unity of ownership; and that the driveways are highly convenient and reasonably necessary for the beneficial use and enjoyment of the shopping center and the apartment complex. Therefore, the plaintiff maintains that, upon severance of unity of title, the defendants took parcel B subject to the servitudes then existing, as the parties are presumed to convey with reference to the existing conditions of the property.

We note at the outset that the attempt here is to establish easements by implied reservation rather than by implied grant. Illinois may be said to follow the generally accepted view recognizing the implication of easements in favor of a grantor as well as a grantee.

On the merits, the crucial issue is whether, in conveying that portion of its property now owned by the defendants (parcel B), the plaintiff retained easements by implication over the driveways in question.

The easement implied from a prior or existing use, often characterized as a "quasi-easement," arises when an owner of an entire tract of land or two or more adjoining parcels, after employing a part thereof so that one part of the tract or one parcel derives from another a benefit or advantage of an apparent, continuous, and permanent nature, conveys or transfers part of the property without mention being made of these incidental uses. In the absence of an expressed agreement to the contrary, the conveyance or transfer imparts a grant of property with all the benefits and burdens which existed at the time of the conveyance of the transfer, even though such grant is not reserved or specified in the deed.

The *Restatement [of Property]* describes a doctrine creating easements "by implication from the circumstances under which the conveyance was made." This implication "arises as an inference of the intention of those making a conveyance." The *Restatement* operates on the basis of eight "important circumstances" from which the inference of intention can be drawn: whether the claimant is the conveyor or the conveyee; the terms of the conveyance; the consideration given for it; whether the claim is made against a simultaneous conveyee; the extent of necessity of the easement to the claimant; whether reciprocal benefits result to the conveyor and the conveyee; the manner in which the land was used prior to its conveyance; and the extent to which the manner of prior use was or might have been known to the parties. These eight factors vary in their importance and relevance according to whether the claimed easement originates out of necessity or for another reason.

In applying the *Restatement's* eight important circumstances to the present case, the fact that the driveways in question had been used by the plaintiff or its predecessors in title since the 1960s, when the respective properties were developed; that the driveways were permanent in character, being either rock or gravel covered; and that the defendants were aware of the driveways' prior uses before they purchased parcel B would tend to support an inference that the parties intended easements upon severance of the parcels in question.

[The] defendants, nevertheless, argue that there are two factors which overwhelmingly detract from the implication of an easement: That the claimant is the conveyor and that the claimed easement can hardly be described as "necessary" to the beneficial use of the plaintiff's properties. Relying on the principle that a grantor should not be permitted to derogate from his own grant, the defendants urge this court to refuse to imply an easement in favor of a grantor unless the claimed easement is absolutely necessary to the beneficial use and enjoyment of the land retained by the grantor. The defendants further urge this court not to cast an unreasonable burden over their land through imposition of easements by implication where, as here, available alternatives affording reasonable means of ingress to and egress from the shopping center and apartment complex allegedly exist.

While the degree of necessity required to reserve an easement by implication in favor of the conveyor is greater than that required in the case of a conveyee, even in the case of the conveyor, the implication from necessity will be aided by a previous use made apparent by the physical adaptation of the premises to it.

The requirement that the quasi-easement must have been "important for the enjoyment of the conveyed quasi-dominant [or quasi-servient] parcel" is highly elastic. Some courts say that the use must be one which is "reasonably necessary to the enjoyment of the [conveyed or retained] land." Others demand a use which is necessary for the beneficial, convenient, comfortable or reasonable enjoyment of such land.

Notwithstanding their difference in use of terminology, the authorities agree that the degree or extent of necessity required to create an easement by implication differs in both meaning and significance depending upon the existence of proof of prior use. Hence, given the strong evidence of the plaintiff's prior use of the driveways in question and the defendants' knowledge thereof, we must agree with the appellate court majority that the evidence in this case was sufficient to fulfill the elastic necessity requirement.

The evidence, moreover, regarding the difficulty of making deliveries to the front of the shopping center was sufficient to demonstrate the unreasonableness of such an alternative measure.

Affirmed.

Case Questions

1. Who originally owned all the parcels of land?
2. How was each parcel used?
3. Could delivery trucks find an alternate means of access to the shopping center?
4. Did the buyers know of the use of the driveway by the trucks?
5. Were the driveways mentioned in any of the deeds?
6. What eight factors does the court examine as "important circumstances" in deciding the case?
7. Does the standard of proof differ if there is a claim for an easement by implied reservation as opposed to one implied by grant?
8. Does the court use a standard of absolute necessity?

EASEMENTS BY NECESSITY

An **easement by necessity** is one that can arise solely on the basis of necessity, and the requirements of prior use need not be established. However, this type of easement lasts only so long as the necessity continues, whereas an easement by implication may go on in perpetuity. In some states, condemnation procedures are available to assist landowners who need to obtain access to their property. In other states, an easement is automatically given when landlocked property is transferred.[1]

In Figure 3.1, B's circumstances could be changed to require an easement by necessity if the properties were surrounded by water. Then A's only method of access to the street would be through B's land, unless and until a bridge or causeway to B's land was constructed.

Some states have begun to follow doctrines on easements by implication and necessity that are less complex. For example, in *Carter v. County of Hanover,* 496 S.E.2d 42 (Va. 1998), the court found that without any deed restrictions, the "grantor of property conveys everything that is necessary for the beneficial use and enjoyment of the property."

Practical Tip

Rights of ingress and egress and their scope should be determined prior to listing, sale, or purchase of property. Personal observations of trespassers and others on the property should lead to an investigation of their origins, motivations, and rights (if any).

Christine and Steve Mallock buried their son in a burial plot purchased at Southern Memorial Park, Inc. Each year the Mallocks conducted a memorial service for their son at his burial plot. On the seventh anniversary of their son's death, the Mallocks went to their son's grave at 11:00 A.M. for the annual service, which

Consider 3.3

---

1.   Fla.Stat. § 704.01; *see also* Prestatement of Property § 476 and Colo. Const. art. II § 14. Other states may not have a statute or condemnation procedures but follow strong public policy in favor of an easement. *Big Sky Hidden Village Owners Ass'n v. Hidden Village, Inc.,* 915 P.2d 845 (Mont. 1996).

3.3, continued

generally took 30 minutes. When they arrived they discovered that a tent and chairs set up for funeral services on the plot next to their son's grave were actually resting on his gravesite. The Mallocks asked Southern's management if the tent and chairs could be moved until they could conduct their service. The managers refused, and the Mallocks went ahead with their ceremony, cutting it to five minutes, after they moved the chairs and tents by themselves.

Southern's managers called the police and had the Mallocks evicted. Southern claims the Mallocks had no rights on the property except for the grave. Their deed for the plot does not award an easement for access. Do the Mallocks have the right to access to the gravesite? *Mallock v. Southern Memorial Park, Inc.*, 561 So.2d 330 (Fla. Ct. App. 1990)

Consider 3.4

At one time, the parcels shown in the diagram below were owned by Harry Borst, who built the garage and used it for his car.

In 1947, Hunt purchased plot 1; in 1951, the Zimmermans purchased plot 2. Hunt had leased the garage from Borst until the sale to the Zimmermans in 1951. Hunt tried to rent the garage from the Zimmermans but was refused. The Zimmermans used the driveway on the Hunts' land to gain access to the garage. After numerous disputes and gates, the Zimmermans brought suit to stop the Hunts from blocking the driveway. The Zimmermans claim that they have an easement because there is no other way to use the garage. There is no mention in the deeds of any driveway or easement. Do the Zimmermans have an easement? *Hunt v. Zimmerman*, 216 N.E.2d 854 (Ind. Ct. App. 1966)

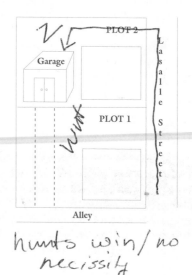

hunts win/ no necissity

EASEMENTS BY PRESCRIPTION

Obtaining an easement by **prescription** is somewhat similar to obtaining title to property through adverse possession. However, the term *adverse possession* (discussed in Chapter 13) is inappropriate for easements because easements are nonpossessory land interests. Several elements must be established before an easement by prescription is created:

1. *The easement must be used for the appropriate prescriptive period.* The prescriptive period will vary from state to state but generally corresponds to the state's adverse possession period, which ranges from five to 20 years throughout the United States.

2. *The use of the easement must be adverse (not permissive).* If the landowner has given the prescriptive taker an oral license of passage, such use is permissive and will not qualify for prescription. The permissive use must be mutually agreed upon—a landowner's posting of a permission sign will not prevent prescriptive rights.

3. *The use of the easement must be open and notorious.* In most states, this requirement means that the prescriptive taker must use the property in such a way that a

landowner would, under ordinary circumstances, be aware of the use. Because actual knowledge of use is not required, landowners who do not periodically inspect their property run the risk of having a prescriptive use accumulate.

4. *The use of the easement must be continuous and exclusive.* This requirement forces the prescriptive user to confine use to a particular area. The user is required to use the same strip of land or access route consistently.[2]

A prescriptive claim can be based only on the user's use and not on use by others. An exception is the rule of tacking, which permits those in privity of contract (buyers and sellers) and those who inherit title to land to add their use to that of the seller or deceased in making up the prescriptive period. For example, a father using an easement for five years and then passing his property to his son by will also passes his five years of prescriptive use of the easement.

To prevent a prescriptive taking, the landowner may take several steps, most of which are recognized by the majority of states. Written protest is one method of interrupting the prescriptive period, as is physical interruption (for example, the use of a gate). Perhaps court-obtained injunctive relief is the best alternative, because such action provides the landowners with full records for establishing a cutoff of the prescriptive period. The following case deals with multiple issues in a claim of an easement by prescription.

Carnahan
v. Moriah Property Owners Association, Inc.

716 N.E.2d 437 (Ind. 1999)

[handwritten: couldn't use water craft on the lake that wasn't there (that they used for years)]

Facts

Prior to 1972, Charles and Julia Drewry owned a 22-acre lake and the surrounding property. In November, 1972, Donald and Joyce Carnahan purchased a one-acre lot from the Drewrys and the purchase included a portion of the lake bed. The Carnahans used the lake for recreational activity including ice skating, fishing, swimming, and the use of various watercraft on the lake. In the spring of 1973, the Carnahans placed a houseboat on the lake and lived on it intermittently until 1976 when they finished building their lakeside home on their lot. They used a ski boat on the lake until 1986 and wave runners and jet skis through the summer of 1993.

In 1984, the Carnahans purchased an adjacent one-acre plot, one-fifth of which was bed in the lake. Subsequent to this purchase the lake and adjoining lands were surveyed and platted into lots for subdivision additions to Lake County. In 1987, the Carnahans acquired another adjacent lot of 1.2 acres, one-eighth of which was lake bed. With their original purchase and the two subsequent ones, the Carnahans owned over half an acre or 2.5% of the 22-acre lake bed.

In 1991, the Moriah Property Owner's Association (Moriah) obtained the property rights to the majority of the lake bed including nearly all the water suitable for use by watercraft. Moriah then prepared restrictive covenants that were rules for use of the lake. One rule was "No motors are allowed on the lake except electric trolling motors powered by no more than two 12-volt batteries."

When the Carnahans received a copy of the new restrictions, they filed suit to establish their prescriptive easement in the lake. They also alleged interference with their real property, easement, and riparian rights. Moriah counter-claimed that the Carnahans' use of the lake was a threat to adults and children who swam there.

---

2. The Restatement (Third) of Property (Servitudes) has four theories listed for granting prescriptive easements: (1) sufficiently long use can lead to entitlement; (2) use to perfect a flawed title meets the requirements; (3) long-term use is evidence of a right lost that must be restored; and (4) prescriptive claims arise and can exist but must be advanced within a limited time frame.

The trial court ruled that the Carnahans had a prescriptive easement but found that the restrictive covenants were valid. The court of appeals agreed that there was a prescriptive easement but reversed on the restrictive covenant validity. Moriah appealed.

Judicial Opinion

Sullivan, Justice. Prescriptive easements are not favored in the law, and in Indiana, the party claiming one must meet "stringent requirements." . . .

Adverse use has been defined as a "use of the property as the owner himself would exercise, disregarding the claims of others entirely, asking permission from no one, and using the property under a claim of right." The concept of adversity was developed in the context of establishing use rights over static paths or roads that crossed the property of adjoining landowners. The Court of Appeals affirmed the trial court's conclusion as to adversity by citing a prototypical path or road case for the proposition that "an unexplained use for 20 years is presumed to be adverse and sufficient to establish title by prescriptive easement."

We agree with the reasoning in the *Mitchell, Fleck,* and *Reder* decisions that "an unexplained use for 20 years" of an obvious path or road for ingress and egress over the lands of another creates a rebuttable presumption that a use was adverse. However, we are unwilling to recognize such a presumption in favor of a party trying to establish a prescriptive easement for the recreational use of a body of water. This is because recreational use (especially of a body of water) is of a very different character from use of a path or road or ingress and egress over land. Recreational use (especially of water which leaves no telltale path or road) seems to us likely to be permissive in accordance with the widely held view in Indiana that if the owner of one land "sees his neighbor also making use of it, under circumstances that in no way injures the land or interferes with the landowner's own use of it, it does not justify the inference that he is yielding to his neighbor's claim of right or that his neighbor is asserting any right; it signifies only that he is permitting his neighbor to use the land."

We thus conclude that claimants seeking to establish an easement based on the "recreational" use of another's property must make a special showing that those activities were in fact adverse; they will not be indulged a presumption to that effect.

Because the facts involve a conveyance of the servient estate during and near the end of the 20-year prescriptive period, we focus on the relationship between the Carnahans and the Drewrys, which comprised over 18 years of the relevant period.

The trial court's findings do not address whether the Carnahans' recreational use of the lake was adverse to the Drewrys. They only track the Carnahans' periodic change in the use of recreational equipment over the years. Therefore, the findings of fact do not support the court's conclusion that the Carnahans' recreational activities constituted the "'adverse seasonal use of Lake Julia."

On the other hand, the record does contain ample evidence supporting the inference that the Carnahans' use of the lake was both non-confrontational and permissive in recognition of the Drewry's authority as title holders to a majority of the lake bed. For example, Mr. Carnahan testified that Mr. Drewry "would wave" to them as they anchored their houseboat in "plain sight of his house," but that they kept the houseboat "in the middle" as opposed to the "south side of the lake" so as not "to bother anybody." When asked why they retired their ski boat in 1986, Mr. Carnahan responded that they "didn't want to tick off the neighbors." There are other examples of the Carnahans' non-adversarial use of the Lake, such as Mr. Carnahan's statement that it had " been under his driving force that if people were on the lake fishing, the Carnahans stayed off," and Mrs. Carnahan's statement that "if there are children in the lake, we are either not out there or we are at the opposite end."

We find the evidence establishes that the Carnahans' use of Lake Julia was not adverse and was insufficient to overcome the special showing required with respect to establishing a recreational easement. The Carnahans were engaged in a nonconsumptive, leisurely use of Lake Julia which neither diminished nor adversely altered the quantity or quality of the water. We recognized that the law did not require an affirmative act of hostility of [*sic*] the part of the Carnahans; nevertheless, we conclude that their occasional, recreational use was not inconsistent with the Drewry's title as majority owners of the property underlying Lake Julia. We also note that the Carnahans' use of the lake was clearly distinguishable from De Rose's adversarial use of Center Lake at issue in *Sanders.* ("De Rose anchored his boats for hours under a claim of right . . . in defiance of Sanders's protest and request to depart, . . . while asserting that Sanders did not own the land so covered with water and had no right to exercise any control over the same . . . "). Accordingly, as a matter of law the trial court's judgment was not sustained in its findings nor on the record on the basis that the Carnahans established a prescriptive easement.

We reverse the trial court's finding that the Carnahans had established a prescriptive easement.

Case Questions

1. What did the Carnahans own and when did they own it?
2. How did the Carnahans use the lake and how much did they use?
3. Was there adverse use by the Carnahans?
4. Does the court find there is an easement by prescription?

Would putting up a gate and posting a "No Trespassers" sign for two years be enough to stop an easement by prescription? *Kessinger v. Matulevich,* 925 P.2d 864 (Mont. 1996)

The Zuni Indians, as part of their religion, make a periodic pilgrimage at the time of the summer solstice, on foot or horseback, from their reservation in northwest New Mexico to the mountain area the tribe calls Kohlu/wala:wa, which is in northeast Arizona. The Zuni believe Kohlu/wala:wa is their place of origin, the basis for their religious life, and the home of their dead. The pilgrimage has occurred since the fifteenth century.

The pilgrimage crossed over the rather large landholdings of Earl Platt. In 1985, Mr. Platt declared that he was going to prohibit the Zuni from crossing his lands during their pilgrimage. The United States government intervened in the dispute on behalf of the Zuni. A woman from St. Johns, Arizona (located in the northeast part of the state), has testified that she remembers watching the pilgrimage as a girl in 1938. Can Mr. Platt stop the Zuni? Do the Zuni have any rights? *U.S. on Behalf of Zuni Tribe of New Mexico v. Platt,* 730 F.Supp. 318 (D. Ariz. 1990)

Scope and Extent of Easements

The extent of permissive use of an easement is determined according to the type of easement. If an express easement has been created, determining the extent of the easement is simply a task of interpretation of the deed or contract granting the easement. A court must undertake this task of interpretation and will employ the **rule of reason** in executing its task. The rule of reason prohibits a court from imposing unreasonable burdens when the parties have expressed their desires and intentions in general terms. Under the rule of reason, a court cannot impose a strained construction on the language used by the parties.

http://

Visit Alaska's Division of Mining, Land, and Water to view proposed regulations for public easements at: **http://www.dnr.state.ak.us/land/11aac51.htm**.

For example, if the parties expressly provide for an easement across servient land in a definite location, then the court may not impose a different route for the easement upon the parties. On the other hand, an express easement for a pipeline that does not specify depth can be interpreted to permit the dominant estate holder to move the pipe to a greater depth because of technological changes and necessities. Likewise, the grant of an easement to use a beach "for the purpose of boating, bathing, fishing, or other recreation" does not include the right to use the beach for the purpose of commercial boat rental. An easement for "foot passage" will not be expanded to permit vehicles, but an easement for "the right to pass" may be properly interpreted to permit vehicular traffic.

The extent, location, and use of a prescriptive easement is determined according to the type of use made during the prescriptive period. For example, a prescriptive right acquired through foot use does not include the right of vehicular use, and a vehicular private prescriptive use does not include an expansion to commercial use.

The task of determining the extent, use, and location of easements is perhaps the most difficult in easements by implication. With this type of easement, an assumption is made that the parties would recognize the normal development of the dominant estate. Normal development is defined according to the initial use of the property. For example, if the dominant estate is used for residential purposes, it is within the normal development that such land may be subdivided for numerous residences. However, it is not within the normal development for the property to be used as a commercial rock bed with the accompanying use of large trucks. The use of an easement by implication cannot be expanded to benefit properties other than the dominant estate.

However, all types of easements may be enlarged in their scope through prescription. For example, an easement "for the purpose of transporting milk to a factory" may be used for all purposes for a prescriptive period and thus expand to a general easement. All elements of prescription must be present for the prescriptive period for the expansion of an easement through prescriptive use.

The following case illustrates some of the difficulties encountered in determining the scope and extent of an easement.

Wetmore v. Ladies of Lorretto, Wheaton

220 N.E.2d 491 (Ill. 1966)

Facts

Since 1928, Wetmore (plaintiff/appellee) and his family have owned an 80-acre parcel of land near Wheaton, Illinois. In 1946, Wetmore sold 10 acres of the land to the Ladies of Lorretto (Ladies/defendants/appellants), a convent and a nonprofit corporation. The diagram below depicts the location of the parcels of property involved.

The Ladies improved the parcel with a large mansion house, swimming pool, sunken gardens, and various outbuildings. Because the 10-acre parcel was landlocked, Wetmore granted to the Ladies an express easement across the remainder of the tract to the east. The easement was an existing driveway that ran in front of Wetmore's house.

Wetmore negotiated the sale of the 40-acre tract (as shown) to the Ladies in 1957. The Ladies had originally wished to purchase a 33-foot strip for a road to Orchard Drive, but Wetmore would agree only to the sale of the entire tract. Wetmore asked the Ladies to give up a small strip near Hawthorne Lane and they declined; however, they stated that when their new 33-foot road was built, they would direct their traffic to that road.

Prior to the road's completion in 1960, relations between Wetmore and the Ladies deteriorated substantially.

Throughout the 1950s, the Ladies conducted kindergarten and music classes on the 10-acre tract. The result was that 40 to 50 vehicles and pedestrian traffic passed by Wetmore's house daily. Occasionally, the Ladies had picnics, parties, and garden parties, which resulted in hundreds of cars passing by Wetmore's house in a single day.

After their road was completed in 1960, the Ladies made verbal requests and sent out maps and directions asking that Wetmore's driveway not be used. Traffic on the driveway was reduced to five vehicles per day.

Still unsatisfied, Wetmore hired a deputy to turn back vehicles, and at times, Wetmore had confrontations with the Ladies and visitors, which frightened these parties. On one of Wetmore's complaining visits to the convent, the sheriff had to be called to have him removed.

Wetmore installed a gate with a bell and alarm on the driveway to alert him to those using it.

In 1962, the Ladies built a House of Studies partially on the 10-acre tract and partially on the 40-acre tract (see diagram). This new building and its purpose of holding classes caused an increase in traffic.

Wetmore objected to use of the driveway for the House of Studies on the grounds that it was an unintended

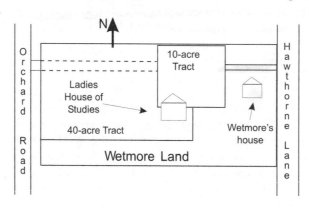

expansion of the easement for use by the 40-acre tract. The Ladies alleged they had an implied easement for both tracts. The trial court found for Wetmore and issued an injunction against the Ladies, and the Ladies appealed.

Judicial Opinion

Davis, Justice. The essential elements of an easement by implication are: (1) The existence of a single tract of land so arranged that one portion of it derives a benefit from the other, the division thereof by a single owner into two or more parcels, and the separation of title; (2) before the separation occurs the use must have been long, continued, obvious or manifest, to a degree which shows permanency; and (3) the use of the claimed easement must be essential to the beneficial enjoyment of the parcel to be benefitted.

We believe that the first two requirements are clearly present in this case. The plaintiff owned the entire 80 acre tract in 1946, and after the conveyance to the defendant of the 10 acre tract, still owned the 70 acre tract, which he severed in 1957. At the time of the conveyance of the 10 acre tract to the defendant in 1946, there was a well-defined roadway—extending from the north where the driveway was located—over which an express easement had been granted, within and along the east side of the 10 acre tract to its south edge, where a corner of the 40 acre tract adjoined.

The roadway was surfaced with some semi-permanent material, was clearly visible, and had been long and continuously used.

We do not believe, however, that the third requirement—that the easement be essential to the beneficial enjoyment of the land—is present.

Where alternative means of access to property are available without passing over the lands of another and the use of such means does not result in an unreasonable burden, courts should exercise due continence in implying and imposing a burden over the lands of another. The land conveyed to the defendant gave it direct access to a public road. Under such circumstances an easement by implication was not sanctioned.

The plaintiff obtained an injunction preventing the continued use of the express easement appurtenant to the 10-acre tract by reason of its use for the benefit of the nondominant 40-acre tract. The defendant contends that not every extension of the use of an easement to an additional tract is a misuse, and that it is only where the extension materially changes the burden on the servient estate, either as to the type of use or the amount, that there is a misuse.

We do not understand that to be the law. If an easement is appurtenant to one tract of land, any extension thereof to another tract of land is a misuse.

While the erection of the House of Studies building on part of the 40 acre tract results in a technical misuse of the easement granted appurtenant to the 10 acre tract, such trivial and inconsequential misuse neither justifies the issuance of an injunction restraining defendant's right to use the easement expressly granted, nor warrants the authorization granted to plaintiff to close Hawthorne Lane as a means of access to defendant's property.

Defendant is entitled, however, in view of plaintiff's past conduct, to an injunction restraining the plaintiff and his agents from wrongful entry upon defendant's property and from interfering with defendant's proper use of the express easement.

Reversed.

Case Questions

1. Who originally owned all of the land in question? *West mor*
2. Had the Hawthorne driveway been in use at that time?
3. What types of activities were conducted by the Ladies of Lorretto on their property?
4. How much traffic was there on the Hawthorne driveway prior to the construction of the 33-foot road? How much traffic was there after the road construction?
5. What actions did Wetmore take to inhibit the use of the Hawthorne driveway?
6. Where was the House of Studies built? Why is its location critical?
7. Who won at the trial court level? What relief was awarded the prevailing party?
8. What type of easement exists according to the appellate court?
9. Did access for the House of Studies constitute an impermissible use of the easement?
10. Who wins at the appellate level? What did the court give as a remedy?

Rights and Obligations of Estate Holders in an Easement

Each of the parties in an easement relationship has certain legal responsibilities and rights. It is the responsibility of the easement owner (dominant estate) to keep the easement on the servient estate in repair. This responsibility of repair exists even though the servient estate owner is responsible for damages or the state of disrepair in the easement. The easement owner has the right to enter the servient land for purposes of repair. Furthermore, the easement owner may improve the easement with pavement or gravel when the easement is a right of passage.

The owners of servient estates have the right to use their property in any way not interfering with the dominant holder's use of the easement. For example, the servient owner may grant more than one easement to more than one party.

Servient estate owners may also construct fences along the easement and install gates so long as there is no interference with the easement owner's use of the easement.

The dominant estate has the right to transfer an easement. An easement is transferred along with the dominant estate even though it is not specifically mentioned in the deed. An "all other appurtenances" clause serves to transfer an easement. Likewise, a servient estate is sold subject to any prior-acquired easements.

Termination of Easements

The termination or extinguishment of an easement may be accomplished in several different ways depending on the type of easement involved. An easement is terminated when there is one owner for the dominant and servient estates or when the nonpossessory and possessory interests become united in one owner.

As discussed earlier, an easement by necessity is terminated when the necessity terminates.

All easements can be terminated through abandonment. Abandonment occurs through prescriptive nonuse. Two elements are required to establish abandonment: (1) the easement owner must possess the intent to abandon; and (2) the intent to abandon must be accompanied by conduct indicating the intent to terminate. For example, the owner of a railroad easement who removes the tracks and destroys the shipping factory using the railway has manifested the intent to abandon through conduct. Permitting an easement to fall into a state of disrepair may constitute sufficient conduct manifesting an intent to abandon. For example, allowing an irrigation ditch to become inoperable is an example of disrepair indicating intent to abandon.

All easements may be terminated if the servient owner successfully prevents the dominant holder's use of the easement for the required prescriptive period. Thus an easement may be created and terminated through prescription.

Some easements are created for a specific time or purpose and are terminated upon the expiration of time or elimination of purpose. For example, a right-of-way given so long as the dominant land is used for a stable would terminate if the land becomes used for other purposes.

An easement may be terminated through *estoppel*. This occurs when the servient owner, believing there has been abandonment, constructs improvements over the easement in reliance upon the abandonment. The idea supporting this theory of termination is that the easement owner should notify the servient landowner that such improvements interfere with the easement. If the easement owner were not required to object, then the servient landowner would make costly changes only to have them eliminated after completion. Estoppel requires prompt action to minimize expense.

PROFITS

A **profit** (or *profit a prendre*) is an easement plus the right of removal. A profit gives the holder the right not only of access to another's land, but also to remove oil, minerals, water, or some other part of the real property. (See Chapter 2 for more discussion of oil and gas rights.) A profit is not the same as the ownership of subsurface rights because such ownership is exclusive and unlimited. More than one party can hold a profit in a piece of property, and a profit can be limited by the types of minerals that may be taken, or the time allowed for taking.

A profit is not the sale of personal property, because the landowner does not sever the mineral or soil—the profit owner does. For example, the right to remove coal is a profit, whereas the right to buy coal after removal is the sale of personal property.

A profit can be appurtenant, as in the right to remove water for use on an adjoining tract; or it can be in gross, as when an oil company that owns no property in the area is given the right to remove oil from a particular parcel.

Apart from these definitional differences, the creation, rights, and obligations of the parties in a *profit a prendre* relationship are governed by the same principles of law discussed in the easement portion of this chapter.

One of the most frequently used profits is one for timber. Timber is considered a part of the real estate but can be severed through the award of a profit in the timber. Under the **Uniform Commercial Code (UCC)** (as adopted in most states), a contract for the sale of timber to be removed by the buyer is considered a contract for the sale of goods, but it is important to understand that title to the timber does not pass to the buyer unless and until it is identified or removed from the land.

LICENSES

A **license** is a right to use land in the possession of another, but it passes no land interest and does not alter or transfer property. A license only makes certain conduct on another's land lawful, such as hunting, fishing, or simply being on the property.

A licensee holds a privilege, and that privilege may be revoked at any time by the landowner. A license may be created by an oral agreement, since it is not an interest in land. If the parties attempt to create an easement by oral agreement, a license results.

In 1974, Beaufort County (the County) leased property located at the Hilton Head Airport to Hilton Head Air Service (Air Service). Air Service has operated an aviation business on the leased premises, providing services to the flying public such as maintenance and repair of aircraft. Air Service has also allowed rental car companies to operate on its leased premises.

In May 1979, the County and Air Service entered into a 25-year lease agreement. The lease agreement provided that the county would develop the airport according to a Master Plan Study accepted by the Federal Aviation Administration (FAA). A dispute arose regarding the presence of the rental car companies, which were not specifically or generally authorized by the plan. Air Service claims it can have the rental car companies removed at any time because there are no leases, many of their agreements are oral, and they hold only a license. Is Air Service correct in its characterization of the agreements with the car rental companies? *Hilton Head Air Service v. Beaufort County*, 418 S.E.2d 849 (S.C. 1992)

Consider 3.7

COVENANTS

A **covenant** is a restriction placed in a deed that is, in effect, a nonpossessory interest in land. Covenants serve to restrict or control some aspect of the use of the land. The common law rule with respect to such covenants is that they are enforceable against the grantor and grantee but not against any subsequent transferees. For example, a covenant in a grant of land for a railway requiring the construction of a depot and station would be enforceable against the grantee but not against subsequent transferees. For this reason, covenants are not effective in enforcing residential use restrictions. However, **equitable servitudes** may provide a solution. Equitable servitudes are restrictions on building and the use of land. These restrictions are enforceable against subsequent transferees in the restricted areas.

The recognition of equitable servitudes results from the need of residential home buyers for assurance that areas will remain residential and at a certain quality and level. These zoning laws are also helpful in restricting land use. Zoning laws are discussed at length in Chapter 18, and covenants and equitable servitudes are discussed in Chapter 21.

CAUTIONS AND CONCLUSIONS

If all persons involved in real estate transactions were knowledgeable and cautious enough to provide for easements, much of the discussion and many of the quoted cases in this chapter would be unnecessary. In applying the tools and risks described in this chapter, those involved in a sale transaction should answer the following questions:

1. Is the property accessible or is it landlocked?
2. If the property is accessible, where is the access and who owns it?
3. If the property is landlocked, how can access be obtained?
4. Where is the access route (or where should it be) located?
5. How large an access route is necessary?
6. What types of uses can be made of the access route?
7. Is the access route recorded in any of the land records?
8. Will the deed in the transaction provide for an easement?
9. What parties are using the property, why, when, and for how long?
10. Who will be responsible for maintenance?

If buyers, sellers, agents, brokers, and financiers would take the time to check land records and physically inspect the property involved, many of the expensive easement litigations noted in this chapter could be avoided. The cases used in this chapter demonstrate the types of strong feelings and reactions that can result from misunderstandings on property use. This expensive hostility might be avoided by determining answers to the previous 10 questions.

Key Terms

easement, 46
easement appurtenant, 47
easement in gross, 47
affirmative easement, 47
negative easement, 47
conservation easement, 48
dominant tenement (estate), 48
servient tenement (estate), 48

easement by express grant, 48
easement by express reservation, 48
easement by implication, 50
quasi easement, 50
easement by necessity, 53
prescription, 54
rule of reason, 57
profit, 61

profit a prendre, 61
Uniform Commercial Code (UCC),
   61
license, 61
covenant, 62
equitable servitudes, 62

Chapter Problems

1. Charlotte Minogue and John Monette are sister and brother. Each inherited a home from their father through his last will and testament. Charlotte inherited her father's actual residence at 90 Hawthorne Avenue in Albany, New York. John inherited the contiguous parcel located at 88 Hawthorne Avenue.

A blacktop driveway, approximately 10 feet wide, runs between the two houses. A survey in 1988 showed the driveway to be located on John's property. A concrete cinder-block garage is located at the rear of Charlotte's two-family home. The driveway had provided access for her father to the garage and to Charlotte and her tenants until John blocked such use in 1988.

Charlotte filed suit seeking a declaration of easement for ingress and egress over the driveway. Is she entitled to one? What theory could she use? What type of easement might she have? *Minogue v. Monette,* 551 N.Y.S.2d 427 (1990)

2. Alfonso owned a tract of land depicted in the diagram below. He could no longer afford the property taxes and decided to sell the western half of the property to Billy. In the deed, no mention was made of the access road on Alfonso's eastern half. Billy wishes to use the access road, but Alfonso refuses. The highway on the eastern side goes directly to town (three miles). The highway

on the western side is a major travel route with the nearest exit 25 miles away.

   a. Does Billy have a right to use the access road?

   b. Suppose Alfonso had told Billy he could use the access road. Would the result be different?

   c. Suppose Alfonso had told Billy he could use the access road; then Alfonso transferred the property to Sam; and Sam refused Billy's request to continue using the access road. What would be the result?

3. Rachael owns a small tract of land in Idaho but lives in Boston. Rachael's Idahoan neighbor, Big Bob, has been using a path on Rachael's tract of land to transport his potatoes for 15 years. Rachael has not visited the property for 16 years but has paid taxes on it. Everyone in the area knows of Big Bob's use of Rachael's land. Upon discovery of Big Bob's use, Rachael wishes to know her rights.

   a. What are Rachael's rights?

   b. Suppose Rachael discovered the problem after three years and put up a fence with a locking gate, which Big Bob then kicked down to continue his use. What would be the result?

   c. Suppose Rachael discovered the problem after three years and put up a sign that read: "No trespassing. Keep out. This means you, Big Bob." What would be the result?

   d. Suppose Rachael discovered the problem after three years and wrote Big Bob a note (sent certified mail) that read, "Please feel free to use my adjoining property, Big Bob." What would be the result?

   e. Suppose Big Bob increased the size of his dam and the pond behind it (both located on his property) and flooded Rachael's property several times each year for 32 years. Does Big Bob have any rights in Rachael's property as a result? *Chittenden v. Waterbury Center Community Church,* 726 A.2d 20 (Vt. 1998).

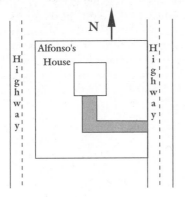

4. American University acquired a parcel of land (Lot 806) from Aetna Life Insurance Company. The university was given a Declaration of Easement and Agreement that provided that the grantor:

> conveys to the owners from time to time of [Lot 806 and their] tenants, occupants, guests and business invites, a nonexclusive easement for vehicular parking of not less than 236 automobiles on the parking areas located from time to time upon [Lot 807].

New owners of Lot 807 decided to regulate parking and limit the number of spaces available to American University. Can a private agreement like this or regulations change the terms and scope of an easement? *Burka v. Aetna Life. Ins. Co.,* 945 F.Supp. 313 (D.D.C. 1996)

5. In 1962, Temco sold property located at 900 South Wakefield Street to Harvey and Rosabelle Wynn. The purchase contract contains the following provision: "use of apartment swimming pool to be available to purchaser and his family." The Wynns were told that subsequent purchasers of their property would also have use of the swimming pool, which is located in an apartment complex next to the Wynns' home. No reference to use of the swimming pool was made in the Wynns' deed.

In 1969, the Bunns purchased the Wynns' home. The Bunns were told of their right to use the pool but upon moving in were denied access. The Bunns insisted on access but were still denied. They filed suit against the owner of Temco, Offutt, seeking a declaration of the easement rights. Do the Bunns have easement rights? *Bunn v. Offutt,* 222 S.E.2d 522 (Va. 1976)

6. Sylvia Tenn owns a six-story building that has air conditioners in the windows. 889 Associates, Ltd., is planning to construct a 12-story building next to Tenn's building. The result will be that Tenn's window air conditioners will no longer be effective. Tenn claims that she has had the air conditioners for more than 20 years and that she has acquired a prescriptive easement for the air conditioners. Is she correct? *Tenn v. 889 Associates, Ltd.,* 500 A.2d 366 (N.H. 1985)

7. Pacific Theatres and Supply Company, Limited, acquired title to a lot in Waikiki near Seaside and Kalakaua Avenue. The lot deed also provided:

> TOGETHER with the perpetual right of ingress and egress over the 10-foot strip of land on the Western side of Lot 2-B.

Consolidated Amusement bought Pacific's lot and has operated a movie theater there since 1936. Waikiki Business Plaza acquired title to an adjacent lot and planned to construct the Plaza Building and set up vendors' booths in the area. Before the vendors began business and during building construction, Consolidated and the Plaza agreed to allow a "pedestrian passageway" for Plaza activities when the Plaza commenced commercial business with the various booths. Consolidated maintains the booths interfere with its easement for theater patrons. Plaza claims that a small passageway is sufficient. Who is correct? Can the easement be reduced by agreement? *Waikiki Business Consolidated Amusement v. Plaza,* 719 P.2d 1119 (Haw. 1986)

8. Asa E. Phillips owned property in Seal Harbor, Maine. His deed included a 20-foot right-of-way over property owned by Kate Gregg and W. Layton Stewart. The right-of-way had long been reduced to a five-foot wide footpath and was largely overgrown with trees. Gregg and Stewart had placed gates and warning signs along the path to discourage Phillips's use. Phillips brought suit for an injunction to prevent Gregg and Stewart from interfering with his use of his right-of-way. Gregg and Stewart claimed he had abandoned his easement through nonuse. Who is correct? How should the court determine abandonment? *Phillips v. Gregg,* 628 A.2d 151 (Me. 1993)

9. Paul Atkinson purchased land from Donald Mentzel that included an easement across Mentzel's land so that Atkinson could have access to his garage. Atkinson wished to install telephone cable along the easement so that he could more fully use his garage. At the time of the conveyance the Atkinson property did not have utility service. The easement was described as a right-of-way and including the following:

> The purpose of this easement is to provide access from Lake Shore Drive to the following described real estate and shall allow access for all uses of said property other than retail sales.

Should Atkinson be permitted to install the telephone cable along the easement? *Atkinson v. Mentzel,* 566 N.W.2d 158 (Wis. App. 1997)

10. The Freeds and Margaret Sterner are owners of adjacent lots. Mrs. Sterner has used a driveway across the Freedses' land for access to her garage. The driveway has been there since 1957, when the Freedses' and Mrs. Sterner's lots were owned by a Mr. William Weaver as one parcel. In 1988, the Freeds erected a barrier and Mrs. Sterner could no longer use the driveway. Does Mrs. Sterner have any rights? Does she have an easement? If so, what type? *Sterner v. Freed,* 570 A.2d 1079 (Pa. 1990)

Internet Activities

1. For more information on easements that affect residential purchases in the state of Oregon, go to: **http://www.teleport.com/~garski/easement.htm**.

2. For more information on conservation easements, go to:

http://www.mtlandreliance.com

http://www.allianceforamerica.org

http://www.r6.fws.gov/pfw/r6pfw8b.htm

http://www.mnland.org/easement.htm

http://www.epa.gov/safewater/dwsrf/ffland.html

3. For information on utility easements in residential property go to: **http://www.homeadvisor.msn.com/dl/highlight/qa/5020.asp**.

4. For information on easements in rural property, go to: **http://www.tetranet.net/~triad/tipsbook.htm**.

NEBRASKA DEPARTMENT OF

PA&T

PROPERTY ASSESSMENT AND TAXATION

REAL PROPERTY REGULATIONS

Numerical Index

REG. NO.	SUBJECT	DATE	REG. NO.	SUBJECT	DATE
Reg-10-001	Definitions	7/00	Reg-10-004	Record Keeping	7/00
Reg-10-002	Procedures	7/00	Reg-10-005	Improvements on Leased Land	7/00
Reg-10-003	Manuals	7/00			

REG-10-001 DEFINITIONS

001.01 Real property shall mean all land, buildings, fixtures, improvements, certain mobile homes, mineral interests, and all privileges pertaining to real property.

001.01A Fixtures shall include any item of property that is:

001.01A(1) Annexed or physically attached to or incorporated into the real property;

001.01A(2) Applied or adapted to the use or purpose of the real property to which it is attached, which shall mean that the real property cannot be used for its intended purpose without the item and the item cannot be used for its intended purpose without the real property; and

001.01A(3) Intended to be annexed to the real property. Intention shall be inferred from the nature and extent of the annexation and adaptation, unless the owner of the item or the owner of the real property provides documentation that the intention is otherwise.

Chapter 4
Fixtures

Is the refrigerator included with the house?

The American Home Buyer

Every lawyer knows that cases can be found in this field that will support any proposition.

Powell, Real Property

A **fixture** is real property that was once personal property. It becomes attached to the real property and becomes a part of it. This chapter answers the questions: What is a fixture and when does personal property become a fixture? How is the title to a fixture transferred? What rights do creditors have in fixtures?

DEFINITION OF A FIXTURE

Whether a particular item of personal property will become real property depends on several factors discussed in the following sections. No single factor controls; rather, the different factors must be considered together in their entirety in order to determine whether an item is real or personal property. The distinction between real and personal property is critical in two primary areas: First, it will control whether an item passes with the real property or if it may be removed prior to the title transfer. Second, it will affect the determination of the creditor's rights, that is, how much the mortgage holder is entitled to and how much belongs to the personal property creditor.

Degree of Annexation Test

The degree of annexation test is the first factor to be considered in determining the status of an item of property, and its purpose is to examine the fixture's degree of attachment. Under the English rule for fixtures, annexation was the controlling factor, and anything attached by mortar, nail, screw, or bolt was classified as a fixture.

Currently, annexation is defined as attachment to the realty with a use or purpose related to the realty. A furnace in a home is an example that meets the degree of annexation necessary for a fixture because the home cannot function without the presence of the furnace (which was once personal property). On the other hand, a ship or boat does not become part of the real property of a dock simply because an anchor is dropped, because its attachment to the realty is unrelated. A painting on a wall can be hung on any wall, but the sculptures within building columns are a part of the building and hence meet this annexation test.

The degree of annexation test applies to personal property attached to realty but not to accessions. Accessions are those items of personal property that are used in the construction of a building and become so integrated into the building that their identity is lost. Examples of accessions are lumber, bricks, and beams.

Applying the degree of annexation test to each of the following, determine the likelihood of having the item treated as a fixture.

Consider 4.1

a. Roger W. Marsh, d/b/a [doing business as] Bestmade Wood Products, constructs wooden cabinets on special order and installs them in homes (usually new homes under construction). He installs the cabinets by placing them in the house and nailing them to the walls and floors. The Department of Revenue wished to collect sales tax from Marsh on the grounds that the cabinets were the sale of personal property. Marsh maintains the property is real estate once installed, he does not receive payment until after installation, and thus is not liable for sales tax for the sale of personal property. Who is correct? *Marsh v. Spradling*, 537 S.W.2d 402 (Mo. 1976)

b. J.K.S.P. Restaurant, Inc., purchased a prefabricated dining car from Pullman in 1965. The diner was transported in three sections from New Jersey to New York, where it was unloaded, assembled, and installed on a foundation that had been built in the ground. The three sections of the diner were bolted in place. J.K.S.P.'s president stated that the purpose of designing diners in this way was to retain their character and personality and allow for easy removal and movement. Nassau County has included the value of the diner in its assessment of J.K.S.P.'s real property value. Is this correct? *J.K.S.P. Restaurant, Inc. v. Nassau County*, 513 N.Y.S.2d 716 (1987)

Nature and Use of the Property

The unique nature of the property attached is also examined to determine its necessity in relation to the effective functioning of the building. For example, storm windows are especially built and installed for a particular home and work

http://

Fixtures are defined at
Nebraska's Department
of Property Assessment
and Taxation at: **http://
pat.nol.org:80/
reg/10.htm**.

to help control heat in the home. Likewise, a pipe organ in a church with the pipes serving as decoration for the building has an intricate relation to the building. In a garage, an air compressor that is used to hoist cars for repair is central and necessary to the function of that building.

Relationship Between Annexor and Premises

Another factor to be examined is what type of land interest the party attaching the personal property (the annexor) owns. In brief, the higher the degree of interest in the land, the more likely it is that the item or property will be treated as a fixture. For example, a small cottage or bungalow placed on cement blocks on the land by a fee simple owner is a fixture. That same bungalow placed on leased land by a tenant will probably retain its characteristics of personal property.

A tenant does not hold as great an interest in the land as a life estate holder or a fee simple holder. Therefore, annexations by tenants are less likely to be treated as fixtures. Two additional questions to examine in analyzing this factor are: (1) Did the tenant intend the item to be a gift to the landlord (that is, did the tenant intend to leave the property at the termination of the lease?); and (2) will removal of the property cause substantial damage? For example, a floor replaced with a new covering by a tenant will be substantially damaged if the covering is removed upon termination of the tenancy. On the other hand, removal of temporary wall bookshelves may not cause irreparable damage and would be classified as a tenant's personal property.

Intent

The intent of the parties can be the controlling factor in cases where the issue of fixture versus personal property is a close decision, as well as in cases where the parties have reached an agreement (or have placed a provision in their contract or lease) covering the issue of whether an item will be real or personal property. For example, the refrigerators may be included in the sale of residences or apartments, and according to the parties involved may be considered a fixture. Likewise, washers and dryers may be part of the real estate according to the terms of the parties' agreement.

Trade Fixtures

The term **trade fixture** is a misnomer. This term covers a special rule for machines and equipment that treats items used in a trade or business as personal property, even though their degree of annexation may result in some damage upon removal. In the absence of an agreement between the parties, title to the equipment or machinery does not pass with the sale of the factory or business. For example, a large printing press bolted to the floor is a trade fixture and thus personal property. Likewise, display counters in stores are attached but are classified as trade fixtures.

Consider 4.2

Cliff Ridge Skiing Corporation is in bankruptcy, and a priority dispute has arisen among creditors because of a question as to whether Cliff Ridge's chairlifts are fixtures. The chairlifts were attached to the real property Cliff Ridge had mortgaged to First National Bank. There were concrete pads poured into the realty, towers were bolted to the concrete pads, cables were strung between the towers, and about 100 chairs were attached to the cables. However, one creditor maintains that the chairlifts can be easily removed from the land and sold as a package to another ski resort. Another creditor maintains that the pads, towers, and cables are specifically designed to fit the topography of a particular ski resort and cannot be easily modified for another resort. Who is correct? *In re Cliff's Ridge Skiing Corp.*, 123 B.R. 753, 13 UCC Rep.2d 1309 (Mich. 1991)

4.2, *continued*

Who Wants to Know?

Although the treatises on real property do not list this factor as one to be used in the determination of real versus personal property, the question of "who wants to know" has affected judicial decisions in this area. This factor permits differing results depending on what party is seeking to determine the classification for an item of property.

For example, in litigation between a buyer and seller, the buyer is favored because the seller usually presents the form contract and has failed to make all intentions clear in that contract. In an eminent domain valuation procedure, the landowner is favored with a liberal finding of fixtures because just and fair compensation is the court's concern in these circumstances. If a question arises on the application of real property insurance for certain items, the insured will be favored with liberal fixture treatment because of the insurer's failure to clarify coverage provisions. In taxation valuations, fixtures are more liberally found because of the increased value of the property when the fixtures are included in the valuation determination.

The following cases are examples of courts applying the various factors used in the determination of whether an item is real or personal property. Note that the first two cases deal with the same fixture, but reach different results.

Adams Outdoor Adv. Ltd. Part. v. Long
483 S.E.2d 224 (Va. 1997)

Facts

Robert E. Long owned land in the City of Hampton that he leased to Adams Outdoor Advertising Limited Partnership. Adams had an advertising billboard placed on the property. On October 6, 1993, Long notified Adams that he was terminating the lease. Adams accepted the termination and told Long that it would have the electrical service disconnected and would schedule demolition of the billboard for the first week in November. Long wanted to use the billboard to advertise his own business and filed suit to enjoin Adams from destroying the billboard. Long maintained the billboard was part of the land and belonged to him. Adams asserted that it owned the billboard as a lessee. The trial court found for Long and Adams appealed.

Judicial Opinion

Lacy, Justice. The billboard at issue is a structure permanently affixed to the land. Whether such a structure remains personalty, owned by the person who erected the structure, or becomes part of the realty, and thus owned by the landowner, is determined either by an agreement establishing the nature and ownership of the structure or, in the absence of agreement, by applying the three-part test enunciated by this Court in *Danville Holding Corp. v. Clement,* 16 S.E.2d 345 (Va. 1941). The record in this case establishes that the lease agreements between successive landlords and tenants addressed the issue of ownership rights in the billboard.

The billboard was erected more than 65 years ago by Consolvo & Cheshire, an advertising agency. At that time,

Consolvo & Cheshire negotiated a lease which provided that "[a]ll boards and materials placed on the premises" by the lessee were the property of the lessee and that the lessee could "remove their boards" from the premises on the termination of the lease. Similar language regarding ownership was contained in leases executed between Consolvo & Cheshire and successive landowners in 1938 and 1945. Subsequent leases executed in 1949, 1957, 1968, and 1977 between successor landowners and different lessees, stated that "signs, structures and equipment" erected by the lessee were the property of the lessee and could be removed by the lessee.

Adams claims to be the owner under the terms of the 1977 lease or, alternatively, under the *Danville* test, because all the leases show an intent that the lessee retain ownership of the billboard. We agree that each lease does address the ownership of the billboard, but places ownership in the lessee *who erected the billboard.* Consolvo & Cheshire erected the billboard in this case, and, therefore, Adams does not qualify as the owner of the billboard under the terms of any lease. Because the lease agreement clearly addresses ownership of the billboard, application of the test enunciated in *Danville* is unnecessary, and the trial court correctly rejected Adams' ownership claim.

The trial court also correctly held that Long was the owner of the billboard. When tenants retain ownership of structures they erect on property and are allowed to remove the structures, the removal generally must occur within a reasonable period after the end of the tenancy. If the structure is not removed, it becomes the property of the landlord because it is affixed to the land. This rule is based on a presumption of abandonment and protects subsequent parties from interruption by a tenant who returns to remove the fixtures. The entry of a former tenant on the land to remove the structure would itself constitute a trespass.

In this case, the tenant that constructed the billboard, Consolvo & Cheshire, did not remove it at the conclusion of its tenancy or within a reasonable time thereafter. Consequently, the billboard, which was permanently affixed to the land, became part of the realty and the property of the landowner. When Long acquired the land, he acquired the billboard as part of the land purchased.

Affirmed as to the finding that the billboard belongs to Long.

Case Questions

1. What did the original lease provide in terms of rights to the billboard?
2. Why is it important who erected the billboard?
3. Why is it important that Consolvo & Cheshire did not remove the billboard?
4. Who gets the billboard now?

R. C. Maxwell Company v. Galloway Township

679 A.2d 141 (N.J. 1996)

Facts

R. C. Maxwell is a New Jersey corporation that has conducted outdoor advertising since 1894. At the time of the case, Maxwell had 900 outdoor advertising displays in New Jersey.

Maxwell leased property owned by Scola, Inc., in Galloway Township for the purpose of erecting four billboards. Maxwell's billboards have traditionally been taxed by the state as business personal property. Maxwell also pays licensing and permit fees to the state pursuant to the Outdoor Advertising Act, and more recently the Roadside Sign Control and Outdoor Advertising Act.

On November 25, 1991, the Attorney General issued an advisory opinion on behalf of the Director, Division of Taxation, that the billboards were taxable as real property. The result was that Galloway Township's assessment for Scola's real property increased from $86,700 to $90,400. Maxwell and Scola challenged the assessment, but the Board of Taxation upheld the assessment. Maxwell and Scola appealed, but the tax court granted summary judgment for Galloway Township. The court of appeals affirmed and Maxwell and Scola appealed.

Judicial Opinion

Handler, Justice. The taxpayers contend that billboards are personal property that is exempt from taxation as real property. Subsection (a) of N.J.S.A. 54:4-1 classifies improvements "consisting of personal property" that are "affixed to the real property" as "within real property" and therefore taxable.

The taxpayers argue that under this statutory framework, billboards should be classified not as improvements to realty but only as personal property because (1) they can be removed without material injury to either the real property to which they are affixed or to the billboard itself, and (2) they are ordinarily not intended to be affixed permanently to real property.

Maxwell's billboards are comprised primarily of wood with some metal components such as bolts and nails. The advertising copy is located on what is known as the face of the billboard, which rests on a grid of vertical planks known as uprights and horizontal planks known as stringers. Backbracing connects the uprights to anchors, which are planks that are almost entirely stuck to the ground. Three of the billboards in this case have 12-foot by 25-foot faces and one has an 8-foot by 15-foot face.

Illuminated billboards also have the following additional components: (1) a one hundred amp service panel with timer clock; (2) six quartz or fluorescent fixtures; (3) a maximum of 110 lineal feet of rigid pipe; (4) a service entrance cable; and (5) a ground rod.

Because approximately 85% of Maxwell's billboard signs are made of wood, there is a constant need for new or recycled replacement parts. Maxwell regularly repairs or replaces its billboard parts that either are damaged by the elements or succumb to rot. Maxwell contends that if a billboard location is lost, it is able to disassemble the billboard and salvage a high percentage of its wooden parts for reuse at another site.

On close review, we determine that Maxwell's wooden billboards can be removed without being materially injured. A billboard's utility is not destroyed when it is removed. Approximately 80% of a billboard's support structure is salvageable on removal. The advertising face, which is the key component of a billboard, is not damaged by removal and is normally completely reusable.

The ultimate determination depends on an objective view of what the "ordinary intent" was for installing the billboards.

The actual history of the billboards suggests that they might have been intended to be affixed permanently. The billboards have been at their current sites for ap-proximately thirty-five years. Post-installation history of property has been considered to support a finding that the ordinarily [sic] intention was one of permanence.

The course of billboard industry practices demonstrates that the ordinary intent for the billboards is not to have them permanently affixed to the land. First, billboard owners typically do not own the land on which their displays are constructed. Second, billboard leases are generally short-term ones. Third, wooden billboards are regularly constructed without a concrete foundation. Fourth, billboards often relocate on short notice due to State land condemnations and landlords' decisions not to renew leases.

Billboards remain the property of the billboard company and do not ordinarily pass with title to the realty on which they are erected. Billboard companies do not leave billboards when their leases end and they vacate a location; rather, they remove them and erect them at new sites. Billboards are frequently resold separately from real property. Every year, hundreds of billboards are sold in New Jersey from one company to another.

Accordingly, we determine on the record in the case that billboards are not ordinarily intended to be affixed permanently to the land.

Of course, there are some billboards of steel and concrete that may not qualify for the tax exemption. We focus here on traditional wooden billboards and do not determine whether steel and concrete billboards can be removed without being materially injured or were not ordinarily intended to be affixed permanently to the real estate.

Reversed.

Case Questions

1. List the factors the court reviews in determining whether the billboards are real or personal property.

2. Why does the court not determine whether steel and concrete billboards are also exempt from real property taxation?

3. List some parties you think would have been involved as amicus curiae (friend of the court) in this case and would have intervened for purposes of having the taxation issue determined.

4. What is different about this case from the *Adams* case?

Specialty Restaurants Corporation v. County of Los Angeles

136 Cal. Rptr. 904 (1977)

The Queen Mary is taxable

Facts

Specialty Restaurants Corporation and PSA Hotels, Inc. (plaintiffs), are lessees of premises on the *Queen Mary*, a stationary vessel owned by the City of Long Beach, California. In 1973, 1974, and 1975, the assessor of the County of Los Angeles assessed the leasehold interests of Specialty and PSA on the grounds that those interests were possessory interests in real property or improvements to real property.

Specialty and PSA paid the taxes levied under protest and filed an application with the Assessment Appeals Board, contending that the *Queen Mary* was personal property and that their possessory interests were not real property and hence not subject to taxation.

The Assessment Appeals Board (the Board) held that the interests were personal property and not subject to taxation. Specialty and PSA then filed for refunds and were denied the refunds by the trial court, and they appealed.

Judicial Opinion

Ford, Presiding Justice. Two of the ship's original four engines have been completely removed. The two remaining engines, located in the "after engine room," form part of an exhibit in "the museum." The ship has no propulsion power; it was towed from its former mooring place to Pier J. The ship could not be safely towed outside the harbor "because of its alterations since it came to Long Beach." The rudder of the ship is welded so that it cannot be operated. All twenty-three of the ship's boilers have been removed. The ship's fuel tanks are intact but are not used as such; their purpose is to "maintain their [*sic*] buoyancy and stability of the ship."

Captain Lynch testified that he doubted "very seriously" that the *Queen Mary*'s original propulsion system could be restored.

The wharf structure which provides ways onto and off of the *Queen Mary* was designed specifically for the *Queen Mary*. Captain Lynch testified that "[t]he whole site of the ship, of course, was planned on the basis that the *Queen Mary* would be moored there." He further testified that it was "not inconceivable" that the wharf could be adapted to the dimensions of another large ship.

After the execution of the lease numerous improvements were made with respect to the site. A total amount of $10,750,474 was spent on improvements to the site to accommodate the *Queen Mary* as a tourist attraction.

Revenue and Taxation Code section 104 provides that "real estate" or "real property" includes improvement. Revenue and Taxation Code section 105 defines "improvement" as including "[a]ll buildings, structures, fixtures, and fences erected on or affixed to the land, except telephone and telegraph lines." Civil Code section 660 provides that a "thing is deemed to be affixed to land when it is attached to it by roots, as in the case of trees, vines or shrubs; or imbedded in it, as in the case of walls; or permanently resting upon it, as in the case of buildings; or permanently attached to what is thus permanent, as by means of cement, plaster, nails, bolts, or screws; . . . " Revenue and Taxation Code section 106 provides that " '[p]ersonal property' includes all property except real estate."

Defendants contend that plaintiffs' possessory interests in the *Queen Mary* are possessory interests in real property because the *Queen Mary* is in improvement, being either a structure or fixture affixed to the land within the meaning of Revenue and Taxation Code section 105. In *Simms v. County of Los Angeles*, 35 Cal.2d 303, at page 309, 217 P.2d 936, at page 940, the court stated three tests to be applied in determining whether an article is a fixture or an object affixed to the realty: "(1) the manner of its annexation; (2) its adaptability to the use and purpose for which the realty is used; and (3) the intention of the party making the annexation." For taxation purposes the intention which is determinative is not the subjective intention of the party making the annexation, but the intention apparent from the physical facts.

In this case the City of Long Beach's intention to make the *Queen Mary* a permanent addition to the realty is clearly manifested by the physical facts. The *Queen Mary* houses a museum, a hotel, restaurants and various shops. Extensive sums of money were expended by the city to develop the *Queen Mary* and its site at Pier J as a tourist attraction. A large rock dike encloses the *Queen Mary*. A system has been established to protect the underwater hull of the *Queen Mary* and to eliminate the necessity of moving the ship to a dry dock to maintain its underwater surfaces. An extensive system of utilities has been established to supply the ship with such items as water, steam, sewage disposal, electricity and communication. A power plant was built to service the *Queen Mary* exclusively. An extensive system of gangways reached by means of elevators and escalators was built to allow access to the ship by tourists and other patrons. A large parking facility was established to accommodate visitors and large sums of money were expended on access roads and bridges. A consideration of the physical facts compels the inference that the city intended the *Queen Mary* to be a permanent addition to real property.

Great expense involved in removal of heavy equipment and the difficulty attending its removal are indicative of intended permanence. The fact that the evidence showed that with the expenditure of considerable time and effort the *Queen Mary* could be removed from its location at Pier J is not determinative as to its nature for purposes of taxation. "The mere fact that said doors can be removed without material damage to the vaults by chipping away with a chisel, jack hammer, or compressed air hammer, the cement grouting which attaches them to the vaults, does not alone establish their character as articles of personalty. A door or window in an ordinary dwelling house can be removed with very little damage to the realty. It also may be replaced by one of different design or by a new one if the former should become broken or defective, but no one would contend that either was not a part of the realty by reason of these facts alone."

The second test mentioned in *Simms v. County of Los Angeles,* is the "adaptability" of the article to the "use and purpose for which the realty is used." "The most favored indicia of implied intention of permanence of annexation, for general purposes, are the various circumstances surrounding the use of the property. The question most frequently asked is whether the real property is peculiarly valuable in use because of the continued presence thereon of the annexed property."

In the cases presently before us the fact that the *Queen Mary* is integral to the purpose for which the land is used appears to be beyond question. All the improvements made to the land were designed to accommodate the *Queen Mary* as a tourist attraction. It is manifest that the area of real property permanently by the *Queen Mary* is "peculiarly valuable in use" because of the *Queen Mary's* presence.

Turning to the question of the manner in which the *Queen Mary* has been annexed to the land, it is manifest that the annexation is substantial.

In making its finding that the *Queen Mary* was personal property the trial court stressed the fact that "the *Queen Mary* floats in the ocean." However, we do not think that that fact is determinative. The *Queen Mary* is securely fastened to the wharf and its movement is minimal. Captain Lynch testified that the decision to allow the ship to float in its enclosed basin was to protect against possible earthquake damage; that manner of placement in no way indicates an intention on the city's part to make the *Queen Mary* other than a permanent addition to the land.

The uncontradicted testimonial and documentary evidence presented in this matter with respect to the proper classification of the *Queen Mary* for tax purposes clearly fails to support the trial court's determination that the *Queen Mary* is personal property.

Applying the law as set forth herein with respect to the proper classification of property for tax purposes to the undisputed facts in this case, we hold that the trial court erred as a matter of law in determining that "the *Queen Mary* was and is personal property" and that "the possessory interests of plaintiffs in, on and to the *Queen Mary* were and are possessory interests in personal property" and as such are nontaxable. We hold that the respective possessory interests in plaintiffs' Specialty Restaurants Corporation and PSA Hotels, Inc., in, on and to the *Queen Mary* are possessory interests in improvements to real property and as such are subject to taxation.

Reversed.

Case Questions

1. Explain how the *Queen Mary* is attached to the Long Beach pier.

2. Is the *Queen Mary* capable of being seaworthy again?

3. Is the *Queen Mary* personal property or real property?

4. Will the *Queen Mary* be subject to real estate taxation?

5. Is the *Queen Mary* a trade fixture?

Applying the factors for determining what constitutes a fixture and the preceding cases, determine the status of each of the following:

Consider 4.3

a.   Floor-to-ceiling bookcases installed in an apartment by a tenant

b.   Automatic garage door opener control

c.   Landscaping

d.   Electric ceiling fans

e.   Stove and refrigerator purchased by the debtor for her mortgaged home (*In re Rolle,* 218 B.R. 636 (Bank v. S. D. Fla 1998)

f.   Modular commercial building attached by concrete pad by tenant (*Hot Shots Burgers and Fries, Inc. v. FAS FAX Corp.,* 169 B.R. 920 (E. D. Ark. 1994)

4.3, continued

g. Partitions nailed to the floor in an office building
h. Paneled refrigerator (paneled to match kitchen cabinets)
i. Bank vault door
j. Murphy bed (bed that folds into wall)
k. Seats and screens in a theater
l. Ski lifts at a ski resort
m. Storage bins on a farm
n. Display cases in a department store
o. Bus passenger shelter on a sidewalk
    (*Ali v. City of Detroit,* 554 N.W.2d 384 [Mich. App. 1996])

Practical Tip

When in doubt, ask! Brokers should verify what is included in a property sale to avoid such items becoming an issue of negotiation and/or contention. Sellers should make clear their intentions and possibly remove any items that could confuse buyers and sale terms. Buyers should list, count, and verify to be sure they know what they're getting.

A Word on Precautions

Once again, the cases in this chapter have demonstrated that emotions and litigation can arise very easily over what appear to be insignificant items. Also, most of the confusion, emotion, and litigation again could be avoided if parties would clearly determine their positions at the outset through written agreements. Figure 4.1 summarizes the questions that should be addressed in various types of land transactions to cover the issue of fixtures.

Attachments

Apart from fixtures, there are many other attachments to land. For example, most property contains trees, bushes, and grasses, which are referred to as *fructus naturales* and are considered part of the real property. When land is sold or mortgaged, these naturally growing elements are simultaneously sold or mortgaged.

Some property contains growing crops or *fructus industriales* (or **emblements**). These crops are not treated as part of real property; they are classified as personal property. If a tenant grows crops on leased property, the crops belong to the tenant even though they may not be ready for harvest at the time the tenant's lease terminates. This right of removal of crops planted by a tenant is called the **Doctrine of Emblements.**

Consider 4.4

Rainier National Bank held a mortgage on property owned by Fred and Evelyn Wall. The Walls leased the property to Ronald Ritter, who grew Christmas trees on the property. Ritter gave a security interest in all crops from the land to Security State Bank. Ritter defaulted on his loan from Security, and a dispute began as to whether Rainier had priority because the Christmas trees were real property and Rainier had recorded its real property mortgage first. Who is correct? Who has priority? Are the Christmas trees real or personal property? *Rainier National Bank v. Security State Bank,* 796 P.2d 443 (Wash. Ct. App. 1990)

Real

TRANSFER OF TITLE TO FIXTURES AND PERSONAL PROPERTY

If property is classified as a fixture and part of the real property, title to it will pass with the deed transferring title to the property. However, for items not classified as fixtures, some method of transferring title is necessary. Whenever a

FIGURE 4.1   *Fixture Analysis*

Parties	Questions to be Answered (important)
Landlord/Tenant	1. Does the lease contain a provision on what types of attachments the tenant may make and remove?
	2. Does the lease contain a provision on payment for damages for removal?
	3. Does the lease require prior notification before a tenant attaches property?
Buyer/Seller	1. What items are included with the real property?
	2. Are any items specifically excluded?
	3. Does the contract list questionable items, such as drapes?
	4. Does the contract prevent substitution or removal of fixtures before closing?
	5. Is a bill of sale drawn up for questionable items such as washers, dryers, and refrigerators?
Creditor/Attacher	1. Who owns the land where the property is being attached?
	2. How permanent will the attachment be?
	3. Can removal occur without damage to the property?
	4. Are there other creditors with protected interests in the real property?

question exists as to whether an item is real or personal property, a bill of sale should be used to assure complete transfer of title.

CREDITORS' RIGHTS IN FIXTURES

One of the reasons given for the determination of whether an item is personal property or a fixture was that creditors' rights are affected by the determination. Each state has provisions to protect creditors' interests in personal property that becomes attached to real estate and is then classified as a fixture.

This protection is afforded under **Article 9 of the Uniform Commercial Code (UCC).** The UCC is a set of laws drafted by a group of scholars, attorneys, and businesspeople with the idea of having state-to-state uniformity in commercial transactions.

Article 9 covers creditors' rights and responsibilities in collateral pledged by debtors for loans. All of the states have adopted some version of Article 9. However, there have been revisions and technical amendments to Article 9 over the years that have been adopted in some states. In July 2001, a substantially revised Article 9 takes effect in 28 states. The new changes are covered in the sections below.[1] Each state has made some variations and the actual Article 9 language discussed in this portion of the chapter will vary from state to state.

---

1.   Section numbers are new to Article 9.

Scope of Article 9

Article 9 of the UCC governs the use of personal property or the use of fixtures as collateral. The concern in this book will be fixtures because of their relationship to real estate law.

Article 9 permits the creditor to obtain a **security interest** in the collateral which provides the creditor with certain rights, opportunities, and priorities.

Creation (Attachment) of Security Interest (9-203)

There are three requirements for creating a valid security interest: a security agreement, a debtor with rights in collateral, and value given by the creditor.

SECURITY AGREEMENT (9-105)

[handwritten margin note: Must be in clear Writing Debtor]

A security interest begins with the execution of a **security agreement** by the creditor and debtor (9-203). A security agreement has several requirements: (1) it must be in writing; (2) it must be signed by the debtor (under Revised Article 9, the agreement must be "authenticated," which allows for signing via electronic record); (3) it must contain language indicating that a security interest is being created; and (4) it must contain a description of the collateral that reasonably identifies it. Since fixtures will be attached to real property, a description of the real property involved is helpful in clarifying the identity and location of the property. Form security agreements, available in each state, generally meet all of the requirements for a valid security agreement.

DEBTOR'S RIGHTS IN COLLATERAL (9-202)

In some cases, the debtor may already own the collateral and is simply pledging such property as security for a debt. In most fixture cases, however, the creditor is selling goods to the buyer, and the buyer is pledging the purchased goods as collateral. In these cases, the debtor has rights in the collateral at the time of delivery so that the pledge can be properly made. For example, a seller of air conditioners who has the buyer execute a security agreement will have a valid security interest when the buyer takes possession of the air conditioner. The security agreement can be executed in advance and become effective upon the buyer's possession.

VALUE GIVEN BY CREDITOR (9-203)

In the preceding example, the creditor gives value through the binding commitment to extend credit. A creditor may give value in any way that would constitute consideration in a simple contract. In the case of fixtures, the promise to extend credit is most frequently given as value by the creditor.

Once all three requirements are met (authenticated security agreement, collateral interest, and value), the security interest attaches. Just having a security interest gives the creditor certain rights to a superior position over that of other creditors. A secured creditor is always given priority over unsecured creditors. Also, the creation of a security interest entitles the creditor to repossession of the secured property in the event the debtor defaults on payments for the collateral. However, for the creditor to enjoy the most complete protection available under Article 9, **perfection,** a process of creating notice of a security agreement, must be obtained.

Purchase Money Security Interest in Fixtures (9-103)

Creditors with a **purchase money security interest (PMSI)** obtain more complete protection. A PMSI is given to secure all or part of the purchase price of the item purchased. For example, when a home owner or business purchases an air conditioner on credit from a seller or manufacturer of such units and the seller or manufacturer takes a security interest, a PMSI exists. The distinction between a PMSI and a security interest is important because the PMSI creditor is entitled to certain priorities in the event the debtor (buyer) defaults on payments for the future.

Perfection of Security Interest (9-301)

Financing Statement (9-502) Perfection (when fixtures are involved) is obtained through the filing of a financing statement. A **financing statement** is a written form that will vary from state to state but must include the following items:

1. Names of the debtors and the secured party
2. Signature (authorization under Rev. Article 9) of the debtor
3. Address of the secured party from which information can be obtained
4. Mailing address of the debtor
5. A statement describing the items of collateral

Fixture financing statements must be filed in the real estate records. Most of the information required on the financing statement is self-explanatory, but the description item is critical, including a property description for fixtures. While there have been substantial Article 9 changes on perfection, the fixture perfection has remained the same because of the need for filing with real property records.

FILING THE FINANCING STATEMENT

A valid or authenticated financing statement must be filed for fixtures locally, generally at the county level where land records are kept.

Article 9 fixture filings are local because fixtures are land interests, and all records of creditors' interests in land should be reflected in the same records. An accurate land description is needed to make clear where the fixture is located and for proper notification of all parties interested in the land.[2]

Upon filing of the financing statement in the proper office, the creditor's interest is perfected. This perfection entitles creditors to priority over subsequent creditors and even priority over some prior creditors. These priorities are discussed in the next section.

LENGTH OF PERFECTION (9-515)

A filing under the UCC is good in most states for a period of five years. However, if the debt is paid prior to that time, the financing statement and security interest can be terminated. If necessary, the creditor may renew the financing statement any time during the final six months of the five-year term and will thus receive the protection for another five years.

---

2.   In *Webb v. Interstate Land Corp.*, 920 P.2d 1187 (Utah 1996), a court held that a fixture financing statement filed without a description of the real property on which the sign is located was "totally ineffective to protect its interest in the sign against anyone except buyer of sign who saw it affixed."

General Rules of Priority Among Secured Creditors (9-317)

To determine priorities among creditors in the event of the debtor's default, certain rules and exceptions will be applied. These general rules are the starting point for determining the priorities in payment rights when a debtor is in default on loans secured by mortgages and security interests in fixtures:

1. A secured creditor has priority over an unsecured creditor.
2. A perfected secured creditor has priority over an unperfected secured creditor.
3. A perfected secured creditor has priority over subsequent real estate interests. (For example, a filing on January 3 gives the secured party priority over filings occurring later in that month or simply later in time.)
4. A prior real estate interest (mortgage, deed of trust, lien, or judgment) has priority over a subsequently filed security interest.
5. Between perfected secured creditors the date of filing is controlling, with the first creditor to file having priority.

Exceptions to General Rules

PMSI EXCEPTION (9-324)/(9-334)

A PMSI creditor may take priority over prior real estate encumbrances if the financing statement is filed before the goods become fixtures or within 20 days after they become fixtures. This priority applies even though language in the mortgage provides that all after-attached property and fixtures are subject to the mortgage. To illustrate, suppose that a homeowner has a mortgage on his property, which was filed in August 1998. The homeowner is in need of a solar water-heating system. The system is purchased from Solar Systems Company on credit, and a security agreement is executed and a financing statement filed on June 3, 2000. The solar system is then attached and installed. Solar Systems Company (as a PMSI) would have priority over a 1998 mortgage holder.

The reason for the PMSI exception is that without some form of special priority for the secured party, creditors would be hesitant to finance improvements and added fixtures to existing structures still subject to a mortgage.

Consider 4.5

The La Mesa Restaurant was started in 1979 in a building on property mortgaged to First National Bank (FNB) on June 1, 1979. La Mesa performed well until the 1990 recession in the Phoenix area. Business was very slow and, in addition, the restaurant required new ovens, stoves, and refrigerators. La Mesa purchased the equipment from Kelvinator. Kelvinator executed a security agreement with La Mesa and properly filed a financing statement on August 14, 1990.

By January 1992, La Mesa was five months behind on its mortgage payment and FNB foreclosed. The amount due on the mortgage was $57,000. The amount due to Kelvinator was $31,000. The foreclosure sale, after expenses, brought in $60,000. How much will Kelvinator be paid? How much will FNB receive?

CONSTRUCTION MORTGAGE EXCEPTION

A construction mortgage is a mortgage used for the construction on and improvement of land. It has priority over fixture security interests for fixtures installed during construction.

READILY MOVABLE EXCEPTION

Secured creditors with perfected interests in readily removable office or factory machines or in replaced consumer goods and appliances have priority over conflicting real estate interests. Readily removable office equipment includes items such as fax machines, photocopy machines, and computers. These personal property interests are not real estate and hence are not subject to a mortgage (a real property interest).

CONSENT EXCEPTION

Subsequent perfected secured parties may obtain priority by obtaining the consent of others holding encumbrances against the subject property. The reason for this exception is to allow parties involved to reach an agreement on priorities if they are able.

TENANT EXCEPTION

Creditors of tenants who have attached fixtures to leased property have priority over other prior and subsequent real estate encumbrances so long as the tenant has the right to remove such items upon termination of the lease. For example, a secured creditor of a tenant who attaches the financed, movable air conditioner to the landlord's property has priority over a mortgage on the property executed by the landlord.

GOOD-FAITH PURCHASER EXCEPTION

Good-faith purchasers (9-320) who purchase realty or fixtures in the ordinary course of business will have priority over secured parties so long as they purchase for value. Purchasers of real estate with fixtures covered by security interests are thus protected when the creditor or secured party does or does not file the required financing statement.

Figure 4.2 summarizes the Article 9 priorities and exceptions.

> **Consider 4.6**
>
> Mrs. Kellerman remodeled her kitchen. Since her built-in oven needed to be replaced, she purchased an oven from Al's Appliance and TV. Mrs. Kellerman financed the purchase, and she and Al executed a security agreement on June 30, 2000. Mrs. Kellerman's property has a mortgage on it that was filed in 1995 to secure the financing of her home.
>
> 1. Is Al's interest perfected? *Yes*
> 2. Can Al obtain priority over the 1995 mortgage? *Only*
> 3. Is Al required to file a financing statement to obtain priority over the mortgage?
> 4. Would the result be different if the mortgage covered all after-attached property and fixtures?
>
> See *Capitol Federal Savings and Loan Association v. Hoger*, 880 P.2d 281 (Kan. App. 1994).

Default by Debtor and Rights of Secured Party (9-604)

If a secured party has priority and the debtor has defaulted, the secured party has the right to remove the collateral from the real estate but must reimburse the owner or other encumbrances for the cost of repairing any injury to the property. Under Revised Article 9, the fixture creditor now has the right to any non-judicial foreclosure provided for the state where the secured party's fixture is

FIGURE 4.2   *Priorities in Fixtures Under Article 9 (9-313)*

Type of Party	Priority Over	Exceptions to General Priority Rules
Secured party	Unsecured party, secured party whose interest attached after	Good faith purchasers
Perfected secured party	Secured party, unsecured party, subsequently filed real estate encumbrances (mortgages, deeds of trust, liens, judgments, security interests)	Good faith purchasers
PMSI perfected secured party	Secured party, unsecured party, subsequently filed real estate encumbrances	Construction mortgages with advancements yet to be made; Good-faith purchasers
	Prior perfected security interests and real estate encumbrances if financing statement filed before annexation of the fixture or within 20 days of annexation	
Construction mortgage	All subsequent encumbrances and security interests	
Secured party for: readily removable office or factory machines.	No fixture filing required; perfection required	Construction
Secured party for a tenant	Priority over all real estate encumbrances (prior and subsequent)	
	Priority over all real estate encumbrances regardless of perfection so long as tenant holds the right to remove property	
Good faith purchaser	Prior security interests if purchase is made in the ordinary course of business. For real estate, filing on fixtures gives creditor priority	

located. However, the security agreement may provide that the debtor is responsible for paying the cost of repair. Neither the debtor nor the secured party is responsible for paying any decrease in value caused by the removal of the fixture. For example, if mirrors are removed from a wall, the cost of repair may be $30 for restoring the wall surface. However, the $1,000 decrease in value of the property need not be paid.

Maplewood Bank and Trust v. Sears, Roebuck and Co.

625 A.2d 537 (N.J. Super. A.D. 1993)

Facts

Edward and Terre Capers bought their home with a purchase money mortgage from Maplewood Bank and Trust (plaintiff). The mortgage was entered into on September 20, 1988, and recorded on October 5, 1988. The original amount of the mortgage was $121,000.

On May 31, 1989, Sears, Roebuck and Company (Sears) filed a financing statement covering a completely new kitchen for the Capers consisting of "new countertops, cabinets, sinks, disposal unit, dishwasher, oven, cooktop and hood" installed. Sears filed a financing statement on the Caperses' property after the Capers gave Sears a security interest in their home as security for the remodeling of their kitchen on credit.

On August 18, 1989, the Capers executed a second mortgage on their home to Savings Bank for the sum of $34,000. That mortgage was recorded on August 23, 1989.

When the Capers defaulted in their payments to Maplewood and Sears, Maplewood declared the entire balance of its loan due. Maplewood filed for foreclosure of its mortgage on November 5, 1989. Sears filed an answer and counterclaim for the amount of its security interest in the kitchen remodeling.

Sears' claim was dismissed and the foreclosure for Maplewood was entered. Sears appealed the dismissal of its claim.

Judicial Opinion

Coleman, Presiding Judge. It is undisputed that the new kitchen Sears installed and financed satisfies the definition of fixture. It is also undisputed that Sears obtained a purchase money security interest in the fixture to secure full payment. Sears perfected its security interest by filing a financing statement covering the fixtures in the Hunterdon County Clerk's Office where the first mortgage held by plaintiff was recorded.

The purchase money interest of Sears attached to the goods or chattels before they became affixed to the realty as fixtures. By perfecting the security interest, Sears was able to make its security interest in the fixtures permanent, or until paid or discharged. The point to be made is that Sears' security interest is limited to the fixtures and does not extend to the realty otherwise.

By statute, Sears' purchase money security interest, when perfected, "has priority over the conflicting interest of an encumbrancer or owner of the real estate. . . ." This means the purchase money security interest of Sears in the goods or chattels which became fixtures gives it a "super priority" as to those goods or chattels which became fixtures.

Next we must focus upon the remedies available to a purchase money security interest lien holder upon default by the debtor. Sears contends it should be entitled to receive from the proceeds obtained at the foreclosure sale, the difference between the value of the realty with the new kitchen and the value of the realty after the new kitchen has been removed. We reject this entire approach as an inappropriate remedy absent authorization by statute.

The Uniform Commercial Code, as adopted in New Jersey, provides:

> When the secured party has priority over all owners and encumbrancers of the real estate, he may,

on default, subject to the provisions of subchapter 5, remove his collateral from the real estate but he must reimburse any encumbrancer or owner of the real estate who is not the debtor and who has not otherwise agreed for the cost of repair of any physical injury, but not for any diminution in value of the real estate caused by the absence of the goods removed or by any necessity of replacing them.

Thus based on the plain language of § 9-313(8), Sears has two options: removal of the fixtures or foregoing removal of the fixtures.

The most compelling authority supportive of Sears' position is an article, "An Integrated Financing System for Purchase Money Collateral: A Proposed Solution to the Fixture Problem Under Section 9-313 of the Uniform Commercial Code" by Morris G. Shanker. 73 Yale L.J. 795 (1964)

The article cite[s] certain instances where the fixture secured party may prefer not to exercise his removal rights. For example, if an elevator was designed for a specific building, it would have little or no value apart from that building. Other cited examples include situations where a fixture secured party should be *required* to use judicial foreclosure proceedings even though he has the right of removal. For example a secured party should not be free to remove a heating system in a large apartment building in the dead of winter, even where the debtor defaulted.

[Shanker] states that limiting the remedy to the right to remove or choosing not to remove, in no way detracts from the fixture secured party's paramount security interest in his collateral; it merely requires him to enforce his security interest in a sensible and equitable fashion.

We decline to adopt the creative approach articulated by Professor Shanker. Such action, in our view, would be legislating. To adopt Sears' argument in the absence of legislation, would mean that a mortgagee's security interest could be impaired substantially without the Legislature pronouncing an intention to do so.

We are also persuaded that Sears is not entitled to any remedy, other than removal of the fixtures, based on equitable principles. Sears knew its remedy was limited to removal upon default. Indeed, the Retail Installment Contract and Security Agreement prepared by Sears and signed by the Capers provided that the Capers were giving Sears a "security interest under the Uniform Commercial Code in all merchandise purchased under this contract . . . [and] *the security interest allows Sears to repossess the merchandise"* in the event the Capers did not make payments as agreed.

Summary judgment in favor of plaintiff is affirmed.

Affirmed.

Case Questions

1. List the creditors in the Capers's property.
2. Where was Sears in the list of creditors in terms of priority?
3. What rights did Sears have upon default?

4. Why does the court not adopt a right not to remove under Article 9?
5. Explain the elevator example in Professor Shanker's reasoning that is referred to by the court. Do you agree with his point and analysis?

Ethical Issue

In the *Maplewood* case, re-examine the time between when the Caperses entered into the three credit contracts and their default. Were the Caperes overextended? Is it the creditors' responsibility to decline credit in these circumstances? Why don't laws place limitations on the amount of credit individuals can obtain? Is there an ethical component to the use and extension of credit? What responsibilities should both sides to a credit arrangement have beyond what the law requires?

CAUTIONS AND CONCLUSIONS

Article 9 affords creditors tremendous protection in collateral rights and priorities. However, creditors need to be certain of their positions; the following questions should help ensure them the best position and best available protection for their secured debt:

1. Is there a written security agreement with all of the necessary information?
2. Has value been given?
3. Has the security interest attached?
4. To whose property is the item being attached?
5. What other creditors have interests in that property? Is there a construction mortgage? Have the land records been checked?
6. Is the financing statement complete? Is the legal description included and accurate? Is the collateral sufficiently identified?
7. Has the financing statement been filed and in the correct place?
8. Has the financing statement been filed within the appropriate time limits (20 days on a PMSI)?
9. Is renewal necessary? When?
10. Can removal damage be minimized?

By answering these questions and following through on tasks at the outset, creditors can avoid the problems of forgotten filings, incomplete documents, and the resulting lack of protection.

For those involved in a real property transfer, the presence of Article 9 interests is to be checked and provided for in the parties' contract. If an Article 9 interest is not disclosed or is overlooked, the door for litigation and liability is immediately opened. The following checklist is suggested for buyers, sellers, brokers, agents, and others involved in real estate transactions:

1. Have the records been checked to determine if a perfected security interest exists?
2. If a perfected interest does exist, who is the creditor? What property is covered? How much is owed? What payments are made? Is all of the paperwork proper? Does this creditor have priority?

3. Does an unperfected security interest exist on any items on the property? Who is the creditor? How much is owed? What payments are made? Is all of the paperwork proper?

4. Who will pay the balance due? Will it be paid from sale proceeds? Is the buyer to assume responsibility for payments?

5. Is there a provision in the contract for the disposition of debts and collateral pledges?

Key Terms

fixture, 66
trade fixture, 68
fructus naturales, 74
fructus industriales, 74
emblements, 74

Doctrine of Emblements, 74
Article 9, 75
Uniform Commercial Code (UCC), 75
security interest, 76

security agreement, 76
perfection, 76
purchase money security interest (PMSI), 77
financing statement, 77

Chapter Problems

1. Determine whether each of the following would constitute a fixture. Discuss any further information that would be helpful in making the determination.
   a. A marble monument with a cement foundation in a cemetery
   b. Bookshelves in a library
   c. Wall mirrors installed by a tenant
   d. A furnace that is bolted to the floor in a factory
   e. A hog house (with a cement foundation) on a farm
   f. Ceiling fans in a home
   g. A printing machine in a college copy center
   Reynolds v. State Bd. Community Colleges, 937 P.2d 774 (Colo. App. 1996)

2. Bill leased an apartment from Windmere Apartments, Inc. Under the lease agreement, Bill is permitted to remove all fixtures installed on the property. Bill arranged to have custom bookshelves placed along one wall (the shelves are attached to the wall). Bill financed the shelves with Carl's Cabinetry, and Carl's filed a valid financing statement for the fixtures on December 1, 2000. Windmere has had a mortgage on the property since 1992.
   a. If Bill defaults, may Carl's remove the shelves?
   b. What obligations does Carl's have?
   c. If Windmere defaults, does its mortgagee get the shelves?
   d. What would the position of Carl's be if no filing was made?

3. William and Virginia Britton own a one-acre parcel of land near Detroit's Metropolitan Wayne County Airport. They operate several small industrial businesses in the industrial building located on their land. In 1992, Wayne County began acquiring a total of 550 acres around the airport for expansion purposes. Wayne County offered the Brittons $188,580 for their property. The Brittons disputed the amount for not including the value of their trade fixtures. Listed as trade fixtures were the following: tanks, air compressors, forklifts, scales, storage racks, hose-braiding machines, pipe-threading machinery, hydraulic pumps, grinding machinery, and work tables. It also included such miscellaneous items as a coat tree, an electric clock, a first-aid kit, file cabinets, a refrigerator, a metal folding chair, a flatbed truck, trash drums, and lawn mowers. Should the county be required to compensate the Brittons for these items in a taking of real property? *Wayne County v. Britton*, 563 N.W.2d 674 (Mich. 1997).

4. The Michigan Tax Tribunal held that Michigan National Bank's night depository equipment, drive-up window equipment, vault doors, and remote transactions units, which were physically integrated with the bank's land and buildings, were fixtures and subject to taxation as realty by the city of Lansing. Is the Tax Tribunal correct? Should the drive-up facilities be classified as fixtures or personal property? *Michigan National Bank, Lansing v. City of Lansing*, 293 N.W.2d 626 (Mich. App. 1980); aff'd 322 N.W.2d 173 (Mich. 1982)

5. Harry owns Harry's Discount Clothiers, Inc. Harry has a five-year lease on the building in which his store is located. The building had concrete flooring, which was not appropriate for a clothing store, so Harry had parquet flooring installed. The flooring was installed in the same fashion as tile flooring. Determine whether the flooring will be treated as a fixture, trade fixture, or as personal property in the following situations:
   a. When the lease terminates, Harry wants to take the flooring with him. What is the result?

b. Harry purchases the building and then sells it to Bob who claims that the flooring goes with the building. What is the result?

c. Harry's fire insurance policy covers personal property but no real property. What is the result?

d. The county tax assessor wishes to increase the value of the property on the basis of the value added by the floor. What is the result?

6. On January 20, Tom purchased a new hot water tank for his home from Tanks, Inc. Tanks agreed to carry Tom on part of the price of the tank and took a security interest in the tank. The tank was then installed. On February 1, Tom borrowed money from First Federal, and First Federal took a second mortgage on the house. On March 1, Fiesta Funtime Pools obtained a judgment against Tom and his house for the unpaid balance due on Tom's pool.

a. Who has priority?

b. What would be the result if Tanks had filed a financing statement on January 31?

c. What relation would a first mortgage have in the situation?

d. If Tom defaults to Tanks, what can be done under Article 9?

7. Mr. and Mrs. Lester Coy purchased a mobile home and gave a security interest in it to Bernard Parsons, who financed the purchase of the home. Their agreement provided that the mobile home would remain personal property regardless of the degree of attachment to any real property. Parsons filed the financing statement as if the mobile home were personal property and not a fixture. The Coys placed their mobile home on a lot purchased with funds loaned by Western World Properties, which had a recorded mortgage on the property. The Coys defaulted on their mortgage, resulting in a foreclosure sale. The issue that arose was whether the land only could be sold or the mobile home and land could be sold because the mobile home had been attached to the property. The mobile home rests on concrete footing and has concrete stairs leading to its doors. There are gas, electricity, water, and telephone hookups to the mobile home. Is the mobile home part of the real property or did it remain personal property? *Parson v. Lender Service, Inc.*, 801 P.2d 739 (Pa. 1986)

8. a. Would an above-ground swimming pool be considered personal property or a fixture? *Farrier v. Old Republic Insurance Co.*, 61 B.R. 950 (Pa. 1986)

b. Would bulk barns used to store tobacco and other products on farms be considered fixtures or personal property? The barns are often leased out when not being used by the tobacco farmer owner. *U.S v. Gaskins*, 748 F. Supp. 366 (E.D.N.C. 1990); *Casper v. Cape Mercantile Bank & Trust Co.*, 156 B.R. 794 (S.D. Ill. 1993)

c. Would windows and gutters added to a house be fixtures? *In re Hinson*, 77 B.R. 34 (Md. 1987)

d. Would catfish in a leased pond be considered real property or personal property? *In re Findley*, 76 B.R. 547 (Miss. 1987)

9. During construction of the Grand Beach Inn, heating and air-conditioning units were installed in the rooms and are part of the walls for each room. The Grand Beach Inn was to be a hotel with individual guest rooms with individually controlled heat and air-conditioning. In a foreclosure on the never-opened inn, the issue of whether the units are included in the real property has arisen. Are the heating and air-conditioning units personal property or fixtures? *Lewiston Bottled Gas Co. v. Key Bank of Maine*, 601 A.2d 91 (Maine 1992)

10. The Godins owned land in Halifax, Vermont, and gave a mortgage on that land to Greenfield Savings Bank on October 27, 1972. The Godins purchased a mobile home in New Hampshire for the lot on May 10, 1973. Hartford National Bank & Trust financed the purchase. The Godins then moved the mobile home to Halifax, Vermont, and Hartford filed a UCC financing statement with the Halifax town clerk on July 1, 1975.

Next, the Godins installed the mobile home on their lot. A concrete-block foundation supported the mobile home, and there were attached steps, a connecting septic system, and encasement of the foundation in aluminum foundation siding. The Godins defaulted on their payments to Hartford, and Hartford brought suit to repossess the mobile home. Greenfield objected on the grounds that the home was a fixture, part of the realty, and subject to their prior mortgage. Who has priority? *Hartford National Bank & Trust Co. v. Godin*, 398 A.2d 286 (Vt. 1979)

Internet Activities

1. For each state's version of Article 9, definition, security interests, and transfer of interests in fixtures, go to: **http://www.law.cornell.edu/uniform/ucc.html#a9**.

2. For a look at progress on the national financing statement forms, go to **http://www.intercountyclearance.com/ra9/ra9.html**. For UCC forms samples, go to **http://www.sos.state.tx.us/siteindex.shtml**.

HB1661	Allows certain political subdivisions to have a mechanic's lien when they pay mechanics to perform abatement work on derelict real property.		
Sponsor:	*Gambaro, Derio L. (65)*	Effective Date:	00/00/0000
CoSponsor:	*Kennedy, Harry (66)*	LR Number:	2595L.01I
Last Action:	COMMITTEE: **MUNICIPAL CORPORATIONS**		
	03/01/2000 - Executive Session Held (H)		
	VOTED DO PASS		
	HB1661		
Next Hearing:	Hearing not scheduled		
Calendar:	Bill currently not on calendar		

ACTIONS	HEARINGS	CALENDAR
BILL SUMMARIES	BILL TEXT	FISCAL NOTES
BILL SEARCH	HOUSE HOME PAGE	

Available Bill Summaries for HB1661 Copyright(c)
* Committee * Introduced

Available Bill Text for HB1661
* Introduced *

BILL SUMMARIES

COMMITTEE

Chapter 5
Liens

One thing Charles Keating, former CEO of a defunct California savings and loan, left behind is mechanic's liens. Nonpayment of subcontractors on his Phoenician Resort has created a ripple effect in terms of economic impact. The resort was a project of American Continental Corporation, the owner of the savings and loan. Court records list 61 subcontractors as being owed money, including $120,000 for metal work, $303,000 for glass and windows, $2,400,000 for electrical work, $31,000 for painting, and $18.5 million to the general contractor.

Mechanic's liens—the big squeeze

A special encumbrance that makes real property the security for the payment of a debt or obligation is a **lien**. In some cases, property owners place liens on their property voluntarily as security for a loan. In other cases, creditors have the right to create liens on property because of contracts or work they have performed. This chapter focuses on the second type of lien—the liens of third parties attached for nonpayment.

In this chapter, several questions about liens are answered. What types of liens exist? How are liens created and enforced? How can liens on real property be satisfied and removed from the property? By the end of the chapter, you will understand the significance of the facts in the epigraph.

TYPES OF LIENS

Statutory Liens

A **statutory lien** is a lien that exists because of an enabling statute. For example, a mechanic's lien is a statutory lien. **Mechanic's liens,** sometimes called materials and labor liens or construction liens, are created by statutes and enable those furnishing labor and materials for construction and improvement of real property to file a lien against that property for debt or payment security. Mechanic's lien statutes have existed since colonial times and exist now in all states, plus Puerto Rico and the District of Columbia. Some states, like California, afford these liens constitutional protection.[1] There are also state statutes that permit the attachment of a lien on real property when taxes are not paid.

Equitable Liens

An **equitable lien** is created pursuant to a mortgage arrangement. Sometimes referred to as a **contractual lien,** or voluntary lien, these liens are created as a method for securing repayment of money borrowed to purchase the property or borrowed against the property.

Voluntary v. Involuntary Liens

A **voluntary lien** is agreed to in advance by both parties; a mortgage is an example. Both parties agree to the placement of the lien on the property as security for the advance of money to purchase the property or simply as security for a loan of money.

An **involuntary lien** is attached to the property but is not pursuant to any contractual arrangement. Involuntary liens are placed on property for satisfaction of property, state, or federal taxes (see Chapter 22).

Judicial Liens

A **judicial lien** arises from some action taken by a court. For example, there are many cases that a plaintiff wins, but winning and collecting the judgment are two separate issues. To collect the judgment, the plaintiff must attach the defendant's property. Plaintiffs can attach wages, bank accounts, equipment, inventory, and, more relevantly here, real property. A judicial lien is the means by which the defendant's property is sold to satisfy or secure the plaintiff's judgment.

Once a judgment is recorded against real property, it becomes a creditor's lien. If the property is sold, then the plaintiff with the judgment has the priority of a secured creditor in the proceeds from the sale. The priority of the judgment or judicial lien is determined on the basis of "first in time is first in right." If the property is already subject to a mortgage, then the plaintiff is a secured creditor with priority after the mortgagee. In some cases, the plaintiff can initiate sale action by foreclosing on the judicial lien. Even without foreclosure, the plaintiff's lien is recorded against the property, and the title will not be passed or insured until the judgment has been paid or otherwise resolved between the parties.

---

1.   Cal. Const. Art. XIV, § 3 (1992) provides: "Mechanics, persons furnishing materials, artisans, and laborers of every class, shall have a lien upon the property upon which they have bestowed labor or furnished material for the value of such labor done and material furnished."

Most states permit either the judgment that awards damages or an abstract of the judgment to be recorded in the land records, so that the lien is effective against any property owned by the judgment debtor.

Mechanic's and Materials Liens

Mechanic's and **materials liens** arise because persons have supplied labor, material, or both for the construction, improvement, alteration, or repair of real property or real property structures. This type of lien is the focus of the remainder of this chapter.

The laws on mechanic's liens vary significantly among the states. At one point in the late 1920s, a Uniform Mechanic's Lien Act was proposed. By 1943, the Commissioners on Uniform State Laws withdrew the proposal because "varied conditions made uniformity impossible." However, the purposes of the laws are clear—to prevent unjust enrichment of property owners who do not pay for improvements.

In 1987, the National Conference of Commissioners on Uniform Laws adopted its Uniform Construction Lien Act. The Act answers three basic questions: Who is entitled to a lien? Who has priority among lien holders? and What are the landowner's rights with respect to payment and liens? The Act has not yet been adopted by any states.

CREATION OF MECHANIC'S LIENS

Who Is Subject to Lien?

Any property owner who contracts expressly or by implication with another person for the improvement of land or furnishing of materials is subject to the provisions of that particular state's mechanic's lien provisions. However, it is important to note that such a party must be the property owner or must be acting as an agent or representative of the owner. For example, a lessee having improvements made on the leased premises does not have the authority for the imposition of a lien unless the landlord consents or the lessee is acting as an agent for the landlord. In the following case, the issue of liability among landlord, tenant, and lienor is resolved.

http://

Read Missouri's proposed bill on mechanic's liens at: **http://www.house. state.mo.us/bills00/ bills00/HB1661.htm**.

Kansas City Heartland Construction Co. v. Maggie Jones Southport Cafe, Inc.

824 P.2d 926 (Kan. 1992)

Facts

Maggie Jones Southport Cafe, Inc. (Maggie Jones), leased space in a shopping mall owned by 95th & Nall Associates. The leased space had been operated as a restaurant and the Maggie Jones lease provided for operation as another restaurant.

Maggie Jones obtained a loan from the Small Business Administration (SBA) that was secured by the leaseholder improvements made to the leased premises. Maggie Jones contracted with Kansas City Heartland Construction Company (Heartland) for renovation of the restaurant site.

Maggie Jones became insolvent and went into bankruptcy. At the time of its bankruptcy, Maggie Jones owed Heartland $104,000. 95th & Nall did not realize Maggie

Jones owed any money to contractors until after the Maggie Jones restaurant closed. The SBA sent notice to 95th & Nall that it would be enforcing its secured interest in the restaurant improvements through a public auction. A public auction was held.

Heartland performed its last work on March 26, 1987. On July 16, 1987, Heartland filed its lien statements against Maggie Jones and 95th & Nall. Heartland obtained permission from the bankruptcy court to file suit in state court to determine whether 95th & Nall should be required to pay the $104,000 due to Heartland. The trial court found for Heartland and ordered 95th & Nall to pay $104,000 plus interest for a total of $136,933. The Court of Appeals affirmed the judgment and 95th & Nall appealed to the Supreme Court.

Judicial Opinion

Abbott, Justice. The general rule is where a mechanic's lien arises under a contract with a tenant, such lien attaches to the leasehold or tenant's estate only, and not to the reversion, fee, or the estate of the landlord. The rights of the mechanic's lien claimant can rise no higher than those of the person with whom he has contracted or to whom he has furnished labor or materials. . . . *Without the authority of the landlord, or his consent, or some act of the landlord to make his estate liable,* a tenant cannot charge the land with a lien for labor or materials for constructing or improving a building thereon.

The estate of the owner cannot be subjected to a lien for work done or materials furnished at the instance of the lessee *unless the lessee may be regarded as an agent or trustee of the owner.* Such may be express or implied from the conduct and acquiescence of the owner and from all the circumstances, which estop the landlord from denying agency.

The question, then, is whether Maggie Jones had express or implied authority to act as the agent for 95th & Nall. The trial court never directly addressed whether an agency relationship existed between Maggie Jones & 95th & Nall.

An agent has express authority if "the principal has delegated authority to the agent by words which expressly authorize the agent to do a delegable act." Here, there is no evidence to support an express agency. Article 26 in the lease between Maggie Jones and 95th & Nall specifically stated that "[t]his Lease does not create the relationship of principal and agent . . . the sole relationship between Landlord and Tenant being that of landlord and tenant . . . " Furthermore, according to testimony at trial, there was no written (or implied) agreement between Maggie Jones and 95th & Nall that Maggie Jones would act as 95th & Nall's agent. Larry Gaines, President of Maggie Jones, never represented himself or Maggie Jones as the agent of 95th & Nall. Reginald Armstrong, manag-

ing partner of 95th & Nall, never authorized Gaines to act as 95th & Nall's agent. Additionally, Gaines understood from the beginning that Maggie Jones was responsible for paying for improvements to the property.

The evidence does not support a finding of express warranty; the question remaining is whether an implied agency existed on these facts.

On the question of implied agency, it is the manifestation of the alleged principal and agent as between themselves that is decisive, and not the appearance to a third party or what a third party should have known. An agency will not be inferred because a third person assumed that it existed.

Implied agency is based on an implied intention to create an agency. It arises upon facts for which the principal is responsible. It arises when, from the statements and conduct of the parties, it appears that the principal, or the principal and the 'agent,' intended to make it appear to others that the acts of the 'agent' were authorized by the principal.

95th & Nall argues that because the trial court did not make a specific finding regarding agency, the trial court must have ruled "the landlord's *knowledge* of the construction and *implied authorization* of the work created an agency relationship."

95th & Nall claimed that because it did not give prior written approval, Heartland's lien did not attach to 95th & Nall's property. Article 29 [of the lease] specified that "[w]henever under this Lease, provision is made for Tenant securing the consent or approval by Landlord, such consent or approval shall be in writing."

. . . [t]he Court of Appeals noted "the lease in question also included a provision that required the lessee to surrender all improvements to the lessor upon termination of the lease. Since all improvements were to be surrendered under the lease, the lessee becomes the lessor's agent and a mechanic's lien can attach to the lessor's real estate."

The lease, however, did not require Maggie Jones to surrender *all* improvements. Article 23 authorized Maggie Jones to remove any trade fixtures, signs or carpeting from the premises.

. . . [t]he crux of the matter is whether the landlord benefitted from the improvements. Here, the trial court's finding that 95th & Nall did not benefit from the renovations is supported by substantial competent evidence. When Maggie Jones went bankrupt, the SBA forced its secured interest in the improvements through a public auction.

Article 36 of the lease specified that in terms of liens, 95th & Nall would have a subordinate position. This was done so that the lessee could obtain an SBA loan. At the time of the sale, the new tenant of the restaurant property made arrangements to buy some of the leasehold improvements from the SBA; the new tenant did not purchase the improvements from 95th & Nall. The SBA also financed the new tenant and when the new tenant subsequently went bankrupt, the SBA again held a public auction. This time, the interior was gutted.

Heartland also argues that Gaines' testimony supports finding that 95th & Nall assumed authority for the renovations by abating rent while renovations were being completed. 95th & Nall did not assume authority for payment of the renovations by abating rent.

Additionally, neither apparent agency nor equitable estoppel are applicable here. Apparent [or ostensible] agency is based on intentional actions or words of the principal toward third parties which reasonably induce or permit third parties to believe that an agency relationship exists.

Mike White, a general contractor doing business as Heartland, testified he negotiated and contracted with Gaines for Heartland to do the remodeling. White did not negotiate with 95th & Nall. White did not ask 95th & Nall to approve any of the work. Any payments Heartland or subcontractors received were received from Maggie Jones. In fact, 95th & Nall only became aware that Heartland was doing the renovation work when the work was half-way completed.

White testified he discussed work with Armstrong regarding an exterior paint job. (The lease specified that 95th & Nall was responsible for this work.) That discussion involved both Gaines and Armstrong. Gaines, not

Armstrong, authorized White to go ahead with the paint job, which only cost a few hundred dollars. Armstrong subsequently reimbursed Maggie Jones for the paint job, and Maggie Jones paid Heartland.

White, as Heartland's representative, was not induced to enter into the contract with Maggie Jones because of an alleged agency. White also did not rely in any way upon an alleged agency. White never saw the lease between Maggie Jones and 95th & Nall.

There is not substantial competent evidence to support a finding that Maggie Jones acted as the agent for 95th & Nall. Consequently, the trial court's and the Court of Appeals' conclusions of law are erroneous.

Reversed.

Case Questions

1. What terms of the lease were particularly significant for the court?

2. Who were the creditors left unpaid when Maggie Jones went into bankruptcy?

3. What are the differences among express, implied, and apparent authority?

4. What lessons should landlords learn from this case and the high cost of litigating the finding that there was no agency relationship?

Suppose that a property owner who originally contracted with a builder sold his property and the new owner signed nothing but allowed the builder to continue construction. Is the new owner subject to a lien? *Thomas Hake Enterprises, Inc. v. Betke*, 703 N.E.2d 114 (Ill. App. 1998)

> **Consider 5.1**

Any person who may validly contract may be subject to the imposition of a lien (the party subject to the lien is called the **lienee**). Corporations owning property are subject to mechanic's liens on contractually improved corporate property. In the absence of a specific statutory provision, a lien may not be imposed against the United States government or any of the state governments. The idea behind this governmental exemption is to prevent the taking of state land for the satisfaction of a mechanic's lien. Thus, construction of schools and public buildings such as courthouses and office complexes would be exempt from the attachment of mechanic's liens. For quasi-public entities, such as utilities, some states recognize an exemption, while others do not.

Practical Tip

Some commercial landlords require contractors to register with them. Upon registration, the contractors are given a statement that limits the landlord's liability and explains that their contract is with the tenant and not the landlord.

Most state lien statutes require that the **lienor** have an underlying contractual arrangement to enforce a lien. However, the degree and type of contractual arrangement varies significantly from state to state: Some states require only an express or implied agreement before a lien may be attached (**consent statutes**). Others require the owner of the property to sign a contract for the work or materials (**contract statutes**). The difference between these contract and consent statutes is that under the contract statutes, the lienor must establish the existence of a contract to attach a lien. Under the consent statutes, the lienor need only establish that the owner consented through circumstances such as an owner permitting work to continue after witnessing the work being initiated or continued.

The formalities required in the contract vary significantly in the states, but the following items should be included. Compliance with this list will satisfy the requirements of any of the states following the contract requirements:

1. Amount due under the contract (for labor, materials, and so on)
2. Amount of time within which work is to be completed
3. Amount of time permitted for payments and any schedule of payments
4. Description of the real property involved
5. Description of the work to be completed
6. Signature of the parties. (If the property is community or held in tenancy by the entirety, then both spouses' signatures are required.)
7. If the property being repaired or improved is consumer property, Regulation Z (12 C.F.R. § 226) requires the following disclosure to be made:

> The buyer may cancel this transaction at any time prior to midnight of the third business day after the date of this transaction.

Under Regulation Z, the contract must also include cancellation information such as how and to whom cancellation notice must be given.

8. Provisions for breach of the agreement (i.e., nonpayment or nonperformance), such as withholding payment or obtaining another contractor.

It is possible, particularly in construction contracts, to have an open-end agreement so that supplies are purchased as necessary. It is also possible for a contract executed by an agent of the owner to be valid against the owner, so long as the agent held proper authority to enter into the contract. Care should be taken when lienors are dealing with unincorporated associations such as churches and foundations to make sure that the person signing holds proper authority for the transaction of the business. Without such proper authority, the property of the church or foundation is not subject to a lien. Trustees and executors of estates may also have authority to make improvements on real property that is part of the trust or estate, but such authority should be verified by the lienor so that the property may be properly liened.

The description of the liened property is critical because the lien is recorded in the real property records and only with an accurate description of the property will creditors be able to tell what interest in which property is held by lienors. In the following case, a slight slip in description by a lienor created a great deal of litigation.

Practical Tip

Verify who is working for whom. Verify title holders if you are a contractor, subcontractor, or supplier. Verify the subcontractors and suppliers if you are the property owner. Be certain you know the role of all potential parties.

Mull, et al.
v. Mickey's Lumber & Supply Co., Inc.

461 S.E.2d 270 (Ga. App. 1995)

Facts

Ricky and Karen Mull (appellants/defendants) purchased lots 20 and 21 in the Camelot Subdivision in Walton County. The lots were side by side and located at the end of a cul-de-sac. It was determined that lot 20 could not be built upon, so the Mulls built their home on lot 21. The lots were taxed separately.

The Mulls obtained a building permit for lot 21 and entered into a construction contract with a general contractor, Waterport Construction Company (which is now in bankruptcy). No construction was performed on lot 20 and all materials from Mickey's Lumber & Supply Co., Inc. (appellee), were delivered to lot 21.

Within five days prior to the closing of the permanent loan on the Mulls' property, Mickey's Lumber recorded a materialmen's lien. A legal description of the Mulls' property was included but lot 20, rather than lot 21, was specified as the subject property.

The trial court found the description to be legally sufficient. The Mulls appealed.

Judicial Opinion

Birdsong, Presiding Judge. The sufficiency of a property description in a legal document gives rise to a question of law for the court. Appellants contend that the lien is void as the inclusion within the property description of the erroneous lot number "20" establishes that the lien was applied to and attached to the wrong property.

OCGA Section 44-14-361.1 prescribes in pertinent part the statutory procedure for filing a materialmen's lien; this statute is in derogation of common law and must be strictly construed. Failure to follow the mandatory procedures would render the lien unenforceable. The test for sufficiency of a description in a legal document is whether it makes possible the identification of the real or personal property described. The issue therefore is whether the property description in question failed to identify sufficiently the real estate against which the lien was claimed. A description in a deed, contract for sale of land, or a claim of lien on real estate, in order to be valid must identify the land or must contain a key by the use of which the description may be applied by extrinsic evidence.

We must now determine whether the claim of lien did contain an adequate key, when aided by extrinsic evidence, so as to render the property description sufficient. In this regard, it suffices if the "key" leads definitely to the identification of the property being described *when aided by extrinsic evidence*. In the case sub judice the "key," even when aided by extrinsic evidence, fails to lead definitely to the identification of lot number 21 as the property subject to the lien. Although the lien document references a deed which has two lots on it, the document also references a plat which clearly identifies lot 20 as a separate lot, and does not infer that the lot 20 in the lien document could apply to any other lot but lot 20 of the plat.

Courts are not at liberty to revise contracts under the guise of professing to construe them. Moreover, statutes involving a materialmen's lien must be strictly construed in favor of the property owner and against the materialman. Here the lien document, due to a unilateral mistake by the appellee, inaccurately described the property subject to the attempted lien, and no adequate "key" can be found in this instance to remedy this fatal deficiency. The appellate process affords this Court no latitude to make adjustments for the ill-earned good fortune of the lucky or the heart-rendering misfortune of the unlucky.

We decline to determine whether the appellee may still amend its complaint to seek recovery against appellants on a claim of unjust enrichment.

Reversed.

Case Questions

1. How were the Mulls's two lots treated by the tax records?
2. Why doesn't Mickey's Lumber obtain payment from the general contractor?
3. Against whom are the materialmen's statutes strictly construed?
4. What does the court mean when it discusses "ill-earned good fortune?"

Ethical Issue

In the *Mull v. Mickey's Lumber & Supply Co.* case, the Mulls did use the lumber in the construction of their home. Because of the bankruptcy of their general contractor, Mickey's, as a sub, has not been paid. Is it unfair for the Mulls to enjoy the benefit of the lumber and not pay Mickey's? Didn't the Mulls already pay for the lumber through their payments to their general contractor? Does it seem unfair to have the case turn on the technicality of a lot number when the lots are both owned by the beneficiary? What would happen in future cases if the court made an exception?

Consider 5.2

Laurel Nursing Services entered into a contract with Centerbrook, Architects and Planners, for engineering work as well as their services in aiding Laurel in obtaining permits for the operation of a day-care center on property located in Old Saybrook, Connecticut. Laurel entered into the contract with Centerbrook on July 14, 1989, but did not have an actual written contract to purchase the subject property until July 28, 1989.

When the closing on the land occurred on October 16, 1989, Centerbrook had not been paid for its services and it filed a lien against the property on December 7, 1989. When Centerbrook brought an action to foreclose on its lien, Laurel objected on the grounds that it did not have an interest in the land at the time the contract was entered into and that the then-owner/seller of the land was not a party to the Centerbrook contract and had not consented to the services. Laurel maintained the lien was invalid. Is Laurel correct? Must the contracting party have an interest in the land at the time the contract is entered into for a lien to be valid against that land? *Centerbrook v. Laurel Nursing Services,* 620 A.2d 127 (Conn. 1993)

Who Is Entitled to a Lien?

The classes of persons entitled to place liens on real property will vary from state to state but will be set forth in the applicable mechanic's lien statutes. Ordinarily, the right is given to mechanics and laborers, but state statutes have extended the availability of the right to others. In some states, the right of lien is given to contractors, subcontractors, those furnishing materials, those acting in a supervisory capacity, and in some cases to architects. In each of these instances, the coverage may be limited, or it may require that special notice be given to the landowner or that the landowner be aware of the work of all of those claiming a lien. In some states, only those who are properly licensed (if licensing is required) are entitled to levy liens on property. In the following case, an issue about the types of lienors is resolved and occurred because of environmental statutes not anticipated at the time many mechanic's lien statutes were drafted.

Haz-Mat Response, Inc. v. Certified Waste Services Limited

910 P.2d 839 (Kan. 1996)

Facts

Coastal Refining and Marketing contracted with Certified Supply Corporation and Chief Supply Corporation to dispose of up to 500,000 pounds of Coastal's hazardous waste located on Coastal's property in four containers: two above-ground emulsion breaking tanks, one API separator, and one in-ground tank. Certified and Chief subcontracted with Haz-Mat Response, Inc. (plaintiff), to perform the work.

Problems arose during performance of the contract, and although Haz-Mat removed the waste from the storage tanks, it was not disposed of as required by contract. Coastal hired other contractors to complete the work. Coastal refused to pay Certified and Chief, who in turn refused to pay Haz-Mat. Haz-Mat filed a mechanic's lien and thereafter filed suit against Certified, Chief, Coastal, and CIC Industries, the owner of the real property on which Coastal conducted business. Haz-Mat asked for foreclosure of the mechanic's lien it had filed against the property.

Coastal filed a motion for summary judgment claiming that hazardous waste removal would not support a mechanic's lien because such removal is not improvement of the real property. Coastal also claimed that a subcontractor may not recover against a property owner on the basis of unjust enrichment in the absence of privity of contract. The trial court granted summary judgment for Coastal on both issues, and the court of appeals affirmed the decision on the mechanic's lien but reversed on the issue of unjust enrichment. Haz-Mat appealed.

Judicial Opinion

Davis, Justice. We agree with the Court of Appeals' conclusion that the removal of hazardous waste in the circumstances of this case was not lienable.

Our mechanic's lien law is remedial in nature, enacted for the purpose of providing effective security to any persons furnishing labor, equipment, material, or supplies used or consumed for the improvement of real property under a contract with the owner. The theory underlying the granting of a lien against the property is that the property improved by the labor, equipment, material, or supplies should be charged with the payment of the labor, equipment, material, or supplies.

At the same time, a mechanic's lien is purely a creation of statute, and those claiming a mechanic's lien must bring themselves clearly within the provisions of the authorizing statute.

There is no dispute that Haz-Mat complied with all the statutory requisites in filing its mechanic's lien, that it provided labor and materials used in the removal of hazardous waste on the owner's real property, and that it has not been paid under its subcontract. The question before the trial court and on appeal is whether Haz-Mat's waste-removal activities constituted an *improvement of real property*.

The phrase "improvement of real property" is not defined in the Kansas mechanic's lien statute. The only reported Kansas case interpreting the term "improvement" as used in our mechanic's lien statute is *Mark Twain Kansas City Bank v. Kroh Bros. Dev. Co.*, 798 P.2d 511 (Kan. App. 1990). The question presented in *Mark Twain* was whether the architectural and engineering services provided by subcontractors constituted lienable labor resulting in an improvement to real property when construction was never commenced and there appeared no visible or physical manifestation of the subcontractors [*sic*] work on the property. *Mark Twain* held that the professional services provided were never used or consumed in any improvement of the real property within the meaning of the [statute].

Mark Twain concluded that there is a requirement of "[s]ome visible improvement" or some "visible effect on the real estate" in order to put those who seek to acquire an interest in the land on notice that building has commenced on the property.

Black's Law Dictionary's definition most closely reflects what is meant by use of the phrase "improvement of real property": "A valuable addition made to real property (usually real estate) or an amelioration in its condition, amounting to more than mere repairs or replacement, costing labor or capital, and intended to enhance its value, beauty or utility to adapt it for new or further purposes."

Applying the above definition, we find no evidence that the removal of the hazardous waste was part of an overall plan to improve the property or that removal would necessarily enhance the value of the real property. We agree with the Court of Appeals that the removal was not lienable because it was part of a maintenance program that was necessary in the normal course of Coastal's business.

The sole basis for the trial court's decision that a claim for unjust enrichment would not lie was the lack of privity between the owner, Coastal, and the subcontractor. Our past cases establish that recovery under quasi-contract or unjust enrichment is not prohibited simply because the subcontractor and the owner of the property are not in privity of contract.

Although Haz-Mat has submitted an affidavit stating that its president "believed" Coastal was responsible for the bill along with the prime contractor, Haz-Mat did not present any evidence nor did it claim that this supposed belief was based on any statement or promise by Coastal.

Moreover, the undisputed facts fail to establish that Coastal misled Haz-Mat to its detriment, that Coastal in some way induced a change of position in Haz-Mat to its detriment, or that any fraud existed. We conclude that the undisputed facts require affirmance of the trial court's decision that the theory of unjust enrichment was not available to Haz-Mat.[2]

Affirmed in part and reversed in part.

Case Questions

1. List the parties involved in the case and their relationships.
2. What is the key definitional issue for purposes of determining whether Haz-Mat has a lien?
3. Is the removal of hazardous waste an improvement? Doesn't such removal increase the value of the property?
4. Why is there no claim for unjust enrichment allowed?

Consider 5.3

GRW Engineers, Inc., entered into a contract to furnish architectural and engineering services to Chateau Royale, Inc. Chateau Royale was turning a historic building into a restaurant and hired GRW to prepare plans and specifications for the renovation and conversion. GRW worked on the plan and specs over a period of months. Bills were submitted to Chateau, but not paid. Chateau's attorney finally contacted GRW and said its bills were "out of reason." The attorney then offered GRW $25,000 to settle the account. The original contract amount was $340,000–$365,000 (depending on some contingencies in the work). GRW refused and filed a lien. Chateau claims GRW did not have the right to lien its property for services. Is Chateau correct? *GRW Engineers, Inc. v. Elam,* 504 So.2d 117 (La. 1987)

The question of who is entitled to a mechanic's lien is in large part controlled by whether the state is a contract state or a consent state, or whether specific provisions have been made for those other than lienors in direct contract with the landowner. For example, if a property owner who has construction done actually hires and has a direct contractual relationship with the contractor—there is privity of contract between them. On the other hand, the owner does not have a direct contractual relationship or privity with others involved in the construction project such as subcontractors, suppliers, and laborers. Thus, in the absence of some specific provisions in the applicable state statutes, the ability to lien stops at the direct contractual relationship.

To provide payment assurances for subcontractors, suppliers, and laborers not in privity with the landowner, state statutes usually permit them to place a lien on property provided they meet some notice and other preliminary requirements prior to the time the lien is filed. Basically, the statutes permit them to lien if the property owner is aware of their work.

In some states, it is possible that if all claims (of subcontractors, suppliers, and so on) are pursued and made into liens, the landowner could have liens in excess

---

2. In *Tpst Soil Recyclers v. W. F. Anderson,* 957 P.2d 265 (Wash. App. 1998), the court held that a subcontractor's removal treatment and disposal of contaminated soil was not an improvement qualified for mechanic's lien protection.

FIGURE 5.1   *Amounts of Lien Claims by State*

Recovery Only to Extent of Amount Unpaid to General		Direct Lien for Full Amount	
Alabama	Massachusetts	Alaska	New Hampshire
Arkansas	Michigan	Arizona	New Jersey
Connecticut	Minnesota	California	New Mexico
Delaware	Mississippi	Colorado	North Dakota
District of Columbia	Nebraska	Hawaii	Oregon
Florida	New York	Idaho	Pennsylvania
Georgia	North Carolina	Indiana	Rhode Island
Illinois	Tennessee	Kansas*	South Dakota
Iowa*	Utah	Louisiana	Texas*
Kentucky	Virginia	Maryland	Vermont
Maine	West Virginia	Missouri	Washington
		Montana	Wisconsin
		Nevada	Wyoming

*Indicates some variation or limitation

of the contract price. Other states follow the New York rule and limit the amount of the liens to the contract price less any amounts paid to the general contractor. Figure 5.1 is a summary of state laws on this issue.

Some states provide an exemption for residential property, that is, the owners of residential property cannot have liens in excess of the contract price with the general contractor. In the following case, the court deals with an issue of the application of the residential exemption to a lien by a supplier.

Bee Spring Lumber Co. v. Pucossi

943 S.W.2d 622 (Ky. 1997)

Facts

Edward and Elena Pucossi reside in Louisville, Kentucky, and purchased a lot on Nolin Lake in Edmonson County, Kentucky. They contracted with a builder to construct a lake house for them for a total contract price of $20,400. When the Pucossis had paid a total of $16,050 to the builder, the builder abandoned the project and could not be located. The lake house was never completed and was never occupied.

Bee Spring Lumber had furnished $8,292.68 in lumber and materials for the Pucossi project to the builder. Bee Spring Lumber had a lien against the property and brought suit to collect on that lien. The Pucossis claimed

that they could not be held liable for more than the contract price because this was residential construction. The trial court held that the statutory exemption did not apply and held the Pucossis liable for the full amount ($8,292.68) owed Bee Spring Lumber. The court of appeals reversed and held that the statutory residential exemption applied. Bee Spring Lumber appealed.

Judicial Opinion

Wintersheimer, Justice. The question presented is one of first impression regarding the legal effect of the 1988 amendment to KRS 376.010. Bee Spring Lumber contends that Subsection (4) should not apply to a second or vacation home. The Pucossis argue that the statute protects them when payment is made to a defunct builder. The 1988 amendments were adopted in response to the Court of Appeals cases of *Kinser Sheet Metal, Inc. v. Morse,* 566 S.W.2d 179 (Ky. App. 1978) and *Smith v. Magruder,* 566 S.W.2d 430 (Ky. App. 1978).

The statute allows a dollar-for-dollar credit when a property owner has paid a defaulting contractor against any materialman's or mechanics' liens filed by suppliers. Apparently the legislative intent was to include owners of property who are having homes constructed pursuant to a construction contract and who intend to use the property as a dwelling once the structure was completed and to afford them certain protection and relief under the language contained in Subsection (4). The language in question is the last sentence of the subsection:

> This subsection shall apply to the construction of single or double family homes constructed pursuant to a construction contract with a property owner and intended for use as the property owner's dwelling.

The purpose of KRS 376.010, the Mechanics' and Materialman's Lien Statute, was to provide the suppliers and laborers of building materials some financial security in collecting their contract price by allowing the real property to be encumbered for the amount of the debt. In *Kinser, supra,* the Court of Appeals construed the phrase "owner-occupied" to mean that actual physical occupancy was necessary to trigger the additional protection provided to homeowners by Subsection(4).

As stated in *Smith* and *Campbell & Summerhays, Inc. v. Greene,* KY., 381 S.W.2d 531 (1964) it has been the policy of Kentucky law to construe mechanics' lien laws liberally to protect those who furnish labor and materials. As stated in *Smith,* the legislature has recognized the possibility of an abuse which would be to the detriment of some small homeowners and has identified an exception to the mechanics' lien laws for those premises that are owner occupied. The new statutory language applying the subsection to single or double family homes "intended for use as the owner's [*sic*] dwelling" when read in context extends the notice requirement for an existing owner occupied dwelling to a dwelling undergoing construction which is to be occupied by the owner when it is ready for such occupancy.

It has always been a matter of concern to this Court as to what balance should be maintained between the small homeowner and the small vendor, both of whom are defrauded by a defaulting general contractor. It is tragic that a small homeowner would be required to pay twice for the same services or materials, but on the other hand, the small vendor has no real ability to sustain a loss once his

material and labor are expended. The real villain escapes by the route of default or bankruptcy.

Here, the question becomes "Did the legislature intend to protect those persons who have the opportunity of owning a vacation or second home in addition to their primary residence?"

Mechanics' lien statutes protect laborers and suppliers because once the labor and materials are expended they lose their value to the supplier but increase the property value of the premises for the benefit of the landowner. The Pucossis expended $16,050 of the original $20,400 contract price, and they have benefited from the physical improvements to their Nolin Lake real estate.

The mechanics' and materialman's statutes are to be construed according to their common and approved language usage. KRS 446.080(4). In interpreting the statutes, we must take a liberal view toward promoting the legislative intent. KRS 446.080(1). Mechanics' lien statutes are to be interpreted liberally to protect those who furnish labor and materials. *Campbell & Summerhays, Inc., v. Greene, supra.*

The property covered includes an owner-occupied dwelling and related improvements to the real property on which the owner-occupied dwelling is located, and to the construction of a home intended for use as the property owner's dwelling even if not yet occupied. Here, the building was not occupied and never completed. The crucial language in the statute is the last sentence of Subsection (4).

The plain meaning of the words intended for use as "the" (emphasis added) property owner's dwelling means primary residence or principal dwelling. Any fair reading of the statute makes it clear that the term "dwelling" is used in the statute to apply to owner-occupied dwelling. If the legislature had wanted to expand the protection of the last sentence of Subsection (4), they might have included language such as "intended for use as the property owner's primary dwelling or vacation home or second home." We do not intend to speculate on what the General Assembly could have added to the statute. We are obliged to interpret what they did in context with the long-standing provisions of mechanics' and materialman's statutes.

It is the holding of this Court that KRS 376.010(4) is not applicable to second homes or vacation homes, and the dollar-for-dollar credit provided by that subsection of the statute does not apply to such properties.

The decision of the court of Appeals is affirmed.

Affirmed.

Case Questions

1. Describe the history of the construction and lien.
2. Why do such residential lien exemptions exist?
3. Why is there an issue of whether the residential exemption applies to a second home?

FIGURE 5.2   *Basics of Mechanic's Lien Rights*

What Property Is Subject to Liens?
- All real property
- Exemptions:
    - Public property
    - Railways
    - Property devoted to public use
    - Property of quasi-public corporations

Who Can Claim Liens?
- Original or principal contractors
- Subcontractors
- Persons supplying labor
- Persons supplying materials

Types of Claims
- Written contracts
- Implied contracts (some states)

What Property Is Subject to a Lien?

Once a lien is obtained, it applies to the whole of the real property and not simply the portion of the structure that was the subject of the lienor's work, labor, or materials. The lien attaches to both the building and the lot on which the building is located (subject to the exemptions-noted page). A lienor could lien individual lots in a subdivision for work performed on each of those lots. Figure 5.2 summarizes the generic basics of lien rights.

PROCEDURAL ASPECTS OF OBTAINING A LIEN

Because mechanic's liens are statutory, the procedural aspects for creating and enforcing a lien will vary from state to state, but the fundamentals are the same. Since the lien is a land interest, it will be recorded in the appropriate governmental land-record office. In most states, liens are probably filed in the same office as financing statements for fixtures (see Chapter 4). See Web Exhibits 5.1 and 5.2 for sample lien forms. Note that a place is provided on the first page of the form (not shown) for a real property description.

The times for filing, perfection, and period of validity for liens are areas of difference among the states. The length of time allowed for filing a lien also varies, as does the date that the allowed time period begins. Some statutes begin the 60- or 90-days' period for filing the lien on the date the work is completed or on the date the supplies are delivered. Even completion of work is defined differently from state to state: it may mean the end of work or the completion of the project with the issuance of an architect's certificate.

Many states follow a prenotification procedure, especially for those performing work who do not have a direct contractual relationship with the property owner. Those without such a contract who desire lien protection must file a

Practical Tip

Establish a payment mechanism for the contractor, subcontractors, and suppliers that ensures payment gets to the proper parties. Draws by the general contractor very often do not end up in the hands of the subcontractors and suppliers. Maintain adequate controls over payments so that your funds do not end up in the internal business of the general contractor instead of being paid to the subs and suppliers whose completed work is the basis for the draw.

preliminary notice within a certain period of time after their work has begun or their supplies have been delivered. Such notice is served on the owner of the property, the contractor (who has a contractual agreement with the property owner), and the construction lender. Basically, the notice serves to alert all concerned to the possibility of a lien. Because this notice gives a right to an eventual lien, the party giving the notice should be able to prove that such notice was sent, to whom it was sent, and when it was sent. In some states, the notice must be served personally or sent certified mail. This notice is not a lien; it simply makes all three parties aware of those working on the project, what they are doing, and the supplies and costs involved. The preliminary notice gives only the right to execute a lien in the future. In those states requiring the preliminary notice, failure to give the notice may cost the lienor the right of the lien.

The time period for which the lien, once filed, is effective also varies. In some states the period of effectiveness is six months (measured from the date of filing). If payment is not made by the owner or other assigned party during the time the lien is effective, then the lienor will bring suit (a form of foreclosure suit) to execute upon the lien to satisfy the payment due. If suit is not brought within the statutory period of effectiveness, the lien is lost.

PRIORITY OF LIEN INTERESTS

Attachment of Lien

In the prior discussion, the method of perfecting a mechanic's lien was established, but the times and dates of perfection may also be important in terms of the priority of the recorded lien. In the majority of states, a lien for the construction of a building ordinarily dates back to the commencement of construction. Thus, if construction begins on January 1, 2001, and is completed on June 1, 2001, and a lien is filed on July 1, 2001 (assuming a proper filing time), then the priority of the lien dates back to January 1, 2001, when construction began. If new financing were obtained for the building in June, the new lender's mortgage would be second in priority to the contractor's lien, because the contractor's lien has a priority date of the start of construction, or January 1, 2001. This principle is critically important for construction lenders, who must be certain construction has not begun prior to the recording of their mortgage in order not to lose priority. For permanent lenders, this means that all construction costs and subcontractors must be paid and all liens must be satisfied before the lenders record their mortgage or lend the money (so that they are not last in priority behind all those who have worked on the project and who have not yet been paid).

In another group of states, the priority date for liens is the date the particular lienor began work, not the date overall construction was begun.

In the final group of states, the lien is effective from the date of filing. For example, if the lender records the mortgage before the liens are filed, the lender would have priority because the liens would not date back to the time the construction was begun.

Rights of Purchasers

Whether a bona fide purchaser of property is subject to a preexisting lien or free from that lien will depend on the state's rule regarding attachment. For states that have a rule on attachments dating back to the time construction was commenced, a purchaser would be subject to the lien. In other states, the purchaser would be subject to the lien only if the lien were filed and recorded prior to the time of the purchase and the recording of the deed transferring title. In some states, a residential property exemption prevents the placement of liens on newly constructed residences when the home has been purchased in good faith from a contractor for use as a residence.[3] This exemption protects the buyers even if the priority of liens dates back to the start of the home's construction. The following case represents one state's view on purchaser rights versus mechanic's liens.

Sundance Mechanical & Utility Corporation v. Atlas

880 P.2d 861 (N.M. 1994)

Facts

Marvin and Carole Atlas (defendants/appellees) entered into a contract with R. J. Eden Construction Company on November 19, 1985, for the construction of a residence on real property owned by the Atlases. The original contract payment amount was $331,554.09. The contract required Eden to furnish labor, services, and materials for construction of the house.

On December 31, 1985, Eden, acting as general contractor, entered into a written contract with Sundance Mechanical & Utility Corporation (plaintiff/appellant) for Sundance to perform subcontract work on the Atlas house. Between September 2, 1986, and October 13, 1986, Eden and Sundance performed work on the Atlas residence.

On October 13, 1986, before construction was completed, the Atlases terminated Eden's contract as general contractor and began personally supervising construction of the residence. Between September 19, 1986, and June 18, 1987, the Atlases paid various subcontractors and suppliers $43,412.20 for work and materials.

Sundance completed its work on October 30, 1986. At this time Eden owed Sundance $14,637.80 for the work performed. On October 31, 1986, Sundance filed a claim of lien against the Atlases in the County Clerk's office in Bernalillo County. On February 17, 1987, the Atlases paid Sundance $3,000 to reduce the claim to $11,637.80.

On March 13, 1987, Sundance filed suit to foreclose on its lien. Sundance filed for a motion for summary judgment, which the trial court granted. The Atlases settled the payment with Sundance by paying $18,557.39, the amount awarded by the trial court. They then filed a motion to have the judgment set aside. The trial court then found that the Atlases had paid Eden in full at the time it was discharged and that they were entitled to the statutory protection of a residential homeowner and exemption from any subcontractors' liens. Sundance's lien was declared invalid and Sundance was ordered to refund the money that had been paid. Sundance appealed.

Judicial Opinion

Baca, Justice. Section 48-2-10.1(A) first requires that an owner pay the general contractor "all amounts due and owing" before the owner can avail itself of the benefit of the statute. We have interpreted payment of "all amounts due and owing" to mean final payment rather than partial payment. According to the facts stipulated by the parties prior to trial, the amount due on the contract between the Atlases and Eden was $331,554.09. The uncontroverted facts show that the Atlases paid Eden $279,615.69 on the contract. These facts establish that the Atlases failed to make full and final payment to Eden under the contract between the parties.

---

3.   Fla. Stat. Ann. § 627. 7842(c)

Our interpretation of Section 48-2-10.1(A) requires that the owner be an "innocent owner" in order to obtain the benefit of the statute. An "innocent owner" is defined as an owner "who had no notice, actual or constructive, of intervening claims by unpaid materialmen." Here the Atlases were not only aware of Sundance's claim of debt but also its claim of lien. The Atlases had paid Sundance $3,000 to reduce the claim of lien to $11,637.80 on February 17, 1987. The Atlases, having actual notice of debt and lien, cannot be considered "innocent owners."

Reversed.

Case Questions

1. Why do the Atlases not qualify as "innocent owners"?
2. What should the Atlases have done before firing Eden?
3. Why did the trial court and appellate court differ on their conclusions?
4. Of what significance is the Atlases' payment of $3,000 to Sundance?

Practical Tip

Mechanic's liens and the sale of residential property are a risky combination. Suppliers and subcontractors should be aware of their lien limitations. Buyers should do background checks on builders and observe the property to be certain lien claims do not arise, even though ultimately defeated. All parties should know their state statutory protections for lien holders and buyers alike.

Priority Among Mechanic's Liens

The statutes on the priority among mechanic's liens are widely varied but can be grouped as follows:

1. Statutes in which all liens are treated equally, as if all began work at the start of the project
2. Statutes in which liens are given priority according to the time the liens were perfected
3. Statutes in which liens are given priority according to the time individual work began
4. Statutes in which liens are given priority on the basis of the lienor's status

The common law rule, which more than half the states follow, is that all mechanics are on equal footing and there is no priority among them. Thus, under common law, all liens go back to the time when construction of the project first began. The reason for this rule under common law was to protect those furnishing labor and materials at the end of a project from always being left without payment or recourse. For example, if first workers or suppliers were given priority, the foundation workers would always be paid but the carpet layers would not.

This method of dating all liens back to the time construction was begun puts all on an equal basis with an equal opportunity for recovery. The criteria for determining when construction began varies from state to state, but at common law the construction began with "the first stroke of the ax or spade." Many construction lenders will have the property inspected before a mortgage is recorded, so that they can be assured that no work has begun and that they will have priority over all other lienors who will enjoy equal footing from the time construction begins.

If there are insufficient funds available to pay lienors on an equal footing, a mathematical formula is used. Suppose that $15,000 is left to be distributed, and the following amounts are due to lienors Akron, Barkley, and Clark:

Akron	= $15,000
Barkley	= $10,000
Clark	= $ 5,000
Total liens	= $30,000

The method of distribution is based on proportions. Since the total amount of liens is $30,000, the proportions for the parties are as follows:

Akron   = 15,000 ÷ 30,000, or ½

Barkley   = 10,000 ÷ 30,000, or ⅓

Clark   = 5,000 ÷ 30,000, or ⅙

Therefore, the $15,000 would be distributed as follows:

Akron   = ½ × 15,000 = $7,500

Barkley   = ⅓ × 15,000 = $5,000

Clark   = ⅙ × 15,000 = $2,400

In the second group of states, priority of lienors is determined by the times each lienor's project or portion of the work began. Again, this gives lienors involved with the initial stages of construction a greater chance of payment.

In the remaining two groups of states, claims are paid according to the time the lien is filed. Laborers may be given special priority over other lienors, or subcontractors may obtain relief after general contractors have been satisfied.

Mechanic's Liens and Fixture Filings

It is possible for an Article 9 UCC fixture filing to have priority over a mechanic's lien. When the security interest is a purchase money security interest (see Chapter 4) and the filing was completed before the item became a fixture or within 20 days after its annexation as a fixture, then the Article 9 interest takes priority, even over previously filed mortgages and (in this case) previously filed or attached mechanic's liens.

Mechanic's Liens and Homestead Exemption

Some states provide for property protection for residential dwellers, called a **homestead exemption.** This exemption provides protection from the attachment of mechanic's liens or at least from the forced sale of property for the satisfaction of a mechanic's lien. Likewise, in those states with dower protection, a mechanic's lien may not attach to a dower or curtesy interest (see Chapter 10), or cause the sale of that interest. The homestead exemption can also preclude foreclosure on a judicial lien.

Mechanic's Liens and Mortgages

As mentioned in the discussion of attachment, whether or not a mortgage (construction or permanent) will have priority over a mechanic's lien depends on the state's law regarding the time of attachment. If the priority of liens dates back to the time construction was commenced, then the mortgage must have been recorded prior to that time in order to enjoy priority. If the time of attachment is determined from the date of filing, then the mortgage must have been recorded prior to the time the lien was filed in order to enjoy priority. This priority also applies to mortgages in which the funds are to be advanced in a series of construction draws over a period of time.

TERMINATION OF MECHANIC'S LIENS

Waiver or Release by Agreement

A mechanic's lien may be eliminated by agreement of the parties. The first type of agreement is called a **waiver agreement,** in which a party waives the right (either before, during, or after construction) to file a lien for work on materials furnished. A sample waiver agreement is found in Web Exhibit 5.3. Some states recognize waivers in original contracts, which makes the waiver automatic and enforceable, while other states require the execution of a separate waiver agreement. Waivers executed during and after construction are recognized as valid in all states.

Some states have certain statutory language required for lien waivers. For example, California requires the following language in bold type on the lien waiver:

> NOTICE: THIS DOCUMENT WAIVES RIGHTS UNCONDITIONALLY AND STATES THAT YOU HAVE BEEN PAID FOR GIVING UP THOSE RIGHTS. THIS DOCUMENT IS ENFORCEABLE AGAINST YOU IF YOU SIGN IT, EVEN IF YOU HAVE NOT BEEN PAID. IF YOU HAVE NOT BEEN PAID, USE A CONDITIONAL RELEASE FORM. Cal. Civ. Code § 3262 (3) and (4).

The purpose of this language is to help subcontractors and contractors understand the distinction between a conditional or limited release and an unconditional release. An unconditional release means that once the signing party is issued a check, all liens are released. Under a conditional or limited release, only the materials and work furnished to the date of the lien are released. The signing party still has lien rights for future work and materials.

Another type of release is the subordination release, which entitles the signing party to a lien, but the lien is secondary to other interests in the property such as those of the construction lender and any other named secured parties.

LIEN ALTERNATIVES

The complexity of liens and the problems that arise for property owners as well as the cost of enforcement have caused many states to attempt resolution of construction payment issues through non-lien methods. A number of jurisdictions[4] now have some form of **stop notice statutes** or **trapping statutes.** These statutes were passed with the subcontractor and supplier interests in mind. Under these statutes, suppliers and subcontractors can give notice to those who are disbursing funds for the project to stop payment to the general contractor until their rights, interests, and payments have been reviewed.

The statutes create many additional issues beyond the complexities of mechanic's liens. For example, what is the liability of the fund holder if payment is not stopped? Also, the result can often be that no one is getting any money once the stop payment notice is given. These relatively new statutes have issues that require resolution that must come through case law.

---

4.   Alabama, Arizona, California, Colorado, District of Columbia, Florida, Indiana, Louisiana, Michigan, Mississippi, New Jersey, New Mexico, New York, North Carolina, Ohio, Oklahoma, Pennsylvania, Rhode Island, South Dakota, Texas, and Washington.

CONSTITUTIONALITY OF MECHANIC'S LIENS

Several state and federal courts have examined the issue of whether mechanic's lien statutes are constitutional. Most have found them to be constitutional so long as adequate notice is given to the landowner of the lien or potential lien. In recent years, challenges have been brought to lien statutes on a due process theory that the landowner is being deprived of a land interest. The basis for these challenges is that a lien may be filed without prior judicial action, thereby affecting the title of the land without a chance for the owner to rebut the lien. However, most courts faced with this due process issue have held that no significant property interest is taken, because although the lien decreases the property value, there is a corresponding increase in value for the improvements made. The liens are also upheld because the owner is given a chance to be heard before the amount of the lien is paid or the property is subjected to foreclosure.

CAUTIONS AND CONCLUSIONS

The discussions in this chapter affect three parties: property owners, lienors, and lenders. Each group should take appropriate precautions to ensure that liens affect them in only a positive manner.

For property owners, the following questions should be answered:

1. Are licensed, reputable contractors being used?
2. If a general contractor is involved, what guarantees exist for payment of subcontractors and material suppliers? Is there adequate payment supervision?
3. Are there preliminary notice requirements for liens other than those by the general contractor?

For lienors, the following questions should be answered:

1. Who owns the property?
2. Is there a prior mortgage? a construction mortgage?
3. Is preliminary notice of a lien required? If so, how is it properly given?
4. Are there time limits for filing a lien?
5. How long is the lien effective?
6. How long may a lienor wait before foreclosing on a lien?
7. What priorities exist among lien holders?

For lenders, the following questions should be answered:

1. Who owns the property?
2. Is there a prior mortgage? Are there current liens?
3. Has construction or work already begun?
4. Are preliminary notices required?
5. Was the mortgage filed prior to the beginning of the work?
6. Who is the general contractor? What payment supervision is provided?

By assessing their positions and determining their rights and obligations at the outset, property owners, lienors, and lenders can often avoid the pitfalls of liens and enjoy the protections and benefits offered by them. Figure 5.3 provides a summary of the issues in mechanic's lien rights, waivers, and collections.

FIGURE 5.3   *Issues in Mechanic's Lien Rights, Waivers, and Collections*

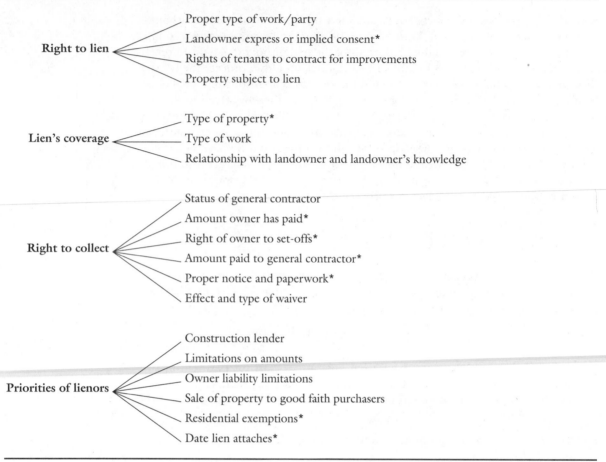

Right to lien
- Proper type of work/party
- Landowner express or implied consent*
- Rights of tenants to contract for improvements
- Property subject to lien

Lien's coverage
- Type of property*
- Type of work
- Relationship with landowner and landowner's knowledge

Right to collect
- Status of general contractor
- Amount owner has paid*
- Right of owner to set-offs*
- Amount paid to general contractor*
- Proper notice and paperwork*
- Effect and type of waiver

Priorities of lienors
- Construction lender
- Limitations on amounts
- Owner liability limitations
- Sale of property to good faith purchasers
- Residential exemptions*
- Date lien attaches*

*Varies by state

Key Terms

lien, 85
statutory lien, 86
mechanic's liens, 86
equitable lien, 86
contractual lien, 86
voluntary lien, 86

involuntary lien, 86
judicial lien, 86
materials liens, 87
lienee, 89
lienor, 89
consent statutes, 90

contract statutes, 90
homestead exemption, 101
waiver agreement, 102
stop notice statutes, 102
trapping statutes, 102

Chapter Problems

1. In 1977, Chagnon Lumber Company agreed to sell building materials on credit to Stone Mill Construction Corporation. Stone Mill had purchased land and intended to build houses on the property with Chagnon's and other suppliers' materials.

John and Ann Breiten purchased one of the Stone Mill homes. At closing of the sale, the Breitens were given an affidavit signed by an officer of Stone Mill that stated that the corporation had paid for all materials used in the house. The Breitens paid the purchase price and took title to the house.

Within 90 days after their last delivery of materials, but after the Breitens' closing, Chagnon filed in court for permission to attach a lien to the Breitens' property.

The Breitens objected to the lien on the grounds that they had no knowledge that any bills remained unpaid. Are the Breitens correct? Do they have any protection against the lien? *Chagnon Lumber Co., Inc. v. Stone Mill Construction Corp.,* 474 A.2d 588 (N.H. 1984)

2. In October 1981, Robert E. Hinkle leased to Raymond Arington the Dixie Plaza in Upshur County, West Virginia. The lease agreement contained the following clause:

Any improvements made to the leased premises shall, upon termination of this lease or the termination of any extension thereof, become the property of the lessor.

Arington hired Dunlap and others to do electrical and carpentry work to a building located on the premises. Arington went out of business shortly thereafter, owing Dunlap money for wages and materials.

On March 3, 1982, Dunlap filed a mechanic's lien against the property. That same day he filed a suit to enforce the lien against Arington and Hinkle. Can Arington and Hinkle be subject to a mechanic's lien and its foreclosure? *Dunlap v. Hinkle,* 317 S.E.2d 508 (W.Va. 1984)

3. Robert and Janet Barker had signed an installment contract to purchase a home from Roland and Gloria Barker and Eugene and Sandra Barker. Robert and Janet moved into the home in May 1975, and in December 1975, the home was partially destroyed by fire. Robert and Janet moved out of the home for five months so that repairs and restoration could be completed. Robert contracted with Tri-County Builders to repair the house. Robert paid $19,000 of the $20,000 contract price to Tri-County, but Tri-County did not complete the project and also failed to pay Brownsburg Lumber Company (the supplier of the lumber for the home repairs). Brownsburg filed a timely lien notice but notified only Robert and Janet of his supplier role. He did not notify the other Barkers who, under the terms of Robert and Janet's purchase contract, still held title to the house until the full purchase price was paid. Brownsburg filed suit to enforce its lien. Roland and Eugene claim that lien is invalid because they had no notice of Brownsburg's supplier role. Who is correct? Can Brownsburg collect on the lien? *Barker v. Brownsburg Lumber Co., Inc.,* 399 N.E.2d 426 (Ind. 1980)

4. A is a carpenter and has completed the framing of eight homes for G, the general (prime) contractor. Prior to A's work, B had leveled and graded the property; C had put in the foundation; D had staked out the driveways and homes; and E had partially installed the plumbing fixtures. The tasks were completed on the following dates:

  A, November 22, 2000
  B, August 1, 2000
  C, September 15, 2000
  D, August 15, 2000
  E, August 30, 2000

All parties properly served a preliminary notice. A construction mortgage was filed August 1, 2000. No one has been paid, and A, B, C, D, and E have all filed liens by December 1, 2000. Who has priority, the mortgage company or the lienors? What order of priority exists among the lienors? What happens if there is not enough money to pay the lienors?

5. Fifteen couples purchased homes in the Green Meadows subdivision, and they had all moved in by August 2000. Two days before Christmas, workmen's liens were filed against the homeowners' properties. Under state law, the filing of the liens dated back to the time construction began, May 2000. The homeowners wish to know their rights. What is the result? Would the result be different in your state?

6. Bank One filed a mortgage on May 31, 1989 on property owned by Sam and Grace Malz. The mortgage secured a $2,400,000 loan Bank One had made to the Malzes for purposes of constructing ten six-unit buildings on the property. At the time the mortgage on the property was filed, Schalmo Builders, Inc., the contractor hired by the landowner to construct the buildings, had performed soil tests and staked out the locations for the buildings. The Malzes did not pay the builder and defaulted on the loan. The builder foreclosed on its lien and Bank One claimed priority. Who has first claim to the proceeds from the foreclosure sale of the property? *Schalmo Builders, Inc. v. Malz,* 629 N.W.2d 52 (Ohio App. 1993).

7. Allen Betke contracted with Thomas Hake Enterprises, Inc., to construct a home in Carpentersville, Illinois. As construction progressed, Betke was unable to pay, so he arranged for Charlotte Birck and her son,

Jason Birck, to buy the house Charlotte and Jason paid Betke $68,000, and Betke continued to supervise construction and hire subcontractors although Charlotte wrote checks for payment and channeled them through Betke for the contractors, subs, and suppliers.

The house was resold by Charlotte for $175,000 to the Coffmans. However, there were liens on the property from various parties not paid by Betke. The sale could not close until the lien issues were resolved. Charlotte claims she and Jason are not subject to the liens because they had no contracts with the lienors. Is she correct? *Thomas Hake Enterprises, Inc. v. Betke,* 703 N.E.2d 114 (Ill. App. 1998).

8. A contractor's lien covers which of the following?

    a. The constructed building

    b. The lot on which the building is located

    c. An existing parking garage on the lot

    d. A PMSI in the blinds hanging on the windows of an office building

9. Contractor A has contracted to build a recreational building for the First Avenue Baptist Church, an unincorporated association. The church moderator signs the contract. When the church refuses to pay because the moderator acted without authority, contractor A attempts to place a lien on the property but the church officers object. Who is right and why?

10. Are architects and engineers entitled to liens for the work they perform prior to construction? *Korsunsky Kank Erickson Architects, Inc. v. Walsh,* 370 N.W.2d 29 (Minn. 1985)

Internet Activities

1. For filing deadlines for liens in the state of Mississippi, go to: **http://www.kwik-net.com. lien-ms.htm**.

2. For filing deadlines for liens in the state of California, go to: **http://cmaccom.com/articles/art091.html**.

3. For mechanic's liens forms and statutes in Ohio visit: **http://www.fklaborlaw.com/Ohio-mechanic's-liens.htm**.

4. For information on California mechanic's liens, go to: **http://www.sbxchange.com/main.htm**.

5. For a state-by-state view of mechanic's liens, go to: **http://www.kwik-net.com/lien-st**.

6. Compare and contrast the deadlines for filing liens in the states. Which is more favorable to claimants.

Chapter 6
Describing Land Interests

I hereby transfer 32 acres more or less in the southwest of lot no. 105 in the 13th District and 2nd section of my county.

   Matthews v. Logan, 247 S.E.2d 865 (Ga. 1978)

[A deed must] comprehend the certainty of the land or tenements to be conveyed.

   Sir Edward Coke

An accurate, legally sufficient description of a land interest being transferred is critical. An error in a description can have generational impact. Also, certain minimum requirements are set by statute and judicial precedent for deed descriptions. Only those descriptions complying with the requirements will be legally sufficient to pass title to property.

In this chapter the following questions are answered: What are the methods used to describe land? What precautions should be taken in drafting and checking land descriptions?

METHODS OF DESCRIBING LAND INTERESTS

Metes and Bounds

The metes and bounds method is a technique of describing the boundary lines of a particular parcel. **Metes** refers to distance, while **bounds** refers to the direction of the distance to be taken.

A **metes and bounds description** consists of a series of instructions that could be followed to walk out the boundary lines of the land parcel. A permanent beginning point can be natural (such as a stream or river) or artificial (such as a bridge). Monuments are frequently used as starting points for metes and bounds descriptions.

For example, a metes and bounds description of the shaded portion in Figure 6.1 would be as follows:

> *Beginning at a point on the south side of Gary Street, 200 feet east from the corner formed by the intersection of the south side of Gary Street and the east side of Hale Street, then proceeding south parallel to the east side of Hale Street 100 feet; then proceeding east parallel to the south side of Gary Street 50 feet; then proceeding north parallel to the east side of Hale Street 100 feet to the south side of Gary Street; and then proceeding west on the south side of Gary Street, 50 feet or to the beginning point.*

Because of their dependency on starting points (which can be moved) and because of the potential for inaccurate measurement, metes and bounds descriptions may result in problems when land is transferred.

The following case deals with the adequacy of a metes and bounds description.

> ### Practical Tip
>
> Physical inspections help verify the accuracy or inaccuracy of descriptions. Compare physical boundaries with deed descriptions.

> ### Practical Tip
>
> Many metes and bounds descriptions have been handed down over the years as property has been transferred. As in the *Foreman* case, old descriptions are often used and relied upon mistakenly in the transfer of land. However, the mere sale or transfer of the land does not mean that the description is accurate or valid. Further, maps are insufficient for description and transfer of title without identifying marks on them.

FIGURE 6.1   *Sample Land Parcel for Metes and Bounds Description*

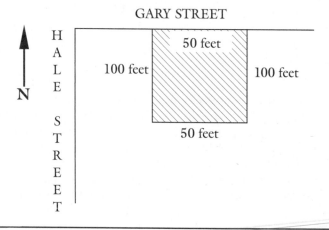

Foreman v. Sholl

Forman Bought property
title suit
heirs won

439 S.E.2d 169 (N.C. App. 1994)

Facts

Kenneth and Mary Foreman (Mr. and Mrs. Foreman, plaintiffs), spoke with Jeseppo Perrone in 1979 and indicated that they were interested in locating the heirs of "people who had bought property in Buncombe County, North Carolina, from the Mountain Retreat Association in 1907 or shortly afterwards" for the purpose of buying property from them.

In 1981, Mr. Perrone called Mr. Foreman and told him he had located the heirs and had a deed. Mr. Perrone offered to deed over, by quitclaim deed, title to the land. Mr. Perrone met Mr. Foreman on the sidewalk in front of the Radisson Hotel in Charlotte, North Carolina, on September 15, 1983. Mr. Foreman paid Mr. Perrone $2,400 and Mr. Perrone handed Mr. Foreman an envelope containing a quitclaim deed, which Mr. Foreman examined. The deed named "Kenneth J. Foreman, Jr., Trustee" and conveyed 59 tracts, 41 of which are described by reference to a 1906 drawing recorded in the Buncombe County Register of Deeds.

The drawing shows over 1,000 lots; distances are shown on some of the lots but there are no markers from which the distances can be measured. The bearings of the lines are not depicted. The radius or arc distance or chord length, chord bearing, and tangent distance of any arc are not shown. Nothing in the drawing refers to anything that can be located or identified with certainty.

In 1990, the Foremans, pursuant to a dispute with a number of landowners claiming title to the tracts (defendants), brought suit to quiet title to the land conveyed to them by Mr. Perrone. The trial court held that the description was insufficient and that the Foremans were not the title holders of the tracts. The Foremans appealed.

Judicial Opinion

Greene, Judge. All conveyances purporting to be color of title, including deeds, must contain, as an essential element of the conveyance, "a description identifying the land." The description must be "either certain in itself or capable of being reduced to a certainty by a recurrence to something extrinsic to which the deed refers." It is the deed that must speak . . . [and] oral evidence must only interpret what has been said therein. In other words, a description, although indefinite, is sufficient if the court can, with the aid of extrinsic evidence which does not add to, enlarge, or in any way change the description, fit it to the property conveyed by the deed.

When it is apparent upon the face of the deed, itself, that there is uncertainty as to the land intended to be conveyed and the deed, itself, refers to nothing extrinsic by which such uncertainty can be resolved, the description is said to be patently ambiguous. A patent ambiguity is such an uncertainty appearing on the face of the instrument that the Court, reading the language in light of all the facts and circumstances *referred to in the instrument,* is unable to derive *therefrom* the intention of the parties as to what land was to be conveyed. Parol evidence may not be introduced to remove a patent ambiguity since to do so would not be a use of such evidence to fit the description to the land but a use of such evidence to create a description by adding to the words of the instrument.

Whether a description is patently ambiguous is a question of law. In this case, the deed upon which plaintiffs rely to establish color of title describes the property with reference to a drawing recorded in the Buncombe County Register of Deeds and known as the Drawing. Thus the Drawing becomes a part of the deed as if it were written therein. The question, therefore, is whether the Drawing provides a description having the same degree of certainty as [is] required of a description appearing only in the deed itself. The Drawing without question is not sufficient in itself to describe the land conveyed. The Drawing does not have any ascertainable monuments, does not indicate the size of the tracts of land shown, does not indicate any courses and very few distances, and has no ascertainable beginning points. The only issue is whether the description in the deed is capable of being reduced to certainty by use of something extrinsic to which the deed refers. We do not believe it is. The Drawing simply does not refer to anything extrinsic that would be of aid in identifying the property with certainty. The four surveyors, offered by plaintiffs, testified that they could, by reference solely to the Drawing, identify the property on the ground. This testimony, however, added to and enlarged the description given in the Drawing and was thus not competent.

Affirmed.

Case Questions

1. What do you think about the circumstances surrounding the acquisition? List the circumstances in the parties' conduct and conveyance that seem different from the usual land transfers.
2. What were the problems with the Drawing?
3. Was the Drawing incorporated as part of the deed?
4. Was there a sufficient description? Do the Foremans hold title?
5. Why wasn't the testimony of the surveyors permitted?

http://
Visit the Nebraska State
Surveyor's Office Website
at: **http://www.sso.state.
ne.us/bels/minstand.
htm**.

Plat Map

Probably the most frequently used method for describing property in residential areas is the **plat map.** In this form of description, a map of a subdivision is recorded at some state or local agency responsible for property records. Each plat map contains the size and shape of each lot, the numbers of blocks and lots, the names of all streets, indications of alleys and easements, and a list of covenants and restrictions. A sample plat description would be, "Lot 27 of Candlelight Estates IV, as per plat recorded in Book of Maps 30, page 80, in the Office of the County Recorder of Holim County, Utah."

Consider 6.1

Corner Cupboard Craft Shop acquired title to real property from James and Shirley Smith. The legal description in the deed contains a metes and bounds description that contains several distance calls followed by the phrase "more or less" and general directions such as "northwesterly." A plat map is attached to the deed with the metes and bounds description. Is the legal description sufficient to pass title? *Lawyers Title Insurance Corp. v. Nash,* 396 S.E.2d 284 (Ga. 1990)

The plat map itself must have certain minimal information to be considered a valid description. For example, county and town are critical information. If the deed description relies on an attached map, the map must be labeled with direction, street names, and lot numbers. The following case deals with a problem that arose because of the failure to comply with the statutory requirements for plat maps.

McDonald v. Jones

852 P.2d 588 (Mont. 1993)

Facts

Irene H. Jones owned 12.63 acres of land in the Seeley Swan valley. The land had various improvements, including a house constructed by Jones. Ownership of America approached Jones and requested that she convey two undeveloped acres from the 12-acre tract in exchange for Ownership's stock. There was no agreement specifying which two acres were to be conveyed.

A deed prepared by a friend, Vernon H. Peterson, on April 13, 1981, contained the following land description:

> That portion of Lot numbered Seven (7) of Section Six (6) in Township Twenty (20) North of Range Sixteen (16) West of Montana Principal Meridian, Montana, lying West of Federal Aid Secondary 209 right-of-way and containing two acres more or less and further accurately described by plat on file with the party of the first part and the party of the second part. Party of the first part herein reserves all minerals under the above description.

The deed did not specify which two undeveloped acres were to be conveyed, and no plat was ever filed with

the Missoula County Clerk and Recorder. The Missoula County Clerk and Recorder erroneously treated the conveyance as a transfer of the full 12.63 acres. The Missoula County Treasurer changed the tax notice address and all notifications from that time were sent to Ownership.

In 1985, Missoula County transferred title to the property to Lee McDonald pursuant to a tax sale for Ownership's failure to pay property taxes. McDonald had notice of the two-acre limitation, but said nothing when the same deed description was used. Nonetheless, McDonald went to Ownership and asked for a quitclaim deed. Ownership did quitclaim any interest it had to McDonald in exchange for a $2,000 piece of property McDonald conveyed to Ownership.

Irene Jones, now married to Vernon Peterson, conveyed the remainder of the 12.63 acres to the Irene H. Peterson Limited Partnership.

The parties finally came face-to-face on the property, and McDonald filed suit to clear title. The trial court found for Jones on the grounds that there was an invalid description in the deed to Ownership and title had not passed. McDonald appealed.

Judicial Opinion

Hunt, Justice. Section 76-3-14 of MCA (1979), states that a subdivision shall be comprised of parcels less than 20 acres which have been segregated from the original tract. Jones' warranty deed to Ownership was an attempt to subdivide a parcel of land by segregating a two-acre parcel from the original 12.63 acre tract. The attempted subdivision violated the Montana Subdivision and Platting Act because the Act requires that a plat be filed of record before title to subdivided ground can be sold or transferred in any manner. In addition, the Act requires that the clerk and recorder reject any instrument that purports to transfer title to a parcel that is required to be surveyed.

The record shows that the parties intended to transfer only two acres of undeveloped land out of the 12.63 acres of land. No plat was recorded describing the two acres even though the deed did make a reference to such a plat. The deed should have been rejected.

A deed will be considered void for uncertainty if the identity of the property can not be ascertained by reference to extrinsic evidence. We consider the property description contained in a deed adequate if it contains sufficient information to permit the identification of the property to the exclusion of all others.

In this instance, the parties failed to come to a meeting of the minds regarding which two acres of land Jones was to convey to Ownership. No extrinsic evidence was available for the District Court to identify which two acres the parties contemplated to be conveyed. Therefore, we hold that the deed was void for uncertainty. Because the warranty deed was ineffective in conveying any portion of the 12.63 acres, the subsequent deed from Ownership to McDonald conveyed no interest in property. We hold that the District Court was correct as a court sitting in equity in holding that the original conveyance between Jones and Ownership was void for failure to comply with the Montana Subdivision and Platting Act.

Inasmuch as Jones had continued to pay property taxes, the county tax sale was invalid. Jones and Peterson had the proper chain of title.

Affirmed.

Case Questions

1. What was the problem with the description in the original deed from Jones to Ownership?
2. Do you think the parties were trying to avoid the cost of a plat map?
3. How did the property come to be sold by the County Treasurer?
4. Who has title to the property now?

In the *McDonald* case, the parties avoided the cost of a survey and plat designation. However, the buyer also lost its interest, as did others who purchased the property with the title defect in the original deed. What are the consequences of legal circumvention of a statute on subdivision?

Did Irene Jones make a double gain here? Didn't she intend to convey the land and then just take it back? Are Ownership and McDonald owed anything? Does it make a difference that McDonald knew of the description problem and said nothing?

> Ethical Issue

Government Survey

HISTORY

Another method for describing a land interest is by the **United States government survey.** This survey was done in 1785 because there was such a vast section of land west of the original 13 colonies, and so many claims were being made for it. The purpose of the survey was to provide a uniform system for describing property that is based on dividing the vast lands into rectangular segments.

PRINCIPAL MERIDIANS AND BASELINES

The geographer for the United States who was assigned the survey task had to develop a system for the survey that would compensate for the Earth's curved surface.

mardi Gras

The survey began with the establishment of **prime** or **principal meridians** and **baselines.** These first guidelines serve as the solution for the curvature of the Earth's surface. The lines were positioned at uniform distances apart so that the curve would not affect the accuracy of the survey. Thirty-five prime or principal meridian lines run north to south, and 32 baselines run east to west. The meridians are named according to their locations: Chickasaw, Michigan, Willamette, and Tallahassee are examples of principal meridians.

GUIDE MERIDIANS AND PARALLELS

Between each of the baselines and principal meridians, the surveyors placed correction lines to further compensate for the Earth's curved surface. **Guide meridians** were placed between principal meridians, and **parallels** were placed between baselines. These supplementary lines were placed every 24 miles. The result is that the surveyed land is divided into a **grid** of 24-mile squares.

TOWNSHIPS AND RANGES

This grid of 24 miles is broken down even further with **township** lines placed every six miles between the parallels and **range** lines placed every six miles between the guide meridians. The divisions are illustrated by Figure 6.2. In the figure, the six-mile squares (townships) are identified by their distances (in the number of squares) from the principal meridian. This distance is labeled as either east or west of the principal meridian. For example, in Figure 6.2 the upper right-hand square is one square west of the principal meridian, or R1W. However, because all squares adjacent to the meridian will have that same label, the townships are further identified according to their distance from the baseline. The upper right-hand square is the fourth square north of the baseline, or T4N.

Consider 6.2 | Label each of the 21 blank squares in Figure 6.2 according to their location with respect to the Salt Lake Meridian and the baseline.

FIGURE 6.2   *Twenty-Four-Mile Grid of U.S. Government Survey*

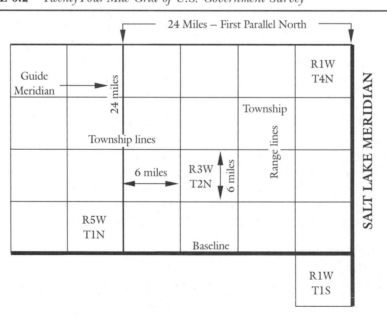

Each six-mile square or township in Figure 6.2 is further broken down into 36 one-mile squares. Each one-mile square is called a **section.** Sections are numbered in a serpentine fashion starting at the upper right-hand corner and proceeding left (see Figure 6.3).

Each section is one-mile square or a total of 640 acres, and each section can be broken down into fractional portions to more precisely describe the land involved. These fractional portions are described according to directional locations. Figure 6.4 is an example of a section with fractional portions labeled. To start, each section can be divided into quarters. The upper right-hand corner is the northeast quarter, and the lower left-hand corner is the southwest quarter. In the same manner, each quarter can be broken into quarters and labeled.

In Figure 6.4, finish filling in the descriptive names of the unmarked portions (A, B, C, D, and E) of each section.

Consider 6.3

FIGURE 6.3   *Sample Township*

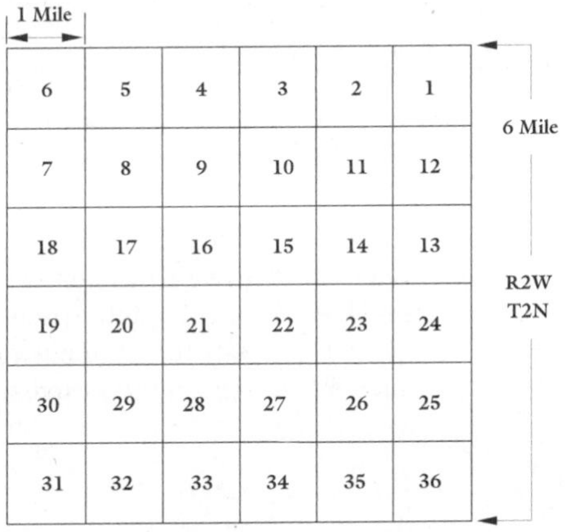

FIGURE 6.4   *Sample Section*

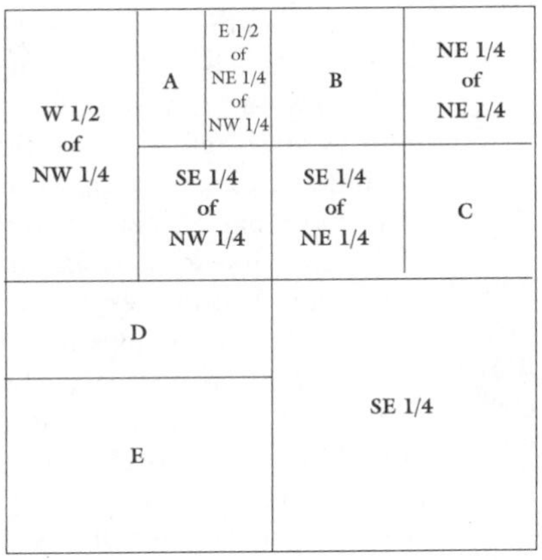

Practical Tip

The *Triplett* case shows how important it is for the description in a deed to be accurate, right down to the word "of." In this situation, 60 years of confusion resulted because of inadequate descriptions. Regardless of the means used for describing the property, make sure the description meets the legal tests for sufficiency under that method.

DESCRIPTION AND SIZE

Pulling together all divisions of the government survey, a sample land description would be "SE 1/4 of Section 12, Township 3 North, Range 2 East of the Salt Lake Meridian, Iron County, State of Utah." The addition of the county and state helps in determining which baseline is involved.

Because the government survey is uniform, it is possible to determine the size of a described parcel of land once the exact description is known. For example, if the land described is the NE 1/4 of a section, then the size of the parcel is 1/4 of 640 acres (the size of a section), or 160 acres. If the land described were the NE 1/4 of the NE 1/4, then the parcel would be 1/4 of 160, or 1/16 of 640, or 40 acres.

The following case deals with problems that result when the land is referenced to the government survey but still not adequately identified.

Triplett v. David H. Fulstone Co.

849 P.2d 334 (Nev. 1993)

Facts

In 1907, 35 acres of land located in Lyon County and abutting the Walker River were owned by the Mason Townsite Company. In 1935, because of the failure of Mason Townsite to pay assessed taxes, the property was conveyed to Lyon County by tax deed. The property was described in the 1935 deed as follows:

> Frac. W 1/2 of the SE 1/4; Frac. SW 1/4 of NE 1/4, Sec. 28, T. 13, N.R. 25 E., water only, for the total purchase price of $90.05.

In 1937, Lyon County conveyed title to Everett and Edna Triplett's predecessor in title. That deed contained the following description:

> Fr. W 1/2; Fr. SE 1/4; Fr. SW 1/4; Fr. NE 1/4, Sec. 28, T. 13N., R. 25 E., M.D.B. & M., 60 acres, formerly assessed to Mason Townsite Company.

The word "of" was omitted twice in the first line of the 1937 deed and replaced with "Fr."

In 1939 and 1941, Lyon County, apparently not realizing it had conducted a tax sale of this land, held additional tax sales of the undisputed property. These deeds were to those who are the predecessors in title to the David H. Fulstone Company. The description in these deeds was almost identical to the 1935 deed conveyance to Lyon County. These deeds did not contain the omission of the words "of," as did the 1937 deed.

The Fulstones have paid taxes on the property and have used the property for pasturing, hunting, and wood-cutting for 15 years. The Tripletts (plaintiffs/appellants) claimed title. The trial court held that the description in the deed for the Tripletts' predecessor in title was inadequate to transfer title to them and that the Fulstones had adversely possessed the property.

Judicial Opinion

Per Curiam. The first issue presented is whether the 1937 tax deed to the Tripletts' predecessors in interest was a valid conveyance of the disputed property. This court has held that an inadequate legal description of the land in a deed may be remedied by extrinsic evidence.

The correct legal description of the 1937 deed can be easily ascertained by reference to the Lyon County assessment rolls. The 1937 tax deed specifically referenced land "formerly assessed to Mason Townsite Company," and because reference to the tax rolls establishes a description which encompasses the disputed property, we conclude that the holders of the first deed to the property have title to it. Because the deed to the Tripletts' predecessor in interest was validly conveyed and filed, it follows that this conveyance takes precedence over the subsequent conveyances to the Fulstones' predecessors in interest. Finally, although it appears that the 1937 deed should have provided sufficient warning for subsequent purchasers to be on notice of a previous conveyance, because this issue was not raised at the trial level or on appeal, we express no opinion with regard to this issue.

The Fulstones have occupied and claimed the property for at least fifteen years. Because we believe the evidence adduced below affirmatively established adverse
possession by clear and competent proof, we affirm the
judgment of the district court.

Affirmed.

Case Questions

1. Which of the descriptions was sufficient under the
government survey method?
2. What was different about the 1937 deed from Lyon
County?
3. Were the 1939 and 1941 deeds valid? Why?
4. Who ends up with title to the property and why?

> **Consider 6.4**

Since 1958, Ray and Barbara Mensen have leased on a month-to-month basis a
house owned by Helen and Clarence Haines. (Clarence died in 1984.) In 1963,
discussions began between the two couples about the possibility of a purchase of
the home. The Haineses had hoped the Mensens would look after them in their
old age since the Haineses had no known relatives.

Several drafts of the deed were produced, along with discussions that the
property was being deeded to the Mensens in exchange for care and assistance
for the Haineses. The deed giving the Mensens "the farm" was transferred to them
sometime in December 1980 or January 1981 and recorded on January 13, 1981.
The deed also included the following language:

> Part of the Northeast Quarter of the Northeast Quarter of Section 9 Town-
> ship 16 North Range 13 East all in Douglas County Nebraska as recorded
> in the Douglas County Register of Deeds office.

The Mensens did not deliver the promised care, and Helen Haines brought
suit to have the deed declared void for failure of consideration and inadequacy
of the description. Is the description adequate? *Haines v. Mensen*, 446 N.W.2d 716
(Neb. 1989)

ADEQUACY OF DESCRIPTIONS

When properly followed, the three methods of description just discussed provide
legally sufficient descriptions. However, many other different methods of description are used, some of them legally sufficient and others only creating confusion
and causing litigation. The most important criterion in evaluating the legal sufficiency of a description is whether the land is described in such a manner that
only one possible tract can be identified from the description.

Description by Popular Name

Often a popular name such as "my ranch, the Double T" is used as a description
for conveying land. This type of description may or may not be sufficient, depending on whether the landowner holds one or several tracts of land.

In the following case, the issue of the legal sufficiency of a description by popular name is addressed.

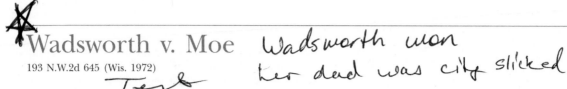

Wadsworth v. Moe

193 N.W.2d 645 (Wis. 1972)

Wadsworth won her dad was city slicked

Test

Facts

L. W. Anacker owned two parcels of land in the town of Stanton, Dunn County. One parcel consisted of a 130-acre farm with a dwelling and a number of other buildings. The other parcel was a 1-acre piece of land with a remodeled schoolhouse in which Anacker lived. The schoolhouse was enclosed by a fence and was located 1/8 mile from the other buildings.

After his wife's death in 1962, Anacker became depressed and stopped farming. He lived in the schoolhouse near his daughter, Mabel Moe (appellant).

Anacker decided to sell the farm without the schoolhouse, and the farm was listed for $18,000. Wadsworth (respondent) learned of the listing, and he and Anacker went to a bank and had a real estate option document drawn up. (A standard legal form was used.)

In the blanks provided, the real estate was described as "The L. W. Anacker farm in the town of Stanton." Wadsworth paid Anacker $1,500 for the option and could buy the property by paying an additional $14,000 by January 4, 1968. The contract also provided:

> Party of the second part may occupy the land and other buildings from this date forward. Party of the first part may occupy the dwelling and keep possession of the same up to November 1, 1968. Present insurance to be assigned to party of the second part free. The electric stove in the kitchen to remain for party of the second part.

On December 18, 1968, Wadsworth informed Anacker of his intention to exercise the option.

When Mabel Moe learned of the option she refused to let her father convey title, claiming that the legal description in the option was inadequate.

The trial court entered a judgment for Wadsworth and granted him specific performance. Mrs. Moe appealed.

Judicial Opinion

Wilkie, Justice. An option to purchase real estate which does not conform to the statute of frauds is void and a nullity. To comply with the statute, the contract or memorandum must be reasonably definite as to the property conveyed. Here the trial court determined that the description of the real estate as "the L. W. Anacker farm in the town of Stanton" was not sufficiently definite but that the entire document, considered as a whole together with the stipulation of facts by the parties, did comply with the statute of frauds and was, therefore, valid.

The trial court was entirely correct in deciding that the bare description on the option did not comply with the statute of frauds. When an individual owns more than one parcel of land in the same general locality, the description in the document must be sufficiently definite so that a person might know to a reasonable certainty to which parcel or parcels the document relates.

The trial court did find, however, that although the option description was not sufficient, the whole option when taken together with information in the stipulation of facts was sufficient to meet the statute of frauds. All the terms of a contract may be considered when deciding whether the document conforms to the statute of frauds.

The land description in the option document was admittedly vague as to what constituted the "L. W. Anacker farm." The extent of the land is not shown. The other terms of the option contract do not clear up this ambiguity, neither does the stipulation. The extrinsic evidence shows either that both the farm and all of the schoolhouse land were conveyed; that only the schoolhouse land was conveyed; or that the farm, but not the schoolhouse was conveyed. In short, the contract, even when considered together with this extrinsic evidence, continues to be vague about the extent of the land sold.

In the end, the option contract here does not sufficiently show the extent of the land conveyed and for that reason must be held null and void.

Reversed and remanded for dismissal of the complaint.

Case Questions

1. Describe the size, nature, amenities, and locations of Anacker's land.
2. Where did Anacker reside?
3. Did Anacker farm the land?
4. Who is Mabel Moe?
5. What type of agreement did Anacker and Wadsworth execute?
6. How was the land described?
7. What is the significance of the stove clause?
8. Did Wadsworth exercise the option to purchase?
9. What were Mrs. Moe's objections to the agreement?
10. Who won at the trial court level?
11. Is the description legally sufficient?
12. Did the court examine extrinsic evidence?
13. What is the appellate court's decision?

On December 13, 1945, Percy C. Harris conveyed by warranty deed to P. H. Coleman some land described as "twenty (20) acres out of the southwest quarter of
Section 7 . . . containing one hundred sixty acres."

Harris actually owned the west half of the northeast quarter and the west half
of the southeast quarter of Section 7.

Coleman claims that he now owns the full 160 acres because Harris was conveying the full parcel and the 20-acre reference was because he thought that he
owned segments of various quarters. How much does Coleman own? *Mounce v.
Coleman,* 650 P.2d 1233 (Ariz. 1982)

> **Consider** 6.5

Description by Street Number

Many times in residential sales, the description used for the property being conveyed is the street address. Although this type of description may be used as a supplement, it should not be used as the sole description. One reason is that street
numbers and names may change. Also, the use of the street address alone does
not describe the exact segment of land being transferred.

General Conveyances

Sometimes a legal description such as "all my real estate" is used. Such a description is inadequate because it does not provide the location, extent, and boundaries of the interest being conveyed.

Impermanent Descriptions

Often metes and bounds descriptions use a starting point that is impermanent in
its character, such as "pile of rocks" or "fences." These types of descriptions create problems because there can be movement or even destruction of the beginning point, thus rendering the description invalid.

Interpretation of Descriptions

In determining the adequacy or meaning of a description, courts follow certain
rules that are uniformly applied:

Rule 1 The language of the description is construed against the grantor
(seller) of the property and in favor of the grantee. This rule is based
on the idea that the grantor drafted the deed and had the opportunity to check it for accuracy.

Rule 2 If there are two descriptions, one ambiguous and one nonambiguous,
the nonambiguous description prevails so that a legally sufficient
description is found.

Rule 3 Ambiguities may be clarified by reference to other portions of the document and to oral testimony. This clarification by outside evidence is
permissible only if there is a latent as opposed to a patent ambiguity
in the deed. A latent ambiguity is one that is not apparent to the parties when the deed is written. Examples of latent ambiguities are typing errors or the simple carryover of an erroneous legal description of
which the parties are unaware. A patent ambiguity (as in the *Wadsworth*
case) can be clarified only by reference to other parts of the deed or
document and not by reference to extrinsic evidence.

The following case brings together all of the problems that can arise with a description combining metes and bounds with plat map description and ambiguities in both creating interpretation issues.

Withington v. Derrick

572 A.2d 912 (Vt. 1990)

Facts

James and Madeline Withington (plaintiffs) and Asa and Vivian Derrick (defendants) dispute the ownership of a piece of land located at the confluence of the parties' properties (as pictured here*). On October 10, 1959, in two separate transactions, two brothers, as common grantors, deeded the two pieces of property located in the Village of Wilder, Town of Hartford, Vermont, to the Withingtons and the Derricks. The Derricks' deed provides as follows:

Being Lot #36 as delineated on Hazen's Survey and Plan of Lots in the Village of Wilder, so-called, and which lot is bounded on the East by Lot #29, now owned by the grantees herein; on the north by Lot #35, now owned by the Benedicts; on the west by land now of Hoff; and on the south by the street known as Chandler Terrace.

The phrase in the Derricks' deed describing the western boundary of the property is incorrect: there was no adjacent landowner by the name of Hoff. At the time of the conveyance, people named Haff did own several lots about a block away. Even assuming that the drafter of the instrument was referring to Haff, the Haff property could not possibly have been the western boundary of lot 36. The Withingtons' deed includes the following description:

Also an irregular parcel of land described as follows: Beginning at a point marking the southeasterly corner of the Haff premises, and thence proceeding northerly along said Haff premises to the corner of Fern Street; thence easterly along Fern Street to the Benedict premises and St. John premises and the boundary of the right of way to said premises to Lot #36; thence southerly along the westerly boundary of Lot #36 to Chandler Terrace; thence westerly along the southerly boundary of the premises herein conveyed to the corner of Lot #44 which is the point of beginning.

This description has two problems. First, the Benedict and St. John deeds do not mention any

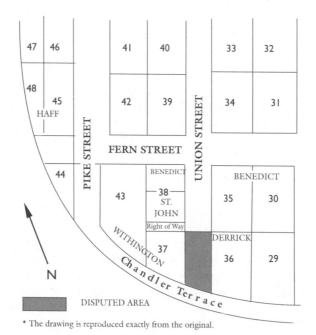

DISPUTED AREA

* The drawing is reproduced exactly from the original.

right-of-way leading to or adjoining their land; however, it is uncontested that a narrow strip of land on the southerly end of the St. John premises separately existed as a right-of-way. Second, the last part of the description does not close the deeded property. Further, Fern Street and Union Street were never accepted as municipal roadways.

The trial court held that the grantors had intended to deed to the defendants the portion of the never-accepted Union Street directly west of lot 36 but that the drawer of defendants' deed has mistaken lot 44 for lot 37 and accordingly named the Hoff (meant to be Haff) property as the western boundary of lot 36. The trial court awarded title to the piece of property at issue to the Derricks, and the Withingtons appealed.

Judicial Opinion

Gibson, Justice. Essentially, only two facts vaguely support the trial court's theory. First, since Union Street was not really a street at the time of the deed, one might infer that the grantors intended lot #36 to include the parcel of land adjoining lot #36 inaccurately marked as a street. Nonetheless, in addition to the fact that this is purely conjecture, we note that the same grantors had granted land in prior deeds (the Benedict and St. John properties) which adjoined, but did not include, Union Street. Thus, there is no reason to assume that Union Street would normally be considered part of one of its adjoining lots simply because it had never been accepted as a street.

Second, the trial court's theory, though attenuated, does provide an explanation of why the description in plaintiffs' deed does not close their property. Nevertheless, since the boundary of the "closing" segment of plaintiffs' land is not in dispute, the fact that plaintiffs' deed description does not close is of little consequence. Where there are several manifest errors and the proffered interpretation hinges on nothing more than speculation, that interpretation cannot prevail without first applying the established rules of construction to determine the intent of the parties.

"In construing a deed, we initially look at the instrument itself, which is deemed to declare the understanding and intent of the parties." Thus, it is the intention expressed by the words of the deed, not the unexpressed intention that the parties may have had, which prevails. Generally, a particular description will govern over a general description, but less significant aspects of a description will "[become] the controlling influence in determining the identity of premises where other parts of [the] description are not sufficiently certain," or are nonexistent. For instance, in *Spiller v. Scribner* 36 Vt. 365 (1863), where the deed described land as "being lots No. 22 and 23" and as "our home farm," this Court held that the disputed land, which was inside the home farm but outside lots No. 22 and 23, was not part of the deeded land because "land conveyed . . . by clear and well defined metes and bounds . . . shall prevail . . . over any general words of description that may have been used in the deed." *Id* at 256. The Court pointed out that an additional, more particular description could have overridden the reference to specific lot numbers, but that *the description of a lot by reference to its [number] is a description in its legal effect according to the lines of such lot as surveyed and established in the original division of town, and is just as definite, although not so particular, as it would be if the lines were given, and should receive the same construction and have the same legal effect, in one case as the other, and such description in this case must be the controlling description, and determine the extent of the land conveyed*

In the instant case, the descriptions referring to the land of adjoining property owners are particular descriptions. Further, "[w]here an ambiguity or error exists with regard to the description in a deed, an attached map or survey relating to the ambiguity or error will control."

When there is a conflict between a specific description by metes and bounds and a lot as shown upon a map by which a tract of land is conveyed, the latter provision will control. When a deed the lot intended to be conveyed is properly designated by its number on a recorded plot, but the deed, in attempting to give a more particular description, incorrectly or inaccurately sets forth the dimensions of the same, such designation by lot number will prevail over such other description in the deed.

In the instant case, defendants' deed unambiguously describes their property as "[b]eing Lot 36 as delineated on Hazen's survey and Plan of Lots in the Village of Wilder," and plaintiffs' deed unambiguously describes the disputed property line as continuing "southerly along the westerly boundary of Lot #36." In contrast, the more detailed description of the disputed boundary line in defendants' deed is incorrect and ambiguous. Consequently, the unambiguous description by lot number should prevail over the erroneous reference to an adjoining property owner. The trial court's theory, created in an attempt to reconcile the ambiguities and inaccuracies in the deeds' description, is not supported by any evidence in the record and cannot supplant the plain meaning of the lot descriptions in the deeds.

Reversed and remanded.

Case Questions

1. What deed language created the confusion about ownership?
2. To whom does the trial court award title and why? What does the appellate court do?
3. In reviewing the deeds and the ambiguities, what rules does the appellate court follow?
4. What is the significance of the map?
5. What is the significance of "Haff" vs. "Hoff"?

CAUTIONS AND CONCLUSIONS

In preparing or proofreading a land description, too much caution is never an issue. A sale of land may have been negotiated to the final detail, but if the deed description is inaccurate, litigation, liability, and other difficulties will result. The following questions are suggested for consideration by anyone involved in a land transaction and should help avoid the difficulties of mistakes, inadequacies, or inaccuracies:

1. Is a legal description used? Is there more than a street address or common description?
2. If a metes and bounds description is used, is a better description available? If not, are permanent beginning points used?

What You Should Know About Surveys

A private survey is more than a sketch of the boundaries of a parcel. A survey is apt to contain, in addition to the legal description of a parcel, information on the status of title to the parcel not disclosed by the usual title examination or title commitment and information on the ability to develop the property. A survey may disclose any of the following:

- Acreage content. The acreage content is important not only for purposes of determining the price of the property but is also important regarding information that must be furnished to many governmental agencies in any permitting process.
- Encroachments on the property. An examination may reveal that encroachments have ripened into established claims to a portion of the property or may indicate potential litigation that may delay development.
- Encroachments on adjoining property. An investigation may indicate that these encroachments may be a cause for potential litigation with the adjoining property owner.
- Public and private easements not of record. These easements may represent potential matters for litigation or may interfere with the plan of development.
- Undedicated roads. A claim of access across the client's property may be evidenced by an undedicated road. This claim may represent potential litigation or interference in the plan of development.
- Legal access. The survey may indicate that the property in question does not have legal access. If the survey does not reflect a dedicated road adjoining the property, an examination may determine that the property does not have legal access. Your client may therefore have to sue to obtain legal access.
- Gaps between parcels believed to be contiguous. The gaps may prevent your client from developing the parcels as a single parcel.
- The location of utility easements. These easements may interfere with the plan of development and may require relocation to proceed with development.
- The high water line of any water boundary. The high water line may indicate limits of ownership regardless of the legal description.
- Variations in the legal description of the property. Variations must be reconciled with previously utilized descriptions and may represent potential litigation.
- Fences upon the property. Fences may be evidence of adverse claims or boundary lines by agreement or acquiescence contrary to the title information.
- Agricultural use which may be evidence of possession inconsistent with record ownership.
- Historical or archeological sites which, in some areas, may not be disturbed and therefore will interfere with any plan of development.
- Existence of wetlands that may indicate the property cannot be developed.
- Existence of filled lands which may not physically be able to support the planned improvements. Further, an investigation may indicate that the requisite governmental permits to fill the property were not obtained, representing a potential matter for litigation.

3. If a government survey description is used, are all portions present? Is the prime meridian included?

4. If a plat map is used, is the location of the plat map in the land records accurately identified?

5. If two or more parcels are being conveyed, are they described separately? Are the descriptions distinct and run together?

6. Have two or more persons proofread the description?

The boxed excerpt (opposite) from an article by Lewis Kanner lists the important factors to examine when a survey of property is done.

Key Terms

metes, 108
bounds, 108
metes and bounds description, 108
plat map, 110
United States government survey, 111

prime meridians, 112
principal meridians, 112
baselines, 112
guide meridians, 112
parallels, 112

grid, 112
township, 112
range, 112
section, 113

Chapter Problems

1. Diagram each level of the following descriptions:
   a. SW 1/4 of the SW 1/4 of Section 27, T2N, R3E of the Gila Salt River Meridian.
   b. N 1/2 of the E 1/2 of the E 1/2 of the SW 1/4 of Section 12. How many acres of land does this describe?
   c. NE 1/4 of the NW 1/4 of Section 14, T3N, R4W, Gila Salt River Meridian.

2. Using metes and bounds, describe the property at the junction of Ash and Elm Streets as shown below. What happens if a metes and bounds description is not closed? *Undernehr v. Sandlin*, 827 S.W.2d 164 (Ark. App. 1992)

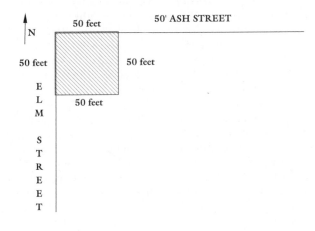

3. The Smiths have just purchased a home, and the description of the residence on the deed is, "Lot 14 of Hohokam Estates II, Book of Maps 31, page 445, Clark County, Nevada, and also known as 2322 Seville Street." Is the description sufficient?

4. Determine and discuss the legal sufficiency of each of the following descriptions. In the applicable instances, determine if there is a patent or a latent ambiguity.
   a. "The real estate owned by the sellers and located in the town of Oak Grove, now known as the 'Dobie Inn,' and used in the business of sellers."
   b. "My house at Little Chicago."
   c. A metes and bounds description beginning with, "to an iron pipe and a line sighted with a gate marker."
   d. "All my property in Monroe County, Indiana." See *Partnership Props. Co. v. Sun Oil Co.*, 552 So.2d 246 (Fla. App. 1989).
   e. "All my real estate wherever situated."
   f. "My farm, Willamena Estates."
   g. "Two acres in SE corner of SE 1/4 of SW 1/4 of Section 12."

5. The San Antonio Independent School District entered into a lease agreement with South Texas Sports, Inc., for the lease of Alamo Stadium and other tracts of land nearby. The validity of the lease was challenged by several homeowners' associations, including River Road. The homeowners were challenging the lease on administrative grounds, potential nuisance effect and the

insufficiency of the lease agreement itself. The description in the lease was as follows:

> that certain tract of land located in Bexar County, Texas, together with all improvements located thereon, such land and improvements being more particularly described and shown on the plot plan attached hereto as Exhibit 'A'.

Exhibit A is a map on which eight tracts of land are marked. Alamo Stadium is not shown as one of the tracts being leased. Is the description along with Exhibit A sufficient for a valid lease? *River Road Association v. South Texas Sports,* 720 S.W.2d 551 (Tex. 1986)

6. Joe Tanner, Commissioner of the Department of Natural Resources, brought suit against employees of the Department of Natural Resources (DNR), who were responsible for the management of Sapelo Island. Tanner brought suit because the employees prevented Tanner and others from landing their planes on two lots on Sapelo Island. The DNR employees claimed the state owned the lots (lot 7 and lot 4) and Tanner's claim to any interest or title in the lots was void. DNR claimed that the description in the deed to Tanner was insufficient to pass title. The legal description of lot 4 in the plaintiffs' deed is as follows:

> All of that certain lot, tract or parcel of land situate, lying and being in the 1312 District, G.M., McIntosh County, Georgia, at Raccoon Bluff on Sapelo Island, containing Twenty-One (21) Acres, more or less and being Lot (4) Four of the Raccoon Bluff Subdivision of William Hillary. Said property being bounded Northerly by Lot 3, Easterly by Blackbeard Island River; Southerly by Lot 5; and Westerly by the out line [*sic*] of Raccoon Bluff Tract. This being that same property conveyed to Ben Brown by deed and plat from William Hillary dated July, 1882 and recorded in Deed Book 'U' at Page 298 and 299, to which said deed and plat reference is hereby made for all intents and purposes.

What type of description is this? Do you think it is sufficient to pass title to the property? *Brasher v. Tanner,* 353 S.E.2d 478 (Ga. 1987)

7. Diagram the following: Commencing at a point on the south side of Hale Street, 200 feet from the intersection of the south side of Hale Street and the east side of Gary Street; from thence south 10 feet parallel to the easterly side of Gary Street; from thence east 5 feet parallel to the southerly side of Hale Street; from thence north 10 feet parallel to the easterly side of Gary Street; from thence 5 feet west on the southerly side of Hale Street to the beginning point.

8. The following description appears in a deed: "Fairbrother farm recorded at West Fairlee Land Records Book 16, page 107." Is the description sufficient?

9. R. L. Shelton, by will probated in 1952, devised all his real estate to his wife for life or during widowhood, with remainder in fee to his 12 children. Included in his estate was a farm located in Pittsylvania County southwest in Gretna. In 1957, Lottie Shelton Amos, one of Shelton's children, and her husband executed a deed conveying their property to B. E. Coffey described as "all of those certain tracts or parcels of land . . . in or near the town of Gretna." Following the metes and bounds description of the parcels in Gretna (the residue of property Mrs. Shelton had acquired from her husband), the deed provided:

> It is the intention of the parties of the first part to convey to the party of the second part all the real estate which they now own in Pittsylvania County, Virginia, including but not restricted to the lands described above.

The interest Shelton's widow held in the farm expired with her death in 1979, and the Shelton children had the farm sold at auction. When Coffey learned about the 1957 deed, he questioned title and refused to close.

Mrs. Amos filed a quiet title action asking the court to construe the 1957 deed as conveying only the real estate located in Gretna and to declare that she is the owner of a one-twelfth interest in the farm.

At trial, it was established that, in 1957, Mr. and Mrs. Amos were in Florida and had trouble managing the Gretna property. Mr. Coffey, who bought the land from Mr. and Mrs. Amos while vacationing in Florida, said, "I've bought something, I don't know what I bought, I don't know where it is, I'll probably never see it, it'll probably never amount to anything." Mr. Coffey also argued about the price but was told by Mr. Amos that the transaction included an interest that Mrs. Amos had inherited from her father.

The trial court ruled that Mrs. Amos had conveyed to Mr. Coffey her one-twelfth interest in her father's farm. Is this correct? *Amos v. Coffey,* 320 S.E.2d 335 (Va. 1984)

10. The Twain Harte Homeowners Association brought suit to quiet title in a recreational easement they alleged they held in the land of Earl Patterson. The easement provides for "recreational use and enjoyment for the benefit of the Twain Harte Tract." Patterson says the description of the dominant estate is inadequate because he remains uncertain as to who actually holds the easement. He maintains the grant of the easement is void because of an invalid description. The Association maintains that the description is sufficient to indicate they as home owners are the owners and beneficiaries. Who is correct? *Twain Harte Homeowners Association v. Patterson,* 239 Cal. Rptr. 316 (1987)

Internet Activities

1. For an overview of land description methods and related sites, go to: **http://www. flatsurv.com/legaldes.htm**.
2. Write a land description of your place of residence employing the three different methods described at **http://www.flatsurv.com/legaldes.htm**.
3. View a plat map at **http://www.buyersresource.com/Bglossary.html** and **http://www. emeraldpt.com/plat.asp**.

KENTUCKY LEGISLATURE

Kentucky Revised Statutes

List by Section

Statutes Last Updated August 30, 2000

Includes Enactments through the 2000 Regular Session
This page was produced on 09/06/2000 at 11:28:31 AM

Terms & Conditions | PDF Viewer

KRS Chapter 132.00

- **.010 Definitions for chapter.**

- **.011 Repealed, 1992.**

- **.012 "Abandoned urban property" defined -- Classification as real property for tax purposes.**

Chapter 7
Land Interests:
Present and Future

Land is, like any other possession, by natural right wholly in the power of its present owner; and may be sold, given or bequeathed, absolutely or conditionally. But natural law would avail little without the protection of the law.

Samuel Johnson

Rents in the upstate New York town of Salamanca were cheap 100 years ago and have barely gone up since. Back in 1892 the Seneca Indians agreed to rent the 1,700 acres of their tribal land, on which most of the hamlet is built, for only $17,000 a year. Now the 99-year lease is about to expire, and the Senecas want a rent increase—to $800,000 annually. Salamanca's 6,600 residents, who own their houses but lease the land, point out that hard times have already wiped out half the town's small businesses. Many residents claim they will leave rather than see typical rents leap from $7/year to $4,700. Says Realtor Shirley Weast: "What they're proposing is an absolute death sentence."

The landlords have taken the reaction with calm and a certain pleasure. Says Seneca Nation President Dennis Lay: "When they negotiated the original leases, they thought we weren't going to be here at the end. I guess we fooled them."

"Revenge of the Senecas," *Time.* © 1990 Time, Inc. Reprinted by permission.

So far, this book has covered what land is. The focus now shifts to how someone "owns" or "possesses" land and all its components (see Chapter 2). Land, unlike other forms of property ownership, has different levels and types of ownership or title. Because of its permanent nature, title to land can exist in the present or in the future. Title to land can also be for a partial interest in that land. Likewise, land possession can be transferred without an accompanying transfer of title. This chapter explains the various types and degrees of interests and title in land.

As both opening quotes for this chapter demonstrate, what interest you actually have in land is extremely important in determining your rights. The major question answered in this chapter is, how can an owner hold title to property? Additional related questions are, how long can an interest be held? and can interests be transferred? The degree and extent of ownership are the focus of this chapter's discussion. Figure 7.1 depicts the full extent and the interrelationships of land interests.

LAND INTERESTS—FREEHOLD ESTATES AND ACCOMPANYING FUTURE INTERESTS

Freehold Estates

The terms **freehold** and **fee,** adopted from English common law, hold significance for understanding the methods of land ownership. Freehold means that an interest in land is uncertain or unlimited in duration. Fee here means that an interest in land is inheritable. Fee freehold estates are both uncertain or unlimited in duration and inheritable by others upon the death of the interest holder.

Fee Simple Absolute Ownership

A **fee simple absolute** estate (a form of freehold estate sometimes referred to as a fee simple) is an interest in land representing the greatest extent of property ownership available. In lay terms, the fee simple absolute estate would be described as absolute ownership. The owners of fee simple absolute estates are free to transfer their interests to others at any time, including upon death.

At common law, a fee simple absolute estate was created when the transfer or grant made by the owner or grantor read: "To A and his heirs," with "and his heirs" used to indicate the inheritability of the interest. However, in three-fourths of the states, the language requirement of "and his heirs" has been eliminated so that a fee simple absolute estate can be created simply by using "To A" language.

Fee Simple Defeasible

A **fee simple defeasible** is an interest in land that is uncertain or unlimited in duration and that has the potential of being terminated. There are two types of fee simple defeasible estates—the fee simple determinable and the fee simple subject to a condition subsequent.

FIGURE 7.1 *Land Interests*

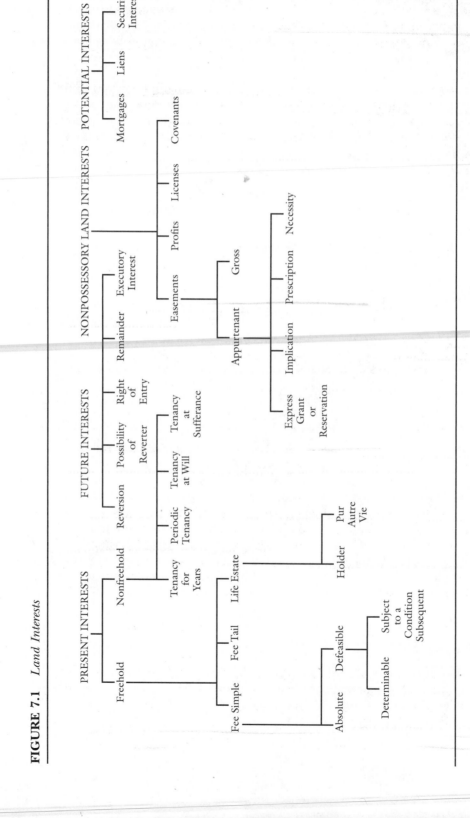

Fee Simple Determinables and Possibility of Reverter

This land interest is uncertain and inheritable. In **fee simple determinable,** the grantor is giving the grantee full title and right to the property so long as the grantee complies with an attached restriction. An example of language creating a fee simple determinable is "To A so long as the premises are used for school purposes." The most important characteristic distinguishing a fee simple determinable from a fee simple absolute is that A's interest will terminate if the property is not used for school purposes. If A does not comply with the restriction, title to the property will revert to the grantor. Upon reversion to the grantor, the grantor's future interest becomes a present interest.

Possibility of Reverter—The Fee Simple Determinable Future Interest

What if, after a fee simple determinable is created, the grantor's expressed desire is violated and the grantee's interest terminated? For example, suppose the grant is made, "To A so long as the property is used for residential purposes." A builds a factory. What happens to the land interest? The rule for fee simple determinable requires that upon A's violation of the restriction, A's interest terminates and title to the property reverts to the grantor. This potential loss of title is a future interest called the **possibility of reverter.**

At common law, grantors are free to transfer their possibilities of reverter any time while alive *(inter vivos),* and their reverters pass upon their death **(testamentary)** to their heirs or devisees. Many states have now passed statutes regulating the possibility of reverter. In some states, this future interest cannot be transferred or inherited. In others, statutes have been enacted that restrict the possibility of reverter by placing a time limit on validity of the interest—in many states the maximum is 40 years. Still other states require the grantor or holder of the interest to periodically rerecord a notice that the interest exists. All of these state-enacted statutes are notice systems, which are tremendous helps in land transactions because the future interests of others can be determined without having to examine the granting language in each deed transferring title to the property. The constitutionality of these statutes has been questioned in some court cases.

Kinney Land and Cattle Company conveyed, by warranty deed, to the state of Kansas 790 acres of land for use as a state park. There was a paragraph in the deed called "Clause of Reversion," which required the state to build and maintain a lake of a minimum of 150 acres. The failure to maintain the lake caused title to "revert to the grantor, successors or assigns." From 1934–1970, the state maintained a lake on the property, but the lake was never 150 acres in size. Shareholders of Kinney Land and Cattle have brought suit to quiet title to them in the 790 acres. Will they be given title? *Kinney v. State of Kansas and Kansas Fish and Game Commission,* 710 P.2d 1290 (Kan. 1985)

Consider 7.1

Fee Simple Subject to a Condition Subsequent

A grantor can accomplish the same purposes as a fee simple determinable grant through the use of a grant of a **fee simple subject to a condition subsequent.** This interest is created with slightly different language such as, "To A on the condition that the land be used for school purposes and if the land is ever not used for school purposes, O (the grantor) may reenter and repossess the land." The fee simple subject to a condition subsequent is similar to a fee simple determinable in that A will lose the interest if there is not compliance with the restriction. The difference between the two is that the violation of a fee simple determinable restriction terminates A's interest immediately, whereas violation of a condition subsequent grant requires some action on the part of the grantor (O) before the interest of A terminates.

Right of Entry/Power of Termination

When the present interest of a fee simple subject to a condition subsequent is created, the grantor is permitted to reenter the property and take possession if the grantee violates the terms of the condition. For example, the following language creates a fee simple subject to a condition subsequent in the grantee but also reserves an interest for the grantor: "To my niece Sally on the condition that liquor never be served on the premises, and should liquor ever be served, I reserve the right to reenter and take possession of and title to the property." Sally holds the present interest of a fee simple subject to a condition subsequent, but the grantor/uncle holds a future interest called a **right of entry** or **power of termination**.

The distinction between right of entry and the possibility of reverter is that right of entry requires some action on the part of the grantor to be effective, whereas the grantor's rights are automatic with a possibility of reverter.

At common law, the right of entry could not be transferred *inter vivos* (while the grantor is alive) but could be transferred at death. Some states have passed statutes that vary these common law rules. However, at common law and in most states, the grantor is permitted to transfer the right of entry to the present interest holder of the fee simple subject to a condition subsequent. If such a transfer is made, the present and future interests merge, and the present holder of the fee simple subject to a condition subsequent will then hold a fee simple absolute interest. In the example, if Sally's uncle conveyed his interest to her, Sally would then have a fee simple absolute. As with the fee simple determinable, many states have passed time limitations and recording requirements for the continuing validity of the future right of entry interest. The restrictions and recording requirements are similar or identical to those described for possibilities of reverter.

It may be difficult to distinguish between the creation of a possibility of reverter and a right of entry. When reentry language is used as part of the grant, the task of determining the type of future interest created is easy. However, in the absence of such language the distinction is a fine one, and several judicial rules for interpretation have developed. First, the courts will examine the entire document to determine the grantor's intent. They will also look for certain phrases and words that are used as keys in determining the type of interest created. For example, language such as "until," "so long as," or "for so long" indicates a possibility of reverter. Language such as "but," "provided that," or "on the condition

Practical Tip

Restrictions on land use are enforceable. If a restriction is to be imposed as part of a transfer, have it drafted carefully to reflect intent and all the constraints. If property is being sold, listed, or purchased, verify the existence of restrictions, compare property use, and clarify ambiguities.

Practical Tip

Verify rights of those who are in possession of property: How long have they been there? What are the terms of their presence? Are they there by lease rights or some other form of grant? What rights do they have for renewal or options?

that" indicates a right of entry. In many states, the issue of which type of interest is created is resolved by a presumption in favor of the right of entry, because this type of future interest requires some action on the part of the parties to affect title to the property and does not have the immediate effect on title that a possibility of reverter would have.

In the following case the court deals with a question about the type of land interest created.

Dennis v. Bird

941 S.W.2d 486 (Ky. 1997)

Facts

In May 1977, Herbert and Maxine Bird purchased a 113-acre farm. They conveyed one acre of the land to Rayford Blackburn and his daughter, Glenda Dennis (Rucks). The deed from the Birds to Blackburn and Dennis contained an option for the Birds to repurchase the property in the event Rayford and Glenda stopped living on the property.

Shortly after the conveyance, Rayford died and Glenda was declared incompetent and unable to live by herself on the property. Herbert Bird tendered a check to Charles Dennis and Jeanna Johnson, the administrators of the estate of Rayford and co-guardians for Glenda (appellants), and requested that title to the one-acre parcel be turned over to him. Dennis and Johnson refused and the Birds filed suit. The trial court granted the Birds summary judgment and Dennis and Johnson appealed.

Judicial Opinion

Schroeder, Judge. The facts of this case present a future interest problem worthy of a law school exam. What interest was conveyed by the original deed? We start with the premise that the grantors (O) owned a fee simple absolute in a freehold estate, a 113-acre farm. By general warranty deed, a conveyance of some interest was made of one acre (blackacre), to Glenda Dennis (A) and Rayford Blackburn (B) as joint tenants with rights of survivorship. The language of the deed says, "[a] fee simple title. . . ." Following the legal description is a reservation of an easement and another reservation or option to repurchase:

> It being hereby mutually covenanted and agreed by and between the parties hereto that in the event the parties of the second part, Rayford Blackburn and Glenda Dennis, cease to live upon the hereinabove described premises or are desirous of selling the same that the party of the first part, Herbert H. Bird, shall be given the first and prior option to purchase the same at the price of Four Hundred Dollars ($400.00).

What estate was being conveyed to A & B—a life estate, a fee simple determinable, or a condition subsequent? Does O have a reversion, a possibility of reverter, or a power of termination/right of re-entry?

We know from *Phelps v. Sledd*, Ky., 479 S.W.2d 894 (1972) that construction of a deed is a matter of law, and that the intentions of the parties are to be gathered from the four corners of the instrument. *Sherman v. Petroleum Exploration,* 280 Ky. 105, 132 S.W.2d 768, 771 (1939) adds: "This entire instrument is to be considered in the light of attendant circumstances . . ." and "[n]o clause or word in a deed was used without meaning or intent." We also know from *Transylvania University v. Rees,* 297 Ky. 246, 179 S.W.2d 890 (1944) that reversions, remainders, and other future interests may be reserved in a deed without the necessity of a grantee signing off. This is not a conveyance back to O, but a conveyance of less than the fee simple absolute by O to A & B. As such, there is no Statute of Frauds (KRS 371.010(6)) problem with the grantees not signing the deed. Acceptance of a deed of less than a fee gives the grantees only that interest conveyed, with a reversion, etc. in O. The Statute of Frauds deals not with reversions but contracts or options *back* to O.

Nor is there a problem with the rule against perpetuities (codified as KRS 381.215) which requires that in order to be valid, an interest in property must necessarily vest in interest within a period measured by 21 years following the termination of lives in being at the time of creation of the interest. A reversion in O, as well as the possibility of reverter, power of termination/right of re-entry are all vested interests (although not vested in possession) at the time of creation. The "rule against perpetuities" and the "doctrine of worthier title" apply to remainders, that is, in cases in which O doesn't convey the entire fee simple absolute but holds back something for a third party, not himself. Even if we were dealing with a remainder, both A and B were lives in being at the time of creation and the "wait and see doctrine" would have no application.

With the foregoing, we look at the four corners of the deed and say that O did not intend to get the property back automatically after the deaths of A and B, so a life estate in A & B with a reversion in O was not intended. That leaves a fee simple of some sort. Would it automatically terminate if A & B moved or wanted to sell (fee simple determinable with a possibility of reverter), or would O have to take affirmative action to enforce his right (fee simple on condition subsequent with a power of termination/right of re-entry)? We believe the requirement that O pay $400.00 manifests an intention to require O to take affirmative action to enforce his interests. Therefore, a fee simple on condition subsequent was intended to be conveyed to A & B with a power of termination/right of re-entry in O.

Since O reserved a right of re-entry, there is no restraint on alienation of property for less than market value as appellants contend. Again, that concept presupposes that a fee simple absolute was conveyed to A & B with a subsequent option back to O. This never happened. O kept his right of re-entry from the very beginning. Appellants are confusing deeds with options to purchase. Whether the rights retained by O discourage A & B from making improvements, etc. is also of no consequence nor inequitable. We have long recognized life estates and their automatic termination without the need to compensate the life tenants, heirs or estate for improvements. Indeed, a whole body of law exists which defines what repairs, improvements, waste, etc. can or even must be done by a life tenant and the rights and remedies of remaindermen. The rights of O as a holder of the right of re-entry are similar.

Therefore, we affirm the judgment.

Case Questions

1. Who conveyed what to whom?

2. Why did the grantor think he was entitled to have the property back?

3. What type of interest does the court determine existed here?

4. After you have read the section on the Rule Against Perpetuities, determine why the court finds it is inapplicable here.

Consider 7.2

In 1949, Log Cabin Association, Inc., conveyed to Jackson County Board of Education a parcel of land using the following language:

> TO HAVE AND TO HOLD the above-released premises, subject to the right of way reserved therein, unto the party of the second part and its successors and assigns to it and their only proper use and behoof forever; so that neither the party of the first part nor any other person in its name and behalf shall or will hereafter claim or demand any right or title to said premises or any part thereof by virtue of any claim or right now existing in the party of the first part shall, by these presents, be excluded and forever barred, upon condition that in the event a new public school building is not erected upon the above described land within a period of two (2) years from the date of this deed or in the event that at any time thereafter the premises hereby dedicated should cease to be used for public school purposes, then and in either of those events, the premises hereby dedicated shall revert to the party of the first part, its successors and assigns.

In 1962, Log Cabin Association conveyed by warranty deed its interest in the school property "subject to the restrictions" noted in the deed to Kelley W. Byars. In 1964, Byars transferred his interest to C. Shelby Dale. Also in 1964, Dale conveyed the interest to Anderson.

In 1963, Log Cabin Association was dissolved, and it provided that all assets be distributed to the Samuel H. Kress Foundation. In 1978, the Kress Foundation executed a deed purporting to give its "contingent reversionary interest" originally held by Log Cabin Association to the Jackson County School Board.

Who owns what? Could the school board now sell a clean title to the property? *Anderson v. Jackson County Board of Education*, 333 S.E.2d 533 (N.C. 1985)

Determine what types of future and present interests are created by the following language:

Consider 7.3

a. "To A so long as the premises are used for church purposes."
b. "To A and his heirs provided that the premises never be used for commercial purposes."
c. "To Cal Trans so long as the land is used for the construction of an off-ramp for access to Harrah's Club Casino."

Fee Tail Ownership

The position of **fee tail** interest in Figure 7.1 establishes it as an uncertain or unlimited estate that is inheritable. However, the distinction between fee simple and fee tail is that fee tail is inheritable only by lineal descendants or direct descendants of the grantee. Lineal descendants are children, grandchildren, great-grandchildren, and so on.

Fee tail interests present substantial problems because of the transfer restrictions and because finding lineal heirs can be cumbersome and confusing. To alleviate the problems of fee tail, many states have passed statutes that convert fee tail grants into fee simple absolutes. Some states retain the fee tail interest (Iowa, South Carolina, and Oregon). Other states permit holders of fee tails to eliminate the fee tail restrictions through a series of transfer transactions. Still other states permit fee tail grantees to hold a life estate and then pass title to the land to their heirs at death. Fee tails created prior to legislative changes are still recognized as valid.

http://

See a state's fee tail statute at: **http://www. azleg.state.az.us/ars/ 33/00201.htm**.

Life Estate Ownership

CREATION

Another type of freehold estate is the **life estate,** which is an interest in land valid only for the life of the holder or for some other measured life. A life estate is uncertain in its duration because termination occurs upon the death of the measuring life. A conventional life estate is created with the language "To A for his life." A's interest will automatically terminate at death. This type of life estate is one measured by the life of the holder of the interest. A second type of life estate, measured by a life other than that of the holder, is created by language such as "To A for the life of B" and is called a **life estate** *pur autre vie.*

http://

Search for more information on life estates and other land interest issues at: **http:// www.lrc.state.ky.us/ search.htm**.

The life estate appears to be an odd method of land ownership, but it is used effectively as an estate planning tool so that estate taxes may be postponed or reduced. For example, a wife who predeceases her husband might have a will granting her husband a life estate in some property with the provision that the property be given to the children at the termination of the husband's life interest. The husband holds a lesser interest only for life, and the distribution will be taxed at the time of the children's receipt of the property held by the husband as a life estate.

Also, some states provide for the automatic creation of legal life estates in certain instances. Marital rights such as dower and curtesy are rights afforded surviving spouses to entitle them to some portion of their deceased spouse's property. In some states, these marital rights are given to the surviving spouse in the form of a life estate imposed by statute. (A complete discussion of dower and curtesy rights appears in Chapter 10.)

Viva Parker Lilliston died in 1969 and in her will provided as follows:

> *Item Twelve: I give and devise my farm situated on the Seaside from Locustville,*
> *in the county of Accomack, State of Virginia . . . to my daughter, Margaret Lillis-*
> *ton Edwards, upon the conditions, set out in Item Fourteen. . . . Item Fourteen: all*
> *gifts made to my daughter, Margaret L. Edwards, individually and personally,*
> *under Items Eleven and Twelve of the Will, whether personal estate or real estate,*
> *are conditioned upon the said Margaret L. Edwards keeping the gift or devise here-*
> *in free from encumbrances of every description, and in the event the said Margaret*
> *L. Edwards shall attempt to encumber some or sell her interest, or in the event any*
> *creditor or creditors of Margaret L. Edwards shall attempt to subject her interest in*
> *the gift or devise herein made to the payment of the debts of the said Margaret L.*
> *Edwards, then and in that event the interest of said Margaret L. Edwards therein*
> *shall immediately cease and determine, and the gift or devise shall at once become*
> *vested in her children, viz: Betty Bell Branch, Beverly Bradley, John R. Edwards,*
> *Bruce C. Edwards, Jill A. Edwards, and Jackie L. Edwards, in equal shares in fee*
> *simple . . .*

In 1979, Margaret tried to obtain the consent of her children to sell the farm. Beverly Bradley, one of the listed children of Margaret, refused to give such consent. Margaret died in 1980 and left $1.00 to Beverly and directed that the farm be sold and the proceeds distributed among her other children. Beverly challenged the will, claiming that her interest had vested and could not be taken away. She claims that Margaret had a life estate and she and the other children had a remainder. Margaret's lawyer claims that Margaret held a fee simple subject to a condition subsequent that she could convey at her death in the manner that she did.

What types of interests did Margaret and her children hold? *Edwards v. Bradley,* 315 S.E.2d 196 (Va. 1984)

RIGHTS OF LIFE TENANTS

The holders of life estates, referred to as **life tenants,** have certain rights in the use and possession of their property. Holders of life estates have the right of undisturbed possession during the time of their estate. However, life tenants do have the obligation not to waste or destroy the property interest because of the rights of accompanying future interest holders (noted below). For example, cutting timber on the life estate property for the purpose of building fences or for fuel is appropriate conduct for a life tenant; however, cutting timber for commercial sale would be inappropriate because there is a dissipation of the value of the property and the interests of the future holders of title.

While alive, life tenants can transfer their interests, but buyers of such interests should be aware of the restricted time of the life estate: a transferee's interest lasts only as long as the tenant/transferor is alive. Any attempt by a life tenant to convey an interest at death is invalid. Similarly, creditors of the life tenant can have security in the property only until the life tenant's death. Issues of the responsibility of payment for taxes between life tenants and reversioners are treated differently among the states.

Reversions

A **reversion** is a future interest in the grantor arising when the grantor has given someone else a lesser estate, that is, something less than a fee simple absolute. For example, when the grantor makes the grant "To A for life," the present life estate of A will terminate upon A's death. At that point, the land must be transferred to someone, and in this case it will transfer or revert to the grantor. Thus, all during A's life estate, the grantor has a future interest called a reversion. Other types of conveyances that would give the grantor a reversion include fee tails and the nonfreehold estates. For example, at the termination of any type of tenancy, the land reverts to the grantor.

Remainders

A **remainder** is a future interest created in one other than the grantor. It is also a future interest that must follow a life estate or a fee tail. An example of language creating a remainder would be "To A for life, then to B." B holds the remainder interest, which is a future interest, because the interest becomes possessory only upon the death of A. In this example, the grantor has given what would have been a reversion to another, thereby creating a remainder. Two types of remainders may be created: vested and contingent.

VESTED REMAINDERS

A **vested remainder** is one given to persons ascertained and in existence who have the immediate right to the land interest upon termination of the prior freehold estate. In the example "To A for life, then to B," B holds a vested remainder because (1) B is ascertained and in existence at the time of the grant, and (2) B will have the immediate right to the estate upon A's death. B's remainder is an example of one that is absolutely vested. Two other types of vested remainders that may be created are **vested remainder subject to partial divestment** and **vested remainder subject to complete divestment.**

To illustrate vested subject to partial divestment, the following grant can be used: "To A for life, then to the children of B." A vested remainder exists if B is dead and has one child. However, if B is alive, the possibility exists that B will have additional children during A's life estate. B's child holds a vested interest but could be divested of one-half or two-thirds of the interest should B have one or two more children before A's death. If A dies when B has three children, each child would receive a one-third interest. If A dies when B has one child, that child would receive the full interest. The potential for loss of part of the interest is referred to as divestment. Since the child of B who is alive at the time of the grant will never lose the full interest, the divestment can be only partial. The vested remainder created in the example when B is still alive is a vested remainder subject to partial divestment.

Vested remainder subject to complete divestment is illustrated by the language "To A for life, then to B, but if B is not married, then to C." At the termination of A's life interest, B, ascertained and in existence at the time of the grant, will have a possessory interest. However, B could lose the interest by not marrying prior to A's death. In this instance, B not only is divested of a portion of the interest, but also loses the entire interest if the marriage requirement is not fulfilled at the time of A's death. This type of remainder in B is a vested remainder subject to complete divestment.

CONTINGENT REMAINDERS

A **contingent remainder** is the opposite of a vested remainder. That is, a contingent remainder is one in which the taker of the interest is unascertained or the interest has a condition precedent to its existence and will not pass automatically upon the termination of the prior estate. An example of a contingent remainder that is classified as such because its takers are unascertained would be "To A for life, remainder to the children of B [a bachelor with no children]." It is possible that B may have children at the time of A's death and the children would be entitled to their interest, but at the time of the grant the takers (nonexistent children) are unascertained.

An example of a contingent remainder that is classified as such because of a condition precedent would be "To A for life, then if B is married, to B." In this example, B's interest does not automatically follow A's death, for B must comply with the condition precedent of marriage to obtain the interest. There is a fine distinction between a condition precedent contingent remainder and vested remainder subject to a complete divestment. That distinction is that a condition preceding the remainder makes the remainder contingent, whereas a condition following the remainder makes the remainder subject to complete divestment.

If a contingent remainder fails (B is not married or has no children), the interest would revert to the grantor. When a contingent remainder future interest is created, a reversion or interest in the grantor is also created.

All types of remainders are transferable both *inter vivos* and at death. Obviously, a conveyance at death would be invalid if a condition of survival were attached to the remainder.

Consider 7.5

Determine what types of present and future interests are involved in the following grants. Be sure to classify remainders according to their type, vested (partial or complete divestment) or contingent:

a. "To A for life, then to B" — *Remainder*
b. "To A for life, then to B and her heirs" *Fee simple Absolute*
c. "To B for life, then if A is married, to A" — *Contingent remainder*
d. "To A for life, then to B's heirs" (B is alive.) *Partial Divestment*
e. "To A for life, then to B, but if B does not survive A, to C"
    Subject to Complete divestment

Executory Interests

In the preceding example e, a third party, C, has an interest that cannot be identified from the prior discussions of future interests. In this example, C holds an executory interest. An **executory interest** is a future interest created in one other than the grantor that is not a remainder. An executory interest is not vested at the time the grantor makes the grant and is considered to be vested only when it becomes possessory. An executory interest usually arises in one of three circumstances. The first circumstance is when a fee simple determinable or a fee simple subject to a condition subsequent is given to two parties at the same time. For example, a grant "To A, so long as the premises are never used for commercial purposes and if they are so used, then to B" creates a fee simple defeasible interest in A and an executory interest in B. B's interest does not follow a life estate and is not a remainder. Further, B's interest is similar to a right of reversion or right of entry, but B is not a grantor; hence, B's interest must be an executory interest.

The second circumstance that causes an executory interest occurs when the grantor creates a gap between present and future interests. An example would be "To A for life, then one year after A's death, to B." B does not have a remainder because there is no immediate vesting of B's interest. The gap of one year causes B to hold an executory interest.

FIGURE 7.2   *Interrelationship of Present and Future Interests*

Present Interests	Creation Language of Future Interests	Future Interests Created in Grantor	Others' Future Interests
Fee simple absolute	"To A" "To A and his heirs"	None	None
Fee tail	"To A and the heirs of his body" "To A and the female heirs of her body" "To A and the heirs of his body and his wife J"	Reversion if no heirs	None
Fee simple determinable	"To A so long as the property is used for church purposes"	Possibility of reverter	Executory interest
Fee simple subject to a condition subsequent	"To A on the condition that the property is used for church purposes"	Right of entry/ Power of termination	Executory interest
Life estate/holder	"To A for life"	Reversion	Executory interest Remainder

The third circumstance occurs when the grantor creates some future freehold estate, for example, "To A in 10 years." No present interest is created, and the 10-year interest cannot be classified as a grantor's interest because A is not the grantor. The interest is not a remainder because it does not follow another estate. A holds an executory interest. Figure 7.2 summarizes the future interests and their interrelationships with the present interests.

SPECIAL RULES GOVERNING INTERESTS IN LAND

Three rules or doctrines relating to land interests developed as common law in England and still apply to the construction and use of future interests: the Rule in Shelley's Case, the Doctrine of Worthier Title, and the Rule Against Perpetuities.

Rule in Shelley's Case

The **Rule in Shelley's Case** applies to grants made with the language "To A for life, remainder to the heirs of A." If the rules set forth in the preceding discussion were followed, A would have a life estate and the heirs would have a contingent remainder since heirs are unascertainable until the death of A. The Rule in Shelley's Case requires the merger of the present and future interests, with the result that A will have a fee simple absolute. Some states have passed legislation eliminating the effect of the Rule in Shelley's Case so that the present and future interests are not merged. The following case illustrates how the Rule in Shelley's Case and the state statutes abolishing it work.

Lusk v. Broyles

694 So.2d 4 (Ala. Civ. App. 1997)

Facts

In 1949, Andy Lusk and Mary Eliza Lusk executed a deed conveying certain rights in 130 acres (Parcel One) to Howard Lusk, who was the direct lineal ancestor of Elizabeth Broyles, Charles Lusk, and Homer Lusk (plaintiffs). The deed from Andy and Mary contained the following language:

> KNOW ALL MEN BY THESE PRESENTS: That we Andy Lusk and his wife Mary Eliza Lusk . . . have this day . . . given, and granted, and by this instrument do give, grant and convey to . . . Howard Lusk for and during his natural life and at his death to the heirs of his body per stirpes

[Parcel One] . . .

> To have and to hold the foregoing described lands unto the said Howard Lusk for and during his natural life, and at his death, the right and title to said lands to vest in the heirs at law of said Howard Lusk. . . .

In 1952, Andy and Eliza Lusk executed a deed conveying to Howard an interest in an additional 40 acres of land (Parcel Two). This instrument is a printed form with typewritten additions to render it complete, and reads as follows:

> KNOW ALL MEN BY THESE PRESENTS, that we, Andy Lusk and his wife, Eliza Lusk, parties of the first part, in consideration of the sum of One Hundred Dollars and other valuable consideration to us in hand paid by R.H. Lusk during his natural life and then to his bodily heirs, party of the second part, the receipt of which is hereby acknowledged, do hereby grant, bargain, sell and convey unto the said party of the second part, the following described property—to-wit:

[Parcel Two]

> It is the intention of the grantors to convey to said R.H. Lusk only a life estate in and to said lands herein described, with the remainder to his bodily heirs.

> Together with all and singular tenements, hereditaments, rights, members, privileges, and appurtenances thereunto belonging, or in any way appertaining, to have and to hold the same unto the said party of the second part, and to his heirs and assigns, forever; and we hereby warrant the title to the same against all claims whatever.

In 1994, one year before his death, Howard executed a deed conveying a fee simple interest in Parcels One and Two to himself and Ruth Lusk, his wife (grantee), as joint tenants with right of survivorship.

Upon his death, the plaintiffs filed suit for title to the property. The court found for the descendant plaintiffs, and Ruth Lusk appealed.

Judicial Opinion

Robertson, Presiding Judge. In light of these facts, we must consider whether Howard, at the time he executed the 1994 deed to the grantee, possessed a fee simple title to Parcels One and Two or only a life estate, with remainders vested in his bodily descendants (which include the plaintiffs). The grantee contends that the 1949 and 1952 deeds from Andy and Eliza to Howard conveyed common law estates in fee tail, which by operation of statute are converted to estates in fee simple absolute. The plaintiff heirs argue that the deeds instead conveyed life estates to Howard and remainders in fee simple to the heirs of his body, and that Howard therefore could not have conveyed to the grantee anything more than his own life estates (which necessarily terminate upon his death).

At common law, when an ancestor by any gift or conveyance took an estate of freehold, and in the same gift or conveyance the estate was limited to his or her heirs in fee or in tail, the words "the heirs" were deemed as a matter of substantive law to be words of limitation and not of purchase. See *Wolfe v. Shelley*, 72 Eng. Rep. 490 (1581). This is the famous, or infamous, principle of property law known as the "Rule in Shelley's Case." However, this rule of the common law is not followed in Alabama because it has been superseded by statute. Section 35-4-230, Ala. Code 1975, provides as follows:

> Where a remainder created by deed or will is limited to the heirs, issue or heirs of the body of a

person to whom a life estate in the same property is given, the persons who, on termination of the life estate, are the heirs, issue or heirs of the body of such tenant for life are entitled to take as purchasers by virtue of the remainder so limited by them.

Thus, the Rule in Shelley's Case would have operated to convert automatically a conveyance of a life estate to a grantee with remainder in fee to the grantee's heirs into a conveyance of a fee in the grantee. However, 35-4-230 alters this arbitrary rule, requiring that a grantor's intent to sever a grantee's life estate interest from the grantee's heirs' remainder interest be honored according to the express terms of the conveyance.

We now turn to the precise language of the 1949 and 1952 deeds themselves to determine whether they may be classified as expressly giving Howard a life estate and his bodily heirs a remainder. The granting clause of the 1949 deed to Parcel One conveys Parcel One to Howard Lusk *for and during his natural life*. Moreover, the same clause specifically grants Parcel One "to the heirs of his body per stirpes" at Howard's death. This language expressly conveys both a life estate to Howard and a remainder interest in his bodily heirs. Similarly, the granting clause of the 1952 Parcel Two deed, while less artfully drafted, conveys Parcel Two to Howard *during his natural life,* and conveys a remainder interest to his *bodily heirs.* Indeed, the grantors' intent to do this is evidenced by their statement in the deed that it was their intention "to convey to said R. H. Lusk *only a life estate* in and to [Parcel Two], with remainder to his bodily heirs." Thus, as a matter of law, Howard, in 1994 could have conveyed only his life estates in Parcels One and Two to the grantee, which life estates necessarily terminated upon his subsequent death.

The trial court correctly concluded that the grantee held no interest in Parcels One and Two after Howard's death.

Affirmed.

Case Questions

1. What type of interest was granted to Howard Lusk?
2. How does Ruth Lusk claim an interest?
3. What does the Rule in Shelley's Case do to a grant such as the one to Howard?
4. What does the Alabama statute do to the grant to Howard Lusk despite the Rule in Shelley's Case?

Doctrine of Worthier Title

The **Doctrine of Worthier Title** applies to grants with the language "To A for life, remainder to the heirs of the grantor." Following the future interest rules, A would have a life estate and the heirs would have either a vested remainder or contingent remainder (depending on whether the grant was *inter vivos* or testamentary). However, under the Doctrine of Worthier Title, A has a life estate, the heirs have no interest, and the grantor holds a reversion. Legislation in some states has eliminated this doctrine or has permitted courts to determine the grantor's true intent in making the grant.

Practical Tip

The complexities of real estate law and real estate ownership can be confusing, and mistakes about notions of title and interest can be costly. Be certain sellers, buyers, brokers, and lenders understand the implications of various interests in real estate. Legal advice is often necessary to create, clarify, and interpret form of ownership.

Rule Against Perpetuities

The basic idea of the **Rule Against Perpetuities (RAP)** is to limit the length of time during which grantors may control the transfer, conveyance, and vesting of land interests. The purpose is to ensure that property is not tied to the grave and its transferability and flexibility in use restricted. However, the rule is arbitrary in application, applying only to contingent remainders and executory interests.

Generally stated, the rule provides that an interest is good only if it vests no later than 21 years after the death of the last individual who is part of the group of measuring lives for the grant. A measuring life is defined as the lifetime of individuals named in the grant. Vesting is defined as the absolute right to receive property, not actual possession. If the 21-year vesting rule is violated by a grant, the grant is lost and title reverts to the grantor or the grantor's estate to be distributed according to the grantor's desires or according to state law if no will exists.

To understand the application of the rule, it is best to explain each portion of it in the context of an example. Here we will use the grant, made in a will, "To my children for life, remainder to any and all of my grandchildren who reach age 21" as the example for working through the rule's application:

Step One—Determine the type of interest involved. The children have a life estate. The grandchildren are unascertained (more could be born during the children's life estate) and therefore hold a contingent remainder. Furthermore, because there is a potential gap between the life estate of the children and the grandchildren (who must be 21), the grandchildren's interest could be classified as an executory interest.

Step Two—Determine whether the Rule Against Perpetuities is applicable. Because the Rule Against Perpetuities applies to both contingent remainders and executory interests, the rule is applicable to the grandchildren's interests.

Step Three—Determine when the interest would vest. The interest would vest when the last grandchild reached age 21.

Step Four—Determine the measuring lives in being. At the time of the will's grant, the children are alive and thus would be the measuring lives for purposes of the 21-year rule for vesting.

Step Five—Determine whether all interests will vest within 21 years after the death of the last measuring life. Consider all possibilities of birth and survival. Upon the death of the last child, there can be no more grandchildren. Thus, the longest it can take for a grandchild's interest to vest is 21 years after the death of the last child. (Gestation periods are not included in the 21 years.)

Step Six—Determine if the Rule Against Perpetuities is violated. Because all grandchildren will have the interest vested within 21 years after the lives in being of the children, the Rule Against Perpetuities is not violated and the grant is valid.

Consider 7.6 | Determine whether the Rule Against Perpetuities is violated by the following grant made while the grantor is alive: "To my children for life, remainder to any and all of my grandchildren who reach age 21." Be sure to use the six steps in your analysis.

Because this complex rule could present difficulties in wills and other transfers, some states have passed statutes eliminating the rule or restricting its harsh effects. Even in states without such legislation, the effect of the Rule Against Perpetuities can be avoided simply by placing a **saving clause** in the will or grant of property. A saving clause either provides an alternative for distribution should the grant violate the rule or provides that the grant is to be interpreted so as to avoid violation of the rule. To make confusion about the rule less embarrassing, consider that violation of the Rule Against Perpetuities in drafting wills and trusts is the largest area of malpractice litigation for estate-planning attorneys.

A Uniform Statutory Rule Against Perpetuities has been adopted in 24 states and this uniform rule reduces some of the more complicated provisions in the rule such as its application to nonvested interests.

Figure 7.3 summarizes the future interests, their related present interests, their language of creation, and the rules that govern them.

FIGURE 7.3   *Summary of the Creation and Rules of Future Interests*

Future Interest	Related Present Interest	Sample Language of Creation	Applicability of Rules
Possibility of reverter	Fee simple determinable	"To A so long as the property is used for church purposes"	Some state limitation and filing requirements
Right of entry/ power of termination	Fee simple subject to condition subsequent	"To A on the condition that the property is used for church purposes"	Some state limitation and filing requirements
Revision	Life estate/fee tail	"To A for life" "To A for the life of B"	Doctrine of Worthier Title
Vested remainder	Life estate	"To A for life, then to B"	Rule in Shelley's Case; Doctrine of Worthier Title
Vested subject to partial divestment	Life estate	"To A for life, then to B's children" (B is alive with two children)	Rule in Shelley's Case; Doctrine of Worthier Title
Vested subject to complete divestment	Life estate	"To A for life, then to B, but if B is not married, to C"	
Contingent remainder	Life estate	"To A for life, then to B's children" (B is a bachelor) "To A for life, then if B is married, to B"	Rule Against Perpetuities
Executory interest	Life estate Fee simple defeasible Fee tail	"To A for life, then in 10 years to B" "To B in 10 years"	Rule Against Perpetuities

The Rule Against Perpetuities causes a great deal of confusion whenever long-term property interests arise. In the following case the court clarified the issue of lease options and the Rule Against Perpetuities.

Texaco Refining and Marketing, Inc. v. Samowitz

570 A.2d 170 (Conn. 1990)

Facts

Sam Samowitz (plaintiff) leased property from Texaco Refining and Marketing (defendants) in 1964. The lease term was 15 years with three options to renew for periods of five years each. The lease gave Samowitz "the exclusive right, at lessee's option, to purchase the demised premises . . . at any time during the term of this lease or an extension or renewal thereof, from and after the 14th year of the initial term for the sum of $125,000."

On August 14, 1987, Samowitz gave notice, via certified mail, to Texaco that he desired to exercise his right to purchase the property. Texaco refused to convey the property on the grounds that the RAP was violated, and Samowitz brought suit. The trial court found for Samowitz and Texaco appealed.

Judicial Opinion

Peters, Chief Justice. The defendants rely on the common law rule against perpetuities as their second argument for the unenforceability of the plaintiff's option to purchase their property. The rule against perpetuities states that "[n]o interest is good unless it must vest, if at all, not later than twenty-one years after some life in being at the creation of the interest." J. Gray, The Rule Against Perpetuities (4th Ed. 1942) p. 191; *Connecticut Bank & Trust Co. v. Brody*, 174 Conn. 616, 623, 392 A.2d 445 (1978). The defendants maintain that the option in this case did not vest within the time span mandated by the rule. We disagree.

The trial court determined that the option in the lease agreement did not violate the rule against perpetuities by construing the lease agreement as a series of discrete undertakings, first for an initial fourteen year term, and thereafter for each renewal term. Because the option could be exercised only within one of these discrete terms, none of which exceeded twenty-one years in length, the court held that the interest in the option would necessarily vest within the time period specified by the Rule Against Perpetuities.

Whatever might be the merits of the trial court's construction of the lease agreement, we prefer to consider a more basic question: do options in long-term leases fall within the jurisdiction of the Rule Against Perpetuities? Our precedents indicate that the rule applies to an unrestricted option to purchase real property; *Neustadt v. Pearce*, 145 Conn. 403, 405, 143 A.2d 437 (1958); *H.J. Lewis Oyster Co. v. West*, 93 Conn. 518, 530, 107 A. 138 (1919); but not to an option to renew the term of a real property lease. *Lonergan v. Connecticut Food Store, Inc.*, 168 Conn. 122, 124, 357 A.2d 910 (1975). We have not, however, previously considered the relationship between the rule against perpetuities and an option to purchase contained in a long-term commercial lease of real property.

The defendants have offered no reason of policy why we should extend the ambit of the rule against perpetuities to cover an option to purchase contained in a commercial lease. "The underlying and fundamental purpose of the rule is founded on the public policy in favor of free alienability of property and against restricting its marketability over long periods of time by restraints on its alienation." *Connecticut Bank & Trust Co. v. Brody, supra*, 174 Conn. at 624, 392 A.2d 445; 4 Restatement, Property (1944) pp. 2129–33. An option coupled with a long-term commercial lease is consistent with these policy objectives because it stimulates improvement of the property and thus renders it more rather than less marketable. 3 L. Simes & A. Smith, *The Law of Future Interests* (2d Ed. 1956) p. 162. Any extension of the rule against perpetuities would, furthermore, be inconsistent with the legislative adoption of the "second look" doctrine, pursuant to which an interest subject to the rule may be validated, contrary to the common law, by the occurrence of events subsequent to the creation of the interest. See General Statutes § 45–95; *Connecticut Bank & Trust Co. v. Brody, supra*, at 627–28, 392 A.2d 445.

We therefore conclude that an option to purchase contained in a commercial lease, at least if the option must be exercised within the leasehold term, is valid without regard to the rule against perpetuities. This position is consistent with the weight of authority in the United States.

The plaintiff's option in this case was, therefore, enforceable.

There is no error.

Case Questions

1. What land interest did Samowitz have?

2. What was the maximum length of the Samowitz/Texaco lease?

3. Does the lease violate the Rule Against Perpetuities? Explain.

4. Does the option to purchase violate the Rule Against Perpetuities?

5. Who ends up with title and possession in the case?

Consider 7.7 | Would a 97-year lease violate the Rule Against Perpetuities? *Matter of Ferguson*, 751 P.2d 1008 (Colo. 1987)

Consider 7.8 | Would a tenant's right of first refusal on property in the event the owner ever decided to sell the property and that runs in perpetuity violate the Rule Against Perpetuities? *Hornsby v. Holt*, 359 S.E.2d 647 (Ga. 1987); *Fallschase Development Corp. v. Blakey*, 696 So.2d 833 (Fla. App. 1997)

LAND INTERESTS—NONFREEHOLD ESTATES

The nonfreehold estate is one limited in duration and noninheritable. Four types of nonfreehold estates are examined in Chapters 8 and 9 in more detail. In lay terms, nonfreehold estate refers to the landlord-tenant relationship.

Determine what types of estates are created by the following language and examples:

Consider 7.9

a. "To A for life"   *Fee simple absolute*
b. "To A and his heirs"
c. "To A"
d. "To A and B"
e. "To A and his female bodily heirs"   *Contingent*
f. "To A provided the premises are never used for the sale of liquor"   *Reverter*   *Fe Reverte simple Determinable*
g. "To A on the condition that the premises are never used for a dance hall"   *Reverter*
h. "To A so long as the premises are used for church purposes"   *Simple D*
i. "To my husband, Ralph, for life"   *Life estate*
j. "To the trustee for First County Church so long as the premises are never used for the playing of bingo"   *S*
k. "To my granddaughter, Alfreda, and all of Alfreda's female issue"   *Contingent & Life   Fee tail*
l. "To my daughter, Sara, for the life of my brother, Sam"
m. "To my granddaughter so long as the premises are used for a library for Whitman College"
n. "To my son, John, and his bodily heirs"
o. "To Jess S. Long, and the children of his body begotten, and their heirs and assigns forever"
p. "To A for the period the land is used for a golf course"

ECONOMICS OF LAND INTERESTS

To this point, the discussion of land interests has focused on the legal rights and responsibilities provided for each type of interest. These legal protections are a central concept in the law of real property. However, the basis for these protections can be traced to economic factors. The boxed excerpt "An Economic Theory of Property Rights" by Richard Posner (see page 142) explains the economic rationale for real property rights and protections.

CAUTIONS AND CONCLUSIONS

Knowledge of this chapter will be most useful in situations where land titles are being transferred. In the case of a transfer, all parties (buyers, sellers, brokers, agents, and financiers) need to analyze the transfer by checking the following issues:

1. What type of interest does the seller hold?
2. What restrictions are on the transfer? Could the land title be lost?
3. Does the seller have the right and ability to transfer the property? Can the seller transfer full title or simply a lesser interest, such as a life estate?
4. What type of language is being used in the conveyance? Is the buyer getting a fee simple absolute or a life estate? Are restrictions being imposed upon the buyer?

An Economic Theory of Property Rights

Imagine a society in which all property rights have been abolished. A farmer plants corn, fertilizes it, and erects scarecrows, but when the corn is ripe his neighbor reaps it and sells it. The farmer has no legal remedy against his neighbor's conduct since he owns neither the land that he sowed nor the crop. After a few such incidents the cultivation of land will be abandoned and the society will shift to methods of subsistence (such as hunting) that involve less preparatory investment.

This example suggests that the legal protection of property rights has an important economic function: to create incentives to use resources efficiently. Although the value of the crop in our example, as measured by consumer willingness to pay, may have greatly exceeded the cost in labor, materials, and foregone alternative uses of the land, without property rights there is no incentive to incur these costs because there is no reasonable assured reward for incurring them. The proper incentives are created by the parceling out among the members of society of mutually exclusive rights to the use of particular resources. If every piece of land is owned by someone in the sense that there is always an individual who can exclude all others from access to any given area, then individuals will endeavor by cultivation or other improvements to maximize the value of the land.

The creation of exclusive rights is a necessary rather than sufficient condition for the efficient use of resources. The rights must be transferable. Suppose the farmer in our example owns the land that he sows but is a bad farmer; his land would be more productive in someone else's hands. The maximization of value requires a mechanism by which the farmer can be induced to transfer rights in the property to someone who can work it more productively. A transferable right is such a mechanism.

An example will illustrate. Farmer A owns a piece of land that he anticipates will yield him $100 a year, in excess of labor and other costs, indefinitely. The value of the right to a stream of future earnings can be expressed as a present sum. Just as the price of a share of common stock expresses the present value of the anticipated earnings to which the shareholder will be entitled, so the present value of a parcel of land that yields an annual net income of $100 can be calculated and is the minimum price that A will accept in exchange for his property right. Farmer B thinks he could net more than $100 a year from working A's land. The present value of B's higher expected earnings stream will, of course, exceed the present value calculated by

A. Assume the present value calculated by A is $1000 and by B $1500.

Then the sale of the property by A to B will yield benefits to both parties if the price is anywhere between $1000 and $1500. At a price of $1250, for example, A receives $250 more than the land is worth to him and B pays $250 less than the land is worth to him. Thus, there are strong incentives for the parties voluntarily to exchange A's land for B's money, and if B is as he believes a better farmer than A, the transfer will result in an increase in the productivity of the land. Through a succession of such transfers, resources are shifted to their highest valued, most productive uses and efficiency in the use of economic resources is maximized.

The foregoing discussion suggests three criteria of an efficient system of property rights. The first is universality. Ideally, all resources should be owned, or ownable, by someone, except resources so plentiful that everybody can consume as much of them as he wants without reducing consumption by anyone else (sunlight is a good, but not perfect example—why?). No issue of efficient use arises in such a case.

The second criterion . . . is exclusivity. We have assumed so far that either the farmer can exclude no one or he can exclude everyone, but of course there are intermediate stages: the farmer may be entitled to exclude private individuals from reaping his crop, but not the government in time of war. It might appear that the more exclusive the property right, the greater the incentive to invest the right amount of resources in the development of the property.

The third criterion of an efficient system of property rights is transferability. If a property right cannot be transferred, there is no way of shifting a resource from a less productive to a more productive use through voluntary exchange. The costs of transfer may be high to begin with; a legal prohibition against transferring may, depending on the penalties for violation, make the costs utterly prohibitive.

Discussion Questions

1. How do property rights serve to protect and "incent" landowners?

2. Why is it sometimes more economically efficient for a property owner to transfer property?

3. What are the three criteria for an efficient system of property rights?

Note: For the answer to the question on the exclusivity of sunlight, see Chapter 3.

An examination of the land records (discussed in Chapter 13) should provide the parties with answers to most of the above questions. The important point is that the answers be found before the transaction is completed.

Key Terms

freehold, 125
fee, 125
fee simple absolute, 125
fee simple defeasible, 125
fee simple determinable, 127
possibility of reverter, 127
inter vivos, 127
testamentary, 127
fee simple subject to a condition
    subsequent, 127
right of entry, 128

power of termination, 128
fee tail, 131
life estate, 131
life estate *pur autre vie,* 131
life tenants, 132
reversion, 132
remainder, 133
vested remainder, 133
vested remainder subject to partial
    divestment, 133

vested remainder subject to
    complete divestment, 133
contingent remainder, 133
executory interest, 134
Rule in Shelley's Case, 135
Doctrine of Worthier Title, 137
Rule Against Perpetuities (RAP), 137
saving clause, 138

Chapter Problems

1. Tom and Doyle Proctor were deeded 20 lots of land in a Florida subdivision with the understanding that they would construct an incinerator on the property. The deed contained no specifics on the incinerator or the Proctors' responsibilities. The developer claims a right of reentry. The Proctors claim the land is theirs as a fee simple estate. Who is correct? *Proctor v. Inland Shores, Inc.,* 373 S.E.2d 268 (Ga. 1988)

2. What type of interest is created by the following language?

> IN CONSIDERATION of Ten Dollars . . . Grantor hereby grants . . . to Grantee, its successors and assigns, the entire interests in the Property . . . reserving and excepting unto Grantor the Production Royalty and Ten Cent Wheelage Royalty, both described below; subject only to the production royalty reserved in the Delcarbon Deed, to Grantor's right of re-entry for condition broken, as described below . . .
>
>   If Grantee defaults in the payment of annual fees . . . then Grantor shall be entitled to a reconveyance of the Property and delivery of exclusive possession thereto. *Jelen and Son v. Kaiser Steel, Inc.,* 807 P.2d 1241 (Colo. 1991)

3. Refer to the chapter opening quote on the Senecas' 99-year lease. What type of land interest was created by the Senecas? Was it a fee interest? a freehold interest?

4. In each of the following, determine what type of present and future interests are created, and also the applicability of any of the three rules: the Rule in Shelley's Case, the Doctrine of Worthier Title, and the Rule Against Perpetuities.

(G = grantor; L/E = life estate; rem = remainder)

   a.   G ──→L/E ──→   A
                   ──→ L/E ──→ A's widow
                                 Rem to A's children at the
                                 death of the widow

   b.   G ──→L/E──→   A

   c.   G ──→A and her heirs on the condition that
             liquor never be sold on the premises

   d.   G ──→L/E ──→   A──→Rem to B and his
                               heirs if B shall survive A
     Suppose A (during her lifetime) gave D the right to use the land for 10 years. What type of estate would be created?

   e.   G ─────────→   A so long as liquor is not
                               sold on the premises
     Suppose G later left all his interest to A. What type of estate would be created?

   f.   G ─────────→   A when A reaches age 25

   g.   G ──→L/E ──→   A (80 years old)
                       └──→ L/E ──→ children
                              for life
                              Rem to grandchildren

h. G ——→L/E ——→   A ——→B and his heirs
                                  but if B shall
                                  predecease
                                  A
                                  └——→ C

i. G ——→ L/E ——→   A ——→ heirs of A

j. G ——→ L/E ——→   A ——→ B if B lives to
                                  attain the age
                                  of 30 years
                                  (B is 5 years old)

5. W. E. Collins executed and delivered to the Church of God of Prophecy a warranty deed with the following language:

> This transfer or deed is made with the full understanding that should the property fail to be used for the Church of God, it is to be null and void and property to revert to W. E. Collins or heirs.

What type of interests were created in the deed? Do any of the interests violate the Rule Against Perpetuities? *Collins v. Church of God of Prophecy,* 800 S.W.2d 418 (Ark. 1990)

6. A deed and contract provided that Dempsey, Carter, and Burton Layne would all hold title to 375 acres of land in Pittsylvania County, Virginia. Under the terms of the agreement, when one brother died, the remaining brothers or their heirs had the opportunity to purchase the deceased brother's one-third interest through a right of first refusal. Does the right of first refusal here violate the Rule Against Perpetuities? *Layne v. Henderson,* 351 S.E.2d 18 (Va. 1986); What about an option to repurchase property reserved by the grantor? *Dennis v. Bird,* 941 S.W.2d 486 (Ct. App. Ky. 1997)

7. Richard J. Long and Mary Long, his wife, conveyed by warranty deed dated September 30, 1949, to the Pompey Fire Department a parcel of land (called P-1). The deed, which was properly recorded in the Onondaga County Clerk's Office on November 15, 1949, stated that the grant of the parcel was given for the purpose of "erecting thereon a fire house." The deed also included the following language:

> In the event that the said premises are no longer used to house a fire department, then and in that event the land and building erected thereon is to revert to Richard J. Long and Mary Long, or their heirs and assigns.

Shortly after the conveyance, a firehouse was erected on P-1. The building is a two-story structure with a cinder block first floor and a wood frame second floor. The first floor contains three large bays to house fire trucks and equipment. The building was used continuously from 1950 to 1985 to house the Fire Department. In 1984, the Fire Department acquired another parcel of land (P-2) located about 300 yards from P-1. P-2 had an elementary school that was remodeled to include vehicle bays and other features of a well-equipped firehouse. In November 1985, the Fire Department moved its essential equipment and the majority of its functions to the P-2 facility. Does the fire department still own the land conveyed by the Longs? *Long v. Pompey Hill Volunteer Fire Dept.,* 539 N.Y.S.2d 1014 (1989)

8. What types of interest are created by the following language?

> To my daughter, Edna M. Arehart, to have and to hold same for and during her lifetime, and at her death to her issue in equal shares, or if she shall have no issue, then to the Odd Fellows Home at York, Nebraska, provided, if my said daughter, Edna M. Arehart, shall be left a widow, then upon her becoming a widow, I give and devise all my real estate to her, by absolute title, believing she may need the same for her maintenance. *Dover v. Grand Lodge of Nebraska Ind. Order of Oddfellows,* 206 N.W.2d 845 (Neb. 1973)

9. Hixon, by his will, made the following grant:

> To my wife, Alice, for her life, the net income from my property and upon her death said property to be distributed equally among my heirs.

What interests were created? Are they valid? *Harris Trust & Saving Bank v. Beach,* 495 N.E.2d 1170 (Ill. 1986)

10. Higbee Corporation and Kennedy both claimed title to a narrow strip of property located in Bethel Park, Allegheny County, Pennsylvania. Higbee filed suit to quiet title. The original grant on the property to Kennedy provided as follows:

> *To have and to hold the said piece of land above-described the hereditaments and premises hereby granted or mentioned and intended so to be with the appurtenance unto the said party of the second part his heirs and assigns to and for the only proper use and behoove of the said party of the second part his heirs and assigns forever provided the party of the second part his heirs and assigns wishes to make use of it for the purpose of a road. THE PARTY OF THE SECOND PART AGREES TO KEEP A GOOD FENCE AROUND THE ABOVE-MENTIONED LOT, FAILING TO DO SO FORFEITS HIS CLAIM, whenever the party of the second part wishes to give up his claim to said lot he is to have full privilege to remove all fencing materials whenever the party of the second part his heirs and assigns fails to fulfill this agreement the land is to revert to the party of the first part.*

What type of land interest was created?

Internet Activities

1.   See Hampden County Massachusetts registry of deeds for a glossary of terms used in this chapter: **http://registryofdeeds.co.hampden.ma.us/glossary.html**.

2.   Fee simple ownership is a distinctive matter in Hawaii. First visit **http://www.capitol. hawaii.gov/hrscurrent/Vol12/hrs516/HRS_516-1.htm** to see how the State defines fee simple terms. Then visit **http://www.maui.net/~wmta/lease.html** and read about the controversial issues involving fee simple versus leasehold estates.

Chapter 8
The Landlord-Tenant Relationship

Who is responsible for paying the damages caused by a fire in my apartment—me or my landlord? What happens if I move out early—before my lease expires? Can my landlord, without my permission, enter my apartment while I'm gone?

All the above questions are asked frequently by tenants leasing apartments, homes, and trailers. Although a rental agreement seems like a simple transaction—the tenant pays the rent and the landlord allows the tenant to live on the premises—there are many rights and responsibilities of both parties that should be clearly understood by them before execution, during performance, and after termination of the lease agreement. This chapter answers the questions, What types of lease agreements exist? What terms should be included in the lease agreement? What rights and responsibilities do each of the parties have? In answering these questions, common law and majority views are covered along with the provisions of the Uniform Residential Landlord Tenant Act (URLTA), which has been adopted in about one-third of the states. This chapter concentrates on residential leases, and Chapter 9 deals with commercial leases. The residential tenant has more protections and rights than does the commercial tenant.

TYPES OF TENANCIES

The four types of tenancies that existed at common law are *tenancy for years, periodic tenancy, tenancy at will,* and *tenancy at sufferance.* These tenancies will apply to both commercial and residential leases to the extent there are no specific statutory changes in the state. A lease agreement can provide for its own type of lease and terms, but there are categories that common law still recognizes.

Tenancy for Years

A **tenancy for years** is created by a lease, which will run for a time period specified in that lease. Other language used to describe the tenancy for years includes "estate for years," "tenancy for a term," or " tenancy for a period." Every tenancy for years has fixed beginning and ending dates and is created by language such as "To A for 7 years" or "To A from 31 March 2000 until 30 June 2001." When the termination date is reached, this land interest automatically terminates.

In a tenancy for years, the parties involved have a continuing relationship and should have a written agreement setting forth all their rights and obligations. A tenancy for years that runs for a period longer than one year is required to be in writing. (Details on the content of such written agreements are discussed later in this chapter.)

Periodic Tenancy

A **periodic tenancy** has no definite ending date: it continues until one of the parties takes proper legal steps to terminate the interest. A periodic tenancy can be expressly created, and an example of language used to create such an interest is "To A on a month-to-month basis beginning 30 June 2000."

The periodic tenancy or estate from period to period can also result or be implied from the conduct of the parties as opposed to being created expressly. A periodic tenancy will result in the following circumstances. One party moves into another's property on an oral lease agreement that is to run for 24 months. In the jurisdiction in which the parties reside, lease agreements running for longer than one year must be in writing to be enforceable. According to the writing requirement in the law, the parties do not have a valid lease agreement, but once the landowner accepts the tenant's rent, a periodic tenancy results and is terminated only through the proper actions of the parties.

Proper actions required for termination of a tenancy are specified by statute in each state, but the key to termination in all states is notice. The type or length of notice will vary, but the requirement of notice is universal. The typical period, both at common law and by state statute on a month-to-month tenancy, is a full period's notice, or one month.

Tenancy at Will

A **tenancy at will** can be created expressly and arises when the parties agree to the lease of property but provide no time period for the lease. Language to create a tenancy at will would be "To A at O's discretion or will."

In a tenancy at will, both parties have the right to terminate the tenancy at any time and are not required to provide advance notice of such termination. In some states, statutory provisions have changed this freedom and require some form of notice to terminate. In such states, the tenancy at will is in essence a periodic tenancy by statute.

Tenancies at will can arise in situations with a financed property, where there is a default by the party possessing the property. For example, suppose A leases the land on which her mobile home is located, and her mobile home is financed through a bank. A leaves and the mobile home remains on the leased land. If A defaults on her payment and the bank is forced to repossess the mobile home, then the bank becomes a tenant at will on the land.

Tenancy at Sufferance

This final nonfreehold interest, **tenancy at sufferance,** arises when a tenant from a properly created tenancy holds over on the landlord's property for a period beyond that authorized. For example, suppose a landlord leased a building to a tenant for two years with a lease termination date of March 31, 2001. The tenant should vacate the premises by the termination date, but if the tenant remains, he or she is nothing more than a trespasser. A landlord may have such a holdover tenant evicted. However, if the tenant chooses to remain on the property at the landlord's sufferance and if the landlord accepts rent after the termination date, a periodic tenancy then results.

TERMS OF LEASE AGREEMENT

Need for Lease Agreement

Certain types of leases, under the Statute of Frauds, must be in writing. Typically, a lease must be in writing if it runs for a period longer than one year. In some states, the writing requirement may be imposed at six months. This requirement applies to both residential and commercial leases.

To satisfy the Statute of Frauds, the writing may be informal—in the form of a letter, memorandum, or series of documents. The basics needed are the parties, the signatures of the parties, a description of the leased premises, the term of the lease, and the amount of the rent. See Web Exhibits 8.1 and 8.2 for samples.

Consider 8.1

Edson found, through Perry Development, an apartment in New York City. Edson told the leasing agent at Perry that he wanted a three-year lease. Perry's business manager wrote a letter to Edson confirming the location of the apartment, the dates of the lease term, the rent, and to whom the rent would be paid. After Edson had occupied the apartment for three months, he received a notice from Perry that the lease would terminate at the end of the fourth month. Edson objected, but Perry maintained that a lease for longer than a year must be in writing, and without anything in writing, Edson was a month-to-month tenant only. Edson wishes to know his rights.

Practical Tip

Be certain the lease agreement is in writing before the tenant takes possession of the property. Be certain both parties, the landlord and the tenant, understand the terms of the lease.

Even though the Statute of Frauds requires only that leases of certain durations be in writing, all leases should be in writing so that the parties' rights and responsibilities are clearly established. In addition to the minimum requirements for a written lease already mentioned, there are many issues and details in leases. The following sections cover various terms and areas of difficulties in leases.

If the parties do not deal specifically with these issues in a written lease agreement, statutory or common law provisions will apply, and the parties may not have the protection or obtain the results they expect.

Habitability

At common law, when tenants leased property, the doctrine of caveat tenant applied: Tenants leased the premises at their own risk and there were no warranties, covenants, promises, or guarantees that the premises were habitable. The common law did not impose an obligation on the landlord to deliver habitable premises. The effect of this lack of protection was that many tenants entered into leases for uninhabitable properties. They were then obligated to the lease and faced with the often difficult task of obtaining repairs and services from the landlord.

To prevent the devastating effects of this doctrine, particularly in areas where there were housing shortages, many cities and state legislatures enacted laws that require landlords to deliver premises to tenants in habitable condition. For example, the following statutory language would prohibit the rental of uninhabitable premises.

> *No persons shall rent or offer to rent any habitation, or the furnishings thereof, unless such a habitation and its furnishings are in a clean, safe and sanitary condition, in repair, and free from rodents or vermin.*

The effect of a regulation such as this is to make a lease for uninhabitable premises void and thereby excuse the tenant from performing by it (see also Chapter 1, pages 8–10).

Even in jurisdictions without a statute that applies specifically to leases, some tenants have been excused from performing lease agreements on other grounds. Leases of premises found to have building or fire code violations have been held void, and courts have excused tenants from performing on the grounds of illegality. For example, in *Pines v. Perssion*, 111 N.W.2d 409 (Wis. 1961), four college students leased a home for use as their residence for the school year. The landlord promised that the premises would be repaired in time for the start of the fall semester. When the students arrived for the fall semester, the house was in a state of complete disrepair. An attorney advised the students to have the home inspected, and a building inspector found many violations including inadequate wiring, broken plumbing, faulty stair handrails, and lack of windows and screens. The court excused the students from performing on the grounds that the violations of the building code made a lease of the premises void.

Under a third and final theory for requiring landlords to deliver habitable premises, some states, through statute or judicial decision, create an **implied warranty of habitability** in all lease agreements. The URLTA includes an implied warranty of habitability. For case illustrations of the implied warranty of habitability, refer to Chapter 1.

Consider 8.2

A 60-unit cooperative apartment building on West 142nd Street in Manhattan was severely damaged by fire on February 7, 1994, and rendered uninhabitable by the Department of Buildings. No action was taken to demolish or renovate the building, and in November, 1994, the owners brought suit seeking a court order requiring the Owners Corporation and its managing agent to restore the premises to a safe and habitable condition. However, the property had not been adequately insured, and the Owners Corporation declared bankruptcy on November 23, 1994.

8.2, continued   The Owners Corporation defended its inaction on the grounds that the cost of restoration would exceed the market value of the property. The owners maintain there is a statutory requirement for a landlord to keep his property in a safe and habitable condition. Could the warranty of habitability be used to mandate the reconstruction of a building? Should it be so used? *Bernard v. Scharf,* 656 N.Y.S.2d 583 (Sup. Ct. 1997)

Consider 8.3   Dennis and Bonnie Adams leased a mobile home from James Gaylock for $175 per month. When they moved in, they discovered that window glass was missing, the front door would not lock, the rear door left a gap when it was closed, two burners on the stove did not work, and a foul odor caused by a poor drainage system for the kitchen and bathrooms came from beneath the mobile home. When they used the furnace for the first time, there was a strange odor. The fire department came to inspect and told the Adamses not to use the furnace again. Has the landlord breached his implied warranty of habitability to the Adamses? *Adams v. Gaylock,* 378 S.E.2d 297 (W. Va. 1989)

Not all states have passed statutes on habitability or follow the idea of implied habitability. Therefore, tenants desiring protection against uninhabitable premises in states not affording protections should provide for habitability as a term for performance in their lease agreement. The clause may be simple, as the following language indicates: "Owner (landlord) agrees to deliver premises to tenant in a fit and habitable condition."

If the tenant has the opportunity to inspect the premises prior to entering into the lease agreement, a clause may be added requiring the landlord to make certain repairs and adjustments prior to the tenant's taking possession. To the just-mentioned habitability clause, the following language might be added: "Owner (landlord) agrees to repair the following or make the following changes prior to the date of the tenant's possession: . . . "

Ethical Issue   In some cases landlords are resistant to making repairs to properties that do not meet the standards for habitability. Many courts have undertaken creative remedies to this problem of resistance. For example, in Phoenix, Arizona, Sherwin Seyrafi, called a "slumlord" by various news organizations, was charged with misdemeanor violations for the conditions of his various properties and then ordered by a judge, as part of his sentence, to live in one of his properties for 30 days. What is the ethical standard the sentencing judge is applying to the landlord's conduct? Do you agree or disagree with the sentence?

Some states have specific statutory requirements on certain conditions in rental property. For example, the presence of lead-based paint in residential property is now highly regulated. In some states, the landlord is required to remove the lead paint and repaint the apartment. In other states, the presence of a child under seven in rental property with lead-based paint imposes a near strict liability on the landlord for any resulting injury to the child. In addition to the breach of the warranty of habitability, tenants may have statutory remedies when the habitability issue is one caused by the presence of this type of paint.

Under the Residential Lead-Based Paint Hazard Reduction Act of 1992, 42 U.S.C. §§ 4851–4856, both the Environmental Protection Agency (EPA) and the Department of Housing and Urban Development (HUD) were charged with disclosure standards for lead paints on their properties. Under the HUD/

EPA rules, landlords must disclose the presence of lead paint on their property and provide a pamphlet explaining the hazards of lead-based paint (40 C.F.R. § 745.100 *et seq.* and 24 CFR § 35.80 *et seq.*). The effect of the rule has been that landlords are eliminating the lead paint because the disclosure makes properties difficult to rent.

Deposits

Most tenants are required to make some type of deposit when initially entering into a lease agreement. The types of deposits include security deposit, cleaning deposit, and prepaid rent.

SECURITY DEPOSIT

The deposit most frequently required is the **security deposit.** Its purpose is to protect the landlord in the event of property damage or an early termination of a lease agreement by a tenant. The money held on deposit as security may be used to cover expenses or damages and may even be specified as liquidated damages.

In some states, security deposits are regulated to a great extent; in other states, it is the responsibility of the parties to agree on the purpose and effect of the security deposit. For example, under the **Uniform Residential Landlord Tenant Act (URLTA),** a provision limits the amount of a security deposit that the landlord is permitted to demand. Section 2.101(a) provides, "A landlord may not demand or receive security, however denominated, in an amount or value in excess of (one) month['s] period."

Once landlords have obtained a security deposit, they have possession of it until the termination of the underlying lease agreement. There are considerable differences among the states as to landlords' uses and obligations regarding security deposits received by tenants. The common law rule is that the landlord is a debtor to the tenant for the security deposit and is free to use the funds as if they were the landlord's own. However, some states have enacted legislation requiring landlords to pay tenants a minimum amount of interest (such as 5 percent) for the time the deposit is held. Some states also require landlords to keep the security deposits in special trust accounts and maintain and submit periodic records of their balances and deposits received.

States also differ in their definitions of what constitutes a security deposit. For example, in some states prepaid rent is considered part of the security deposit, and in other states the landlord is not required to follow security deposit procedures on funds labeled prepaid rent.

The security deposit may encourage a tenant to perform according to the terms of the lease; for if the tenant breaches the lease agreement, the landlord may, according to the lease provisions, keep the security deposit as liquidated damages. Parties to a lease are free to agree on damage provisions, and a liquidated damage clause is an advance agreement between the parties of how a breach will be determined and what the breach damages will be. The lease may provide that the liquidated damages for breach will be the security deposit. For example, if a tenant leases an apartment for $800 per month for a six-month period and abandons the premises at four months, the landlord is entitled, with a proper liquidated damage provision in the lease, to keep the security deposit as damages for early termination by the tenant. When early termination occurs, it is unclear whether the landlord will suffer any damages (the apartment could be rerented the next day or could sit vacant for the remaining two months of the terminated

tenancy). An agreement to keep the security deposit as damages is a valid liquidated damage clause because it is unclear how much the damages (if any) will be.

In some states and under the URLTA, if the landlord chooses the remedy of
keeping the security deposit, then he is limited to the amount of the security
deposit as damages. To attempt to collect actual damages as well as keeping the
security deposit as damages would be assessing a void penalty for breach. A landlord is not entitled to both liquidated and actual damages. Also under the URLTA,
retention of the security deposit requires the landlord to account for the reasons
and the amounts to the tenant.

Leases should specify what amounts are being taken and for what purposes.
The following language is an example of the type of clause necessary to establish
that funds are being taken as a security deposit:

> *SECURITY: In order to guarantee Resident's faithful performance of the terms and
> conditions contained herein, Resident hereby deposits with owner the sum of
> $_____ as a security deposit to be applied to the payment of accrued but unpaid
> rent and any other damages suffered by reason of Resident's noncompliance or
> breach of any terms and conditions of the Rental Agreement.*

If there are no statutory provisions governing security deposits in the state, the
parties should specify in the lease agreement their rights to the security deposit,
including procedures and time limitations for its use and return and its effect as
a provision for liquidated damages.

Consider 8.4

Barbara Kent and her roommate, Sheila Barnes, have signed a nine-month lease
on an apartment. The rent is $650 per month, and the roommates were required
to make a $500 security deposit. At the end of four months, they decide to move
to a house closer to their places of employment. The apartment owner is unable
to lease the apartment for three months, and the apartment is vacant for that
time. Discuss the use of the security deposit to cover damages according to the
laws of your state.

CLEANING DEPOSIT

In addition to security deposits, which are intended to secure rental payments,
landlords may require tenants to make other deposits before occupying the leased
property. A **cleaning deposit** is a typical lease requirement and may take the form
of a nonrefundable fee that all tenants are required to pay. Under the URLTA, a
nonrefundable cleaning deposit must be stated as such in the lease agreement.
The following is a sample clause from a lease: "Additionally, Resident hereby pays
the sum of $_____, which is a NONREFUNDABLE redecorating fee." The fees
paid may be called cleaning, refurbishing, redecorating, or restoration fees, but
they all require advance disclosure of retention under the URLTA.

Some cleaning fees are taken with the idea that they will be used, if necessary,
at the time the tenant vacates the premises. The theory behind this type of deposit
is that tenants will have greater incentive to keep the premises clean and well
maintained and not destroy items of property. For example, some leases contain
addenda that specify cleaning costs to be assessed if, at the end of the lease and
upon the landlord's inspection, particular cleaning tasks are necessary. Specific
items such as drapery cleaning or wall repainting may be represented as a dollar
amount, so that tenants will know the potential assessments in advance.

PREPAID RENT

Many landlords require tenants to pay the first and last months' rent prior to taking possession of the property. Such a provision is for the protection of the landlord in the event the tenant vacates the premises without paying rent. However, the URLTA and many other states' provisions limit the amount of prepaid rent or total deposits that may be required of the tenant initially, and the limit may be as small as 1½ times the monthly rent. The lease agreement or an addendum to it should specify exactly what amounts are being received from the tenant and the purpose and application of those amounts. These limitations are not applicable in commercial leases.

Amount of Rent

In addition to specifying the amounts of deposits, the lease agreement should specify the monthly rental fee. The amount of rent becomes more of an issue in commercial leases where landlords are entitled to portions of profits (see Chapter 9). Residential lease agreements should specify how much rent is to be paid, the date the rent is due, to whom the rent is to be paid, and if there are any fees associated with late rental payments. The following is a sample rental fee clause that includes the necessary terms for rental payments.

> *RENTAL: The rental shall be $_____ per month, plus sales tax thereon at the rate in effect from time to time, payable in advance on the FIRST day of each month at the on-site manager's office. An equitable proration of the first month's rent shall be made if the term of this Rental Agreement commences other than on the first day of the calendar month. A late charge of $10.00 per day shall be added as additional rent to any rent payment not paid in full on or before the due date. A $25.00 fee will be charged for all checks returned from the bank unpaid. Management reserves the right to demand that all sums due under the lease be paid in cash and to return any check previously accepted by Management and demand cash.*

Rent Control

New York City and San Francisco are examples of cities with **rent controls** on landlords. These rent controls limit the amount of rent landlords can charge to tenants. Nearly two-thirds of the rental market in both cities is rent regulated. Under rent regulation, a housing authority sets rates and determines any exceptions. A lease in violation of such rent control or rent stabilization statutes is void. A tenant cannot be evicted for refusal to pay more than the maximum rent permitted by the housing authority.

In areas where there is a rent stabilization regime, some landlords have converted their properties to "hotels" and charge higher rates to their occupants. However, rent control provisions also define what constitutes a "housing accommodation," and factors such as length of time of occupation, whether a key is retained on a regular basis by the occupant, what types of belongings the occupant has on the property, and whether the occupant does have a residence other than the occupied property are critical in defining housing. Even though the property owner may call the living area a "hotel," and collect rent on a weekly basis, it may still be subject to rent controls given the factors listed above (*Gracecor Realty Co., Inc. v. Hargrove*, 683 N.E.2d 326 [Ct. App. NY 1997]).

Other landlords have tried putting waivers of rent stabilizations in their lease agreements with tenants. These types of waivers have been declared void by courts

http://

Learn more about New York's rent regulation systems at: **http://www. dhcr.state.my.us/ora/ ora.htm**.

as contravening the purpose of rent stabilization in providing affordable housing for city dwellers (*Draper v. Georgia Properties, Inc.*, 660 N.Y.S.2d 556 [Sup. Ct. 1997]).

Still others have tried to circumvent rent controls by arguing that there is a housing shortage. However courts have not intervened and deferred to others' judgment (*Santa Monica Beach, Ltd. v. Superior Court*, 968 P.2d 993 [Cal. 1999]).

The following case provides the U.S. Supreme Court view on rent controls.

Fisher v. City of Berkeley California

475 U.S. 260 (1986)

Facts

In June 1980, the city of Berkeley passed an initiative entitled Ordinance 5261-NS, Rent Stabilization and Eviction for Good Cause Ordinance (hereinafter Ordinance). The stated purposes of the ordinance were:

> to regulate residential rent increases in the City of Berkeley and to protect tenants from unwarranted rent increases and arbitrary, discriminatory, or retaliatory evictions in order to help maintain the diversity of the Berkeley community and to ensure compliance with legal obligations relating to the rental of housing. This legislation is designed to address the City of Berkeley's housing crisis, preserve the public peace, health and safety, and advance the housing policies of the City with regard to low and fixed income persons, minorities, students, handicapped and the aged.

To accomplish the goals, the ordinance enacted strict rent controls. All rental properties (23,000) in Berkeley were given a base rate as of the May 1980 rental rate, and increases were permitted only pursuant to an annual general adjustment of rent ceilings by the Rent Stabilization Board or pursuant to a special petition approved by the same board. Failure to comply with the rent ceilings could result in suits by the tenants, the withholding of collected rents from the landlord, criminal penalties, or a combination.

Shortly after the ordinance was passed, a group of landlords (appellants) brought suit in California Superior Court challenging the ordinance as unconstitutional because it preempted federal antitrust laws. The Superior Court upheld the ordinance, and the Court of Appeals reversed. The California Supreme Court held that there was no conflict between the Ordinance and the Sherman Act. The landlords appealed.

Judicial Opinion

Marshall, Justice. Recognizing that the function of government may often be to tamper with free markets, correcting their failures and aiding their victims, this Court noted that a state statute is not pre-empted by the federal antitrust laws simply because the state scheme may have an anticompetitive effect. We have therefore held that a state statute should be struck down on pre-emption grounds only if it mandates or authorizes conduct that necessarily constitutes a violation of the antitrust laws in all cases, or if it places irresistible pressure on a private party to violate the antitrust laws in order to comply with the statute.

Appellants argue that Berkeley's Rent Stabilization Ordinance is pre-empted because it imposes rent ceilings across the entire rental market for residential units. Such a regime, they contend, clearly falls within the per se rule against price fixing, a rule that has been one of the settled points of antitrust enforcement since the earliest days of the Sherman Act. That the prices set here are ceilings rather than floors and that the public interest has been invoked to justify this stabilization should not, appellants argue, save Berkeley's regulatory scheme from condemnation under the per se rule.

Certainly there is this much truth to appellants' argument: Had the owners of residential rental property in Berkeley voluntarily banded together to stabilize rents in the city, their activities would not be saved from antitrust attack by claims that they had set reasonable prices out of solicitude for the welfare of their tenants. Moreover, it cannot be denied that Berkeley's Ordinance will affect the residential housing rental market in much the same way as would the philanthropic activities of this hypothetical trade association. What distinguishes the operation of Berkeley's Ordinance from the activities of a benevolent landlords' cartel is not that the Ordinance will necessarily have a different economic effect, but that the rent ceilings imposed by the Ordinance and maintained by the Stabilization Board have been unilaterally imposed by government upon landlords to the exclusion of private control.

The distinction between unilateral and concerted action is critical here. Adhering to the language of § 1, this Court has always limited the reach of that provision to unreasonable restraints of trade effected by a 'contract, combination . . . or conspiracy' between separate entities. The ordinary relationship between the government and those who must obey its regulatory commands whether they wish to or not is not enough to establish a conspiracy. Similarly, the mere fact that all competing property owners must comply with the same provisions of the Ordinance is not enough to establish a conspiracy among landlords.

There may be cases in which what appears to be a state- or municipality-administered price stabilization scheme is really a private price-fixing conspiracy, concealed under a "gauzy cloak of state involvement." This might occur even where prices are ostensibly under the absolute control of government officials. However, we have been given no indication that such corruption has tainted the rent controls imposed by Berkeley's Ordinance. Adopted by popular initiative, the Ordinance can hardly be viewed as a cloak for any conspiracy among landlords or between the landlords and the municipality. Berkeley's landlords have simply been deprived of the power freely to raise their rents. That is why they are here. And that is why their role in the stabilization program does not alter the restraint's unilateral nature.

Because under settled principles of antitrust law, the rent controls established by Berkeley's Ordinance lack the element of concerted action needed before they can be characterized as a per se violation of § 1 of the Sherman Act, we cannot say that the Ordinance is facially inconsistent with the federal antitrust laws. We therefore need not address whether, even if the controls were to mandate § 1 violations, they would be exempt under the state-action doctrine from antitrust scrutiny.

Affirmed.

Case Questions

1. Is there preemption of the Berkeley ordinance by the federal antitrust laws?
2. What arguments do the landlords make on their behalf?
3. Who is setting rent prices?
4. Do the landlords have any control?
5. Is the Ordinance constitutional?

Note: Several other U.S. Supreme Court decisions indicate this type of activity is subject to scrutiny because property rights are affected.

In San Francisco and New York, the following discoveries have been made:

> ### Consider 8.5

a. two-thirds of residential rental property is under rent controls and the average rent is $650.
b. The rent for the remaining one-third properties is $1,500–$2,000, the apartments are small, in poor condition, and have a waiting list.
c. Landlords under rent control are converting their properties to commercial facilities or condominiums.
d. There is little tenant turnover in rent-controlled property with relatives taking leases upon tenants' deaths.

What explains the price differences and problems? Give the economic analysis.

Lease Term

The portion of the lease agreement that specifies the term may simply state the beginning and ending dates of the lease. However, additional language is necessary if the tenant is to be given the option to renew. The option to renew should specify when the option must be exercised, how it is to be exercised, and how the rental amount for the option period is to be computed. In addition, the length or maximum length of the option period should be specified.

Attorneys' Fees

In spite of careful drafting and execution of lease agreements, there is still the possibility of litigation. All leases should make provision for the payment of costs and attorneys' fees in the event litigation on the lease becomes necessary. The following clause is an example of an attorneys' fee provision:

In the event legal action is necessary for the enforcement of rights and obligations granted under this agreement, the prevailing party shall be entitled an award including attorneys' fees and all attendant court costs regardless of the stage to which the legal action proceeds.

In states where attorneys' fees cannot be collected in contract actions, these clauses are unenforceable.

Rules and Regulations

Particularly in apartment complexes, it is necessary for smooth functioning of joint facilities and for each tenant's peaceful enjoyment of the property that all residents comply with certain rules and regulations on the use of the property. Under the URLTA and most state statutes, landlords are permitted to promulgate rules by which tenants must abide for the smooth operation of the rented property. Section 3.102 of the URLTA permits rules and regulations that promote the convenience, safety, or welfare of the tenants, prevent the landlord's property from abusive use, or provide for a fair distribution of services and facilities held out for the tenants generally. The rules must apply to all tenants, be disclosed to all tenants, and not be applied unfairly. Rules and regulations cannot allow the landlord to avoid responsibilities or eliminate tenants' rights. Rules and regulations may be incorporated into the lease agreement in two ways:

Practical Tip

A violation of the rules and regulations imposed by the landlord is also grounds for eviction. Most landlords provide tenants with notice of a violation before proceeding to an eviction.

1. They may actually be written into the section of the lease agreement on the applicability of rules and regulations.
2. They may be incorporated as an addendum or a schedule to the lease agreement or referenced in the lease. If they are referenced, the tenant is entitled to a copy.

The types of rules and regulations that are typical and meet the standards of the URLTA are hours of pool use, use of laundry facilities, parking regulations, and noise and pet restrictions. (A notice of change in the rules should be sent directly to each tenant.)

The following case deals with the reasonableness of a landlord's rule.

Berlinger v. Suburban Apartment Management

454 N.E.2d 1367 (Oh. 1982)

Facts

Gary R. Berlinger (plaintiff/appellant) was a tenant in an apartment managed by Suburban Apartment Management (SAM/landlord/appellee). His security deposit was $420, and his monthly rent was $210.

In his lease agreement was the following paragraph:

No animals, birds, pets, motorcycles, waterbeds, trucks, jeeps, or vans shall be kept on the premises at any time.

The rule provided for a $50 fine for each violation. Berlinger had a motorcycle on his patio on October 10, 13, and 24, and November 7, 1979.

SAM notified Berlinger of the violation and the $200 fine. Berlinger did not pay the fine and moved out. SAM kept Berlinger's security deposit for a $200 fine, $210 in rent, and $10.50 in interest. Berlinger objected on the grounds that the fine was excessive and the rule was arbitrary. Berlinger sued to have his security deposit returned. The trial court awarded him $20 based on the following:

Security deposit	$420.00
Plus interest	+ $10.50
Subtotal	$430.50
Less rent (for unpaid last month)	$210.00
Less 4 × $50 (four days of motorcycle)	$200.00
Total	$20.50[1]

Berlinger appealed.

Judicial Opinion

Jackson, Judge. It does not appear that the $50 per diem charge for the presence of a motorcycle was in the nature of a fee for parking or storage. The lease was not modified to permit possession of a motorcycle on the premises. Instead, the charge is in the nature of liquidated damages. It is a matter of common knowledge that motorcycles, if operated loudly, can be objects of great annoyance. This effect is magnified in densely populated places such as apartment complexes. Thus, it is not unconscionable for a landlord to prohibit the bringing of motorcycles on the premises.

A different issue is presented, however, by the liquidated damages clause. To be valid, a provision for liquidated damages must meet three criteria, expressed in the following excerpt from *American Financial Leasing v. Miller* (1974) 41 Ohio App.2d 69, 73, 322 N.E.2d 149 [70 O.O.2d 64] (quoting from 16 Ohio Jurisprudence 2d 155):

> [I]t must, according to most cases, appear that the sum stipulated bears a reasonable proportion to the loss actually sustained; that the actual damages occasioned by the breach are uncertain or difficult to ascertain; and most important of all, that a construction of the contract as a whole

evinces a conscious intention of the parties deliberately to consider and adjust the damages that might flow from the breach.

Actual damages occasioned by a breach of the "no motorcycle" provision of the lease are difficult to ascertain. However, the sum of $50 per day (which in a thirty-day month would amount to $1,500) does not bear a reasonable relationship to any loss which might foreseeably be sustained. A court could take judicial notice that the operation of a motorcycle might cause great damage to a landlord, because tenants who object to loud noise might move out. However, no evidence was introduced tending to show the amount of damages which might foreseeably result from the mere presence of a motorcycle.

The liquidated damages clause contained in the Disposition Advice is therefore invalid under the common law and under R.C. 5321.14, and is hereby ordered stricken from the lease.

In the absence of a valid provision for liquidated damages, the appellee was entitled to recover only the monetary equivalent of the actual damages caused by the appellant's breach. Again, however, the appellee failed to adduce any evidence tending to show that it sustained actual damages as a result of the presence of the motorcycle on the property, even if the motorcycle was there for one month, as claimed by appellee. In the absence of any evidence on this subject, compensatory damages may not be awarded.

The appellee did prove beyond any doubt that the appellant breached his promise not to bring a motorcycle on the property. The appellee is therefore entitled to judgment on its claim for breach of contract, and an award of nominal damages in the sum of one dollar.

The appellant proved that he was entitled to the return of his security deposit ($420) plus interest ($10.50) less one month's rent ($210), for a total of $220.50.

Reversed.

Case Questions

1. The trial court actually miscalculated and hence made the award at $20.00 as opposed to $20.50.

1. What rule was at issue?
2. Was the fine excessive?

Paul Salmonte leased Richard and Mildred Eilertsons' Florida home in 1985. The Eilertsons lived in Houston, Texas, but sometimes returned to inspect the house. The Eilertsons also had an exterminator go to the home on a monthly basis. By May 1986, Salmonte decided that the inspections and extermination were occurring too often and began refusing regular access. The Eilertsons discovered that Salmonte had breached the terms of the lease agreement that prohibited changes in carpeting, wallpaper, and locks and then went to inspect the home and pets. The Eilertsons noticed that one of their rugs had been moved to the garage and had a car parked on it. They then filed a complaint for eviction for breach of the lease agreement. Could the Eilertsons have Salmonte evicted for violations of the rules? *Salmonte v. Eilertson*, 526 So.2d 179 (Ct. App. Fla. 1988)

Consider 8.6

Landlord's Right of Access

Although landlords own the property, tenants have the exclusive rights of possession even as against the landlords so long as a valid lease agreement exists. This principle of exclusive possession was applied at common law and has been codified in many states to protect tenants from landlords' unauthorized entry onto leased premises. Under Section 3.103 of the URLTA, a landlord can enter a tenant's dwelling if:

a.   The tenant consents and the purpose is repair or services; and
b.   In case of emergency (even without the tenant's consent). Except in emergencies the landlord must give the tenant at least (2) days' notice and must come at reasonable times.

In the lease agreement, the parties are free to agree to other terms of entry and arrangements for entry, and in most states these terms will be enforceable so long as the tenant has not been required to give up any statutory rights. With consent required, the tenant must act reasonably.

Assignments and Subleases

Assignments and **subleases** are similar in that they both bring third parties into the landlord-tenant relationship. However, there is a distinction between the two processes: In an assignment, tenants actually transfer their leasehold interests to third parties who will take over all obligations and assume all benefits associated with the original lease. In a subleasing arrangement, the tenants give up only a portion of their leasehold estate. For example, a tenant with a three-year lease sublets the leased premises to someone who resides there while the tenant is studying in Europe for one year. But if the tenant remains in Europe and the other party takes over the remaining one and one-half years on the lease, then an assignment has occurred. Regardless of the label the parties give to the transfer of interest, the issue of whether an assignment or a sublease has occurred is one for the courts.

A leasehold interest at common law was freely alienable; both subleases and assignments were permitted and honored. However, the parties may restrict transfers through the terms of their agreement. For example, some leases declare any transfer void, although the enforceability of such a provision is questionable. Another type of transfer restriction is a provision whereby tenants forfeit their leasehold interests if they attempt to transfer those interests to others. Under this type of provision, the assignment or sublease is not void, but the landlord has terminated both the original party's interest and the subtenant's or assignee's interest. Finally, the lease agreement may simply contain a provision by which the tenant promises not to sublet or assign. If the tenant violates the provision and the landlord has resulting damages, those damages are collectible from the breaching tenant. In some leases, the sublease or assignment is not prohibited, but the tenant is first required to obtain the landlord's approval for the transaction. If the landlord does not approve, one of the other types of provisions just mentioned would take effect. The following clause is an example in which prior consent is required: "Resident may not assign this Rental Agreement or sublet the premises, in whole or in part, without the prior written consent of management."

This consent to assignment was established as an ongoing right by the 1603 **Rule in Dumpor's Case,** which provided that if the landlord consented to one assignment, all other assignments were also deemed valid. In other words, at common law, once the landlord waived rights to prohibit an assignment, the right to prohibit was lost. Most states have abolished the effect of this rule.

RIGHTS AND RESPONSIBILITIES OF PARTIES TO A LEASE ASSIGNMENT

Although an assignment is a complete relinquishment of the tenant's leasehold interest, the tenant's obligations do not end with an assignment. The tenant remains obligated to the landlord; if the assignee does not perform according to the terms of the lease agreement, the original tenant will be liable for damages.

The assignee is not responsible for the obligations of the original tenant unless the assignee assumes these obligations. The assumption of responsibilities is not generally a problem since the assignee will be the recipient of the benefits—the right to the leasehold interest. The assignee does have the right to require the landlord to perform according to the terms of the lease agreement, as well as the right of suit in the event of nonperformance. If an assignment is to be permitted, the lease agreement should specify all details on assignment, such as methods of payment and communication.

The assignor remains liable for performance on the contract and is not released from obligations simply because a third party is now involved. In the event of nonperformance or breach, the landlord can pursue remedies from either the original tenant or the assignee. Although the landlord does not have privity of contract with the assignee, the landlord is still obligated to perform obligations as established by law or by the original parties' lease agreement.

RIGHTS AND RESPONSIBILITIES OF PARTIES TO A SUBLEASE

In a sublease, the subtenant becomes a tenant of the original lessee and not a tenant of the landlord. There is no legal relationship between landlord and subtenant and no rights of enforcement by one party against another. Any rights the parties have must be exercised indirectly through the tenant with whom they have a contractual relationship. For example, if a landlord who is required to maintain insurance on the leased premises fails to do so and a subtenant loses property because of it, the subtenant could proceed against the tenant. Although the tenant could then proceed against the landlord for recovery, the subtenant would have no direct cause of action against the landlord because the landlord's obligation to insure is to the tenant and not to the subtenant.

Unconscionability

As with most consumer contracts, leases are subject to judicial standards of fairness in language and bargaining power. Under the URLTA, a rental agreement is unconscionable if the tenant is required to waive any of the rights, remedies, or protections afforded under the act.

Other areas in lease agreements found unconscionable by courts include excessive cleaning deposits, excessive assessment of cleaning fees, excessive security deposit requirements, prohibitions on the right to organize, and waivers of judicial process. The basic standard in all cases is one of bargaining power and fairness to the parties involved.

RIGHTS AND RESPONSIBILITIES OF PARTIES TO LEASE AGREEMENT

Each party in a lease has certain required responsibilities of performance as well as rights. The sections below cover those rights and responsibilities.

Responsibilities of Landlords and Rights of Tenants

MAINTENANCE OF THE PREMISES

At common law, a lease was viewed as a transfer of a land interest with no obligation of maintenance and repair for the landlord once the tenant began the leasehold interest or lease period. Just as the doctrine of habitable premises has changed considerably, so has the doctrine governing the landlord's duty of repair. Several theories have now been used by courts or codified by states that require the landlord to keep the leased premises in repair. The theories are (1) constructive eviction, (2) self-help, (3) tort liability, and (4) lease termination.

1. Constructive Eviction One theory used to require repairs and thereby ensure the tenant of continued habitability is the doctrine of **constructive eviction.** For this doctrine to apply, the tenant must be able to establish that the landlord had an obligation to repair either through a covenant in the lease agreement or through some statutory or judicially imposed duty. Under URLTA Section 2.104, landlords are required to comply with building codes, make the repairs necessary to keep the leased premises habitable, keep the common areas clean and safe, keep all services and facilities in working order, arrange for trash collection and removal, and supply running water (hot and cold) and heat in winter and according to outside temperatures.

Once the tenant has established that the landlord was responsible for maintenance of the premises, the tenant must also prove that the landlord has failed to perform according to the statute or agreement. Furthermore, it must be shown that the failure to perform has made it difficult or impossible for the tenant to continue living on the premises. Under the doctrine of constructive eviction, the tenant in these circumstances is evicted constructively by the landlord and by moving out is excused from performance of the lease. The greatest problem with the doctrine is that the tenant must move out for the doctrine to apply. In areas where housing shortages exist, particularly for low-cost units, this requirement of moving out imposes hardships. In some states, the courts have permitted tenants who can establish all of the elements of constructive eviction to fix the problem areas and remain in the leased premises, deducting the cost of the repairs from their rent.

The following case presents an example of constructive eviction and illustrates one state's statutory remedies for the problem.

Minjak Co. v. Randolph

528 N.Y.S.2d 554 (1988)

Facts

Diane Randolph and her roommates (respondents) leased a loft space from Minjak Company (petitioner) in 1976. Although the building was primarily used for residential purposes, Minjak had Randolph and the others sign a commercial lease. Their loft consisted of 1700 square feet. Two-thirds of the square footage was used for Mr. Kikuchi's music studio, where he composes, rehearses, and stores his very expensive electronic equipment and musical instruments.

Late in 1977, the fifth-floor tenant began to operate a health spa equipment business that included the display of fully working jacuzzis, bathtubs, and saunas. All the equipment was filled to capacity with water for display purposes. From November 1977 through February 1982, Randolph experienced at least 40 separate water leaks from the fifth floor. At times, water literally poured into their bedrooms and closets. Water leaked into the kitchen and onto Mr. Kikuchi's grand piano and other musical instruments. Randolph's complaints went unheeded by Minjak.

Sandblasting done by the fifth-floor tenant in 1978 caused dust to fall into the loft, their food, their eyes, and their beds. Construction on the stairs and elevators produced so much dust that the tenants were wearing masks, and Mr. Kikuchi ceased using the loft for his music studio in 1981. Randolph, Kikuchi, and the others ceased rent payment in 1981. In 1983 Minjak filed suit for nonpayment of rent. The tenants responded that they were unable to use two-thirds of the loft space, that there was a breach of the warranty of habitability, and that the landlord had failed to provide essential services.

Rent totals were $12,787.00, including $200 for October 1981, $450 for each month from November 1981 through December 1982, and $567 per month since January 1983. The jury awarded the tenants a rent abatement of 80 percent for part of the period, 40 percent for another part and 10 percent for breach of the implied warranty of habitability. The jury also awarded $20,000 punitive damages and $5,000 in attorneys' fees. The appellate court reversed, holding that constructive eviction was not a defense to nonpayment of rent. The parties appealed.

Judicial Opinion

Memorandum Decision. We reverse and hold that the tenants were entitled to avail themselves of the doctrine of constructive eviction based on their abandonment of a portion of the premises and that the award for punitive damages was permissible and warranted by these facts.

We agree with the holding and reasoning of *East Haven Associates v. Gurian*, 64 Misc.2d 276, 313 N.Y.S.2d 276, that a tenant may assert as a defense to the nonpayment of rent the doctrine of constructive eviction, even if he or she has abandoned only a portion of the demised premises due to the landlord's acts in making that portion of the premises unusable by the tenant. The rule of *Edgerton v. Page*, 20 N.Y. 281, the first decision to establish the requirement of abandonment of premises as a condition to asserting the defense of constructive eviction, is not undermined by our acknowledgement of a defense for partial constructive eviction. *Edgerton v. Page, supra,* emphasized that the tenant's obligation to pay rent continues as long as the tenant remains in possession of the entire premises demised. . . . It is not contrary to this rule nor against any established precedent to hold that when the tenant is constructively evicted from a portion of the premises by the landlord's actions, he should not be obligated to pay the full amount of the rent. Indeed, compelling considerations of social policy and fairness dictate such a result. None of the cases cited by the landlord reaches or warrants a contrary conclusion.

As for petitioner's argument on appeal that the tenants never abandoned any portion of the premises and, in fact, continued to use the entire loft even up until the day of trial, we note that this assertion is unaccompanied by any citation to the record. This was no mere inadvertent error, for there is absolutely nothing in the record to support such a claim. The evidence at trial fully supported a finding that respondents were compelled to abandon the music studio portion of the loft due to the landlord's wrongful acts [which] substantially and materially deprive[d] the tenant[s] of the beneficial use and enjoyment of the loft.

The award for punitive damages, as reduced by the Civil Court to $5,000, should be reinstated as well. Although no exception to the court's charge permitting the jury to award punitive damages was made, we discuss the issue of the propriety of submitting this issue to the jury in light of petitioner's argument that the award subjects it to a liability for which there is no support in the law and in light of Appellate Term's inconclusive comment on whether or not punitive damages could, as a matter of law, be awarded in habitability cases.

Although generally in breach of contract claims the damages to be awarded are compensatory, in certain instances punitive damages may be awarded when to do so would deter morally culpable conduct.

The determining factor is "not the form of the action, . . . but the moral culpability of the defendant, and whether the conduct implies a criminal indifference to civil obligations."

With respect to this State's strict housing code standards and statutes, made enforceable through civil and criminal sanctions and other statutory remedies, it is within the public interest to deter conduct which undermines those standards when that conduct rises to the level of high moral culpability or indifference to a landlord's civil obligations. Therefore, it has been recognized that punitive damages may be awarded in breach of warranty of habitability cases where the landlord's actions or inactions were intentional and malicious.

Accordingly, the issue of punitive damages was properly submitted to the jury, and we are satisfied that this record supports the jury's finding of morally culpable conduct in light of the dangerous and offensive manner in which the landlord permitted the construction work to be performed, the landlord's indifference to the health and safety of others, and its disregard for the rights of others, so as to imply even a criminal indifference to civil obligations.

One particularly egregious example of the landlord's wanton disregard for the safety of others was the way in which the stair demolition was performed: steps were removed and no warning sign even posted. The landlord's indifference and lack of response to the tenants' repeated complaints of dust, sand and water leak problems demonstrated a complete indifference to their health and safety and a lack of concern for the damage these conditions could cause to the tenants' valuable personal property. Such indifference must be viewed as rising to the level of high moral culpability. Accordingly, the award of punitive damages is sustained.

We likewise reject petitioner's argument that respondents cannot rely on their lease in order to recover attorney's fees pursuant to the provisions of Real Property Law Sec. 234. This statute has the effect, *inter alia*, of implying into a lease for residential property which contains a provision permitting the landlord to recover attorney's fees in a summary proceeding brought pursuant to the lease a similarly binding covenant by the landlord to pay the tenant's reasonable attorney's fees incurred in the successful defense of a summary proceeding commenced by the landlord arising out of the lease.

The Civil Court judgment should be reinstated.

Case Questions

1. What type of property was leased?
2. How was the property used?
3. Describe the problems with the fifth-floor tenant.
4. Was the landlord aware of the problems with habitability?
5. Is constructive eviction a defense to nonpayment of rent?
6. Does the fact that the tenants did not move out affect their case?
7. Why were punitive damages awarded?

---

2. Self-help Common law did not permit the **repair and deduct** self-help method of remedying leased premises in disrepair. However, under the URLTA, this remedy of **self-help** has been adopted by an increasing number of states. Under Section 4.103 of the URLTA, the tenant can make repairs (up to $100) if the landlord does not respond within 14 days of a written demand for repair. The tenant can then send the landlord an itemized statement on the repair costs and deduct that amount from his rent. Tenants may not make repairs at the landlord's expense if the tenant or family member caused the condition.

Under this section of the URLTA, the tenant is given the statutory right to repair and deduct the cost of property problems that are not self-induced. Notice must first be given to the landlord under the URLTA provisions.

3. Tort Liability In the absence of the statutorily or judicially imposed self-help right, tenants have another theory under which to correct problems and recover the cost from the landlord. In some decisions, the tenant has not been permitted to repair and deduct but has been permitted to repair and recover in tort for the damages caused or alleviated through the tenant's corrective actions. The difficulty with this remedy is that it necessitates legal action by the tenant for recovery. This remedy provides the tenant with an opportunity for damages and remedies beyond just nonpayment of rent or a reduction in rent.

4. Lease Termination A final option available to a tenant faced with a lease of uninhabitable premises is to treat the state of disrepair as constructive eviction, vacate
the premises, and regard the lease and the obligation to pay rents as terminated.
This right of termination through constructive eviction was a common-law right
that exists in all states in common law or statutory form. In the event a statute
regulates constructive eviction, it is important for the tenant to comply with all
procedural requirements before vacating the premises.

RETALIATORY ACTION BY LANDLORDS

If a tenant is able to exercise any of the rights and remedies afforded by self-help
statutes, implied covenants, or tort liability, it is possible that the landlord may, in
response to the tenant's action, retaliate with eviction. Because the purposes of
these theories would be defeated if eviction resulted, the URLTA and many state
statutes provide that landlords may not engage in retaliatory eviction against tenants who choose to exercise their self-help rights. For example, Section 5.101 of
the URLTA provides that a tenant cannot be evicted and that a tenant's rental fee
cannot be raised or his or her services decreased as a result of any of the following: (1) filing a complaint with housing authorities, (2) organizing or joining a
tenant's union, or (3) using self-help procedures and remedies. If a tenant has
engaged in these activities, there is usually a period during which the landlord's
eviction would be presumptively retaliatory. For example, the URLTA presump-
tive retaliatory period is one year after the tenant has engaged in any of the protected activities. The effect is that it becomes the landlord's burden to establish
that the tenant was evicted for reasons other than the exercise of statutorily protected rights. Naturally, the presumption can be overcome or held inapplicable in
cases where the tenant has not paid rent or has in some way breached the lease
agreement.

The following case deals with an issue of retaliatory conduct in response to a
tenant's complaints about noise.

Casa Blanca Mobile Home Park v. Hill

963 P.2d 542 (N.M. App. 1998)

Facts

Barbara Hill was a resident of Casa Blanca Mobile Home
Park. Shannon Kearns was a resident of an apartment
owned by Fair Plaza Associates. Both Hill and Kearns had
month-to-month rental agreements with the property
owners.

Hill began complaining in May 1996 about the level
of noise from her neighbor's television. The manager of
the mobile home park where she lived testified that he
was awakened on 15 occasions between the hours of
12:30 and 1:00 A.M. to investigate the TV disturbances.
Hill also complained during the day in July about the television set. At that point the manager served Hill with a
30-day notice of termination on her lease.

Kearns had sent two letters of complaint to the manager of her apartment complex about the noisy neighbors above her. Her manager also sent her a 30-day notice
of termination.

Hill and Kearns filed suit (the cases were consolidated for the same issues) alleging that the actions by
their landlords were retaliatory and a violation of
Uniform Owner-Resident Relations Act (UORRA). Both
property owners won at trial with the court concluding
they had the right to terminate the leases of Hill and
Kearns for their complaints about noise. Hill and Kearns
appealed.

Judicial Opinion

Hartz, Chief Judge. Section 47-8-39 of the UORRA states:

Owner retaliation prohibited.

A.   An owner may not retaliate against a resident who is in compliance with the rental agreement and not otherwise in violation of any provision of the [UORRA] by increasing rent, decreasing services or by bringing or threatening to bring an action for possession because the resident has within the previous three months:

> (1)   complained to a government agency charged with responsibility for enforcement of a minimum building housing code of a violation applicable to the premises materially affecting health and safety;
>
> (2)   organized or become a member of a residents' union, association or similar organization;
>
> (3)   acted in good faith to exercise his rights provided under the [UORRA], including when the resident makes a written request or complaint to the owner to make repairs to comply with the owner's obligations under Section 47–8–20 NMSA 1978;
>
> (4)   made a fair housing complaint to a government agency charged with authority for enforcement of laws or regulations prohibiting discrimination in rental housing;
>
> (5)   prevailed in a lawsuit as either plaintiff or defendant or has a lawsuit pending against the owner relating to the residency;
>
> (6)   testified on behalf of another resident; or
>
> (7)   abated rent in accordance with the provisions of Sections 47–8–27.1 or 47–8–27.2 NMSA 1978.

B.   If the owner acts in violation of Subsection A of this section, the resident is entitled to the remedies provided in Section 47-8-48 NMSA 1978 [permitting recovery of attorney fees and a civil penalty equal to twice the monthly rent] and the violation shall be a defense in any action against him for possession.

The Residents rely specifically on paragraph (3) of Subsection A, which prohibits retaliating against a resident by bringing an action for possession "because the resident has within the previous three months . . . acted in good faith to exercise his rights provided under the [UORRA]." The question before us thus becomes: Is complaining about noisy neighbors a "right provided under the UORRA"?

Although based on the Uniform Residential Landlord and Tenant Act (URLTA) approved by the National Conference of Commissioners on Uniform State Laws in 1972, the UORRA has a number of unique provisions. [T] he URLTA contains nothing comparable to the general prohibition against retaliation for exercising rights provided under the UORRA.

No specific provision of the UORRA gives a resident the right to complain about noisy neighbors. Indeed, no specific provision requires the owner to keep residents from being too noisy. Although the UORRA has several provisions granting a resident rights against the owner, the provisions relating to maintenance or operation of the premises appear only in Section 47–8–20(A), which states:

Obligations of owner.

A.   The owner shall:

> (1)   substantially comply with requirements of the applicable minimum housing codes materially affecting health and safety;
>
> (2)   make repairs and do whatever is necessary to put and keep the premises in a safe condition as provided by applicable law and rules and regulations as provided in Section 47-8-23 NMSA 1978;
>
> (3)   keep common areas of the premises in a safe condition;
>
> (4)   maintain in good and safe working order and condition electrical, plumbing, sanitary, heating, ventilating, air conditioning and other facilities and appliances, including elevators, if any, supplied or required to be supplied by him;
>
> (5)   provide and maintain appropriate receptacles and conveniences for the removal of ashes, garbage, rubbish and other waste incidental to the occupancy of the dwelling unit and arrange for their removal from the appropriate receptacle; and
>
> (6)   supply running water and a reasonable amount of hot water at all times and reasonable heat except where the building that includes the dwelling unit is not required by law to be equipped for that purpose, or the dwelling unit is so constructed that heat or hot water is generated by an installation within the exclusive control of the resident and supplied by a direct public utility connection.

The Residents acknowledge that the UORRA itself does not explicitly spell out the right to complain about noise. But they contend that this right is "provided under" the Act because (1) the right is recognized by the common law and (2) the Act incorporates by reference that proposition of common law.

Their argument has some appeal, but it is not convincing.

Hill makes an additional argument in support of the proposition that her alleged right to complain about noisy neighbors is a right "under the UORRA." She contends that her rental agreement, through the owner's rules and regulations, gives her a "right to quiet enjoyment." We need not decide however, whether a right contained in a rental agreement is a right "under the UORRA." We have examined the rules and regulations cited by Hill. They set forth various prohibitions and requirements that the tenants must honor. None imposes a duty on the owner. The cited provisions of the rental agreement did not confer upon the residents a right to quiet enjoyment, much less a right to complain to the owner.

Finally, Kearns argues that the UORRA itself implicitly grants residents the right to complain about noisy neighbors. She points to two specific provisions of the Act. First, Section 47–8–24 sets strict limitations on the owner's access to the rented promises. Kearns apparently contends that because these restraints on the owner are traditionally encompassed by the resident's right to quiet enjoyment of the premises, the UORRA has recognized that right in its most expansive sweep—that is, to include a right to peace and quiet (and the right to complain about its absence). The second provision she relies on is Section 47–8–22, entitled "Obligations of resident," which contains a subsection requiring the resident to "conduct himself and require other persons on the premises with his consent to conduct themselves in a manner that will not disturb his neighbors' peaceful enjoyment of the premises." Contending that the Act is "not designed to allow residents to enforce any rights, including their right of quiet enjoyment, amongst themselves." Kearns suggests that the Act implicitly imposes a duty of enforcement on the owner (and apparently a further right of the resident to complain to the owner).

Even assuming, without deciding, that Section 47–8–39(A)(3) protects against retaliation for exercising rights *implicitly* provided by the UORRA, we disagree with Kearns' analysis. Rather than supporting her position, the two cited sections rebut it. When a statute goes so far and no further, we infer that conduct beyond the line is not governed by the statute. We do not infer, as Kearns would have it, that because a statute takes two steps, it implicitly takes the third. In particular, the statutory provision imposing a duty on residents not to disturb their neighbors demonstrates that the Legislature considered the problem of noisy neighbors. By imposing a duty on the resident but not the owner, the statute clearly gives the owner the power to deal with disruptive tenants but leaves the exercise of that power to the owner's discretion.

This result is not senseless. [W]hen leases are month-to-month, noisy residents are likely to damage severely the economic interest of the owner by making it difficult to retain and attract other tenants. The owner is well-advised to take action against the noisy resident. The Legislature may have seen no great need to impose a statutory duty on the owner to control noisy residents.

Moreover, even were we to recognize a duty upon an owner to its residents to take action against other noisy residents (which may in fact arise under the common law), it does not follow that we must recognize a defense of retaliatory eviction when a resident complains about noisy neighbors. Failure by the owner to control noisy residents may entitle the beleaguered resident to termination of the lease, abatement of rent, or damages. But we have been directed to no authority, nor have we found any, that an owner must continue a lease with a resident who complains of noisy neighbors. Although the Legislature may wish to create such a right, thus far it has not, and perhaps with good reason. Even an enlightened owner may have difficulty resolving a dispute between a marginally inconsiderate resident and a marginally oversensitive neighbor, and such an owner may decide that the best solution is for one resident to depart. We note that in its order affirming the metropolitan court, the district court in Kearns' case found that Fair Plaza "was put in the untenable position of having to resolve a dispute between two tenants." Given that the cost of litigation can quickly add up to the equivalent of several months' rent, the Legislature could determine that recognition of a cause of action for retaliation because of complaints of noisy neighbors could do more harm than good—increasing rents because of increased litigation costs to owners, while doing little to improve the quality of life for residents. Such a determination would not be an anomaly.

We conclude that the UORRA does not provide a right to complain about noisy neighbors. In particular, Section 47–8–39(A)(3) does not protect a resident from an otherwise proper termination of a rental agreement and action for possession motivated by retaliation for such complaints.

We affirm.

Case Questions

1. Why were Hill and Kearns evicted from their leased premises?

2. Do you think the notice of termination by the landlords was retaliatory?

3. Does the New Mexico statute provide protection against retaliation in this case?

4. Do you think tenants should enjoy protection against retaliation for complaining about noise? Is a noise-free apartment part of a tenant's rights under a lease?

MAINTENANCE OF THE COMMON AREAS

Regardless of any state's position on the landlord's responsibility to maintain individual dwelling units, all states obligate the landlord to maintain the common areas of a building. Common areas are those used by all tenants, such as staircases, halls, and laundry facilities. Although tenants may not be entitled to terminate their leases for disrepair of these areas, the landlord will be held liable for injuries resulting from the disrepair.

DUTY TO MAINTAIN PREMISES TO PREVENT INJURIES

The landlord has responsibility and liability for conditions on the leased premises. In many situations, the landlord has dangerous items and structures on the property that can cause injury to tenants even though those structures are not the leased premises and not technically part of the common areas of a building.

The following case involves an issue of landlord liability.

Errico v. LaMountain

713 A.2d 791 (R.I. 1998)

Facts

In September 1989, Kimberly Errico (plaintiff/tenant), then a senior at Providence College, began living with two friends in a three-bedroom rental apartment in Providence. The apartment was located in the second story of a house owned by Joseph and Eileen LaMountain (defendants) and included a front balcony that was four feet deep and extended across the entire front of the house's second floor. The balcony had a wood railing and could be accessed only through the Errico apartment.

On September 18, 1989, Errico went onto the balcony to look for one of her roommates. She placed her left hand on the railing to brace herself as she leaned over to look below. As she did so, the railing gave away immediately; she plummeted 15 feet below to the ground level and sustained various injuries including head lacerations, a concussion, and multiple fractures to her pelvis.

In 1991, Errico filed suit against the LaMountains alleging that the balcony area was to be maintained by them and was left in an unsafe and defective condition. At trial, the jury awarded Errico $100,000. The LaMountains appealed.

Judicial Opinion

Flanders, Justice. At common law a landlord was not liable for injuries sustained by a tenant or a guest on the leased premises unless the injuries resulted either from a latent defect known to the landlord but not to the tenant or from the landlord's breach of a covenant to repair in the lease. The defendants urge that their conduct in this case was "clearly governed" by this line of authority and that application of the common-law rule should have

shielded them from any liability. They further claim that their lease agreement with Errico contained no express covenant to repair, that there was insufficient evidence of a defect in the balcony railing or, if the railing was defective, the defect was latent and they were unaware of any railing problem when they entered into the lease with Errico. For the reasons explained below, defendants' reliance on the common law rule is misplaced because it no longer serves to immunize residential landlords from liability for their failure to put and keep the leased premises in a fit and habitable condition.

The defendants' duties to Errico were defined and governed by the act, which took effect on January 1, 1987, and applies to rental agreements for residential dwelling units entered into, extended, or renewed after that date. The LaMountains' 1989 lease with Errico was such a rental agreement. In passing the act the Legislature hoped to "[s]implify, clarify, modernize and revise the law governing the rental of dwelling units and the rights and obligations of landlords and tenants." Thus the act's intended and actual effect is to supersede any common-law rules relating to residential tenants and landlords in conflict with its provisions. Among those obligations that the act imposes on landlords is the duty to "[m]ake all repairs and do whatever is necessary to put and keep the premises in a fit and habitable condition" (§ 34–18–22[2]). This duty, one of several set forth in the act as part of a landlord's ongoing responsibility to maintain the leased premises, is a continuing one, and the act does not provide that it ceases when the tenant takes possession of the leased premises. Hence we agree with Errico that § 34–18–22(2) created a duty that the

LaMountains owed to her by operation of law and that this duty was in full force and effect when the railing on her apartment balcony collapsed.

We agree with the trial justice that the evidence introduced at trial was sufficient to justify a finding that the wooden railing had deteriorated "well, well before the events of the Fall of 1989." Testimony established that just after the accident the ends of the railing's wooden spindles appeared to be rotten at the very point where they became detached during Errico's fall. Photographs introduced at trial further substantiated the railing's visible deterioration. And the unobjected-to evidence that defendants replaced the entire railing with new wood several months after the accident (and then reinforced the new railing by installing metal corner brackets) was also corroborative of the railing's unfit condition at the time of the fall.

To buttress their position that the railing had not been defective and that in any event they made reasonable inspections thereof, defendants rely in part upon the trial testimony of Mrs. LaMountain. She testified that "every year" she inspected the balcony, making a visual and tactile check of the railing ("I would just give it a good shake and test it"). She further testified that as a result of her inspection she believed the railing to be "perfectly safe." However, we note that the trial justice concluded that Mrs. LaMountain "was not a credible witness" and that "[h]er testimony in particular about her inspections and testing of the porch rail were not credible." The defendants also point to the testimony of Mr. LaMountain, whom the trial justice acknowledged was a "somewhat more credible" witness than his wife. He had inspected the railing during the course of painting it. Indeed he said he had given it a "good hard brush." But Mr. LaMountain, who knew the house was sixty years old when he purchased it, only painted the railing twice while he owned the structure, never leaned against it to test a person's weight, and never had the toe rail checked by a carpenter before the accident. We conclude that the observable evidence of the railing's physical deterioration, in conjunction with defendants' admission that they had inspected the railing at various times before the accident occurred, supports the conclusion of the jury and the trial justice that the railing was structurally unsound when Errico fell and that defendants either knew of this condition or failed to inspect the railing properly to detect this structural problem, thereby breaching their statutory duty to Errico. In light of the evidence supporting defendants' breach of their duty to repair and to maintain the leased premises in a fit and habitable condition, we conclude that none of the other alleged misstatements in the trial justice's negligence instructions—if in fact they were erroneous—constituted reversible error.

The defendants also argue that the trial justice committed error when she instructed the jury on the applicability of the doctrine of res ipsa loquitur to the case at bar. They contend that the doctrine is inapplicable here because other causes for Errico's injuries were not sufficiently eliminated by the evidence. In particular, they claim that the balcony railing that caused Errico's injuries was within the exclusive control and possession of Errico and her roommates at the time of the fall and for some three months before the accident.

Res ipsa loquitur is not a rule of either procedural or substantive tort law but is rather a form of circumstantial evidence. Where applicable, the doctrine "establishes inferential evidence of a defendant's negligence, thus making out a prima facie case for a plaintiff, and casts upon a defendant the burden of rebutting the same to the satisfaction of the jury. * * * [T]he burden of proof remains on the plaintiff, but the defendant has the burden of going forward with the evidence."

In *Parrillo v. Giroux Co.*, 426 A.2d 1313, 1320 (R.I. 1981), this Court explicitly adopted the approach taken by the Restatement (Second) of Torts § 328(D), at 156 (1965) for determining when this circumstantial-proof-of-negligence doctrine may be employed.

This approach disavows an earlier requirement of first having to establish a defendant's exclusive control of the premises for the doctrine of res ipsa loquitur to apply, thus parting company with Rhode Island's former rule that a plaintiff had to demonstrate that the defendant at the time of the accident exclusively controlled the instrumentality of the plaintiff's injury. "All that is required is that the plaintiff produce sufficient evidence from which a reasonable [person] could say that, on the whole, it was more likely than not that there was negligence on the part of the defendant." Thus, Errico was not required to establish that defendants were in exclusive control of the second-floor balcony in order to obtain a jury instruction on res ipsa loquitur. As previously referenced, the photographic and physical-inspection evidence suggested that the railing had been defective even before this tenancy began and had been in this condition when defendants conducted their inspections. Moreover, the act would have allowed defendants to obtain access to Errico's premises at reasonable times during the tenancy to conduct repair work and to take any other necessary steps to keep this railing fit and the balcony area habitable. And despite the LaMountains' suggestion that Errico was also negligent because she had been heaving garbage bags from the balcony when it collapsed, the mere presence of garbage bags at the scene was insufficient to lend any credence to this otherwise unsupported defense theory. Because the evidence in the record supported a jury charge on res ipsa loquitur and because that charge correctly followed the Restatement approach we adopted in *Parrillo*, we reject defendants' argument that the trial justice committed reversible error in instructing the jury on this issue.

Finally, the defendants dispute the trial justice's instruction that the jury could award Errico compensation for her alleged future impairment and disability from the injuries she suffered in the fall. They claim that there was no competent medical testimony to substantiate such an instruction. However, we need not decide whether medical testimony normally would have been a necessary condition precedent to such an instruction because Errico testified without objection that she learned during a visit to her orthopedic physician that the continuing pain she was experiencing "would be permanent." Having failed to object or to move to strike this testimony at trial, the defendants are unable to challenge on appeal the uncontested evidentiary predicate for this challenge to future-loss instruction to the jury.

For these reasons, the defendants' appeal is denied and the judgment of the Supreme Court is affirmed.

Affirmed.

Case Questions

1. What happened to Errico and how did it happen?
2. Who is responsible for maintenance of the balcony?
3. Was the inspection of the balcony enough?
4. What is *res ipsa loquitur*?

DUTY TO COMPLY WITH STATUTES AND REGULATIONS: THE AMERICANS WITH DISABILITY ACT

In addition to compliance with state and federal statutes already discussed, landlords must also be in compliance with the Americans with Disabilities Act (ADA) (42 U.S.C. §§ 12181-12189). The ADA requires the removal of "architectural barriers in places of public accommodation when those barriers are readily removable." While landlords must comply with ADA, the act does permit the landlord and tenant to allocate the compliance responsibility under the terms of their lease. In residential leases, the landlord makes the accommodations in the common areas and the tenant makes his accommodations in his individual dwelling. (See Chapter 9 for more details on commercial properties and the ADA.)

Practical Tip

When a landlord undertakes the responsibility of providing facilities, he or she must be certain those facilities remain in good repair and that no additional risks are created by the presence of the facilities.

Consider 8.7

Daniel Enriquez, an eight-year-old boy, was killed when he was struck by an automobile on a frontage road in the vicinity of the apartment complex where he lived with his grandparents. In the complex there was a playground built by the owner, the Cox Estates, for use by the children in the complex. The play area was enclosed by a fence. Immediately outside the fenced-in playground was a flood ditch, the frontage road, and the Interstate 25. A hole in the fence allowed the children to escape from the playground into the street area.

Fred Calkins, the personal representative for Daniel's estate, filed suit against the property owner/landlord for its negligence in failing to maintain the fence. Should the owner be held liable? *Calkins v. Cox Estates*, 792 P.2d 36 (N.M. 1990)

LIABILITY TO THIRD PARTIES

In addition to the tenants, other parties may enter the common areas of leased property or enter the dwelling units of tenants' guests. For injuries occurring to third parties in the common areas, the landlord is liable in the same way as with tenants—that is, is expected to exercise reasonable care in the maintenance of common areas.

The landlord's liability for injury to third parties while the third parties are actually in a dwelling unit varies according to the terms of the lease agreement. If the landlord has accepted the burden of repair and upkeep but fails to meet that burden, then resulting injuries to third parties are the responsibility of the land-lord. On the other hand, if the tenant has undertaken the responsibility of repair and upkeep, then such injuries to third parties are the responsibility of the tenant.

Sometimes both the landlord and the tenant are liable. For example, in a case where the landlord is to maintain and a nonremedied problem exists (such as a loose step), the tenant must warn third parties of the problem until the landlord has the chance to repair. If the tenant fails to warn visitors of the problem dur-ing the interim, both landlord and tenant could be held liable.

If the leased premises have code violations, the landlord is responsible for injuries to third parties resulting from such violations. Furthermore, even if the landlord has no statutory or contractual duty to repair, it is his or her responsi-bility to warn the tenant of any hidden defects and to post notices for third par-ties who might enter the property.

Today, landlords may have liability for the failure to provide adequate security or to screen those entering their property. The following case deals with the issue of the landlord's liability for injury to the tenants caused by others who enter the property.

Tenney v. Atlantic Associates

594 N.W.2d 11 (Iowa 1999)

Facts

Patricia Tenney arrived home early in the morning of December 5, 1993. She was raped by an unknown in-truder who had gained access to her apartment by use of keys on either December 4 or early on December 5. Tenney's apartment had two locks, including a dead bolt, and both locks required keys. There was no sign of a forced entry to the apartment.

When Tenney moved into her apartment, a Park Towne (the dba for Atlantic Associates) employee gave her the two master keys to her apartment because the tenant keys she was originally given for the apartment did not work. The employee said he would have to have the master keys to make copies because, with the tenant keys not working, they were the only keys to Tenney's apart-ment. Tenney's locks were not changed after the former tenant moved out so the same keys continued to open the locks to her apartment despite the change in tenants.

Tenney filed suit against Park Towne alleging negli-gence on its part in failing to maintain key records and se-curity on key access as well as its failure to change the locks upon the change in tenants. The district court en-tered summary judgment for Park Towne (Atlantic) and Tenney appealed.

Judicial Opinion

Larson, Justice. The district court ruled that, even assum-ing Park Towne and its tenant had a "special relation-ship," Park Towne still owed no duty of care to the

plaintiff to prevent her injuries at the hands of a third party. The reason given by the court was that

> [a] landlord must know or should know of an un-reasonable risk of injury [to owe a duty of care]. A landlord is not required to take precautions against a sudden attack from a third person which it has no reason to anticipate [and] [t]here is nothing in the record in this case which would place Park Towne on notice of po-tential criminal activity, let alone the type of as-sault which Tenney suffered.

Whether a duty exists is a question of law that may be properly resolved in a summary judgment proceeding.

A. *The duty.* A landlord is not an insurer against every conceivable act by a third party but is required to provide reasonable security against the injury under the circum-stances shown by the record. But

> [t]he fact that the actor realizes or should realize that action on his part is necessary for another's aid or protection does not of itself impose upon him a duty to take such action.
> Restatement [Second] of Torts § 314.

The Restatement provides a short list of special rela-tionships that, despite the general rule, create a duty to aid or protect others. This includes the relationship between an innkeeper and his guest. The innkeeper-guest relationship, because of its similarity to the landlord-tenant relationship, has prompted an evolution in the law of landlord-tenant relationships.

> Prior to 1979, there was no general tort duty on landlords to protect their tenants against criminal theft or attack. The situation began to change in that year, however, with the landmark decision of *Kline v. 1500 Massachusetts Avenue Apartment Corp.*, which imposed a duty of reasonable care upon the owner of an urban multiple unit apartment dwelling to protect its tenants from foreseeable criminal assaults. A growing number of courts have imposed similar duties of reasonable protection upon landlords to protect their tenants, and to protect others perhaps as well, from criminal attack, provided that such assaults are reasonably foreseeable and preventable *(Prosser & Keeton § 63, at 442–43 [footnotes omitted; emphasis added]).*

Kline, the case referred to by Prosser & Keeton, involved facts similar to those in this case, although in *Kline* a tenant was assaulted and robbed in a common hallway, not in her own apartment, as in this case. When Ms. Kline first moved into her apartment, doormen provided security at the entrances and the lobby desk was staffed at all times. Within a few years the doormen were gone, and the desk was left unattended much of the time, "in the face of an increasing number of assaults, larcenies, and robberies being perpetrated against the tenants in and from the common hallways." *Kline*, 439 F.2d at 479. The court noted that responsibility for providing security at the main entrance and in the common hallways and elevators was in the landlord, and the lessees of individual apartments were not in a position to provide it.

Kline discussed the rationale driving the rule denying recovery by tenants: generally a private person has no duty to protect another from a criminal attack; the criminal act is a superseding cause of the harm; it is difficult to assess foreseeability of criminal acts; any standard that the landlord must meet would be vague; adverse economic consequences would be incurred by the landlord; and public policy favors allocating protection of citizens to the government.

The court in *Kline* explained the rationale for the changed attitude of courts toward the landlord-tenant relationship:

> This court has recently had occasion to review landlord-tenant law as applied to multiple family urban dwellings. In *Javins v. First National Realty Corporation* the traditional analysis of a lease as being a conveyance of an interest in land—with all the medieval connotations this often brings—was reappraised, and found lacking in several respects. This court noted that the value of the lease to the modern apartment dweller is that it gives him "a well known package of goods and services—a package which includes not merely walls and ceilings, but also adequate heat, light and ventilation, serviceable plumbing facilities, secure windows and doors, proper sanitation, and proper maintenance." It does not give him the land itself, and to the tenant as a practical matter this is supremely unimportant.

> We conclude that a landlord, just as any other actor, owes a duty of due care to protect its tenants from reasonably foreseeable harm and

>> must act as a reasonable person under all of the circumstances including the likelihood of injury to others, the probable seriousness of such injuries, and the burden of reducing or avoiding the risk. . . . The questions of control, hidden defects and common or public use, which formerly had to be established as a prerequisite to even considering the negligence of a landlord, will now be relevant only inasmuch as they bear on the basic tort issues such as the foreseeability and unreasonableness of the particular risk of harm.

> We agree that this "'reasonable care in all the circumstances standard will provide the most effective way to achieve an allocation of the costs of human injury.'" This standard

>> should help ensure that a landlord will take whatever precautions are reasonably necessary under the circumstances to reduce the likelihood of injuries from defects in his property. "It is appropriate that the landlord who will retain ownership of the premises and any permanent improvements should bear the cost of repairs necessary to make the premises safe. . . . "

> A duty of care arising out of a landlord-tenant relationship, like that of an innkeeper and guest under Restatement section 314A, does not make the landlord an insurer. Nor will the rule of law be equally applicable in every case.

>> The duty in each case is only one to exercise reasonable care under the circumstances. The defendant is not liable where he neither knows nor should know of the unreasonable risk, or of the illness or injury. He is not required to take precautions against a sudden attack from a third person which he has no reason to anticipate, or to give aid to one whom he has no reason to know to be ill. He is not required to take any action where the risk does not appear to be an unreasonable one. . . .

> This rule of liability, which requires reasonable foreseeability, must be distinguished from premises liability under Restatement section 344, which arguably presupposes foreseeability.

For the reasons discussed, the plaintiff must eventually establish that the risk of harm by a third party was reasonably foreseeable to the defendant in order to establish a duty.

In the present case, the issue is whether the plaintiff's resistance to summary judgment presented evidence generating a genuine issue of fact on foreseeability. The plaintiff's resistance included answers to interrogatories that we believe generated a genuine issue of fact.

The plaintiff's own answers stated, in part:

> I saw a cabinet in the office containing many keys every time I entered which was always unlocked and often unattended.
>
> When I moved in, I was given 1 key that did not work (they had 2 keys when they showed [the] apartment). When I went back, they gave me 2 keys and stated that they were the only keys in existence and they would need possession of my keys later to copy for the master set. They never contacted me. I had a problem with the heat and the faucets and both times someone had entered my apartment with a key to work on [the] problem and left a note. This despite my being told there would be no entry without notice.
>
> When I received the 2 keys, a key ring identified for my apartment was taken off a hook in the cabinet. That key ring had numerous keys on it, at least 2 or 3 more.
>
> There is no doubt that I was assaulted by someone who gained entry with a key.

The answer to interrogatories regarding the plaintiff's two experts not only outlined their opinions as to the acts of negligence on the part of the defendant; they also made it clear that at least one prior act of attempted assault had happened on the premises. One witness, Phillip Schneider, is a professional appraiser experienced in facilities of this type. According to him, the defendant failed to respond adequately after a groundskeeper at Park Towne had entered an apartment with a key and attempted to sexually assault a tenant. (Park Towne continued to employ him for two years afterward.) In addition, Schneider noted the following factors that could reasonably be expected to lead to third-party crimes: failure to do appropriate background check of employees, failure to control access to master keys, failure to change locks prior to new occupancy, failure to maintain adequate security of regular keys, failure to establish and communicate policies to employees regarding keys, failure to maintain written policies with regard to keys, and failure to maintain written policies or communicate policies to employees regarding security.

Thomas Costello's opinions were also included in the plaintiff's answers to interrogatories. Costello is a certified public housing manager and a certified property manager. He is a former president of the St. Louis chapter of the Institute of Real Estate Management. His report highlighted the defendant's failure to adequately respond to the previous attempted sexual assault at Park Towne. He stated that the defendant "failed to act in conformity with the standard of conduct of a reasonably prudent apartment manager" by failing to take reasonable steps to prevent unauthorized access to the plaintiff's apartment. Further, according to him, the defendant lacked a proper management plan and was negligent in providing an on-site manager only about ten percent of the time. According to him, this is insufficient for a 400-unit apartment complex. In addition, the defendant failed to adequately secure keys and failed to change locks in nine years, "despite incidents that would cause provident [persons] to change the locks." In addition, his opinion was the master locks and keys were not properly accounted for.

We conclude that the court erred in finding as a matter of law that this defendant did not owe a duty of care to the plaintiff.

The defendant's motion for summary judgment did not allege the lack of material fact on proximate cause, but the court found as a matter of law that proximate cause could not be established because the intruder's action was a superseding cause. We address this issue, even though it was not raised in the motion for summary judgment, because it will likely arise at trial.

> The general rule is that [i]f the likelihood that a third person may act in a particular manner is the hazard or one of the hazards which makes the actor negligent, intentionally tortious, or criminal does not prevent the actor from being liable for harm caused thereby.

Restatement (Second) of Torts § 449, at 482. Further,

> [t]he happening of the very event the likelihood of which makes the actor's conduct negligent and so subjects the actor to liability cannot relieve him from liability. The duty to refrain from the act committed or to do the act omitted is imposed to protect the other from this very danger. To deny recovery because the other's exposure to the very risk from which it was the purpose of the duty to protect him resulted in harm to him, would be to deprive the other of all protection and to make the duty a nullity

Restatement (Second) of Torts § 449 cmt.b, at 483.

In the present case, the plaintiff's claim is that the violent acts of the intruder were reasonably foreseeable.

In *Stevens v. Des Moines Independent School District*, N.W.2d 117 (Iowa 1995), a middle school student sued the school for failing to protect him from injury by another student. We held that the willful act of the aggressor could not be considered a superseding cause under the rule just discussed. We conclude the district court erred in finding a superseding cause of injury as a matter of law.

We conclude the defendant is not an insurer of its tenants' safety, but it owed a duty of care to protect the plaintiff from reasonably foreseeable harm; the defendant failed to establish the absence of a genuine issue of fact regarding foreseeability; and the court erred in finding a lack of proximate cause as a matter of law.

We reverse and remand.

Case Questions

1. List some of the security issues you see in the way the keys for Tenney's apartment were handled.
2. Does it matter that a third person and not the landlord caused the harm to Tenney?
3. Does it matter that the landlord is held liable for criminal conduct?
4. Were Tenney's injuries foreseeable?
5. Did the landlord cause the injuries to Tenney?

Ethical Issue

Suppose that a landlord is aware that illegal drug activity is taking place on his leased property. What should he do? Should he evict the tenant? Can a lease contain a clause that permits eviction for illegal activity? What if the landlord can't lease the property to anyone except those who engage in illegal activity?

USE OF EXCULPATORY CLAUSES

To attempt to avoid liability to both tenants and third parties, landlords frequently include exculpatory or hold-harmless clauses in leases. These clauses provide that the landlord will not be liable for any injuries or damages occurring on the premises because of the landlord's negligence or the negligence of any other parties. Although these clauses can be found in many lease agreements, their legal effect is minimal. In other words, landlords cannot by provisions in agreements hold themselves harmless for injuries caused by their failure to maintain the premises or to comply with building and safety codes. The courts have interpreted such clauses, at least in residential leases, to be unconscionable and unenforceable, or in some decisions, void. Some states have enacted specific statutes that prohibit exculpatory clauses; and in states that have adopted the URLTA, the section on unconscionability has been used to invalidate exculpatory clauses. The following is an example of an exculpatory clause in a residential lease:

> *Lessor and his Agent shall not be liable for any damage or inconvenience to either person or property, that may be sustained by Lessee, his family, invitees, licensees, or guests on or about the premises herein leased, including damage or inconvenience resulting from breakdown or delays.*

Landlords may take two precautions to help reduce their potential liability for injuries caused to tenants and to visiting third parties. The first precaution is for landlords to obtain adequate insurance. The second is for leases to specify who is responsible for repair and maintenance. A repair and maintenance clause may alleviate the effect of repair and deduct actions by tenants and may also serve to determine who is liable in the event disrepair causes an injury to a third party.

Consider 8.8

Benson was a lessee in a building owned by Centennial Mills. A water pipe in the building burst, and water poured into Benson's apartment, destroying Benson's furniture, clothing, appliances, rugs, and draperies. It has been established that the pipe burst as the result of faulty maintenance. Benson has brought suit against

Centennial to recover damages for the loss of personal property. Centennial's defense is an exculpatory clause in the lease that says the landlord is not responsible for damages. What is the result? On the day the pipe burst, Benson had a guest staying with him, and the guest's personal property was also damaged. Does the guest have any rights against Centennial?

8.8, *continued*

Rights of Landlords and Responsibilities of Tenants

Landlords have several basic rights under the lease agreement that, in turn, constitute the tenants' responsibilities under the agreement. The purpose of leasing property is to have the property produce income; thus, fundamental is the right of landlords to receive timely rental payments pursuant to the terms of the lease agreement.

Tenants have an obligation to make timely rental payments according to the method and place of payment specified by the landlord. If a tenant does not make timely payment, there has been a breach of the lease agreement, and the landlord is permitted to take steps to minimize damages. Under URLTA Section 4.201, the landlord must give the tenant a written notice of nonpayment that states that the lease terminates within a specified period after receipt of the notice if rent is not paid. Although some states have changed the time constraints, the URLTA specifies that if rent is not received within 14 days from the time the tenant receives the notice of nonpayment, the lease will terminate within 30 days from receipt of the notice.

Most states provide specific procedures for having nonpaying tenants evicted from leased premises. Two names for this procedure are **forcible detainer** and **action for dispossession.** A distinct feature of these specialized procedures is that the defenses a tenant may assert are limited, so that the landlord is not kept in litigation for long periods while the tenant remains in possession of the property. For example, tenants may assert reasons for nonpayment that are justified under their states' landlord-tenant acts. Under the URLTA, defenses to nonpayment of rent are the landlord's failure to supply heat or water or the tenant's exercise of the right to repair and deduct for maintaining habitability of the premises. However, the right of asserting these defenses for nonpayment is limited to states that have recognized the right of habitability as being interrelated to the payment of rent and the existence of a valid lease agreement. In states not recognizing the doctrine of habitability, uninhabitability is not a defense to a landlord's action for possession.

In seeking to evict a tenant for nonpayment of rent, landlords must be able to establish that they have not waived their rights to timely payment. That is, if they have waited until the eighth day of the month for rent due on the first and have accepted the late payment, they will be bound by the delay period in the future unless they serve tenants with formal notice of the intent to exercise the right to timely payment.

In some states, landlords are afforded other remedies for nonpayment of rent. For example, in some cases a tenant abandons the premises and leaves personal property. Some states give the landlord a lien, an interest, or a right to possession of that personal property. Although some landlords attempt the private remedy of changing locks for a truly short dispossession action, the courts have invalidated such conduct on the grounds that the tenant has been denied due process.

In some cases, a tenant stops paying rent upon vacating the premises prior to the expiration of the lease term. The landlord has possession of the premises but no tenant to produce rental income. In these circumstances, the landlord has a right of action for breach of contract against the tenant to collect the lost rents and associated expenses of the property sitting vacant. However, most states do require the landlord to mitigate damages, which means that if it is possible, the landlord must rent the premises and recover from the tenant only for the period during which the apartment was vacant.

Consider 8.9

If a tenant abandons a leased apartment after performance of three months on a six-month, $650-per-month lease, and the landlord is able to rent the apartment for one of the three remaining months, what are the landlord's damages?

Nonpayment of rent is the typical reason for a landlord's action for dispossession, but any breach of the rental agreement by the tenant may result in a termination notice and dispossession action by the landlord. Examples of other breaches include breaking the rules and regulations, failing to maintain the premises according to the lease agreement, and performing illegal activities on the premises.

Tenants are also under obligation to use the landlord's property in such a way that is not destructive of its future value. In the absence of express agreement or permission, tenants cannot destroy vegetation, reconstruct buildings, or destroy existing structures. Their basic right is use without change or destruction. The parties to the lease should agree in advance on the addition of fixtures and what will happen to the fixtures at the end of the lease term, so that their placement or removal is not interpreted to be a waste of the landlord's property.

Consider 8.10

Richard Taylor was a resident of a Kenai low-income housing project owned by Gill Street Investments known as the Gill Street Apartments. Taylor's apartment badly needed cleaning and exuded a bad odor of which the neighbors complained. Taylor has admitted that he leaves his drapes open and walks around his apartment nude, and his apartment is located near the children's play area in the complex. Taylor was known to sit in his car for extended periods of time and honk his car horn if someone had parked in his parking space, and would continue honking until the car in his place was moved. Taylor was frequently drunk and frightened children when he was intoxicated. Taylor was current in his rent, but Gill Street Investments served him with an eviction notice. Could Taylor be evicted? *Taylor v. Gill Street Investments,* 743 P.2d 345 (Alaska 1987)

CAUTIONS AND CONCLUSIONS

In negotiating a lease, the following factors should be provided for, or at least considered:

1. What is the lease term? Must the lease be in writing? (Usually, leases for longer than one year must be in writing.)
2. When the lease expires, is there an option to renew? Can a month-to-month tenancy then exist?
3. How much notice, if any, is required for termination by both the landlord and the tenant?
4. Are there provisions for attorneys' fees? Does the tenant waive any legal rights?
5. Are pets and children permitted? Are water beds permitted?
6. Are there rules and regulations on noise, pool use, and so on?
7. Is there an exculpatory clause? If so, what is its effect?

8. Who is responsible for maintenance in the dwelling unit and in the common areas?

9. What provision is made for fixture placement and removal?

10. Are assignments and subleases permitted?

11. When may the landlord enter the tenant's dwelling unit without permission?

12. How much is required in deposits? What is the purpose of each deposit? Are deposits refundable?

13. How are utilities paid?

14. Is there a warranty of habitability? Do any items need repair or replacement prior to the beginning of the lease term?

15. Are there late penalties for rental payments?

Although the list does not include all areas that should be covered in the lease, it serves as a checklist for the areas causing both landlords and tenants the most problems and the most litigation.

Key Terms

Chapter Problems

1. Louis Varnado, a four-year-old child, sustained serious bodily burns from boiling water being carried in a pot by his grandmother from the kitchen to the bathtub of their apartment. The hot water in the apartment complex did not function and the landlord had not repaired the defective water heater despite complaints from the tenants. As a result, the tenants boiled water in their kitchens and carried it to their bathrooms in order to enjoy warm baths and basin water. Andrea Varnado brought suit against the landlord for her son's injuries that she says were caused by his failure to repair the water heater. Do you agree? Would you hold the landlord liable? *Bennett M. Lifter, Inc. v. Varnado*, 480 So.2d 1336 (Fla. 1985)

2. Garcia lived in a tenement house in the East Harlem section of Manhattan with his two young children. The paint in one of the rooms and in the bathroom was flaking off the walls, and Garcia's children were eating the paint and the flakes. In spite of Garcia's several complaints, the landlord did not remedy the problem. Garcia then expended $29.53 for materials and $70 for labor to replaster and repaint the walls in the rooms. He brought suit for the recovery of these amounts from his landlord. Could he recover these amounts from his landlord? *Garcia v. Freeland Realty, Inc.*, 314 N.Y.S.2d 215 (1972)

3. Thomas Campbell and Bonnie Glenn owned the apartment building located at 102-104 Bellevue Street, in the Dorchester section of Boston. Campbell was the day-to-day manager, supervising any renovations and collecting the rents.

On April 2, 1987, a Boston police officer, after observing heavy foot traffic in the building, made a drug-related raid and arrest in the building.

Break-ins were common at apartment no. 104-3. Following one of the break-ins, a different door was installed to apartment no. 104-3. The door had a hollow "peephole" below the traditional peephole and two "two by fours" were used to bar the inside of the door. After the new door was installed, transactions could occur by having the buyer put money through the lower peephole in the door. Drugs were pushed out the same hole to the buyer.

Campbell collected rents in the building. When he collected from apartment no. 104-3, he would be met by different individuals who claimed to be the occupant's cousin or brother. Campbell was never able to see inside apartment no. 104-3.

Three weeks after the new door was installed, Detective Sherman Griffiths of the Boston Police Department was shot and killed during the course of a raid on apartment no. 104-3. His widow (plaintiff) brought suit against Campbell and Glenn for their negligence in the operation and maintenance of their building. Are they liable? *Griffiths v. Campbell*, 679 N.E.2d 536 (Mass. 1997)

4. Mary Weatherall was a tenant in the Yorktown Townhome complex. She fell on the ice and snow accumulated outside her leased apartment and fractured her ankle. Can she recover from the landlord for her injury and the landlord's failure to maintain the premises? *Weatherall v. Yorktown Homeowner's Assn.,* 852 P.2d 815 (Okl. 1991)

5. In December 1989, Jack Vinson rented a home from Robert Hamilton under an oral month-to-month agreement. When Vinson moved in, he found the home to be in considerable disrepair. Vinson made some of the repairs in exchange for rent credit. He was willing to do more extensive repairs on the house, but, in return for his labor, he wanted a one-year lease plus rent credit. Vinson claimed that Hamilton agreed to these two demands.

Vinson then continued repairs, replacing a broken living room window, cleaning out the cluttered yard, and painting the exterior of the house.

By September 1990, the relationship between Vinson and Hamilton had deteriorated. While Hamilton was still willing to give Vinson a rental credit for his work, he disputed the accuracy of the bills for the repair work. Soon thereafter, Hamilton gave Vinson a 30-day notice of termination of the month-to-month lease. Vinson received a summons and complaint for a forcible entry and detainer (an action for eviction) on November 7, 1990. Can Vinson be evicted or does he have any defenses? *Vinson v. Hamilton,* 854 P.2d 733 (Alaska 1993)

6. Mr. and Mrs. John Julian, Sr., rented a home from Mr. and Mrs. Donald Linden for $150 per month in Silverhill, Alabama. In March, when it came time to mow the grass around the home, Mrs. Julian inquired of the Lindens about the yard and was told to assume responsibility for mowing "from the bushes to the highway, to the dirt road, from the highway back to the pecan trees." Within this area was a thicket, dense with undergrowth and small trees, that concealed an old shed.

In September 1985, Johnny Julian, the Julians' ten-year-old son, chased his puppy into the thicket and encountered the shed, rotting and dilapidated, for the first time. When his puppy ran into the shed, Johnny pulled himself up on an outside wall to try to see inside; some bricks over the opening where he had placed his hands to lift himself dislodged as the shed collapsed, and three of his fingers were severed.

The Julians filed suit against the Lindens on the theory that they had negligently failed to warn of a known hidden danger. Should the Julians win? *Julian v. Linden,* 545 So.2d 23 (Ala. 1989)

7. Ella terminated her six-month lease agreement at the end of three months by abandoning her apartment. Her monthly rent was $400. Although the landlord had several opportunities to rent the apartment, he refused, stating, "Why hassle with another tenant when I can sue and collect the $1,200 from Ella?" Is the landlord correct in his assumption?

8. Because of the landlord's refusal to fix a window in their apartment, the Haineses have had unusually high heating bills. They wish to know if they can either have the window repaired and deduct the repair costs from their rent or deduct the additional heating costs from their rent. Explain to them their rights under the URLTA.

9. Adam Armstrong rented Apartment 103-A located at 441 Kanekapolei Street in Honolulu from Jack Cione. The apartment was originally part of a two-bedroom unit within a cooperative building called the Waikiki Regent, which was constructed in 1959 and contained nine identical units.

On April 12, 1982, Armstrong's right hand and wrist were injured when a glass panel in the apartment's shower door shattered as he attempted to close it. The shower door was installed when the apartment was originally built and was constructed of three glass panels with hinged aluminum frames on an aluminum track. Safety glass was not used.

Cione says he was unaware of a crack in the door and Armstrong knew the door was difficult to close but never complained to Cione about the problem. Is this a breach of the warranty of habitability? *Armstrong v. Cione,* 736 P.2d 440 (Haw. 1987)

10. Margaret Skinner owned two adjacent parcels of land. She lived on one and leased the other to Bud Wellington on a month-to-month basis. The Bradys lived on the other side of Wellington. Skinner gave Wellington permission to keep two mules on the property. One was named Martin Luther and the other was named King. King acted like a typical, ornery mule. Basically he did not like anyone and would put his ears back and shy away when anyone got close to him. On the other hand, Martin Luther acted more like a horse than a mule. He was playful and friendly. The mules were docile and neither had ever kicked, bitten, or tried to injure anyone. They were no more dangerous than any other mules, but like other mules, they were unpredictable.

One day Arthur Brady, Jr., who was four years old at the time, was kicked by one of the mules. No one seems to know which mule kicked him. The Bradys filed suit. Is Skinner liable? *Brady v. Skinner,* 646 P.2d 310 (Az. 1982)

Internet Activities

1. For an overview of Landlord Tenant Law, go to: **http://www.law.cornell.edu/topics/landlord_tenant.html#menu**.

2. To see state adoptions and the text of the statute of the Uniform Residential Landlord and Tenant Act, go to: **http://www.law.cornell.edu/uniform/vol7%2ehtml#lndtn**.

3. For access to state landlord rights, statutes on eviction, security deposits, and other issues, go to: **http://www.rentlaw.com**.

4. For a site that details tenants rights, go to: **http://little.nhlink.net/nhlink/housing/cto/know/kyrr.htm**.

5. Using information obtained from the websites provided, which states are more favorable to tenants? landlords?

6. View various landlord and tenant forms and leases at **http://rhol.org/rental/forms.htm**.

7. Review the accuracy of tenant rights at **http://www.liv.asn.au/public/rights/rights-Landlord.html**.

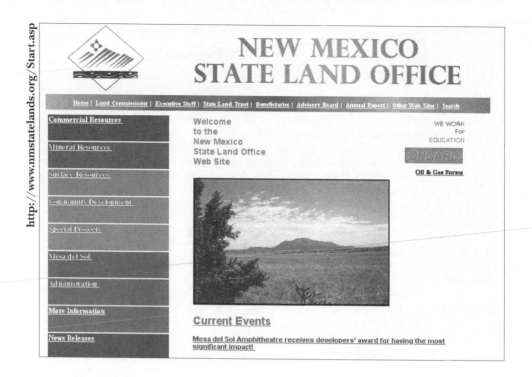

NEW MEXICO
STATE LAND OFFICE

Home | Land Commissioner | Executive Staff | State Land Trust | Beneficiaries | Advisory Board | Annual Report | Other Web Sites | Search

Commercial Resources

Mineral Resources

Surface Resources

Community Development

Special Projects

Mesa del Sol

Administration

More Information

News Releases

Welcome
to the
New Mexico
State Land Office
Web Site

WE WORK
For
EDUCATION

ONGARD

Oil & Gas Forms

Current Events

Mesa del Sol Amphitheatre receives developers' award for having the most
significant impact!

Chapter 9
Commercial Leases

All leases are negotiable.

David Kirk, Boston Financial Group[1]

Beware the clause and its effect.

Phillip M. Perry, Attorney[2]

Commercial leases are complex beasts. From office space in the World Trade Center to the neighborhood shopping center, commercial leases must address additional issues and topics not contemplated in the residential lease. Also, the statutory provisions and protections discussed in Chapter 8 for residential leases do not exist in commercial transactions. Many states continue to rely primarily on case law for their commercial lease law, interpretation, and protections. In this chapter the following questions are addressed: What are the requirements for the formation of a commercial lease? What topics and issues should a lessor and lessee address? What facts and information should be studied prior to entering into a commercial lease?

1., 2. "Clause and Effect," *Country Sampler and Country Business,* June 2000, p. 44.

FORMATION OF THE COMMERCIAL LEASE

Negotiations

While residential leases can be complex, commercial leases have additional issues that are often contingent upon business conditions, timely completion of construction, and compliance with agreements with other tenants. Accurate information is critical for the potential tenant. Who are the other tenants? What is the rental amount? How are the other tenants doing? In the negotiation stage, the rules for contract formation on misrepresentation and fraud apply. However, reliance on representations by leasing agents and landlords is risky. In commercial lease negotiations, independent verification of information is important, as the following case illustrates.

Practical Tip

Due diligence, or the examination of all aspects of a transaction, is as necessary in commercial leasing as it is in sales of land. Lessees should verify the accuracy of square footage, sales, and income claims. They should look into demographics and planned changes in the area that might affect the sales base. Reliance on rental agents' and landlords' information is misplaced.

Herring-Marathon Master Partnership B v. Boardwalk Fries, Inc.

979 F.2d 1326 (8th Cir. 1992)

Facts

Marathon owns and operates the Park Plaza Mall in Little Rock, Arkansas. The mall opened in July 1988, and on March 21, 1989, Boardwalk entered into a ten-year Lease Agreement with Marathon to operate a Boardwalk Fries restaurant in the Mall's food court.

Boardwalk, with Marathon's approval, sublet the Park Plaza Mall space to Ken Rittmueller and James Tandy as franchisees. Rittmueller and Tandy opened their mall restaurant on May 21, 1989.

In March 1990, Rittmueller and Tandy closed the mall restaurant and abandoned the premises due to poor sales. Marathon filed suit against Boardwalk for unpaid rents, and Boardwalk filed a third-party claim against Rittmueller and Tandy for the rent.

Boardwalk claimed that Marathon had misrepresented the sales of other tenants during the lease negotiations. When the annual rent was revealed to be $40,000 for the restaurant space, William Morris, Marathon's leasing agent explained, "Look, this mall is opening gangbusters. . . . We've got a couple of players in this food court that are going to do more than a million bucks." Jack Csicsek, Boardwalk's vice president for Franchising and Leasing, Rittmueller, and Tandy all described sales as the "only deciding factor" in their decision to lease in Park Plaza.

The trial court entered judgment for Marathon, and Boardwalk appealed.

Judicial Opinion

Loken, Circuit Judge. Boardwalk based its fraud defense primarily upon the trial testimony of Rittmueller and Tandy. Rittmueller testified that he had more than a dozen conversations with Morris between October 1988 and the signing of the lease in March 1989. During four or five of those conversations, Morris orally provided sales figures for other tenants of the newly opened food court. According to Rittmueller, Morris sent him a typewritten sheet listing four months' sales for four or five of the food court tenants—a document Rittmueller subsequently lost—but never showed him a Cumulative Monthly Sales Report. If Rittmueller's testimony is believed, the sales figures that Morris provided were substantially inflated. Tandy's trial testimony supported Rittmueller. However, Rick Smith, manager of the franchise restaurant, testified that he, Tandy, and Rittmueller were given a Cumulative Monthly Sales Report.

Morris testified that he discussed the sales volumes of other food court tenants with Rittmueller and Tandy before the lease was signed and that he responded truthfully to Rittmueller's and Tandy's inquiries about sales figures. Specifically, he told Rittmueller that Chick-Fil-A reported $130,000 in sales in August 1988, and that Sbarro's pizza restaurant reported sales of $77,000 to $80,000 for part of November and December 1988—figures that are consistent with the Cumulative Monthly Sales Reports for that period.

On appeal, Boardwalk contends that the district court erred in finding that Marathon's agent, William Morris, committed no misrepresentation. The monthly sales of other food court tenants declined significantly between the Park Plaza Mall's opening in July 1988 and the signing of Boardwalk's lease in March 1989. Boardwalk argues that Morris had a continuing affirmative duty to disclose that fact. In addition, Boardwalk claims that Morris at least had an obligation to disclose those declining sales in response to repeated requests for sales figures by Rittmueller and Tandy over the course of the lease negotiations.

We reject Boardwalk's contention that, under Arkansas law, Marathon had an affirmative duty to disclose the declining sales experienced by other food court vendors. "As a general rule there is no duty between vendor and purchaser to disclose any information affecting the value of property in an arm's length transaction." There was no special relationship between these parties giving rise to such a duty. As the district court found, Boardwalk is an experienced and knowledgeable restaurant franchising company that can be expected to know what information it needs to obtain in negotiating leases of this type. In these circumstances, Arkansas law imposes no affirmative duty to disclose other tenants' declining sales figures over the course of the lease negotiations.

Arkansas law does impose a duty on parties negotiating a real estate transaction to respond truthfully to material inquiries:

> [W]hen parties . . . deal at "arm's length" and in no confidential relationship, the prospective purchaser is under no obligation to volunteer information to the vendor; but if in such a situation, the vendor makes inquiry of material matters and the purchaser undertakes to make answers, then such answers must be truthful, unequivocal and non-evasive.

Relying on the testimony of Rittmueller and Tandy, testimony the district court expressly rejected, Boardwalk asserts that, in response to repeated inquiries, Morris provided Rittmueller and Tandy with a list of inflated sales figures. However, they claimed to have lost that list and, as the district court observed, "their explanation for the loss of this very important document is unconvincing and unsatisfactory."

Rittmueller and Tandy also testified that they never saw a computerized Cumulative Monthly Sales Report until after the lease was signed.

Morris testified that he responded truthfully to all inquiries about other food court vendors' sales, and the district court credited that testimony. The sales figures that Morris testified he provided orally to Tandy and Rittmueller were consistent with the Cumulative Monthly Sales Reports. On this record, we cannot conclude that the district court's finding that credited Morris's recollection of these conversations, rather than Rittmueller's and Tandy's, is clearly erroneous.

Finally, we note that the testimony of Boardwalk's vice president, Csicsek, provides independent support for the district court's decision. Csicsek testified that he, not the prospective franchisees, Rittmueller and Tandy, was solely responsible for negotiating the lease's economic terms. Csicsek testified that he made the decision to enter into the lease based upon one phone call to Morris. Csicsek admitted that he never saw a computer generated printout of other tenants' sales volumes, nor the document Rittmueller claimed to have received from Morris listing the sales figures for various tenants. In these circumstances, we agree with the district court that Boardwalk made an inadequate inquiry before signing the lease. If Boardwalk considered the prior sales of other tenants in the newly opened food court material, it should have unambiguously requested that Marathon provide the required information. Thus, Boardwalk's defense of fraud in the inducement is without merit.

Affirmed.

Case Questions

1. Who entered into the lease agreement?
2. Why was there a sublease and to whom?
3. What misrepresentation is alleged to have occurred?
4. What information should the lessees have examined before entering into the lease?
5. Does a leasing agent owe any duty to a prospective tenant in terms of disclosure?

(Ethical Issue)   While the court in the *Boardwalk Fries* case did not find misrepresentation, do you think there was adequate disclosure of information about the mall's sales performance? Does the statement about the mall opening "gangbusters" accurately reflect its performance? Was it unfair to only answer specific questions? Is affirmative disclosure necessary?

The Lease Agreement

As odd as it may seem, many commercial tenants are operating under oral lease agreements. Lease agreements, whether commercial or residential, need only be in writing according to the state's statute of frauds. Generally, that requirement runs from six months to one year. A lease with a term in excess of those periods must be in writing. However, a month-to-month commercial lease would not be covered by the statute even though the lease may run on for years. Despite the minimum requirement for a writing, all commercial tenants should have a lease agreement in writing. Reliance on oral representations of a landlord can be risky because courts cannot enforce oral promises unless there are exceptional circumstances. See Web Exhibit 9.1 for a sample commercial lease.

TOPICS IN THE COMMERCIAL LEASE

A successful landlord/tenant relationship in a commercial lease is the result of careful attention to details in the lease negotiations and in the lease itself. This section covers the typical provisions in a commercial lease.

http://

For information about commercial leasing opportunities in New Mexico, see: **http://www.nmstatelands.org/Start.asp**.

The Lease Term

Commercial leases carry peculiarities in terms of start or beginning dates that residential leases will not have. For example, many commercial properties have tenants with lease agreements before the property is constructed. In the Phoenix area, a developer who had taken on the responsibility of revitalizing the downtown section had commitments from businesses to be tenants in buildings that were to be constructed based on those commitments. Thus, the lease agreements existed before the buildings existed. Such arrangements are also typical with shopping centers and malls. The developer obtains commitments from large or anchor tenants prior to construction of the center or the mall, and the remaining tenants sign on for the yet-to-be-constructed stores on the basis of the anchor tenant's commitment.

In these types of leases, the start date of the leases is tied to completion of construction. However, completion of construction can change as the project progresses. The tenant will want protections for these fluctuations for purposes of planning and inventory holdings. Tenants in malls and shopping centers will want to negotiate their start dates around seasonal swings to avoid opening a business or moving a business to a new location during a slow period in the sales year. For example, retail outlets have highest sales from October through January, so that commencing a lease in October would be a profit maximizer. On the other hand, commencing a lease in February begins an obligation during a slow period, with a long wait for increased sales.

Another issue to arise with beginning dates is whether the tenant is allowed to move in before actual completion of the unit or the common areas and, if so, when rent will become due. Because of the uncertainty involved, it is probably best for the parties to put an outside date in the contract, that is, a date by which there must be occupancy or the lease is terminated. With an outside date, contingencies such as noncompletion, bankruptcy, and delays are covered. The developer is not tied to a specific date of completion but has a range, and the tenant has a latest possible occupancy date for planning purposes. The lease may even provide an option for the tenant to extend the outside date if the date passes and the tenant still desires to continue with the lease.

Premises Condition

The implied warranty of habitability or usability does not exist in commercial leases. If a tenant wants a guarantee that the leased premises will be delivered with certain repairs, conditions, or improvements, a warranty for these items must be in the lease agreement. Problems such as faulty heating or air-conditioning, leaking roofs, and broken windows should be described in the lease as repairs that are conditions precedent to the tenant's performance under the terms of the lease.

In recent years, the courts have become more helpful to commercial tenants, finding in some instances that the condition of the premises is sufficiently bad to constitute constructive eviction of a commercial tenant.[3]

Consider 9.1

Sandra and L. G. Hamilton leased an 11,584-square-foot residential property located at 1512 West Plato Road, Duncan, Oklahoma. The Hamiltons intended to operate their business, a recording studio, from the premises. When problems developed with the condition of the property, the Hamiltons sought remedies under the Oklahoma Residential Landlord Tenant Act. The landlord claimed that the residential remedies were not available to the Hamiltons because they were also using the property for commercial purposes. Who is correct? Does residential landlord/tenant law apply, or is this a commercial tenant transaction? *FDIC v. Hamilton,* 58 F.3d 1523 (10th Cir. 1995)

In addition to the initial condition of the premises, the parties should agree on which party will be responsible for maintenance. The landlord may want to specify that the obligation to repair does not arise until the tenant brings the condition of disrepair to the landlord's attention through a written notice. Some obligations of repair may be imposed upon the tenant, such as keeping trade fixtures in good working condition. For example, many tenants have an electronic sign outside their business; the obligation of repair and upkeep of that sign belongs with the tenant.

The parties may also wish to make a provision for emergency repairs—an authorization for immediate work in circumstances where the parties are unable to contact each other and the repair is absolutely necessary. Water leaks are an example wherein immediate action may save later costs and damage, and an emergency repair by either party without the other's approval can save money for both.

An additional complication of repairs on the premises is that of business interruption. During the course of renovation, the tenant may experience an interruption of customer traffic or may lose ease of accessibility because of

---

3.   *See* for example, *Truetried Serv. Co. v. Hager,* 691 N.E.2d1112 (Ohio.App. 1997) and *Echo Consulting Services, Inc. v. North Conway Bank,* 669 A.2d 227 (N.H. 1995).

construction blockage or hazards. The following case deals with this issue of a tenant frustrated by construction interruption of business and the limited common law protection available to these commercial tenants.

Bijan Designer For Men, Inc. v. St. Regis Sheraton Corporation

536 N.Y.S.2d 951 (1989)

Facts

The St. Regis Hotel (defendant), located at Fifth Avenue and 55th Street in Manhattan, was originally built in 1904. In November 1988, the hotel was designated by the Landmarks Preservation Committee as an official New York City landmark. The committee required that the hotel's heating, ventilating, air-conditioning, electrical, plumbing, and fire safety systems be installed or replaced.

Bijan Designer for Men (plaintiff) leases a two-story retail space situated in the St. Regis. Bijan has its own entrance from Fifth Avenue as well as entrances directly from the hotel's lobby and mezzanine. Bijan sells luxury-quality men's apparel and accessories, by appointment only, to a group it describes as "a distinguished and select domestic and international clientele of extremely well-to-do and renowned patrons." Bijan's lease commenced in 1981 for a period of 16 years. Bijan selected the site in the St. Regis because of the hotel's reputation, clientele, layout, security, and ambiance. Both parties expected Bijan to draw clientele from among the hotel's guests.

On June 30, 1988, the St. Regis was temporarily closed to commence the necessary reconstruction and renovation. The work was planned to take 14 to 18 months. The main doors to the hotel lobby were boarded up and access to the hotel lobby involved entering through a defunct restaurant and being cleared by a security guard.

Upon notification of the closure, Bijan informed the St. Regis that its rent would be paid into an escrow account. The St. Regis demanded payment, and Bijan filed suit to prevent the acceleration of rent.

Judicial Opinion

Saxe, Justice. It is the plaintiff's position that by closing the St. Regis, the landlord rendered useless Bijan's contractually provided-for access to the hotel, resulting in an actual partial eviction of Bijan. An actual eviction, whether partial or complete, suspends in its entirety the tenant's obligation to pay rent.

The Defendant relies on paragraph 14.A of the lease, which permits the lessor to, *inter alia*, "make such decorations, repairs, alterations, improvements or additions as lessor may deem necessary or desirable either to the Hotel or the demised premises" and further on provides that "the rent shall in no way abate while the decorations, repairs, alterations, improvements or additions are being made and Lessor shall not be liable to Lessee by reason of loss or interruption of the business of Lessee because of the prosecution of any such work or otherwise."

For its part, Bijan points out that the very first paragraph of the lease promises the tenant that "[t]he first floor of the premises shall have access to the Hotel's main lobby" and also that "[t]he second floor of the premises shall have access to the Hotel's mezzanine." Its position is that this right of access may not be abrogated by the landlord's right to repair. In addition, the tenant contends that the implied covenant of good faith and fair dealing prohibits the actions taken by the landlord.

These motions confront the court with competing policies. Restoration and renovation of an old landmark building should be welcomed and encouraged, and in fact, here, the landlord attempted to contractually provide for that right. On the other hand, the rights accorded a tenant, such as the negotiated-for right of direct access to the hotel lobby, must be carefully protected from undue interference, particularly where, as here, that right provides a substantial economic benefit to the tenant.

Here, the tenant certainly consented to renovations; it is less clear, however, whether that consent was so broad as to permit its right of access to be subsumed or negated by those alterations or improvements.

More recently, in *Broadway Copy Service, Inc. v. Broad-Wall Co.*, 77 A.D.2d 827, 431 N.Y.S.2d 13, where a landlord painted over the clear glass doors leading from the rear of a tenant's store to the building's lobby, it was held as a matter of law that this act did not constitute an actual partial eviction which would excuse the tenant from paying rent. Noting, however, that painting over the glass door prevented prospective customers from knowing the nature of the tenant's business and potentially deprived the tenant of possible sales, the court indicated that the tenant might have a cause of action for compensatory damages.

It is apparent that a landlord's breach of an express or implied lease term does not necessarily result in an actual eviction, but merely gives rise to a cause of action for damages.

The tenant points to several cases in which a landlord's acts constituted an actual partial eviction. For instance, where a landlord sealed and blocked off a freight elevator which opened directly into tenant's store, it was found that this action constituted an actual partial eviction.

When the facts alleged by the plaintiff are viewed in light of the foregoing cases, it is apparent that the plaintiff's theory of actual eviction cannot be supported. The plaintiff agreed to repairs, alterations or improvements either in the store or in the hotel, and that the landlord would not be liable for loss or interruption of Bijan's business due to such work. If extensive alterations made upon consent *within* the leased premises cannot amount to an eviction, I fail to see how extensive renovations made upon consent *outside* the leased premises can be said to constitute an eviction. Moreover, where the exculpatory clause is so broad, for the court to construe the clause to permit extensive work except where the hotel must be closed to customers would constitute a re-writing of the contract by the court. Furthermore, although sealing off contracted-for access has been held to constitute actual eviction, whereas the defendants point out the plaintiff continues to have access to the lobby and mezzanine, albeit a lobby and mezzanine which are part of a hotel undergoing renovations.

It is apparent that the parties, particularly the tenant, did not contemplate that any building renovation might necessitate a lengthy closing of the hotel. I therefore take the opportunity to note that especially where—as here—the value of the leasehold takes into account the presence of the landlord's clientele, tenants are well advised to provide for the eventuality of temporary closing for renovation, or at least to specify some limits to the exculpatory clause concerning repairs.

In the absence of such a provision, Bijan is left with a situation which may clearly have a negative impact on the value of the leased premises, but which just as clearly does not constitute an actual partial eviction. This is not to say that a tenant in the plaintiff's position is necessarily without recourse. Notwithstanding the exculpatory clause permitting renovations, a right to compensatory damages may exist if the landlord exceeded the rights granted by the lease, and if its actions constitute a breach of another term of the lease, such as a right of access or an implied covenant of good faith or quiet enjoyment.

There was no partial eviction.

Case Questions

1. Describe the layout of Bijan's leased premises.
2. Why was the hotel closed?
3. How long was the closure expected to last?
4. What arguments does Bijan make to justify its nonpayment of rent to St. Regis?
5. Will Bijan be given any relief?
6. What protections should have been drafted into the lease?

Rent and Rent Terminology

One unique aspect of the commercial lease is its terminology. Rental payments' terms and fees are very different from the flat monthly rates of residential leases. Although some older commercial leases do have flat per-month rates, called **gross rent,** this type of arrangement has been phased out over the past 30 years. Even if it is a part of the lease rent, the tenant will have some form of **escalation clause** that is a formula for extra rent beyond the base rent.

The most common form of commercial lease that has replaced the gross rent lease is the **triple net** or **net-net-net.** Under this arrangement, the tenant pays directly or reimburses the landlord for taxes, insurance, and maintenance expenses for the property and then pays the landlord a flat rate or **fixed rent** above and beyond the "net" amount paid for taxes, insurance, and maintenance.

For purposes of the triple net lease, *taxes* includes real property taxes and assessments including those on fixtures regardless of whether the landlord or tenant owns them. *Insurance* includes fire, casualty, and liability insurance to cover the tenant's operations. *Maintenance* includes not only maintenance and repair but also operational expenses such as utilities and other services.

Even the fixed rent lease may be subject to adjustment. Many retail centers carry a **Consumer Price Index (CPI) adjustment clause.** This clause ties the flat rate to the

CPI and allows the landlord to increase the fixed rent by the amount of increase in the CPI for the year. The lease may provide for a cap or a maximum increase that stipulates the rent will increase by the CPI increase or a maximum of six percent.

Some leases contain **specific happenings increase provisions.** For example, a lease may contain a provision that allows a rent increase in the event the developer or landlord is required to pay increased taxes.

As the popularity and hence size of shopping centers has grown, new rent payment ideas have been created to cover the costs of maintaining these large centers. For example, many tenants are responsible for their prorated share of **common area maintenance (CAM)** (sometimes called **operating expenses**).

Operating expenses can be a tricky part of lease negotiations for a tenant. Landlords have included everything from marketing expenses to elevator repairs in the operating expenses for their facilities. Some tenants negotiate out of their CAMs operating expenses the landlord's costs incurred because of the risk of operating a commercial facility. Excluded expenses would include the marketing expenses because they increase when consumer spending is down. Other tenants rely on the landlord for promotion of a center or mall that they could not provide for themselves to generate business. Some expenses, such as those related to the elevators, may be capital improvements and should be amortized, as opposed to expensed all at once.

At a minimum, tenants should negotiate full access to the landlord's operating expense records so that they can see what is being included. These expenses can increase the rent substantially. For example, it would not be unusual for a base rent in a commercial building to be $32 per square foot; with expenses the payment increases to $46 per square foot. Some leases place caps on expenses with base year restrictions or expenses being no greater than 5 percent above those of comparable properties.

Once the operating expenses are clearly defined, the tenant should negotiate carefully for the percentage of operating expenses he or she will pay. The allocation of operating expenses, or CAM, can be complex with the following representing one formula:

$$\frac{\text{Rental area of the tenant's premises}}{\text{Total of all rentable areas on the property}} \times \frac{\text{Total common}}{\text{area maintenance}} = \frac{\text{Tenant's}}{\text{monthly fees}}$$
$$\text{(gross leasable area)} \qquad \text{costs or CAM}$$

The language used in the formula is critical. If, for example, the formula used "rented areas" as opposed to "rentable areas," then the effect would be to transfer to the occupying tenants the costs of CAM instead of having the landlord carry those costs until the premises are leased. The definition of even "rentable areas" may need clarification such as whether mezzanines, basements, and other areas are included and the effect of having movable (cart) tenants selling smaller items in a mall.

Shopping center and mall leases usually carry a **percentage rent** that entitles the landlord to a given percentage of the tenant's gross receipts. When drafting a gross-percentage provision, the parties should remember the following details to facilitate collection of the intended fees.

1. A definition of gross sales should be included and should specifically state what is and is not included in the computation of gross sales.
2. Record-keeping obligations of the tenant should be specified, along with the landlord's right of examination and right to talk with the preparer and to have an independent auditor examine the records.

3. Details of how often the percentage is to be paid, when it is to be paid, and whether the tenant is required to submit periodic reports on sales should all be included.
4. The landlord should have a covenant of secrecy for the right of access. That is, the landlord should be permitted to examine books and records, but should be subject to suit and damages if such information is disclosed to others.

One difficulty in commercial leases is the definition of "gross sales." The following case illustrates the complexity of determining "gross sales."

Circle K Corporation v. Collins

98 F.3d 484 (9th Cir. 1996)

Facts

Circle K Corporation leased property from landowner Frank Collins and agreed to pay rent calculated at 2 percent of "gross sales" on the premises, with some exceptions specified. The lease was a 20-year lease and also provided for a minimum base rent. The lease went into effect in 1975. The lease clause on rent provided as follows:

Lessee shall pay annually as hereinafter provided as additional rent, the amount, if any, by which two percent (2%) of Lessee's "gross sales" (as hereinafter defined) exceeds the guaranteed minimal annual rent plus the sum of the real estate taxes and insurance premiums on the leased premises for such year. Said additional rent is hereinafter referred to as "percentage rent."

The lease defined "gross sales" as follows:

Gross receipts of every kind and nature originating from sales and services on the demised premises, whether on credit or for cash, in every department operating on the leased premises, whether operated by Lessee, or by a Sublessee, or concessionaire excepting therefrom any rebates and/or refunds to customers, refundable deposits on beverage bottles, telephone tolls, gasoline sales, money order transactions, the transfer or exchange of merchandise between the stores of Lessee if any, . . . and the amount of any sales, privilege license, excise or other taxes on transactions collected and/or paid either directly or indirectly by Lessee to any government or governmental agency.

In July 1981, Arizona instituted a state lottery. In August 1981, Circle K sent a letter to Collins, advising him that Circle K wished to sell lottery tickets at the store located on Collins's property. At the bottom of the letter was the following statement and a place for Collins to sign:

I, _____, the Lessor (or agent for same) do hereby accept and agree to allow participation in the Arizona Lottery by the Circle K Corporation upon and from the property/ies leased from me. I further agree to exempt and exclude any commissions and computation of sales of Arizona Lottery tickets from the calculation of any percentage rentals.

Collins did not sign the letter or return it to Circle K. Circle K began selling lottery tickets and did not pay Collins a percentage rate based on lottery ticket sales. Circle K filed for Chapter 11 bankruptcy in 1990. The bankruptcy court originally held that lottery proceeds were property of the state and should not be included in gross sales, but did include Circle K's commissions from the state for being a lottery agent. The Bankruptcy Appellate panel reversed and included gross sales revenue and Circle K appealed.

Judicial Opinion

Canby, Circuit Judge. This case requires us to interpret a contract. Although contract interpretation involves mixed questions of law and fact, the application of contractual principles is a matter of law.

It is a close question whether the Collins lease provides for percentage rent of two percent of Circle K's commissions from lottery sales, or two percent of total ticket sales price. We conclude, however, that the bankruptcy court's view is the correct one: percentage rent should be calculated only on the commissions. The parties have made comparisons to other types of receipts covered or not covered by the terms of the lease, but in our view state-sponsored lottery ticket sales fall into a class by themselves. They are quite unlike the general run of commercial operations mentioned in the lease. The State of Arizona has made Circle K one of its sales agents. State regulations require Circle K to pay over to the state its total proceeds from sales, less commissions and prizes awarded. The commission rate was originally five percent of ticket sales, and is now six percent.

In the hands of the State, lottery proceeds are used for various public purposes in the manner of tax revenues. In its ticket sales, Circle K acts more nearly as a tax collector for the State than as a retailer. It sells chances and takes custody of receipts, in which it has no interest beyond its commission, and remits them to the State. It is paid for its services by commission, and that commission is properly considered a "gross receipt" from "services" performed on the premises. We do not, however, interpret the lease as reaching the total funds received for the State in its calculation of percentage rent.

The only two cases squarely in point agree with this interpretation of similar leases. In *Cloverland Farms Dairy, Inc. v. Fry,* 587 A.2d 527 (1991), the Maryland Court of Appeals dealt with a lease, entered before Maryland authorized its lottery, that contained a clause as broad as the one before us. The lease provided for a percentage rent on "gross sales made in the store." It also provided that in computing "gross sales," the lessee was to take the total amount of sales of every kind made in the store and deduct therefrom the following, to the extent that same are included in such total amount: (1) refunds made to customers, (2) sales, excise and gross receipts taxes, and (3) proceeds from sale of money orders (fee received for issuance of money orders shall not be deducted).

Despite this broad language, the Court held that gross lottery sales did not fall within the percentage rent clause. The Court recognized that reasonable persons "would have thought that the additional rental percentage clause encompassed the sale of any and all items, not expressly excluded, which *Cloverland* would sell in its store in the course of its business activities." Lottery sales did not fall in that category.

The Maryland Court in *Cloverland* relied in part on the only other case cited to us that dealt with the same issue, *Anest v. Bellino,* 151 Ill. App.3d 818, 104 Ill. Dec. 861, 503 N.E.2d 576 (1987). *Anest* held that gross lottery sales did not fall within a percentage rental clause applying to "all gross sales." The Court stated:

Although the restaurant actually handled the money, that portion of the money belonging to the lottery system was not intended by the parties to be included in gross sales. Only the commissions and bonuses belong to the restaurant, and only those amounts increase the restaurant's sales.

Arizona has no decisions in point, but we have no reason to believe that its courts would diverge from these two decisions that are the only ones to have dealt with the lottery issue in connection with percentage rent clauses. The same factors that led Maryland's and Illinois' courts to exclude total lottery sales exist in this case. The money collected by Circle K, except for commissions, belongs to the State. Lottery sales were not part of the Circle K's regular business in the reasonable contemplation of the parties at the time the lease was entered into; they are in a class by themselves. If the parties had foreseen the future legalization of lottery sales, and had addressed the question specifically in the lease, the nature of other exceptions suggests that total proceeds other than commissions would have been excluded from "gross sales." The arguable-comparable activity of money order transactions was so excluded, as were receipts from refundable deposits on beverage bottles, and sales taxes that Circle K collected but transferred to the State. Thus the same kinds of considerations that led to the decisions in *Cloverland* and *Anest* are present here.

We conclude that the term "gross sales" in the percentage rent term of the lease agreement did not include the total sales price of state lottery tickets. "Gross sales" included only the commissions that Circle K received in exchange for its services in selling the tickets. The decision is therefore reversed.

Reversed.

Case Questions

1. When was the lease negotiated? How were "gross sales" defined?

2. What have other states done with the issue of lottery sales with respect to rental percentage clauses?

3. Why is the issue of the sale of money orders similar?

4. Is it significant that Collins did not sign the letter on the lottery sales?

On June 7, 1968, Sears entered into a "Shopping Center Lease" (lease) with Honey Creek Square, Inc. (Honey Creek), to lease space in its mall, Honey Creek Square Shopping Center. The lease became effective on November 1 of that year for a term of 30 years plus four 5-year options.

Consider 9.2

9.2, *continued*

The lease is a standard Sears form that was modified pursuant to negotiations between Honey Creek and Sears. Rent due from Sears under the lease is based solely on a percentage basis of Sears' net sales made on the Honey Creek Store, with no guaranteed minimum. The monthly amount is calculated according to paragraph 8 of the lease, which reads in pertinent part:

(a) Tenant, in consideration of said demise, does covenant and agree with Landlord to pay as rental for all of said demised premises (including the above mentioned retail store and attached Tire Service Station) a sum equal to three per cent (3%) of so much of "Net Sales" (as herein defined), made by Tenant upon the demised premises during any Lease Year (as herein defined) during the first three (3) years of the term hereinabove provided, as are not in excess of Eight Million Dollars ($8,000,000), and a sum equal to two and one-half per cent (2½%) of so much of such Net Sales made by Tenant upon the demised premises during any Lease Year commencing with the fourth year of said term and continuing thereafter to the end of said term, as are not in excess of Eight Million Dollars ($8,000,000), and a further sum, applicable during the entire lease term, equal to one and one-half per cent (1½%) of such Net Sales as are in excess of Eight Million Dollars ($8,000,000), said rentals to be paid in monthly installments within fifteen (15) days after the end of each calendar month during the term hereof.

(b) The words "Net Sales" as used herein mean gross sales made upon the demised premises by Tenant and its departmental sublesses, concessionaires and licensees occupying space upon said demised premises, but deducting or excluding, as the case may be, the following: (i) Sales of departments or divisions not located upon said demised premises; (ii) The amount of all sales, use, excise retailers' occupation or other similar taxes imposed in a specific amount, or percentage upon, or determined by, the amount of retail sales made upon said demised premises; (iii) Returns and allowances, as such terms are known and used by Tenant in the preparation of Tenant's profit and loss statements; (iv) Delivery, rental, installation and service charges; (v) Amounts in excess of Tenant's (or of its sublessees', concessionaires' and licensees'), cash sales price charged on sales made on credit or under a time payment plan; (vi) Sales of merchandise ordered through the use of Tenant's catalog order channels, regardless of the place of order, payment, or delivery; (vii) Policies of insurance sold on said demised premises and the premiums collected on policies of insurance; (viii) Sales made through the Commercial and Industrial Sales Department of Tenant.

Sears paid rent to Honey Creek Square, Inc., without incident until December 1981, when Honey Creek requested and carried out an audit in accordance with the terms of the lease. The auditor's report stated that in December 1981, Sears did not include in net sales the following:

9.2, *continued*

Alteration sales	$ _____
Gift-wrapping sales	$1,262
Bike set-up sales	$112
Auto labor sales	$16,269
Service contract (maintenance agreement) sales	$53,513
Service center sales	$13,217

Sears admits that these amounts were not included in its report of net sales for December 1981. Sears stated that it had never included income from these categories in its net sales figure, except auto labor, which had been included from November 1977 through September 1981, because of a misunderstanding on the part of its in-store controller.

Can Honey Creek recover rent based on the above exclusions from net sales? *Washington National Corporation v. Sears, Roebuck & Co.,* 474 N.E.2d 116 (Ind. 1985)

Other topics that should be covered in the rental portion of a commercial lease include the place payment is to be made, to whom payment is to be made, whether there are penalties for late payment, and how much those penalties will be.

Security deposits are typical in commercial leases and can be substantial, so that the landlord is assured of payment. Because there is no uniform act on commercial leases, the parties should specify the purpose of the security deposit, whether it will be returned, on what grounds it can be retained, and whether there will be any time limits for returning the deposit upon termination of the lease.

Fixtures and Alterations

In most cases, the commercial premises being leased consist of walls, a roof, and a door. Generally, very little has been done to improve, finish, or decorate the interior of each retail space. There are substantial cost issues as to who will make the necessary improvements, alterations, and construction to render the premises usable for a retail operation. It is generally the responsibility of the tenant to make the interior ready for operation because the landlord does not know the operation or needs of the tenant's business as well as the tenant does. This requirement of completion, plus any restrictions the tenant may have in altering the premises (because of building codes or the landlord's hesitancy or preference), should be set forth in the lease agreement. If the landlord wants limited or movable wall installation, such a restriction should be specified in the agreement.

An issue directly related to the tenant's responsibility of improvement and completion is what happens to all the improvements the tenant has made once the lease is terminated. In other words, are the improvements treated as trade fixtures or do they become permanent fixtures and property of the landlord? Although legal guidelines determine what a trade fixture is and what remains as the landlord's property (see Chapter 4), it is best for the parties to specifically provide for this.

One method of providing for all phases of tenant alterations is to place a provision in the lease that requires the tenant to obtain prior written approval of the landlord for all proposed alterations. Under this arrangement, the tenant supplies the landlord with a written proposal that includes specifications for what constitutes a fixture in the proposed alteration and what will remain the property of the tenant as a trade fixture.

Operations

Commercial leases should list the hours of day-to-day operations as well as the days of closure. For example, many office buildings will be open for operation from 6:00 A.M. until 9:00 P.M. on weekdays, with limited access on Saturdays and Sundays. Many leases list specific holidays in which there will be no access or available amenities. In Arizona, critical portions of office building leases include those days during which the air-conditioning for the facility will not be running. In the summer months, the buildings would not be usable on those days. Commercial tenants must negotiate specific days, holidays, and hours for operation.

Shopping center leases contain additional provisions, such as hours of operation. It does small tenants little good to be open for business if the large tenants in the center have different hours of operation and are not open to attract the foot traffic. The hours of operation are particularly critical for shopping malls, since access will be controlled at the doors to this closed environment.

Consider 9.3

Thomas Wingard and seven other dealers who operate service stations in the Columbia, South Carolina area, pursuant to franchise lease agreements with Exxon Co., USA, brought suit against Exxon seeking relief from a clause in their leases that requires them to operate their stations 24 hours per day and seven days per week.

Exxon had established a uniform 24-hour operation provision in its leases in 1988 as part of a marketing strategy. All stations with a minimum of 30,000 automobiles per day nearby a competing station open 24 hours per day, or another 24-hour traffic generator in the area, had to operate 24 hours per day and seven days per week. The clause was offered on a "take it or leave it" basis to the dealers, but they were given the opportunity to review the lease and take it to an advisor before signing. Exxon did require each dealer to initial the 24-hour operations clause.

The dealers claim the clause is unfair, unconscionable, and unenforceable. Are they right or can Exxon require 24-hour operations from its lessees/franchisees? *Wingard v. Exxon Co.*, 819 F. Supp. 497 (D.S.C. 1992)

Common Areas

MANAGING ACCESS

Commercial leases should contain specific provisions on the responsibilities and liabilities for maintenance and safety of the common areas. Businesses and offices will have operational difficulties themselves if the common areas are unsafe, unclean, or simply inaccessible. The landlord should assume responsibility for maintenance and security of these areas. Further, the lease should provide for tenant rights in the event the landlord fails with respect to this responsibility. A critical area in shopping center leases is the availability of parking for those using the tenants' offices and businesses. Conflicts can result when there is shared parking among commercial tenants, and lease provisions should address overflow issues and accommodations. For example, some tenants have specifically designated spaces in the center parking lot so that customers can gain access.

Consider 9.4

Douglas Theater Corporation (Douglas) operates the Ivanhoe Theater in Chicago. Gold Standard Enterprises, Inc. operates a liquor store. Both were tenants of a common landlord and shared a parking lot. Gold Standard's lease was dated May 22, 1978, and ran to September 30, 2003. The Douglas lease was dated March 15, 1982, and ran to June 30, 1987.

9.4, *continued*

In 1982, Gold Standard purchased its underlying property as well as the common parking lot, subject to all tenants' rights under their leases. In 1987, Douglas exercised an option to purchase its underlying theater property. On June 30, 1987, Douglas entered into a parking lot lease with Gold Standard to run until September 30, 2003. The lease gave responsibility for maintenance and operation to Gold Standard. The use of the parking lot was granted in common on a first-come-first-serve basis.

Gold Standard was open for business from 10:00 A.M. to 10:00 P.M. weekdays and Saturdays and on Sundays from noon to 6:00 P.M.. The theater was open 40 weeks per year, with shows running from 8:00 to 10:00 P.M. Tuesday through Saturday with 2:00 P.M. matinees on Saturday and Sunday. The theater was doing well, with the result that exits and access to Gold Standard were blocked. Both parties began having cars towed, and eventually the parties went to court over the issue. What should the court do? Has the landlord failed in his responsibilities? *Douglas Theater v. Gold Standard Enterprises, Inc.,* 544 N.E.2d 1053 (Ill. 1989)

MANAGING FREE SPEECH

One of the interesting aspects of shopping center operation is the presence of individuals who are seeking support for particular political causes. Their presence provides an interesting interaction between their First Amendment rights and the rights of the shopping center owners. Currently there is much litigation and debate over this issue, but the U.S. Supreme Court gave demonstrators certain rights in *Pruneyard Shopping Center v. Robins,* 474 U.S. 74 (1980), and various state and local regulation of such demonstrators' rights remains a topic of constitutional litigation. In the U.S. Supreme Court decision in *Hurley v. Irish-American Gay Group of Boston,* 515 U.S. 557 (1995), the Court held that interference with private speech rights by requiring public accommodation of all views presents First Amendment violations. States must be cautious in mandating speech rights of certain groups on commercial properties.

Twelve of the 17 states that have reviewed the issue of demonstrators' access to shopping centers have permitted the shopping center owners to restrict that access. California, Colorado, New Jersey, Massachusetts—the Massachusetts law was reviewed in the *Hurley* case—and Washington permit free speech on commercial properties but do vary in the type of speech allowed. For example, some permit only the solicitation of signatures for ballot propositions and candidates under the theory that the modern commercial center is the equivalent of the town square where free speech was practiced and protected.[4]

MANAGING SAFETY

The liability of commercial landlords for injuries to tenants and tenants' employees by third parties who enter the leased property is an area of increasing litigation. The standard, as the following case illustrates, is similar to the residential landlord standard of foreseeability of the conduct of third parties.

---

4.   For a look at some of the shopping center and free speech cases, see *New Jersey Coalition v. J.M.B. Realty Corp.,* 650 A.2d 757 (N.J. 1994); *Bock v. Westminster Mall Co.,* 819 P.2d 55 (Colo. 1991); *Betchelder v. Allied Stores Int'l, Inc.,* 445 N.E.2d 590 (Mass. 1983) and *Alderwood Associates v. Washington Environmental Council,* 635 P.2d 108 (Wash. 1981). Washington has a latter limiting case: *Southcenter Joint Venture v. National Democratic Party Committee,* 780 P.2d 1282 (Wash. 1989).

Sharon P. v. Arman, Ltd.

65 Cal. Rptr. 643 (Cal. App. 1997)

Facts

Sharon P. (plaintiff) was an employee at a business located in the Coast Savings building located at 1180 South Beverly Drive, Los Angeles. On Thursday, April 8, 1993, Sharon P. entered the underground parking garage of the building at 11:00 A.M. and parked in her assigned space. While she was leaning back into her car to remove some items from her back seat, a man with a gun who was wearing a ski mask approached her. She was forced back into her car and sexually assaulted.

In the months preceding her attack, the condition of the parking garage had deteriorated. Lights were out (the lights were out in the immediate area of her attack that day), areas of the garage smelled of urine, and security cameras in the garage had not worked for months. In some places there were cots set up where apparently the homeless had moved into the garage.

Sharon P. brought suit against Arman, Ltd. (defendant), the owner of the building and garage, and APCOA (defendant), the manager of the parking garage. APCOA's responsibilities were collection of revenues from those using the garage. The trial court entered summary judgment for Arman and APCOA. Sharon P. appealed.

Judicial Opinion

Croskey, Acting Presiding Judge. To prove that she has a valid cause of action against defendants for negligence, plaintiff must show (1) defendants owed her a duty of care, (2) defendants breached that duty, and (3) she suffered injuries which were proximately caused by defendants' breach of duty. (*Ann M., supra,* 6 Cal.4th at P. 673, 25 Cal.Rptr.2d 137, 863 P.2d 207.)

Landowners are required to "maintain land in their possession and control in a reasonably safe condition. . . . " In the case of a landlord, this general duty of maintenance, which is owed to tenants and patrons, has been held to include the duty to take reasonable steps to secure common areas against *foreseeable* criminal acts of third parties that are likely to occur in the absence of such precautionary measures. [Citations omitted.]."

Regarding the primary factor of foreseeability, a landowner's "duty to take affirmative action to control the wrongful acts of a third party will be imposed only where such conduct can be reasonably anticipated." In this, as in other areas of tort law, foreseeablity is a crucial factor in determining the existence of duty. However, a landowner has a duty "to exercise reasonable care to discover that criminal acts are being or are likely to be committed on its land."

Restatement Second of Torts, section 344, comment (f), details the "foreseeability" circumstances under which the duty of a landowner to protect others from the wrongful acts of a third party arises:

'Since the [owner of land] is not an insurer of the visitor's safety, he is ordinarily under no duty to exercise any care until he knows or has reason to know that the acts of the third person are occurring, or are about to occur. He may, however, know or have reason to know, from past experience, that there is a likelihood of conduct on the part of third persons in general which is likely to endanger the safety of the visitor, even though he has no reason to expect it on the part of any particular individual. If the place of character of his business, or his past experience, is such that he should reasonably anticipate careless or criminal conduct on the part of third persons, either generally or at some particular time, he may be under a duty to take precautions against it, and to provide a reasonably sufficient number of servants to afford reasonable protection.'

In *Ann M.,* the court determined that the scope of duty owed by the defendant to the plaintiff did not include providing security guards for the common areas of the shopping center. The court based its conclusion on the absence of prior incidents similar to the one which injured the plaintiff. Plaintiff had been raped while working in a store in the shopping center. The store, a photo processing service, was located in a secluded area of the shopping center. The shopping center generally contained about 25 commercial tenants. The lease between the photo processing service and the defendant owner of the strip mall gave the defendant the right to police the common areas of the mall, but did not impose a duty on the defendant to do so. The plaintiff was raped, and the store robbed, at 8 A.M. There was evidence that prior to the assault, there had been incidents of bank robberies, robberies of shoppers, violent purse snatchings, break-ins and assaults by a man who would come up behind women shoppers and pull down their pants. The defendant responded with evidence that its records contained no references to violent criminal acts in the shopping center prior to the rape of the plaintiff and that it was defendant's standard practice to record instances of violent crimes. There was also evidence that prior to the rape, employees and tenants in the shopping center were concerned about their safety because of transients who loitered in the common areas; and the police had been called twice about such persons. The tenants discussed hiring foot patrols but determined it would be too expensive. They asked defendants to provide patrols but defendant declined. Ultimately, the tenants hired a security company to drive by the center several times a day. Plaintiff was raped thereafter. There was no evidence that the rapist was a loitering transient.

The court stated that the heart of the case was whether the defendant "had reasonable cause to anticipate that criminal conduct such as rape would occur in the shopping center premises *unless it provided security.*"

The *Ann M.* court found that the evidence presented by the parties in that case precluded a finding that violent criminal assaults were sufficiently foreseeable to impose a duty on the landlord to provide security guards in the common areas. First, even assuming the landlord knew of the previous criminal activities at the shopping center, they were not similar in nature to the crime plaintiff suffered—rape. Second, none of the plaintiff's other evidence (the presence of transients and the statistical crime rate in the surrounding area) was "sufficiently compelling to establish the high degree of foreseeability necessary to impose upon [the landlord] a duty to provide security guards in the common areas."

Our conclusion that a lack of prior *similar* incidents is not dispositive of this appeal is supported not only by *Ann M.*'s narrow focus on the existence of a duty to provide security guards, but also upon the fact that the court expressly left open the question of "whether some types of commercial property are so inherently dangerous that, even in the absence of prior similar incidents, providing security guards will fall within the scope of a landowner's duty of care." The court specifically mentioned two particular types of such commercial property—all-night convenience stores *and parking garages.* The court stated that the plaintiff had "offered no evidence to show that, *like a parking garage* or an all-night convenience store, a retail store located in a shopping center *creates 'an especial temptation and opportunity for criminal conduct.'*"

Absent sufficient and desirable mass transit, parking garages are, and will continue to be, as common as vehicles themselves. The need for such facilities can hardly be avoided, especially given California's love affair with the automobile and its lack of effective mass transportation. Therefore, they should be made to be both functional and safe. However, as they are located on private property, they are not routinely, or even sporadically, patrolled by the police. Public policy dictates that persons who

profit from owning or managing facilities, which by their very nature create "an especial temptation and opportunity for criminal conduct," should supply at least the minimal amount of security warranted under the particular circumstances of the case. Whether or not there is moral blame attached to defendants' conduct in the way they operated and managed the parking garage, the finding of a duty of care furthers public safety.

As for the economic consequences of such a duty of care, there is no evidence that the cost of providing sufficient protection cannot reasonably be passed on to the persons who utilize the parking garage. For example, there is no evidence that such tenants cannot bear the added expenses themselves or pass it along to their customers. The "cost" of parking should include its entire cost, including reasonable security measures.

Defendants argue that there was "no effective way" to keep out persons who might engage in criminal conduct and that any requirement for the posting of a security guard would impose "an unreasonable burden." With respect to the first point, it is not necessary to succeed in order to persevere. That the task of making the garage reasonably safe might well have been difficult of achievement, cannot justify doing nothing. As to the second point, there is nothing in the record to demonstrate that any "unreasonable burden" would necessarily be involved; it is not at all clear that security guards would have been required.

We have concluded that a criminal assault on plaintiff was reasonably foreseeable and . . . we hold that defendants owed to plaintiff a duty of care to provide reasonable security.

Whether the defendants, in their management and operation of the garage, met their duty to plaintiff, and if not, whether the breach of that duty was a substantial factor in plaintiff's injuries are issues which will have to be addressed on remand.

Reversed.

Case Questions

1. What are the differences between parking lots in strip malls and parking garages?
2. Are parking garages inherently dangerous?
3. Was Sharon P.'s assault foreseeable?
4. Who is liable to Sharon P.?
5. Who will pay for the costs of additional security in parking garages?

Consider 9.5

One of the difficult issues many shopping center malls face is the presence and access of teenagers to the mall. Referred to as "mall rats," these teenagers often become aggressive and harass tenants and customers alike. They "travel" in groups in the malls and often congregate in intimidating large groups. Their activities can stretch through an entire day. What actions could a landlord take with regard to mall rats? Should a landlord take any action? Do tenants need protection against their presence? Do the mall rats present any security risks?

Americans with Disabilities Act

THE BASICS OF THE LAW

The **Americans with Disabilities Act (ADA)** (42 U.S.C. § 12007 [1990]) was passed "to provide a clear and comprehensive national mandate for the elimination of discrimination against individuals with disabilities," and to establish "clear, strong, consistent enforceable standards" for "scrutinizing such discrimination."

Section 302 of the ADA provides that "no individual shall be discriminated against on the basis of disability in the full and equal enjoyment of the goods, services, facilities, privileges, advantages, or accommodation by any person who owns, leases (or leases to), or operates a place of public accommodation."[5]

Those who fit the categories of owner, operator, lessee, and lessor must make "reasonable modifications" in "policies, practices, or procedures" that are necessary to allow individuals with disabilities access to their goods, services, or facilities.

The following case deals with an unusual ADA disability issue.

Staron v. McDonald's Corporation

51 F.3d 353 (2d Cir. 1995)

Facts

Matthew Staron and others who joined him in this suit (plaintiffs) went to both a McDonald's and Burger King restaurant (defendants) in Connecticut. They found the air in both to be full of tobacco smoke. Because of their various physical conditions, including asthma, they were unable to enter these places without encountering breathing difficulties.

They registered complaints with the State of Connecticut Human Rights Commission and received no results to their satisfaction. They filed suit seeking a judicial declaration that the smoke-filled restaurants were violations of the ADA and that the restaurants were required to adopt "No Smoking" policies in order to comply with the law.

The District Court dismissed the suit and the plaintiffs appealed.

Judicial Opinion

Walker, Circuit Judge. The ADA was promulgated "to provide a clear and comprehensive national mandate for the elimination of discrimination against individuals with disabilities," as well as to establish "clear, strong, consistent, enforceable standards" for scrutinizing such discrimination . . . [d]efendants do not dispute that the section applies to them as owners and operators of public accommodations. They also concede at this point that plaintiffs qualify as "individuals with disabilities"

---

5.   Examples of the traditional form of real property accommodations under ADA include sufficient width in aisles and restrooms for wheelchairs (*Pinnock v. International House of Pancakes*, 844 F. Supp. 574 [S.D. Cal. 1993]); permitting guide dogs for the visually-impaired (*Crowder v. Kitagawa*, 842 F. Supp. 1257 [D. Haw. 1994]), installation of elevators (*Tyler v. City of Manhattan*, 849 F. Supp. 1429 [D. Kan. 1994]); resurfacing of streets and sidewalks to remove potholes and ensure smooth surfaces for wheelchairs (*Kinney v. Yerusalim*, 9 F.3d 1067 [C.A. 3 1993]); and reversal of policy prohibiting wheelchairs on the Little League field (*Anderson v. Little League Baseball, Inc.*, 794 F. Supp. 342 [D. Ariz. 1992]).

under the ADA. The basis of the magistrate judge's Recommended Ruling, and the principal contention of McDonald's and Burger King on appeal, is that a total ban on smoking does not constitute a "reasonable modification" under the ADA.

The ADA and cases interpreting it do not articulate a precise test for determining whether a particular modification is "reasonable." However, because the Rehabilitation Act, which applies to recipients of federal funding, uses the same " reasonableness " analysis, cases interpreting that act provide some guidance.

The Supreme Court, addressing the issue of the reasonableness of accommodations under the Rehabilitation Act in the employment context, stated that "accommodation is not reasonable if it either imposes 'undue financial and administrative burdens' . . . or requires 'a fundamental alteration in the nature of [the] program.' " [O]ther courts have articulated factors that they consider relevant to the determination, including the nature and extent of plaintiff's disability.

Although neither the ADA nor the courts have defined the precise contours of the test for reasonableness, it is clear that the determination of whether a particular modification is "reasonable" involves a fact-specific, case-by-case inquiry that considers, among other factors, the effectiveness of the modification in light of the nature of the disability in question and the cost to the organization that would implement it.

While there may be claims requesting modification under the ADA that warrant dismissal as unreasonable as a matter of law, in the cases before us a fact-specific inquiry was required. None has occurred at this early stage of the suits. The magistrate judge instead concluded— and the district court agreed—that plaintiffs' request for a ban on smoking in all of defendants' restaurants was unreasonable as a matter of law. The magistrate judge offered two grounds for this conclusion: first, that "the ADA, by itself, does not mandate a 'blanket ban' on smoke in 'fast food' restaurants," and second, that "it is not reasonable, under the ADA, to impose a blanket ban on every McDonald's [and Burger King] restaurant where there are certain restaurants which reasonably can accommodate a 'no-smoking' area." We believe that neither ground justifies dismissal of the complaints.

The magistrate judge correctly noted that the ADA on its face does not ban smoking in all public accommodations or all fast-food restaurants. Defendants carry this point a significant step further, however, and argue that the ADA precludes a total smoking ban as a reasonable modification. They assert that Congress did not intend to restrict the range of legislative policy options open to state and local governments to deal with the issue of smoking. Their argument rests on § 501(b) of the ADA:

Nothing in this chapter shall be construed to invalidate or limit the remedies, rights, and procedures

of any Federal law or law of any State or political subdivision . . . that provides greater or equal protection for the rights of individuals with disabilities than are afforded by this chapter. Nothing in this chapter shall be construed to preclude the prohibition of, or the imposition of restrictions on, smoking . . . in places of public accommodation covered by subchapter III of this chapter.

42 U.S.C. § 12201(b). The magistrate judge echoed a sentiment similar to defendants', stating that "the significant public policy issues regarding smoking in 'fast food' restaurants are better addressed by Congress or by the Connecticut General Assembly. . . . "

It is plain to us that Congress did not intend to isolate the effects of smoking from the protections of the ADA. The first sentence of § 501(b) simply indicates that Congress, states, and municipalities remain free to offer greater protection for disabled individuals than the ADA provides. The passage does not state, and it does not follow, that violations of the ADA should go unredressed merely because a state has chosen to provide some degree of protection to those with disabilities.

Cases in which individuals claim under the ADA that allergies to smoke constitute a disability and require smoking restrictions are simply subject to the same general reasonableness analysis as are other cases under the Act.

The magistrate judge's principal objection to plaintiffs' proposed modification was that plaintiffs were seeking a total ban on smoking in all of defendants' restaurants even though "there are certain restaurants which reasonably can accommodate a 'no-smoking' area." We do not think that it is possible to conclude on the pleadings that plaintiffs' suggested modification in this case is necessarily unreasonable.

To be sure, the few courts that have addressed the question of reasonable modification for a smoke-sensitive disability have found a total ban unnecessary. Yet these courts only reached this conclusion after making a factual determination that existing accommodations were sufficient

Plaintiffs in this case are entitled to prove that a ban on smoking is a reasonable modification to permit them access to defendants' restaurants. Given that McDonald's has voluntarily banned smoking in all corporate-owned restaurants, the factfinder may conclude that such a ban would fully accommodate plaintiffs' disabilities but impose little or no cost on the defendants. The magistrate judge's unsupported assumption that certain restaurants "reasonably can accommodate a 'no-smoking' area" does not obviate the need for a factual inquiry. Plaintiffs have alleged that, regardless of the different structural arrangements in various restaurants, the environment in each establishment visited by the plaintiffs contained too much smoke to allow them use of the facilities on an equal basis as other nondisabled patrons. These allegations belie the magistrate judge's assumption that no-smoking areas offer a sufficient accommodation to plaintiffs.

In addition, we note that plaintiffs do not solely request a ban on smoking. Their complaints ask that defendants be enjoined "from continuing or maintaining any policy" that denies plaintiffs access to their restaurants, as well as "such other and further relief as it may deem just and proper." While plaintiffs bear the eventual burden of showing that particular modifications are reasonable, we do not think that it is necessary at this point in the lawsuit to bind plaintiffs to the one specific modification they prefer. If plaintiffs should fail in their quest for an outright ban on smoking, they may still be able to demonstrate after discovery that modifications short of an outright ban, such as partitions or ventilation systems, are both "reasonable" and

"necessary," *42 U.S.C. § 12182(b)(2)(A)(ii),* and plaintiffs should be allowed the opportunity to do so.

Reversed and remanded.

Case Questions

1. What disability do the plaintiffs allege?
2. Does the court find that the ADA applies in these circumstances?
3. What must the plaintiffs establish when the case is remanded for trial?
4. Does the ADA address the issue of smoking?

Practical Tip

In conducting a review of potential leased premises, the tenant should check for access routes, appropriate restroom facilities, automatic doors, drinking fountain heights, and elevators, and evaluate the costs of compliance.

ADA Lease Provisions

Without specific provisions on the ADA, legal requirements for access and alterations will be allocated under other lease terms such as those on alterations or repair. The ADA does apply to commercial facilities, referred to as "places of public accommodation" (PPA). Included in the PPA under the ADA would be shopping centers, medical offices, banks, and other professional service office buildings such as those for accountants, lawyers, and architects. The types of requirements for PPAs would include the removal of barriers and the presence of paths of entry for those with disabilities. Many of these requirements are being met by modifications taking place in facilities throughout the country with the installation of automatic doors and ramps.

Prior to entering into a lease, a tenant should conduct a form of due diligence review in which the premises are examined for ADA compliance. If modifications are required, the tenant should negotiate their addition and cost allocation. The lease agreement should allocate the costs of future compliance with the ADA and other laws as well as the cost of upkeep.

Landlord's Right of Entry

As in residential leases, commercial tenants have the right to the quiet use and enjoyment of their property, but on occasion, the landlord will need access. The lease should specify the hows and whens of the landlord's access, including when the landlord may enter the tenant's premises and for what purpose; how much notice is required before the landlord may enter, what form that notice must take, and how it is to be delivered; and whether notice provisions may be waived during emergency situations.

Destruction and Damage to Premises

The parties need to make provisions for what would happen to their relationship in the event that an accident or catastrophe destroys the shopping center property. For example, the 1993 bombing of the World Trade Center in New York City left many tenants without office facilities for substantial periods of time. Many tenants had contingency plans for operations. Other tenants filed suit against the landlord (the Port Authority) for the interruption of their leases and businesses.

Several questions must be answered: If the premises are damaged or destroyed to the point of being unusable by the tenant, does the responsibility of rent abate? (During the time of nonuse, provision should be made for the tenant to stop paying rent.) May the tenant cancel the lease? At what point are the premises completely destroyed? Allowing the common law to cover these issues is inviting the ambiguity of the doctrine of impossibility and does not provide the parties with sufficient guidelines for their conduct.

In some cases, the parties incorporate into the lease an obligation of the landlord to rebuild the premises. Because of the unique nature of the shopping center, in which prime location can be the key to a successful business, this obligation to rebuild can be extremely important to the tenant. The tenant may not want to terminate the lease but may want to be back in business as soon as possible and can provide for time limitations on rebuilding. If a construction clause is imposed on the landlord, provision should also be made to require the landlord to carry appropriate insurance to cover reconstruction costs.

Breach

The last topic of concern to both parties in the commercial lease is what constitutes a breach and what the damages are in the event of a breach. For the landlord, nonpayment of rent is the major problem, and remedies should be specified. If the remedies are not specified, the law affords the same protections in commercial leases as it affords in residential leases. If rental payments are not made in a timely manner, the landlord may bring an action to dispossess the tenant. If the tenant breaches the lease agreement by terminating business prior to the lease expiration date, the landlord may have the responsibility to mitigate the situation by trying to find another tenant. But the parties could specify otherwise and could provide for a liquidated damage figure. In cases of breaches in other areas (such as failure to maintain or failure to grant access), the parties may agree to submit matters to arbitration prior to suit.

Consider 9.6

Austin Hill Country Realty negotiated a five-year lease with Palisades Plaza, Inc., for an office suite for a monthly base rent of $3,128 for the first year, $3,519 for years two and three, and $3,910 for years four and five. The lease also provided for a plan for improvements to the suite and that the lease would commence at the time the improvements were completed. The lease was negotiated and signed in September 1992 and the parties anticipated the occupation and lease would begin in November 1992.

Problems with the improvements resulted when Palisades could not get directives from Hill on completion of construction. Construction was halted because of disagreements about the improvements. Palisades sent a letter to Hill stating that its failure to cooperate on the improvements was an anticipatory breach. Palisades advertised a vacancy in the suite in the local newspaper but was unable to locate a new tenant. Palisades then sued for the lost rent under the contract. Hill maintains that Palisades could have done more to locate a tenant such as advertising in commercial property listings. Must Hill pay the full amount of rent due under a five-year contract? *Austin Hill Country Realty, Inc. v. Palisades Plaza, Inc.,* 948 S.W.2d 293 (Tex. 1997)

If a suit is required to collect damages for breach of a lease agreement, provision for payment of costs and fees to the party who prevails would also be made in the lease agreement.

Practical Tip

Because of potential liability for infringement for the unauthorized sale of trademarked goods or for the sale of knock-off goods, landlords will need to put a clause in the lease prohibiting such sales and also take precautions in screening tenants and knowing what activities are going on in the leased premises.

Landlord's Responsibility for Tenant's Conduct

A recent development in commercial leases is one of holding landlords responsible when their tenants are engaged in trademark infringement. For example, many landlords lease properties to stores that sell knock-off goods or goods that the stores are not licensed to sell. Such tenants are often found in outlet malls. To protect their trademarks, some manufacturers have joined together to bring suits against landlords so that landlords are more cautious about their tenants and the tenants' activities. For example, in *Polo Ralph Lauren Corp. v. Chinatown Gift Ship,* 855 F.Supp. 648 (S.D. N.Y. 1994), Polo Ralph Lauren, Rolex Watch USA, and Louis Vuitton brought suit against a landlord who was leasing property to three retailers who were selling goods that infringed on their trademarks for their clothing, watches, and leather goods, respectively. The court held that there was a cause of action against the landlord for its vicarious liability under federal law for facilitating the infringement by the tenants.

Assignment of Leases

Most states readily permit the assignment of leases by tenants. But in nearly all commercial leases that have been drafted by the developer, assignments are prohibited unless approval from the developer is obtained. Even if a lease does not contain an assignment prohibition, the type of assignment may be severely limited by the use restrictions clause. Since the tenant remains liable on the lease, the tenant would be responsible for a breach if an assignment were made to a retailer who sold goods that were unauthorized by the use provision.

Commercial leases involve complexities in assignments and subleases because of tenant mix. Many commercial leases have restrictions on assignments or require landlord approval because the landlord would breach his non-compete clauses with other tenants if, for example, an assignment meant there were two drugstores in one shopping center.

SHOPPING CENTER LEASES—SPECIFIC PROVISIONS

A successful shopping center is the result of a careful mix of tenants. To maximize the return on not just the owner's investment but also the profits earned by the individual tenants, the tenants need to complement rather than compete with one another. This section offers background on obtaining that mix.

The Anchor Tenant

Long before a center opens its doors and, in some cases, long before construction of the center begins, the developer or owner negotiates with an **anchor tenant** to begin creating the mix of tenants. The anchor tenant is generally the grocery store in a freestanding center or a major department store for a mall. In the case of a shopping mall, there may be two to five anchor tenants. The anchor tenants are responsible for drawing the majority of the customers to the center or mall and will do a significant amount of advertising that also brings in customers. The terms under which these anchor tenants will come to the center are critical because other tenants and lease terms will be controlled by the demands of the anchor tenant. For example, if a chain drugstore is to be the anchor tenant in a freestanding shopping center, the developer will not be able to lease to a small and locally owned drugstore a smaller space in the center. Likewise, if a discount clothing store is the anchor tenant, it would be difficult to lease the smaller spaces to retail clothing stores.

Commercial leases tend to be significantly longer than residential leases largely because of the degree of investment made by the developer and the time required for recoupment of the investment in the property. Periods of 15 to 20 years for the initial term of the lease are not unusual and are generally accompanied by four to five 5-year renewal options.

A portion of every commercial lease will cover restrictions on the developer's other tenants and future leases. For example, if a center will have a bakery, the bakery tenant will want a clause in the lease that prohibits both the landlord from leasing to another bakery and other tenants from assigning their leases to other bakeries.

One of the difficulties that can arise for a shopping center developer or owner occurs when an anchor tenant is signed and then fails to open for business. Because the developer is dependent upon the mix of tenants, and the tenants and their customer traffic are drawn by the anchor tenant, the failure of an anchor tenant to commence operations, even when rent is paid, can be devastating for the center. The following case deals with the issue of an anchor tenant's failure to open for business.

Slater v. Pearle Vision Center, Inc.

546 A.2d 676 (Pa. 1988)

Facts

Maurice Slater and Peter Kanton are the owners and developers of Bloomsburg Shopping Center (the shopping center/appellant/lessor). Pearle Vision Center (Pearle/lessee/appellee) is a tenant in this strip-type shopping center and has paid rent for its facilities but has never opened for business. Slater and Kanton, concerned about having such a large vacancy in their center, brought suit seeking an injunction requiring Pearle to occupy its premises and open for business.

Pearle filed a motion for summary judgment maintaining there was no breach of the lease agreement because there was no express provision in the lease agreement that required Pearle to occupy and use the premises. The trial court granted Pearle's motion, and Slater and Kanton appealed.

Judicial Opinion

Beck, Judge. Shopping Center argues that the lease contains both an express and an implied requirement that Pearle occupy the premises. The express requirement is alleged to be found in Section 10 of the lease, which states:

> A. Tenant covenants and agrees that it shall use the Premises solely as a "Pearle Vision Center" or such other name as is used by the other Tenant's businesses within the State of Pennsylvania for the retail sale and repair of eyeglasses, lenses and other optical merchandise and optical services, and eye examination and lens grinding and preparation and for no other purpose. . . .

The quoted language on its face would appear to impose an obligation on Pearle to occupy the premises and to use it as a vision center. However, Pennsylvania case law requires us to interpret such language in commercial leases to mean only that no use other than the use specified in the lease is permitted. The language does not address the question of the lessee's duty to occupy the premises.

In the seminal case of *Dickey v. Philadelphia Minit-Man Corp.*, 377 Pa. 549, 105 A.2d 580 (1954), the lease provided that the leased premises were to be occupied by the lessee in the business of washing and cleaning automobiles and for no other purpose. The lease also provided for rent based on a percentage of gross sales, with a fixed minimum annual rental. The defendant tenant occupied and used the premises for a number of years in accordance with the lease, but then limited its business to waxing cars and largely eliminated the car washing aspect of its business.

The lessor argued that in a lease where the rental is based upon gross sales, there is an implied obligation of the tenant to continue the business on the premises to the fullest extent possible. The Court rejected this argument, finding that the tenant's decision to change its business was made in good faith and in the exercise of legitimate business judgment and was not forbidden by an implied term of the lease. Interestingly, in so holding, the Court specifically distinguished a Louisiana case where a tenant had completely vacated the leased premises and conducted its business elsewhere.

Thus, the holding of *Dickey* would appear to be that a use covenant like that presented here cannot be read as an express requirement that the tenant use the premises for the precise permitted business purpose. Moreover, *Dickey* holds that there is no implied obligation that the tenant under a percentage lease refrain from conducting its business in good faith and in accordance with sound business judgment simply because doing so may decrease the rent payable.

More pertinent to the instant case is the fact that *Dickey* specifically does not address a situation where the tenant conducts no business on the leased premises. It also does not address a lease for premises which are part of a strip of stores where the economic health of each store may be dependent on the others.

Since there is no other directly controlling Pennsylvania precedent, we must necessarily rely on more general principles of lease construction.

Thus, where it is clear that an obligation is within the contemplation of the parties at the time of contracting or is necessary to carry out their intentions, the court will imply it.

[W]e find ample evidence in this lease that these parties may well have contemplated and intended that Pearle was obligated to occupy and use the premises. For example, sub-paragraph 9(E) of the lease provides that the tenant agrees to "open the Premises for business to the public not later than ninety (90) days after Landlord's approval of tenant's plans and specifications." Although we recog-

nize that Shopping Center's complaint does not specifically allege when or if it ever approved Pearle's "plans and specification," thus triggering this provision, the complaint does allege that Pearle "failed to open the premises and utilize it in accordance with" this provision.

Moreover, we find that there are other provisions in the lease that suggest that actual occupancy and use of the premises by Pearle was in the contemplation of the parties when they executed the lease. Section 10(B) states that the tenant agrees "that it will conduct its business in the entire Premises." Section 30 includes "abandonment" as an Event of Default and contains the following noteworthy exception:

> Notwithstanding anything to the contrary herein, Tenant may allow the demised premises to be vacant for a period not exceeding sixty (60) days, provided Landlord is given not less than ninety (90) days written notice that such vacancy will occur: said vacancy being necessary due to repairs or remodeling of the demised premises or transfer of possession to a franchisee or assignee pursuant to the terms of this lease.

This exception appears in type that differs from the body of the lease, which otherwise appears to be largely based on a standard form thus creating at least the suggestion that this provision was a separately negotiated term. The necessary implication of this provision, which severely circumscribes Pearle's ability to leave the premises vacant, is that except under the circumstances specifically outlined, Pearle cannot allow the premises to be vacant.

Finally, the lease contains references to the obligations of Pearle vis-a-vis the viability of the shopping mall as a whole. The "affirmative obligations" of Pearle set forth in Section 20(A) refer to Pearle's obligation to keep the premises in a manner consistent with the general character of the shopping mall and to refrain from any action or practice that "may damage, mar or deface the Premises or any other part of the Shopping Center."

In the face of such provisions, we cannot agree with the trial court's conclusion.

Reversed.

Case Questions

1. Describe the landlord and tenant.
2. Did the tenant ever open for business?
3. Does the lease expressly require the tenant to open for business?
4. Does the lease imply that the tenant will open for business?
5. Does Pennsylvania have an exact case on point?
6. Is the intention of the parties important?
7. How does the court determine intention?

On January 17, 1975, A & P entered into a 20-year commercial lease with Jerome Schostak, d/b/a Midland Venture for property A & P intended to use for operation of a grocery store. The lease provided for a fixed rent of $8,630 per month plus an additional 1 percent of all sales in excess of $10,356,000.00. A & P did not have sufficient sales to owe the 1 percent until 1979. In July 1990, A & P ceased its operations on the property, but continued to pay its fixed rent. In November 1990, A & P subleased the store to Dunham's Athleisure Corporation. Dunham's lease provided that it would pay 2 percent of its gross sales in excess of $3,000,000. Dunham also has never had sales sufficient to kick in the percentage portion of rent.

A & P has simply continued to pay the fixed monthly rent. Dunham maintains that A & P owes more because the contract was negotiated with the underlying assumption that A & P would stay in business. Should A & P be required to pay more rent? *Plaza Forty-Eight, Inc. v. Great Atlantic & Pacific Tea Company, Inc.,* 817 F.Supp. 774 (E.D. Wis. 1993).

> **Consider 9.7**

In many cases, anchor tenants pay a minimal or at least lower amount of rent than the other tenants. If the large spaces in the center go unoccupied, then all of the remaining tenants suffer. Tenants who occupy smaller units in the center do so with the idea that their services and goods will be unique to that center and that the landlord will not reduce their business by leasing to a competing venture in the same center. These ideas of traffic from anchor tenants and non-competition are marketing tools that must be guaranteed by lease terms.[6]

JCPenney is a tenant in the Quaker Village Shopping Center in the Borough of Leetsdale in Allegheny County, Pennsylvania. As part of its operations, Penney has a Thrift Drug Store within its store as a means of attracting foot traffic. Customers who would not otherwise come to Penney's shop there as they wait for their prescriptions to be filled. Penney has a clause in its lease with Quaker Village, Inc., that Quaker Village will not lease to any drugstore or any business that fills prescriptions.

In 1992, Quaker Village entered into another lease agreement with Giant Eagle Market, Inc., for Giant Eagle to occupy a grocery store space in the Village Shopping Center. However, Giant Eagle does have a pharmacy in its stores.

Penney filed suit to enjoin the operation of Giant Eagle and its pharmacy. Should Penney be entitled to an injunction against its landlord and Giant Eagle? *JCPenney Co., Inc. v. Giant Eagle, Inc.,* 813 F.Supp. 360 (W.D. Pa. 1993).

> **Consider 9.8**

Business Restrictions

The makeup of a shopping center can be an important factor in its financial success. An appropriate mix of merchants will draw shoppers because they can accomplish more at one center with a good variety of stores. However, the proximity of the various businesses raises intense issues of competition, which have dotted the antitrust case law for the past 15 years. The lessees in the shopping center may want to control the makeup of the center or even the types of merchandise sold by each retailer. Indeed, in some instances, the anchor tenant stipulates that it

---

6. Recent decisions have some courts implying a covenant of continuing operations, particularly for anchor tenants. When a significant portion of the rent is tied to revenues, courts have held that the tenant must continue operations (*East Broadway Corp. v. Taco Bell Corp.,* 542 N.W.2d [Iowa 1996]).

must review and approve all potential lessees for a center. For example, in some leases, anchor tenants have clauses that disallow the leasing of space to discount merchants. This is to prevent the anchor tenant from being undersold on certain items because a store in the same center has been leased to a discount merchant of those items.

The issue that arises from these clauses that limit the types of business operations is whether the clauses violate federal or state antitrust laws. Many such clauses have been challenged by the Federal Trade Commission and the Justice Department in an effort to eliminate them.

At this point, it is difficult to determine what clauses do or do not violate antitrust laws. Because the issues of the type of market, location, and competition vary from city to city, the validity of these clauses also varies. But for the most part, if the clauses are reasonably necessary for shopping center survival, they should be insisted upon by tenants. In the following case, the issue of use restriction is critical.

Child World, Inc. v. South Towne Centre, Ltd.

634 F.Supp. 1121 (S. D. Oh. 1986)

Facts

Child World, Inc. (plaintiff), operates large retail toy stores throughout Ohio and other states called "Children's Palace." South Towne Centre, Ltd. (defendant), is a limited partnership in the state of Ohio and leases space in its South Towne shopping center complex to a Children's Palace store. Section 43(A) of the lease, executed in February 1976, provided as follows:

Except insofar as the following shall be unlawful, the parties mutually agree as follows:

A. Landlord shall not use or permit or suffer any other person, firm, corporation or other entity to use any portion of the Shopping Center or any other property located within six (6) miles from the Shopping Center and owned, leased or otherwise controlled by the landlord (meaning thereby the real property or parties in interest and not a "straw" person or entity) or any person or entity having a substantial identity of interest, for the operation of a toys and games store principally for the sale at retail of toys and games, juvenile furniture and sporting goods such as is exemplified by the Child World and Children's Palace stores operated by Tenant's parent company, Child World, Inc. at the demised premises and elsewhere.

The lease was a 20-year lease and was signed by Barbara Beerman Weprin, the sole general partner of South Towne. Mad River Ltd. is another limited partnership in which Weprin is the sole general partner. Mad River owns

another parcel of land approximately one-half mile from the South Towne Center. On December 24, 1985, Mad River entered into an agreement to sell the parcel of land to Toys "R" Us, Inc. Toys "R" Us intends to construct a retail facility similar to the description in the above-noted lease clause. When Children's Palace was informed of the sale, they brought suit seeking to enforce the covenant not to lease or sell to a competitor of Children's Palace.

Judicial Opinion

Rice, Circuit Judge. The consensus of the federal courts which have considered covenants in shopping center leases is one with which this Court can agree; namely, that the varying terms, conditions, and economic justifications for such restrictions render them inappropriate subjects for application of the per se rule. Defendants have not alleged nor proven anything about Section 43(A) of the lease which would indicate that it has only anticompetitive consequences. Indeed, in Finding of Fact #9, Defendants agree that Section 43(A) was negotiated as an inducement for Plaintiff to erect a Children's Palace store on Defendants' premises and to enter into a twenty-year lease. This economic justification for exclusivity clauses such as Section 43(A) have not been found to be per se illegal, but rather have been found consistent with the public interest in economic development. Such laws can induce tenants to establish stores and to enter into a particular marketplace, often then encouraging the entry of other, often smaller, merchants.

A number of factors have been considered by the courts which have excluded restrictive covenants in shopping center leases: (1) the relevant product and geographic markets, together with the showing of unreasonable impact upon competition in these markets, due to the restrictive covenant; (2) the availability of alternate sites for the entity excluded by the operation of such a covenant; (3) the significance of the competition eliminated by the exclusivity clause, and whether present or future competitors were the parties excluded; (4) the scope of the restrictive covenant and whether it varied depending on particular circumstances; and (5) the economic justifications for the inclusion of the restrictive covenant in the lease.

Defendants have made no attempt to address the majority of these factors and to introduce evidence as to the markets affected by Section 43(A), the nature of the competition in these markets, and the like. Rather, Defendants focus exclusively upon the breadth of Section 43(A) and its prohibition of sale or lease by Defendants to competition of Plaintiff within a six-mile radius of the South Towne Centre shopping center. Defendants remind the Court that in none of the cases cited by Plaintiff was a restrictive covenant with a six-mile radius upheld under the rule of reason.

Due to the particular facts of this case, however, the Court needs not, and specifically does not, reach the validity of the six-mile limitation contained in Section 43(A). Regardless of possible overbreadth, a restrictive covenant challenged as unreasonable under Section 1 of the Sherman Act will be upheld to the extent that a breach of the covenant has occurred or is threatened to occur within a reasonable geographic area and time period. The parties have agreed, in Finding of Fact #12, that the parcel which Defendants seek to convey to Toys "R" Us is approximately one-half mile from the Children's Palace store covered by the Lease. The Court finds that Section 43(A) is lawful and enforceable to the extent of one-half mile, as required by the facts of this case.

Defendants have the burden of establishing that Section 43(A), enforced to the extent of one-half mile, would constitute an unreasonable restraint of trade. Defendants have not, however, presented any evidence to discharge their burden of demonstrating unreasonableness. Furthermore, the facts in this case, both those proven by the parties and those of which the Court takes judicial notice, tend to underscore the reasonableness of Section 43(A) as applied. Considering the latter set of facts first, this Court is quite familiar with the area of Miami Township within which the South Towne Centre is located. The Court takes judicial notice of the manner in which the real property in the Centre's vicinity has been developed, the rate at which economic development has proceeded, and the physical relationship of shopping centers, one to another, in this area. These current economic and geographic characteristics, of which judicial notice is taken, are among the factors which tend, even apart from Defendants' failure to meet their burden of showing unreasonableness, to support the enforceability of Section 43(A) to the extent of one-half mile.

Turning to the impact which enforcement of Section 43(A), as applied in this case, would have upon the Defendants, the burdens of enforcement are not unduly great. As noted *supra,* Section 43(A) does not appear to preclude rental or sale, even within a one-half mile radius, to any number of stores which can compete with a Children's Palace toy and game store but which are not "copycat" stores. On the financial level, there is testimony from a representative of Defendants in the record to the effect that the value of the parcel in question increases almost daily. Moreover, Defendants believe that they will have no difficulty in finding another purchaser, should Section 43(A) preclude their sale of the parcel to Toys "R" Us.

Enforcement of Section 43(A) to the extent of one-half mile would also not appear to foreclose the entry of Toys "R" Us into competition with Plaintiff's store in the environs of the South Towne Centre shopping center. In his deposition, J. Tim Logan indicated that, even were Section 43(A) upheld, presumably in its entirety, Toys "R" Us would still establish a store in the vicinity of Plaintiff's store.

Other courts have believed that restrictive covenants of a scope of one-half mile or more, albeit less than six miles, are legitimate lures by landlords in order for shopping center tenants to enter particular marketplaces and to thereby enhance the economic development of the community. The public has surely benefited from the development of South Towne Centre. As a restriction of six miles appeared reasonable to Defendants' predecessors at the time of bargaining, enforcement of Section 43(A) of the Lease to the extent of one-half mile is consistent with that original calculation of value, and certainly reasonable.

Judgment for plaintiff.

Case Questions

1. Who leased what from whom?
2. What restrictions were there in the lease agreement?
3. How did Toys "R" Us become involved?
4. Is the sale a violation of the anticompetition clause?
5. Is the same shopping center involved?

☀CAUTIONS AND CONCLUSIONS

The commercial lease carries a unique set of legal problems from antitrust to liquidated damages to store hours. A checklist for commercial lease negotiations is a necessity, and the headings in this chapter can be used as a guideline in making sure all possible legal issues are covered. As is true with other areas of real estate, an investigation can never be too complete.

The following is a checklist for commercial leases.

1. Amount of rent. If there is a profit-sharing arrangement, specify exact terms. Is it gross or net profit? What percentage? Where is it paid?
2. In the case of a shopping center lease, what competition will be permitted?
3. Who is responsible for maintaining the common areas? Who will carry liability insurance for the common areas?
4. Can the lease be assigned? Is approval for assignment required?
5. Who will make repairs? Who pays?
6. Who will make improvements?
7. Are there mandatory hours of operation?
8. Is there an understanding on fixtures? Who keeps them?
9. What deposits are required? Are they refundable?
10. Is there compliance with all applicable laws, including ADA?

Key Terms

gross rent, 184

escalation clause, 184

triple net, 184

net-net-net, 184

fixed rent, 184

Consumer Price Index (CPI) adjustment clause, 184

specific happenings increase provisions, 185

common area maintenance (CAM), 185

operating expenses, 185

percentage rent, 185

Americans with Disabilities Act (ADA), 194

anchor tenant, 198

Chapter Problems

1. In April 1965, Berkeley Heights Shopping Center leased 11,514 square feet of space to A & P Supermarkets. Under the terms of the lease, Berkeley agreed not to lease any other shopping-center space to another grocery store. On April 16, 1977, A & P informed Berkeley that it was ceasing operations and subleasing the premises to Drug Fair, a modern chain drug store that also sells foodstuffs. In 1985, Berkeley sought to lease other space in the center to another grocery store, and Drug Fair objected on the grounds of the covenant not to compete. Berkeley maintains the covenant only applies when the premises Drug Fair occupies are used as a grocery store operation. Who is correct? *Berkeley Development Co. v. Great Atlantic & Pacific Tea Co.*, 518 A.2d 790 (N.J. 1986)

2. MacDonald Group, Ltd., owned and operated the Fresno Fashion Fair Mall and leased space to Edmond's, a California retail jeweler. The lease contained a

covenant that limited MacDonald to one additional jewelry store as a tenant in the mall. The lease was entered into in 1969. In 1978, MacDonald was involved in the construction of an expansion to the mall and began negotiations to include a retail jeweler in the new expansion. Edmond's objected and brought suit. The covenant provides that only two jewelry stores would be tenants in the Fresno Fashion Fair Mall. The expansion would still be part of the Fresno Fashion Fair Mall and would not have a separate name. Would the covenant apply to the new addition to the mall? *Edmond's of Fresno v. MacDonald Group, Ltd.*, 217 Cal. Rptr. 375 (1985)

3. Brophy College was a devisee in the will of Anastasia Nealon and received title to two parcels of real property through the probate of her will: lots 2337 and 2339 located on East McDowell Road in Phoenix. The Tovars claimed the right to occupy these lots under a purported lease agreement they had with Nick Mercer (purported to be the husband of Anastasia). The Tovars operated an adult bookstore and theater on the premises.

In 1977, most of the property on lots 2337 and 2339 was destroyed by fire, and Brophy College gave the Tovars notice of the right of termination on lot 2337 and notice of termination of a periodic tenancy on lot 2339. The notice on 2337 was pursuant to a lease agreement that permitted the tenant to terminate if there was a fire; and the notice for lot 2339 was a period's notice to terminate the periodic tenancy on that lot.

The Tovars claimed there was a lease for lot 2339 included in the lease for lot 2337, since there was a longhand addition to the lease that stated, "These premises primarily for expansion of Empress Theater 2339 E. McDowell." During their occupancy, the Tovars had spent $1,500 making improvements on lot 2339, including a stage, dressing room, sign, and carpeting. They did not use lot 2339 for six to eight months prior to the fire because of poor business but did pay rent for its use. Tovar testified that he and Mercer had orally agreed that the lease on lot 2337 applied to lot 2339.

The Tovars failed to vacate the premises, and Brophy College brought action in forcible detainer to require the Tovars to leave. The trial court found for the Tovars. Is the decision correct? *William Henry Brophy College v. Tovar,* 619 P.2d 19 (Ariz. 1980)

4. E. H. Webb and Ann Thomas Webb own a shopping center in Davidson County, Tennessee, and leased one of its spaces to Scooter Stores, Incorporated, in 1971. In 1975, Scooter assigned the lease to Borchert Enterprises. The Webbs approved the assignment, but various controversies arose between the parties, and Borchert filed suit. The Webbs counterclaimed for rent due under a clause in the lease, which required a payment of 2 percent of gross sales as additional rent. The clause provided as follows:

> *Lessee, in addition, agrees to pay to Lessor as additional rental a sum equal to two (2%) percent of the gross sales in excess of Two Hundred Thousand ($200,000) Dollars per annum, excluding sales tax and money order sales, said payments to be made annually, within forty-five (45) days from each annual anniversary of this Lease. Lessee agrees to provide to Lessor annually a Certified Public Accountant's report of sales to substantiate the payments made hereunder.*

Borchert was engaged in the operation of a convenience market and installed several pinball machines. The Webbs contended that Borchert had failed to pay the 2 percent due on the pinball revenues, and Borchert contended that revenue from the pinball machines was not included in the term *gross sales*. The trial court held that the pinball income was part of gross sales, and Borchert appealed. How should the case be decided? *Borchert Enterprises, Inc. v. Webb,* 584 S.W.2d 208 (Tenn. 1979)

5. Thom Rock Realty Company developed an interior design showroom center. The center, created by I. M. Pei & Partners was to total almost one million square feet and be devoted exclusively to showroom tenants. Herman Miller, Inc., a designer and manufacturer of high-end office furniture, leased space in the showroom facility. The 10-year lease was signed in 1986 and contained a clause that the facilities would "be used for showrooms and other related uses."

There was a downturn in the economy in the late eighties, and the demand for contract furniture and showrooms declined. Thom Rock lost many tenants and began leasing the space in its showroom facility to video production firms and other types of companies. Herman Miller sued Thom Rock for breach of its rental agreement on the grounds that the lease contained a restrictive use clause. Can such a clause be enforced? How does the goal of the design center compare with the mix of a shopping center? *Herman Miller Inc. v. Thom Rock Realty Co.,* 46 F.3d 183 (2nd Cir. 1995)

6. Hanson Natural Resources Company subleased its 41,000 square feet of office space to Automated Communications, Inc. The lease that ACI signed contained the same clauses that Hanson had in its lease, namely that the property would be used "as general offices only." ACI's president had a well-documented habit of bringing one of her many dogs to work with her. When the landlord complained about the dog's presence being a violation of the business only clause, Hanson brought a forcible entry and detainer action to have ACI removed from the premises. Can ACI be removed for breach of the lease agreement? Does the presence of a dog breach the "general offices" only covenant? *Hanson Natural Resources Company v. Automated Communications, Inc.,* 926 P.2d 176 (Ct. App. Colo. 1996)

7. David Gotlieb and Taco Bell Corporation entered into a 20-year lease on August 15, 1991 for the purpose of building a Taco Bell Restaurant in Brooklyn, New York. There was a due diligence provision in the lease, and Taco Bell was permitted to cancel the lease if it could not obtain the necessary permits for the construction of the fast-food facility. Shortly after the lease was signed, community and religious groups began an organized effort to oppose the construction of the Taco Bell and any other fast-food franchises in the area. Taco Bell worked with community leaders for six months but was unable to make any progress. Taco Bell never applied for the permits but did cancel the lease. Gotlieb objected and sued Taco Bell for lost rents. What are Gotlieb's responsibilities upon Taco Bell's repudiation of the lease? What are Taco Bell's responsibilities? *Gotlieb v. Taco Bell Corporation,* 871 F.Supp. 147 (E.D.N.Y. 1994)

8. Elaine Barton entered into a five-year lease with the Mitchell Company for retail store premises for the purpose of operating her patio furniture store. The lease began November 1, 1985. In October 1984, the Mitchell Company leased the space adjoining Ms. Barton's store to Body Electric. Body Electric operated an exercise studio. Loud music, screams, shouts, and yells accompanied the operation of Body Electric during business hours. The intensity and volume of such caused the walls of Ms. Barton's space to vibrate. Paintings fell off the walls. Ms. Barton lost customers and salespersons because of the noise.

Ms. Barton complained of the noise, and Mitchell promised to add insulation to the walls. Nothing was done and the noise levels made it impossible for Ms. Barton to continue her operation. She vacated the premises on August 3, 1985. Mitchell then brought suit against Barton for rent due on the unexpired portion of the lease. Can Mitchell recover the rent? *Barton v. Mitchell Company*, 507 So.2d 148 (Fla. 1987)

9.   Could a tenant who has agreed to a rental fee based on total number of square feet utilized withhold from his usual amount of rent when he discovers that the landlord has misrepresented the total amount of square feet? Or is it the tenant's responsibility to verify square footage? *MTS, Inc. v. 200 East 87th Street Associates,* 899 F.Supp. 1180 (S.D.N.Y. 1995)

10. F. W. Woolworth was leasing property to Century 21., Inc., for a branch realty office. Before the lease closing occurred, F. W. Woolworth sent Century 21 a letter describing the presence of asbestos in the property. The letter further indicated that Century 21 should conduct additional investigations to determine the amount of asbestos exposure in the building. Century 21 claims the asbestos discovery and removal is a cost that Woolworth as the landlord should assume. Woolworth maintains that the condition of the premises does not carry a warranty in commercial leases. Who is correct? *Century 21, Inc. v. F. W. Woolworth Co.,* 582 N.Y.S.2d 101 (1992)

Internet Activities

1.   For news releases about a variety of topics, including commercial leases and terms, go to: **http://recenter.tamu.edu/news/**.

2.   Search for good provisions for leases at **http://www.legaldocs.com**.

3.   Review a sample commercial lease at **http://www.gahtan.com/prec/Real_Estate/ leases/commercial**.

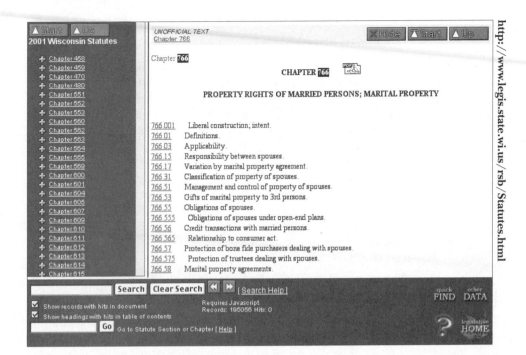

Chapter 766

CHAPTER 766

PROPERTY RIGHTS OF MARRIED PERSONS; MARITAL PROPERTY

Chapter 10
Co-Ownership
of Real Estate

Prenuptial Agreement

*TO ALL WHOM this may come to affect or may concern, know yet that it is understood that on the fourth day of February, Nineteen Hundred and Ninety-Five, that **Jim Morrissey** (hereafter known as the **First Party**) and **Jeanne Fulton** (hereinafter known as the **Second Party**) are entering into a contract of wedlock.*

The following constitutes a full, legal and binding arrangement of said properties set before this date. This agreement shall be executed in multiple copies.

*The following below is a full, detailed breakdown of said agreement regarding all properties of consequence shared by the **First Party** and the **Second Party**.*

HIS	*HERS*
Season tickets	*Everything else*

Adapted from a 1997 Seagram's Ad

Often, title to real property is held by two or more people. Married couples hold title together to their homes. Children inherit a parcel of land from a parent as equal co-owners. Partners hold title to their office building and the land on which it is located. **Co-ownership** is very common in holding title to real estate.

Since so much of real property ownership consists of ownership by more than one person, it is necessary to understand the forms and rights of co-ownership. The questions to be answered in this chapter are: How can title be held among several owners? What are the rights of each of the owners? What are the responsibilities of each of the owners? What action or actions may be taken in the event difficulties arise between or among the parties?

METHODS OF CO-OWNERSHIP

In this chapter, four methods of co-ownership are discussed: tenancies in common, joint tenancies, tenancies by the entirety, and tenancies in partnership. Marital co-ownership rights are also discussed.

Practical Tip

The way title is carried has significant implications for the listing, sale, and purchase of property. Title insurers will not issue policies for property transfers attempted without the consent of all joint tenants. The rights and identity of all co-owners should be determined prior to marketing, buying, or selling property.

Tenancies in Common

When parties hold title to property as tenants in common, they hold separate interests in a single portion of property. The tenants in common may hold equal or unequal shares in the land. For example, two tenants may hold a one-half interest in a tract of land or they may hold a one-third/two-thirds portion of the property. Tenants in common may acquire their interests at different times and may convey their interests to others. The conveyances can be made *inter vivos* (while the tenant in common is alive) or by will. For example, if X and Y hold title to a piece of property and X passes away, leaving, by will, his property to sons W and Z, then Y, W, and Z are all tenants in common.

Under a **tenancy in common,** each tenant is entitled to equal possession of the whole of the property. To the extent one cotenant has exclusive possession, the other cotenants are entitled to payment for their loss of use. For example, if cotenant A leased the property she owns with B and C to an architectural firm and kept the rent, B and C would be entitled to recover their share of the rental proceeds from A.

In the majority of states, the language necessary to create a tenancy in common is simply "To A and B." When this language is used, A and B will each have a 50 percent interest in the property. To create unequal interests, the amount of ownership must be specified. For example, "One-third of the above described property to my son B and two-thirds of the same to my daughter C" would be the language needed to create a tenancy in common with different shares or interests in the property.

(For a discussion of the co-ownership of subsurface rights, see Chapter 2.)

Joint Tenancies

http://

Read about marital property rights in http://www.legis.state. wi.us/rsb/Statutes.html.

A **joint tenancy** is a form of co-ownership in which the parties hold equal shares and possess unique rights of ownership through survivorship. That is, when one joint tenant dies, title to the property remains with the surviving joint tenants. A joint tenancy interest cannot be given away by will because at the moment of death, title vests in the remaining joint tenants. If A, B, and C are joint tenants and C dies, A and B remain joint tenants and hold title to the property. C's heirs

FIGURE 10.1   *The Severance of a Joint Tenancy*

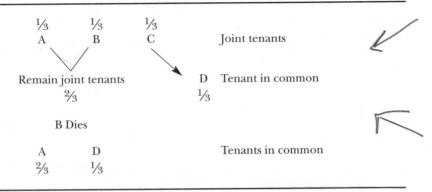

have no rights or interest in the property. If B then dies, A will hold full title to the property and B's heirs have no rights or interest in the property.

An interesting issue that arises in joint tenancy title is whether a joint tenant can make a valid *inter vivos* conveyance of his or her interest. Suppose, for example, that in the A, B, C joint tenancy, C conveys her interest to D. The result is that the unity of title is broken and the joint tenancy is partially severed. The result will be that D becomes a tenant in common with a one-third interest and A and B remain joint tenants for the remaining two-thirds of the property. Figure 10.1 illustrates the impact of joint tenancy transfers.

The Language of a Joint Tenancy

There are several requirements for the creation of a valid joint tenancy interest. The first requirement is the use of clear language to create a joint tenancy. Some states require the use of the phrase "as joint tenants with right of survivorship." Other states may simply require the use of the term "joint tenants." The following case deals with the creation of a joint tenancy and then whether it was severed.

Estate of Gulledge

673 A.2d 1278 (D.C. App. 1996)

Facts

Clayton and Margie Gulledge owned a house at 532 Somerset Place (the Somerset property). They had three children: Bernis Gulledge; Johnsie Walker; and Marion Watkins. After Margie Gulledge died in 1970, Clayton remarried, but the second marriage was not successful.

While the divorce proceedings were pending, and because of his fear of losing the house, Clayton borrowed money from his son, Bernis, in order to pay off the financial demands of the second Mrs. Gulledge. In exchange, Clayton created a joint tenancy of the Somerset property, naming himself and Bernis as joint tenants. Bernis expected, as a joint tenant with right of survivorship, that

he would, upon his father's death, take full title to the Somerset property and that his loan to his father would be satisfied.

In 1988, Clayton conveyed his interest in the Somerset property to his daughter, Marion Watkins, "in fee simple tenants in common."

In 1991, Clayton died, survived by his three children. However, Bernis died in 1993 and Johnsie died in 1994. The three estates were consolidated and there ensued quite a battle at the probate court level over the Somerset property. Bernis' personal representative, Deborah Walker (appellant), argued that Bernis was the sole owner of the Somerset property at Clayton's death. Marion Watkins argued that Clayton's conveyance to her severed the joint tenancy and she and Bernis were tenants in common at the time of Clayton's death and that she, therefore, owned one-half of the Somerset property. The trial court agreed with Ms. Watkins and Ms. Walker appealed.

Judicial Opinion

Schwelb, Associate Judge. The parties agree that Clayton Gulledge's interest in the joint tenancy was alienable. They disagree only as to the nature of the interest which Clayton transferred to Ms. Watkins. The Estate of Bernis Gulledge (the Estate) argues that an owner cannot convey to a third party a greater interest than his own, and that because Clayton Gulledge's interest was subject to Bernis' right of survivorship, the interest which Ms. Watkins received from Clayton must be similarly restricted. Ms. Watkins contends, on the other hand, that Clayton's conveyance to her converted the joint tenancy into a tenancy in common by operation of law, and she received from Clayton an undivided one-half interest in the property.

The question whether a joint tenant severs a joint tenancy by ultimately conveying his interest to a third party without the consent of the other joint tenant has not been squarely decided in the District of Columbia. The issue is one of law, and our review is therefore de novo. This applicable rule in a large majority of jurisdictions is that either party to a joint tenancy may sever that tenancy by unilaterally disposing of his interest, that the consent of the other tenant is not required, and that the transfer converts the estate into a tenancy in common.

Although no decision by a court in this jurisdiction is directly on point, the discussion of joint tenancy that can be found in District of Columbia cases is consistent with the majority approach.

[The parties' cited] authorities do not conclusively settle the question before us, they provide no support for the notion that this court should reject the majority rule.

Nevertheless, the Estate contends, Sections 45-301 and 45-305 of the District of Columbia Code (1990 Repl.) supersede the common law rule authorizing the unilateral severance of joint tenancies. Section 45-301 states, in relevant part, that "[a]ny interest in or claim to real estate whether entitling to present or future possession and enjoyment, and whether vested or contingent, may be disposed of by deed or will, . . . " Section 45-305 provides that "[a]ny person claiming title to land may convey his interest in the same, . . . " The Estate argues that if we hold that Clayton Gulledge's transfer of his interest in the joint

tenancy unilaterally converted the joint tenancy into a tenancy in common, then we will be permitting Clayton to convey something that he does not have, namely, an interest not restricted by Bernis' right of survivorship.

Statutes in derogation of the common law are subject to strict construction. The Estate has cited no statutory language or history suggesting a legislative design to alter the common law with respect to the severance of a joint tenancy.

The Estate also argues that even if this court adopts the majority rule and recognizes Clayton Gulledge's common law right to sever the joint tenancy, the deed creating the joint tenancy constituted a contract. It was a breach of that contract, according to counsel for the Estate, for Clayton to take any action—here, the transfer of his interest to Ms. Watkins—which had the effect of terminating Bernis' right of survivorship without Bernis' consent. The Estate contends that Bernis furnished valuable consideration to his father in order to secure the right of survivorship, and that the termination of joint tenancy denied Bernis the fruits of the agreement reflected in the deed. We are not persuaded.

Bernis and Clayton agreed to the creation of a joint tenancy. That was their sole agreement. The rights of a joint tenant are governed by District of Columbia law, and Bernis thus acquired the rights of a joint tenant as defined by that law. Had the parties intended to create a right of survivorship that was not severable by either cotenant without the other's consent, they could have expressly so provided. Instead, they agreed to hold the property as joint tenants, and Bernis was bound by the legal consequences of that estate. One of these consequences was that, if Clayton transferred his interest to a third party, a tenancy in common would be created. The occurrence of that eventuality did not deny Bernis any legitimate expectation or infringe upon his rights in any way.

For the foregoing reasons, we conclude that when Clayton Gulledge conveyed his interest to Ms. Watkins, she and Bernis Gulledge both became owners of an undivided one-half interest in the property as tenants in common. Upon Bernis' death, his estate replaced Bernis as a tenant in common with Ms. Watkins.

Affirmed

Case Questions

1. Who conveyed what to whom and when?
2. Was the joint tenancy severed?
3. Who owns the Somerset property?
4. Do you think the result was Clayton's intent? Was it fair to Bernis?

Althea Lynley and Agnes Peach hold title to a 640-acre section in Montana as joint tenants with right of survivorship. The two acquired the property in their younger days with the idea that they would always be there for each other, and that the survivor would carry on with the property's development as a ranch.

Within five years of their acquisition, Althea married and moved to San Diego, and Agnes was left in Montana, where she married and developed the property with her husband. The title to the property remained the same as it was when the deed was originally recorded. Agnes died in June 1994. Her husband and children assumed they would inherit the land because Agnes's will left everything she owned to them. However, Althea, who returned for Agnes's funeral, claims the land belongs to her. Who is correct?

Consider 10.1

Other Requirements for Joint Tenancy Creation: The Unities

There are four other requirements for valid formation. They are referred to as the **unities** of a joint tenancy and they are time, title, interest, and possession.

Unity of Time This condition means that joint tenants must take their title to the property at the same time. For example, if O conveyed Blackacre to A and B on December 30, 2000, then A and B meet the unity of time requirement because they acquired their interest at the same time. However, if O conveyed half of Blackacre to A on December 30, 2000 and then conveyed the other half to B on June 30, 2001, then A and B cannot be joint tenants because they acquired their interests at different times. They are tenants in common.

In some states, this unity of time requirement presents problems when one party owns property prior to marriage and then after marriage seeks to hold the property with a spouse as joint tenants. For example, suppose Jane owns a home prior to marriage and upon marrying Bob seeks to transfer the property so that she and Bob will hold the property as joint tenants. If Jane transfers the property, the unity of time is not satisfied because Jane would have acquired her interest previously. This problem is overcome by setting up what is called a **strawman transaction.** In this transaction, Jane transfers the property to a third party (the strawman), who then transfers the property back to Jane and Bob. Jane and Bob have thus satisfied the requirement of unity of time for joint tenancy. Although this transaction is simply procedural, it is necessary if this unity is to be satisfied. Some states have eliminated the requirement of unity of time in circumstances like Jane and Bob's and have passed statutes indicating the strawman transaction need not be conducted for the joint tenancy to be valid.

Unity of Title Parties are not joint tenants unless they derive their title from the same source or grantor. For example, if O conveys Blackacre to A and B, A and B can be joint tenants. However, if B then conveys his interest to C, A and C cannot be joint tenants since A derived her title from O and C derived his title from B. A and C are tenants in common.

George Herring and his wife had property conveyed to them as "Mr. and Mrs. Herring" with the following language:

Consider 10.2

> TO HAVE AND TO HOLD unto said parties of the second part, and the Survivor
> of them, his heirs and assigns forever. It is the intention of this conveyance that
> said parties of the second part are to be vested with title as joint tenants, with the

incident of survivorship, and not as tenants in common; so that upon the death of either said parties of the second part, the entire fee simple absolute title in and to said property shall ipso facto become vested in the Survivor of said parties of the second part.

Mrs. Herring conveyed her interest in the property to her son from a previous marriage, Clarence Carroll. Mr. Herring brought suit to have the conveyance set aside. During the judicial proceedings, Mr. Herring died and his children, Marshall Herring and Beatrice Midkiff, as Mr. Herring's sole heirs, continued the case, claiming they were entitled to receive title to the property. Mr. Carroll claims the conveyance by Mrs. Herring to him was valid and made him a tenant in common with Marshall and Beatrice. Who is correct? Herring v. Carroll, 300 S.E.2d 629 (Ct. App. W. Va. 1983)

Unity of Interest This unity requires that joint tenants have equal interests in the property. For example, A and B each holding a one-half interest qualifies for joint tenancy. However, if A holds a one-third interest and B holds a two-thirds interest, then A and B can be only tenants in common.

Unity of Possession This requirement holds true for a valid tenancy in common as well. Under unity of possession, the parties must have equal rights to possess the property, and one party cannot dispossess the others of the land. If the land is divided either geographically or by time (into present and future interests; see Chapter 7), then the parties are no longer co-owners, and unity of possession is lost. For example, if O conveys Blackacre to A for life and then to B and C, B and C may be any type of tenants in the future, but they are not joint tenants with A because their interest in the property is divided.

Tenancies by Entirety

A **tenancy by entirety** requires the presence of the same four unities as for a joint tenancy plus one additional unity: unity of person. Unity of person requires that the tenants be married.

Tenancy by entirety also carries with it the right of survivorship; spouses are not permitted to dispose of the property by will. Severance of this tenancy requires the signature of the nonsevering spouse, and the property itself may be subject to dower and curtesy rights (discussed later in the chapter). Upon divorce of the parties (or dissolution of the marriage), tenancy by entirety is severed. In some states, this results in a conversion to joint tenancy; in others, to tenancy in common.

Tenancy in Partnership

A **tenancy in partnership** exists either when partners have contributed property to the partnership or when the partnership has purchased property with partnership funds. The partners hold title to such property as co-owners or as tenants in partnership. A tenancy in partnership has the characteristics of a joint tenancy. Upon the death of one of the partners, the remaining partners are entitled to the deceased partner's share. Heirs and devisees of the partner have no rights to the partnership property itself, but they may be entitled to payment for the value of the deceased partner's share or interest in the partnership.

Although laws vary from state to state, a tenancy in partnership has characteristics common to all of the tenancies. Each partner has the right to possession and use of the property for partnership purposes, and one partner cannot dispossess the other partners or the partnership of the property. In many states, transfer of partnership property requires the signature of all partners. Parties engaging in a land transaction with a partner should verify how title is held and whether the partner has authority to transfer the property. (More information on partnerships and limited partnerships can be found in Chapter 22.)

CREDITORS' RIGHTS AND CO-OWNERSHIP

Because there is more than one method of co-ownership, creditors' rights in property vary. The extent of the creditor's rights in terms of repossession and sale are limited according to the rights of the cotenant. In a tenancy in common, tenants may mortgage, lien, or pledge their share of the property; and in the event of one tenant's default on the underlying debt, the creditor could become a tenant in common or could sell the tenant's portion of the property to satisfy the debt. It is important to recognize that tenants may pledge only so much of the property as they own and that a creditor cannot foreclose on the entire property when one of the tenants defaults.

Creditors who accept pledges of property from joint tenants must realize the limitation of their interests. Because the estate is subject to survivorship, it is possible that their security will be lost if their debtors predecease other joint tenants. If a joint tenant defaults on an underlying debt secured by joint tenancy property, the creditor takes possession and title by foreclosure (or other method) and thus becomes a tenant in common.

In a tenancy by the entirety, creditors have no rights in the property unless the underlying debt is a joint debt of the husband and wife. Thus a creditor cannot validly enforce a pledge of the property made unilaterally by one of the spouses.

A creditor taking only a partial property pledge from a co-owner should be aware of problems in priority that may arise if later all tenants pledge their interests to another creditor. In those circumstances, it is possible that the first partial creditor will be second in priority to a later full-pledge creditor.

Figure 10.2 compares the various kinds of tenancies—their creation, transfer, and creditor relations.

RIGHTS AND RESPONSIBILITIES OF COTENANTS

Rents

Since in all of the tenancies each tenant has the equal right of possession, nonpossessing tenants are not permitted to collect rent from the tenant who is in possession of the property. However, the possessing tenant does not have the right to exclude the other tenants from the property (see discussion on partition and ouster). If the tenant in possession is collecting rents and profits from third parties who are using the property, such receipts should be shared with the other tenants. The general rule is that the nonpossessing tenant is entitled to his or her share of the fair market rental value but must also honor the terms of the lease entered into by the tenant in possession.

FIGURE 10.2   *Comparison of Methods of Co-Ownership*

Characteristics	Methods of Co-Ownership			
Unities	**Tenancy in Common**	**Joint Tenancy with Right of Survivorship**	**Tenancy by the Entireties**	**Tenancy in Partnership**
		1. Time 2. Title 3. Interest 4. Possession	1. Time 2. Title 3. Interest 4. Possession 5. Person (marriage)	3. Interest 4. Possession 5. Person (partners)
	4. Possession			
Transferability	*Inter vivos* Testamentary transfer	*Inter vivos* (severs tenancy) No testamentary transfer	One spouse cannot sell Surviving spouse	One partner could sell Title goes to surviving partners
Creditors' Rights	Rights survive debtor Creditor can become tenant in common	Limited to rights of survivorship Creditor can become tenant in common	Must be debt of husband and wife	Only partnership debts

Consider 10.3

In 1966, Rheta and William Rogers purchased a drugstore in Hayesville, North Carolina, while married. They acquired their interest as tenants by the entirety. In 1980, Rheta and William were divorced. As part of the property settlement agreement in the divorce, Rheta received the house and 12 acres of land and William received the remaining property with the provision that he pay Rheta half of their value.

Following the divorce, Mr. Rogers leased the drugstore property to Mr. and Mrs. Richard Kelly in June 1981. The Kellys operated a drugstore on the premises called "Kelly's Pharmacy." Mr. Rogers allowed the Kellys to take possession of the property and required that they pay rent only as they could. The Kellys made two rental payments of $840 during 1981 and in 1982 paid rent from January until June.

Mrs. Rogers filed suit to (1) regain possession of the drugstore property; and (2) collect half of the fair rental value of the property. What is Mrs. Rogers's interest in the property? Can she evict the Kellys? Is she entitled to half the rent? How should the rent be determined? *Rogers v. Kelly,* 311 S.E.2d 43 (N.C. App. 1984).

Expenditures

When cotenants do not pay equal amounts for the purchase of property, most courts have ruled that the shares in the property are not equal and have apportioned title according to the portion of the purchase price contributed.

Some payments are necessary to keep the land or its title clear, for example, taxes and mortgage payments. Cotenants are required to share in these expenses according to their proportionate share of title in the property. The proportion of these payments may be offset, in some states, if one of the cotenants has been in exclusive possession.

Expenditures for improvements are made solely at the discretion of the improving cotenant; there is neither a right to require contribution from the other tenants nor a right to offset costs by reducing the portion of mortgages and taxes paid by the improving cotenant. Expenditures for repairs are treated in the same manner because of the difficulty in trying to distinguish between repairs and improvements.

Partition and Ouster

Partition is the physical division of co-owned property whereby co-owners become adjoining landowners or neighbors. Severance, on the other hand, merely changes the form of co-ownership. Partition results in separate owners of adjoining parcels of land.

A partition can be made voluntarily when co-owners agree upon a geographical division of the property or it can be made by a court when circumstances require. The following circumstances require the partition of co-owned property: (1) when one tenant has dispossessed the other tenant or tenants and refuses to allow access (ouster), (2) when a tenant refuses to contribute for necessary expenditures, (3) when a tenant refuses to distribute rents and profits earned from exclusive possession (at common law), or (4) when other circumstances arise where the court deems a partition appropriate (such as feuding relatives).

If it is impossible or illogical to physically divide the property, a court may order the property sold and the proceeds divided among the cotenants according to their proportionate interests. For example, if a piece of property has water on only one portion, a division would be unfair but a sale would allow the parties to realize the value of their interests.

> **Consider 10.4**
>
> X and Y own equal shares of a one-acre parcel of land in the White Mountains of Arizona. Y has built a cabin on it at a cost of $62,000. Y has also managed to rent the cabin for 50 of the 52 weeks in 2001 at $350 per week. Mortgage payments on the cabin are $520 per month. Utilities vary from summer to winter but average about $90 per month. Taxes on the property are $80 per month with the cabin, but were $40 without it. Insurance is $270 per year. X has demanded an equal share of the profits. Y refuses but says X is responsible for half of the mortgage, utilities, taxes, and insurance. What is the result? Would the result be different depending upon what type of tenancy exists?

MARITAL PROPERTY RIGHTS— CO-OWNERSHIP BY MARRIAGE

In every state, there are provisions to protect married persons holding title to property with their spouses. Tenancy by the entirety is one example, and other provisions and protections include dower and curtesy rights in some states and community property rights in other states.

The Common Law—Dower Rights

Under common law, **dower rights** existed for the protection of a widow. The common law rule was that a widow is entitled to a one-third interest for her life in any and all real property her husband owned at any time during their marriage.

Because of probable confusion and complications associated with dower rights, many states have changed dower rights to simply protect a surviving spouse by requiring that one-third to one-half of the deceased spouse's property of any character (real or personal) be given to the surviving spouse. Such statutes help prevent the problem of disinheritance by giving some property to the surviving spouse, but outright instead of in the form of a life estate interest. Some states have homestead exemptions that provide the surviving spouse with a minimum amount of property such as a residence, some personal property, a living allowance, and vehicles. This minimum amount is given to the surviving spouse before any distributions of property and before any creditors' obligations are satisfied.

Regardless of the form dower takes, it is a well-protected interest of a spouse. In the following case, the complexities of dower create a cloud on the title of another "wife."

Funches v. Funches

413 S.E.2d 44 (Va. 1992)

Facts

Gisele Funches was married to Robert Funches until his death in March 1990. However, following Robert's death, Gisele discovered that Robert had married, at least by ceremony, Pranee Funches. Gisele and Robert had never been divorced.

Gisele (plaintiff/appellant) learned that during the course of his bigamous marriage to Pranee (defendant/appellee), Robert and Pranee had purchased real property near Alexandria, Virginia and took title as "tenants by the entirety with right of survivorship." Upon Robert's death, Pranee claimed she had full title to the land. Gisele claimed that because they could not be legally married, Pranee and Robert could not hold title as tenants by the entirety. According to Gisele's suit, Pranee and Robert were thus tenants in common and Gisele, as Robert's heir, was entitled to one-half of the property.

The trial court held that Robert and Pranee did not have a tenancy by the entirety because they were not married but rather held title to the land as joint tenants with right of survivorship and that Gisele had no dower interest in the land. Gisele appealed.

Judicial Opinion

Compton, Justice. The decision in this case is controlled by the principles which we recently enunciated in *Gant v. Gant,* 237 Va. 588, 379 S.E.2d 331 (1989). Indeed, the first sentence of the *Gant* opinion states the crucial issue in the present case: "In this appeal, we consider the effect of a deed purporting to convey an estate by the entirety, with words of survivorship, to parties who are not married."

In *Gant,* after a married couple divorced, they acquired a house and lot by a deed which purported to convey the property to the unmarried couple "to be held and owned by them . . . as tenants by the entireties with the right of survivorship as at common law. . . . " Later, the man married another woman. Upon his death, his widow and their daughter filed a partition suit naming the ex-wife, among others, as a party defendant. We affirmed the trial court's ruling that, upon the decedent's death, the property had passed to the ex-wife by survivorship and that the widow and her daughter had no interest in the property.

In *Gant,* we stated: Tenancies by the entirety are based upon five unities: those of title, estate, time, possession, and persons. The unity of persons relates to marriage and embodies the common law fiction that husband and wife are one. A tenancy which lacks the fifth unity but is based upon the other four is a joint tenancy, for which the first four unities are also prerequisite." We held that parties who are not married to each other, even though "they lack one of the essential unities prerequisite to the creation of a tenancy by the entirety, . . . may become joint tenants, and if the instrument creating the estate manifests the requisite intention, the joint tenancy will be clothed with the common law right of survivorship."

Only slight elaboration beyond the analysis of *Gant* is necessary to demonstrate that Gant's principles govern the result in this case. Obviously, the deed which purports to establish a tenancy by the entirety between these persons who are not married to each other creates a joint tenancy. Clearly, the words of survivorship expressly manifest the requisite intent that the joint tenancy is clothed with the common law right of survivorship. And, this express manifestation of survivorship necessarily excludes plaintiff's dower interest.

Furthermore, the interest of the defendant, the surviving joint tenant, is superior to the dower interest of the plaintiff, the wife of the other joint tenant. "One joint tenant's right in the joint estate is superior to the contingent or inchoate dower of the wife of the other joint tenant. Joint tenants are seized *per mi et per tout*,—that is, each of them has the entire possession of his part as well as of the whole. One of them has not a seizen of one-half and the other the remaining half. Neither can one be exclusively seized of one acre and the other of another acre. Each has an undivided moiety of the whole, not the whole of an undivided moiety. The possession and seizen of one joint tenant is the possession and seizen of the other."

Finally, the plaintiff contends that the trial court erred when it did not recognize her dower interest and failed to modify the deed to reflect a tenancy in common "when the deed arose out of a criminal and illegal incident of bigamy." The complete answer to this contention, assuming as we must on demurrer that the decedent committed bigamy by marrying the defendant, is that the "marriage" did not confer the ownership or survivorship interests in the property. Instead, the deed created the right of survivorship in the defendant.

Here, survivorship was expressly created by the parties in the deed; no property rights were acquired by any wrongful acts. Thus, the fact of a void marriage affects neither defendant's ownership of the property nor her right of survivorship.

Affirmed.

Case Questions

1. What is the relationship between and among Robert, Gisele, and Pranee?
2. What type of interest did Robert and Pranee create with their deed language?
3. What type of interest does Gisele say they had? Why?
4. What unity was lacking on the tenancy by the entirety? What is the effect of this missing unity?
5. How does the court deal with the issue of the underlying bigamous marriage?

Suppose that someone married her stepfather who then passed away. Would she, under the holding in the *Funches* case, be entitled to her dower interest in his property? *Rhodes v. McAffee*, 45 S.W.2d 522 (Tenn. 1998).

> **Consider 10.5**

The Common Law—Curtesy Rights

Curtesy is a surviving husband's protection that, at common law, gave the husband a life estate in all real property owned by his wife during their marriage. However, the **curtesy rights** existed only if there were issue born of the marriage. This right has been modified by the states today, and the above discussed statutory protections now eliminate common law provisions on dower and curtesy but still protect surviving spouses.

Statutory Marital Law—Community Property

Community property is a system of ownership by spouses that has Spanish origins and exists, in some form, in 11 states with many others adopting its 50-50 ownership principles. In states where community property is the basis for marital property rights, unless the parties agree and specify otherwise, property is held as community property.

The basic principle governing this system of co-ownership is that both partners in the marriage work for the benefit of the community and do so on an equal basis and therefore own half of all property acquired during the course of the marriage. This half-ownership principle is true regardless of whether the spouses were employed or unemployed during the course of the marriage.

Over the past few years, a new type of marital property interest has been created to provide couples with the benefit of community property rights while allowing them the ease of transfer that joint tenancy or tenancy by the entirety provide with automatic transfer of title upon death. Called *community property with right of survivorship*, this new interest allows a married couple in community property states to hold title to property as a community asset but still permits the 50-50 ownership principle to apply. The result is that the tax basis for property can be stepped up to help minimize estate taxes (see Chapter 22). This new interest is created by statute, is not yet recognized in all community property states, and still has some tax issues pending with the Internal Revenue Service.

In some states, the basic principles of community property rights have been applied in cases where the parties were not married but lived as husband and wife. Courts in community and noncommunity property states have allowed unmarried cohabitants rights in their partner's property acquired during the course of cohabitation. The basis for allowing these property recoveries has been a contract, express or implied, or a quasi-contract found to exist between the unmarried partners.

The following case deals with the difficulties of property rights when the parties are not married.

Champion v. Frazier

977 S.W.2d 61 (Mo. App. 1998)

Facts

Leroy Frazier (defendant) and Helen Champion (plaintiff) began to see each other during the late 1970s. During the entire time of their relationship, they have been married to other people. Prior to 1989, they maintained separate apartments, but in 1989, they moved into a house together on Lalite Street in St. Louis (Lalite property). Only Leroy's name was on the title and bank loan for the Lalite property.

In May 1994, Leroy moved out of the Lalite property and Helen continued to live there with her two adult children and two grandchildren.

In June 1994, Helen brought suit against Leroy for, among other things, breach of contract with regard to Helen's rights in the Lalite property. Helen said that Leroy promised that she would own half of the property. The trial court found that there was a contract and awarded Helen half of the value of the Lalite property or $20,000 of the $40,000 appraised value. Leroy appealed.

Judicial Opinion

Hoff, Judge. Plaintiff alleges Defendant breached a contract to share equally in all benefits obtained through ownership of the Lalite property. Plaintiff testified Defendant made two statements to indicate her ownership interest in the Lalite property.

Plaintiff testified Defendant took her to see the house and told her if she liked it "he would get it" for her. She understood this to mean that they would live together there and save money by not paying for two of everything. Plaintiff also testified that Defendant asked her to sign a "bank statement" for the loan to pay for the house. When she asked why she should sign it because he

had not taken her to get the deed, she testified Defendant said, "Don't worry about that. Before I get the title I'll make sure your name is on it." Defendant denied making any of these statements. Defendant testified the only document Plaintiff ever signed from the bank was to put her name on his checking account. There were no other witnesses to corroborate the statements on which Plaintiff relied. Furthermore, Plaintiff concedes she is not obligated to pay the outstanding mortgage on the Lalite property.

An oral contract for specific performance to convey real estate cannot be based on conversations too loose or casual. The alleged statements that Plaintiff relied on are too loose and casual to indicate Defendant's intention to convey an interest in the Lalite property to Plaintiff. Defendant's alleged statements do not constitute an explicit promise to share equally in all benefits obtained through ownership of the Lalite property. We agree there was no express contract between the parties.

However, the trial court did find an implied-in-fact contract between the parties. Our research indicates the only Missouri case finding an implied-in-fact contract between unmarried cohabitants is *Hudson*. It explains courts should look to the conduct of the parties to determine whether there exists an implied contract between them. In *Hudson*, the court found an implied-in-fact contract based on the nature of the relationship between the parties. Marshall F. Hudson and Brigitte DeLonjay were unmarried cohabitants. They purchased a residence together, with both names on the title, and each financially contributed to the purchase. They owned a number of joint bank accounts to which each contributed. They paid most of their household expenses from the joint funds.

Additionally, the parties in *Hudson* created a business corporation, Affiliated, financed by both their joint checking account and a loan on which both parties were jointly obligated. Each party personally guaranteed the loan and their residence was pledged as security. Both parties worked at the business and each owned stock in the corporation. Various financial statements showed the parties owned all of their assets jointly. They also formed another business, Dollco, from jointly held capital.

This business purchased various equipment and a piece of real estate. Title to the real estate was taken in the name of Hudson d/b/a Dollco. There was "voluminous documentary evidence" of the jointly held assets.

The trial court in *Hudson* entered judgment in favor of DeLonjay based on an implied-in-fact contract, breach of a confidential relationship, constructive fraud, and constructive trust. The trial court awarded DeLonjay an "equal share of the residential property, one half the stock of Affiliated, one half the value of the Dollco assets, an equal share of money deposited in the registry of the Court, certain money appropriated by Hudson, and the balance in a joint bank account." This court affirmed the trial court's judgment.

A review of the conduct between Plaintiff and Defendant here indicates the evidence is insufficient to support a finding of an implied-in-fact contract to share equally in the Lalite property. The following facts are undisputed. Plaintiff's name was not on the title to the Lalite property nor was her name on the bank loan. In 1995, Plaintiff declared bankruptcy under Chapter 7. She did not indicate any interest in the Lalite property in the bankruptcy filing. A proposal for a new roof for the Lalite property was made out in the name of both Plaintiff and Defendant; and both Plaintiff and Defendant signed a remodeling contract for the property.

Defendant added Plaintiff's name to his checking account sometime between June 1989 and August 1990. Plaintiff wrote out all the checks for the bills. Defendant worked as a Deputy Sheriff for the City of St. Louis at a salary of $24,000. His paycheck was deposited in the joint account. Defendant also received income from rental properties. Plaintiff received $207 per month as child support from the state for her two children. That money was also deposited in the joint account. Plaintiff did not file any income tax returns until 1995. Plaintiff received food stamps which were used by Defendant to purchase groceries for the household.

The record also reveals the following. Defendant discovered he had glaucoma in 1984 and by 1991 he was no longer able to drive. Plaintiff testified she drove Defendant around for his job after he could no longer drive

and without her help Defendant would not have been able to keep his job. However, Defendant testified ninety percent of the time he drove with Willie Smith. Willie Smith testified he and Defendant worked together most of the time and Willie drove during this time.

Although it is apparent Plaintiff contributed to the household, the conduct between Plaintiff and Defendant does not support a finding of an implied-in-fact contract to share equally in the Lalite property. Plaintiff did not substantially contribute to the purchase of the Lalite property nor is her name on the title or bank loan. The facts in this case are distinguishable from the facts in *Hudson*. Here, there is no "voluminous documentary evidence" of jointly held assets nor is there "extensive testimony" concerning the assets held by the parties to indicate an implied-in-fact contract between them. Moreover, Plaintiff and her family have continued to live in the Lalite property without paying rent since Defendant moved out in May 1994.

Here, Plaintiff and Defendant had a family relationship. Plaintiff did not introduce any evidence that she expected to be paid for the services she rendered. In addition, both parties benefited from Plaintiff's services. For instance, Plaintiff helped Defendant keep his job which was at a much higher salary than Plaintiff was able to obtain. As a result, Defendant could pay the mortgage and insurance on the Lalite property. Under the circumstances, Plaintiff's rendition of services alone does not justify a monetary award because there was no express contract or actual understanding between the parties that she would be paid for such services.

Upon review of the record, there is no substantial evidence to support the trial court's finding of an implied-in-fact contract. In addition, there is no substantial evidence to support the existence of an express contract.

We reverse and remand for the trial court to enter judgment in favor of Defendant on the breach of contract claim.

Reversed and remanded.

Case Questions

1. What was the nature of the relationship between Helen and Leroy?

2. What was their understanding on the Lalite property?

3. What evidence does Helen point to in order to establish her rights?

4. Do you think the fact that Helen and Leroy were married to other people at the time influenced the appellate court's decision? Why or why not?

Consider 10.6

In 1981, William Hurt and Sandra Jennings began living together in New York City. Mr. Hurt was a movie actor, and Ms. Jennings was an accomplished member of a ballet company. In 1982, Ms. Jennings accompanied Mr. Hurt to South Carolina where he was filming a movie. They lived together as husband and wife during the filming of the movie. Mr. Hurt was still married to another woman at that time, with the divorce becoming final in December 1982.

The relationship was volatile, but Mr. Hurt stated that "as far as he was concerned, we were married in the eyes of God" and "more married than married people." Ms. Jennings gave birth to a child later verified to be Mr. Hurt's. She then filed suit in 1988 seeking to establish her rights in Mr. Hurt's property and earnings. She claimed that Mr. Hurt had promised to support her if she would have his child and give up her career.

Should the court support an award of property and support for Ms. Jennings? *Jennings v. Hurt,* 554 N.Y.S.2d 220 (1990)

If community property law is applicable to a marriage relationship, then all property acquired during the course of the marriage is classified as community property and is half owned by each spouse. However, the spouses may still have some separate property to which they hold complete title. For example, any property owned prior to marriage that is brought into the marriage is separate property. Also, gifts and inheritances received by individual spouses during the marriage are separate property. If, for example, a wife receives an inheritance from her father, the money would be her separate property and would not belong to the community.

Debts are also considered community obligations, and each spouse is responsible for 50 percent of the debts entered into for the benefit of the community.

Those dealing in real estate in community property states need the signature of both spouses for the listing, mortgaging, improvement, or sale of real property. Real estate partnerships operating in these states must obtain a waiver from the spouses of all partners, so that the property can be transferred without the risk of a spouse's interest being exercised at a later time. In noncommunity property states, the same practice should be followed for dower and curtesy rights.

One of the benefits of the community property system is that both spouses acquire some property rights during the course of the marriage. In noncommunity property states, marriage for a lifetime does not guarantee a 50 percent share of the property acquired during the marriage. To equalize the states' laws on marital property, the **Uniform Marital Property Act** was drafted but has been adopted only in Wisconsin. The purpose of the act is to bring community property principles to noncommunity property states.

Consider 10.7

The very public divorce of Lorna Wendt, the wife of a GE executive, presented a test of property rights in Connecticut. Mrs. Wendt was awarded $20 million of the $100 million her husband had accumulated as a GE officer. Mrs. Wendt claimed she gave up her career as a music teacher in order to serve as a corporate wife. She had requested half of the $100 million. What is the nature of a marital partnership? What public policy issues are at stake in marital property divisions? Mrs. Wendt worked as a music teacher to allow her husband to obtain his MBA. Does she have any rights with respect to that investment?

Premarital or Antenuptial Agreements

In recent years, and particularly with second marriages, many couples have entered into agreements minimizing or waiving their marital property rights. These agreements, called **premarital, prenuptial,** or **antenuptial agreements,** are subject to strict review by courts to determine if they are fair and were entered into voluntarily. Presently, 15 states have adopted the **Uniform Premarital Agreement Act,** which supports upholding these agreements. Most other states have some form of legislation that recognizes them.

The area of prenuptial or antenuptial agreements has been clarified by courts and legislation over the past decade. The following excerpt from *Forbes* provides a good summary of the areas of concern in these agreements. See also Web Exhibit 10.1 for a sample prenuptial agreement.

Practical Tip

Marital and quasi-marital property rights are complex and carry significant impact in terms of real property interests and titles. The status of couples should be verified for both buyers and sellers prior to listing, selling, or buying property. Individuals should have their rights, obligations, and nuptial agreements reviewed by an attorney. The validity of such agreements should be verified according to individual state law.

Ten Steps to an Airtight Prenup

1. Make sure there's no hint of coercion. To nail this down, make sure your spouse-to-be has his own lawyer. The American Academy of Matrimonial Lawyers will gladly supply a list of its members.
2. A lawyer for Donald Trump, Stanford Lotwin, says you can limit disclosure by stating merely that you have certain assets exceeding a certain value. Make sure you don't lie. If your spouse can prove you were hiding assets, you could be in big trouble.
3. Be prepared for a few surprises. Some are pleasant, some not.
4. Avoid any appearance of forcing a deal at the last minute. Sign at least a month before the wedding. Later than that an aggrieved spouse could claim he was made to sign under pressure.
5. Don't give the prospective spouse the idea that you regard your assets as more precious than her. "The more stringent and self-protective, the more likely the marriage is going to blow up in their faces," warns Beverly Hills lawyer Alexandra Leichtner.
6. Don't throw in anything mean: like the provision Stan Lotwin recently saw imposing a $1,000 penalty for every pound a wife gained. No court would enforce that kind of provision, and it could spur the judge to toss the whole thing out.
7. Consider increasing your spouse's cut over time to make the agreement more equitable. New York

divorce litigator Carl Tunick recalls a phone call from a woman eager to divorce her husband immediately. Tunick pointed out that she was entitled to an extra $1 million for every year she stuck it out. "Can't you wait until Jan. 1?" asked Tunick. She did, and they're still married.
8. See that your spouse stands to inherit something if you die first. Without such a provision, taxes could soak up everything—including your 401(k).
9. Don't count on escaping alimony payment. In New York and a few other states, a spouse can waive the right to alimony. If the judge thinks it's unfair, he can order you to pay anyway, no matter what the agreement might say.
10. Be very careful about mixing premarital and postmarital assets. Because if you cannot absolutely prove what was yours before the marriage, you could stand to lose it.

Discussion Questions

1. List three things you *should not* do in negotiating, drafting, or signing a prenuptial agreement.
2. What public policy issues do you see in honoring prenuptial agreements?

From "Ten Steps to an Airtight Prenup," by McMenamin. Reprinted by Permission of Forbes Magazine, © 2001 Forbes, 1996.

> **Ethical Issue** | Discuss the public policy and ethical issues in prenuptial agreements. One lawyer has commented, "I've never seen a marriage with a prenuptial agreement last." Why this observation?

The following case involving two well-known partners discusses the validity of an antenuptial agreement.

Delorean v. Delorean

511 A.2d 1257 (N.J. 1986)

Facts

John Z. DeLorean (husband/plaintiff) and Cristina DeLorean (wife/defendant) entered into an antenuptial agreement on May 8, 1973 (only a few hours before they were married), that provided the following:

> [A]ny and all property, income and earnings acquired by each before and after the marriage shall be the separate property of the person acquiring the same, without any rights, title or control vesting in the other person.

The marital assets (such as future earnings) could have exceeded $20 million, and practically all of them were in the name of the husband. Without this agreement and considering that the marriage lasted 13 years and resulted in two minor children, the wife would ordinarily be entitled to 50 percent of the marital assets at the time of divorce.

On the husband's petition for divorce, the wife alleged that the agreement was invalid because she was not given full information about the extent of her husband's financial affairs before she signed and that her husband exercised undue influence on her in getting the agreement signed. The trial court upheld the validity of the agreement, and Mrs. DeLorean appealed.

Judicial Opinion

Imbriani, J.S.C. Initially, it is clear that "antenuptial agreements fixing post-divorce rights and obligations [are]. . . . valid and enforceable" and courts should "welcome and encourage such agreements at least 'to the extent that the parties have developed comprehensive and particularized agreements responsive to their peculiar circumstances' " (*D'Onofrio v. D'Onofrio*, 200 N.J.Super. 361, 366, 491 A.2d 752 [App.Div. 1985]). In determining whether to enforce an antenuptial agreement there are at least three requirements that have to be met.

First, that there was no fraud or duress in the execution of the agreement or, to put it another way, that both parties signed voluntarily. The wife alleges she did not sign voluntarily because her husband presented the agreement to her only a few hours before the marriage ceremony was performed and threatened to cancel the marriage if she did not sign. In essence she asserts that she had no choice but to sign. While she did not have independent counsel of her own choosing, she did acknowledge that before she signed she did privately consult with an attorney selected by her husband who advised her not to sign the agreement. Yet, for whatever reasons, she rejected the attorney's advice and signed.

While her decision may not have been wise, it appears that she had sufficient time to consider the consequences of signing the agreement and, indeed, although she initially refused to sign it, after conferring with her intended spouse and an attorney, she reconsidered and decided to sign it. Concededly, the husband was 25-years older and a high-powered senior executive with General Motors Corporation, but she was not a "babe in the woods." She was 23-years old with some experience in the modeling and entertainment industry; she had experienced an earlier marriage and the problems wrought by a divorce; and she had advice from an attorney who, although not of her own choosing, did apparently give her competent advice and recommended that she not sign. While it may have been embarrassing to cancel the wedding only a few hours before it was to take place, she certainly was not compelled to go through with the ceremony. There was no fraud or misrepresentation committed by her husband. He made it perfectly clear that he did not want her to receive any portion of the marital assets that were in his name. At no time did she ever make an effort to void the agreement and, of course, it was never voided. Under these circumstances the court is satisfied that the wife entered into the agreement voluntarily and without any fraud or duress being exerted upon her.

Second, the agreement must not be "unconscionable." This is not to say that the agreement should be what a court would determine to be "fair and equitable." The fact that what a spouse receives under an antenuptial agreement is small, inadequate or disproportionate does not in itself render the agreement voidable if the spouse was not overreached and entered into the agreement voluntarily with full knowledge of the financial worth of the other person. So long as the spouse is not left destitute or as a public charge the parties can agree to divide marital assets in any manner they wish. Mrs. DeLorean presently enjoys substantial income from her employment as a talk-show television hostess and was given a life interest in a trust of unknown amount created by Mr. DeLorean, which he testified had assets of between $2 and $5 million. She will not be left destitute. The court is unaware of any public policy which requires that the division of marital assets be made in what the court believes to be fair and equitable if the parties freely and voluntarily agree otherwise. In the final analysis it is for the parties to decide for themselves what is fair and equitable, not the court. So long as a spouse had sufficient opportunity to reflect on her actions, was competent, informed, and had access to legal advice and that of any relevant experts, a court should not, except in the most unusual case, interject its own opinion of what is fair and equitable and reject the wishes of the parties. Since the wife voluntarily agreed to this division of the marital assets and she will not become destitute or a public charge, the agreement is not unconscionable.

Third, the spouse seeking to enforce the agreement made a full and complete disclosure of his or her financial wealth before the agreement was signed. Obviously, one cannot make a knowing and intelligent waiver of legal and financial rights unless fully informed of all of the facts; otherwise one cannot know what is being waived. The husband asserts that the wife acknowledged that she received a full and complete disclosure of his financial wealth because the agreement states:

> Husband is the owner of substantial real and personal property and he has reasonable prospects of earning large sums of monies; these facts have been fully disclosed to Wife.

However, that statement is not very meaningful and is insufficient to satisfy his obligation to make a full and complete disclosure of his financial wealth. While several states hold that a full and complete disclosure is not synonymous with a detailed disclosure, those cases can be distinguished because they impose upon each spouse a duty to inquire and investigate into the financial condition of the other. However, as far as this court can ascertain, New Jersey imposes no such duty.

A conflict arose as to precisely what financial information was disclosed by Mr. DeLorean. However, the court is satisfied that even if it accepted as true the testimony of Mr. DeLorean he did not satisfy his legal obligation to make a full and complete disclosure.

While the wife was aware that Mr. DeLorean was a person of substantial wealth, there was no way that she could have known with any substantial degree of certainty the extent of his wealth. This is important because one can appreciate that while a wife might waive her legal rights to share in marital assets of $1 million, she might not be willing to do so if she knew the marital assets were worth $20 million. And the suggestion that Mrs. DeLorean had a duty to investigate to ascertain the full nature and extent of his financial wealth is both unfair and unrealistic. How many people when about to marry would consider investigating the financial affairs of their intended spouse? How many people would appreciate or tolerate being investigated by an intended spouse? And how many marriages would be canceled when one of the parties is informed of an investigation being conducted by the other? Such a requirement would cause embarrassment and impose a difficult burden.

The only way that Mrs. DeLorean could knowingly and intelligently waive her legal rights in Mr. DeLorean's assets was if she was fully and completely informed what they were. And for Mr. DeLorean to merely state that he had an interest in a farm in California, a large tract of land in Montana, and a share in a major-league baseball club fell far short of a full and complete disclosure.

However, it is argued that California, not New Jersey, law should be applied. When the agreement was executed the parties had substantial contacts with California and reasonably expected to retain many of them which, indeed, has been the case. For these reasons the law of California must be applied in this case. California does not treat a party to an antenuptial agreement as a fiduciary. As this court reads California law, the disclosures made by John DeLorean appear to be sufficient.

Affirmed.

Case Questions

1. When was the antenuptial agreement signed?
2. Describe the circumstances surrounding the signing of the agreement.
3. Was Mrs. DeLorean represented by her lawyer at the time the agreement was signed?
4. What is the extent of the assets involved?
5. Why does the court use the term "babe in the woods"?
6. Is the agreement under California or New Jersey law?
7. Was there undue influence?
8. Is the agreement valid?

FIGURE 10.3 *Prenuptial Agreements of the Rich and Famous*

Name	Terms	Results
Donald Trump and Marla Maples	No alimony if adultery; child support; limited dollar amount	Prenup honored in divorce; Maples awarded limited amount.
Barry Bonds (San Francisco Giants) and Susan Branco	Agreement (14 pages) signed on the way to the wedding.	Judge held agreement void because Mrs. Bonds didn't know what she was signing. $10,000 per month alimony.
Steven Spielberg and Amy Irving	Scrap of paper prenup, but Irving had no lawyer. Gave Irving no interest in Spielberg rights, royalties, revenues, and properties.	Judge set agreement aside for Irving's lack of representation. Spielberg settled for $100 million (4-year marriage).
Melinda and Bill Gates	Unknown	Still married

Consider 10.8

William Pajak married his third wife, Audrey, one day after they entered into a prenuptial agreement by which Audrey waived any and all interests in William's estate. William had four children from his two previous marriages and wished for his property to go to them. Audrey was a secretary at Carolina Furniture Company, William's business. She had a tenth-grade education and did not read the agreement before signing it. The agreement was drafted by William's lawyer, and the lawyer was present while Audrey signed the agreement. Audrey also indicated she knew William owned the furniture store, but she knew of no other holdings. In fact, William's property and estate were quite extensive. Shortly after their marriage, William passed away. Audrey claimed an interest in the estate because the prenuptial agreement was invalid. The children claim Audrey understood the agreement and chose not to seek advice. Should Audrey be entitled to a spouse's share of the estate? *Pajak v. Pajak*, 385 S.E.2d 384 (W.Va. 1989)

Figure 10.3 provides a summary of famous prenuptial agreements.

CAUTIONS AND CONCLUSIONS

Whether a party is a seller, buyer, or creditor, the status of property co-owners must be determined. Questions to be answered before entering into an obligation regarding the co-owned property are:

1. Who are the co-owners?
2. What type of co-ownership exists?
3. Is one co-owner authorized to transfer title or to give a lien?
4. How much of an interest does the co-owner have?
5. Are additional signatures (spouses') required?

Key Terms

Chapter Problems

1. On a deed dated November 1, 1928, an acre of land located on Gap Road near Peak Mountain in Rockingham County, Virginia, was conveyed to Add Shoemaker and his wife Bessie Shoemaker with the following provision:

It is hereby mutually understood and agreed, that the grantees herein named are to have and to hold the said land and tenements as joint tenants, and not as tenants in common.

Add Shoemaker died intestate (without a will) in 1951 and was survived by Bessie and several children. Bessie, at some point after Add's death, conveyed to Wilmer A. Shoemaker (one of her sons) a 0.542-acre portion of the land she and Add had acquired in the 1928 deed. Bessie died in 1984.

Wilmer died testate (with a will) sometime before 1988 and by his will devised the 0.542-acre tract of land to Shelby Jean Moubray. Moubray conveyed the tract to David Martin Smith and Vivian Secrist Smith on January 28, 1988.

On February 19, 1992, Susan Shoemaker Hoover, Catherine G. Shoemaker Smith, Sarah P. Shoemaker Pennington, and Margie C. Shoemaker Hoover (collectively, the Hoovers), the children of Add and Bessie, filed suit against Alvin Shoemaker, Nellie Craun, and Charles Shoemaker, also children of Add and Bessie (collectively, the Smiths). The suit alleged that by the language of the 1928 deed, Bessie and Add were tenants in common only and that upon Add's death his interest in the tract of land should have passed by intestate succession to his children. The children also asked that the land be sold and its proceeds distributed because it was not convenient to partition the land. Are the children right? *Hoover v. Smith,* 444 S.E.2d 546 (Va. 1994)

2. A, B, and C were partners in the operation of a grocery store. The partnership's major assets were the store and the land on which it was located. C has passed away, and the executor of C's estate now wants to sell the estate's one-third interest in the store and the land. A and B claim they now own the land. What is the result?

3. Barbara Laudig and Robert Laudig were married in 1972. In 1987, Mr. Laudig discovered that Mrs. Laudig was involved in an extramarital relationship. Mr. Laudig left their home, but returned later that year and agreed to stay if Mrs. Laudig would sign a postnuptial agreement. The agreement provided that Mrs. Laudig, in exchange for $10,000, would waive all rights to marital property if she had an extramarital affair anytime during the next 15 years. The agreement was signed by both parties in August 1987.

In December 1988, Mrs. Laudig renewed her relationship with her former paramour, and Mr. Laudig filed for divorce in May, 1989. Mr. Laudig sought to enforce the postnuptial agreement and be awarded all the marital property. Mrs. Laudig objected on the grounds that their postnuptial agreement was against public policy. Who is correct? *Laudig v. Laudig,* 624 A.2d 651 (Pa. 1993)

4. Bill bought a house on September 3, 1999, for $160,000 with $15,000 down and a $145,000 mortgage. On November 5, 1999, Bill was married and deeded the property to "William H. Smith and Jane D. Smith, husband and wife, not as tenants in common, and not as community property estate, but as joint tenants with right of survivorship." What type of co-owners are Jane and Bill?

5. In February 1952, James and Syvilla Ballantyne acquired title, as joint tenants, to a lot in the city of Minot. They lived there in a house located on the lot. On April 10, 1959, James Ballantyne died, leaving a will that purported to devise the lot to his wife, Syvilla, for life, with the remainder to his eight children by a previous marriage. James and Syvilla had no children of their marriage, and the probate court awarded Syvilla a life estate and a remainder to the eight children as part of the final distribution of James's estate.

Syvilla occupied the home and paid the taxes on it until her death on May 11, 1973. She did not remarry and left a will that did not mention the lot but left the residue of her estate to her sisters (appellants) and her brother. After Syvilla's death, James's eight children took possession of the property and attempted to sell it. At that time, the discovery of the joint tenancy was made, and Syvilla's sisters brought suit. What interest was created and who owns what and how following Syvilla's death? *Cranston v. Winters,* 238 N.W.2d 647 (N.D. 1976)

6. Mr. Lichtenstein and his son, Albert, owned a department store in downtown Corpus Christi. Because of their disagreements over leasing, payments, and maintenance, the two sought to have their tenancy in common partitioned. The court found the property could not be fairly and equitably divided and ordered a sale, with the distribution of proceeds to the Lichtensteins. Was the court correct in its action?

7. Robert and Bernice Fick lived together beginning in 1981. In 1984, they were married. Shortly before their wedding, they both signed a prenuptial agreement that had been drafted by Robert. Among other things, the agreement waived both parties' rights to alimony upon divorce. The agreement incorporated by attachment both Bernice's and Robert's financial statements of property ownership and debts. However, Robert's statement was not attached at the time the agreement was signed and was not produced for Bernice until a year after their wedding. In 1989, Bernice filed for divorce and asked that the prenuptial agreement be set aside. Robert maintained that the agreement was valid because Bernice signed voluntarily and was represented by counsel. Bernice says she was mislead because Robert did not attach his financials and she signed without complete information. Should the court set aside the prenuptial agreement

and award Bernice the alimony and property she is requesting? *Fick v. Fick,* 851 P.2d 445 (Nev. 1993)

8. Carolyn Cummings had been awarded a medical retirement and disability benefits from the state of Alaska during the 1970s. She then met and married Gary Cummings and continued to receive her benefits from Alaska because of her disability. She used the funds to purchase various items for their household as well as a camp trailer. During an action for divorce, Carolyn claimed the furnishings and the trailer were her separate property. Gary claimed the commingling of the funds made those items community property. Who is correct? *Cummings v. Cummings,* 765 P.2d 697 (Id. 1988)

9. Otto and Oscar Olson built a footbridge on their property across the Smith River in 1949. A document called "Footbridge Access" was signed "Olson Brothers by Otto Olson" and gave E. G. Dunn the right to use the footbridge. A dispute later arose between the parties regarding the right to use the bridge. Oscar says Otto could not convey the access without his signature. Is he correct? *Smo v. Black,* 761 P.2d 1339 (Or. 1988)

10. Dr. Stuart G. Moraitis and Dr. George R. Galluzzo practiced dentistry together in a building they owned. After a dispute, Dr. Galluzzo changed the locks on the building and Dr. Moraitis had to begin his practice elsewhere. Dr. Moraitis brought suit, alleging he was a tenant in common who had been ousted and was entitled to the imputed rental value of the premises based on the ouster. Is Dr. Moraitis correct? *Moraitis v. Galluzzo,* 511 So.2d 427 (Fla. 1987)

Internet Activities

1. For the statutory text of the states that have adopted the Uniform Premarital Agreement Act, go to: **http://www.law.cornell.edu/uniform/vol9.html#prema**.

2. For a look at state-by-state resources on family law and resources, visit: **http://www.divorcenet.com**.

3. For information on community property laws, go to: **http://recenter.tamu.edu/pubs/catcpro.html**.

4. Review the states with community laws at: **http://www.1040.com**.

Chapter 11
Multiunit Real Estate Interests

According to the latest statistical abstract of the United States, 17.7 percent of those who purchased residential property purchased a condominium.

Statistical Abstract of the United States, 1998

The limited supply of land has resulted in alternative means of home, and hence of real estate ownership. When the supply of surface properties is limited, as discussed in Chapter 2, we turn to the air rights as a way of maximizing property use. Acquiring air rights has resulted in several types of home ownership in a group setting. The condominium, townhouse, cooperative, time-sharing, and recreational lease forms of housing are all answers to the home or second-home ownership dream for those with limited funds or for those in areas with limited capability for expansion. For many, these forms of ownership have represented all the tax benefits of owning a home without the upkeep and maintenance. Since 1979, these alternative forms of housing and real estate ownership have made up over half of the housing starts in the United States.

This chapter examines these alternative forms of multiunit real estate interests and answers the following questions: What are the definitions of and distinctions among condominium, townhouse, cooperative, and time-sharing properties? How is each of the multiunit housing arrangements created? Who is responsible for the common areas? How do multiunit developments function?

APPLICABLE LAWS

Each state has its own statutes to govern each of the methods of real property ownership just discussed, and the statutes vary significantly from state to state. This concept of individual ownership of parts of buildings did not exist until the 1950s because of the relative ease with which a single-family dwelling could be built or purchased. Puerto Rico passed the first applicable laws in 1958 with the adoption of its Horizontal Property Act.

In 1961, Congress authorized the Federal Housing Administration (FHA) to insure mortgages on condominium units; subsequently, the attractiveness of condominiums was substantially enhanced, and state laws were passed. At the end of 1963, 39 states had some form of legislation; by 1969, all states had adopted some form of regulation on condominium and townhouse developments.

The tremendous growth in these multiunit forms of real estate ownership has resulted in some scrambling on the part of legislatures and uniform law conferences to establish laws on these unique forms of real estate holdings. The oldest uniform law is the **Uniform Condominium Act,** which has been adopted in 10 states. States without the Uniform Condominium Act may still have legislation on ownership, but it may be referred to as regulation or law relating to **horizontal property regimes.** In some states, the laws are referred to as **horizontal property acts.**

Laws continue to evolve to address the complex issues that result from these creative forms of ownership. There is a **Model Real Estate Cooperative Act** and a **Model Real Estate Time-Share Act.** To cope with issues of common interest ownership and liability, there is the relatively new **Uniform Common Interest Ownership Act.** In 1994, the Uniform Common Interest Ownership Act was proposed as a model code for all forms of land ownership in which the owners of individual units also have an interest and/or obligation to pay for maintenance of other land areas. This new model code is still being studied and reviewed by states and has been adopted by a few. These last three model laws enjoy only limited state adoption.

The methods of ownership covered in this chapter have one thing in common: They are not the traditional forms of real estate ownership. There are different rights and obligations associated with each. Further, the laws on these forms of real property ownership vary from state to state. Even the names associated with various forms of multiunit housing vary. However, the following sections cover the various forms of multiunit housing and the generally applicable principles of law.

CONDOMINIUMS

Definition and Characteristics

A **condominium** can take many physical forms: It can be a townhouse, an apartment, or part of a freestanding duplex house. However, the physical form of the condominium has no effect on the owner's legal status or rights. The owner owns a fee simple interest in the actual dwelling unit and is entitled to all the rights of a fee simple holder: The condominium may be sold, leased, or mortgaged and is subject to foreclosure, power of sale, and homestead rights. The owner is also given an undivided joint interest in all the common areas of the building. The owner of a condominium unit in the form of an apartment in a multistory building would have an undivided interest in areas such as the halls, stairs, lobby, and any recreational facilities.

Although the condominium unit owner has an interest in the common areas, only the actual dwelling unit may be mortgaged or pledged, and creditors of the unit owner may foreclose only on a per-unit basis, not on the entire unit. Also, although the unit owner holds a fee simple interest, there may be restrictions on the use and decoration of the condominium unit.

Creation of Condominium

A condominium development must be carefully created for several reasons. First, the ownership structure and related issues exist at two levels: All unit owners hold fee simple title and an undivided interest in the condominium common areas. Second, much of the success of the condominium development depends on the development's organizational structure and the control that the organization has on the modification of units, collection of fees, neighborhood courtesies, and so on. Finally, in many states, when an apartment complex is converted to condominiums, laws require adequate notification procedures and set limitations on conversion costs. The documents and steps typical to the creation of a condominium development are discussed in the following sections. (Note that the steps and documents may vary from state to state.)

http://

Read the Illinois Condominium Property Act at **http://www.state.il.us/ state/legis/**.

CONVERSION RESTRICTIONS

Because of the large number of conversions of apartments to condominiums, many states have passed statutes and regulations requiring minimum notice periods before conversions can take place. The purpose of **conversion restrictions** is to give tenants the opportunity to decide whether to purchase the condominium unit in which they live or to move. Tenants thus have the opportunity to plan and are not forced into a rapid decision on the conversion issue. The typical notice requirement of conversion statutes is 120 days. Also, most statutes provide that if, within the notice period, the tenant declines the opportunity to purchase the condominium unit, then the tenant must be given an additional period of time within which to vacate the premises. Many conversion statutes require that such tenants be permitted to live out existing leases at their option.

Practical Tip

The use and development of the common areas of multiunit housing should be addressed in the bylaws if the owners want limitations. Further, the bylaws should specify the nature of approval required for association action such as a majority or two-thirds vote of approval.

The Ciega Verde Condominium Association held an announced meeting, the purpose of which was to discuss the parking problem at their building and the bid for roof repairs. At the meeting, it was proposed that the condominium tennis court be converted into a parking lot to solve the parking overcrowding. Several unit owners have objected on the grounds that they should have a vote on conversion of common areas. Are they correct? *Young v. Ciega Verde Condominium Association, Inc.*, 600 So.2d 528 (Fla. 1992)

Consider 11.1

DECLARATION OF CONDOMINIUM OR MASTER DEED

The prerequisite for the creation of a condominium development is the fee simple ownership of a lot or lots of an existing building or buildings. The fee simple ownership may be held by an individual, several individuals, or a corporation. The owner (or owners) begin the condominium development by drafting and recording a master deed or a **declaration of condominium.** This **master deed** describes the real property involved and states the number of units located therein. Every deed to every condominium unit owner will refer to this master deed for a complete legal description of the unit owner's interest. In some states, this initial document is called a **declaration of horizontal property regime and covenants.** In general terms, and with state variations, the declaration contains the following items:

1. Legal description of the property.
2. Detailed description of the building or buildings making up the complex and the number of stories, basements, and units.
3. Mailing address of each unit and a physical description including the number of rooms, method of access, and other identifiable characteristics.
4. Detailed description of the common areas.
5. Limitations on the use of common areas.
6. Monetary value of the building and each unit.
7. How votes are to be assigned—per unit basis or per value basis.
8. Restrictions on land use; for example, all-adult restrictions.
9. Name and address of legal representative for the development.
10. Voting procedures.
11. Methods for amending the declaration of condominium.

In many states, the declaration or master deed for a condominium project may be called a **declaration of covenants, conditions, and restrictions (CC&Rs or CCRs).**

Although the items on the list appear to be routine, it should be noted that once the declaration is filed, it becomes a permanent reflection of the rights of all unit owners, and variations in the uses and structure of the property are not permitted unless the amendment procedures specified in the declaration are followed.

INCORPORATION

Although it is not authorized in all states, the next step is the incorporation of the development. There are valid reasons for incorporation: Title to the common areas can be held by the corporate entity, with each unit owner having a share or interest in the corporation. This corporate ownership of the common areas alleviates some of the liability problems discussed later in this chapter. Corporate ownership also affords an opportunity for a system of controlling the common areas through voting with rules on meetings, methods of voting, quorums, and so on. One of the difficulties with condominium living is the inability of unit owners to agree on operations. Corporate ownership of common areas provides the parties with rules for determining operational methods. When disputes arise, there are far more legal precedents in corporate law than there are rights and procedures afforded under a declaration of condominium.

DEEDS

Also needed for condominium creation are the individual deeds for each unit, which will be given to buyers to evidence their ownership. Condominium deeds should comply with all requirements for real-property deeds (see Chapter 12) in addition to the following specifics:

1. Legal description (includes a reference to the declaration of condominium and where it is recorded)
2. Mailing address
3. Use restrictions (may be a reference to another document)
4. Title warranties

BYLAWS

Once the declaration and incorporation (if desired) are complete, the condominium developer must adopt **bylaws** for the unit owners. One purpose of bylaws is to provide rules and regulations for the unit owners and for the day-to-day operation of the units. The bylaws also include the rules for the homeowners' association, which is the governing body for the dwelling units once the developer has sold all units and withdrawn. An effective homeowners' association is responsible for dealing with issues of noise, property use, property upkeep, and maintenance of the common areas. However, condominium homeowners' associations frequently end up in litigation because of the need for balance in managing common living conditions and individual property ownership. The following case deals with such an issue.

Nahrstedt v. Lakeside Village Condominium Association, Inc.

878 P.2d 1275 (Cal. 1994)

Facts

Natore Nahrstedt owned a condominium in a 530-unit complex called Lakeside Village in Culver City, California. The 530 units are spread throughout 12 separate three-story buildings. The residents share common lobbies and hallways in addition to laundry and trash facilities.

The Lakeside Village has CC&Rs that were included in the developer's declaration recorded with the Los Angeles County Recorder on April 17, 1978, at the inception of the development project. The CC&Rs include a pet restriction as follows:

> No animals (which shall mean dogs and cats), livestock, reptiles or poultry shall be kept in any unit. [Domestic fish and birds are excluded].

In January 1988, Nahrstedt (plaintiff) moved into her Lakeside Village condominium with her three cats. When the Association learned of the cats' presence, it demanded their removal and assessed fines against Nahrstedt for each month that she remained in violation of the pet restriction.

Nahrstedt then brought suit against the Association, its officers, and two of its employees asking the trial court

to invalidate the assessments, to enjoin future assessments, to award damages for violation of her privacy when the Association "peered" into her condominium unit, to award damages for infliction of emotional distress, and to declare the pet restriction "unreasonable" as applied to indoor cats (such as hers) that are not allowed free run of the project's common areas. Nahrstedt said she did not know of the restriction when she purchased her unit.

The trial court dismissed Nahrstedt's complaint and she appealed. The court of appeal reversed the dismissal, and the Association appealed.

Judicial Opinion

Kennard, Justice. Because a stable and predictable living environment is crucial to the success of condominiums and other common interest residential developments, and because recorded use restrictions are a primary means of ensuring this stability and predictability, the Legislature in section 1354 has afforded such restrictions a presumption of validity and has required of challengers that they demonstrate the restriction's "unreasonableness" by the deferential standard applicable to equitable servitudes. Under this standard established by the Legislature, enforcement of a restriction does not depend upon the conduct of a particular condominium owner. Rather, the restriction must be uniformly enforced in the condominium development to which it was intended to apply unless the plaintiff owner can show that the burdens it imposes on affected properties so substantially outweigh the benefits of the restriction that it should not be enforced against any owner.

Use restrictions are an inherent part of any common interest development and are crucial to the stable, planned environment of any shared ownership arrangement. The viability of shared ownership of improved real property rests on the existence of extensive reciprocal servitudes, together with the ability of each co-owner to prevent the property's partition.

Restrictions on property use are not the only characteristic of common interest ownership. Ordinarily, such ownership also entails mandatory membership in an owners association, which, through an elected board of directors, is empowered to enforce any use restrictions contained in the project's declaration or master deed and to enact new rules governing the use and occupancy of property within the project. As Professor Natelson observes, owners associations "can be a powerful force for good or for ill" in their members' lives. Therefore, anyone who buys a unit in a common interest development with knowledge of its owners association's discretionary power accepts "the risk that the power may be used in a way that benefits the commonality but harms the individual." Generally, courts will uphold decisions made by the governing board of an owners association so long as they represent good faith efforts to further the purposes of the common interest development, are consistent with the development's governing documents, and comply with public policy.

Thus, subordination of individual property rights to the collective judgment of the owners association together with restrictions on the use of real property comprise the chief attributes of owning property in a common interest development.

One significant factor in the continued popularity of the common interest form of property ownership is the ability of homeowners to enforce restrictive CC&R's against other owners (including future purchasers) of project units.

Restrictive covenants will run with the land, and thus bind successive owners, if the deed or other instrument containing the restrictive covenant particularly describes the lands to be benefited and burdened by the restriction and expressly provides that successors in interest of the covenantor's land will be bound for the benefit of the covenantee's land. Moreover, restrictions must relate to use, repair, maintenance, or improvement of the property, or to payment of taxes or assessments, and the instrument containing the restrictions must be recorded.

In California our Legislature has made common interest development use restrictions contained in a project's recorded declaration "enforceable . . . unless unreasonable."

Although no one definition of the term "reasonable" has gained universal acceptance, most courts have applied what one commentator calls "equitable reasonableness," upholding only those restrictions that provide a reasonable means to further the collective "health, happiness and enjoyment of life" of owners of a common interest development. Others would limit the "reasonableness" standard only to those restrictions adopted by majority vote of the homeowners or enacted under the rulemaking power of an association's governing board, and would not apply this test to restrictions included in a planned development project's recorded declaration or master deed. Because such restrictions are presumptively valid, these authorities would enforce them regardless of reasonableness.

An equitable servitude will be enforced unless it violates public policy; it bears no rational relationship to the protection, preservation, operation or purpose of the affected land; or it otherwise imposes burdens on the affected land that are so disproportionate to the restriction's beneficial effects that the restriction should not be enforced.

To allow one person to escape obligations under a written instrument upsets the expectations of all the other parties governed by that instrument (here, the owners of the other 529 units) that the instrument will be uniformly and predictably enforced.

Refusing to enforce the CC&R's contained in a recorded declaration, or enforcing them only after protracted litigation that would require justification of their application on a case-by-case basis, would impose great strain on the social fabric of the common interest development. It would frustrate owners who had purchased their units in reliance on the CC&R's. It would put the owners and the homeowners association in the difficult and divisive position of deciding whether particular CC&R's should be applied to a particular owner. Here, for example, deciding whether a particular animal is "confined to an owner's unit and create[s] no noise, odor, or nuisance" is a fact-intensive determination that can only be made by examining in detail the behavior of the particular animal and the behavior of the particular owner. Homeowners associations are ill-equipped to make such investigations, and any decision they might make in a particular case could be divisive or subject to claims of partiality.

Enforcing the CC&R's contained in a recorded declaration only after protracted case-by-case litigation would impose substantial litigation costs on the owners through their homeowners association, which would have to defend not only against owners contesting the application of the CC&R's to them, but also against owners contesting any case-by-case exceptions the homeowners association might make. In short, it is difficult to imagine what could more disrupt the harmony of a common interest development than the course proposed by the dissent.

Under the holding we adopt today, the reasonableness or unreasonableness of a condominium use restriction that the Legislature has made subject to section 1354 is to be determined not by reference to facts that are specific to the objecting homeowner, but by reference to the common interest development as a whole.

Accordingly, here Nahrstedt could prevent enforcement of the Lakeside Village pet restriction by proving that the restriction is arbitrary, that it is substantially more burdensome than beneficial to the affected properties, or that it violates a fundamental public policy.

We conclude, as a matter of law, that the recorded pet restriction of the Lakeside Village condominium development prohibiting cats or dogs but allowing some other pets is not arbitrary, but is rationally related to health, sanitation and noise concerns legitimately held by residents of a high-density condominium project such as Lakeside Village, which includes 530 units in 12 separate 3-story buildings.

Our conclusion that Nahrstedt's complaint states no claim entitling her to declaratory relief disposes of her primary cause of action challenging enforcement of the Lakeside Village condominium project's pet restriction, but does not address other causes of action (for invasion of privacy, invalidation of assessments, injunctive relief, and seeking damages for emotional distress) revived by the Court of Appeal. Because the Court of Appeal's decision regarding those other causes of action may have been influenced by its conclusion that Nehrstedt had stated a claim for declaratory relief, we remand this case to the Court of Appeal so it can reconsider whether Nahrstedt's complaint is sufficient to state those other causes of action.

Reversed.

Case Questions

1. What did the pet restriction provide?

2. Why does Nahrstedt believe her pets should be exempt?

3. Of what importance is the fact that Nahrstedt said she did not have direct knowledge of the restriction at the time she purchased her unit?

4. What does the supreme court conclude about the cats and the restriction on pets?

Was it fair for Nahrstedt to continue to keep her pets while the Association assessed fines? What interests are being balanced with the rule? Would it be acceptable just to keep pets in secret?

(Ethical Issue)

The bylaws are generally drafted by the developer but may be adopted by the unit owners once the developer has sold all the units. The bylaws should contain rules for the following areas:

1. Composition of a governing board or committee for the association and the methods and requirements for election of its members.
2. Details for meetings, such as place, time, notice, quorum, requirements, and voting processes.
3. Procedures for day-to-day maintenance authorization, equipment replacements, and routine repairs.
4. Amount of any association fees to be collected from unit owners for maintenance of common areas, and so on; the methods for collecting such fees; and the penalties for late payment or nonpayment. (In some states, the association is entitled to a lien on the unit owner's property in the event of a failure to pay association fees.)
5. Procedures for amending the bylaws.
6. Use restrictions, such as adult-only restrictions and limitations on transfer and rental.

REGULATIONS

Because condominium living is similar to renting and many condominium complexes are converted apartment buildings, occupants must be governed by regulations in order to ensure smooth functioning of the unit. The regulations should contain provisions on items such as pets and the use of the pool, laundry room, and other recreational rooms and equipment. It is perhaps also necessary for the bylaws to contain provisions for the development of and amendment to the regulations. Many bylaws or regulations also establish enforcement procedures. For example, committees may be placed in charge of enforcement or enforcement may be placed in the hands of the officers or directors of the condominium organization. Legal action for violations may be established in the rules as well as a provision for recovering attorneys' fees from a violating occupant.

Bylaws, CCRs Regulations, and Condominium Homeowners' Associations: The Conflicts

The area of frequent litigation in condominium ownership is that of sorting through the rights, powers, and authority in the bylaws, the CCRs, and those put in charge of management of condominiums, the homeowners' association. The battles over who has superior authority and what each has authority over have been frequent and expensive. There are some basic principles for condominium owners to keep in mind as they try to determine their rights and obligations. First, the CCRs take priority over bylaws. A homeowners' association cannot take away rights given in the CCRs. Those CCRs are actually property rights and cannot simply be voted away at a board meeting for the association. For example, in *Woodside Village Condominium v. Jahren,* 754 So.2d 831 (Fla. App. 2000), the court declared an amendment to the CCRs of a condominium project void. The amendment would have prohibited owners of the units from leasing their units for more than 9 months in any 12-month period. Originally, the CCRs provided that the unit owners could not lease or rent without prior approval for one year or less. While the court noted that the goal of the homeowners' association was a noble one of keeping the value of their properties from deteriorating due to too many tenants, the association simply could not change a property right those owners had through the CCRs when they purchased their units. They had a right to lease their real property interest and that interest was being partially taken away without the process required for taking a real property interest. Likewise, a bylaw cannot impose requirements on unit owners that are not part of the CCRs, as in *Shorewood West Condominium Ass'n v. Sadri,* 992 P.2d 1008 (Wash. 2000) where the court held that the homeowners' association could not put lease restrictions in its bylaws when there were no such restrictions or authority for them in its CCRs.

Another area of contention is that of the use of condominium units. In these situations, the homeowners' association, the bylaws, and CCRs often collide with public policy or even antidiscrimination laws. For example, in *Quinones v. Bd. of Managers of Regalwalk,* 673 N.Y.S.2d 450 (N.Y. A.D.1998), the court held that a board did not have the authority to prohibit the operation of a day care center for adults in one of the condominium units because of the state's interest in promoting such homes and that such an interpretation of the CCRs was too restrictive.

Another issue that arises and often results in litigation based on antidiscrimination statutes is that of adult-only covenants in the CCRs for condominiums. The age restrictions vary and generally limit occupation of units to those above a certain age with 12, 18, and even 60, being typical ages for such restrictions. These restrictions have been declared constitutionally valid and are covered in Chapter 20.

Finally, an issue of contention is changing the appearance or structure of individual units. In many bylaws, provision is made for the creation and operation of an architectural control committee. Its purpose is to maintain uniformity in the appearance of condominium units. Particularly with regard to freestanding units, it is important that the units remain somewhat similar in appearance and that owners' changes in colors, structure, or appearance not detract from the overall appearance of the development. The architectural control committee reviews proposed construction changes and then either approves or disapproves them. It may also be given the responsibility for periodically checking the neighborhood to ensure that unauthorized and unapproved changes are not being made.

In the following case, there is a tense interaction among a condominium owner and her construction project, the association board, and city government.

LaSalle National Trust, N.A. (Carma McClure) v. Board of Directors of the 1100 Lake Shore Drive Condominium

677 N.E.2d 1378 (Ill. 1997)

Facts

Carma McClure, as the beneficiary of a trust, was the owner of a penthouse condominium located in the Lake Shore Drive Condominium located at 1100 North Lake Shore Drive. Her condominium consists of units 39A, 39B and 40B which have always been sold as one unit. An earlier owner added a roof house on the 41st floor that became part of McClure's penthouse. McClure had purchased the penthouse on March 20, 1991, for $1.4 million knowing that it was not in good condition. McClure and her husband, James Martin, decided to completely renovate the penthouse. They began in 1991 by demolishing its interior. McClure began this work without first notifying the Board of Directors of the Lake Shore Condominium (Board) (defendant). She also did not obtain the necessary city permits for the demolition.

The demolition resulted in the Board being cited by the city of Chicago for failure to obtain a permit. Also, an elevator cab was damaged, the alarm system in the building was cut off for a day, yard boxes and dumpsters were placed and removed illegally, and two other units in the building were damaged as a result.

McClure paid for the damage to the elevator cab. She also paid $16,552 to Elizabeth Rann, the owner of one of the damaged units as well as the president of the Lake Shore Condominium Association (association). McClure maintained Rann inflated her damages because of financial difficulty but that she paid them in order to get construction moving on her penthouse.

Demolition was complete in July 1991. McClure provided the Board and the city with a complete set of plans for the renovation in October 1991. Had the Board approved the plans, the work could have started and been completed in 26 weeks, or in May 1992.

On September 24, 1991, the Board passed a resolution that provided *"[a]ll expenses incurred by the Board in connection with the modification by a unit owner to his unit or adjacent living [sic] comment [sic] elements shall be assessed to the unit owner. Expenses which will be assessed include, but are not limited to engineering, architectural and attorney fees and the cost of documents, plans and specifications."*

The Board refused to approve McClure's plans unless and until she agreed to assume responsibility for the roof. McClure offered to pay one-third of the cost of replacing the main and machine room roofs if the Board would approve her plans.

Having still not approved the plans in March 1992, the Board proposed to McClure that she pay the Board expenses in reviewing the plans ($10,969); place money in escrow for covering any damages during renovation; repair, replace, and maintain the roof; and have a full time on-site representative at the penthouse during construction.

Another unit was under renovation at the same time, and its owners were required to sign a similar agreement but were not assessed expenses of review nor required to assume the costs of repairing common elements.

McClure disagreed with many of the proposals but signed an agreement in May 1992 so that she could get her renovation started.

Once renovation began, the building began having infiltration problems. The Board maintained McClure had caused the problems with her construction. McClure said the infiltration was caused by cracks in the side of the building. Because of the infiltration problem, McClure could not finish her renovation in 1992, 1993, or 1994.

The parties were at a standstill until August 1994 when the Board and McClure entered into an agreement whereby she would pay for one-half the cost of installing a new roof. The new roof was installed, but the water infiltration continued. A contractor indicated the infiltration would not stop until the Board caulked the walls of the building.

McClure then filed suit against the Board on several grounds including breach of fiduciary duty by the Board in withholding its approval, which amounted to constructive fraud. The trial court found for McClure and awarded her $896,609.52. The Board appealed.

Judicial Opinion

Wolfson, Presiding Judge. The Condominium Declaration provides the Board can be liable to a unit owner only for "any acts or omissions found by a court to constitute gross negligence or fraud." Since there was no claim of gross negligence, and since there were no allegations or evidence of actual fraud, says the Board, there can be no liability. . . .

Condominium boards and board members owe a special duty to apartment owners. The Condominium Property Act provides:

> "In the performance of their duties, the officers and members of the board *** shall exercise the care required of a fiduciary of the unit owners."

This fiduciary duty is owed by boards as well as their individual members. The decisions make no distinction between a board and its members when describing fiduciary duty.

The failure of condominium board members to act in a manner reasonably related to their fiduciary duty results in "liability for the Board and its individual members."

The scope of that fiduciary duty can be limited by the declaration. In this case, the relevant part of the Declaration of Condominium is:

> "Neither the directors, Board, officers of the Association, Trustee, nor Developer shall be personally liable to the Unit Owners for any mistake of judgment or for any other acts or omissions of any nature whatsoever as such directors, Board, officers, Trustee or Developer, *except for any acts*

or omissions found by a court to constitute gross negligence or fraud." (Emphasis added.)

The first issue we must decide is whether the limitation of liability to acts or omissions that "constitute gross negligence or fraud" applies to McClure's count II. Gross negligence is not an issue in this case, but the Board contends the word "fraud" in the exclusion applies to actual fraud, not to the constructive fraud found by the trial court.

This case concerns a Declaration clause that seeks to exculpate the Board and its members and officers from personal liability except in narrow circumstances. Generally, exculpatory clauses "are not favored and are strictly construed and must have clear, explicit and unequivocal language showing that it was the intent of the parties."

If the Board wanted to limit its liability to actual fraud, it should have said so. Constructive fraud is a well-established doctrine in this State.

Constructive fraud does not require actual dishonesty or intent to deceive. "In a fiduciary relationship, where there is a breach of a legal or equitable duty, a presumption of fraud arises."

We find that the word "fraud" in the exculpatory clause includes both actual and constructive fraud. A holding to the contrary would virtually wipe out the Condominium Property Act's creation of a fiduciary duty between the Board and unit owners. If the Board were able to limit itself to actual fraud, there would be no liability for violation of its fiduciary duty. That is so because constructive fraud springs from the breach of a fiduciary duty.

Count II does not use the words "constructive fraud." Instead, it set out various ways the Board knowingly and willfully breached its fiduciary duty to Mrs. McClure. The allegations were fact-specific and, if believed, established a picture of delay, lack of cooperation, and obstruction.

To state a cause of action based on constructive fraud, "the facts constituting the alleged fraud must be set forth in the complaint."

Clearly, count II alleges that the Board breached its fiduciary duty to McClure. Where there is a breach of a legal or equitable duty arising out of a fiduciary relationship, a presumption of constructive fraud arises.

We find that the plaintiff adequately pled a constructive fraud.

McClure placed her confidence in the Board, which, by statute, owed her a fiduciary duty. In return, according to the trial court's findings, the Board virtually held her penthouse for ransom. This Board did not "act in good faith with due regard to the interests of the other."

We conclude the record supports the trial court's findings that: the Board's obstructive acts and lack of cooperation contributed to substantial delays in construction; damages for loss of use of the penthouse apartment, in the form of fair rental value, were recoverable and were properly proved.

Affirmed.

Case Questions

1. Prepare an outline of the events in the penthouse renovation project.
2. What did the Board do wrong according to the court?
3. What does the court mean when it states that the Board held McClure's penthouse for ransom?
4. What is constructive fraud?
5. Who is liable to McClure?

> **Consider 11.2**
>
> The Village by the Sea condominiums are two-story condos located near a bay. Some of the condos have a third floor to them, known as lofts. The lofts are directly above the first two floors of the condo units. One of the owners of a condo with a loft, Michael Garrity, put in a pull-down staircase and finished the loft with some sheetrock and used it as an extra sleeping area. The association objected to the use of the loft as a taking of a common area. Two of the units had finished lofts completed by the developer and were sold that way to the original owners. Who owns the loft areas in the units? *Villas by the Sea Owners Ass'n v. Garrity*, 748 A.2d 457 (Me. 2000)

Homeowners' Association Board Liabilities

Because the governing boards of homeowners' associations for condominiums often make decisions on contentious issues, impose increases in association fees, and halt construction by individual unit owners for noncompliance with CCRS, they are often defendants in lawsuits brought by unit owners. Courts have had to determine association liabilities, defenses, and immunities. They have borrowed the standards for governing boards for liability from general corporation law.

The boards of homeowners' associations are protected by what is known in corporate law as the **business judgment rule.** So long as boards act in good faith and for articulated purposes related to the well-being of the property and unit owners, courts will not substitute their judgment for that of the board. Figure 11.1

FIGURE 11.1   *Rules of Thumb in Condominium Ownership and Management*

---

1. The CCRs represent property rights and cannot be taken away or changed except in the same fashion that covenants on land parcels are changed or according to procedures outlined in the CCRs themselves.

2. Homeowners' associations and boards govern subject to the CCRs; they do not override the CCRs.

3. Bylaws cannot override CCRs; homeowners' association boards cannot override bylaws or CCRs except by proper process and procedure not in violation of unit owners' property rights.

4. All changes by homeowners' association boards require notice to unit owners and proper vote including raising association fees.

5. CCRs, bylaws, and homeowners' associations cannot pass or enforce rules and restrictions in violation of antidiscrimination laws or public policy.

6. Boards must be consistent in their enforcement of CCRs and bylaws; selective enforcement can be the basis of discriminatory conduct or the loss of protections under the CCRs for lax enforcement.

is a checklist for both condominium owners and boards of their homeowners' association to abide by in performing their various roles in multiunit ownership.

The following case deals with an issue of management and oversight by the condominium association.

Randol v. Atkinson

965 S.W.2d 338 (Mo. App. 1998)

Facts

The Woodmoor Condominiums were created in 1990 and are managed by the Woodmoor Condominium Association (association). Woodmoor consists of 10 units with wooden decks.

On April 3, 1993, Susan Jochens (now Atkinson), who owned a condominium in Woodmoor, used her barbecue to make dinner for herself and her boyfriend. After finishing with the grill, neither Jochens nor her boyfriend went back onto the deck.

At approximately 2:00 A.M., fire swept through the condominium project and all 10 units were destroyed. The source of the fire was the grill on Jochens' deck.

Mr. and Mrs. Randol and others (appellants) filed suit against Jochens, the association, and the original development corporation, Wind River. They submitted an affidavit from a former fire marshal of Kansas City, Missouri, that indicated the use of charcoal grills on wooden decks was dangerous and a known fire hazard. The Randols and others who lost their units in the fire contend that the association should have adopted bylaws or rules prohibiting such use. The lower court dismissed the case, finding that there was no duty on the part of the association. The Randols and other owners appealed.

Judicial Opinion

Howard, Judge. Appellants allege five theories for their argument that the Association and Wind River owed a duty of care to the condominium owners. Appellants first contend that the Association and Wind River owed a duty of care to the condominium owners under the Declaration of Condominium and bylaws for the Woodmoor Condominiums, as well as under Missouri statutory law.

We first address whether the bylaws or the Declaration created a duty on the part of the Association and Wind River to ban the use of charcoal grills by the unit owners. Condominium bylaws constitute the rules and regulations that govern the internal administration of the condominium complex. *Wescott v. Burtonwood Manor Condominium Ass'n Bd. of Managers,* 743 S.W.2d 555, 558 (Mo.App. E.D.1987). The bylaws must be strictly construed. To support their argument, Appellants rely on a provision in the bylaws granting the Association and

Wind River the power "to adopt, repeal or amend Rules and Regulations for the Woodmoor Condominiums." Appellants also rely on the section in the Declaration that regulates the use of limited common elements. We find nothing in the bylaws or the Declaration that, by itself, imposed a duty on the Association and Wind River to ban the use of charcoal grills.

We next address whether the Association and Wind River had a statutory duty to ban charcoal grills. Because the Woodmoor Condominiums were created after September 28, 1983, the Uniform Condominium Act, §§ 448.005 to 448.210 RSMo 1994, applies. Appellants argue that § 448.3–103.1 of the Uniform Condominium Act imposed a duty on the Association and Wind River to prohibit charcoal grills. Section 448.3–103.1 provides, in pertinent part, that "[i]n the performance of their duties, the officers and members of the executive board are required to exercise (1) if appointed by the declarant, the care required of fiduciaries of the unit owners, and (2) if elected by the unit owners, ordinary and reasonable care." Although the facts are unclear, we will assume for the purpose of analysis that both Wind River and the Association were in control of the Woodmoor Condominiums at the time of the fire. That being the case, this section clearly imposes a fiduciary duty on Wind River and a duty of ordinary and reasonable care on the Association. However, we find that the Respondents' duties did not require them to ban the use of charcoal grills. Appellants presented no convincing evidence that the use of charcoal grills was such a dangerous practice that the failure of Respondents to ban the grills amounted to negligence.

Next Appellants contend that the Association and Wind River owed a duty of care to the owners of the Woodmoor Condominiums under a common law analysis of duty based on foreseeability, fairness, and public policy. However, the duties owed by the Association and Wind River to the unit owners are limited to those duties included in the bylaws and the provisions of Chapter 448 RSMo. Therefore, an analysis of common law duty is not appropriate in this case.

Third, Appellants contend that the Association and Wind River owed a duty of ordinary care to the owners of the Woodmoor Condominiums because condominium associations are analogous to landlords, who have a duty of ordinary care to their tenants. No Missouri court has found that condominium associations are analogous to landlords for the purpose of determining whether a duty is owed. We decline to make that analogy in this case.

Fourth, Appellants contend that the Association and Wind River owed a duty of care to the owners of the Woodmoor Condominiums because the Association and Wind River undertook the management of the Woodmoor Condominiums for the benefit of the condominium owners. However, where the existence of a duty is established, it is not one to protect against every possible injury which might occur. *Hoover's Dairy. Inc. v. Mid-America Dairymen, Inc./Special Products, Inc.,* 700 S.W.2d 426, 431 (Mo. 1985). Rather, it is generally measured by whether or not a reasonably prudent person would have anticipated the danger and provided against it. In this case, it was not the duty of the Association or Wind River to protect the owners from all potential sources of harm, particularly those caused by the negligence of third parties.

It is not negligence to fail to anticipate that another will be negligent, because one is entitled to assume and act upon the assumption that others will exercise due care for their own safety, in the absence of notice to the contrary. *Buck v. Union Elec. Co.,* 887 S.W.2d 430, 434–35 (Mo.App. E.D. 1994). The Appellants have not alleged that either the Association or Wind River had notice that any of the unit owners were being negligent in the use of their grills. Therefore, Respondents cannot be found negligent in their failure to anticipate Susan Jochens' negligence.

Fifth, Appellants contend that the Association and Wind River owed a duty of care to the owners of the Woodmoor Condominiums because the Association and Wind River had a special relationship with the condominium owners, who relied on the Association and Wind River to provide a place of safety. However, the condominium association-unit owner relationship is not recognized in Missouri as a special relationship which, by itself, gives rise to a duty. The judgment of the trial court is affirmed.

Affirmed.

Case Questions

1. Who was responsible for the fire and how did the fire occur?

2. What theories do the owners of the units destroyed in the fire say apply in the case?

3. How does the court handle the theories?

4. Give a summary of the law on associations' responsibilities given the decision in this case.

Louis Croce purchased 49 units in the Glenwood Park condominiums at a foreclosure sale in the mid-1970s. Through subsequent acquisitions, he was able to purchase more of the units and now owns 58 of the 60 units in the complex. Mr. Croce sent out a notice to all owners and lessees that he was raising the association fees from $30 to $160 per month. Josephine Artesani, one of the owners, says that she knew of no association meeting in which the increase was discussed. Can Mr. Croce raise the fees in this manner? *Artesani v. Glenwood Park Condominium,* 750 A.2d 961 (R.I. 2000)

> **Consider 11.3**

COOPERATIVES

Nature of Cooperatives

Ownership of a **cooperative** is not a fee simple ownership of real estate. A cooperative is a living arrangement in which the dwellers own an undivided joint interest in the land and buildings that make up the cooperative. Ownership is most likely held by the cooperative as a nonprofit organization, with each cooperative unit assigned a certain number of shares in the corporation. A cooperative unit dweller does not own a real estate interest but rather a share or shares in a corporation that owns the entire complex. Accompanying this share ownership are the rights to lease of the dwelling unit and to exclusive occupancy of that unit. In essence, the corporation of which the tenant is a shareholder is the landlord for all units in the cooperative.

Another distinction between the cooperative method of land interest ownership and traditional fee simple ownership is the possibility that the cooperative
shareholder may be restricted in the transfer of shares. Although cooperative unit
owners may be free to sell their leasehold interests or shares, they may be required
to offer their interests first to the corporation and may even be restricted in how
the property can be disposed of upon their death.

In the following case, the court deals with the issue of the nature of ownership in a cooperative.

Kadera v. Superior Court and Consolidated Cooperative of Scottsdale East, Inc.

931 P.2d 1067 (Az. App. 1996)

Facts

On January 22, 1993, Krag and Erin Kadera (petitioners)
purchased one share of stock in Consolidated Cooperative of Scottsdale East, Inc. (respondent) from a former
shareholder, paying $21,000 for their share. The Kaderas
were required to sign a form designating how they were
taking title to their interest, which they did in joint tenancy with right of survivorship.

When the Kaderas took possession of the unit, they
were required to pay a $200.00 per month "carrying
charge." This figure represented a proportionate one-
twelfth of the cooperative's annual expenses.

After the Kaderas moved into their unit, they were
served with a Notice of Default, Intention to Terminate
Agreement, and Demand for Possession of the Premises.
The cooperative, through its manager, alleged that the Kaderas had violated the nonfinancial terms of their occupancy agreement because they had a nonrelative living in
their unit and were operating a babysitting service from it.

On August 16, 1995, the cooperative filed a forcible
entry and detainer action seeking to have the Kaderas
evicted from their unit. The Kaderas claimed they were
not tenants but owners, and could not be evicted under
landlord/tenant law. The trial court denied the Kaderas'
motion to dismiss and they appealed.

Judicial Opinion

Grant, Judge. The legislative purpose behind the Arizona
Residential Landlord and Tenant Act ("ARLTA") is expressed in section 33-1302: ARLTA was passed both to
"simplify, clarify, modernize and revise the law governing
the rental of dwelling units and the rights and obligations
of landlord and tenant," and to "encourage landlord and
tenant to maintain and improve the quality of housing."

ARLTA undisputedly is inapplicable to the facts of
this case. The legislature unequivocally excluded from

the reach of ARLTA a residential occupant who is also an
"owner of a proprietary lease in a cooperative."

Respondent Corporation does not argue it is entitled
to exercise the ARLTA provisions; rather, it argues it is entitled to bring an action for forcible entry and detainer
against Petitioners under A.R.S. section 12-1171 *et seq.*
The forcible entry and detainer proceeding contained in
this statute applies to a "holdover by a person to whom
lands, tenements, or real property were let." Section 12-
1171 *et seq.* applies only to landlord-tenant relationships.

While the legislature authorized the use of summary
proceedings in the residential landlord-tenant context, it
excluded a holder of a proprietary lease in a cooperative
from the reach of these proceedings.

The legislature recognized that although the cooperative is a hybrid property arrangement wherein the line
between ownership and leasehold blurs, the cooperator
has a real property ownership interest. The term "proprietary lease," used frequently to identify the relationship
between the cooperator and cooperative corporation, is
oxymoronic. The cooperative corporation may indeed
hold title to the real property, nevertheless, the cooperator also owns a real property interest. Precisely because
the legislature recognized that hybrid property arrangements carry with them ownership interests, section 33-
1308(6) of ARLTA excludes from its reach not only
cooperatives, but also condominiums.

Petitioners argue since ARLTA's special detainer action, which incorporates section 12-1177, excludes cooperatives neither proceeding is appropriate. We agree. To
hold otherwise would give cooperators far fewer protections than tenants are guaranteed under ARLTA. Surely
the legislature did not intend this result. While an ordinary tenant may forfeit a deposit upon breach, the cooperator has considerably more at stake because the total
investment is so much greater. Thus, we find ARLTA and

summary proceedings inappropriate in the context of residential cooperative housing.

Respondent Corporation argues that since it has title to the real property, Petitioners cannot own a real property interest. We disagree. Respondent Corporation was established for the sole purpose of selling real property interests on a non-profit basis in the cooperative housing complex it owns, and Petitioners purchased such an interest. It was not necessary that title pass in order for Petitioners to have a real property interest. Moreover, the fact that this interest in land was not conveyed by a real estate sales contract is not fatal to the sale.

This court has clearly stated that with respect to real estate sales, we will not exalt form over substance.

With the exception of a title transfer, there are all of the indications of a residential real estate transaction here. Petitioners chose the location and neighborhood in which they wanted to live. No doubt their decision was partially based on Respondent Corporation's description of the benefits of cooperative ownership over renting in its "Introduction to Living at Consolidated Cooperative of Scottsdale East, Inc.":

> Membership in Consolidated Co-Ops provides the member with many *advantages of home ownership but without the mortgage liability and accompanying responsibilities.* The most often cited advantage of Co-op living is economic. Co-ops are founded on the premise that cooperation leads to better services at lower cost and *Co-op charges are usually lower than those for similar rental units. Cooperators pay actual housing costs, not a landlord's profit. Pride of ownership and sense of community also contribute to reduced housing costs.*
>
> *Co-Op [sic] housing offers its members the opportunity to help determine the kind of community they will live in, the quality of services it will provide and the way it will develop. Many members see this degree of control over their housing circumstances as an even greater advantage* than the continuing financial bargain in housing that Co-ops offer. (Emphasis added).

Respondent argues that because Petitioners are its shareholders, they have no right, title, or interest in corporate property, and therefore they may not interfere with Respondent.

Given that Petitioners paid a large initial down payment and entered into a contract which requires that they pay on a monthly basis the principal and interest on the mortgage, as well as other operating costs, their real property interest is clearly in the nature of an ownership or fee interest.

When the legislature held that cooperatives are to be excluded from ARLTA, it excluded cooperatives from all summary proceedings, including those brought for forcible entry and detainer under A.R.S. section 12-1177 *et seq.*

Thus, we hold that a cooperative corporation's remedy for breach by a cooperator/shareholder lies in Arizona's real estate law.

Reversed and Remanded.

Case Questions

1. What interest did the Kaderas acquire?
2. Why did the cooperative want them out?
3. Can the cooperative use landlord/tenant law on the eviction of tenants?
4. Will the Kaderas be able to stay?
5. Who pays for the costs of this litigation?

Creation of a Cooperative

Because a cooperative is a different type of real property interest, the documents needed for its creation vary from the documents necessary for a condominium's creation. The basic documents include the articles of incorporation and evidence of incorporation (certificate of incorporation or corporate charter), the bylaws, and the proprietary lease.

ARTICLES OF INCORPORATION AND EVIDENCE OF INCORPORATION

Since ownership of a cooperative is really ownership of an interest in a corporation, the first documents necessary for formation of a cooperative are the incorporation papers. These documents vary according to state corporation law. Most states do require the filing of articles of incorporation before a certificate of incorporation or corporate charter is issued. The following information is generally required for incorporation:

1. Corporate name
2. Purpose of the corporation (cooperative)
3. Share structure, including voting rights and transferability
4. Name of legal agent or representative
5. Structure of the board of directors and makeup on initial board
6. Provisions for amendment to the articles

BYLAWS

The bylaws for a cooperative are similar to those for both corporations and condominiums: their purpose is to specify how the operation is to be run. The bylaws provide the details for meetings, including place, time, notice, quorums, and voting requirements. Finally, the bylaws contain the procedures for transferring ownership rights to cooperative members and usually provide instructions for developing and executing the proprietary lease.

PROPRIETARY LEASE

A **proprietary lease** is very similar to an ordinary lease in that it covers many of the topics and issues arising in the landlord-tenant relationship. However, the following factors distinguish the two.

1. *Length:* If the proprietary lease provides for a termination date at all, the date will be a long time into the future. Otherwise, the termination of the lease is tied to the transfer of the tenant's interest in the cooperative corporation.
2. *Rent:* No provision for rent is made in a proprietary lease; instead, the tenant pays a maintenance fee to the board of directors or officers. A provision is made for possible increases in the maintenance fee and may even provide for percentage increases according to a cost-of-living scale.

The proprietary lease should also cover certain contingencies, such as the owner's option to sell if maintenance fees increase substantially and the owner's rights in the event the cooperative unit is uninhabitable for a period of time.

TOWNHOUSES

Nature of Townhouses

The owner of a **townhouse** owns the land on which the townhouse is located, the actual dwelling unit, and an undivided joint interest in the common elements of the development such as a swimming pool, clubhouse, and so on. Actual ownership of the land on which the townhouse is located distinguishes this form of multiunit housing from the others, where there is simply ownership of space. It is possible for the owners in a townhouse development to form a corporation or a homeowners' association. The organization and structure of townhouse development is discussed in more detail later in the chapter.

Creation of Townhouses

As already discussed, a townhouse is different from a condominium in that the real property on which the townhouse is located is part of the owner's interest. In many states, other differences exist in the procedures for creating a townhouse development. In the following sections, the various documents needed for this method of multiunit development are discussed.

DECLARATION OF COVENANTS, CONDITIONS, AND RESTRICTIONS
Similar to a master deed or declaration of condominium, the declaration of covenants, conditions, and restrictions (CC&Rs or CCRs) is the first step in developing a townhouse area. The CCR contains all of the rights and responsibilities of the individual owners. Since the CCRs are recorded, everyone is presumed to know their content even though they may not have been read. Once recorded, the CCRs serve as constructive notice of the operation and regulations of the development. Many times, all-adult restrictions are part of the CCRs. In the event of a conflict, the CCRs are the final authority for correcting ambiguities or clarifying legal rights.

ARTICLES OF INCORPORATION
The decision to incorporate is discretionary in some states as simply a more convenient way of holding title. Other states require that a corporation must be formed to hold title to common areas, and each owner is given a certain percentage share of the corporation. The articles are not recorded with the land records but are usually found in the state's corporate formation document section.

BYLAWS
The bylaws deal with the need for smooth day-to-day functioning of the development, with attendance to repairs and maintenance and compliance with all restrictions. Although the bylaws set up voting procedures, such procedures must be consistent with the articles of incorporation to be valid. The bylaws may also establish various committees to aid in the enforcement of restrictions—an architectural control committee, for example.

REGULATIONS
The purpose of the regulations in a townhouse development is the same as for those in a condominium development: to keep common facilities in repair and reasonably available to residents in the development.

TIME-SHARING INTERESTS

Nature of Time-Sharing Ownership

In resort areas, the concept of **time-sharing** ownership or recreational ownership has become popular. The owner of a time-share owns a fee simple interest but can exercise the right of possession only for a limited time each year and during the same period of time each year. For example, a time-share may be the right to the use of a two-bedroom apartment in San Diego from June 1 to June 8 every year in perpetuity. This right of use may be transferred *inter vivos* or by will or intestate succession. The limitation on the property is the time of use. In addition to the right to use the dwelling unit, the owner is also given the right to use all common areas, including any recreational facilities such as pools, game rooms, and saunas.

Time-sharing units require clarification of whether a unit owner will always have a particular unit at a given time or whether a unit will simply be available for the buyer's use at the time purchased. The time-share regimen should specify how the time units are divided, the length of each owner's time unit, and whether a specific unit was assigned. A sample length-of-use clause appears below to illustrate the complexity of this task:

> Week No. 1 is the seven consecutive days commencing at noon on the first Saturday of each year and continues till noon on the following Saturday. Week No. 2 is the seven consecutive days next succeeding Week No. 1. Successive weeks up to and including Week No. 51 are computed in a like manner. Week No. 52 contains the seven consecutive days next succeeding Week 51 together with any additional days not otherwise assigned continuing until the commencement of Week No. 1 of the following year. From Martin, *Timesharing in Colorado,* 11 *Colorado Lawyer* 2804 (1982)

Some states permit a method of time-sharing ownership known as the **recreational lease,** whereby owners have the same rights of use but are lessees paying over time for the right of use. Generally, these recreational leases have rent-escalation clauses that increase the rent according to some scale over the perpetual period of the lease.

Creation of Time-Sharing Interests

A time-sharing interest may take the form of a recreational lease, a proprietary lease, or a limited fee simple interest. A recreational lease is a financing device that allows the lessee to spread out over time the payment for use of another's recreational property. The lease may be a true lease with a landlord-tenant relationship between the parties, or its character may depend more strictly on the terms of the agreement. Ninety-nine-year leases or those without a specific termination date are more likely to be proprietary leases for a cooperative form of ownership. Leases where the rental payment is determined according to a formula that is based on expenses of operation are also more likely to be proprietary leases for a cooperative form of ownership. Thus, time-sharing interests may be landlord-tenant relationships or they may be cooperative interests.

Time-sharing interests may also be interests in perpetuity but limited in use to a specified period during each year. It is possible for a time-sharing interest to be a fee simple interest with limited use rights.

The **vacation license** is an arrangement in which the developer retains a fee simple interest in the property and grants licenses for use for certain periods during the year. This type of arrangement has been held to constitute the sale of securities by the Securities and Exchange Commission (SEC) and is subject to registration requirements.

Some projects refer to the time-sharing interest as a tenancy in common with an agreement to use for a specified block of time. Other projects refer to time-sharing interests as **interval-ownership grants** that give the purchaser a recurring estate for a given period of time.

In some areas, time-sharing owners have developed time-sharing networks in which the owners trade off interests in one location for interests in another. In any of the arrangements, the documents should specify responsibilities and the liabilities for the cost of maintaining the premises.

Many states simply regulate their time-sharing properties through their condominium laws (California, Colorado, Maine, New Hampshire, New Mexico, Pennsylvania, Rhode Island, Utah, and West Virginia). Other states have enacted separate statutes to govern time-sharing projects (Arizona, Connecticut, Florida, Hawaii, Louisiana, Nebraska, New Mexico, South Carolina, Tennessee, and Virginia).

HYBRIDS

In some states, hybrid forms of ownership can be found under various labels such as **patio homes, garden homes,** and **attached homes.** In these hybrid forms, the owners may own the land and the entire dwelling but will have a party wall agreement for the joint wall between properties. The laws governing these hybrids vary from state to state. In some states, joint wall properties are treated as townhouses, while in others they are labeled condominiums.

LIABILITY ISSUES IN MULTIUNIT INTERESTS

> ## Practical Tip
>
> Townhouses and condominium and cooperative buildings may look very much the same. Sellers, buyers, lenders, and brokers should verify through the legal documents associated with a multiunit interest what type of ownership rights exist. Appearances are not controlling in terms of the rights afforded. For example, in *Orchard Glen East v. Bd. of Sup'rs*, 492 S.E.2d 150 (Va. 1997), what looked like an apartment complex was really a condominium and its owner would pay real property taxes.

Owners of single-family dwellings buy insurance to cover liabilities they may have for injuries occurring on their premises. With single-family dwellings, it is clear that there is liability in ownership and that the liability rests with the homeowner. It is the owner's responsibility to maintain and repair the premises. However, in multiunit housing arrangements, the nature of multiple ownership makes the issues of liability and responsibility less clear.

Contractual Liability of Unit Owners

Three issues of contractual liability of multiunit housing are of major concern and should be clarified by anyone seeking to purchase, develop, or rent a multiunit housing project or unit. These issues are the liability of owners for (1) unpaid bills of the developer, (2) assessment and maintenance fees, and (3) improvement and repair costs of common elements and individual units.

LIABILITY FOR UNPAID BILLS OF DEVELOPERS
Generally with multiunit developments, there comes a time when control of the development is turned over to a corporation, a homeowners' association, or a board of directors for operation. The point in time at which this turnover is made varies—some articles of incorporation or bylaws provide for a number turnover point (e.g., when three-fourths of all units have been sold), while others provide for an absolute point (when all units have been sold). When control is turned over to the development residents, the developer not only is no longer in control but also is no longer responsible for maintenance and repair costs.

One possible problem with turnover is when all construction elements of the development are not owned free and clear (when there are outstanding debts). In most cases, the developer would be responsible for payment of such obligations, since the corporation or homeowners' association probably would not have existed at the time of the debt contract. However, there are potential problems in spite of the developer's liability. First, the developer may not be able to pay, and fixtures may be repossessed from the development or liens may be placed on it. Second, even if the developer can pay, a lawsuit may be required to establish liability.

In many multiunit housing projects, problems with the developer's delivery of promised services and quality of construction arise and the owners or their association are left to pursue legal remedies such as breach of the implied warranty of habitability. States vary in their willingness to permit such recovery in multiunit housing.

LIABILITY FOR ASSESSMENT AND MAINTENANCE FEES

In multiunit housing, all unit owners are responsible for the costs of maintaining common areas. Funds for the costs of repair and maintenance come from the assessment of monthly fees and perhaps periodic capital assessment payments made by the unit owners. The amount of these fees may be specified in the declaration or bylaws and may be subject to change upon a vote or according to a formula included in the declaration or bylaws.

Every unit owner is required to pay these fees. In many cases, the fees are paid to the mortgagee, who in turn pays the association (since the mortgagee has an interest in keeping the property, which is held as security, well-maintained). If an owner does not make the required maintenance or assessment payments, the association may have several alternatives, depending upon the particular state law. One alternative is to cut off services to the unit: running water, heat, and so on. Another alternative is to place a lien on the unit.

LIABILITY FOR IMPROVEMENT AND REPAIR COSTS OF COMMON ELEMENTS

Whenever a multiunit housing development undertakes the improvement or repair of common elements, the owners are liable for the costs. Some of the issues arising in this area of liability are what constitutes a common element, whether limitations on amount of liability exist, and how assessments for such repairs can be changed, agreed to, or modified. Ideally, all these issues are resolved in the bylaws, articles of incorporation, or declaration so that improvements do not become major legal issues.

Tort Liability of Unit Owners

INDIVIDUAL UNITS

Each unit owner is responsible for the maintenance and safety of his or her dwelling unit and is thus liable for torts occurring within it. A unit owner is expected to have insurance on the dwelling unit, just as a homeowner is expected to have insurance on the single-family dwelling.

COMMON AREAS

A major issue in multiunit housing law and a major concern for owners of these units is the liability for injuries occurring in common areas. If the development has a corporation, such as a nonprofit homeowners' association, then that corporation should carry insurance for liability in the common areas. Regardless of incorporation, the owners of the dwelling units are liable together and individually (jointly and severally) for torts occurring in common areas. The corporate organization with insurance simply makes the liability easier to bear, and the premium costs can be part of the assessment to each unit owner.

The liability for injuries occurring in common areas extends to visitors, repairpersons, governmental personnel (such as fire and medical personnel), and any others authorized to be on the premises, including unit owners. The responsibility of maintaining common areas extends to the responsibility for injuries resulting from faulty repair or lack of maintenance.

The following case deals with an issue of condominium associations' liability for harm to third parties in their common areas.

Martinez v. Woodmar IV Condominiums

941 P.2d 218 (Ariz. 1997)

Facts

Carlos Martinez (plaintiff) was attending a graduation party at the Woodmar IV 152-unit condominium project (defendant) as a guest of one of the unit owners. After 15 minutes of being at the party in the unit, Martinez and two fellow party-goers left to go to the complex's parking lot to check on their cars. They found a group of local ruffians sitting on the car of one of Martinez's friends. A "discussion ensued."

At some point, Martinez ran from the "discussion," and was shot in the back as he ran. The group scattered and no one has been charged with the Martinez shooting.

From descriptions given to the live-in security officer for the complex, the security officer concluded that the group was a gang of young people from a neighboring complex. This group would often gather in the Woodmar parking lot to sell drugs and "participate in other unsavory activities." The security guard would disperse the group when he saw them. However, because of budget constraints he was the only security guard and patrolled between the hours of 8 and 9 P.M. until 5 or 6 A.M. The shooting in the parking lot occurred one hour before the guard began his duties.

Martinez filed suit against the homeowners' association of Woodmar for its negligence in failing to provide adequate security. The trial court granted a motion for summary judgment, the court of appeals affirmed, and Martinez appealed.

Judicial Decision

Feldman, Justice. We focus on Defendant's status with relation to the land rather than the presence or absence of a special relationship between it and the tortfeasor or Plaintiff. We are concerned only with the question of whether Defendant, occupying a status similar to that of a landlord, had a duty of reasonable care to maintain the safety of its common areas because it had control over the land.

We believe this distinction is contrary to existing law when, as in this case, the danger causing the injury is located on property in the exclusive control of the landlord or condominium association. In Arizona, if there is no statute or case law on a particular subject, we have traditionally followed the Restatement of Laws. RESTATEMENT § 360 states:

> A possessor of land who leases a part thereof and retains in his own control any other part which the lessee is entitled to use as appurtenant to the

part leased to him, is subject to liability to his lessee and others lawfully upon the land with the consent of the lessee or a sublessee for physical harm caused by a dangerous condition upon that part of the land retained in the lessor's control, if the lessor by the exercise of reasonable care could have discovered the condition and the unreasonable risk involved therein and could have made the condition safe.

We note Defendant in this case is not a lessor but a new type of possessor—a condominium association that has retained in its control common areas, such as the parking lot, that unit owners are entitled to use as appurtenant to their unit.

The element of control, we believe, is essential to a finding of duty for the condominium association. Like a landlord who maintains control and liability for conditions in common areas, the condominium association controls all aspects of maintenance and security for the common areas and, most likely, forbids individual unit owners from taking on these chores. Thus, if the association owes no duty of care over the common areas of the property, no one does because no one else possesses the ability to cure defects in the common area. We do not believe the law recognizes such a lack of responsibility for safety. We therefore hold that with respect to common areas under its exclusive control, a condominium association has the same duties as a landlord.

Thus, if we apply the rules of RESTATEMENT § 360 and RESTATEMENT (SECOND) OF PROPERTY § 17.3, a condominium association has a duty not only to the unit owners and their tenants but also to those who are on the land with their consent and who will inevitably be expected to use common areas such as the parking lot. This element of control creates an "affirmative obligation to exercise reasonable care to inspect and repair such parts of the premises for the protection of the lessee; and the duty extends also to members of the tenant's family, his employees, his invitees, his guests, and others on the land in the right of the tenant."

The duty to maintain the safety of common areas applies not only to physical conditions on the land but, we believe, also to dangerous activities on the land.

The court of appeals noted the Restatement rule but stated that "given plaintiff's legal status [as a licensee], Woodmar only owed a duty to 'refrain from knowingly letting him run upon a hidden peril or wantonly or willfully causing him harm.'" The court found the gang hanging out in the parking lot was not a hidden danger, stating the "transient harm created by third persons who commit crimes" is distinguishable from a dangerous physical condition that a landowner must make safe. The duty to those using the common areas with consent of the association, its unit owners, and their tenants, includes the use of reasonable care to prevent harm from criminal intrusion.

For the purpose of this section, the unreasonable risk of harm from criminal intrusion constitutes a dangerous condition, so that where the landlord could by the exercise of reasonable care have discovered the unreasonable risk of criminal intrusion and could have made the condition safe from such unreasonable risk of criminal intrusion, he is subject to liability for physical harm caused by criminal intrusion if he had not taken the necessary precautions. As regards parts of the property retained [under] [*sic*] the landlord's control, common entranceways, fire escapes, halls and other approaches to the leased property are included.

It is well recognized at present that failure to provide adequate lighting, door locks, or other security measures may subject certain landowners to liability for harm caused by a criminal attack on persons to whom the owner owes a duty of care.

Logically, it cannot be otherwise. If one owes a duty of reasonable care to those on one's land with permission, then the circumstances will dictate what is reasonable to protect others from foreseeable and preventable danger. The category of danger neither creates nor eradicates duty; it only indicates what conduct may be reasonable to fulfill the duty.

Our case is the type in which courts are tempted to blur the concepts of duty and negligence. As we have previously indicated, we disapprove of attempts to equate the concepts of duty with specific details of conduct. Duty is an issue "of the relation between individuals which imposes upon one a legal obligation for the benefit of the other. . . . " As the possessor of the common areas, Defendant has a relationship, similar to that of a landlord, with unit owners, their tenants, and persons on the land with consent and permission to use the common areas. That relationship required Defendant to use reasonable care to avoid causing the injury to those it permitted to use the property under its control. The relationship between Defendant, its unit owners, and persons given permission to enter the common areas thus imposed an obligation on Defendant to take reasonable precautions for the latter's safety. The type of foreseeable danger did not dictate the existence of duty but only the nature and extent of the conduct necessary to fulfill the duty. The true issue on summary judgment in this case, therefore, was not the question of duty but rather the question of negligence. We turn, then, to the specific facts to determine whether the trial judge correctly granted summary judgment.

In the response to the motion for summary judgment, there is evidence presented that Defendant knew of the incursion by gangs in the parking lot and other common areas of its property, knew the gangs engaged in drug dealing and other criminal activity, was warned by its own security guard of the need for 24-hour patrols, had hired a second guard for a short period but terminated him because of expense considerations, and knew a neighboring condominium complex had hired off-duty Phoenix police officers to patrol. We therefore hold there is sufficient evidence from which a jury could find the danger foreseeable and Defendant negligent.

On this record, also, we cannot say as a matter of law Defendant could not have taken reasonable measures that probably would have prevented the attack. It may be that increased security patrols, better fencing, calls for police control, or other measures might have prevented injury. This question of causation in fact is, of course, one especially for the jury.

Although Defendant did not owe Plaintiff a duty of care based on Defendant's special relationship to control the attacker in this case, with respect to the common areas under its control it had a duty like that of a landlord to maintain its property in a reasonably safe condition. This included the duty to take reasonable measures to protect against foreseeable activities creating danger, including criminal attacks, on the land it controlled.

Accordingly, summary judgment was improper. Therefore, we vacate the court of appeals' opinion, reverse the trial court's grant of summary judgment, and remand to the trial court for proceedings consistent with this opinion.

Reversed and Remanded.

Case Questions

1. What happened and when?
2. What kind of security did Woodmar have available?
3. Did the homeowners' association have any duty to Martinez?
4. Does the court discuss any other duties the association may have?
5. What is the duty of condominium associations with regard to criminal activity on their premises?

Compare and contrast the finding in the following additional case on liability of condominium associations for criminal activity.

Medcalf v. Washington Condominium Ass'n

747 A.2d 532 (Conn. App. 2000)

Facts

Mechelle Medcalf (plaintiff) and a friend, Deborah Michelson, arrived at 1633 Washington Boulevard in Stamford, Connecticut, to visit their friend, Tracy Skiades, who resides at the Washington Heights Condominiums.

Ms. Medcalf parked her car in the street level parking lot and walked to the lobby doors. The lighting in the parking lot was dim. She picked up the intercom and called Ms. Skiades. Ms. Skiades' brother-in-law answered and informed Skiades that Ms. Medcalf was downstairs. Ms. Skiades then tried to let Ms. Metcalf in using the electronic buzzer system. The system did not work and Ms. Skiades indicated she would come down and open the door. As she traveled down to the lobby, Ms. Medcalf was attacked and injured by Kenneth Strickler.

Ms. Medcalf filed suit against Washington Heights Condominium Association and Professional Property Management Company, Inc., its managing agent (defendants). Ms. Medcalf alleged that their failure to maintain the buzzer system was the cause of her assault and injuries. The jury found for Ms. Medcalf and the association and managing agent appealed.

Judicial Decision

Mihalakos, Judge. The dispositive issue in this appeal is whether there is a causal connection between the assault and the failure of the security system. We conclude that the jury could not reasonably have found that the failure to maintain the intercom security system was the proximate cause of the assault.

The elements in a negligence cause of action are duty, breach of that duty, causation and damages. "The first component of legal cause is causation in fact. Causation in fact is the purest legal application of . . . legal cause. The test for cause in fact is, simply, would the injury have occurred were it not for the actor's conduct."

The second component is proximate cause. "Proximate cause establishes a reasonable connection between an act or omission of a defendant and the harm suffered by a plaintiff." "The Connecticut Supreme Court has defined proximate cause as [a]n actual cause that is a substantial factor in the resulting harm. . . . The substantial factor test reflects the inquiry fundamental to all proximate cause questions, that is, whether the harm which occurred was of the same general nature as the foreseeable risk created by the defendant's negligence." Proximate cause is a question of fact to be decided by the trier of fact, but it becomes a question of law when the mind of a fair and reasonable person could reach only one conclusion. "Lines must be drawn determining how far down the causal continuum individuals will be held liable for the consequences of their actions. . . . This line is labeled proximate cause." In issues involving proximate cause analysis, this court has held that "an intervening intentional or criminal act relieves a negligent defendant of liability, except where the harm caused by the intervening act is within the scope of risk created by the defendant's conduct or where the intervening act is reasonably foreseeable. . . . As a general rule, the act of a third person in committing an intentional act or crime is a superseding cause of harm to another resulting therefrom. . . . In such a case, the third person has deliberately assumed control of the situation, and all responsibility for the consequences of his act is shifted to him." Recovery is barred in a negligence action where there is a lack of causal connection between the defendant's wrongful conduct and a plaintiff's injury.

In *Doe v. Manheimer*, 563 A.2d 699, our Supreme Court was not persuaded that the owner of a property should reasonably foresee that an overgrowth of vegetation would provide an inducement for the commission of a violent crime by a stranger. The court held that the overgrown vegetation was an incidental factor and not a substantial factor that would establish proximate cause.

In the present case, the plaintiff offered no evidence that the malfunctioning intercom system was designed to provide security to a person outside the building. The defendants' failure to maintain the intercom system was inconsequential and was not the proximate cause of the assault. The injury may likely have occurred without any negligence with respect to the intercom system.

The defendants could not have reasonably foreseen that a malfunctioning intercom system might provide a substantial incentive or inducement for the commission of a violent criminal assault on their property by one stranger upon another.

We rule that, as a matter of law, the jury could not reasonably have found that the assault on the plaintiff and the resultant injury were within the foreseeable scope of risk created by the defendants' failure to maintain the intercom system. Therefore, the plaintiff failed to establish the necessary causal relationship.

The judgment is Reversed.

Case Questions

1. What happened and when?
2. What does Ms. Medcalf allege is the cause of her injuries?
3. What is the difference between causation and proximate cause?
4. Is this case different from the *Woodmar* case? Do the two states' laws differ on injuries to visitors from third parties?

Consider 11.4

Donna Marie Morgan lived in the condominium building owned by 253 East Delaware Condominium Association (Delaware) and managed by Joseph Moss Realty (Moss). On September 18, 1986, at about 8:30 P.M., Morgan walked from her class at Loyola University's downtown campus to the building where she entered the lobby. She observed a man talking with the doorman when she first entered the building and was checking her mail. The man followed her onto the elevator.

When the elevator arrived at the tenth floor, the man poked a gun in her back and forced her off the elevator and into the stairwell. He pushed Morgan down to the ninth floor, robbed and beat her with the gun and caused severe injuries.

Morgan filed suit alleging that Delaware and Moss were negligent for their failure to protect her from criminal acts of unknown parties. Should Delaware and Moss be held liable? *Morgan v. 253 East Delaware Condominium Association,* 595 N.E.2d 36 (Ill. 1992)

Because of the potential liability to all who might be within the common areas, associations for multiunit housing should carry liability insurance to ensure coverage and prevent the liability of individual owners for such torts.

CAUTIONS AND CONCLUSIONS

Like other real estate purchases, multiunit housing can be a good investment, but it is important to study before buying. The following questions should be answered before an investment is made.

For a condominium conversion:

1. What is the status of the building? What repairs are necessary? Who will make the repairs? Who will pay for the repairs?
2. When will the developer turn over control of the building operation? Who or what organization will control the building operation at that point? What system of government, maintenance, and repair has been set up?
3. Is there a provision to opt out (back out) if the units do not sell?
4. Will the developer finish repairs? Are there any outstanding liens?

For an existing development:

1. Is there an association? If so, how does it work and is it effective?
2. Are there assessments? If so, how much are they, and do the unit owners pay them?

3. What provisions for operations and restrictions are made in the declaration, charters, bylaws, and regulations?
4. Are the common areas well maintained?
5. What elements are included in the common areas, and what elements are the responsibility of individual unit owners?
6. How do other unit owners feel about the assessments and how the development is functioning?
7. Are there any pending lawsuits?
8. Is there adequate insurance coverage for the common areas?
9. Are the units rented or owner-occupied?

For any type of multiunit purchase:

1. Is it possible to obtain financing?
2. What type of ownership interest is being obtained?
3. Are there restrictions on transferability?
4. Are there use and age restrictions?
5. Are the units subject to architectural control?

The quality of a multiunit investment is tied to the quality of the investor's investigation of the development. The investigation can never be too thorough.

Key Terms

Uniform Condominium Act, 228	conversion restrictions, 229	cooperative, 239
horizontal property regimes, 228	declaration of condominium, 230	proprietary lease, 242
horizontal property acts, 228	master deed, 230	townhouse, 242
Model Real Estate Cooperative Act, 228	declaration of horizontal property regime and covenants, 230	time-sharing, 243
		recreational lease, 244
Model Real Estate Time-Share Act, 228	declaration of covenants, conditions, and restrictions (CC&Rs or CCRs), 230	vacation license, 244
		interval-ownership grants, 244
Uniform Common Interest Ownership Act, 228	bylaws, 231	patio homes, 245
		garden homes, 245
condominium, 228	business judgment rule, 237	attached homes, 245

Chapter Problems

1. Betty Grey and other condominium unit owners in Hawkins Landing brought suit against Coastal States Holding Company and others who also owned units in the Hawkins Landing condominium project for their expansion of their units by the construction of a second story onto each of their units. Grey and the others maintained that the defendants had thereby appropriated the airspace above their units, a common element belonging to the Hawkins Landing Association, Inc. Is Grey correct? *Grey v. Coastal States Holding Company*, 578 A.2d 1080 (Conn. 1980)

2. Roundtree Villas Association, Inc., is a nonprofit corporation whose primary function is to own and administer the common elements of the condominium project called "Roundtree Villas." Roundtree Corporation, Inc., was the original owner of a parcel of real estate that filed a deed under the Horizontal Property Act. Republic Mortgage Investment Services, Inc., was the financier of the project. Mortgage Investment Services, Inc., was an advisory service employed by Republic Mortgage, the lender.

The condominium project was constructed by Miles and Teal Builders at a time when money was short and sales were slow. Miles and Teal sold what they could and then 4701 Kings Corporation, a company created by Republic Mortgage to accept title to Roundtree Villas in lieu of Republic's foreclosure, took over the property. Shortly after the acquisition, the owners of the units began to complain about problems with the units' roofs and balconies. The lender attempted to remedy the problems, but only with stopgap measures. The problems continued.

The homeowners' association for Roundtree filed suit against Republic, the lender, and 4701 Kings Corporation for breach of the implied warranty of habitability and sought damages for the repair of the roofs and balconies. The jury entered a verdict against the lender and the lender appealed. Should the lender be held liable? *Roundtree Villas Association, Inc. v. 4701 Kings Corporation,* 321 S.E.2d 46 (S.C. 1984)

3. Melvin R. Luster and Harold E. Friedman formed a partnership to convert the 20 East Cedar property from rental property to condominium units. Deeds to each unit provided purchasers with title for the designated unit plus an undivided percentage of the "common elements." In each sales agreement, the partnership agreed to complete certain repair and rehabilitation work in the building.

In 1970 (during the conversion process), Luster and Friedman leased a canopy from White Way Electric Sign and Maintenance Company with a down payment of $6,128 and 60 monthly payments of $261.76 each. The canopy was ornamental and was installed at the front entrance of the 20 East Cedar building.

In 1973, the unit owners formed their own association, and Luster and Friedman were relieved of their responsibilities. After the release, the unit owners discovered the liability remaining on the canopy lease as well as several other unpaid expenses incurred by Luster and Friedman in the rehabilitation of the building.

The association brought suit, seeking a complete accounting and monetary relief from Luster and Friedman. The trial court ordered Luster and Friedman to pay for the canopy, and Luster and Friedman appealed. Who is liable? *20 East Cedar Condominium Association v. Luster et al.,* 349 N.E.2d 586 (Ill. 1976)

4. Jay Johnson purchased a condominium in November 1978 but failed to pay the monthly maintenance fee after August 1979. The Condominium Declaration for his condominium apartments provided that the homeowner's council (First Southern) has a lien on each apartment for any unpaid assessments and authorized the council to enforce the lien through "non-judicial foreclosure through a power of sale."

Using the authority in the declaration of condominium, First Southern foreclosed on Johnson's unit. Johnson claimed he enjoyed a homestead exemption protection and that the council could not foreclose. Can the council foreclose? *Johnson v. First Southern Properties, Inc.,* 687 S.W.2d 399 (Tex. 1985)

5. William B. Miller, an owner of a condominium in San Antonio's Villa Del Sol, has failed to pay his share of common element assessments and owes $3,604.51 in back assessments. The bylaws authorize the directors to enforce

the assessments by whatever means necessary. The directors shut off Mr. Miller's electricity. Is this proper under their bylaws? *San Antonio Villa Del Sol Homeowners Association v. Miller,* 761 S.W.2d 460 (Tx. 1988)

6. The Island House Association, Incorporated, a homeowners' association formed for the operation of the Island House condominiums and villas, assessed each unit for maintenance fees. The association required condominium owners to pay more for maintenance than villa owners because the condominium building was larger, had more units, and required more frequent repairs. The provision for fees was in the bylaws and had been voted on by the owners and approved by a majority. Thiess, a condominium owner, refused to pay his fees and claimed the assessment was inequitable and unfair. What was the result?

7. George E. Western is the owner of a condominium unit in Chardonnay Village. Chardonnay Village Condominium Association, Inc., is the association of condominium unit owners that governs and manages the condominium project. Under the Louisiana Condominium Act, associations are empowered to collect expenses of administration, maintenance, repair, and replacement of the common elements. The condominium declaration of Chardonnay Village authorizes the association to collect the costs of utilities for each unit as well as for the common areas.

Western has failed to pay the assessments for the common areas for approximately three years for a total of $4,962.08, which included late fees of $25.00 per month.

On October 1, 1986, the association turned off Western's water supply for failure to pay the assessment. Western filed for a temporary restraining order to prevent the water turnoff and was awarded such by the trial court. What should be the result? *Western v. Chardonnay Village Condominium Association, Inc.,* 519 So.2d 243 (La. 1988)

8. Silver purchased a condominium unit in a new building and less than six months after moving in, he and several other owners discovered that the air-conditioning units were defective. They sued the developer on a breach of implied warranty for new home construction. The developer maintained that the warranty applied only to single-family sales. What was the result?

9. Ronald and Roseanne Ebner are shareholders and tenants under a proprietary lease of an apartment in a Manhattan multiple dwelling owned by 91st Street Tenants Corporation. The Ebners sought to assign their shares and their lease to Janusz Gorzynski. They made application to the corporation's board of directors, but the consent to transfer was denied on the grounds that Gorzynski is a psychiatrist who intends to use the apartment primarily for treating patients and only secondarily as a residence. The board also pointed out that Gorzynski would allow other physicians to use his residence when he is out of the city.

The Ebners then used Article II, Section 6, of the proprietary lease, which permits a tenant to make an assignment without the consent of the board so long as there is written consent from a majority of lessees owning capital stock. The Ebners believe they have obtained such consent, but they have obtained only one signature in many cases when the shares are jointly owned. Describe the types of interests involved in this situation and advise

the parties on their rights. *Ebner v. 91st Street Tenants Corp.*, 481 N.Y.S.2d 198 (1984)

10. Robb, a resident of North Townehome Park, installed evaporative coolers in the windows of his townhouse, and the homeowners' association complained, citing architectural nonconformity. Is it permissible to prevent such an installation or require it to be removed?

Internet Activities

1. For the statutory text of the states that have adopted the Uniform Common Interest Ownership Act, go to: **http://www.law.cornell.edu/uniform/vol7.html#comin**.

2. For the statutory text of the states that have adopted the Uniform Condominium Act, go to: **http://www.law.cornell.edu/uniform/vol7.html#comin**.

3. See **http://www.cnyc.com/index.html** for information on condominium ownership issues in New York City.

4. Explore Michigan's condominium act: **http://www.libofmich.lib.mi.us/law/publicacts/condominium.html**.

5. For current legal issues in condominium sales, visit: **http://orlink.oldrepnatl.com/** and click on Bulletins, then on Condominiums.

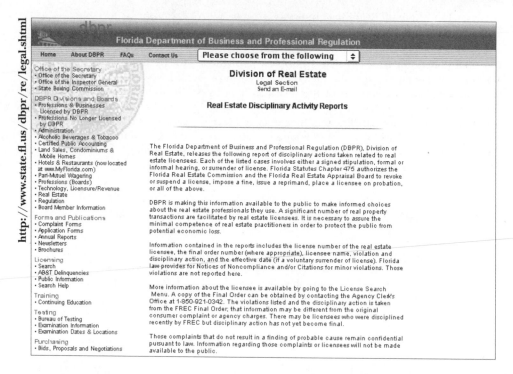

Chapter 12
The Broker's Role in the Transfer of Real Estate

If Megan Kanka's parents had known that their house was across the street from Jesse Timmendequas, she might still be alive. If property values fall . . . well, little girls' lives are more important.

Tom Davey of *Buyer's Voice* addressing the responsibility of brokers and agents to direct buyers to sex-offender registration records that reveal the residences of convicted sex offenders (the statutory requirement for registration of sex offenders and notification when they move into neighborhoods is often referred to as "Megan's Law," named for Megan Kanka, who was killed by Jesse Timmendequas, a convicted sex offender and neighbor).

These opening quotes reflect the tension that brokers face in trying to sell property, while at the same time being fair to buyers. Balancing those interests requires brokers to understand the legal and ethical issues involved in the transfer of property.

Over the past few years the role of broker has been evolving as new dilemmas and questions arise. Does the broker represent the seller or the buyer in the transaction? Is the broker responsible for defects the seller fails to disclose? Is the broker entitled to be paid when a sale falls through? The broker is both the buyer's and the seller's key to an efficient market in real estate, because brokers have the market information and access to bring buyers and sellers together. This chapter focuses on the role of the broker in real estate transactions and answers the following questions: What is the agency relationship of the broker? What responsibilities and liabilities does the broker have as an agent? What ethical constraints should a broker follow? What areas should a broker focus on when listing and selling a property?

NATURE OF BROKER'S/AGENT'S ROLE

Definition

A **broker** is an agent[1] hired either by the owner of a property to aid in its sale or by a potential owner (buyer) to find property suitable for specified needs. A broker is the middle person acting to bring buyer and seller together. Generally, a broker works on a commission basis rather than on salary. That commission is usually specified as some percentage of the sales price and will probably not be paid until the actual sales transaction is complete (see consideration discussion in this chapter).

Traditional Principal/Agent Concepts vs. Principal/Broker Roles

Under the traditional principal/agent relationship, the agent works on behalf of the principal, owes a duty of loyalty to the principal, would not breach confidences of the principal, and would not profit at the principal's expense. The principal and the agent are a team, working together with a common interest. However, the real estate broker relationship, because of the nature of property transactions, creates flowing, instead of rigid, relationships. Interactions and methods of conducting business blur the traditional lines and rules of agency. While the industry is still evolving with respect to the role of brokers, there are certain types of broker relationships that are common in the industry. Those types of relationships are found in the following section.

Practical Tip

The courts and professional organizations continue to struggle with the unique problems of the principal/agent relationship in broker/seller listings. Some possible resolutions include going beyond existing disclosure requirements and possibly seeking further legislation on disclosure. Yet another proposal is to introduce a type of limited agency that would be specifically designed for the unique broker/seller/buyer relationship. Under this proposal, the duties of the listing broker and selling broker would be specifically delineated to alleviate the conflicts with general agency law. Still another proposal is to develop a different relationship among the parties along the lines of a consultant or independent contractor. Under this proposal, the nature of the relationship would be limited by title and responsibilities and would not be a traditional principal/agent relationship. The broker would serve as a facilitator and offer expertise but would not be a fiduciary for either party.

---

1.   Note: The term *broker* is used here in a generic sense to reflect that person hired to represent either the seller or buyer in a real estate transaction. *Broker* and *agent* have distinct meanings in the real estate industry, with differing training and education requirements. A real estate agent must work for a broker but can serve as an agent in the legal sense for seller or buyer. That real estate agent's broker is also a legal agent for the listing seller or the represented buyer. The terms *broker* and *agent* are used interchangeably throughout the chapter.

THE TYPES OF REAL ESTATE BROKER RELATIONSHIPS

The Listing Agent

The listing agent works directly with the seller to list the property, advertise it, and contribute other marketing services. However, even the listing broker will be involved in showing property to buyers and hence has dual contact with buyer and seller. A 1998 survey established that even though the listing agent is the only one involved in a sales transaction, 72 percent of purchasers of real estate still believed in those circumstances that the listing agent represented them and not the seller.

The Dual Agency

Given the confusion of buyers with respect to the role of brokers, many states have addressed the issue through the allowance of a dual agency. A **dual agency** in real estate is a concept borrowed from agency law that permits an agent to represent two parties so long as the parties are aware of the dual representation.

Making the parties aware of either the dual or singular role of the real estate agent has required legislation and regulation. Nearly all states have some form of mandatory disclosure requirements. That is, before the buyer or seller signs a broker for representation, they must be told of the role the broker plays. In addition, the **National Association of Realtors (NAR),** the professional association for brokers and agents, requires under its code of ethics that NAR members make specific disclosures to all parties. (NAR's Code of Ethics and Standards of Practice are available at **http://nar.realtor.com/about/ethics.htm.**)

If these disclosures are not made, the real estate broker will lose the commission or be required to pay back the commission. Web Exhibits 12.1 and 12.2 are sample disclosure forms for Massachusetts and Florida.

In the case of dual representation, the disclosure form, known as a "Consent to Act," must be signed by the parties hiring the broker. Web Exhibit 12.3 is a sample dual representation consent form.

The Buyer Broker

Under a new trend, an agency relationship in which the buyer is represented by a broker has taken hold. The buyer broker generally requires a nonrefundable up-front fee that ranges from $100 to $500 and then works with the buyer to find the property. However, the buyer broker is paid a percentage of the commission from the eventual property sale. An issue of conflict arises since compensation is tied to the purchase price: Will the buyer broker negotiate the lowest possible price when compensation increases as the price increases? There is disagreement in the industry about the propriety of buyer brokers. The Realtors' code of ethics requires buyer brokers to disclose their relationship with their buyer when they have their first contact with the seller. See Web Exhibit 12.4 for sample open and exclusive listings

| Ethical Issue | Tom Caines is acting as an agent for Luci and Neil Dayton, a couple looking to purchase a home. Tom has located a home in Ventura Canyon that nearly perfectly suits the needs Luci and Neil have described to him. Tom approaches the owner, Mel Cusack, and explains that he is representing Luci |

and Neil Dayton as buyers. Tom then adds, "Look, you have what they want. You can pretty much get your asking price. It helps me because I am on commission in addition to the fee they paid up front." Has Tom acted ethically? What conflict does Tom have in acting as a buyer broker and earning a commission?

The Open Listing Agency

An **open listing** agreement is used when an owner lists the property to be sold with more than one broker. Under this form of listing, the seller owes only one commission to the broker who actually sells the property. Furthermore, the seller retains the right to sell the property personally; and if the seller does produce the buyer, no commission is owed to any broker.

The open listing agreement in no way prohibits the seller from selling the property directly. The seller retains the right to sell property to anyone not first contacted by the broker, and the seller need not pay the broker a commission. The seller retains the right to list the above described property with any other broker(s).

Other brokers are free to solicit listings from sellers who have open listing arrangements with other brokers, and the only commission paid will be the one to the broker who actually produced the buyer.

The Exclusive Agency

An **exclusive agency listing** arrangement is one in which the seller is required to pay a commission to the listing broker if that broker sells the property. However, the seller still retains the right to sell the property independently; and if the seller does sell the listed property, the listing broker earns no commission. If the seller hires another broker, the original broker retains the right to commission and the seller will be obligated for two commissions.

The major distinction between the open listing agreement and the exclusive agency listing agreement is that the open listing permits the seller to list the property with other brokers. Under the exclusive agency listing, sellers should not list with other brokers, because they will still be responsible to the exclusive broker for the commission and may end up paying more than one commission. In both types of listings, the seller may still sell the property independently without being required to pay the commission.

The Exclusive Right-to-Sell or Exclusive Listing-to-Sell Agency

Under the **exclusive right-to-sell** or **exclusive listing-to-sell** arrangement, the seller agrees to pay a commission to the broker regardless of who produces a buyer. The broker earns the commission even if the seller produces a buyer independently of the broker. This type of listing agreement, which is beneficial to the broker, is the one used most frequently in the real estate industry.

Multiple Listing Agency

The **multiple listing** agreement is not really a form of agency between seller and broker, but rather a service available to brokers who are members of some of the multiple listing services. An example of a **multiple listing service** is the **MLS,** a network of exclusive right-to-sell listings that affords brokers and sellers a larger market for their properties. Through MLS, broker members are able to show the listed properties of other brokers. The listing broker then shares in the commission if a nonlisting broker obtains a buyer for the broker's listed property. The split commission is prenegotiated and determined by the MLS members. Since there is still only one listing agreement, the seller is liable for only one commission. The MLS is a marketing tool enabling brokers to assist each other in finding buyers and to split fees accordingly.

The Subagency

The subagency theory has come about because of the MLS. Under an MLS listing, there is the listing broker (who represents the seller) and then, quite often, the selling broker (who brings the buyers who eventually buy the property). Members of the industry have labeled the selling broker a subagent of the seller because the selling broker derives his/her authority from the listing broker. However, perception by buyers is that the selling broker represents them; 72 percent of all buyers in an FTC survey indicated this belief. Further, 82 percent of sellers believed the selling broker was working for the buyer rather than for them. In 1993, NAR changed its position that subagents were mandatory agents of the seller, and the result has been a shift to more buyers' agents in MLS listings.

Net Listing Agency

In the **net listing** agreement, the seller and broker may have any of the previous types of listing arrangements for determining who is entitled to the commission. This arrangement merely provides a different method for determining the amount of commission the broker is entitled to receive. Generally, the commission is some percentage of the selling price. However, in net listings, the sellers set forth a predetermined amount that they must receive from the sale of the property after expenses, insurance, and so on. The broker's commission is anything received above that predetermined amount. For example, if the seller sets the net figure for receipt at $40,000 and $41,500 remains after expenses, the broker is entitled to receive $1,500 as commission. Again, this form of commission determination may be coupled with an open listing, exclusive agency listing, or exclusive right-to-sell format.

The Designated Agency

A **designated agency** relationship arises when one firm represents both the buyer and seller in a transaction. The broker for the firm designates one salesperson to represent the seller and another sales person to represent the buyer. While it is a form of dual agency, its character is slightly different because both agents work for one company.

The Nonagent Broker

A **nonagent broker** may be known as a **transaction broker, intermediary, limited agent,** or **statutory broker.** Only 10 states recognize this relationship in which brokers represent both buyer and seller in closing a transaction but have no fiduciary obligations. They are simply facilitators for closing. States vary on their requirements for creating a nonagency relationship.

The Internet as an Agent

Stocks, bonds, and antiques have sold well over the Internet. The free market exchange of information and quick transactions have produced selling booms in everything from books to toys. The idea of matching buyers and sellers of real estate with an Internet data base seemed to be a possibility that would eliminate the need for any type of agent or broker. However, those responsible for Microsoft's Internet site for home buyers, **http://www.HomeAdvisor.com**, have conceded that agents play a critical role in the buying and selling of real estate, particularly when it comes to homes.

The most successful Internet real estate sites are those that partner with agents. Such a site is **http://www.Realtor.com.** The site's partnering with agents gives potential buyers a wide-ranging data base from which to select properties and an agent who can walk them through the properties as well as provide advice on putting in offers. Real estate buyers are not yet ready to negotiate the purchase of a home without a physical view and not prepared enough to handle the contracting and negotiations by themselves.

Internet listing services are not so different from other types of listings or even the MLS. The seller lists property with the Internet service, which plays the role of the listing broker. Buyers may come to the site with their own agent or broker, or they may use an agent or broker offered by the site. That broker or agent then is entitled to split the commission with the Internet listing service.

Since the dominant Internet site began in 1996 (**http://www.Realtor.com**), there have been 1.2 million listings there. This site, along with **http://www. HomeStore.com,** accepts listings only from licensed real estate agents who have registered with the service. The commission rate on both sites is always 6 percent. Other sites have begun and offer discount commissions such as **http:// www.yhd.com** (also known as "your home direct" and only in New Jersey) and **http://www.eHomes.com** (California). EHomes offers different types of listings, including, for example, for sale by owner (a flat fee of $95), and agent assistance (4.5 percent commission). There is one site that consists of listings by sellers (**http://www.Homegain.com**). **http://www.Homebytes.com** offers a flat-rate $499 commission, **http://www.eRealty.com** offers a 4.5 percent commission with a 1 percent rebate to buyers who are represented by eRealty. The newest entrant with national markets is **http://www.zipRealty.com,** which offers a 4.5 percent commission, with buyers receiving a rebate of half that commission if they are represented by zipRealty (up to $15,000). ZipRealty follows a new business format in which agents are assigned to the office to field calls and handle buyers and sellers, while other agents are assigned to the field for purposes of showing the properties.

What types of disclosures do you think Internet sites would have to make to buyers and sellers? How could they be certain these parties understood their commission rates and their responsibility for payment of commission? Could it all be done via computer?

Consider 12.1

LISTING AGREEMENTS FOR HIRING BROKERS/AGENTS

The first step taken to ensure success in real estate transactions is for the parties to execute a contract of agency (a contract for hiring an agent) appropriately specifying their rights, duties, and responsibilities. This agency arrangement between broker and seller is called a **listing agreement.** State requirements for valid listing agreements vary, but the parties should be cautious about including certain fundamental topics so that their positions are made absolutely clear.

Agreements in Writing

Nearly all states require that the listing agreement be in writing. In fact, in most states, the failure to have listing agreements in writing will cost the broker or salesperson the commission for the listing agreement. Oral agreements for real estate agency contracts are unenforceable in most states. Even if a broker sells the property pursuant to an oral agreement, the seller need not pay the commission. Courts impose a duty on brokers and agents to get their commission agreements in writing.

Signature by Owner

The listing agreement must be signed by the owner of the property. Brokers should be certain that the true owner has signed the agreement and that if there is more than one owner, all owners have signed. In the case of land owned by a corporation or partnership, brokers should verify that the officer, director, or partner signing the listing agreement has authority to do so. The authority of a trustee, executor, administrator, or personal representative should also be verified, along with any restrictions on the authority to transfer title to the property. For example, some executors of estates may have authority to list the property but not to sell it without prior court approval.

Importance of Careful Drafting

Both brokers and sellers should be cautious in drafting the listing agreement so that the type of listing is clear and the commission issue is not clouded with ambiguities. Generally, with greater prices in real estate, brokers stand to receive substantial sums as commissions when buyers are found. With so much money involved, it is only natural that many legal battles have been fought and are pending in the courts over the issue of who is entitled to receive a commission. The best way to avoid such litigation is to make sure the listing agreement is carefully and unambiguously drafted.

Expiration Date

Most states have some type of law or regulation requiring a definite expiration date to be set forth in the listing agreement. In those states where such a limitation is required, listing agreements not meeting the requirement are treated as unenforceable contracts and may cost the broker the commission in spite of the sale and in spite of the existence of a written listing agreement. Some states impose maximum time limits for listing agreements with 90 days being a typical maximum length.

Brokers may put a clause in the listing agreement that entitles them to a commission for a certain period of time after the expiration of the listing agreement for sale to prospective buyers originally introduced to the property by the broker during the listing period.

A sample clause follows:

If within ninety (90) days after the expiration of this listing agreement, a sale is made directly by the broker to any person to whom this property has been shown by you or the broker or an agent of the broker, the same fee shall prevail, unless this listing is renewed or the property is relisted on the same basis with another broker, and in that case, this stipulation shall be void.

In some states there are statutory requirements for the right to earn a commission on a listing agreement that has expired if a sale is made to a prospect the broker brought to the seller. Requirements often include the broker providing a seller with a list of "protected persons," or those persons to whom the property has been shown, so that the seller is aware of the broker's claim for a commission should a sale to any of them occur. This list must be a formal document and generally has an applicable time limit, such as within 72 hours after the listing agreement ends.

One additional danger in having a listing agreement without an expiration date and extension clause, even in those states recognizing the validity of such listings, is that the seller may cancel the agreement at any time. Such a right of cancellation is often used to avoid paying a commission. The courts have implied a duty of good faith on the part of the parties to an indefinite-duration listing agreement to preclude commission avoidance.

Clauses covering the expiration date and extension clauses should also cover the rights of termination under the listing agreements. Issues that should be covered in the clauses include whether the listing may be terminated, how termination occurs, what type of notice of termination is required, and what damages will be due and owing, if any.

The following case deals with a termination and commission issue on a listing agreement.

Island Realty v. Bibbo

748 A.2d 620 (N.J. App. 2000)

Facts

Island Realty (plaintiff/appellant) listed Susan Bibbo's (defendant) property in Loveladies, New Jersey. The listing agreement was an MLS exclusive right to sell effective from May 13, 1998, until November 13, 1998. The listing price was $359,000 and the commission for Island was 6 percent.

On July 23, 1998, Ms. Bibbo notified Island that she wanted to remove her house from the market. She confirmed that decision the next day with a letter to the Island offices.

On July 27, 1998, Island faxed to Bibbo an unsigned, illegible agreement for sale for the listing price from a buyer produced by another realtor. A legible version was faxed the next day, but the actual agreement was not signed by the buyer until July 29, 1998. Bibbo never received a signed copy of the purchase agreement and she did not sign either document that she received. In short, Bibbo refused to sell the property. She also refused demands by Island for its commission.

Island filed suit for its full commission of $21,540. The lower court granted Bibbo's motion for summary judgment and Island Realty appealed.

Judicial Opinion

Kestin, Judge. In a written statement attached to the dismissal order, Judge Ford expressed her reasons for granting defendant's motion for summary judgment and dismissing the complaint. The statement recited in part: Mrs. Bibbo did not sign the agreement, since she felt she had removed the house from the market, and further, since she found the terms to be unacceptable; although the offer was for full price, the initial deposit of $1,000 and the additional deposit of $35,900 were not paid, and the offer had not been signed by the prospective purchaser. . . .

The listing agreement does not address the issue of termination in the event that the seller, as is purported occurred here, has a change of heart. For purposes of this motion, however, I am assuming that the listing agreement was in effect and the question is whether or not the right to a commission, setting aside the enforceability of the agreement, ever occurred. It appears that it was within the prerogative of the seller to reject even a full price offer based upon unacceptable terms, in this case, the deficiency of the down payment, and the failure of the purchaser to follow through with the offer.

Therefore, there was not a ready, willing and able buyer making a bona fide offer, and thus the right to receive the commission never accrued. Since there is no factual dispute to be resolved, summary judgment is appropriate.

In denying plaintiff's motion for reconsideration, Judge Ford expressed her reasons in an oral opinion:

> . . . I agree that somebody could make a full price offer knowing that someone is not going to accept it for whatever reason, and under this theory they could always guarantee themselves a source of income because to say that just as long as somebody offers the full price, then that triggers the commission. I don't think . . . I agree.

What this is governed by is what was the agreement between the parties. And the agreement was that Island Realty would market the property for sale. I think that the ultimate decision about whether or not to accept a contract always resided with the seller of the property and no matter what the circumstances were, the decision about whether or not to sell the property was always reposed with the seller.

I don't think that by entering in a listing agreement that the seller intends to surrender that aspect of the ownership of the property because otherwise they would be, in effect, surrendering all of the decision making for the sale of the property. And I think that's something that goes with the incident of ownership of property that resides with the seller. What they are giving up is the right to market the property. And when there is a meeting of the minds in terms of a transaction and even if that transaction doesn't consummate in an actual sale, if there's a meeting of the minds and if the seller backed out of that, then there would be a right to some type of real estate commission. And I agree that Island Realty would then be entitled to the commission it would have realized on the transaction which in this case would have been approximately $10,000, not the full commission but the commission that they would have realized because they would have split it with the other—they're the listing broker and there was a broker here that actually produced this potential customer. But for whatever reason, there was no meeting of the minds in terms of the terms and conditions of this contract. And there may be some question as to whether or not this particular [purchaser] rose to the level of being a ready, willing, and able [purchaser] and whether or not the terms were acceptable to the [seller].

But in any event, because of the seller's personal circumstances she decided to take this property off the market. And so long as she did not go to another agency and market it, if she was taking it off the market at that point in time, then I think that it is implicit within her agency agreement that she have the right to do that. This again doesn't do violence to the right of Island Realty to get a commission on a sale or where they produce a ready, willing, and able buyer. But here because there just wasn't a meeting of the minds and because a reasonable seller cold disagree with certain terms and conditions of this contract, then I think that my initial decision was accurate and that the application for a commission is denied. . . .

In general, the seller is liable for the commission where, during the listing term the realtor was the "efficient producing cause" of an actual sale.

Where the property has been withdrawn from the market before the broker's efforts have produced a buyer who stands ready to consummate the transaction, the owner is responsible to the broker only for such damages as may be established for breach of contract or on a quantum meruit basis for special services rendered in connection with reasonable efforts to sell the property, undertaken before it was withdrawn from the market.

Instead of seeking the full sales commission where no sale had occurred, plaintiff could have sought damages based on breach of contract or on quantum meruit. Even though one cannot prevail on both a contract claim and a quantum meruit (implied contract) claim covering the same services, our liberal approaches to pleading practice permit a party to seek relief on alternative grounds. However, when questioned at oral argument before us on the subjects of quantum meruit and breach of contract damages, plaintiff expressly disavowed any interest in pursuing a claim other than for its full commission, notwithstanding that count four of the complaint, viewed with the customary liberality employed in construing the scope of pleadings. We note, as well, that during the pendency of this matter plaintiff never asserted that it had incurred damages from defendant's alleged breach of contract apart from its loss of the full sales commission.

Affirmed.

Case Questions

1. When was the listing agreement signed? When was it terminated?

2. When was the offer faxed? When was it signed?

3. Does a seller have the right to refuse an offer for the full listing price?

4. Is the broker entitled to the commission in this case? Is the broker entitled to damages in this case?

Amount of the Commission

Particularly in multiple listing arrangements, commissions charged have tended to be uniform. This uniformity in commission rates has caused the Justice Department to bring suit alleging a conspiracy to fix prices. In an effort to countermand these suits, a clause containing language similar to the following frequently appears in form listing agreements: "The commissions payable for the sale, lease, or management of property are not set by any board of Realtors, multiple listing service, or in any manner other than between the broker and the client."

While there has not been a judicial decision directly addressing real estate commissions and their antitrust implications, the United States Supreme Court has ruled in *McClain et al. v. Real Estate Board of New Orleans, Inc. et al.*, 441 U.S. 942 (1980) that real estate brokerage has a sufficient impact on interstate commerce for it to be subject to federal antitrust laws such as the Sherman Act and its prohibition on price fixing.

Consider 12.2

The newly elected president of a professional organization of real estate agents held a dinner at an exclusive country club. He invited his colleagues who would help him manage the organization during his tenure of office. Their discussion at dinner centered around a new membership drive and the organization of committees. The new president then stood at the meeting and said the following:

> My business is dying fast. I have already borrowed $75,000 to keep afloat. If I am going bankrupt at 6 percent, I might as well go bankrupt at 7 percent. I don't care what the rest of you do, that is what I am going to do.

Has there been an antitrust violation?

Because the MLS listing enables brokers to tap into an entire community's market, its accessibility is often critical for success in the business. Sales statistics indicate that 80 percent of all residential purchases involve a multiple listing service broker. However, in recent years these organizations have, like other trade and professional associations, faced review of their anticompetitive effects. Membership restrictions for such boards are particularly suspect when the result is that those denied memberships, on the basis of unjustified criteria, are effectively precluded from the business benefits and activities afforded members.

With the advent of the Internet, the anticompetitive impact of both commission uniformity and the powerful MLS listing has been diminished. Buyers have ease of access to information, and antitrust cases related to MLS membership and broker commissions have decreased substantially.

When Commission Is Due and Owing

Most form listing agreements provide, and the majority of courts hold (in the absence of an agreement to the contrary), that the broker is entitled to the commission when a purchaser who is ready, willing, and able to meet the terms of the listing agreement has been brought to the seller. Actual closing of the deal is not necessary for the broker to collect the commission.[2]

Several legal issues arise from this time framework for the awarding of commissions. The listing agreement should state that the commission is due and payable when a purchaser's offer that complies with the listing agreement terms is presented by the broker and that the commission is not payable from sales proceeds or escrow funds only.

Also, the listing agreement must contain and clearly set forth all of the material terms and conditions for sale of the property, since the broker's entitlement to commission is tied to those terms. And since the seller becomes liable if all terms are met, the seller must be certain that all necessary provisions desired for the sale of the property are established in the listing agreement.

Producing a buyer who is ready and willing simply means that a buyer is ready to purchase according to the seller's listing terms and has made necessary deposits on the property. The *able* portion of the test for commission entitlement requires the broker to establish that the buyer had the financial ability, credit, or resources necessary to go through with the transaction.

Once such a buyer is produced and the seller chooses to back out of the transaction, the commission is still due and owing. Furthermore, if the seller contacts the buyer directly and gets the buyer to cancel, this attempt to thwart the transaction will be ineffective and the broker's commission will still have to be paid.

The most important factor to remember about the ready, willing, and able standard for the broker's commission is that it is not contingent on the sale's actually closing and the buyer's actually paying the funds.

Consider 12.3

Palmer and Elva Loyning entered into a real estate listing agreement with Property Brokers, Inc., to sell their ranch near Roberts, Montana. The agreement employed Property Brokers "to sell or exchange" the property, and would give them an 8 percent commission under the following circumstances:

> *In the event that you or any other brokers cooperating with you, shall find a buyer ready and willing to enter into a deal for said price and terms, or such other terms and price as I may accept, or that during your employment you supply me with name of or place me in contact with a buyer to or through whom at any time within 180 days after the termination of said employment I may sell or convey said property, I hereby agree to pay you in cash for your services a commission equal in amount to 8 percent of the above-stated selling price.*

The agreement was entered into on June 25, 1979, and was to expire June 25, 1980.

Vern Schoulte and a broker cooperating with Property Brokers showed the Loyning ranch to John and Anyce Gerhardt. The Gerhardts and Loynings entered

---

2.   Some states do follow, however, a "no deal, no commission" rule (Oregon, Idaho, Kansas, Massachusetts, and Nebraska). Louisiana remains unclear on its standard, while Vermont and Alaska point to the virtues of "no deal, no commission" while adhering to the "ready, willing, and able" standard.

into a buy–sell agreement on October 23, 1979. An earnest money deposit of $1,000 was given to Schoulte to hold until closing.

The buy–sell agreement was made entirely contingent upon the sale of the Gerhardts' property near Sidney, Montana. Meanwhile, the Gerhardts would take possession of the Loyning ranch as tenants. The buy–sell agreement, including the tenancy provision, was to expire March 31, 1980. If another buyer was found prior to March 31, 1980, the Gerhardts would have 72 hours to finalize their agreement.

The Gerhardts were not able to sell their property near Sidney before March 31, 1980, and no other buyer was found. The Loynings allowed the Gerhardts to stay at their ranch as tenants beyond the March 31 deadline. On August 6, 1980, however, the $1,000 earnest money deposit was forfeited.

On December 31, 1980, the Gerhardts eventually sold their property near Sidney, and were then able to buy the Loyning ranch. On January 29, 1981, the Gerhardts finalized the purchase of the Loyning ranch.

Property Brokers and Schoulte brought suit for their commission. Are they entitled to their commission? *Property Brokers, Inc. v. Loyning,* 654 P.2d 521 (Mont. 1982)

<aside>**12.3,** *continued*</aside>

The Juneaus signed a three-month exclusive right-to-sell listing agreement with Welek for the sale of their home in the Lake of the Ozarks area of Missouri. Welek showed the property to Joe Lawrence, who made an offer of $49,500 (the listing price) with a $500 earnest money deposit. Welek talked with Mr. Juneau, who orally assented to the contract but asked for $1,500 additional earnest money. Lawrence complied. The Juneaus received the contract but never signed it and withdrew the property from the market. Lawrence bought another home in the area and Welek brought suit for the commission. The trial court entered judgment for Welek, and the Juneaus appealed.

What should the court decide? *Welek Realty, Inc. v. Juneau,* 596 S.W.2d. 495 (Mo. 1980).

<aside>Consider **12.4**</aside>

In some states, courts have rendered decisions that eliminate the ready, willing, and able standards and require the actual closing of a deal before the broker is entitled to a commission. These states are limited, and again if the parties desire such an effect, a **no deal, no commission clause** may be put in the listing agreement.

Description of Property and Sale Terms

Because the listing agreement will be the basis for advertising the property and a representation of its quality, size, location, and so on, it is important that the broker obtain accurate information about the property to be sold. Raw land parcels should be carefully described so that there is no error about size or which parcels are actually being conveyed.

Furthermore, the broker's right to commission is tied to presenting an offer from a ready, willing, and able buyer that meets the seller's terms set forth in the listing agreement. This turning point of the transaction should therefore be accurately and fully set forth. Obvious terms to be included are price, method of financing, date property may be transferred, fixtures included and not included, seller's agreement to furnish good title, any conditions for rental or occupancy of the property, any easements or other use restrictions, and any required court approval if the property is part of an estate. A provision should also be included on what becomes of the earnest money in the event of a buyer's default. The fewer details left undiscussed at the time of the listing, the easier it will be for the broker to obtain an appropriate offer and the less confusion will arise at the time an offer is presented. Careful attention to details at the time of the listing may save the broker time and earn a commission more easily at a later date.

Conditions Precedent

A **condition precedent** is a happening or event that must occur before the party or parties to a contract are required to perform their obligations under that contract. Conditions precedent may be inserted in the listing agreement as prerequisites for the broker earning the commission. For example, court approval of a sale of estate property may be inserted as a condition precedent to sale, to payment of the commission, or to both. Financing being obtained by the buyer may also be used as a condition precedent to the seller's performance under the listing agreement.

Liability Limitations

Many brokers insert clauses in their listing agreement limiting their liability to the seller to the amount of commissions paid under the listing agreement. In some cases, such limitations are effective, but when the seller has suffered tremendously because of the broker's negligence, such a clause may be ineffective. (Brokers' duties of care were discussed earlier in this chapter.) Furthermore, with new theories that third parties should recover damages directly from brokers, these liability limitations are often irrelevant (discussed later in the chapter).

Other Details

The listing agreement should also contain permission clauses allowing the broker to advertise, place signs on the property, bring prospective buyers to the property, and use a multiple listing service to market the property.

Figure 12.1 is a checklist for preparing an effective listing agreement

RESPONSIBILITIES OF BROKERS/AGENTS

Authority

Through the listing agreement, the broker is given only the authority to market the listed property and bring prospective buyers to the seller, unless additional authority is specified. Any restrictions and limitations of the broker's authority should be put in the listing agreement. Brokers who engage in conduct beyond the scope of their authority will be held liable for any damages or obligations incurred in excess of that authority. For example, a broker who reduces the listing price without the seller's consent would be liable for the price difference. A broker who accepts an offer for a seller without authority to do so would be liable for damages caused the buyer.

Antisolicitation Statutes

Some states have enacted antisolicitation statutes that prohibit brokers and agents from soliciting property owners to list their properties for sale. In many cases,

FIGURE 12.1

*Checklist for a Effective Listing Agreement**

1. Name of owner
   a. Are they authorized?
   b. Who holds title?
   c. Is there more than one owner?
   d. Signatures

2. Type of listing agreement
   a. Open
   b. Agency
   c. Exclusive right to sell
   d. Net
   e. Multiple listing

3. Duration of the listing
   a. Length
   b. Extension clause for buyers intro-
      duced to the property by the
      broker
   c. Termination: reasons, methods,
      notice, damages

4. Entitlement to commission
   a. Ready, willing, and able
   b. No sale, no commission
   c. Fraud or bad faith by the seller

5. Description of the property
   a. Accurate legal description
   b. Correct parcels

6. Selling Terms
   a. Price
   b. Financing
   c. Date of transfer
   d. Good title
   e. Rental or occupancy
   f. Easements

7. Conditions precedent
   a. Court approval
   b. Buyer financing
   c. Sale of other property

8. Marketing rights
   a. Advertise
   b. Place sign on property
   c. Showings
   d. Multiple listing

9. Rights upon buyer's default
   a. Earnest money
   b. Effect on listing

10. Liability limitations

*Should be written

these antisolicitation statutes are enacted to prevent "blockbusting," which is the practice of controlling the racial composition of neighborhoods by soliciting listings and sales through the ploy of alleging a change in the neighborhood's racial composition (see Chapter 19 for a more complete discussion). Illinois' antisolicitation statute provides as follows:

It shall be unlawful for any person or corporation knowingly:

**

(d) to solicit any owner of residential property to sell or list such residential property at any time after such person or corporation has notice that such owner does not desire to sell such residential property. For the purpose of this subsection, notice must be provided as follows:
(1) The notice may be given by the owner personally or by a third party in the owner's name, either in the form of an individual notice or a list, provided it complies with this subsection.

**

(3) The individual notice, or notice in the form of a list with the accompanying affidavit, shall be served personally or by certified or registered mail, return receipt requested.

Antiblockbusting statutes that attempt to restrict access of real estate agents to certain areas for purposes of obtaining listings have not survived constitutional challenges (*New York State Association of Realtors, Inc. v. Shaffer,* 27 F.3d 834 (2nd Cir. 1994). A restriction such as that in Illinois that permits the property owner to prevent *future* contacts by agents would survive constitutional challenges. However, prohibitions on solicitations in certain areas would be an infringement of commercial speech rights.

DUTY OF CARE

http://

Visit Florida's Division of Real Estate Legal Section to learn about their Disciplinary Activity Reports: **http://www.state.fl.us/ dbpr/re/legal.shtml.**

A broker is required to exercise care in listing the seller's property, presenting offers, and handling the details of closing.

This duty of care requires the broker to list the property at a reasonable fair market value figure. There is much temptation to underappraise properties and list them accordingly so that a rapid, easy sale and commission can be obtained. But the listing price must be accurately set to assist the seller in the sale and also to ensure a fair return. The broker must be cautious in making overzealous statements about sales potential and abilities, because inflated expectations of the seller can cause problems for the broker later.

If the seller needs to net a certain minimum from the transaction, the broker must be cautious in computing the corresponding sales price. Care must be taken to add contingencies such as payment of points and the costs of the transaction such as escrow fees, title insurance, and termite inspection. The broker also must check the terms of the seller's loan to verify assumability and any transfer fees or prepayment penalties that might affect the seller's net.

Once the listing agreement is executed, the broker's duty of care to the seller continues. The broker should evaluate the soundness of all offers and inform the seller (particularly the unsophisticated) of the hazards or pitfalls involved in each offer. All implications should be explained, including the form and adequacy of the down payment, the security or need for security in the financing, the advantages and disadvantages of financing alternatives, and any contingencies involved in the sale. Although the broker must never advise which offer to take, weaknesses and strengths should be explained.

In explaining offers, the broker must be cautious not to cross the fine line between exercising care and practicing law. A broker may explain to a seller the customs and practices of the real estate industry but should limit remarks to that sphere. Since offering opinions on legal rights and responsibilities could prove costly to the broker, legal details should be referred to an attorney.

Consider 12.5

J. Pagel Realty and Insurance Co. acted as real estate brokers for the sale of property owned by Clifton and Mary Morley. The brokers arranged for the sale of a home in Bisbee, Arizona, with the buyers paying for the home with a down payment and a $12,500 note to the Morleys. The phrase "This note is secured by a mortgage on real property" was crossed off the note. The brokers, as permitted by Arizona law, completed all of the paperwork for the transaction but did not discuss the need for a mortgage to enforce the note. The buyers defaulted on the note and sold the house to another party. The Morleys sued Pagel for damages, claiming that they should have been told of the need for a mortgage. Pagel defended on the grounds that such advice would have been practicing law. Should the mortgage issue have been discussed? *Morley v. J. Pagel Realty & Insurance,* 550 P.2d 1104 (Ariz. 1976).

The broker should also assume the responsibility of proofreading documents such as the listing agreement, the offer, and the eventual contract for errors in figures, descriptions, and dates. Closing papers should also be carefully scrutinized to ensure that the correct terms appear. In states in which brokers may fill out contracts, brokers must exercise care to make sure all the terms are present, carefully drafted, and accurately stated. Forms should be scrutinized to make sure they comply with the parties' intentions.

Brokers can maintain better client relationships by prequalifying prospective buyers. Presenting an offer from a financially unqualified buyer or even taking the time to show property to financially unqualified buyers is a waste of time on all sides. Furthermore, the presentation of an offer from an unqualified buyer spells liability for the broker.

Often, clauses will be used in listing agreements to try to avoid liability for breach of the duty of care. These clauses are invalid for brokers, as they are for accountants, lawyers, engineers, and other professionals. No professional may be exculpated by a clause for failure to exercise the standards of care established in that profession.

Practical Tip

In exercising their duties of care, brokers should answer these questions as a self-check:

- Is the property properly priced?
- Is the net accurate and does the seller understand it?
- Is the listing agreement accurate?
- Are potential buyers qualified? Do they have adequate savings and income?
- Are the offers sound? What are the pitfalls?
- Has there been adequate communication with the seller?
- Are the escrow papers being drawn? Are they accurate?
- Are clients being kept informed of the progress of escrow?
- Are deadlines being met?

Fiduciary Duty

Once a broker is employed by a principal, that broker is expected to act only in the best interests of the principal, regardless of the negative effects and consequences that may result for the broker.

Brokers must not lead their sellers into unsound transactions for the sake of a commission and should inform their sellers when problems arise in the negotiation or closing of a transaction. All aspects of the transaction should be represented accurately and disclosed in a timely manner. Any changes affecting the principal's rights or interests must be revealed immediately.

Most states impose a separate fiduciary duty upon brokers with respect to earnest money deposits. Money that belongs to the seller should not be commingled with the broker's own funds. Most states require that deposits be placed in trust accounts or escrow accounts, or else require the establishment of escrow funds within a short time after receipt. Brokers in these states who retain deposits for unreasonable lengths of time may be held liable for this loss and may face license revocation or suspension.

Duty of Loyalty

A broker may not work both ends of the transaction by representing both parties unless there has been full disclosure and both parties consent to such dual representation. See pages 255–256.

A broker may not profit secretly from a transaction involving the principal. Brokers must disclose to their clients all they know about all parties involved in the transaction. If a broker chooses to deal in listed property, a full and complete disclosure of the interests must be made to the client. If a broker is a partner, shareholder, or relative of a party to the transaction, such a relationship must be disclosed. If a broker does not make the appropriate disclosure and hence realizes a secret profit, that profit must be returned to the principal.

Consider 12.6

The Taylors listed their property with ARE Realty, with Jensen Timber as the broker and Pamela Creighton as the agent salesperson. The listing was unsuccessful, and seven days prior to its expiration, Creighton submitted an offer to the Taylors naming herself or her nominee as the buyer. The Taylors accepted the offer. When the final papers were presented for closing, the Taylors noted that Creighton was not buying the property; instead a Walter Wake and wife were the buyers. Walter Wake was also listed as a broker for ARE Realty. The Taylors discovered the Wakes were Creighton's parents and that the down payment of $5,000 was being made with Wake's and Creighton's commission. The Taylors refused to go through with the transaction, and the Wakes brought suit for specific performance. What is the result?

Under dual agency relationships, the duty of loyalty becomes complicated. For example, suppose that a broker representing both buyer and seller knows that the buyer is a credit risk? Does the duty of loyalty require the broker to disclose that to the seller? Does such a disclosure breach the duty of loyalty to the buyer? Most states that permit dual agency also list categories of information the dual agent must keep confidential such as: (1) the seller being willing to take less than the asking price; (2) the buyer's willingness to pay more than the asking price; (3) the motivation of the parties in buying and selling; and (4) the willingness of either party to accept less favorable financing terms. Dual agency duties and disclosure often require legal help.

Ethical Issue

Given the credit risk example for a dual agent, is it possible to be loyal to both parties? Does one side suffer in a dual agency relationship? Is the dual agent simply protecting information the buyer would never gain access to if there were separate agents?

LEGAL DUTIES AND RESPONSIBILITIES TO THIRD PARTIES

The broker and the buyer from whom offers are obtained do not have a direct contractual relationship. However, the broker may still have liability to the buyer for misrepresentations as to the condition of and defects in the real property being sold. This liability is based on the common law tort of misrepresentation. This liability has also been expanded dramatically in the last 5 years.

Practical Tip

Buyers should fully review inspection reports for details on the inspection beyond just hearing that there had been a "clean" report. Further, all chemicals used on the property should be disclosed and discovered for purposes of personal safety and the potential of environmental liability.

Misrepresentation

Misrepresentations about the subject property generally fall into two categories: (1) those made intentionally and (2) those made negligently. Intentional misrepresentation occurs when the broker knows of a fact and then either misstates it to the purchaser or simply fails to disclose it to the purchaser. Negligent misrepresentation is established by showing (1) that the broker failed to make a reasonable effort to determine whether the fact represented was true or false and (2) that the purchaser justifiably relied on that misrepresentation in purchasing the property.

Thus, under the theory of negligent misrepresentation, a broker making statements without a sufficient knowledge base may be held liable. An example of negligent misrepresentation is when the broker makes statements about the cost of heating, air-conditioning, or electricity and does so without a statement of cost from the seller or without an actual investigation or verification of the cost.

In negligent misrepresentation, ignorance of whether a statement is true or false is no excuse for escaping liability; it is the broker's responsibility to determine the truth or falsity of statements. When the prospective buyer asks if city sewer, water, and gas are available for the property, the appropriate response for a broker without such knowledge is, "I don't know, but I can check."

NONDISCLOSURE

Misrepresentation occurs when the broker is aware of the problems or defects in property but fails to disclose such material information to prospective buyers. Cosmetically covered wall cracks and foundation cracks of which the broker is aware should be disclosed. The traditional water-in-the-basement problem should also be disclosed. The fact that an existing property use violates the city code is another example of a fact requiring disclosure.

SALES PUFFING

Misrepresentation is even found to exist in the sales-puffing techniques often used by brokers and salespersons. The classic line given to induce a purchase is "if you are going to do anything, you had better do it quickly because I have another buyer on the line for this property." The statement is innocent enough so long as there is, in fact, another buyer. If no other buyer exists, it has been held that such statements serve to inflate the value and desirability of the property and constitute misrepresentation to the buyer rushed into a purchase by such statements.

SAFETY STANDARDS

A broker may be held liable for conditions on a property that violate codes or are unsafe if the conditions are not disclosed to prospective buyers or remedied prior to the closing of a deal. It is also a good idea for the broker to check for hazards while showing the property, so that new developments or hazards are noted and disclosed.

The following case deals with issues of broker/agent liability and misrepresentation.

Robinson v. Grossman

67 Cal. Rptr.2d 380 (Cal. App. 1997)

Facts

John Helm, an architect, designed and built a large home in 1989. Anne Marie Grossman was a co-owner of the home and property with Helm. Because the home was built on hilly terrain, Helm used a pier and grade beam foundation. Helm and Grossman moved into the home in 1990 and listed it for sale with California Prudential Realty with Marti Gellens-Stubbs as the listing agent.

On the real estate disclosure form, Helm and Grossman stated that they were unaware of any significant defects in the foundation, exterior walls, windows, ceilings or other parts of the home. When Ms. Gellens-Stubbs inspected the property, she noticed hairline stucco cracks, which Helm assured were only cosmetic. Ms. Gellens-Stubbs did not note the cracks on her portion of the disclosure statement but did write, "property appears to be in good condition . . . I see nothing to contradict what the seller has mentioned. . . . " Later, Gellens-Stubbs noticed that the interior paint was peeling near a dining room window. Helm explained that the peeling had been caused by water infiltration during construction, but that the problem had been remedied. Gellens-Stubbs did not note this information either.

Mark and Susan Robinson looked at the home several times in 1991 and noticed the stucco cracks. When they discussed the cracks with their agent, Gracinda Maier, she recommended that they have the home professionally inspected. Helm told the Robinsons that the cracks "were caused by the finish of the house, which is called a Santa Barbara finish, and there was a product called elastomeric that . . . would alleviate the stucco cracks."

Helm and Grossman accepted an offer of $653,750 from the Robinsons. The purchase contract of May 22, 1991, required Helm and Grossman to furnish the Robinsons with a geological report by Ninyo & Moore. The contract permitted the Robinsons to cancel the agreement if any of the geological reports or testing commissioned by the Robinsons revealed problems they would be unwilling or unable to correct.

On May 24, 1991, Maier added the following to the disclosure statement:

> My visual inspection found numerous cracks in the house. Buyer's agent recommends buyer to have property inspected by a professional home inspector and have the land checked by a geologist.

Gellens-Stubbs then added the following:

> Stucco cracks on home are cosmetic in nature according to the seller because of finish and type of stucco.

The Robinsons hired Ameritec Home Inspection Service. Robert Brand, an employee, listed the "very old" water stain in the dining room and "normal settling cracking" of the stucco. Brand found no soils-related distress and the report concluded, "the house was very well built, . . . [and] was not going anyplace. . . . "

During final inspection in July 1991, Mrs. Robinson noticed more water stains in the ceiling and wall of the entryway. There were patched stucco cracks and some water damage on the deck. Grossman assured that the cracks were cosmetic and the small hole in the deck had been repaired. The final inspection report included the phrase "per seller—stucco cracks are cosmetic." Gellens-Stubbs sent Mr. Robinson a letter stating, "The ceiling and wall in the downstairs sitting area will be repainted where the stains are and according to seller, the stucco cracks are cosmetic in nature and were patched with a stucco and glue mixture." Escrow closed.

A few weeks after moving into the home, as they were attempting to have a swimming pool installed, the entire excavation around the house collapsed. The Robinsons sued Helm, Grossman, Gellens-Stubbs, Prudential, and others for professional negligence, and negligent and intentional misrepresentation.

The trial court dismissed the fraud accusations against Prudential and Gellens-Stubbs. The jury found there had been negligent misrepresentation, professional negligence and awarded the Robsinson $16,827. They had asked for the value of the home or $719,130 (if it had been as represented plus the approximate cost of reconstruction). The jury found Grossman had no liability and awarded her attorney's fees of $10,980.13 from the Robinsons. The Robinsons appealed.

Judicial Opinion

Kremer, Presiding Judge. In *Easton v. Strassburger* (1984) 152 Cal. App.3d 90, 199 Cal.Rptr. 383, the court first pronounced the duty of the seller's broker to potential purchasers to both inspect and disclose. "[T]he duty of a real estate broker, representing the seller, to disclose facts . . . includes the affirmative duty to conduct a reasonably competent and diligent inspection of the residential property listed for sale and to disclose to prospective purchasers all facts materially affecting the value or desirability of the property.

In *Easton,* agents of the seller's broker observed "red flags" indicative of soils problems, but did not obtain a soils report or inform the buyer there were potential soils problems. The purchaser sued after massive movement of fill soils caused the foundation to settle and resulting damages; the jury found the broker and others had been negligent. In concluding the jury's verdict was supported by substantial evidence, the appellate court reasoned:

> Real estate agents hold themselves out to the public as professionals, and, as such, are required to make reasonable use of their superior knowledge, skills and experience within the area of their expertise. Because such agents are expected to make use of their superior knowledge and skills, which is the reason they are engaged, and because the agents in this case were or should have been alert to the signs of soils problems earlier described, the jury was well within the bounds of reason when it concluded that a *reasonably diligent and competent inspection of the property would have included something more than a casual visual inspection and a general inquiry of the owners.*

In response to *Easton,* and at the urging of the California Association of Realtors, the Legislature added a new article to the Civil Code entitled "Duty to Prospective Purchaser of Residential Property."

"It is the intent of the Legislature to codify and make precise the holding of *Easton.* . . . It is not the intent of the

Legislature to modify or restrict existing duties owed by real estate licensees."

The *Easton* duty is set forth in section 2079 as follows: "(a) It is the duty of a [licensed] real estate broker or salesperson, . . . to a prospective purchaser of residential real property . . . to conduct a reasonably competent and diligent visual inspection of the property offered for sale and to disclose to that prospective purchaser all facts materially affecting the value or desirability of the property that an investigation would reveal."

In 1985 the Legislature added another article to the Civil Code (§ 1102 *et. seq.*) entitled "Disclosures Upon Transfer of Residential Property." Before execution of a sales contract, the seller is required to deliver a statutory Real Estate Transfer Disclosure Statement to the buyer, which contains a checklist to give notice of problems or potential problem with the property, and cautions that the representations are made by the sellers, not the real estate agents, and that the potential buyers may wish to obtain professional advice or inspections of the property. An agent representing the seller must also complete his or her portion of the disclosure form. The disclosures and acts required under the article "shall be made in good faith," which means "honesty in fact in the conduct of the transaction."

We find no support for the Robinsons' argument section 2079's disclosure duty included a duty to independently verify or disclaim the accuracy of the seller's representations, and we do not interpret section 2079 in that manner. In enacting section 2079, the Legislature sought to foster availability of professional negligence insurance by eliminating the implication in *Easton* that a seller's agent could have negligence liability for relying in good faith upon the seller's representations or failing to discharge a vague obligation to obtain professional inspections or reports.

Under the post-*Easton* statutory scheme, once the sellers and their agent make the required disclosures, it is incumbent upon the potential purchasers to investigate and make an informed decision. In making the required disclosures, the sellers' agent is required only to act in good faith and not convey the sellers' representations without a reasonable basis for believing them to be true.

It is undisputed the Robinsons had *actual* knowledge of each of the three "red flags" of which they now complain well before escrow closed. They saw the stucco cracks during pre-offer site visits, during which Helm, not Gellens-Stubbs, explained their cause. Gellens-Stubbs noted on the disclosure statement the stucco cracks were cosmetic *"according to seller, . . . "* and on the buyer's disclosure statement, *"per seller—stucco cracks are cosmetic."* (Italics added.) Gellens-Stubbs also sent Mr. Robinson a letter again advising "[a]*ccording to seller,* the stucco cracks are cosmetic in nature and were patched with a stucco and glue mixture." (Italics added.)

During Ameritec's inspection, which Mr. Robinson attended, it was Helm, not Gellens-Stubbs, who explained the paint peeling around the dining room window was caused by a leak which had been remedied. Likewise, it was Grossman, not Gellens-Stubbs, who later assured Mrs. Robinson the water staining in the entryway was caused by a leak which had been fully repaired. Under the circumstances, the Robinsons could not have reasonably believed the representations came from Gellens-Stubbs, or that she either verified them or vouched for their accuracy. Moreover, both Gellens-Stubbs and Maier, the Robinsons' agent, encouraged them to obtain independent inspections to verify the causes of the "red flags." The Robinsons failed to obtain a geotechnical inspection, and their home inspector confirmed Helm's and Grossman's representations.

The Robinsons' geologist, Ralph K. Jeffery, testified the pool excavation failure was caused by an unstable ancient landslide and creeping soils, the latter of which also caused interior wall cracks and uneven floors in the home. Jeffery admitted, however, that during initial visits to the property he saw no soils-related distress in the home; rather, such manifestations did not appear until 1992.

When asked whether the stucco cracks were nonetheless "signs of possible earth-movement damage to the home." Jeffery responded. "That would be one explanation for them." However, he had done no destructive testing to determine what caused the cracks, and they could be attributable to "too thin of stucco coat, improper waterproofing, a whole litany of architectural things and probably some things I can't even guess what they are because I don't have expertise . . . as an architect." Robert K. Burkett, the Robinsons' civil and structural engineer, agreed it could not be determined whether the stucco cracks were related to earth movement without performing testing. Peter Curry, the defense structural engineer, testified that even in 1993, he saw no stucco cracking attributable to foundation movement.

In sum, the Robinsons well knew the representations regarding the "red flags" were exclusively those of Helm and Grossman, and they have shown no detrimental reliance upon anything Gellens-Stubbs disclosed or failed to disclose. Thus, under any scenario the Robinsons' arguments fail.

Reversed as to the agents and brokers' liability.
Affirmed as to Grossman.

Case Questions

1. Give a history of the negotiations and disclosures leading to the escrow closing.
2. Was there any misrepresentation by Gellens-Stubbs?
3. Was there any misrepresentation by Helm and Grossman?
4. Was any information withheld from the Robinsons?
5. Did the Robinsons obtain sufficient expert opinions before buying the house?

The law on broker liability for concealment or the failure to disclose material information to potential buyers varies. In Alaska, the District of Columbia, Illinois, Minnesota, South Carolina, Texas, Utah, and Wisconsin, the brokers are held liable for innocent misrepresentations. Some states impose liability for only intentional or negligent misrepresentation. For example, Washington does not hold brokers liable for innocent misrepresentation because the result would be "strict liability" for brokers.

Consider 12.7 | Suppose a broker misrepresented the length of time that a piece of property had been listed. Would such a misrepresentation be a basis for liability? Does the broker harm a seller by such a disclosure? *Beard v. Gress,* 413 N.E.2d 488 (Ill. 1980)

"As Is" Clauses

Often property will be sold with a provision in the contract that says it is sold **as is,** meaning that the buyer is taking the property as it stands with all existing defects and no promises of repair. Such a clause would appear to relieve the broker of liability for latent defects and the failure to disclose material information. However, the courts have held that the use of the as is clause is not a blanket of immunity for the broker from allegations of fraud. If a broker actively misrepresents the condition of the property or fails to disclose true facts, the "as is" clause will have no effect, and the broker will still be held liable for the silent or affirmative misrepresentation. A dilapidated building sold "as is" will not provide immunity from liability for the broker who failed to disclose that the building had been condemned.

Disclosure, Discrimination, and Silence

Over the past five years, brokers and agents have faced increasingly complex issues of disclosure with respect to properties they are listing or showing. Should the fact that a crime has been committed on the property be revealed? Should the fact that someone with HIV/AIDS owned the property previously be revealed? What if, as the quotes opening this chapter discuss, there is a registered sex offender living in the neighborhood where the property is located? In some of these disclosure situations, brokers and agents have statutory duties imposed that prohibit them from affirmatively disclosing the information about the property. In other situations, an affirmative duty to disclose is imposed by statute. However, even in those situations in which the information is protected by statute and the broker is prohibited from affirmatively disclosing it, the broker or agent cannot lie in the event the buyer asks a question and the broker or agent has the information.

The presence or absence of criminal activity on a property or the presence of a released sex offender near a particular property is deemed to be material information because it does affect the value of the property.

NAR has adopted a position on the issue of sex offender information that provides, *all public disclosures should emanate directly from the appropriate law enforcement agency, and no affirmative disclosure duty regarding the location of released sex offenders should be placed on real estate licensees as a result of state public notification programs.*

In NAR's position statement, information on sex offenders must come from the government records themselves and not from brokers or agents. Brokers and agents need only respond to questions from buyers by referring them to the public records.

All states currently have some form of statute on the responsibility for disclosure of sex offender information. Some states exempt real estate agents from disclosure, while others include required language in contracts referring buyers to appropriate agencies for information.

Insurance Protection

The number of suits against brokers by third parties for misrepresentation is skyrocketing. Liability, in the form of actual and punitive damages, which may be imposed upon brokers for either intentional or negligent misrepresentation, is tremendous. As noted earlier, a broker may be held liable under a pretense of knowledge even when the broker has no actual knowledge. As a result of these cases, insurers now offer **errors and omissions insurance** coverage, which is a form of malpractice insurance for brokers and salespersons in the real estate industry. Such coverage is essential when most commercial transactions involve seven-digit figures and hence seven-digit liability.

The coverage may be purchased for an individual or for a real estate company, its broker, and its salespersons. The amount of coverage available usually begins at $100,000 with a deductible of $1,000 for small claims. In choosing coverage, brokers and salespersons should check the policy provisions on legal defense (Will local or company attorneys be used?), including how legal defense costs are treated in terms of policy coverage; what activities are covered (sales, management, and so on); and whether acts committed prior to the policy validity date will be covered.

Self-Protection

Perhaps the best protection a broker may obtain against a suit for misrepresentation is preventive protection. Preventive protection includes understanding the property to be sold and all of its defects, restrictions, and limitations.

Web Exhibit 12.5 will link to a seller's disclosure form used by brokers and agents to try and be certain that they know all the material information they are expected to know about a property they have listed. "I didn't know" is no longer a defense for brokers and agents with regard to property conditions and issues affecting the value of the property. Brokers' and agents' liability is determined by whether they *should* have known and not whether they actually did know.

Practical Tips

The following is a checklist for brokers undertaking a new listing and handling prospective buyers of that property:

- Ask about the property repair record.
- Ask about the utilities.
- Ask about the condition of appliances, roof, walls, and basement.
- Include pertinent information about physical condition in the listing agreement.
- Make an independent investigation of the property, carefully looking for recent cover-ups, redecorating, and hidden defects.
- Consider a warranty policy for the home.
- Make no statement that is not based on your firsthand information or knowledge.
- Have available a list of addresses and phone numbers for municipal, state, and country offices, so that the prospective buyer may make independent checks on information.
- Do not fail to disclose pertinent information, and do not participate with the seller in a nondisclosure scheme.
- Take measurements to verify room sizes and square footage.
- Follow up on the buyer's questions for which you have no answer or knowledge.

LICENSING REQUIREMENTS FOR BROKERS/AGENTS

In all states and the District of Columbia, some requirements must be met and a license obtained before a person may act as a broker. Such licensing requirements serve to protect two groups. First, licensing affords protection to the public by requiring real estate practitioners to meet certain uniform standards of competency and practice. Second, such requirements afford protections to existing licensees from unscrupulous or illegal conduct by new entrants into the field.

Every state has a statute that establishes licensing requirements for those seeking status as real estate practitioners. In each state statute, some type of administrative agency is created to be responsible for the issuing of licenses to real estate practitioners and will have a title such as the real estate board, board of real estate, real estate commission, or department of real estate. These administrative agencies are responsible for establishing licensing procedures and qualifications or for enforcing statutorily imposed licensing procedures and qualifications. Agencies also serve to clarify and interpret applicable legislative provisions. In addition, they are usually responsible for the supervision of licenses, investigations of alleged misconduct, and appropriate disciplinary measures such as license revocation or referrals for criminal prosecution.

Requirements for Obtaining Licenses

Two types of agents may work for the principal buyer or seller in the real estate transaction. Brokers are licensed to operate their own real estate brokerage businesses. A **salesperson** (sometimes called an **agent**) is licensed only to work for a broker, with the broker assuming responsibility for the salesperson's actions. Licensing requirements for brokers are more stringent than those for salespersons, and a salesperson's license is almost universally a prerequisite for a broker's license.

Most state license laws follow the model license law written by the National Association of Real Estate License Law Officials (NARELLO). Each state will have its own variations, but the following list of requirements is part of the NARELLO model.

a. *Educational requirements.* State educational prerequisites for licensing vary from none to an accredited college or university degree. Most states impose a requirement of a high school diploma and a minimum number of classroom hours in real estate education.

b. *Experience.* This requirement is limited to broker licenses. Most states require two years' experience as a salesperson or two years' experience in the real estate field as a prerequisite for licensing as a broker. The requirement of experience is coupled, in many states, with classes taken at an accredited college or university in real estate topics (finance, law, appraisal, and so on).

c. *Examination.* All states require both salespersons and brokers to pass examinations to obtain licensing. More than half of the states use a standardized test accompanied by an additional section that covers laws and practices of the particular state. Examinations for brokers cover significantly more material than do examinations for salespersons.

d. *Sponsorship.* About half of the states require candidates for salespersons' licenses to be sponsored by a licensed broker who will be responsible for the salesperson when the license is awarded.

e. *Minimum age.* In most states, the minimum age for licensure is the age of majority in the state (about half of the states list 18 years of age). In some states, the minimum age for brokers may be higher than for salespersons.

f. *Citizenship.* Some states still require United States citizenship status as a prerequisite for licensing; however, this requirement with respect to other forms of licensing has been struck down on constitutional grounds.

g. *Residency.* Some states require that license applicants be residents of the state for 30 to 90 days before application may be made. Again, such requirements for other license cases have been subject to constitutional challenges.

h. *Criminal record.* Nearly all of the states have provisions prohibiting licensing if the applicant has been convicted of a felony. However, these states usually restrict the length of time for which a license may be denied on this basis.

i. *Application.* All states require potential licensees to submit a completed form provided and developed by the regulating agency. Completion and delivery of the form to the agency is required 30 to 60 days prior to examination. Commonly, the application will require the applicant to give character references from persons in the community or from persons already established in the real estate business.

j. *Payment of fees.* All states require the payment of a licensing fee upon original application. Furthermore, a renewal fee is required to be paid at intervals established by the states.

Issuance of Licenses

Once applicants have satisfied the requirements, their state license will be issued. In all states, all licenses must be displayed in the agent or broker's place of business. Some states also have a requirement whereby licensees must carry pocket cards indicating their licensed status. Some states require the return of the salesperson's license to the state agency upon the termination of that salesperson's employment with a particular broker. When the salesperson is hired by another broker, that broker may request the salesperson's license from the agency.

Doing Business Without Licenses

Attempting to act as a salesperson or broker without proper licensing is illegal. The licensing of brokers and salespersons is a regulatory scheme, and any contract for commission between an unlicensed salesperson or broker and a seller would also be void. Court enforcement of such a contract is not available. In addition, a fee paid to an unlicensed salesperson or broker may be recovered.

License renewals have become significant over the past few years, with many states requiring evidence of continuing education as well as the payment of license fees. Continuing education requirements may include college course credits as well as professional seminars. Some states require training both initially and for renewals in fair housing laws.

The following case deals with a commission issue when a broker's license expires.

Douglas v. Schuette

607 N.W. 2d 142 (Minn. App. 2000)

Facts

Terry Lee Douglas (appellant) listed the property of Dennis and Lucille Schuette (respondents). The property consisted of 420 acres of land in Sherburne County. On April 29, 1990, Beverly A. Aubol signed a purchase agreement for the property with escrow to occur on or before September 15, 1990.

On June 30, 1990, Douglas's real estate license expired. On July 9, 1990, the listing agreement between Douglas and the Schuettes expired and was not renewed. Under Minnesota law, a broker or agent can provide the sellers with a list of "protected persons," or those persons to whom they have shown the property in order to protect the commission in the event the property is sold to one of those prospects. Douglas did not provide the Schuettes with such a list.

In late spring 1990, Aubol began to question Douglas's business practices. Because she had planned to purchase the property to develop it jointly with Douglas, she notified the Schuettes that she would no longer be willing to buy the land because of what she had discovered about Douglas.

The Schuettes then listed their property with another agent and Aubol notified them on November 11, 1990, that she was once again interested in the property. Aubol and the Schuettes signed a purchase contract for the property which closed on April 18, 1991.

On August 2, 1995, Douglas brought suit against the Schuettes demanding his commission on the property. The trial court granted summary judgment to the Schuettes and also awarded them sanctions against Douglas in the amount of $18,500. Douglas appealed.

Judicial Opinion

Foley, Judge. The listing agreement provides that appellant is entitled to a commission

> upon the happening of any of the following events:
> (1) the closing of the sale, (2) [seller's] refusal to close the sale, or (3) [seller's] refusal to sell at the price and terms required in this contract.

Appellant is also entitled to a commission if respondents sell the property to a person (1) who during the listing agreement showed an interest in the property or was shown the property by appellant and (2) whose name was on a protective list provided by appellant within 72 hours after the end of the listing agreement.

Under the listing agreement, appellant was entitled to a commission if a closing occurred. Appellant admitted, however, that there was never a closing under the first purchase agreement. Under the stipulated facts, the first purchase agreement was cancelled on October 30, 1990. While the property was eventually sold to the same buyer on April 18, 1991, (1) that sale was governed by a different purchase agreement, (2) it was arranged with another agent, (3) the listing agreement between the parties had already expired, and (4) appellant's real estate license was no longer in effect.

The listing agreement also provided that if the seller refused to close, appellant would be entitled to a commission. Respondents did not refuse to close. Aubol stated in her December 17, 1997, affidavit that "she was no longer willing to purchase the property because [she] was ending [her] association with [appellant]." After learning of Aubol's unwillingness to purchase the property, respondents agreed to cancel the purchase agreement. Because there is no evidence in the record of

collusion between respondents and the buyer to cancel the purchase agreement in order to prevent appellant from earning his commission, the district court properly concluded that it was Aubol, not respondents, who refused to close.

Appellant could also have earned a commission if respondents had refused to sell the property at the price and terms required under the contract. However, in her affidavit Aubol states that she was not willing to buy the property. Because appellant failed to produce a buyer willing to purchase the property at the price and terms required in the listing contract, appellant cannot rely on this provision to retain a commission.

By complying with the override clause of the listing agreement, appellant could have recovered a commission. The override clause stated:

> If within 180 days after the end of this contract [respondents] sell or agree to sell the property to anyone who:
> (1) During this contract made inquiry of [respondents] about the property and [respondents] did not tell [appellant] about the inquiry; or
> (2) During this contract made an alternative showing of interest in the property or was physically shown the property by [appellant] and whose name is on a written list [appellant gives respondents] within 72 hours after the end of this contract, then [respondents] will pay [appellant a] commission on the selling price, even if [respondents] sell the property without [appellant's] assistance.

The record shows that appellant failed to provide respondents with a list of protected persons. Under Minnesota law,

> licensees shall not seek to enforce an override clause unless a protective list has been furnished to the seller within 72 hours after the expiration of the listing agreement. Minn.Stat. § 82.195, subd. 4 (1998).

Because appellant failed to provide a protective list within the statutory period, appellant is precluded from recovering his commission under the override clause.

Appellant claims that the purchase agreement served as a substitute for the protective list. This court has explicitly held that a purchase agreement cannot substitute for a protective list.

The listing agreement stated:

> I understand that I do not have to pay your commission if I sign another valid listing contract after the expiration of this contract, under which I am obligated to pay a commission to another licensed real estate broker.

The district court concluded that because respondents entered into a listing agreement with another licensed real estate agent after their listing agreement with appellant had expired, appellant is barred from seeking a commission under this provision. We agree.

Appellant claims that because he procured the buyer who eventually bought the property, he is entitled to a commission. However, this court has held that a real estate agent cannot recover a commission by relying on the procuring-cause doctrine. Here, the listing agreement included a provision that relieved respondents of any obligation to pay a commission to the appellant if, after the expiration of the listing agreement with appellant, respondents entered into another listing agreement with a different agent. The district court did not err in its determination that no commission was earned.

Appellant argues that the district court erred in concluding that he did not have standing to bring suit for his commission because he was not a licensed real estate agent when the sale between respondents and Aubol was consummated.

> No person shall bring or maintain any action in the courts of this state for the collection of compensation for the performance of any of the acts for which a license is required under this chapter without alleging and proving that the person was a duly licensed real estate broker, salesperson, or closing agent at the time the alleged cause of action arose. Minn.Stat. § 82.33, subd. 1 (1998)

"This section is penal in nature and will defeat a claim for commissions if a plaintiff fails to allege and prove that [he or she was] duly licensed."

On June 30, 1990, appellant's real estate agent license expired. Appellant is thus precluded from asserting any cause of action arising from facts that took place after that date. Appellant had no cause of action until the contract was allegedly breached. Thus, appellant did not have a cause of action until respondents either (1) closed

the sale, (2) refused to close the sale, (3) refused to sell at the price and terms required in the contract, or (4) sold to someone to whom appellant had shown the house and who was also on a protective list timely furnished to respondent.

The record proves that respondents never (1) closed under the first purchase agreement, (2) refused to close, or (3) refused to sell the property at the price and terms required under the listing agreement. In addition, appellant failed to provide respondents with a list of protected persons within the statutory period and thus cannot recover under the override clause. Therefore, the only dates on which any cause of action of appellant could have arisen were December 13, 1990, when the second purchase agreement was signed, or April 18, 1991, when the property was eventually sold to Aubol. Because appellant was not a licensed real estate agent on either of these dates, he had no standing to raise a claim.

Appellant argues that so long as he was licensed when he began his services, he can recover a commission. Appellant cites no Minnesota law to support this proposition.

Appellant also argues that the statute does not preclude his claim because his partner was a licensed real estate agent. The evidence demonstrates that respondents dealt exclusively with appellant, who was not licensed at the time of the sale.

Affirmed.

Case Questions

1. Give the sequence of events on the listing and sale of the property.
2. Why did Aubol not go forward with the original purchase of the property?
3. What did Douglas fail to do that might have entitled him to a commission?
4. What happens if a real estate agent is not licensed at the time of closing?

Ceas Mortgage Company brought suit against Walnut Hills Associates, Ltd., for an unpaid commission. Ceas alleged that it was a real estate broker for the sale of property to Walnut Hills. Ceas Mortgage did not have a real estate broker's license, but an employee of Ceas who handled the transaction was a licensed broker. The transaction took place in Illinois where the following statute governs the payment of real estate commissions:

> No action or suit shall be instituted, nor recovery therein be had, in any court of this State by any person, partnership, limited liability company, or corporation for compensation for any act done or service performed, the doing or performing of which is prohibited by this Act to other than licensed brokers or sales persons unless such person, partnership, limited

Consider 12.8

12.8, *continued*

liability company, or corporation was duly licensed hereunder as a broker or sales person at the time that any such act was done or service performed which would give rise to a cause of action for compensation.

Should Ceas collect a commission? Is there a legal or ethical obligation to pay the commission? *Ceas Mortgage Co. v. Walnut Hills Associates, Ltd.,* 726 N.E.2d 695 (Ill. App. 2000)

Exemptions from Licensing

All states have some exemptions from the licensing requirement. For example, individuals selling real estate for themselves need not be licensed. In all states, attorneys acting for clients in real estate transactions are not required to be licensed as brokers. Those acting as personal representatives, executors, administrators, or trustees for estates need not be licensed to sell or offer to sell property of the estate. All states also have exemptions for public officials dealing with land and its purchase and sale as part of their official duties and responsibilities.

Professional Organizations

Although state licensing is a prerequisite for brokers and salespersons to conduct real estate transactions, membership in professional organizations of real estate practitioners is not required. However, many such organizations have codes of ethics and responsibility, so that membership is indicative of a willingness to subscribe to those standards.

The largest professional association in the real estate industry is the National Association of Realtors (NAR). Only those who are members may use the designation **Realtor,** which is a registered trade name of the association. When used by real estate practitioners, this term indicates that they subscribe to the code of ethics of NAR. NAR also promotes and provides educational opportunities for Realtors, and local and state chapters often have publications mailed to members that provide updates and information on changes in the field of real estate.

There are also affiliates of NAR for specific real estate professions. The following list is not comprehensive but indicative of the various specialized affiliates of NAR:

1. American Institute of Real Estate Appraisers (AIREA)
2. Institute of Real Estate Management (IREM)
3. Realtors National Marketing Institute (RNMI)
4. Society of Industrial Realtors (SIR)
5. Women's Council of Realtors

BROKER'S/AGENT'S LEGAL DUTIES AND RESPONSIBILITIES TO STATE

State

The penalties discussed have been private penalties imposed by the courts when those harmed by the conduct of brokers have brought suit for damages. However, because they are licensed by the state, brokers must also comply to state laws and regulations. Their failure to comply results in the state-imposed penalties of revocation or suspension of license and the possible imposition of fines or penalties.

http://

Read the text of the Code of Ethics and Standards of Practice of the NAR at: **http://nar.realtor.com/ about/ethics.htm**.

Suspension or Revocation of Real Estate License

Each state has its own requirements and penalties for forms of illegal conduct, but certain types of conduct are universally prohibited by the states and usually result in suspension or revocation of license.

1. *Commingling of funds.* All states have some provision prohibiting brokers from commingling clients' funds with their own funds and require the maintenance of separate escrow or trust funds.
2. *Discriminating practices.* Refusing to show property on the basis of a prospect's race, color, sex, or national origin may bring about not only a loss of license, but also the imposition of federal penalties and other state penalties for violations of the fair housing laws. Discriminatory practices include *steering* (where brokers direct certain races to certain areas and away from other areas) and *redlining* (where sales or listings are agreed to on the basis of the neighborhood racial composition). (See Chapter 19 for a full discussion of these issues.)
3. *Conviction of a felony.* Just as a felony conviction may preclude initial licensing, it may also result in the loss of license.
4. *Advertising.* Placing media advertising that contains misrepresentations will result in disciplinary action in all states. Some states require the written consent of the owner for advertising.
5. *Splitting commissions with an unlicensed party.* Only licensed individuals may split commissions.
6. *Failure to deliver required documents.* Those who fail to deliver required copies of documents to clients, such as purchase contracts and listing agreements, are subject to the suspension or revocation of their licenses.
7. *Failure to submit all offers.* All offers received prior to written acceptance must be submitted to the seller.
8. *Breach of duties to seller and unethical conduct.* Although private action is available to those harmed, the state also may discipline violating parties.
9. *The unauthorized practice of law.* Some states permit brokers to fill in purchase contract forms and closing documents, while other states require attorneys. Brokers exceeding the type of work permitted in their state are subject to disciplinary action by both the agency administering licensing and the state bar.

Rights upon Suspension or Revocation

Since the suspension or revocation of a license, or the imposition of other fines and penalties, adversely affect income, brokers have constitutionally afforded rights in proceedings to impose such penalties. However, the constitutional standards of due process are satisfied with administrative proceedings. That is, the agency responsible for licensee supervision may conduct appropriate hearings and impose penalties even though such an agency is not part of the judiciary.

Although suspension and revocation proceedings are not criminal prosecutions, the alleged violator does have the right to be informed of the charges and to appear and defend the charges and present witnesses. The alleged violator is also entitled to advance notice of the hearing date so that adequate preparation time is available. Additionally, the alleged violator is entitled to advance notice of those witnesses who will be called to testify against him or her in the hearing, so that preparation may be directed toward the specific evidence.

The following case involves a broker's suspension and the issues of fitness for continued licensing.

Dearborn v. Real Estate Agency

997 P.2d 239 (Ct. App. Or. 2000)

Facts

On October 4, 1996, Harold Dearborn (petitioner), then a licensed real estate agent, broker, and designated broker, was arrested at his home. Police officers found small amounts of cocaine and methamphetamine in his home. Police officers were at his home pursuant to an investigation of Dearborn's sexual activities with transients in exchange for drugs. One of the transients with whom he had sexual relations was a 17-year-old. Dearborn was indicted for possession of controlled substances as well as prostitution, endangering the welfare of a minor, and furnishing obscene materials to a minor. Dearborn entered a guilty plea to two counts of possession of a controlled substance and the other counts were dismissed. He was placed on probation for 18 months, ordered to serve 10 days in jail, perform community services, and pay a $500 fine. He was also ordered to have no contact with juveniles without prior approval from his probation officer.

The Real Estate Commissioner began proceedings to have his broker's license suspended. At the time of the hearing, Dearborn had paid his fine, performed his community service, had his driver's license reinstated (which had been suspended upon the guilty plea), and had his probation changed to unsupervised probation. The Commissioner ordered that Dearborn's license be suspended pending successful completion of the terms of his probation. Upon successful completion of probation, his broker's license would be revoked and he would be issued a limited salesperson license for two years. Assuming no further difficulties, he could then have an unrestricted license. Dearborn appealed the agency's decision.

Judicial Opinion

Linder, Justice. The Commissioner suspended petitioner's real estate broker's license based on the conclusion that he had violated ORS 696.301(26) and (31). That statute provides that the Commissioner may suspend or revoke the license of any real estate licensee, reprimand any licensee, or deny the issuance or renewal of the license of any applicant, "who has done any of the following":

> Entered a plea of nolo contendere, or has been found guilty of, or been convicted of, a felony or misdemeanor substantially related to the licensee's trustworthiness or competence to engage in professional real estate activity.

> *****

> Any act or conduct, whether of the same or of a different character specified in this section

which constitutes or demonstrates bad faith, incompetency or untrustworthiness, or dishonest, fraudulent or improper dealings.
ORS 696.301

Petitioner argues that those statutory subsections, and ORS 696.301 as a whole, permit suspension of a real estate license or other discipline of a licensee only for "actions that were part of and directly impact his duties as a real estate licensee or broker." Petitioner contends that conviction of two counts of possession of a controlled substance cannot satisfy that standard, at least where the drug possession is not shown to have had any relation to or effect on real estate activity as such.

In support of his argument, petitioner notes that the other subsections of ORS 696.301 all appear to deal with ethical violations or improper practice directly related to a licensee's real estate activity.

As the Commissioner's order acknowledges, ORS 670.280 also is relevant here. That statute states that, with the exception of the suspension or revocation of a teacher's or a school administrator's license, "no licensing board or agency shall deny, suspend or revoke an occupational or professional license or certification solely for the reason that the applicant or licensee has been convicted of a crime [.]" (Emphasis added.) The statute further provides, however, that a licensing board or agency may nevertheless "consider the relationship of the facts which support the conviction and all intervening circumstances to the specific occupational or professional standards in determining the fitness of the person to receive or hold such license or certificate."

The agency admits that, at a minimum, ORS 696.301 requires a "substantial nexus" between the conduct that led to the disciplinary action and "the licensee's future activity as a broker" or salesperson.

We agree with the agency's position in that regard. ORS 696.301(26) permits disciplinary action based on a criminal conviction only if the conviction is "substantially related to the licensee's trustworthiness or competence to engage in professional real estate activity." Even if that statute does not require that the conviction have [*sic*] been directly related to past real estate activity, it does require a nexus between the conviction and the licensee's future conduct "in professional real estate activity." Any other reading of the statute would be contrary both to its express terms and to the terms of ORS 670.280, which provides that, with certain exceptions not pertinent here, no professional or occupational license can be suspended, revoked or denied "solely for the reason that the applicant or licensee has been convicted of a crime[.]" Some connection is required between the conviction and past or future occupational or professional conduct.

The Commissioner appears to have read the statute in the same way. In his final order on reconsideration, the Commissioner identifies and relies on two purported connections between petitioner's criminal convictions (and the conduct that led to those convictions) and his trustworthiness and competence to engage in real estate activity. Those two connections are: (1) the risk that petitioner would have improper contact with persons under 18 years old, and (2) the risk that petitioner's drug use would lead to misbehavior in his real estate practice. In the abstract, such concerns might well be both related to a licensee's trustworthiness or competence as a real estate broker or salesperson and sufficient to warrant disciplinary action. In this case, however, there is no factual support for the link that the Commissioner identified between petitioner's conviction and his real estate activity, past or future.

In the section of his final order that explains the reasoning that led to his decision, the Commissioner suggested that because at least one of petitioner's sexual partners in the past was under 18 years of age, a "significant" risk was created for "the unsuspecting real estate consumer and family[.]" The Commissioner acknowledged that "there is no evidence of [petitioner's] use of his position as a real estate licensee for soliciting sexual partners or of his approaching clientele or their families for such purposes[.]" Nevertheless, the Commissioner found the risk of such behavior to be "unacceptable" based on the Commissioner's speculation that petitioner might "indiscriminately seek sexual liaisons with strangers," apparently including individuals he encountered in his real estate business, "who could be juveniles, and entice them with drugs, which he also uses."

There is no factual support in this record for the nexus that the Commissioner identified between petitioner's convictions, on the one hand, and his trustworthiness and competence to engage in professional real estate activity, on the other. Instead, that nexus is based purely on supposition. As the Commissioner acknowledged in his order, nothing in the record suggests that petitioner ever used his position as a real estate licensee as a basis for soliciting sexual partners. Nothing suggests that he ever approached any client or any member of any client's family for an illicit purpose. Although his solicitation of transients as sexual partners and his offer to exchange drugs for sex may be reprehensible and even criminal, any link between that behavior and petitioner's real estate activity is, on this record, based on pure conjecture. The Commissioner described petitioner's choice of sexual partners as "indiscriminate," which may be apt. Nevertheless, the record indicated that petitioner always kept his sexual behavior, and his drug use, separate from

his work. As the agency admits in its brief, some link between criminal behavior and real estate practice, past or future, is required. None is established here.

The Commissioner also was concerned that petitioner might have contact with persons under age 18 due to petitioner's work in the real estate profession, which was forbidden under the terms of petitioner's probation. The Commissioner evidently believed that suspension of petitioner's license therefore was necessary to ensure petitioner's compliance with his probation conditions. We need not decide whether suspension of a real estate license would be authorized on such a rationale. Here, by the time that the Commissioner issued his final order on reconsideration, petitioner's probation apparently had ended, and the probation condition prohibiting him form having contact with juveniles, with his probation officer's consent, was no longer in effect.

In his final order, the Commissioner also identified a link between petitioner's drug use and a future risk to his real estate clients. The Commissioner opined that "a licensee using drugs, who has access to people's homes, also has access to any prescription drugs, cash, or other things convertible to cash found in a home. To allow such an individual this type of access," the Commissioner concluded, "is an unacceptable risk." Again, while such a concern about a drug user might be justified in the abstract, nothing in the record supports that concern here. Petitioner had been licensed for decades and had never before been the subject of any disciplinary action. Nothing, other than imagination, suggests that he would use or ever had used his position as a real estate licensee to take drugs, cash, or anything else from a client's home.

In sum, we reverse and remand in this case because we find no factual support in the record to justify the concerns identified in the Commissioner's final order. Although a conviction for possession of a controlled substance may possibly be linked to a licensee's trustworthiness or competence to engage in professional real estate activity, here the facts simply do not support the nexus between past criminal conduct and future risks that are cited by the Commissioner.

Reversed and remanded.

Case Questions

1. Describe the nature of the real estate broker's criminal convictions.

2. Is a criminal conviction grounds for not issuing a license? When is a criminal conviction grounds for revocation or suspension of a license?

3. Will the suspension of the license and subsequent sanctions be upheld in this case?

4. What does the court say is missing from the Commissioner's finding?

RELATIONSHIPS AMONG BROKERS/AGENTS

In this final section the focus of discussion is on duties and responsibilities among the interrelationships of those acting within the industry.

Broker–Salesperson Relationship

A broker will probably have salespersons working in a common office. With such an arrangement, care should be taken to make clear the rights of principals and also the rights among salespersons. First, there should be a contract between broker and salesperson that establishes their rights and obligations. A salesperson is generally classified as an independent contractor, and the agreement should confirm that relationship. The topics that should be covered in such an agreement are included in the following list:

- Broker will maintain a properly equipped office.
- Salesperson is licensed and will maintain licensing status (including the payment of fees).
- Broker will make all listings available to salesperson.
- Broker may supply information to salesperson for prospective listings.
- Broker may not dictate which parties salesperson will solicit.
- Salesperson will work diligently for sales and listings.
- Salesperson and broker will abide by the Code of Ethics of the National Association of Realtors, as well as state, national, and local laws.
- The commission-splitting arrangements will be set and followed.
- Termination of agreements will be limited to certain circumstances.
- Arbitration procedures (if arbitration is agreed upon) are set.

Salesperson–Salesperson Relationship

Because there is generally more than one salesperson per office, the broker should establish rules and regulations governing their interrelationships. For example, provision should be made for handling a commission split when more than one salesperson is involved in the sale. Also, a policy should be established for distributing information on prospective listings so that prospects are evenly divided. A policy on who will handle office business or walk-ins should also be formulated.

Broker–Broker Relationship

Often in open listing agreements, the issue of who actually obtained a buyer for a sale—and, hence, who is entitled to a commission—becomes critical. The standard used for determining this is the **procuring cause of the sale standard.** To be entitled to a commission under this standard, the broker need not be the one to obtain the actual sale terms but must establish that he or she brought seller and buyer together.

Bringing seller and buyer together can result from direct contact or newspaper advertisement. If the broker finds and introduces to the principal a person who is ready, willing, and able to purchase or exchange the property according to the principal's terms, the commission is earned. It is immaterial if the final contract is made without the presence or knowledge of the procuring broker.

The following case deals with a dispute over commissions and the procuring cause of the sale.

Telluride Real Estate Company v. Penthouse Affiliates, LLC

996 P.2d 151 (Co. Ct. App. 1999); *cert. denied*

Facts

Jeffrey Brooks and Prospect Real Estate listed the Revenue Penthouse (defendants) in Telluride, Colorado, on MLS. In September 1995, Steven Hilbert (plaintiff) was introduced to Richard Furlaud (defendant), a potential purchaser of the property. Hilbert showed Furlaud and his wife several properties in the Telluride area, including the Revenue Penthouse.

The Furlauds were interested in the Penthouse and made a follow-up appointment with Hilbert to see the property again. At that time they asked questions about taxes, homeowners' fees, and the amount of an offer.

The Furlauds returned to New York, and Hilbert gave them his cell phone and fax number because he would be on a trip for the next few days. He also gave the Furlauds the name of another agent in his office for them to reach for further questions if he could not be reached. Hilbert called Brooks that evening and told him he had a definite prospect for the Revenue Penthouse.

On the flight home, Furlaud had decided against the Penthouse, but called a friend who owned property in Telluride and expressed dissatisfaction with Hilbert. Furlaud's friend spoke with Brooks and asked Brooks to call Furlaud. Furlaud and Brooks then reached a "handshake deal" for Furlaud to purchase the Penthouse.

No one returned Hilbert's calls and Hilbert sent a letter confirming his right to a commission. Both Brooks and Furlaud responded that they were "dissatisfied" with Hilbert's services. The property closed and Hilbert and his firm brought suit for their commission. The trial court awarded them $70,000 and Brooks and Furlaud appealed.

Judicial Opinion

Rothenberg, Judge. The doctrine of procuring cause has long been a part of the common law in Colorado. Under this doctrine, the determination whether a broker is the procuring cause rests on whether the broker set in motion a chain of events which, without break in continuity, resulted in a sale. When the buyer and seller involved in a real estate contract intentionally exclude a broker from negotiations, they are precluded as a matter of law from defending on the basis that the broker was not the procuring cause. *Winston Financial Group, Inc. v. Fults Management, Inc.*, 872 P.2d 1356 (Colo.App. 1994). Application of the procuring cause doctrine does not depend on the existence of a written agreement.

In 1993, the General Assembly enacted, effective January 1, 1994, "An Act Concerning Brokerage Relationships in Real Estate Transactions." Defendants assert that the 1994 Act was intended to supplant completely existing law pertaining to brokerage relationships. However, the trial court concluded that there was nothing in the statutory scheme addressing the issue of procuring cause and, therefore, that it was not an issue considered or addressed by the statutory amendments. We agree with the trial court that the plain language of the statutory scheme does not support defendants' assertion.

Statutes in derogation of the common law must be strictly construed. The legislative declaration contained in the 1994 Act states:

> (1) The general assembly finds, determines, and declares that the public will best be served through a better understanding of the public's legal and working relationships with real estate brokers and by being able to engage any such real estate broker on terms and under conditions that the public and the real estate broker find acceptable. This includes engaging a broker as a single agent, subagent, dual agent, or transaction-broker. Further, the public should be advised by the general duties, obligations, and responsibilities of a real estate broker in any particular real estate transaction.
>
> (2) This part 8 is enacted to govern the relationships between real estate brokers and sellers, landlords, buyers, and tenants in real estate transactions.

Thus, the expressed purpose of the legislation is to protect consumers in their interactions with real estate professionals. The 1994 Act does not address comprehensively the area of commissions and/or compensation earned by brokers. In addition, the parties have agreed that there was no mention of the procuring cause doctrine in the legislative history surrounding the 1994 Act. Accordingly, we conclude, as did the trial court, that the Act did not eradicate the common law concept of procuring cause.

Applying the principle of procuring cause to the facts here, the trial court found that:

> Hilbert showed the unit, provided information, diligently attempted to provide assistance but was 'frozen out' by Defendants who all expected that

this would save $70,000 to all concerned in the transaction . . . 'But for' Hilbert's three showings (two of the Revenue unit) this transaction would not have occurred.

There is record support for the trial court's determination that Hilbert was the procuring cause of the transaction and defendants do not dispute that fact. Rather, their assertion, which we have rejected, is that the realty agents cannot prevail as a matter of law because the Act eradicated the common law concept of procuring cause.

In view of our conclusion that the procuring cause doctrine still permits recovery, we need not reach the separate issue whether under § 12-61-803(2), C.R.S. 1998, Hilbert also was a "transaction-broker," given the undisputed fact that he failed to comply with § 12-61-808(2)(a)(I) and § 12-61-808(2)(d), C.R.S. 1998. See 12-61-802(6), C.R.S. 1998 (defining "transaction-broker" as: a broker who assists one or more parties throughout a contemplated real estate transaction with communication, interposition, advisement, negotiation, contract terms, and the closing of such real estate transaction without being an agent or advocate for the interests of any party to such transaction).

In summary, we uphold the trial court's determination that the realty agents were entitled to a commission as the procuring cause of the sale.

On cross-appeal, the realty agents contend the trial court erred in refusing to award them damages for tortious interference with contract and for civil conspiracy.

Tortious interference with a contract requires that: (1) the plaintiff have a contract with another party; (2) the defendant knew or should have known of such contract's existence; (3) the defendant intentionally induced the other party to the contract not to perform the contract with the plaintiff; and (4) the defendant's actions caused plaintiff to incur damages.

Here, the realty agents maintain that all of the required elements were met, and that the trial court misapplied the law to the facts. Specifically, they point to the trial court's finding that Furlaud had participated in "freezing out" Hilbert in order to save $70,000 in commissions. However, the court also found that Furlaud was dissatisfied with Hilbert, that a buyer is entitled to work with any real estate professional he or she chooses, and that the required element of intentional inducement had not been proven.

Affirmed.

Case Questions

1. Who brought the Furlauds to the property? Who was the listing agent?

2. Who finished the deal with Furlaud?

3. Does the statute eliminate the doctrine of "procuring cause of the sale"?

4. Does Hilbert get his commission?

✳CAUTIONS AND CONCLUSIONS

The real estate broker plays an integral role in the transfer of real estate. The role is not only complex in terms of the knowledge requirements and duties of the broker and agent, it is also complex in its relationships with the various parties in a real estate transaction. Because of these complexities, brokers and agents should be certain that their relationships are clear and established by written agreement.

Those relationships and agreements should cover whom the agent or broker represents, how long that relationship will last, how compensation is to be paid, and when that compensation is due. Even relationships between and among agents and brokers in their own firms should be clearly established in written agreements so that issues such as commission arrangements are clear.

All states have statutory requirements for agent and broker licensing and most have statutory requirements for disclosures to clients on representation. Brokers and agents should be very careful to comply with the requirements when there is a dual representation of both buyer and seller.

Brokers and agents should be cautious in their descriptions of and representations about the properties they show to potential buyers and the listings they take. All statements and representations should be verified by physical inspection or by asking the seller. Full disclosure, with certain statutory exemptions, is expected of brokers and agents.

Brokers and agents can bring professionalism and experience to aid both buyers and sellers. However, all need to be certain that they work with each other with an understanding of their statutory and contractual obligations that are carefully negotiated and drafted.

Key Terms

broker, 255
dual agency, 256
National Association of Realtors (NAR), 256
open listing, 257
exclusive agency listing, 257
exclusive right-to-sell, 257
exclusive listing-to-sell, 257
multiple listing, 257

multiple listing service (MLS), 257
net listing, 258
designated agency, 258
nonagent broker, 258
transaction broker, 258
intermediary, 258
limited agent, 258
statutory broker, 258
listing agreement, 260

no deal, no commission clause, 265
condition precedent, 266
as is, 274
errors and omissions insurance, 275
salesperson, 276
agent, 276
Realtor, 280
procuring cause of the sale standard, 284

Chapter Problems

1. Lucy Mae Jones entered into a contract to purchase a home listed by Century 21 Mary Carr & Associates Realty. The contract had a clause that required Jones to promptly apply for financing for the property. The loan was approved by Home South Mortgage Corporation on the condition that Jones pay off the balance due on a Visa account. Jones refused, although she had the funds available, because the account belonged to her boyfriend and he was unemployed and could not pay. The result was that the financing was not granted. The realty brought suit for its commission alleging bad faith on the part of Jones. Should the agency be able to collect its commission in this case? *Century 21 Mary Carr & Assoc. v. Jones,* 418 S.E.2d 435 (Ga. 1992)

2. Fines and Earnestine Hagans purchased a home through Woodruff & Associates Realty. After the Hagans moved into their home, they discovered there was a fault in their neighborhood. The subdivision streets had different levels, and they began to notice separations in their home, between the entry door, in the den, between the garage door, and in the air conditioning unit. The Hagans filed suit against Woodruff for their failure to disclose the presence of a fault line through the neighborhood. Woodruff did not know of the presence of the fault. The Hagans maintain it was Woodruff's responsibility to find these things out because buyers rely on real estate agents for information. Should Woodruff be held liable? *Hagans v. Woodruff,* 830 S.W.2d 732 (Tx. 1992)

3. Gibson Bowles, Incorporated, was the listing broker on the Montgomerys' property. A buyer's offer obtained by Gibson Bowles was accepted by the Montgomerys. The buyer had to qualify for VA financing, but Montgomery told him to delay so that the sale would fall through. After several postponements, Gibson Bowles sued for the commission. What is the result?

4. Ballard signed an open listing agreement with Barrett for the sale of real property. Barrett ran an advertisement in the local newspaper. In response to the advertisement, Scilley visited the property and talked directly with Ballard. The two were able to reach an agreement. When Ballard refused to pay the commission, Barrett brought suit. Barrett maintains she was the procuring cause of the sale. What is the result?

5. Buffington signed an exclusive listing agreement with Clements Realty. Mosier and Westby were the agents handling the listing for broker Eugene Clements. Haas, another broker, brought in an offer on the Buffington property from State Investment Corporation. Buffington accepted the offer and the transaction closed. State Investment was to make monthly installment payments on the property, but Buffington had no security in the property for the payments. When State Investment defaulted, Buffington sued Mosier, Westby, Clements, and Haas for failing to tell her of the need for security. Who is liable and on what basis?

6. Rosen, a broker selling desert land in Nevada, advertised that the area's population would be 50,000 in 10 years. The state predicted a population increase of 4,000 for the area. The state licensing agency sought to suspend Rosen's license. What is the result?

7. Lori Hanegan's broker's license was up for renewal in 1994. In Colorado, a broker applying for renewal is required to complete a minimum of "twenty-four hours of credit, of which shall be credits developed by the real estate commission." Ms. Hanegan completed 36 hours of continuing education but those hours did not include the mandatory eight hours developed by the real estate commission.

Hanegan's failure to take the mandated eight hours was discovered in an audit of licensee's continuing education units. Disciplinary proceedings were initiated and following a hearing, Hanegan was fined $50 and a public censure was recommended. Is the punishment appropriate? *Colorado State Real Estate Commission v. Hanegan,* 924 P.2d 1170 (Co. Ct. App. 1996)

8. Andrew Letsos listed his property for sale with Andrew Brusha, an agent with Century 21-New West Realty, on June 15, 1990. The property was listed at a price of $229,000, and Letsos agreed to pay a 6 percent commission. After eight consecutive listing renewals and no buyers, the property was listed again at a price of $129,000 on September 16, 1992. Following a listing period at the new price that ran one and one-half years with no success, Mr. Brusha contracted with Mr. Letsos to buy the property for $92,000 on March 9, 1993. Sometime later in March 1993, Mr. Brusha met Anthony Hernandez, another real estate broker. In May, Mr. Brusha and Mr. Hernandez contracted for the sale and purchase of the Letsos property for $115,000, with closing to take place on or before July 27, 1993.

Letsos and Brusha closed their deal on the property in July 1993. When Letsos's attorney called Brusha for a follow-up payment, Brusha asked for some time because he would have the money as soon as his sale of the property to Hernandez closed. Letsos's attorney then told Letsos about the Hernandez sale and Letsos filed suit against Brusha and Century 21 alleging breach of fiduciary duty by Brusha in his failure to disclose the sale to Hernandez. Should Letsos recover for breach of fiduciary duty? *Letsos v. Century 21-New West Realty,* 675 N.E.2d 217 (Ill. App. 1996)

9. Leticia Easton purchased a one-acre parcel of land in the city of Diablo, California, with a 3,000-square-foot home, swimming pool, and a large guest house for $170,000 in May 1976 from the Strassburgers through Valley Realty.

Shortly after Easton purchased the property, there was a massive earth movement and subsequent slides in 1977 and 1978 that destroyed a portion of the driveway. Experts testified that the slides occurred because a portion of the property was fill that had not been properly engineered and compacted. The slides caused the foundation of the house to settle, which in turn caused cracks in the walls and warped doorways. After the damage, the value of the property was set at $20,000. Cost estimates for repairs were $213,000.

Agents Simkin and Mourning represented Valley Realty and inspected the property several times prior to sale. "Red flags" indicated problems, but the agents did not have soil tests done and did not mention to Easton any potential soil problems.

Easton filed suit against the Strassburgers and Valley Realty. Is Valley Realty liable to Easton? Are the Strassburgers liable? *Easton v. Strassburger,* 199 Cal. Rptr. 383 (1984).

10. Kohn is a licensed real estate broker associated with his father's firm, Louis T. Kohn Realty. As managing agent for the Levee Building at the Laclede's Landing area of St. Louis, one of Kohn's responsibilities was to seek tenants for the building. One of the building owners suggested Kohn look into the possibility of Spaghetti Factory locating a restaurant in the building. The following sequence of events took place.

- *April 1975:* Kohn visited Denver's Spaghetti Factory and presented the idea to the executives.
- *May 1, 1975:* Kohn presented the idea to the Spaghetti Factory home office in Portland.
- *May 22, 1975:* Kohn met with three representatives of the Spaghetti Factory at the Levee Building. The Levee Building was determined to be unacceptable in size. Kohn took the three to Cohn's (defendant/appellee) office to examine his building. Spaghetti Factory executives asked for a floor plan. Kohn, in the presence of Cohn, said he would take care of the details.
- June 26, 1975: Kohn and Cohn met, and Kohn indicated he was seeking a tenant for Cohn's building. Cohn said he would go to Portland, but did not go.
- *October 1975:* Kohn and Spaghetti Factory executives met.
- *October 23, 1975:* Cohn and Spaghetti Factory executives met.
- *October 29, 1975:* Spaghetti Factory executives wrote Kohn and declined to lease the Cohn building.
- *September 16, 1976:* Cohn and Spaghetti Factory reached a five-year lease agreement.

Assuming there is no written agreement, could Kohn collect a commission in your state? *Kohn v. Cohn,* 567 S.W.2d 441 (Mo. 1978)

Internet Activities

1.   Learn more about the brokerage business by visiting the National Association of Realtors home page at **http://www.Realtor.com/**.

2.   Find out more of the duties and responsibilities of the real estate broker in the sale of a home. Go to: **http://www.hud.gov/fha/res/sc2secta.html**.

3.   To check out the brokerage regulatory roles in selected states, go to: **http://mktg.sba. uconn.edu/fin/realest/other/other.htm#FederalGovernmentLinks**.

4.   Jacques Werth is the author of *High Probability Selling*. He profiles the top 1 percent of all sales people from the last 30 years and finds some common traits in their behavior and style. Visit his Web site at: **http://www.highprobsell.com**.

5.   Visit the Internet listing sites and compare and contrast the terms of using these sites. See p. 259 for a list of the Internet home listing sites.

WISCONSIN DEPARTMENT OF REVENUE

Contact Us | E-Services | Employment | Events/Training | FAQs | Forms | Home
Links | Newsroom | Publications | Reports/Data | Search | Survey | Tax Professionals

Real Estate Transfer Information

Most of our forms, instructions, reports, etc. are in the Adobe Acrobat Portable Document Format (PDF). Before viewing these documents, you will need to install or upgrade to the free **Acrobat Reader version 4 with Search**. ***Having Problems?***

NEWSLETTERS

The following DOR "Newsletters" pertain to general interpretations of the Wisconsin Administrative Code and Statutes.

- October 2000
- February 2000
- October 1999
- June 1999
- April 1999
- October 1998
- June 1998
- February 1998
- October 1997
- January 1997

GUIDELINES / CRITERIA

- Guidelines for Real Estate Transfer Fee and Return (10/98)
  The Guidelines is a summary of the Newsletters published since 1983.

- Criteria for a Completed Real Estate Transfer Return (PE-500 R. 1-2000) (PE-100 R.01-2000) The Criteria will assist in making a judgement as to when a particular return is incomplete to warrant rejection of the conveying document from recordation.

HOW TO OBTAIN TRANSFER FORMS

○ Write to:

Forms Request Office
Wisconsin Department of Revenue
PO Box 8903
Madison, WI 53708-8903

OTHER INFORMATION

- **Form P-520** Real Estate Transfer Fee Transmittal (11/00)

Chapter 13
Methods of Transfer and Conveyance in Real Estate

A New Orleans lawyer provided the FHA with an Abstract of Title for a client's loan. The abstract traced title back only to 1803 and the FHA demanded a search back to its origins. The lawyer responded:

Your letter regarding title in Case 189156 has been received. I note that you wish to have title extended further than the 194 years covered by the present application. I was unaware that any educated person in this country, particularly those working in the property area, would not know that Louisiana was purchased by the U.S. from France in 1803, the year of origin identified in our application. For the edification of uninformed FHA bureaucrats, the title to land prior to U.S. ownership was obtained from France, which had acquired it by Right of Conquest from Spain. The land came into possession of Spain by Right of Discovery made in the year 1492 by a sea captain named Christopher Columbus, who had been granted the privilege of seeking a new route to India by then reigning monarch, Isabella. The good queen, being a pious woman and careful about titles, almost as much as the

FHA, took the precaution of securing the blessing of the Pope before she sold her jewels to fund Columbus' expedition. Now the Pope, as I'm sure you know, is the emissary of Jesus Christ, the Son of God. And God, it is commonly accepted, created this world. Therefore, I believe it is safe to presume that He also made that part of the world called Louisiana. He, therefore, would be the owner of origin. I hope to hell you find His original claim to be satisfactory. Now, may we have our damn loan?

According to Internet legend, the client got the title abstract approved and the loan.

W hen people think of the transfer of title to real property, they often think of it as a buyer and seller exchanging paperwork. However, title to property may be transferred in many ways other than through a sales transaction and the formalities of closing (see Chapter 15) these include transfer by adverse possession. Whether property is transferred through a sales transaction or any other means, the transfer must meet minimum legal requirements for the transfer to be effective. Also, certain precautions should be taken in any transfer to assure the transferee that the title obtained is good and will remain protected. In this chapter, the following questions are answered: What methods exist for transferring property? What rules and requirements are applicable to the methods of transfer? What protections for transfer of title exist?

http://

Check your own state's Website or see the state of Wisconsin's Real Estate Transfer Information at: **http://www.dor.state.wi.us/ust/retn/html.**

TRANSFER OF PROPERTY BY DEED

In England, the transfer of title was originally accomplished by a ceremony of symbolism called the **livery of seisin.** In the ceremony, the grantor and grantee stood with witnesses on the property to be transferred, and the grantor gave the grantee some portion of the property such as a clump of dirt or a twig to symbolize the conveyance of the land. The grantor also spoke certain words at the time of this physical transfer to indicate what land and what type of interest (such as simple or fee tail) was being conveyed. This method of conveyance created difficulties in establishing who owned what parcels and where the boundaries were located (see discussion of adverse possession in this chapter).

With the passage of the Statute for the Prevention of Frauds and Perjuries in 1677, England required that a written instrument be used to convey title to property. This written instrument of conveyance is the **deed**. Today, each state has its own writing requirement for deeds, now called the Statute of Frauds. The writing or the deed must meet certain requirements to be valid. There are also variations in the types of deeds that may be used and the promises or warranties of the grantor associated with each.

Requirements for Valid Deed

The general requirements of all types of deeds are: (1) grantor with legal capacity, (2) signature of the grantor, (3) grantee named with reasonable certainty, (4) recital of consideration, (5) words of conveyance (items 4 and 5 are referred to as the **premises**), (6) habendum or type of interest conveyed, (7) description of land conveyed, (8) acknowledgment, (9) delivery, and (10) acceptance.

GRANTOR WITH LEGAL CAPACITY: AGE AND MENTAL CAPACITY

The states have varying rules as to what is required to establish capacity on the part of the grantor. For grantors who are natural persons, the requirements are a minimum age (the age of majority) and a sound mind. For purposes of the deed, a sound mind generally means that grantors understand three things: the legal significance of a deed conveyance, to whom the property is being conveyed, and the nature and value of the property being conveyed. Legal capacity may still be found to exist in spite of old age and eccentric habits.

When the competency of the grantor is at issue, the issue of undue influence in a confidential relationship also arises; and the two issues generally go hand in hand in court proceedings on the validity of deeds. A confidential relationship exists where one party places continuous trust in another party and relies on that party for his or her skill, judgment, integrity, and assistance in carrying out business transactions or day-to-day activities. If mental weakness is accompanied by a factual situation in which the grantor has a confidential relationship with the grantee, most courts place a presumption of undue influence on the conveyance and require the grantee to overcome that presumption.

Typically, a confidential relationship arises between parent and child when the parent is elderly; and it arises between others, such as client and attorney, when the party who is afflicted or weak is being cared for by a younger, stronger, and capable party. Undue influence exists when the stronger party uses the trust to obtain transfer of property.

Consider 13.1

Gladys Whatley was hospitalized for blindness, diabetes and various problems with her hips. At the time of her admission, hospital personnel described her as "considerably impaired" mentally. She received various medications while in the hospital and the medical records refer to her as "ill" and "appearing very weak."

While she was in the hospital, her daughter Kay brought to her and had Gladys execute a new will in which some beach property owned by Gladys was conveyed to Kay and her husband. After Gladys was released from the hospital to Kay's care, Kay had a deed drawn up in which the beach property was conveyed to Kay and her husband outright. When the remaining children learned of the conveyance, they sought an easement so that they could use the beach on the property. When Kay refused, they sought to have the will and deed set aside for undue influence. Can they succeed? *Avery v. Whatley*, 670 A.2d 922 (Me. 1996)

GRANTOR WITH LEGAL CAPACITY: IDENTIFICATION OF GRANTOR

Individual grantors should be sufficiently identified in the deed so that their identity is clear. The spelling of the grantors' names should be accurate. In addition, care should be taken to have the grantor's name appear in the deed of conveyance in the same way as the grantor's name appeared as grantee in the instrument conveying title to him. For example, "John Edward Doe" is not the same as "J. E. Doe"; using both can create later problems in tracing title claims. Titles such as "Mrs. James Doe" should not be substituted for the grantor's name.

In many states, the status of the grantor is important because married grantors may not legally convey title to real property unless joined in the conveyance by their spouses. In addition to correctly stating the name of the grantor, the deed should also delineate the status of the grantor, such as, "unmarried male" or "single female." Previously, single women were referred to as "widow" or "spinster." The term "divorced and not remarried" is used to clarify the presence or absence of marital rights. These status clauses serve to ensure that the deed is executed with proper authority. If the grantor is acting on another's behalf, that also should be indicated. For example, an executor for an estate would have a status description clause as follows: "Paul H. Ramsay as executor for the Last Will and Testament of Mary R. Ramsay, whose will was admitted on <u>date</u> in <u>court</u> in case #_____."

In many cases, the grantor is not an individual but some form of business organization. Business organizations may possess the legal capacity necessary to hold title to property and may be grantors with proper capacity. For example, a corporation may hold and convey title in the corporate name. In this instance, the corporation is the actual grantor, but an agent of the corporation will perform the physical act of executing the deed. It is important to make sure that the corporation may properly transfer title to the property and that the conveyance is not an extraordinary corporate transaction requiring shareholder approval. Most title companies require a board resolution when a corporation is transferring property.

Under the **Uniform Partnership Act (UPA)** and in many states, partnerships may hold legal title to property and are thus grantors with legal capacity. In some states, title to partnership real property may be held only in the individual partner or partners' names. Again, it is important that the conveyance be made with authority, whether the title is in the partnership or individual partner's name. Proof of such authority should be demanded. In the case of a limited partnership, the general partner or partners must be the grantor. In the following case, the parties became terribly confused and cost themselves a great deal of time and money because their deeds were executed using the wrong grantor.

Michaelson v. Michaelson

939 P.2d 835 (Colo. 1997)

Facts

Ervin and Ruth Michaelson were married in 1946. During their marriage they formed a Colorado corporation called Michaelson's Originals, Inc. They each owned 50 percent of the corporation with 2,500 shares of stock each.

The Michaelsons were divorced on November 10, 1965, but the permanent orders on the division of their marital property were not entered until 1989. The reason for the delay was a great deal of confusion over three parcels of land. Ruth Michaelson quitclaimed the three parcels to Ervin.

No stock in the corporation was exchanged.

In 1990, following Ervin's mismanagement of some assets of the corporation, Ruth filed suit against him for breach of fiduciary duty. Ervin claimed that Ruth was no longer a shareholder and could not bring suit. The trial court held that Ruth was a shareholder and could bring suit. The trial court further held that Ruth's quitclaim conveyed only her interest in the land and not in the corporation and that she was entitled to compensation for

the value of the land quitclaimed. The Court of Appeals dismissed the case and Ruth appealed.

Judicial Opinion

Hobbs, Justice.   The [trial] court found that Ruth Michaelson's share of the post-1965 increased value of the corporate property was $277,093. The court ruled that Ruth Michaelson was also entitled to $78,665, which amount was one-half of new assets acquired by the corporation after 1965.

The court of appeals reasoned that Ruth Michaelson had already received a settlement for the properties for their increase in value from 1965 to 1989 and had conveyed, by the quitclaim deed, her equitable interest in the real property. We do not agree. To the contrary, the marital property award included a corporate property valuation only up to the date of the divorce, November 10, 1965, and did not include post-1965 appreciation on the corporate property, nor did the quitclaim deed operate to alter Ruth Michaelson's rights as a shareholder, including her *pro rata* share in all of the property and assets of the corporation upon dissolution, after creditors were satisfied. Accordingly, we reverse the judgment of the court of appeals.

The case before us deals primarily with the effect of Ruth Michaelson's quitclaim deed. The court of appeals determined that, upon dissolution of the corporation, equitable title to corporate property passes to all record shareholders. Therefore, the execution of the quitclaim deed by Ruth Michaelson operated to divest her of any claim she had to the corporate properties enumerated in the deed. We disagree. Under Colorado law, title to corporate property remains in the corporation upon dissolution. The quitclaim deed had no effect on Ruth Michaelson's status as a shareholder or the distribution of corporate property and assets to which she was entitled as a *pro rata* participant.

In construing any deed, our purpose is to give effect to the instrument. Unless ambiguity exists, "the intent should be determined from the four corners of the instrument." We must consider the deed in its entirety, harmonize all its provisions, and give force and effect to all of its language if possible. We must not ascertain intent from "portions presented in isolated sentences and clauses," but from the deed as a whole.

With these principles in mind, we examine the language of this quitclaim deed. The granting clause states:

> WITNESSETH, That the grantor for and in consideration of the sum of other valuable consideration and Ten and no/100 DOLLARS the receipt and sufficiency of which is hereby acknowledged, has remised, released, sold, conveyed and QUIT CLAIMED, and by these presents does remise, release, sell, convey and QUIT CLAIM unto the grantee [Ervin Michaelson], his heirs, successors and assigns, forever, *all the right, title, interest, claim and demand which the grantor has in and to the real property,* together with improvements, if any, situate, lying and being in the City and County of Denver and State of Colorado. . . .

(Emphasis added.) The property to be conveyed was described as follows:

> Lots 1 through 13, Block 1, Norwood Addition;
> Lots 9 through 15, Block 2, Norwood Addition; and
> Lots 9 through 15, Block 6, Sumners Addition to Denver
> also known by street and number as:
> 123-135 South Kalamath
> 164-176 South Kalamath
> 401-435 Santa Fe Drive
> 931-935 West 4th Avenue

Ervin Michaelson argues that the language of the deed indicates an intent on the part of Ruth Michaelson to convey not only her then present individual interest in the parcels of property, but also her "equitable title" in the properties as a shareholder upon dissolution of the corporation. We disagree. The grant constituted a clear and unambiguous conveyance of her individual ownership interest, if any, in the three enumerated parcels of land.

The language of the deed does not convey Ruth Michaelson's shares of the corporation or her right to receive a shareholder distribution upon dissolution. To determine what Ruth Michaelson conveyed, we must identify what interest she owned in the three parcels, if any, at the time of the conveyance. Two of the three properties listed on the quitclaim deed were owned by the corporation; the titles to Norwood, Block 1, and Sumners, Block 6, were in the name of Michaelson's Originals, Inc. Ruth Michaelson had no ownership interest in those two parcels and conveyed none by reason of the quitclaim deed. Rather, she was a shareholder of the corporation that owned those two parcels. However, Norwood, Block 2 was held by the Michaelsons individually as partners, not the corporation. When she executed the quitclaim deed, Ruth Michaelson conveyed her ownership interest in Norwood, Block 2, to Ervin Michaelson. The trial court correctly did not include this property in the damages for breach of fiduciary duty.

Although ownership of two of the properties remained in the corporation after dissolution, Ervin Michaelson nevertheless argues that Ruth Michaelson obtained an equitable title to the parcels and conveyed that interest to him.

In Colorado, "equitable title" to real property owned by a corporation does not pass to the shareholders upon dissolution of that corporation. Title remains in the corporation pending distribution to the shareholders of the remaining assets, in cash or in kind, after creditors of the corporation are satisfied.

Likewise, no merit exists in Ervin Michaelson's claim that the quitclaim deed on November 22, 1989, operated to waive Ruth Michaelson's claim for breach of fiduciary duty. The 1965 divorce action did not terminate the corporate existence. Ruth Michaelson did not transfer her shares of stock to Ervin Michaelson, and she continued to be a shareholder of record.

As an officer and director of Michaelson Originals, Inc., Ervin Michaelson had a fiduciary duty to act in good faith and in a manner he reasonably believed to be in the best interests of the corporation and all of its shareholders, in this case Ruth Michaelson. The record is replete with evidence of Ervin Michaelson's breach of fiduciary duty to Ruth Michaelson.

The court of appeals determined that Ruth Michaelson had already "been paid the value of her share of the real estate plus an appropriate amount for the increase of value of the real estate from 1965 to 1989," and so negated her award. However, the record does not support this determination.

Two relationships existed here. The first was the marital relationship which existed between 1946 and 1965. In this regard, the marital property division reflected: (1) the value of marital property up to the 1965 divorce date; and (2) the corporate property valued only from 1952 up to the 1965 divorce date. The second was the corporate relationship. The corporate property's *increase* in value from 1965 to 1989 was not included in the marital property division, nor were any properties acquired by the corporation after 1965.

Reversed.

Case Questions

1. What did Ruth have the authority to convey?
2. Did Ruth give up title to the land?
3. Was Ruth entitled to compensation for giving up the title?
4. Does a deed convey title to the stock shares?
5. Do you think Ervin believed he owned the land and could manage it as he pleased? What deed would transfer to Ervin the property and the right of control and who would be the grantor?

An example of a grantor without legal capacity is a charitable organization that is an unincorporated association. In most states, associations such as these have no legal existence and hence may not hold or convey title to property. In these associations, title must be held and conveyed through the association officers or trustees, unless there is a specific state statute authorizing the holding of legal title by unincorporated associations (see footnote h, Figure 13.1, p. 296).

Governmental bodies have no inherent authority to convey title; and must be authorized by statute to do so. They must strictly adhere to the guidelines and restrictions set up in their statutory authorizations.

Executors, guardians, trustees, and administrators have legal authority to convey title on behalf of their estates or protected persons but must do so according to the terms of the will or trust and possibly only with court approval.

GRANTOR'S SIGNATURE

A grantor with proper capacity must sign the deed, and if the grantor is not signing as an individual there must be an indication of any representative or agent capacity. If two persons hold title, both signatures are required. Again, in most states the signatures of both spouses are required to convey title even in cases where only one holds such title. Verification of authority to sign should always be obtained, particularly for those who sign for business organizations, estates, minors, and so on.

If a party is signing on behalf of an individual grantor, a power of attorney should be furnished. In some states, that power of attorney must be recorded along with the actual deed. The power of attorney should be either a general one, conveying upon the signer all authority, or one specifically authorizing the transfer of real estate or the transfer of the particular parcel.

If the party is incapable of signing, an *X* may be placed along with a verification clause to indicate who placed the *X*. The name may be typed in for the grantor.

In the case of a corporate agent signing for a corporation, many states require that the corporate seal also be placed on the deed. The signature must indicate that the deed is being executed on behalf of the corporation.

Figure 13.1 summarizes the types of grantors and the identification and signatures necessary for meeting the requirements for a valid deed.

FIGURE 13.1 *Grantor Capacity, Identification, and Signatures*

Grantor	Sample Identification	Signature
Individual	"John Edward Doe, a single man"	"John Edward Doe"
	"John Edward Doe, and Mary Frances Doe, his wife."	"John Edward Doe/Mary Frances Doe"
	"Eileen Jones Doe, a widow"	"Eileen Jones Doe"
Incompetent	"John Edwards Doe, as conservator for the estate of Eileen Jones Doe, an adult protected person" (an incompetent)	"Eileen Jones Doe by John Edward Doe, conservator for the estate of Eileen Jones Doe"[a]
Partnership	"ABC Partnership, a partnership organized and authorized to do business under the laws of the State of Arizona."	"ABC Partnership by John Edward Doe, general partner"[b]
Corporation	"LMN Company, Inc.,[c] a corporation incorporated and authorized to do business under the laws of the State of Arizona with its principal place of business in Phoenix"	"LMN Company, Inc., by John Edward Doe, president[d] (corporate seal)"[e]
Executor	"John Edward Doe, as executor of the last will and testament of Eileen Jones Doe, deceased at Mesa, County of Maricopa, State of Arizona"	"John Edward Doe as executor of the last will and testament of Eileen Jones Doe"[a]
Minor	"John Edward Doe, a minor under the age of 18 years"[f]	"John Edward Doe by Willard Scott Doe, as legal guardian of John Edward Doe, as minor"
Individual with power of attorney (attorney in fact)	"John Edward Doe, a single man"	"John Edward Doe by Willard Scott Doe, his attorney in fact"[g]
Illiterate	"John Edward Doe, a single man"	"X," with verification clause to indicate who made the "X." Name of grantor should be typed below the "X."
Unincorporated Association[h]	Need individual(s) signatures	"John Doe"

a. Court approval may be required for transfer.
b. Authority of partner to convey as general partner should be confirmed.
c. Use name under which it was incorporated.
d. Authority to transfer should be verified; board resolution required;
    check to see if it is an extraordinary corporate transaction (additional approval requires).
e. Should be attested to or verified by corporation's secretary.
f. Or whatever age of majority happens to be.
g. Power of attorney must authorize real property transfers.
h. Ten states have adopted the Uniform Unincorporated Nonprofit Association Act, an act that qualifies
    nonprofit associations as a legal entity (Alabama, Arkansas, Colorado, Delaware, Hawaii, Idaho, Texas,
    West Virginia, Wisconsin, and Wyoming) and the signature would be "Tri-City Arts League, by John Doe,
    President."

The following language appears in a deed:

> THIS DEED OF CONVEYANCE, *made and entered into this 8th day of April, 1975, between* LOGAN MIDDLETON, *President of the V.T.C. Lines Incorporated, Harlan, Harlan County, Kentucky, party of the first part, and* JOHN CHRISTIAN, *Evarts, Harlan County, Kentucky, party of the second part.*

The signatory portion of the document in its entirety appears thusly:

> /s/ Logan Middleton
> *Logan Middleton, President*
> *V.T.C. Lines, Incorporated*

The only other reference to the corporate entity is contained in the attestation clause:

> *Subscribed, sworn to, and acknowledged before me by Logan Middleton, President, V.T.C. Lines, Incorporated, to be his own free act and deed, and the act and deed of said corporation on this the 8th day of April 1975.*
>
> /s/ Mary Alice Hutbank
> Notary Public
> My Commission Expires: 2/27/79

Christian is now attempting to convey the property to Johnny Pace. The Johnsons have levied the property as creditors of V.T.C. Lines. Christian claims he is the property owner and that the levy is improper. Using Figure 13.1 and the chapter discussion, determine if title was conveyed to Christian. *Christian v. Johnson,* 556 S.W.2d 172 (Ky. 1977)

GRANTEE NAMED WITH REASONABLE CERTAINTY

Identifying the grantees with reasonable certainty is required because the validity of public records on land transfers depends on the accuracy of the spelling and identity of the parties involved in the transaction. Accurate spelling will control how effective the indexing system for land transactions will be. If there are any aliases or AKAs (also known as), they should be noted on the deed.

The status of the grantee should also be included in the deed. For example, individuals should be identified as single or married, and corporations should be identified as to their location and place of incorporation. Again, the grantee must have legal capacity for title to pass effectively.

The interests and forms of ownership being conveyed to the grantees should also be noted. For example, the proper language should be used if the grantees wish to be joint tenants (see Chapter 10). If the grantees are taking unequal shares, the shares should be specified, for example, "one-third to John Edward Doe, a single man, and two-thirds to Jane Elizabeth Doe, a single woman, as tenants in common."

Some states have statutory presumptions for how title will be taken in the event no form of ownership is specified for the grantees. For example, in many states, grantees who are married will take the property as tenants by the entireties unless the deed specifies otherwise.

RECITAL OF CONSIDERATION

The requirement for a recital of consideration in a valid deed does not require the parties to actually include the price paid for the land in the deed. In fact, deeds that convey title to real property as gifts generally have a simple recital of consideration, such as, "for the consideration of ten dollars, and other good and valuable consideration" (see Web Exhibit 13.1 for a sample warranty deed and the recital clause). The use of a nominal sum presents no problems for the deed's validity. So long as some consideration was actually paid, the deed's transfer of title may be enforced.

WORDS OF CONVEYANCE

The recital of consideration and words of conveyance portions of the deed are referred to as the premises of the deed. The purpose of requiring words of conveyance is to ensure that the grantor clearly expresses the intent to transfer some title or interest in the property. The words of conveyance also serve to establish any limitations the grantor is imposing in passing title to the property (see discussion of warranties later in this chapter). Standard form deeds use language such as "do hereby grant and convey," "do hereby grant," "do hereby convey and specially warrant," or "do hereby quitclaim." These words effect the transfer and also control the warranties or promises made by the grantor to the grantee in the transferring of the property.

HABENDUM THE TYPE OF INTEREST CONVEYED (HABENDUM)

This requirement for a deed relates to the Part I discussion of land interests as fee simple, fee tail, fee simple defeasible, and so on. In this part of the deed, the grantor indicates which land interest is being conveyed. The language used in the **habendum clause** of the deed is discussed in Chapter 7:

- *Fee simple:* "To A," "To A and her heirs"
- *Fee simple determinable:* "To A so long as the premises are used for a school"

Any restrictions or encumbrances such as easements or liens should be noted following the habendum clause, and these restrictions generally begin "subject to."

DESCRIPTION OF LAND CONVEYED

The requirement for a land description in the deed relates to the Chapter 6 discussion of what constitutes an adequate legal description of property. The grantee's protection of title for the property rests upon this description, which for this purpose appears in the public records.

ACKNOWLEDGMENT

The purpose of the **acknowledgment clause** of the deed is to establish that the act of conveying was indeed the act of the grantor. Actually, in most states the deed need not be acknowledged to be valid between the parties to the deed, but acknowledgment is required before the deed may be recorded in the public land records.

An acknowledgment occurs when the parties to a deed appear before a notary (or otherwise authorized state official) in order to sign their names and to indicate that such signatures are made willingly and that the parties signing are, in fact, the parties to the deed.

The acknowledgment should appear immediately after the signature. Venue (the county and state) should also be stated. Most states require the following information in an acknowledgment: (1) the date, (2) the name of the notary or other official, and (3) that the person (grantor) signing is identified as the same described in the deed. In most states, a notarial seal is also required.

The requirement of witnesses varies from state to state, with some states requiring witnesses in addition to the acknowledgment and others requiring only acknowledgment. In some states, deeds that lack acknowledgment may be established as authentic through use of the testimony of witnesses who were present at the time of the deed's execution.

DELIVERY

Delivery is required to complete the transfer of title by deed. In the majority of transactions, this step is a simple one in which the deed is given in exchange for a purchase price. Delivery can be actual or constructive. In determining whether delivery has been accomplished, the intent of the grantor is critical. If the deed is delivered to a third party, delivery to the grantee is complete only if the grantor has relinquished all control. If the deed is placed in escrow with instructions to convey it to the grantee upon receipt of funds, there again is no delivery because a condition is attached. Often deeds are executed and placed in a safe-deposit box, with instructions given to relatives for removal of the deed after the grantor's death. Such a transfer is not delivery. The standards for delivery of deeds are the same as the standards for delivery of deeds as gifts discussed later in the chapter.

Most states provide that if a deed has been executed, acknowledged, and recorded (discussed later in this chapter), there is a presumption that the deed was delivered. However, it is possible to rebut the presumption through the production of evidence in a legal proceeding.

Once delivery is accomplished, the grantor's destruction of the deed, change of mind, or conveyance to another is of no legal significance.

Mary Blettell was in poor health and went to live with her daughter, Darlene Snider. Herman, Mary's second husband and stepfather to Darlene, continued to live in a house owned by Mary. Hw was unable to care for Mary and Mary wanted him to live at the house she owned even though he was not on the title for the property.

Mary instructed Darlene to bring her all the deeds to her property. She signed over the deed to the home where Herman lived and told Darlene to record the deed after Mary died. Darlene then took the deed and placed it in her own safe deposit box and held onto it for two years until Mary died in 1989. The day after Mary died, Darlene recorded the deed. Herman was not aware of Mary's conveyance to him until after Mary died and Darlene had recorded the deed.

Mary's heirs filed suit contending that there was not a valid transfer of the property to Herman and that they were entitled to the property as heirs to her estate. The lower court held there had been a valid transfer and the heirs appealed. Who has title to the property? Was there a valid conveyance? *Estate of Mary Blettell v. Snider*, 834 P.2d 505 (Or. App. 1992)

> **Consider 13.3**

ACCEPTANCE

Title to property cannot be thrust upon grantees, but acceptance is presumed if the transfer of property is beneficial to the grantee. This presumption works even when the grantee has no knowledge of the conveyance. If the grantee has possession of the deed, acceptance is again presumed.

TYPES OF DEEDS

The type of deed used by the grantor controls the number and the significance of promises about the title made by the grantor. The types of deeds that may be used are: (1) quitclaim deed, (2) warranty deed, (3) special warranty deed, (4) deed of bargain and sale, and (5) judicial deed.

Quitclaim Deed

A **quitclaim deed** is a deed of no promises. It does not purport to transfer or convey title to the property therein described. What is conveyed by a quitclaim deed is any right, title, and interest the grantor may have in the described property, although there is no promise by the grantor that any right, title, or interest exists. A quitclaim deed is often referred to or used as a release for purposes of clearing a cloud on a title or correcting title defects. This form of deed is also used to convey lesser land interests such as life estates. The language of conveyance used in a quitclaim is "I (grantor) hereby quitclaim to . . . " or "I (grantor) hereby remise, release, and quitclaim unto . . . "

In the *Michaelson v. Michaelson* case (pp. 293–295), a quitclaim deed was used, but with regard to several of the properties, the grantor did not have title. A quitclaim deed passes title, if, in fact, the grantor has title. But the grant makes no promises that he or she has title.

Warranty Deed

Most land transactions require the grantor to transfer title by warranty deed. The **warranty deed** is so named because it contains several warranties that the grantor makes to the grantee in the transfer. In most states, these warranties arise because of the language used by the grantor in the words of conveyance, which usually includes "warrant" but according to state statute may instead include "grant" or "convey." Other states may require that the warranties given be set forth in definite language in the deed.

At common law, six warranties were given by the grantor in the warranty deed: seisin, right to convey, freedom from encumbrances, covenant of warranty, quiet enjoyment, and further assurances. In most states, the warranty or covenant of seisin is a promise that the grantor has title to the property. In other states, it is currently a warranty that the grantor is in possession of the property. This warranty is not breached by the presence of easements or encroachments.

The right to convey is simply a warranty that the grantor has the authority to pass title to the property. In states where seisin means only possession, this warranty is important in that the right to transfer is guaranteed.

Freedom from encumbrances is a warranty that ensures the title is free from defects. Under this provision, the grantor warrants that the property is free from encumbrances upon the title and free from physical encumbrances upon the property. However, the deed may include a list of any encumbrances that the grantor is passing along, such as an outstanding mortgage or an easement. The types of title defects warranted against (unless specifically mentioned) are: mortgages, unpaid taxes, assessments, leases, judgment liens, right of redemption, and dower rights. Physical defects warranted against (unless specifically mentioned) are: building restrictions, encroachments, easements, profits, party wall agreements, fences, and mineral rights.

The covenant of warranty requires the grantor to compensate the grantee for any loss experienced because of the grantor's failure to convey title to the property described in the deed. If a grantee loses title to the conveyed property or is required to pay an amount to retain title, the grantor agrees to indemnify the grantee for such loss, costs, and expenses. In the following case, the court deals with an issue of damages when a grantor who conveyed title by warranty deed has conveyed a defective title.

Schorsch v. Blader

563 N.W.2d 538 (Wis. App. 1997)

Facts

On April 30, 1985, Anton F. Schorsch and his son purchased a schoolhouse and 1.8 acres of land from the Wautoma Area School District for $20,400. The District signed a warranty deed transferring property to the Schorsches.

In 1993, the Schorsches entered into an agreement to sell the property but their purchasers refused to close when it was discovered that James, Chester, and Louise Blader held title to .8 of an acre of the property. The Blader portion of the land included the parcel's only access to State Highway 22. The Schorsches brought suit against the Bladers for adverse possession of the .8 acre and against the District for misrepresentation and breach of warranty. At trial, the Schorsches lost on the adverse possession claim but prevailed on the breach of warranty. After a separate trial on damages, the trial court awarded the Schorsches $13,600 in lost profits and $12,243 in attorney fees and litigation expenses. The District appealed, challenging the damage award.

Judicial Opinion

Roggensack, Judge. The Schorsches maintain that the common law measure of damages for a breach of warranty of seisin is irrelevant, because it has been superseded by § 706.10(5), STATS., which they assert requires the use of the common law of damages for breach of contract. No citation is offered for their assertion, and the District disputes that they are correct.

When we are asked to apply a statute whose meaning is in dispute, our efforts are directed at determining legislative intent. In attempting to determine the intent of the legislature, we begin with the plain meaning of the language used in the statute.

The Schorsches rely on the following words from § 706.10(5), STATS., for their theory of damages: "A conveyance . . . shall be construed according to its terms, under rules of law for construction of contract." They argue that because § 706.10(5) requires deeds to be construed

as contracts, the common law of damages for breach of contract applies, not the common law of damages for breach of warranty of title. Their argument requires us to decide whether the phrase "construction of contracts" refers to the process of determining the meaning of words used in the deed or whether that phrase refers to the types of damages awardable for breach of specific covenants.

A deed must also be interpreted to determine its meaning. It may contain several types of promises or covenants, which are collateral to the conveyance of property. At common law, a deed was construed according to rules of construction for other written documents.

If a warranty deed is given without a stated exception, at common law, the grantor of a warranty deed, his heirs and personal representatives, covenanted with the grantee, his heirs and assigns, that: (1) the grantor is lawfully seized of the premises and has the right to convey the same; (2) the grantee shall have quiet enjoyment of the property; (3) the property is free from encumbrances; and (4) the grantor will defend the grantee's title and right of possession.

Section 706.10(5), STATS., codified certain common law covenants for the benefit of the grantee, which sometimes had been excepted from deeds, and established a rebuttable presumption that they were included, unless the terms of the deed provided to the contrary. It was upon these warranties that the Schorsches sued.

Section 706.10(5), STATS., did not change the rules which were used to interpret the meaning of deeds. Stated another way, § 706.10(5) confirms that the rules of law for construction of contracts are to be used to determine the substance of the covenants from the grantor to the grantee of a deed. Nothing in the language of the statute implies any change whatsoever in the measure of damages for a breach of any covenant. Therefore, we conclude that the common law measure of damages for breach of warranty of title was not changed by § 706.10(5).

We now examine the Schorsches claim, under the common law of damages for breach of warranty of title. They were entitled to recover the portion of the purchase price which they proved to be attributable to the .8 of an acre of land to which title failed, plus statutory interest on that amount from the date of purchase. This recovery includes the intrinsic value of the .8 of an acre, as well as any extrinsic value the trial court finds it provided to the parcel on which good title was conveyed, on the date of purchase.

The Schorsches paid $20,400 for the schoolhouse and 1.8 acres of land. Its then current tax assessment was $20,500, with $2,500 attributable to the land. There was testimony that the .8 of an acre, standing alone, was worth $5,000 on the date of trial. However, there was also testimony that the current market value of the parcel, as a whole, was $36,000 and the .8 of an acre represented 45% of that amount. There was no direct testimony about what part of the purchase price the .8 of an acre represented. We remand to the trial court to make that determination and thereafter to calculate interest on that amount at the statutory rate from the date of purchase.

The amount so determined, together with the attorney fees and costs already awarded, are the Schorsches damages for breach of warranty of title of the .8 of an acre.

For the reasons set forth above, we set aside $19,203.50 of the $35,002.67 damage award, and remand for a determination of additional damages measured by that portion of the $20,400 purchase price, which is attributable to the .8 of an acre on which title failed, and interest thereon at the statutory rate, from the date of purchase.

Reversed and remanded.

Case Questions

1. What warranty of title did the District breach?
2. What is the common law method for computation of damages?
3. What damages are the Schorsches awarded and why?
4. Can the Schorsches sell a portion of the property and warrant good title?

Under the warranty of quiet enjoyment, the grantor is making the same promise as under the covenant of warranty. That is, the grantor will reimburse the grantee for expenses and losses incurred if a problem with title arises.

The warranty of further assurances requires the grantor to execute documents or institute suits to protect any defects in title that might exist and which the grantee desires corrected.

In the majority of states, these six common law warranties have been combined into three basic warranties, which are:

1. The grantor possesses an indefeasible fee simple estate, or the grantor has good title and the transfer is proper.
2. There are no encumbrances against the property except those specifically noted.
3. The grantee shall have quiet enjoyment of the property, and the grantor will warrant and defend title against all claims.

If there is an unbroken chain of warranty deeds conveying title to the property, each grantor is liable to all subsequent grantees on the warranties provided (see Web Exhibit 13.1 for a sample warranty deed).

Special Warranty Deed

A **special warranty deed** offers the same warranties as a warranty deed but limits the time of application. Under a special warranty deed, a grantor's warranties apply only for the period of that grantor's ownership. A grantor who owns property from June 1, 1998, to June 1, 2000 and conveys title with a special warranty deed would warrant only for the same period of time and would provide no warranties for defects and encumbrances created or arising prior to that period of ownership. In a special warranty deed, the covenants are not listed, and the language used is similar to the following: "Grantor hereby covenants that he has not done anything whereby the above described property has been encumbered in any way whatsoever." Some states allow shortened language in the granting clause, such as "do hereby specially warrant and convey."

Deed of Bargain and Sale

This form of deed is another name, in some states, for a special warranty deed. A **deed of bargain and sale** offers warranty protection limited to events occurring during the grantor's ownership.

Judicial Deed

A **judicial deed** is a deed executed pursuant to court orders. Examples include the deeds of the following: executors and administrators of estates, conservators of estates, guardians of minors or incompetents, and sheriffs. **Sheriffs' deeds** are issued to parties who have purchased properties at foreclosure sales and are issued after the period of the debtor's right of redemption (see Chapter 15). Assuming all legal procedures are followed, these deeds serve to convey good title.

A deed contained the language, "I, Jacob Smith, of Washington County, warrant and defend unto Christena Smith . . . the following real estate. . . . " Although the deed included all the necessary requirements, the parties are now unclear as to the type of deed given and what warranties, if any, were given. Discuss. *Hummelman v. Mounts,* 87 Ind.178 (1882)

> **Consider 13.4**

TRANSFER OF PROPERTY BY ADVERSE POSSESSION

Acquiring title to real property through **adverse possession** (often called **squatter's rights**) can be traced to the Middle Ages. It arose during that time because there was no proper system for keeping records of land titles, and property owners inevitably lost important documents establishing ownership rights. Adverse possession helped establish title by allowing owners to prove title through possession for a certain period of time. The doctrine arose for a very practical reason.

> **Practical Tip**
>
> Even for those who are occupying land with permission, some form of written agreement about their presence can avoid complication and possibly adverse possession. The presence of possession by permissive use should be clarified, if not by agreement, at least by a letter memorializing the arrangement.

Even when the American colonies were first settled, the use of adverse possession continued because recording systems were nonexistent or unsophisticated and important documents were still being lost by landowners. Also, the doctrine was important in establishing boundary lines for those who owned large tracts and were seldom sure of the exact boundaries of their properties. When boundary disputes arose, the doctrine of adverse possession was used to help settle them.

Adverse possession continues to be a method of acquiring title because of its application in cases where title and boundary disputes arise and building encroachments are discovered.

The process of obtaining title to property through adverse possession is similar to the process of obtaining an easement by prescription (discussed in Chapter 6). In acquiring title to real property through adverse possession, there is no exchange of a document of title and no closing or deed conveyance. Instead, the acquirer gains title through certain types of actions related to land. The conduct and possession required varies from state to state because adverse possession is a statutory doctrine. However, if the prerequisites of conduct and possession are met, the acquirer will hold title as though there had been a conveyance through the traditional methods of deed transfers. The requirements for adverse possession are:

- Actual and exclusive possession
- Open, visible, and notorious possession
- Continuous and peaceable possession
- Hostile and adverse possession
- Possession for the required statutory period

The adverse possessor has the burden of proving the coexistence of each of the requirements, which are discussed individually in the following sections.

Actual and Exclusive Possession

Actual and exclusive possession means that the acquirer must have sole physical occupancy of the property. The extent of physical occupancy required is controlled by the nature of the land being possessed. Generally, the extent of physical occupancy must correspond with the customary and appropriate uses made on land of that nature and size. The issue of what constitutes possession is a question of fact and within the province of the jury, but several common case factors in this area help illustrate the standards for customary and appropriate uses.

For residential property, the adverse possessor is required to take up residence in the appropriate structure on the premises; for farmland, the adverse possessor is required to farm the acres sought to be acquired; and for ranch or grazing property, the adverse possessor is required to use the land for the grazing of livestock. In possession of open acreage, such as farm or ranch land, the fencing in of the possessor's acreage is a commonly recognized method of establishing a customary and appropriate use of the property.

Consider 13.5

The Kapinskis owned and occupied lot 18 from 1935 to 1950. In 1950, the lot was conveyed to the Wyroskis. The Laurins purchased lot 19 in 1954. The lots were the sites of summer homes. A row of lilac bushes marked the boundary between lots 18 and 19, and the Kapinskis and Wyroskis put in and maintained a lawn and flower bed that bordered the lilacs. A boathouse for lot 18 was also located next to the lilac bushes. Laurin claimed the boundary line was too far on his property and in 1960 brought an action to clear title. The Wyroskis claimed they had obtained title by adverse possession. What is the result? Is there sufficient actual possession? *Laurin v. Wyroski,* 121 N.W.2d 764 (Wis. 1963)

Open, Visible, and Notorious Possession

Under this requirement, the adverse possessor must use the property in a manner that is open to the public and sufficient to put those who would pass the property on notice that there is occupation. This possession must not be secret or clandestine; it must be obvious to those who customarily see or pass the property. Open and visible possession is "calculated to apprise the world that the land is occupied and who the occupant is; and such an appropriation of the land by claimant as to apprise, or convey visible notice to the community or neighbor-hood in which it is situated that it is in his exclusive use" (*Marengo Cave Co. v. Ross*, 10 N.E.2d 917 [Ind. 1937]). Courts have labeled this element as one of the disseisor (adverse possessor) unfurling a flag over the land and keeping it flying so the owner can see the enemy and the planned conquest.

Continuous and Peaceable Possession

To show continuous and peaceable possession, the adverse claimant must be in possession for the requisite statutory period without being evicted either physi-cally or through court action. The requisite statutory period varies from state to state and is discussed on page 306. This continuity of possession may be estab-lished even if the property is used only for certain periods during the year, so long as those periods are consistent and regular.

The adverse possessor may employ the doctrine of tacking to establish con-tinuous possession. This doctrine allows a purchaser or someone inheriting a land interest to incorporate the adverse use of the predecessor into meeting the required statutory period. Tacking may be used between predecessor and adverse possessor where there is privity. Privity requires the parties to have a reasonable connection such as a contract, will transfer, or intestate distribution of the predecessor's interest. For example, if A is adversely possessing tract 1 and dies leaving all his property to B after having completed five years on tract 1, B could incorporate those five years in meeting the statutory period of continuous possession.

Hostile and Adverse Possession

This element of adverse possession requires that the adverse possessor establish that the property possession was against the rights of the property's true owner and such action is inconsistent with the title of the true owner. However, the adverse possessor (disseisor) need not establish ill will, bad feelings, or hatred toward the true owner.

The state of mind of the possessor is the issue in establishing this requirement. The appropriate state of mind may be drawn from the concept of either claim of right or color of title. Under claim of right, the possessor claims to be the owner of the property whether or not such claim has any justification. Under color of title, the possessor has an instrument that is believed to convey title, when in real-ity such instrument is ineffective or inoperative. Unless specified differently by statute, the claimant may establish hostile and adverse possession under either one of these mental intents. In some states, adverse possession may be established regardless of the presence of either of these two mental states.

Often, factual circumstances arise in which an adverse claim is maintained because there has been a mistake in the placement of a boundary line, and the parties wish to base their claim on that mistaken boundary for the requisite statu-tory period. Most states find that a mistaken belief about a boundary line is enough to meet the intent requirements for adverse possession.

Consider 13.6

Robert and Barbara Harmon purchased a tract of land in 1983 and hired a sur-veyor to mark their property lines. They then constructed a fence based on that survey. In 1985, James and Deanna Colfer purchased the tract of land adjoining the Harmons'. The Colfers wished to build a condominium project on their land,

FIGURE 13.2 *Number of Years Required for Adverse Possession**

State	Years	State	Years	State	Years	State	Years
Alabama	20	Illinois	20	Montana	5	Rhode Island	10
Alaska	10	Indiana	10	Nebraska	10	South Carolina	10
Arizona	10	Iowa	10	Nevada	5	South Dakota	20
Arkansas	7	Kansas	15	New Hampshire	20	Tennessee	7
California	5	Kentucky	15	New Jersey	30	Texas	3
Colorado	18	Louisiana	30	New Mexico	10	Utah	7
Connecticut	15	Maine	20	New York	10	Vermont	15
Delaware	20	Maryland	20	North Carolina	20	Virginia	25
District of Columbia	15	Massachusetts	20	North Dakota	20	Washington	7
Florida	7	Michigan	15	Ohio	21	West Virginia	10
Georgia	20	Minnesota	15	Oklahoma	15	Wisconsin	20
Hawaii	20	Mississippi	10	Oregon	10	Wyoming	40
Idaho	5	Missouri	10	Pennsylvania	21		

* These figures represent the general time period. Many states have variations depending on issues such as payment of taxes, possession of deed, etc. For example, Texas periods run from 3 to 25 years.

13.6, *continued*

and the city of Reno approved the construction, provided a crash wall was constructed between their land and the Harmons'. As the Colfers prepared to construct their crash fence, they discovered that the Harmons' fence encroached on their property from 2 to 6 inches in certain spots. The fence had to be knocked down in those spots to put up the crash fence and the result was that all of the Harmons' block fence was destroyed. The Harmons brought suit for trespass. Will the Harmons win? *Colfer v. Harmon,* 832 P.2d 383 (Nev. 1992)

If a party is given permission by the true title holder to use the property, such permission prevents the user from asserting an adverse claim because permissive use is not hostile and adverse. Thus, where the true owner grants a license or easement or gives permission for some other use of property, the user or possessor's use or possession may not ripen into an adverse claim.

It is possible for co-owners of property to make adverse claims against one another. Thus a cotenant may oust others of their possession and gain title by possessing the entire interest for the requisite statutory period.

Possession for Required Statutory Period

The possession of the property with the requisite characteristics previously listed must occur for a certain statutory period of time. Although times vary from state to state, the typical adverse period is 20 years. In some states, such as Arizona, the period is as short as 10 years (see Figure 13.2). The adverse claimant must maintain possession continuously for the period of time specified by state statute.

The following case deals with several of the elements of adverse possession and the rights of the parties.

Schultz v. Dew

564 N.W.2d 320 (S.D. 1997)

Facts

On April 11, 1946, Lawrence and Pearl Pepka obtained a warranty deed for their residential property, which was Outlot 37 and a portion of Outlot 40 of Big Stone City. In 1991, the Pepkas conveyed their property to their children, holding back a life estate for themselves [see Chapter 7 for more information on life estates].

The Dews' chain of title is somewhat more complex but involves the remaining two-thirds of Outlot 40 and was eventually conveyed to Thomas C. Dew and Denise A. Dew as husband and wife (the Dews).

The Pepkas believed their driveway on Outlot 40 was on their property and they used it without the Dews' permission. However, as the Outlot existed at the time of the Pepkas' acquisition, their driveway was actually located well onto the Dews' property. Lawrence Pepka put gravel on the driveway and then later paved it with asphalt. He also mowed the lawn for six feet west of the driveway because he believed that to be the boundary point between his property and the Dews'. Sometime in the 1960s, Lawrence and his son Bernard planted seven evergreen trees along the driveway in the area now disputed. Bernard had received the trees as a gift from a local minister for serving as an altar boy.

The Pepkas did not put up a fence and the Dews and Pepkas had a good relationship. As the Pepkas aged, Tom Dew helped them maintain their property by mowing their law and shoveling their snow. Pearl took the Dews baked goods in exchange for the help. Tom even put up the snow fence for Pearl after Lawrence passed away and the snow fence was located along what she believed to be the boundary line for their properties.

In 1993, Pearl decided to sell the property. Because of a survey that revealed the true boundary line to be different from that used by the Pepkas, the Dews asserted ownership of the property through the Pepkas' driveway. Pearl attempted to settle the matter and even offered to purchase the disputed strip. When no agreement could be reached, Pearl filed suit to clear title to the strip by adverse possession. The trial court found no disputed facts and declared the Pepkas the owners of the property. The Dews appealed.

Judicial Opinion

Miller, Chief Justice. The relevant law governing adverse possession in this case is found in SDCL 15–3–13. That statute provides:

> For the purpose of constituting an adverse possession by a person claiming title not founded upon a written instrument, or judgment, or decree, land shall be deemed to have been possessed and occupied in the following cases only:
>
>> (1) Where it has been protected by a substantial inclosure; or
>>
>> (2) Where it has been usually cultivated or improved.

Since these provisions are stated in the disjunctive, a claim of adverse possession may succeed if the claimant establishes either a substantial enclosure or cultivation or improvement. It is the application of these two subsections to the undisputed facts that is at issue here.

First, Dews claim there was no substantial enclosure sufficient to establish the necessary intent to claim exclusive right to the property. Admittedly, there was no fence. However, natural barriers may also satisfy the requirement of a substantial enclosure. In *Cuka*, we adopted the rationale of courts in Oregon and Florida which held:

> 'The land claimed in the instant case is unfenced, but because of the water boundary the peninsula can be considered for all practical purposes as enclosed,' and 'the sufficiency of the enclosure is a question of law for the court.' We hold, therefore, that under the facts of this case the James River formed a substantial enclosure.

Here, Pepkas claim the trees planted along the driveway constitute a barrier or enclosure sufficient to satisfy the statute. Their position has logical appeal. If a naturally occurring river, the boundaries of which are susceptible to change over the years may constitute an enclosure, surely natural elements such as trees which are deliberately placed by the person claiming adverse possession may also serve as a boundary. It might be claimed the tree line is not as complete of a barrier or enclosure as a river, but as pointed out in *Cuka*, the James River actually provided access (rather than denied it) during the winter months when the river was frozen. Surely, the enclosure need not be absolutely secure to satisfy subsection (1) of the statute. Further, the trees might actually be more in the nature of an enclosure than the river because, although both can be naturally occurring, the tree line is decidedly a more deliberate enclosure because Pepkas intentionally planted and maintained the trees. As a matter of law, then, the tree line does constitute a substantial enclosure.

Next, Dews claim the facts do not support the conclusion that the strip of land was "usually cultivated or improved" by Pepkas. Dews claim that:

a continuous planting or a continuous cultivation would be required but was not the case in this instance where it was simply planting seven trees and then allowing them to grow. Some water may have been put on those trees for a few years, but there is no testimony that 'usual cultivation' by any stretch of the imagination was performed.

Pepkas not only planted the trees in the 1960's and encouraged them to grow, but Pearl testified by deposition that they had cleaned debris out of the strip on which the driveway and gravel road exist, and mowed the strip as part of the yard surrounding their house, garage, and shed regularly since the 1940's or 1950's. Even Tom Dew conceded that Pepkas had mowed the area until 1988. As a matter of law, mowing the strip of land (in a residential area on the outskirts of town) and planting and maintaining trees on the strip constitutes cultivation.

Similarly, the undisputed facts also establish Pepkas improved the land. Pepkas initially improved the driveway to their garage by putting gravel over the surface. Later, the surface was upgraded to asphalt or black top. These facts are not disputed. Dews argue the black top had not been sealed or regularly maintained, and thus was not enough of an improvement to satisfy the statute. However, the fact remains that the strip of land is not unimproved; the driveway and landscaping are plain evidence support-ing this conclusion. As a matter of law, the gravel and later asphalt driveway, together with landscaping, constitute an improvement to the land, indicating Pepkas were in possession of the disputed strip of property.

As a defense, Dews also assert that Pepkas have disclaimed title to the property. This contention lacks merit. As Pepkas note, a disclaimer exists only if it is a knowing relinquishment of an asserted property right and a single act, standing alone, is insufficient to establish a disclaimer. Here, the aging and recently widowed Pearl Pepka decided to sell her property, at which time it was discovered that record title to the disputed strip was owned by Tom Dew. When approached about the matter, Dews refused to sell the strip or grant an easement for the driveway, necessitating this action. Pepkas' attempts to settle the matter short of litigation can hardly be said to be the equivalent of the four separate disclaimers.

Case Questions

1. List the things the Pepkas had done to the property in question.
2. Is the failure of the Pepkas to build a fence a problem? What kinds of things qualify as fences?
3. Did Pearl lose any rights by offering to buy the strip of land from the Dews?
4. Who owns the property in question?

Observations About Adverse Possession

One question often brought out in adverse possession cases is, Who was paying the taxes during the alleged period of adverse possession? Unless a state's statute specifies, the adverse possessor is not required to pay taxes to be allowed to claim title. California's statute, for example, does require the payment of taxes for an adverse claim to be successful. In some states, the failure to pay taxes weakens but does not destroy a claim for adverse possession.

When a title holder is faced with an adverse claimant, the proper method for halting such a claim is to bring a legal action in trespass to have the claimant removed by court order or injunction. This removal serves to interrupt the claimant's continuous possession and thus ends the adverse period. Once judicial action is brought, the claimant's right to possession stops. The filing of the suit stops the adverse period. Such a proceeding may be brought by seeking an injunction or in the form of a quiet title action in which the court will determine the parties' rights and interests in the property. A **quiet title action** requires that notice be given to all interested in the property in advance of a hearing on the property. Once title is quieted in the record holder of title, the adverse claimant would have to begin anew to establish the requisite statutory period.

TRANSFER OF PROPERTY BY INTER VIVOS GIFTS

Title to property may be transferred through an *inter vivos* **gift** from **donor** (grantor) to **donee** (grantee), that is, the gift is made while the donor is alive. A gift is defined as a voluntary transfer of property by donor to donee where there is no consideration or compensation for the transfer. For title to transfer by gift, three elements must be present. There must be (1) donative intent by the donor or grantor, (2) delivery of the gift, and (3) acceptance by the donee or grantee.

Donative Intent

To establish donative intent, it must be shown that the donor intended to pass title absolutely and irrevocably and to relinquish all rights in the property.

In establishing donative intent, the party seeking to prove that a gift was made is best able to do so through the production of a written instrument conveying title. Occasionally, because of the equities of the situation, the courts will enforce an oral gift of land, but for the most part a written conveyance is required.

Delivery

Delivery of a deed to the donee does not necessarily require a physical transaction, but this requirement is met by proving that the donor intended to part with possession, control, and ownership. In most cases, delivery is accomplished by the simple physical transfer of possession of the written instrument (the deed) from the donor to the donee.

However, delivery can be actual (physical) or constructive delivery. Actual delivery occurs when the donee is given the deed. **Constructive delivery** occurs when the deed is available for the donee and the circumstances are such that only the donee would have access to it. For example, if the donor locks the deed in a desk and gives the donee the only key, there has been constructive delivery.

Constructive delivery can also occur when an instrument or document is transferred to a third person on behalf of the donee. However, in such cases the delivery must be unconditional, and any attempt by the donor to maintain control over the property will cause the gift to fail. In some instances, a donor will deliver the deed to a third party with instructions that the deed be delivered to a designated donee upon the donor's death. Such a delivery is ineffective because the donor retains control while living. If, however, the donor no longer retains control over the deed, then such a delivery is an effective gift.

In other cases, the donor will deliver a document to an attorney or another third party, indicating the desire that a particular donee have the property described in the document but that the instrument not be recorded for a period of time. Again, an effective gift results if control is relinquished, and the gift fails if the donor maintains control.

In yet other cases, the donor will place a document in a safe-deposit box specially obtained for housing the document and jointly held with the donee. In most circumstances, the placement of a deed in a joint facility is not delivery.

Consider 13.7

Holstein wanted his niece to have a parcel of land upon which she could build a home after her completion of law school. Holstein signed and executed a deed for a small parcel that he owned and turned it over to his attorney with instructions that the deed be recorded upon the niece's graduation. Holstein told his niece of the pending gift to inspire her in her last year of law school, but he died before the niece graduated. Both the niece and other heirs claim the parcel. Who wins?

Acceptance

The final requirement for a valid gift of realty is acceptance by the donee. For the most part, this element of a gift is presumed unless the donee makes a clear refusal, as by tearing up the deed or refusing to accept the appropriate paperwork.

Gifts may be set aside on some of the same grounds used to set aside apparently valid contracts. For example, a donor (grantor) who executed a deed under duress (force or threat of force or wrongful act) or undue influence may have the gift set aside. Or in the event of the donor's death, heirs or devisees may petition to have the gift deed set aside on these bases. **Undue influence** exists when a party in a confidential relationship is able to exert great influence over the donor for the party's own benefit.

TRANSFER OF PROPERTY BY WILL OR INTESTATE SUCCESSION

Title to property may be transferred upon the death of the title holder by the provisions in the title holder's will; or if no will was executed, it may be transferred pursuant to a state statutory scheme of distribution for those dying intestate. The passage of title by will and intestate succession are covered in detail in Chapter 17.

TRANSFER OF PROPERTY BY EMINENT DOMAIN

Eminent domain is the taking of private property by a governmental entity for use for the general public good. Such a taking is permissible and serves to transfer full and complete title to the state if the state provides the existing owners with appropriate compensation. The issues of the taking of property and appropriate compensation are discussed in detail in Chapter 19.

PROTECTION OF TITLE

From the discussions of deeds, adverse possession, and other methods of transfer of real estate, one can see that confusion could arise with respect to who has title to property. The deed and the possessory rights are between the parties. However, the issue of third parties and their rights with respect to the land arises if there is no notice of the rights of grantor and grantee. This portion of the chapter focuses on the means used to protect title and determine title in the event a dispute arises.

Recording

The process of **recording** as a method of title protection has been practiced in the United States since the days of the colonies. Indeed, the Massachusetts Bay Act of 1634 required records of land transfer to be filed with the court so that an accurate record of land ownership could be maintained. These early acts required the extra work of copying every instrument of conveyance. Every state now has some form of recording act. Although the acts differ, the same topics are covered in each: (1) the documents required to be recorded, (2) the mechanics of recording, (3) a system for maintaining and organizing records, and (4) a method for determining priorities of interests.

> ## Practical Tip
>
> Recording the deed is a necessary part of every land transaction. As the *Gensheimer* case illustrates, one day of waiting can make all the difference in terms of who gets title to the land.

DOCUMENTS REQUIRED TO BE RECORDED

All of the recording acts basically provide that all instruments affecting title to land are to be recorded. These instruments include deeds, mortgages, liens, judgments, and, as discussed in Chapter 4, Article 9 financing statements. New York's statute requires the following instruments to be recorded (Real Property Law, Sec. 290):

> . . . every written instrument, by which any estate or interest in real property is created, transferred, mortgaged or assigned, or by which the title to any real property may be affected, including an instrument in execution of a power, although the power be one of revocation only, and an instrument postponing or subordinating a mortgage lien; except a will, a lease for a term not exceeding three years, an executory contract for the sale or purchase of lands, and an instrument containing a power to convey real property as the agent or attorney of the owner of such property.

The recording of a land-related document affords both protection and public notice. Not everyone could be expected to have actual knowledge or notice about every land transaction. Recording serves to give everyone the chance to verify transactions. Recording is constructive notice to everyone of the rights of the parties in the land.

MECHANICS OF RECORDING

Recording is accomplished at statutorily designated offices. Offices may be local, such as a county recorder office, or may be a state agency or a town clerk. As discussed in Chapters 3, 4, and 5, other documents such as easements, liens, and fixture filings are recorded in the same place. In most states, recording is accomplished at a county office for the location of the property. Some states may have a separate land records office in counties where the population is high.

The difference between filing and recording is that in filing, the document is retained by the governmental agency. In recording, the document is copied and the copy is retained by the governmental agency in an appropriate organizational system (discussed later in this chapter).

Every state requires the party desiring the instrument to be recorded to pay a fee before the instrument is entered on the records. The fees are set according to the type of document and the number of pages in it.

When the fee is paid, the party seeking to record the instrument is given a receipt with the date and time stamped on it. The document being recorded will also have a stamp of date and time. Since many documents are accepted at the same time, each document will also be numbered (the number is sometimes called a *fee number*) to indicate the exact order of filing. Each document also indicates where in the agency's records it will be filed, such as "Book 425 of Deeds, p. 585" or "Docket 300 of Book of Maps, p. 700."

SYSTEM FOR MAINTAINING AND ORGANIZING RECORDS

With the great number of documents filed annually, every state must have some system for organizing the records so that information about title to a piece of property can be readily obtained. The purposes of such recording systems are to provide a method whereby the chain of title for a particular piece of property can be effectively traced and to provide title protection. Chain of title simply provides a history of how a piece of real estate has been transferred over the years between successive owners. To establish ownership of property today, the current owner must establish that the chain of title is unbroken; in other words, that title has been conveyed without any breaks through successive owners.

To be able to trace chains of title, the records must follow an index system. States have either a grantor/grantee system of indexing, a tract system, or both. Most states have a grantor/grantee system, which is easy to understand but more difficult to use when establishing the chain of title. In a **grantor/grantee index system,** the agency responsible for recording maintains a running index of transactions alphabetized by the grantor's and grantee's names.

Figures 13.3 and 13.4 are sample grantor and grantee index entries. Suppose the Joneses were purchasing lot 388 from the Jenningses. The Joneses could establish the chain of title by first looking for the Jenningses in the grantee index (Figure 13.4) and then verifying the transfer by looking at American Continental in the grantor index (Figure 13.3). To trace further back, they would check American Continental in the grantee index to find its grantor and so on. The presence of the docket or volume number and the page number in the index permits the tracing party to turn to the records and actually examine the joint tenancy deed of conveyance.

FIGURE 13.3 *Sample Grantor Index*

Date of Recording	Grantor	Grantee	Type of Document	Brief Land Description	Docket or Volume	Page
4/9/90	American Continental Corporation	Terry H. and Marianne Moody Jennings	Joint Tenancy Deed	Lot 388 of Hohokam Village, Unit Two	14342	913

FIGURE 13.4 *Sample Grantee Index*

Date of Recording	Grantee	Grantor	Type of Document	Brief Land Description	Docket or Volume	Page
4/9/90	Terry H. and Marianne Moody Jennings	American Continental Corporation	Joint Tenancy Deed	Lot 388 of Hohokam Village, Unit Two	14342	913

Although the tracing of the chain of title is uncomplicated here, many titles require more thorough searches. Also, the grantor/grantee system of indexing has inherent problems: the use of different names, initials, or married names can cause confusion and an apparent break in the chain of title. (See earlier discussion of grantor and grantee.) Title obtained in other ways such as by will may not appear in the land records. Also, not all title defects such as judgments and tax liens will appear in the grantor/grantee index.

The second system of indexing, called the **tract index system** (also known as *block indexing* or *numerical indexing*), avoids some of the inherent problems of the grantor/grantee system. Many states have both systems, but title companies, which sell insurance for chains of title, use the tract index system to avoid the problems in the grantor/grantee system. Furthermore, tracing the chain of title under the tract index system is much faster than under the grantor/grantee system. Under the tract index system, the entire county is divided into tracts and the chain of title for each tract is traced back to the time when the land was given in a government grant. Each piece of land is then indexed to a tract, so that every piece of property can have its origins traced quickly to the origination of title.

METHOD FOR DETERMINING PRIORITIES OF INTERESTS

State recording acts provide a method whereby land transfers and interests can be made public. All have constructive notice of its existence and the rights of the parties. Once a document is recorded, everyone has notice of the recorded interest even without seeing a recorded document.

Unscrupulous grantors have conveyed the same land interests to different parties. When this occurs, who is entitled to the property and who is left to collect damages from the fraudulent grantor on the basis of breach of warranty? State statutes employ three different methods for determining priority: (1) pure race, (2) notice, and (3) race/notice.

1.   *Pure Race* North Carolina's statute is a pure race statute and provides as follows:

§47-18. Conveyances, contracts to convey, options and leases of land.
(a)   No (i) conveyance of land, or (ii) contract to convey, or (iii) option to convey, or (iv) lease of land for more than three years shall be valid to pass any property interest as against lien creditors or purchasers for a valuable consideration from the donor, bargainor or lessor but from the time of registration thereof in the county where the land lies, or if the land is located in more than one county, then in each county where any portion of the land lies to be effective as to the land in that county

A **pure race statute**[1] means first to record is first in right, or the first party to record the instrument in the proper place will hold title to the property. This rule applies even though deeds may have been executed to the parties prior to the time the recording party received the same interests. An example follows.

- *Day 1:* Grantor conveys Blackacre to A.
- *Day 2:* Grantor conveys Blackacre to B.
- *Day 3:* B records interest.
- *Day 4:* A records interest.

1.   Pure race states are Louisiana and North Carolina

In a pure race jurisdiction, B takes title as the first to record even though the interest in Blackacre was conveyed first to A.

2.   *Notice* Arizona's statute [ARS §33-412] is an example of a notice statute:

    A.   All bargains, sales and other conveyances whatever of lands, tenements and hereditaments, whether made for passing an estate of freehold or an estate for a term of years, and deeds of settlement upon marriage, whether of land, money or other personal property, and deeds of trust and mortgages of whatever kind, shall be void as to creditors and subsequent purchasers for valuable consideration without notice, unless they are acknowledged and recorded in the office of the county recorder as required by law.

    B.   Unrecorded instruments . . . as to all subsequent purchasers with notice thereof, shall be valid and binding.

The key to understanding the system of priorities in notice states[2] is the term **good faith purchaser** or **bona fide purchaser (BFP).** The **notice statutes** entitle the last good faith purchaser to keep the land interest. However, if a deed is not recorded in a notice state, the purchaser may lose title to a subsequent bona fide purchaser. A good faith purchaser is defined as one who has no knowledge of a prior conveyance either constructive (no prior recorded interest) or actual (no knowledge of a transfer or sale). A notice example follows.

- *Day 1:* Grantor conveys to A (a BFP).
- *Day 2:* Grantor conveys to B (a BFP).
- *Day 3:* Grantor conveys to C (a BFP).

In this case, since A and B did not record, C takes title. This would be true even if A and B recorded their interests on day 4 before C recorded on day 5. In a notice jurisdiction, the failure to record may cost the parties their interests.

3.   *Race/Notice* New York is a jurisdiction following the **race/notice system** of priorities (Real Property 291):

A conveyance of real property . . . may be recorded. . . . Every such conveyance not so recorded is void, as against any person who subsequently purchases or acquires by exchange or contracts to purchase or acquire by exchange, the same real property or any portion thereof . . . in good faith and for a valuable consideration, from the same vendor or assignor, his distributees, or devisees and whose conveyance, contract, or assignment is first duly recorded. . . .

Race/notice statutes entitle the property to go to a good faith purchaser, but it will go to the good faith purchaser who is the first to record. An example would be as follows.

- *Day 1:* Grantor conveys property to A (BFP).
- *Day 2:* Grantor conveys property to B (BFP).

---

2.   Notice states are Alabama, Arizona and Colorado (race/notice by judicial decisions), Arkansas (except mortgages), Connecticut, Delaware, Florida, Illinois, Kansas, Kentucky, Maine, Massachusetts, Missouri, New Hampshire, New Mexico, Ohio (except mortgages), Oklahoma, Rhode Island, South Carolina, Tennessee, Texas, Vermont, Virginia, and West Virginia.

- *Day 3:* Grantor conveys property to C (BFP).
- *Day 4:* B records.
- *Day 5:* A records.
- *Day 6:* C records.

In a race/notice jurisdiction[3], B would take title to the property because B was the first BFP to record the interest; in a notice system, C would take title; and in a pure race system, B would take title. However, if B were not a BFP, in a race/notice jurisdiction A would take title; in a notice jurisdiction, B's status is irrelevant and C would still take title; and in a pure race jurisdiction, B would still take title.

The following case provides a discussion of priorities for title.

Gensheimer v. Kneisley

778 S.W.2d 138 (Tex. 1989)

Facts

On May 15, 1985, Gilbert and Vivian Beall executed a general warranty deed to Mark Gensheimer. On September 9, 1985, Kevin Kneisley obtained a judgment against Gilbert Beall for $124,895.90. Kneisley recorded an abstract of the judgment on October 28, 1985. On October 29, 1985, Gensheimer's deed from the Bealls was recorded. Kneisley filed suit against Gensheimer, who had already been living in the property, claiming superior title. The court found for Kneisley and Gensheimer appealed.

Judicial Opinion

Bleil, Justice. Gensheimer further maintains that the trial court erred in granting Kneisley's summary judgment because the abstract of the judgment acquired by Kneisley against Gilbert Beall failed to include Vivian Beall's name. Since her name was not included on the judgment, Gensheimer argues, no lien exists on the property; alternatively, if a lien exists at all, it is only as to the community one-half interest of Gilbert Beall. Tex.Prop.Code Ann. § 52.004(b)(2) (Vernon 1984) provides that an abstract of judgment must be recorded and indexed alphabetically showing the name of each defendant in the judgment. No requirement exists that an abstract show the names of the parties to the suit or the names of the defendants in the suit; the only requirement is that the defendants against whom a judgment was taken be listed. Although Vivian Beall was named as a party, the judgment was taken only against Gilbert Beall. The abstract of

the judgment shows the name of the party against whom the judgment was taken—Gilbert Beall. Community property subject to a spouse's sole or joint management, control, and disposition is subject to the liabilities incurred before or during marriage. Therefore, the abstract of judgment against Gilbert Beall constituted a valid lien against the entirety of the property held in community by Gilbert and Vivian Beall.

Kneisley's judgment against Beall was on file when Gensheimer recorded his deed from Beall. Kneisley recorded first, on October 28, 1985; Gensheimer's deed from Beall, dated May 15, 1985, was not *recorded* until October 29, 1985. A lien of a judgment creditor who has fixed a lien upon real estate by abstracting a judgment takes precedence over a prior unrecorded deed executed by the judgment debtor, unless the creditor has notice of the unrecorded deed at or before the time the lien was fixed on the land. Kneisley stated by affidavit that he had no knowledge or notice of a deed dated May 15, 1985. Gensheimer did not controvert this fact. A valid lien against the property was established and foreclosed upon, and Kneisley's recorded judgment lien takes precedence over Gensheimer's prior unrecorded warranty deed, thus vesting superior title to the property in Kneisley.

Nevertheless, Gensheimer also complains that the trial court erred in granting judgment because a fact issue exists as to whether Kneisley had knowledge of the warranty deed dated May 15, 1985, from the Bealls to Gensheimer. When Kneisley abstracted his judgment on

---

3.   Race/notice states are Alaska, California, Georgia, Hawaii, Idaho, Indiana, Maryland, Michigan, Minnesota, Mississippi, Montana, Nebraska, Nevada, New Jersey, New York, North Dakota, Oregon, Pennsylvania (except mortgages), South Carolina, South Dakota, Utah, Washington, Wisconsin, Wyoming, and the District of Columbia.

October 28, 1985, Gensheimer's warranty deed was not in his chain of title, since it was not recorded until the following day. An unrecorded deed does not give constructive notice. Kneisley's uncontroverted affidavit established that he had no actual knowledge or notice of the deed.

Affirmed.

Case Questions

1. Write out a chronology of events with respect to the title and recording interests.
2. Was there actual notice of the Gensheimer deed?
3. Was there constructive notice of the Gensheimer deed?
4. Does the judgment take priority over a warranty deed?
5. Who has title to the property in this case?

Consider 13.8

Day 1. O conveys to A (BFP).
Day 2. O conveys to B (BFP).
Day 3. A records.
Day 4. B records.

In the above example, who takes title under all three types of recording statutes?

Torrens System

Another method of title protection used instead of a recording system is the **Torrens system**—named after Sir Robert Torrens, who introduced it in Australia in 1858. The system is one of land title registration; that is, documents of transfer are not recorded, but title to land is registered once by making an entry reflecting the owner. That owner is then given an official certificate of title. If the owner wishes to transfer title to the land, the certificate and a deed are given to the purchaser. The purchaser then takes these documents to the land registration office where the old certificate is surrendered, a change of ownership is entered, and a new certificate is issued to the purchaser. This system eliminates the need for establishing the chain of title.

Initial registration under the Torrens system requires a form of quiet title action, so that all parties with interests or potential interests may be heard before title is registered.

Title Abstracts

In many states, parties transferring property interests will hire attorneys to trace the chain of title on a piece of property and then issue an opinion on that chain. That opinion, in written form, is called an **abstract of title** and is defined as a concise statement of the substance of documents or facts appearing on the public records that affect the title.

The abstract begins with the legal description of the property, often called a **caption** or **head,** and then proceeds with copies of all documents, in chronological order, affecting title. Acknowledgments and signatures are not included so long as the abstractor views them as being in order and proper.

Part of the abstract also includes the **abstractor's certificate,** which summarizes what the abstractor did not examine. For example, it would be very typical for the abstractor to state that zoning violations may affect the title's marketability but that information on such violations is not available from the recorder's records. The abstractor then directs the users to the appropriate agency for determining whether zoning violations exist.

The buyer's attorney then examines the abstract and issues an opinion that includes a description of the property and time covered by the abstract, who holds title to the property, what defects or imperfections exist, and any recommendations for clearing up these defects and imperfections. The abstract will include summaries of items such as deeds, mortgages, deeds of trusts, *lis pendens* (pending legal action on the property), sheriffs' sales certificates, liens, taxes, assessments, judgments, and bankruptcy petitions.

Title Insurance

Recording and title abstracts still do not provide protection if a title defect arises. Neither system of title protection offers a guarantee that no problems will arise. In most parts of the United States today, **title insurance** affords the property purchaser financial protection in the event certain types of defects arise in the property.

A title insurer may operate in one of two ways. First, it may hire an attorney to do an abstract and then issue insurance on the basis of that opinion. Second, the title insurer may be a complete operation by actually doing the search and abstract and then issuing insurance. Those insurers operating the second type of business maintain a title plant for conducting their operations. A title plant consists of copies of documents taken from the public records. Generally, title companies will organize their records pursuant to a tract index system.

Title insurers issue different policies according to the type of applicant for insurance and the use to be made of the property. For example, there are different policy forms for commercial and residential property. Also, different policies are issued for owners of property and for those who wish insurance as mortgage lenders. Neither policy is issued until the insurance company has had an opportunity to examine the records and establish the chain of title.

PROCESS OF ISSUING A POLICY

In many contracts for the sale of real estate today, the condition of delivery of marketable title through the purchase and issuance of a title insurance policy is a prerequisite to closure of the transaction. **Marketable title** is one free of problems related to the chain of title, the quality of title, and the seller's right to convey the property. Although the definition of marketable title may vary, adding a requirement that a title insurer issue a policy gives the buyer assurance and financial backing in the event of a problem. A policy will not be issued unless the insurer is reasonably sure no loss will be incurred.

The seller applies for a policy with a title insurance company. The title company prepares an abstract, and any defects are considered by the title examiner, who decides whether the defects are a risk or whether the property is insurable. If there is a favorable decision, the title insurer issues a preliminary binder that is not a policy but a commitment to insure contingent upon the transaction's closing and the title's being delivered to the buyer.

If the company finds defects that make the property uninsurable, the seller may be given the opportunity to correct those defects and thus make the title insurable. For example, the title abstract will provide a list of all judgments against persons having the same name as the seller. The seller may by affidavit establish that he or she is not the same person as named in those judgments. Tax liens may be removed through payment. When such corrections are made, the insurer will then issue the preliminary binder.

A fee may be charged for the preparation of the abstract and also for the issuance of the policy. In many states, the fee charged will be based on an escalating scale set by a state regulatory body, which allows the fee charged to increase with the value of the property. The reason for the escalating scale is that a title problem on a more expensive piece of property will cost the insurer more in terms of correction or compensation.

Many companies will physically inspect the property to be insured in order to determine any adverse possession or occupancy not reflected in the public records. Also, when insuring a construction lender, the title insurer must be certain that construction or work has not begun prior to the recordation of the mortgage. As noted in Chapter 5, any start of construction from the presence of equipment to the digging of one shovelful of dirt will place the mechanics in first priority if those acts are done prior to recording.

COVERAGE AFFORDED BY THE TITLE POLICY

Title insurance differs significantly from ordinary fire or auto insurance in covering only defects in title in existence at the time of the transfer. Title insurance does not afford protection for new problems developing after the closing of the transaction and the transfer of title to the buyer.

The Title Policy

The American Land Title Association (ALTA) has developed the most widely used form policies and the ones used by major title insurers.

ALTA issues policy forms for lender's, owner's, construction lender's, and leaseholds. The basic title policy includes the following sections:

1. Insuring clauses (outline the coverage) which covers
   a. failure of title to the property
   b. defects in title such as liens
   c. lack of right of access
   d. unmarketable title
2. Exclusions (outline those items not covered) (see below)
3. Schedules, generally A and B (which outline the added protections or endorsements purchased by the policy holder)
4. Conditions (requirements for the issuance of the policy such as removal of liens)
5. Stipulations (certain statements of fact that the parties agree are part of their assumptions for the policy such as the new definition of what constitutes a "public record")

The ALTA policies also include a mandatory arbitration clause under the American Arbitration Association and a coinsurance clause that will require higher policy values to be purchased when a building is to be constructed on raw land. Title policy buyers must now purchase title insurance based on the proposed value of the land with completed construction and not simply based on the value of the raw land. An 80 percent coinsurance clause means the liability of the title insurer will be limited if the value of the land increases 20 percent or more over the amount of the insurance purchased and results in lesser recovery for partial claims.

The ATLA Policy also requires that the title insurer undertake its obligation to defend a title "diligently." This change adds an element of good faith to the title insurer's role in pursuing claims against the insured property.

EXCLUSIONS IN TITLE INSURANCE COVERAGE

Exclusions from coverage are listed in what is called schedule B of the policy. It is important to remember that title insurance insures only the accuracy of the recording system.

Most matters that would be discoverable by survey, such as inaccurate boundary lines, are not covered by title policies. Furthermore, any facts, rights, or claims that are not noted in the public records but are ascertainable by inspection are not covered in the policy. Zoning restrictions are not covered, nor is eminent domain (unless proceedings are noted in the records). Unpatented mining claims and defects not in the public records but known to the insured are likewise excluded.

The following are additional exclusions:

- Violations of environmental laws unless recorded in the public records (see Chapter 20 for a discussion of these environmental laws)
- No payment of litigation defense costs for items excluded under schedule B exceptions
- The insured property owner must be a bona fide purchaser to be entitled to policy protections
- Public records are more narrowly defined to include only property records as designated by the state as the proper filing place for matters affecting property. Without a specific clause, for example, federal rights-of-way would not be covered.
- More clear definition of "unmarketablility of title" (see Chapter 14)
- Problems with title based on usury (see Chapter 15) in the underlying financing of the transaction
- Mechanic's liens (see Chapter 5) that arise from work contracted for and commenced after the date of the policy
- Eminent domain rights (see Chapter 19) are not covered unless notice of such appears in the public records prior to the date of the policy.

THE ENHANCED TITLE POLICY—
SPECIAL PROTECTION THROUGH ENDORSEMENTS

Additional coverage to limit exclusions may be purchased. For example, mechanic's lien protections may be added to a policy. Encroachment protection may be purchased as a rider, so that if a building on the insured's property encroaches on another's property, the policy will cover the damages.

Other types of endorsements include coverage for violation of protective covenants (see Chapter 22), violation of zoning laws, and location endorsements that protect the buyer against faulty surveys. The California Land Title Association policy, which is becoming more popular outside California, can include hundreds of endorsements available to title policy purchasers. Sometimes referred to as "the California 100," these endorsements give purchasers a wide choice of options for protections. Some states, such as Texas, do not permit the use of these complex endorsement policies.

Other types of special endorsements would include a tax easement endorsement that provides protection for an easement appurtenant (see Chapter 3) if the owner of the servient estate fails to pay taxes on the property. Corporations purchase a successorship and assignment endorsement that allows them to transfer the policy protection to subsidiaries or newly formed corporations that result from mergers and consolidations so that the policy rights are not lost to corporate reorganizations. Also, like ordinary property and casualty insurance, title insurance can carry an inflation endorsement that will afford protection for replacement costs as opposed to a given value or original cost.

WHO IS PROTECTED UNDER TITLE POLICY?

The policy affords protection to the insured (or insureds) named in the policy (a mortgagee or buyer). If the mortgagee is protected and a loss of property results from a title defect, the insurer will pay the balance due on the mortgage, thereby relieving the owner of liability for the mortgage. However, the owner will lose the property and any existing investment or equity. Title policies are not transferable, and the protection afforded a buyer in one transaction may not be passed along to the next buyer.

The seller of the property is afforded no protection by the purchaser's title insurance policy. The seller remains liable to the buyer for breach of any warranties if defects in title arise. In fact, it is not unusual for a title insurer to pay the buyer the loss resulting from the title defect and then through subrogation proceed against the seller for the seller's breach of warranty to the buyer.

DAMAGES

All title policies will have a section dealing with the determination and payment of losses. Under the standard policy, the loss is defined as the least of:

1. The actual loss of the insured claimed; or
2. The amount of the insurance set forth in the policy; or
3. If the policy is for a mortgagee, the amount necessary to pay off the mortgage debt.

In addition to actual loss, the title insurer will pay the costs, attorneys' fees, and expenses imposed upon an insured in litigation carried out by the insurer for the insured. The following case deals with the complexities of title insurance and its coverage.

Somerset Savings Bank v. Chicago Title Insurance Company

649 N.E.2d 1123 (Mass. 1995)

Facts

Somerset Savings Bank agreed to finance a 72-unit condominium project and Chicago Title issued a policy for Somerset's $9.5 million mortgage. After the title policy was issued, the city of Revere, Massachusetts refused to issue a permit for the project because of issues with existing zoning laws, including a railroad right of way through the property. Somerset was left with a $9.5 million mortgage on condominiums that would never be built. Somerset brought suit against Chicago Title for its failure to note the zoning issue. The trial court held that the zoning issue was not covered under the policy, the court of appeals reversed on one issue, and Somerset appealed.

Judicial Opinion

Lynch, Justice. The title insurance policy issued to the plaintiff, policy number 22-0468-02-000026, provides, in pertinent part:

> SUBJECT TO THE EXCLUSIONS FROM COVERAGE, THE EXCEPTIONS CONTAINED IN SCHEDULE B AND THE PROVISIONS OF THE CONDITIONS AND STIPULATIONS HEREOF, CHICAGO TITLE INSURANCE COMPANY . . . insures . . . against loss or damage . . . sustained or incurred by the insured by reason of:
>
> (1) Title to the estate or interest described in Schedule A being vested otherwise than as stated therein;

(2) Any defect in or lien or encumbrance on such title

(4) Unmarketability of such title. . . .

The policy contained an integration clause which provides:

This instrument together with all endorsements and other instruments, if any, attached hereto by the Company is the entire policy and contract between the insured and the Company.

Any claim of loss or damage, whether or not based on negligence, and which arises out of the status of the lien of the insured mortgage or of the title to the estate or interest covered hereby or any action asserting such claim, shall be restricted to the provisions and conditions and stipulations of this policy.

The exclusions from coverage provides in pertinent part as follows:

(1) (a) Governmental police power.

(b) Any law, ordinance or governmental regulation relating to environmental protection.

(c) Any law, ordinance or governmental regulation (including but not limited to building and zoning ordinances) restricting or regulating or prohibiting the occupancy, use or enjoyment of the land, or regulating the character, dimensions or location of any improvement now or hereafter erected on the land, or prohibiting a separation in ownership or a change in the dimensions or area of the land or any parcel of which the land is or what a part.

(d) The effect of any violation of the matters excluded under (a), (b) or (c) above, unless notice of a defect, lien or encumbrance resulting from a violation has been recorded at Date of Policy in those records in which under state statutes, deeds, mortgages, *lis pendens*, liens or other title encumbrances must be recorded in order to impart constructive notice to purchasers of the land for value and without knowledge; provided however, that without limitation, such records shall not be construed to include records in any of the offices of federal, state or local environmental protection, zoning, building, health or public safety authorities.

The judge began her analysis of the contract claims with the observation that, in general, building and zoning laws are not treated as encumbrances. She went on to rule: "Even assuming, however, that the restriction on use created by G.L. c. 40, § 54A is an encumbrance on the property or renders title unmarketable, there is no cover-

age under the policy because the exclusions clearly apply."

When the provisions of a policy are plainly and definitively expressed, the policy must be enforced in accordance with the terms. Absent ambiguous contractual language in the policy, custom and practice evidence cannot be used to vary the provisions of the policy. However, pertinent custom and usage are, by implication, incorporated into a policy and are admissible to aid in policy interpretation, not as tending to contradict or vary a contract, but on the theory that usage forms part of the contract.

It is well established that building or zoning laws are not encumbrances or defects affecting title to property. Such restrictions are concerned with the use of the land. There is a difference between economic lack of marketability, which concerns conditions that affect the use of land, and title marketability, which relates to defects affecting legally recognized rights and incidents of ownership. An individual can hold clear title to a parcel of land, although the same parcel is valueless or considered economically unmarketable because of some restriction or regulation on its use. A title insurance policy provides protection against defects in, or liens or encumbrances on, title. Such coverage affords no protection for governmentally imposed impediments on the use of the land or for impairments in the value of the land.

The insurance policy provided coverage for losses sustained as the result of a defect in or lien or encumbrance on the title to the property and for unmarketability of the title. Although they may have impaired the property's market value or caused a halt to construction on the property, the requirements of G.L. c. 40, § 54A, have no effect on the marketability of the title nor did they create a defect, lien, or encumbrance on the title. The existence of the statutory restriction, therefore, does not give rise to coverage under the policy.

The plaintiff also alleges that the defendant failed to examine, review, and analyze the title to the premises and to notify the plaintiff of any facts regarding title. We agree with the judge, as apparently did the appeals Court, that no such contractual obligation exists. The plaintiff did not request a report from the defendant regarding the status of title to the property. The defendant was not employed to examine the title, rather, the plaintiff purchased a policy to insure against existing defects and encumbrances on the title. The defendant has demonstrated that proof of a contract to examine and analyze the status of the title, an essential element to the plaintiff's claim for breach of contract is unlikely to be presented at trial.

The judge ruled that the defendant had no duty to disclose the prior use of the property as a railroad right-of-way of the applicability of G.L. c 40, § 54A, and further ruled that the defendant had not voluntarily assumed such a duty. Therefore, the judge granted summary judgment for the defendant on the plaintiff's negligence claims. The Appeals Court concluded that, whether the defendant had assumed an obligation, not cast on it by the terms of the policy, to disclose matters affecting the property that an examination of the registry would reveal is a matter for further development. We concluded that the granting of summary judgment was not appropriate on these claims because there is a factual dispute whether the defendant voluntarily assumed a duty to inform the plaintiff of these matters.

The plaintiff argues that the issuance of a policy places a duty on a title insurance company to search for, and to disclose to the insured, any reasonably discoverable information that would affect the insured's decision to proceed with the purchase. As a general rule, we decline to impose such a duty. A title insurance company's duty to the insured is governed by the terms of the policy. Its liability is limited to the policy, and it will not be liable for negligence in searching the records. Id. However, if the title insurance company agrees to conduct a search and to provide the insured with an abstract of title, it may expose itself to liability for negligence as a title searcher, in addition to any liability under the policy. A title insurance company thus may be found liable on a negligence claim if the act complained of was a direct result of duties voluntarily assumed by the insurer, in addition to the contract to insure title. The plaintiff met its burden in opposition to the allowance of summary judgment on this issue. It offered evidence that the defendant's advertising claimed knowledge of local laws and practices, and might fairly be interpreted as an assurance that all matters recorded at the registry which might influence the decision to buy the property would be called to the insured's attention. This evidence might warrant the finding that the defendant assumed a duty to notify the plaintiff.

We reject the defendant's argument that it cannot be liable for any loss or damage resulting from its negligence because of the language in the policy's integration clause, which limits liability to the provisions and conditions set forth in the policy. In most instances, an insurance contract is not a negotiated agreement, rather its conditions are predominantly dictated by the insurance company to the insured. In this context, we must look at whether the clause exculpating the defendant from loss arising from its own negligence is unfair or unconscionable.

This analysis requires a balancing of the freedom of contract against possible harm to the public resulting from allowing such exculpation. In recognition of the needs and expectations of the purchaser of the policy, his or her lack of bargaining power, and the public policy implications of allowing such a disclaimer of liability, we conclude that a claim based on a breach of duty to exercise due care in notifying an insured of matters discovered in a title search voluntarily assumed outside the policy is not barred by the integration clause.

Affirmed in part and reversed in part.

Case Questions

1. What "defect" does the mortgage company say existed in the property?
2. Is the policy clear on its exclusions?
3. What is the difference between title policy liability and contractual liability?
4. Is it possible that a title company might be held liable in this case? What is the court's decision, and what new theory does it advance for holding title companies liable despite exclusionary language?

UNIFORM LAWS AND PROPOSALS

The complications of deeds, title, and recording have produced several uniform acts. Two of them, the Uniform Simplification of Land Transfers Act and the Uniform Marketable Title Act, both drafted for use in 1990, have not yet been adopted in any states. The Uniform Recognition of Acknowledgments Act, which applies to both deeds and wills, has been adopted in 16 states.

CAUTIONS AND CONCLUSIONS

Transferring title to property requires a great deal of detailed work on the paperwork and on the background of the property itself. Parties involved in a tranfser of title by deed should check the following:

1. Does the grantor have the authority to tranfer the title to the property?
2. Does the grantor have full and complete title to the property?
3. Is the description for the property accurate?
4. Are there any boundary issues that are evident from a physical inspection of the property?
5. Do the public records reveal any title issues such as judgments or liens?
6. Are there restrictions on the use of the land such as zoning or covenants?
7. Can I obtain title insurance for the property?
8. What will the title insurance cover?
9. How does recording work in my state and is my title protected if I am first to record my deed?
10. What type of title am I getting and do I get any warranties with my title?
11. Is there a good chain of title? Do I need a title abstract?
12. Have I checked the rights of those occupying the property and are there any possible claims for title by adverse possession?
13. Have I proofed the deed for correct spelling and adequate descriptions of the property?
14. Have I met the formal requirements for signature?

The devil is in deeds and these questions should help the parties walk through those potential pitfalls in transferring title.

Key Terms

livery of seisin, 291
deed, 291
premises, 291
Uniform Partnership Act (UPA), 293
habendum clause, 298
acknowledgment clause, 298
delivery, 299
quitclaim deed, 300
warranty deed, 300
special warranty deed, 302
deed of bargain and sale, 303
judicial deed, 303

sheriff's deed, 303
adverse possession, 303
squatter's rights, 303
quiet title action, 308
inter vivos gift, 309
donee, 309
donor, 309
constructive delivery, 310
undue influence, 310
recording, 311
grantor/grantee index system, 312
tract index system, 312

pure race statute, 313
good faith purchaser, 314
bona fide purchaser (BFP), 314
notice statutes, 314
race/notice system, 314
Torrens system, 316
abstract of title, 316
caption (head), 316
abstractor's certificate, 316
lis pendens, 317
title insurance, 317
marketable title, 317

Chapter Problems

1. William Small purchased three lots located in the El Encanto subdivision in Tucson, Arizona, from the Mullins. Small had the lots reconfigured so that he could build a certain style and positioned home, but then changed his mind. The plat map still carried the original lot lines. Over the course of 12 years, three homes and two swimming pools along with patio home walls between each of the lots were added. Architects for the homes used the plat maps. The result was that the homes, pool, and walls encroached on the boundary lines of the other lots, according to the legal description Small had put on the deeds. Could the deeds be changed for the present owners to reflect their improvements and assumptions about the lot boundaries? *United Bank of Arizona v. Ashland Development Corp.,* 792 P.2d 776 (Az. 1990)

2. The following is an actual deed recorded on page 215 of volume 40, Cass County, Illinois, deed records.

I, J. Henry Shaw, the grantor, herein

   Who lives at Beardstown the county within,

For seven hundred dollars to me paid today

By Charles E. Wyman, do sell and convey

Lot two (2) in Block Forty (40), said county and town,

Where Illinois River flows placidly down,

And warrant the title forever and aye,

Waiving homestead and mansion to both a goodbye,

And pledging this deed is valid in law

I add here my signature, J. Henry Shaw

[Seal]   Dated July 2 1881

The acknowledgment on the deed is as follows:

I, Sylvester Emmons, who lives at Beardstown,

A Justice of Peace of fame and renown,

Of the county of Cass in Illinois state,

Do certify here that on the same date

One J. Henry Shaw to me did make known

That the deed above and name were his own,

And he stated he sealed and delivered the same

Voluntarily, freely, and never would claim

His homestead therein, but left all alone,

Turned his face to the street and his back to his home.

[Seal]   S. Emmons J.P.   Dated August 1, 1881

Is this a valid deed? What type of deed is it?

3. Under each of the three types of recording systems, who takes title?

- *Day 1:* O conveys to A (BFP).
- *Day 2:* A conveys to B (BFP).
  B records.
- *Day 3:* O conveys to C (BFP).
  C records.

4. Clarence and Lillian Ellison and Clifford and Mary Grace Bearden are adjoining landowners with a dispute regarding the location of the boundary line between their properties. A fence built by the Beardens has separated the two parcels of property for more than 40 years. The Ellisons have raised gardens, cut timber, grazed cattle, and otherwise used the property on their side of the fence for more than 38 years. An error in the location of the fence was discovered, but the Ellisons claimed title to the land up to the fence through adverse possession. The Beardens' son knocked down the southernmost portion of the fence, and the Ellisons filed suit. The trial court found the Ellisons held title to the disputed boundary property and ordered a survey to have the deed reformed. Is this a correct outcome? *Bearden v. Ellison,* 560 So.2d 1042 (Ala. 1990)

5. Prepare a deed on the basis of the following information. Be sure to attach to it any comments on missing information or information that is not necessary.

   a. *Land to be conveyed.*

   b. *Grantors.* Mr. and Mrs. Paul S. Smith living in a home on the pictured lot, 4141 Waverly Street, Phoenix, Arizona, 85003. They own the property as joint tenants. Mrs. Smith's name is Helen.

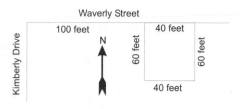

   c. *Grantees.* Mr. and Mrs. Samuel P. Polk, 3232 Holly Drive, Phoenix, Arizona 85204. They wish to own the property as joint tenants. Mrs. Polk's name is Janice.

   d. *Date of transaction.* September 12, 2000.

   e. *Amount Polks will pay to Smiths.* $152,500.00.

   f. A neighbor of the Smiths, Thomas Jones, is a notary public who will furnish his services for free. His commission expires September 15, 2004.

   g. The Smiths wish to warrant title only for the time they have held the property.

   h. The Smiths have lined up their neighbors, Brad Georges and Bill Daves, to witness the transaction.

   i. A school water pipeline runs through the back two feet of the property. There are no other easements, encumbrances, unpaid taxes, or liens on the property.

   j. The Polks are paying cash.

6. Determine who gets title to the property under each of the three types of jurisdictions in the following circumstances.

   Day 1: O conveys to A (BFP).

   Day 2: O conveys to B (not BFP).

   Day 3: O conveys to C (BFP).

   Day 4: B records.

   Day 5: A records.

7. Irene Franzen and Joseph and Shirley Cassarino are neighbors. As is often the case, the boundary line between their properties is described one way in their deeds but appears to be physically different. Indeed, part of the Cassarinos' garage is on Franzen's property, and the Cassarinos have used other parts of the area in dispute as a vegetable garden. They have also mowed the yard in the disputed area and planted trees and shrubs. They have so used the land since they moved into their home in 1964. Irene Franzen claims title to the strip of land through her deed. The Cassarinos counterclaim for the land on the grounds of adverse possession. Who holds title to the land strip? *Franzen v. Cassarino,* 552 N.Y.S.2d 789 (1990)

8. In 1968, Colonial Motel Properties, Inc., acquired title to a 7.746 acre tract of land next to land owned by Marathon Petroleum. Colonial decided to expand its motel business by appealing to trailer truck drivers. The southern portion of its acreage and .27 acres of Marathon's property were covered with dirt and gravel for use for parking by the drivers. Since 1970, trucks have parked on this lot. A sign that read as follows was posted:

> *Free Parking for Colonial Inn Motel Guests Only. All Others $20.00 per night. Violators impounded at owner's expense. All vehicles must register.*

The motel also employed a security guard for the lot to ensure that all vehicles were registered. The lot, the sign, and the security guard were all visible from Marathon's property.

In 1985, Marathon was approached by a buyer for its property and the .27 acre encroachment was discovered. Colonial claimed title through adverse possession. Is Colonial correct? *Marathon Petroleum Co. v. Colonial Motel Properties, Inc.,* 550 N.E.2d 778 (Ind. 1990)

9. William Bryant constructed an air strip on what he believed to be was his property. He used the airstrip for landing his plane, but he also permitted other pilots in the area to land there. The airstrip was used for 40 years and was located on land that was primarily used for timber and mining. When Bryant brought suit against the coal mining company that owned the land seeking to establish title to the airstrip by adverse possession, the coal company defended itself by noting that Bryant's use was not exclusive and not sufficiently open and notorious to qualify for a taking by adverse possession. Does Bryant have title by adverse possession? *Bryant v. Palmer Coaking Coal Co.,* 936 P.2d 1163 (Wash. App. 1997)

10. When Florence Bucalo Walsh's first husband, Frank Bucalo, died in 1986, she created a life estate interest in their property and gave the remainder to her son, Robert Bucalo. Sometime later Florence told Robert that she wanted to marry Jim Walsh. Robert disapproved of Walsh and refused to give his blessing to the marriage. Florence told Robert that if he didn't change his attitude that she would take him out of the will. Robert was intransigent and the new Mrs. Walsh not only changed her will, she brought suit to have the remainder interest she had conveyed to Robert set aside on the grounds of undue influence. What would Mrs. Walsh have to prove to establish undue influence? Could she do it if Robert knew nothing about the conveyance before his mother had completed it? *Walsh v. Bucalo,* 620 A.2d 21 (Pa. Super. 1993)

Internet Activities

1. Go to: **http://www.willhall.com/geninfopg4.html#tyitletakingtitle** for details on taking title to property in the state of California.

2. For an article on the Torrens system of land title registration, go to: **http://www.murdoch.edu.au/elaw/indices/subject/4.html**.

3. Search for a deed in the Louisa County Virginia Deed Search system at **http://trevilians.com/deedinde.htm**.

4. Visit the Texas state government Website for explanations of title insurance **http://tdi.state.tx.us/consumer/cbo58.html**.

HOME   FAQ   SITE TOUR   SEARCH/INDEX   E-MAIL

own a home

topics

hud news
audience groups
own a home
rental help
homeless
your community
business
contracts
consumer info
complaints
about hud
reading room
handbooks/forms
kids
let's talk
local info
fed one-stops

own a home
buyer's kit
homes for sale
buy a hud home
home improvements
refinancing

housing counseling
senior citizens
keep your home
hud refunds
selling your home

Homebuyer's Kit: Sure - buying a home is a big deal. But if you understand the process and know what to expect, it won't be overwhelming. Don't think you can afford a home? Read through our kit - you might be surprised to find out how easy it is for you to become a homeowner.

Homes for sale: See listings of HUD homes for sale, plus properties being sold by other federal agencies. One might be right for you!

Buy a hud home: When someone with a HUD insured mortgage can't meet the payments, the lender forecloses on the home; HUD pays the lender what is owed; and HUD takes ownership of the home. Then we sell it at market value as quickly as possible. A HUD home can be a very good deal - check it out!

Home improvements: Whether you want to fix a faucet or add a new addition to your home, you need to know the facts and the pitfalls of home improvements. Here are some sources that can help.

Refinancing: Sometimes, refinancing your mortgage can really save you money. You may be able to pay less interest, lower your monthly payment, or convert from a 30-year loan to a 15-year loan (and build your equity faster!). But be sure that refinancing is right for you.

Housing counseling: Contact one of the HUD-funded housing counseling agencies - they can help you sort through your housing options.

VISIT OUR PAGES FOR:

First Time Homebuyers
Senior Citizens
Veterans
Women
People With Disabilities
Farmworkers
Native Americans
Policy Analysts/
Researchers
Lenders
Real Estate Brokers
Appraisers
Empowerment Zones
PHAs/Tribes
Non Profits
Grantees
Community/Interfaith Groups
Elected Officials
Multifamily Industry
Homeless Assistance Providers
Fair Housing/Civil Rights
Black Colleges/ Universities
Small Businesses
International Partners
Health Care Facilities Providers

Chapter 14
The Purchase Contract

May 10, 1947. Received from Lucky Hertel $80.00 (eighty dollars) earnest money on lot and house number 960 Union Street. Price $5,000 (five thousand dollars) and balance of $4,920.00 to be paid when papers and title insurance are completed. It is understood this deal would be closed and house vacated on or before June the 10th. All the furniture except personal belongings included in this transaction.

It would be interesting to discover whether Lucky Hertel had an enforceable contract for the purchase of real property. This chapter discusses the formation of contracts for the sale of real estate, the required and suggested content of such contracts, and the remedies for nonperformance of valid real estate contracts.

COMMON LAW PRINCIPLES OF FORMATION AS APPLIED TO REAL ESTATE CONTRACTS

Although contracts for the purchase and sale of real estate have certain specific requirements, they are still subject to the general requirements for formation of all contracts. A contract does not exist until there has been an offer, acceptance, and consideration; and these prerequisites do not change because real estate is involved.

Offer

The **offer** is the first step in the real estate transaction. Generally, the offer is made by the buyer. Listing agreements, advertisements, auction flyers, and notices of public sales are treated as invitations for offers. These marketing tools are employed to make the buyer aware of the property offering and to catch the buyer's attention.

ELEMENTS

To be valid, an offer must indicate a present intent to contract, it must be certain and definite in its terms, and it must be communicated to the offeree (the party receiving the offer). Most offers for real estate purchase are made when the buyer actually fills out, signs, and presents to the seller a form or contract of purchase. The language in such forms contains definite evidence of intent to contract: "_____ as seller, agrees to sell to _____ as buyer, and buyer agrees to purchase from seller the following described property. . . . "

The intent to contract is obvious when form contracts are used, but often contracts are negotiated and entered into through very informal procedures. For example, the buyer's offer may come in the form of a letter or memorandum, and so long as the language used evidences present intent to contract, a valid offer exists. However, language such as, "I'm considering buying," "Would you consider selling?" or "What would your asking price be?" is not indicative of present intent to contract and could only be construed as inquiries or invitations for offers.

Likewise, memoranda or correspondence from seller to buyer must also indicate present intent to contract to be considered offers. Language such as "I might sell," "I'd consider selling," "I'm thinking of offering," or "In December, I'll offer" is too conditional and not indicative of a present desire to enter into a binding sales contract.

Not only must the offer have the proper intent language in order to become the basis of the contract, it must also contain sufficient information and details: the identity of the parties, the description of the property, the price, and the terms (to be discussed in detail). This criterion is easily satisfied when a form purchase contract is used because the form lists all required information. If one of the basic requirements for formation is missing, then the offer will not be treated as an offer but as an invitation for an offer or simply as a step in the negotiation process. A contract may not be formed on the basis of indefinite terms. A complete sales contract can be seen at the text Web site for this chapter.

The final element for a valid offer is that it must be communicated to the offeree. In usual cases, this is accomplished by delivering the purchase contract form with the buyer's signature to the seller or an agent of the seller. Delivery of the offer to the seller's broker or salesperson, as the seller's agent(s), is sufficient communication.

http://

See a sample real estate contract at: **http://www.aami.net/html/aami_sales_contract.htm**.

Consider 14.1

Determine if the following language from a letter by Thompson to Hale (the lot owner) meets the requirements for a valid offer:

> *I am very much interested in your lot, zoned C-2, which is located at the south-eastern corner of Gilbert and Southern Roads. If the price is $475,000 or less, I can pay cash. I will need it for construction by 6/1/01.*

> */s/ Walter Thompson*

TERMINATION

Since an offer is but one part of the contract formation process, it is not legally binding and may be revoked or withdrawn at any time prior to acceptance by the offeree. When an offer is voluntarily withdrawn prior to acceptance, the offeror has no liability for any damages others may have incurred in relying on the offer.

It is possible to limit an offer so that it terminates upon the expiration of its time of validity. For example, a valid offer may include as one of its terms, "This offer good only until noon on April 5, 2001." This offer would automatically terminate at that time and date unless there is acceptance by the offeree prior to that time. By law, even offers without specific time limits terminate after the passage of a reasonable amount of time, although it is probably best for the offerors to withdraw or revoke any long-outstanding offers. The determination of reasonable time varies according to the nature and location of the property and the terms of the offer.

The death of either an offeror or the offeree serves to terminate the offer (with an exception noted in the next section: Options). At the moment of death, the offer is automatically terminated or withdrawn.

Rejection of the offer by the offeree terminates the original offer. A rejection is generally in the form of a negative response, such as, "No, I'm not interested." But in real estate transactions, a rejection may be given indirectly. If an offeree makes the acceptance of an offer conditional on certain additional terms and requirements, the acceptance is in reality both a rejection of the original offer and a **counteroffer,** placing the original offeree in an offeror position. The following sequence of excerpts from correspondence illustrates this point.

a. Offeror: *"I will buy Blackacre (legal description) from you for $10,000 cash, to close 6/1/01."*
b. Offeree (counteroffer): *"I accept your offer, but must have cash in hand by 5/1/01."*
c. Offeree (original offeror): *"That is agreeable."*

When the offeree conditioned acceptance on a change in closing date (b), the acceptance was in reality a counteroffer that the original offeror, now an offeree, was free to accept or reject.

In practice, when brokers and salespersons run between buyer and seller with changes in terms and addenda to the purchase contract, they are engaging in a series of events where the parties are constantly changing roles as offerors and offerees. It is important to note that the offeree must accept all of the offeror's terms without change or qualification for the contract to exist. Any material change results in a rejection and a counteroffer, which must be accepted by the other party.

Consider 14.2

Terry and Marianne Jennings listed their home for sale with Stapley Realty. When the listing agent, Brad Reed, came to the home, he asked if there was anything that was attached to the house that would not be sold with the house.

Mr. Jennings pointed to an original Hunter ceiling fan and said it would not stay with the house since he had installed it himself. Reed told the Jenningses that it would be best to remove the fan and replace it with another lighting fixture or fan. They agreed and planned to do the replacement on Saturday. On Friday afternoon, the "For Sale" sign and the lock-box for real estate agent access went on their property. On Saturday morning another agent taking a couple to another home noticed the Jennings's house, which had not yet appeared in the multiple listing. He took the couple through it and that night they made an offer on it. The Jenningses accepted all the terms because they had only 90 days to sell their home and move to another one. Mr. Jennings noted above his signature, "Ceiling fan in family room is not included." The buyers then refused to go through with the sale. The Jenningses wish to know if they have any rights. Is there a contract?

14.2, *continued*

Options

REQUIREMENTS

Often a buyer is unsure about purchasing property and wants time for investigation. However, since an offer may be revoked by the offeror any time prior to acceptance, the opportunity to purchase may not be available when the eventual decision is made. The buyer requires some type of guarantee that the offer will remain open for a stated period of time. However, simply having the seller include a time provision in the offer ("This offer to remain open until June 15, 2001") is insufficient because the seller is still able to revoke the offer provided there is proper notice to the offeree.

However, if the buyer obtains an option from the seller, this problem is alleviated. An **option** is a contract for time whereby the seller agrees to hold an offer open for a specified period in exchange for consideration (payment). Either a buyer or seller can turn an offer into an option with proper consideration from the offeree.

The important aspect of the option, which distinguishes it from the ordinary offer, is that the offeror is given consideration to keep the offer open. If consideration is not given, the offeror is free to revoke the offer at any time. However, if an offeror has been paid for an option on property and sells the property to another party, the offeror is in breach of contract and will be required to pay damages to the option holder. The amount of consideration is not important so long as it is actually paid. The following case deals with the issue of consideration in options.

Board of Control of Eastern Michigan University v. Burgess

206 N.W.2d 256 (Mich. 1973)

Facts

On February 15, 1966, Burgess (defendant/appellant) signed a document that provided Eastern Michigan University (EMU/plaintiff/appellee) a 60-day option for the purchase of Burgess's home. The document, drafted by an agent of Burgess, indicated receipt of "one and no/100 Dollar ($1.00) and other valuable consideration."

The dollar was never paid. On April 14, 1966, EMU notified Burgess of its acceptance, but Burgess refused to close and deliver title. EMU brought suit for delivery of the property or specific performance. The trial court found for EMU, and Burgess appealed.

Judicial Opinion

Burns, Judge. Options for the purchase of land, if based on valid consideration, are contracts which may be specifically enforced. Conversely, that which purports to be an option, but which is not based on valid consideration, is not a contract and will not be enforced. In the instant case defendant received no consideration for the purported option of February 15, 1966.

A written acknowledgment of receipt of consideration merely creates a rebuttable presumption that consideration has, in fact, passed. Neither the parol evidence rule nor the doctrine of estoppel bars the presentation of evidence to contradict any such acknowledgment.

It is our opinion that the document signed by Burgess on February 15, 1966, is not an enforceable option, and that Burgess is not barred from so asserting. In the instant case Burgess claims that she never received any of the consideration promised here.

That which purports to be an option for the purchase of land, but which is not based on valid consideration, is a simple offer to sell the same land. An option is a contract collateral to an offer to sell whereby the offer is made irrevocable for a specified period. Ordinarily, an offer is revocable at the will of the offeror. Accordingly, a failure of consideration affects only the collateral contract to keep the offer open, not the underlying offer.

A simple offer may be revoked for any reason or for no reason by the offeror at any time prior to its acceptance by the offeree. Thus, the question in this case becomes, "Did defendant effectively revoke her offer to sell before plaintiff accepted that offer?"

Defendant testified that within hours of signing the purported option she telephoned plaintiff's agent and informed him that she would not abide by the option unless the purchase price was increased. Defendant also testified that when plaintiff's agent delivered to her on April 14, 1966, plaintiff's notice of its intention to exercise the purported option, she told him that "the option was off."

Plaintiff's agent testified that defendant did not communicate to him any dissatisfaction until sometime in July 1966.

If defendant is telling the truth, she effectively revoked her offer several weeks before plaintiff accepted that offer, and no contract of sale was created. If plaintiff's agent is telling the truth, defendant's offer was still open when plaintiff accepted that offer, and an enforceable contract was created. The trial judge thought it unnecessary to resolve this particular dispute. In light of our holding the dispute must be resolved.

An appellate court cannot assess the credibility of witnesses. We have neither seen nor heard them testify.

Accordingly, we remand this case to the trial court for additional findings of fact based on the record already before the court.

Reversed and remanded.

Case Questions

1. How long was the option?
2. What property was involved?
3. How much was the consideration?
4. Was the consideration paid?
5. Was there a valid option?
6. What issue remains to be determined?

TERMINATION

Another distinguishing feature about the option provision is that, unlike an ordinary offer, it does not terminate with the death of the offeror or the option holder. In other words, the estate of an option holder could elect to exercise the option for the estate. Likewise, the estate of the offeror is required to honor the option if the option holder decides to exercise the right after the death of the offeror.

Another issue in options is what happens when the option holder rejects the option prior to the time it is scheduled to terminate. For example, A gives B an option on some property to run from February 1, 2001, to March 2, 2001, and B pays A $100 for the option. On February 16, 2001, B notifies A of rejection of the offer. The following questions arise: (1) Must A still hold the offer open until March 2, 2001? (2) Is B entitled to a refund of a portion of the option payment? (3) Must A refund a portion of the option payment in order to sell the property prior to March 2, 2001?

The jurisdictions are split on the answers to the questions raised by the option holder's rejection prior to expiration of the option term. One view is that rejection is rejection, that is, an option is an offer that terminates once rejected by the option holder (offeree). The majority view is that a rejection before the option term has no effect on the option, that is, that the option continues for the specified period unless the offeror has materially changed position. Under this view, if the parties agreed to a partial refund and signed a mutual release terminating the option, then the offeror would be free to sell the property to another. Under the first view, release and refund would not be required for the offeror to be free to transfer the property.

In light of the split among the courts on how options are to be handled in the event of rejection prior to their expiration, it is probably best for the parties to put a clause in their option agreement dealing with the problem of early rejection, the offeror's rights in such circumstances, and the option holder's right of refund. Clarifying the result by agreement may prevent a tenuous legal position for the offeror and may be less costly for an offeree who is able to make an early purchase decision.

Consider 14.3

On February 7, 2001, A entered into negotiations with B for the purchase of B's farm. After consulting with an attorney and having the property appraised, B agreed to sell for $150,000. A and B agreed in writing that in exchange for $300 then received from A, B would hold the offer open for nine months. After six months, A wrote B that he was no longer interested in buying the farm. Several days later, A received notice from B that he was negotiating with C to sell the farm for $250,000. A immediately called B, who suggested that if A would agree to pay $175,000 and conclude the deal within 10 days, then B would still be willing to sell to A. A protested that B was driving a hard bargain, but finally agreed by telegram that evening to buy the farm for $175,000 within 10 days. A purchased the farm as agreed and then sought to recover $25,000 from B or alternatively to rescind the purchase (in other words, get out of the contract). What result and why?

The difficulty encountered with the early rejection of options can be eliminated by careful drafting of agreements. The items in the following checklist should be included when negotiating and drafting option agreements:

- Legal description of the property
- Proper names of the parties
- Signatures of the parties
- Length of the option
- Beginning and ending dates of the option period
- Amount of consideration to be paid
- Destiny of the consideration if
  a. the option is exercised: Can it be a down payment?
  b. the option expires without acceptance: Does the offeror retain the money?
  c. the option holder rejects prior to expiration: Will there be a prorated refund?
  d. the property is destroyed during the option period
  e. one of the parties dies
- Recording of the option in the public records, and its removal if not exercised
- Procedures and notifications required for exercise of the option
- All terms or provisions of the sales contract:
  a. marketable title (type of deed, insurance, and so on)
  b. rights of lessees
  c. presence of mortgages and new liens during the option period
- Assignability of the option

Options should not be confused with earnest money deposits accompanying offers by buyers for the purchase of real estate. **Earnest money** is appropriately named because it is customarily required to show the offeror's good faith and is actually part of the payment for the purchase price. Options generally come from sellers and are promises to hold offers open for periods of time. Payment for an option is not necessarily a payment of part of the purchase price. Furthermore, consideration is required for an option to be valid, whereas earnest money is not required for a valid contract to purchase (although it may be good business practice).

Acceptance

Acceptance is the conduct on the part of the offeree that indicates a willingness to assent to the terms of the offer. Acceptance is the second part of the so-called meeting-of-the-minds requirement for formation of a contract. Like the offer, acceptance has certain requirements: (1) it must be by the party with the power of acceptance; (2) it must be absolute, unequivocal, and unconditional; and (3) it must be communicated to the offeror.

POWER OF ACCEPTANCE

The only party with the power of acceptance is the party to whom the offer is made. Offers are not transferable. Options are an exception to this rule. Options, like all nonpersonal contracts, are transferable. An assignment of an option right entitles the assignee to exercise the rights afforded by the option.

ABSOLUTE, UNEQUIVOCAL, AND UNCONDITIONAL ACCEPTANCE

This element of acceptance was already briefly explained in the section about the termination of offers. The offeree must accept the offer on its terms and must not change them or condition acceptance upon some new or different terms. If the offeree does make any changes in the terms, then there is no acceptance; rather, there is a counteroffer that the original offeror (now offeree) is free to accept or reject.

Practical Tip

The fax machine is a convenience used frequently to expedite offers, co-offers, and other contractual opportunities. However, faxes are not generally legally sufficient evidence for the purpose of formalizing an agreement. Fax signatures fade and can be forged. If you use a fax for communication, be certain to follow up with the formal documents. Be sure to allow time in your offers for such required responses.

Practical Tip

Although the federal government now recognizes e-mail as valid proof of acceptance (signature), parties should always follow up on such acceptances to be sure that the party accepting is really the party sending the e-mail.

COMMUNICATION OF ACCEPTANCE TO OFFEROR

The signature on the purchase contract alone is insufficient acceptance: A copy of that agreement must be delivered to the offeror or the offeror's agent for a valid contract to exist.

Many times an offer will dictate the means of acceptance. It may require acceptance to be by mail or personal delivery, or to be given within a certain period of time. The offeree must comply with these requirements for the acceptance to be valid; otherwise, noncompliance with the terms is a counteroffer.

The following case deals with an issue of compliance with an offer's terms as well as the timing rules for an acceptance.

Gilmore v. Lujan

947 F.2d 1409 (9th Cir. 1991)

Facts

Reed Gilmore (plaintiff/appellant) filed an oil and gas application for Parcel NV-148 in June 1987 with the Bureau of Land Management (BLM). His application was selected in a computerized random drawing. BLM notified Gilmore by an August 26 letter sent certified mail that included the following language:

> Enclosed is the original and two copies of Form No. 3100-11, "Offer to Lease and Lease for Oil and Gas" for your execution. The applicant (or the applicant's attorney-in-fact, as provided by 43 C.F.R. [§] 3112.6-1(a) and (b) [(1986)]), must manually sign and date each copy on the reverse side of the form.
>
> All copies of the lease form must be properly executed and filed in this office within thirty (30) days from your receipt of this decision, which constitutes a compliance period. Failure to do so will result in the rejection of your offer without further notice.

Gilmore received the letter on August 29, 1987. He signed the copies and sent them certified mail from his office in Kimball, Nebraska, on September 21, 1987, with a return receipt requested. On the morning of September 28, 1987, Gilmore's secretary, Debra Bohac, noticed that she had not yet received the return receipt card. September 28 was the 30-day deadline.

Bohac called the BLM and spoke with Joan Woodin to see if the forms had been received. While there was subsequent disagreement about the full content of the conversation, Woodin and Bohac agreed that Woodin told her the forms had not been received.

Bohac then tried to book a flight for Gilmore to Reno, but there were no flights available that would get Gilmore there before the BLM office closed. Bohac then called the BLM back and spoke with Bernita Dawson, a Land Law Examiner in the BLM. Bohac offered to telefax (fax) the lease forms and maintains Dawson agreed to take the faxes as acceptance. Dawson denies making such a statement.

Gilmore then sent a telecopy to Robert McCarthy, a Reno attorney, who delivered it to the BLM at 11:15 A.M. on September 28. The mailed originals were received in the BLM office the next day, September 29. BLM informed Gilmore on September 29 that his offer was rejected for failure to comply with the terms. The decision was affirmed by the overall agency and Gilmore filed suit in federal district court. The district court dismissed the case, and Gilmore appealed.

Judicial Opinion

Nelson, Circuit Judge. For what would seem a minor detail to the uninitiated, there is an abundance of administrative decisions involving the requirement of a holographic signature on lease applications. Of particular significance to this case is *W.H. Gilmore,* 41 IBLA 25 (1979) (no apparent relation to appellant here) published prior to the regulations in effect in this case. W.H. Gilmore, who was the second priority applicant, protested the award of the lease to the first applicant who had used a rubber-stamped signature in his filing. The Board refused Gilmore's petition because the only pertinent regulation in effect at that time, 43 CFR 3102.6-1, (1979) coupled with a prior Board decision, clearly allowed rubber-stamped signatures. The Board admitted administrative headaches would probably result from its decision but stated:

> We fully recognize that our holding in the instant case exposes the Department to another method by which the reasonable efforts of the Department to insure fair play and compliance with the law can be made more difficult, and we deplore the proclivity of some leasing services to exploit every conceivable loophole in the letter of the regulations without any discernible regard for their spirit and intent.

Nevertheless, the Board was compelled to allow the rubber-stamped signature. The regulation itself was ambiguous but *Mary I. Arala,* 4 IBLA 201, 78 I.D. 397 (1971) (*Arala I*) had earlier held that such ambiguity must be construed in favor of the applicant. The *W.H. Gilmore* Board commented further that the BLM had not only the right, but the duty, to inquire into individual cases where questions arose regarding the legitimacy of the lease application.

As the result of *W.H. Gilmore,* the BLM promptly amended the regulations. In June 1980, the BLM added 43 CFR 3102.4 which read in part, "[a]ll applications [and] the original offers . . . shall be holographically signed in ink by the potential lessee. . . . Machine or rubber stamped signatures shall not be used."

The BLM regulation was validly promulgated following notice and comment. It gave fair notice to all applicants that failure to comply would result in denial of their applications. Such is the case here. The telefaxed application submitted by appellant was not holographic, and it was created by a machine—both violations of the plain language of the regulation. It was within the discretion of the Secretary not to depart from the regulation in this case.

While in this instance, denial produces a harsh result, a telefaxed signature is a machine produced signature. It is the exact situation the amended regulations sought to address.

Because appellant had ample notice that only a holographic signature would suffice, his estoppel argument fails as well. Appellant has alleged only that BLM did not tell him that it planned to deny his non-conforming application. For BLM to be estopped from enforcing its own regulations, however, appellant must demonstrate affirmative misconduct on the part of the government which goes beyond a mere failure to inform or assist. Gilmore has made no such showing here.

The decision we reach here is compelled by the narrow scope of the court's review of agency decisions. Obviously the equities favor Gilmore, as he is guilty of no omission but use of the United States mails. Eight days for delivery of mail from Nebraska to Nevada far exceeds the time it should take. Indeed, the Pony Express could have covered the distance with time to spare.

Justice Holmes observed that citizens dealing with their government must turn square corners. *Louisiana Railway Co. v. United States,* 254 U.S. 141, 143, 41 S.Ct. 55, 56, 65 L.Ed. 188 (1920). Gilmore turned all but the last millimeter, but that millimeter, whose traverse is jealously guarded by the BLM, was his undoing. Relief to Gilmore in this narrow case would expose BLM to no fraud or risk of fraud, as his bona fides are beyond question. If Gilmore and those other few luckless applicants whose documents are stored rather than delivered by the Postal Service are to get any relief, it must come at the hands of the BLM. As shown by this case, those hands are more iron than velvet. We can only suggest to BLM that the body politic would not be put at risk by the granting of relief in these narrow and rare situations.

Affirmed.

Case Questions

1. What is the subject matter of the contract?
2. Give a list of the chronology of events through September 29.
3. Does the court find a facsimile signature is sufficient?
4. Who will get the property?
5. Does the court believe the result is harsh? Does the court believe the result is a necessary part of government regulations or transactions?

Practical Tip

Deal with one party at a time. Multiple offers create confusion and liability. Make sure there is only one outstanding valid offer at a time. Don't extend another offer until an outstanding offer is revoked.

PROBLEM OF MULTIPLE OFFERS
Because acceptance is effective upon communication to the offeror, an offeror who has made more than one offer may find two acceptances being communicated before one or both of the offers can be revoked. It is a major legal risk for an offeror to have more than one offer outstanding. Consider the following sequence of events as an example.

Day 1: Buyer A submits an offer to seller.
Day 2: Seller counteroffers to buyer A. Buyer B submits an offer to seller.
Day 3: Seller counteroffers to buyer B. Buyer A accepts. Before seller can revoke, buyer B accepts.

The seller in the example has formed two valid contracts and would have to convey the property to one buyer and pay damages for breach to the other buyer.

Consider 14.4

Cynthia has listed her home with We Sell 'Em Realty, Incorporated. Buyer A conveys a written offer of $183,000 to Cynthia on March 1, 2001. Buyer B conveys an offer of $184,000 to Cynthia on March 2, 2001. On March 2, 2001, Cynthia issues counteroffers of $185,000 to both A and B. On the counteroffers, Cynthia adds the following: "This offer good until March 4, 2001, 6 P.M."

Suppose Buyer A accepts on March 3, 2001 (written forms signed) and communicates the acceptance to Cynthia at 7 P.M. that day. Cynthia then contacts Buyer B and says, "I revoke the counteroffer." What is the result?

a. Suppose that before Cynthia contacts B, B contacts Cynthia and accepts at 2:15 P.M. (written forms signed). What would be the result?

b. Suppose that B paid Cynthia $50 to hold the offer open until March 4, 2001, 6 P.M. What would be the result?

c. Suppose same facts as part b except that B calls Cynthia at 1 P.M., March 3, 2001, and states, "I reject," whereupon Cynthia receives A's acceptance. What would be the result?

14.4, *continued*

Consideration

The third and final requirement for formation of a valid contract is consideration. **Consideration** is something of value given up by each party to the contract. In most cases involving a sale of real property, consideration is easily established: The seller gives up title to the property; and the buyer gives up money, assumes a mortgage, or both in order to pay for that property.

Consideration need not be money. As noted, the buyer's promise to take over a loan is sufficient consideration. The traditional earnest money deposit received from buyers in a real estate transaction is a form of consideration but is not required for the contract to be valid and binding. Provided that both parties have promised to give something up in the transaction, those promises constitute sufficient consideration. However, earnest money does demonstrate sincerity and good faith on the part of the buyer and may be used as a source of funds for damages in the event of a problem.

The amount of consideration is not of legal concern to the courts, so long as there is consideration and it passes from one party to the other. Therefore, a promise to pay $5,000 for property worth $20,000 is valid consideration provided that each party voluntarily agrees to the terms.

The following case deals with the sufficiency of consideration in a real estate purchase agreement.

Trengen v. Mongeon

206 N.W.2d 284 (N.D. 1973)

Facts

On May 9, 1967, Louis and Margaret Mongeon executed a warranty deed conveying approximately 960 acres of land to their son Ernest and his wife, Pearl (defendant/appellee). The deed contained an acknowledgment of the receipt of $38,400 as consideration for the conveyance. At the same time, the parties entered into an agreement whereby Earnest and Pearl agreed to pay to Louis and Margaret the sum of $1,800 annually for as long as both or the survivor of them shall live. At the time of the agreement, Louis was 87 and Margaret was 83. Ernest's sister, Elaine Trengen (plaintiff/appellant, as guardian for her parents), brought suit seeking to set the deed aside on the grounds of lack of consideration. The trial court found for Ernest and Pearl, and Elaine appealed.

Judicial Opinion

Teigen, Judge. In the present case the consideration is of an indeterminable value. Monetarily, payment of the sum of $1,800 was made in the fall of 1967, and that sum will continue to be payable on or before November 1 of every year for as long as both or the survivor of the plaintiffs shall live. Payments received by the plaintiffs to the present time total $10,800.

. . . Since adequacy of consideration is not necessary to sustain a deed, and any valuable consideration, however small, is sufficient, the consideration need not equal the value of the property conveyed, especially where no creditor's rights are affected. Indeed, the merely nominal consideration of one dollar, which is frequently recited in deeds, evidences a sufficient consideration. So, where, as compared with the actual value of the property or interest received, the consideration is adequate, the deed will stand, whether such consideration be merely a valuable one without any monetary payment or a valuable one coupled with pecuniary advances. Adequacy of monetary consideration is not an important element in a conveyance which has for its principal purpose the conferring of a gift or endowment rather than financial gain. The adequacy of consideration is not to be viewed with hindsight, but it should rather be considered from the viewpoint of the parties at the time the deed was executed. The ordinary standard for testing the adequacy of consideration to support a transfer of property is not applicable to a deed conveying realty on condition that the grantee care for the grantor during the remainder of the grantor's life because of the uncertainty of life involved in such agreements. In considering the adequacy of consideration of a promise to care for and support a grantor for the remainder of his life in exchange for a conveyance of land, conditions existing at the time the contract is made are controlling, and subsequent events, such as the early death of the person to be cared for cannot be used to determine the adequacy of the consideration.

The trial court also found that the plaintiff's love and affection for their son Ernest was both a motivating factor and part of the consideration for the transaction.

Natural love and affection has always been held to be sufficient consideration for a deed where the relationship of the parties is such as to justify the presumption that love and affection exists.

The love and affection the plaintiffs (parents) felt toward Ernest is evidenced by the fact that, as stated in the agreement, the land in question had been devised to Ernest by the wills of both Louis and Margaret, and nine days after the land was conveyed to Ernest and the defendant (Pearl), Louis and Margaret executed new wills, each of which contained this provision:

> I have purposely omitted my son, Ernest Mongeon, as a devisee or legatee under this Will, for the reason that my [wife, Margaret Mongeon] [husband, Louis Mongeon] and I have made disposition of substantial farmlands to him during our lifetime for a fair consideration . . . [emphasis added].

We conclude that, in the absence of a finding of fraud or undue influence, the evidence is sufficient to support a finding that there was adequate consideration to uphold the conveyance of the land from the plaintiffs to Ernest and the defendant.

Affirmed.

Case Questions

1. What was the relationship between Louis and Margaret and Ernest and Pearl?
2. How much land was conveyed?
3. What was the total price?
4. How was the price to be paid?
5. How old were Louis and Margaret at the time of the conveyance?
6. Was there consideration?

SPECIFIC REQUIREMENTS FOR REAL ESTATE CONTRACTS

In addition to meeting the common law requirements just discussed, parties desiring to execute a valid real estate purchase contract must also meet certain specific requirements that apply to real estate contracts in particular. These requirements are: (1) that the contract be in writing, (2) that the signatures of the parties appear on the contract, and (3) that the description of the property be included and adequate.

Writing Requirements

As discussed in Chapter 13, contracts and deeds relating to the transfer of property must be in writing under what is termed the Statute of Frauds. Oral agreements for the transfer of property are unenforceable. Every state has some provision in its Statute of Frauds governing real estate contracts and the need for them to be in writing.

The writing need not be a formal contract: A contract and its terms may be pieced together from informal writings so long as all the requirements for formation are met and the necessary elements are present. The use of e-mail for contract formation is also possible. However, the party claiming a valid contract using e-mail proof will need to establish that the communications forming the contract were actually sent by the party they seek to hold to that contract.

> What ethical issues are involved when there is an oral agreement that requires a writing to be enforceable at law? While such agreements are not legally binding, should they be morally binding? What ethical obligation exists to continue performance under an oral agreement?

Ethical Issue

One of the exceptions to the writing requirements for land contracts under the Statute of Frauds is the doctrine of part performance. Under this doctrine, a party may be entitled to enforce an oral agreement for the sale of property if certain conduct can be established. Under Section 197 of the *Restatement of Contracts,* the party seeking to invoke the protection of the doctrine of part performance must establish one of the following:

1. That valuable improvements have been made to the property; or
2. That there has been full or partial payment of the purchase price and that the paying party has possession of the property.

The reasoning behind this exception is that establishing that either criterion has occurred provides some tangible physical evidence that an agreement exists. In other words, if a contract did not exist, why would the improvements have been made, or why was payment accepted and a party permitted to possess the property? While some states do not recognize the doctrine of part performance at all, some states recognize variations. For example, some states require possession only while other states require payment, or improvements, or both.

Hancock Construction maintained that it had an oral agreement to purchase property from Kempton & Snedigar Dairy. On the basis of the oral contract, Hancock had engineering studies done on the property and arranged to obtain a loan for $292,830. Kempton & Snedigar refused to go through with the contract, alleging a defense of the Statute of Frauds. Hancock brought suit for specific performance relying on the doctrine of part performance. What was the result?

Consider 14.5

Marriott Corporation entered into a real estate purchase contract with Creyts Complex, Inc., for the purchase of some land located in Oak Creek, Wisconsin. Marriott wished to construct a Courtyard Hotel on the site. Their agreement was contingent upon Creyts Complex being able to purchase a parcel contiguous to the land it owned, called the Moss-Glowacki parcel (named for its two owners). Marriott wanted the full parcel of both the Creyts Complex tract and that of Moss-Glowacki. The agreement provided that time was of the essence and closing was to occur within 60 days. Marriott extended the agreement twice. Problems in securing title to the Moss-Glowacki parcel arose when the City of Oak Creek stepped in and demanded certain accommodations in exchange for its approval of Marriott's proposed use. The efforts to buy the property continued along with negotiations with the city for a year after the expiration date of the contract. The last written agreement on the closing date for the sale put that date as October 3, 1988. In September 1989, Marriott refused to renegotiate its contract terms in order to permit the Moss-Glowacki acquisition as well as the city's approval. Creyts Complex alleges Marriott breached its contract. Marriott claims its contract

Consider 14.6

14.6, *continued* expired on October 3, 1988, and that there was no writing indicating an extension of the agreement. Must an extension for a land sale contract be in writing? *Creyts Complex, Inc. v. Marriott Corporation,* 98 F.3d 321 (7th Cir. 1996)

Signature of Parties

One requirement of a written contract is that the signatures of the parties must appear. If several writings are used to satisfy the contract requirement, the signatures of the parties must be found somewhere in each of those writings.

Perhaps the most important aspect of obtaining signatures for a contract is to make sure that all signatures necessary to bind the party appear. In the case of joint owners, both signatures are necessary, and in many states the signatures of both husband and wife are required.

In the case of business organizations such as partnerships and corporations, the parties signing on their behalf must have the authority to transfer property and must indicate the capacity in which they are signing. For example, a corporate officer signing for the corporation should have the following signature line:

ABC Company, Inc.

by _____

                                        Steven Doe, President

Attest _____

                                        John Doe, Secretary

Adequate Description of Property

To satisfy the Statute of Frauds, the property to be conveyed must be identified. Although in most states including the legal description is not required for the purchase contract, it is perhaps the best way to reasonably identify the property and avoid confusion. If the description used does not clearly indicate what land is being conveyed, then the writing will not satisfy the Statute of Frauds, and the contract will be unenforceable. (Methods of description are found in Chapter 6 and more details on property identification are found in this chapter at p. 339.)

http://

For information on home inspection, visit **http:// www.freddiemac.com/ sell/consumerkit/english/ index.html**.

TERMS OF PURCHASE CONTRACTS

In addition to satisfying the minimum requirements for contract formation, buyers and sellers must also carefully set forth the details and terms of the sale. Although the Statute of Frauds permits the enforcement of fairly simple agreements, the desires of the parties may demand more detail.

A complete contract begins with a careful review and inspection of the property. Figure 14.1 is a checklist for buyers to complete before purchasing any property.

Many parties elect to sign a binder followed by a formal purchase contract. Such binders can be hazardous for two reasons: On one hand, it may be so loosely drafted that the parties really have no protections and no locked-in price or terms. On the other hand, it may be drafted carefully enough to legally bind the parties without containing all the terms desired, and the parties may be bound by a general agreement that does not reflect their understanding. The parties should have

FIGURE 14.1   *Checklist for Negotiation Real Estate Contracts*

1. Determine exact boundaries of buildings, driveways, and fences.

2. Determine easements and underground utilities.

3. Determine zoning laws and other governmental regulations applicable to property.

4. Determine future or present uses of surrounding property.

5. Determine quality of available utilities and fire protection.

6. Determine rights-of-way or easements if necessary for use of property.

7. Determine locations of schools, public transportation, churches, and shipping centers.

8. Determine physical condition of building: termites, plumbing, electric, and water in basement.

9. Determine traffic conditions on street and surrounding streets.

10. Determine possible changes in traffic and street structure (such as a proposed freeway).

11. Determine possible nuisances: factories, aircraft, playgrounds, smoke, fumes, and noise.

12. Determine title: judgments and assessments.

13. Determine status of inhabitants (if any).

14. Determine soil suitability if intention is to build.

15. Determine if seller is married or was previously married.

16. Determine utility costs.

17. Determine reputation of builder if new development, verify warranties, approval, conformity with Interstate Land Sales Full Disclosure Act (ILSFDA), bonding, and licensing of builder.

18. Determine if any warranty protection is available.

19. Determine whether any toxic wastes exist or have existed on the property and whether any environmental agencies have actions pending.

20. Determine whether the property is located in a natural hazard area: faults, floodplains, and/or shifting soil.

an agreement that irons out all their understandings and details, so that a contract based on their desires either will or will not go through. The following sections cover specific issues.

Property Identification

In most purchase contracts (other than those for acreage), the street address will be given, followed by a clause such as, "and more particularly described as" or "more fully described as" and then the legal description. In many cases, brokers or salespersons will take the description from the listing agreement; however, the best source for the description is straight from the seller's deed.

Following the legal description, a general protection clause (found in many form contracts) should be inserted and reads as follows:

> . . . *together with all the right, title, and interest of the seller in and to the land lying in the street in front of or adjoining the above described property, to the center lines thereof respectively.*

Any personal property being conveyed, should be listed in the contract. A clause reading "together with the following personal property . . . " may be inserted along with a list of the personal property. This clause is particularly important in the purchase of multiunit dwellings. Since the standards for what constitutes a fixture may vary, it is best to list the property included if there is any doubt. It is important to verify that the seller actually owns the personal property and whether there are any Article 9 security interests in the property. (See Chapter 4 for a full discussion of security interests.) Identification of the property by serial number may assure the buyer that the same personal property that was viewed is transferred.

Because a deed transfers title to real property only, title to personal property should be handled through a bill of sale, which is in effect a deed for personal property.

If there are any title limitations in the property being transferred, such as assessments, easements, or rights-of-way, they should also be noted in the contract. In many forms, a general provision appears after the description, which reads: "subject to rights, rights-of-way, easements, including those for public utilities, water companies, alleys, and streets; assessments and other encumbrances of record." If there are restrictive covenants on the property, they too should be noted in the provision. If the seller needs to reserve or grant an easement, a clause to that effect should also follow the description.

Practical Tip

Be sure to carefully identify the parties to the contract. Below is a checklist.

1. Name: full name, aliases, and AKAs (also known as). How does seller's name appear on deed granting title?
2. Marital status.
3. If legal entity (corporation) is involved:
   a. Place incorporated and proper corporate name.
   b. Name of president.
   c. Name of secretary.
   d. Authority of individual signing.
4. If partnership is involved:
   a. Proper partnership name.
   b. Type of partnership (general or limited).
   c. Name of partner.
   d. Authority of partner.
5. If executor for estate is involved:
   a. Name of estate.
   b. Executor's name and aliases.
   c. Executor's appointment and authority.
6. If agent acting for another is involved:
   a. Name of agent and aliases.
   b. Authority of agent (power of attorney).

Note: Numbers 3–5 are critical so that the correct name(s) are used in the transaction and deed.

Earnest Money

As discussed earlier, this payment is not required for the validity of the purchase contract but does demonstrate the buyer's good faith. The amount should be indicated in the contract along with the name of the person who is to hold the deposit for the parties. For example, the following phrases could be used:

1. $500.00 earnest deposit payable to Security Title.
2. $500.00 cash or check drawn to the order of _____ to be held in escrow by _____.

Financing

This element of the purchase price is critical. For example, suppose a buyer purchases a home for $110,000 and the earnest money is $1,000 with an additional payment of $19,000 at closing. The remaining amount to be paid is $90,000 and this $90,000 of consideration may be paid in a number of ways. The payment methods used most often are: (1) assumption of an existing mortgage, (2) purchase money mortgage by the seller, (3) new financing, or (4) any combination of the first three.

ASSUMPTION OF AN EXISTING MORTGAGE

In order to pay the remaining $90,000 of the purchase price, the buyer could agree to assume responsibility of the $90,000 mortgage on the property, or take over the seller's payments on the property. (The problems and liabilities of assumption are discussed in Chapter 15.) A sample clause providing for such an assumption is:

> *As part of the total purchase price, the Buyer agrees to assume and pay the existing first mortgage on the property described above with (mortgagee) and having an approximate balance of _____ dollars ($ .00), with said balance to be established by Seller furnishing a mortgagee's statement with payments of principal, interest, taxes, and insurance of $ _____ per month with an annual interest rate of _____ % and running until _____, 20_____.*

Some drafters prefer to list the exact balance at drafting and provide for an update at closing. It is important that the monthly payments, rate, and ending date of the loan are accurate.

If approval by the mortgagee is required for an assumption, then a clause stating "subject to the mortgagee's approval" should be inserted. Furthermore, some states permit the mortgagee to increase the interest rate upon assumption, and such an increase should also be stated in the contract.

PURCHASE MONEY MORTGAGE BY THE SELLER

In some land transfers, the seller will act as the lender either by retaining title until the money is paid or by taking a mortgage on the property. In the example, if there were no mortgage to be assumed and the $90,000 still remained to be paid, the seller could finance the buyer's purchase. The language used would be as follows:

> *As part of the total purchase price, Seller agrees to take a purchase money note secured by a mortgage covering the above described property in the amount of _____ dollars ($ .00), with the principal amount of the note being that sum and the rate of interest being _____ % per annum, with both principal and interest payable in the amount of $_____ on the _____ day of each month beginning on the _____ day of _____, 20_____, and continuing until _____, 20_____, when the balance shall be paid in full.*
>
> *It is further agreed that the Buyer will execute the necessary note and mortgage reflecting these terms at or before closing on the property.*

The seller may ask the buyer to furnish a balance statement or credit report as a condition to the granting of the note and mortgage. If the seller provides financing, the seller will need to comply with the federal **Truth in Lending Act** and make certain disclosures on financing cost (see Chapter 15).

NEW FINANCING

To complete payment of the purchase price, the buyer may agree to obtain new financing for the balance due ($90,000 in the example). At the time the parties agree to the terms of the sale, the buyer's ability to obtain financing may be unknown. This portion of the purchase contract must be phrased as a condition precedent to performance or contingency.

A condition or contingency, known as a condition precedent, is an event that must occur before the parties or one party is obligated to perform under the contract. If a condition precedent never occurs, then the parties are

Practical Tip

Use caution in drafting the conditions. They are often the turning points of closure on a sale and a lack of specifics can burden both parties in the transactions. For buyers, financing terms help clarify how much they must do in order to exercise good faith in meeting the condition. For sellers, details help them free the property when the terms of the condition are not met.

not obligated to perform but are released from their contractual obligations. Although the contract is binding and creates legal obligations, conditions or contingencies control whether those obligations must be performed.

At a minimum, such a conditional financing clause should contain the most important terms, such as the principal amount, interest rate, maturity date, amount and frequency of installments, number of points (lender's commitment fee), and source of the financing (bank, trust company, or other source). Also, the clause should place time limitations on the buyer: "The loan application must be made within 14 days of the agreement," plus a maximum time for qualification. The following is a typical conditional financing clause:

> *This agreement is subject to the Buyer's securing a new first mortgage loan on the property described in this agreement in an amount of not less than* _____ *dollars ($ .00) from* (bank, savings and loan, Federal Housing Administration, or other source*), principal and interest payable in equal monthly payments of not more than $*_____ *at an interest rate of not more than* _____ *% per annum, said mortgage loan being all due and payable* _____ *years from date of consummating this agreement.*

A conditional financing clause gives the buyer a specified period within which to obtain financing and then gives the seller the opportunity to find financing for the buyer. Such an arrangement should have carefully drafted time limits and notification requirements.

Consider 14.7

Highlands Plaza, Incorporated, entered into an agreement to purchase property from Viking Investment Corporation. The purchase was conditioned upon Highlands obtaining a $125,000 mortgage on the property. Highlands was able to obtain the $125,000 only through a first and second mortgage with different institutions, but still sought to go through with the sale. Viking refused on the grounds that the financing condition was not met. Highlands has brought suit for specific performance. What is the result?

[handwritten margin note: Win → got the finance]

COMBINATIONS OF FINANCING METHODS

The buyer can pay the purchase price through a combination of the various methods of financing. Thus, in the same example of a buyer purchasing a home for $110,000, the financing might be arranged as follows: If the property was already mortgaged for $78,000, the buyer could pay $1,000 earnest money, put $19,000 down, and assume the $78,000 mortgage; and the seller could take a second mortgage and carry the remaining $12,000. The arrangements could be written in the contract as follows:

> *The purchase price of one hundred ten thousand dollars ($110,000) is to be paid as follows:*
>
> a. *$1,000.00 Earnest money to be deposited with ABC escrow in the form of cash or check.*
>
> b. *$19,000.00 Additional down payment to be paid on or before the close of escrow.*
>
> c. *$78,000.00 Approximate balance of first mortgage with California Pacific Mortgage to be assumed by the buyer with monthly payments of principal, interest, taxes, and insurance of* _____ *due and payable on the* _____ *day of each month and an annual rate of* _____ *%, with final payment being made on* _____, *20*_____.

d.   *$12,000.00 Buyer agrees to execute note and second mortgage to seller on the above described property in the amount of $12,000 at a rate of _____ % per annum payable in monthly installments of _____ on the _____ day of each month beginning on the _____ day of _____, 20_____.*

Property Reports

Often buyers contract to purchase property before actually knowing the condition (in detail) of the property. However, the contract may require, as conditions precedent to the buyer's performance, expert reports on the property.

PROPERTY CONDITION REPORTS

One such condition often inserted in the contract is a clean termite report. An example of such a clause is as follows:

> *The Sellers shall, at their expense and prior to closing, furnish the Buyers with a certificate from a reputable exterminator (a) certifying that the building(s) are free and clear from infestation and any resulting damage caused by termites or other wood-boring insects, and (b) guaranteeing such status for a period of one year from the date of closing. If such infestation or damage is found, buyer shall have the option of terminating all rights and obligations under this contract or requiring the sellers to cure and/or repair any infestation or damage on the property caused by termites or other wood-boring insects.*

Another type of report buyers may require in conditional form is a soil report, particularly in circumstances where buyers are purchasing land for development and construction. The quality of the soil will control the feasibility of constructing homes or other buildings on the property.

In recent years, it has become critical for buyers to verify the status of the property with respect to its condition and with regard to certain environmental concerns. In many transactions, it has become standard procedure for the parties to make inquiries of governmental agencies regarding the presence of toxic waste on the property or its previous use for toxic waste disposal. State and federal environmental agencies are asked to check their files to determine whether any actions or investigations regarding the property are pending or have been taken. (See Chapter 20 for discussion of asbestos, radon, and toxic waste.)

Also, many parties to purchase contracts will request geological reports to determine whether the property is a risk because of its location in a fault or floodplain.

Federal Disclosure Requirements

In the 1960s, because of an increase in available leisure time and disposable income, more and more Americans sought to purchase land for the construction of recreational, second, or vacation homes. Unfortunately, many purchases of such land were made sight unseen, with buyers purchasing mail-order lots. Most buyers had no idea what they were purchasing but were led on by colorful and often misleading brochures that depicted the property as part of a lush vacation spot, when in fact it was nothing but raw, undeveloped land often lacking roads, utilities, and water.

Practical Tip

Check state and federal regulations on land sales before developing promotional materials, listings, and contracts. Be certain you are in compliance with all filing and disclosure requirements. If you believe an exemption applies, be careful to analyze why you can claim an exemption.

Because of the large number of frauds being perpetrated, Congress passed the **Interstate Land Sales Full Disclosure Act (ILSFDA)** (15 U.S.C. §1701 *et seq.*)—see Appendix E—which regulates sellers of undeveloped properties while still permitting them to sell the land. The basic purpose of the act is to provide full and accurate information so that buyers are in an equal bargaining position with sellers when making purchase decisions. The ILSFDA is administered by the Office of Interstate Land Sales Registration (OILSR), a division of the **Department of Housing and Urban Development (HUD).**

WHO IS COVERED UNDER THE ILSFDA?

Since the ILSFDA is a federal enactment, it applies only to sales of land involving or affecting interstate commerce—generally, to the sale or lease of 50 or more unimproved lots in interstate commerce. The act defines what constitutes interstate commerce in a negative manner by excluding those sales it does not cover:

a. Sales or lease of real estate pursuant to court order
b. Sales of securities by real estate investment trusts
c. Sales or lease by governments or government agencies
d. Sales of cemetery lots
e. Sales or leases in subdivisions with fewer than 25 lots
f. Sales or lease of lots 20 acres or more in size
g. Sales of lots where there is a residential, commercial, or industrial building

The ILSFDA also provides an exemption for intrastate land developers if the developer complies with the following requirements:

a. Prospective buyers or spouses make on-site inspection of the lots before purchasing.
b. Sales contract (1) identifies who will be responsible for roads and utilities, (2) provides deeds free and clear of any blanket encumbrances, and (3) grants a rescission period of seven business days.
c. Good faith estimates of cost of getting services such as electric, water, sewer, and gas and when they will be complete.

The intrastate residential subdivision exemption requires the developer to file a written affirmation of compliance with the rules and full information about the purchasers or lessees.

CONTENT OF FILING REPORTS FOR NONEXEMPT DEVELOPERS

If a developer is nonexempt, a **statement of record** must be filed. It must include the following information:

a. Names and addresses of the developers and their interests in the property
b. Legal description of the topography, climate, nuisances, subdivision map, permits, and licenses
c. General terms and conditions of the lot offer, including selling price and buyer's right of revocation for 48 hours
d. Access to nearby communities and roads
e. Availability of utilities; and if the utilities are developer-controlled, estimates for completion
f. Copies of articles of incorporation, partnership, or other entity creation of the developers and the development

The registration statement takes effect in 30 days unless HUD determines it is incomplete. HUD's notification stops the running of the 30 days and the developer must comply with HUD's requests.

In addition to filing a statement of record, the developer is required to file a copy of the **property report.** A copy of the property report must also be given to every buyer before the buyer signs a contract for purchase. The report is set up in an easily understood question-and-answer format. It includes the same basic information as the statement of record but in a more readable manner, and does not include articles of incorporation for developers. No property reports can be distributed until the registration statement is effective.

PENALTIES FOR VIOLATION OF ILSFDA

Developers failing to comply with the disclosure requirements face both civil and criminal penalties. Parties who purchase from violating developers may sue the developers for damages, specific performance, or any other relief the court deems fair, just, and equitable. Purchasers may also sue to recover interest, court costs, attorneys' fees, appraisal fees, and cost of travel to and from the lots. Recovery for fraud or misrepresentation in the property report is available, whether or not there is actual reliance on the report. The criminal penalties for willful violations of the Act are $10,000, five years' imprisonment, or both. Civil penalties range from $1,000 to $1,000,000.

In addition to regulation by the ILSFDA, all developers (even those exempt under the federal act) may be required to comply with state land sales acts and disclosures. These state acts may also require the filing of reports and documents prior to the negotiation of sales.

Would the ILSFDA apply to:

a. The sale of condominium units?
b. The sale of mobile home lots?
c. The sale of 200 40-acre parcels?
d. The sale of homes in a tract subdivision with 375 lots?
e. A developer who has filed with the state?

> **Consider 14.8**

Condition of Premises

To provide assurance for the buyer that the property will not be substantially damaged between the time of purchase and the time of closing, a conditional clause on the property's condition should be put in the contract. In addition, any repairs the buyer feels must be made should also be included as conditions to the buyer's performance. The following clause would be appropriate:

> *The Sellers agree to keep the property in the same condition as it exists as of the date of the contract. Sellers further agree to repair the following items: _____ _____ _____. If such repairs are not completed or if the condition of the property has deteriorated, the buyers shall have the option of terminating all rights and obligations under this contract, or having said repairs made, or having conditions corrected at the sellers' expense, or requiring sellers to make said repairs or remedies.*

In recent years, the issue of whether warranties are made from the seller to the buyer in the transfer of real property has been frequently litigated.

IMPLIED WARRANTY OF HABITABILITY

The **implied warranty of habitability** protection is currently limited to purchasers of new homes and is applied only to builders and vendors. The cases decided on the issue have several consistent standards for habitability, summarized as follows:

1. It is possible for a new home to be in substantial compliance with building codes and still be uninhabitable.
2. The primary function of a new home is to shelter its inhabitants from the elements. If a new home does not keep out the elements because of a substantial defect of construction, such home is not habitable within the meaning of the implied warranty of habitability.
3. Another function of a new home is to provide its inhabitants with a reasonably safe place to live, without fear of injury to person, health, safety, or property. If a new home is not structurally sound because of a substantial defect of construction, such a home is not habitable within the meaning of the implied warranty of habitability.
4. If a new home is not aesthetically satisfying because of a defect of construction, such a defect should not be considered as making the home inhabitable.

Consider 14.9

On the basis of the four statements on the warranty of habitability, determine whether the following defects would be a breach of the warranty. (Assume all buyers purchased new homes.)

a. A septic tank that does not function properly
b. Water seepage into a home
c. A mudslide damaging a home owner's patio area
d. A cracked foundation
e. Cracked basement walls

Many states have passed statutes that specifically dictate when warranties are made and also codify the judicially afforded protection of the implied warranties. Over the past five years, there have been new issues related to the implied warranty protection. One issue is whether the warranty of habitability extends to purchasers of homes beyond just the original purchaser from the builder. While some states have permitted the extension of the warranty, most states provide that the warranty applies to the original purchaser only. Many sellers, in order to avoid litigation over their properties, are selling their homes "as is" (see Chapter 12), that is, they are disclosing that there may be defects but that they are not responsible for them and buyers have been given the opportunity to inspect the property for any problems. In addition, many buyers are purchasing a warranty policy for their homes so that should problems arise, they will have insurance protection for repairs and renovation.

Another issue has been the statute of limitations for recovery under the implied warranty of habitability. For the most part, the states have treated the cases as ones in contract that are subject to contractual breach statutes of limitations. However, exceptions have been made in cases where the builder is also guilty of misrepresentation or fraud.

A final issue is whether the implied warranty of habitability can be disclaimed. States that permit such disclaimers require that the buyers be aware of the limitation. That awareness can come from conspicuous language, actual signing of a disclaimer, or any other type of conduct that shows the buyers knew of the limitation before they purchased the home. Some states permit a disclaimer of the implied warranty only if some other type of warranty is given in exchange. An example of a disclaimer upheld in a New York case follows:

> It is further understood that THE SPONSOR MAKES NO HOUSING MERCHANT IMPLIED WARRANTY OR ANY OTHER WARRANTIES, EXPRESS OR IMPLIED, IN CONNECTION WITH THIS PURCHASE AGREEMENT OR THE UNIT, AND ALL SUCH WARRANTIES ARE EXCLUDED EXCEPT AS PROVIDED IN THE LIMITED WARRANTY ANNEXED TO THIS PURCHASE AGREEMENT. THE EXPRESS TERMS OF THE ANNEXED LIMITED WARRANTY ARE HEREBY INCORPORATED IN AND MADE A PART OF THIS PURCHASE AGREEMENT; THEY SHALL SURVIVE THE CLOSING OF TITLE; AND THERE ARE NO OTHER WARRANTIES WHICH EXTEND BEYOND THE FACE THEREOF.

The types of problems generally covered under the warranty include cracking floors, leaking basements, defective materials, sewage backups, and drainage problems.

Consider 14.10

Richards and others purchased homes in the Indian Hills subdivision near Casa Grande between 1975 and 1977. The houses had been built by Powercraft beginning in 1974. Richards bought his home not directly from Powercraft, but as a repossessed home offered for sale by Farmers Home Administration (FHA).

After living in the home for a while, Richards discovered numerous defects including faulty water pipes; improperly leveled yards that resulted in pooling and flooding; cracking of interior and exterior walls; separation of floors from the walls; separation of driveways; and sidewalks, carports, doors, and windows that were stuck closed or could not be locked because of misalignment. Powercraft was notified, and repair attempts brought only temporary relief.

Richards filed a complaint with the Registrar of Contractors. The Registrar found that Powercraft had failed to follow certain plans and specifications when building the homes and that it had failed to properly compact the soil beneath each home before the building began. Powercraft's license was revoked on December 6, 1978.

Richards filed suit against Powercraft, alleging a breach of the implied warranty that houses be habitable and constructed in a workmanlike manner. Can he recover under the warranty theory? *Richards v. Powercraft Homes, Inc.*, 678 P.2d 427 (Ariz. 1984)

NEW DAMAGES AND THE IMPLIED WARRANTY

Liability theory with respect to home buyers is evolving in California with the imposition of damages for emotional harm to buyers when their homes are defective. In *Salka v. Dean Homes of Beverly Hills, Inc.* (22 Cal. App.2d 902(1993)), the owner of a home that became waterlogged because of a defective foundation recovered not only the economic damages, but also $50,000 for emotional harm. The appellate court in affirming the emotional harm award stated:

> The purchase of a home isn't only the largest investment people make in their lifetime, it is also a highly personal choice concerning how and where one lives his or her life. Generally, no other material acquisition is of equivalent personal importance.

HOME WARRANTY POLICIES

There are really two uses of the term *home warranty*. The first use is that covered by state statutes in which the builder is required, for specified times, to offer a

Practical Tip

In addition to the areas covered, include the following in your contract.
1. How will the buyer(s) take title? joint tenants? tenants in common?
2. Can the contract be assigned?
3. When will possession be given to the buyer?
4. What leases exist? What rights do the tenants have?

warranty on construction of the house. The second use is that often seen on listing signs placed on property, such as "one-year warranty available." This protection is for the buyer and is a form of insurance that covers defects and problems on the home for one year from closing.

If a buyer is not in a position of being protected by either a statutory or implied warranty, the purchase contract may still be drafted to afford protection in the event defects arise. One way to obtain such protection is to require the seller to purchase one of the available home warranty protection plans. Most policies for used homes will run for a period of a year, but varying coverage exists. The buyer should specify in the contract what type of protection is sought. Another protection can be obtained by requiring the seller to personally warrant the property. A sample seller's warranty clause follows:

Homeowners Warranty

> *The Seller warrants that the plumbing, heating, air conditioning, and electrical systems in the buildings on the property are in good working order and condition, and will be in good working order and condition at the time of closing. In the event such items are not in working order at closing, the Seller agrees to deduct the cost of repair or replacement from the amount due from the buyer at settlement.*

A warranty clause such as this may be coupled with a warranty policy.

Environmental Contingency Clause

Because of so many issues regarding environmental hazards (see Chapter 20), many contracts now have environmental inspections as conditions precedent to performance. These **environmental contingency clauses** require inspection of the property for problems relating to the presence of toxic waste, radon, asbestos, and other toxins. Some states have adopted legislation with respect to these issues. For example, Rhode Island and Florida now require radon-disclosure notices in residential sales contracts. These disclosures simply state in the contract that radon may be present on the property. The parties would have to add the requirement that the removal be a contingency or that inspection be conducted prior to closing. In some contracts, the cost of remedial action to reduce an elevated level of radon is charged against the seller at closing. This issue will continue to evolve as more steps are taken at the federal level regarding public education and mitigation of radon exposure. Even developers of new properties will want to consider soil testing before purchasing undeveloped land to determine high radon levels in the soil.

Risk of Loss

not true in IL (opposite)

In most jurisdictions, the risk of loss by fire or other casualty is with the buyer from the time the purchase contract is executed. The buyer has an insurable interest at the time of the contract execution and may hold a valid policy on the property even though there is no title or possession.

However, in most cases, the seller will maintain insurance on the property until closing. To avoid the duplication of insurance and costs, parties should agree that the seller will maintain insurance on the property until closing. If the parties do agree to such an arrangement, the buyers should be added to the existing policy along with a notation establishing the buyer's interest in the property.

Recording the Contract

The purchase contract need not be recorded to be effective between the parties. The obvious danger is that without recording, the property may have liens attached and other interests recorded that would have priority over the buyer's interests. Nonetheless, throughout the country the recording of the sales contract is very uncommon. One reason for not recording is a very practical one: The contract has conditions and contingencies that might not be met; therefore, it is always subject to the buyer's default. If the recorded contract falls through, the seller is not free to sell to anyone else until a release is signed and the contract is somehow stricken from the records. Without the defaulting purchaser's signature on a release, clearing the contract could be an expensive matter requiring a court hearing. It is best to put a clause in the agreement prohibiting recording.

Closing Date and Escrow Instructions

Although the purchase contract establishes the terms of the sale, it does not contain all the details for the execution of documents, transfer of title, and payment of money. The purchase contract will provide a date for the closing of escrow, such as in the following clause:

1. *Closing shall take place within* _____ *days of the date of this agreement.*
2. *Closing shall be on* _____, *20____.*

In many states, the closing is handled by a third party (see Chapter 16), and a contract is required among the buyer, seller, and third party to properly complete the transaction. It is necessary to have a clause in the purchase contract that requires the parties to execute such an agreement, and the standard forms provide:

> *Buyer and Seller shall execute escrow instructions to fulfill the terms hereof and deliver the same to the escrow agent within 15 days of the date of execution of this agreement.*

Also, if applicable, a simple clause such as "time is of the essence in the performance of this agreement," may be included to indicate the parties' intention that delays mean the contract will not go forward. This will save the parties later problems with extensions in the execution of the contract. Without an indication of the parties' intent, the courts are likely to permit reasonably timely performance that may not comply with the time limits the parties wished to be absolute.

Apportionments

Property is not always transferred at times when taxes, insurance, and rent are due. Usually, the property is transferred after the parties have prepaid insurance premiums or taxes or after they have received advance rent from lessees. To be absolutely fair to the parties, the amounts involved must be apportioned between the buyer and seller as of the date of transfer of title. Specific clauses may be used for the apportionment of each type of fund or a general apportionment clause may be used. The following are examples of specific types of clauses:

1. *Proration of Rent* All rent on any and all portions of the property shall be pro-rated to the date of closing, with the seller receiving all rents due to the date of closing and the buyer receiving all rents due thereafter. All prepaid rents shall be prorated in the same manner.
2. *Taxes* All taxes due and owing on the property shall be prorated to the date of closing, with the seller paying all taxes due to the date of closing and the buyer paying all taxes due thereafter. Any prepaid taxes shall be prorated in the same manner.

Marketable Title

The clause on **marketable title** in the purchase contract is a condition precedent to the buyer's performance that requires the seller to deliver a certain quality of title. The clause may be very simple, requiring the seller to furnish a title insurance pol-icy, or it may be demanding and restrictive, by requiring the seller to remove liens or obtain zoning changes. The following are examples of the title clauses:

1. *In the event title to said property herein described is found by a title insurance company to be unmarketable at the time of closing, the purchaser is excused from performance.*
2. *Title to the premises shall be good and marketable and free and clear of all liens, restrictions, easements, encumbrances, leases, tenancies, and other title objec-tions, and shall be insurable as such at ordinary rates by any reputable title insurance company selected by the buyer.*

Marketable title is generally defined as one a prudent person would accept even with full knowledge of all facts about the property. Marketable title is a title that is free from reasonable doubt or controversy and which is not subject to any liens or encumbrances. An unmarketable title is one that has defects or the ques-tion of defects that could cause the purchaser to be subjected to adverse claims or litigation. The determination of whether a particular title meets the standard of marketability is made on a case-by-case basis. One general standard applied in reviewing the marketability of a title is, Would a prudent person accept this title in exchange for a fair purchase price?

In many purchase contracts, the seller is given a time limit within which to cure defects in title discovered before closing. For example, if the preliminary title report shows a defect, the seller may be given an extension on closing of 30 or 60 days to cure the defect. Figure 14.2 provides a list of marketable title issues.

Consider 14.11

The following clause is part of a sales contract for the purchase of real property.

Title is to be conveyed free from all encumbrances except: Any state of facts an accu-rate survey may show, provided same does not render title unmarketable.

Upon a title search, it was discovered that a telephone easement was record-ed for the property, and that the height of the sidewalk on the property violated a city ordinance, although a waiver had been obtained for its construction. The title company offered to insure title except for the sidewalk waiver and the tele-phone easement. The buyers refuse to perform on the grounds of lack of mar-ketable title. What is the result?

Many states have adopted the **Uniform Marketable Title Act,** which provides that a person who has unbroken record title for 50 years has marketable title.

FIGURE 14.2   *Marketable Title*

Affects Marketable Title[*]	Does Not Affect Marketable Title
Unrecorded easements	Zoning
Easements (unless visible)	CC&Rs
Quiet title litigation pending	Visible easements
Liens	
Leases	
Encroachments	
Mortgages	
Tenancies	
Water rights	
Tax issues	
Disputes among heirs on property rights	
Land contracts	
Prescriptive and adverse possession rights	

[*]   The buyer could agree to accept title subject to any of these and such willingness would be noted in the contract.

There are certain exceptions to the act, but it was designed to create a 50-year statute of limitations on various title claims and provide a mechanism whereby titles could be cleared of unrenewed and unenforced clouds.

Remedies

LIQUIDATED DAMAGES

The purchase contract can include provisions to control what will happen if either party does not fulfill the obligations created under the contract. Many contracts provide that the earnest money or deposit will be used for damages in the event of a breach by one of the parties. That deposit should be large enough to cover damages. The following is an example of such a clause:

> Should the undersigned Buyer fail to carry out this agreement, all money paid hereunder, including any additional earnest money, shall, at the option of the Seller, be forfeited as liquidated damages and shall be paid to or retained by the Seller, subject to deductions of broker's commission and disbursements, if any. In the event neither party has commenced a law suit within one (1) year after the closing date set forth herein, the broker is authorized to disburse the earnest money as liquidated damages, and if the Seller has not notified the Buyer of election to consider the earnest money as liquidated damages within six (6) months of said closing date, broker is authorized to refund all earnest money to the Buyer.
>
> Should the Seller be unable to carry out this agreement by reason of a valid legal defect in title which the Buyer is unwilling to waive, all money paid hereunder shall be returned to the buyer forthwith, and this contract will be void.

In most cases, the courts will enforce the earnest money retention as a valid **liquidated damages** clause; that is, a clause in which the parties agree on the amount of damages before any breach of contract occurs. However, the seller may not attempt to keep the earnest money deposit and collect actual damages in addition, for then the remedy would be viewed as a penalty and void. Also, the amount of liquidated damages must be reasonable or reflective of the potential loss the seller will suffer because of the buyer's breach.

Because of so much litigation over the validity of liquidated damage clauses, some states have passed statutes requiring that specific language be used in order to have a valid and enforceable provision for liquidated damages. Many of these statutes also require that the parties sign or initial the clause in the contract so that a court can be certain the parties were aware of its existence. Still other states require a "second look" at liquidated damages clauses.

The following case deals with the issue of the reasonableness of a liquidated damages clause and the second-look doctrine.

Kelly v. Marx

705 N.E.2d 1114 (Mass. 1999)

Facts

On March 18, 1994, John and Pamela Kelly (plaintiffs) signed an offer to purchase residential property from Steven and Merrill Marx (defendants) for $335,000. The Kellys gave $1,000 earnest money with the offer.

By early May, 1994, the Kellys and Marxes had signed a purchase and sale agreement and deposited another $16,750. Clause 18 of their agreement provided:

> If the BUYER shall fail to fulfill the BUYER'S agreements herein, all deposits made hereunder by the BUYER shall be retained by the SELLER as liquidated damages.

The closing date was set as September 1, 1994, but the Kellys never purchased the property because they were unable to sell their house. The Kellys notified the Marxes on August 9, 1994, that they would not be closing on the transaction.

On August 24, 1994, the Marxes accepted another offer to purchase and eventually sold the property on September 20, 1994, to new buyers for a purchase price of $360,000. The Marxes kept the Kellys' total deposit of $17,750 and the Kellys brought suit to recover it. The trial court granted the Marxes' motion for summary judgment and the court of appeals reversed. The Marxes appealed.

Judicial Decision

Ireland, Justice. Liquidated damages clauses which provide for the seller of real estate to retain the buyer's deposit are recognized in Massachusetts, and, as both parties concede here and the Appeals Court concluded, they are a common real estate practice. The question before us is whether enforceability of a liquidated damages

clause is to be tested by analyzing the circumstances at contract formation, the prospective or "single look" approach, or when the breach occurs, the retrospective or "second look" approach.

This question has created confusion in our courts, and originates from ambiguous language in the leading, most recent case of this court on liquidated damages in the context of the purchase and sale of real property. *A-Z Servicenter, Inc., v. Segall,* 334 Mass. 672, 675, 138 N.E.2d 266 (1956). Many decisions, following *A-Z Servicenter,* have concluded that liquidated damages should be measured, first, by assessing the reasonableness of the liquidated damages in light of the parties' ability to anticipate damages at contract formation, and, second, against the actual damages resulting from the breach.

A judge, in determining the enforceability of a liquidated damages clause, should examine only the circumstances at contract formation. Our position is that "where actual damages are difficult to ascertain and where the sum agreed upon by the parties at the time of the execution of the contract represents a reasonable estimate of the actual damages, such a contract will be enforced." *A-Z Servicenter, Inc. v. Segall, supra* at 675. Liquidated damages will not be enforced if the sum is "grossly disproportionate to a reasonable estimate of actual damages" made at the time of contract formation.

This approach most accurately matches the expectations of the parties, who negotiated a liquidated damage amount that was fair to each side based on their unique concerns and circumstances surrounding the agreement, and their individual estimate of damages in event of a breach. We agree with the reasoning of the dissenting Justice (at the court of appeals), who pointed out that the "second look reveals nothing that the parties had not contemplated" when they entered their contract. *Kelly v. Marx, 694 N.E.2d 869, 214 Mass. App. at 833* (Spina, J., dissenting).

In addition to meeting the parties' expectations, the "single look" approach helps resolve disputes efficiently by making it unnecessary to wait until actual damages from a breach are provided. By reducing challenges to a liquidated damages clause, the "single look" approach eliminates uncertainty and tends to prevent costly future litigation. The "second look," by contrast, undermines the "peace of mind and certainty of result," the parties sought when they contracted for liquidated damages. It increases the potential for litigation by inviting the aggrieved party to attempt to show evidence of damage when the contract is breached, or, more accurately, evidence of damage flowing from the breach but occurring sometime afterward. In other words, "the 'parties must fully litigate (at great expense and delay) that which they sought not to litigate.'"

The plaintiffs argue that application of a "second look" approach would allow the court to guard against undue windfalls, such as the one the defendants would receive here if they were to keep the deposit, because the defendants suffered no loss from the breach of the sale. We disagree. In essence, the plaintiffs want to undo the agreement between the parties, who expect to receive stipulated damages, not damages resolved by a court examining postbreach circumstances. The parties agreed to the extent of their damages when they agreed on a liquidated damages clause. "The proper course is to enforce contracts according to their plain meaning and not to undertake to be wiser than the parties, and therefore that in general when parties say that a sum is payable as liquidated damages they will be taken to mean what they say and will be held to their word."

Turning to the present case, we conclude the plaintiffs are not entitled to the return of the deposit they paid to the defendants. The potential damages were difficult to predict when the agreement was made. As another court has correctly noted: "The parties could not know what delays might ensue, what might occur in the real estate market, or how a failed sale might affect the seller's plans. Real estate purchase and sale agreements are precisely the type of contracts that are amenable to liquidated damages provision."

Viewing the facts at the time of contract formation, the liquidated damages were a reasonable estimate of the damage to the defendants. The deposit, five per cent of the purchase price, was a reasonable forecast of the defendants' losses that would result if the buyers were to breach the agreement. These costs could arise from a host of issues relating to finding another buyer and waiting for an uncertain period of time before selling their property, and in light of the risk of an undeterminable loss that is dependant on many factors (primarily the shape of the real estate market at the time of the breach). The sum is not grossly disproportionate to the expected damages arising from a breach of the sale agreement, nor is it "unconscionably excessive" so as to be defeated as a matter of public policy. As the Appeals Court conceded, "Were our inquiry limited to the circumstances obtaining at the time the parties entered into their agreement, we would permit the sellers to retain the deposit, amounting to five percent of the purchase price."

The summary judgment of the superior court in favor of the defendants is affirmed.

Case Questions

1. What was the amount of the deposit the Kellys made?
2. What damages did the Marxes experience as a result of the Kellys' failure to close on the house?
3. What is the second-look doctrine? Why did it develop?
4. Will the Marxes be allowed to retain the deposit of the Kellys?

ACTUAL DAMAGES

The decision to keep the earnest money as damages is often left to the discretion of the seller. In other words, the seller may elect to proceed and collect the actual damages sustained by the buyer's breach. Such damages could include all the monies expended by the seller in preparing for closing, such as the cost of reports. It could also include a commission to the broker or lost rental value if the property remains vacant or if a lease is terminated in anticipation of the buyer's takeover.

Likewise, the buyer may opt to collect actual damages for the seller's breach, which could include the costs of preparation for closing in the form of loan origination or commitment fees, appraisal fees, survey costs, and so on.

The party who is suing for actual damages has the burden of establishing proof of the amount of the damages and that those damages were suffered as a result of the other party's breach.

If the action for actual damages is brought for nontimely performance in a time-is-of-the-essence agreement, the party bringing the action must show damages that resulted from delay. Examples of such damages are a higher interest rate on a loan, a loss of rent, and the cost of renting another property.

The **Uniform Land Transactions Act (ULTA),** drafted for passage by the states in 1975, has several sections providing formulas for determining actual damages in the event of a breach of a land sales contract. For example, a seller reselling at a lower price than that provided in the breached contract recovers from the breaching buyer the difference in price plus the incidental costs of resale.

SPECIFIC PERFORMANCE

Specific performance is a remedy generally granted to buyers that requires the seller to go forward with the transaction according to the terms of the contract.

Generally, specific performance is not awarded to sellers who have breaching buyers; in such cases sellers are left to the remedies of actual damages or the collection of liquidated damages.

RESCISSION

Rescission is a remedy that entitles the parties to rescind their agreement and return to the positions they were in before they entered into the contract. The buyer is given back any compensation paid and the seller is no longer obligated to sell the land. Rescission is most commonly used in cases where the seller is guilty of misrepresentation or fraud regarding the land or its condition.

Consider 14.12	The Willistons signed a purchase agreement for the construction and purchase of a new home from United Homes. They paid $1,000 earnest money. The contract provided that in the event the Willistons did not qualify for their loan of the property, only $800 would be returned and $200 would be retained by United for paperwork and processing. The Willistons did not qualify, and United kept $200. The Willistons maintain the retention of the $200 is unfair and illegal. What is the result?

MISREPRESENTATION

There are times when parties have executed a complete written agreement, but the contract is set aside because one of the parties entered into it because of a misrepresentation by the other party.

Misrepresentation can be innocent; that is, one party through misinformation or lack of knowledge provides the other party with inaccurate and misleading information. Misrepresentation can also be fraudulent, as when one party intentionally provides inaccurate information for purposes of inducing a sale. Finally, misrepresentation can occur because of a party's failure to disclose information that would have affected the purchasing decision. Upon discovery of misrepresentation, the party may rescind the agreement. However, all types of misrepresentation require proof of the following common elements before rescission is available as a remedy.

In real property, some defects are obvious, such as a well-worn roof and a buyer takes subject to those visible problems. However, the seller must not conceal or fail to disclose latent defects such as cracked foundations, leaky roofs, and unstable soil conditions. The misrepresentation results when the seller has a duty to disclose and fails to do so. That duty to disclose arises for latent, material problems with the property.

The following are the elements of misrepresentation by a seller:

1. A statement of material fact has been made or omitted—the type of information involved would affect the buying decision.
2. There is reliance on the statement of fact—the buyer uses the fact in making the decision of whether to buy.
3. There is detriment—the buyer suffers through loss of property value or cost of repair.

The following case illustrates the application of the three elements in a case in which the misrepresentation was a fraudulent one about a latent defect in the property.

Practical Tip

Avoid misrepresentation issues:
1. Don't state unverified information.
2. Don't predict the future for property conditions or equipment (e.g., "This air conditioner will last 10 years").
3. Get independent confirmation of material information.
4. Carefully and visually inspect the property.
5. Document what you say and the questions you answer.
6. Know the "red flags" of real property (see Chapters 12 and 19).
7. Disclose all material issues, defects, and conditions.

Reed v. King

193 Cal. Rptr. 130 (1983)

Facts

Dorris Joni Reed (plaintiff/appellant) purchased a house from Robert King through his real estate agents (defendants/respondents). No one informed Reed that a woman and her four children had been murdered in the house 10 years earlier. When Reed learned of the murders, she brought suit seeking rescission and damages. The trial court dismissed the suit and Reed appealed.

Judicial Opinion

Blease, Associate Justice. In the sale of a house, must the seller disclose it was the site of a multiple murder? Neither King nor his agents told Reed that a woman and her four children were murdered there. However, it seems "truth will come to light; murder cannot be hid long." (Shakespeare, *Merchant of Venice*, Act II, Scene II.) Reed learned of the gruesome episode from a neighbor after the sale.

King and his real estate agent knew about the murders and knew the event materially affected the market value of the house when they listed it for sale. They represented to Reed the premises were in good condition and fit for an "elderly lady" living alone. They did not disclose the fact of the murders. At some point King asked a neighbor not to inform Reed of that event. Nonetheless, after Reed moved in neighbors informed her no one was interested in purchasing the house because of the stigma.

Reed paid $75,000, but the house is only worth $65,000 because of its past.

Does Reed's pleading state a cause of action? Concealed within this question is the nettlesome problem of the duty of disclosure of blemishes on real property which are not physical defects or legal impairments to use.

Reed seeks to state a cause of action sounding in contract, i.e., rescission, or in tort, i.e., deceit. In either event her allegations must reveal a fraud. "The elements of actual fraud, whether as the basis of the remedy in contract or tort, may be stated as follows: There must be (1) *a false representation* or concealment of a material fact (or, in some cases, an opinion) susceptible of knowledge, (2) made with *knowledge* of its falsity or without sufficient knowledge on the subject to warrant a representation, (3) with the *intent* to induce the person to whom it is made to act upon it; and such person must (4) act in *reliance* upon the representation (5) to his damage."

The trial court perceived the defect in Reed's complaint to be a failure to allege concealment of a material fact. "Concealment" and "material" are legal conclusions concerning the effect of the issuable facts pled. As appears, the analytic pathways to these conclusions are intertwined.

Concealment is a term of art which includes mere non-disclosure when a party has a duty to disclose. Reed's complaint reveals only non-disclosure despite the allegation King asked a neighbor to hold his peace. There is no allegation the attempt at suppression was a cause in fact of Reed's ignorance. Accordingly, the critical question is: does the seller have a duty to disclose here? Resolution of this question depends on the materiality of the fact of the murders.

In general, a seller of real property has a duty to disclose: "where the seller knows of facts *materially* affecting the value or desirability of the property which are known or accessible only to him and also knows that such facts are not known to, or within the reach of the diligent attention and observation of the buyer, the seller is under a duty to disclose them to the buyer. This broad statement of duty has led one commentator to conclude: 'The ancient maxim *caveat emptor* ('let the buyer beware') has little or no application to California real estate transactions.'"

Whether information "is of sufficient materiality to affect the value or desirability of the property . . . depends on the facts of the particular case." Materiality "is a question of law, and is part of the concept of right to rely or justifiable reliance." Accordingly the term is essentially a label affixed to a normative conclusion. Three considerations bear on this legal conclusion: the gravity of the harm inflicted by non-disclosure; the fairness of imposing a duty of discovery on the buyer as an alternative to compelling disclosure, and its impact on the stability of contracts if rescission is permitted.

Numerous cases have found non-disclosure of physical defects and legal impediments to use of real property are material. However, to our knowledge, no prior real estate sale case has faced an issue of non-disclosure of the kind presented here. Should this variety of ill-repute be required to be disclosed? Is this a circumstance where "non-disclosure of the fact amounts to a failure to act in good faith and in accordance with reasonable standards of fair dealing[?]"

The paramount argument against an affirmative conclusion is it permits the camel's nose of unrestrained irrationality admission to the tent. If such an "irrational" consideration is permitted as a basis of rescission the stability of all conveyances will be seriously undermined. Any fact that might disquiet the enjoyment of some segment of the buying public may be seized upon by a disgruntled purchaser to void a bargain. In our view, keeping this genie in the bottle is not as difficult a task as these arguments assume. We do not view a decision allowing Reed to survive a demurrer in these unusual circumstances as endorsing the materiality of facts predicating peripheral, insubstantial, or fancied harms.

The murder of innocents is highly unusual in its potential for so disturbing buyers they may be unable to reside in a home where it has occurred. This fact may foreseeably deprive a buyer of the intended use of the purchase. Murder is not such a common occurrence that buyers should be charged with anticipating and discovering this disquieting possibility. Accordingly, the fact is not one for which a duty of inquiry and discovery can sensibly be imposed upon the buyer.

Reed alleges the fact of the murders has a quantifiable effect on the market value of the premises. We cannot say this allegation is inherently wrong and, in the pleading posture of the case, we assume it to be true. If information known or accessible only to the seller has a significant and measurable effect on market value and, as is alleged here, the seller is aware of this effect, we see no principled basis for making the duty to disclose turn upon the character of the information. Physical usefulness is not and never has been the sole criterion of valuation. Stamp collections and gold speculation would be insane activities if utilitarian considerations were the sole measure of value.

Reputation and history can have a significant effect on the value of realty. "George Washington slept here" is worth something, however physically inconsequential that consideration may be. Ill-repute or "bad will" conversely may depress the value of property. Failure to disclose such a negative fact where it will have a foreseeably depressing effect on income expected to be generated by a business is tortious. Some cases have held that *unreasonable* fears of the potential buying public that a gas or oil pipeline may rupture may depress the market value of land and entitle the owner to incremental compensation in eminent domain.

Whether Reed will be able to prove her allegation the decade-old multiple murder has a significant effect on market value we cannot determine. If she is able to do so by competent evidence she is entitled to a favorable ruling on the issues of materiality and duty to disclose. Her demonstration of objective tangible harm would still the concern that permitting her to go forward will open the floodgates to rescission on subjective and idiosyncratic grounds.

A more troublesome question would arise if a buyer in similar circumstances were unable to plead or establish a significant and quantifiable effect on market value. However, this question is not presented in the posture of this case. Reed has not alleged the fact of the murders has rendered the premises useless to her as a residence. As currently pled, the gravamen of her case is pecuniary harm. We decline to speculate on the abstract alternative.

Reversed.

Case Questions

1. What happened in the house?
2. How did Reed discover it?
3. What effect did it have on the value?
4. Is concealment fraud? When?
5. Can Reed proceed with her case?
6. Give examples of other types of disclosures that would be necessary.

Would the failure to disclose a problem with errant golf balls landing on the roof of a house be misrepresentation? What if the house is located across the street from a golf course? *Murray v. Crank*, 945 S.W.2d 28 (Mo. Ct. App. 1997)

Consider 14.13

Remedies for misrepresentation include rescission, actual damages, and, if fraudulent, punitive damages. If a real estate agent or broker colludes with a party to defraud or misrepresent, the agent or broker faces license suspension or revocation.

DISCLOSURE STATUTES

Because of many problems with innocent and intentional misrepresentation in the sale of property, the National Association of Realtors and other groups, have succeeded in obtaining passage of disclosure laws. In Maine and California, sellers are required to fill out questionnaires to disclose any known defects including problems with plumbing, the electrical system, walls, floors, insulation, and the home's foundation. Over half of the remaining states recommend such disclosure. Known as **transfer disclosure statements (TDS),** these forms, in the states where they are required, must be presented to potential buyers *before* they enter into a purchase contract. The result of these mandatory disclosure forms has been growth of real estate inspection firms and the warranty industry that affords buyers protection for defects that arise despite all the caution in inspection and disclosure.

The duty of disclosure has also been recognized by many courts regardless of statutory obligations, and all relevant information that would affect a decision to purchase should be disclosed by the seller.

Practical Tip

Issues of disclosure often conflict with sellers' and brokers' duties under the Fair Housing Act (see Chapter 19). In other words, answering a question may result in a pattern of not selling certain properties. Some real estate agents answer buyers' questions about stigmatized (psychologically impacted) property as follows: "It is the policy of our firm not to answer inquires of this nature one way or the other. In addition, any type of response to such inquiries by me or other agents may be a violation of federal fair housing laws. If you believe that this information is relevant to your decision to buy the property, you must pursue this investigation on your own."

Practical Tip

Professor Thomas John Rhoads has offered the following advice to sellers and their agents in making their decision to disclose information: "Seek out all the information that you would want to have yourself and remember the simple rule, "If you don't want to disclose, then you probably should."[1]

Decide whether the following statements would or would not be a basis for misrepresentation in a real estate contract.

Consider 14.14

a. "The test/scores for this area's public schools are the highest in the state."
b. "This roof has a 30-year warranty."
c. "This well could never run dry."
d. "That easement is not recorded, but it's valid."
e. "This property was certified in 1990 as termite free."
f. "The crime rate is very low here."
g. "The city has no plans for a stadium next to this house."
h. "The value on this house just keeps going up."
i. "Basements in this area don't leak."

---

1. Thomas John Rhoads, "Caveat Venditor: Seller Disclosure in California Residential Real Estate Transactions," 2 *Journal of the Pacific Southwest Academy of Legal Studies in Business 45* (1996).

Psychological Disclosure Statutes

A new form of disclosure statute has resulted from cases such as *Reed* and because of additional issues that could have a psychological impact on the buyer and possible resulting reduction in value.[2] More appropriately named nondisclosure statutes, these laws shield sellers and their agents from liability for the nondisclosure of murder, suicide, or other felonies committed on the property or that a resident or former resident suffers from the human immunodeficiency virus (HIV). Currently, 17 states have some form of liability shield statutes for nondisclosure of this information with psychological impact. However, the statutes often leave open the question as to the seller's or agent's response if the buyer specifically asks a question about such activity on the property. Most legal experts agree that if there is a specific question from a buyer, the seller or his agent cannot lie about the property and would be required to disclose such information.

Consider 14.15

Roberts purchased a home through a realty. When she learned that one of the sellers had died of hepatitis and the other from pneumonia, she suspected that the sellers had AIDS and she brought suit against their estates and the realty for their failure to disclose this psychologically important information about the property. Should Roberts be permitted to rescind the contract? Do you think she has the right to that information about the sellers? If you were the real estate agent, would you feel an obligation to disclose such information? What response is appropriate in those states where the agent is prohibited from disclosing whether the seller had AIDS?

Consider 14.16

In 1989, Jeffrey and Patrice Stambovsky bought an 18-room mansion in Nyack, New York for $650,000. They talked with a local architect who said, "Oh, you're buying the haunted house." The Victorian house has had gifts left by ghosts and the Amazing Kreskin has sought to hold a seance there. The Stambovskys were not given this information before they signed the contract, and they now wish to have their earnest money returned ($32,500). In fact, the house had been written up in *Reader's Digest* in 1977; in the article the owner described a ghost who looked like Santa Claus. In a description in a house tour book, the house description read: "riverfront Victorian—with ghost." Mr. Stambovsky feels he and his wife are the victims of "ectoplasmic fraud." Is he correct? *Stambovsky v. Ackley,* 572 N.Y.S.2d 672 (1991)

Ethical Issue

What ethical issues exist in nondisclosure of information about the property? Is there a moral obligation to disclose material information? What happens when a statute prohibits disclosure unless a buyer specifically asks?

2.   For example, Connecticut's statute provides (at Conn.Gen.Stat. 20-329cc) "'psychologically impacted' means . . . , but is not limited to: (1) the fact that an occupant of real property is, or was at any time suspected to be, infected or has been infected with the human immunodeficiency syndrome, as defined in section 19a-581; or (2) the fact that the property was at any time suspected to have been the site of a homicide, other felony or suicide."

§ 20-329dd provides: "(a) The existence of any fact or circumstance which may have a psychological impact on the purchaser or lessee is not a material fact that must be disclosed in a real estate transaction.(b) No cause of action shall arise against an owner of real estate or his agent for the failure to disclose to the transferee that the property was psychologically impacted, as defined in § 20-329cc."

☀ CAUTIONS AND CONCLUSIONS

To be certain a real estate contract is complete and enforceable, the parties must not only follow the basic contract rules for formation, they must be certain they have covered all the contingencies and issues. This chapter has explained the most common pitfalls in real estate contracts which include:

- The danger of multiple offers and having two parties accept
- The need to have minds meet on all the terms, whether material or immaterial
- Providing for contingencies so that performance is not required until certain events occur, such as the buyer obtaining financing, the seller being able to deliver marketable title, or experts concluding the property is termite free
- Covering the details of transfer, such as how the buyer will take title, how the rent and taxes will be apportioned, who will carry insurance until closing, and how the condition of the property will be preserved
- Establishing damages in advance through a liquidated damages clause so that the earnest money becomes the damages for breach
- Being certain there is adequate disclosure about the property's nature and history that will include everything from soil conditions to whether there was a murder there
- Making sure that the contract complies with applicable federal laws such as the ILSDFA and the Truth in Lending laws

A contract for the sale and purchase of real estate may seem like a simple exchange of title, but it is a complex transaction with many layers that requires careful negotiation and drafting, contingencies for problems that arise, compliance with applicable laws, and steps to be certain good title passes.

Practical Tip

Before buying property, talk to the neighbors. Find out about noises and check with others for the history of the property. Have experts check the physical condition of the property for everything from leaky roofs to malfunctioning air conditioners.

Key Terms

Chapter Problems

1. The following excerpts from letter negotiations on land occurred between Magnus Matthews and Elaine Brown.

January 4, 2001

Dear Magnus

I am interested in buying that lot you showed me last Saturday. You talked about $40,000 as a price. That sounds good to me. Let's meet Wednesday at Frisco Kid's to iron out details.

    Elaine

January 4, 2001 (via fax)

Elaine,

$40,000 is the price. Cash only. I'll see you Wednesday at 5:30.

    Magnus

On January 5, 2001, a developer came to Magnus with $40,000 cash and asked to buy the lot. Magnus signed a contract and accepted a $4,000 earnest money deposit. On January 6, 2001, Magnus met Elaine at Frisco Kid's and said when he first spotted her, "Sorry, kid. I sold the lot yesterday. Cash straight up. Let's talk about any of my other lots." Did Magnus and Elaine have a contract?

2. Reese Aherns signed a contract to purchase a mountain home from Mr. and Mrs. Jack Johnson. The contract included the following condition (handwritten in an addendum signed by both parties):

Closing is subject to buyer's inspection of property by him and his designated specialist and complete satisfaction of specialist with property condition.

Aherns's specialist inspected the property and said he thought the roof would need to be replaced in a few years. He also felt some wood near the front of the cabin should be replaced. Aherns demanded that the Johnsons fix these items or he would not close. The Johnsons maintain they did not agree to any repairs; the condition was for Aherns' protection so that he could opt out of the agreement. Aherns has threatened to sue for breach of contract. Who should win?

3. State which of the following defects would be covered under the implied warranty of habitability (assuming new-home purchasers):

    a. Defective air-conditioning system

    b. Use of ungalvanized nails in walls

    c. Variations in the color of carpet (one color ordered)

    d. Sagging roof

    e. Lack of insulation

4. Tommy Smith negotiated the sale of what was called the "Smith Farm" to Alex Boone. Tommy negotiated separately with Boone and had agreed to deliver to Boone option contracts from all of his relatives who held an interest in the Smith Farm. Boone had agreed to pay Tommy for obtaining the agreements and signature of his relatives who all held an interest in the Smith Farm. Boone represented a kaolin company. Kaolin is a mineral that had been discovered in great quantities beneath the Smith Farm. The minerals rights for the Smith Farm had been leased for a number of years, but no company had ever done any significant amount of mining of that subsurface area.

After the relatives had signed all the agreements to sell and the transaction had closed, they were told of Boone's relationship with a kaolin company and his payments to Tommy in exchange for Tommy assuring the relatives that the $85,000 price obtained was the best that they could hope for. The relatives brought suit to have the transaction set aside because of misrepresentation by the buyer in the transaction. Is this possible? Can a buyer be guilty of misrepresentation? Do you think Tommy had any duty to disclose what he was doing to his relatives? Did Boone have any duty to disclose who he was representing? *O.L. McClendon v. Georgia Kaolin Co., Inc.,* 837 F. Supp. 1231 (M.D. Ga. 1993)

5. Otto and Frank Mattuschek owned a ranch in Montana consisting of 3,540 acres. Carnell, a real estate broker, discovered their interest in selling the ranch, and the following instrument was executed:

PLAINTIFF'S EXHIBIT "A"

APPOINTMENT OF AGENT

I hereby appoint E. F. Carnell of Lewistown, Montana whose office is located in said City and State, my agent with the exclusive right to sell the following property:

    Our Ranch property 3540 acres,
    T.23 & 22-R-19 & 20-Fergus County Mont.

For the Sum of $30,000.

    Conditions and terms of the sale are as follows:

    Cash to seller. Possession Dec. 1-1953, seller retain 5% landowner Royalty. Seller pay 1953 taxes, seller transfers all lease land to buyer.

    And I agree to furnish a title as outlined in the following paragraph:

A. An abstract of title showing a good merchantable title to said property together with a warranty deed properly executed.

    Said sale may be made for a less amount if hereafter authorized by me; you are further authorized to receive a deposit on the sale price. I agree to pay a commission of

continued

$1000—on the sale price and the commission shall be payable as soon as the sale is made and a down payment has been made, or sale price paid in full at the time of sale, and, or as soon as a binder fee has been collected on the sale, whichever be first.

This authorization is to remain in effect and full force for 30 days and thereafter until revoked by me in writing.

Dated at Lewistown, Montana this 14th day of May 1953—

x <u>Otto Mattuschek</u>
x <u>Frank Mattuschek</u>

Carnell then met Ward, a prospective buyer, and accepted from him a check for $2,500 as a binder. The check looked as follows:

93-73/921

PLAINTIFF'S EXHIBIT B

1st Bank Stock Corporation
First National Bank of Lewistown

Lewistown, Montana, May 20 1953   No. _____

Pay To The Order of ____*Red Carnell*____ $2500xx
____twine five hundred and no/100 Dollars____

                              s/s E. E. Ward

For down Payment on land
Mattuschek
(Endorsement E. F. Carnell)

At the same time Carnell had the following executed on his letterhead:

PLAINTIFF'S EXHIBIT "C"
(Defendant's Exhibit no. 1)

Real Estate	Fergus Realty City	Property
Insurance	213 Main St. Phone 598	Farms
Rentals	Lewistown, Montana	Ranches

May 20 – 1953

I hereby agree to buy the Mattuschek place in accordance with the terms of the agreement between E. F. Carnell and the Mattuscheks. Dated

May 14, 1953.
/s/ E. E. Ward

To Buy or Sell—See "Red" Carnell

Carnell drove to the ranch and advised the Mattuscheks of the sale. They asked if Ward would be willing to lease back the property. When the closing was attempted, the Mattuscheks refused to convey the property, and the Wards filed suit seeking specific performance and damages. Is there a contract? Are any damages or remedies appropriate? *Ward v. Mattuscheks,* 330 P.2d 971 (Mont. 1958)

6.   Carl and Cleo Nordstrom entered into a contract to purchase 480 acres of farmland from John Lee and Marilee Miller. The purchase price was $480,000. The advertisements for the property described it as "irrigated cropland" and stated that the property had two wells. One advertisement read:

> *480 acres of Prime Developed irrigation land located northwest of Garden City in Finnery County, Kansas. Two irrigation wells and approximately 14,000 ft. of underground pipe. This land is flood-irrigated and all runs are one-half mile long.*
> *THIS IS ONE YOU HAVE TO SEE TO BELIEVE.*

Robert Legere, a real estate broker, contacted the Nordstroms and showed them the property. Nordstrom inspected the land, the buildings, and the wells. The Nordstroms paid $15,000 down, sold their home and store in Colorado, and purchased the property and moved in on March 2, 1976.

During the summer of 1976, one of the irrigation wells went dry. On further investigation, Nordstrom discovered that insufficient water was available to supply either well and the farm could no longer be operated owing to its geological limitations.

Nordstrom confronted the defendants with the information, and the defendants offered to drill another well and change the contract payment terms. The Nordstroms refused and brought suit for fraud and misrepresentation seeking rescission of the agreement. Should they win? *Nordstrom v. Miller,* 605 P.2d 545 (Kans. 1980)

7.   The Rosens contracted to purchase from the Luttingers some property in Stamford for $85,000 and paid an $8,500 deposit. The contract contained the following contingency:

> *. . . subject to and conditional upon the buyers obtaining first mortgage financing on said premises from a bank or other lending institution in an amount of $45,000 for a term of not less than twenty (20) years and at an interest rate which does not exceed 8½ percent per annum.*

The Rosens agreed to use due diligence in attempting to obtain such financing. The parties further agreed that if the Rosens were unsuccessful in obtaining financing as provided in the contract, and notified the Luttingers within a specific time, all sums paid on the contract would be refunded and the contract would terminate without further obligation of either party.

In applying for a mortgage that would satisfy the contingency clause in the contract, the Rosens relied on their attorney, who applied at a New Haven lending institution for a $45,000 loan at 8¼ percent per annum interest over a period of 25 years. The Rosens' attorney knew that this lending institution was the only one that would at that time lend as much as $45,000 on a mortgage for a single-family dwelling. A mortgage commitment for $45,000 was obtained with "interest at the prevailing rate at the time of closing but not less than 8¾ percent." Since the commitment failed to meet the contract requirement, timely notice was given to the Luttingers, and demand was made for the return of the down payment. The Luttingers' counsel thereafter offered to make up the difference between the 8¾ percent interest rate offered by the bank and the 8½ percent rate provided in the contract for the entire 25 years by a funding arrangement, the exact terms of which were not defined. The Rosens did not accept this offer and, on the Luttingers' refusal to return the deposit, an action was brought. Who should win? *Luttinger v. Rosen,* 316 A.2d 757 (Conn. 1972)

8. Patrick and Laurie Doyle submitted a form real estate purchase contract to Tom Ortega to purchase his property for $28,000. Ortega countered for $30,000. The Doyles accepted his counteroffer but changed a checked box on who would pay escrow fees. Ortega then agreed to the revisions and sent back the form changing the escrow agent from Rock Springs National Bank to an Idaho Bank. Do the Doyles and Ortega have a contract? *Doyle v. Ortega,* 872 P.2d 721 (Idaho 1994).

9. Would an oral modification of a real estate contract be enforceable? *Bradshaw v. Ewing,* 376 S.E.2d 264 (S.C. 1984).

10. Must a seller disclose to a buyer that his neighbors are unusually noisy, i.e. that their parties sometimes cause the seller's house to shake? *Shapiro v. Sutherland,* 76 Cal. Rptr. 2d 101 (1998)

Internet Activities

1. Explore the complete resources of HUD at **http://www.hud.gov/**.

2. For the full statutory text of the ILSFDA (Interstate Land Sales Full Disclosure Act), go to: **http://www.hud.gov:80/fha/sfh/ils/ilsstat.html**.

3. Go to **http://www.freddiemac.com/community/homebuy.htm** for information on how to conduct a consumer inspection of a proposed home purchase.

4. For a detailed explanation of a California transfer disclosure statement, go to: **http://www.willhall.com/geninfopg13.html#conditionsofrealpropertytransferdiscstat**.

Home Loan Guaranty Services

Veterans Benefits & Services

VA Home Loans - A quick guide for homebuyers and real estate professionals

Information on the Home Loan Program

Am I Eligible for a VA Loan?

Property Management

Lenders & Servicers

Contact VA Loan Guaranty Service

Forms

Loan Guaranty HomePage

VBA HomePage

VA Privacy Policy/Notices

◆ Why a VA loan?　　　　　　　　　◆ Had a VA loan before?

◆ Five easy steps to a VA loan　　　　◆ How to get a VA loan

◆ VA financing - a good deal for veterans　◆ Requirements for loan approval

◆ What is a VA-guaranteed loan?　　　◆ Costs of obtaining a VA loan

◆ What can a VA loan be used for?　　　◆ Need more information?

◆ Who is eligible?

WHY A VA LOAN?

The more you know about our home loan program, the more you will realize how little "red tape" there really is in getting a VA loan. These loans are often made without any downpayment at all, and frequently offer lower interest rates than ordinarily available with other kinds of loans. Aside from the veteran's certificate of eligibility and the VA-assigned appraisal, the application process is not much different than any other type of mortgage loan. And if the lender is approved for automatic processing, as more and more lenders are now, a buyer's loan can be processed and closed by the lender without waiting for VA's approval of the credit application.

Additionally, if the lender is approved under VA's Lender Appraisal Processing Program (LAPP), the lender may review the appraisal completed by a VA-assigned appraiser and close the loan on the basis of that review. The LAPP process can further speed the time to loan closing.

Back to top

FIVE EASY STEPS TO A VA LOAN

1. Apply for a Certificate of Eligibility.
   A veteran who doesn't have a certificate can obtain one easily by completing VA Form 26-1880, Request for a Certificate of Eligibility for VA Home Loan Benefits and submitting it to one of our Eligibility Centers with copies of your most recent discharge or separation papers covering active military duty since September 16, 1940, which show active duty dates and type of discharge.
2. Decide on a home the buyer wants to buy and sign a purchase agreement
3. Order an appraisal from VA. (Usually this is done by the lender.)
   Most VA regional offices offer a "speed-up" telephone appraisal system. Call the local VA office for details.
4. Apply to a mortgage lender for the loan.
   While the appraisal is being done, the lender (mortgage company, savings and loan, bank, etc.) can be gathering credit and income information. If the lender is authorized by VA to do automatic processing, upon receipt of the VA or LAPP appraised value determination, the loan can be approved and closed without waiting for VA's review of the credit application. For loans that must first be approved by VA, the lender will send the application to the local VA office, which will notify the lender of its decision.
5. Close the loan and the buyer moves in.

Chapter 15
Financing in the Transfer of Real Estate

TEST YOUR KNOWLEDGE

Do you know the meanings of the most commonly used terms in buying a home? Check this list and then take the test at the end of the chapter (pages 408–409).

point	ARM	conventional loan
deed of trust	caveat emptor	balloon payment
lock	loan-to-value ratio	setback
annual percentage rate	creative financing	hazard
amortization	earnest money	insurance
escrow	FHA	walk-through
government loan	prepaids	PITI

Financing the purchase of real property is a complex critical element of our business and professional lives and a key part of any economy. This chapter discusses the methods of financing the purchase of land, and the rights and remedies of borrowers and lenders under each method.

THE MORTGAGE

Ancient civilizations such as Egypt and Babylonia employed the concept of pledging property to finance its purchase or to secure loans for other purposes. Called *fiducia* in ancient Rome, the process of obtaining security in real property required the borrower to transfer title to the lender, who retained such title until the borrower had completely repaid the loan. Later, under the concept of *pignus,* the borrower retained title, but the lender was entitled to take possession at any time if the borrower defaulted.

Although the Roman concepts of *fiducia* and *pignus* were used later in Europe as methods for financing the purchase of real property, the term **mortgage** was not introduced into the English legal system until after the 1066 invasion of England by William I (William the Conqueror). Mortgage is derived from the French word *mort,* which means dead or frozen (to indicate that the borrower could not transfer the property freely), and *gage,* which means pledge.

The following is a current definition of mortgage from *Black's Law Dictionary* (1996):

> a pledge or security of a particular property for the payment of a debt or the performance of some other obligation, whatever form the transaction may take, but is not now regarded as a conveyance; a written instrument providing security for payment of a debt.

This basic definition applies to all forms of mortgages and mortgage theories adopted by each of the states. However, the details on the creation, enforcement, and rights of parties do vary.

Parties to the Mortgage

A mortgage is a two-party relationship. The borrower who is buying or pledging property is referred to as the **mortgagor.** The mortgagor may be borrowing the funds to purchase the property being pledged, called a **purchase money mortgage** (see page 380). Alternatively, the mortgagor may be pledging property already owned as security for a loan for other reasons.

The lender who advances the mortgagor the funds for the loan is referred to as the **mortgagee.** In a mortgage relationship, one of these two parties (mortgagor or mortgagee) will hold title to the property and the other will have an interest in the property.

Title Theory versus Lien Theory

Although all states permit the use of the mortgage to enable the mortgagee to secure repayment of the underlying debt by the mortgagor, each state has a different theory of how that security is accomplished. However, each of the state theories can be classified as a title theory, a lien theory, or an intermediate theory (a combination of the two).

Title theory states follow the idea that a mortgage actually gives the mortgagee some type of legal title to the property. This theory is the older of the two and is used primarily in the eastern states. Under title theory, the mortgagee has the right to possession and the right to collect rents on the property.

In **lien theory** states, the mortgagee has only a lien on the property and is entitled to possession and rents only upon foreclosure. Under this theory, the mortgagor actually holds title to the property. The lien theory is followed by the majority of states west of the Mississippi.

Some states follow an intermediate theory, which is a combination of the title and lien theories. In these states, the mortgagee is entitled to possession and rents upon the default of the mortgagor. However, unlike the lien theory, the mortgagee is not required to wait until after foreclosure; and unlike the title theory, the mortgagee does not hold title until after completion of proceedings mandated by statute but short of full foreclosure.

The following case illustrates the effect of a lien theory mortgage when a mortgagor is in default. The language of the court clarifies the principle that title and all its rights remain with the mortgagor until a court process is held.

Siffring Farms, Inc. v. Juranek

561 N.W.2d 203 (Neb. 1997)

Facts

Donald Juranek was in default on the mortgage on his property held by Farm Credit Bank of Omaha, and a decree of foreclosure was signed on March 20, 1992. The mortgaged property was sold to Siffring Farms at a foreclosure sale held on September 3, 1993. The sale was confirmed on October 8, 1993, and a sheriff's deed to the Juranek property was delivered to Siffring on November 16, 1993.

In April 1993, Juranek and his son had entered into an agreement with J.C. Robinson Seed Company to grow seed corn. Juranek and his son grew the seed corn on the property that was subject to a mortgage. The seed contract was signed by both Juranek and his son, as well as by a representative of Robinson. While the contract provided that Robinson would supply the seed and would at all times remain owner of the crop unless Robinson chose to release it, the grower was required, among other things, to plant and fertilize according to Robinson's timing and specifications; to "rogue out" volunteer corn near the seed acreage; to protect the crop against insects, weeds, and other conditions that could damage it; and to destroy all male plants. Payment under the contract was based upon a formula and the work that had been required by Robinson. The contract further provided that the payment would be divided, with 20 percent going to Juranek's son as the grower and 80 percent to Juranek as the landlord. Under the formula for payment, the grower had the ability to establish a settlement price (or prices)

per 5,000 bushels at any time (or times) between May 1, 1993, and April 21, 1994. Regardless of when the settlement price was determined; however, payments under the contract could not be made before December 16, 1993.

On November 10, 1993, Siffring filed suit against the Juraneks, Robinson, and Farm Credit for payment under the Robinson contract. Robinson deposited the money with the court and participated no further in the litigation. The lower court held that because the seed corn crop had been harvested prior to November 16, 1993, the date of the delivery of title to the property, the proceeds from the sale to Robinson had already become the personal property of Juranek and that the money from Robinson belonged to Juranek. Siffring appealed.

Judicial Opinion

Flowers, District Judge. Siffring claims the district court erred in (1) finding that the payment due Juranek under the Robinson contract was personal property and not rent, (2) failing to find that the payment due Juranek was rent and that the right to it passed to Siffring with the delivery of the sheriff's deed, and (3) finding the lease to be a crop share arrangement.

The first question we must decide is whether the payment due Juranek under the Robinson contract is rent. Juranek and *amicus curiae*, Farm Credit Services of the

Midlands, suggest that it is something different. The contracts identifies Juranek as the landlord and his son as the grower. The contract imposed no obligations upon Juranek. The payment due him was for the use of the land. While the testimony at trial shows that Juranek may not have been as passive as the Robinson contract contemplated, it does not necessitate a different conclusion. In this case, the payment due Juranek was for the use of his land, which, by definition, is rent.

The next question is whether the rent was unaccrued at the time the sheriff's deed was delivered to Siffring. At the time the sheriff's deed was delivered, Juranek and his son had done all that was required of them to receive payment. The seed corn had been grown, harvested, and delivered to Robinson. The right to receive payment was a fully vested and enforceable right, and Robinson was no longer using Juranek's land for any purpose under the contract. We find that under the circumstances the rent had accrued, even though the time for payment had not yet arrived. Siffring cites *Conservative Sav. & Loan Assn. v. Karp*, 218 Neb. 217, 352, N.W.2d 900 (1984), for the proposition that a purchaser at a judicial sale is entitled to all rents collected after the date the purchaser receives the sheriff's deed. What *Conservative Sav. & Loan Assn.* actually held was that the purchaser was entitled to all rents collected for the period after the date of the sheriff's deed. The case says nothing about the right to receive rents that had accrued for a prior period but had remained unpaid. In the instant case, the rent due Juranek was for the 1993 corn crop season. That season ended

with the harvest of the seed corn, which was prior to the delivery of the sheriff's deed to Siffring. Robinson was no longer using Juranek's land when Siffring took title, and there was no rent due under the contract for the period that commenced on November 16, 1993.

Because the rent had accrued prior to the date Siffring took title and was for a period of time during which Juranek was the owner, we need not determine whether the rent was crop share or cash, or what difference, if any, that would make.

The payment due Juranek for the crop grown under the contract with Robinson covered a period of time prior to Siffring's ownership and had accrued prior to November 16, 1993. The payment did not pass to Siffring with the sheriff's deed.

Affirmed.

Case Questions

1. Even though Juranek was in default during the period in which he contracted with Robinson, why does he get to keep the proceeds from the contract with Robinson?

2. What would have happened in the case if the foreclosure had occurred prior to the harvest of the seed corn?

3. What clauses could be put in a mortgage to allow the mortgagee to collect the benefits of any contract entered into during a time of default or foreclosure?

4. Who had title to the property between April 1993 and November 16, 1993? Why?

Creation of Mortgage Relationship

WRITING REQUIREMENT

As with all real estate transactions, the mortgage must be in writing. In addition to compliance with the Statute of Frauds, the rights of the mortgagee in the property are to a certain extent protected by public notification of the mortgagee's interest. Such public notification comes through the recording of the mortgage instrument with the appropriate governmental unit—the same governmental unit where deeds (Chapter 13) and security interests (Chapters 4 and 5) are recorded. Mortgages are complex land interests and a written document helps to ensure that all interests, rights, and remedies are clearly established; a written document is the only method whereby such clarification is possible.

UNDERLYING DEBT REQUIREMENT

The Debt Instrument A mortgage is invalid unless there is some underlying debt. In other words, a mortgage cannot be enforced unless the mortgagor owes some debt to the mortgagee. Generally, and particularly in the sale and purchase of residential property, that underlying debt is evidenced by a **promissory note.** The promissory note is the actual contractual arrangement between the parties for the loan of funds. It is usually a very simple instrument specifying the principal

FIGURE 15.1   *Promissory Note*

$ _____ City, State _____ 20_____

For value received _____ promises (s) to pay

to _____ or order, at _____

the sum of _____ DOLLARS ($ _____).

Should default be made in the payment of any installment when due, then the whole sum of principal and interest shall become immediately due and payable at the option of the holder of this note, with interest from date of such default at the highest legal rate until paid on the entire unpaid principal and accrued interest.

Should any installment due hereunder not be paid as it matures, the amount of such installment which has matured shall, at the option of the holder of this note, bear interest at 10 percent per annum from its maturity date until paid.

Principal and interest payable in lawful money of the United States of America.

Should suit be brought to recover on this note _____ promise(s) to pay as attorneys' fees a reasonable amount additional to the amount found hereunder.

The makers and indorsers hereof severally waive diligence, demand, presentment for payment and protest, and consent to the extension of time of payment of this note without notice.

This note is secured by a mortgage upon real property.

_____   _____

_____   _____

---

amount, the rate of interest, and the payment terms. Also, the promissory note indicates that its payment is secured by a mortgage or deed of trust. Figure 15.1 is an example of a note secured by a mortgage.

The promissory note usually contains terms that make it negotiable—a quality that enables the lender to easily transfer and sell the note to third parties. Also, the note contains various clauses relating to acceleration, default, and attorneys' fees. These provisions are closely tied to the rights afforded mortgagees and are discussed later in this chapter in conjunction with appropriate mortgage terms. Without an underlying debt, there can be no mortgage and resulting security for a lender, as the following case illustrates.

First American Bank of New York v. Sloane

651 N.Y.S.2d 734 (Sup. Ct. App. 1997)

Facts

Leon Zeibert had given his nephew, Alan Sloane, large amounts of cash over the years. Zeibert maintained that Sloane and his wife, Gloria, had signed a mortgage on their home as security for the loans. However, Zeibert did not have a copy of the note.

Zeibert claimed priority over other creditors of Sloane in a state receivership proceeding. First American Bank objected to Zeibert's claim of a mortgage. The lower court held that there was no mortgage because Zeibert's cash advances were gifts not intended to be secured by a mortgage. Zeibert appealed.

Judicial Opinion

Carpinello, Justice. At the hearing before the court-appointed Referee, Zeibert, who is the uncle of the co-owner of the subject premises, testified that he had given his nephew $40,000 in 1978 and another $40,000 in 1983.

These advances were purportedly secured in 1983 by an $80,000 mortgage signed by defendants Alan A. Sloane and Gloria M. Sloane, incumbering the subject premises. Although Zeibert testified that a note had been executed essentially contemporaneously with the mortgage, Zeibert was unable to produce any note at the hearing.

The Referee found (and Supreme Court confirmed) that Zeibert had made advances of hundreds of thousands of dollars to his nephew over the years, some of which had been repaid sporadically. Based upon the totality of the circumstances, including but not limited to the fact that Alan Sloane was Zeibert's "favorite nephew" for whom he "would do anything", the Referee concluded that the advances by Zeibert were gifts and not loans secured by the mortgage and on that basis disallowed Zeibert's claim to any of the surplus moneys.

[While i]t is true that a mortgage is not invalidated by the absence of the note or bond manifesting the debt. Nonetheless, in order to be enforceable as a lien on real property, the mortgage must be supported by valid consideration and "[a] transaction intended to be in the nature of a gift, there being *** no intention that the mortgagor would be called upon to pay the 'mortgage', is not a mortgage."

Since the Referee's determination disallowing Zeibert's claim was based upon substantial support in the record, Supreme Court's decision to confirm the report should be affirmed.

Affirmed.

Case Questions

1. Why did the court find there was no mortgage?
2. Do you think the result would have been different if Sloane had a signed note?
3. What problems would result if creditors could claim valid mortgages without underlying debt?

Federal Regulation of Mortgage Debt Instruments
FEDERAL DISCLOSURE REQUIREMENTS IN MORTGAGE DEBT

Federal Disclosure Regulations Perhaps one of the most significant concerns faced by all lenders in properly executing the note underlying a mortgage is whether the note complies with all applicable federal regulations. The **Truth-in-Lending laws** were passed by Congress in 1968 as part of the **Federal Consumer Credit Protection Act.** To carry out the basic provisions of the act, the Federal Reserve Board promulgated specific regulations on compliance, which are referred to in their entirety as **Regulation Z** (12 C.F.R. § 226 *et seq.*). If Regulation Z is applicable in a mortgage transaction, certain disclosures must be made to the party or parties signing the note.

Lending institutions engaged in mortgage lending are subject to Regulation Z. The applicability of Regulation Z to brokers and other private parties participating in installment sales and other creative financing methods is discussed later in this chapter. Regulation Z does not apply to the following:

1. Business transactions
2. Commercial transactions
3. Agricultural transactions
4. Organizational credit transactions

If Regulation Z is applicable to a lender and to the particular credit transaction involved, the lender is required to make certain disclosures. The following information must be furnished to the borrower:

1. Identity of creditor
2. Cash price
3. Annual percentage rate
4. Finance charge including any prepaid finance charges
5. Amount financed and itemization

6. Total payment amount
7. Number of payments
8. Amount per payment
9. When the payments are due
10. Late payment charges

These disclosures are usually made on a statement separate from the promissory note and mortgage documents. Figure 15.2 is an example of a Regulation Z disclosure statement for a mortgage-secured note. If the note has a variable interest rate, there is a special disclosure form that appears at the bottom of Figure 15.2.

Federal Debt Rescission Regulations Although Regulation Z provides for a three-day rescission period for security interests and second mortgages, this period does not apply to **residential mortgage transactions.** The exception to the three-day rescission period and notice of that period is for first notes and mortgages on property being purchased by a consumer for use as a residence. However, the consumer who executes a second note and mortgage on his residence is permitted to cancel that transaction within the three-day period. In these types of financings, the lender must disclose the right of cancellation and must also provide, in written form, procedures for exercising the right of cancellation. Figure 15.3 is a sample from the regulations.

Federal Debt Credit Advertising Regulation One additional issue under Regulation Z is the advertisement of the credit terms the lender has available. Regulation Z defines an **advertisement** as "a commercial message in any media that promotes, directly or indirectly, a credit transaction." Advertisements must be accurate and state only those terms that are actually available. Any advertisements including finance charges must also state those charges in terms of an annual percentage rate (APR). The APR is an expression of the cost of credit according to its yearly rate. Formulas for computing the APR are set forth in the regulation, along with tables that can be used in such computations.

Regulation Z also provides that if certain **triggering language** is used in advertisements, then additional disclosures must also be included. Triggering language includes:

1. Amount or percentage of any down payment
2. Number of payments or period of repayment
3. Amount of any payment
4. Amount of any finance charge

The additional disclosures that must be made in advertisements using triggering terms are as follows:

1. Amount of percentage of down payment
2. Terms of repayment
3. Annual percentage rate
4. Disclosures of any increases in payments or rates that may occur

Two examples of down payment triggering language are "total move-in costs of $1,000" or "as low as 10 percent down." The phrase "30-year loan" is an example of a triggering term because it indicates the repayment period. "Payable in monthly installments of $550" is triggering language related to the amount of the

FIGURE 15.2   *Sample Mortgage Disclosure Statement Graduated Payment*

Convenient Savings and Loan   Account number 4862-85

Michael Jones

300 Walnut Court, Little Creek, USA

Annual Percentage Rate	Finance Charge	Amount Financed	Total of Payment
The cost of your credit as a yearly rate	The dollar amount the credit will cost you	The amount of credit provided to you or on your behalf	The amount you will have paid after you have made all payments as scheduled
15.37	$177,970.44	$43,777	$221,548.44

Your payment schedule will be

Number of Payments	Amount of Payments	When Payments are due
12	$446.62	Monthly, beginning 6/1/81
12	$479.67	Monthly, beginning 6/1/82
12	$515.11	Monthly, beginning 6/1/83
12	$553.13	Monthly, beginning 6/1/84
12	$593.91	Monthly, beginning 6/1/85
300	Varying from $637.68 to $627.37	Monthly, beginning 6/1/86

Security: You are giving a security interest in the property being purchased.

Late Charge: If a payment is late you will be charged 5% of the payment.

Prepayment: If you pay off early, you

❏ May   ❏ will not   have to pay a penalty.

❏ May   ❏ will not   be entitled to a refund of a portion of the finance charge.

Assumption: Someone buying your home cannot assume the remainder of the mortgage at the original terms.

See your contract documents for any additional information about nonpayment, default, any required repayment in full before the scheduled date, and prepayment refunds and penalties

e means an estimate

Special disclosure for variable interest rate mortgage loans

You are not required to complete this agreement merely because you have received these disclosures or have signed a loan application. If you obtain this loan, the lender will have a mortgage on your home. You could lose your home, and any money you have put into it, if you do not meet your obligations under the loan.

The annual percentage rate on your loan will be _____ %.

Your regular _____ (frequency) _____ payment will be $ _____

(Your interest rate may increase. Increases in the interest rate could increase your payment.

The highest amount your payment could increase to is $_____.)

Form #H15 from 12 C.F.R. 226 App. H15.

payments. Triggering language related to the finance charge includes "total cost of credit is . . . " and "$90,000 mortgage with two points." Use of any of these phrases requires the advertising lender to include the additional information.

General language such as "no down payment," "years to repay," and "monthly installments to suit your budget" may be used without triggering the additional disclosure requirements.

FIGURE 15.3   *Rescission Form (for Refinancing)*

Your Right to Cancel

You are entering into a transaction that will result in a [mortgage/lien/security interest][on/in] your home. You have a legal right under federal law to cancel this transaction, without cost, within three business days from whichever of the following events occurs last:

(1) the date of the transaction, which is _____; or

(2) the date you received your Truth in Lending disclosures; or

(3) the date you received this notice of your right to cancel.

If you cancel the transaction, the [mortgage/lien/security interest] is also cancelled. Within 20 calendar days after we receive your notice, we must take the steps necessary to reflect the fact that the [mortgage/lien/security interest] [on/in] your home has been cancelled, and we must return to you any money or property you have given to us or to anyone else in connection with this transaction.

You may keep any money or property we have given you until we have done the things mentioned above, but you must then offer to return the money or property. If it is impractical or unfair for you to return the property, you must offer its reasonable value. You may offer to return the property at your home or at the location of the property. Money must be returned to the address below.

If we do not take possession of the money or property within 20 calendar days of your offer, you may keep it without further obligation.

How to Cancel

If you decide to cancel this transaction, you may do so by notifying us in writing, at

(creditor's name and business address)

You may use any written statement that is signed and dated by you and states your intention to cancel, or you may use this notice by dating and signing below. Keep one copy of this notice because it contains important information about your rights.

If you cancel by mail or telegram, you must send the notice no later than midnight of

(date)

(or midnight of the third business day following the latest of the three events listed above)

If you send or deliver your written notice to cancel some other way, it must be delivered to the above address no later than that time.

I WISH TO CANCEL

_____   _____
Consumer's Signature   *Date*

Consider 15.1

Harry and Wilma are purchasing their first home, which is to be constructed over the next six months. They will put down $10,000 and borrow the remaining $90,000 of the purchase price. First Savings and Loan will be lending the $90,000 to Harry and Wilma.

a. With what provisions of Regulation Z must First Savings and Loan comply?
b. Suppose that one year after moving in, Harry and Wilma decide to borrow money to construct a swimming pool. They sign a note and second mortgage with Hank's Bank. With what provisions of Regulation Z must Hank's Bank comply?

Consider 15.2

Do the following advertisements contain any triggering language requiring further disclosure?

a. NEW LISTING—Exciting three-bedroom home. Excellent Northeast Mesa location. Pool and tennis court. Low rates and low down payment.
b. 5% DOWN, 12½% INTEREST LOAN—Country style two-bedroom and guest house.

FEDERAL REGULATION OF HOME EQUITY LOANS

Credit card and personal loan interest are not an income tax deduction. However, interest on home mortgages is deductible. Lenders for home equity lines of credit have been aggressively marketing their services and urging consumers to convert their debt into a home equity loan. Regulation Z includes disclosure standards for these credit lines and requires that the following information be given to the homeowner:

1. That the line of credit creates a security interest in their home and that they could lose their home if the obligation is not repaid.
2. That they need to consult a tax advisor regarding limitations on the deductibility of the interest.
3. What charges are incurred in obtaining the line of credit (such as application fees, points, and annual maintenance fees).
4. All the standard Regulation Z disclosures regarding rates, rate changes, minimum payments, APR, and the right of rescission (also three days for all lines of credit and loans that create a security interest in a debtor's home).

Model disclosure forms have been developed by the Federal Reserve Board for these types of credit arrangements as well. Web Exhibit 15.1 is a sample disclosure form for a home equity credit line.

FEDERAL REGULATION OF THE DECISION TO EXTEND CREDIT FOR REAL PROPERTY FINANCING

The federal government has an extensive regulatory scheme governing lenders in their decisions to extend credit for the owner's purchase of real property. Those regulations control everything from the lending criteria to the statistical reports profiling borrowers.

Equal Credit Opportunity Act Mortgage lenders are also subject to the provisions of the **Equal Credit Opportunity Act (ECOA)** (15 U.S.C. § 1691), which prohibits lenders from refusing loans or discriminating in lending on the basis of sex, marital status, race, religion, or national origin. Penalties for violations include private suits as well as fines. Both federal and independent mortgage lenders must be cautious in reviewing loan applications and must base their decisions on issues of creditworthiness that can be substantiated.

The application of the ECOA to real estate loans is different from its application to unsecured loans or credit card agreements. The ECOA requires creditors to make the decision to extend credit on the basis of individual creditworthiness and not on the basis of race, sex, marital status, and so on. However, as a practical matter, the lender may be required to obtain the signature of the spouse for the mortgage or deed of trust to ensure protection of its security in real property for the loan. This signature is simply necessary for the creditor to enforce sale and foreclosure rights and ensure compliance with state marital property protections and is not an ECOA violation (*Evans v. Centralfed Mortgage Co.,* 815 F.2d 348 [5th Cir. 1987]).

Fair Housing Act and Community Reinvestment Act Under the **Home Mortgage Disclosure Act,** lenders are required to furnish to the federal government information about the nature of loan applicants and their approval rates for loans by race. The latest figures (1997) show the following rates for loan denials: Whites (26%); Asian Americans (13%); Blacks (53%); Native Americans (52%); and Hispanics (38%). The reporting requirements are designed to prevent such lending practices as "redlining" or the red circling of certain areas on a map for the reason that lenders target high-risk areas and use location as their lending criterion as opposed to individual qualifications (see Chapter 19 for more details on redlining). There is continuing federal focus on loan bias and prosecution for violations.

The 1977 **Community Reinvestment Act (CRA)** requires banks to meet the lending needs of their community, including loans to both individuals and small businesses in low-income areas. The Federal Reserve Board, responsible for the enforcement of CRA, requires great detail in reports filed by lenders on their loan portfolios including information on loans for multiunit housing, small businesses, and rehabilitation of neighborhoods.

> ## Practical Tip
> Lending bias remains a significant public and legal issue. Lenders should keep accurate records, maintain high levels of community involvement, and work with shareholder groups on disclosure policies.

Additionally, many institutional shareholders are asking for loan information from banks and requesting proxy proposals for disclosure to shareholders of bank compliance with the CRA.

Debtor's Rights in Mortgage Credit Transactions

Finding financing for a real property purchase is often difficult, involves complex paperwork, and too often requires meeting deadlines. Courts have imposed liability on lenders who are not cautious in handling loan applications and decisions. Lenders have an obligation of good faith and fair dealing and have been held liable to buyer borrowers for negligence in responding to loan applications. The doctrine of **lender liability,** holds lenders liable for the lack of timely approval or the withdrawal of an approval for financing already issued.

DEBTOR'S RIGHTS ON INTEREST RATES: USURY
One additional problem lenders need to be concerned with in the creation of a debt underlying the mortgage involves the amount of interest charged. Most states have laws fixing the maximum interest rates that may be charged legally. If the lender charges a rate in excess of that statutory maximum, then **usury** is present.

The usury rate varies significantly from state to state and also according to changes in the economic climate and the type of credit transaction involved.

Although most lenders would never use an interest rate that exceeds the statutory maximum, they may engage in usury by charging fees in addition to the interest collected on the loan. These fees include financier's charges and points. However, certain charges may be made legally in addition to the maximum legal interest rate without having the loan made usurious. The following list explains such charges:

a. *Charges for costs actually incurred.* It is a general rule that additional charges by a lender for necessary expenditures actually made in rendering the loan will not make the transaction usurious. These charges include appraisal fees, credit report fees, survey costs, title search and insurance costs, recording fees, and actual costs incurred in the preparation of loan documents.

b. *Charges for commissions by loan brokers.* Brokers, in negotiating a loan between parties, may charge commissions even though the loan is negotiated for the statutory maximum. The payment of such a commission will not render the loan usurious. By law, such a charge must be paid to a third party and not the lender.

c. *Standby commitment charges.* Often a builder will have obtained a construction loan for a project but not permanent financing. Instead, the builder will usually arrange to have a standby commitment for permanent financing from a lender. Because the standby commitment requires the lender to produce the money upon the builder's demand, with no guarantee that the builder will make such a demand, the lender's funds are tied up for a period of time. The lender is permitted to charge a commitment fee in addition to the maximum legal interest rate for the loan because of the legitimate service rendered.

d. *Late charges.* Late fees are not considered usurious because of the expense, time, and paperwork involved in collecting and posting late payments.

e. *Government loan charges.* When a borrower seeks a government insured loan (such as a Federal Housing Administration [FHA] loan) there is additional paperwork involved, and the lender is required to pay a premium for government loan insurance. These expenses may be charged to the borrower in addition to the maximum legal interest rate without being considered usurious.

f. *Construction loan charges.* Construction lenders generally have more paperwork and tasks associated with their loans than in consumer loans. The principal amount of the loan is paid in various installments as construction progresses, and the lender may be required to inspect before releasing funds. Also, additional paperwork is required to handle liens (e.g., mechanic's liens as discussed in Chapter 5) and payment of subcontractors and suppliers. Fees for these services may be charged in addition to the maximum legal interest rate without resulting usury problems.

g. *Life insurance premiums.* Many lenders require the borrower to maintain life insurance, with the benefits to be used to retire the note debt. Payment of the premiums for such insurance is not included in the computation of interest charges.

h. *Prepayment penalties.* The issue of whether early loan repayment charges are included in the total interest charges varies from state to state. However, even in states where prepayment penalties are not included in the interest rate, the amount of the charges may be limited by state statutes.

i. *Brundage clauses.* A **Brundage clause** requires the borrower to pay any tax that may be imposed on the lender's mortgage. However, in some states the loan will be usurious if the tax plus the interest charged exceeds the statutory maximum.

Each state provides that certain types of lenders and transactions are exempt from the usury laws. For example, all states with usury laws have some type of exemption for business loans, and many states exempt FHA-insured loans from their usury statutes.

The penalties for charging a usurious rate vary from state to state. In some states, the lender forfeits all interest and recovers only the principal. In others, the lender forfeits only that amount of interest above the maximum. In yet other states, the entire contract is void, and the lender forfeits both interest and principal.

The area of second mortgages has been a focus for usurious loan practices. Five major lenders have entered into settlement agreements with state officials for excessive interest rates on second home mortgages, particularly in low-income areas in inner cities. The Union Neighborhood Assistance Corporation, based in Boston, focuses its efforts on finding such high-interest loans and offering homeowners assistance in obtaining legal relief from them.

Practical Tip

Lenders should be cautious in putting loan packages together. All fees must fit within the state law maximums for fees and interests. For example, a Federal Express charge for delivery to a borrower that is then passed along to the borrower is considered a loan fee and could put the lender in the position of exceeding maximum fees charged for loans.

Debtor's Rights with Recording

A mortgage need not be recorded to be valid. However, an unrecorded mortgage gives rights only between the borrower (mortgagor) and the lender (mortgagee). In order to protect the mortgagee against others' rights or to give the mortgagee priority in relation to other creditors, the mortgage must be recorded in the government office where deeds and other documents affecting land interests are recorded. The process of recording gives the lender priority over subsequently recorded and unrecorded land interests. (See discussion of priorities later in this chapter.)

Terms of the Mortgage

As with contracts for the sale and purchase of real property and with brokerage agreements, the basics of the relationship are only the beginning. Many additional terms are needed in the mortgage agreement to protect and define the rights of the parties. Although many of these terms could also be a part of the underlying debt agreement, it is wise to have corresponding provisions in the mortgage and promissory note documents.

ACCELERATION CLAUSE

Usually, the **acceleration clause** appears only in the promissory note. The purpose of the acceleration clause is to permit the mortgagee to accelerate the maturity date of the note in the event of a default by the mortgagor. The second paragraph in Figure 15.1 on page 367 is a typical example of an acceleration clause. The acceleration clauses in that sample note are exercisable at the option of the holder of the note.

The reason virtually all mortgage notes contain an acceleration clause is that without them the mortgagee's only recourse for default would be a suit to collect the amount of payments missed or a partial foreclosure for the amount of the mortgagor's default. The mortgagee would be required to bring suit each time there was a default. One dispositive suit could not be used.

Practical Tip

A "prior forbearance" clause is one that allows the lender to accelerate a loan when payment is late even if late payments have been made in the past. Under a prior forbearance clause, the lender does not need to reinstate his or her right to prompt payment before declaring the loan in default and accelerating the loan for the full amount due.

Acceleration clauses are recognized as valid in all states and are also permitted to government-insured loans for real estate.

One of the common issues with acceleration clauses is whether the lender can accelerate the loan when there has been a history of allowing late payments. Suppose, for example, that your mortgage payment was due on the first of each month. You have never paid before the 15th of the month and have occasionally paid a late penalty. Your mortgage company has always accepted your late payments. One month you pay on the 16th of the month, with the late fee, and the lender declares you in default and accelerates your loan. In some states, the lender would be required to give notice that it was insisting on timely payment. Such a notice would require postponing acceleration until the next late payment. Some lenders have eliminated the problems of the interaction of late payments and acceleration by putting a clause such as this in their mortgages:

> *Holder may exercise this option [to accelerate] during any default by maker regardless of any prior forbearance.*

Consider 15.3

Joseph Loiacono loaned money to Morris and Janice Goldberg and secured the loan with a mortgage on the Goldbergs' home. The original mortgage provided that payment of the mortgage debt could be accelerated on default only upon the option of the mortgagee. When the Goldbergs defaulted, a modification agreement was entered into by the parties whereby the mortgage debt "shall become immediately due and payable" if the mortgagor's default continues for a period of 10 days. The addendum further provided that "this Agreement does not in any way impair the rights of the [mortgagee] under [the mortgage]" and that the mortgagee had the right to renew, extend, or modify the amount due without notice to the mortgagors. The Goldbergs defaulted in October 1988. Loiacono began foreclosure proceedings in 1990, which were dismissed for failure to seek a default judgment. Loiacono refiled for foreclosure in 1993, but that action was dismissed for failure to make proper service of process upon the Goldbergs. Loiacono re-served the Goldbergs and obtained a default judgment that was later vacated because Loiacono had not obtained a new index number for the case. Loiacono filed again for foreclosure in 1995, but the Goldbergs asked that the case be dismissed because the mortgage became due and owing in 1988 and the statute of limitations on contract was six years, which barred Loiacono from bringing suit since more than six years had passed since their default. Should the default be measured from 1988? Had Loiacono waived default? *Loiacono v. Goldberg,* 658 N.Y.S.2d 138 (Sup. Ct. 1997)

INTEREST ACCELERATION CLAUSE

The **interest acceleration clause** also generally appears in the underlying note for the transaction. This clause allows the increase of the interest being paid on the debt to either the maximum amount permitted by law or some other amount established in the clause. This increase results when the mortgagor has defaulted on the payments. An example of the language used to create such a right follows:

> *Should default occur and acceleration of the full amount of the entire indebtedness is called for, interest on the entire amount of the indebtedness shall accrue thereafter at*

the maximum rate of interest then permitted under the laws of the state of
_____ *or continue at the rate provided herein, whichever of said*
rates is greater.

BALLOON PAYMENT CLAUSE

Usually, a mortgage is amortized over a certain number of years, so that the full amount of the mortgage loan and the interest are paid when the term of the mortgage has expired. For example, after 30 years of a typical residential 30-year mortgage, the mortgagor will have paid the full amount of the debt and interest due on the mortgage. However, when the mortgage contains a **balloon payment clause,** the result will not be the same.

Under a mortgage with a balloon payment clause, the mortgagor is still required to make periodic installment payments, but those payments do not fully amortize the amount of the loan; hence, the mortgagor will be required to pay the balance of the amount due at the end of the term of the mortgage. The lump sum due at the end of the mortgage term is called a **balloon payment.**

Although the balloon payment provision is very typical in commercial transactions, it is unusual and often prohibited in residential mortgages. For example, government-insured loans cannot include balloon payment provisions.

PREPAYMENT PENALTY CLAUSES

The mortgagee has the right to earn the interest on the money invested and loaned to the mortgagor for the term of the mortgage. Unless the note or the mortgage specifically provides, the mortgagor has no right to prepay the amount due on the loan in advance of the mortgage term.

Most mortgages will thus contain a clause that requires the mortgagor to pay a penalty in order to prepay the amount due on the loan. The penalty is justified on the grounds that prepayment makes it necessary for the lender to find a new investment outlet and to incur the expenses associated with finding and making that reinvestment. The penalty may apply to the entire period of the loan or may be applicable only during the first 5 to 10 years of the mortgage. The following is an example of a **prepayment penalty clause:**

> *In the event of a default hereunder, or in the event that said mortgagor desires by reason of sale or otherwise to prepay the total amount due and owing at the time of any of the above described prepayments, the mortgagee shall have the right to assess and collect a premium of* _____ *(_____ %) of the then principal balance. The right of the mortgagee to assess and collect such premium shall continue for a period of 10 years from the time the amortization of the above described indebtedness begins.*

The prepayment penalty clause is recognized as valid in all states; however, it should be noted that on certain types of government-insured loans, a prepayment penalty cannot be part of the mortgage agreement or the note. Also, if loans are to be sold or transferred to certain government corporations, the loan arrangement cannot include a prepayment penalty.

LATE PAYMENT CLAUSE

To help the mortgagee receive payments on time and to avoid the problems of collecting payments after the agreed-upon mortgage payment deadlines, late payment clauses are usually included in mortgage documents, promissory notes, or both. These clauses enable the mortgagee to charge a late fee for payments received a certain number of days after the due date. The purpose of the fee is to cover the bookkeeping expenses of having to post late payments. Late payment clauses are legal in all types of loans. The following is an example of a late payment clause from a mortgage:

> *If any payment due hereunder is received later than fifteen days after the due date of the payment, a late charge of _____ (_____ %) of the amount then overdue may be charged by the mortgagee for the purposes of defraying costs of collection and posting of the account.*

Acceptance of a late payment and late payment fee may or may not waive the right to acceleration.

DUE-ON-SALE CLAUSE

The **due-on-sale clause** is a provision in the mortgage agreement that is similar to the acceleration clause. The difference is that it takes effect not upon the default of the mortgagor, but upon the attempted sale of the property by the mortgagor to a buyer who will take over mortgage payments. The due-on-sale clause gives the mortgagee the right to call the entire balance of an indebtedness due and payable if the borrower sells the mortgaged property. The following is an example of a due-on-sale clause:

> *TRANSFER OF THE PROPERTY; ASSUMPTION. If all or any part of the property or an interest therein is sold or transferred by Borrower without Lender's prior consent, excluding (a) the creation of a lien or encumbrance subordinate to this deed of trust; (b) the creation of a purchase money security interest for household appliances; (c) transfer by devise, descent, or by operation of law upon the death of a joint tenant; or (d) the grant of any leasehold interest of three years or less not containing an option to purchase, LENDER MAY, AT LENDER'S OPTION, DECLARE ALL SUMS SECURED BY THIS DEED OF TRUST TO BE IMMEDIATELY DUE AND PAYABLE. Lender shall have waived such option to accelerate if, prior to the sale or transfer, Lender and the person to whom the property is to be sold or transferred reach agreement in writing that the credit of such person is satisfactory to Lender and that the interest payable on the sums secured by this deed of trust shall be at such rate as the Lender shall request. If Lender has waived the option to accelerate provided in this paragraph and if the Borrower's successor in interest has executed a written assumption agreement accepted by Lender, Lender shall release Borrower from all obligations under this Deed of Trust and note. If Lender exercises the option to accelerate, Lender shall mail Borrower notice of such acceleration at least 30 days prior to the time Lender will declare such sums due and payable.*

As interest rates increase, such a clause becomes more helpful to the mortgagee because mortgage notes at older, unprofitable rates can be eliminated and the outstanding funds reinvested at higher rates. However, the clauses do create problems for the mortgagor attempting to sell property in a period of high interest rates. If the buyer cannot take over an existing loan and the cost of borrowing is prohibitive, then the seller will experience great difficulty in transferring the property.

Because of the increase of interest rates during the 1970s and early 1980s, many lenders sought to enforce their due-on-sale clauses when mortgagors attempted to sell their property. Both buyers and mortgagors had objections to the legality of the clauses, and from 1970 until 1980 more than 20 different cases involving the issue of due-on-sale clauses were heard by state appellate courts. Some states recognized the clauses as valid, while others declared them unenforceable.

Although there was much confusion and debate over the validity of due-on-sale clauses during the economic downturn of the early 1980s, the issue was settled when the U.S. Supreme Court held in *Fidelity Federal Savings and Loan v. de la Cuesta,* 458 U.S. 141 (1982), that the clauses were valid and could be enforced in federally related mortgage loans. State laws declaring the clauses invalid were preempted by the federal standards that permitted enforcement.

On October 15, 1982, Congress enacted the Garn-St. Germain Depository Institutions Act of 1982 (called the Garn Bill; 12 U.S.C. § 226), which provides that states may not restrict the enforcement of due-on-sale clauses with respect to real property loans except to protect home buyers who relied on due-on-sale restrictions and reasonably believed they had assumable loans. The purposes of the Garn Bill were to aid buyers who might have relied on assumability and to clarify the types of transfers under which the due-on-sale clause may be enforced.

Types of Mortgages

GOVERNMENT-INSURED MORTGAGES—FHA AND VA MORTGAGES

The acronyms **FHA** and **VA** are used widely in advertisements, discussions, and news about the housing market. Both terms signify a government-backed loan, which means that if the borrower defaults on repayment of the loan, the lender can recover the loan amount from the federal agency insuring the loan. The Federal Housing Administration and the Veterans Administration, respectively, serve as the insuring agencies for these types of loans.

These loans have restrictions, most of which are imposed for the protection of the mortgagor. For example, the interest rate on such loans is set by the federal government, and the borrower must qualify for the loan through the insuring government agency. Also, the terms of the mortgage and note are regulated by the federal government, and certain types of clauses discussed above are prohibited. For example, as mentioned earlier, the balloon payment provision is prohibited in FHA and VA loans.

In addition to the benefits of the government's acting as an insurer, a mortgagee giving a government-insured loan also enjoys the benefits of having a secondary market for these mortgages through government-owned corporations. These government-owned corporations, such as the **Federal National Mortgage Association (FNMA** or **Fannie Mae)** and the **Government National Mortgage Association (GNMA** or **Ginnie Mae)**, purchase blocks of government-insured mortgages and in some cases conventional mortgages. These secondary-market corporations were created to encourage primary lenders to participate in the home mortgage market.

There are additional restrictions on government-insured mortgages. For example, both FHA and VA carry maximum loan amounts, so that these loans are not available for higher-priced residences. Also, the borrower is required to pay the premium for the government insurance, which is a fixed percent of the outstanding balance for the life of the loan. There may also be down-payment requirements on certain loans.

There are many different types of FHA loans that have been developed to enable buyers to qualify for and afford home purchases. For example, FHA

http://
For more information on VA home loans, visit **http://www.homeloans. va.gov/lgyinfo.htm**.

introduced the graduated-payment mortgage (FHA 245), which provided for a lower beginning monthly payment that is gradually increased each year over the next five years until reaching a level payment in the sixth year of the loan. Additional features were introduced by FHA for the purchase of low-income housing, including lower interest rates and lower down payments, to help those in lower-income brackets purchase homes.

FEDERAL REGULATORY AGENCIES FOR MORTGAGE LENDING

In 1989, the **Financial Institutions Reform, Recovery and Enforcement Act of 1989 (FIRREA)** was passed as part of a sweeping reform of the federal thrift industry. The act made substantial changes in the structure of the federal regulatory scheme of those financial institutions primarily responsible for real estate loans. FIRREA made three changes: it (1) reorganized regulatory bodies, (2) enhanced regulatory powers, and (3) expanded real estate appraisal requirements.

Both the **Federal Home Loan Bank Board (FHLBB)** and the **Federal Savings and Loan Insurance Corporation (FSLIC),** original regulators of federal savings and loans, were dissolved, with their responsibilities given to the **Office of Thrift Supervision** and the **Federal Deposit Insurance Corporation (FDIC).** The **Resolution Trust Corporation (RTC)** was created to temporarily manage thrift institutions placed in conservatorship or receivership. Though originally intended to run only through 1991, the RTC remained an active force in the real estate industry through 1996. All remaining RTC issues are handled by the FDIC.

The FIRREA requires federal agencies (including FHA and VA) to establish standards to govern real estate appraisals. Also, federal financial institutions will be required to reevaluate their internal procedures for appraisals and evaluation of the qualification of appraisers for specific real estate transactions.

As a result of the role appraisers played in the problems that led to the demise of many savings and loans, not only was the FIRREA passed with its requirements for appraisers and appraisals, but also courts have now established professional liability standards for appraisers. Appraisers have been held liable for negligence to third parties who rely on their appraisals in the same manner that accountants are held liable to certain third parties for their financial opinions (*First State Savings Bank v. Albright Associates of Ocala, Inc.,* 561 So.2d 1326 (Fla. App. 1990).

CONVENTIONAL MORTGAGES

The **conventional mortgage** is a mortgage made by a private lender that is not insured by a government agency and, hence, not subject to the restrictions imposed on lenders seeking government insurance. The conventional mortgage may be offered by the same institutions offering FHA and VA loans.

Financing property by a conventional mortgage is different from financing by a government-insured mortgage in that the interest rate will probably be higher; the down payment required will probably be greater; and the lender will be able to incorporate additional terms in the mortgage agreement such as balloon payments, interest acceleration clauses, and other terms restricted or regulated in government loans.

PURCHASE MONEY MORTGAGES

The purchase money mortgage is one in which the funds are being borrowed to finance the purchase of the property, and the property is pledged as security for the loan. In most residential home purchases, the lender obtains a purchase money mortgage for the buyer, who borrows funds for the purchase of the residence.

MASTER MORTGAGES

With all of the possible clauses that may be used in a mortgage, it is likely that the mortgage will be long and complex. Furthermore, a lender may be using the same mortgage forms for all mortgages given and will be recording the same document each time in the appropriate governmental office. To avoid this duplication of recording, some states have enacted **master mortgage** statutes, which permit lenders to record one master mortgage. Then, to record a newly created mortgage, the lenders simply record a document that refers to the location of the recorded master mortgage and gives the description of the subject property.

STRAIGHT TERM MORTGAGES

A **straight term mortgage** is a mortgage in which there is no provision for the amortization of principal over a period of time. Rather, the borrower makes interest payments at various intervals and then repays the unpaid principal along with any accrued interest at the end of the term (usually three to five years). The balloon payment clause creates a form of a straight term mortgage. This type of mortgage can be used effectively by the seller in alternative financing techniques (see page 402).

SUBORDINATE OR WRAP-AROUND MORTGAGES

A **subordinate mortgage** (or **wrap-around mortgage**) is created in property that is already subject to another mortgage. It has been used effectively by sellers who act as lenders for their buyers who cannot afford a loan from a commercial lender because of high rates. This type of mortgage is discussed in detail in the alternative financing section of this chapter.

ANACONDA OR DRAGNET MORTGAGES

An **Anaconda mortgage** or **dragnet mortgage** contains a clause that provides that the mortgage secures all items of indebtedness that the mortgagor may, at any time during the period of mortgage, owe to the mortgagee. Under such an agreement, the lender may acquire all the debts of the mortgagor at a discount and then collect 100 percent through the mortgage transaction.

ADJUSTABLE RATE MORTGAGES

A trend in home financing is the **adjustable rate mortgage (ARM).** The adjustable rate mortgage is one that has a fluctuating interest rate throughout the life of the loan. The fluctuations result from the loan's rate being tied to some index such as the FHA rate, the treasury securities index, or treasury bill rates. The fluctuations will vary according to the terms of the note or loan agreement, but the following factors should be covered to ensure that the borrower knows the extent of the fluctuations.

1. What index will be used? Short-term indices (like treasury bills) tend to be more volatile. The only restrictions on use are that the index be public and not controllable by the lender.
2. What will be the margin? The margin is the difference between the index rate and the contract rate. In other words, the borrower's rate is the index plus the margin. The margin could be from 1 to 4 percent.
3. What adjustment period will be used? Will the ARM be adjusted every six months? Every year? Shorter periods are more beneficial for the lender.
4. Is there a rate cap? Is there a maximum interest rate for the loan?

5. If the loan is assumed, is the cap readjusted upon assumption?
6. Is the rate for loan qualifying different from the rate for the first year? If so, there may be negative amortization, which means the monthly payments are low the first year but the size of the mortgage increases during that time.

REVERSE MORTGAGES

With an increasing retired population with large amounts of equity in their homes, lenders have developed the **reverse mortgage.** Reverse mortgages allow retired homeowners to supplement their retirement income by borrowing on the equity in their homes. The mortgage company in a reverse mortgage makes monthly payments to the owners of the property according to the mortgage terms and amount. The owners need not repay the loan until they have died and the house is sold. Out of the proceeds of the sale, the reverse mortgagee is repaid the principal plus interest. Because of overcharging on mortgage fees and inadequate disclosure of the nature of these mortgages in many transactions, the Department of Housing and Urban Development has filed suit against aggressive mortgagees and has developed disclosure requirements for such mortgages.

COMMERCIAL MORTGAGES

The focus of this chapter has been primarily on residential mortgages, but commercial buildings are financed using a **commercial mortgage** with the same format and relationships. However, commercial loans require that additional issues be addressed in the mortgage document, such as what happens to the lessees in the building and whether there will be assignment of rents presently or in the event of a default. Additionally, commercial lenders must be concerned about prior and current uses of the property for purposes of environmental issues and liabilities.

Rights and Responsibilities of Mortgagor and Mortgagee

Most of the responsibilities of the mortgagor and the mortgagee should be covered in the written and executed mortgage agreement between the parties. But in case the parties fail to specify all the necessary terms of their relationship, the law does provide certain rules for governing the relationship.

RENTS AND LEASES

The rights of the parties with regard to the rents received from the property will vary (as discussed earlier) according to whether the property is located in a title or a lien theory state. In the title theory states, the mortgagee has the right to the rents upon execution of the mortgage. In the lien theory states, the mortgagee is not entitled to rents or possession until after default and the successful completion of court proceedings for foreclosure.

However, in some lien theory states, the parties are permitted to put a clause in their mortgage agreement that gives the mortgagee the right to possession and rents immediately upon default by the mortgagor. In other lien theory states, such a clause is treated as void.

In any state where the mortgagee is properly in possession of the mortgaged property and collecting rents, the mortgagee does have the responsibility for accounting to the mortgagor for the rents received during the period of possession. In some lien theory states, the rents received while the mortgagee is in possession must be applied to the reduction of the mortgage debt.

One final issue that remains in the area of the leasing of mortgage property is that of the tenant's rights. The rights of tenants of mortgaged property will vary according to the time the lease was executed. For those leases that antedate the mortgage, the mortgagee is required to honor the tenant's rights, even when the mortgagee forecloses. In a postdated lease, the mortgagee is permitted to terminate the lease simply because of the mortgagor's default. Of course, the mortgagor and the mortgagee could have a clause in the lease that made tenants' rights subject to all mortgages. If a lease is entered into after the mortgage has been executed, the mortgagee is permitted to extinguish the rights of the tenant upon default and foreclosure.

Both tenants and mortgagees should carefully scrutinize the other documents before entering into their transactions. For example, a tenant leasing subsequent to a mortgage execution should check the mortgage for termination and cancellation provisions to fully appreciate the rights available. A mortgagee taking a mortgage on property subject to existing leases should carefully review the terms of the leases prior to execution of the mortgage to determine if any additional protections or clauses need to be built into the mortgage.

The following case illustrates the rights of mortgagor, mortgagee, and tenants upon default by the mortgagor. After reading the case, determine whether the result would be the same under the theory of mortgages followed by your state.

Comerica Bank-Illinois v. Harris Bank Hinsdale

673 N.E.2d 380 (Ill. App. Ct. 1996)

Facts

Affiliated Bank/North Shore National issued a first mortgage on the Family Square Shopping Center in Hillside, Illinois (mortgagor). Comerica Bank-Illinois is the successor to Affiliated. Upon taking over the loan, Comerica recorded both a mortgage and an assignment of rents as security for the loan. The assignment provided that Comerica could collect rents from the property without taking possession of the property, and without exercising any of its other options under the property. Chicago Title and Trust held a second mortgage on the same property.

The mortgagor paid the first installment of real estate taxes on the property in 1990, but failed to make further payments. Comerica first learned of the tax delinquency in 1993 when a real estate buyer notified Comerica that it had purchased the property at a public sale. The tax obligation on the property exceeded $600,000. The mortgage agreement did require the mortgagor to make the tax payments to a Comerica escrow, but Comerica had waived the requirement.

Comerica was free to foreclose at that time, but, instead, in April 1994, Comerica notified the mortgagor that it was in default and that Comerica would exercise its legal remedies if the default was not cured. The mortgagor did not cure the default and Comerica chose to exercise its rights under the assignment of rents clause in

the mortgage. Comerica began collecting rents from the tenants in the property without foreclosing on it. By collecting rents, Comerica was able to reduce the debt on the property without assuming responsibility for the large tax obligation.

On May 20, 1994, Comerica filed for an accounting and relief against the mortgagor and its guarantors. The mortgagor filed a counterclaim seeking the appointment of a receiver and mandating Comerica's maintenance and operation of the mortgaged property. The trial court dismissed the counterclaim. On August 5, 1994, Chicago Title filed an action for foreclosure on its second mortgage and appointment of a receiver for an accounting of the rents. The trial court found that the rents collected by Comerica belonged to the mortgagor. Comerica appealed.

Judicial Opinion

Theis, Justice. The trial court awarded the rents to the mortgagor. On appeal, Comerica claims that the trial court erred in awarding the rents to the mortgagor as Comerica should have been allowed to exercise its right to collect rents under the assignment of rents.

The trustee first argues that Comerica's assignment of rents, which permits Comerica to collect the rents without any other action, cannot supersede the common law requirement of possession. In resolving this issue, we have relied on Illinois case law. However, we have also found relevant bankruptcy decisions and Federal case law to be thorough and persuasive. Because the Supreme Court has required bankruptcy courts to apply State law in determining mortgagee's entitlements to rents, we find bankruptcy decisions useful in resolving this issue.

Courts will not enforce private agreements that are contrary to public policy. At common law, it was strictly held that the mortgagee must take actual possession before he was entitled to rents. "[A] clause in a real estate mortgage pledging rents and profits creates an equitable lien upon such rents and profits of the land, which may be enforced by the mortgagee upon default by taking possession of the mortgaged property."

The possession requirement reflects the public policy in Illinois which seeks to prevent mortgagees from stripping the rents from the property and leaving the mortgagor and the tenants without resources for maintenance or repair. Applying Illinois law, the court in Monarch stated that:

> To obtain the benefits of possession in the form of rents, the mortgagee must also accept the burdens associated with possession—the responsibilities and potential liability that follow whenever a mortgage goes into default. The mortgagee's right to rents, then, is not automatic but arises only when the mortgagee has affirmatively sought possession with its attendant benefits and burdens. *In re J.D. Monarch Development Co.,* 153 B.R. 829, 833 (Bankr.S.D.Ill. 1993).

We recognize that there is a modern trend in this area of the law which permits a mortgagee to collect rents once it has taken constructive, as opposed to actual, possession of the property. Courts have recently allowed mortgagees to collect rents after taking some affirmative action to gain possession of the property such as obtaining judicial intervention by way of injunctive relief. Similarly, courts have ruled that mortgagees may be entitled to rents once a receiver has been appointed.

While the trustee concedes that actual possession is not necessary to collect rents, it argues that Comerica failed to take the affirmative action which would constitute constructive possession of the property. In the absence of such action, Comerica's enforcement of the assignment of rents permits Comerica to strip the property of its value without accepting responsibility for its maintenance. The trustee claims that such conduct contravenes Illinois' public policy. We agree.

We find that even under the more progressive "affirmative action" cases, a mortgagee still needs to obtain a court's authorization before he may collect rents without taking possession. Such a requirement ensures that the [*sic*] all of the parties' interests will be before the court, and will not be subject to the unilateral acts of the mortgagee. We agree with the trustee's claim that actual or constructive possession of the property is required before a mortgagee may collect rents. Because Comerica's assignment of rents permitted Comerica to collect rents in contravention of Illinois public policy, we refuse to recognize that provision of the agreement.

This is not the end of our discussion, however, as the trustee argues that it took the necessary affirmative action and that it is therefore entitled to the rents. The trustee claims that filing a foreclosure action and seeking the appointment of a receiver constitute the necessary affirmative action which entitled it to the rents.

We find that the mere filing of the foreclosure action or request for a receiver is not sufficient to trigger the mortgagee's right to collect rents. First, in a foreclosure action, the mortgagee is not entitled to rents until judgment has actually been entered unless the mortgage agreement permits the mortgagee to obtain prejudgment possession. Similarly, the mere request for the appointment of a receiver is not sufficient. "[T]he mortgagee is not entitled to the rents until the mortgagee or a receiver appointed on the mortgagee's behalf has taken actual possession of the real estate after default." Accordingly, we find that it is not the mere filing of certain pleadings, but rather the trial court's affirmative ruling on such filings which entitles the mortgagee to the rents.

It is undisputed that the trustee did not obtain prejudgment possession of the property. The rents in dispute were collected during the time that the mortgagor was in possession of the property but before the receiver was appointed. Therefore, we find that the trial court was correct in ruling that the rents collected properly belong to the mortgagor.

Affirmed.

Case Questions

1. Outline the parties and their roles in the transaction.
2. Why did Comerica want to collect rents and not proceed with foreclosure?
3. What reasons are given for requiring possession before collection of rents is permitted?
4. What effect does this case have on assignment of rent clauses in mortgages?

Property Covered by the Mortgage

Unless otherwise specified, the mortgage will include all real property located on the land described in the mortgage document. The mortgage covers all buildings, fixtures, easements, and any other items classified as real property.

Often mortgagees will include as a provision in their mortgage agreement an **after-acquired property clause.** The purpose of such a clause is to have the mortgage include any buildings, fixtures, or other attachments that might be made to the land subsequent to the time of the mortgage. The clause also protects the mortgagee in that if substantial changes occur in the structures already existing on the land or any additions to those structures, the mortgagee would be prevented from effectively exercising rights in that property.

To clarify the exact property included in the mortgage, the mortgagee should specify any questionable items that might be construed as personal instead of real property. The following clause is an example of a thorough inclusion clause (which can cover after-acquired clause property) that would follow the legal description of the property in the mortgage agreement.

> *TOGETHER with all articles and fixtures used in occupying, operating, or renting the building on the premises, including but not limited to gas and electric fixtures, radiators, heaters, washers, driers, engines and machinery, boilers, ranges, elevators, escalators, incinerators, motors, bathtubs, sinks, pipes, faucets, and other heating and plumbing fixtures, air conditioning equipment, mirrors, cabinets, refrigerators, stoves, fire prevention and extinguishing devices, furniture, shades, blinds, curtains, draperies, drapery and curtain rods, rugs, carpets and all other floor coverings, lamps, wall hangings and pictures, and all replacements thereof and additions thereto from this point on and such additions and replacements shall be deemed to form a part of the realty and are thus covered by the lien of this mortgage.*

Transfers and Assignments by Mortgagor

In many property purchases made through the use of a purchase money mortgage, the mortgagor will not remain in possession or use of the property for the entire term of the mortgage. In residential and commercial transactions, it is often necessary for the original mortgagor to sell or transfer the mortgaged property. In the following sections, the methods of transfer and the rights and duties of the parties involved in the transfer are discussed.

THE ASSUMPTION

In many cases, the original mortgagor's interest rate is lower than the rates available at the time the transfer of the property becomes necessary. If the buyer can purchase the property by agreeing to assume the responsibility for repayment of the original mortgage, the seller will have a much better chance of being able to market the property at a good price.

The following factual example helps to illustrate how this method of transferring the mortgage debt as part of the purchase price of the property works:

> *Hal Wood purchased a small home for $75,000 in 1991. In 2001, Hal had to sell the home. Hal had a mortgage balance of approximately $65,000 on the home, and he advertised to sell the home for $98,000. Bob Freeman has made an offer to purchase the home for $95,000, with Bob paying Hal $30,000 cash and agreeing to assume responsibility for repayment of the $65,000 mortgage.*

The following is a diagram of the example:

FIRST MORTGAGEE ⟵——————⟶ HAL WOOD, MORTGAGOR

BOB FREEMAN, BUYER

Practical Tip

The assumption of a loan is often a more efficient way to transfer property. However, the creditworthiness of the transferee is a critical issue in such a transfer. Also, knowing the state's position on deficiency judgments in the event the transferee defaults is important information to have prior to sale. Absent statutory protection, if the transferee defaults, the transferor remains liable for the balance of the loan.

The transaction is a simple assignment of contract benefits and a delegation of contract duties. Bob will enjoy the benefits of residing in the property but will assume responsibility for the mortgage payments. The transaction is referred to as an **assumption,** or, frequently, as a **cash-to-mortgage sale,** since Bob is paying enough cash down to be able to assume the mortgage.

The transaction raises several questions as to the liability of each of the parties involved. Bob, as the buyer or assignee, becomes liable on the mortgage by executing an assumption agreement. An assumption agreement specifies the amount of the mortgage balance, the name of the mortgagee, and that the buyer agrees to assume responsibility for repayment of the mortgage amount. Such an agreement does not, however, relieve the original mortgagor (Hal) of liability under the mortgage arrangement. The mortgagor remains liable for repayment of the debt and may be turned to if the buyer defaults. The mortgagee has the right to enforce repayment against either one of the parties and always retains the right of foreclosure in the event both parties default (discussed later). The buyer is primarily liable on the mortgage and the seller is secondarily liable, so the lender is required to proceed against the parties in a certain order.

The only way the mortgagor can be relieved of liability under the mortgage agreement is if the mortgagee consents to such a release. Many mortgages have provisions that require a release once the mortgagee has qualified or is satisfied with the purchaser and has consented in writing to the transfer and assumption.

Not all mortgages may be assumed and, as discussed earlier, many are subject to a due-on-sale provision, which effectively prevents the mortgagor from transferring the rights available under the mortgage.

THE SUBJECT-TO SALE

In a sale of property by a mortgagor to a buyer in which the buyer takes *subject to* the existing mortgage, the mortgagor remains personally liable on the mortgage; the buyer undertakes no personal responsibility for payment of the mortgage; and the property remains subject to the foreclosure rights of the mortgagee. In a **subject-to sale,** the seller continues to be responsible for the payments on the mortgage. The mortgagee's rights are not affected by a transfer of property subject to its existing mortgage. The subject-to sale can be used very effectively in some of the alternative financing techniques discussed later in the chapter.

REFINANCING

In some property sales where the cash-to-mortgage balance is too high for the buyer, the buyer will be required to finance the purchase of the property by borrowing the money under a new note secured by a new mortgage. This new mortgage is called **refinancing** the purchase of the property. The result is that the original mortgagee is paid the full amount due on the mortgage, the seller is given the cash difference between the sale price and the mortgage balance, and a new mortgage is created in the property. Upon payment, the seller is no longer liable and the mortgagee no longer has any rights in the property.

Transfers and Assignments of Mortgages by Mortgagees

Many property owners are confused when they receive notification that their mortgage has been sold. Some believe that their loan or credit rating will be affected by such a transfer. Actually, the assignment of a mortgage has been and remains motivated by a thriving secondary market for mortgages. A mortgage may be sold several times over the course of the loan period. Because of the savings and loan crisis of the 1980s, many homeowners have experienced seven or more transfers over the terms of their mortgages as the now disbanded RTC worked through the holdings of these firms.

Upon an assignment by a mortgagee of a mortgage loan, the mortgagor's rights remain the same. The change in payment, in terms of party and place, is required only after the mortgagor is notified of the assignment and where future payments should be made. The loan terms cannot be changed by the assignment, and the assignment has no effect on the mortgagor's credit rating.

Satisfaction of the Mortgage

As discussed earlier, a mortgage is valid only if it is supported by some underlying debt. Once that debt is repaid, the mortgage is no longer valid and must be terminated. The termination of the mortgage and hence the mortgagee's interest is accomplished through the execution and recording of an agreement called a **satisfaction of mortgage.**

The satisfaction of mortgage requires only an adequate description of the property and the signature of the mortgagee (usually notarized). Figure 15.4 is an example of the simple language that may be used to satisfy the requirements for clearing title to the property of the mortgage.

The satisfaction of the mortgage document should be recorded where all other land interests are recorded because it serves to clear the title of the mortgage lien in lien states or to vest title in the mortgagor in title states. All states have some type of statutory penalty that is imposed upon mortgagees who wrongfully refuse to execute a release or satisfaction of the mortgage. Ordinarily, the penalty is minimal, but in some states the fine may be imposed on a weekly basis, such as $50 per week for each week the release or satisfaction is not given.

FIGURE 15.4   *Satisfaction of Mortgage*

KNOW ALL MEN BY THESE PRESENTS: That the mortgage executed by _____ to _____ dated _____ and recorded _____ in Docket _____ pages _____ in the Office of the County Recorder of _____ County, _____, together with the debt thereby secured, is fully paid, satisfied, and discharged.

DATED THIS _____ day of _____, 20 _____

_____

MORTGAGEE

Foreclosure

DEFAULT OF THE MORTGAGOR

Foreclosure requires a default by the mortgagor. A **default** occurs when the mortgagor fails to comply with some provision of the mortgage agreement. Generally, default occurs when the mortgagor has failed to make timely payments in accordance with the schedule agreed to under the terms of the underlying note or in the mortgage agreement itself. However, it is possible for default to occur whenever the mortgagor breaches the agreement through violation of any of the other provisions of the mortgage. For example, most mortgagees require the mortgagor to maintain hazard insurance on the property and to make timely payments of taxes and assessments. Failure to comply with these provisions also constitutes a default.

In case the mortgagor engages in conduct that causes destruction, devaluation, or general decline of the property, usually a provision in the mortgage agreement prohibits such activities, known as *waste,* and the mortgagee may declare such conduct to be a default.

It is important that the provisions in the mortgage agreement establish what constitutes default. Although all states afford remedies for mortgagees upon the mortgagor's default, very few of the statutes define what actually constitutes default. The mortgagee must rely on the written mortgage agreement to establish default. The mortgage acceleration clause and default provisions are usually tied to violations of the mortgage terms, such as maintaining hazard insurance or making timely payments.

PROCESSES OF FORECLOSURE

As mortgages existed initially in England, the mortgagor was required to make payment of the debt by a certain date. If the payment was not made, the mortgagor lost all right and interest in the property to the mortgagee. Today, upon the mortgagor's default, it is quite possible that the mortgagor will lose all interest in the property, but the loss will not occur without substantial judicial procedures and notification plus a second chance or two for the mortgagor to regain the interest in the property.

Upon default, the mortgagee is entitled to foreclose on the property. This **foreclosure** may be accomplished in different ways according to state law. Each state has different procedures for the mortgagee to follow in exercising foreclosure rights, but basically the methods can be divided into two groups.

JUDICIAL FORECLOSURE

Under **judicial foreclosure,** the mortgagee is required to bring suit in the appropriate court to have the rights of the interested parties determined. The court then orders the sale of the property to satisfy the total amount then due and owing on the debt. If the mortgagee is to have good title pass through the judicial foreclosure sale, there must be proper compliance with all procedural requirements; otherwise the entire proceeding may be set aside.

1. Filing the Petition Judicial foreclosure begins with the mortgagee or the mortgagee's attorney filing a petition in the proper court, usually in the state and county where the property is located. The petition must adequately state the factual basis for the foreclosure action, including the dates and amounts of all defaults, the exact amount of principal then due on the underlying debt, and the requested relief such as a judicial sale.

2. Required Parties After the petition is filed, it must be served upon all parties who will be affected by the foreclosure action. In addition to the mortgagor, other parties included are tenants, second or junior mortgagees, holders of mechanic's liens, UCC Article 9 secured creditors, any government agencies having tax claims, and all other statutory lienors. Determining the parties who need to be served with notice of foreclosure is best accomplished by conducting a search of the land records for all possible land interests.

3. Filing the Notice of Action (Lis Pendens) Because of court backlog and required statutory waiting periods, it may be some time before the foreclosure sale can actually be ordered and carried out by the courts. Public notification of the pending foreclosure is necessary to prevent the creation of additional interests in the property between the filing of the petition and the actual sale of the property. To accomplish this, the mortgagee files a notice in the land records that an action has been filed. This notice is called a *lis pendens,* and it serves as adequate notification to all dealing with the property or the mortgagor that a foreclosure suit is pending. The notice is filed under all parties' names so that the records establish whose interest existed prior to the filing of the action.

4. Foreclosure Trial or Hearing The only elements required to be established at the actual hearing for foreclosure are that there has been a default and that the mortgage agreement authorizes the judicial action and sale. Generally, such a hearing is simply a formality and the mortgagor may not even appear to challenge the proceedings.

5. Strict Foreclosure Once the court finds that the foreclosure is appropriate, an order for foreclosure will be entered. In strict foreclosure states, the judge enters an order that permits the mortgagor a certain time period (usually three to four months) within which to pay the total amount due and owing and thereby reacquire the property in question. If the mortgagor is not able to pay the amount due within that time, the order provides for a sale of the property. The mortgagor thus loses forever all interest in the property and the right to reacquire the property.

6. Foreclosure with Statutory Redemption In other states, a sale will be held as soon as possible after the judge finds default and orders foreclosure, but the mortgagor is still given one last chance to redeem the property interest. For a statutory period ranging from six months to a year after the property is sold, the mortgagor is given the right to pay the full amount due and regain right to the property (even if the property has in fact been sold). This right to pay the debt after the judicial sale is referred to as the **statutory right of redemption.** The effects of the statutory period are twofold: (1) the mortgagee is required to wait before closing the case file completely and (2) the purchaser of the property is required to wait before actually obtaining full and complete title.

7. The Judicial Sale Upon order in most state courts, the mortgaged property is offered at a public sale for which notice has been published. The sale is carried out by an officer of the judiciary, such as a sheriff, and is conducted as an auction with the property being transferred to the highest bidder. In strict foreclosure states, the purchaser is given a **sheriff's deed,** which serves to convey title but does not include any warranties of title. The deed is only as good as the judicial procedures were proper. In statutory redemption states, the purchaser is given some type of document such as a certificate of sale as evidence of the purchase, but the purchaser cannot be given title to the property until the period of statutory redemption has passed. At the end of the statutory redemption period, the purchaser is given a sheriff's deed (also called a **judicial deed**).

Most challenges to foreclosure proceedings by mortgagors arise because of complaints about the judicial sale. The sale must be adequately advertised and bidding conducted in a fair and proper manner. Often mortgagors feel that the price obtained for the property was inadequate. Such a complaint is seldom a basis for setting aside the transaction because the very nature of the transaction results in lower bids. This is especially true in states where redemption is possible and the investment is tied up for the statutory period with no guarantee of title being transferred. Because foreclosure involves the loss of property interests, courts are strict about procedural compliance.

The following case involves issues of procedural requirements for foreclosure.

Rao v. Towers Partners, L.L.C.

688 So.2d 709 (La. App. 1997)

Facts

Mary Lee Wade and her husband, Lt. James Rao, United States Navy, (the Raos) purchased a six-unit complex in Algiers, Louisiana, from Orleans Bank and Trust (OBT) in 1988. The Raos executed a demand note to OBT for $60,000 with fixed interest at a rate of 10 percent, payable monthly in $640 payments. The note was secured by a mortgage and pledge of a demand note in the amount of $100,000. The Raos made extensive repairs to the property because of its poor condition and had expended over $20,000 in renovation of the units.

The Raos made their monthly payments until OBT failed and was taken over by the FDIC. In September 1992, Lt. Rao wrote the FDIC and asked that the property mortgage be discounted to $40,000–$45,000 in order that he could refinance the property. The FDIC appraisal showed the property to then be worth $80,000 and the FDIC refused to take a discount of more than 1 or 2 percent. Lt. Rao was then stationed outside the New Orleans area and tried to sell the property. The Raos spent another $4,800 trying to fix it up. Because of an economic downturn in the area, the Raos had no success in selling the property and in a year of having the property listed for sale they had only one offer they could not accept because it required the Raos to serve as the financiers for the buyer's purchase.

The FDIC sold the Raos' note to Towers Partners, L.L.C, a limited liability company consisting of David Caballero and Lawrence Roe Dodd. Lt. Rao contacted Caballero and offered to pay down the mortgage and continue paying on the note. The Raos missed their payments for December 1992, and January and February 1993. Caballero refused to accept a check from the Raos for $1920 sent via Express Mail.

On February 3, 1993, Towers sent the Raos a letter demanding payment of the full amount of the debt. The demand letter stated that "The reason for this acceleration of your indebtedness [*sic*] is the creditor's lack of security in your collateral."

On March 23, 1993, Dodd filed a petition for foreclosure on the property. According to the petition:

1. The Raos are indebted to Tower in the sum of $51,185.32 with interest at an annual rate of 12% from 11 January 1988 until paid plus 25% attorneys' fees;
2. The payments due on the note for the month of 9 October 1992 and payments due thereafter have not been made despite amicable demand (Paragraph 9).

The attestation clause on the verification of the petition is blank and lacks the signature of a notary public.

On Towers's motion, the trial court on March 30, 1993, appointed Towers keeper of the properties and authorized Towers to take possession of the premises and to manage, operate, and conserve the value thereof and to collect the rents, issues, and profits in accordance with law. The tenants were directed to pay rent only to Towers. At that time all units were rented at a total monthly rental of $1,700.

By letter of April 7, 1993, counsel for the Raos advised Dodd of the error in the executory process petition relative to the alleged default in payment and asked that the writ be recalled and the rents released, failing which an injunction suit would be filed. On September 16, 1993, the Raos filed the petition in the instant case for damages and injunctive relief against Towers, Caballero and Dodd.

On February 11, 1994, Eric Oliver Person enrolled as counsel for Tower and Caballero. On November 18,

1994, the trial court granted Towers's motion to dissolve the temporary restraining order preventing foreclosure sale of the property.

The property was appraised for $40,000 in connection with the sheriff's sale held on March 9, 1995, and was adjudicated to Towers Partners for $28,000.

Judicial Opinion

Waltzer, Judge. The trial court erred in determining that the procedure required by law for an executory proceeding had not been followed and that a wrongful seizure occurred.

Executory process has many technical requirements that must be observed scrupulously, and it is one of the few areas of law wherein there is a rational basis for giving form precedence over substance. Seizure pursuant to executory process is wrongful if the procedure required by law for an executory proceeding has not been followed.

Tower made demand for payment of the demand note and had the right to execute on that basis. The Raos have not shown that payment was not due under the demand note, and did not avail themselves of any of the procedural remedies available to them to defend against the executory process suit.

The end result would have been the same to the Raos: the property would have been seized (as, in fact, it was), managed by Tower (as it was) and eventually sold (as it was). The seizure that took place was made on a petition that failed to state the correct grounds, but was a legitimate exercise of Tower's right to proceed under executory process based on the note's demand feature. The technical deficiency of the petition did not cause anything to happen that would not have happened had the proper grounds been stated. Thus, the Raos can show at most a technical infirmity of the petition, but no damages attributable to that deficiency. Although it is true that a party aggrieved by a wrongful seizure is entitled to general and special damages, he must nevertheless prove that he did sustain damages. Rao did not and cannot sustain that burden of proof. Therefore, we reverse the trial court's judgment awarding damages for wrongful seizure.

In light of our reversal, the remaining assignments of error are moot.

Reversed.

Case Questions

1. Were the Raos harmed by what happened?
2. Was Towers permitted to refuse the three months' worth of payments when it did?
3. What was the flaw in the petition?
4. Was notice given in a proper and adequate fashion?

Edward Knudsen owned a nine-acre ranch, adjacent to a country club, that was appraised at $900,000. Knudsens's monthly mortgage payments of $4,008 became too burdensome, and he defaulted. The mortgage company, after public notice, sold the ranch for $214,460—a mere $5.66 more than the mortgage on the property. Has the mortgage company acted properly?

Consider 15.4

8. *The Soldiers and Sailors Relief Act (50 U.S.C. §501)* This federal act can have a substantial effect on mortgage foreclosure proceedings. It requires that special notice be given to mortgagors who are currently in active military service. The act also permits the court to postpone foreclosure proceedings if the default of the mortgagor results from a pay reduction because of induction into the armed services.

The **Soldiers and Sailors Relief Act** was passed to protect those drafted into the military service from losing their homes while they served. The act provides further protection in statutory redemption states because the period of the mortgagor's active military service is not included in computing the statutory period. In other words, the period does not begin until active service terminates. The Persian Gulf War of 1991 saw this act applied to reservists who were called to active duty and experienced economic hardship.

FORECLOSURE BY POWER OF SALE

Many states permit mortgagees to include in their mortgage agreements provisions that permit them to sell the property, upon the mortgagor's default, without court proceedings. This **power of sale** is a characteristic of the deed of trust financing arrangement (discussed later).

Under this method of foreclosure, a rather quick and nonjudicial sale may be held. All states permitting foreclosure by this method have set up statutory procedures with which the mortgagee must comply before the sale is recognized as valid.

1. Notice and Advertisement All states recognizing the power of sale as a method of foreclosure require the mortgagee to furnish notice to all interested parties (the mortgagor, secondary or junior creditors, lienors, and so on) and also to advertise or publish notice of the impending sale, including time and place of the sale. In some states, the notice of sale is so important that this method of foreclosure is referred to as **foreclosure by advertisement.** The notice and advertisement must be accomplished within a certain time period before the sale takes place. (Many states require that notice and advertisement be given 90 days prior to the date of sale.)

In many states recognizing power of sale, the ease with which foreclosure can be accomplished is not without some cost to the mortgagee. This is because, in many states, the mortgagee loses the right to a deficiency action by exercising the power of sale. In other words, the mortgagee is entitled to a speedy foreclosure; but if the sale does not bring enough to satisfy the mortgagor's obligation, the mortgagee is not permitted to sue the mortgagor for the amount of the deficiency.

Because the power of sale foreclosure is not judicially instituted or supervised, mortgagors frequently bring challenges to the adequacy of notice, the conduct, and the propriety of the actual sale.

2. Right of Redemption An additional distinction between the power of sale and foreclosure procedures is that under the power of sale, the debtor loses the statutory redemption period. The debtor has only up until the time of the sale to redeem the property. Once the property is sold at the advertised sale, full title is conveyed, and the debtor does not have a six-month or one-year period (as under judicial foreclosures) to redeem the property. Again, this distinction emphasizes the speed with which a nonjudicial procedure can clear the property of the debtor's interest.

3. The Soldiers and Sailors Relief Act This act also affords protection for those in active military duty from the power of sale foreclosure. Under the Soldiers and Sailors Relief Act, the procedures must simply be postponed for all those who qualify. The postponement runs for the period of active service.

DEED IN LIEU OF FORECLOSURE

Chances are that before foreclosure procedures of any type are initiated by the mortgagee, substantial effort has been made to work with the mortgagor in an effort to correct the default. On government-insured loans, the average duration of default before foreclosure is initiated is six months. If there is an effort by the mortgagor to correct the default—in most cases by making up back payments—the average duration of default before foreclosure is 10 months. Thus, the lender works with the borrower before instituting proceedings. The mortgagor is encouraged to try to sell the property during this time in an effort to save any interest it may have in the property.

After the mortgagee has extended all possible accommodations and there is no hope for recovery, the parties may still reach an agreement to avoid the costs and delays of foreclosure. The agreement the parties reach will be for the mortgagor to quitclaim the property to the mortgagee. Often the mortgagee will agree to pay the mortgagor for such a deed, although it may be a minimal amount such as $500. When the mortgagor turns over title in this manner, the transaction is called a **deed in lieu of foreclosure.** When the deed is signed over by the mortgagor, the underlying debt is canceled. Perhaps one of the most famous deed-in-lieu-of transactions occurred in 1994 when Sears turned over the deed to the Chicago Sears Tower to a trust set up for the benefit of all the mortgage holders on the property. After facing mounting costs and years of declining real estate values, Sears walked away from the financings and cost involved.

In some states, for the mortgagee to be a bona fide and protected purchaser, there must be some payment in addition to cancellation of the debt so that the mortgagee is a purchaser for value and entitled to full protection as a transferee. The transaction must also be free of coercion on the part of the mortgagee toward the mortgagor. The mortgagee must be able to establish that the mortgagor entered into the transaction voluntarily.

To avoid difficulties and questions about voluntariness, particularly if the mortgagor subsequently declares bankruptcy, the parties should sign an agreement explaining their transaction or at least have the mortgagor execute an affidavit explaining the reason for the transfer and the consideration being paid for it. Such an agreement will answer any questions that might arise.

The following case provides some insight into the complexities of mortgages and the relationship between lenders and borrower as well as the effect of layered mortgages.

Hull v. North Adams Hoosac Savings Bank

730 N.E.2d 910 (Mass. App. 2000)

Facts

Before his marriage to Kathleen Hull (Harry) had a variety of real estate investments, including one acquired in 1985 and located at East Quincy Street and another also acquired in 1985 at Millard Avenue. The Quincy Street property had a first mortgage to the sellers and the Millard Avenue property had a first mortgage to North Adams Bank.

Following his marriage to Kathleen, Harr conveyed the properties to himself and Kathleen as tenants by the entirety and subject to the mortgages. Immediately upon conveyance to them jointly, the two used the properties to obtain an additional property, located on Yale Street, subject to a mortgage. The Hulls lived in a rental unit in the Millard Avenue property. The diagram (opposite) illustrates the Hulls' complex mortgage relationships.

By 1988, and still more mortgages later, the marriage was over and Harry had all loans in default. The banks threatened foreclosure and Kathleen borrowed $15,000 from her parents to bring the payments on the properties current.

Harry filed for divorce in 1989 and conveyed his interests in the East Quincy and Yale properties to Kathleen, subject to the mortgages. Kathleen also agreed to assume the payments for these properties. The divorce court awarded her the Millard Avenue property.

Kathleen fell into arrears trying to make payments on all three properties and asked the bank to separate them out. The bank maintained the liens were indistinguishable and filed for foreclosure shortly after Kathleen filed suit to have her rights under the mortgages determined and for the bank's bad faith in its refusal to separate the loans and properties.

The jury at the trial court awarded Kathleen $300,000 and the trial court judge granted the bank's motion for judgment n.o.v. Kathleen appealed.

	Millard Avenue	East Quincy Street	Yale Street
1985 loan (to Harry)	1st mortgage (from Harry)		
1986 loan (to Harry & Kathleen)	2d mortgage (from Harry & Kathleen)	1st mortgage (from Harry & Kathleen)	
1988 loan (to Harry)	3rd mortgage (from Harry)		1st mortgage (from Harry)

Judicial Opinion

Kass, Judge. We have laid out the facts in some detail and at some length to test the correctness of the grant of judgment n.o.v. Kathleen's primary contention is that the bank owed her a duty to explain that she was not liable on Yale Street. Failing to do so, she says, saddled her with operating and attempting to maintain mortgage service on all three properties, a burden that was her undoing. The jury found (by special verdict) that the bank's insistence on payment of mortgages on all three properties was a failure on the part of the bank to exercise good faith in the bank's dealings with Kathleen and that this inflicted $300,000 in damages on her.

The facts do not admit of the finding of failure by the bank to exercise good faith; the question of damages falls by the wayside with that conclusion. Although Kathleen was not on the Yale Street mortgage note in October, 1988, when the bank first asked her for payment on that property along with the other two loans, she had already acquired an undivided interest in the primary security for that note, i.e., the Yale Street property, by deed from Harry dated February 16, 1988. In addition, the Yale Street loan from the bank was cross-collateralized by a third mortgage loan on Millard Avenue. Consequently, a default on Yale Street triggered a default on Millard Avenue. In turn, a default on Millard Avenue caused a default on East Quincy Street because those two properties had been mortgaged to the bank together to secure the September 9, 1986, loan. On the basis of the loan documents between the bank and the Hulls, the bank was quite within its rights in asking that the loans involving all three properties be made current, on pain of foreclosure if they were not.

Had there been any doubt about Kathleen's interest in Yale Street, that was resolved by her accepting sole title to it on May 31, 1989, with a proviso in the deed that the grantee, by accepting the deed, assumed and agreed to pay the mortgage to the bank. She then became personally liable on the Yale Street debt. She also acquired the title to the Millard Avenue and East Quincy Street properties.

Between the time of Kathleen's acquisition of sole title to the three properties on May 31, 1989, more than five years went by before the bank foreclosed on the three loans in November, 1994. The forbearance of the bank did not work a waiver of its rights as a mortgagee under the loan documents nor was it inequitable for the bank to exercise its contractual rights under the governing documents.

If follows that the judge correctly allowed the motion for judgment n.o.v.

Affirmed.

Case Questions

1. Why did the bank treat all the loans as one?
2. Did Kathleen agree to assume personal liability? Were all the properties subject to foreclosure?
3. Does it matter that Kathleen was not an original party to all the mortgages?
4. Does Kathleen still owe the money if she wants to keep the property?

Loan Workouts

The economic conditions of the late 1980s and early 1990s have brought the term *workout* to the real estate industry. A **workout** is a negotiated restructuring of a real estate loan between the borrower and lender that is used as an alternative to foreclosure, litigation, or bankruptcy. Typically, a workout results when there is reduced market or rental value to a property pledged as security for a loan. These events occur because of a general market downturn, the loss of a major local industry, overbuilding, or an economic boom in a nearby area that draws away growth.

A workout can involve an extension of the loan repayment and amortization period; a temporary suspension of loan payments; a reduction or elimination of accrued future loan interest; additional security; a reduction in the loan's principal; personal guarantees from officers or directors; or additional or new control on borrower operations, cash disbursements, or accounts receivables.

Many lenders use the workout period as a way to avoid lender liability suits that are usually brought as counterclaims by borrowers in foreclosure actions. These counterclaims often allege malice or bad faith on the part of the lender in dealing with an ailing borrower who can establish that recovery and repayment were possible. Many lenders have borrowers waive these liability claims as part of the workout conditions.

Lenders must exercise caution in workouts to not issue idle threats, while at the same time not forcing the borrower into an unfair renegotiation. In *State National Bank v. Farah Manufacturing Co.*, 678 S.W.2d 661 (Tex. 1984), the court imposed tort liability on a bank for its excesses in handling a troubled debtor.

Proceeds and Priorities upon Foreclosure

One of the most important issues in mortgage law is the priority of parties holding interests in the mortgaged property. The priority of the parties will determine rights of foreclosure and will also determine who will be entitled to payment first upon sale of the mortgaged property at a foreclosure sale. Very often when a mortgagor defaults, more than one creditor has an interest in the property. The priority of the various creditors will determine the order of distribution of the proceeds from the sale of the property.

RECORDED INTERESTS
As mentioned earlier, a mortgage is valid even if not recorded, but only as between mortgagor and mortgagee. An unrecorded mortgage takes last position against any interests in the mortgaged property that are recorded either prior to the mortgage execution or subsequent to it.

If a mortgage is recorded, the general rule for priority of interests is: first in time is first in right. That is, the mortgage recorded first will enjoy priority over junior or second mortgages recorded later in time. Generally, the same rule applies for the priority of mortgage interests over other recorded land interests such as lien or security interests: If the mortgagee recorded the mortgage prior to the recording of these other interests, then the mortgagee will have priority. There are exceptions as discussed in Chapters 4 and 5. For example, purchase money security interests (PMSIs) in fixtures take priority over previously recorded mortgages if the PMSI is recorded before annexation of the fixture to the land or within 10 days after its annexation; and mechanics' liens take priority over previously recorded mortgages if work on the land began before the mortgage was recorded.

M gave a mortgage to C1, who recorded the mortgage that day (May 30, 2001) at 8 A.M. in the county recorder's office. M had previously given a mortgage to C on May 15, 2001, which C recorded at 11 A.M. on May 30, 2001. Who, between C and C1, has priority?

Consider 15.5

APPLICATIONS OF PROCEEDS FROM FORECLOSURE
The determination of priority among the various interest holders is the preliminary step in determining who will or will not be paid in the event foreclosure on the property becomes necessary. It is very likely that only a minimal amount will be received at a foreclosure sale—perhaps simply the amount of the outstanding debt. However, the order of the distribution of funds is as follows:

1. Payment of the costs of sale: court costs, fees, notice and publication costs, and so on
2. Payment of the mortgage debt having first priority
3. Payment of any junior liens, claims, or mortgages in the order of their priority
4. If there is any surplus, it is distributed to the mortgagor

Although the preceding list makes the law appear fairly clear as to the order of distribution, there are times when the issue becomes complicated because of the types of mortgages involved and the clauses found in them.

There are some exceptions to the general priority rule of first in time is first in right. One such exception relates to the priority of liens for federal and state taxes. Although the mortgage recorded prior to the filing of the lien will enjoy priority, the expenses associated with foreclosure may be subordinate to the tax lien filed prior to foreclosure.

Consider 15.6

A foreclosure sale on a parcel of property took place on September 11, 2001. The amount received from the sale is $75,000. The following list indicates the parties holding interests in the property sold. Distribute the funds according to the priority of the parties.

- First Federal: balance of $32,000 due on note secured by mortgage recorded January 21, 1996
- Great Western: balance of $8,000 due on note secured by mortgage recorded October 16, 1997
- Federal tax lien: balance of $22,000 due, with notice of lien recorded on January 5, 1998
- First Federal's costs and expenses of foreclosure: $5,000
- Judgment lien against the property owner for $10,000 recorded December 23, 1986
- American Finance: purchase money security interest in solar water heater, filed before attachment on December 1, 1996, in the amount of $3,000

The foreclosure sale extinguishes all mortgages and liens on the property regardless of whether the sale proceeds were sufficient to cover all of them.

Postforeclosure Remedies—The Deficiency Judgment

In many cases, the sale of the mortgaged property at a foreclosure sale does not bring sufficient funds to satisfy the mortgage debt and expenses associated with the foreclosure. Therefore, many states allow a **deficiency judgment,** or allow the mortgagee to collect the deficiency from the mortgagor in the form of a personal judgment in addition to the permitted foreclosure process.

In some states, a personal judgment is given against the mortgagor at the same time the court enters the decree of foreclosure. In other states, an action for deficiency cannot be brought until the foreclosure sale is held and the exact amount of the deficiency is known. In yet other states, a deficiency judgment is not permitted in certain types of mortgages, particularly in purchase money mortgages for residential property.

Practical Tip

Rights in foreclosure vary significantly from state to state and for residential as opposed to commercial transactions. Prior to foreclosure, lenders should determine state laws on deficiencies and their relationship to foreclosure proceedings.

Statistics indicate that deficiency actions, particularly in the case of residential purchase money mortgages (even where permitted), are not frequently used because of the appearance of taking more from debtors who have just lost their residences to foreclosure.

In some states, mortgagees are required to proceed in a certain manner in order to preserve their rights to deficiency judgments. That is, the mortgagee must establish that the security for the underlying note was exhausted or that the foreclosure remedy has been pursued. In some states, if the mortgagee proceeds directly on the note in order to obtain a personal judgment against the mortgagor, the right of foreclosure is forfeited.

DEEDS OF TRUST

The typical mortgage involves only two parties: the mortgagor and the mortgagee. The **deed of trust** (also known as the trust deed form of securing debts with real property) is a type of mortgage or security agreement that includes three parties. In this arrangement, the property owner (buyer/trustor) conveys title to a third party (trustee) who then holds title for the benefit of the lender (beneficiary).

This three-party financing arrangement holds several advantages for the lender. First, the lender in most states has the right of foreclosure in the event of default, but without proceeding through the courts (a process called the **power of sale**). The power of sale is generally exercised by notice to the trustor and publication of the proposed sale date. Although there is a statutory minimum waiting period before the sale may be conducted, it is a much shorter period than that required for foreclosure. Also, exercising the power of sale is less costly than instituting and conducting judicial foreclosures.

A second advantage for the lender is that the lender's involvement can be kept secret, since only the trustee's name need appear in the records. Further transferees of the note can also keep their identities a secret.

Another advantage is that the deed of trust facilitates the borrowing of large sums. Sales of bonds and other debentures by corporations to many parties can be secured by one deed of trust on corporate property, which will be held by a third party.

Relationship to Mortgages

Even though a deed of trust may be used instead of a mortgage to secure an underlying debt, the rights and relationships of the parties with the exception of foreclosure remain the same. That is, the trustor still has the obligations of timely payment, nonwaste, insurance, and so on. Furthermore, the deed of trust contains the same types of clauses and provisions discussed under the mortgage sections of this chapter.

The lender must be cautious about the language used to create the deed of trust so that the proper relationship is set up, or in many states the setup will be treated as a mortgage. Perhaps the most important idea to be included in the deed of trust instrument is the notion of the separation of title. The actual title to the property is held by a third party, the trustee, and upon satisfaction of the debt the title must be conveyed to the trustor.

A provision in the deed of trust, which provides that the deed of trust becomes null and void upon satisfaction of the debt, has caused many courts to rule that the instrument was instead a mortgage.

In mortgages, the mortgagee is given the right of foreclosure in the event of default. In deeds of trust, the trustee is given the power of sale. As already discussed, there are definite time advantages associated with the power of sale. There is also the benefit of the elimination or limitation of the redemption rights of the trustor. Under the deed of trust, the borrower is usually given a right of reinstatement, which is the right to pay the amount due and owing the trustor at any time prior to the time of the sale and thereby redeem the property. The distinction between this right and the right of redemption is that reinstatement must take place prior to the sale. Under a deed of trust, the sale terminates all rights of the trustor; under a mortgage, the period of redemption actually begins at the time of the sale and runs for six months to a year afterwards. Strict foreclosure applies to mortgages, not deeds of trust.

In some states, reinstatement requires the trustor to pay only the amount due in back payments plus costs and expenses. In other words, when the power of sale is exercised, the right of reinstatement may be exercised without the trustor paying the full, accelerated amount of the loan then due. This type of provision permits borrowers to reinstate more easily.

Duties and Responsibilities of the Trustee

The trustee in a deed of trust financing arrangement is acting for the benefit of both parties and is therefore required to act impartially. The trustee is under no duty to check title or verify recording of the trust instrument, but is merely the administrator responsible for carrying out the financing arrangement according to the terms set forth.

In many states, a statute specifies what parties are permitted to serve as trustees in a financing arrangement. In all states recognizing this form of financing, the trustee must be someone other than the lender. Typically, those authorized to serve as trustees are lawyers, brokers, title insurers, and escrow companies.

When conflicts arise between the parties or when a default has occurred, it is the responsibility of the trustee to honor the provisions of the trust agreement and conduct a sale pursuant to the terms of the agreement and according to any statutory procedures provided in the state where the property is located.

Consider 15.7 Fill in the chart to indicate the distinctions between mortgages and deeds of trust. Be sure to list under the mortgage sections the provisions applicable in title theory and lien theory states.

	NUMBER OF PARTIES	TITLE	REMEDIES UPON DEFAULT	RIGHT OF REDEMPTION
Mortgages				
Deeds of Trust				

INSTALLMENT LAND CONTRACTS

The **installment land contract** is an alternative method of financing the purchase of property to a mortgage or a deed of trust. It is frequently used when the buyer is unable to obtain financing, when the buyer cannot come up with a large enough down payment, or when the rate at which financing can be obtained is simply exorbitant. Often called a **contract for deed** or a **long-term land contract,** the installment contract is also used to finance the purchase of property in areas where lenders have been reluctant to lend because of problems with maintaining their interest in the secured property.

Each state has different statutes and regulations regarding the land contract, but all states follow the basic nature of this method of financing the purchase of property. The installment land contract is not a purchase contract in which earnest money is received and the primary purpose is to establish the rights and responsibilities of the parties between the time the agreement is reached and the closing of the transaction. Rather, the installment land contract is an agreement covering the parties for the life of the debt, which is being carried by the seller and repaid by the buyer. The installment land contract may not be executed until the date of closing.

The Forfeiture Aspect

One of the unique features of the installment land contract is that in some states the seller has a very strong remedy in the event of the buyer's default: **forfeiture.** In other words, some states recognizing the validity of installment contracts provide that a buyer who defaults will forfeit all interest acquired in the property to the seller.

The forfeiture takes place without judicial procedures and within a certain period of time after the default. For example, some states provide that if a defaulting buyer has paid less than 20 percent of the property's purchase price, then that buyer's interest is forfeited within 30 days after the notification of the default. The 30 days is deemed to be a grace period during which the buyer has the opportunity of redemption by paying what is then due and owing. The length of the grace period varies according to the amount of payment made by the buyer; in some states it may last up to a year.

A seller who wishes to exercise the forfeiture provisions must be cautious in accepting late payments from the buyer. If the seller has been customarily accepting late payments, the forfeiture provisions cannot be invoked on the basis of late payments unless the seller provides the buyer with notice of the reinstatement of timely payments. In order for the forfeiture statutes to be constitutional, some form of notice of default and intent to exercise forfeiture rights must be given to the defaulting buyer.

Some states still require a form of foreclosure proceedings for a forfeiture of interest to take place. In these states, the courts have been concerned with the protection of the buyers; thus, they have required sellers to give buyers a chance for redemption rather than subject them to the time limits of strict forfeiture.

Title Problems

When a mortgagee is involved in financing the purchase of property, chances are that the mortgagee will verify that there is a good title vested in the seller of that property, for a clean title is the secret to the stability of the mortgagee's security. However, in an installment contract, no third party is involved who may be interested in protecting the business. The parties have only to deal with each other, and there is a good chance that title will not be examined. Many buyers using the installment method of finance may find that they have purchased property with tax liens and other possible deficiencies that would ordinarily be discovered by the lender.

Furthermore, without the involvement of a third-party lender, many buyers neglect to record the installment contract and their rights become subject to other interests that may be recorded after the fact. The time span of the contract may also create problems with title because bankruptcy could occur, the vendor could pass away, and title issues would exist in the transference of the credit.

For the seller of the property, the recording of the land contract can present problems if the buyer defaults and forfeits all interest in the property. The seller would have a recorded land contract as a defect on the title to the property, and a quiet title action would be required to remove the cloud of the forfeited contract from the records.

Tax Consequences

One of the benefits of using the installment method of financing the purchase of property is that the seller may defer recognition of gain made on the sale of the property to the buyer. By meeting certain requirements set forth in the Internal Revenue Service regulations, the seller avoids having to report an entire gain on the sale of property in one year. The specific tax benefits available in installment sales are discussed in Chapter 22 but were limited significantly under the Tax Reform Act of 1986.

Regulation Z Application

The seller in an installment contract is required to comply with certain disclosure requirements if Regulation Z (12 C.F.R. § 226) is applicable to the property sale. Many lots for second or resort homes are purchased on an installment basis and hence federal regulations are applicable (see Appendixes E and F).

The seller covered by Regulation Z must be certain to comply with two major disclosure provisions under the regulations. First, the buyer must be notified of the right of rescission. For example, in the purchase of nonprimary residential property, the buyer is entitled to the 72-hour rescission period and must be given a form to sign indicating that the right exists and how it can be exercised.

The seller must also be concerned with disclosing all minimum requirements for a closed-end transaction under Regulation Z. (Minimum disclosure requirements were discussed earlier and include such information as the amount of the payments, the number of payments, the annual percentage rate, and so on.)

SUBDIVISION TRUSTS

The **subdivision trust** is available only in a limited number of states. This method of financing is a three-party arrangement that involves a trust relationship, but the parties have different roles than in the deed of trust financing arrangement. Both the buyer and the seller are beneficiaries of a trust managed by a third-party trustee. The seller transfers title to the property to the trustee, and the buyer and seller execute a note or other contract that contains the payment terms and other provisions governing the parties' relationship.

In addition, the parties will execute a trust agreement that will contain the provisions explaining the duties and responsibilities of the trustee, who will hold title to the property. The trust agreement in this method of financing is critical because it will determine when the trustee may take action and how payments are to be made. In essence, the trust agreement determines how effective the seller's security in the property will be. The diagram shows the subdivision trust relationship.

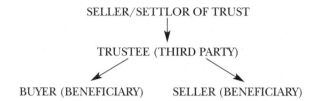

SELLER/SETTLOR OF TRUST

TRUSTEE (THIRD PARTY)

BUYER (BENEFICIARY)   SELLER (BENEFICIARY)

If the buyer defaults on the payments due, the trust agreement will provide the trustee with the right of sale of the property, or perhaps with the right of reconveyance of title to the seller with a forfeiture of the buyer's interest in the property. This method of financing permits the seller quick relief in the event of a buyer default.

Typically, the subdivision trust is used by developers (buyers) with great ideas but little cash for the development of land parcels. Under this arrangement, the buyer and seller have the protection of a third party holding title, and the benefit of having the trust continue once the developer is able to sell or lease the development; thus, both buyer and seller can benefit from the profits obtained upon completion of the development. The trust agreement permits an arrangement in which the seller not only is paid a certain amount for the property, but also is entitled to collect a certain portion of the development profits after the buyer begins to earn on the investment.

An example of a subdivision trust arrangement is when a farmer sells a substantial portion of prime-location real estate to a shopping center developer. During the construction of the shopping center, the farmer would take minimal or no payments for the property. Upon completion of the shopping center, the leasing of the property, and the collection of rents and perhaps percentages of the sales of tenants, the farmer would collect the purchase price of the property, an additional share of the profits received for a certain period of time, or both. The relationship is shown in the diagram.

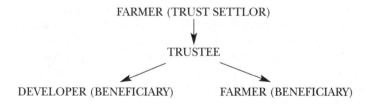

FARMER (TRUST SETTLOR)

TRUSTEE

DEVELOPER (BENEFICIARY)   FARMER (BENEFICIARY)

In many of the states recognizing the subdivision trust as a method of financing the purchase of property, the rules on foreclosure, redemption, power of sale, and reinstatement rights are simply inapplicable. Rather, the parties are governed only by the law of trusts for that jurisdiction. In these states, the parties are often free to insert provisions in their trust agreements for the trustee to follow in the event of nonpayment or any other form of default.

ALTERNATIVE FINANCING METHODS

During poor economic conditions, price increases and high interest rates have created financial barriers to the purchase and ownership of residential, income-producing, and commercial properties. These barriers were large down payments and high monthly payments, which effectively prevented many willing buyers from participating in the real estate market. To ease some of the burden and open the market, many lenders, sellers, buyers, and brokers instituted methods of financing the purchase of property that combined traditional methods, created new methods, and often combined the two. In the following sections, some of the methods used quite frequently are discussed.

Shared-Appreciation or Equity-Participation Financing Mortgages

The **shared-appreciation mortgage** or **equity-participation financing** is a creation of the commercial lender that involves a trade-off: The lender offers lower monthly interest rates in exchange for a share in the appreciation of the property pledged as security. Under this approach, the lender will finance a loan at say 7 percent as opposed to 8 percent and, upon the borrower's sale of the property, will receive some percentage of the profit made—usually no more than 40 percent. The lender thus experiences a gain on the transfer of the property, and the buyer enjoys the benefit of lower monthly payments by giving up a portion of the property appreciation.

Wrap-Around Mortgages

This type of financing arrangement is used in the purchase of property that already has financing not subject to a due-on-sale clause upon transfer. The wrap-around mortgage is similar to an assumption except that the seller is afforded more security.

For example, suppose that a residence is being sold for $85,000, and there is an existing mortgage balance of $50,000 on the property. The buyer can afford to put $10,000 down. In an assumption, the buyer would then assume the $50,000 obligation, and the seller would take a second mortgage on the property to secure the buyer's repayment of the $25,000 to him. Under a wrap-around arrangement, the buyer simply takes title to the property subject to the mortgage. The buyer is given a loan by the seller for $75,000, which is secured by an all-inclusive mortgage. The seller will continue to make the payments on the $50,000 loan, and the buyer will make payments to the seller on a full $75,000 at a lower-than-market rate. The seller will retain that portion of the buyer's monthly payment that is above the amount due on the $50,000 mortgage.

One way the seller can make a profit on the transaction is to charge a higher rate on the entire wrap-around mortgage. If the $50,000 loan is at 9 percent, the seller could carry the full $75,000 at 12 percent and would make 12 percent on $25,000 and an additional 3 percent on the original $50,000 obligation.

Exchange or Trades

In a property exchange, the parties involved swap the equity in their properties as a means of purchasing each other's property. This type of financing is used more commonly in commercial transactions. It is frequently used when employees in the same firm are being transferred to each other's respective location.

Each needs a house in the other's location, and the equities are simply swapped as a means of purchase.

The primary concern of the parties to a property exchange is that the equities are even. If the equities in the exchanged properties are not even, one of the parties must pay the other the difference in cash.

Lease-Purchase Agreements

If it is difficult for the buyer to obtain financing at the time the parties desire to enter into a transaction, and if the seller does not wish to become involved in carrying the buyer's purchase, then the parties may enter into an agreement of sale and simultaneously execute a lease agreement. The purchase agreement will have a delayed closing date.

The parties will agree to the purchase price and to a future date for closing the sale when financing will be more reasonable. Usually, the buyer will make a deposit toward the down payment and will also make monthly rental payments to the seller. The amount of the monthly rental payments will cover at least the underlying mortgage debt for which the seller is responsible, and it may exceed that amount as a benefit to the seller carrying the lease or as partial payment of the eventual down payment that will be required.

With the **lease-purchase mortgage,** the buyer has a definite purchase price locked in at the current market price as well as the opportunity to wait for better loan terms. The seller enjoys the tax benefits of leasing the property (discussed in Chapter 22) and has a sale guaranteed at some future date. The seller also has the generally afforded remedy of retaining the buyer's deposit in the event the sale is not executed or the buyer terminates the lease.

A variation of this method of financing is the lease with an option to buy. Under this type of arrangement, the parties do not actually enter into a purchase contract, but the buyer is given the right to exercise an option to purchase at any time during the period of the lease. The parties' agreement may also provide that the rental payments may be used toward the down payment if the option to purchase is exercised.

The Broker, Regulation Z, and Alternative Financing

Alternative methods of financing carry with them complexities that require the assistance of brokers and lawyers in making the methods work effectively for both parties in the transaction. In addition, these methods of financing may also carry with them hidden legal pitfalls for the broker assisting a seller or a buyer in arranging the method of financing.

The broker who is regularly involved in the arrangement of credit must meet all of the disclosure requirements under Regulation Z. *Regularly involved* in credit arrangements means that the broker has participated in the arrangement of credit for "more than 5-secured by a dwelling" financing arrangements, or for more than 25 transactions in which a dwelling was not used as credit. However, all of these transactions must meet the basic Regulation Z criteria of a finance charge or financing payable in more than four installments for the broker to be required to comply, in which case the broker must see that the buyer is furnished with all of the disclosure statements discussed earlier.

The brokers should also consult with an attorney to determine whether the acts of individual salespersons in arranging credit transactions can be attributed to them in determining whether they have met the transaction criteria for application of Regulation Z. A broker may also be required to make disclosures if the salespersons working in the same office have met the criteria for the firm as a whole.

In addition to real estate brokers and their work on alternative financing mechanisms, there are also mortgage brokers who serve as a link between potential customers and lenders who will eventually underwrite the loan. These **mortgage brokers** are independent businesses that do not represent any particular company. Their job is to shop for the customer and find the best mortgage interest rate. Whether they are able to find the best rate or guarantee such results is a matter for individual screening and evaluation.

| Ethical Issue | What are the ethics of disclosure when a real estate professional is dealing with an inexperienced borrower or buyer? Is it the job of the mortgage broker or real estate broker to inform the borrower/buyer of all his or her rights? What are the ethics of obtaining a higher interest rate from a borrower because of his or her inexperience? |

CAUTIONS AND CONCLUSIONS

The many complexities and loopholes of all the methods of financing discussed in this chapter are potentially costly to one or both of the parties to the transaction. It is important that all parties involved in the financing arrangement for the purchase of real property consider the following questions before entering into an agreement, so that problems and pitfalls can be avoided initially rather than encountered during the course of performance.

- Is there some form of security for loan repayment?
- What constitutes default under the agreement? Is it defined?
- Are late payments permitted? Is it possible for the acceptance of late payments to cause rights to be waived?
- Is Regulation Z compliance required? Who must comply?
- Are there other secured interests in the property? Who has priority?
- May the security instrument be recorded for protection?
- If there is a default, will the debtor be given some type of grace period?
- What happens if the property is transferred?
- What tax benefits or implications exist?
- Does the written document (or documents) reflect all desires and intents?

Key Terms

mortgage, 364
mortgagor, 364
purchase money mortgage, 364
mortgagee, 364
title theory, 365
lien theory, 365
promissory note, 366
Truth-in-Lending laws, 368

Federal Consumer Credit Protection Act, 368
Regulation Z, 368
residential mortgage transactions, 369
advertisement, 369
triggering language, 369
Equal Credit Opportunity Act (ECOA), 372

Home Mortgage Disclosure Act, 373
Community Reinvestment Act (CRA), 373
lender liability, 373
usury, 373
Brundage clause, 374
acceleration clause, 375
interest acceleration clause, 376

Chapter Problems

1. A purchased B's home through a cash-to-mortgage arrangement with A assuming B's $40,000 Federal Housing Administration (FHA) loan. Three months after the purchase, A has lost his job and is unable to meet the monthly payments. The mortgagee has turned to B for the payments, and B protests, claiming he is no longer liable on the underlying mortgage note. The mortgagee, complying with proper procedures, forecloses on the property and sells it for $25,000. The mortgagee is now interested in obtaining a deficiency judgment and has therefore sued both A and B. Has the mortgagee acted properly under the circumstances? Is B correct about his liability? Is a deficiency judgment possible under the circumstances? Would it make any difference if a deed of trust arrangement were involved?

2. The following summarizes the sequence of events involved on a parcel of property located in Nevada and owned by the Lundgrens:

- *November 30, 1970:* The Lundgrens executed a note in favor of Nevada Wholesale Lumber in the amount of $7,767.44, secured by a deed of trust, with Title Insurance and Trust Company as trustee.
- *May 8, 1972:* The Lundgrens, without notifying Nevada Wholesale, conveyed fee simple title to Rampart Corporation.
- *December 6, 1972:* The Lundgrens executed a second note to Nevada Wholesale for $12,126.99. The note was secured by a dragnet clause in the November 30, 1970, deed of trust.

- *January 16, 1973:* Rampart Corporation executed a note and deed of trust to Myers Realty.
- *February 7, 1973:* Nevada Wholesale recorded a notice of default and election to sell the property.
- *February 12, 1973:* Nevada Wholesale filed suit on the $12,126.99 note.
- *June 28, 1973:* Default judgment was awarded Nevada Wholesale on suit and the land was attached.
- *August 17, 1973:* Myers Realty filed notice of foreclosure on its deed of trust from Rampart Corporation.

Assuming the sale of the property does not bring enough to satisfy all parties in the transactions, who has priority?

3. W. J. Minderhout has entered into a lease agreement with Coast Bank under which Minderhout will lease an office building (worth $200,000) from Coast for rental payments of $25,000 per year. The agreement also provides that at the end of the 10-year lease period established in the agreement, Minderhout will have the option to purchase the building for $40,000. Minderhout wishes to know if the arrangement is a mortgage or a lease and what rights both he and Coast will have in the event he defaults on the lease payments. *Coast Bank v. Minderhout,* 392 P.2d 265 (Calif. 1964)

4. Seven Palms Motor Inn obtained financing from Commerce Mortgage Company for the purchase of a motel. Commerce secured the purchase through a duly recorded mortgage on the property, which contained an after-acquired property clause. Seven Palms then contracted, through a security agreement perfected by the filing of the financing statement, with Sears, Roebuck and Company for the purchase of drapery rods, drapes, and matching bedspreads for each of the rooms in the motel. Seven Palms defaulted and Commerce foreclosed. Sears claimed priority in the items it furnished, since the items were personal property. Commerce claimed the items were fixtures and were covered by the mortgage. What was the result? *Sears, Roebuck & Co. v. Seven Palms Motor Inn, Inc.,* 530 S.W.2d 695 (Mo. 1975)

5. Dr. Lindsey Scott purchased an office building and borrowed the funds for the purchase from Amato, Incorporated. Amato took and recorded a mortgage on the property. Scott had hired Essex Cleaning Contractors to perform janitorial services in the building. Scott defaulted, and Amato took possession of the building and collected and retained all rents. Amato did not pay Essex, contending that Scott had entered into the contract with them and that Scott was therefore liable even after Amato took possession. Scott maintains Amato enjoyed possession and benefits and was therefore liable to Essex. What is the result? *Essex Cleaning Contractors, Inc. v. Amato, Inc.,* 317 A.2d 411 (N.J. 1974)

6. Lynley and Samuel Crabtree purchased their first home in 1986 for $95,000. Their purchase was financed by Western Mortgage and secured by a deed of trust. Two years later, the Crabtrees decided to put in a swimming pool. They were given a loan by Valley National Bank for pool construction. The loan was secured by a second deed of trust. In 1992, the Crabtrees sold their home to John and Julia Gardner. The Gardners assumed the Western Mortgage. The Crabtrees agreed to carry the Valley pool loan in the form of a wrap-around financing. Valley was not notified of the sale of the property.

Both of the Gardners were victims of layoffs in their companies, and they fell behind on all their payments. Western has begun foreclosure proceedings. The property is worth $114,000. The Gardners owe $7,000 in back payments. The mortgage amount due is $89,000. The pool loan balance is $10,000. The expenses of the sale are $7,000 (including a real estate agent's commission). The property is sold for $112,000. How will the amounts be distributed?

7. Stuckenberg, through a straw party, purchased a ranchette-style apartment building with five apartments under one roof. Stuckenberg purchased the property with funds from a note signed with First Federal, which was secured with a deed of trust on the property. Paragraph 7 of the deed of trust provided:

> First Federal shall have power and authority to take possession of the said real estate and to manage, control and lease the same and collect all rents, issues and profits therefrom for the purpose of paying the note secured by the deed of trust.

The full amount of the loan was due in February 1969, and Stuckenberg defaulted on both the January

and February 1969 payments. After the default, First Federal notified Stuckenberg's son of its intention to exercise its rights under paragraph 7 and requested information on the tenants, the rental amounts, and the rental due dates. First Federal then sent to Stuckenberg, his attorney, and all the tenants a notice of First Federal's rights under paragraph 7 and its intent to exercise those rights. A management corporation was hired by First Federal, and personal service of the letter was given to three of the five tenants in the building (the other tenants could not be reached). Can First Federal collect the rents and take over the property in this manner? *In re Stuckenberg,* 374 F.Supp. 15 (Mo. 1974)

8. Do any of the following statements contain triggering terms that require further disclosure under Regulation Z?

    a. "$70,000 balance payable in 120 monthly installments"

    b. "Total interest payments are $40,000 less"

    c. "Fantastic assumption terms available"

    d. "Assume low-interest FHA loan"

9. A construction lender had an obligation to loan $250,000 to a builder/mortgagor. The mortgage was recorded upon execution of the note. The funds were to be dispersed to the mortgagor as follows: 20 percent when the foundation was set, 20 percent when the building was roofed in, 20 percent when the interior plaster was set, 20 percent when the certificate of occupancy was issued, and 20 percent 30 days later. Will the lender have priority at the time of recording or at the time and amount of each advance? *Larson Cement Stone Co. v. Redlem Realty Co.,* 137 N.W.2d 241 (1965)

10. Dynamic Development Corporation (Dynamic) is a developer that builds and sells residential and commercial property. In May 1985, Mid Kansas Federal Savings and Loan Association of Wichita (Mid Kansas) loaned Dynamic $803,250 for the construction of ten "spec" homes in a subdivision Dynamic owned in Prescott, Arizona. There were ten separate loans made, with a note and deed of trust (see page 397) on each of the 10 lots.

By January 1986, Dynamic needed additional funds to complete the homes and Mid Kansas loaned another $150,000, which was secured by a second note and deed of trust on seven of the lots for the spec homes that had not been sold.

The first and second notes were both due in the summer of 1986. Two more lots were sold and released from the deeds of trust. In fall 1986, Mid Kansas notified Dynamic that the five remaining properties would be sold at a trustee's sale if the total debt owed was not paid. Dynamic could not pay the loan amount but did sell one additional lot and applied the proceeds to the loans.

Mid Kansas gave notice of a trustee's sale on the four remaining lots. At the time of the sale, Dynamic owed Mid Kansas $102,000 on the second note and $425,000 on the first note. Mid Kansas foreclosed on the second notes and bought the properties for a credit balance at the sale. Mid Kansas never foreclosed on the first notes, but brought suit, waiving the security, against Dynamic for the efficiency. Can the deficiency be collected? *Mid Kansas Federal Savings and Loan Association of Wichita v. Dynamic Development Corporation,* 804 P.2d 1310 (Ariz. 1991).

Internet Activities

1.   For an overview on mortgages and the law go to: **http://www.law.cornell.edu/topics/ mortgages.html**.

2.   For information on financing residential purchases from the federal government including FHA, VA, consumer protection legislation and different types of governmentally backed mortgages (FANNIE MAEs, etc.), go to: **http://www.hud.gov/**.

3.   For information on homeowner's financing, interest rates, calculations of monthly payment, etc., go to: **http://www.homeowners.com/**.

4.   A complete guide to financing of residential homes for Veterans can be found at: **http://www.va.gov/vas/loan/**.

Test Your Knowledge of Home Buying Terms

Think you are ready to buy a home? There's more to it than looking through a myriad of floor plans and qualifying for a loan. This quiz will test your real estate savvy. There are 20 commonly used real estate terms: Pick the answer that most closely defines the boldfaced word or words.

1. **POINT**
   (a) A fact or idea made by a loan officer.
   (b) A charge that equals 1 percent of the loan amount.
   (c) A discount offered on the loan.
   (d) An upfront charge derived from the mortgage interest rate.

2. **DEED OF TRUST**
   (a) Used instead of a mortgage in Arizona.
   (b) A note signed by the borrower indicating intent to purchase.
   (c) A note signed by the mortgage company indicating it believes the borrower will repay the loan.
   (d) A deed entrusting the borrower to pay the closing costs.

3. **LOCK**
   (a) An electronic security device that restricts access to a home until after closing.
   (b) A period of time for which a certain interest rate is good.
   (c) Securing a certain lot in a subdivision.
   (d) A chamber of compressed air within a house.

4. **ANNUAL PERCENTAGE RATE**
   (a) The percentage of the principal that is paid off yearly.
   (b) The relationship between the principal to the interest paid annually.
   (c) The percentage of the borrower's annual income needed for the mortgage payments.
   (d) The effective rate of interest.

5. **AMORTIZATION**
   (a) Repayment of a mortgage through payments made over a set period of time at regular intervals.
   (b) Prepayment of a loan.
   (c) A deed that lists principal and interest payments of a mortgage.
   (d) A schedule listing how much interest is due.

6. **ESCROW**
   (a) Fancy, scrolled molding.
   (b) Property used as collateral.
   (c) An agreement made between the buyer and the builder.
   (d) Property, documents, and/or money held for safekeeping until specified terms of a sales contract are completed.

7. **GOVERNMENT LOAN**
   (a) A loan given to governmental agencies for construction of affordable homes.
   (b) A loan awarded to the highest bidder for a foreclosed-upon home offered through the U.S. Department of Housing and Urban Development.
   (c) A loan insured or guaranteed by a government housing agency, such as the Veterans Administration.
   (d) A mortgage issued to government workers.

8. **ARM Stands for:**
   (a) Annualized-ratio mortgage.
   (b) Annualized-rate mortgage.
   (c) Adjustable-rate mortgage.
   (d) Arbitrary-rate mortgage.

9. **CAVEAT EMPTOR is Latin for:**
   (a) "Let the buyer beware."
   (b) "Let the seller beware."
   (c) "Home is where the heart is."
   (d) "Let the emperor eat caviar."

10. **LOAN-TO-VALUE RATIO**
   (a) The relationship between the mortgage amount and the amount of appreciation a home is expected to have.
   (b) The mortgage amount compared with the value of other homes in a given neighborhood.
   (c) A comparison of loan terms among various lenders.
   (d) The amount borrowed compared with the appraised value or sales price of a home.

Test Your Knowledge of Home Buying Terms, *continued*

11. CREATIVE FINANCING
  (a) New and innovative types of lending institutions.
  (b) New and innovative types of loans.
  (c) New and innovative ways that borrowers come up with down-payment money.
  (d) A loan specifically geared for artists.

12. EARNEST MONEY
  (a) Money given by a builder to a lending institution showing a buyer's intent to purchase a home.
  (b) Money that is set aside by a builder in case a buyer defaults.
  (c) Money given by a buyer to a seller or builder showing intent to buy the home.
  (d) 20 percent of a purchase price of a home.

13. FHA Stands for:
  (a) Federal Housing Administration.
  (b) Federal Home Association.
  (c) Federal Home Administration.
  (d) Federal Housing Association.

14. PREPAIDS
  (a) A reserve of interest and tax payments set aside in an impound account.
  (b) Prepayment of a mortgage.
  (c) Earnest money applied to the down payment.
  (d) Payments made before a home is built.

15. CONVENTIONAL LOAN
  (a) A loan for a standard three- or four-bedroom, two-bathroom home.
  (b) A loan not insured by the Veterans Administration or guaranteed by the FHA.
  (c) A mortgage worded in easy-to-understand language.
  (d) A loan for a conventional single-family home, not a town home or condo.

16. BALLOON PAYMENT
  (a) Mortgage payments that rise gradually over the life of the loan.
  (b) The final payment of a loan, celebrating the ending of the debt.
  (c) The last payment of a mortgage, with the amount of that payment being much greater than that of the previous payments.
  (d) A second mortgage that is paid in one lump-sum payment.

17. SETBACK
  (a) An interruption in the loan process.
  (b) The amount of money the borrower has to pay out for closing costs.
  (c) The number of feet a patio extends into the back yard.
  (d) The distance from a street that a house must be placed, as required by zoning laws.

18. HAZARD INSURANCE
  (a) Insurance against theft.
  (b) Insurance against physical damage due to fire, storms and other hazards.
  (c) Insurance given to lenders to protect against borrowers defaulting on their loans.
  (d) Insurance given to builders to protect against natural disasters occurring while a home is under construction.

19. WALK-THROUGH
  (a) The initial viewing of a floor plan by the prospective buyers.
  (b) An inspection by a city building inspector of a home under construction.
  (c) An inspection by the builder of a newly constructed home.
  (d) An inspection of a new home by the buyers just before closing.

20. PITI Stands for:
  (a) Principal, interest, taxes and insurance.
  (b) Payments of interest, taxes and insurance.
  (c) Principal, interest, title and investment.
  (d) Property, investment, taxes and insurance.

Score: 20 correct: You've mastered home buying. Pass Go and move into your new home. 17-19: You're ready to buy. 16 or below: Is someone else buying a home for you? Better do some home-buying research.

Answers

1-b, 2-a, 3-b, 4-d, 5-a, 6-d, 7-c, 8-c, 9-a, 10-d, 11-b, 12-c, 13-a, 14-a, 15-b, 16-c, 17-d, 18-b, 19-d, 20-a.

Susan Doerfler, "The Language of Real Estate Loans," *Arizona Republic*, October 1, 1994, AH1. Reprinted with permission.

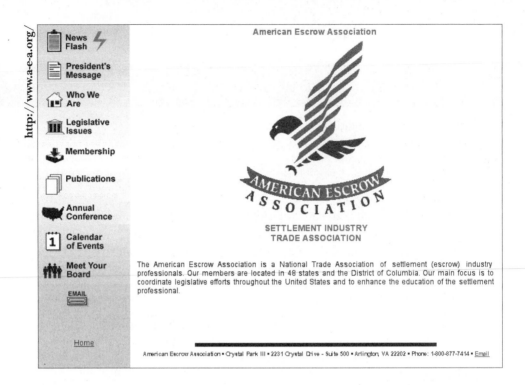

Chapter 16
Closing the Deal

It ain't over until it's over.

Attributed to Yogi Berra

"Close of escrow" shall mean the day documents are filed for record. The exterior landscaping to be the responsibility of the buyer herein. Buyer agrees to provide Seller with landscaping rendering within sixty (60) days, seller herein to approve of same. Buyer and Seller to walk though subject property on or before March 31, 2001 to review and approve finishing details. Buyers are aware flooring allowance is $50,000, any additional costs shall be buyers [sic] expense. Seller herein agrees to provide buyer with a copy of the appraisal of Lot 60, completed by _____ MAI in the amount of $2,150,000. Buyer acknowledges that there is currently a construction loan in the amount of $1,300,000.00 on subject property.

These excerpts from a set of escrow instructions provide some insight into the complexity of bringing a buyer and seller together to close a real estate deal.

Buying property isn't the same as buying Raisinets at the grocery store. That transaction is simple, done face-to-face with title and payment passing at the same time.

410

However, a piece of property is not as neat and compact as a box of candy. The issues of others' interest in the land, financing, and property inspections must all come together somewhere, sometime, and somehow for the sale to take place. "It ain't over until it's over" applies in real estate, but it ain't over until the closing. This chapter covers all the issues related to closing a real estate transaction: How is a closing done? What documents are necessary for closing? What parties will be involved in closing? What are their responsibilities during the closing process?

THE NATURE OF CLOSING

Where?

The nature of a closing varies from state to state, and even within states. In some states a closing is held at the government office responsible for recording land documents, such as county clerk, county recorder, or recorder of deeds. The closing may be held during the hour after the office closes (or the time permitted for recording that day ends) so that the problems of title covered in Chapter 13 do not occur.

In other states, title company offices are used for the closing, again usually at a time when the title search can be closed off, as when the recording office is closed.

In many states, closing will occur at the office of one of the attorneys representing one of the parties to the transaction. Again, the time will be controlled by closure on the title search.

In still other states, there are escrow companies established exclusively for the purpose of handling the documents, funds, and people necessary for the transaction to close.

What?

In some states, closing is a formal process in which the parties gather in a room for signing and exchanging documents. In other states, a party designated, such as an escrow agent or title company, gathers the necessary documents and signatures, and sets a date for closing.

Regardless of the method or place, there is one consistent factor among all the states' methods of closing: getting all the conditions for closing met. Regardless of how, the closings all occur at the same time: when all parties have fulfilled their obligations under the contract and the closing agreement or escrow instructions.

Who?

The closing or **escrow** setup generally involves three or four parties. The buyer and seller who set up the escrow arrangement are the first two parties. If there is a lender involved either in the financing or assumption of financing of the property, the lender is also a party to the transaction. The final party is an independent party (as noted above) who handles the collection of necessary documents and the actual transfer of funds and title.

While the term *escrow* is used throughout the remainder of the chapter, it is used for convenience. Regardless of the method for closing, the parties must designate an agent to handle the preparation for the closing. The agent selected, regardless of name, has the same obligations as an escrow agent. Further, the parties must establish a contractual relationship with this third party no matter how the physical closing takes place.

The party responsible for gathering the documentation, funds, and condition checks could be an attorney, a title company, an escrow company, or anyone else authorized by the state to handle property closings. For example, in some states, insurance companies and certified public accountants are permitted to handle closings.

The party chosen to act as the escrow agent should be carefully screened so that the parties do not subject themselves to a substantial loss because of the agent's lack of integrity. There is nothing that requires a buyer or seller to use a particular company or escrow agent for closing; and if one side has objections or reasons for doubt as to the agent's honesty, such objections and reasons should be made before the transaction is turned over to the escrow agent. Some background checking on the proposed agent may be appropriate.

Since the transfer of property inevitably involves the transfer of large sums of money, such sums should not be turned over to an agent who has not been recommended, checked, or verified as a trustworthy business or businessperson.

THE CLOSING SET-UP

Requirements for Setting Up the Escrow or Closing

VALID AND ENFORCEABLE CONTRACT FOR
PURCHASE AND SALE OF REAL ESTATE

http://

For the latest legislative news on escrows, visit the American Escrow Association at **http:// www.a-e-a.org**/.

An escrow or closing arrangement is set up to formally carry out the provisions of a real estate contract. For an escrow to be valid, there must be an underlying valid contract between the parties. Without such a contract, the third party is only carrying out an agency relationship that has no binding effect on either of the parties, since there is no direct contractual relationship between them. Many parties attempt to consummate a sale quickly by going directly to escrow instructions, but such a timesaving step can be costly in that there is no enforceable contract between buyer and seller—only an agency contract between the escrow agent and buyer and seller. The two can be combined, as when the parties sign a "Purchase Agreement and Escrow Instructions."

DEPOSIT OF DEED WITH AN AGENT

This requirement emphasizes a more general requirement for a valid escrow, which is that the parties set up the transaction as irrevocable. Irrevocability requires that the parties are not permitted to withdraw their funds and documents at will, but that such withdrawals or returns will occur only if the provisions in their contract and escrow instructions are not met. If the seller is free to revoke the deed at any time or if the buyer is able to withdraw the funds at any time, the transaction could never be closed and the agent's responsibilities would be frustrated and liabilities complicated. The seller must deposit a validly executed deed with the escrow agent so that the agent is able to transfer title.

VALID ESCROW INSTRUCTIONS

Even the irrevocable deposit of the deed with the third party will not create an escrow unless the agent and the other two or three parties execute a contract called **escrow instructions,** which will direct the agent or third party on the hows, whens, and whats of closing the property transaction. The third party is authorized to do only what is prescribed in the contractual escrow instructions; without instructions, the third party has no authority to consummate a sale.

Contents of Escrow or Closing Instructions

MANDATORY MATTERS

Because the escrow involves the transfer of a land interest, the authority of the third party must be in writing. In addition, every set of escrow instructions should include these mandatory items:

1. Name of the agent, third party, or depository
2. Names of the buyer (buyers) and seller (sellers) and their proper designation (partnership, corporation, married couple, single person, and so on)
3. Legal description of the property to be transferred
4. Purchase price of the property
5. Conditions of transfer and payment
6. Allocation of expenses, costs, insurance, taxes, assessments, and so on
7. Signatures of the buyer and seller

RECOMMENDED PROVISIONS

In both brokerage contracts and contracts for the sale of property, the minimum requirements do not always provide for the contingencies that can arise in the process of closing a property transaction. The parties are wise to include additional provisions to govern various aspects of closing. Although many states and regions have customs in the area of property closings, it is often a dispute over such customs that results in expensive and time-consuming litigation.

Allocating Costs The escrow instructions should specify who will pay which costs associated with closing the transaction. Again, there are many customs for such allocations, but it is easier and legally binding to list such cost breakdowns as part of the escrow instructions. The following list is indicative of the typical costs associated with closing that should be assessed by the parties in the transaction:

1. Escrow fee
2. Fees for title search, title abstract, title insurance, and attorneys associated with title
3. Recording fees for the deed, mortgage, deed of trust, and any documents required to complete the transaction
4. Mortgage transfer or release fees
5. Loan origination fees
6. Termite inspection report
7. Appraisal or survey fees
8. Credit report fees
9. Loan discount points
10. Attorneys' fees for drafting documents and so on

By agreeing to the allocation of costs in advance, the parties avoid possible confusion and delay in the closing process. However, the parties should not violate any restrictions the lender has placed on closing costs. For example, with certain government-insured loans, federal regulations specify which party must pay certain parts of the costs listed above. With some government loans, the seller is required to pay the loan discount points.

One of the ongoing concerns about closing arrangements is the fee charged for them. Someone—an attorney, a title company, or an escrow firm—will collect a fee for closing the transaction. In the case of title companies used as escrow agents, there is a fee for both the closing and the title insurance policy. In many states, those fees are set by statute or regulation; that is, the title companies' fees are regulated. In some of those states the fees are established by a board composed of members of the title industry in that state.

The presence of an industry regulatory body and the fixed fees caught the attention of the Federal Trade Commission, and in 1990 it brought an action against six of the nation's largest title companies charging them with horizontal price fixing. The title companies and the FTC eventually went to the United States Supreme Court. In *F.T.C. v. Ticor Title Ins. Co.*, 504 U.S. 621 (1992), some of the state regulatory price mechanisms were upheld, but in two of the states the Supreme Court held that there was price fixing because the regulation was not meaningful. Those states simply had a "rubber stamp" approval process and there was no regulatory oversight of pricing. As a result of this decision, many property purchasers were given refunds under a class action litigation settlement.

Practical Tip

The decision in the *Ticor* case requires boards responsible for setting prices to review the market and all increase requests with complete information and input prior to making a decision to allow the price increase. Members of the industry should require such boards to take such proactive postures in order to ensure the fairness of the oversight and the pricing. Some states will need to change their regulatory processes in order to comply with the standards established in the *Ticor* decision.

Prorating Prepaids Property transfers do not usually occur at times when taxes, insurance premiums, and rents are due. At the time of nearly every closing, the seller has prepaid taxes or insurance but will not enjoy the property for the period for which payment has been made. A seller may have paid a $120 insurance premium in January that covers insurance on the property until June, with the property being transferred to the buyer in March. The escrow instructions should provide how those funds will be **prorated** so that the buyer pays for the coverage from March until June.

In many areas, formulas are customarily used to prorate prepaid amounts as to the date of transfer. Basically, the formulas follow along one of two general theories. Theory 1 breaks the year into 360 days with 12 months of 30 days each. Theory 2 holds that the year consists of 365 days and prorates prepaids on a daily basis of 1/365th of the total annual cost. Assuming the closing took place on March 15, in the example above, under theory 1 the seller would receive a credit of $70 or 3 months at $20 plus a half-month at $10. Under theory 2, the seller would receive a credit of $.66 per day (240 ÷ 365). Taking the number of days from March 15 to June 30, the total credit would be $70.62 (107 × $.66).

Consider 16.1

A seller has prepaid both taxes and insurance on the property about to be transferred. The taxes are $600 per year, and the insurance premiums are $300 per year. The seller prepaid both in January for the entire year through December 31. The closing on the property will take place on March 15, and the parties wish to know what formulas can be used to prorate these prepaids. Explain the results to them under both the 360-day year and the 365-day year formulas.

Sale of Personal Property If any personal property such as appliances or furniture is being transferred with the property, the parties should so specify in their agreement. Also, the seller should furnish the escrow agent with a bill of sale in order to transfer title to the property. The bill of sale should accurately describe the property being transferred, preferably including model number and serial number if available. If furniture is being transferred, as in the sale of an apartment complex, the description should be as specific as possible including the size, color, and purpose of the furniture; for example, "one 96-inch green and yellow plaid living-room sofa." The bill of sale should also include warranties from the seller that the seller has title to the property and is authorized to transfer title, and that there are no liens or encumbrances on the transferred property.

Practical Tip

More and more closing agreements include mandatory arbitration clauses. These clauses are helpful in situations in which the parties disagree over compliance with the conditions and the escrow deposit sits in limbo. Arbitration is a much faster way of resolving the dispute than litigation.

Documents to Be Delivered by Each Party

Although a minimum requirement for escrow is that the seller deposit the deeds for transfer, there are other documents associated with the property transfer that both seller and buyer must deposit for the closing to take place. The following list is not comprehensive but is indicative of the detail that should be provided in the escrow instructions.

1. By the seller
   a. Title documents: abstract, opinion, and insurance
   b. Most recent tax bill
   c. Insurance policies
   d. Plans and specifications for original construction and modifications
   e. Warranties on any appliances, heating systems, and so on
   f. Uniform Commercial Code (UCC) bulk sale affidavit for business transfer
   g. Soil, termite, and other property condition reports including reports from environmental agencies
   h. Keys
   i. Notes, mortgages, deeds of trust, UCC Article 9 security agreements and financing statements
   j. List of tenants and copies of leases
   k. Building code inspection and compliance

2. By the buyer
   a. Earnest money check
   b. Loan commitment
   c. List of defects to be remedied prior to closing
   d. Corporate authorization if corporate buyer is involved

3. By the lender
   a. Mortgage, deed of trust, and promissory note
   b. Truth-in-lending statement (see Chapter 15)
   c. Real Estate Settlement Procedures Act (RESPA) statement (see later for discussion)
   d. Required forms if Federal Housing Administration (FHA) or Veterans Administration (VA) loan
   e. Required inspections if FHA or VA loan

Cancellation of Escrow

Because the escrow agent is permitted to consummate the transaction only upon the completion of certain conditions specified in the instructions, it follows that if those conditions are not met, the parties are excused from their performance under the contract and the entire escrow arrangement must be canceled.

Practical Tip

The escrow or closing instructions are a binding contract. The escrow agent must follow the instructions as the parties drafted them. An escrow agent is not in a position to make a "close enough" decision. Either the documentation and requirements have been met or they have not. Any change in the conditions requires a modification of the instructions signed by both parties. The parties together must make a "close enough" decision. One party cannot talk an escrow agent into making that decision.

Many states have provisions for cancellation, but it is best for the parties to specify when cancellation may occur and how such cancellation is to be accomplished. In drafting the cancellation clause, the parties should carefully specify three items. First, the grounds for cancellation should be set forth. The grounds may be a simple statement such as "if either party fails to comply with the terms hereof," or they may be specifically listed. Second, the parties should specify the method of cancellation. The parties are free to agree on what form the cancellation notice should take (in writing, for example) and how such notice is to be delivered (either personally, through the escrow agent, or by mail). Third, the cancellation clause should include time specifications: when the cancellation takes effect and whether the other party will be allowed a certain amount of time within which to comply before the cancellation becomes effective.

Cancellations, Contingencies, and Contract Performance

"It ain't over until it's over" is a most apt description of the closing arrangement. Complex issues on the contract provisions and contingencies often create confusion among the parties. The following sections highlight some key issues.

RELATIONSHIP BETWEEN PURCHASE CONTRACT AND ESCROW INSTRUCTIONS

In the majority of real estate transactions, form agreements are used for both the purchase contract and the escrow instructions. One difficulty with form agreements that are not carefully cross-compared is that they may include contradictory terms. Often the parties will have problems in complying with their conditions, and the contract may have a remedy or procedure different from that specified in the escrow instructions. The question of which document is controlling becomes a critical one, and the answer varies from state to state. Some states hold that the escrow instructions control, since they were executed later in time and can be viewed as superseding the contract. Other states hold that the contract is better evidence of the parties' intent, since the escrow agreement is merely a set of instructions to a third party and not the true purchase and sale agreement.

The following case illustrates one state's solution to the conflict in agreements.

Allan v. Martin

574 P.2d 457 (Ariz. 1978)

Facts

Kirby and Felicienne Allan (defendants/appellants), both licensed real estate agents, approached George and Pamela Martin (plaintiffs/appellees) about purchasing the Martins' property, which was located in Mesa, Arizona. The Martins wished to sell the property to obtain funds to complete and move into a home they were building in the mountains. The parties entered into a purchase and sale contract, which provided that escrow would close on or before July 31, 1974. The Martins needed the funds by that date so that their mountain home could be completed and they could be in it before cold weather began. Escrow instructions were prepared by a title company and signed by both parties.

The closing did not take place on July 31, but the Martins agreed to a 15-day extension. The Martins checked with the title company on August 15, the last day of the extension, and discovered that the money necessary to purchase their property had not been deposited into escrow. The Martins sent a telegram to the Allans which read, "Due to delay in the sale to you of our home we will no longer sell as the contract expired 7-31-74." The Allans received the telegram on August 15.

The next day, the Martins signed a "thirteen day letter," which instructed the title company to cancel the escrow if the Allans did not comply with the escrow instructions within 13 days from the date of the letter. The 13-day provision for notice and compliance was part of the escrow instructions. The Martins indicated that they believed the 13-day notice was given only for the purpose of canceling the escrow. The Allans complied within the 13 days, but the Martins refused to sell. The Martins brought suit seeking cancellation of the contract. The trial court found for the Martins, rescinding the contract and awarding them $1,000 in damages. The Allans appealed.

Judicial Opinion

Hays, Justice. A contract to sell real estate and an escrow arrangement are not the same thing. There must exist a binding contract to sell the real estate which is the subject of the escrow, or the escrow instructions are unenforceable. An escrow primarily is a conveyance device designed to carry out the terms of a binding contract of sale previously entered into by the parties. Therefore, the escrow instructions are not a part of the underlying real estate sales contract and the terms of the instructions cannot alter or modify the sales contract unless the parties specifically and clearly state such alteration or modi-

fication in writing with specific reference to the fact it changes the original contract.

The appellants (Allans) base their appeal almost entirely upon a fine print form provision in the escrow instructions:

CANCELLATION

16. If either party, who has duly performed hereunder, elects to cancel these instructions because of the failure of the other party to comply with any of the terms hereof within the time limits provided herein, said party so electing to cancel shall deliver to Escrow agent a written notice to the other party and Escrow agent demanding that said other party comply with the terms hereof within thirteen days from the receipt of said notice by Escrow agent or that these instructions shall thereupon become canceled.

This term clearly applies only to the procedure for canceling the escrow instructions; it has nothing to do with how and under what circumstances the real estate contract may be rescinded. The time for performance of the contract was the date designated in the contract for the close of escrow. The latest date agreed upon by the parties was August 15, 1974. The sales contract stated that time was of the essence, and appellees [Martins] informed appellants that the time for the closing of the transaction was very important to them. The latest date for closing was a bargained for term, clearly material in this case. The cancellation provision in the escrow instructions cannot be construed to permit the appellants to perform their contract obligation any later than August 15, 1974.

On August 15 the appellant still had not complied with the sales contract; the money to purchase the property had not been delivered to the escrow agent. When time for performance is material to a contract and one party fails to perform by the contract deadline date, the other party may treat the contract as ended. Thus, when the purchase price was not paid into escrow on the last day agreed upon for closing, the appellees had the legal right to refuse to convey their property and to cancel the contract. They notified appellants they were exercising this right by telegram on August 15.

When appellees exercised their right to treat the contract as ended, the escrow instructions became unenforceable because there was no longer a binding contract to sell the property which was the subject of escrow. The "thirteen day letter" canceling the escrow then became only a formality to prove that the escrow was now void. The fact that the quoted provision on cancellation of the escrow instructions gives a party thirteen days to comply with the terms of the escrow does not mean that one may belatedly comply with the breached sales contract when the non-breaching party has given notice that he elects to treat the contract as ended. Nothing in the escrow instructions can revive an already dead underlying contract.

Appellants also urge that by signing the "thirteen day letter" appellees elected the escrow cancellation remedy and thus are bound to convey the property because appellants met their obligations under the escrow within thirteen days. As explained previously, this is incorrect because the escrow was already void at the time the letter was issued and also because the escrow cancellation procedure does not apply to a sales contract.

Affirmed.

Case Questions

1. Who are the buyers in the transaction? Who are the sellers?
2. What was the original closing date as provided in the purchase contract?
3. Why was a timely closing important to the Martins?
4. What happened when closing did not occur on the original closing date?
5. What happened when closing did not occur on the second date?
6. What is the significance of the "thirteen day letter" in the escrow instructions?
7. Did the Allans comply with the thirteen day provision?
8. Is the thirteen day provision controlling?
9. Which document controls, the contract or the escrow instructions?

MUTUAL CANCELLATION PROVISIONS

In addition to the unilateral cancellation provision in the escrow instructions, the parties may wish to provide methods for cancellation by mutual agreement. A form should be used explaining the parties' mutual action, releasing them from liability, and providing for the return or distribution of deposited funds.

The provisions in the escrow instructions for the distribution of funds and costs in the event of cancellation should be consistent with the contractual provisions. Otherwise, the parties should insert a clause in the escrow instructions indicating their intent to have the escrow instructions control. For example, the following clause could be used to give the escrow instructions control so that cancellation procedures, forms, and refunds are clearly established:

> In the event of any conflict in the provisions of these escrow instructions and the underlying sales agreement, it is the intent and desire of the parties that the terms of these escrow instructions be controlling.

CONTINGENCIES FOR CLOSING

The parties should carefully include all requirements that must be met before the escrow agent may deliver title to the buyer and funds to the seller. The contingencies vary significantly from transaction to transaction, but there are many examples that appear repeatedly in both residential and commercial transactions. For example, a requirement that the seller establish compliance with building codes and zoning restrictions may be a condition to the consummation of the sale. As discussed in Chapter 14, delivery of marketable title is a condition to the completion of the sales transaction on all land transfers.

Other contingencies that may be required are the assignment of all lease and service contracts associated with the property, the furnishing of a favorable pest report, evidence of repair of items agreed to be repaired by the seller, the furnishing of an architect's certificate of completion on a newly constructed building, the completion of a final property inspection, the verification of boundaries by survey, and for business sales the furnishing of audited financial statements. The number and types of contingencies are limitless, but in drafting the escrow instructions, all parties should think of how they can be fully protected before transfer occurs to avoid any surprises once the escrow agent has carried out the actual transfer of title and payment of funds.

RESPONSIBILITIES OF THE LENDER IN CLOSING— THE REAL ESTATE SETTLEMENT PROCEDURES ACT

As noted in the preceding discussion of the documents required for closing, the lender, if one is involved, must furnish certain documents for the transaction to be completed. The lender will furnish the promissory note, the Truth-in-Lending disclosures statement, and also the document that will be recorded to evidence the lender's security: the mortgage or deed of trust. However, the lender may be required to make further disclosures and comply with additional provisions created and required under a federal act passed in 1974: the **Real Estate Settlement Procedures Act (RESPA)** (12 U.S.C. § 2601 *et seq.*). If the lender is covered under RESPA, then additional forms, paperwork, and procedures are required before the closing of the transaction is permitted to take place.

RESPA was amended in 1992 (effective 1993) and again in 1995 (see below) to expand its coverage. Also, in 1992, RESPA's final accompanying regulations were promulgated by the **Department of Housing and Urban Development (HUD).** These regulations, referred to collectively as Regulation X, give additional enforcement mechanisms to HUD and expanded HUD's coverage of various aspects of closing. These changes in the law and regulations are covered in the sections following.

Purpose of RESPA

The Real Estate Settlement Procedures Act was passed by Congress in reaction to evidence obtained through hearings that indicated buyers of residential property were surprised at closings with additional fees and expenses that were not disclosed to them in advance. The result was that neither buyers nor sellers could meet these substantial additional costs, or if they could meet them, there was a loss on the expected return on the sale. The first section of RESPA (12 U.S.C. § 2601 *et seq.,* or Regulation X) states the four purposes of the act:

1. To provide more effective advance disclosure to home buyers and home sellers of settlement costs.
2. To eliminate kickback or referral fees that tend to increase the costs of settlement services.
3. To reduce the amounts buyers are required to pay into escrow for taxes and insurance.
4. To reform local record keeping and land title information.

Application of RESPA

RESPA applies to "federally related mortgage loans," which includes first and second mortgages, refinancings, home equity loans, and lines of credit using a home as security for the loan. The required RESPA information (discussed below) must be furnished at the time the lender makes a commitment to offer any of these types of loans. RESPA does not apply to loans for commercial transactions but does apply to refinancings or home equity loans.

http://
FAQs about RESPA issues are answered at **http:// www.hud.gov:80/fha/ sfh/res/resconsu.html**.

Consider 16.2

DiPietro purchased a house that had been rezoned for commercial use for purposes of housing his barbershop. The barbershop did not perform as well as was planned, and DiPietro declared bankruptcy. DiPietro claims that excessive closing costs on his loan should be refunded, and that he should be granted damages under RESPA. Is DiPietro correct? *In re DiPietro,* 135 B.R. 773 (Pa. 1992)

Disclosures Under RESPA

BUYERS INFORMATION HANDBOOK

When a lender covered under RESPA receives a loan application, the applicant must be furnished with a borrower's information handbook within three days. The handbook may be printed by the lender or purchased from HUD. Written by HUD, the handbook includes explanations of RESPA, the selection of an escrow agent, the role of the real estate broker, and the lender's responsibilities. It also contains sample disclosure forms and explanations for fees charged.

GOOD FAITH ESTIMATE OF SETTLEMENT COSTS

As originally passed, RESPA required lenders to make advance disclosures of closing costs to buyers. However, an amendment to the act calls for the lender to make only an estimate of the charges expected at closing. The items required in the good faith estimate can be found in Figure 16.1.

Because all transactions will not include all of the fees listed, RESPA requires the lender to make a good faith estimate for only those figures that the lender "anticipates the buyer will pay at settlement based upon the lender's general experience as to which party normally pays each charge in the locality." Those charges that could arise but are contingent must also be disclosed to the buyer as possibilities, as well as a figure for each charge if it is assessed.

Although HUD offers no precise formula for determining what constitutes a good faith estimate, the estimate must be expressed as a dollar amount. The only other standard for determining compliance is that the estimate must bear "a reasonable relationship to the charges the buyer is likely to experience at closing." In the case of figures that may change substantially between application and closing (such as points), HUD suggests that the lender also include a disclosure regarding the possible fluctuation with the good faith estimate.

It is permissible for the lender to use HUD's **Uniform Settlement Statement** (**USS**, discussed pn page 422) or HUD's sample good faith estimate form (see Figure 16.1). Specifically, RESPA requires that the good faith estimate meet the following four criteria:

1. The form must be clear and concise.
2. The form must include the lender's name.
3. The form must include the following statement or its equivalent in boldface type:

   THIS FORM DOES NOT COVER ALL ITEMS YOU WILL BE REQUIRED TO PAY IN CASH AT SETTLEMENT, FOR EXAMPLE, DEPOSITS IN ESCROW FOR REAL ESTATE TAXES AND INSURANCE. YOU MAY WISH TO INQUIRE AS TO THE AMOUNTS OF OTHER SUCH ITEMS. YOU MAY BE REQUIRED TO PAY OTHER ADDITIONAL AMOUNTS AT SETTLEMENT.

4. The names of the charge in the estimate should be identical or as near as possible to the names used in the Uniform Settlement Statement.

FIGURE 16.1   *Form of Good Faith Estimate*

[NAME OF LENDER][1]

The information provided below reflects estimates of the charges which you are likely to incur at the settlement of your loan. The fees listed are estimates—the actual charges may be more or less. Your transaction may not involve a fee for every item listed.

The numbers listed beside the estimates generally correspond to the numbered lines contained in the HUD–1 or HUD–1A settlement statement that you will be receiving at settlement. HUD–1 or HUD–1A settlement statement will show you the actual cost for items paid at settlement.

ITEM[2]	HUD–1	Amount or Range
Loan Origination Fee	801	$ _____
Loan Discount Fee	802	$ _____
Appraisal Fee	803	$ _____
Credit Report	804	$ _____
Inspection Fee	805	$ _____
Mortgage Broker Fee	[Use blank line in 800 Section]	$ _____
CLO Access Fee	"	$ _____
Tax Related Service Fee	"	$ _____
Interest for [X] days at $ _____ *per day*	901	$ _____
Mortgage Insurance Premium	902	$ _____
Hazard Insurance Premiums	903	$ _____
Reserves[3]	1000–1005	$ _____
Tax and Assessment Reserves		$ _____
Settlement Fee	1101	$ _____
Abstract or Title Search	1102	$ _____
Title Examination	1103	$ _____
Document Preparation Fee	1105	$ _____
Attorney's Fee	1107	$ _____
Title Insurance	1108	$ _____
Recording Fees	1201	$ _____
City/County Tax Stamps	1202	$ _____
State Tax	1203	$ _____
Survey	1301	$ _____
Pest Inspection	1302	$ _____
[Other fees—list here]		$ _____

_____   _____
Applicant   Authorized Official

_____
Date

These estimates are provided pursuant to the Real Estate Settlement Procedures Act of 1974, as amended (RESPA). Additional information can be found in the HUD Special Information Booklet, which is to be provided to you by your mortgage broker or lender, if your application is to purchase residential real property and the lender will take a first lien on the property.

---

1. The name of the lender shall be placed at the top of the form. Additional information identifying the loan application and property may appear at the bottom of the form or on a separate page. Exception: If the disclosure is being made by a mortgage broker who is not an exclusive agent of the lender, the lender's name will not appear at the top of the form, but the following legend must appear:
    This Good Faith Estimate is being provided by _____, a mortgage broker, and no lender has yet been obtained.
2. Items for which there is estimated to be no charge to the borrower are not required to be listed. Any additional items for which there is estimated to be a charge to the borrower shall be listed if required on the HUD–1.
3. As an alternative to using aggregate accounting with no more than a two-month cushion, the estimate may be obtained by using a single item accounting with no more than a one-month cushion.

(As amended Jan. 21, 1998)

Note that both the handbook and the good faith estimate must be delivered within three days of loan application regardless of whether the lender ultimately approves the loan of the applicant.

While originally Congress provided buyers/borrowers with a private right of suit for the failure to comply with the good faith estimate requirements, that provision was eliminated in the RESPA amendments, and federal courts have since held that there is no private cause of action for the violation of the RESPA's good faith estimate requirements. Enforcement against violators is handled by HUD. (*Collins v. FMHA-USDA,* 105 F.3d 1366 [11th Cir. 1997] *cert. denied,* 521 U.S. 1127 [1998])

Disclosures Relating to Assignments

The 1990 amendments to RESPA require certain disclosures on the possible assignment, sale, or transfer of the loan servicing of an account. At the time of the loan application, the following information must be given to the potential borrower(s):

- Whether the loan may be assigned, sold, or transferred.
- For each of the most recent three calendar years completed, the percentage of loans made for which servicing has been assigned, sold, or transferred.
- If the person making the loan does not engage in the servicing of loans, that there is a present intent to assign, sell, or transfer the loan.

These disclosures must be made on a sheet bearing the borrowers' signatures to verify that they have read and understood the disclosures. The RESPA amendments also provide procedures for notification of borrowers in the event that a sale, transfer, or assignment does occur, and notification must be made within 15 days after the effective date of the transfer. Further procedures are provided for the borrowers to object to any inaccuracies in figures and balances submitted to the transferee of the loan. The disclosures relating to assignments can be seen in Web Exhibits 16.1 and 16.2.

UNIFORM SETTLEMENT STATEMENT AND ADVANCE DISCLOSURE

The purpose of the Uniform Settlement Statement (USS) required under RESPA is to provide the buyer with a final summary and explanation of all costs paid at the closing. Upon request, the buyer is permitted to inspect the USS one day in advance of the settlement. If the request is made, then the escrow agent must furnish the buyer with a completed USS. Any buyer who does not request the USS in advance is entitled to receive a copy at the time of closing, or if the buyer is not present at closing, as soon as is practicable thereafter.

The form used for the USS was developed by HUD, and a sample appears in Web Exhibit 16.3. All of the charges listed on the form must be disclosed. In some circumstances, the buyer will be required to pay a fee before closing, but such a fee is required by the lender, not by HUD. In cases of outside payment such as for pest inspection, the cost must still be noted on the USS but will be followed by the abbreviation **poc (paid outside closing)**.

The USS is not required if the buyer is to pay one flat fee at closing, so long as the fixed fee is given to the buyer as a dollar amount at the time of the loan application. This exemption is generally applicable in situations where the buyer is purchasing a new home from the developer, who is offering fixed closing costs as an incentive for purchase.

PENALTIES FOR FAILURE TO MAKE DISCLOSURES

The Real Estate Settlement Procedures Act does not provide any express penalties for failure to make the disclosures. As a federal agency, HUD, charged with enforcement of RESPA, would have the usual remedies of complaint, injunction, and other forms of civil enforcement mechanisms to stop violations.

RELATIONSHIP OF STATE LAWS

The act invalidates only those state laws that are inconsistent with its provisions. It is possible for lenders and escrow agents to be required to comply with even higher standards of disclosure and possible penalties if their states' laws require further disclosures and procedures. Lenders must comply with both RESPA and any applicable state regulations and statutes.

Prohibited Conduct Under RESPA

Another stated purpose of RESPA was to eliminate the kickback and referral costs, which were increasing the cost of closing for buyers. Certain forms of conduct between members of the real estate industry are now prohibited under RESPA.

KICKBACKS AND UNEARNED FEES

Prior to the passage of RESPA, it was common practice for escrow agents to pay fees for business referred to them by lenders, brokers, and salespersons. Such fees were often payable in the form of a percentage commission. However, RESPA prohibits the giving or accepting of "any fee, kickback, or thing of value" for the referral of business. Therefore, cash payments, special discounts, stock, and special prices are all prohibited.

REQUIRING THE USE OF A SPECIFIC TITLE COMPANY

The act also prohibits sellers from requiring "as a condition to selling the property, that title insurance be purchased by the buyer from any particular title company." This provision regulates developers who were given substantial discounts in their title policies in exchange for the promise to send all of their purchasers to the title insurer for their policies.

Prohibitions on kickbacks extend to referrals on refinancings, lines of credit, and home equity loans.

CONTROLLING BUSINESS ARRANGEMENT AND RESPA

One of the more intricate RESPA issues that Regulation X addresses is the referral to a mortgage company or title firm in which the real estate agent or attorney or lender owns an interest. There is no kickback or referral fee for the business sent, but the agent, attorney, or lender receives a fee in the form of higher earnings and perhaps dividends from the title company or mortgage firm. Under Regulation X, a referral by someone who owns a 1 percent or greater interest in the company receiving the referral must include a disclosure to the buyer/borrower. These referrals are not prohibited under RESPA, but the buyer must be furnished with the following information:

1. That the referring party owns a controlling interest in the provider;
2. A separate piece of paper must be used to make this disclosure;
3. An estimate of the charges the provider will make;
4. The disclosure must be provided no later than the time of the referral; and
5. A statement that use of the provider is not mandatory.

Web Exhibit 16.4 is a sample Affiliated Business Arrangement Disclosure Statement form developed by HUD.

Those real estate firms providing in-house computerized loan origination services will be required to disclose not only their charges for such services, but also any interests they hold in the service or any mortgage firms included in the databases.

Consider 16.3

Alan Brown owns 100 percent of the stock of Brown Realty, Inc. He owns 51 percent of the stock of Western Mortgage Company and 12 percent of the stock of Lincoln Title and Escrow Company. All of Brown's agents are instructed to recommend to buyers both Western and Lincoln for purposes of closing the deals on their homes. List for Alan the RESPA requirements for such a referral.

Consumer Rights on Questions on Mortgage Accounts

Consumers have the right under RESPA to make inquiries about the servicing of their loans. If they make a written inquiry on their loan, the mortgage service provider must acknowledge receipt of the consumer request within 20 days and take action on the request within 60 days. The type of action required is an investigation that results either in a credit to the consumer's account for any errors or a full explanation in response to the consumer's question. Violations of these sections of RESPA carry civil class action remedies of up to $1,000 for each litigant, not to exceed $500,000 or 1% of the net worth of the loan service company, whichever is less.

Consider 16.4

Jacqueline P. Walker and Kevin R. Franklyn took out a second mortgage on their 4,000-square foot home so that they could obtain the funds they needed to replace their carpeting. They signed the paperwork for the loans and the carpet was installed. Jacqueline Walker signed a certificate of completion on the carpet and the mortgage service company released the funds to the carpet company. Kevin Franklyn called to object to the release of the funds because Jacqueline had no ownership interest in the property and did not have the authority to sign. He demanded a return of the carpet funds to his escrow account there. The mortgage service company refused and after six months, Franklyn filed suit under RESPA. Does RESPA apply? Did the mortgage service company violate Franklyn's rights?

PENALTIES

Unlike the disclosure sections of RESPA, the prohibition sections contain specific penalties for violation. The penalty for violating the kickback section is a fine of $10,000, one year of imprisonment, or both; plus liability to the harmed party in the amount of three times the kickback paid or received; plus court costs and attorneys' fees. The penalty for requiring the use of a particular title company is three times the amount charged for the title insurance (paid to the buyer), plus court costs and attorneys' fees. The treble recovery is permitted even if the charge for the policy was reasonable and conformed to charges acceptable within the area.

The following case deals with issues of whether RESPA violations took place.

Durr
v. Intercounty Title Co. of Illinois

826 F. Supp. 259 (N.D. Ill. 1993); cert.den., 513 U.S. 811 (1994)

Facts

Kenneth Durr, in the course of purchasing property, was furnished with a Uniform Settlement Statement (USS) that reflected charges in excess of actual costs of closing. Durr, along with other property purchasers, filed a class-action suit alleging violation of RESPA by Intercounty Title Company. Durr's alleged errors were that he was charged a $25 deed recording fee, when in fact the deed recording fee was $23, and that he was charged $37 for recording of his mortgage when in fact that recording fee was $31.50.

Durr alleged that the collection of such fees above actual charges incurred constituted a violation of RESPA in that Intercounty was thereby accepting a charge for services other than those actually rendered. Intercounty filed a motion to dismiss.

Judicial Opinion

Shadur, Senior District Judge. As for the motion to dismiss, here is the statute (RESPA § 2607(b)) invoked by Durr:

> **(b) Splitting charges**
> No person shall give and no person shall accept any portion, split, or percentage of any charge made or received for the rendering of a real estate settlement service in connection with a transaction involving a federally related mortgage loan other than for services actually performed.

Although a statutory heading is not part of the statute itself, the caption is consistent with the exceedingly plain meaning of the statute as one targeting only the *division* of charges where the giver is involved in rendering a "real estate settlement service" and the acceptor gets paid "other than for services actually performed." Here is how our Court of Appeals has confirmed the clear meaning and purpose of RESPA § 2607(b) in *Mercado v. Calumet Fed. Sav. & Loan Ass'n.*, 763 F.2d 269, 270–71 (7th Cir. 1985):

> We affirm because the complaint does not allege that Calumet gave or received "any portion, split, or percentage of any charge" to a third party. Section 8 of RESPA is an anti-kickback statute. The statute requires at least two parties to share fees. As the Senate Report explained, § 8 "is in-

tended to prohibit all kickback and referral fee arrangements whereby any payment is made or 'thing of value' furnished for the referral of real estate settlement business. The section also prohibits a person that renders a settlement service from giving or rebating any portion of the charge to any other person except in return for services actually performed." S.Rep. 93-866, 93d Cong., 2d Sess. (1974), reprinted at 1974 *U.S.Code Cong. & Admin.News* 6551. The complaint does not allege the presence of any "other person."

Mercado, id. at 271 goes on to say:

> Congress considered and explicitly rejected a system of price control for fees; it concluded that the price of real estate services should be set in the market. See 1974 *U.S.Code Cong. & Admin. News* 6549-50. It directed § 8 against a particular kind of abuse that it believed interfered with the operation of free markets—the splitting and kicking back of fees to parties who did nothing in return for the portions they received.

Durr's attorney Harris points to the earlier decision in *United States v. Gannon,* 684 F.2d 433 (7th Cir. 1981) (*en banc*)—though cited and meaningfully distinguished in *Mercado*—as leading to a different reading. It does not. *Gannon* treated a counter attendant at the Cook county Torrens section as a RESPA violator for having exacted payments for filing in an amount beyond what the state law authorized—a "gratuity" for doing the very job that the counter attendant was hired to do. But that was done on the legal fiction that Gannon was wearing two hats—the "official capacity" hat and his own as an individual—and was therefore both "giver" and "acceptor" when he pocketed the unauthorized amounts (684 F.2d at 438):

> We believe a single individual *can* violate § 2607(b) by receiving in his official capacity a "charge" for the rendering of settlement services, but personally keeping a portion of the charge in fact for something other than the performance of those services.

That sharp distinction between *Mercado* and *Gannon* has been well expressed in *Duggan v. Independent Mortgage Corp.,* 670 F.Supp. 652, 653-54 (E.D.Va. 1987).

Here the claimed misconduct of Intercounty simply does not come within the limited scope of RESPA § 2607(b). Durr's payment was made to Intercounty—clearly *they* were not the giver and acceptor who split a real estate settlement service charge. As for the other payment involved—from Intercounty to the Recorder of Deeds—it involves the exact opposite of the statutory prohibition, for there was no *acceptance* by the Recorder of a portion of the charges originally paid by Durr "other than for services actually performed." This case is as non-actionable under RESPA § 2607(b) as were *Mercado* and *Duggan*.

Durr's Complaint and this action are therefore dismissed for their failure properly to invoke the jurisdiction of this Court under RESPA § 2607(b).

Motion granted. Case dismissed.

Case Questions

1. How much did Durr allege he was overcharged?
2. How does he characterize these charges as a violation of RESPA?
3. Is there any violation of RESPA?

Ethical Issue

When there is an error in a settlement statement, should the parties resolve the error or resort to litigation under RESPA? What would you do if you spotted the error? Would you say nothing and wait for closing and a possible violation? Does it help the purpose of the RESPA regulations to allow self-correction?

Consider 16.5

Hollis Grissom was president of State Savings and Loan of Clovis, New Mexico, in June 1983. He was asked by a principal of Eaton Investors, Thomas Hartley, if State Savings would finance construction of a medical building in Denver, Colorado. Grissom also owned 72 percent of the stock of State Savings. On July 5, 1983, Grissom wrote Hartley a six-month financing commitment for $450,000. The loan commitment provided for a 2 percent origination fee, half of which was payable upon Hartley's acceptance of the commitment.

Hartley sent an acceptance letter and a check for $4,500 (1 percent of the commitment). The check was made out to Grissom personally rather than to State Savings, apparently the result of a clerical error. Grissom applied the check to his personal use, allotting part of it to a personal loan and taking the remainder in cash.

In November 1983, the Federal Savings and Loan Insurance Corporation (FSLIC) placed State Savings into receivership. FSLIC refused to honor the loan commitment because there was no record that State Savings had ever received the 1 percent origination fee. Grissom refused to discuss the matter and was thereafter indicted for embezzlement and RESPA violations. He was convicted and appealed on the grounds that the $4,500 was earned as compensation for services he performed. Was Grissom guilty of a violation of RESPA? *U.S. v. Grissom*, 814 F.2d 577 (10th Cir. 1987)

Consider 16.6

Security Escrow kept $250,000 in an account with Southwestern Savings and Loan at no interest. Southwestern was a substantial residential mortgage lender in the area and had all of its borrowers use Security Escrow to close their residential purchases. Would this no-interest account present any problems under RESPA?

Limitations on Escrow Deposits Under RESPA

The final purpose of RESPA was to eliminate the excessive prepaids and deposits required of buyers before escrow could close. The reasons for the prepaid amounts required by lenders were to make sure that the property was insured and that tax liens did not arise immediately after closing. For the buyer, the prepaids were forced savings, but they also created difficulties in coming up with the cash necessary for closing. To solve this conflict, RESPA limits the amount that the lender may require to be deposited at the time of escrow and also limits the amount that may be required monthly.

At escrow, the maximum payment is calculated as the amount that would normally have been paid into escrow from the date the charge would have been last paid until (but not including) the date of the first full mortgage payment, plus the equivalent of two-months' payment (actually, the wording of the statute is one-sixth of 12 months). For example, suppose annual taxes on the property are $1,200 (or $100 per month), due on April 30. Closing on the property will occur on July 15, and the first full mortgage payment will be made on September 1. Under RESPA, the maximum deposit would be $600, computed as follows: $100 would be paid on May, June, July, and August 1 before the first full mortgage payment is due, for a total of $400. The two-month cushion is $200, so the total is $600.

After settlement, RESPA prohibits the lender from requiring large monthly deposits for taxes and insurance. Monthly payments for taxes and insurance are limited to 1/12 of the amount that will become due during the year on such charges. Deposits on hand cannot exceed one-sixth of the 12-month totals. New guidelines on escrow accounts went into effect in 1995. The two-month maximum cushion for insurance and taxes still applies, but borrowers must now be sent both beginning and end-of-year statements that provide full information about the payments that could be required and then a final accounting of how the payments made were used. The 1995 rules also limited the number of escrow accounts per home to one. Many lenders were using separate insurance and tax accounts and, in effect, double-charging their customers. About one-third of the states have regulations that require debtors to be paid the interest on their escrow accounts earned during the year.

There are no civil or criminal penalties stated in RESPA for violation of these deposit limitations, but there have been several suits by harmed buyers in which federal district courts have taken jurisdiction and have held that the buyers do have a civil remedy under the act for their actual damages.

The Calhouns are purchasing property. The taxes on the property are $600 per year, and the insurance is $300 per year. Both taxes and insurance are due on June 30. Closing on the property will take place on September 15, with the Calhouns' first mortgage payment due on November 1. How much is the lender permitted to be paid at closing? How much may the lender require in monthly deposits?

Consider 16.7

ESCROW AGENT'S RESPONSIBILITIES

Perhaps the greatest area of concern and liability in the closing process lies with the party responsible for conducting the closing: the third party or escrow agent. The difficulty with the role of the escrow agent is that the relationship is not a true agency, since both parties' interests are carried forth by the agent. A trust relationship is not established because a trust is not created. The unique position of the agent in closing is established by a series of duties and responsibilities created specifically for this arrangement necessary for real estate transfers.

Escrow Agent's Duty to Follow Instructions

The escrow agent is given an assignment to perform according to the provisions established in the escrow instructions. The agent can do no more and no less than what is specified in that agreement because the only authority possessed by the agent is that given in the escrow instructions. Agents exceeding their authority are liable, as are agents not performing the required functions. For example, if an agent is required to pay all tax liens on the property before turning funds over to the seller and fails to do so, the agent is liable to the buyer for the amount of the tax liens.

The escrow agent often faces the same difficulties the buyer and seller face if it is not made clear which document controls—the escrow instructions or the contract. In the absence of a provision to the contrary, the agent must follow only the terms and conditions set forth in the escrow instructions, for that is the only agreement to which the agency is a party. The following case illustrates this principle of limiting the duties of the agent to the escrow instructions.

First Montana Title Company of Billings v. North Point Square Association

782 P.2d 376 (Mont. 1989)

Facts

Loyd Kimble was the owner of a parcel of land in Yellowstone County, Montana. He borrowed $3,000,000 from Commerce Mortgage Company for which he executed to Commerce a note and mortgage on the land parcel on May 12, 1980. The note and mortgage were assigned to American Guaranty Life Insurance Company, and the assignment was recorded on June 4, 1981. Loyd Kimble also borrowed an additional $150,000 using the same land parcel as security, and he executed a note and mortgage to Commerce Mortgage Company, which mortgage was recorded on July 1, 1981.

Loyd Kimble defaulted on his loan payments, and the mortgages went into default. American and Commerce obtained a judgment against Kimble on the mortgage loans on July 3, 1986. There was no sheriff's sale of the land.

On July 21, 1986, Kimble entered into an option agreement for the purchase of the land parcel by North Point Square and others (defendants/appellants). The option was exercisable on or before January 24, 1987. An abstract of the option was recorded on July 24, 1986.

The escrow agreement with First Montana Title Company provided that First Montana (plaintiff and respondent) would hold a partial release of *lis pendens* (legal document recorded to indicate litigation pending on a parcel of land), a release of the judgment in the foreclosure, and a release of American Guaranty's and Commerce's mortgages to clear the title to parcel if the option was exercised. In exchange, American and Commerce would receive the sale proceeds from the exercise of the option.

On August 22, 1986, First Interstate Bank of Billings obtained a judgment lien on the parcel for $77,041.01, and First Interstate Bank of Missoula obtained a judgment lien on the parcel for $27,000 on September 30, 1986. Interstate Production Credit Association obtained yet another judgment on the same parcel.

On January 21, 1987, North Point Square exercised the option by timely delivery of $336,674.05 to First Montana Title Company. Paragraph 6 of the escrow agreement provided:

> Escrow agent is hereby authorized to use said funds to clear title to the property and to then distribute the balance of the funds to the two underlying mortgagees as follows:
> (a) To American Guaranty Life Insurance Company—97%
> (b) Commerce Mortgage Company—3%

When the option agreement had been exercised and the money received, First Montana Title took the position that under paragraph 6 it must pay off the judgment liens before distributing the balance of the funds to American and Commerce. American and Commerce disagreed with this interpretation. First Montana then interpleaded (deposited) the funds with the district court for a determination of which parties were entitled to them. The trial court entered a judgment for the judgment lien holders and against the mortgagees, and the mortgagees appealed.

Judicial Opinion

Sheehy, Justice. The position of American Guaranty Life Insurance Company and Commerce Mortgage Company is that an option which is recorded prior to the establishment of judgment liens on the same property gives the holder of the option a priority over such subsequent judgment liens. They contend that the escrow agreement had the effect of an assignment for consideration prior to the entry of the judgments and that therefore under the escrow agreement the funds should pass to American Guaranty and Commerce Mortgage Company free of said judgment liens.

The controlling issue in this case is the contractual effect of the language in the escrow agreement. If the escrow holder was required to "clear title" before the mortgagees could receive the balance of the funds, the relative priorities between a recorded option and judgment liens become irrelevant. We hold it was the escrow holder's duty to clear title for the optionee under the escrow agreement.

It is clear to us that the decision in this case should turn on the language of the escrow agreement, as a matter of contract. Under paragraph 6 above quoted, the escrow agent was authorized by all of the parties to the agreement to "use said funds to clear title to the property," and then to distribute the proceeds to the mortgagees.

In *Ogg v. Herman, et al.* (1924), 71 Mont. 10, 15-16, 227 P. 476, 477, this Court said:

> While provision is made that plaintiff shall furnish an abstract showing clear title, good title, and a marketable title, it is apparent that these terms were used interchangeably, and that they are in fact synonymous. A clear title means that the land is free from encumbrances. (Citing authority.) A good title is one free from litigation, palpable defects and grave doubts, comprising both legal and equitable titles, and fairly deducible of record. (Citing authority.) A clear title means a good title (citing authority) and a good title means a marketable or merchantable title. (Citing authority.) A contract to convey in fee simple, clear of all encumbrances, implies a marketable title (citing authority), and a marketable

title is one of such character as assures to the purchaser the quiet and peaceable enjoyment of the property and one which is free from encumbrances. (Citing authority.)

This Court further noted in *Gantt v. Harper* (1928), 82 Mont. 393, 405, 267 P. 296, 298, the following:

> Webster's definition of the word "clear" as here employed is "free from encumbrance, obstruction, burden, limitation," etc., and the word "title," in the sense here used, "the union of all elements which constitutes ownership, at common law, divided into possession, right of possession, and right of property, the last two now, however, being considered essentially the same."

> In our opinion, the words, "clear title" as employed in the plaintiff's letter, denied admission in evidence, means title to the property free from any encumbrance, burden or litigation, uniting all the elements constituting ownership, including right of possession and right of property—i.e., fee-simple title. Such was in effect the contract upon which the defendant agreed to pay a brokerage commission on the sale of the property, and a tender of the performance was complete as in accordance with the defendant's terms.

The contractual duty of the escrow agent in this case, agreed to by all the parties, was that the escrow holder should distribute the funds so as to deliver clear title to the optionee upon the exercise of the option. The judgment liens were indeed clouds on the title, and clear title could not be delivered until those judgment liens were satisfied and removed.

Affirmed.

Case Questions

1. Give a list and chronology of events regarding the parcel of land.
2. What did paragraph 6 require the escrow agent to do?
3. What was disputed about the escrow agent's obligation under paragraph 6?
4. What definition of clear title does the court use?
5. Who will get paid first? How much will be left over for American and Commerce?

Escrow Agent's Fiduciary Responsibilities

Along with the duty of following instructions, the escrow agent also has the responsibility of acting for the benefit and only in the best interests of the parties to the transaction. The agent cannot jeopardize either party's rights by closing for the sake of obtaining the closing fee if the required terms and conditions of the instructions have not been met. The consequence of the breach of this fiduciary responsibility by the agent will be the imposition of liability by the party who experiences a loss as a result of the agent's conduct.

Embezzlement of deposited funds by the escrow agent is definitely a breach of the fiduciary duty, but the problem is that usually the agent has disappeared or the funds cannot be recovered from the agent. This lack of remedy leaves the parties to the underlying sales contract to determine who will absorb the loss of the embezzled funds. The risk of loss will be determined according to the degree of compliance with the contract contingencies. That is, if the buyer has complied with all contingencies and the money has been deposited with the agent, then title to the money technically belongs to the seller, who would absorb the loss. Likewise, if the money has been deposited but the contingencies necessary for transfer have not been completed (e.g., the buyer does not qualify), title to the funds (and hence the risk of loss) would remain with the seller. The following case deals with the issue of misconduct by an escrow agent.

Baker v. Stewart Title & Trust of Phoenix, Inc.

5 P.3d 249 (Ariz. App. 2000)

Facts

Ben Friedman, an attorney, obtained investments from Baker and others (plaintiffs) for a number of limited partnerships he created. However, the limited partnerships were a scam for Friedman to reap secret profits.

Friedman would find a property, and, using a fictitious name, buy it through an escrow established at a title company. While the escrow for the property was open, he would create a limited partnership and solicit investors for the down payment. After the escrow closed, he would then sell the property to the partnership for a far greater price than the purchase price he had paid to the seller of the property. By using fictions names and shell entities, he was able to conceal the fact that he was making substantial gains each time a partnership was created.

However, Friedman required assistance in making these transactions work. He had that help from Bonnie DeAngio, an employee of Stewart Title & Trust (defendant/appellee). Ms. DeAngio handled at least eight of the Friedman escrows and on at least one of the escrows she notarized the signature of a fictitious person on a deed of trust. On another escrow she helped Friedman impersonate a fictitious buyer in a face-to-face meeting with the seller. DeAngio also handled the transfer of the properties to the limited partnerships and the affidavits of value in these transfers showed the fictitious buyer, who DeAngio knew to be Friedman, was receiving the profits from the transfer. Following each closing and transfer, an associate of Friedman's, Tom Lynch, paid DeAngio several hundred dollars.

There is no evidence to indicate that Stewart Title knew of DeAngio's fraudulent actions. DeAngio did leave Stewart Title and went to work for Chicago Title where she continued her work for Friedman.

When the limited partnerships failed, all of the investors (plaintiffs/appellants) filed suit against Stewart Title alleging its liability for the fraud of its employee. The trial court granted Stewart Title summary judgment on this issue as well as their racketeering claim (alleged violation of federal RICO statutes). The investors appealed.

Judicial Opinion

Berber, Judge. An employer is vicariously liable for the negligent or tortious acts of its employee acting within the scope and course of employment. Conduct falls within the scope if it is the kind the employee is employed to perform, it occurs within the authorized time and space limits, and furthers the employer's business even if the employer has expressly forbidden it.

Here, De Angio's actions fell within the scope of her employment because she typically notarized documents and opened and closed escrows. Opening escrows using fictitious names by itself is legal; De Angio's opening of these escrows was thus not wrongful unless she knew that Friedman was acting with intent to defraud.

DeAngio's more apparent wrongful actions involved notarizing documents for Friedman that she knew he had signed under fictitious names and then concealing his fraudulent signature. Tom Lynch gave her cash after these closings. When Friedman was asked in his deposition, "So basically, anything that you asked her to do with respect to the defrauding of the investors, she [DeAngio] did?" he answered "yes." He also described her as "a very important facilitator" in his schemes. Though Stewart Title argues that appellants cannot show that DeAngio knew of Friedman's actions, the parties' depositions suggest that she may well have knowingly engaged in misconduct while at Stewart Title by notarizing signatures she knew to be false.

Stewart Title further claims that it would have received escrow fees, collection account fees and title insurance fees even if DeAngio had acted legitimately and, further, that the increase in purchase prices of properties due to her malfeasance did not affect its fees. Nevertheless, DeAngio's activity benefitted and furthered the business of Stewart Title because of the repeat business that she generated with Friedman. In fact, DeAngio stated that Stewart Title encouraged its escrow officers to procure new clients and develop business with existing clients. These clients would usually follow the escrow officers when they changed employment. Generating such benefits may suffice for liability. Due to DeAngio's conduct furthering its business, Stewart Title may incur vicarious liability. Whether Stewart Title would have received the same fees if she had acted properly is irrelevant.

The appellants claim that DeAngio is liable for conspiracy to defraud and, therefore, Stewart Title incurs liability under respondeat superior for all fraud-based claims. We address Stewart Title's liability for conspiracy as it applies to each group of plaintiffs and to each summary judgment.

The preliminary issue is whether DeAngio herself is liable for conspiracy. "For a civil conspiracy to occur two or more people must agree to accomplish an unlawful purpose or to accomplish a lawful object by unlawful means, causing damages."

However, the central issue remains whether Stewart Title could be liable under respondeat superior for DeAngio's acts in furthering the Friedman conspiracy. We find no case that holds an employer liable for its employee's acts to perpetuate a conspiracy to defraud under respondeat superior. The absence of such case law may result from the term "conspiracy" generally indicating vicarious liability for concerted action. If Stewart Title is liable for conspiracy through respondeat superior, two layers or "double" vicarious liability would result: DeAngio would be liable for a concerted action she did not personally perform and Stewart Title would be further liable. The nexus between Stewart Title and all the appellants thereby becomes too remote.

Reversed and remanded.

Case Questions

1. Explain what scheme to defraud existed and what the title company employee's role in it was.

2. What is respondeat superior and how does it apply in this case?

3. Will the title company be held liable for the problems with the investment?

4. Do you think DeAngio understood what she was doing?

Escrow Agent's Duty of Care

The escrow agent has a duty to exercise reasonable care and skill in the performance of the closing function. Thus, an agent is expected to understand and comply with title procedures, insurance documents, and recording requirements. In other words, the agent is held to the professional standards of those who are involved in the real estate industry and familiar with its terms and procedures. The following case illustrates the difficulties an escrow agent can encounter as a result of an oversight.

Boatright v. Texas American Title Company

790 S.W.2d 722 (Tx. 1990)

Facts

Philip and Linda Boatright negotiated for the purchase of 2.013 acres of land from Meadowbrook, Ltd. The Boatrights paid cash and executed a note payable to Meadowbrook for $63,200. A deed of trust secured the note, and Meadowbrook executed a general warranty deed to the Boatrights. Texas American Title acted as escrow agent for this transaction.

The Boatrights immediately entered into a "flip trans-action," meaning that they found an immediate buyer for the property. Akro-Tex was the buyer, and Texas American was again designated as the escrow agent. Akro-Tex paid $33,000 cash and executed two promissory notes: (1) one for $63,200 and (2) one for $36,025. The escrow agree-ment provided that the notes would be secured by deeds of trust, and the Boatrights executed a general warranty deed. However, the warranty deed failed to mention the Akro-Tex lien. Only the deed of trust for the $63,200 note was recorded by Texas American. Unknown to the Boatrights, the $36,025 deed of trust was never recorded.

Akro-Tex made only three payments on the $36,025 note and defaulted. The Boatrights hired Harold F. Harris to pursue collection of the note. The lack of the deed of trust was then discovered, and the Boatrights had additional difficulties in their relationship with Meadowbrook as a result of the default and lack of deed of trust. The Boatrights sued Texas American for breach of fiduciary duty. The trial court granted a judgment notwithstanding the verdict for Texas American, and the Boatrights appealed.

Judicial Opinion

Fuller, Justice. When an escrow agent undertakes to act in an escrow relationship with the parties by performing such actions as preparing the escrow papers, advising both par-ties and accepting and cashing checks, a fiduciary duty arises between the escrow agent and both parties.

Donald R. Conoway, senior vice president and gen-eral counsel for Southern, testified that title companies such as Texas American perform escrow functions in the ordinary course of their business and agreed that they hold critical real estate documents and money in escrow.

Dan Oliver, an attorney offered as an expert by the Boatrights, testified that title companies acting as escrow agents owe a fiduciary duty to both closing parties. He testified that he would not perform a closing without the deed of trust and that a breach of fiduciary duty occurred to the seller if the escrow agent in the title company failed to deliver one of the two deeds of trust. Texas American

admitted that a deed of trust covering the $36,025.00 note was never recorded.

Patricia Sweisthal, an escrow officer with Texas American that handled the Boatright–Akro-Tex transac-tion agreed that it is part of the function of an escrow offi-cer to match the real estate documents just to see that everything has been done. She could not swear there was ever a deed of trust for the $36,025.00 note. She was asked: "And part of your responsibility as an escrow officer is see-ing that you have the proper deeds of trust securing the notes involved?" She agreed and was then asked: "That much was not done?" She answered: "Evidently not." There was sufficient evidence before the jury to find Texas American negligent. The elements needed to provide neg-ligence, duty, breach and injury were presented.

Gerald Anthony Colbert, a real estate broker, testi-fied that all of the papers, including the deeds of trust were present at the closing. Texas American was to for-ward the documents to Akro-Tex.

There was sufficient evidence for submission of the issues as to the negligence of Texas American for jury de-termination and sufficient evidence to justify the jury's findings as to Texas American's negligence and the ac-tual damages suffered by the Boatrights. We also find there was evidence that supported the jury's finding that Texas American was grossly negligent in failing to see that all supporting documents were executed and properly recorded, thereby indicating a conscious indifference as to the Boatrights' welfare.

The trial court should have entered judgment for the Boatrights against Texas American.

Reversed.

Case Questions

1. Describe the series of sales and deeds of trust.
2. What is a "flip transaction"?
3. What document was missing and in what transaction?
4. What was the effect of the missing document?
5. Is the escrow agent a fiduciary for both parties?
6. Was the escrow agent negligent here?

✳ CAUTIONS AND CONCLUSIONS

The devil is once again in the details. Closing a property transaction is a matter of careful attention to the paperwork and timing. When preparing to close on a property:

1. Be sure you have all the necessary paperwork.
2. Make sure the paperwork is signed by someone with authority.
3. Make sure the paperwork is dated.
4. Make sure the paperwork has all the blanks complete.

5. Make sure that you have placed deadlines and timelines in your closing agreement.
6. Be sure to choose a reputable company and parties for handling the closing.
7. Be sure that you have complied with all the required paperwork for federal and state laws in the closing documents.
8. Make sure your escrow and closing instructions are detailed enough for the agent to handle all issues and handle them so that your risk is minimized.
9. Be sure you are clear on the relationship between your contract and the closing agreement or escrow instructions.
10. Keep copies of all closing documents.

Key Terms

escrow, 411
escrow instructions, 412
prorated, 414
Real Estate Settlement Procedures Act (RESPA), 419

Department of Housing and Urban Development (HUD), 419
Uniform Settlement Statement (USS), 420
poc (paid outside closing), 422

Chapter Problems

1. Herbert Walsh is the owner of valuable commercial/industrial acreage located near a municipal airport. Sam Stanton is interested in purchasing the property and informs Walsh that he has deposited $25,000 with First American Escrow, along with signed escrow instructions to purchase the property for a total cash price of $750,000. If Walsh signs the escrow instructions, do the parties have an enforceable contract?

2. Gladys Pickrell entered into a contract to purchase property from the Wades for $40,000. Pickrell and the Wades signed a purchase and sale agreement and also signed escrow instructions that would permit closing upon Pickrell's qualifying for a loan. Pickrell deposited $1,500 earnest money with the escrow agent. A judgment creditor of Pickrell garnished the earnest money prior to Pickrell's qualifying for the loan. The Wades protest that the money belonged to them. What is the result?

3. Dearborn paid United Financial Mortgage $100 rent for every closing that it conducted at United's office that involved United as a lender. Dearborn paid $300 rent for every closing that involved another lender. Is this a RESPA violation? *Lawyers Title Ins. Corp. v. Dearborn Title Corp.,* 118 F.3d 1157 (7th Cir. 1997); remanded at *22 F. Supp2d* 820 (N.D. Ill. 1998).

4. First Trust was the escrow agent designated to handle a property closing for Reinhold as seller and Cazalet as buyer. Escrow instructions were executed and provided for payment to Reinhold in one lump sum upon the satisfaction of certain contingencies. Shortly after the instructions were executed, Cazalet wrote to First Trust and asked that payment be made in three installments rather than in a lump sum and that payment be delayed. First Trust complied with Cazalet's letter and Reinhold objected. What was the result?

5. Jeff and Kathy Briggs obtained a mortgage loan from Madison Equity Mortgage Company, Inc. Madison Equity lent the Briggses funds that they used to refinance their residence. Madison Equity is a mortgage broker, and once the loan had been made to the Briggses, Madison transferred the loan to Countrywide Funding Corporation in exchange for a $528.75 payment. Countrywide maintains that the payment is simply a yield spread premium all lenders pay to brokers and that the Alabama state legislature has authorized such payments from lenders to brokers. The Briggses maintain the fee is a kickback that violates RESPA. Who is correct? Do you think state law or federal law will govern the payment? *Briggs v. Countrywide Funding Corp.,* 931 F.Supp. 1545 (M.D. Ala. 1996)

6. Prepare a good faith estimate of closing costs and a settlement statement from the following information:

- *Sales price:* $70,000
- *Term of loan:* 30 years
- *Loan:* $63,000; 90 percent FHA loan; $450 origination fee; 2 percent discount
- *Principal and interest:* $652
- *FHA insurance:* 1 percent
- *Location of property:* 5730 E. Grand Ave., Mesa, AZ 85203, Maricopa County
- *Tax information:* $1,200 per year for city, county, and state taxes; taxes due July 1, 2001
- *Estimated settlement date:* June 15, 2001 with first payment on August 1, 2001

What additional information is needed to complete the good faith and settlement statement?

7. Which of the following loans and lenders would be subject to RESPA?

    a. A loan for a single-family dwelling by First Federal Savings and Loan

    b. A loan for the purchase of one condominium unit for use as a residence in a complex consisting of 450 such units

    c. A loan for the purchase of a 20-unit apartment complex by a bank insured by the Federal Deposit Insurance Corporation (FDIC)

    d. A loan secured by a second mortgage for the construction of a swimming pool in the backyard of a residence

    e. A loan for the purchase of a cooperative that was formerly an apartment

    f. Refinancing a home mortgage to take advantage of lower interest rates

    g. Home equity line of credit with funds to be used for a child's college education costs

    h. A loan for the purchase of a mobile home (*Campbell v. Machias Sav. Bank,* 865 F.Supp. 26 [D. Me. 1994])

8. Is an escrow company liable for embezzlement by an employee?

9. William R. Bliss agreed to sell George P. Salemo, Jr. (and later his nominee, Catherine Salemo, his wife), a piece of residential property in the Phoenix area for $795,000. U.S. Life Title Company of Arizona was employed as the escrow agent for the transaction. Written escrow instructions were executed and delivered to U.S. Life Title.

The buyer's agent gave a certified check for $114,023.80 to U.S. Life Title at the time of closing. The certification was forged, and Chase Manhattan Bank, on which the check was drawn, refused payment. Before the forgery was discovered, U.S. Life Title delivered the closing documents, including the deed, from Bliss to Salemo and disbursed $74,422.28 to Bliss. U.S. Life Title recorded a *lis pendens* and brought suit against Salemo for the amount of the forged check. The suit was later amended to include Bliss as an additional defendant on the grounds of an indemnity provision in the escrow instructions.

After the forgery was discovered on October 22, Bliss purchased a home from the Tillotsons and as part payment assigned the note he had received from Salemo. That note was secured by a deed of trust on the property. Tillotson foreclosed on the deed of trust and resold it to Bliss, who in turn sold it to another buyer for $755,000. Thus, Bliss received $49,745 from Salemo through escrow and $74,422.28 at closing and then recovered the property that he had sold. Bliss therefore received benefits of $310,000 to $375,000 from the various transactions. Who will bear liability for the forgery? *U.S. Life Title v. Bliss,* 722 P.2d 356 (Ariz. 1986)

10. From September 1975 through May 1979, Graham Mortgage Corporation provided Rose Hill Realty, Inc., with interim financing of Rose Hill's purchase, rehabilitation, and resale of Detroit-area residences. For each loan it received, Rose Hill agreed to refer to GMC two mortgage loan applicants from its brokerage business, in addition to referring the purchaser of the rehabilitated house. In turn, GMC, when making FHA or VA mortgage loans to purchasers of the rehabilitated residences sold by Rose Hill, charged Rose Hill fewer points than it charged other sellers. To recoup the income lost through the reduction in points charged to Rose Hill, GMC increased the points charged to buyers of residences referred to Rose Hill and financed by FHA or VA loans.

Richard E. Chapin, executive vice president and director of GMC; Thomas P. Heinz, a vice president and manager of GMC; and Manford Colbert, president of Rose Hill Realty, were charged along with GMC with violations of Section 8(a) of RESPA. (Kickbacks Section)

GMC moved at the trial court to have the indictment dismissed on the grounds that the making of a mortgage loan is not "a real estate settlement service." Is this correct? *U.S. v. Graham Mortgage Corp.,* 740 F.2d 414 (6th Cir. 1984)

Internet Activities

1. For more information on RESPA, go to: **http://www.hud.gov/fha/sfh/res/respa_hm.html** for FAQs, statutory text, and related links to this act.

2. For explanation and an example of a settlement statement, go to: **http://www.hud.gov/fha/sfh/res/resappa.html**.

3. For an explanation of the operation of escrow settlement accounts in the state of Oregon, go to: **http://www.valleybrokers.com/ag0/escrow.shtml**.

Wills & Living Trusts

ON THIS PAGE: What You Should Know | For More Information

If you are like many people you probably wonder about the differences between a will and a living trust, and whether you need one or the other, or both. To figure out whether you should use either or both of these documents to pass on your property when you die, you need to understand their important characteristics, as well as the probate process.

Related Topics:

About Money

Financial Planning

Related Links:

Funerals & Burials

Widowed Persons Service

AARP Legal Services Network

Press Release

Congressional Testimony

What Should I know?

A will gives instructions about how you want your property distributed after your death. It lists the people or organizations (your beneficiaries) you want to receive your property and what part of your estate should pass to each. You also appoint someone (an executor) to administer your estate after your death. That person makes sure your property is distributed as you had intended, and pays any outstanding debts and taxes.

Like a will, a revocable living trust lets you direct how your property will be distributed after your death. You appoint someone (your trustee) to administer your trust. Unlike a will, you can also establish how your property will be managed during your lifetime, if you become disabled. Another difference with a trust is that it allows your property to pass to your beneficiaries without going through the probate process, described below. As a result, your trust property passes more easily to your beneficiaries.

Chapter 17
Transferring Real Estate after Death: Wills, Estates, and Probate

Let's talk of graves, of worms, and epitaphs;
Make dust our paper, and with rainy eyes
Write sorrow on the bosom of the earth.
Let's choose executors and talk of wills.

William Shakespeare,
King Richard II, Act III, Scene 2

- Malcolm Forbes left $1,000 each to owners of nine New York restaurants, including Lutece, the Four Seasons, and Mortimer's; and $1,000 each to 30 motorcycle clubs.
- Bob Fosse left $25,000 to be divided among 66 friends including Dustin Hoffman, Lisa Minelli, and Neil Simon "to go out and have dinner on me."
- Cole Porter left his clothes to the Salvation Army.

- Lillian Hellman gave her Toulouse-Lautrec poster to Mike Nichols.
- Jim Morrison left everything to his wife, who died three years later, so Morrison's estate went to his father-in-law.
- Alan Jay Lerner, among other bequests in his will, left $1,000 to two friends: "The purpose of this modest remembrance is to defray the cost of one evening's merriment to be devoted to cheerful recollections of their departed friend."
- Philip, fifth Earl of Pembroke, used his will to get back at a friend: "I give to the Lieutenant-General Cromwell one of my words . . . which he must want, seeing that he hath never kept any of his own."
- John Lennon's will disinherited anyone who contested it.
- Judy Garland left $250,000 to each child to be paid twice at ages 25 and 35, but the probate located only $40,000 in assets and $1,000,000 in debts.[1]

Death is inevitable, but what happens to your property can be dictated by you or by the law. The law of wills and estates makes the determination of who gets what when you die.

All of the above information about odd wills and estates raises questions about your property and what happens to it when you die. Can a will direct any disposition of property? Can you disinherit a spouse, children, or other relatives? How are creditors paid? What if there are insufficient assets to pay the creditors? Will taxes be paid first? What if there is no will, what happens to my property? This chapter answers these questions and others about your property and its transfer and disposition upon death.

LAW OF WILLS, ESTATES, AND PROBATE

In all areas of law relating to real estate discussed so far, it has been clear that the specific laws for various subjects often vary significantly from state to state. This degree of variation is greatly exaggerated in the law of wills, estates, and probate—so much so that it would take an entire series of texts to fully explain all of the variations. This chapter does not attempt to explain each state's provision but deals with the subject in general terms.

However, there is a uniform law in the area, called the **Uniform Probate Code (UPC),** which by 2001 had been adopted in some form by sixteen states.[2] Because of the likelihood of expanded adoption of the UPC and because of its simplicity, the provisions of this code are discussed throughout the chapter.

INTESTATE ESTATES

If a person dies without a valid will or fails to dispose of certain items of property in a will, the person is said to have died **intestate** or partially intestate. In the case of an intestate death, the property of the decedent is distributed according to the

1. Sources: Stephen M. Silverman, *Where There's a Will* (HarperCollins 1991), and Jeff Stryker, "Poison-Pen Wills: They Couldn't Resist: Oh, One Last Thing," *The New York Times,* May 31, 2000, WK 7.
2. Not all states have the same version of the UPC. The predominant form of the UPC continues to be the 1969 version, but the 1990 version is increasingly popular. The states with some form of the UPC are Alaska, Arizona, Colorado, Florida, Hawaii, Idaho, Maine, Michigan, Minnesota, Montana, Nebraska, New Mexico, North Dakota, South Carolina, South Dakota, and Utah.

state's law on **intestate succession.** The method of distributing the intestate's property differs between each of the states, but in all states it is controlled by the decedent's familial situation at the time of death.

Intestacy with Surviving Spouse

Generally, each state statute begins by attempting to leave the property of the decedent to the closest living relatives. All state intestacy statutes begin by giving all or
some portion of the property to the surviving spouse if there is one. In some states,
the surviving spouse will share the amount of the estate with any surviving children. As early as 1670, England's statute of distribution gave
one-third of the intestate's property to the surviving spouse
and two-thirds to the surviving children.

> ## Practical Tip
> Everyone should have a will. The problems
> with intestate distribution are complex and
> waste resources of the estate. Even those
> who have minimal property would benefit
> from the presence of a will because it expe-
> dites the process of property distribution.

Under the UPC (as modified in 1990), the surviving
spouse of the intestate will inherit the entire estate if no
parent survives the decedent and there are no surviving
children or their descendants. However, if there are surviving children and they are all children of the surviving
spouse and the surviving spouse has no other children, the
surviving spouse will still receive the full estate. This last
portion comes from the "Cinderella" problem. The theory is that a surviving
spouse left with children from two marriages might favor the children from a previous marriage and shortchange the decedent's children.

Certain marital property rights in some states may supersede intestate formulas for distribution. For example, in community property states (see Chapter 10),
the surviving spouse would always be entitled to his or her one-half of all community assets. The UPC distribution systems make it clear that the more complex
the family relationships, the greater the need for a will to clarify your desires with
respect to these family members.

> ### Consider 17.1

Ralph married Cora in 1949. Ralph and Cora had two children, Steven and Alice.
Cora died in 1959, and Ralph married Susan in 1963. Ralph and Susan had two
children, Alan and Erica. Ralph has just died intestate and his estate is valued at
$800,000. How would Ralph's property be distributed under the intestacy laws of
your state? How would it be distributed under the UPC?

Intestacy with No Surviving Spouse but with Descendants

Under the UPC, if a decedent has no surviving spouse, the estate property will
pass to his or her descendants. The UPC uses the terms "descendants" to refer to
children, grandchildren, and other direct lineal descendants of the intestate
decedent. The UPC follows the policy that, where possible, property should pass
to future generations and not back to older generations. The terms and amounts
of distribution among the descendants is covered later in this chapter.

Intestacy with No Surviving Spouse and No Descendants

If the decedent has no surviving spouse or descendants, the estate property goes
back to his or her parents in equal shares. If there is one parent, that parent will
receive the full estate.

If the decedent has no surviving spouse, no descendants, and no parents, the property is then inherited by the descendants of the parents, or, in lay terms, the brothers and sisters of the decedent and their descendants (the decedent's nieces and nephews) will inherit the property.

If there are no descendants of the parents, the grandparents of the decedent inherit the property, with one-half going to the maternal grandparents and one-half going to the paternal grandparents. Likewise, the descendant rules apply here so that if the grandparents are deceased, their descendants (or the aunts and uncles of the decedent) would inherit the property.

Consider 17.2

Ron, a single young man, has just passed away. Survivors include his parents, a brother, a sister, both sets of grandparents, and two uncles. How would Ron's property be distributed under the laws of intestacy of your state? How would it be distributed under the UPC?

Intestacy with No Surviving Relatives

All states have some provision governing the destiny of the property of a decedent who has no surviving relatives. At some point in all of the state statutes, the property will go to the state or some public fund, or will **escheat** to the state. The degree to which a state statute permits distant relatives to inherit varies. Under the UPC, the property will escheat if there are no lineal descendants of the maternal or paternal grandparents; thus, the UPC does not permit second or collateral heirs to inherit.

The escheat provisions of state intestate statutes are often referred to as **laughing heir statutes** because an escheat is required before distant heirs, who may not have known the decedent, inherit the decedent's property.

Intestacy Terminology and Special Provisions

Some terms and special provisions used in intestacy statutes affect how the property is distributed. The following sections define and discuss some of those terms and provisions.

Practical Tip

Will contests, even among families with the best of feelings, are not uncommon. Clarity in language is critical. Careful drafting avoids confusion and will contests.

PER STIRPES VERSUS PER CAPITA DISTRIBUTION

As each of the formulas for distribution of intestate property was discussed, it was clear in some of those circumstances that many relatives would be involved as heirs. A question that arises is who gets how much?

There are basically three theories for distribution of property along descendant lines. Under a **per capita** theory, the parties take an equal share. Under a **per stirpes** theory, the parties take by degree of relationship. Under the UPC theory (for which there are pre- and post-1990 versions that result in different distribution even across UPC states since not all states have adopted the 1990 modifications), the results for distribution are somewhat of a cross between per capita and per stirpes.

The best way to understand these theories of distribution is by an example and variations of it. Suppose that G is the intestate grandfather (decedent) and he has three children: A, B, and C. C has two children, Y and Z. B has one child, X. A has no children. The family relationships are diagrammed as follows:

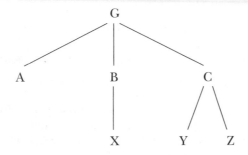

Suppose that all three children have survived G. In this case, all three systems reach the same solution: A, B, and C take one-third each.

Suppose that one child, C, predeceases G. The other two children survive G. Under a straight per capita distribution, A, B, Y, and Z each take one-fourth of the estate. Under per stirpes and the UPC, A and B take one-third each and *Y* and Z have one-half of one-third, or one-sixth of the estate of G for each.

Suppose that all three children predecease G. Under the per capita and pre-1990 and post-1990 UPC, the result is the same: X, Y, and Z each take one-third of the estate. However, under the per stirpes method, *X* takes one-half, and *Y* and Z each take one-half of one-half, or one-quarter.

Suppose A and B predecease G, but C survives G. Under the pre-1990 UPC, which is the same as per stirpes distribution, the result would be that C and X would each take one-half of G's estate. The result is the same under a per capita distribution because there are only two surviving heirs. Under the 1990 UPC revision (per capita at each generation), the solution is often debated. One view is that C would take one-half of the estate, with the remainder (one-half) combined into a single share and distributed equally among the surviving grandchildren of G (with the exception of C's children), so that X would get one-half of the estate. Another view is that after C's one-half interest, the remaining one-half is distributed equally among all the grandchildren so that X, Y, and Z would receive one-third of one-half of the estate or one-sixth of G's estate.

H and W were married in 1949. They had four children, A, B, C, and D. H died in 1990 and left all of his property to W. W passed away two months ago, intestate. A died in 1989 but had three children, X, Y, and Z. B, C, and D are alive at the time of W's death. B has one child, R; and C has two children, T and S. How would the property of W be distributed in your state? How would the property be distributed by per stirpes distribution under the UPC?

Consider 17.3

RELATIVES BY MARRIAGE
In most states, relatives by marriage other than the surviving spouse are not entitled to receive property through intestate distribution. Stepchildren, nieces, nephews, and spouses of predeceased children are all part of this excluded group.

HALF-BLOOD RELATIVES
No state has a provision that absolutely excludes half-blood relatives of the intestate from taking a share under the statutory scheme of distribution. Many states and the UPC treat a half-blood relative the same as a full-blood relative. Other states have provisions requiring half-blood relatives to take a lesser proportion of the estate than full-blood relatives.

POSTHUMOUS HEIRS

At common law and under all state statutes and the UPC, children born after the intestate's death are still treated as heirs.

Some states stipulate that the **posthumous** or **afterborn heir** must be born within 10 months of the decedent's death in order to be treated as an heir. The states vary significantly on posthumous relatives who are not children of the decedent or lineal descendants of the decedent. Some states do not permit any such posthumous relatives to take property under intestate distribution; other states stipulate that these relatives must be in the embryonic stages of development at the time of the intestate's death to be eligible to take property. The UPC specifies that an afterborn heir live for a minimum of 120 hours in order to inherit.

ILLEGITIMATE CHILDREN

Under the UPC and in all states, illegitimate children who have not been adopted by anyone are treated as natural children of their mothers and are entitled to inherit from their mothers and their mothers' relatives. Unless legitimized, these children are not treated as the natural children of their fathers.

ADOPTED CHILDREN

The legislative trend has been for adopted children to be treated as the natural children of the parents adopting them. The UPC also follows this doctrine for purposes of intestate distribution.

ALIENS

Aliens are entitled to receive property through intestate distribution. Their citizenship is not an issue in their right to inherit.

CONVICTS

A convict is permitted to inherit property and have it distributed through intestate succession at the time of death. Conviction status does not result in the escheat of the convict's property to the state.

MURDER

Under the UPC and in most states, an heir convicted of murdering (intentionally and feloniously) the intestate is not entitled to the intestate share of property that ordinarily would be awarded. State provisions vary as to the type of conviction required before the inheritance is lost. The following case deals with an issue of murder and inheritance.

In the Matter of the Estate of Morris P. Van Der Veen

935 P.2d 1042 (Kan. 1997)

Facts

On or about April 30, 1993, Kent Van Der Veen murdered his parents, Morris and Deanne Van Der Veen. Kent was 19 years old at the time and had fathered a child two years earlier who had been legally adopted by persons not identified in the court proceedings. Morris and Deanne were not aware of the existence of Kent's child prior to their deaths.

The 1989 joint will of Morris and Deanne Van Der Veen provides for the following distribution of their estate after debts and obligations are paid:

Upon the death of the survivor of us, each of us hereby gives, devises, and bequeaths all of the rest, residue, and remainder of our property of every kind, character, and description, and wherever located, unto our children, Laura Ann Van Der Veen and Kent Phillip Van Der Veen, equally and per stirpes.

Kent Van Der Veen was disqualified from inheriting any portion of his parents' estate under Kansas's slayer statute. Kent's child, the biological grandchild of Morris and Deanne, petitioned to inherit one-half of her biological grandparents' estate. The grandchild is identified in the case only as D.B.B. The trial court denied the grandchild any interest in the estate, and the grandchild appealed.

Judicial Opinion

Allegruccci, Justice. In their will, the Van Der Veens bequeathed one-half of their estate to each of their children, Laura and Kent. It is agreed that Kent is statutorily disqualified from inheriting property from his parents. At all pertinent times, it has been provided by statute:

No person convicted of feloniously killing, or procuring the killing of, another personal shall inherit or take by will[,] by intestate succession, as a surviving joint tenant, as a beneficiary under a trust or otherwise from such other person any portion of the estate or property in which the decedent had an interest. K.S.A. 1996 Supp. 59-513.

This appeal challenges the district court's determination that the statute prevails over the express terms of the Van Der Veens' will, resulting in D.B.B.'s being disinherited. The argument made on behalf of D.B.B. by her guardian *ad litem* is that the language of her grandparents' bequest to their children, "equally and per stirpes," must be construed to give what would have been Kent's share, if he had not been disqualified, to his heir, D.B.B. D.B.B.'s guardian *ad litem* further argues that D.B.B.'s adoptive status is irrelevant because K.S.A. 59-2118(b) provides that "[a]n adoption shall not terminate the right of the child to inherit . . . through the birth parent."

Appellee Laura Van Der Veen counters that the language of 59-2118(b), on which D.B.B. relies, was added in 1993 and became effective after the Van Der Veens' deaths. If the effective date of the amendment does not prevent it from applying in the present case, appellee further argues, the statute should be construed to restrict inheritance "through the birth parent" to instances where the birth parent has died. In other words, it should be interpreted so as to exclude inheritance through a birth parent who is alive but disqualified. In appellee's words, the statute should be interpreted so that the disqualified killer is treated as if he never existed rather than as if he had died.

We first address whether D.B.B.'s adoption affects her right to inherit from her biological grandparents. There is no doubt that the legislature intended that 59-2118(b), at all pertinent times, permitted an adoptee to inherit from and through his or her biological parents.

In that enactment, the sentence, "An adoption shall not terminate the right of the child to inherit from or through the birth parent," was added to 59-2118(b).

The Court of Appeals in [*In re Estate of Hirderliter*, 882. P.2d 1001 (Kan. 1994)] quoted from House Judiciary Attachment #4, which the Judicial Council offered in support of the amendment. It confirms that the early cases 'hold that, absent a statue to the contrary a child inherits from both natural and adoptive parents.' Thus, the Court of Appeals concluded that the 1993 amendment to 59-2118 merely codified existing law so that the rule should be given effect whether decedent died before or after the effective date of the statutory amendment, July 1, 1993.

We find the Court of Appeals' rationale persuasive and conclude that D.B.B.'s adoption would not bar her from inheriting from or through her biological parent.

We next consider whether Kent's being barred from inheriting from his parents prevents the inheritance from passing through him to his child. This was the basis for the trial court's decision and has not been decided by the appellate courts of this state. The question has arisen in other jurisdictions, however, and has been pondered by commentators, scholars, and the National Conference of Commissioners on Uniform State Laws.

With regard to the UPC, the Tennessee Court of Appeals, in *Carter v. Hutchison*, 707 S.W.2d 533, 537 n. 10 (Tenn.App. 1985), noted:

A vast majority of states enacting the forfeiture statutes have patterned them after the model statute proposed by Dean Wade in 1936, see J. Wade, [*Acquisition of Property by Willfully Killing Another—A Statutory Solution*, 49 *Harv. L.Rev.* 715, 753-55 (1936)], or the Uniform Probate Code. Thus, in twenty-nine states there is a statutory presumption that the victim's property passes to his estate as if the slayer had predeceased the decedent. Four states provide for forfeiture but are silent as to distribution. Tennessee is among ten states that provide for forfeiture and for distribution to the decedent's heirs through the laws of intestate succession. The eight remaining states without statutes have forfeiture provisions by court decision.

It appears that Kansas is one of the few states that does not expressly provide for distribution of the forfeited share.

Turning to the present case, it is clear that under either version of the UPC, appellee would take one-half of the estate of her parents. The other half would be taken by her disqualified brother's minor child.

The disposition of the slayer's share is one of four issues identified as unresolved by 59-513 and discussed in a 1984 law review article. Kuether, *Barring the Slayer's Bounty: An Analysis of Kansas' Troubled Experience*, 23 *Washburn L.J.*, 494, 495, 519-26 (1984). In introducing the topic, Professor Kuether stated:

> Some jurisdictions have held [that the slayer's share] should pass as though the slayer predeceased the victim. It would thus pass to the victim's other heirs, including those who would be the slayer's heirs if they also would be the victim's heirs. Others have barred all those who would take through the slayer. 23 *Washburn L.J.* at 519.

Professor Kuether did not cite case law to support his assertions. He also stated that there was scholarly opinion favoring both dispositions.

Kuether continued:

> Taking by representation and the antilapse statute both represent the state's policy regarding the decedent's presumed intent if the primary taker, the slayer, cannot take. In most cases this will be accurate, as where a grandchild takes from the victim grandparent's estate as a representative of the slayer-child. It is unlikely the grandparent would wish to punish the innocent grandchild. 23 *Washburn L.J.* at 521.

Professor Kuether undertook to show why two possible objections to considering the slayer to have predeceased the victim were not significant. The first is that the slayer might act in order to benefit his heirs. He suggests that "[t]his will be rare since it is a very costly gift by the slayer." Furthermore, to bar all taking by representation and any antilapse with the exceptional slayer in mind would be unjust and typically contrary to the victim's intent. The second "is Kansas' traditional position that those who take by representation take subject to the equities against their ancestors." Kuether's analysis why this principle is not applicable in the case of a slayer/beneficiary is convincing. He states that the principle was developed in cases where an heir claims through a person who was indebted to the decedent. The shares of the other beneficiaries were reduced by the amount of the indebtedness. In contrast, the other beneficiaries' shares have not been reduced by the slayer's killing the decedent. In fact, their benefits have been accelerated. Thus, just treatment of the other beneficiaries does not demand that the slayer's heirs be disqualified or penalized. To illustrate this proposition in the circumstances of the present case, we need only look at appellee's situation. She would take one-half of her parents' estate if they had died from natural causes, and she would take the same if Kent is disqualified for killing their parents and his share passes as if he predeceased them. In contrast, if Kent's child were disqualified because Kent killed his parents, the innocent child would be penalized, and appellee would take twice what the testators intended and what she expected.

We conclude that the better rule where the slayer's heir or heirs are wholly innocent would be to dispose of the disqualified slayer's share as if the slayer predeceased the victim(s).

The Van Der Veens intended for their daughter to take one-half of their estate. Their knowledge of Kent's troubled nature is reflected in a provision of the Van Der Veens' will that nominates Laura to serve as Kent's guardian and conservator. Nonetheless, they bequeathed one-half of their estate to him. There is nothing in the instrument from which the court could conclude that the Van Der Veens intended for Laura to receive the entire estate in the event of Kent's incapacity or disqualification. By extension, it may reasonably be inferred that they would not have intended for Kent's innocent child to be disqualified in order for Laura to receive the entire estate.

Appellee invites the court to speculate that the Van Der Veens would not have intended for their unknown, illegitimate grandchild to share in their estate. We decline the invitation and note there is no factual support in the record for such a speculation.

The judgment of the district court is reversed.

Case Questions

1. What is a "slayer statute"?

2. What does the court find about adopted children inheriting from their biological parents?

3. What does the court find about grandchildren of murderers inheriting the barred murderer's share of an estate?

4. Is Laura's position different from what it would have been if the inheritance by the grandchild were disallowed?

5. Why does the court discuss the concept of innocence?

Ethical Issue | What ethical and public policy issues exist in the dilemma of slayers, beneficiaries, and decedents? What concerns are courts and legislators trying to address with slayer statutes?

ADVANCEMENTS

At common law, the doctrine of **advancements** required that any gifts to heirs made by the intestate while alive had to be subtracted from that heir's share before distribution of the intestate estate was made. For example, suppose three heirs were entitled to receive equal shares of a $90,000 estate. If one heir had received $10,000 as an *inter vivos* gift, that heir would get only $20,000 under the doctrine of advancements. The remaining two heirs split the extra $10,000. Some states still follow the doctrine, but it is recognized under the UPC only if there is some writing indicating an intent to follow it.

PROPERTY INTERESTS NOT PASSING BY INTESTATE SUCCESSION

Some estates in land will not transfer by intestate distribution because of their characteristics. These interests, which were discussed in Part I, are life estates, joint tenancies by the entireties, and rights under dower and curtesy (discussed in Chapter 10). These interests automatically pass title at the time of death of one of the parties involved and thus are not subject to the rules of intestacy. Life insurance benefits also pass according to the party or parties named as beneficiaries under the policy, and the distribution of proceeds is not governed by the laws of intestacy.

SIMULTANEOUS DEATH

In cases of accidents and air disasters, it is frequently true that a husband and wife, who would ordinarily receive each other's estates, will perish together or will die under circumstances where it is impossible to tell who predeceased the other. Some states have survival period requirements that must be met before an heir may inherit through intestate distribution. Under the UPC, heirs must survive by 120 hours before they are permitted to inherit. The reason for survival clauses is efficiency. For example, a husband might survive his wife in an auto crash by only a few hours or a day and then pass away. In the absence of a survival provision, the property of the wife would pass to her husband's estate, which would in turn pass according to the remaining rules of intestate succession. With a survival provision, the property of each would be directly distributed to those next in line.

Some states have passed a uniform law related to the UPC, the **Uniform Simultaneous Death Act (USDA),** which provides that if a married couple dies under circumstances where it is impossible to determine the order of their deaths, then property of each spouse is distributed as if the other spouse had predeceased them. Thus, the wife's property would be distributed as if she died without a surviving spouse and the husband's property would be distributed in the same manner. Again, the purpose of the statute is to avoid the multiple distributions that might be required if the order of death had to be determined.

WILLS

Purpose of a Will

A **will** is a series of written instructions that sets forth what is to be done with the decedent's property upon death. The will cannot serve to transfer any property so long as the maker of the will (testator) is alive. As discussed in the intestacy section, the law does provide for the distribution of property in the event of an intestate death, but the law's method of distribution may not be desirable or may not be the wish of the decedent.

Practical Tip

Everyone needs a will. It saves time and the assets of the estate. However, the number of Americans with a will is limited:

Age Group	Percent with a Will
35–44	41%
45–54	63%
55–64	62%
65 and older	75%

Source: U.S. Bancorp/Pipper Jaffray (2000)

A will can expedite the distribution of property. Under the UPC, the procedures provided for probating a will require a minimal number of court appearances and substantially reduce paperwork, court costs, and attorneys' fees.

A will also may more accurately reflect the decedent's desires. For example, the will can name who will be responsible for handling and distributing the property, who should be appointed as guardian for minor children, who will make funeral arrangements, and what type of funeral arrangements are to be made.

Trusts to protect the income of minor children and trusts to save on estate taxes assessed at the time of death may also be created by a will.

Requirements for a Valid Will

The requirements for executing a valid will vary from state to state as significantly as do the methods of intestate distribution. However, all of the states deal with the following topics in their provisions that govern the requirements for a will: writing, testamentary capacity, signature, witnesses, and acknowledgment.

WRITING

Like all other documents conveying interests in real property, a will is generally required to be in writing to be recognized as valid. The writing requirement is true for wills even if the testator is not disposing of any real property in the will. A few states do recognize oral or **nuncupative wills,** but often such wills are limited to the disposal of personal property and must be created under circumstances of near death. In many states, the nuncupative will requirements are similar to the gift in contemplation of death (gifts *causa mortis*) requirements.

Perhaps the most frequently litigated issue under the writing requirement is the issue of whether the document actually constitutes a will or is an attempt to substitute some other document for a will. The following sections discuss the validity of such will substitutes.

Holographic Will Most wills are thought of as formally typed documents drafted by attorneys, backed by blue paper, and written in very formal language. However, other types of writings can qualify as wills that have none of those characteristics. Many states and the UPC recognize the holographic will as valid. The **holographic will** is a will that is written entirely in the handwriting of the testator and signed by the testator. Some states now permit holographic wills placed on a preprinted form.

Some states require that the holographic instrument be witnessed to be valid, while others recognize the will as valid so long as it is signed. In many cases, letters with proper execution have qualified as wills for the testator. One problem with the holographic will, particularly in states where the will need not be witnessed, is establishing the authenticity of the handwriting and the signature as that of the testator. The long-lasting probate battle over the will of millionaire Howard Hughes was the result of trying to establish whether and which of several purported holographic wills were authentic.

The following language was found in a holographic will left in the residence of William P. Avery and Deborah Smalling who were unmarried but lived together in the house they had built with their earnings and savings:

> *I would like Deborah to have my home and property to maintain and keep with the hope that she may find the comfort and independence that has been denied me. She has been my love and faithful consort and has given me untold support and happiness. Words fail me.*
>
> */s/William P. Aver*

Does the will qualify as a holographic will? Does the language have any ambiguities? Would the will also pass to Deborah the 32 acres of land on which the house sat? *Smalling v. Terrell*, 943 S.W.2d 397 (Tenn. App. 1996)

Consider 17.4

Contracts to Make Wills and Joint or Mutual Wills Often, particularly between husbands and wives, contracts will be executed for the parties to make joint or mutual wills that will serve to dispose of the property belonging to the two in a certain way. Such expression of intent cannot be changed or revoked by either party through a change in the will provisions unless the change is mutually agreed upon.

The contract to make the wills cannot itself be recognized as a will. However, once the wills are executed, the terms of both the agreement and the wills can be enforced. Theoretically, each party is bound even after the death of one of the parties to the agreement. In practice, litigation results.

To be enforceable, the agreement to make a will must be supported by consideration. Such consideration is furnished in the case of husband and wife by their mutual relinquishment of the right to distribute their property according to their desires.

A **joint will** is one in which the same document is executed by different parties as their own will. **Mutual wills** are the separate wills of parties that are reciprocal in their provisions and are probably based on a mutual agreement, understanding, or contract to make a will. States vary in their recognition of the validity of joint wills, but all states recognize mutual wills. Because of their nature, mutual wills are often the subject of will contests.

One of the issues often arising in the case of a mutual will is whether its provisions can be revoked. The provisions can be revoked with the mutual consent of the parties. Unilateral revocation usually brings litigation by the heirs or potential heirs.

Content of the Writing There are no requirements for specific provisions in a valid will (with the exception of execution requirements discussed later). However, all persons executing wills should remember the purpose of their wills and clearly set forth their intentions and desires for the distribution of their property and the handling of their affairs upon death.

Generally, wills can be broken down into the following topics, although the topics and their content may vary from state to state and according to the needs of the testator's family.

1. *Declaration clause:* Declares the age, capacity, and residence of the testator and that the document is a will.
2. *Definition clause or clauses:* Lists wife, husband, children, and so on. Defines terms such as *children* and *issue*.

3. *Funeral and burial arrangements clause:* If desired, specifies funeral procedures.
4. *Debt clause:* Provides for payments of all debts, estate and inheritance taxes, and so on.
5. *Appointment clause or clauses:* Appoints the party responsible for the administration of the estate. May also specify the powers of the appointed person.
6. *Gift clause or clauses:* Disposes of the estate property, by either specific dispositions or a general disposition.
7. *Execution and signature clauses:* See discussion later in this chapter.

TESTAMENTARY CAPACITY

There are two requirements for **testamentary capacity:** age capacity and mental capacity.

1. Age Capacity Every state has a statute that fixes the minimum age requirement for executing a valid will. In most states, the age of testamentary capacity is the age of majority, which in most states is 18 or 21. The age computation is made at the time the will is executed; thus, age capacity is required before a valid will can be executed and is not determined as of the time of death.

2. Mental Capacity Many wills begin their declaration clause with "I, _____, being of sound mind. . . . " This establishes the mental capacity requirement for the execution of a valid will, which is that the testator must be of sound mind. Mental capacity is not synonymous with intelligence, logic, or distributing property only to relatives. Rather, mental capacity is established when the testator is able to understand the following:

1. The nature or extent of his or her property
2. What persons would be the natural recipients
3. What disposition is being made of the property
4. The relationship between items 1 to 3
5. How to form an orderly distribution of property

Thus, the presence of eccentricity or old age is insufficient in and of itself to establish a lack of testamentary capacity. Each case on testamentary capacity presents a different set of factual circumstances and requires the court to apply each of the five factors listed according to the familial situation of the individual testator. The following case illustrates how the determination of testamentary capacity is made.

Bracewell v. Bracewell

20 S.W.3d 14 (Tex. App. 2000)

Facts

Irene Bracewell was married to W.T. Bracewell and they had two children, Bobbie, born in 1932, and Charles, born in 1936. In 1961, Irene executed a will that left all of her estate to Charles. During the 1960s, Irene left W.T., who had named a lake on their ranch, Lake Irene, and moved in with Charles at his home in Houston, Texas. Irene returned to W.T. in 1975 and executed another will that left everything to W.T. if she died first. W.T.'s will left everything to her if he died first.

During the 1970s, Irene suffered from nervousness anxiety, hypertension, hypothyroidism, and degenerative joint disease. In 1984, Irene was hospitalized with Parkinson's disease. She added to her long list of medications, including tranquilizers, prescriptions for Parkinson's.

While Irene loved both W.T. and Charles, all agreed that W.T. and Charles did not get along. In 1989, W.T. executed another will that left all of his property to Bobbie. Irene, upon learning of this change, deeded property to

Charles and executed a new will. Following the execution of the will, Irene's mental and physical health deteriorated and she died in 1995 following a year in a nursing home.

W.T. wanted the 1975 will probated and Charles petitioned to have the 1989 will recognized as valid. A jury agreed with W.T.'s position that Irene lacked competency to execute the 1989 will and the judge then admitted the 1975 will to probate. Charles appealed.

Judicial Opinion

Wanda McKee Fowler, Justice. In the instant appeal, Charles complains that the evidence adduced at trial is legally and factually insufficient to support the jury's finding that Irene lacked testamentary capacity to execute a valid will on August 17, 1989.

In his brief, W.T. contends that the trial record shows that Irene lacked testamentary capacity on the day the 1989 will was executed. At trial, W.T. testified that Irene was hospitalized in 1984. According to W.T., Irene was "sick a lot" from that time on, and that she was a different woman. W.T. stated that, following her diagnosis with Parkinson's Disease, Irene quit driving a car, quit going to church, and "didn't want no company." W.T. concluded that, in 1989 " Irene was in pretty bad shape." In addition to his own testimony, W.T. offered the following witnesses in support of his contention that Irene was not legally competent to execute the 1989 will: (1) Bobbie Bracewell Rigby; (2) Linda Grisset; (3) Dr. Luke Scamardo; and (4) Dr. Gary Newsome. That testimony is summarized below.

W.T. and Irene's daughter, Bobbie Bracewell Rigby, testified on W.T.'s behalf. According to Bobbie, Irene's health "got bad in 1984." She added that, although Irene had been a devout woman previously, her mother quit going to church because of her condition. Bobbie stated further that, after 1984, Irene socialized with other people less frequently. Bobbie reported that, during 1987, and most of 1988, she visited Irene every day so that she could bathe her mother, brush her teeth, and fix her hair. Bobbie added that Irene "acted like a little child" while her daughter brushed her teeth for her. Bobbie testified that Charles sent a letter to "Dr. Jankovic" in Houston, Texas, in October of 1987, which recited Irene's medical history. In that letter, Charles reported that his mother had been taking "pain pills, tranquilizers, and sleeping pills" for thirty years or "maybe longer." Charles wrote further that Irene's Parkinson's Disease was "continu[ing] to get worse."During the summer of 1989, Bobbie and her husband traveled to Pennsylvania to pursue his work in the oil pipeline industry. Bobbie noted that she "didn't think" that Irene was "of sound mind" during the 1989 time period "because the way she was about church and everything."

Linda Grisset is Bobbie's youngest daughter and W.T.'s granddaughter. Linda described her relationship with her grandmother, Irene, as a "close" one. Linda testified that, from 1975 through 1979, Irene never missed a single Sunday church service, and that she went to the beauty parlor every Wednesday. In addition, Irene helped out at her church by cleaning, vacuuming, wiping song books, and doing "whatever needed to be done." During that time, Irene loved to read and would help Linda with her schoolwork. Linda, described Irene as a "nervous lady." Linda testified that, in 1984, after a stay in the Madison County Hospital, Irene stopped driving and quit going to church altogether. Linda was married on August 21, 1989. Linda testified that she visited Irene on the afternoon of Thursday, August 17, 1989, to tell her grandmother about her wedding plans. According to Linda, Irene would not "respond to anything" and "couldn't relate" to her granddaughter at all on that day. Linda testified further that Irene was "absolutely not" in a sound frame of mind on August 17, 1989, that she was in that same condition "[m]ost of the time, and had been for awhile."

Dr. Scamardo testified that he prescribed the "minor tranquilizer" Librium to treat Irene's anxiety and, later, Diazepam, which is a relative of Valium. In addition, Dr. Scamardo prescribed Sinequan, which he described as a "major tranquilizer," for Irene's anxiety. Dr. Scamardo also prescribed Valium to treat Irene's anxiety disorder. During the course of her treatment for anxiety, Irene was also taking pain killers for degenerative joint disease in addition to thyroid medication. After she was diagnosed with Parkinson's Disease, Dr. Scamardo prescribed Sinemet and a number of other medications to treat symptoms related to that condition.

Dr. Scamardo testified that he was informed by Charles, in 1987, that Irene was experiencing "periods of incoherence" at home. Dr. Scamardo added that Irene's family had to supply information for her when she came in for treatment because she was incoherent "ninety-nine percent" of the time.

After W.T.'s counsel instructed Dr. Scamardo on the applicable legal standard, Dr. Scamardo testified that, in his opinion, Irene would not have had testamentary capacity on the day she executed the 1989 will. Dr. Scamardo explained that he based this opinion on Irene's "anxiety course" during her entire treatment history. He elaborated further that, during the time he treated Irene, she had periods in which she would become "more anxious," [and] more incoherent." According to Dr. Scamardo, on August 17, 1989, Irene would have been unable to "keep up with all the complicated dealings of making out a will, [and] dealing with business dealings."

Dr. Newsome reviewed Irene's medical records dating from the 1970s, and he also reviewed records from the Clouser Pharmacy for the year 1989. Dr. Newsome observed that Irene was "taking some pretty heavy duty medication" during the time she signed the 1989 will. He noted further that "she was having evidence of confusion" as early as 1984. Dr. Newsome explained that people who are diagnosed with Parkinson's Disease later in life have a "much greater incidence of . . . having significant depression, dementia and even worse psychiatric symptoms of delusions and hallucinations and paranoia." Dr. Newsome added that Irene's condition may have been worsened by the fact that Irene misused her medication.

In Dr. Newsome's opinion, Irene's lack of competency wasn't even a "close" question. Dr. Newsome added that, given the medications described in the Clouser Pharmacy records, he was "not sure if [he] would know what planet [he] took these medicines." Dr. Newsome commented further that Irene's decision to lock herself in the bathroom for the purpose of executing her will could be considered an indication of the level of her paranoia at the time. Dr. Newsome also noted that Irene's decision to leave the bulk of her estate to Charles showed that she was unaware of her "bounty" and unaware that she had any children "other than Charles Bracewell."

The overall evidence supports the doctors' testimony. In 1984, Irene was diagnosed with a serious, degenerative illness. As a result of the illness, she changed. Parkinson's Disease is an illness that is progressive in nature, and its impact on individuals such as Irene, who are diagnosed later in life, can be more mental than physical.

Therefore, we hold that the verdict was supported by legally sufficient evidence and overrule the challenge by Charles on that issue.

Notwithstanding the facts recited above, even Charles testified that his mother was experiencing incoherence in 1987, and that her Parkinson's Disease was progressing in severity at that time. Nell Halley, who witnessed the 1989 will, could only "assume" that Irene knew what she was doing when she signed the will because Irene did not discuss her plans. The voluminous medical records and the testimony given by Dr. Scamardo and Dr. Newsome also demonstrate that Irene was on "heavy duty medication" in 1989, and that she would not have been able to "keep up with all the complicated dealings of making out a will," or participate meaningfully "with business dealings" at that time. After reviewing all of the evidence, we do not consider the jury's finding so contrary to the overwhelming weight of the evidence as to clearly wrong and unjust. Accordingly, we overrule Charles's factual sufficiency challenge.

Affirmed.

Case Questions

1. Are health problems alone grounds for a finding of lack of mental capacity for executing a will?
2. Is age alone grounds for a finding of lack of mental capacity for executing a will?
3. Explain what testimony was the basis for a finding of a lack of mental capacity.
4. What lessons do you learn about multiple wills, health issues, and family relationships from this case?

SIGNATURE

All states require, as part of the formal prerequisites for a valid will, that the will be signed by the testator. The signature requirement is straightforward when the testator is able to sign. However, there are circumstances when the testator, because of disease or hospital equipment, is unable to personally sign the will. In these circumstances and under the UPC, the testator may direct someone else to sign the will so long as the testator acknowledges the will and is present at the signing of it.

Those who are unable to write may still authenticate a will by placing an *X* on the signature portion of the will, witnessed by others as being placed by the testator.

The signature of the testator should appear at the end of the will to make clear what portions and provisions were intended to be included in the will. As a matter of practice or law, the testator should also initial each page of the will to prevent pages from being added or altered after the execution occurs.

| Consider 17.5 | Burnell Young died on December 18, 1995, leaving a will that left all of his property to his daughter, Martha Young. Freeman Young, his son, challenged the validity of the will on the grounds that Burnell could not read. Should a will be set aside because the testator cannot read? *Succession of Young*, 692 So.2d 1149 (La. App. 1997) |

WITNESSES

The witness requirements for a valid will vary from state to state. The number of witnesses required for a valid will is either two or three; under the UPC, the requirement is two. In addition, some states require that the witnesses be disinterested parties; that is, the witnesses must not be beneficiaries under the will. The UPC does not impose this requirement of having disinterested witnesses. Often the issue of whether the witnesses are disinterested arises because of indirect benefits obtained.

George Baxter Gordon executed a will that provided that the Church of Christ of New Boston, Texas, would receive a substantial amount of his property. The will was executed with two members of the church serving as witnesses for the will. Upon Gordon's death, several heirs contested the admission of the will to probate on the grounds that the witnesses were interested parties. What was the result? *In re Estate of Gordon*, 519 S.W.2d 902 (Tx. 1975)

Consider 17.6

Many states not only prescribe the number and quality of witnesses required for the execution of a valid will but also specify the manner in which the witnesses witness the transaction. For example, some states require that all of the witnesses be present in the same room at the time the testator signs the will, and that the witnesses sign in the presence of the testator and in the presence of one another. Other states and the UPC do not require the witnesses to actually witness the signing by the testator so long as the testator indicates the signature is authentic before the witness signs.

ACKNOWLEDGMENTS

Many states and the UPC provide all testators with the opportunity to execute a **self-proving will.** In a self-proving will, the signatures of the testator and the witnesses are notarized following a clause that is a form of affidavit for the parties. If the proper acknowledgment procedures are followed, then the will is presumptively valid, meaning that there is a presumption that the will was validly executed and meets all formalities required for proper execution. Figure 17.1 is an example of an acknowledgment clause used in a UPC state. The clause is inserted in the will after the testator and the witnesses have already signed.

Will Contests

The validity of a will may be challenged by anyone who might have an interest in the estate of the decedent—someone named in the will or an heir omitted from the will. Some of the grounds for such challenges have already been discussed. For example, it is possible to have a will set aside if the testator lacked testamentary capacity. Or a will may be set aside if the formalities of execution were not met, as in the cases where the witnesses were interested parties or where there were no witnesses. Lack of the testator's signature is another ground for having the will set aside.

However, one very common ground for having a will set aside that has not yet been discussed is that of **undue influence.** Under this type of contest, the party challenging the will does not dispute the valid execution of the will or the testator's capacity, but rather raises the defense that the will was not executed of the testator's own free will and choice—that someone else was directing the testator.

FIGURE 17.1 *Sample Will Acknowledgment*

STATE OF _____   )

SS. ACKNOWLEDGMENT/AFFIDAVIT)

County of _____   )

We, _____, _____, and _____, the Testator
and the witnesses, respectively, whose names are signed to the foregoing instrument,
being first duly sworn, do hereby declare to the undersigned authority that the Testator
signed and executed the instrument as his Last Will and Testament and that he signed
willingly, and that he executed it as his free and voluntary act for the purposes therein
expressed, and that each of the witnesses, in the presence of the Testator, signed the
will as witness and that to the best of their knowledge the Testator was at that time
eighteen or more years of age, of sound mind, and under no constraint or undue influence.

Testator _____

Witness _____

Witness _____

Subscribed and sworn to and acknowledged before me by _____, the

Testator, and subscribed and sworn to before me by _____, and

_____, witnesses, this _____ day of _____ 20____

Notary_____

Undue influence is a difficult concept to define. It need not amount to force
but must be something more than advice, persuasion, and kindness. The following elements must be established for the court to set aside a will on the grounds
of undue influence:

1. The testator must be established as a person who could be subject to undue
   influence.
2. A party must be shown to have had the opportunity to exercise undue
   influence.
3. A party must have been disposed to exercise undue influence.
4. There must be a will that reflects the results of undue influence.

Undue influence, like testamentary capacity, is based on the factual circumstances in each individual case. Classically, the finding of undue influence occurs
when an elderly party becomes dependent on a friend or relative for assistance
in day-to-day living, then executes a will leaving all or the majority of their estate
to that person while other relatives are ignored in the testamentary disposition.

Relationships of dependency and trust are called *confidential* relationships. In
many states, there is a presumption that undue influence was involved in the execution of a will if there is a confidential or fiduciary relationship between the testator and the party who is a major beneficiary and who also procured the execution of the will.

The following case deals with an issue of undue influence.

Ramsey v. Taylor

999 P.2d 1178 (Or. App. 2000)

Facts

John C. Ramsey Sr. (Senior) executed a will in the last months of his life that left the bulk of his estate to Melody Taylor, his paramour. Senior's relationships with his son and grandsons were strained and his will included the following clause:

> I have intentionally provided significant, yet smaller amounts for my son and grandsons because they have for several years alienated my affections by being irresponsible, contentious, and constantly seeking financial support from me rather than providing for themselves.
>
> I have made provisions for MELODY J. TAYLOR because MELODY J. TAYLOR provides me care and support.

Senior was suffering from cancer and renal failure and his pain was extraordinary. His doctors prescribed high doses of morphine which Melody administered. Senior died from an overdose of morphine.

John Ramsey Jr. (John II), Senior's son, challenged the validity of the will on the grounds of undue influence as well as felonious killing of a testator by a beneficiary. The trial court found there was undue influence and refused to admit the will to probate. Melody appealed.

Judicial Opinion

De Munz, Presiding Judge. We agree with the trial court that a confidential relationship existed between Senior and Taylor. Evidence in the record establishes not only that Taylor and Senior spent most of their time together in the last few months of his life but also establishes that Taylor took increasing responsibility over that time in managing all aspects of Senior's day-to-day life, including procuring and administering his medications, arranging and driving him to medical and business appointments, caring for his house and clothes, providing his food, and managing his checkbook. Taylor and First Interstate argue that no confidential relationship has been established because there is no direct proof that Taylor offered, or Senior accepted, business or financial advice from her. They further point out that an abundance of evidence demonstrates that Senior had strong opinions and ideas about what to do with his money. As to the question of direct evidence that Taylor gave business or financial advice, we disagree that direct evidence is necessary to establish a confidential relationship under these circumstances. Unrebutted evidence establishes that Senior reposed confidence in Taylor to handle most aspects of his daily life, including his finances.

The question, then, is whether "suspicious circumstances" are present that would require Taylor to go forward with "'evidence sufficient to overcome the adverse inference'" of undue influence. *In re Reddaway's Estate*, 329 P2d 886 (or. 1958).

A.   *Procurement*

This factor concerns whether the beneficiary participated in the preparation of the challenged will: There is evidence that, before Senior's meeting with his attorneys on August 7, Taylor assisted Senior in preparing a revision of the previous trust document, substituting herself for Philomena King as a beneficiary. It is undisputed that the documents that Senior actually signed on August 10 did not reflect the same changes in the disposition of his estate as did the changes that Taylor assisted in preparing. However, it also is undisputed that the documents actually executed on August 10 did, in fact, give a greater amount of Senior's estate to Taylor than did the revision that Taylor helped to prepare. In sum, we find that there is sufficient evidence of "procurement" to suffice as a "suspicious circumstance."

B.   *Independent Advice*

This factor concerns whether Senior "had the benefit of the independent advice of his own attorney in drawing up the new will" that benefited Taylor. Evidence in the record establishes that Senior met with his attorneys on two occasions to prepare his final will and trust and that Taylor was not present at those meetings. Although we have found it to be a suspicious circumstance where a testator is taken to a beneficiary's attorney rather than his or her own attorney to prepare a will, it is undisputed that Senior consulted his own attorneys, who had previously prepared a will and trust for him. Moreover, one of the attorneys testified that Senior told him that Taylor had been of no help to him in deciding how to dispose of his estate. Also, the attorneys discussed with Senior his intent to benefit Taylor and the reasons why he was benefitting Taylor to a greater extent than he was benefitting his family. We conclude that no "suspicious circumstance" was present regarding whether Senior received independent advice concerning his last will and trust.

C.   *Secrecy and Haste*

This factor concerns whether there was "secrecy and haste attendant on the making of the will." We do not find that there was any secrecy attendant on the making of Senior's final will and trust. Senior attempted to talk to both John II and John III about the changes he planned to make to his will and trust on August 4, several days before consulting his attorneys. There is no evidence from which it can be inferred that Senior's final will and trust were prepared in secrecy. Given Senior's history of threatening and following through on his threats to cut family members from his will, it is entirely consistent with Senior's past behavior that he would inform his family of his intent to reduce their prospective inheritances. As to haste, the evidence shows that Senior's final will and trust were prepared in relative haste, undoubtedly due to his deteriorating physical condition. We do not believe however, that haste in preparing and executing a will because the testator understands that he is terminally ill is the type of haste that the court had in mind when it declared that "haste and secrecy" could be a "suspicious circumstance."

D.　*Change in Decedent's Attitude Toward Others*

This factor concerns whether there has been an unexplained change in the testator's "attitude toward those for whom he had previously expressed affection[.]" The court found that, although Senior had had negative feelings toward his family before Taylor even met Senior, "Senior had been kept away from his family and friends by Ms. Taylor during the last two months of his life which had an effect on his attitude toward his family." There was evidence that Senior spent a great deal of time with Taylor in June and July 1995 and therefore often was not at home. He also spent a great deal of time with Taylor in August during his final illness when she stayed at his home with him. There also was evidence that Senior did not wish to see John II, as shown by his statement on August 4 to his nurse that "I haven't talked to him in a long time and I don't want to talk to him now."

There was evidence that Taylor was protective of Senior, that she was upset by John II's behavior in causing Senior to cry on August 4, and also when John III pulled Senior from his bed on August 16th, causing him pain. However, there also was evidence that John II, John III, and Ron Ramsey (a nephew) all had occasion to be alone with Senior during the last month of his life without Taylor's interference (although there is no evidence that Ron Ramsey made any effort to visit Senior until the day before his death). There also was evidence that Taylor facilitated visits by Senior's friend Jill Brogdon and his niece Nan May during the final week of his life, at his request. The evidence does not support the trial court's conclusion that Taylor kept Senior from his family and friends during the final months of his life.

E.　*Change in the Testator's Plan of Disposing of His Property*

This factor concerns whether there is "a decided discrepancy between a new and previous wills of the testator; and continuity of purpose running through former wills indicating a settled intent in the disposition of his estate[.]" Frankly, the only continuity of purpose that can be gleaned from Senior's prior wills and trusts is his purpose of disinheriting beneficiaries with whom he had recently fought and disinheriting or reducing the inheritance of those to whom he had already given substantial gifts. To summarize: In the mid to late 1980s, Senior had Brogdon write out revisions to his will on several occasions after threatening to cut off family members who either asked for or received funds from him. In 1990, after buying a house in which he allowed John III's family to live, Senior executed a will leaving John III 10 percent less than he was leaving John II and Ron Ramsey. After giving the house to John III in 1991, Senior disinherited him entirely in his next will. After John II moved out of Senior's new house in 1991 due to their disagreements, Senior disinherited him, as well. Evidence showed that Senior provided living accommodations to his granddaughter Davis around that time and that the next trust, the one prepared but never executed in 1993, disinherited Davis, but reinstated John II, John III and Ron Ramsey as minor beneficiaries. There was evidence that Senior gave money to his granddaughter Zabel and that she later was omitted from the 1994 will and trust. It is also notable that the will and trust benefitting Taylor was not the first to provide generous benefit to one of Senior's "significant others."

In short, over the last decade of his life, Senior's various wills and trusts did not reveal any settled intent as to the disposition of his estate. Although all of them, including the last, benefited family members to some extent, which family members were benefitted varied greatly, apparently based on Senior's most recent dealings with them.

F.　*Unnatural or Unjust Gift*

Here, the testator has chosen to favor a "significant other," or mistress. Moreover, the testator had known this "significant other" for only a little more than two months at the time of his death. Also, although there is no direct evidence that Taylor generated Senior's affection "solely for the purpose of inducing" him to make gifts, we can infer from the circumstances that Senior's generosity toward her may have had something to do with her willingness to show him affection. We take into account the fact that Senior was in his 80s at the time he met Taylor and clearly was not easy to get along with and the fact that Taylor was in her 30s. We also take into account that, within weeks of meeting Senior, Taylor took a vacation with him and began accepting very generous gifts of cash from him. We conclude that this evidence is sufficient to describe Senior's choice to benefit Taylor as a "suspicious circumstance" under the test of *Reddaway*.

G.　*Donor's Susceptibility to Influence*

By comparison, the evidence in this case shows that Senior remained fairly physically active until the last few days of his life, when the pain of his cancer rendered him relatively immobile. Although he clearly was deteriorating quickly due to the rapid spread of his cancer, he was not physically helpless or feeble until after he executed his final will and testament. Concerning Senior's mental susceptibility to undue influence, we find no evidence of senility or instability or that his mental condition made him an "easy mark." Also, there is no evidence that he was confused, disoriented, or suffering from memory loss.

The testimony of a great number of the fact witnesses, and even the expert testimony of Dr. Luther who opined that Senior *was* susceptible to influence, convinces us that Senior was not, in fact, susceptible to undue influence. The evidence demonstrates that Senior had, for approximately the last decade of his life, consciously chosen to get attention, indeed homage, from others either by giving them generous gifts or promising them generous parts of his estate. He appears to have been fully aware that he was using his money to obtain attention from his family and friends. We do not agree with Dr. Luther's assessment that Senior's use of his money in this manner demonstrates vulnerability to undue influence. Rather, it demonstrates that Senior was intent on influencing others, not that he was influenced by others.

II. DID TAYLOR OVERCOME THE ADVERSE INFERENCE?

Under the rubric provided by *Reddaway,* we have concluded that Taylor had a confidential relationship with Senior and that two suspicious circumstances were attendant on the making of his final will and trust. The question, then, is whether there is evidence in the record to overcome the adverse inference that must be drawn from our findings thus far. We believe that there is.

The first suspicious circumstance that we found was that Taylor assisted Senior in drafting revisions to his 1994 trust before he consulted his attorneys in August 1995. In light of other evidence in the record, however, we find that any adverse inference to be drawn by this circumstances has been overcome. We conclude that Taylor has overcome any adverse inference to be drawn from her participation in preparing a preliminary draft of Senior's final will and trust.

The other suspicious circumstance that we have found to be present in this case is that Senior's choice to benefit a "significant other" whom he had known for only a few months rather than leave his entire estate to family members and that this may be termed an "unnatural" disposition under the *Reddaway* test. In this case, the record reflects that, under most of his previous wills and trusts, Senior wished John II either to receive nothing or to receive a relatively small portion of the estate. Even the previous will and trust most beneficial to John II allocated to him only 36 percent of the estate. There is no indication in the record that Senior ever intended John II to be the primary beneficiary of any will and trust.

Second, the record amply demonstrates that Senior did not perceive John II as either "deserving" or "faithful" for a long period of time before Taylor came on the scene.

In his final assignment of error, John II argues that the trial court erred in failing to set aside all of the *inter vivos* transfers to Taylor. Although John II did not assign error to the trial court's conclusion that Taylor did not feloniously kill Senior by administering the prescribed morphine, John II argues that, as a matter of "equity and good conscience," Taylor should not be entitled to keep any money that she received from Senior because she "was the person who administered or directed the administration of the morphine." We reject John II's argument. We agree with the trial court's conclusion that Taylor administered the morphine in the amounts prescribed by Senior's physicians. We also agree with its conclusion that that amount of morphine was required to control the excruciating pain that Senior was experiencing during the last days of his life. The record shows that, although it was common medical knowledge that administering such an amount of morphine to a terminal cancer patient suffering from renal failure could lead to the result seen here, physicians are known to use morphine in these circumstances anyway, in order to ease the suffering of dying patients.

We have concluded that Taylor did not exercise undue influence over Senior when she received *inter vivos* gifts from him or when he made her a major beneficiary of his final will and trust. We do not find that "equity and good conscience" require us to deprive Taylor of those gifts on the ground that she and Senior's physicians carried out his wishes that he receive only palliative care during his final illness.

Reversed and remanded.

Case Questions

1. Describe Senior's relationships at the time of his death.
2. Was there a confidential relationship?
3. Was there undue influence?
4. What factors does the court look at in determining whether there is undue influence?
5. Will Senior's will naming Melody the primary beneficiary be probated?
6. What of Melody's administration of a lethal dose of morphine?

Consider 17.7

Bill Cruxton died in November 1992. He was widowed, childless, and past 80. In his will he left $500,000, the bulk of his estate, to a 17-year-old waitress who had been kind to him as part of her job as a waitress at Dink's Restaurant in Chagrin Falls, Ohio. Cruxton had lunch and dinner there every day for 13 months preceding his death. He was very public about leaving the money to her because he knew that her father had died and that she wanted to attend college. Cora Bruck, Cruxton's 86-year-old sister, is challenging the will as Cruxton's only relative. Cruxton left her only sufficient funds to cover her funeral expenses. Mark Fishman, Bruck's attorney, has stated, "Mr. Cruxton's longtime friends all agree that this was not the same guy. The Bill Cruxton that they knew was a very conservative and down-to-earth guy. This is the last thing they would have expected from the true Bill Cruxton." Are there valid grounds for challenging the will?

Consider 17.8

James G. Newkirk left his wife and daughter in 1951. Shortly thereafter, he met Pauline Knight and began living with her; they held themselves out as husband and wife in all places where they resided. In 1952, Newkirk executed a will that left all of his property to Pauline and made no provision for his wife or daughter except the following clause:

> *Third: I have a daughter, Joan Janick, who is married, and for whom I have heretofore provided, and I do not wish her to participate in my will.*

Newkirk died in 1964, and Pauline presented the will for probate. Newkirk's daughter challenged the will on the grounds of undue influence because the will had been made less than a year after Newkirk left and was made at a time when he was still married and had a child to provide for. What was the result? *In re Estate of Newkirk*, 456 P.2d 104 (Ok. 1969)

Disinheritance and Limitations on Distribution

Most states have provisions that prevent **disinheritance** of certain family members. In fact, all states have some protections for the surviving spouse. Although a will may purport to disinherit a surviving spouse, the surviving spouse will be entitled to one or more of the following depending on the state's system of property allocation between husband and wife.

1. *Dower:* In some states, the wife is entitled to a certain portion of her husband's estate. If she is not provided for in the will, she will still receive her statutory dower percentage.
2. *Curtesy:* In some states, the husband is entitled to a portion of the wife's estate, and the result will be the same as in the dower situation above.
3. *Community property:* In community property states, the surviving spouse is entitled to half of the community property even if the testator spouse has attempted to disinherit by the terms of the will.
4. *Homesteads, exemptions, and family allowances:* Most states have some provision that requires that the home and often specific personal property (usually furnishings) pass to the family (spouse and children) of the decedent. These items are thus given to the family regardless of disinheritance provisions in the will. Also, many states provide for an allowance to be given to the spouse and children of the decedent for the purposes of support during the probate of the estate.

In some cases, the surviving spouse has been provided for in the will but would be entitled to receive more under the afforded statutory protections. Under these circumstances, many states permit the surviving spouse to elect whether to take what was provided under the will or to take the statutory share as provided by the applicable protections. The election must be formally filed as part of the probate proceedings, usually within a certain limited period.

Relatives other than the surviving spouse may be disinherited. Testators who disinherit relatives should be cautious in making sure that all property is given to others, because if there is any unbequeathed property, it is still possible that the disinherited relative will inherit under the laws of intestate succession. In addition, some states require a clause in the will naming the disinherited relative and the testator's intent to disinherit that relative. Even when such a clause is not required, it may aid in the determination of capacity, by showing that the testator was aware of the familial situation. The clause also aids in interpretation by showing the specified intent of the testator.

Living Wills

In recent years, the term **living will** has been used extensively. A living will is a document that verifies the wishes of the testator to be taken off artificial life-support systems when there is no reasonable prospect of recovery. States that recognize living wills have statutory requirements for their validity. For example, disinterested witnesses and specific language are required in many states. Whatever requirements a state has must be followed if the living will is to be valid. Web Exhibit 17.1 is a sample living will form.

The **Uniform Rights of the Terminally Ill Act,** as approved by the Conference on Uniform Laws and endorsed by the American Bar Association, provides a comprehensive statement of law regarding the rights of the terminally ill. This act gives legal rules for living wills, authorization of appointment of an agent to make healthcare decisions, rules for determination of which family members may make decisions on healthcare for the incapacitated, and rules on immunities and liabilities of healthcare givers in cases covered under the act. Living wills under the act are labeled "Declaration Relating to the Use of Life-Sustaining Treatment."

In *Cruzan v. Director, Missouri Dept. of Health,* 497 U.S. 261 (1990), the Supreme Court issued a decision on the right to be removed from life support systems. That right must be preserved by the individual in advance and is not a decision that can be made by others for the individual. Most states are now responding to that decision with the passage of laws that offer the procedures for establishing that right.

http://

For more detailed information, visit: **http://www.uslivingwill registry.com**.

http://

Additional details on living trusts is available at: **http://www.aarp.org/ confacts/money/ wills-trusts.html**.

Living Trusts

One of the more popular property transfer forms over the past five years is the **living trust.** The living trust is a revocable trust established during the testator's life. It can be revoked at any time and the testator still retains control of the trust assets. However, upon the testator's death, the trust property passes according to the provisions of the trust and probate is avoided.

These trusts must be executed formally and can involve large amounts of paperwork for compliance with the tax laws. While touted as a tax-avoidance

Practical Tip

The living trust is a tricky legal device that requires thought, planning, and work. The creation of a living trust should be done cautiously, methodically, and with a full understanding of the laws that apply.

device, there is nothing accomplished with a living trust that cannot be done through a will and the use of joint tenancy ownership (see Chapter 10).

Revocation of Wills

A will can be revoked in several different ways: (1) by physical destruction of the document, (2) by execution of a subsequent document, or (3) by operation of law.

REVOCATION BY PHYSICAL DESTRUCTION

Revocation can be accomplished by some act of mutilation or destruction of the will document by either the testator or by someone acting on behalf of the testator and at the testator's request. In addition to the physical destruction of the document, the testator must have accompanying intent to destroy the will. The degree of destruction and the permissibility of partial destruction varies according to state law. For example, some states recognize the crossing out of portions of a will as a revocation of those portions of the will, whereas other states treat such an act as a destruction of the entire will.

The types of acts sufficient for physical destruction include cutting, tearing, burning, and writing *void* or *canceled* across the will. If there are copies of the will, some states provide that the destruction of one of the copies constitutes revocation of the will, while other states require the destruction of the original.

Consider 17.9

Charles Uhl executed a will in 1946, and upon his death it was found in his safe-deposit box. The will contained several interlineations and markings made by Uhl in colored pencil, including a notation in the left-hand margin of the first page that stated, "Revise whole mess."

Uhl's sister visited him while he was alive and they found the will. His sister told him the will would not be valid and Uhl replied, "The will is still good and is good anywhere. Oh, nuts! I am going to make a new one. I will get it done. Don't worry about it."

When the will was offered for probate, the sister objected because her share was small and she contended the will had been revoked. What was the result? *In re Estate of Uhl,* 81 Cal. Rptr. 436 (1969)

REVOCATION BY EXECUTION OF A SUBSEQUENT DOCUMENT

A will can be revoked by the subsequent execution of any of several instruments. A second will serves to revoke a prior will. An addition to a will (called a **codicil**), which may contain provisions inconsistent with the original will, also serves to revoke certain portions of the will. And a subsequent contract or agreement that so provides also serves to revoke a will. Revocation by a subsequent document is valid only if the subsequent document is executed with the same formalities required for the execution of the original will.

Generally, a subsequent will contains a clause that provides that the testator "hereby revokes any prior wills and codicils." However, such a clause need not be present for the subsequent will to serve as a revocation of the preceding will. The will that is latest in time of execution serves to revoke prior wills.

In jurisdictions that recognize holographic wills, a holographic will or codicil can serve to revoke a prior formally executed will so long as the holographic instrument complies with all validity requirements.

REVOCATION BY OPERATION OF LAW

Most states have provisions that require the revocation or partial revocation of a will when the familial circumstances of the testator change between the time of the will's execution and the testator's death. For example, many states provide that divorce automatically serves to revoke a will at least with regard to property left to the former spouse. In other states, marriage after the execution of the will entitles the new spouse to at least an intestate share of the property.

Perhaps one of the most common partial revocations of wills occurs when testators have children after execution of the will but before death, so that such children are not provided for under the provisions of the will. Children born or adopted after will execution are called **pretermitted** children. Many states provide that these children are entitled to receive the amount they would have received through intestate succession.

PROBATE

Purpose of Probate

Probate is the name given to encompass all legal proceedings required to accomplish the passing of title of the decedent's property to those for whom it was intended. Probate involves determination of the existence of a valid will and defenses to the will, the existence of heirs if no will exists, the proper construction of the will, the collection of the decedent's assets, the payment of debts, and the distribution of the estate. The procedures and the terminology for the procedures vary from state to state, but the basic processes discussed in the following sections apply to all states.

Appointment of Party to Administer Probate

In every state, some party or parties will be appointed to carry out all administrative details involved in probating an estate. If the decedent died intestate, the party is often called an **administrator** or **administratix.** If the decedent died testate, the party is often called an **executor** or **executrix.** Under the UPC, the party is called a **personal representative** regardless of whether the decedent died testate or intestate.

No matter which name is given to the administrative party, his or her role is the same: carrying out all transfers, payments, and distributions involved in the probate of the estate. In many cases, because these parties are responsible for substantial sums and valuable property, they will be required to post a bond for the period of the estate's administration. Under the UPC and in most states, the bond requirement can be waived in the testator's will or by statute, particularly in cases where the sole beneficiary will act as the personal representative. Waiving the bond can mean a substantial savings in the cost of administering the estate.

The party appointed to this position varies. If the decedent died testate, the party named in the will is appointed personal representative. If the party appointed in the will is unable to serve or if the decedent died intestate, the court is required to appoint a party. Most states have statutes specifying who qualifies as a personal representative and the order of preference for appointment. For example, in many states the surviving spouse has first priority for appointment.

Application for or Opening of Probate

Probate proceedings are opened by the filing of an application or petition with the appropriate court, which is generally the probate division or probate court located in the area of the decedent's domicile. However, other courts may have jurisdiction. For example, if the decedent owned property in a second jurisdiction, the probate court in that area would also be entitled to receive an application or petition for probate. In the case of an estate located in multiple jurisdictions, one probate court will serve as the court for hearings, petitions, and so on, and the other courts will then recognize those proceedings as dispositive with regard to the property distribution and will carry out that court's orders.

Parties who may apply or petition for the opening of probate include heirs, devisees, persons entitled to appointment as personal representatives, and creditors. Basically, any party with an interest in the estate may apply or petition for the estate to be opened.

The application or petition will include a filing of the document alleged to be the will if the decedent died testate. It will either seek to have the will admitted to probate or to have the determination made that the decedent died intestate. The applicant or petitioner is required to serve notice upon potential heirs and interested parties that application has been filed, and the notice includes a hearing date. Because the purpose of the hearing is to determine the validity of the will, any persons wishing to challenge its admission to probate must prepare to present evidence at the hearing. Many of the cases in this chapter involved appeals from hearings wherein a will was found to be valid or invalid.

Collection of Assets

Once the will is admitted to probate or the finding of intestacy has been made, it becomes the job of the personal representative to collect the assets of the estate. Most states and the UPC require the personal representative to file an inventory with the court within a certain period after appointment. The inventory is also sent to heirs and devisees, and its purpose is to fully disclose the extent of the estate and to serve as a beginning reference point for the accounting of the personal representative. It is the responsibility of the personal representative to collect all debts due to the estate and to make sure that all property to which the decedent held title is obtained.

Determination and Payment of Debts

In addition to collecting and reporting assets, it is the responsibility of the personal representative to determine what valid debts exist and should be paid. Most states require the publication of a notice of probate in a public newspaper to alert creditors of their need to file a claim with the estate. For example, under the UPC, the personal representative is required to publish notice of the opening of probate once a week for three weeks in a newspaper of general circulation. Creditors then have four months from the time of first publication to file a claim with the estate or have their claim forever barred from collection.

Once the personal representative receives a creditor's claim, the decision is made to allow and pay the claim or to disallow it. If a claim is disallowed, the creditor always has the opportunity to bring suit against the estate for the purpose of having a judicial determination on the validity of the claim.

Distribution of Estate

Whether the decedent died testate or intestate, the determination must be made as to who will be entitled to what portions of the estate after creditors' claims, taxes, and administrative expenses have been paid.

In the case of intestacy, the court will hold a hearing or trial for the adjudication of heirs. In the case of a testate estate, the court may still be required to construe the provisions of an ambiguous will, and a hearing or trial will be required for that interpretation. In interpreting a will, the court's primary rule is to follow the intent of the testator. If such intent is not clear from the words in the document itself, extrinsic evidence may be used to clarify the intentions of the testator. In determining intent on specific provisions, the court will examine the overall purpose and intent conveyed by the testator in the will as an entire document.

After the determination of heirs and the interpretation of the will, the property will be distributed to the appropriate parties. Different terms are used to describe the types of gifts given to heirs of the decedent. A gift of real property is called a **devise** and the recipient a **devisee;** a gift of money is called a **legacy** and the recipient a **legatee;** a gift of personal property is called a **bequest** (general term that includes legacies).

Occasionally, certain circumstances arise that make the distribution of gifts impossible. For example, a testator may have left a specific item of property or a legacy to an heir who has predeceased the testator. In the absence of the testator's provision or a state statute that permits such a gift to go to the heirs of the predeceased recipient, the gift will **lapse,** become part of the residuary estate, and revert to those who are entitled to that portion of the estate. If there is no clause devising the residuary estate, the specific gift would be distributed according to the laws of intestacy.

Also, there are times when a testator has left a specific item of property to an heir; and although the heir is still in existence, the property is not. For example, a testator may have left a "1986 Honda Accord to my nephew Ralph." If the testator does not own the Honda Accord at death, the gift adeems or fails completely. This doctrine of **ademption** will apply regardless of the intention of the testator.

Closing of Probate

Once all of the preceding steps have been accomplished, the personal representative may proceed to close the estate. The closing of the estate may require a hearing or may be accomplished, as under the UPC, by the informal filing of a closing inventory and accounting. Once the proper procedures have been complied with and the required hearings held, the estate is closed and cannot be reopened for the purposes of relitigating creditors' and heirs' claims. The closing of the estate thus operates as an estoppel for future actions in the absence of any fraud or wrongdoing in the administration of the estate, and assuming proper compliance with all procedural requirements.

Estate Tax Implications

The transfer of property from the decedent to the heirs may involve the payment of taxes on the parts of the estate and the heirs. Several types of taxes may be involved in the passage of title to property through probate. First is the possible estate tax at both the federal and state levels. Before a tax may be imposed upon an estate at either level, the estate must have a certain minimum value.

The amount of tax due on an estate subject to taxation is computed according to tables provided by the federal government, and certain deductions are allowed before the taxable value is actually determined. For example, at the federal level, a marital deduction is given for a probate transfer of property between spouses for the entire amount of the estate. For eight years following 1997, the federal exemption from estate taxes will increase from $600,000 to $1,000,000.[3] Estates valued below the federal maximum are not required to pay federal estate taxes. In addition, there are larger exemptions for family-owned businesses when the death of one of the principals in that business occurs. There are also estate and inheritance taxes at the state level.

In addition to a tax on the estate, an inheritance tax may also be imposed on the heirs. Inheritance tax is computed as a certain percentage of the amount received by the heir. It should be noted that the inheritance tax is not an obligation of the estate but of the heir.

The time limitation for filing a federal estate tax return is nine months, which can be extended upon an estimation of no tax or a payment of the amount estimated to be due.

CAUTIONS AND CONCLUSIONS

There are two ways to die: intestate and testate. If you die intestate, there are laws in each state to provide for the distribution of your estate. Those laws can be complex and may not distribute your property according to your desires. The other way to die, testate, is preferred. The execution of a will not only assures that your property is distributed the way you would like to see it distributed, it can save time and money in the administration of your estate.

A will should be executed with witnesses and at a time when those witnesses can verify that the will is done voluntarily and with a clear enough presence of mind to understand what property is being given away in the will and who the beneficiaries are.

When executing codicils or new wills, use great caution to be certain that the right will and your correct intentions are carried out by the valid document.

Key Terms

Uniform Probate Code (UPC), 436
intestate, 436
intestate succession, 437
escheat, 438
laughing heir statutes, 438
per capita, 438

per stirpes, 438
posthumous or afterborn heir, 440
advancements, 443
Uniform Simultaneous Death Act
    (USDA), 443
will, 443

nuncupative will, 444
holographic will, 444
joint will, 445
mutual will, 445
testamentary capacity, 446
self-proving will, 449

---

3.   The issue of estate tax has become a political one with a strong movement for elimination of the so-called "death tax." Currently, the phase in is as follows: 2001: $675,000; 2002–2003: $700,000; 2004: $850,000; 2005: $950,000; 2006: $1,000,000.

Chapter Problems

1. On August 9, 1983, Mr. Emmett King was taken to the emergency room at Halifax Memorial Hospital with a leaking abdominal aneurysm. He was in extreme pain and suffering from shock from the loss of blood. He was given considerable pain medication including meperidine (Demerol), morphine, and diazepam (Valium). Meperidine and morphine both may decrease mental awareness.

He was placed on a respirator with an intratracheal tube and taken to intensive care. At about 1 P.M., Delores King, one of King's daughters, visited him with Jeff Crowder, King's grandson. Jeff went to the waiting area and asked Patsy West and Rhoda Joyner to come and witness a codicil that King was executing. When they arrived, Delores read the codicil to King and asked him if he understood that he was giving Jeff his business and the real property on which it was located. King nodded that he did. Delores helped guide King's hand across the document for a signature. Patsy and Rhoda signed as witnesses. The witnesses indicated Mr. King was aware of them and what was happening. The codicil was executed at 1 P.M., and King died at 2:15 P.M.. Dr. Richard Frazier, King's doctor, said that King was in a semicoma during most of the morning and had been sedated. Dr. Frazier believed that King would have been incapable of knowingly executing the document.

Prior to the execution of the codicil, King's wife, children, and grandchildren received his estate. With the codicil, Jeff got most of it. The trial court found the will and codicil to be valid, and Thomas King, a son, appealed. Is the will/codicil valid? Discuss all issues. *In the Matter of the Will of Emmett J. King*, 342 S.E.2d 394 (N.C. 1986)

2. In 1984, Alexander Tolin executed a will under which the residue of his estate was to be devised to his friend Adair Creaig. The will was prepared by Steven Fine, Tolin's attorney, and executed in Fine's office. The original will was retained by Fine, and a blue-backed photocopy was given to Tolin. In 1989, Tolin executed a codicil to the will that changed the residuary beneficiary from Creaig to Broward Art Guild, Inc. The codicil was also prepared by Fine, who retained the original and gave Tolin a blue-backed photocopy of the original executed codicil. Tolin died in 1990. Six months before his death, he told his neighbor, Ed Weinstein, who was a retired attorney, that he made a mistake and wished to revoke the codicil and reinstate Creaig as the residuary beneficiary. Weinstein told Tolin he could do this by tearing up the original codicil. Tolin handed Weinstein a blue-backed document that Tolin said was the original codicil. Weinstein looked at the document—it appeared to him to be the original—and gave it back to Tolin. Tolin then tore up and destroyed the document with the intent and for the purpose of revocation. Some time after Tolin's death, Weinstein spoke with Fine and found out for the first time that the original will and codicil had been held by Fine. Tolin had torn up the blue-backed copy that had been given to Tolin at the time of execution. The document that Tolin tore up was an exact photocopy of the will. Tolin's personal representative petitioned the court to have the will and codicil admitted to probate. Creaig filed a petition to determine if there had been a revocation of the codicil. Had there been a revocation of the will? *In Re Estate of Tolin*, 622 So. 2d 988 (Fla. Dist. Ct. App. 1993)

3. The heirs of Vern V. Walls filed a will contest alleging that the last will and testament of Vern V. Walls was the result of undue influence by Cyril DeClercq (brother of Kathryn Walls, Vern's predeceased wife) and Floyd DeClerq (nephew of Kathryn).

Vern V. Walls died on March 31, 1986, at the age of 79. Kathryn had died two months earlier after a long illness. Walls and Kathryn had one child who had predeceased them at age 14. Walls was survived by several brothers and sisters. Cyril is Kathryn's brother. Prior to Kathryn's death, Vern's and Kathryn's wills provided that on the death of the survivor, their estate would be divided equally between the Walls heirs and the DeClercq heirs. On March 15, 1986, Vern, then in the hospital for emphysema, executed a new will that directed the bulk of Vern's estate, valued at approximately $300,000, be given to the DeClercq heirs. Only $34,000 in cash bequests were given to the Walls heirs. Harold Tenney, the original lawyer for the 1985 wills, testified that he represented Vern on a roof problem subsequent to the will execution but that their relationship terminated over the roof problem. Donald G. Baird, Cyril's lawyer, drew up the new will as well as a power of attorney from Vern to Cyril. He was contacted by Cyril to handle these matters for Vern. Is there undue influence? *In the Matter of the Estate of Walls,* 561 N.E.2d 344 (Ill. 1990)

4.   William and Margaret Pearl Phillips, husband and wife, executed a joint will for the disposition of their property. The will contained the following clause:

> *It is the intention of the testators that the surviving testator shall have the right by codicil to change the bequests of equal division referred to said testator's heirs, but may not change the bequests to the heirs of the first deceased testator.*

William died first. Margaret drafted a codicil that changed the distribution of the property to William's heirs. Upon her death, William's heirs challenged the admission of the will to probate on the grounds that the codicil violated a joint contract to make a will. What is the result? *In re Estate of Philips,* 195 N.W.2d 486 (Wis. 1972).

5.   D. W. Elmer died testate, and a provision in his will was as follows: "THIRD: I make no provision for my brothers, Jake N. Elmer, Henry Elmer, nor for my sisters, Lena Elmer, Rachel Martell, and Marie Brown, all of whom are financially so fixed that they can well live without any benefits from my estate."

Unfortunately, D. W. did not dispose of all of his property under the provisions of the will. To whom will the property be given? *In re Estate of Elmer,* 210 N.W.2d 815 (N.D. 1973).

6.   On February 13, 1956, Philip Bogner made his last will and testament. One portion of the will gave a one-half interest in some real and personal property to his daughter Helen Bogner Falgren and her husband, Curtis Falgren. At the time of the execution of the will, Helen and Curtis were married and had eight children. From 1946 to 1956, Curtis was employed by Philip and received a salary of $5,800 as well as a furnished home.

In 1956, the Falgrens moved to Oregon to run a poultry ranch that had been purchased using a loan on an insurance policy Philip had purchased for Helen. Philip repaid that loan when it became evident the Fallgrens would not. Sometime thereafter, a physician and Helen told Philip that Curtis had been involved in depraved moral conduct including incestuous relationships with one of his daughters and that such activity had continued for a number of years.

Helen obtained a divorce from Curtis in 1965 on the grounds of infidelity and returned home to North Dakota with her children to live with her father. Bogner told several people including a family counselor, his sister, and one of his employees that he was going to disinherit his son-in-law. Bogner died on September 3, 1968, and portions of his will read as follows:

THIRD: To my daughter, Helen Bogner Falgren and her husband Curtis Falgren, *or to the survivor of them . . .*

SIXTH: I appoint my daughter, Helen Bogner Falgren, to be my Executrix under this Will, and if she fails or ceases to act, I appoint Curtis Falgren Sr., husband *of my daughter, Helen Bogner Falgren, to be the Executor and successor Trustee of the trust hereinabove provided. If my daughter does not survive me, or dies before a grandchild of mine attains the age of 21 years, without having appointed a guardian of the persons and estates of my grandchildren, I appoint Curtis Falgren, Sr. to be guardian of the persons of such grandchildren and their estates. (Emphasis added.)*

Lines had been forcefully drawn through the emphasized words. The obliterations did not exist at the time the will was originally executed. Has there been an effective revocation? *In re Estate of Bogner,* 184 N.W.2d 718 (N.D. 1971)

7.   Andrew, age 60, made a formal, typed will leaving all of his property to his wife, Wilma. The will was valid in all respects; however, only one witness had signed it. Steven, Andrew's son, claimed this will was void due to insufficient witnesses. Is Steven correct? why or why not?

8.   Tom is in the hospital and is dying, having suffered a stroke that has left him partially paralyzed. Tom's will has been prepared for him (he is of sound mind), but Tom cannot control the movement of his hand to sign or make a mark on the will. Tom's wife guides his hand over the paper, making an X. Is the will valid?

9.   Wilma has passed away intestate and is survived by the following relatives: her mother, Catherine; her sister, Chris; her granddaughter, Elizabeth (daughter of Wilma's deceased daughter Jill); a grandson, Joe (son of Wilma's living daughter Buddy); daughter Buddy; and a single daughter, Diane. Who is entitled to Wilma's estate?

10.   Frances Malnar, a widow, was 74 and suffering from advanced liver disease. Frances had no children but had a sister in Yugoslavia and several nieces and nephews who were the children of her two brothers who had predeceased her. Frances was on good terms with her nieces and nephews, corresponded with them throughout the year, and had visits from them on occasion.

Frances could speak very little English and could write only her name. Her native language was Croatian.

In July 1971, Frances executed a will that left most of her property to her nieces and nephews and a $100 gift to a Catholic church. One of her nephews was named executor of the will.

Frances had severe health problems and was hospitalized several times for gastrointestinal bleeding. When she returned home from hospital stays, she was helpless and was assisted by Genevieve Malnar with groceries, trips to her doctor, and other routine daily activities.

On June 18, 1973, Frances was hospitalized for liver failure and remained hospitalized or in a nursing home until her death. During this period, she was visited frequently by Mary Mishka. On July 30, 1973, Genevieve brought her mother's attorney to Frances in the nursing home for the purpose of drafting a will. Frances had used a different attorney for her original will and for Genevieve's power of attorney and did not know the attorney Genevieve brought to the home. With the attorney present, Genevieve and Frances spoke in Croatian about the disposition of Frances's property. Genevieve then told the attorney that the entire estate was to go to her. The attorney did not speak Croatian. The attorney drafted the will, and Genevieve arranged for the execution and helped prop up Frances so that she could sign an *X* to the will.

Upon Frances's death, Genevieve petitioned to have the will admitted to probate. The nieces and nephews presented the original will and challenged the second will on the grounds of undue influence. The trial court found undue influence and refused to admit the second will to probate, and Genevieve appealed. Was there undue influence? *In re Estate of Malnar,* 243 N.W.2d 435 (Wis. 1976)

Internet Activities

1. For the statutory text on state adoptions of the Uniform Probate Code, go to: **http://www.law.cornell.edu/uniform/probate.html**.

2. For the statutory text on state adoptions of the Uniform Rights of the Terminally Ill Act, go to: **http://www.law.cornell.edu/uniform/vol9.html#teril**.

3. Visit a consumer information page on wills at: **http://www.itslegal.com/infonet/wills/Estate1.htm**.

4. Visit the following sites for more on living wills and estate and probate issues:
http://www.uslivingwillregistry.com/
http://www.mindspring.com/~scottr/will.html
http://www.ca-probate.com
http://www.law.cornell.edu/topics/estate_gift_tax.html
Canada: **http://www.sentex.net/~lwr/**
U.K.: **http://www.euthanasia.org/lwpdf.html**

Chapter 18
Zoning

Property is in its nature timid and seeks protection, and nothing is more gratifying to government than becoming a protector.

John C. Calhoun   March 21, 1834

Local governmental bodies may pass laws to control the use of land within their jurisdiction. These laws are grouped into one term describing their regulatory effect: **zoning.** The zoning on a piece of property can affect its value, price, and marketability. Knowing and understanding the zoning on a piece of property is a preliminary inquiry for any buyer. In this chapter, the following questions are answered: What is zoning? What types of zoning exist? What terms are used in zoning and zoning procedures? Are all forms of zoning constitutional? Is it possible to change or make exceptions?

PURPOSES

Each community is divided into areas, districts, or zones in which certain types of activities are permitted and others prohibited according to their classification. Zoning may control items such as the height of buildings or whether apartments as opposed to single-family dwellings may be constructed. In some cases, zoning prohibits construction of buildings altogether, such as when construction of homes on a mountain side is prohibited. Zoning has been used in many cities as a method of controlling community development. A **general** or **master plan** for the community is created, and then zoning ordinances are passed according to the plan, so that the community develops in an orderly fashion and the problems and nuisances that result from residential areas being too close to factories are effectively precluded.

Zoning laws are for the most part ordinances passed by a local governmental entity such as a city or town. These entities act under an enabling statute that is general in character. In most cases, the enabling statute is based on the **Standard State Zoning Enabling Act,** which was drafted by the United States Department of Commerce in the 1920s. This act authorizes the local governmental entities to pass zoning laws that "lessen congestion . . . promote safety . . . prevent over-crowding . . . avoid undue concentration of population . . . and promote health and general welfare."

AUTHORITY

The purposes of the final authorization to "promote health and general welfare" are to grant broad authority to local government and also to establish the source of that authority. The source of authority for zoning laws is found in the police power clause of the United States Constitution, which provides that governments exist for the promotion of the health, safety, morals, and general welfare of people and that governmental bodies may promote these goals through regulation of the individual citizens. Zoning laws passed for the general welfare purpose fit within this constitutional framework.

Restrictions on the exercise of police power are that the zoning laws passed must, in fact, serve some public health, safety, or morals interest, and that zoning laws cannot be arbitrary or discriminatory. (These issues are discussed later in the "Methods" section.) Another constitutional issue raised when zoning ordinances were first enacted was whether restrictions on use constituted a taking without due process of law as required under the Fourteenth Amendment (see Chapter 19). Zoning laws must serve some legitimate public purpose and not take the form of preference as opposed to regulatory necessity.

In the *Village of Euclid, Ohio v. Ambler Realty Co.*, 272 U.S. 365 (1926), the United States Supreme Court has recognized that zoning is constitutional in general, that the zoning process is permissible under the exercise of police power, and that resulting decreases in land values do not constitute a taking of property requiring compensation (see p. 478). Although it is possible that zoning ordinances as applied to particular tracts of land within a city may be unconstitutional, such determinations must be made on a case-by-case basis.

METHODS

Once a governmental entity has been given authority to enact zoning ordinances, that authority may be used in many different ways and with many different combinations of restrictions. Generally, the governmental body begins, pursuant to the Standard State Zoning Enabling Act, with a master plan in which it divides the geographical area into an appropriate number of districts with varying shapes that will help carry out the purposes of traffic control, safety, and so on. Once these

http://

The city of Cincinnati Municipal Codes can be found at: **http://www. rcc.org/muncode.html**.

districts are decided upon, the governing body may then proceed to pass ordinances for each district. Similar situations must be treated uniformly; for example, all zoning districts must be subject to the same rules and regulations. The following sections address the types of rules and regulations a governmental body might choose in setting up its zoning structure.

Use Restrictions

Generally, land use is regulated by zoning ordinances. Uses can usually be classified into four categories: residential, commercial or business, industrial, and agricultural. A city may divide these categories into several subcategories, as when residential is divided into R-1 for single-family dwellings, R-2 for duplex houses, and R-3 for apartments, mobile homes, or similar structures. Industrial districts may be classified according to the nature of the industry with respect to noise, waste, activity, danger, odor, and so on. When various degrees of each category are established, the number 1 is usually associated with the most restrictive land use as in the example of R-1, which includes generally only single-family dwellings.

Zoning classifications may be cumulative or noncumulative. In a **cumulative classification,** the lesser restricted areas allow all of the activities permitted in more restrictive areas. If cumulative zoning existed in the R-1 example above, then R-2 districts would allow single-family dwellings to be included along with R-2 duplex houses, and R-3 districts would allow single-family dwellings and duplex houses, along with R-3 apartments, and mobile homes.

Cumulative zoning also permits high-ranked activities in low-ranked districts. Classifications are ranked as follows:

1. Residential, single family
2. Residential, multiple family
3. Residential, apartment
4. Commercial, office
5. Commercial, business
6. Industrial

For example, an area zoned commercial could have residential uses within it under cumulative zoning. However, the reverse does not apply and no industrial or commercial activity would be permitted in residential areas.

In a **noncumulative classification,** only the activities specified by the applicable zone are permitted. For example, in R-2 areas, there would be no single-family dwellings. Also, if an area is zoned industrial or commercial, there cannot be residences in these areas under a noncumulative system. Noncumulative zoning serves to prevent nuisance actions by prohibiting the existence of homes and apartments in industrial areas.

In developing their zoning systems, local governments are restricted only by the constitutional restraint of legitimate purpose and reason for the exercise of their police power. One of the issues that has been raised repeatedly in challenging the validity of zoning ordinances is whether zones limited to single-family dwellings can be permitted, with the effect of eliminating other, less costly forms of housing and thus precluding a portion of the population from residing in certain areas.

In the following case, a court was faced with determining the validity of a zoning law that controlled strictly the location of mobile homes.

Petition of Carpenter

699 So.2d 928 (Miss. 1997)

Facts

Stanley Carpenter owns a 92-acre parcel of land in a rural area of Petal, Mississippi. Mr. Carpenter wanted to put a mobile home on a small area of the property located near the road and protected from view by mature trees. Mr. Carpenter would then have his son living there.

Mr. Carpenter's property is located in an RF District, a zoning classification that permits agriculture, farming, forestry, livestock production, nurseries, truck gardens, public or commercial stables and kennels, poultry, livestock and small animal raising; single-family dwellings, two-family dwellings, and accessory uses including home occupations and signs.

Ordinance 1979 (42-A-70) prohibited placement of mobile home units outside of approved mobile home parks:

> The purpose of this Section is for the establishment of areas within Petal, Mississippi, for the development and expansion of mobile home parks. These mobile home parks shall be developed and located so as to provide safe and sanitary living conditions for the occupants and to be convenient to employment, shopping centers, schools and other community facilities, and to prohibit Single Mobile Home Units from being used and utilized within the City Limits unless placement is in an approved Mobile Home Park, as described in this ordinance.

The Board of Aldermen unanimously denied Mr. Carpenter's position. Mr. Carpenter appealed and the circuit court affirmed the Aldermen's decision. Mr. Carpenter appealed.

Judicial Decision

McRae, Justice. Carpenter next asserts that Ordinance (42–A [*sic*] 70) constitutes impermissible exclusionary zoning because it limits the placement of mobile homes to designated mobile home parks, thus prohibiting an individual from locating a mobile home on land he owns and requiring him, instead, to pay rent to the owner of a mobile home park. He further contends that the ordinance, as drafted, bears no reasonable relationship to any legitimate governmental interest. The City of Petal counters that the ordinance is a valid exercise of its police power intended to protect property values in surrounding residential areas.

This Court has held that "[t]he classification of property for zoning purposes is a legislative rather than a judi-

cial matter." *Faircloth v. Lyles*, 592 So.2d 941, 943 (Miss. 1991); *W.L. Holcomb, Inc. v. City of Clarksdale*, 217 Miss. 892, 900, 65 So.2d 281, 284 (1953). Thus, zoning decisions will not be set aside unless clearly shown to be arbitrary, capricious, discriminatory, illegal or without a substantial evidentiary basis. *Faircloth*, 592 So.2d at 943; *Barnes v. Board of Supervisor, DeSoto County,* 553 So.2d 508, 510 (Miss. 1989).

The same standards apply when the constitutionality of a zoning ordinance is challenged. The issue then is whether the ordinance is a valid exercise of the police power, defined as "'that power required to be exercised in order to effectively discharge, within the scope of constitutional limitations, its paramount obligation to promote and protect the health, safety, morals, comfort and general welfare of the people.'"

The Board's assertion that restriction of mobile homes and modular housing to mobile home parks is necessary to protect property values in surrounding residential areas rings hollow. Were individual mobile homes and/or other forms of manufactured housing prohibited only in R-1 and R-2 residential districts, it would, at least, be fairly debatable whether the ordinance, as drafted, was necessary to meet its intended purposes. Prohibiting individual mobile home or even modular home sites in *any* area other than designated mobile home parks, however, bears no relationship to the goal of preserving surrounding residential property values. In the Rural Fringe District, where Carpenter's property is located, permitted land uses include agriculture, farming, forestry and livestock production; nurseries and truck gardens; public or commercial stables and kennels; poultry, livestock and small animal raising; single-family dwellings; two-family dwellings; and accessory uses including signs and incidental home occupations. As the Mississippi Manufactured Housing Association points out,

> In the Rural Fringe District, Petal will allow commercial stables, dog runs, pigpens and chicken yards within 100 feet of a property line, but have [*sic*] refused to allow Mr. Carpenter to locate his manufactured home 550 feet from the street on a 100 by 200 foot tract in the middle of his 92 acres.

* * * * * *

The City of Petal's ordinance, allowing varied poultry, livestock, agricultural and forestry uses but disallowing manufactured housing, cannot be based on aesthetic concerns. There is no requirement for any screening of old forestry equipment such as scooters, worn out tractors or other agricultural equipment, or even pig pens or dog runs.

Further, we fail to see how a blanket prohibition against mobile homes and manufactured housing on individual sites in any zoning district in the City relates to Section 6.111 of the ordinance's stated purpose of developing and locating mobile home parks "so as to provide safe and sanitary living conditions for the occupants and to be convenient to employment, shopping centers, schools and other community facilities." The provision is more restrictive than what is reasonably necessary to meet the purposes stated in Article 2 of the Ordinance.

The Board's assertion that the ordinance is not unreasonable or unduly oppressive because Carpenter could always obtain a permit to establish a mobile home park on his property likewise is without merit. Section 6.112 enumerates the requirements for developing a mobile home park. So stringent are the requirements for a mobile home park that the Board's premise is tantamount to declaring that it is not unduly burdensome to restrict an individual from building a free-standing store on his property, because he's allowed to build a mall or strip shopping center there as long as he provides adequate parking, restaurant and restroom facilities.

Carpenter further asserts that the ordinance constitutes an equal protection violation because it discriminates against "that certain class of persons unable to afford conventional housing and that certain class of persons, who, due to economic status, desire to own land and place thereon affordable housing." Aside from authority supporting his general proposition that no person or class of persons shall be denied equal protection of the law, Carpenter provides neither authority nor evidence to support his argument that the ordinance in question discriminates against a particular class of people. We, therefore, do not consider the argument raised.

Reversed.

Case Questions

1. What did the ordinance in question provide and what did Mr. Carpenter want?
2. Did the Board of Aldermen have a sufficient basis for the restrictions on mobile homes?
3. Did Mr. Carpenter have adequate alternatives?
4. Is the ordinance valid?

Consider 18.1

The town of Chester, New Hampshire, has a zoning ordinance, in effect since 1985, that provides for a single-family home on a two-acre lot, a duplex on a three-acre lot, and excludes multifamily housing from all five zoning districts. Planned residential developments (PRD) would be permitted to have multifamily structures.

Chester consists principally of single-family homes with the majority of its residents commuting to work in Manchester. A bedroom community, Chester, at the time of the case, was projected to have one of the highest growth rates in New Hampshire.

Raymond Remillard, a resident of Chester who owns 23 acres, tried for 11 years to obtain a permit to construct a multiunit housing complex primarily for low- to moderate-income families. He was unsuccessful until he brought suit challenging the validity of Chester's zoning ordinances. Can he challenge the zoning plan successfully? *Britton v. Town of Chester,* 595 A.2d 492 (N.H. 1991)

Intensity Zoning

Intensity zoning regulates the extent to which an area zoned at a certain level may be put to that level's use. Intensity regulations generally take the following forms:

1. Building-height limitations
2. Setbacks for buildings (minimum distance between the street or sidewalk and the structure)
3. Minimum lot sizes (may be total square feet or minimum length and width)
4. Maximum structures per area (often called *density*—specifies, for example, the number of houses that may be built in an R-1 tract)

5. Floor area ratios (sets a maximum amount of floor area per lot; for example, a 10-to-1 ratio would permit a 10-story building to occupy an entire lot or a 20-story building to occupy half the lot.)

Aesthetic Zoning

The purpose of **aesthetic zoning** is to control or improve the beauty of a city or other area subject to a zoning plan. Zoning that exists purely for aesthetics is not valid in a majority of the states. However, if the alleged aesthetic control can be tied to or coupled with a health or welfare purpose, then the aesthetic control is valid. More and more, courts are recognizing the public interest in aesthetic controls and upholding their validity. For example, an aesthetic zoning ordinance may prohibit the construction of homes on the side of a mountain to prevent the beauty of the

> **Practical Tip**
>
> Know not only the zoning ordinances but the community philosophy. That philosophy affects the composition of zoning boards and their decisions. Often what is unwritten is as important in understanding the development of a community as the written zoning plan itself.

mountain from being destroyed. However, if it can be established that there is too much risk in constructing homes on the mountainside because of possible slides that would not only destroy the homes but could injure others at the foot of the mountain and require city safety and rescue equipment, then the ordinance is more of an exercise of police power for safety reasons than an aesthetic control.

Aesthetic zoning has been used to preserve historical towns and portions of cities by controlling the type of architecture, its repair, and alteration. These types of zoning ordinances have been held valid because they preserve not only historical areas but also the tourist business for the localities.

The following case deals with an issue of zoning aesthetics.

Houghtaling
v. City of Medina Board of Zoning Appeals

731 N.E.2d 733 (Ohio App. 1999)

Facts

The Houghtalings are the owners of a travel business known as "Pleasure Cruises." Pleasure Cruises is operated out of the Houghtalings' home on East Liberty Street in Medina, Ohio. Mr. Houghtaling had installed a metal replica of an anchor on the lawn of their home in 1997. The anchor is seven and one-half feet in height and the crossbar is six feet long. Two lights were added to the ends of the crossbar a few months later.

In May 1997, the Medina City Planning Director, Richard Grice, sent a letter asking the Houghtalings to remove the anchor. The letter stated that the anchor violated City Zoning Code 1113.07.

The Houghtalings appealed Grice's decision to the board. The board ordered the sign removed. Lower courts found for the Houghtalings and the board appealed.

Judicial Opinion

Batchelder, Judge. Medina City Zoning Code 1113.07 regulates home occupations in the city of Medina. One of the restrictions on home occupations is that "[n]o sign, advertising the home occupation, will be permitted." Medina City Zoning Code 1113.07(e). The term "sign" is defined in Medina City Zoning Code 1361.03(15).

> "Sign means any structure or natural object such as a tree [*sic*], rock, bush and the ground itself, or part thereof, or device attached thereto or painted or represented thereon, which shall be used to attract attention to any object, product, place, activity, person, institution, organization or business, or which shall display or include any letter, word, banner, flag, pennant, insignia, device

or representation used as, or which is in the nature of an announcement, direction or advertisement. For the purpose of these regulations the word 'sign' does not include the American flag, the insignia of any government, governmental agency or of any charitable organization."

The parties agree that Pleasure Cruises is a "home occupation" within the meaning of the zoning code.

The ultimate issue before this court is whether the anchor violates Medina City Zoning Code 1113.07(e) as a sign that advertises the Houghtalings' home occupation. The matter may be set to rest without deciding whether the anchor meets the definition of "sign" within the meaning of Medina City Zoning Code 1361.03(15). No definition of the term "advertise" appears in the Medina City Zoning Code. Therefore, we will give the term its ordinary and plain meaning. The term has been defined as "[t]o advise, announce, appraise, command, give notice of, inform, made known, publish," or "[t]o call a matter to the public attention by any means whatsoever." Black's Law Dictionary (6 Ed. 1990) 54.

Assuming without deciding that the anchor is a sign, we conclude that the anchor does not advertise the home occupation of the Houghtalings, Pleasure Cruises. The evidence was uncontroverted that there were no markings on the anchor itself that informed the public of the name or telephone number of Pleasure Cruises. There

was much testimony about whether the anchor advertised a business that sold cruise ship vacations. There was testimony that the Houghtalings used the anchor as a reference point for people who came to their home to pick up tickets, by telling the clients to look for the anchor. As one witness aptly noted, the presence of a large anchor in one's lawn indicates some nautical connection. Several witnesses testified that, in their opinion, the anchor advertised Pleasure Cruises, but each of these witnesses had prior knowledge of the existence and nature of the business. However, there is nothing on the face of the anchor or about the anchor itself that declares to the public at large who is without such prior knowledge that a business that sells cruise ship vacations is run out of the Houghtalings' house. The evidence before the common pleas court was uncontradicted in that respect.

Because it does not advertise the Houghtalings' home occupation, Pleasure Cruises, the anchor does not violate Medina City Zoning Code 1113.07(e).

Judgment affirmed.

Case Questions

1. What did the Houghtalings do with their home?
2. Is the anchor a sign?
3. Will the anchor be permitted to stay?

Consider 18.2

Nestled in the Mount Washington Valley, the town of Conway, New Hampshire, historically has been a tourist destination for activities in the White Mountain National Forest. Route 16 links the villages of Conway and North Conway and offers striking views of the mountains and ledges to the west. Substantial commercial development, primarily along this highway, has rendered part of the town a shoppers' Mecca. Hundreds of signs draw tourists in the day and evening hours to the shopping centers, lodging facilities, and restaurants clustered in the villages of Conway and North Conway.

In 1982, the town of Conway passed a zoning ordinance requiring all property owners to obtain a permit from the town zoning officer before erecting a sign. The same zoning ordinance prohibited signs "illuminated from within," but allows signs illuminated by external lights.

Michael Asselin, the owner of Mario's, a restaurant on Route 16, purchased a sign that was illuminated from within and erected it on his property. The town notified Asselin that the sign was in violation of the ordinance. Asselin challenged the authority of Conway to regulate commercial speech (his sign) solely for the purpose of "preserving scenic vistas" and "retaining the character of a country community." Is Conway's restriction of the types of signs for its businesses covered as permissible zoning? *Asselin v. Town of Conway,* 628 A.2d 247 (N.H. 1993)

Exclusionary Zoning ✗

Exclusionary zoning is used to exclude others from the community and prevent increases in population. For such antigrowth ordinances to be invalid, they must be shown to be a permanent block to any use of the land within the locality. Restrictions on the rate of development so that services and governmental organization can grow at an equal rate serve a legitimate public interest and are permissible forms of regulation.

Exclusionary zoning may also be used to prevent certain types of land use. Ordinances passed to eliminate all but single-family dwellings are examples of exclusionary zoning. These exclusionary ordinances are subject to strict judicial scrutiny.

Interim Zoning

It may take a city or town some time to make a study and develop a master plan upon which to base zoning regulations. In the time it takes for such study and planning, developers may enter the community and develop segments so that any plan adopted will be frustrated. To alleviate this problem, cities and towns may adopt **interim** or **hold zoning** to prevent uncontrolled development before a comprehensive plan and ordinances are adopted. The interim zoning may be as simple as a requirement of approval before construction or development begins. This prior approval gives the city or town government discretionary control before permanent zoning takes effect.

Social Issue Zoning

In **social issue zoning,** zoning ordinances are used as a tool in battling social issues. For example, zoning ordinances have been used to disperse adult theaters and bookstores. In *Young v. American Mini Theaters,* 427 U.S. 50 (1976), the United States Supreme Court held that zoning ordinances may classify these types of businesses differently from other movie houses and bookstores for safety purposes, thus upholding the disbursement treatment required by the ordinances at issue in the case. In *City of Renton v. Playtime Theaters, Inc.,* 475 U.S.41 (1986), the United States Supreme Court held that zoning restrictions on adult bookstores are valid under the First Amendment so long as nothing prevents such businesses from locating in other areas of the city. In the following case, a federal appellate court faces the issue of alternative availability.

Lim v. City of Long Beach ✗

217 F.3d 1050 (9th Cir. 2000)

Facts

In 1995, the city of Long Beach passed an ordinance that amended its existing adult entertainment zoning ordinance by prohibiting adult entertainment businesses within 300 feet of a residential zoning district, 1,000 feet of any public or private school, 600 feet of any city park, 500 feet of a church, and 1,000 feet of another adult entertainment business.

Seung Chung Lim and his corporation, Fluffy, Inc., challenged the constitutionality of the newly amended ordinance. He and Fluffy, Inc., own and operate two adult entertainment businesses located within 300 feet of residential districts. The district court found the ordinance to be valid and Mr. Lim appealed.

Judicial Opinion

Michael Daly Hawkins, Circuit Judge. As a threshold matter, we note that it is clear that the burden of proving alternative avenues of communication rests on Long Beach.

The issue before this court—one that is decidedly less clear—is the level of specificity about each particular site Long Beach is required to provide to sustain its burden.

A city allows for alternative avenues of communication if it offers adult businesses a "reasonable opportunity to open and operate . . . within the city . . . ," *Renton,* 475 U.S. at 54, 106 S.Ct. 925. We have applied a two-step approach to determining whether this condition is satisfied: (1) relocation sites provided to adult businesses must be considered part of an actual business real estate market for commercial enterprises generally; and (2) after excluding those sites that may not properly be considered part of the relevant real estate market, there are an adequate number of relocation sites. See *Topanga Press v. City of Los Angeles,* 989 F.2d, 1524, 1529 (9th Cir.1993).

In *Topanga Press,* we noted that "[w]e are left to the simple, yet slippery, test of reasonableness when attempting to discern whether land is or is not part of a market in which any business may compete." We then listed five considerations in making the reasonableness determination: (1) a relocation site is not part of the market if it is "unreasonable to believe that it would ever become available to any commercial enterprise," (2) a relocation site in a manufacturing or industrial zone that is "reasonably accessible to the general public" may also be part of the market; (3) a site in a manufacturing zone that has proper infrastructure may be included in the market; (4) a site must be reasonable for some generic commercial enterprise, although not every particular enterprise, before it can be considered part of the market; and (5) a site that is commercially zoned is part of the relevant market. In addition, a site must obviously satisfy the conditions of the zoning ordinance in question.

Plaintiffs argue that the district court erred in considering sites with restrictive leases banning adult entertainment establishments. Under *Topanga Press,* however, sites must only reasonably become available to some generic commercial enterprise, not specifically to adult businesses. Plaintiffs also argue that the district court improperly considered certain currently occupied property as part of the actual business real estate market. *Topanga Press* stated that the requirement that property potentially become available (the first factor, above) "connotes genuine possibility." Thus, for example, property subject to a long-term lease might not meet the *Topanga Press* test. Plaintiffs contend that under *Topanga Press,* Long Beach should have been required to prove that the currently occupied property would reasonably become available to any commercial enterprise. Long Beach came forward with a list of 115 sites it contended were potentially available. According to the district court opinion, Long Beach provided pertinent, specific and detailed information about each site. Based on this information, the district court found that Long Beach made a good faith and reasonable attempt to prove that it was providing the Plaintiffs with a reasonable opportunity to open and operate.

A city cannot merely point to a random assortment of properties and simply assert that they are reasonably available to adult businesses. The city's duty to demonstrate the availability of properties is defined, at a bare minimum, by reasonableness and good faith. If a plaintiff can show that a city's attempt is not in fact in good faith or reasonable, by, for example, showing that a representative sample of properties are on their face unavailable, then the city will be required to put forth more detailed evidence. But where a city has provided a good faith and reasonable list of potentially available properties, it is for the Plaintiffs to show that, in fact, certain sites would not reasonably become available. There is no reason to conclude that Long Beach acted in bad faith or unreasonably in identifying potentially available properties. The burden of showing that particular sites would not reasonably become available therefore rests with the Plaintiffs.

Once the relevant market has been properly defined in light of any additional evidence presented by Plaintiffs on remand, the district court will have to reexamine whether the market contains a sufficient number of potential relocation sites for Plaintiffs' adult businesses. Because it is unclear how many sites will be part of the relevant market, we cannot determine whether the district court correctly concluded that a sufficient number of sites exist to allow Plaintiffs a reasonable opportunity to open and operate.

Here, there is evidence that Long Beach had a rational reason for enforcing the adult business ordinance and not enforcing other zoning ordinances. Long Beach enforces its adult business ordinance become of its interest in curbing the secondary effects of adult businesses. Long Beach does not have a similar interest in enforcing its other ordinances. As such, the district court did not err in denying Plaintiffs' equal protection claim.

Remanded for further trial on the sufficiency of locations.

Case Questions

1. What does the ordinance restrict?
2. Are there other sites available for adult businesses?
3. Are these sites offered by the city sufficient?
4. What does the appellate court rule must be done?

The city of Tampa passed a zoning ordinance that prohibits the location of an adult business within 500 feet of a residential or office district. The ordinance was passed to revitalize inner-city neighborhoods and was not based on studies of the effects of these businesses on residential neighborhoods. Specialty Malls was denied a permit to operate an exotic dance club in an office district and then filed suit alleging that the ordinance serves no substantial governmental interest. The aldermen of the city maintain that these adult businesses attract transients and were not conducive to a "stable, growing, vibrant neighborhood." Is the zoning ordinance constitutional? *Specialty Malls of Tampa v. City of Tampa,* 916 F.Supp.1222 (M.D. Fal. 1996)

Consider 18.3

The city of Southborough, Massachusetts, passed a zoning ordinance that prohibited the operation of abortion clinics within the town. Framingham Clinic attempted to establish a clinic that would perform first-trimester abortions and challenged the ordinance. Is the regulation permissible? *Framingham Clinic, Inc. v. Board of Selectmen,* 367 N.E.2d 606 (Mass. 1977)

Would it be constitutional for a city to restrict protestors outside abortion clinics? What if the city could establish the protests caused congestion and noise? *Madsen v. Women's Health Center, Inc.,* 512 U.S.753 (1994)

Ethical Issue

One social zoning issue that has emerged over the past few years is the concept of group homes for those with terminal illness or mental or physical disabilities.

The two following cases reflect different views on how requests for such group homes in residential areas are resolved.

State of Nebraska v. Champoux

555 N.W.2d 69 (Ct. App. Neb. 1996)

Facts

On February 7, 1994, a criminal complaint was filed against Steven Champoux alleging that he had unlawfully allowed "more than three unrelated persons to live in a building . . . in violation of the use regulations for the R-2 Residential District." Champoux filed an unsuccessful motion to quash the complaint on the grounds that the zoning ordinance he was charged with violating was unreasonable and arbitrary and in violation of the Due Process Clause of the Constitution. Following a trial on November 17, 1994, Champoux was convicted with the following findings:

Champoux owns and maintains rental property at 1840 Hartley Street in Lincoln. On the date cited in the complaint, January 26, 1994, Champoux was renting the property at issue to five unrelated persons, all of whom lived on the property. This property is one side of a duplex and is located in an "R-2 Residential District," which is zoned for single-family or two-family use. Lincoln Mun.Code § 27.03.220 (1994) defines a family as "[o]ne or more persons immediately related by blood, marriage,

or adoption and living as a single housekeeping unit in a dwelling. . . .A family may include, in addition, not more than two persons who are unrelated for the purpose of this title."

Champoux was fined $25 and appealed.

Judicial Opinion

Irwin, Judge. In passing upon the constitutionality of an ordinance, an appellate court begins with a presumption that the ordinance is valid; consequently, the burden is on the challenger to demonstrate the constitutional defect. To successfully challenge the validity of a zoning ordinance that does not affect a fundamental right or involve a suspect classification, a litigant must prove that the conditions imposed by the city in adopting the ordinance were unreasonable, discriminatory, or arbitrary and that the regulation bears no relationship to the purpose or purposes sought to be accomplished by the ordinance.

The interests set out by the city in support of the ordinance in question are the "sanctity of the family, quiet neighborhoods, low population, few motor vehicles, and low transiency." Champoux argues that although the zoning ordinance was presumably enacted pursuant to legitimate governmental objectives, the city "has provided no evidence that the lack of a biological relationship between the inhabitants of a dwelling increases traffic, parking problems, noise, disturbances, and destroys the character of the single-family neighborhood." As a result, he argues, the city has "failed to show that the ordinance is reasonably related to these objectives." However, as discussed and contrary to Champoux's arguments, Nebraska jurisprudence requires that Champoux demonstrate the constitutional defect in the zoning ordinance.

The U.S. Supreme Court has addressed the constitutionality of a zoning ordinance that defined a family to include any number of related persons or a total of two unrelated persons. The Court held that the ordinance bore a rational relationship to permissible state objectives and, thus, was constitutional. *Village of Belle Terre v. Boraas,* 416 U.S. 1, 94 S.Ct. 1536, 39 L.Ed.2d 797 (1974). The Court reasoned:

> The regimes of boarding houses, fraternity houses, and the like present urban problems. More people occupy a given space; more cars rather continuously pass by; more cars are parked; noise travels with crowds.
>
> A quiet place where yards are wide, people few, and motor vehicles restricted are legitimate guidelines in a land-use project addressed to family needs. This goal is a permissible one. . . . The police power is not confined to elimination of filth, stench, and unhealthy places. It is ample to lay out zones where family values, youth values, and the blessings of quiet seclusion and clear air make the area a sanctuary for people.

Nonetheless, a state may impose higher standards on the basis of state law and may guard individual rights more fervently than the U.S. Supreme Court does under the federal Constitution. The substantive rights provided by the federal Constitution define only a minimum, a floor rather than a ceiling.

Therefore, we must determine whether our state Constitution provides greater due process rights than the U.S. Constitution. This is a matter of first impression in Nebraska. We have reviewed the decisions of other jurisdictions regarding constitutional challenges to zoning ordinances similar to that before us. Our review shows that other jurisdictions are split on this issue.

Jurisdictions that have upheld similar zoning ordinances under their state constitutions generally hold that such ordinances are rationally related to legitimate state interests in that they promote family and youth values

and protect the State's interest in preserving the family and marriage.

In justifying the distinction drawn between related and unrelated living companions, one court stated:

> The transient and separate character of residency by the plaintiffs' tenants is not as likely to stimulate on their part similar concerns about the quality of living in the neighborhood for the long term.
>
> . . . [S]uch occupants . . . are less likely to develop the kind of friendly relationships with neighbors that abound in residential districts occupied by . . . families. . . . [T]hey are not likely to have children who would become playmates of other children living in the area. Neighbors are not so likely to call upon them to . . . perform any of the countless services that families . . . provide to each other as a result of longtime acquaintance and mutual self-interest.

Jurisdictions which have struck down zoning ordinances similar to that before us as violative of the rights encompassed in their state constitutions generally hold that the enactment of such ordinances assumes, without support, that unrelated persons who live together behave differently than traditional families.

When striking down these ordinances, the jurisdictions reason that such ordinances are both over inclusive and under inclusive in that they prohibit a "plethora of uses" that are not contrary to the objectives of such ordinances. According to these jurisdictions, there are less restrictive alternatives available that focus on the size of the dwelling and the number of occupants rather than the relationship of the household members. However, even jurisdictions that have stricken down ordinances similar to that before us acknowledge that a municipality is not

> without authority to regulate the behavior it finds inimical to its concept of a residential neighborhood, including a rational limitation on the numbers of persons that may occupy a dwelling. [A municipality] need not open its residential borders to transients and others whose lifestyle is not the functional equivalent of "family" life. Nor are [municipalities] precluded from distinguishing between the biological family and a functional family when it is rational to do so. . . .

We are not persuaded that Champoux has overcome the ordinance's presumption of validity. In enacting zoning ordinances to provide for the public health, safety, and general welfare, a municipality may consider the quality of living in its community and may attempt to promote values important to the community as a whole. The city's objectives are certainly legitimate. Although the means and ends employed by the city may not be a perfect fit, the zoning ordinance and the city's stated objectives are rationally related. In so concluding, we adopt the reasoning of the Supreme Court in *Village of Belle Terre v. Boraas*, 416 U.S. 1, 94 S.Ct. 1536, 39 L.Ed.2d 797 (1974), and that of other jurisdictions upholding ordinances similar to that before us as discussed above.

We also note that the ordinance's definition of "family" is expansive enough to allow numerous other household relationships in addition to that of a traditional family.

It is said, however, that if [three] unmarried people can constitute a "family," there is no reason why [four or five] may not. But every line drawn by a legislature leaves some out that might well have been included. That exercise of discretion, however, is a legislative, not a judicial, function.

For these reasons, we conclude that the zoning ordinance before us does not violate Champoux's due process rights under the Nebraska Constitution.

Affirmed.

Case Questions

1. With what violation was Champoux charged?
2. What have other states ruled with regard to single-family restrictions?
3. What burden of proof did Champoux have with respect to the zoning restriction?
4. Is the zoning restriction constitutional?
5. Does Champoux's conviction stand?

Contrast the findings in the *Champoux* case with the following case on single-family dwellings.

Eichlin
v. Zoning Hearing Board of New Hope Borough

671 A.2d 1173 (Comm. Ct. Pa. 1996)

Facts

Harry Eichlin (appellant) appealed the decision of a New Hope Borough Zoning & Hearing Board decision to grant a zoning permit to Buck Villa, Inc. (BVI), for use of a single-family dwelling as a group home for eight unrelated HIV-infected persons.

Judicial Opinion

Colins, President Judge. Appellant raises three issues for our consideration: (1) whether the use proposed by the landowner is the functional equivalent of a traditional family, thereby qualifying said use as a family group home; (2) whether a family group home of more than five (5) members is a permitted use only in detached single family dwellings; and, (3) whether the record, including the Board's decision, establishes that the proposed use will be conducted and/or carried on in something other than a detached single-family dwelling.

First, Appellant argues that the use proposed by BVI is not a family group home as contemplated by Section 218(3) of the Ordinance, New Hope Borough Zoning Ordinance No. 1933-2, art. 1 § 1(3), because BVI is only providing housing for individuals infected with the HIV virus and is not creating a family living arrangement that is the functional equivalent of a traditional family. We

note initially that a significant portion of Appellant's argument relative to this issue focuses on the expert testimony of Fred Wicks, Ph.D., a psychologist licensed to practice in the Commonwealth and who concentrates in family practice. However, the opinions offered by Dr. Wicks were rejected by the Zoning Hearing Board in performing its fact-finding function. Our limited scope of review forecloses our investigating that determination; thus, Dr. Wicks's testimony will not be considered anew by this Court on appeal.

Section 218(3) of the Ordinance defines the term "family" to include:

A home for *no more than eight unrelated persons* which is sponsored and operated by a *non-profit group, organization or corporation* for a group of persons to live together in a single communal living arrangement where the residents permanently live together as the *functional equivalent of a traditional family in a non-profit dwelling unit maintaining a non-transient common household with single cooking and dining facilities and sharing a permanent unity of social life*. This shall be referred to as a "family group home". Groups contemplated by this use include, but are not limited to, the handicapped, the elderly, and the disabled, but excludes halfway houses for ex-convicts and for drug or alcohol rehabilitation, or for licensed personal care homes or any other use specifically provided for in this Ordinance. A family group home may have *no more than two residential managers living at the home in addition to the residents.* Residential managers are agents or employees of the agency or organization sponsoring and operating the group home.

New Hope Borough Zoning Ordinance No. 1933-2, art. 1 § 1(3) (emphasis added).

Appellant argues that BVI will not be providing the residents of the subject property with personal care, attendant care, direct care, assistance in the giving and taking of medicines, contact with physicians to ensure compliance with physicians' orders, use of the telephone, and help with the laundry. Further, Appellant argues that the resident manager will not provide any hands-on care or on-site care for the residents, except in a crisis. Appellant also makes much of the leases signed by residents of the home, the fact that residents are charged rent each month, and the residents' ability to leave the home at their preference.

Appellant concludes that based on BVI's omission of these types of care, the contractual nature of the residents' stay in the home, and the residents' ability to leave the home at their preference, the Board erred in finding that the residents of the home will live as the functional equivalent of a traditional family.

In considering whether the residents of this home will "function" as a traditional family, we must be mindful of the undisputed fact that the residents of this home will all be over the age of eighteen and therefore have the legal status of adult citizens.

In the instant appeal, the Zoning Hearing Board concluded that the communal living arrangement proposed by BVI will be the functional equivalent of a traditional family. Specifically, the Zoning Hearing Board found: 19. The residents of the home will live together as the functional equivalent of a traditional family, the Board finds, for the following reasons:

(A) The resident manager will act as the "head of the household" in much the same way as a parent or parents, by assisting in the planning and arranging of the activities of the group home and its residents; dispensing advice, establishing or implementing rules; assuming responsibility in emergency situations, etc.;

(B) The residents will share kitchen and dining facilities in a manner similar to a traditional family. As in any such family with adult mem-

bers, those members shall have an option to cook or eat independently if they choose;

(C) Each resident is responsible for his own living quarters, much as a family member is responsible for his or her own bedroom;

(D) Common chores in the home will be shared by the residents in a fashion similar to the sharing of chores in a family;

(E) Residents will, if they choose, perform communal shopping, pool resources and designate one or more of their group to do the shopping, in a fashion similar to a family;

(F) Residents will make a choice as to the television to be watched and the music to be listened to, presumably with the same amount of disagreement that exists as to these choices in a traditional family;

(G) Common areas of the home are to be maintained by the residents, in the same fashion as members of a family would maintain them.

The Zoning Hearing Board also found that the residents of the home will have weekly meetings for the purpose of sharing information, news, and problems, and to resolve issues, concerns, or disagreements in the best interests of the group.

Appellant argues that the outcome of this case is controlled by this Court's decision in *Owens v. Zoning Hearing Board of Norristown,* 79 Pa.Cmwlth. 229, 468 A.2d 1195 (1983), wherein we held that a Borough may, in the exercise of its police power, prohibit "seven unrelated adults from residing together in a commercial boarding house situate in a single and two family residential district." Appellant's reliance upon *Owens* is misplaced. In *Owens,* this Court recognized that a traditional nuclear family is characterized by a nurturing environment and concluded that a home operated by a profit-motivated operator vastly differed from that of quasi-nuclear families. In the case *sub judice,* the group home does not have a profit motive. Therefore, our analysis in this case is confined to determining whether the living arrangement proposed by BVI conforms to the Ordinance.

Appellant also relies upon our Supreme Court's decision in *In re Appeal of Miller,* 511 Pa. 631, 515 A.2d 904 (1986), arguing that the facts of *Miller* provide no support for the granting of BVI's zoning permit because the property owner in *Miller* provided physical care for the residents, while BVI, admittedly, will not provide such physical care. We, however, in reviewing Miller do not find the provision of physical care the determinative factor to be considered.

In *Miller,* the Supreme Court held that owners of a house that took in boarders of various ages and physical or mental handicaps, notwithstanding the owner's receipt of $200.00 per month from some residents and the residents' lack of permanency, had established that the residents of the house lived together in *a caring familial unit*, and had satisfactorily met the definition of the term family. Mr. Chief Justice Nix, writing for a unanimous Supreme Court, concluded that [d]uring the hearing before the Board, the appellant offered substantial evidence to establish a caring familial unit. The individuals lived and cooked together as a single housekeeping unit. The same furnishings were throughout the house and the activities of the home were shared in by all occupants. *Each occupant had access to all areas of the premises.* There was *only one kitchen, the meals were taken by all as a group at one sitting.* The group attended social and religious functions together and celebrated holidays jointly.

BVI's expert, Ms. Tucker, testified that there is some disagreement on the definition of "family," but sociologists generally agree that three characteristics found in a family are child rearing, affection, and companionship. We conclude that these characteristics substantially conform with the Supreme Court's interpretation that the functional equivalent of a traditional family is a caring, nurturing unit.

Ms. Tucker testified that the "resident manager, in a sense, functions like the head of a household of a traditional home. The resident manager helps the un-related individuals form a cohesive group in planning and arranging activities within this group home." While it is true that "the resident manager . . . will not provide any on-site care or hands-on care . . . .[,] if there is a crisis and an unexpected crisis, the resident manager will help out."

Ms. Tucker's overall opinion was that even though children will not be raised in the home, the group home in this case will exhibit the characteristics of affection and companionship common to a traditional family.

Based on the Zoning Hearing Board's findings of fact and our review of the record, especially the credible testimony and expert opinions of Ms. Tucker, we conclude that the Zoning Hearing Board was correct in concluding that the residents of this group home will function as the equivalent of a traditional family, as defined in Section 218(3) of the Ordinance.

Appellant's second and third arguments go hand-in-hand, in that determination of the second issue requires a resolution of the third issue. In his third issue, Appellant argues that the home as renovated will not satisfy the requirements of a group home set forth in Section 218(3) of the Ordinance because the resident manager will actually be living in a separate apartment,

and consequently will have limited access to the HIV-infected residents. In support of this issue, Appellant argues that the Board found that BVI "proposes to renovate the structure by creating eight (8) bedrooms and related bath facilities on the first floor, in addition to living, dining and kitchen facilities, and an apartment or living unit (absent a kitchen facility) for a residential manager on the second floor."

Section 202 of the Ordinance defines "apartment" as "[a] dwelling unit attached to other dwelling units by a common wall and/or ceiling/floor provided there are no less than three nor more than twelve dwelling units within any structure." A "dwelling unit" is defined in the Ordinance as "[a]ny room or group of rooms forming a single habitable unit with facilities which are used or intended to be used for living, sleeping, cooking and eating by one (1) family." Section 215 of the Ordinance. Based on these definitions, it cannot be said that the resident manager's living quarters would qualify as an apartment under the Ordinance because the Zoning Hearing Board found that these living quarters are not intended to contain cooking or dining facilities; there is substantial evidence of record to support this funding.

While it is true that the Zoning Hearing Board found that the structure would include separate living quarters for the residential manager, the Ordinance requires, *inter alia*, that for the structure to be considered a group home, the structure must be a "dwelling unit . . . with single cooking and dining facilities." Section 218(3) of the Ordinance. Because single cooking and dining facilities are determinative of whether there is a single dwelling unit or multiple dwelling units, and the structure in this case contains only single cooking and dining facilities, we conclude that the home as proposed constitutes a single dwelling unit as defined in this Ordinance.

Affirmed.

Case Questions

1. What is the definition of a family, according to the court?

2. What is the significance of the fact that the home will be renovated prior to the occupancy by the eight residents?

3. What is the significance of the factor of payment of rent by residents in these cases?

4. What is the role of the resident manager and why is that role important?

Zoning as a Taking

Many who have had their permissible land uses restricted by zoning have raised the issue of whether such regulation constitutes a "taking" under the United States Constitution's Fifth Amendment, which would require that they be compensated for the loss in value of their land. (See Chapter 19 for additional details on eminent domain and just compensation.) In *Agins v. Tiburon,* 447 United States 255 (1980), the United States Supreme Court held that "The application of general zoning law to particular property effects a taking if the ordinance does not substantially advance legitimate state interests . . . or denies an owner economically viable use of his land."

One area of **takings issues** that has been the focus of litigation over the past few years has involved the Army Corps of Engineers and its policy under the Clean Water Act to include all wetlands within its regulation. **Wetlands** would include transitional land areas between dry or uplands and water bodies: swamps, marshes, and bogs. In effect, the Corps has adopted a national zoning policy for United States wetlands. Further, the Corps has been active in restraining development of these wetlands and several suits have been brought challenging the Corps' position as a taking of the wetlands property. Further, many states have restrictions on beachfront and wetlands development. In the following landmark case, the United States Supreme Court faced the issue of a "taking" because of development restrictions on wetlands.

Practical Tip

Over the past few years, many wetlands cases have been brought challenging developmental restrictions. Property purchasers considering coastal property should check not only local zoning, but state and federal restrictions as well prior to purchasing.

Lucas v. South Carolina Coastal Council

505 U.S. 1003 (1992)

Facts

In 1986, David H. Lucas (petitioner) paid $975,000 for two residential lots on the Isle of Palms in Charleston County, South Carolina. Lucas intended to build single-family homes on the lots. In 1988, South Carolina's legislature enacted the Beachfront Management Act. The effect of the act was to prohibit Lucas from erecting any permanent habitable structures on his two lots. Lucas filed suit challenging the legislation as a taking under the Fifth and Fourteenth Amendment, which requires that he be compensated. The trial court found that the law rendered Lucas' land valueless. The South Carolina Supreme Court reversed, and Lucas appealed.

Judicial Opinion

Scalia, Justice. Prior to Justice Holmes' exposition in *Pennsylvania Coal Co. v. Mahon,* 260 U.S. 393, 43 S.Ct. 158, 67 L.Ed. 322 (1922), it was generally thought that the Takings Clause reached only a "direct appropriation" of property.

Justice Holmes recognized in *Mahon,* however, that if the protection against physical appropriations of private

property was to be meaningfully enforced, the government's power to redefine the range of interests included in the ownership of property was necessarily constrained by constitutional limits. If, instead, the uses of private property were subject to unbridled, uncompensated qualification under the police power, "the natural tendency of human nature [would be] to extend the qualification more and more until at last private property disappear[ed]." These considerations gave birth in that case to the oft-cited maxim that, "while property may be regulated to a certain extent, if regulation goes too far it will be recognized as a taking."

We have, however, described at least two discrete categories of regulatory action as compensable without case-specific inquiry into the public interest advanced in support of the restraint. The first encompasses regulations that compel the property owner to suffer a physical "invasion" of his property. In general (at least with regard to permanent invasions), no matter how minute the intrusion, and no matter how weighty the public purpose behind it, we have required compensation. For example, in *Loretto v. Teleprompter Manhattan CATV Corp.,* 458 U.S.

419, 102 S.Ct. 3164, 73 L.Ed.2d 868 (1982), we determined that New York's law requiring landlords to allow television cable companies to emplace cable facilities in their apartment buildings constituted a taking, even though the facilities occupied at most only 1-1/2 cubic feet of the landlords' property.

The second situation in which we have found categorical treatment appropriate is where regulation denies all economically beneficial or productive use of land.

As we have said on numerous occasions, the Fifth Amendment is violated when land-use regulation "does not substantially advance legitimate state interests *or denies an owner economically viable use of his land.*"

On the other side of the balance, affirmatively supporting a compensation requirement, is the fact that regulations that leave the owner of land without economically beneficial or productive options for its use—typically, as here, by requiring land to be left substantially in its natural state—carry with them a heightened risk that private property is being pressed into some form of public service under the guise of mitigating serious public harm.

We think, in short, that there are good reasons for our frequently expressed belief that when the owner of real property has been called upon to sacrifice *all* economically beneficial uses in the name of the common good, that is, to leave his property economically idle, he has suffered a taking.

Under Lucas's theory of the case, which rested upon our "no economically viable use" statements, that finding entitled him to compensation. Lucas believed it unnecessary to take issue with either the purposes behind the *Beachfront Management Act,* or the means chosen by the South Carolina Legislature to effectuate those purposes. The South Carolina Supreme Court, however, thought otherwise. In its view, the *Beachfront Management Act* was no ordinary enactment, but involved an exercise of South Carolina's "police powers" to mitigate the harm to the public interest that petitioner's use of his land might occasion. By neglecting to dispute the findings enumerated in the Act or otherwise to challenge the legislature's purposes, petitioner "concede[d] that the beach/dune area of South Carolina's shores is an extremely valuable public resource; that the erection of new construction, *inter alia,* contributes to the erosion and destruction of this public resource; and that discouraging new construction in close proximity to the beach/dune area is necessary to prevent a great public harm."

It is correct that many of our prior opinions have suggested that "harmful or noxious uses" of property may be proscribed by government regulation without the requirement of compensation. For a number of reasons, however, we think the South Carolina Supreme Court was too quick to conclude that that principle decides the present case.

("[T]he problem [in this area] is not one of noxiousness or harm-creating activity at all; rather it is a problem of inconsistency between perfectly innocent and independently desirable uses"). Whether Lucas's construction of single-family residences on his parcels should be described as bringing "harm" to South Carolina's adjacent ecological resources thus depends principally upon whether the describer believes that the State's use interest in nurturing those resources is so important that *any* competing adjacent use must yield.

When it is understood that "prevention of harmful use" was merely our early formulation of the police power justification necessary to sustain (without compensation) *any* regulatory diminution in value; and that the distinction between regulation that "prevents harmful use" and that which "confers benefits" is difficult, if not impossible, to discern on an objective, value-free basis; it becomes self-evident that noxious-use logic cannot serve as a touchstone to distinguish regulatory "takings"—which require compensation—from regulatory deprivations that do not require compensation. *A fortiori* the legislature's recitation of a noxious-use justification cannot be the basis for departing from our categorical rule that total regulatory takings must be compensated. If it were, departure would virtually always be allowed.

Where the State seeks to sustain regulation that deprives land of all economically beneficial use, we think it may resist compensation only if the logically antecedent inquiry into the nature of the owner's estate shows that the proscribed use interests were not part of his title to begin with. This accords, we think, with our "takings" jurisprudence, which has traditionally been guided by the understandings of our citizens regarding the content of, and the State's power over, the "bundle of rights" that they acquire when they obtain title to property. It seems to us that the property owner necessarily expects the uses of his property to be restricted, from time to time, by various measures newly enacted by the State in legitimate exercise of its police powers; "[a]s long recognized, some values are enjoyed under an implied limitation and must yield to the police power."

In the case of land, however, we think the notion pressed by the Council that title is somehow held subject to the "implied limitation" that the State may subsequently eliminate all economically valuable use is inconsistent with the historical compact recorded in the Takings Clause that has become part of our constitutional culture.

On this analysis, the owner of a lake bed, for example, would not be entitled to compensation when he is denied the requisite permit to engage in a landfilling operation that would have the effect of flooding others' land. Nor the corporate owner of a nuclear generating plant, when it is directed to remove all improvements from its land upon discovery that the plant sits astride an earthquake fault. Such regulatory action may well have the effect of eliminating the land's only economically productive use, but it does not proscribe a productive use that was previously permissible under relevant property and nuisance principles.

As we have said, a "State, by *ipse dixit*, may not transform private property into public property without compensation. . . . " *Webb's Fabulous Pharmacies, Inc. v. Beckwith,* 449 U.S. 155, 164, 101 S.Ct. 446, 452, 66 L.Ed.2d 358 (1980). Instead, as it would be required to do if it sought to restrain Lucas in a common law action for public nuisance, South Carolina must identify background principles of nuisance and property law that prohibit the uses he now intends in the circumstances in which the property is presently found. Only on this showing can the State fairly claim that, in proscribing all such beneficial uses, the *Beachfront Management Act* is taking nothing.

The judgment is reversed.

Case Questions

1. What did Lucas purchase and for how much? When?
2. When was the law on beachfront construction passed?
3. Does South Carolina allege an important public purpose?
4. What is the distinction between this case and one in which a landowner is required to remove a business because it is a nuisance?
5. Will Lucas be able to build on his lots?
6. What implications does this case have for future wetlands development?
7. What implications does this case have for government preservation of wetlands properties?

PROCEDURAL ASPECTS

Adoption of Zoning Regulations

As already stated, local governments obtain their authority for zoning from an enabling act, and most states have adopted some form of the Standard State Zoning Enabling Act. This act consists of nine basic sections summarized as follows.

- *Section 1—Grant of power:* In this section, the governmental unit is given the authority to zone on the basis of a need to preserve health, safety, morals, and the general welfare of the community.
- *Section 2—Districts:* In this section, the governmental unit is given the authority to divide its area of jurisdiction into any size, shape, and number of districts for purposes of regulating activities or structures in those districts.
- *Section 3—Purposes in View:* This section requires the governmental unit to exercise its power under Section 2 pursuant to a master plan designed to provide all areas with adequate safety protection, schools, water, sewage, parks, and all other amenities.
- *Section 4—Method of Procedures:* In this section, the governmental unit is authorized to establish procedures for adopting and amending zoning regulations.
- *Section 5—Changes:* This section specifies that changes in zoning may be made but can be stopped if 20 percent or more of the owners of lots in the area in question oppose the change. The 20 percent may also include those who own lots within a certain distance of the area subject to the change. The distance (in feet) is left blank, to be determined by the adopting governmental unit.
- *Section 6—Zoning Commission:* This section establishes the right of the governmental unit to appoint a **zoning commission** to set up the original zoning plan on the basis of studies of the area.
- *Section 7—Board of Adjustment:* The purpose of this section is to allow the local governments to set up a **board of adjustment** that can, in cases and circumstances they deem appropriate, make exceptions to the zoning regulations in particular areas, so long as the exceptions are in keeping with the idea of the master plan and basic district division. These exceptions are called **variances** under the act.

- *Section 8—Enforcement:* In this section, the local governmental body is authorized to call zoning violations misdemeanors and to provide for penalties of either fines or imprisonment. Also, the local governmental body is authorized to bring suit to stop construction or use of property that is in violation of the zoning regulations; in other words, to seek an injunction for violative activity.
- *Section 9—Conflicts:* This section serves to clarify which set of laws will govern in the event two governmental units have established zoning for the same area; for example, if a county has adopted zoning for the county, but the cities within the county have adopted their own zoning ordinances. This section provides that city ordinances will be controlling to the extent they are more strict than the county ordinances.

The Standard State Zoning Enabling Act was drafted in 1922, revised in 1926, and at one time was adopted in most states. Today, although it is still the law in the majority of states by far, it provokes some dissatisfaction. The American Law Institute has drafted a Model Land Development Code that some states have adopted as a supplement to the Standard State Zoning Enabling Act. Although there may be slight variations in adoption forms, the preceding sections summarize the basic ideas, theories, and practice of zoning in local governmental units. Zoning control must be in the hands of a public body, not be subject to individual discretion, and not have unilateral control vested in one party.

Exceptions from Zoning Regulations

Section 7 of the Standard State Zoning Enabling Act provides for a board of adjustment and allows the board to grant exceptions or variances for use in zoned districts. An application for a variance to the board of adjustment must show two things:

1. That the petitioning party would suffer an undue hardship if the ordinance is enforced
2. That the granting of the variance will not be excessively disruptive of the surrounding land or the master plan

Factors considered by boards in making their variance decisions include: the effect of the use on surrounding land, the benefit to the public of the varied use, whether the property for which the variance is sought is different in its surface character from other property in the district, whether loss will be experienced if the variance is not granted, and whether the master plan's purposes would be defeated through the grant of the variance.

One of the most frequently approved variances involves an exception to building-height restrictions. Building height may be limited by ordinance, but it may be economically beneficial to the community and not a burden on surrounding property to permit a large business to build a multistory building in a single-story zoned district.

Another frequently used term that allows an exception to the zoned use is **special permit.** Under a special permit, the board makes an exception such as for the construction of a church or school in a residential area provided certain restrictions or conditions are met. Whether a variance or special permit will be granted is within the discretion of the board and is, more or less, a matter of opinion.

If a variance or special permit is denied, the party or parties seeking the variance have the right to seek judicial review of the board of adjustment's decision on the grounds of abuse of discretion, constitutionality, or arbitrariness. Figure 18.1 summarizes the procedural aspects of zoning.

FIGURE 18.1 *Zoning Process*

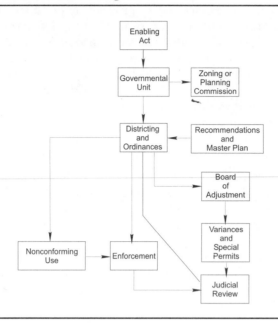

Definitions often become critical in defining uses and granting permits. Group homes for the mentally and physically disabled often raise issues of "family" and how it is defined.

Nonconforming Uses

A **nonconforming use** is the use of property in a way prohibited by a zoning ordinance passed after the use already existed. An example would be a store or business operating in an area that has just been zoned residential. Most zoning ordinances permit the continuation of such uses even though the ordinances would prohibit a new store or similar use from beginning. A nonconforming use also occurs when an existing building does not meet subsequently passed ordinances, such as a building of several stories located in an area that subsequently prohibits multistory buildings.

For a nonconforming use to be immune from newly passed zoning ordinances, it must be in existence at the time the zoning is passed. Furthermore, the activity or structure cannot be expanded but must remain limited to the extent of the nonconforming use at the time the zoning was passed.

A right to nonconforming use can be lost if the nonconforming activity is abandoned or if the nonconforming building is destroyed by fire or natural events. The zoning ordinances may specify a time period for abandonment as well as what constitutes destruction for purposes of ending a nonconforming use.

Recently, many local governments, in an effort to carry out their community planning objectives, have sought to eliminate nonconforming uses over time and have passed ordinances that require amortization of nonconforming uses. These amortization sections require nonconforming uses to be eliminated over a specified period—usually five years. Amortization periods allow landowners some time to convert their property to appropriately zoned activities or buildings. The following case deals with an issue of a continuing nonconforming use.

Money
v. Zoning Hearing Board of Haverford Township

755 A.2d 732 (Pa. 2000)

Facts

David Money (landowner) applied to Haverford Township for a building permit to replace a deteriorated, nonconforming garage/chicken coop with a nonconforming garage that took up less space but that was a larger garage than the current size limits for his property's zoning. Mr. Money petitioned to be allowed to building the garage larger than existing maximums as the replacement of an existing nonconforming use with another nonconforming use.

The Township denied his application and Mr. Money appealed to the Zoning and Hearing Board (ZHB). The ZHB denied his appeal. Mr. Money appealed.

Judicial Opinion

Friedman, Judge. In his appeal to this court, Landowner contends that the ZHB committed an abuse of discretion and an error of law when it denied Landowner a building permit because the area of Landowner's proposed garage exceeds the maximum permitted by section 182-7111. B(2) of the Zoning Ordinance. Specifically, Landowner claims that the ZHB erred in rejecting Landowner's argument that he is entitled to erect the proposed garage as a continuation of a nonconforming use—i.e., the replacement of a lawful nonconforming structure. Landowner also asserts that the trial court erred in relying upon the proposition that the replacement of "one nonconforming structure with another nonconforming structure" is prohibited.

We agree.

Here, the sole issue is whether Landowner abandoned the nonconforming use. The Township contends that Landowner abandoned the nonconforming use by allowing the old garage/chicken coop to fall into a state of disrepair. The Township argues that the dilapidated condition of the garage/chicken coop prevented the structure from being used as a garage for a substantial period of time and supports the conclusion that the use was abandoned.

As the party claiming the abandonment, the Township bears the burden of proving that Landowner abandoned the nonconforming use. To sustain its burden of proof, the Township must show that (1) Landowner intended to abandon the nonconforming use and (2) Landowner actually abandoned the use consonant with his intention. Here, the Township has failed to meet its burden of proving either Landowner's intent to abandon or actual abandonment.

[A] landowner's failure to use property for a period of time designated by a zoning ordinance is evidence of the intention to abandon. *See Latrobe Speedway.* Here, section 182-802.C(1) of the Zoning Ordinance provides, "If a nonconforming use of land or building ceases operations for a continuous period of more than six (6) months, then this shall be deemed to be an intent to abandon such use, and any subsequent use of land shall conform to the regulations of this chapter." The effect of this ordinance is to create a presumption in favor of an intent to abandon where a use is discontinued for more than six months.

Here, however, the Township did not prove that Landowner had failed to use the old garage/chicken coop for more than six months before he applied for the building permit. Indeed, the evidence is to the contrary. At the hearing, Landowner testified that he used the dilapidated garage/chicken coop to store a car, "some wood and . . . couple of cases of . . . coffee mugs." The ZHB did not reject or discredit that testimony; nor did any evidence contradict Landowner's testimony in that regard.

However, we acknowledge that, even where a landowner has used the building within the prior designated time period, structural alterations to a building that are inconsistent with continuance of the nonconforming use may establish both intent to abandon and actual abandonment.

Here, Landowner proposes to replace the old garage/chicken coop with a similar structure—a garage. Because both structures are nonconforming as to area, it cannot be said that Landowner is abandoning the nonconforming use by building the new garage. Landowner's proposed replacement garage is a continuation, not an abandonment, of a nonconforming use.

Courts have permitted landowners to demolish nonconforming structures and replace them with new nonconforming structures.

Reversed.

Case Questions

1. What was the extent of Mr. Money's use of his existing garage/chicken coop?
2. Had Mr. Money abandoned the use of the garage/chicken coop?
3. Is the new garage a change or a continuation?

Some courts have even declared certain nonconforming uses to be nuisances and have had them eliminated by legal action for nuisance. Through the litigation by surrounding landowners, nonconforming use can be eliminated by court injunction. For example, a smelting plant in a residential area could easily be enjoined as a nuisance and the problem of nonconforming use eliminated.

Consider 18.4 | Gannett Outdoor Sign Company had more than 300 billboards in the city of Tempe 20 years ago. Today, Gannett has only 23. Tempe prohibits such outdoor billboards today, but existing signs were protected as nonconforming uses. Gannett alleges that the city has been able to talk property owners into eliminating their leases for the billboards to Gannett when the owners applied for permits for property development. Gannett has filed suit to challenge the practices and the ordinance as unconstitutional. Will Gannett succeed?

CAUTIONS AND CONCLUSIONS

From the information and cases in this chapter, it is not difficult to see that the issue of zoning can be controlling in the value of property and is certainly controlling in the use to be made of property. Before land is purchased or before construction is begun, make a zoning check. In addition, check surrounding tracts and plats to see the effects of growth and expansion and also the resulting effect on property values. Finally, evaluate the master plan to determine any future problems and possible changes or variances that might affect the land's value. When it comes to the issue of zoning, there can never be enough research.

Key Terms

zoning, 464
general plan, 465
master plan, 465
Standard State Zoning Enabling Act,
    465
cumulative classification, 466
noncumulative classification, 466

intensity zoning, 468
aesthetic zoning, 469
exclusionary zoning, 471
interim zoning, 471
hold zoning, 471
social issue zoning, 471
takings issues, 478

wetlands, 478
zoning commission, 480
board of adjustment, 480
variances, 480
special permit, 481
nonconforming use, 482

Chapter Problems

1.   The city of Philadelphia's Department of Licensing & Inspections denied Midnight Sessions, Ltd., a permit for the operation of an exotic dance club because of a history of disturbances and crime when such dance clubs operated. The city, through police department records, was able to establish that there was an increase in noise, trash, drug activity, loitering, and public urination in every area where an exotic dance club was given a permit for operation. In addition, the clubs attracted between 3,000 and

5,000 patrons on weekend event nights, and after the show many of those patrons roamed the surrounding neighborhoods in a state of drunkenness. Could the city prohibit the clubs altogether? *Midnight Sessions, Ltd. v. City of Philadelphia*, 945 F.2d 667 (3rd Cir. 1991)

2.   New Orleans passed an ordinance governing its historical Vieux Carré section that detailed the types of structures and permissible repairs, maintenance, and alterations in the area. The ordinance has been challenged on the grounds that it exceeds the police power. What is the result?

3. Marina Limited Partners applied for a zoning variance to relocate part of their 700-slip marina to a new marina to be constructed at another location on the Geist Reservoir in Hamilton County, Indiana. Marina would move 300 of its slips to the new marina. The construction of the new marina required approval of a variance by the Board of Zoning Appeals for the city of Noblesville. At the hearing, John Allen and others who owned property in the area appeared and objected to the marina's construction. They presented evidence that construction of the marina would lower their property values. There was additional evidence regarding noise, traffic, smoke, fumes, and odors. The board's staff recommended approval, but the board denied the variance. Marina Partners filed suit alleging the finding was arbitrary. Are they correct? *Allen v. Board of Zoning Appeals for the City of Noblesville,* 594 N.E.2d 480 (Ind. 1992)

4. The Township of Brady has zoning restrictions on the number of animals that can be kept on properties in certain areas. More pigs are permitted per acre than cows. A farmer has brought suit alleging that the zoning restriction is arbitrary and not based on a public welfare basis. Township officials say that pig waste does not smell as much as cow waste and hence they permit more pigs than cows. Is the zoning restriction valid? *Richardson v. Township of Brady,* 218 F.3d 508 (6th Cir. 2000)

5. The Madison County Livestock and Fair Association owns a tract of land that has been used as the location for county fairs. The tract is now located in an area in which zoning changes prohibited such uses. The use of the tract as a fairgrounds has been a nonconforming use. The Association filed for a permit to build a race track on the tract. Neighbors objected because they said that such a proposed use could not be grandfathered in under the nonconforming use. Are they correct? *Perkins v. Madison County Livestock & Fair, Ass'n.,* 613 N.W.2d 264 (Iowa 2000)

6. The city of St. Louis passed an ordinance that required all for-sale signs posted on properties within the city to include an indication of the zoning for the property. Green failed to place the zoning on the sign for one of his listed properties and was convicted of a misdemeanor. Green appealed the conviction on the grounds that the ordinance was an excessive exercise of power by the city. What was the result?

7. An ordinance of the city of Palo Alto, a college town, prohibits two or more persons from living together in a single-family residential district unless they are related by blood, marriage, or legal adoption. A tenants' union has brought suit challenging the validity of the ordinance. What is the result?

8. The Stoyanoffs sought to build a home of an ultra-modern design in Ladue, Missouri. The home was to be built in a neighborhood in which all of the homes were of two-story conventional architectural design such as Colonial, French, or English.

The city of Ladue has a zoning ordinance that requires that a proposed structure conform to certain minimum architectural standards of appearance and conformity with surrounding structures, and that unsightly, grotesque and unsuitable structures, detrimental to the stability of value and the welfare of surrounding property, structures and residents, and to the general welfare and happiness of the community, be avoided, and that appropriate standards of beauty and conformity be fostered and encouraged.

Can the city stop construction of the Stoyanoff home? *State of Missouri Ex Rel. Stoyanoff v. Ladue,* 458 S.W.2d 305 (Mo. 1970)

9. Bernard Smookler and his wife purchased a 123-acre tract of land at the intersection of Jolly and Meridian Roads in Wheatfield Township in 1968. Ninety acres were used for agriculture, and 1.5 acres were rented to a tenant for residential use. Two years later, they requested a zoning change from rural agricultural to mobile home park with a 300-foot strip for commercial zoning. The planned mobile home park would be called Wheatfield Acres Mobile Home Park, would include five units per acre, and would have 535 total units.

The 1970 census put the population of Wheatfield Township at 1,117 with 325 housing units. There is no master plan for the township, which is 36 square miles with 18,297 acres and only about 5 percent developed. Three residential areas are in the township, with most of them located in the northern part. The proposed park would be in the northwest section. At the time of the application, Wheatfield had one commercial development: a gas station along Interstate 96. The township had no police or fire department and relied on the adjoining cities, counties, and the state for such services. There are no mobile home parks in the township and nothing that could be characterized as low-cost housing, but there has been some discussion of creating mobile home parks.

The Zoning and Planning Commission denied the plaintiffs' application, stating that the area would be better for residential use, there would be an added burden to police and fire services, and to the schools, and no benefit to the surrounding community.

The Smooklers appealed the commission's decision to the trial court. There the Smooklers and the commission stipulated that there would be no traffic problem nor any problems with the sanitary or sewage systems. The Smooklers alleged at the trial court that the decision of the commission was evidence of a preconceived scheme to eliminate or prohibit mobile home parks. Can zoning be used in this way to control population growth? *Smookler v. Township of Wheatfield,* 232 N.W.2d 616 (Mich. 1975)

10. Jerome Alexander is a financial planner who runs his financial planning business out of his home in Glencoe, Illinois. He has two employees who park their cars on the street outside his home. His neighbors reported him for violation of a local law that prohibits the operation of home businesses. When the law was originally passed, it was designed to prevent businesses such as sweatshops and factories with smokestacks. Mr. Alexander believes that the ordinance cannot be enforced. Is he correct?

Internet Activities

1. For an example of a land use restrictions enforcement statute, go to: **http://www.capitol.state.tx.us/statutes/statutes.html**

2. Go to **http://www.grandoffice.com/location/property.asp** to see a master plan for development in Greensboro, North Carolina.

3. Go to **http://www.cityofalhambra.org**, click on Development Services, then on Zoning, and under Chapters select "23.71 Development Agreements" for the City of Alhambra, California, Development Agreement statute.

Chapter 19
Constitutional Issues
in Real Estate

If there isn't a law, there will be.

  Harold Farber

Previous chapters of this book have emphasized that owning real property consists of rights that are afforded various forms of protection. Owning and transferring title to real property also includes certain constitutional rights that entitle property owners to certain guarantees with regard to their property ownership. The purpose of this chapter is to discuss the constitutional protections afforded real property owners and purchasers.

LAND TITLE AND CONSTITUTIONAL ISSUES—
EMINENT DOMAIN

The right of a governmental body to take title to property for a public use is called **eminent domain.** This right is established in the. Fifth Amendment to the

http://

At the Bureau of Land
Management, see how
public lands are sold:
http://www.blm.gov/

Constitution as well as in certain state constitutions. Private individuals cannot require property owners to sell their property, but governmental entities can require them to transfer title for public projects for the public good. The Fifth Amendment provides that "property shall not be taken for a public use without just compensation." For a governmental entity to properly exercise the right of eminent domain, three factors must be present: public purpose, taking (as opposed to regulating), and just compensation.

Public Purpose

To exercise eminent domain, the exercising governmental authority must establish that the taking is necessary for the accomplishment of a government purpose. When eminent domain is mentioned, use of property for highways and schools is thought of most frequently. However, the right of the government to eminent domain extends much further. For example, the following uses have been held to constitute public purposes: the condemnation of slum housing (for purposes of improving city areas), the limitation of mining and excavation within city limits, the declaration of property as a historic landmark, and the taking of property in order to provide a firm that is the town's economic base with a large enough tract for expansion.

According to the United States Supreme Court, the public purpose requirement for eminent domain is to be interpreted broadly, and "the role of the judiciary in determining whether that power [eminent domain] is being exercised for a public purpose is an extremely narrow one." (*United States ex rel. T.V.A. v. Welch,* 327 U.S. 546 [1946])

Taking or Regulating

For a governmental entity to be required to pay a landowner compensation under the doctrine of eminent domain, it must be established that there has been a **taking** of the property. A taking must go so far as to deprive the landowner of any use of the property. In the landmark case of *Pennsylvania Coal v. Mahon,* 260 U.S. 393 (1922), the Supreme Court established standards for determining a taking as opposed to mere regulation. At that time, Pennsylvania had a statute that prohibited the mining of coal under any land surface where the result would be the subsidence of any structure used as a human habitation. The owners of the rights to mine subsurface coal brought suit challenging the regulation as a taking, and the Supreme Court ruled in their favor, holding that the statute was more than regulation and, in fact, was an actual taking of the subsurface property rights.

Because of the vast amount of technology that has developed since that case was decided, there are many new and subtly different issues in what constitutes a taking. For example, in some areas the regulation of cable television companies is an infringement on air rights. Such specialized areas of real estate rights are particularly difficult to resolve.

In the following case, the Supreme Court was faced with the same issue of regulation versus a taking under eminent domain.

Loretto
v. Teleprompter Manhattan CATV Corp. et al.

458 U.S. 419 (1982)

Facts

A New York statute required landlords to permit cable television companies to install cable facilities on landlords' property so that tenants could subscribe to cable television services. Teleprompter Manhattan CATV (defendant/appellant) installed its equipment on the roof and side of Loretto's (plaintiff/appellant) building. The equipment was to permanently occupy Loretto's property, and Loretto was paid the usual $1 fee to which a landlord is entitled upon installation of such equipment. Loretto filed suit alleging that this minor but permanent physical occupation of her property constituted a taking under the Fifth Amendment without just compensation. The New York Court of Appeals ruled the installation did not constitute a taking, and Loretto appealed.

Judicial Opinion

Marshall, Justice. The Court of Appeals ruled that the law serves a legitimate police power purpose—eliminating landlord fees and conditions that inhibit the development of CATV, which has important educational and community benefits. Rejecting the argument that a physical occupation authorized by government is necessarily a taking, the court stated that the regulation does not have an excessive economic impact upon appellant when measured against her aggregate property rights, and that it does not interfere with any reasonable investment-backed expectations. In a concurring opinion by Judge Gabrielli, it was stated that the law works a taking but concluded that the $1.00 presumptive award, together with procedures permitting a landlord to demonstrate a greater entitlement, afford just compensation.

We conclude that a permanent physical occupation authorized by government is a taking without regard to the public interests that it may serve. Our constitutional history confirms the rule, recent cases do not question it, and the purposes of the Takings Clause compel[s] its retention.

In *United States v. Pewee Coal Co.*, 341 U.S. 114 (1951), the Court unanimously held that the Government's seizure and direction of operation of a coal mine to prevent a national strike of coal miners constituted a taking, though members of the Court differed over which losses suffered during the period of Government control were compensable. The plurality had little difficulty concluding that because there had been an "actual taking of possession and control," the taking was as clear as if the Government held full title and ownership. . . . In *United*

States v. Central Eureka Mining Co., 357 U.S. 155 (1958), by contrast, the Court found no taking where the Government had issued a war-time order requiring nonessential gold mines to cease operations for the purpose of conserving equipment and manpower for use in mines more essential to the war effort. . . . The Court reasoned that "the Government did not occupy, use, or in any manner take physical possession of the gold mines or the equipment connected with them." The Court concluded that the temporary though severe restriction on use was justified by the exigency of war.

The historical rule that a permanent physical occupation of another's property is a taking has more than tradition to commend it. Such an appropriation is perhaps the most serious form of invasion of an owner's property interests.

Constitutional protections for rights of private property cannot be made to depend on the size of the area permanently occupied.

This Court has consistently affirmed that States have broad power to regulate housing conditions in general and the landlord-tenant relationship in particular without paying just compensation for all economic injuries that such regulation entails. In none of the cases, however, did the government authorize permanent occupation of the landlord's property by a third party. Consequently, our holding today in no way alters the analysis governing the State's power to require landlords to comply with building codes and provide utility connections, mailboxes, smoke detectors, fire extinguishers, and the like in the common area of a building. So long as these regulations do not require the landlord to suffer the physical occupation of a portion of his building by a third party, they will be analyzed under the multi-factor inquiry generally applicable to nonpossessory governmental activity.

Our holding today is very narrow. We affirm the traditional rule that a permanent physical occupation of property is a taking. In such a case, the property owner entertains a historically rooted expectation of compensation, and the character of invasion is qualitatively more intrusive than perhaps any other category of property regulation.

The issue of the amount of compensation that is due . . . is a matter for the state courts.

Reversed.

Case Questions

1. What regulation is at issue?
2. What form of physical occupation of property is alleged?
3. Was Loretto paid for the occupation?
4. What public purpose did the New York Court of Appeals find existed?
5. The Supreme Court cites two cases in reaching its decision—what are they? their facts? the decisions?

6. In determining whether a taking has occurred, what is the significance of physical occupation?
7. What distinction is offered between television equipment and items such as smoke alarms and fire extinguishers?
8. How much compensation will Loretto be paid?

As established by the *Lucas* case in Chapter 18, there are times when regulation can constitute a taking for purposes of property owner rights and compensation. The following is a landmark case in the constitutionality of use regulations.

Nollan v. California Coastal Commission

483 U.S. 825 (1987)

Facts

James and Marilyn Nollan own a beachfront lot in Ventura County, California. A quarter-mile north of their property is Faria Park, an oceanside public park with a public beach and recreation area. Another public beach, known as "the Cove," lies 1,800 feet south of their lot. A concrete seawall approximately eight feet high separates the beach portion of the Nollan's property from the rest of the lot.

The Nollans originally leased their property with an option to buy and had only a small bungalow (504 square feet) located on the lot. The Nollans' option to purchase was conditioned on their promise to demolish the bungalow and replace it. To do that, the Nollans had to apply for a coastal development permit from the California Coastal Commission. They filed for such a permit and proposed construction of a three-bedroom home similar to other residences in the area.

The Nollans were informed that their application was on the calendar and the staff had recommended approval provided that the Nollans allow a public easement to make it easier for the public to get to the Cove and Faria County Park.

The Nollans filed suit with the Ventura County Superior Court asking them to invalidate the easement condition. The court agreed and remanded the matter to the commission for a full hearing. The commission found the new house would block the view of the beach and also inhibit the public psychologically from using the beach.

The Nollans filed another suit and said the condition constituted a taking of their property. The trial court agreed and remanded to the commission. The commission appealed, and the appellate court reversed. The Nollans appealed to the United States Supreme Court.

Judicial Opinion

Scalia, Justice. Had California simply required the Nollans to make an easement across their beachfront available to the public on a permanent basis in order to increase public access to the beach, rather than conditioning their permit to rebuild their house on their agreeing to do so, we have no doubt there would have been a taking. To say that the appropriation of a public easement across a landowner's premises does not constitute the taking of a property interest but rather, "a mere restriction on its use," is to use words in a manner that deprives them of all their ordinary meaning. Indeed, one of the principal uses of the eminent domain power is to assure that the government be able to require conveyance of just such interests, so long as it pays for them. Perhaps because the point is so obvious, we have never been confronted with a controversy that required us to rule upon it, but our cases' analysis of the effect of other governmental action leads to the same conclusion. We have repeatedly held that, as to property reserved by its owner for private use, "the right to exclude [others is] one of the most essential sticks in the bundle of rights that are commonly characterized as property."

Given, then, that requiring uncompensated conveyance of the easement outright would violate the Fourteenth Amendment, the question becomes whether requiring it to be conveyed as a condition for issuing a land use permit alters the outcome. We have long recognized that land use regulation does not effect a taking if it "substantially advance[s] legitimate state interests" and does not "den[y] an owner economically viable use of his land." The parties have not elaborated on the standards for determining what constitutes a "legitimate state interest" or what type of connection between the regulation and the state interest satisfies the requirement that the former "substantially advance" the latter. They have made clear, however, that a broad range of governmental purposes and regulations satisfies these requirements.

The Commission argues that among these permissible purposes are protecting the public's ability to see the beach, assisting the public in overcoming the "psychological barrier" to using the beach created by a developed shorefront, and preventing congestion on the public beaches. We assume, without deciding, that this is so—in which case the Commission unquestionably would be able to deny the Nollans their permit outright if their new house (alone or by reason of the cumulative impact produced in conjunction with other construction) would substantially impede these purposes, unless the denial would interfere so drastically with the Nollans' use of their property as to constitute a taking.

The Commission argues that a permit condition that serves the same legitimate police-power purpose as a refusal to issue the permit should not be found to be a taking if the refusal to issue the permit would not constitute a taking. We agree. Thus, if the Commission attached to the permit some condition that would have protected the public's ability to see the beach notwithstanding construction of the new house—for example, a height limitation, a width restriction, or a ban on fences—so long as the Commission could have exercised its police power (as we have assumed it could) to forbid construction of the house altogether, imposition of the condition would also be constitutional. Moreover (and here we come closer to the facts of the present case), the condition would be constitutional even if it consisted of the requirement that the Nollans provide a viewing spot on their property for passersby with whose sighting of the ocean their new house would interfere. Although such a requirement, constituting a permanent grant of continuous access to the property, would have to be considered a taking if it were not attached to a development permit, the Commission's assumed power to forbid construction of the house in order to protect the public's view of the beach must surely include the power to condition construction upon some concession by the owner, even a concession of property rights, that serves the same end. If a prohibition designed to accomplish that purpose would be a legitimate exercise of the police power rather than a taking, it would be strange to conclude that providing the owner an alternative to that prohibition which accomplishes the same purpose is not.

The evident constitutional propriety disappears, however, if the condition substituted for the prohibition utterly fails to further the end advanced as the justification for the prohibition. When that essential nexus is eliminated, the situation becomes the same as if California law forbade shouting fire in a crowded theater, but granted dispensations to those willing to contribute $100 to the state treasury. While a ban on shouting fire can be a core exercise of the State's police power to protect the public safety, and can thus meet even our stringent standards for regulation of speech, adding the unrelated condition alters the purpose to one, which, while it may be legitimate, is inadequate to sustain the ban. Therefore, even though, in a sense, requiring a $100 tax contribution in order to shout fire is a lesser restriction on speech than an outright ban, it would not pass constitutional muster. Similarly here, the lack of nexus between the condition and the original purpose of the building restriction converts that purpose to something other than what it was. The purpose then becomes, quite simply, the obtaining of an easement to serve some valid governmental purpose, but without payment of compensation. Whatever may be the outer limits of "legitimate state interests" in the takings and land use context, this is not one of them. In short, unless the permit condition serves the same governmental purpose as the development ban, the building restriction is not a valid regulation of land use but "an out-and-out plan of extortion."

Justice Brennan argues that imposition of the access requirement is not irrational. In his version of the Commission's argument, the reason for the requirement is that in its absence, a person looking toward the beach from the road will see a street of residential structures including the Nollans' new home and conclude that there is no public beach nearby. If, however, that person sees people passing and repassing along the dry sand behind the Nollans' home, he will realize that there is a public beach somewhere in the vicinity. The Commission's action, however, was based on the opposite factual finding that the wall of houses completely blocked the view of the beach and that a person looking from the road would not be able to see it at all.

Even if the Commission had made the finding that Justice Brennan proposes, however, it is not certain that it would suffice. We do not share Justice Brennan's confidence that the Commission "should have little difficulty in the future in utilizing its expertise to demonstrate a specific connection between provisions for access and burdens on access," that will avoid the effect of today's decision. We view the Fifth Amendment's property clause to be more than a pleading requirement, and compliance with it to be more than an exercise in cleverness and imagination. As indicated earlier, our cases describe the condition for abridgement of property rights through the police power as a "substantial advanc[ing]" of a legitimate State interest. We are inclined to be particularly careful about the adjective where the actual conveyance of property is made a condition to the lifting of a land use restriction, since in that context there is heightened risk that the purpose is avoidance of the compensation requirement, rather than the stated police power objective.

We are left, then, with the Commission's justification for the access requirement unrelated to land use regulation:

Finally, the Commission notes that there are several existing provisions of pass and repass lateral access benefits already given by past Faria Beach Tract applicants as a result of prior coastal permit decisions. The access required as a condition of this permit is part of a comprehensive program to provide continuous public access along Faria Beach as the lots undergo development or redevelopment.

The Commission [believes] that the public interest will be served by a continuous strip of publicly accessible beach along the coast.

The Commission may well be right that it is a good idea, but that does not establish that the Nollans (and other coastal residents) alone can be compelled to contribute to its realization. Rather, California is free to advance its "comprehensive program," if it wishes, by using its power of eminent domain for the "public purpose," but if it wants an easement across the Nollans' property, it must pay for it.

Rewriting the argument to eliminate the play on words makes clear that there is nothing to it. It is quite impossible to understand how a requirement that people already on the public beaches be able to walk across the Nollans' property reduces any obstacles to viewing the beach created by the new house. It is also impossible to understand how it lowers any "psychological barrier" to using the public beaches, or how it helps to remedy any additional congestion on them caused by construction of the Nollans' new house. We therefore find that the Commission's imposition of the permit condition cannot be treated as an exercise of its land use power for any of these purposes.

Reversed.

Case Questions

1. What was the proposed use of the Nollans' land?
2. What condition did the Commission wish to impose?
3. If the Commission could not have the condition, were they willing to grant the permit?
4. Is the condition a taking of the Nollans' property?
5. What arguments did the Commission make?

For additional cases and information on "takings," please refer to pages 478–480 in Chapter 18.

Just Compensation

The final requirement for the proper exercise by a governmental entity of the right of eminent domain is that the party from whom the property is being taken be given **just compensation.** The issue of just compensation is difficult and is always a question of fact. Basic to this determination is that the owner is to be compensated for loss and that the compensation is not measured by the governmental entity's gain. In *United States v. Miller,* 317 U.S. 369 (1943), the Supreme Court held that, in cases where it can be determined, fair market value is the measure of compensation. And in *United States ex rel. T.V.A. v. Powelson,* 319 U.S. 266 (1943), the Supreme Court defined fair market value to be "what a willing buyer would pay in cash to a willing seller."

Possible problems in applying these relatively simple standards include peculiar value to the owner, consequential damages, and greater value of the land because of the proposed governmental project. Basically, the issue of just compensation becomes an issue of appraisal, which is affected by all the various factors involved. In determining just compensation, the courts must consider factors such as surrounding property values and the owner's proposed use.

Consider 19.1

The U.S. Energy Department located its now-failed supercollider project in Ellis County, Texas. Generally, land prices in the area had been $500 to $800 an acre. However, during the two years preceding the announcement of the now-defunct project, as anticipation about the area getting the supercollider project grew, land began selling for as high as $7,000 an acre. The U.S. government's policy is to pay "fair market value" for the land that it needs. How was the fair market value for the nearly 7,000 acres taken by eminent domain for the project determined?

19.1, *continued*

CONSTITUTIONAL ISSUES IN LAND-USE RESTRICTIONS

The use of land is restricted through zoning requirements (Chapter 18), future interests (Chapter 7), and covenants or restrictions in deeds that control the use of the property being transferred (Chapter 21). Because the right to the full use and enjoyment of one's property has been protected so carefully, any imposed restrictions are subject to judicial scrutiny. All three forms of restrictions have met with constitutional challenges, and these are discussed in the following sections.

Practical Tip

Many racially restrictive covenants can still be found in the chain of title for property. Although they are often used for sensational effect, as when the title to United States Supreme Court Chief Justice William Rehnquist's Arizona land was revealed in the newspaper as having a racial restriction, they are simply invalid and unenforceable. No one can control the language in deeds used prior to the time of their ownership.

Zoning

Some constitutional challenges to zoning have already been discussed. For example, the *Nollan* case held that requiring an easement from a property owner constituted a taking requiring compensation under eminent domain. In the *Village of Belle Terre v. Boraas,* 416 U.S. 1 (1974), the Supreme Court upheld a city's right to restrict property use to single-family dwellings under the public welfare interests of traffic, noise, and congestion control. However, in *Cleburne v. Cleburne,* 473 U.S. 432 (1985), the Court ruled that a zoning ordinance had gone too far in its regulation, that a constitutionally protected right had been infringed upon, and that the regulation prohibiting group homes for the mentally retarded was invalid. The grounds for challenges to zoning ordinances are limited only by the rights afforded in the Constitution (see Chapter 18).

A state has passed a law prohibiting the operation of stores "engaging primarily in the sale of drug paraphernalia." When an injunction is issued against the operator of a store selling items such as papers, clips, and pipes, the operator appeals on grounds that the statute is unconstitutionally vague. What is the result?

Consider 19.2

Annexation

The decision of annexation of property to a city is a difficult one that is marked by strong emotions on both sides of the issue. The United States Supreme Court has dealt with the issue of whether a city's annexation process was creating a violation of the federal Voting Rights Act. In *City of Pleasant Grove v. U.S.,* 479 U.S. 462 (1987), the court held that the decision on annexation cannot be race-based.

Future Interests

Although fee simples determinable and fee simples subject to conditions subsequent do restrict the use and transferability of property, the courts have not intervened in these land interests unless the restrictions have violated any of the fundamental rights afforded by the Constitution. One type of restriction that has been subject to constitutional constraints is the restriction on use according to race. In *Capitol Federal Savings and Loan Association v. Smith,* 316 P.2d 252 (Colo. 1957), the Colorado Supreme Court, in a decision followed by other courts, held that racially based fee simples determinable are unconstitutional.

All-Adult Covenants

In many areas, particularly in retirement communities, land purchases are subject to a restrictive covenant that allows only persons above the age of 18 or 21 to reside in a particular area: an **all-adult covenant.** The validity of these all-adult covenants and communities has been an issue before the courts, and the following case is one of those judicial reviews.

Schmidt v. Superior Court (Valley Home Mobile Park Investments as real parties in interest) won

769 P.2d 932 (Calif. 1989)

Facts

Teri Lynn Schmidt and her sister and daughter (plaintiffs) wanted to purchase a mobile home in a mobile home park managed by Valley Mobile Park Investments (defendants). The purchase was conditioned on Valley's acceptance of the Schmidts' application for space. Valley rejected the application, citing a rule that permitted only persons age 25 or older to live in the park. Schmidt then brought suit alleging that her constitutional rights as well as the Unruh Civil Rights Act had been violated. The trial court dismissed the case. The Court of Appeals ruled that the mobile home park was not specifically designated for senior citizens and reversed. Valley appealed.

Judicial Opinion

Arguelles, Justice. In this case we must determine the validity, under California law, of a private mobilehome park rule limiting residence in the park to persons 25 years or older. The trial court found the rule valid, but the Court of Appeal disagreed, concluding that Civil Code section 798.76 barred a private mobilehome park owner from adopting or enforcing such a rule.

In September 1988, while this matter was pending before us, Congress enacted new legislation (Pub.L. No. 100-430 (Sept. 13, 1988) 102 Stat. 1619, 1988 U.S.Code Cong. & Admin. News, No. 8), effective March 1989, which defendant mobilehome park owners acknowledge will render their 25-year or older policy invalid in the future, at least as applied to families with minor children. Contrary to plaintiffs' suggestion, however, the new federal legislation does not render this proceeding inconse-

quential or moot, because plaintiffs seek damages for the mobilehome park owners' enforcement of the 25-years-or-older rule prior to the effective date of the new federal legislation and the validity of the park owners' conduct at that time necessarily turns on the proper interpretation of California law. Furthermore, the interpretation of the applicable California statutes will continue to affect the nature of the residence policies which private mobilehome parks in California may establish in the future in light of the new federal legislation. Thus, the state law issue posed by this case continues to have general significance.

In September 1988, Congress enacted the Fair Housing Amendments Act of 1988 (Pub.L. No. 100-430 (Sept. 13, 1988) 102 Stat. 1619, 1988 U.S.Code Cong. & Admin. News, No. 8), an act which makes substantial changes in the preexisting federal fair housing law. Among other significant changes, the act makes it unlawful for a business which engages in residential real estate related transactions to discriminate on the basis of "familial status," as well as on the previously forbidden grounds of race, color, religion, sex or national origin. (42 U.S.C. § 3605.) "Familial status" is defined to mean families which include children under the age of 18. (42 U.S.C. § 3602(k).)

While the new act generally bars discrimination in housing against families with children under 18, it also creates an exception for "housing for older persons" in which discrimination on the basis of familial status is not prohibited. (42 U.S.C. § 3607(b)(1).) "Housing for older persons," in turn, is defined to include, *inter alia,* housing which is (1) "intended for, and solely occupied by, persons 62 years of age or older," or (2) "intended and operated for occupancy by at least one person 55 years of age or older per unit" provided that such housing is specifically designed to meet the physical or social needs of older persons and meets other specified criteria. (42 U.S.C. § 3607(b)(2)(B) and (b)(2)(C).)

Plaintiffs contend that because, under traditional supremacy principles, the new federal legislation takes precedence over conflicting state law, and because, under the new legislation, defendants' 25-years-or-older rule may not be validly applied to exclude families with children under the age of 18, the issue of state law presented by this case has been rendered insignificant. For several reasons, we cannot agree.

First, and most obviously, the new federal act clearly does not control plaintiffs' damage claim in this case. By its terms, the federal act does not take effect until 180 days after its enactment and nothing in the act purports to govern conduct—such as the actions of the mobilehome park owners at issue here—which occurred prior to the effective date of the statute.

Second, even with respect to the future, the new federal act does not totally eclipse the question of state law presented here. As we shall see, one of the points at issue in this case is whether the relevant California provisions prohibit a mobilehome park owner from adopting any age-based policy other than an 18-years-or-older rule. If state law does limit a mobilehome park owner's discretion in this fashion, then in the future mobilehome parks in California might well be prohibited from adopting the type of more narrowly defined age-based policies—i.e., a 62-years-or-older rule or a properly limited 55-years-or-older rule—which would qualify for the "housing for older persons" exemption under federal law. (See 42 U.S.C. § 3607(b)(2)(B) and (b)(2)(C).) Accordingly, the question of statutory interpretation before us is by no means eliminated by the recent federal enactment.

Section 798.76 provides in full: "The management [of a mobilehome park] may require that a purchaser of a mobilehome which will remain in the park, comply with any rule or regulation limiting residence to adults only."

In asserting that defendants' 25-years-or-older rule is invalid under section 798.76, plaintiffs advance two distinct, and somewhat inconsistent, arguments. First, plaintiffs maintain that the statutory language permitting a park owner to require compliance with "any rule or regulation limiting residence to *adults only*" (emphasis added) should properly be construed to authorize only a rule or regulation limiting residence to "senior citizens," and that the 25-year-or-older rule is invalid because it does not limit residence to senior citizens. Second, plaintiffs alternatively contend that if "adults only" is not interpreted to mean "senior citizens only," then the statute must necessarily be read to permit a mobilehome park owner only to

adopt a rule limiting residence in the park to persons 18 years or older—i.e., the park owner must permit the residence of all "adults"—and that the statute may not be construed to permit a park owner to adopt any rule which limits residence to a subcategory of adults—e.g., a rule limiting residents to those 25 years or older, or 45 years or older or 62 years or older. We conclude that neither of plaintiffs' arguments can be sustained.

With respect to the initial contention, we think it is clear that the plain language of the statute will not bear the meaning plaintiffs propose. "Adult" is, of course, plainly not the equivalent of "senior citizen," and other statutory provisions concerning senior citizens and mobilehomes—enacted contemporaneously with section 798.76—demonstrate that the Legislature has used quite clear and specific language when it has intended to refer to senior or elderly citizens.

Furthermore, there is absolutely no indication in the background or legislative history of section 798.76 to suggest that the Legislature, in adopting this provision, intended to use the term "adults only" in such an unconventional manner. As we have seen, when this statutory language was first adopted in 1975, no case had either held or intimated that age-based housing policies were valid only within the senior citizen context. In this setting, there simply is no realistic basis for reading the "adults only" language of section 798.76 as bearing such an unnatural meaning. We discuss below whether subsequent developments in the interpretation of, and amendments to, the Unruh Act can properly be viewed as altering the effect of section 798.76, but insofar as the meaning of section 798.76 itself is concerned, we find no legitimate ground for interpreting the section to permit only "senior citizens only" rules.

With respect to plaintiffs' alternative contention—that section 798.76 should be read to permit mobilehome parks to enforce only a rule limiting residence to those 18 years or older, and to preclude the enforcement of any other rule limiting residence, for example, to those 25 years or older, or 45 years or older, or 62 years or older—we again conclude that the claim is untenable in light of both the language and legislative history of the section.

Finally, viewing the matter in very practical terms, we cannot reasonably conclude that the Legislature, in adopting section 798.76, intended to prohibit mobilehome park owners from adopting any age-based rule other than an 18-years-or-older rule. A recent survey of mobilehome parks in California indicates that mobilehome parks throughout the state have adopted a great variety of age-based rules or regulations, with minimum age limits ranging from 18 years of age, to 25 years, 45 years, 50 years, and 60 years. (See *Cal. Dept. of Housing & Community Development, Mobilehome Parks in California: A Survey of Mobilehome Park Owners Pursuant to S.B. 1835*

(Feb. 1986) pp. 31, 33.) Although the survey did not seek to determine how long such policies have been in effect, there is nothing to suggest that this variation is only of recent vintage. To read section 798.76 as plaintiffs propose, we would have to conclude that the Legislature, in enacting the predecessor to section 798.76 in 1975, intended to invalidate all age-based rules in mobilehome parks other than 18-years-and-older rules, thus prohibiting a mobilehome park owner from establishing a park reserved, for example, for persons 55 years or over. In light of the language and legislative history of the provision reviewed above, we cannot reasonably ascribe any such intention to the Legislature.

Finally, plaintiffs claim that if section 798.76 permits a mobilehome park owner to enforce a rule excluding persons under 25 from a mobilehome park, as we have held, the statute is unconstitutional, violating their rights of familial privacy and equal protection. In support of their constitutional claims, plaintiffs rely, *inter alia,* on *Moore v. City of East Cleveland* (1977) 431 U.S. 494, 97 S.Ct. 1932, 52 L.Ed.2d 531 and *City of Santa Barbara v. Adamson* (1980) 27 Cal.3d 123, 164 Cal.Rptr. 539, 610 P.2d 436, decisions in which the United States Supreme Court and this court invalidated local zoning ordinances which impinged on an individual's right to live with members of an extended family *(Moore)* or with unrelated persons *(Adamson).* For a number of reasons, plaintiffs' constitutional challenge lacks merit.

First, both the *Moore, supra,* 431 U.S. 494, 97 S.Ct. 1932, 52 L.Ed.2d 531 and *Adamson, supra,* 27 Cal.3d 123, 164 (Cal.Rptr. 539, 610 P.2d 436), decisions are clearly distinguishable from the present case in a crucial respect. The restriction at issue in each of those cases was a state-imposed rule directly limiting an individual's right to live with whom he or she wanted; in each case, a governmental body had made the substantive decision to limit individual living arrangements within a community. In this case, by contrast, the state, in adopting section 798.76, has not itself established a rule limiting living arrangements or restricting housing to particular age groups, but has simply left that decision—in the private mobilehome park context—to the owner of the mobilehome park. Contrary to plaintiffs' contention, it is not true that, absent section 798.76, a private mobilehome park owner

would not have the authority to adopt an age-based housing policy for its park; a park owner's authority to adopt such a rule arises from its general common law property rights in the mobilehome park, rights which clearly pre-existed the enactment of section 798.76. Nothing in *Adamson* or *Moore* suggests that constitutional guarantees are violated by the enactment of a statute which simply recognizes the continuing existence of a private property owner's authority in this respect.

Second, even if plaintiffs were able to successfully surmount the "state action" hurdle in this case, their constitutional challenge to defendants' age-based housing policy would still lack merit. To begin with, although plaintiffs contend that all classifications on the basis of age should be viewed as constitutionally "suspect" and should be subjected to "strict scrutiny" under the equal protection clause, past decisions—both in this state and in other jurisdictions—have declined to consider age classifications on a constitutional par with classifications which treat persons differently because of their race or ethnic origin.

For the reasons discussed above, we conclude that the private mobilehome park rule at issue here—limiting residence to persons 25 years or older—is not invalid under current California law. Although recent federal legislation will in the future apparently affect the validity of such a rule as applied to families with minor children, defendants did not violate plaintiffs' statutory or constitutional rights in applying the rule during the time period at issue in this case.

Reversed.[1]

Case Questions

1. What restriction was placed on residence in the mobile home park?

2. How does the restriction differ from other restrictions?

3. How does the court deal with the issue of providing housing for families?

4. Is the mobilehome park restriction unconstitutional?

5. Do results on these restrictions differ in retirement states?

Consider 19.3   The Judds purchased a home in a subdivision in Arizona that was designated as one for those age "55 and over." The restrictions on the subdivision also provide that only children over the age of 18 can reside with their parents. The Judds' daughter was recently divorced and has asked to live with them for a few months

---

1.   The federal circuits are in agreement with this California decision that all-adult covenants are constitutional. *See Taylor v. Rancho Santa Barbara,* 206 F.3d 932 (9th Cir. 2000)

until she is financially stable again. The Judds' 12-year-old granddaughter will also be moving in. Can the neighbors obtain a court order to require the daughter and granddaughter to move out? *Riley v. Stoves,* 526 P.2d 749 (Ariz. 1974)

19.3, *continued*

On the basis of the *Schmidt* case and the cases cited therein, determine the constitutional validity of the following:

Consider 19.4

a. A city ordinance requiring all-adult residences only.
b. A city zoning master plan that designates certain areas as adult-only residential areas.
c. A state statute that prohibits landlords from refusing to rent property located in all-adult subdivisions to families with children.

CONSTITUTIONAL ISSUES IN TRANSFER OF PROPERTY

One of the major issues in the transfer of property is the requirement that transfers of title be available to all regardless of race, sex, color, or national origin. The Fair Housing Act was passed in 1968 (42 U.S.C. § 3601 *et seq.*), and § 3604a provides that it is

> unlawful to refuse to sell or rent after the making of a bona fide offer, or to refuse to negotiate for the sale or rental of, or otherwise make unavailable or deny, a dwelling to any person because of race, color, religion, sex, familial status, or national origin.

The basis for this statutory regulation is the Equal Protection Clause of the Fourteenth Amendment. As discussed in Chapter 1, the Fourteenth Amendment requires that all citizens be treated equally in the application and enforcement of state laws. The Fourteenth Amendment is the basis for many of the racial, religious, and national origin discrimination cases. The purpose of the amendment is to guarantee all an equal opportunity to be treated alike under state laws.

However, when the issue involved is private action as opposed to the application of state laws to individuals, the Fourteenth Amendment is not applicable. In other words, the Fourteenth Amendment does not prohibit private discrimination, and legislation to prevent private discrimination is required to fill that gap. The Fair Housing Act is an example of a statute passed to prevent private discrimination. The act applies not only to sellers of properties, but also to real estate brokers and salespersons, mortgage lenders, property insurers, and property appraisers. The following sections cover application of the Fair Housing Act and the techniques for discrimination.

Application of the Fair Housing Act

The purpose of the Fair Housing Act is to assure that every person has an equal opportunity to buy, rent, or live in residential real property. The Act applies to residential housing and prohibits discrimination in selling, renting, lending, or insuring residential property on the basis of race, color, religion, sex, handicap, family status, or national origin. Some states may have additional classes protected under state law.

A handicap is defined in the same way it is under the Americans with Disability Act (see Chapters 8 and 9 on leases). A *handicap* is a mental or physical impairment that limits one or more major life activities. Examples of impairment protected under the Fair Housing Act include impairments in sight, mobility, and hearing. Mental illness, heart disease, cancer, cerebral palsy, multiple sclerosis, diabetes, AIDS, HIV, and treatment for substance abuse are also protected. Smokers and current drug users are not protected.

There are some Fair Housing Act exemptions. The owner exemption is one that applies when an owner is selling his or her own home, does not use a real estate agent or broker, does not own more than three single-family homes, and does not use any form of discriminatory advertising. Another owner exemption applies to the owner of a residential dwelling in which he or she also resides and that has four or fewer units that are leased to others. There is also a religious exemption for religious organizations. These organizations can discriminate on the basis of religion in selling and leasing residential properties. Another exemption covered earlier in the chapter is the exemption for senior housing, or housing for senior citizens exclusively. There are a substantial number of requirements for senior housing, such as having 80 percent or more of the units occupied by at least one resident who is age 55 or above.

Types of Discriminatory Conduct Under the Fair Housing Act

ADVERTISING

Brokers, agents, and even newspapers that run residential property ads must use caution in their descriptive terms so that the ads do not suggest limitations on availability of the property to certain protected classes. For example, language that suggests the property is "great for mature person" would be discriminatory. To comply, brokers and agents should try to describe the property, not potential buyers or lessees or the seller or the neighbors. The following is an excerpt from a HUD memo offering guidelines for advertising real property.

The following is policy guidance on certain advertising issues which have arisen recently. We are currently reviewing past guidance from this office and from the Office of General Counsel and will update our guidance as appropriate.

1. *Race, color, national origin.* Real estate advertisements should state no discriminatory preference or limitation on account of race, color, or national origin. Use of words describing the housing, the current or potential residents, or the neighbors or neighborhood in racial or ethnic terms (e.g., white family home, no Irish) will create liability under this section.

    However, advertisements which are facially neutral will not create liability. Thus, complaints over the use of phrases such as master bedroom, rare find, and desirable neighborhood should not be filed.

2. *Religion.* Advertisements should not contain an explicit preference, limitation, or discrimination on account of religion (e.g., no Jews, Christian home). Advertisements which use the legal name of an entity which contains a religious reference (for example, Roselawn Catholic Home), or those which contain a religious symbol (such as a cross), standing alone, may indicate a religious preference. However, if such an advertisement includes a disclaimer (such as the statement, "This Home does not discriminate on the basis of race, color, religion, national origin, sex, handicap, or familial status"), it will not violate the Act.

Advertisements containing descriptions of properties (apartment complex with chapel), or services (kosher meals available) do not on their face state a preference for persons likely to make use of those facilities, and are not violations of the Act.

The use of secularized terms or symbols relating to religious holidays such as Santa Claus, Easter Bunny, or St. Valentine's Day images, or phrases such as "Merry Christmas" or "Happy Easter," or the like does not constitute a violation of the Act.

3. *Sex.* Advertisements for single-family dwellings or separate units in a multi-family dwelling should contain no explicit preference, limitation, or discrimination based on sex. Use of the term master bedroom does not constitute a violation of either the sex discrimination provisions or the race discrimination provisions. Terms such as "mother-in-law suite" and "bachelor apartment" are commonly used as physical descriptions of housing units and do not violate the Act.

4. *Handicap.* Real estate advertisements should not contain explicit exclusions, limitations, or other indications of discrimination based on handicap (e.g., no wheelchairs). Advertisements containing descriptions of properties (great view, fourth floor walk-up, walk-in closet), services or facilities (jogging trails), or neighborhoods (walk to bus stops) do not violate the Act. Advertisements describing the conduct required of residents ("non-smoking," "sober") do not violate the Act. Advertisements containing descriptions of accessibility features are lawful (wheelchair ramp).

5. *Familial status.* Advertisements may not state an explicit preference, limitation, or discrimination based on familial status. Advertisements may not contain limitations on the number or ages of children, or state a preference for adults, couples, or singles. Advertisements describing the properties (two bedroom, cozy, family room), services and facilities (no bicycle allowed), or neighborhoods (quiet streets) are not facially discriminatory and do not violate the Act.

For additional guidance on advertising, see the HUD Advertising Guide reproduced in the *Fair Housing Handbook.*

Evaluate the following language and determine whether there is a violation of the Fair Housing Act in running an ad with these terms.

Consider 19.5

a. "Spacious 1- & 2-bedroom apartments in quiet mature complex. No pets, please."
b. "2-person limit."
c. "Adults pref."
d. "No children."
e. "Mature Christian handyman wanted to share house."
f. "Ideal for professionals."
g. "Mature setting."
h. "For one person."
i. "Within walking distance."
j. "Handyman's dream."
k. "No alcoholics."
l. "Female tenant wanted."
m. "Near church."
n. "Desirable neighborhood."
o. "Call Betsy."
p. "No pets."

BLOCKBUSTING

Blockbusting is a method of controlling the racial composition of neighborhoods and is usually attributed to the actions of real estate brokers or salespersons. For example, in *United States v. Mitchell,* 327 F.Supp. 476 (N.D. Ga. 1971), a real estate agent went from house to house in a neighborhood, informing the residents that "negroes were coming into the neighborhood" and that houses should be sold as quickly as possible. The result was that all of the white residents in the neighborhood sold their homes, and the neighborhood became all black. Mitchell was convicted of violating the Fair Housing Act.

STEERING

Steering is another form of property transfer discrimination that is generally attributed to real estate brokers and salespersons. It is an attempt to direct buyers to specific sections of town that are labeled as either white or black areas. In *Zuch v. Hussey,* 394 F.Supp. 1028 (E.D. Mich. 1975), salespersons found to have violated the act made statements such as, "Do you read the newspapers? Even the police are afraid to live in the area and they are supposed to protect the rest of us" and "You wouldn't want that home, the coloreds have moved in pretty good there." In the same case, salespersons discouraged black buyers from buying in white areas by temporarily taking homes off the market. Through these tactics (which were declared illegal), several real estate firms were able to maintain racially segregated neighborhoods in the Detroit area for a period of time.

REDLINING

Redlining is the refusal by a lender to lend or an insurer to insure on property because of its location within a predetermined geographic area. The name for this practice arose because lenders and insurers were literally drawing red lines on maps around areas in which property loans and insurance should not be made or should be made on less than favorable terms. The Fair Housing Act and many state statutes prohibit redlining; in many cases, they require lending institutions to submit loan figures so that an agency can verify the institutions' lending records. For example, federal institutions are required to submit loan figures under the Home Mortgage Disclosure Act (12 U.S.C. §§ 2801 *et seq.*). Also, the Community Reinvestment Act of 1977 (12 U.S.C. §§ 2901 *et seq.*) imposes an affirmative obligation on federal financial institutions to meet the community's loan needs regardless of property location or area condition.

Redlining can occur in a number of different ways. The most obvious is when lenders openly refuse to make loans in particular areas. Other, more subtle processes still classified as redlining include the arbitrary variation of loan application processes and loan terms. For example, redlining can consist of requiring a higher down payment, higher closing costs, minimum loan amounts, lowered percentage of loan amount to appraised value, or underappraisal of property. The determination of whether a lender has made a predetermined lending decision on the basis of property location is a question of fact that requires litigation.

An interesting development in lending practices has raised concerns about redlining. A new group of lenders is creating "customized" home mortgage loans. The terms of a mortgage are dictated by market specifics. For example, lenders have determined that Cincinnati home buyers keep their homes for longer periods than most home buyers thereby generating more profits on the loans. So, lenders reduce interest rates for Cincinnati home mortgage debtors. The federal regulators are concerned about these geographic breakdowns and differences as a form of redlining, particularly when racial composition varies.

N.A.A.C.P. v. American Family Mutual Ins. Co.

978 F.2d 287 (7th Cir. 1992)

Facts

The NAACP, through its Milwaukee Branch (plaintiffs), brought suit alleging that insurers in the area were engaging in redlining and that such actions violated the Fair Housing Act.

The trial court dismissed the complaint, and the NAACP appealed.

Judicial Opinion

Easterbrook, Circuit Judge. Is redlining in the insurance business a form of racial discrimination violating the Fair Housing Act? "Redlining" is charging higher rates or declining to write insurance for people who live in particular areas (figuratively, sometimes literally, enclosed with red lines on a map).

Plaintiffs contend that a mortgage loan usually is essential to home ownership, and that lenders are unwilling to provide credit unless the borrower obtains insurance on the house that serves as security for the loan. Higher premiums price some would-be buyers out of the market; a refusal to write insurance excludes all buyers. If insurers redline areas with large or growing numbers of minority residents, that practice raises the cost of housing for black persons and also frustrates their ability to live in integrated neighborhoods. Even if they achieve their goal, they pay extra.

According to the plaintiffs, three sections of the Fair Housing Act address insurance sold (or withheld) in connection with the purchase of a dwelling: 42 U.S.C. §§ 3604(a), 3604(b), and 3605. Section 3605 requires the least discussion. It provides:

(a) It shall be unlawful for any person or other entity whose business includes engaging in residential real estate-related transactions to discriminate against any person in making available such a transaction, or in the terms or conditions of such a transaction, because of race, color, religion, sex, handicap, familial status, or national origin.

(b) As used in this section, the term "residential real estate-related transaction" means any of the following:

(I) The making or purchasing of loans or providing other financial assistance—

(A) for purchasing, constructing, improving, repairing, or maintaining a dwelling; or

(B) secured by residential real estate.

(2) The selling, brokering, or appraising of residential real property.

It would strain language past the breaking point to treat property or casualty insurance as "financial assistance"—let alone as assistance "for purchasing . . . a dwelling". Insurers do not subsidize their customers or act as channels through which public agencies extend subsidies. They do not "assist" customers even in the colloquial sense that loans are "assistance" (a lender advances cash, with repayment deferred). Payment runs from the customer to the insurer. Insurance is no more "financial assistance" than a loaf of bread purchased at retail price in a supermarket is "food assistance" or a bottle of aspirin bought from a druggist is "medical assistance." [II] Section 3604 makes it unlawful:

(a) To refuse to sell or rent after the making of a bona fide offer, or to refuse to negotiate for the sale or rental of, *or otherwise make unavailable* or deny, a dwelling to any person because of race, color, religion, sex, familial status, or national origin.

(b) To discriminate against any person in the terms, conditions, or privileges of sale or rental of a dwelling, *or in the provision of services* or facilities *in connection therewith*, because of race, color, sex, familial status, or national origin.

Plaintiffs rely on the portions of these sections that we have [emphasized]. They contend that by refusing to write policies (or setting a price too dear) an insurer "make[s a dwelling] unavailable" to the potential buyer. Lenders require their borrowers to secure property insurance. No insurance, no loan; no loan, no house; lack of insurance thus makes housing unavailable.

Plaintiffs also submit that property insurance is a "service" rendered "in connection" with the sale of the dwelling. If the world of commerce is divided between "goods" and "services," then insurers supply a "service." "[I]n connection" may be read broadly, and should be (plaintiffs contend) to carry out the national goal of removing obstacles to minorities' ownership of housing. There you have it.

Nothing in the text of the statute permits us to reject these proposed readings. The Fair Housing Act does not define key terms such as "service" and "make unavailable". By writing its statute in the passive voice—banning an outcome while not saying *who* the actor is, or *how* such actors bring the forbidden consequence—Congress created ambiguity.

In 1988 Congress enacted amendments to the Fair Housing Act, authorizing the Department of Housing and Urban Development to "make rules . . . to carry out this subchapter." 42 U.S.C. § 3641a. Congress gave the Executive Branch this power with knowledge that since 1987 a succession of Secretaries have believed that "[i]nsurance redlining, by denying or impeding coverage[,] makes mortgage money unavailable, rendering dwellings 'unavailable' as effectively as the denial of financial assistance on other grounds."

Counsel of HUD: The Secretary deployed this new rulemaking power in the predictable way, issuing regulations that include, among the conduct prohibited by § 3604: "Refusing to provide . . . property or hazard insurance for dwellings or providing such . . . insurance differently because of race".

Section 3604 is sufficiently pliable that its text can bear the Secretary's construction. Courts should respect a plausible construction by an agency to which Congress has delegated the power to make substantive rules. We can imagine the response that courts do not defer to administrative constructions when judges, rather than administrators, hold the power of enforcement.

No matter how a court should have understood the Fair Housing Act in 1984, however, the question today is whether the Secretary's regulations are tenable. They are. Section 3604 applies to discriminatory denials of insurance, and discriminatory pricing, that effectively preclude ownership of housing because of the race of the applicant

Reversed as to the Fair Housing Act violations alleged and remanded for trial.

Case Questions

1. What violation of the Fair Housing Act is alleged?
2. Is insurance specifically mentioned in the statute?
3. What happened in 1988 with respect to the Fair Housing Act?
4. Are insurance companies' actions covered under the Act?
5. Did an administrative agency play a role in this judicial finding?

Redlining has also become an issue in setting appraisal values. In the following case, the appraisal standards of the American Institute of Real Estate Appraisers were challenged as violative of the Fair Housing Act.

United States v. American Institute of Real Estate Appraisers

442 F. Supp. 1072 (Ill. 1977) affirmed 590 F.2d 242 (8th Cir.1978)

Facts

The United States filed suit against two organizations, the American Institute of Real Estate Appraisers (AIREA) and the Society of Real Estate Appraisers (defendants), for violation of the Fair Housing Act. The suit alleged that since the effective date of the Fair Housing Act, these two organizations had engaged in unlawful discriminatory practices by promulgating standards that have caused appraisers and lenders to treat race and national origin as negative factors in determining the value of dwellings and in evaluating the soundness of home loans. The suit further alleged that the organizations failed to take adequate steps to correct the continuing effects of past discrimination and ensure nondiscrimination by appraisers and lenders, whose practices are subject to the influence of the organizations.

The United States sought injunctive relief, and after extensive negotiations the United States and the AIREA agreed not to litigate the matter; instead, they asked for

the approval of a settlement order, which would include the adoption of the following statements as policies of the AIREA:

1. It is improper to base a conclusion or opinion of value upon the premise that the racial, ethnic or religious homogeneity of the inhabitants of an area is necessary for maximum value.

2. Racial, religious or ethnic factors are deemed unreliable predictors of value trends or price variance.

3. It is improper to base a conclusion or opinion of value, or a conclusion with respect to neighborhood trends, upon stereotyped or biased presumptions relating to race, color, religion, sex or national origin or upon unsupported presumptions relating to the effective age or remaining life of the property being appraised or the life expectancy of the neighborhood in which it is located.

Opelka and others, as members of the AIREA, brought suit challenging the settlement order on grounds that appraisal was not within the coverage of the Fair Housing Act and that the AIREA has no authority to enter into such a settlement.

Judicial Opinion

Leighton, District Judge. The first and fundamental objection is that the court lacks jurisdiction (to approve the settlement) because the Fair Housing Act does not apply to appraisers. . . . [T]he court takes this opportunity to hold that the Fair Housing Act does apply to appraisers of real estate. . . . The principal argument advanced is that the sections of the Fair Housing Act do not mention appraisers. Section 3604 provides in pertinent part:

It shall be unlawful—

(a) To refuse to sell or rent after the making of a bona fide offer, or to refuse to negotiate for the sale or rental of, or otherwise make unavailable or deny, a dwelling to any person because of race, color, religion, sex or national origin.

It shall be unlawful to coerce, intimidate, threaten, or interfere with any person in the exercise or enjoyment of, or on account of his having exercised or enjoyed, or on account of his having aided or encouraged any other person in the exercise or enjoyment of, any right [granted under this Act].

It is clear from the plain language of the provisions that appraisers are not exempted from their coverage; both sections are unrestricted with respect to the class of persons subject to their prohibition. The "otherwise make unavailable or deny" language has been applied to a variety of conduct to prohibit all practices which have the effect of denying dwellings on prohibited grounds. For example, the Act applies to racially exclusionary land use practices by a municipality. It applies to "redlining" by financial institutions. It applies to delaying tactics and discouragement of rental applications used by resident managers and rental agents, and top management and owners who fail to set objective and reviewable procedures for rental applications.

The "or interfere with" language has been similarly broadly applied to reach all practices which have the effect of interfering with the exercise of rights under the Act. The Act requires a liberal construction if the statute is to prohibit effectively "all forms of discrimination, sophisticated, as well as simple-minded." Given a broad interpretation of these provisions, it becomes clear that the United States has stated a claim for relief under their terms. The promulgation of standards which cause appraisers and lenders to treat race and national origin as a negative factor in determining the value of dwellings and in evaluating the soundness of home loans may effectively "make unavailable or deny" a "dwelling" and may interfere with persons in the exercise and enjoyment of rights guaranteed by the Act.

The settlement order is approved.

Case Questions

1. Who are the defendants in the case?
2. What does the settlement order provide?
3. Who is challenging the settlement?
4. What is the basis of the challenge?
5. Does the Fair Housing Act apply to appraisers?

Section 8 Housing and the Fair Housing Act

One of the complex issues in the area of fair housing arises when there is an intersection of several federal statutes that provide housing rights. For example, the so-called Section 8 housing program now places low-income families in mainstream housing and does so through rent vouchers. Landlords who participate in the program were once required by HUD regulation and federal statute to take all the Section 8 tenants sent their way with the only limitation being HUD's restrictions on the number of Section 8 tenants within a particular apartment complex or area. Known as the "take one, take all" provisions, the impact on landlords and properties was substantial and the requirement was repealed by Congress. A landlord need not take all Section 8 tenants, but the decision not to rent must be based on something other than receipt of public assistance.

http://

The ADA Accessibility Guidelines for Buildings and Facilities (ADAAG) details scoping and technical requirements to be applied during design-construction, and alteration of buildings and facilities. Visit **http://www.access-board.gov/adaag/html/adaag.htm**.

The Americans with Disabilities Act and Fair Housing

Both the Fair Housing Act and the laws and regulations on Section 8 housing prohibit discrimination on the basis of disability. One form of discrimination is the refusal of a landlord to make reasonable accommodations for tenants with disabilities. For example, a landlord must provide a tenant with multiple sclerosis an assigned parking space rather than the usual "first-come, first-serve" policy because of the tenant's difficulty with walking, her incontinence, and the space she needed for negotiating getting in and out of her car. In the following case, a court was faced with yet another wrinkle in a case that combines the discrimination issues of the Americans with Disabilities Act and Section 8 tenants with low income and disabilities.

Salute v. Stratford Greens Apartments

136 F.3d 293 (2nd Cir. 1998)

Facts

Richard Salute and Marie Kravette are individuals with disabilities who are qualified to receive Section 8 housing assistance. They were denied an apartment at the Stratford Greens Garden Apartments (defendants) because the owner refused to take Section 8 tenants. Salute and Kravette filed suit alleging that they were refused an apartment because of their disabilities. The district court dismissed the suit and Salute and Kravette (plaintiffs) appealed.

Judicial Opinion

Jacob, Circuit Judge. The Fair Housing Amendments Act of 1988 ("FHAA") extended the Fair Housing Act's principle of equal opportunity in housing to individuals with handicaps. The Act makes it unlawful,

> [t]o discriminate against any person in the terms, conditions, or privileges of sale or rental of a dwelling, or in the provision of services or facilities in connection with such dwelling, because of a handicap of that person.

Under the FHAA, discrimination includes "a refusal to make *reasonable accommodations* in rules, policies, practices, or services, when such accommodations may be necessary to afford such person *equal opportunity to use and enjoy a dwelling.*" Thus, if the reasonable accommodations provision is triggered, a defendant can be required to incur "reasonable costs" to accommodate a plaintiff's handicap, "provided such accommodations *do not* pose an *undue hardship* or a *substantial burden.*"

Salute and Kravette contend that the defendants' refusal to reasonably accommodate them by accepting their

Section 8 certificates violated the FHAA. This argument presents at least two questions under the statute: (A) Is a landlord's participation in the Section 8 program an accommodation to the plaintiffs' handicaps within the meaning of the statute? (B) If so, is such an accommodation a reasonable one that the landlord is therefore required to make?

We now turn to the more fundamental question of whether a landlord's participation in the Section 8 program should be deemed an "accommodation" (regardless of its reasonableness) within the meaning of the statute. Plaintiffs' claim is a novel one because they do not contend that they require an accommodation that meets and fits their particular handicaps. Rather, they claim an entitlement to an accommodation that remedies their economic status, on the ground that this economic status results from their being handicapped. We think it is fundamental that the law addresses the accommodation of handicaps, not the alleviation of economic disadvantages that may be correlated with having handicaps.

Ordinarily, the duty to make reasonable accommodations is framed by the nature of the particular handicap. The HUD regulations give two examples of when a reasonable accommodation would be required: the lifting of a no-pets rule to allow use of a seeing-eye dog; or the waiver of a first-come, first-serve policy on parking spots to accommodate the impaired mobility of a person suffering from multiple sclerosis. In all of these cases and examples, it is the handicap that is accommodated. Many reported cases under § 3604(f)(3) involve developers' requests for variances of zoning ordinances that would allow the building of housing for handicapped persons. In these cases as well, the duty to accommodate is shaped by the handicap, such as the need of people with certain handicaps to live together in order to share support personnel and to reinforce each other's efforts in creating and maintaining a home.

Plaintiffs seek to use this statute to remedy economic discrimination of a kind that is practiced without regard to handicap. The "opportunity to use and enjoy" language of the FHAA reinforces the ability of people with handicaps to have the same opportunity as similarly situated persons who have no evident handicaps. What stands between these plaintiffs and the apartments at Stratford Greens is a shortage of money, and nothing else. In this respect, impecunious people with disabilities stand on the same footing as everyone else. Thus, the accommodation sought by plaintiffs is not "necessary" to afford handicapped persons "*equal opportunity*" to use and enjoy a dwelling.

Congress could not have intended the FHAA to require reasonable accommodations for those with handicaps every time a neutral policy imposes an adverse impact on individuals who are poor. The FHAA does not elevate the rights of the handicapped poor over the rights of the non-handicapped poor. Economic discrimination—such as the refusal to accept Section 8 tenants—is not cognizable as a failure to make reasonable accommodations. Accordingly, we affirm the district court's rejection of plaintiffs' claims under the "reasonable accommodations" provision of the FHAA.

Under disparate impact analysis, "a prima facie case is established by showing that the challenged practice of the defendant actually or predictably results in . . . discrimination." Discriminatory intent need not be shown. Once a plaintiff establishes a prima facie case, the burden shifts to the defendant to "prove that its actions furthered, in theory and in practice, a legitimate, bona fide . . . interest and that no alternative would serve that interest with less discriminatory effect."

We agree with the Seventh Circuit's observation that because the Section 8 program is voluntary and nonparticipating owners routinely reject Section 8 tenants, the owners' "non-participation constitutes a legitimate reason for their refusal to accept Section 8 tenants and . . . we therefore cannot hold them liable for . . . discrimination under the disparate impact theory."

Case Questions

1. What discrimination is alleged?
2. What reasonable accommodation do the tenants want the landlord to make?
3. Is accommodation of an economic condition required under the FHAA and the Americans with Disabilities Act?
4. What is the disparate impact argument?

Great Eastern Bank has been sued by several members of the Navajo Tribe for redlining on home loans located on the reservation. Great Eastern has supplied statistics indicating that over 75 percent of all home mortgage loans on reservation property end in default and foreclosure. Is Great Eastern's statistic a valid basis for denying future reservation loans?

Consider 19.6

Penalties Under the Fair Housing Act

Enforcement of the Fair Housing Act is accomplished by anyone harmed by a violation through a civil suit, through complaints filed by state agencies, HUD, or by special interest groups on behalf of protected classes. Even testers, or individuals sent out to pose as potential buyers or renters, can bring actions for violations. Administrative law judges assigned to hear complaints brought by HUD have the authority to issue injunctions to halt an activity. They also have the authority to assess fines and penalties which range from $10,000 to $50,000, depending upon the nature of the violation and the violator's past history of violations. When an individual brings suit, he or she can recover damages for emotional distress, mental anguish, and any other damages resulting from the discrimination.

Many cases brought by HUD are settled through a consent decree that requires a remedy for the disparity in housing opportunities. Compliance with the consent decree is critical because the courts have upheld fines against officers and government officials when they fail to comply with the requirements of the decree.

In *Spallone v. U.S.*, 493 U.S. 265 (1990), the city of Yonkers, New York, was charged with engaging in a pattern and practice of housing discrimination. The charges were brought in 1980, and a consent decree was entered into. By 1988, however, the requirements of the decree to remedy past housing discrimination had not been met, and a federal district court held city council members in contempt and imposed a daily fine. The United States Supreme Court eventually reversed the contempt holding and the fines against the individuals as a violation of some portions of the First Amendment but did uphold sanctions against the city for failure to comply. In this case, the authority of the federal government to collect fines from municipalities was made clear.

DUE PROCESS AND REAL PROPERTY

Throughout the preceding chapters, the concept of due process has been mentioned in connection with different topics. For example, mortgage foreclosures require prior notice to the mortgagor, and the opportunity for the mortgagor to object, before title to or interest in financed property may be taken away. With respect to real property taxes, landowners must be given opportunities to object to and be heard on the valuations of their properties. Tax sales require advance notice to the property owner and an opportunity for redemption. All of these protections are afforded through the Fifth and Fourteenth Amendments' due process clauses of the Constitution, which require that before there is any deprivation of a property interest, the parties must be given opportunities to be heard and to object. Due process protections may be satisfied through judicial or administrative proceedings, so long as the opportunity to be heard is afforded.

CAUTIONS AND CONCLUSIONS

In this chapter, only a few issues of constitutional law affecting real property rights were discussed. The opportunities for constitutional challenges to real property rights and procedures are as limitless as the field of constitutional law. Basically, the areas of constitutional law affecting real property are concerned with the issues of fairness, the deprivation of rights in existing property, or the right to own property. Constitutional protections offer security for property owners holding title and provide potential property owners opportunities for purchase.

Key Terms

eminent domain, 487
taking, 488
just compensation, 492

all-adult covenant, 494
blockbusting, 500
steering, 500

redlining, 500

Chapter Problems

1. The Laufmans attempted to purchase property in an area of Cincinnati that was changing in racial composition from white to black. Oakley Building and Loan denied the Laufmans' loan application on grounds that the neighborhood was declining and they would not have sufficient security by taking a mortgage on the property located there. The Laufmans filed suit alleging that Oakley Building and Loan had violated the Fair Housing Act. Is there a violation? *Laufman v. Oakley Building & Loan Co.*, 408 F.Supp. 489 (Ohio 1976)

2. Florence Dolan owns a plumbing and supply store located on Main Street in the Central Business District of Tigard, Oregon. The store covers approximately 9,700 square feet on the eastern side of a 1.67-acre parcel that includes a gravel parking lot. Fanno Creek flows through the southwestern corner of the lot and along its western boundary. The year-round flow of the creek renders the area within the creek's 100-year floodplain virtually unusable for commercial development. The city's comprehensive plan includes the Fanno Creek floodplain as part of the city's greenway system.

Dolan applied to the city for a permit to redevelop the site. Her proposed plans called for nearly doubling the size of the store to 17,600 square feet, and paving a 39-space parking lot. The existing store, located on the opposite side of the parcel, would be razed in sections as construction progressed on the new building. In the second phase of the project, Dolan proposed to build an additional structure on the northeast side of the site for complementary businesses and to provide more parking. The proposal by Dolan is consistent with the city's zoning scheme in the Central Business District.

The City Planning Commission granted Dolan's permit application subject to conditions imposed by the city's Community Development Code (CDC). The commission required, as a condition to approval of the permit application, that Dolan dedicate the portion of her property lying within the 100-year floodplain for improvement of a storm drainage system along Fanno Creek and that she dedicate an additional 15-foot strip of land adjacent to the flood plain as a pedestrian/bicycle pathway. The dedication required Dolan to give up approximately 7,000 square feet, or roughly 10 percent of the property. In accordance with city practice, Dolan could rely on the dedicated property to meet the 15 percent open space and landscaping requirement mandated by the city's zoning scheme. The city would bear the cost of maintaining a landscaped buffer between the dedicated area and the new store. Can the city require Dolan to do this? *Dolan v. City of Tigard*, 512 U.S. 374 (1994)

3. William G. Haas & Company purchased land and procured a site permit from the city of San Francisco for the construction of a high-rise project. The site permit was later invalidated because of violations of the Environmental Quality Act and later because of the rezoning of the property, which prohibited high-rise projects in the area. Haas brought suit claiming the rezoning and the imposition of other land-use restrictions diminished the value of his property to such an extent that the regulations constituted a taking. What was the result?

4. Midwestern Indemnity refused to write insurance policies for homes located in neighborhoods that were predominantly black. Midwestern's reasons were high theft, vandalism, and arson rates in the areas, and company officials had the areas marked on maps in their offices. Several black home owners brought suit, alleging the insurer was redlining. Midwestern maintains insurers are not subject to the Fair Housing Act. What is the result?

5. The Harpers (a black family) purchased a home with financing through Union Savings Association. During the first year, two of the Harpers' payment checks bounced but were immediately covered. Mr. Harper then lost his job and attempted to work out an interim payment schedule with Union. Union refused and foreclosed on the property. An examination of Union's records reveals that it was the first time Union had refused an interim payment plan for a temporarily unemployed borrower. Harper filed suit, alleging Union had violated the Fair Housing Act. Union maintains the Fair Housing Act is applicable only to purchases of homes and loans, not foreclosures. What is the result?

6. The city of Phoenix announced the taking of 60 homes located near the airport for the purpose of expanding the airport runways to support increased air traffic. The home owners claim that the appraisals should reflect the commercial value of their property because of the closer proximity to the airstrips. The city of Phoenix maintains that value is determined before the change. What is the result?

7. In 1927, W. T. Shore and T. C. Wilson gave property to the city of Charlotte "so long as the property was used for municipal parks, golf courses, or playgrounds for whites only." Several black citizens have brought suit, alleging the restriction is unconstitutional. What type of interest was created, and what is the result?

8. Bradley Winker owned a duplex dwelling unit in Brookings, South Dakota. The duplex was located in an "R-2" residential zoning area that permits two-family dwellings but limits the number of unrelated adults who may constitute a "family." An inspection of one unit in the duplex on November 8, 1994, revealed the presence of at least four unrelated adult college students residing in one unit of the duplex. Brookings filed a complaint against Winker, charging him with a violation of the Brookings ordinance that restricts the number of unrelated adults per unit. Winker sued, challenging the Brookings ordinance as a violation of the due process and equal protection clauses with its restrictive definition of family. Is the zoning restriction valid or unconstitutional? Be sure to refer to cases in this chapter and Chapter 18 to help you analyze the question. *City of Brookings v. Winker,* 554 N.W.2d 827 (S.D. 1996)

9. The Montgomery Newspapers, Inc., ran ads for rental properties in their six newspapers with the following language:

a. "mature person"

b. "ideal for quiet and reserved single and/or couple"

c. "professional male . . . only"

d. "quiet mature setting"

Do any of these phrases violate the Fair Housing Act? *Fair Housing Council of Suburban Philadelphia v. Montgomery Newspapers,* 141 F.3d 71 (3rd Cir. 1998)

10. Bert and Cleone Reece own an apartment building near Logan Field in Billings, Montana. Their policy was to refuse to rent any of their apartments to single women who did not have cars. Further, they did not consider alimony or child support in determining whether a woman could meet monthly rental payments. Do their policies create any constitutional problems? *U.S. v. Reece,* 457 F.Supp. 43 (Utah 1978)

Internet Activities

1. For a detailed explanation on how to obtain a variance to a county zoning ordinance, go to: **http://www.co.rockingham.va.us/variance.htm**.

2. For an example of the exercise of eminent domain for public purposes in the state of Minnesota, go to: **http://www.revisor.leg.state.mn.us/slaws/1997/c082.html** (for a state statute relating to capital improvements; authorizing towns to exercise eminent domain and other powers for purposes of wastewater infrastructure).

3. Read some of the issues relating to eminent domain on the following sites: **http://leg.state.mt.us/Services/Lepo/subcommittees/edsub.htm** and **http://www.geocities.com/CapitolHill/Congress/6444**.

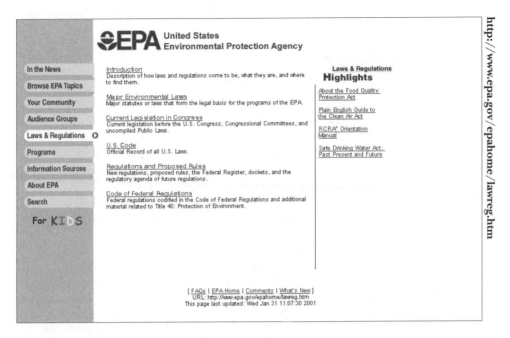

Chapter 20
Environmental Law

The landscape and the language are the same
For we ourselves are landscape and land.

Conrad Aiken, *A Letter from Li Po and Other Poems (1955)*

This chapter discusses both the governmental restrictions on land use and the governmental protections for landowners. The following questions are answered: What types of governmental regulations affect property use and ownership rights? Who is responsible for enforcing governmental regulations? What penalties exist for violation of the regulations? In the event of conflicts between common law rights and governmental regulations, which group of laws will control?

STATUTORY ENVIRONMENTAL LAWS

At the federal level, most environmental laws can be placed in one of three categories: those regulating air pollution, those regulating water pollution, and those regulating land pollution. In addition, the federal regulatory scheme has several laws affecting property rights that do not fit into these categories but are discussed in this section.

http://

Check out the EPA
regulations at: **http://
www.epa.gov/epahome/
lawreg.htm**.

Air Pollution Regulation

EARLY LEGISLATION

The first legislation dealing with the problem of air pollution, the **Air Pollution Control Act,** was passed in 1955. The act did very little in terms of controlling air pollution.

Federal regulation was also largely ineffective in the 1960s. To encourage greater involvement in the air pollution issue, Congress passed the **Air Quality Act** in 1967. Under this act, the Department of Health, Education, and Welfare (HEW) was authorized to oversee the states' adoption of air quality standards and the implementation of those plans. Again, this legislation proved ineffective, for by 1970 no state had adopted a comprehensive plan.

1970 AMENDMENTS TO CLEAN AIR ACT—NEW STANDARDS

Because the states did not take action in the area of air pollution, Congress passed the 1970 amendments to the original but largely ignored 1963 **Clean Air Act** (42 U.S.C. § 7401); these amendments constituted the first federal legislation with any real authority for enforcement. Under the act, the **Environmental Protection Agency (EPA)** was authorized to establish air quality standards. Once those standards were developed, states were required to adopt implementation plans to achieve the federally developed standards. These **state implementation plans (SIPs)** had to be approved by the EPA, and adoption and enforcement of the plans were no longer discretionary but mandatory. The implementation plans, to obtain EPA approval, had to meet deadlines for compliance with the EPA air quality standards, and thus the Clean Air Act established time periods for achieving air quality.

The air quality standards set by the EPA specify how much of a particular substance in the air is permissible. It was up to each state to devise methods for meeting those standards. The first step taken by the states was to measure existing air content of substances such as sulfur dioxide, carbon monoxide, and hydrocarbons. Based on the results, the states then took appropriate steps to reduce the amounts of those substances that exceeded federal standards.

In industrialized states, nearly all manufacturers were required to install pollution equipment. This process proved to be the subject of many suits because industries claimed the equipment was too expensive and often technologically infeasible. Many companies filed suit seeking a delay in equipment installation until pollution control devices could be perfected or at least reduced in cost. The results of the argument for technological infeasibility varied. However, most courts concluded that the Clean Air Act was intended to be technology-forcing. This issue became moot with the passage of Clean Air Act Amendments in 1977 and 1990 and their specific mandates on the technology levels required for companies to achieve compliance.

1977 AMENDMENTS

With the 1977 amendments also came authority for the EPA to regulate business growth in an attempt to achieve air quality standards. With this authority, the EPA classified two types of areas in which business growth could be contained. One was called a **nonattainment area** and included those areas with existing, significant air quality problems, the so-called dirty areas. The second classification was for the clean areas and was called **prevention of significant deterioration (PSD) areas.**

EPA ECONOMIC CONTROLS FOR NONATTAINMENT AREAS

For nonattainment areas, the EPA developed its **Emissions Offset Policy,** which requires three elements before a new facility can begin operation in a nonattainment area:

1. The new plant must have the greatest possible emissions controls. In some cases, this means the plant will be required to meet standards higher than existing standards.
2. The proposed plant operator must have all other operations in compliance with standards.
3. The new plant's emissions must be offset by reductions from other facilities in the area. These offsets have to be greater than the new emissions.

In applying these elements, the EPA follows the so-called **bubble concept,** which examines all the air pollutants in the area as if they came from a single source. If it can be shown that a new plant will have no net effect on the air in the area (after offsets from other plants), then the new facility will not be subject to a veto.

Although the EPA did not regulate initially the construction of plants in areas already meeting air quality standards, environmentalists' protests and suits brought about the application of EPA regulations to PSD areas. Basically, the purpose of PSD regulations is to permit the EPA to have the right to review proposed plant constructions prior to their construction. In their submissions for EPA review, the plant operators are required to establish that there will be no significant effect on air quality and that emissions will be controlled with appropriate devices.

LATEST CONTROLS—CLEAN AIR ACT AMENDMENTS OF 1990

The first comprehensive revision of the Clean Air Act was passed in 1990 as the **Clean Air Act Amendments of 1990.** The amendments to the act focus on issues such as **acid rain,** urban smog, airborne toxins, ozone-depleting chemicals, and regional economic concerns and political problems surrounding these issues.

At the time of the passage of the 1990 amendments, 96 cities had not yet reached their attainment levels under their state implementation plans (required to be reached under the 1977 amendments by 1987), and 41 cities had carbon monoxide levels exceeding the goals in their SIPs. Under the 1990 amendments, the EPA is required to establish a **federal implementation plan (FIP)** within two years of a state's failure to submit an adequate SIP to the EPA. New deadlines were established for polluted areas according to current levels of pollution. Except for Los Angeles, compliance deadlines were set for the year 2000, with annual pollution-reduction goals for cities at 3 to 4 percent per year.

> ## Practical Tip
>
> One of the results of the 1990 amendments to the Clean Air Act has been the development of a market for sulfur dioxide emissions permits. If, for example, one company has an EPA permit to discharge one ton of sulfur dioxide per year, but its equipment allows it to run much cleaner, the company can sell its permit to another utility. The purchase of a particular tract of land may be tied to the buyer being able to obtain the necessary emissions permits. The Chicago Board of Trade deals with emissions permits in much the same way it sells other commodities. The first trading in these emissions permits occurred on March 30, 1993, with a permit for emission of one ton of sulfur dioxide selling for between $122 and $450. Environmental groups currently own about 10 percent of all emissions permits.

The amendments have a substantial impact on smaller businesses such as dry cleaners, paint shops, and bakeries because the definition of a major source of pollution was changed from those businesses emitting 100 tons or more per year to those emitting 50 tons or more per year.

Motor vehicle manufacturers have experienced a substantial impact from the changes. The nine worst nonattainment areas are required to use reformulated gasolines that have reduced emissions by 25 percent by 2000. Tighter tailpipe standards for autos have been phased in to require emission reductions in various pollutants ranging from 30 to 60 percent.

Plants that are major sources of toxic emissions will be required to use **maximum achievable control technology (MACT),** although they can earn six-year extensions if they reduce emissions voluntarily by 90 percent by the time MACT standards are proposed by the EPA.

Utilities are impacted substantially by the new amendments with a cap imposed on sulfur dioxide emissions. Scrubber-installation incentives for utilities mean that putting in scrubbers now will result in a deadline extension for meeting the maximum sulfur dioxide emissions standards.

Administratively, the act contains the new requirements that all major polluting plants have operating permits that contain all of their Clean Air Act requirements. Furthermore, the penalties under the act were increased to allow field citations and civil penalties of up to $25,000 per day in general fines. The act also carries criminal penalties ranging from 1 to 15 years, depending on the nature of the violation and past violations. The EPA is also authorized under the amendments to pay $10,000 rewards to people who provide information leading to criminal convictions or civil penalties.

| Consider 20.1 | Do you think the emissions permits are real or personal property? What issues do you see arising if the permits are classified as real property? What concerns arise if the permits are classified as personal property? |

| Consider 20.2 | Union Electric Company is an electric utility company servicing St. Louis and large portions of Illinois and Iowa. It operates three coal-fired generating plants in metropolitan St. Louis that are subject to sulfur dioxide restrictions under the state of Missouri's implementation plan. Union Electric did not seek review of the implementation plan but applied for and obtained variances from the emissions limitations. When an extension for the variances was denied, Union Electric challenged the implementation plan on the grounds that it was technologically and economically infeasible and should therefore be amended. Will Union Electric succeed in having the plan amended? Be sure to consider the impact of the 1990 Clean Air Act Amendments in answering this question. *Union Electric Co. v. EPA,* 427 U.S. 246 (1976) |

Water Pollution Regulation

In 1965, the first federal legislation on water quality standards was passed—the **Water Quality Act.** The act established a separate enforcement agency—the **Federal Water Pollution Control Administration (FWPCA)**—and required states to establish quality levels for the waters within their boundaries. Because the act contained few expeditious enforcement procedures, only about half of the states had developed their zones and standards by 1970, and none were engaging in active enforcement of those standards with their implementation plans.

Because of the states' lack of involvement and the burdensome enforcement procedures of the 1965 act, new legislation was needed to provide meaningful enforcement. New legislation came not in the form of a new act but in the rediscovery of an old act, the **Rivers and Harbors Act of 1899.** The name of the act is a partial explanation of its purpose: It prohibited the discharge of refuse into navigable rivers and harbors, which caused interference with navigation. Specifically, the act prohibited the release of "any refuse matter of any kind or description" into navigable waters in the United States without a permit from the Army Corps of Engineers. For a time, the act was used to control the issuance of permits and to prosecute those industrial polluters who were discharging without permit. A major problem with the use of this act was the lack of a general prohibition on what was released or the amount of releases, so long as a permit was obtained.

PRESENT LEGISLATION

Not until 1972 was meaningful and enforceable federal legislation enacted with the passage of the **Federal Water Pollution Control Act of 1972** (33 U.S.C. § 1401). Under this act, two goals were set: (1) swimmable and fishable waters by 1983 and (2) zero discharge of pollutants by 1985. The act was amended in 1977 to allow extensions and flexibility in meeting the goals and was renamed the **Clean Water Act.** One of the major changes brought about by the act was the move from local to federal controls of water pollution. Federal standards for water discharges were established on an industry basis and all industries, regardless of state location, are required to comply.

Under the act, all direct industrial dischargers are placed into 27 groups, and the EPA (now responsible for water pollution control since the FWCPA was merged with it) establishes ranges of discharge for each industrial group. The ranges for pulp mills will differ from those for textile manufacturers, but all plants in the same industry must comply with the same ranges.

The ranges of discharges permitted per industrial group are referred to as **effluent guidelines.** In addition, the EPA has established a specific amount of discharge for each plant within an industrial group, which is the effluent limitation. Finally, for a plant to be able to discharge wastes into waterways, it must obtain a **National Pollution Discharge Elimination System (NPDES)** permit from the EPA. This type of permit is required only for direct dischargers, or **point sources,** and is not required of plants that discharge into sewer systems (although these secondary dischargers may still be required to pretreat their discharges). Obtaining a permit is a complicated process that not only requires EPA approval but also state approval, public hearings, and an opportunity for the proposed plant owners to obtain judicial review of a permit decision.

In issuing permits, the EPA may still prescribe standards for release. Generally, the standards that are set depend upon the type of substance the discharger proposes to release. For setting standards, the EPA has developed three categories of pollutants: **conventional, nonconventional,** and **toxic.** If a discharger is going to release a conventional pollutant, the EPA can require it to pretreat the substance with the **best conventional treatment (BCT).** If the pollutant to be discharged is either toxic or nonconventional, the EPA can require the **best available treatment (BAT),** which is the highest standard imposed. In issuing permits and requiring these various levels of treatment, the EPA need only consider environmental effects and not the economic effects on the applicant discharger.

Inland Steel Company applied for a permit from the EPA under the Federal Water Pollution Control Act of 1972. Although Inland was granted the permit, the EPA made the permit modifiable as new standards for toxic releases and treatment were developed. Inland claimed the modification restriction on the permit was invalid because the EPA did not have such authority and also because Inland would be subject to every technological change or discovery made during the course of the permit. Inland filed suit. Was the restriction invalid? *Inland Steel Company v. Environmental Protection Agency,* 574 F.2d 367 (7th Cir. 1978)

Consider 20.3

In 1986, Congress passed the **Safe Drinking Water Act,** which provides for the EPA to establish national standards for contaminant levels in drinking water. The states are primarily responsible for enforcement and can have higher standards than the federal standards, but must at least enforce the federal minimums for drinking-water systems.

Large oil tanker spills, such as the one that resulted from the grounding of the *Exxon Valdez* in Prince William Sound, Alaska, and dumped 11 million gallons of crude oil that coated 1,000 miles of the Alaskan coastline, brought public out-cry for additional federal regulation for pollution of waterways. In 1990, Congress enacted the **Oil Pollution Act (OPA)** of 1990. The OPA applies to all navigable waters up to 200 miles offshore and confers the power for cleanups on the EPA. The EPA may clean up the spill itself and seek compensation from the party deter-mined to be responsible, or it may require the party to do the cleanup and bear the cost of it.

The OPA also established the Oil Spill Liability Trust Fund, which is funded by a five-cent-per-barrel tax that is used to cover the costs of cleanup in those cases where the party responsible does not have the resources to pay for the cleanup.

Penalties under the OPA range from $25,000 per day civil penalties and up to $3,000 per barrel if the spill is willful or negligent. The failure to report an oil spill carries a penalty of $250,000 and/or five years imprisonment for individuals, and $1,000,000 for corporations.

Solid-Waste Disposal Regulation

EARLY REGULATION

The disposal of solid waste (garbage) has been a significant problem in the United States because of the long history and popularity of the open-dumping method of disposal. As with other pollution issues, the disposal of solid wastes initially was per-ceived to be a problem of state and local governments. In 1965, Congress passed the **Solid Waste Disposal Act,** which provided money to state and local govern-ments for research in solid-waste disposal. In 1970, this 1965 act was amended with the passage of the **Resource Recovery Act.** It was this act that encouraged the recy-cling process by offering aid to local governments engaging in recycling projects. The act also provided funds for research and established guidelines for solid-waste disposal, but the law had no real federal power or enforcement provisions.

LATER RESPONSES—TOXIC SUBSTANCE CONTROL

After several major open-dumping problems, such as the Love Canal chemical dumping near Buffalo, New York, two federal acts were passed that granted some enforcement power to the federal government. The **Toxic Substances Control Act (TOSCA)** (15 U.S.C. § 2601) was passed in 1976 and authorized the EPA to con-trol the manufacture, use, and disposal of toxic substances. Under the act, the EPA is authorized to prevent the manufacture of dangerous substances and to stop the manufacture of substances found to be dangerous.

Also passed by Congress in the 1976 reaction to dangerous dumping practices was the **Resource Conservation and Recovery Act of 1976 (RCRA)** (42 U.S.C. § 6901). The two goals of the act are to control the disposal of potentially harm-ful substances and to encourage resource conservation and recovery. A critical part of the act's control is a manifest or permit system that requires manufacturers to obtain a permit for the storage or transfer of hazardous wastes so that the location of such wastes can be traced through an examination of the permits issued.

SUPERFUND

In 1980, Congress passed the **Comprehensive Environmental Response, Compensation, and Liability Act (CERCLA)** (42 U.S.C. § 9601), which authorized the President to issue funds for the cleanup of areas that were once disposal sites for hazardous wastes. Under the act, a **Hazardous Substance Response Trust Fund** is set up to provide funding for cleanup. If funds are expended in such a cleanup, then, under the provisions of the act, the company responsible for the disposal of the hazardous wastes can be sued by the federal government and required to repay the amounts expended from the trust fund. Often called the **Superfund,** the funds are available for governmental use but cannot be obtained through suit by private citizens affected by the hazardous disposals.

In 1986, CERCLA was amended by the **Superfund Amendment and Reauthorization Act.** Under the amendments in that act, liability provisions were included, and the EPA is now permitted to recover cleanup funds from those responsible for the release of hazardous substances. Approximately 700 hazardous substances are now covered (they are listed at 40 C.F.R. § 302). Since the passage of the 1986 amendments, there has been judicial expansion of the concept of "responsibility." Clearly, those who release the substances are liable, but that liability has been expanded to include those who purchased the property without performing adequate checks on its history.

CERCLA LENDER LIABILITY

One of the more intriguing issues that resulted from CERCLA liability was whether a lender has the responsibility of cleanup because it was back in possession of the property due to a foreclosure sale or a deed in lieu of foreclosure. In *U.S. v. Fleet Factors Corp.,* 901 F.2d 1550 (11th Cir. 1990), the court held that a lender could be held responsible and liable for the cleanup of real property it finds itself holding due to a loan default. The finding of the court appeared to create great liability for lenders when they did not have control over the conduct of the mortgagor prior to their repossession or foreclosure. The result was that the EPA promulgated rules on lender liability in 1992. However, the rules did not provide lenders with sufficient guidelines for managing property obtained through default or foreclosure. To clarify liability issues, Congress passed the **Asset Conservation, Lender Liability, and Deposit Insurance Protection Act of 1996.** This new statute provides a specific exclusion for lenders in that the definition of "owner/operator" does not include someone who "holds indicia of ownership primarily to protect his security interest." This new provision has been labeled the "secured lender exemption" from CERCLA liability. However, the new act does provide that a lender can lose its status if it "actually participate[s] in the management or operational affairs of a vessel or facility." But, the "capacity" to assert control does not result in lender liability as the *Fleet Factors* case held. A lender can do the following and still not be subject to environmental liability:

- Monitor or enforce terms of the security agreement
- Monitor or inspect the premises or facility
- Mandate that the debtor take action on hazardous materials
- Provide financial advice or counseling
- Restructure or renegotiate the loan terms
- Exercise any remedies available at law
- Foreclose on the property
- Sell the property
- Lease the property

Practical Tip

When considering a purchase of real property, look into the following issues: Are there asbestos-containing materials and/or asbestos itself on the property? Look in walls, ceiling, and pipes. Is there any lead-based paint on the property? Check for decaying, flaking, and peeling paint as signs of possible lead-paint problems. Lead paint is outlawed now, but many older properties may still have it. Is there a radon problem on the property? The only way to determine whether a property has radon is to have testing done. Radon often enters through foundations or cracks in basement floors. Only experts can detect its presence.

Checking for these environmental hazards prior to purchase is important for safety, for the decision to buy, and for setting the right price for a property that may need some cleaning up.

CERCLA—FOUR CLASSES OF LIABILITY RULES

There are four classes of parties that can be held liable under CERCLA. "Owners and operators" of a contaminated piece of property comprise one group. While "owner" is self-explanatory, "operator" would include those who lease property and then contaminate it, such as those who lease factories, operate storage facilities, and so forth. A second group would be owners and operators at the time the property was contaminated. This group brings under CERCLA jurisdiction those who were responsible for the property contamination, as opposed to present owners who had the problem deeded to them. For example, many gas stations have been converted to other businesses. Suppose that one of the underground gas tanks once used by the gas station has been leaking hazardous materials into the surrounding soil. Not only would the present owners be liable, so also would be all those who owned the gasoline station previously.

The final two groups consist of those who transport hazardous materials and those who arrange for the transportation of hazardous materials. There are virtually no liability exemptions for those who fit into these four groups. Further, it is important to understand that the liability exists under CERCLA for both corporations and corporate officers. For example, the EPA has been successful in criminal prosecutions against officers of corporations who have been ordered to conduct a cleanup but who failed to do so.

CERCLA liability has also extended to corporate board members and corporate successors and officers in cases where a company is purchased by another firm. Those who merge or buy corporations also buy into CERCLA liability—it cannot be avoided by a transfer of ownership. In its 1998 term, the U.S. Supreme Court issued a decision holding parent companies liable for the environmental missteps of their subsidiaries (*U.S. v. Bestfoods,* 534 U.S. 51 [1998].)

Before buying property, a buyer should conduct what is called *due diligence,* which is an investigation into the current and past uses of the land to determine possible CERLA liability. There are three phases in a due diligence review. Phase 1 consists of a search to determine whether there is evidence of past or current environmental problems on the property. Evidence reviewed in a Phase 1 search would be private and public records, aerial photographs, and a site inspection. If Phase 1 reveals some concerns, then the parties proceed to Phase 2, which consists of chemical analysis of soil, structures, and water from the property. If Phase 2 finds the presence of contaminants, the report for Phase 2 will estimate the cost of cleanup. Phase 3 is the actual cleanup plan.

Practical Tip

Due diligence is necessary not only when buying property but also when buying companies with land holdings. Liability under CERCLA transfers via land ownership or corporate ownership.

CERCLA AND THE SELF-AUDIT

One of the issues that many landowners and companies face is whether they should do an internal audit to determine whether there are any environmental hazards on their properties. In the past, companies have been unwilling to do such audits and the cleanup for any problems found because of their fear that disclosure and cleanup might bring them additional liability from environmental officials. Also, companies worried that by volunteering information about contaminated properties they were waiving their attorney/client privilege with the result being that regulators could use privileged and revealing communication about environmental violations in court against the company.

To eliminate these concerns, the EPA developed its **Incentives for Self-Policing, Disclosure, Correction, and Prevention of Violations.**[1] Under the EPA program, those companies that come forward, having met certain conditions, will have their penalties reduced for any violations uncovered in the course of a voluntary audit. The conditions for reduced penalties are as follows:

1. The violations were uncovered as part of a self-audit or due diligence done on property.
2. The violations were uncovered voluntarily.
3. The violations were reported to the EPA within 10 days.
4. The discovery was made independently and disclosed independently and not because someone else was reporting it or there was a threat of reporting.
5. There is correction of the violation within 60 days.
6. There is a written agreement that the conduct will not recur.
7. There can be no repeat violations or patterns of violations.
8. There is no serious harm to anyone as a result of the violation.
9. The company cooperates completely with the EPA.

The EPA will reduce fines and penalties by 75 percent if all but the first two factors are met. Also, if a company falls into the 75 percent mitigation category, the EPA will not recommend criminal prosecution for the violations to the Department of Justice. The documents related to the audit are not entitled to privacy protection and there is the risk of third-party lawsuits for the voluntarily reported violations. However, most companies take advantage of the self-reporting protections offered by the EPA.

Grand Auto Parts Stores receives used automotive batteries from customers as trade-ins. Grand Auto drives a screwdriver through spent batteries and then sells them to Morris Kirk & Sons, a battery-cracking plant that extracts and smelts leads. Tons of crushed battery casings were found on Kirk's land. The EPA sought to hold Grand Auto liable for cleanup. Can Grand Auto be held liable? (*Catellus Dev. Corp. v. United States*, 34 F.3d 748 [9th Cir. 1994]).

Consider 20.4

The Superfund has been used quite frequently since its inception. The result is that more funds are needed to keep it going. Congress has proposed expanding the tax used for funding to include all manufacturers. When expansion of the funding sources for the Superfund has been proposed in Congress, the businesses not currently subject to the superfund tax have opposed additional impositions on them. Do these firms have an obligation to assist in the cleanup? Can some firms claim that they do not affect the environment? Is the cleanup a general business obligation?

Ethical Issue

WHO PAYS FOR CERCLA LIABILITY

One issue that courts continue to face with respect to CERCLA cleanup efforts is whether insurance policies for comprehensive general liability apply to a company's cost of cleanup. The following case deals with the issue of an insurer's liability.

1.   60 Fed. Reg. 66706

Farmland Industries, Inc. v. Republic Insurance Co.

941 S.W.2d 505 (Mo. Banc 1997)

Facts

Farmland Industries, Inc., held general liability policies, umbrella policies, and other excess liability policies from Republic Insurance (Respondents). Farmland found itself in the position of being held liable by the EPA for cleanup at several sites around the country and sought to have Republic pay for the cost of such cleanup. Republic refused, and Farmland filed suit. The trial court held Farmland's CERCLA liabilities were not covered under the insurance policies, and Farmland appealed.

Judicial Opinion

Covington, Judge. The Comprehensive Environmental Response Compensation Liability Act of 1980 (CERCLA), as amended, 42 U.S.C.A. §§ 9601-9675 (West 1995 & Supp.1997), and analogous state statutes impose liability on individuals and companies who own or operate, or formerly owned or operated, facilities from which hazardous substances have been released. 42 U.S.C.A. § 9607(a). The law also imposes liability if an individual or company arranged for the treatment or disposal of hazardous substances at a facility from which hazardous substances have been released.

Farmland purchased comprehensive general liability policies, umbrella policies, and other excess liability policies from Respondents. The policies contain language identical or similar to the following:

> The company will pay on behalf of the Insured all sums which the Insured shall become legally obligated to pay as damages because of . . . property damage. . . .

Some of the policies do not contain a definition of the term "damages." The policies that do define "damages" do not distinguish between legal and equitable damages. The policies that define "damages" do so in the following manner:

> "[D]amages" includes damages for death and for care and loss of services resulting from bodily injury and damages for loss of use of property resulting from property damage.

In its petition, Farmland alleged that it has incurred and/or faces the potential for substantial defense costs and liability for damages arising from alleged property damage and personal injury at and near these sites. Farmland alleged that the EPA and/or state agencies have required Farmland to conduct investigation and/or remediation activities. Farmland presented evidence that it has entered various consent agreements with the EPA and state agencies to respond to hazardous substances at the sites at issue.

The issue, one of first impression for this Court, is whether environmental response costs incurred pursuant to CERCLA and similar state laws are "damages" within the meaning of the policies Respondents issued to Farmland. The parties agree that the environmental responses, when required of a responsible party by the government, are in the nature of equitable relief; the parties disagree on the question of whether the cost of this equitable relief is included within the policy term "damages." Farmland argues that the ordinary meaning of "damages" includes equitable relief. Respondents counter that the term "damages" means "legal damages," payments to third persons when those persons have a legal claim for damages. Respondents assert that "damages" does not include the cost of equitable remedies.

Although the issue presented is one of first impression in Missouri, Missouri's law governing interpretation of language in an insurance policy is settled. When interpreting the language of an insurance policy, this Court gives a term its ordinary meaning, unless it plainly appears that a technical meaning was intended. The ordinary meaning of a term is the meaning that the average layperson would reasonably understand.

The insurance policies at issue do not indicate that the parties plainly intended to give "damages" a technical meaning. In some of the policies at issue, the term "damages" is not defined. The policies that do define "damages" make no reference to a definition that distinguishes between legal and equitable relief. This Court will, therefore, give the term "damages" its ordinary meaning.

Reference to standard English language dictionaries reveals that "damages" means "the estimated reparation in money for detriment or injury sustained." Webster's also defines "damages" as "compensation or satisfaction imposed by law for a wrong or injury caused by a violation of a legal right." These definitions of "damages," those that a layperson would reasonably understand "damages" to mean, are broad and inclusive. The ordinary meaning of damages, therefore, includes environmental response costs required by the government.

Respondents nevertheless argue that "damages" does not include equitable relief even if "damages" is given its ordinary meaning. Respondents contend that the government has ordered that Farmland undertake specific actions in this case, such as investigating, planning, and cleaning up pollution. Respondents argue that such actions are not the "money equivalent for detriment or injuries sustained;" therefore, they are not "damages."

The definitions of "damages" do not distinguish between legal damages and equitable relief. Farmland's cost of undertaking the actions required by the government under CERCLA or similar state laws are "damages" within the ordinary meaning of the term. In other words, the equitable relief at issue is a cost that Farmland is legally obligated to pay as compensation or satisfaction for a wrong or injury.

Respondents argue that "damages" cannot include both legal and equitable relief because that would render the term "damages" superfluous when read in context with the phrase "all sums which the insured shall become legally obligated to pay."

The word "damages" is used to make clear that insurers are obligated to cover both direct and consequential losses because of property damage for which an insured can be held liable, irrespective of whether the claimant itself has sustained property damage. This is evidenced by the fact that the only policies that define "damages" do so by explaining that damages includes "loss of use of property resulting from property damage." Furthermore, unlike response costs, fines or penalties are not included within the ordinary meaning of "damages." The ordinary meaning of a "fine" or "penalty" is not compensation or reparation for an injury; rather, it is a sum imposed as punishment. Because fines and penalties are not "damages," the term limits liability under the policy to something less than "all sums which the insured shall become legally obligated to pay because of property damage."

Respondents assert that because the consent decrees at issue require Farmland to clean up its own property, "the notion that Farmland's liability insurance covers such costs 'as damages' is even more farfetched." Respondents reason that the primary purpose of liability insurance is to protect policyholders against claims for damages by third parties who actually sustain some injury or harm. Respondents argue that the government brings an action under CERCLA to enforce compliance with the statutory and regulatory scheme, not to compensate the government for injuries sustained. Respondents conclude that compliance with the law, even when required by a consent decree, is a cost of doing business and is not damages.

This Court does not find Respondents' argument persuasive. CERCLA permits responsible parties to insure against the cost of actions for which they are liable. *See* 42 U.S.C.A. § 9607(e)(1). Congress has already made the relevant public policy determinations. It is not for this Court to decide the issue on public policy grounds. The question is only whether the term "damages" includes environmental response costs.

Respondents' argument would require the parties to an insurance agreement to be prescient with respect to possible types of relief that the law might provide in the future. It would defy logic to hold that a cause of action is not covered simply because it did not exist at the time the parties entered the insurance agreement.

This Court holds that under Missouri law, environmental response costs incurred pursuant to CERCLA and similar state laws are "damages" within the meaning of the policies Respondents issued to Farmland.

Reversed and remanded.

Case Questions

1. What does the court use to define the term "damages"?
2. What does the insurance company wish to use to define "damages"?
3. How does the court respond to the argument that the insurance policy predated the CERCLA statute?
4. Does it matter that the money Farmland pays is the result not of a civil proceeding but of regulatory action?

Other issues within CERCLA are developing in various types of CERCLA cases. One federal district court declared CERCLA unconstitutional for its retroactive effect (*U.S. v. Olin Corp.,* 927 F.Supp. 1502), but it was reversed (*U.S. v. Olin Corp.,* 107 F.3d 1506 [11th Cir. 1997]). Other courts have begun to examine the issue of causation between the contaminants present on a piece of property and its relation to any injury as a means of a cost/benefit analysis or based on an arbitrary and capricious challenge to an EPA demand for cleanup of a site that is not linked to any danger or a cleanup that exceeds standards for dangerous exposure (*Licciardi v. Murphy Oil U.S.A.,* 111 F.3d 396 [5th Cir. 1997]; *U.S. v. Broderick Investment Co.,* 955 F.Supp. 1268 [D. Colo. 1997]). These cases represent the first time courts have considered been restraints on CERCLA enforcement.

The following case involves an issue of causation and CERCLA liability.

Acushnet Company v. Mohasco

191 F.3d 69 (1st Cir. 1999)

Facts

Sullivan's Ledge, once a popular swimming, hiking, and impromptu gathering area located near New Bedford, Massachusetts, has become little more than an industrial dumping ground for scrap rubber, waste oils, gas, combustion ash, and old telephone poles. The sludge became so toxic, the refuse so thick, and the stench so overwhelming, that the city closed down the area in the 1970s.

The EPA eventually identified a number of business entities and their successors in interest as responsible for the cleanup of the area. Following lengthy negotiations, those businesses entered into a consent decree in 1992 that required them to implement a remediation plan and shoulder the costs of that plan for returning Sullivan's Ledge to a nonhazardous site.

Following the agreement, Acushnet Company and others in the consent decree group (plaintiffs) filed suit seeking financial contribution from Mohasco Corporation and others including American Flexible Conduit (AFC), New England Telephone & Telegraph Company (NETT), and Ottaway Newspapers, Inc.

The trial court found that there was insufficient evidence to find these companies liable under CERCLA and granted them summary judgment. The plaintiffs appealed.

Judicial Opinion

Bownes, Senior Circuit Judge. CERCLA, as we have said on other occasions, sketches the contours of a strict liability regime. Broad categories of persons are swept within its ambit, including the current owner and operator of a vessel or facility; the owner or operator of a facility at the time hazardous waste was disposed of; any person who arranged for the transportation of hazardous substances for disposal or treatment; and anyone who accepted hazardous waste for transportation. *See* 42 U.S.C. § 9607(a)(1)–(4). There are a few affirmative defenses available, but they are generally difficult to satisfy (they include showing that the release or threat of release was caused solely by an act of God or an act of war). By and large, a person who falls within one of the four categories defined in § 9607(a) is exposed to CERCLA liability.

While CERCLA casts the widest possible net over responsible parties, there are some limits to its reach. The courts of appeals have generally recognized that "although joint and several liability is commonly imposed in CERCLA cases, it is not mandatory in all such cases."

The Sullivan's Ledge Group mounts a three-fold attack on the district court's reasoning in resolving the respective motions. Its arguments on appeal are broad-brushed in nature, focusing almost entirely on the legal meaning of "causation" and CERCLA's underlying policy goals. First, plaintiffs insist that reading any causal element into CERCLA is inconsistent with the principle of strict liability. Second, they contend that doing so would run counter to the remedial purpose of CERCLA because, among other things, it will let smaller polluters off the hook and discourage responsible parties from entering into consent agreements with the government. Third, to the extent the district court may have considered equitable factors in ruling in favor of Mohasco, Ottaway, and AFC, plaintiffs claim that the court did so without providing a "full and fair allocation trial" within the meaning of section 9613(f).

Defendants-appellees, for their part, contend that it makes sense to say that a *de minimis* polluter has not caused a responsible party to incur clean up costs; and that, in all events, plaintiffs' contribution claims against them founder for a more fundamental reason: the record did not permit a finding that each should bear a meaningful share of the costs associated with restoring Sullivan's Ledge. In their view, these fatal weaknesses in the plaintiffs' case justified judgment as a matter of law in their favor.

We have strong reservations about interpreting the statute's causation element to require that a defendant be responsible for a minimum quantity of hazardous waste before liability may be imposed. The text of the statute does not support such a construction—CERCLA itself does not expressly distinguish between releases (or threats of releases) by the quantity of hazardous waste attributable to a particular party. At least on its face; any reasonable danger of release, however insignificant, would seem to give rise to liability. On this point the courts of appeals are in unison.

To read a quantitative threshold into the language "causes the incurrence of response costs" would cast the plaintiff in the impossible role of tracing chemical waste to particular sources in particular amounts, a task that is often technologically infeasible due to the fluctuating quantity and varied nature of the pollution at a site over the course of many years.

Moreover, it would be extremely difficult, if not impossible, to articulate a workable numerical threshold in defining causation. How low would a polluter's contribution to the mix have to be before a judge could find, with equanimity, that the polluter was not a but-for "cause" of the clean up efforts? Less than 0.5% or 1%? We do not see how much a line, based on the quantity or concentration of the hazardous substance at issue, can be drawn on a principled basis in defining causation. To even begin down that path, we feel, is to invite endless confusion.

This does not mean, however, that the *de minimis* polluter must necessarily be held liable for all response costs. The approach taken by the second Circuit is instructive. The Second Circuit reaffirmed the Restatement (Second) of Torts approach to fleshing out the scope of CERCLA liability, holding that where environmental harms are divisible, a defendant may be held responsible only for his proportional share of the response costs. In extending the principle a half-step, the Second Circuit went on to say that:

> [A defendant] may escape any liability for response costs if it either succeeds in proving that its [waste], when mixed with other hazardous wastes, did not contribute to the release and cleanup that followed, or contributed at most to only a divisible portion of the harm.

We therefore hold that a defendant may avoid joint and several liability for response costs in a contribution action under § 9613(f) if it demonstrates that its share of hazardous waste deposited at the site constitutes no more than background amounts of such substances in the environment and cannot concentrate with other wastes to produce higher amounts. This rule is not based on CERCLA's causation requirement, but is logically derived from § 9613(f)'s express authorization that a court take equity into account when fixing each defendant's fair share of response casts. We caution, however, that not every *de minimis* polluter will elude liability in this way. As always, an equitable determination must be justified by the record.

There is nothing to suggest that Congress intended to impose far-reaching liability on every party who is responsible for only trace levels of waste. Several courts, albeit taking different paths to a similar result, have rejected the notion that CERCLA liability "attaches upon release of *any* quantity of a hazardous substance."

Allowing a CERCLA defendant to prevail on issues of fair apportionment even at the summary judgment stage, is consistent with Congress's intent that joint and several liability not be imposed mechanically in all cases. Permitting a result that is tantamount to a no-liability finding, is in keeping with the legislative goal that clean up efforts begin in a speedy fashion and that litigation over the details of actual responsibility follow. In fact, to require an inconsequential polluter to litigate until the bitter end, we believe, would run counter to Congress's mandate that CERCLA actions be resolved as fairly and efficiently as possible. On the whole, the costs and inherent unfairness in saddling a party who has contributed only trace amounts of hazardous waste with joint and several liability for all costs incurred outweigh the public interest in requiring full contribution from *de minimis* polluters.

Plaintiffs complain that any consideration of causation is at odds with CERCLA's objectives and would discourage responsible parties from entering into consent decrees. Because we ground the quantum inquiry solidly in § 9613(f), we are satisfied their prophesy will not come to pass. The ultimate failure of a contribution claim because someone did only a negligible amount of harm does not impede enforcement by the EPA or frustrate any of CERCLA's objectives.

Affirmed.

Case Questions

1. Explain why companies are litigating against each other under CERCLA.

2. What is a *de minimis* violation of CERCLA?

3. Does the court require that the standard for liability be based on an amount or number?

4. Will the decision excusing companies from cleanup costs defeat the purposes of CERCLA?

STATE REGULATION OF HAZARDOUS WASTE

Many states have been concerned about hazardous waste disposal and have passed their own regulatory schemes to provide mechanisms and funding for cleanup, and penalties for failure to follow their requirements. All 50 states have some form of hazardous waste regulation, and the definitions of hazardous wastes as well as the penalties vary. Arizona includes garbage in its definition, and Oregon establishes fines on the basis of a fee per animal destroyed as a result of the waste. The death of one mountain goat due to hazardous waste will cost the violator $3,500 in Oregon.

Four states (California, Connecticut, Illinois, and Indiana) now impose mandatory disclosure requirements in certain real estate transactions. New Jersey has similar regulations that cover other types of transfers such as stock sales that might result in the indirect transfer of property. The purpose of these disclosure statutes is to have the seller reveal the types of activities that have occurred on the premises. The goal is to either have the parties then agree to have cleanup done prior to closing, or force the selling party into a cleanup because the disclosure of environmental hazards can permit a rescission of the sales agreement.

Environmental Quality Regulation

Environmental controls of air, water, and waste are directed at private parties in the use of their land. However, as part of the environmental control scheme, Congress also passed an act that regulates what governmental entities can do in the use of their properties. The **National Environmental Policy Act (NEPA) of 1969** (42 U.S. § 4321) was passed to require federal agencies to take into account the environmental impact of their proposed actions and to prepare an **environmental impact statement (EIS)** prior to taking any proposed action.

An EIS must be prepared and filed with the EPA whenever an agency sends a proposed law to Congress and whenever an agency will take major federal action significantly affecting the quality of the environment. The information required in an EIS is as follows:

1. The proposed action's environmental impact
2. Adverse environmental effects (if any)
3. Alternative methods
4. Short-term effects versus long-term maintenance, enhancement, and productivity
5. Irreversible and irretrievable resource uses

Examples of federal agency actions that have required the preparation of EISs include the Alaska oil pipeline, the extermination of wild horses on federal lands, the construction of government buildings such as post offices, and any highway construction built with federal funds. Recently, even the North American Free Trade Agreement (NAFTA) was challenged on the basis that an EIS was required.

The following case involves an issue of whether an EIS was required.

Sierra Club
v. United States Department of Transportation

753 F.2d 120 (D.C. 1985)

Facts

In 1983, the Federal Aviation Administration (FAA) issued two orders amending the operations specifications for Frontier Airlines, Inc., and Western Airlines, Inc. These amendments gave the airlines permanent authorizations to operate Boeing 737 jet airplanes (B-737s) out of Jackson Hole Airport, which is located within the Grand Teton National Park in Wyoming. These two airlines are the only major commercial carriers that schedule flights to and from Jackson Hole.

Private jets have flown into the airport since 1960. Western Airlines has been flying into Jackson Hole since 1941. The airport is the only one in the country located in a national park, and Congress has continually funded expansions and improvements of the once single dirt-runway airport.

In 1978, Frontier applied for permission to fly B-737s into the Jackson Hole Airport. The FAA released its EIS on the application in 1980. The EIS found that B-737s were comparable with C-580 propeller aircraft (the type then being used by Western and Frontier) for noise intrusion, but were substantially quieter than the private jets using the airport. The study also showed that fewer flights would be necessary since the B-737 could carry more passengers and that different flight paths could reduce noise.

Based on this EIS, Frontier was given the right to use B-737s for two years. When Frontier applied for permanent approval, the FAA used the 1980 EIS statement and found that with flight time restrictions, the impact would not harm the environment.

The Sierra Club, a national conservation organization, brought suit for the failure to file an EIS for the 1983 amendments and for the use of national park facilities for commercial air traffic without considering alternatives.

Judicial Opinion

Bork, Circuit Judge. We do not think the FAA violated NEPA by failing to prepare an additional EIS. Under NEPA, an EIS must be prepared before approval of any major federal action that will "significantly affect the quality of the human environment." The purpose of the Act is to require agencies to consider environmental issues before taking any major action. Under the statute, agencies have the initial and primary responsibility to determine the extent of the impact and whether it is significant enough to warrant preparation of an EIS. This is accomplished by preparing an Environmental Assessment (EA). An EA allows the agency to consider environmental concerns, while reserving agency resources to prepare full EIS's for appropriate cases. If a finding of no significant impact is made after analyzing the EA, then preparation of an EIS is unnecessary. An agency has broad discretion in making this determination, and the decision is reviewable only if it was arbitrary, capricious or an abuse of discretion.

This court has established four criteria for reviewing an agency's decision to forego preparation of an EIS. First, the agency must have accurately identified the relevant environmental concern. Second, once the agency has identified the problem, it must take a "hard look" at the problem in preparing the EA. Third, if a finding of no significant impact is made, the agency must be able to make a convincing case for its finding. Last, if the agency does find an impact of true significance, preparation of an EIS can be avoided only if the agency finds that changes or safeguards in the project sufficiently reduce the impact to a minimum.

The first test is not at issue here. Both the FAA and Sierra Club have identified the relevant environmental concern as noise by jet aircraft within Grand Teton National Park. The real issues raised by Sierra Club are whether the FAA took a "hard look" at the problem, and whether the methodology used by the agency in its alleged hard look was proper.

We find that the FAA did take a hard look at the problem. The FAA properly prepared an EA to examine the additional impact on the environment of the plan. The EA went forward from the 1980 EIS. The 1980 EIS, which was based on extensive research by Dr. Hakes of the University of Wyoming, noise testing by the FAA, and data derived from manufacturer information, showed that noise intrusions of B-737 jets over the level caused by C-580 propeller aircraft amounted to only 1 dbl near the Airport and decreased in proportion to the distance from the Airport. The agency, exercising its expertise, has found that an increase this minute is not significant for any environment. In addition, the EIS and Hakes studies were based on a worst case scenario, and it was determined that if certain precautions were taken the actual noise levels could be diminished greatly.

Petitioner (Sierra Club) argues that because Jackson Hole Airport is located within national parkland a different standard—i.e., individual event noise level analysis—is mandated. Both individual event and cumulative data were amassed in preparing the 1980 EIS on which the EAs were based. The fact that the agency in exercising its expertise relied on the cumulative impact levels as being more indicative of the actual environmental disturbance is well within the area of discretion given to the agency. We agree with petitioner that although noise is a problem in any setting, "airplane noise is a problem fundamentally inconsistent with the type of recreational experience Park visitors are seeking" and should be minimized. Here the FAA found that a cumulative noise increase of 1 dbl or less is not significant—even for the pristine environment in which Jackson Hole Airport is located.

Given all of these facts, we think the FAA was not required to prepare yet another EIS before granting permanent authorizations for the use of B-737s.

The orders of the FAA are hereby affirmed.

Case Questions

1. What airport noise is at issue?
2. Who is involved in the case?
3. Was an EIS prepared?
4. What is the basis for the appeal?
5. What has the FAA allowed? Will the authorizations stand?

Other Federal Environmental Regulations

In addition to the major environmental laws, many other specific federal statutes protect the environment.

SURFACE MINING

The **Surface Mining and Reclamation Act of 1977** (42 U.S.C. § 6907) requires those mining coal to restore land surfaces to their original conditions and prohibits surface coal mining without a permit.

NOISE CONTROL

Under the **Noise Control Act of 1972** (42 U.S.C. § 4901), the EPA, along with the Federal Aviation Administration (FAA), can control the amount of noise emissions from low-flying aircraft for the protection of landowners in flight paths.

PESTICIDE CONTROL

Under the **Federal Environmental Pesticide Control Act,** the use of pesticides is controlled. All pesticides must be registered with the EPA before they can be sold, shipped, distributed, or received. Also under the act, the EPA administrator is given the authority to classify pesticides according to their effects and dangers.

OSHA

The **Occupational Safety and Health Administration (OSHA)** is responsible for the worker's environment. OSHA controls the levels of exposure to toxic substances and requires safety precautions for exposure to such dangerous substances as asbestos, benzene, and chloride.

ASBESTOS

Buildings that contain asbestos materials remain a problem for buyers, sellers, and occupants. The **Asbestos Hazard Emergency Response Act (AHERA),** passed in 1986, required all public and private schools to arrange for the inspection of their facilities to determine whether their buildings had asbestos-containing materials (ACMs). Schools are required to develop plans for containment, but other buildings are not regulated. The Clean Air Act does, however, define airborne asbestos as a toxic pollutant, and liability may result from the release of fibers from this known carcinogen. Further, an amendment to the Superfund Act classified asbestos as a **Community-Right-to-Know substance,** which means that there is probably a duty to disclose the presence of asbestos to buyers, tenants, and employees. Numerous ethical questions arise with respect to the presence of asbestos and the obligations of landowners to replace the asbestos given that the phaseout of its use did not end until 1997. Questions such as the impact of the release of asbestos from the walls when tenants, employees, and others hang photos and other objects nailed onto the walls remain. The issues of the degree of harm and the cost of replacement continue to be debated among property owners.

ENDANGERED SPECIES

In 1973, Congress passed the **Endangered Species Act,** a law that has been a powerful tool for environmentalists in protecting certain species through their advocacy of restrictions on commercial use and development when the habitats of certain species are interfered with.

Under the act, the secretary of the interior is responsible for identifying endangered terrestrial species, and the secretary of commerce identifies endangered marine species. In addition, these cabinet members must designate habitats considered crucial for these species if they are to thrive. In many instances, there is litigation concerning what species should or should not be on the list. Once a species is on the list, its critical habitat cannot be disturbed by development, noise, or destruction. The following case is a recent one that has given federal agencies broad authority in protecting endangered species.

Babbitt v. Sweet Home Chapter of Communities for a Great Oregon

515 U.S. 687 (1995)

Facts

Two U.S. agencies halted logging in the Pacific Northwest because it endangered the habitat of the northern spotted owl and the red-cockaded woodpecker, both endangered species. Sweet Home Chapter (respondents) is a group of landowners, logging companies, and families dependent on the forest products industries in the Pacific Northwest. They brought suit seeking clarification of the authority of the secretary of the interior and the director of the Fish and Wildlife Service (petitioners) to include habitation modification as a harm covered by the Endangered Species Act (ESA).

The federal district court found for the secretary and director and held that they had the authority to protect the northern spotted owl through a halt to logging. The court of appeals reversed. Babbitt, the secretary of the interior, appealed.

Judicial Opinion

Stevens, Justice. Section 9(a)(1) of the Endangered Species Act provides the following protection for endangered species:

> Except as provided in sections 1535(g)(2) and 1539 of this title, with respect to any endangered species of fish or wildlife listed pursuant to section 1533 of this title it is unlawful for any person subject to the jurisdiction of the United States to—(B) take any such species within the United States or the territorial sea of the United States[.] 16 U.S.C. § 1538(a)(1).

Section 3(19) of the Act defines the statutory term "take":

> The term 'take' means to harass, harm, pursue, hunt, shoot, wound, kill, trap, capture, or collect, or to attempt to engage in any such conduct. 16 U.S.C. § 1532(19).

The Act does not further define the terms it uses to define "take." The Interior Department regulations that implement the statute, however, define the statutory term "harm":

> Harm in the definition of 'take' in the Act means an act which actually kills or injures wildlife. Such act may include significant habitat modification or degradation where it actually kills or injures wildlife by significantly impairing essential behavioral patterns, including breeding, feeding, or sheltering. 50 C.F.R. § 17.3 (1994).

We assume respondents have no desire to harm either the red-cockaded woodpecker or the spotted owl; they merely wish to continue logging activities that would be entirely proper if not prohibited by the ESA. On the other hand, we must assume *arguendo* that those activities will have the effect, even though unintended, of detrimentally changing the natural habitat of both listed species and that, as a consequence, members of those species will be killed or injured. Under respondents' view of the law, the Secretary's only means of forestalling that grave result—even when the actor knows it is certain to occur—is to use his § 5 authority to purchase the lands on which the survival of the species depends. The Secretary, on the other hand, submits that the § 9 prohibition on takings, which Congress defined to include "harm," places on respondents a duty to avoid harm that habitat alteration will cause the birds unless respondents first obtain a permit pursuant to § 10.

The text of the Act provides three reasons for concluding that the Secretary's interpretation is reasonable. First, an ordinary understanding of the word "harm" supports it. The dictionary definition of the verb form of "harm" is "to cause hurt or damage to: injure." *Webster's Third New International Dictionary* 1034 (1966). In the context of the ESA, that definition naturally encompasses habitat modification that results in actual injury or death to members of an endangered or threatened species.

Respondents argue that the Secretary should have limited the purview of "harm" to direct applications of force against protected species, but the dictionary definition does not include the word "directly" or suggest in any way that only direct or willful action that leads to injury constitutes "harm." Moreover, unless the statutory term "harm" encompasses indirect as well as direct injuries, the word has no meaning that does not duplicate the meaning of other words that § 3 uses to define "take." A reluctance to treat statutory terms as surplusage supports the reasonableness of the Secretary's interpretation.

Second, the broad purpose of the ESA supports the Secretary's decision to extend protection against activities that cause the precise harms Congress enacted the statute to avoid. As stated in § 2 of the Act, among its central purposes is "to provide a means whereby the ecosystems upon which endangered species and threatened species depend may be conserved."

Third, the fact that Congress in 1982 authorized the Secretary to issue permits for takings that § 9(a)(1)(B) would otherwise prohibit, "if such taking is incidental to, and not the purpose of, the carrying out of an otherwise lawful activity," 16 U.S.C. § 1539(a)(1)(B), strongly suggests that Congress understood § 9(a)(1)(B) to prohibit indirect as well as deliberate takings. The permit process requires the applicant to prepare a "conservation plan" that specifies how he intends to "minimize and mitigate" the "impact" of his activity on endangered and threatened species, 16 U.S.C. § 1539(a)(2)(A), making clear that Congress had in mind foreseeable rather than merely accidental effects on listed species.

The Court of Appeals made three errors in asserting that "harm" must refer to a direct application of force because the words around it do. First, the court's premise was flawed. Several of the words that accompany "harm" in the § 3 definition of "take," especially "harass," "pursue," "wound," and "kill," refer to actions or effects that do not require direct applications of force. Second, to the extent the court read a requirement of intent or purpose into the words used to define "take," it ignored § 9's express provision that a "knowing" action is enough to violate the Act. Third, the court employed *noscitur a sociis* to give "harm" essentially the same function as other words in the definition, thereby denying it independent meaning. The canon, to the contrary, counsels that a word "gathers meaning from the words around it." The statutory context of "harm" suggests that Congress meant that

term to serve a particular function in the ESA, consistent with but distinct from the functions of the other verbs used to define "take." The Secretary's interpretation of "harm" to include indirectly injuring endangered animals through habitat modification permissibly interprets "harm" to have "a character of its own not to be submerged by its association."

When it enacted the ESA, Congress delegated broad administrative and interpretive power to the Secretary. See 16 U.S.C. §§ 1533, 1540(f). The task of defining and listing endangered and threatened species requires an expertise and attention to detail that exceeds the normal province of Congress. Fashioning appropriate standards for issuing permits under § 10 for takings that would otherwise violate § 9 necessarily requires the exercise of broad discretion. The proper interpretation of a term such as "harm" involves a complex policy choice. When Congress has entrusted the Secretary with broad discretion, we are especially reluctant to substitute our views of wise policy for his. In this case, that reluctance accords with our conclusion, based on the text, structure, and legislative history of the ESA, that the Secretary reasonably construed the intent of Congress when he defined "harm" to include "significant habitat modification or degradation that actually kills or injures wildlife."

In the elaboration and enforcement of the ESA, the Secretary and all persons who must comply with the law will confront difficult questions of proximity and degree; for, as all recognize, the act encompasses a vast range of economic and social enterprises and endeavors. These questions must be addressed in the usual course of the law, through case-by-case resolution and adjudication.

Reversed.

Case Questions

1. Is habitat modification harming endangered species?
2. Does the Court's interpretation mean no intent is required to violate ESA?
3. Did Congress intend to give the secretary authority to shut down an industry?
4. Is logging prevented now?
5. What ethical issues arise from this case?

Since the time of these head-on confrontations, the logging and paper industries have adopted a "Sustainable Forestry Initiative." The Initiative, adopted by 200 members of the American Forest and Paper Association, supports eco-friendly logging. The Nature Conservancy supports the Initiative, which has had the effect of negotiated solutions to the issue of logging versus environmental protection. No further legislation has been needed at the federal level because of the cooperation between and among these groups.

In the following case, the U.S. Supreme Court interpreted the Endangered Species Act as also permitting lawsuits by landowners who are affected by the statute's application.

Bennett v. Spear

520 U.S. 154 (1997)

Facts

The Fish and Wildlife Services issued an opinion on the operation of the Klamath Irrigation Project and the project's impact on two varieties of endangered fish. The Klamath Project is one of the oldest of the federal reclamation projects and is a series of lakes, rivers, dams, and irrigation canals in northern California and southern Oregon. The opinion concluded that the operation of the project might impact on the Lost River Sucker *(Deltistes luxatus)* and Shortnose Sucker *(Chasmistes brevirostris)* species of fish that were listed as endangered in 1988. The opinion further provided for alternative means of operation for the project that included the maintenance of minimum water levels in certain portions of the project.

Brad Bennett and other ranchers (petitioners) operate their ranches within the areas designated to receive less water pursuant to the biological opinion issued. Bennett filed suit alleging that the opinion was incorrect in its conclusions on the impact of the project on the two species of fish and that the opinion failed to take into account the resulting economic impact of lessening the water levels. Bennett's complaint alleged that the Endangered Species Act (ESA) and the Administrative Procedure Act (APA) required the federal government to take his interests into account in making the determination as to what to do about the project. The federal district court dismissed the complaint and the court of appeals affirmed the dismissal. Mr. Bennett appealed.

Judicial Opinion

Scalia, Justice. We first turn to the question the Court of Appeals found dispositive: whether petitioners lack standing by virtue of the zone-of-interests test. Although petitioners contend that their claims lie both under the ESA and the APA, we look first at the ESA because it may permit petitioners to recover their litigation costs, and because the APA by its terms independently authorizes review only when "there is no other adequate remedy in a court," 5 U.S.C. § 704.

The question of standing "involves both constitutional limitations on federal-court jurisdiction and prudential limitations on its exercise."

Numbered among these prudential requirements is the doctrine of particular concern in this case: that a plaintiff's grievance must arguably fall within the zone of interests protected or regulated by the statutory provision or constitutional guarantee invoked in the suit.

We have made clear, however, that the breadth of the zone of interests varies according to the provisions of law at issue, so that what comes within the zone of interests of a statute for purposes of obtaining judicial review of administrative action under the "'generous review provisions'" of the APA may not do so for other purposes.

The first question in the present case is whether the ESA's citizen-suit provision, set forth in pertinent part in the margin, negates the zone-of-interests test (or, perhaps more accurately, expands the zone of interests). We think it does. The first operative portion of the provision says that "any person may commence a civil suit"—an authorization of remarkable breadth when compared with the language Congress ordinarily uses. Even in some other environmental statutes, Congress has used more restrictive formulations, such as "[any person] having an interest which is or may be adversely affected," or "any person having a valid legal interest which is or may be adversely affected . . . whenever such action constitutes a case or controversy." And in contexts other than the environment, Congress has often been even more restrictive. In statutes concerning unfair trade practices and other commercial matters, for example, it has authorized suit only by "[a]ny person injured in his business or property."

Our readiness to take the term "any person" at face value is greatly augmented by two interrelated considerations: that the overall subject matter of this legislation is the environment (a matter in which it is common to think all persons have an interest) and that the obvious purpose of the particular provision in question is to encourage enforcement by so-called "private attorneys general"—evidenced by its elimination of the usual amount-in-controversy and diversity-of-citizenship requirements, its provision for recovery of the costs of litigation (including even expert witness fees), and its reservation to the Government of a right of first refusal to pursue the action initially and a right to intervene later. Given these factors, we think the conclusion of expanded standing follows.

It is true that the plaintiffs here are seeking to prevent application of environmental restrictions rather than to implement them. But the "any person" formulation applies to all the causes of action authorized by § 1540(g)—not only to actions against private violators of environmental restrictions, and not only to actions against the Secretary asserting underenforcement under § 1533, but also to actions against the Secretary asserting overenforcement under § 1533. As we shall discuss below, the citizen-suit provision does favor environmentalists in that it covers all private violations of the Act but not all failures of the Secretary to meet his administrative responsibilities; but there is no textual basis for saying that its expansion of standing requirements applies to environmentalists alone. The Court of Appeals therefore erred in concluding that petitioners lacked standing under the zone-of-interests test to bring their claims under the ESA's citizen-suit provision.

By the Government's own account, while the Service's Biological Opinion theoretically serves an "advisory function," 51 Fed. Reg. 19928 (1986), in reality it has a powerful coercive effect on the action agency:

> The statutory scheme . . . presupposes that the biological opinion will play a central role in the action agency's decision-making process, and that it will typically be based on an administrative record that is fully adequate for the action agency's decision insofar as ESA issues are concerned . . . . [A] federal agency that chooses to deviate from the recommendations contained in a biological opinion bears the burden of 'articulat[ing]' in its administrative record its reasons for disagreeing with the conclusions of a biological opinion,' 51 Fed.Reg. 19, 956 (1986).

What this concession omits to say, moreover, is that the action agency must not only articulate its reasons for disagreement (which ordinarily requires species and habitat investigations that are not within the action agency's expertise), but that it runs a substantial risk if its (inexpert) reasons turn out to be wrong. A Biological Opinion of the sort rendered here alters the legal regime to which the action agency is subject. When it "offers reasonable and prudent alternatives" to the proposed action, a Biological Opinion must include a so-called "Incidental Take Statement"—a written statement specifying, among other things, those "measures that the [Service] considers necessary or appropriate to minimize [the action's impact on the affected species]" and the "terms and conditions . . . that must be complied with by the Federal agency . . . to implement [such] measures."

The Service itself is, to put it mildly, keenly aware of the virtually determinative effect of its biological opinions. The Incidental Take Statement at issue in the present case begins by instructing the reader that any taking of a listed species is prohibited unless "such taking is in compliance with this incidental take statement," and warning that "[t]he measures described below are nondiscretionary, and must be taken by [the Bureau]." Given all of this, and given petitioners' allegations that the Bureau had, until issuance of the Biological Opinion, operated the Klamath Project in the same manner throughout the twentieth century, it is not difficult to conclude that petitioners have met their burden—which is relatively modest at this state of the litigation—of alleging that their injury is "fairly traceable" to the Service's Biological Opinion and that it will "likely" be redressed—i.e., the Bureau will not impose such water level restrictions—if the Biological Opinion is set aside.

Whether a plaintiff's interest is "arguably . . . protected . . . by the statute" within the meaning of the zone-of-interests test is to be determined not by reference to the overall purpose of the Act in question (here, species preservation), but by reference to the particular provision of law upon which the plaintiff relies. It is difficult to understand how the Ninth Circuit could have failed to see this from our cases. As we said with the utmost clarity in *National Wildlife Federal*, "the plaintiff must establish that the injury he complains of . . . falls within the 'zone of interests' sought to be protected by the statutory provision whose violation forms the legal basis for his complaint."

The Court of Appeals erred in affirming the District Court's dismissal of petitioners' claims for lack of jurisdiction. Petitioners' complaint alleges facts sufficient to meet the requirements of Article III standing, and none of their ESA claims is precluded by the zone-of-interests test. Petitioners' § 1533 claim is reviewable under the ESA's citizen-suit provision, and petitioners' remaining claims are reviewable under the APA.

Reversed.

Case Questions

1. Who has brought the suit and why?

2. Can those affected by the protection of an endangered species bring suit under the ESA?

3. How does the court deal with the issue raised by the government that the opinion is only an opinion and not government action?

4. Do the ranchers have standing to challenge the endangered species protection under the ESA?

5. The court's opinion was unanimous. Do you agree that both sides in an environmental case, those representing the interests of the species and those representing economic interests, should have the right to challenge a finding by the federal government?

The Delhi Sands Flower-Loving Fly (the Fly) is located only in California. It is native to the San Bernardino area and was placed on the endangered species list by the Fish and Wildlife Service (FWS).

Because of the Fly, San Bernardino County was forced to alter plans for a new hospital. The county did so and then proposed modifications to the intersection near the hospital so as to improve emergency vehicle access. The FWS refused to allow the modifications because it would interfere with the Fly's habitat. The county, along with the National Association of Home Builders has filed suit. They have asked for an injunction ordering approval of the proposed construction and intersection modifications. Can the court do so? Does the ESA act apply and can it prevent modifications and construction? *National Association of Home Builders v. Babbitt,* 130 F.3d 1041 (D.C. Cir. 1997).

Consider 20.5

STATE ENVIRONMENTAL LAWS

In addition to the federal enactments, 30 states have enacted some form of environmental laws and have established their own environmental policies and agencies. Some states may require new industrial businesses to obtain a state permit along with the required federal permits for the operation of their plants. As noted earlier, all 50 states have some form of hazardous waste regulation.

ENFORCEMENT OF ENVIRONMENTAL LAWS

Federal environmental law can be enforced through criminal sanctions, penalties, injunctions, and suits by private citizens. In addition to the federal enforcement rights, certain common law remedies exist for the protection of property rights such as nuisance or trespass. This portion of the chapter discusses the various remedies available for environmental violations.

Parties Responsible for Enforcement

Although many federal agencies are involved with environmental issues, the Environmental Protection Agency, established in 1970, is the agency responsible for the major environmental problems of air and water pollution, solid-waste disposal, toxic substance management, and noise pollution. The EPA is responsible for the promulgation of specific standards and the enforcement of those standards with the use of the remedies discussed in the following subsections. The Federal EPA may work in conjunction with state EPAs in the development and enforcement of state programs.

The **Council on Environmental Quality (CEQ)** was established in 1966 under the National Environment Protection Act and is part of the executive branch of the government. Its role in the environmental regulatory scheme is that of policy maker. The CEQ is responsible for formulating national policies on the quality of the environment and then making recommendations to lawmakers regarding its policy statements.

In addition to these major environmental agencies, other federal agencies are involved in environmental issues of enforcement such as the Atomic Energy Commission, the Federal Power Commission, the Department of Housing and Urban Development, the Department of the Interior, the Forest Service, the

FIGURE 20.1   *Penalties for Violation of Federal Environmental Laws*

Act	Penalties	Private Suit
Clean Air Act	$25,000 per day civil penalties and up to 15 years, or both $10,000 rewards	Citizen suits authorized EPA; suit for injunctive relief
Clean Water Act	$25,000 per day, up to one year imprisonment, or both; $50,000 per day, up to three years with knowledge; $100,000/six years for subsequent violations	Citizen suits authorized EPA; suit for injunctive relief
Oil Pollution Act	$25,000 per day civil penalty $3,000 per barrel if willful or negligent $250,000 and/or five years for failure to report	State laws; Private actions in nuisance and negligence
Solid Waste Disposal Act or Resource Conservation and Recovery Act	$250,000 and/or 15 years (for intentional) $1,000,000 corporations $50,000 per day and/or five years	Private actions in nuisance and negligence (after EPA has handled enforcement or failed to enforce); EPA suit for injunctive relief and reimbursement of trust funds

Bureau of Land Management, and the Department of Commerce. Basically, all federal agencies that deal with the use of lands, water, and air are involved in compliance with and enforcement of the environmental laws.

Criminal Sanctions for Violations

Most of the federal statutes discussed above carry criminal sanctions for violations. See Figure 20.1 for penalties. The following case deals with criminal sanctions for environment violations.

United States v. Johnson & Towers, Inc.

741 F.2d 662 (3d Cir. 1984)

Facts

Johnson & Towers repairs and overhauls large motor vehicles. In its operations, Johnson uses degreasers and other industrial chemicals that contain methylene chloride and trichlorethylene, which are classified as "hazardous wastes" under the Resource Conservation and Recovery Act (RCRA) and pollutants under the Clean Water Act.

The waste chemicals from Johnson & Towers' cleaning operations were drained into a holding tank, and when the tank was full, pumped into a trench. The trench flowed from the plant property into Parker's Creek, a tributary of the Delaware River. Under RCRA, generators of such wastes must obtain a permit from the EPA. Johnson & Towers had not received nor even applied for such a permit.

Jack Hopkins, a foreman, and Peter Angel, the service manager for Johnson, were charged with criminal violations of the RCRA and the Clean Water Act. Johnson & Towers was also charged and pled guilty. Hopkins and Angel pled not guilty on the grounds that they were not "owners" or "operators" as required for RCRA violations. The trial court agreed and dismissed all charges against Hopkins and Angel except the criminal conspiracy charges.

The government appealed the dismissal.

Judicial Opinion

Sloviter, Circuit Judge. The single issue in this appeal is whether the individual defendants are subject to prosecution under RCRA's criminal provision, which applies to:

> any person who— (2) knowingly treats, stores, or disposes of any hazardous waste identified or listed under this subchapter either—
> (A) without having obtained a permit under Section 6925 of this title . . . or
> (B) in knowing violation of any material condition or requirement of such permit.

If we view the statutory language in its totality, the congressional plan becomes . . . apparent. First, "person" is defined in the statute as "an individual, trust, firm, joint stock company, corporation (including a government corporation), partnership, association, State, municipality, commission, political subdivision of a State, or any interstate body." Had Congress meant to take aim more narrowly, it could have used more narrow language.

Second, under the plain language of the statute, the only explicit basis for exoneration is the existence of a permit covering the action. Nothing in the language of the statute suggests that we should infer another provision exonerating persons who knowingly treat, store or dispose of hazardous waste but are not owners or operators.

Finally, though the result may appear harsh, it is well established that criminal penalties attached to regulatory statutes intended to protect public health, in contrast to statutes based on common law crimes, are to be construed to effectuate the regulatory purpose.

In summary, we conclude that the individual defendants are "persons" within the RCRA, that all elements of that offense must be shown to have been knowing, but that such knowledge, including that of the permit requirement, may be inferred by the jury as to those individuals who hold the requisite responsible positions with the corporate defendant.

Reversed and remanded.

Case Questions

1. Who is charged with criminal violations?
2. What violations are charged?
3. What violations did the lower court dismiss?
4. Did Congress intend to prosecute corporate employees?
5. Does the appellate court reinstate the charges?
6. What proof is required to show violations by the "persons" involved?

Civil Liability for Violations

INJUNCTIVE RELIEF

Although the criminal sanctions imposed on violators may be costly, it is frequently more beneficial to landowners to have the polluting activity halted. As indicated in Figure 20.1, under each federal statute, the EPA has the authority to bring suit for injunctive relief. In seeking injunctive relief, the EPA brings suit asking the court to order a business to stop an activity or other violation of one of the acts. In addition to the EPA's power to seek injunctive relief, each federal act (except NCRA) allows private citizens to bring suit for damages for violations and also for obtaining injunctive relief.

COMMON LAW RELIEF

In spite of the complex federal regulatory scheme as to the environment, the enforcement of private property rights and elimination of pollution have frequently come through private suits based on the common law doctrine of nuisance. A **nuisance** is defined as the use of one's property in such a manner that it interferes with others' use and enjoyment of their properties (see Chapter 2 for more details).

Typical activities that have been found to be nuisances are feedlot operations, oil refinery operations, and activities that create excessive noise and excessive traffic. If a suit is brought in nuisance, the plaintiff may either seek damages to compensate for property value loss or actual property damage, or seek to enjoin the nuisance activity or both. Whether an activity will be enjoined depends upon a balancing test of the economic benefits of the activity versus the detrimental harm to other property owners.

In some cases, the activity of the landowner is so dangerous that strict liability is imposed for the resulting damage. For example, many courts have permitted landowners living near contaminated sites to recover for damages to their property as a result of the contamination.

In the following landmark case, the New Jersey Supreme Court deals with the issue of whether a purchaser can recover from a seller for the sale of contaminated property.

T&E Industries, Inc. v. Safety Light Corp.

587 A.2d 1249 (N.J. 1991)

Facts

United States Radium Corporation (USRC) owned an industrial site on Alden Street in Orange, New Jersey, where it processed radium from 1917 until 1926. USRC sold the radium for medical purposes and also used it to manufacture luminous paint for instrument dials, watches, and other products. Radium processing only permitted recovery of 80 percent of the radium from the carnotite ore, transported to the plant from Colorado and Utah. The unextracted radium was contained in "tailings" that USRC discarded into unimproved portions of the Alden Street site.

Through a complex series of chemical processes, the discarded radium emits radon, which can cause lung cancer when inhaled. Epidemiological studies had not been done at the time the tailings were discarded, and the federal government did not regulate the disposal of the tailings until 1978. However, many people had suspicions about handling radium and, as early as 1917, USRC employees measured the radioactivity of radium. One story told of how Dr. Van Sochocky, the president of USRC, "hacked" off his fingertip when radium lodged beneath his fingernail because he feared the effects of radium.

Radium processing ceased at the Alden site in 1926, and the site was leased to various commercial tenants until it was sold in 1943 to Arpin, a plastics manufacturer. The tailings were not removed from the site in spite of continually developing evidence about the danger. In fact, Arpin constructed a new portion of plant that rested on the discarded tailings. The property changed hands several times. T&E (plaintiff), a manufacturer of electronic components, leased the premises in 1969 and purchased it in 1974.

The Uranium Mill Tailings Radiation Control Act (1978) calls for the evaluation of inactive mill-tailing sites. New Jersey's Department of Environmental Protection (DEP) inspected the plaintiff's site and found radon levels exceeding state and federal standards. In spite of soil removal and other actions, the site could not be brought into compliance; T&E was forced to move its operations. The site could not be sold until clean-up of the tailings was complete.

In 1981 T&E sued Safety Light Corporation (a successor corporation to USRC) (defendant) and others (all corporations that bought from USRC or its transferees) based on nuisance, negligence, misrepresentation, fraud, and strict liability of abnormally dangerous activity. The trial court dismissed the strict liability claim and found that USRC had no knowledge of the dangers when the tailings were disposed of. The jury found for T&E, but the trial court entered a judgment N.O.V. for Safety Light. T&E appealed. The appellate court reversed the trial court's decision. Safety Light appealed.

Judicial Opinion

Clifford, Justice. At the outset we must determine whether a property owner can assert against a predecessor in title a cause of action sounding in strict liability for abnormally dangerous activities. Defendant suggests that only neighboring property owners, not successors in title, can maintain such a suit, and that successors in the title must rely on contract law to recover from a prior owner. According to defendant, a wealth of case law, including the Third Circuit decision in *Philadelphia Electric Co. v. Hercules, Inc.,* 762 F.2d 303 (1985), and the historical development of the abnormally dangerous-activity doctrine support that distinction.

In *Philadelphia Electric Co.* the court considered whether a property owner could recover damages for toxic-waste contamination from its predecessor in title. Relying on the doctrine of *caveat emptor* and the historical role of private nuisance law, the court concluded that the property owner could not bring a private-nuisance claim against its former owner and could not recover damages.

In reaching that conclusion, the court explained the traditional view of a seller's liability:

> Under the ancient doctrine of caveat emptor, the original rule was that, in the absence of express agreement, the vendor of land was not liable to his vendee, or a fortiori to any other person, for the condition of the land existing at the time of transfer. As to sales of land this rule has retained much of its original force, and the implied warrantees which have grown up around the sale of chattels never have developed. This is perhaps because great importance always has been attached to the deed of conveyance, which is taken to represent the full agreement of the parties, and to exclude all other terms and liabilities. The vendee is required to make his own inspection of the premises, and the vendor is not responsible to him for their defective condition, existing at the time of transfer.

Drawing from the rationale of the *Philadelphia Electric Co.* opinion, defendant argues that we should adopt a similar analysis. Defendant stresses that a successor in title, unlike an innocent neighbor, could have inspected the property or demanded a warranty deed. We are not persuaded, however, that a landowner who engages in abnormally dangerous activities should be liable only to neighboring property owners.

The abnormally dangerous-activity doctrine emphasizes the dangerousness and inappropriateness of the activity. Despite the social utility of the activity, that doctrine imposes liability on those who, for their own benefit, introduce an extraordinary risk of harm into the community.

Because some conditions and activities can be so hazardous and of "such relative infrequent occurrence," the risk of loss is justifiably allocated as a cost of business to the enterprise who engages in such conduct. Although the law will tolerate the hazardous activity, the enterprise must pay its way.

Because the former owner of the property whose activities caused the hazard might have been in the best position to bear or spread the loss, liability for the harm caused by abnormally dangerous activities does not necessarily cease with the transfer of property.

Nor are we satisfied that the doctrine of *caveat emptor* as developed in New Jersey should bar plaintiff's cause of action. Although the principle of *caveat emptor* dictates that in the absence of express agreement, a seller is not liable to the buyer or others for the condition of the land existing at the time of transfer.

A real-estate contract that does not disclose the abnormally dangerous condition or activity does not shield from liability the seller who created that condition or engaged in that activity.

We focus now on the elements of the abnormally dangerous-activity doctrine. That doctrine is premised on the principles that "one who carries on an abnormally dangerous activity is subject to liability for harm to the person, land or chattels of another resulting from the activity, although he has exercised the utmost care to prevent the harm." The *Restatement* sets forth six factors that a court should consider in determining whether an activity is "abnormally dangerous." They are:

(a) existence of a high degree of risk of some harm to the person, land or chattels of others;
(b) likelihood that the harm that results from it will be great;
(c) inability to eliminate the risk by the exercise of reasonable care;
(d) extent to which the activity is not a matter of common usage;
(e) inappropriateness of the activity to the place where it is carried on; and
(f) extent to which its value to the community is outweighed by its dangerous attributes.

Defendant does not dispute that liability can be imposed on enterprisers who engage in abnormally dangerous activities that harm others; but it contends that such liability is contingent on proof that the enterprise knew or should have known of the "abnormally dangerous character of the activity."

Defendant adds that knowledge, or the ability to acquire such knowledge, must be assessed as of the time the enterprise engaged in the activity, not at a later time—that is, if the risk of harm from the activity was scientifically unknowable at that time, an enterprise should not be liable.

We need not, however, determine whether knowledge is a requirement in the context of a strict-liability claim predicated on an abnormally dangerous activity. Even if the law imposes such a requirement, we are convinced, for the reasons set forth more fully below, that defendant should have known about the risks of its activity, and that its constructive knowledge would fully satisfy any such requirement.

That brings us to the question of whether defendant's activity was such as to fall within the meaning of "abnormally dangerous-activity."

Radium has always been and continues to be an extraordinarily dangerous substance. Although radium processing has never been a common activity, the injudicious handling, processing, and disposal of radium has for decades caused concern; it has long been suspected of posing a serious threat to the health of those who are exposed to it.

Furthermore, although the risks involved in the processing and disposal of radium might be curtailed, one cannot safely dispose of radium by dumping it onto the vacant portions of an urban lot. Because of the extraordinarily hazardous nature of radium, the processing and disposal of that substance is particularly inappropriate in an urban setting. We conclude that despite the usefulness of radium, defendant's processing, handling, and disposal of that substance under the facts of this case constituted an abnormally dangerous activity. Plaintiff's property is befouled with radium because of defendant's abnormally dangerous activity. Radiation levels at the site exceed those permitted under governmental health regulations. Moreover, the property has been earmarked as a Superfund site. Because plaintiff vacated the premises in response to the health concern posed by the radium-contaminated site and because the danger to health is "the kind of harm, the possibility of which [made defendant's] activity abnormally dangerous," defendant is strictly liable for the resulting harm.

Despite that wealth of knowledge concerning the harmful effects of radium exposure, defendant contends that it could not have known that disposal of the radium-saturated by-products behind the plant would produce a hazard. That contention appears to rest on the idea that somehow the radium's potential for harm miraculously disappeared once the material had been deposited in a vacant corner of an urban lot, or at the least that one might reasonably reach that conclusion—a proposition that we do not accept.

Surely someone engaged in a business as riddled with hazards as defendant's demonstrably was should realize the potential for harm in every aspect of that dangerous business. If knowledge be a requirement, defendant knew enough about the abnormally dangerous character of radium processing to be charged with knowledge of the dangers of disposal.

Finally, we reflect on the "parade of horribles" argument, namely, that our decision will create such uncertainty as to render it impossible for today's business community to regulate its affairs effectively. We have already noted the limited scope of our holding in that it extends only to that rare form of conduct that meets the criteria of an abnormally dangerous activity. Second, we note that almost without exception any conveyance of industrial property today would be made not in vacuum but in full appreciation of regulatory requirements that would surely embrace a condition such as the one on the Alden Street property. Parties to such transactions will be able to accommodate themselves to the necessities of the situation. A seller of land dealing in an abnormally dangerous activity such as the processing of radium can arrange to have the cost of cure shifted to a purchaser and obtain indemnification from such purchaser against any downstream claims. Although the recording of such an agreement might not create a bar to third-party claims, it will surely alter the equities in respect of any claim of benefit-of-the-bargain damages by a successor in the chain.

Affirmed.

Case Questions

1. Who originally owned the property?
2. How was the property originally used?
3. How did the owners feel about handling radium?
4. What was disposed of on the site?
5. At what point did the government step in and cause the site's evacuation?
6. Will T&E be liable under CERCLA?
7. Is Safety Light liable under CERCLA?
8. What is the basis of this lawsuit?
9. What made the disposal an abnormally dangerous activity?
10. What does the court say about the potential of a "parade of horribles" as a result of its decision?

Consider 20.6 Michael and Lauri Maddy own property located next to Vulcan Materials, Inc., a chemical-processing plant. The Maddys have brought suit alleging that the discharge from the plant is a trespass because their lungs and those of their animals have been damaged by chemicals. Is this a correct theory for their suit? Are there alternative theories? *Maddy v. Vulcan Materials Co.,* 737 F.Supp. 1528 (Kan. 1990)

Other theories that can be used to challenge uses of land include negligence and trespass. In the following case, the landowners filed suit for their damages from the electromagnetic fields on their property from utility wires.

Jordan v. Georgia Power Co.

466 S.E.2d 601 (Ga. App. 1995)

Facts

Larry Jordan purchased property in Douglas County, Georgia, in 1972. At the time of the purchase, Jordan was aware of an easement Georgia Power held in the property. Power lines were built on the property in 1973. Mr. Jordan married Nancy in 1983, and she then moved into his home. In 1985, Nancy Jordan was diagnosed with breast cancer, and in 1989 she was diagnosed with non-Hodgkin's lymphoma. In 1990, the Jordans moved from the property but had a difficult time selling the house. The bank foreclosed on the property because it did not sell, and Larry Jordan could no longer continue to make double payments on their new home and the old one.

The Jordans filed suit in 1991 against Georgia Power Company and Olgethrope Power Corporation, alleging that electromagnetic radiation from the electromagnetic fields (EMFs) created by the presence of the power lines on their property caused Mrs. Jordan's breast cancer and lymphoma. Their suit alleged both trespass and nuisance. The trial court found for the power company, and the Jordans appealed.

Judicial Opinion

Pope, Presiding Judge. The Jordans claim that the court erred in granting summary judgment on their trespass claim. They argue that the court invaded the province of the jury.

In their motion for summary judgment, Oglethorpe and Georgia Power argued that EMFs are not tangible matter and that their alleged presence on the Jordans' property could not constitute a trespass. In response, the Jordans filed the affidavit of Roy Martin, a licensed professional electrical engineer, in which he stated that electromagnetic radiation from high power lines is tangible. Martin further stated that a magnetic field could be detected and measured by appropriate measuring devices and that such fields obeyed physical laws.

In its order granting the motion, the court concluded that although the Jordans claimed that there was a detectable entry on their property by the EMFs, these fields were not tangible as defined by law for purpose of trespass determinations. The court stated: "[I]n Georgia a physical invasion of some kind is required in order to state a cause of action for trespass. There has been no physical injury to the real estate alleged. There has been no physical entry alleged. The plaintiffs allege there is a detectable entry by non-tangible, magnetic fields. However, such fields are not tangible as that term is defined by law for purpose of trespass determination."

OCGA Section 1-3-(20) provides: "'[T]respass' means any misfeasance, transgression, or offense which damages another's health, reputation or property." With respect to injuries to real estate, OCGA Section 51-9-1 defines the cause of action for interference with enjoyment of property, stating: "[T]he right of enjoyment of private property being an absolute right of every citizen, every act of another which unlawfully interferes with such enjoyment is a tort for which an action shall lie."

Although arguably the Jordans' trespass action could present a jury question, we conclude that for policy reasons, the trial court's grant of summary judgment was proper. The scientific evidence regarding whether EMFs cause harm of any kind is inconclusive; the invasive quality of these electric fields cannot generally constitute a trespass. In reaching this conclusion, we do not close the door on the possibility that science may advance to a point at which damage from EMFs is legally cognizable and a trespass action may lie.

The Jordans claim that the court erred by granting a directed verdict on the nuisance and property damage claims. In directing the verdict, the court concluded that there were no measurable damages or injury and that there was no nuisance.

Here, the Jordans argue that the court's conclusion that there was no evidence of property damage ignored the fact that the trial was bifurcated as to damages and causation. They contend that because of the bifurcation, evidence of nominal damages was sufficient to prove their claim.

OCGA Section 41-1-1 defines a nuisance as "anything that causes hurt, inconvenience, or damage to another and the fact that the act done may otherwise be lawful shall not keep it from being a nuisance. The inconvenience complained of shall not be fanciful, or such as would affect only one of fastidious taste, but it shall be such as would affect an ordinary, reasonable man." Moreover, "while a physical invasion is generally necessary, noise, odors and smoke which impair the landowners' enjoyment of his [sic] property are also actionable nuisances, if, and only if, a partial condemnation of the property results."

Here, the trial court properly directed a verdict on the nuisance claim. . . . [T]he present state of science does not authorize recovery based on these facts.

While the court found there was no cause of action for trespass or nuisance, it did reverse the case for error on evidence admissibility and for retrial on the other grounds the Jordans alleged for liability including negligence.

Reversed on other grounds.

Case Questions

1. What do the Jordans allege occurred as a result of the power lines being located on their property?
2. Is it important that the Jordans could not sell their house?
3. What is missing that is needed to establish nuisance?
4. What is missing that is needed to establish a trespass? (For more information on trespass, refer to Chapter 2).

GROUP SUITS—THE EFFECT OF ENVIRONMENTALISTS

In many circumstances, private suits have had the most effect in terms of obtaining compliance with environmental regulations or abating existing nuisances affecting environmental quality. The reason for the success of these suits may be the ultimate outcome of the litigation—possible business shutdowns and, at the least, the payment of tremendous amounts of damages and costs.

In some cases, private suits have been brought by environmental groups that have the organizational structure and funding for the initiation and completion of such suits. In some cases, the environmental groups are formed to protest one specific action, such as Citizens Against the Squaw Peak Parkway. Other groups are national organizations that take on environmental issues and litigation in all parts of the country. Examples of these national groups include the Sierra Club, the Environmental Defense Fund, Inc., the National Resources Defense Council, and the League of Conservation Voters. Some environmental groups represent business interests in environmental issues, as does the Mountain States Legal Foundation, which becomes involved in presenting business issues when private organizations and individuals bring environmental suits.

These environmental groups have not only been successful in bringing private damage and injunctive relief suits, but also have been able to force agencies to promulgate regulations required under the federal laws and to enjoin projects where EISs should have been filed but were not.

CAUTIONS AND CONCLUSIONS

The implications of environmental laws on real property transactions are tremendous. Anyone seeking to purchase property for industrial use must be familiar with the air quality standards and release permit requirements in the area to determine if industrial use is possible, and if it is possible, if it will be more costly because of environmental constraints. Due diligence is required before property is sold. That due diligence includes a look at the property as well as at how it has been used. Property owners must also be diligent in voluntary audits and disclosure to the EPA to minimize liability.

Key Terms

Air Pollution Control Act, 510
Air Quality Act, 510
Clean Air Act, 510
Environmental Protection Agency (EPA), 510
state implementation plans (SIPs), 510
nonattainment area, 510
prevention of significant deterioration(PSD) areas, 510
Emissions Offset Policy, 511
bubble concept, 511
Clean Air Act Amendments of 1990, 511
acid rain, 511
federal implementation plan (FIP), 511
maximum achievable control technology (MACT), 512
Water Quality Act, 512
Federal Water Pollution Control Administration (FWPCA), 512
Rivers and Harbors Act of 1899, 512
Federal Water Pollution Control Act of 1972, 513
Clean Water Act, 513
effluent guidelines, 513
National Pollution Discharge Elimination System (NPDES), 513
point sources, 513
conventional pollutants, 513
nonconventional pollutants, 513
toxic pollutants, 513
best conventional treatment (BCT), 513
best available treatment (BAT), 513
Safe Drinking Water Act, 514

Oil Pollution Act (OPA), 514
Solid Waste Disposal Act, 514
Resource Recovery Act, 514
Toxic Substances Control Act (TOSCA), 514
Resource Conservation and Recovery Act of 1976 (RCRA), 514
Comprehensive Environmental Response, Compensation, and Liability Act (CERCLA), 515
Hazardous Substance Response Trust Fund, 515
Superfund, 515
Superfund Amendment and Reauthorization Act, 515
Asset Conservation, Lender Liability, and Deposit Insurance Protection Act of 1996, 515
Incentives for Self-Policing, Disclosure, Correction, and Prevention of Violations, 517
National Environmental Policy Act (NEPA) of 1969, 522
environmental impact statement (EIS), 522
Surface Mining and Reclamation Act of 1977, 524
Noise Control Act of 1972, 524
Federal Environmental Pesticide Control Act, 524
Occupational Safety and Health Administration (OSHA), 524
Asbestos Hazard Emergency Response Act (AHERA), 524
Community-Right-to-Know substance, 524
Endangered Species Act, 524
Council on Environmental Quality (CEQ), 529
nuisance, 531

Chapter Problems

1. In 1976, Swainsboro Print Works (SPW), a cloth-printing facility, entered into a "factoring" agreement with Fleet Factors Corporation (Fleet) in which Fleet agreed to advance funds against the assignment of SPW's accounts receivable. As collateral for these advances, Fleet obtained a security interest in SPW's textile facility and all of its equipment, inventory, and fixtures.

In August 1979, SPW filed for bankruptcy under Chapter 11 (the corporate-reorganization chapter). The factoring agreement continued until early 1981 when Fleet ceased advancing funds because SPW's debt to Fleet exceeded Fleet's estimate of the value of SPW's accounts receivable. On February 27, 1981, SPW ceased operations and began to liquidate its inventory. Fleet continued to collect the accounts receivable assigned to it under Chapter 11. In December 1981, SPW was adjudicated a bank-

rupt under Chapter 7, and the bankruptcy trustee assumed title and control of SPW's facility.

In May 1982, Fleet foreclosed on its security interest in some of SPW's inventory and equipment and contracted with Baldwin Industrial Liquidators (Baldwin) to conduct an auction of the collateral. Baldwin sold the material "as is" and "in place" on June 22, 1982 with buyers assuming the responsibility for removal of the materials.

On August 31, 1982, Fleet contracted with Nix Riggers (Nix) to remove the unsold equipment in consideration for leaving the premises "broom clean." Nix had performed its work in the facility by the end of December 1983.

On January 20, 1984, the Environmental Protection Agency (EPA) inspected the facility and found 700 55-gallon drums containing toxic chemicals and 44 truckloads of material containing asbestos. The EPA incurred costs of $400,000 in cleaning up the SPW facility. On July 7, 1987, the facility was conveyed to Emanuel County, Georgia, at a foreclosure sale from SPW's failure to pay state and county taxes.

The government sued Fleet and the two principal officers and stockholders of SPW to recover the costs of cleaning up the hazardous waste.

Can Fleet be held liable under CERCLA? *U.S. v. Fleet Factors Corp.*, 901 F.2d 1550 (11th Cir. 1990)

2. A group of landowners situated near the Sanders Lead Company brought suit to recover for damages to their agricultural property from accumulations of lead particulates and sulfur oxide deposits released in Sanders's production process. The landowners' property had increased in value because of its commercial potential in being close to the plant. Sanders employs most of the town residents in its operations. What common law and statutory rights do the landowners have, and what relief can be obtained? *Borland v. Sanders Lead Co., Inc.*, 369 So.2d 523 (Ala. 1979)

3. Reynolds Metal has been held to the same technological standards in its pollution control for can manufacturing plants as those applied to aluminum manufacturers. Reynolds claims the processes are different and that the technology is not yet available for can manufacturing. Does Reynolds have a point? *Reynolds Metals Co. v. EPA*, 760 F.2d 549 (D.C. 1985)

4. The Mitchells lived in a residential section of Beverly Hills, Michigan, and sought to enjoin the operation of a nearby piggery. The pigs were fed in an open field, and any garbage not eaten by the pigs was plowed under by tractors. The odors from the operation, particularly in the spring and summer, were such that the use and enjoyment of the Mitchells' property was impaired. Who will win? Are any federal statutory violations involved? *Mitchell v. Hines*, 9 N.W.2d 547 (Mich. 1943)

5. Chasm Power Company was releasing steam and hot water from one of its plants. The steam and water contained no pollutants, but the level of the water was raised significantly when releases were made into an adjoining stream. Downstream owners brought suit seeking injunctive relief. Who will win? *McCann v. Chasm Power Co.*, 105 N.E. 416 (N.Y. 1914)

6. Albert J. Hubenthal leased approximately 55 acres of property in Winona County, Minnesota, to start a worm-farming operation. Shortly thereafter, he began to collect large amounts of material including waste paper, cardboard, used tires, scrap wood, scrap metal, leather, and other building materials that he contends were essential to the worm-farming operation.

The county attorney filed suit seeking to compel Hubenthal to clean up the property on the grounds that it was a public nuisance. After a hearing, the lower court enjoined Hubenthal from storing solid-waste material that could be a "source of filth and sickness" and from

maintaining a junkyard. The order gave Hubenthal 30 days to clean up, which he failed to do. Two months after the order was issued, county officials took three days to remove the materials accumulated from Hubenthal's farm. Hubenthal filed suit for trespass and violation of his due process rights. Is it a nuisance? Can the government clean it up? *Hubenthal v. County of Winona*, 751 F.2d 243 (8th Cir. 1984)

7. From July 7, 1944 to December 16, 1980, Herschel and Nellie McLeod owned a 117-acre piece of land in the town of California, Maryland, in St. Mary's County (referred to as the California Maryland Drum site or CMD site). During this period of ownership, Maryland Bank & Trust (MB&T) loaned money to the McLeods for the operation of his two businesses: Greater St. Mary's Disposal, Inc., and Waldorf Sanitation of St. Mary's, Inc., which were both trash and garbage businesses. The record indicates that MB&T was aware of the nature of the businesses, but it is unclear when it acquired its awareness.

During 1972 to 1973, the McLeods permitted the dumping of hazardous wastes on their property including lead, chromium, mercury, zinc, and ethylbenzene.

In 1980, the McLeods' son, Mark, obtained a loan from MB&T and purchased the 117 acres from his parents. Mark failed to make payments, and MB&T instituted foreclosure proceedings in 1981 and bought the property at a sale in May 1982.

The EPA discovered the hazardous waste problems and conducted a cleanup of the site at a cost of $551,713.50. The EPA then demanded payment from MB&T. When payment was refused, the EPA brought suit to collect the cost of the cleanup. Can EPA collect from MB&T? *United States v. Maryland Bank & Trust Co.*, 632 F.Supp. 573 (D. Md. 1986)

8. Frezzo Brothers, Incorporated, is a Pennsylvania firm engaged in mushroom farming at a location near Avondale. To produce their mushrooms, Guido and James Frezzo (the two family members responsible for the operation of the business) used a growing medium that consisted of fermented hay and horse manure. White Clay Creek, which flowed alongside of the Frezzo operation, was considerably polluted, and upon analysis the pollutants were found to consist mainly of horse manure. There had been no rain in the area, and the Environmental Protection Agency charged the Frezzos and their corporation with willfully discharging manure into the stream. The Frezzos claim the right to use the stream as riparians, and the United States government claims environmental regulations will control over common law rights. Would discharging manure into a stream be a violation of any environmental laws? *United States v. Frezzo Brothers, Inc.*, 602 F.2d 1123 (3d Cir. 1979)

9. First Capital Life Insurance Company made a loan of $7,300,000 to Schneider, Inc., in 1986. The loan was secured by a mortgage on real property located in

Allegheny County, Pennsylvania. Schneider failed to make payments in 1988, and in 1989 First Capital declared the loan in default. First Capital then sent representatives to the property to conduct an environmental inspection. Schneider employees refused to grant access to the property. There was no provision in the mortgage regarding such inspections upon default. Combining your knowledge from Chapter 15 on financing and this chapter on environmental liability issues, determine whether First Capital should be permitted access to the

property prior to foreclosure. *First Capital Life Insurance Co. v. Schneider, Inc.*, 608 A.2d 1082 (Pa. 1992)

10. The CEO of a corporation hired an expert, upon the advice of his attorneys, to conduct an environmental audit of his firm. The state attorney general has subpoenaed the results of the audit with regard to certain tracts of land it seeks to have cleaned up. Should the attorney general be able to get the audit materials? Does the CEO have criminal liability under CERCLA? *State ex rel. Corbin v. Superior Court*, 777 P.2d 679 (Ariz. 1989)

Internet Activities

1. Go to **http://www.lib.lsu.edu/gov/fedgov.html** for a complete listing of federal government agencies, commissions, and services.

2. Connect to **http://eelink.umich.edu/why.html** for links and advice on Environmental Education on the Internet (EE-Link).

3. Go to **http://www.bergen.org/AAST/Projects/ES/WL/** for statutory and educational resources for Wetland Studies.

4. View the Endangered Species Act at: **http://endangered.fws.gov/esa.html**.

5. For information on forests, see: **http://www.fs.fed.us**.

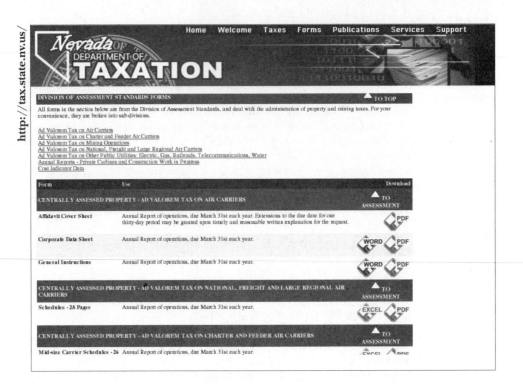

Chapter 21
Tax Aspects of Real Estate Ownership and Transfer

Taxes are what we pay for a civilized society.
  Oliver Wendell Holmes, Jr.

There are three different types of taxes affecting land ownership and transfer. The tax of ownership is commonly called property tax and is paid for a certain period at a rate based on the value of the property. Income tax rates can be affected by real estate ownership and property transfer, helping to make real estate a good investment. Finally, estate, gift, or inheritance taxes (or all three) are paid when property is transferred after the death of the owner (see Chapter 17). The purpose of this chapter is to discuss property taxes and income tax as it relates to real estate ownership and transfer. Questions to be answered include: What is property tax? How is the amount of property tax determined? What happens if property taxes are not paid? Can the amount of the property tax be contested? What effects on income does the sale of property have? Can owning property offer income tax deductions and credits? Are there any exemptions for gains made from the sale of property?

PROPERTY TAXES

The taxing of property has been documented as early as 596 B.C, when the city of Athens levied a tax on the owners of all property within the city. Roman property taxes at one time applied to both real and personal property. During the reign of Henry II in England, a 10 percent tax rate was applied to all "rents and movable properties." In 1697, the first "land tax" was levied in England. When the colonists arrived in North America, they brought with them and exercised forms of taxation: polls, property, and faculty (income earning capacity).

In all of these historical cases, the purpose of levying the tax was to support the government. Property taxes in the United States currently account for 85 percent of the tax revenues of local governments and finance about half of all local government expenditures. Property taxes have been a long-standing source for most local governmental units. As tax rates and valuation have increased, more landowners have been involved in disputes over values. The advantages of property taxes are that there is always property to tax and failure to pay results in a lien or the eventual sale of the property (discussed later in the chapter).

Because of the large amounts of money involved in tax assessments and collections, property tax rates have become a focus of many ballot initiatives. In the following United States Supreme Court case, a new home buyer challenged the property tax rate limits imposed by California's Proposition 13 and its resulting effect on her home purchase.

Practical Tip

Changes and limitations in property taxes have taken effect all around the country. When a listing agreement or property owner provides information on current taxes, be sure to check the valuation rates and procedures to be certain the full financial impact of your purchase is not an unknown that comes after you have closed on the property.

Nordlinger v. Hahn

505 U.S. 1 (1992)

Facts

Stephanie Nordlinger lived in a rented apartment in Los Angeles, never owning any real property until 1988, when she purchased her first home in the Baldwin Hills neighborhood of Los Angeles County for $188,000.

In early 1989, Nordlinger (petitioner) received an assessed value notice for her property from the Los Angeles County Tax Assessor (Hahn/respondent) that reassessed the home upward to $170,100. The new assessed value resulted in a tax increase of $453.60, or a 36 percent increase to $1,701.00. Nordlinger later learned from talking with her neighbors that she was paying five times more in taxes than some of her neighbors who had owned their homes since 1975. For example, an identical house one block away from Nordlinger's had an assessed valuation of $35,820 and a resulting annual tax of $358.20.

This disparity resulted because of the voter passage of California's Proposition 13 (Title XIIIA), a tax-limiting proposal. The maximum amount that any pre-1976 home

owner's assessed value could be increased per year was 2 percent. The amount of the assessed value adjustment was limited to per-year inflation, but the maximum was 2 percent. Thus, a pre-1976 owner of a $2.1 million Malibu home paid only a few dollars more than Nordlinger for property taxes. Nordlinger paid her taxes under protest and filed suit against the assessor on the grounds that her tax was unconstitutional. The trial court dismissed the complaint and the court of appeals affirmed. The California Supreme Court was rejecting all such tax challenges, and Nordlinger appealed to the United States Supreme Court.

Judicial Opinion

Blackmun, Justice. The Equal Protection Clause of the Fourteenth Amendment, § 1, commands that no State shall "deny to any person within its jurisdiction the equal protection of the laws." Of course, most laws differentiate in some fashion between classes of persons. The Equal Protection Clause does not forbid classifications. It simply keeps governmental decision-makers from treating differently persons who are in all relevant respects alike.

As a general rule, "legislatures are presumed to have acted within their constitutional power despite the fact that in practice their laws result in some inequality."

Accordingly, this Court's cases are clear that, unless a classification warrants some form of heightened review because it jeopardizes exercise of a fundamental right or categorizes on the basis of an inherently suspect characteristic, the Equal Protection Clause requires only that the classification rationally further a legitimate state interest.

As between newer and older owners, Article XIIIA does not discriminate with respect to either the tax rate or the annual rate of adjustment in assessments. Newer and older owners alike benefit in both the short and long run from the protections of a 1% tax rate ceiling and no more than a 2% increase in assessment value per year. New and old owners are treated differently with respect to one factor only—the basis on which their property is initially assessed. Petitioner's true complaint is that the State has denied her—a new owner—the benefit of the same assessment value that her neighbors—older owners—enjoy.

We have no difficulty in ascertaining at least two rational or reasonable considerations of difference or policy that justify denying petitioner the benefits of her neighbors' lower assessments. First, the States have a legitimate interest in local neighborhood preservation, continuity, and stability—*Euclid v. Ambler Realty Co.,* 272 U.S. 365, 47 S.Ct. 114, 71 L.Ed. 303 (1926). The State therefore legitimately can decide to structure its tax system to discourage rapid turnover in ownership of homes and businesses, for example, in order to inhibit displacement of lower income families by the forces of gentrification or of established, "mom-and-pop" businesses by newer chain operations. By permitting older owners to pay progressively less in taxes than new owners of comparable property, the Article XIIIA assessment scheme rationally furthers this interest.

Second, the State legitimately can conclude that a new owner at the time of acquiring his property does not have the same reliance interest warranting protection against higher taxes as does an existing owner. The State may deny a new owner at the point of purchase the right to "lock in" to the same assessed value as is enjoyed by an existing owner of comparable property, because an existing owner rationally may be thought to have vested expectations in his property or home that are more deserving of protection than the anticipatory expectations of a new owner at the point of purchase. A new owner has full information about the scope of future tax liability before acquiring the property, and if he thinks

the future tax burden is too demanding, he can decide not to complete the purchase at all. By contrast, the existing owner, already saddled with his purchase, does not have the option of deciding not to buy his home if taxes become prohibitively high. To meet his tax obligations, he might be forced to sell his home or to divert his income away from the purchase of food, clothing, and other necessities. In short, the State may decide that it is worse to have owned and lost, than never to have owned at all.

Petitioner and *amici** argue with some appeal that Article XIIIA frustrates the "American dream" of home ownership for many younger and poorer California families. They argue that Article XIIIA places start-up businesses that depend on ownership of property at a severe disadvantage in competing with established businesses. They argue that Article XIIIA dampens demand for and construction of new housing and buildings. And they argue that Article XIIIA constricts local tax revenues at the expense of public education and vital services.

Time and again, however, this Court has made clear in the rational-basis context that the "Constitution presumes that, absent some reason to infer antipathy, even improvident decisions will eventually be rectified by the democratic process and that judicial intervention is generally unwarranted no matter how unwisely we may think a political branch has acted" (footnote omitted). *Vance v. Bradley,* 440 U.S. 93, 97, 99 S.Ct. 939, 942–943, 59 L.Ed.2d 171 (1979). Certainly, California's grand experiment appears to vest benefits in a broad, powerful, and entrenched segment of society, and, as the Court of Appeal surmised, ordinary democratic processes may be unlikely to prompt its reconsideration or repeal. Yet many wise and well-intentioned laws suffer from the same malady. Article XIIIA is not palpably arbitrary, and we must decline petitioner's request to upset the will of the people of California.

* Friends of the court; interested parties filing briefs.

Affirmed.

Case Questions

1. When did Nordlinger buy her property and for how much?

2. When did the property get reassessed?

3. Discuss and compare Nordlinger's property taxes with those in her neighborhood and other California areas.

4. What two reasons does the court give as a rational basis for the difference in treatment of home owners?

5. How does the court respond to Nordlinger's point about the American dream?

6. Does the court uphold California's property tax scheme?

Assessment

The tax **assessment** is the estimation of the value of all parcels of land for the purposes of taxation. The amount of tax is calculated on the basis of a predetermined factor, such as $10 per $1,000 valuation. This is usually referred to as a millage rate; one mill equals 1/10th percentage of the assessed value, and the assessed value of property for tax purposes is generally 35–50 percent of the property's market value. Property owners pay at the same rate but in different amounts depending on the assessed value of their property. For example, if the tax rate is $10 per $1,000 of valuation and a property is valued at $100,000, then the tax would be $1,000. However, someone with property valued at only $50,000 would pay property tax of $500.

The real property tax is thus called an ***ad valorem* tax** because it increases as property values increase. It is not based on ability to pay or on the amount of services received from the governmental agency that administers the property tax revenues. This type of taxation has been held constitutional so long as the uniform rate structure just illustrated is applied.

To administer the tax program, each county has a tax **assessor** or other official prepare a list of all properties in the county and their owners. This list is often referred to as a **property tax roll** and includes all property that will be subject to the tax. Once the list is completed, it becomes the job of the assessor (who is usually an elected official) to determine the valuations for all properties on the list.

Many assessors prepare land value maps to outline various areas for purposes of assessing values. Thus, the location of schools, shopping, transportation, and other factors affecting land values can be easily determined. In arriving at the final figure for assessment, the assessor may use any of the methods or combinations of methods used by appraisers in their valuations such as comparable property sales prices, replacement cost, or potential rental income. The assessment figures vary significantly from state to state because each state has its own wording as to the basis for assessment value.

In some states, only fee holders are subject to the *ad valorem* tax on real property, whereas other states tax leasehold interests as well as some form of real-property interests.

Each state has its own standards for valuation of property and for assessed value, with some states using the full value and others using only a certain percentage of the value.

Because of statutory limitations on tax rates, some local governments have become creative in collecting new revenues. In the following case, a taxpayer challenged the collection of transfer fees as an unauthorized means of property taxation.

http://
The Division of Assessment Standards at the Nevada Department of taxation lists its specific duties at: **http:// tax.state.nv.us/doas.htm**.

C. R. Campbell Construction Co. v. City of Charleston

481 S.E.2d 437 (S.C. 1997)

Facts

The City of Charleston, South Carolina (respondent) passed an ordinance effective January 1, 1994, imposing a transfer fee equal to .25 percent of the purchase price on the conveyance of real property. All of the revenue generated by the transfer fees is used for acquiring, maintaining, and operating parks and public recreation facilities. In adopting the ordinance, the city council made the finding that the presence of parks increases the value of real estate in the city.

C. R. Campbell (appellant/taxpayer) purchased a lot for $15,000 and paid, under protest, the transfer fee of $37.50. He then brought suit challenging enforcement of the ordinance as an illegal tax. The trial court found the transfer to be valid, and Campbell appealed.

Judicial Opinion

Moore, Justice. The issue before us is a narrow one: Is the transfer fee a uniform service charge or a tax? Taxpayer concedes there is no challenge to the transfer fee if it meets the definition of a uniform service charge. If, on the other hand, the transfer fee is actually a tax, Taxpayer contends it violates S.C. Const. art. X, § 6, which requires that "[p]roperty tax levies shall be uniform in respect to persons and property within the jurisdiction of the body imposing such taxes." As a property tax, Taxpayer contends the transfer fee is unconstitutional because it applies only to property that is conveyed and not otherwise. We need not address this constitutional challenge since we find the transfer fee is a uniform service charge and not a tax.

Our recent decision in *Brown v. County of Horry*, 308 S.C. 180, 417 S.E.2d 565 (1992), is dispositive on this issue. In *Brown*, we upheld a $15 road maintenance fee on all cars registered in the county as a valid uniform service charge under S.C.Code Ann. § 4-9-30(5)(a) (Supp.1995). Similarly, under S.C.Code Ann. § 5-7-30 (Supp.1995), municipalities are authorized to impose uniform service charges. If the transfer fee meets the criteria set forth in *Brown* to constitute a uniform service charge, it is valid.

Under *Brown*, a fee is valid as a uniform service charge if (1) the revenue generated is used to the benefit of the payers, even if the general public also benefits (2) the revenue generated is used only for the specific improvement contemplated (3) the revenue generated by the fee does not exceed the cost of the improvement and (4) the fee is uniformly imposed on all the payers. In this case, it is undisputed the transfer fee is used only for parks and recreational facilities, the payers benefit because their real property values are enhanced, the transfer fee does not generate more revenue than that spent on such facilities, and all payers pay a uniform percentage of the sale price of property conveyed. According to the facts in the record, the transfer fee is a uniform service charge and therefore valid under *Brown*.

Affirmed.

Case Questions

1. Why do you think the council decided to raise money in this fashion?

2. Is the transfer fee discriminatory in any way?

3. Do nonlandowners use the parks?

4. Why is the finding that parks increase land value important?

(Ethical Issue)   Do you think the city council was trying to work around state law on taxation? Do you think their action was fair?

Methods of Valuation for Assessment

The assessment of property involves a great deal of discretion, and many criticisms of the property tax are aimed at this part of the system. However, assessed values tend to be lower than market values, and a recent survey indicated that the average national assessment figure for properties was 30 percent of market value.[1]

The timing of an assessment can affect the assessment figure. Furthermore, many assessors' offices are limited in the amount of time and personnel that can be devoted to the assessment task. In many areas, assessments are not done on an annual basis but biennially or as infrequently as every three or four years. The frequency of valuations will affect the amount of revenue raised since property values tend to rise.

In some cases, raw land is being assessed, but a subdivision or some other type of development is imminent because of surrounding property usage. Some assessments will value the property as if it were capable of being in use at the time (the highest and best-use concept) and will, of course, cause a higher tax

1.   Patrick Rohan, *Real Estate Tax Appeals*, 1988.

on the property. Sometimes, this type of future value assessment serves to force development because the owner of raw land cannot afford the assessed value tax.

Three different approaches are used for valuation of property. The **market approach** bases the value of the property on an analysis and correlation of actual transaction prices. That is, the assessor examines sales and purchases of property similar to the one being assessed. In comparing the sales of land, the assessor will consider factors such as physical characteristics, the time of the sale, special financing, and other unique terms of the sale.

Under the **income approach,** the value of the land is based upon prospective income that will be earned by the land. In using this approach, the assessor can examine net income, net operating income, gross or net rental income, and gross or net cash flow.

When the **cost approach** is used, the assessor is simply making the determination of what it would cost to replace the buildings on the property. The assessor examines information such as the total replacement cost of the building and then subtracts out factors such as deterioration of the premises and whether the facility is obsolete.

Under any of the formulas, the task of assessment is complex, with room for disagreement about the numbers used and the projections in those formulas where some estimating is involved. Lawyers who specialize in assessment appeal assist clients in appealing the value assessed to their properties.

The following case deals with one of the more complex valuation issues that confront appraisers today.

Mitsui Fudosan (U.S.A.), Inc. v. County of Los Angeles

268 Cal. Rptr. 356 (1990)

Facts

The County of Los Angeles adopted a redevelopment plan for the Central Business District Redevelopment Project. The plan limited Mitsui Fudosan (U.S.A.), Inc. (Mitsui), to a maximum floor area ratio of six square feet of building area to one square foot of parcel area. However, Mitsui could exceed that level through transfer of other unused floor area ratios from other parcels within the project area. Making use of these so-called transfer development rights (TDRs), Mitsui, in 1983, purchased from several adjacent landowners at a cost of $8,209,000 sufficient TDRs to permit it to construct an additional 490,338 square feet of building area, more than doubling the density originally permitted.

Beginning in the 1984–85 tax year, the county assessor increased Mitsui's base assessment by $8,209,000 to reflect the value of the TDR transactions. This resulted in increased taxes of $266,821.10 for the 1984–86 tax years. Mitsui paid the taxes under protest and appealed to the county appeals board. The appeals board labeled the issue a legal question and summarily denied the applica-

tion. The trial court granted Mitsui's motion for summary judgment and ordered a refund. The county appealed.

Judicial Opinion

Gates, Associate Justice. For purposes of taxation "this '[p]roperty' includes all matters and things, real, personal, and mixed, capable of private ownership." (§ 103.) "Real estate" or "real property," in turn, encompasses "[t]he possession of, claim to, ownership of, or right to the possession of land." (§ 104, subd. (a).)

The word "land" is not specifically defined by the Revenue and Taxation Code or related property tax regulations. However, no purpose would be served by attempting to force relatively recent three-dimensional land use concepts such as TDRs into one of the cubicles reserved for traditional interests in real property. Virtually since its inception it has been the law of this state that "[t]he sort of property in land which is taxable under our laws is not limited to the title in fee".

Whether or not TDRs are actually embodied within the definition of air rights, which already have been classified under the heading "land," or represent something entirely separate, they are appropriately viewed as one of the fractional interests in the complex bundle of rights arising from the ownership of land. As the density in urban areas increases, diminishing the number of sites available for new construction, the ability to exploit air space in various ways to achieve vertical expansion becomes essential. Property rights which evolve as a means of furthering such goals are properly subject to taxation.

The transactions in the instant case bear all the hallmarks of a transfer of real property. The owners of the donor parcels received valuation consideration, over eight million dollars, in fact, in return for divesting themselves of a portion of their own property interests, interests which are now possessed and owned by Mitsui.

In addition, in conjunction with the conveyances escrows were opened, escrow instructions and purchase and sale agreements were executed, title reports and insurance issued, property surveys were obtained and covenants restricting development were recorded against the donor parcels.

We find unpersuasive Mitsui's suggestion that it merely purchased some type of "zoning variance." As the County quite correctly observes, "[i]n a typical situation of rezoning, an owner does not negotiate with nearby property owners for the acquisition of property rights. A change in zoning does not entail title reports, sales contracts, brokerage commissions, etc." The mere fact that future zoning changes might diminish the value of a TDR is essentially irrelevant since the same fate could befall any property purchased for purposes of development.

The transactions here under review were intended to, and did, involve the transfer of a most significant present, beneficial property interest. The terms of that transfer, as well as the price paid by Mitsui, amply supports an inference that the entire fee interest in the TDRs was transferred. In the absence of substantial and convincing evidence to the contrary, the assessor was entitled to rely upon the purchase price for purposes of determining their full cash value.

The judgment is reversed.

Case Questions

1. What additional assessment was made against Mitsui?
2. What are TDRs?
3. Are TDRs property? Why or why not? Explain their characteristics.
4. What is the significance of increasing urbanization?
5. Is the additional assessment upheld?

ENVIRONMENTAL ISSUES AND ASSESSMENT
An assessment issue that has arisen recently because of EPA mandates on cleanups (see Chapter 20) is the effect on valuation of property for tax purposes of a finding of hazardous waste on the property and a government-imposed requirement for cleanup. Clearly, the presence of CERCLA substances and liability diminishes the value of the property. In the following case the issue is addressed.

Matter of Commerce Holding Corp. v. Board of Assessors of the Town of Babylon

673 N.E.2d 127 (N.Y. App. 1996)

Facts

Commerce Holding Corporation owns a parcel of industrial property in the town of Babylon in Suffolk County. The property, purchased by Commerce in 1984, consists of 2.7 acres of land improved with a one-story industrial building that is presently divided into 37 rental units. A former tenant on the property performed metal-plating operations on the premises and discharged wastewater containing copper, lead, cadmium, zinc, and other metals into on-site leaching pools, ultimately resulting in severe subsurface contamination.

As a result of the contamination, the property was designated as a Superfund site in 1986, making the owner strictly liable for its cleanup. In 1988, Commerce entered into a consent decree with the EPA to remediate the site.

From 1986 to 1991, assessors for the Town valued Commerce's property at between $1.5 million and $2.6 million each year. Commerce filed timely challenges to each yearly assessment on the grounds of excessive valuation. The lower court held that the value of the property has declined because of environmental issues, and the Town appealed.

Judicial Opinion

Ciparick, Justice. In a hearing before Supreme Court, real estate experts for both Commerce and the Town primarily used the income capitalization method to determine the value of the property as if unaffected by contamination, and then subtracted a cost to cure from that value. Specifically, Commerce's expert valued the property by using an income capitalization approach, with a sales approach for the land only, and then subtracted from the property's value in each year the total remaining cost to cure all the contamination. The outstanding cost to cure was calculated in 1991 dollars, trended back to account for inflation in each of the prior years, and reduced by any sums actually spent on remediation that particular year. By contrast, the Town's expert valued the property in an uncontaminated state based on comparable sales data "blended" with an income capitalization approach, and then subtracted from the property's value only the amount actually expended by Commerce in the year the costs were incurred.

The cardinal principle of property valuation for tax purposes, set forth in the State Constitution, is that property "[a]ssessments shall in no case exceed full value". As this Court has stated, the "ultimate purpose of valuation . . . is to arrive at a fair and realistic value of the property involved".

The concept of "full value" is typically equated with market value, or what "a seller under no compulsion to sell and a buyer under no compulsion to buy" would agree to as the subject property's price. In view of this market-oriented definition of full value, the assessment of property value for tax purposes must take into account any factor affecting a property's marketability (accord, RPTL 302[1] ["The taxable status of real property . . . shall be determined annually according to its condition"][emphasis added]). It follows that when environmental contamination is shown to depress a property's value, the contamination must be considered in property tax assessment.

The Town nevertheless asks this Court to adopt a per se rule barring any assessment reduction for environmental contamination. Otherwise, the Town contends, polluters would succeed in shifting the cost of environmental cleanup to the innocent taxpaying public in contravention of the public policy of imposing remediation costs on polluting property owners and their successors in title.

Whatever the merits of the Town's argument, the "full value" requirement is a constitutional mandate that cannot be swept aside in favor of the asserted environmental policy. As the State Board of Equalization and Assessment has recognized, the public policy "argument, while possessing superficial appeal, runs afoul of the requirement found in . . . New York's Constitution, that real property may not be assessed at more than its full (fair market) value". The high courts of Massachusetts and New Jersey have ruled likewise, concluding that statutory and constitutional full value requirements cannot be subordinated to environmental policy concerns.

Thus, in response to the Town's contention that assessment reductions for environmental contamination will encourage landowners to delay remediating their property, this policy argument cannot eviscerate the constitutional directive. Moreover, the Town's concern appears to be overstated; whatever tax benefit Commerce might obtain by deferring implementation of remedial measures pales in comparison to Commerce's potential liability for failure to take appropriate remedial action, including severe penalties under CERCLA (see, 42 USC § 9607[c][3]) and $2,000 in daily penalties for noncompliance with the consent order.

We also reject the Town's argument that because Commerce, by consent order, has agreed to pay the cleanup costs even if it sells the property, the property's market value would be unaffected by the presence of contamination. This contention is belied by the reality that a purchaser of the site, on notice of the environmental contamination, nevertheless would be liable for the cleanup costs under CERCLA (see, 42 USC § 9607[a]). Moreover, that Commerce has agreed to remediate the property does not resolve the question of whether, and to what extent, the contamination in fact affects the value of the land. As Commerce's expert opined, a buyer of the property would have demanded an abatement in the purchase price to account for the contamination notwithstanding the existence of the consent order. Whether a property owner's agreement to pay the cleanup costs would affect the property's value in a given case is a factual matter for the assessment board, but it cannot be said, as a matter of law, that the existence of the consent order in this case precluded an assessment reduction.

While it is not possible to prescribe any one method to assess the effects of environmental contamination, there are certain factors that should be considered. These include the property's status as a Superfund site, the extent of the contamination, the estimated cleanup costs, the present use of the property, the ability to obtain financing and indemnification in connection with the purchase of the property, potential liability to third parties, and the stigma remaining after cleanup.

Against this backdrop, we cannot say that the methodology here employed was erroneous as a matter of law. The valuation of Commerce's property was accomplished by the use of the income capitalization approach to determine the value in an uncontaminated state of this income-producing property, combined with a downward environmental adjustment in the amount of outstanding cleanup costs. While cognizant of the potential of this valuation method to overstate the effects of environmental contamination, we nevertheless conclude that cleanup costs are an acceptable, if imperfect, surrogate to quantify environmental damage and provide a sound measure of the reduced amount a buyer would be willing to pay for the contaminated property.

The Town next argues that even if the entire remaining cost to cure was properly deducted in connection with each yearly assessment, this amount should have been discounted to its present value. However, Commerce's expert testified that the estimated cleanup costs were present value estimates, which he described as the present financial impact of the cleanup on the property's value. The Town failed to introduce any controverting evidence and its challenge is thus precluded.

In conclusion, we hold that based on the record in this case, the reviewing court properly considered the effects of environmental contamination in assessing the value of Commerce's property and applied an acceptable valuation technique.

Affirmed.

Case Questions

1. What happened to the property to cause it to be designated as a Superfund site?
2. Why was the problem with the Superfund designation not considered in valuation?
3. Did the Superfund designation affect market value?
4. How will the land be valued for purposes of taxation?
5. Do you agree with the court's decision? What public policy implications follow from it?

Consider 21.1

What if the environmental damage is caused negligently or intentionally by the owner? Must the property be valued in light of the damage that has occurred given the owner's role? *Reliable Electronic Finishing Co. v. Board of Assessors of Canton,* 573 N.E.2d 959 (Mass. 1991)

Consider 21.2

Cecos International, Inc., was the owner and operator of a former hazardous waste facility now subject to an EPA cleanup and litigation regarding liability. Cecos has proposed deducting the cost of the cleanup from the valuation, which would render the property valueless. The assessor has proposed simply a reduction in fair market value. Which method should be followed? *Vogelgesang v. Cecos International, Inc.,* 1993 Ohio App. Lexis 1478 (Ohio App. March 15, 1993); *Inmar Associates v. Borough of Carlstadt,* 549 A.2d 38 (N.J. 1988)

EXEMPTIONS FROM ASSESSMENT AND TAX

All states have some land exempt from assessment and tax. Land exempted must include federal properties unless there is consent from the federal government. Some states that have large amounts of federal lands receive a percentage of profits from mineral operations on the land, but these receipts are not the equivalent of what a property tax would have yielded. State and local government property is also generally exempt from assessment and taxation. Examples include governmental buildings, parks, and preserves. Most states provide tax exemptions for properties held by nonprofit and charitable institutions. The definitions of exempt organizations vary from state to state.

Some states have used their property tax structure to attract new business to the state. For example, businesses may be given a 5- or 10-year exemption from payment of tax or they may be taxed at a lower rate. This type of favorable treatment can affect decisions made by companies on the placement of plants or storage facilities.

OBJECTIONS TO ASSESSED VALUE

The due process clause requires all states to give property owners the opportunity to object to or protest the assessed values of their properties. All procedures for protesting assessed value are statutory and include several basic steps:

1. Property owners must be notified of the assessed value of their property.
2. Property owners must be given a reasonable amount of time after assessment to gather information and prepare a protest.
3. Property owners must have a procedure for filing a protest and must be given instructions for the hows and whens of such a filing.
4. The local governmental body must provide a hearing forum: an administrative body or some form of judicial review for the property owners' presentation of protests.
5. Property owners have the burden of proof, during the hearing, to show the overvaluation of the property.

Property owners are entitled to all of the above procedural protections before the tax on the property becomes due and owing. No tax can be constitutionally imposed or made final until the property owner has had the opportunity to object. Once the hearing has been held and an adverse decision rendered, the property owner must pay the taxes but may then seek judicial review of the administrative action and challenge the assessment and tax in court.

Collection of Taxes

Accompanying the assessment notice given to all property owners is information on the rate of tax, the total amount of tax due, and the date the tax is due. Most states provide a grace period and then a period during which the tax may be paid along with a penalty. In the case of residential properties subject to a mortgage or deed of trust, the mortgagee or trustee or an assigned servicing agent generally pays the taxes for the property owner through monthly withholdings included in mortgage payments according to the initial loan agreement.

TAX LIENS

Because property tax is not a personal obligation but an obligation of the property, the nonpayment of the tax may result in a lien on the property. Once the tax is not paid, it becomes purely a procedural responsibility for the enforcement agency to execute and file a lien upon the property. Each state's statutes must provide for the procedure of translating nonpayment of property taxes into a lien and must authorize some official or agency to execute the lien; in other words, all **tax lien** procedures are regulated by state statute. In some states, nonpayment results in an automatic lien on the property without any action of filing or recording. In these states, title cannot be cleared or insured until the tax records are checked to be sure there are no property tax delinquencies.

The effect of a tax lien, in most states, is to make all other liens and mortgages inferior and to give the tax lien first priority for payment above all other prior-existing liens. The tax lien may be removed only by payment of the tax due plus any delinquencies and statutory penalties that may accrue through nonpayment. (See Chapter 5 for a discussion of other liens.)

TAX SALES

Since property tax is not a personal tax and the state's enforcement is through the tax lien, the procedure for collecting on a lien is sale of the property, with proceeds being distributed according to priority of parties with security in the property. The authority to foreclose on a lien or sell property for satisfaction of delinquent taxes is within the authority of local governments. The key factor in the **tax sale** of real property is compliance with due process requirements. In other words, before a tax sale may be held, adequate notice must be given to property holders, who must be allowed an opportunity to respond to the proceedings.

Consider 21.3

Indiana's tax sale statute requires that the notice of sale be sent to the property owners' "last known address." The Auditor of Marshall County sent Urbano and Irma Elizondo a notice of sale, which was returned by the post office for an incorrect address. However, the auditor had access to the Elizondos' current address through public records. No follow-up mailing was made. When the Elizondos protested the sale, the statute of limitations had expired. They claim they were denied due process because they did not receive the notice. Are they correct? *Elizondo v. Read*, 556 N.E.2d 959 (Ind. 1990)

Satisfaction of due process requirements does not mandate judicial proceedings prior to the tax sale. Thus, the local government need not obtain a judgment against the property before proceeding to a tax sale. Although the procedures for tax sales vary from state to state, they usually begin with the filing of notice, the delivery of notice to the property owner, and the publication of notice of sale.

When the sale is held, anyone may be present and bid, for the sale is required to be public. The proceeds from the sale are applied first to satisfy the taxes due, interest accrued during nonpayment, any applicable penalties, and the costs of the sale. After those amounts have been satisfied, payment is made according to the priority of any parties having security in the property. (See Chapters 4, 5, 13, and 15 for a complete discussion of priorities.)

In most states, the tax sale is not a final resolution of the property owners' rights, for there usually exists a right of redemption in the delinquent property owner. This right may be exercised in two ways, but whichever method a state follows, it is important to understand that purchase of property at a tax sale does not result in a taking of full and complete title. The rights obtained by a buyer at a tax sale are subject to the property owner's right of redemption. In other words, the owner of the property is given a certain period of time within which to pay amounts due and redeem or regain the property.

Under one method of redemption, the buyer is given a deed to the property, but the deed conveys only defeasible title. This means that at any time during the statutory redemption period, the title of the buyer can be defeated if the property owner is able to pay all amounts due in taxes, interest, penalties, and costs. Once the statutory period expires, the defeasible title becomes full fee simple title. The statutory period varies from state to state in a range of six months to six years.

Under the other method of redemption, the buyer at a tax sale is given only a certificate of sale, which is simply evidence of the purchase. Once the redemption period has expired, the buyer is given a deed to the property.

Under either method, the deed given is called a **tax deed** and is issued by the appropriate tax agency or official in the jurisdiction. The deed will usually indicate that all steps required for a tax sale have been complied with and that the agency or official has the right to conduct the tax sale. However, the tax deed, like a sheriff's deed, has no warranties either express or implied; the buyer's title is only as good as the agency's or official's compliance with all requirements for a valid tax sale. If there is noncompliance, the buyer runs the risk of having the sale set aside by a property owner who has been denied due process.

> **Consider 21.4**
>
> Connor failed to pay the property taxes on his half acre of undeveloped property because he protested the valuation and assessment of the property as excessive. When Connor received notice of a pending sale of his property for taxes, he protested on the grounds of unconstitutionality. Was Connor correct?

INCOME TAX AND REAL PROPERTY

Although income tax is a personal tax and is tied not to ownership of property but to earning of income, real estate ownership and transfer does affect the net income of an individual.

Home Interest Deduction

Congress permits the deductibility of home mortgage interest plus that of one other residence, that the taxpayer uses as a second home under **Internal Revenue Code (IRC)** definitions. The IRC also permits the deductibility of taxes on those properties. There is a limitation on the amount of debt that qualifies for the interest deduction. Because of economic changes, many home owners have been refinancing their residences at lower rates but were also taking advantage of the low-cost funds by pulling out their equity in the home in addition to refinancing the original mortgage. The amount of interest that is deductible in a refinancing is the amount the taxpayer paid plus any improvements. If the taxpayer takes out more equity than the basis in the house, the interest attributable to that portion of the loan is not deductible as home mortgage interest. For example, homeowner A bought her home for $170,000 and has landscaped and added a pool at a cost of $22,000. The market value of her home is $300,000, but she can only refinance $192,000 to have the full amount of the loan interest be deductible. If she borrows more, she will be required to fill out a special form breaking out the deductible interest from the nondeductible interest.

In addition, an original loan amount has interest deductible only to the extent of the fair market value of the home, up to a maximum of $1,000,000 for married couples. Both of these interest deduction limitations were designed to prevent manipulation of one of the few real estate tax benefits that remained in the IRC. For example, this provision prevents someone from buying a home for $180,000 and financing $200,000 in an attempt to obtain a loan with deductible interest. With the gradual elimination of the personal debt interest, closing this loophole became important.

The Revenue Act of 1987 clarified the extent of the deductibility of home interest. Referred to as **qualified residential interest,** the pre-1986 rules allowed interest deduction for all mortgage debt on a first or second home or both so long as the debt did not exceed the cost of the home plus the cost of improvements made to it. The new rules break residential interest into two categories: **acquisition indebtedness** and **home equity indebtedness.** The maximum acquisition indebtedness that can qualify for deductible interest is $1,000,000 ($500,000 for married persons who file separately). The maximum home equity indebtedness is $100,000

($50,000 for marrieds who file separately). Any interest paid in excess of these amounts is considered personal interest and was subject to the phaseout rules of the now completely undeductible credit card and other loan interest. Beginning in 1992, if interest on a loan is paid to an individual, as in a carry-back arrangement (see Chapter 15), that individual's name and social security number must be disclosed on the borrower's return.

Installment Sales

The IRC limits the use of the installment sales method of reporting income from certain property sales. Although the section does not apply to personal residence sales (hence the wrap-around mortgage can remain as an effective means of financing), it does apply to business sales. It eliminates the deferral aspect of installment sales that the IRC carried in the past that permitted the seller to carry forward the gains made by the sale of the property. Such deferrals continue to be available for installment sales of personal use (residence) property.

Sales of Property and Basis

To determine whether there is taxable income when real property is transferred, the key figures used for that determination will be **basis** and sale price. The basis in a home is the cost if it was purchased or the cost of construction if it was built plus additions, improvements, special assessments paid for local improvements, and costs of repair of casualty damage.

For commercial properties, the basis is, again, the cost in terms of price paid or construction costs, plus improvements, but less the **depreciation** taken over the life of the property. Depreciation is a business expense for wear and tear on the building, and it is subtracted from the value of the property for purposes of determining the property's basis.

To determine the gain on a property sale, the expenses of the sale and the basis are taken from the selling price to arrive at the figure. An example using numbers follows:

Gain Realized Calculation

Selling price of property		$97,000
Minus: Selling Expenses		3,000
Amount realized		$94,000
Basis of property		
Cost	$75,000	
Depreciation	10,000	
Improvements	2,000	
Adjusted basis	$87,000	
Gain realized	$ 7,000	

Residential Property Sales, Basis, and Exclusions

The basis for residential property in which the taxpayer resides is computed in the same way as discussed above, with price paid plus improvements. However, depreciation is not available for homeowners.

The computation of gains in the sale of residential property is, however, very different from that same computation for commercial property or property held for investment. With changes in the tax law, every married couple can exclude up to $500,000 in gain from the sale of residential property in which they have lived for at least two of the five years prior to the sale of the residence. That exclusion can be repeated every two years. For single taxpayers, the exclusion is $250,000.[2]

Depreciation Issues in Real Estate

There are many methods for computing property depreciation, such as the straight-line method (the value of the property is divided by the number of years it will be used and it is then depreciated at that rate for each of those years); the sum-of-the-years digits method (the number of years of property use are added together and then used as a denominator in a fraction applied each year); or the double-declining balance method (more depreciation is taken in the early years and declines as the property ages). However, under the tax code, the **Maximum Accelerated Cost Recovery System (MACRS)** method is required for real estate for all property placed into use after 1986. Property placed into use prior to 1986, but after 1980, may be depreciated under the depreciation rules in existence under the tax code at that time.

Under MACRS, real estate is depreciated over a 3, 5, 7, 10, 15, 20, 27.5, 31.5 or 39-year period. The amount of time for the depreciation is controlled by the type of real estate, and all categories are spelled out under the tax code. These classifications for depreciation do have some public-policy purposes. For example, properties used for solar, geothermal, or wind energy production can be depreciated as 5-year properties. Furniture and appliances in rental properties can also be depreciated over a 5-year period. Apartment buildings are subject to a period of 27.5 years, while farm buildings have the 20-year depreciation life. The tax code also contains depreciation tables that provide the annual depreciation figure for property values at given year rates.

Property Exchanges

Some residential property owners and developers exchange parcels of land. For example, transferred employees often find another employee of their company in their new location and are able to simply swap homes. An exchange of like-kind property (commercial for commercial or residential for residential) results in a gain only if cash or other property is received. For example, if Developer A exchanges property he bought for $10,000 for $4,000 cash and similar property worth $12,000, his gain of $6,000 is reported only to the extent of the cash received. Developer A reports $4,000 gain. His basis in the new property is his basis in his old property ($10,000) minus the cash he received ($4,000) plus the gain he reported ($4,000). So, his basis remains as $10,000.

---

2.   There are also provisions under the tax code for single individuals who then marry and sell their residence owned prior to marriage, rules for exclusion in the event of divorce, and hardship relief for couples who are transferred because of employment and have lived in their home less than the required period.

Capital Gains

Capital gains result when property is sold at a profit after a designated holding period that is simply "more than 12 months."[3] Through the 1997 Tax Act, Congress established a cap of 20 percent on the amount of tax on capital gains.[4] Capital losses in sales can be used to offset capital gains. There are many complicated aspects to capital gains transactions that require professional tax advice.

Low Income Housing Credit

The IRC provides tax credits for **low income housing.** These tax credits provide incentives for developers to construct, for example, apartment complexes that will accept Section 8 (low income voucher-program) tenants. The credit is predetermined for buildings placed in service before 1987 at 9 percent for nonfederally subsidized housing and 4 percent for federally subsidized housing. For buildings placed in service after 1987, the amount of the credit is determined by the earnings level on federal long-term bonds and has hovered around 8.9–9.2 percent for nonfederally subsidized housing and 3.8–3.97 percent for federally subsidized housing. The credit can be claimed annually for a 10-year period and can generate one of the few remaining significant tax savings in owning real estate. It is important to note that qualifying for the credit requires that rent in such projects be set according to formulas established by the federal government according to standards of living and income in the area where the project is located, or that the owners accept the Section 8 tenants' vouchers as the maximum rent. HUD sets rents by the market rates. In other words, strict controls govern how much money can be made when this credit is available to low income housing developers. Further, the credit cannot be used by owners of buildings that are in violation of local health, safety, and building codes. The credit can only be used to offset passive income but can be carried forward to future years because of the 1990 changes. In addition to federal tax credits, state and local governments also provide tax benefits for developers who construct low income housing.

Real Estate Investment, Income, and Deductions

The depreciation deductions for real property can be substantial. Prior to tax reform in 1986, many real estate investors were taking their large depreciation deductions from their real property investments and deducting them from their other income. The result was that many taxpayers during the 1980s were showing little income, no income, or, in many cases, paper losses because of the extensive depreciation deductions offsetting their income.

This rather large loophole in the tax code was closed when the IRC was amended to make a distinction between passive and active income and losses. **Active income** exists when the taxpayer "materially participates" in the business, as in those situations where the taxpayer earns a wage from the business or owns the business as a sole proprietor. **Passive income** results from partnership earnings from real estate investments. Indeed, the federal tax laws include a presumption that all

---

3.   There was a wrinkle during 1997 and 1998 that required an 18-month holding period, but the 12-month period was restored by the IRS Restructuring and Reform Act of 1998.
4.   That rate is 10 percent for those in the 15 percent bracket. A special lower rate of 18 percent applies (for those in higher tax brackets) to transactions after December 31, 2000, if the asset sold was held for more than 5 years.

income from real estate partnerships is passive. Since most real estate investments are in the form of limited partnerships, the extra benefit for real estate investors of being able to use their real estate losses to offset other income is not available. The losses, often called **suspended losses,** may be carried forward indefinitely but cannot be used to reduce other income. For example, a loss on a real estate investment could not be taken against the active salary income of the individual investor.

The limits on passive losses apply to individuals, estates, trusts, personal service corporations, and most closely held corporations. Even a taxpayer who materially participates in real estate rental activity can deduct only up to $25,000 in losses from other income.

Material or active participation is not defined in the act and is left to the regulations. But it is clear that active participation is more than just management activities, as defined elsewhere in the Internal Revenue Code. There is, however, an exception for low income housing investments that permits the $25,000 deduction even when the taxpayer does not materially participate in the activity. Also, the intent of Congress in allowing these exemptions was to offer some relief for the moderate income investor. The $25,000 exemption is reduced by 50 percent (never below zero) of the taxpayer's adjusted gross income that exceeds $100,000. Thus, those taxpayers whose adjusted gross income exceeds $150,000 do not enjoy the $25,000 exemption. The effect of these **passive loss** changes are illustrated in the following example:

Taxpayer has an investment interest in three rental properties definitely passive). The performance results on the properties are as follows:

PROPERTY	YEAR	INCOME (LOSS)
1	1	($50)
	2	($100)
	3	($30)
2	1	($10)
	2	($20)
	3	($19.50)
3	1	($90)
	2	0
	3	($40.50)

Taxpayer has passive income as follows:

1	$30
2	$90
3	$150

For year one, taxpayer has a loss of $120 ($150 less the $30 in income). For year two, taxpayer has an additional $30 in losses. In year three, there is no loss.

What would be the result if taxpayer had $150 in income in year one (other figures remain the same)? Discuss the results if taxpayer had $150 in income in year two.

Consider 21.5

In addition to not being able to take the losses against personal income, taxpayers will have to allocate the carry-forward losses according to the proportions for each passive activity. Hence, the carry-forward loss in year one is $40 to property one, $8 to property two, and $72 to property three.

Consider 21.6 | Suppose that the taxpayer in the previous example had all three investments in low-income housing. Would the result be different? Suppose that the taxpayer lived as the manager and did all maintenance work at property one and held no other job. Would the result be different?

AT-RISK RULE

Real estate investment activities are subject to the **at-risk rules.** Real estate investors are at risk for only those borrowed funds for which they have personal liability. The amount a taxpayer has at risk is the initial capital contribution plus any borrowed amounts as long as the taxpayer has personal liability for repayment or has pledged property that is not used in the activity as collateral for the loan. Even these two tests will not put the taxpayer at risk if the lender is also involved in the activity in some way other than as a creditor. Again, interest losses cannot be taken in real estate syndications when the syndicating entity or partnership was the lender for the operating partnership. Investors are not really at risk when the syndicator is the lender.

If the taxpayer is not at risk, the losses must be taken from that activity and not from other income. Again, the losses can be carried forward indefinitely.

INVESTMENT INTEREST—ANOTHER LIMITATION

Interest for indebtedness on a taxpayer's investment activity can only be deducted from the taxpayer's investment income generated by nonpassive investment. Investment interest is deductible only if the indebtedness money is used to purchase any property held as a nonpassive investment.

CAUTIONS AND CONCLUSIONS

A practical note for the discussion on property taxes is that the amount of taxes must be verified and a title search should be done (to determine whether any tax liens are involved) before any transactions on the property are completed. For property owners, notice should be taken of assessment and valuation notifications, so that any discrepancies can be properly and timely challenged.

Regarding the effect of real estate ownership on income tax, buyers and sellers should always investigate the tax consequences of their real estate transactions before entering into contracts. In some cases, the sale may be structured to maximize benefits. In the case of property ownership, the parties should be certain that all possible deductions are being taken so that the return on their investment is maximized.

No property transaction is complete without a tax-effect investigation—both on the property and on the income of the parties involved.

Key Terms

assessment, 543
ad valorem tax, 543
assessor, 543
property tax roll, 543
market approach, 545
income approach, 545
cost approach, 545
tax lien, 549
tax sale, 550

tax deed, 550
Internal Revenue Code (IRC), 551
qualified residential interest, 551
acquisition indebtedness, 551
home equity indebtedness, 551
basis, 552
depreciation, 552
Maximum Accelerated Cost
    Recovery System (MACRS), 553

capital gains, 554
low income housing, 554
active income, 554
passive income, 554
suspended losses, 555
passive loss, 555
at-risk rules, 556

Chapter Problems

1. Galena Oaks Corporation constructed apartment units for the purpose of renting them. Because of a factory shutdown in the area, most of the tenants left and the apartments were difficult to rent. Galena sold the units and treated the gain as a capital gain. The IRS claims the gain is ordinary income. What is the result?

2. Otis and Ethel Wade are considering purchasing a second home in the Catskills. The home will be an A-frame cabin, and they plan to spend 6 to 10 weeks plus 5 to 6 weekends there per year. Currently, the Wades own a home in New Rochelle and have paid off 10 years of their 30-year mortgage. They wish to finance the purchase of the cabin but are concerned that the interest may no longer be deductible. Offer Otis and Ethel an explanation of the deductibility of interest payments on second homes.

3. Myron and Glenda Warren are interested in refinancing their home. The home has been appraised at $250,000. They bought it for $150,000 and added a pool for $20,000. Their landscaping cost $17,500, and drapes and flooring cost $8,000. The lender will refinance up to 80 percent of the appraised value. The Warrens want to be certain the full amount of their loan is deductible. How much can they finance and still have fully deductible interest?

4. Roberta Hathaway is a limited partner in a partnership that runs a shopping center. The center had a loss of $600,000 during its first year because tenants were hard to find. Roberta's share of the loss is $50,000. She will have personal income of $62,000. Can she take the loss? If so, how much?

5. Suppose that Hathaway was a limited partner in a HUD low-income housing development. Would the result be different?

6. Will the general partner/operating partner in the shopping center be able to deduct his $200,000 portion of the loss? What additional information would you need?

7. A and B each own homes in the same area. A's home is 1,550 square feet, and B's home is 2,200 square feet. Although the rate of tax is the same, B's assessment is higher than A's. B claims these valuations are unfair because the lots are of the same size and are in the same neighborhood. Is B correct?

8. Glenda Johnson purchased her home in 1987 for $145,000. In 1990, she added a swimming pool that cost $20,000. Her landscaping cost her $2,800, and her draperies and shutters were $3,100. In 2000, Glenda decided to sell her home because she had found a larger home in a better neighborhood. She was able to sell her house for $293,000. What will she owe in taxes on this sale? Can you compute her basis?

9. A purchased a parcel of property at a tax sale and was given a certificate of sale. A wishes to construct a building on the property, but no lender will lend on the basis of the certificate. Explain why.

10. Dade County's property appraisal adjustments board assessed the value of the property of the Bath Club, which brought a trial court action challenging the assessments. The trial court refused to reduce the assessments, and the Bath Club appealed on several grounds, one of which was that the board's authority to appoint special masters to take testimony and make recommendations denied procedural due process since taxpayers could not appear and offer testimony. Are the taxpayers correct? *Bath Club, Inc. v. Dade County,* 394 So.2d 110 (Fla. 1981)

Internet Activities

1.   Go to: **http://www.irs.ustreas.gov/prod/search/index.html** to search for tax forms, filing instructions, and statutory text regarding reporting of passive income for real estate investments.

2.   Go to: **http://www.taxweb.com/index.html,** which claims to be the first consumer-oriented tax site on the Internet, for federal, state, and local tax issues.

3.   See **http://www.cnyc.com/index.html** for consumer-oriented information on property taxes in New York City.

City of Topeka, ks

Search
Search the site
Updates
News Releases
City Bids Online
List of Mayoral and Council Candidates
Street Closings
Employment
Weekly City Calendar (in .pdf format)
Cable TV City 4 Schedule
Community Calendar of Events
Report a street light that is out
Special Items
Resources
City Codebook Online
City Departments
Mayor, City Council, CAO
Maps
City Council Minutes
City Council Agenda
Recent Ordinances
Recent Resolutions
Topeka Web Site Links
Weather
Current Topeka Weather

Business &
Community
Information

Fun
Stuff

City
Government
Information

Talk
To Us

This website is maintained by the City of Topeka Information Technology Department. Contact the webmaster with questions or comments.

Chapter 22
Legal Issues in Land Acquisition, Finance, and Development

Plans get you into things, but you got to work your way out.

    Will Rogers

If a builder builds a house for a man and does not make its construction firm, and the house which he has built collapses and causes the death of the owner of the house, the builder shall be put to death.

    Hammurabi's Code

A s the quotes indicate, real estate planning, development, and construction are not easy tasks. In fact, the development of real estate requires that all the topics covered in the first 21 chapters of this book be brought together along with some new considerations. The laws affecting real estate are all integrated when someone undertakes the development of real estate. From interaction with zoning and planning commissions to obtaining financing and handling construction of homes or complexes, a developer faces law at every turn in the complex maze of real estate development.

This chapter covers the stages of real estate development and the various laws that apply and affect those stages of development. From construction law to syndication to an integration of zoning and planning law, development requires constant interaction and compliance with the law. Figure 22.1 provides a flow-chart look at the process of land development.

LAND ACQUISITION

Market Analysis

Because real estate investments have been so profitable in the past few years, the idea of doing a market analysis on buying and developing land seems redundant. However, many subdivisions have experienced bankruptcy because the units constructed were too expensive or were inappropriate for the needs of people in the area. Before acquiring land or deciding on the type of subdivision, a developer should determine the economic and physical needs of people living in or moving to the area. The purpose for this type of preliminary study is to determine the location and type of housing that can sell readily. For example, some areas of cities have the greatest concentration of families residing in them, and a subdivision with larger, single-family homes would most likely be profitable. In that same area, townhouses and condominiums might not sell. In college towns, on the other hand, smaller housing units would sell very well because investors and students tend to purchase smaller homes for rental properties or temporary residences.

This initial step of understanding the market may determine the subdivision's ultimate success. Other factors that can be determined in the study include the economic status of residents and how much they can afford to pay for housing. With these factors in mind, construction costs can be appropriately budgeted.

Governmental Analysis

It is also at this stage of development that the developer must work with governmental agencies and within government regulation. Several steps are critical.

ANNEXATION

In some cases, no land parcels that are large enough for subdivision are located within city limits. However, the developer will have a difficult time selling properties in the subdivision if the city emergency services and utility services are not available to the buyers of the units. One alternative is to have a private corporation furnish these services, but a better and more frequently used alternative is to have the subdivision parcel annexed by the city.

The process of **annexation** is similar to a change in zoning and requires application, notice of a hearing, and a public hearing. The public hearing affords all interested parties an opportunity to object (see Chapter 19).

INTERSTATE LAND SALES

http://

For more on interstate land sales, visit HUD's Website at: **http://www.hud.gov/fha/sfh/ils/ilsstst.html**.

The developer should also begin preparing (or have prepared) all documents necessary for compliance with any governmental agencies that might have jurisdiction over the sales. For example, if unimproved lots are being sold, the Interstate Land Sales Full Disclosure Act (ILSFDA; 15 U.S.C. § 1701 *et seq.*) will apply, and the developer must file statements of record and property reports with the

FIGURE 22.1   *Steps in Land Development*

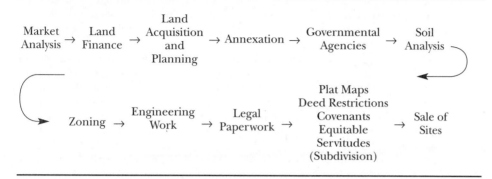

Department of Housing and Urban Development (HUD) (see Chapter 14). Approval of these documents can take time, so the developer should anticipate the possible delay.

FEDERAL LOAN APPROVALS FOR SALES
If improved lots with dwellings or multiunit housing units are to be sold, the developer may wish to have Federal Housing Administration (FHA) and Veterans Administration (VA) financing available for buyers. To do so, the developer must obtain FHA and VA approval for the subdivision. Again, obtaining approval in advance will alleviate the problem of having to wait while buyers are ready to buy.

THE COST OF DEVELOPMENT—IMPACT FEES
In recent years, governmental agencies have required developers to bear some of the costs of creating subdivisions. Subdivisions bring families in at rapid rates, and the cost of new schools is a burden local governments often cannot carry at accelerated paces. Many states have passed laws requiring developers to pay **impact fees** to provide local governments with needed funds to provide for expansion of services such as schools, police, and fire departments that are needed as a result of the development.

   As the following case indicates, these fees have been challenged on the basis of strict interpretation of statutory authority. While the fees themselves are generally valid, the government agencies imposing them must have the clear authority to collect them, and they must be used in an appropriate and legal manner.

Southern Nevada Homebuilders Association, Inc. v. City of North Las Vegas

913 P.2d 1276 (Nev. 1996)

Facts

The City of North Las Vegas (respondent/cross appellant) adopted an ordinance requiring payment of a fee when an applicant applied for a city building permit. The fee proceeds were earmarked for the funding of fire protection and emergency medical services within the City. Southern Nevada Homebuilders Association (SNHBA) filed a complaint asserting that the Ordinance was invalid. SNHBA then filed a motion for summary judgment on the grounds that the city's special building permit fees constituted an unlawful tax that substantially benefitted those who were not subject to the payment of such fees. The district court granted summary judgment and the city appealed.

Judicial Opinion

Per Curiam. On July 7, 1993, the City adopted Ordinance No. 1089. The Ordinance was entitled "Fee for Enhancement and Expansion of Fire and Emergency Medial Services," and required a payment of five cents per square foot of newly constructed building space upon application for issuance of a building permit within the City. Proceeds from the fee would help finance a portion of the cost for developing additional fire protection and emergency medical services ("EMS") "for the people who live and work in the City of North Las Vegas," and mitigate demands on existing fire protection and EMS resources caused by development.

The City contends that NRS 278B.160 is not exclusive, but allows impact fees to be assessed for projects other than those enumerated. We disagree.

NRS 278B.160 provides, in pertinent part:

> A local government may by ordinance impose an impact fee in a service area to pay the cost of constructing a capital improvement or facility expansion necessitated by and attributable to new development.

"Impact fee" is defined as "a charge imposed by a local government on new development to finance the cost of a capital improvement or facility expansion by and attributable to the new development." "Capital improvement" is defined as

1. Drainage project;
2. Sanitary sewer project;
3. Storm sewer project;
4. Street project; or
5. Water project.

"Facility expansion" is defined as "any natural and artificial watercourses, water diversion and water storage facilities, including all appurtenances and incidentals necessary for any such facilities."

We conclude that the language of NRS 278B is clear on its face, allowing impact fees only for the enumerated projects. However, even if NRS 278B were considered ambiguous, the legislative history of the statute clearly reflects an intent to restrict the projects for which impact fees could be imposed.

Several statements made during committee hearings clearly indicate that the language of NRS 278B was intended to limit the projects for which impact fees could be imposed. In the March 30, 1989 hearing, a specific question was asked concerning whether the impact fees would cover a fire station. William Thomas, who had been charged with advising the legislature on the purpose of the bill, answered that he believed fire and police were excluded. Moreover, a question was asked whether there would be "anything in addition to roads and underground to be covered by impact fees." Thomas responded, stating, "according to the way the enabling legislation was written, in what he [Thomas] believed to be section 3 [now NRS 278B.020], that was the limiting factor to determine exactly what impact fees could be used for." *Id.* Again, in the April 14, 1989 Minutes of Assembly Committee on Government Affairs, Assemblywoman Myrna Williams clearly stated the intent of the legislation:

> Throughout [the] country, there seems to have been an adverse relationship between private development and local governments. Local governments, who are struggling to meet their infrastructure needs, look upon new development as a source of funding to take care of their infrastructure needs. Private development claims they are getting hit too hard and object. Problem ends up in court. Decision has to be made who pays for infrastructure.
>
> AB 372 [NRS 278B] provides for a predictable amount of impact fees on new development. It will help to keep cost of new development down. At [the] same time, it will allow local governments to have a predictable formula in source of funding for basic infrastructure needs. . . .
>
> Subcommittee's intention was to work out compromise on both sides in an effort to keep cost as low as possible while allowing local governments to impose impact fees to fund infrastructure that would be necessary as a result of new development.

The above quotes provide examples of a general understanding expressed at the hearing, to the effect that the list of projects subject to impact fees was to be exclusive.

Affirmed.

Case Questions

1. What authority was given to permit the City of North Las Vegas to assess the fees?
2. What was the purpose in allowing the fees?
3. Was fee use limited to specific categories?
4. Why were specific categories given as a limitation by the legislature?

In 1974, the Board of Supervisors of San Diego County adopted a land-use policy called I-43 to help ensure orderly growth in the face of rapid and widespread development in the area. Among other things, the developers would be required to present a "school-availability" letter from the appropriate school district to the Planning Commission and Board of Supervisors to obtain approval to proceed with their proposed development. After Grossmont Union High School District (respondent) indicated in several proposal proceedings that additional developments would cause overcrowding, the board called for additional promises and provisions from developers.

In the fall of 1977, Candid Enterprises, Inc. (plaintiff/petitioner), entered into an agreement with Grossmont to pay for additional school facilities, and the district would then issue an availability letter.

In the interim, the School Facilities Act was passed by the California Legislature, which authorized cities and counties to require developers to pay fees for temporary school facilities. The San Diego Board adopted ordinance 5120, which permitted it to enter into agreements with developers for payments of the fees authorized by the state legislation.

Some fees were collected and some commitments were made, but in 1980 enrollments declined and the board monitored development but was not requiring availability letters or fees. Candid then asked to be released from its $23,500 commitment to Grossmont because the funds were no longer needed. The request was refused by the board. Can the board refuse such a request? Must the fees be needed at the time of collection or the time of use? *Candid Enterprises, Inc. v. Grossmont Union High School District*, 705 P.2d 876 (Cal. 1985)

USE RESTRICTIONS

It is important to recall the discussions in Chapter 7 about use restrictions that result from fee simple defeasible grants. The following case deals with the important point that a grantor's restriction on land use controls not only the developer's plans but also the government's authority in working with the land and developers.

In the following case, a governmental agency faced the issue of use restrictions in its proposed plan for new development.

White v. Metropolitan Dade County

563 So.2d 117 (Fla. 1990)

Facts

In 1940, several members of the Matheson family deeded three tracts of land located on the northern portion of Key Biscayne to Dade County. The 680 acres came to be known as Crandon Park. In the recorded deeds, the grantors expressly provided:

This conveyance is made upon the express condition that the lands hereby conveyed shall be perpetually used and maintained for public park purposes only; and in case the use of said land for park purposes shall be abandoned, then and in that event the said grantor, his heirs, grantees

or assigns, shall be entitled upon their request to have the said lands reconveyed to them.

Since the time of the original grant, several amendatory deeds have been issued by the grantors to allow ancillary uses such as the construction of public roads, public utilities, and a firehouse. However, the grantors did refuse to allow the building of a cable satellite dish.

In 1986, the Dade County Board of County Commissioners entered into an agreement with Arvida International Championships, Inc. (Arvida), and the International Players Championship, Inc. (IPC), to construct a permanent tennis complex on the property. The complex consisted of 15 tennis courts, service roads, utilities, and landscaping and took up 28 acres. The agreement with Arvida and IPC provided that for two weeks each year the complex would become the site of the Lipton International Players Championship Tennis Tournament (Lipton tournament).

In February 1987, the first Lipton tournament was held before approximately 213,000 people. A permanent clubhouse was then erected, with plans calling for a 12,000 seat stadium. The facilities are closed to the public for periods of time before and after the Lipton tournament (three weeks before and one week after) for site preparation and dismantling. When additional parking space became necessary, the grantors' heirs refused to give consent for more parking, and a suit resulted seeking an injunction against the Lipton tournament on the grounds that the deed restriction was violated and the master plan for Dade County was violated because the park was designated as an "environmentally sensitive parkland." The trial court found for Dade County, and the grantors' heirs and environmental groups (appellants) appealed.

Judicial Opinion

Gersten, Judge. Appellant/heirs first contend that the construction of the tennis complex violates the deed restriction. As previously stated, the deed provides that the "lands hereby conveyed shall be perpetually used and maintained for public park purposes only."

"In construing restrictive covenants the question is primarily one of intention and the fundamental rule is that the intention of the parties as shown by the agreement governs, being determined by a fair interpretation of the entire text of the covenant." Similarly, "the terms of dedications of land for park purposes where the lands are conveyed by private individuals are to be construed more strictly than is the case where the lands are acquired by the public body by purchase or condemnation."

Appellant/heirs argue that it was the intent of the Matheson family to limit the use of Crandon Park to passive activities such as picnicking, swimming, and the like. We glean no such intention from the language of the deed. Further, the Florida Supreme Court has adopted a very broad definition for what a "park" encompasses. The court has stated:

[A] park is considered not only as ornamental but also as a place for recreation and amusement. Changes in the concepts of parks have continued and the trend is certainly toward expanding and enlarging the facilities for amusement and recreation found therein.

The court further explained that the permissible uses for a public park include:

[T]ennis courts, playground and dancing facilities, skating, a swimming pool and bathhouse, horseshoe pitching, walking, horseback riding, athletic sports and other outdoor exercises . . . golfing and baseball . . . parking facilities . . . provided always that a substantial portion of the park area remains in grass, trees, shrubs and flowers, with seats and tables for picnicking, for the use by and enjoyment of the public.

We conclude that the construction of the tennis complex did not violate the "public park purposes only" provision of the deed restriction.

Appellant/heirs next argue that turning the tennis complex over to a commercial operator violates the deed restriction. We do not agree. Florida courts have consistently ruled that commercial benefit does not defeat a park's purposes.

Finally, appellant/heirs contend that the operation of the Lipton tournament violates the deed restriction because it deprives the public of the use and enjoyment of Crandon Park, including the use and enjoyment of tennis facilities. We are persuaded by this argument and rule that the holding of the Lipton tournament violates the deed restriction because it virtually bars the public uses of Crandon Park during the tournament, and does bar public use of the tennis complex, for extended periods of time.

In ruling that the holding of the Lipton tournament violates the deed restriction, we note that a distinction must be made between "park purposes" and "public purposes." Assuming *arguendo* that the Lipton tournament is an economic success which brings innumerable benefits to Dade County and its citizens, such an undeniable public purpose is not consistent with a deed restriction mandating the narrower "public park purposes only."

In addition, the word "only" in the deed restriction at issue further buttresses our ruling that the operation of the Lipton tournament, as presently constituted, violates the restriction.

Dade County contends that the tennis complex is consistent with the "public park purposes" restriction provided for in the deed. In support, Dade County argues that the complex is open to the public when the tournament is not being held, the site of the tennis complex utilizes less than 5 percent of Crandon Park, and that a valid park purpose is served by "spectating." Dade County also points to the benefits derived by Dade County from having the Lipton tournament in Dade County.

Here, the public, in fact, is deprived from using these tennis facilities for a period of three to four weeks during the Tournament Period. Further, under the contract as to the 1987 tournament, Arvida had the right to exclude the public for as long as five months.

Dade County argues that the use of the property as a tennis complex is better than its previous use as a dump. While we agree that a tennis complex in a public park, is better than a dump in a public park, we note that the County's previous use of the site as a dump, was also in violation of the deed restriction. We do not congratulate Dade County for shifting from one impermissible use to another.

Finally, Dade County argues, and we agree, that it is well settled that "equity abhors a forfeiture," that "such restrictions are not favored in law if they have the effect of destroying an estate," and that they "will be construed strictly and will be most strongly construed against the grantor."

Appellants/heirs, however, clearly represented to the court and the trial court that they were not seeking a reversal. What appellant/heirs want is a declaratory judgement that the present use of the park is in violation of the deed restriction and an injunction to prevent any further erosion of the "public park purposes only" deed restriction.

We therefore declare Dade County to be in violation of the deed restriction. We reverse the trial court order as to the deed restriction, and remand for entry of an order enjoining Dade County from permitting the Lipton tournament to proceed as it is presently held. Our ruling does not prevent Dade County from using the tennis complex for tennis tournaments. It merely seeks to insure that in holding such tournaments, public access to the rest of Crandon Park is not infringed; and use of the tennis complex is not denied to the public for unreasonable periods of time.

We reverse the trial court order on this point and remand for entry of an order enjoining any further development at the site.

Case Questions

1. What type of land interest was created with the grant to Dade County?

2. How does the court interpret the "park only" requirement?

3. Of what significance is the fact that the public cannot use the courts before, during, and after the tournament?

4. Did Dade County violate other restrictions apart from the deed restrictions?

5. Do the heirs of the grantors want the land returned to them?

6. Must the complex be removed because of environmental concerns?

Governmental Approval

ZONING

Although a zoning check is part of the property purchase checklist, the purchase may have been made knowing that a zoning change could be obtained. For example, the type of residential zoning may need to be changed for its density. Some cities limit the number of housing units per acre, and if the developer is planning a condominium development or single-family dwellings on minuscule lots, the density restrictions may need to be waived. (See Chapter 18 for a discussion of obtaining zoning variances.)

PROTESTS OF RESIDENTS EXERCISING RIGHTS

Today, a developer may face groups involved in municipal improvements that will need to approve the project. These groups include watchdog groups such as those for parks, historic preservation, beachfront and coastal zones, and environmental groups. Their support may be necessary for approval by the governmental bodies. They also enjoy some protection and due process rights in the development process.

Practical Tip

Although obtaining municipal approval sounds as if it is a one-step process, it is actually a layered process. The proposed development may require approval of a planning commission. If the proposed subdivision will vary from existing zoning, the developer may have to appear before the board of zoning appeals. Often cities have plat committees or subdivision control boards that have specific jurisdiction over the division of large parcels of property into smaller lots. Further, the developer will require building permits, road construction permits, transportation permits, and signage permits.

To satisfy others' demands, many developers find that a more extensive **master-planned community,** reached through negotiations with the planning or zoning board, is required. A trend in recent years has been for developers to engage in larger-scale projects that are actually the development of an entire community as opposed to simply a subdivision; this is sometimes referred to as a **planned unit development (PUD).** The community plan envisions parks, commercial and office facilities, and a completely preplanned layout. To obtain approval for the concept, the developer may be required to guarantee the use of the land in a certain way and thus may present a full package of covenants that will govern the community. For example, the developer may agree that certain areas will forever remain as parks for the planned community, or that only single-family residences will be constructed in certain areas of the community or in the community as a whole.

OTHER AGENCY APPROVALS

Water, transit, and drain authorities will also have to approve any subdivision project, and their approval is separate and apart from the other government entities even though they may be housed in the same facility and report to the same city council.

(Ethical Issue) | Suppose that a member of the city council who is scheduled to vote on a particular zoning application is the beneficiary of a family trust that owns property in the area near where the proposed project will be built. The effect of the project going forward will be a substantial increase in value of the surrounding properties. Should the city council member participate in the discussions and vote on the zoning for the proposed project? What issues do you see in such a scenario?

LAND FINANCE

Financing a real estate development is often not as simple as going to the bank and obtaining a mortgage loan. A developer may have to be more creative and bring together a pool of investors to finance the project. These investors will want something more than interest as a return on their funds; they will want to join in on the profits made from the development project. **Real estate syndication** is a generic term for the process of investor ownership of real estate projects. Real estate syndication allows developers to acquire nontraditional funding for a project through groups of individual investors. Syndication can be something as simple as pooling funds to buy an apartment complex or as complex as the development of raw land into a planned community or commercial complex. The following sections cover the forms of and laws that apply to the various forms of syndications.

The Basics of Real Estate Syndication

The primary party in a real estate syndication is the entrepreneur or syndicator. Those who invest in the syndicate are referred to as *unit purchasers.* The form of the syndicate may be a partnership, a corporation, a limited liability company (LLC) or a real estate investment trust (REIT).

Investors in syndicates should understand that syndication units are often high-risk investments. While the returns can be quite high, they are so because of the higher risk involved. Even if returns come, those returns are subject to the volatile nature of the real estate markets. Further, syndicate units are not highly liquid assets. In addition to their restrictions on transferability (see page 572) the units are not often easily sold to others.

Real estate syndications have complex documents and tax issues (see pages 573–574) that require thorough review by both legal and accounting experts. Even with perfection in the documents, unit purchasers must also be cautious about the history, reputation, and ability of the syndicator. Background checks for the planned land development are important prior to investing, but so also are background checks on the syndicator.

Francine Weiss and a number of other Maryland residents invested in the BJV real estate syndication. After she and the others lost most of their investment, they sued the principals in the syndication. During the course of the lawsuit they discovered that the property interests they purchased were at prices two to two and one-half times their actual market value. The BJV principals claim that the prices charged were to permit Francine and the other investors a great tax break by allowing them more to depreciate. How could Francine and the others have avoided the loss of their investment? *Weiss v. Lehman*, 713 F.Supp. 489 (D.D.C. 1989)

Consider 22.2

Syndication Forms—General Partnerships

A **general partnership** is a form of doing business that can be used for syndication so that all the profits and losses flow through to the individual partners. Defined as a voluntary "association of two or more persons as co-owners in a business for profit," a partnership also places the partners at full liability risk. Their personal assets are all subject to the creditors of the partnership.

CREATION

Governed by the **Uniform Partnership Act (UPA),** a uniform law adopted in 49 of the 50 states, partnerships are created by a document called the **articles of partnership.** Each partner makes a capital contribution, the investment in the syndicate, and each partner has an ownership interest in the property acquired by the partnership.

The Internal Revenue Code (IRC) recognized partnerships as an aggregate of the partners only and permits each partner to report his or her share of the partnership's income, gains, and losses. In a real estate investment, this attribute of partnership taxation enables the partners or unit owners to enjoy the full benefit of deductions for depreciation.

TAXATION

Income Tax The basic principle of taxation of partnerships is that the partnership does not pay taxes, the partners do (Internal Revenue Code; 26 U.S.C. § 701). Each partner is responsible for reporting his or her proportionate share of loss or income on his or her individual tax returns. The loss or income of the partnership is determined by subtracting deductions from income, which includes rental income, sales (capital gains), interest, and any other sources of partnership income.

Property Tax In real estate partnerships, issues of taxation arise regarding the property contributed to, sold by, or developed by the partnership. If property is contributed to a partnership by a partner, there is no gain or loss. Thus, if a

Practical Tip

**A Checklist for Those Interested
in Getting into Syndication**

1. Check the current market value of the properties involved.
2. The current leases, rental fees, payment histories, and terms.
3. Check the property and syndicator's expenses.
4. Perform a cash flow analysis.
5. If there are vacancies, why? How does the market look?
6. Check title, taxes, assessment, public records.
7. Check on the tax implications.
8. Check the zoning.
9. Check for environmental issues, liability, and targets.
10. Check terms of underlying loan agreements, mortgages, deeds of trust, and other contracts.
11. Determine whether state and federal securities laws apply to the syndication.
12. Check the background and experience of the syndicator(s).
13. Review the paperwork for the syndication structure and, if applicable, of the syndicator.
14. Are sales people licensed real estate agents? Are they licensed securities dealers?
15. Verify brokerage fees and other commissions for sales of interest in the syndication.

partnership is formed to develop property and one partner's contribution is a piece of property, there is no taxable event to the partnership or partner upon that initial contribution.

Another issue of property taxation is the partnership's basis in property contributed to the partnership by partners as their initial capital contribution. Two categories of tax concerns arise from this type of property contribution: The first comprises the tax consequences for the partnership and the partnership basis in the property. The second comprises the tax consequences for the contributing partner, the type of interest that partner holds, and that partner's basis in the property.

As just discussed, there are no tax consequences to the partnership upon the contribution. However, the basis issue for the partnership remains. The basis of the property is, very simply, the cost of the property plus what has been put into the property. For purposes of a real estate partnership, the basis of contributed property is the partner's basis. Thus, if A, B, and C form the ABC partnership and A contributes a piece of property with a basis of $30,000, the partnership basis is $30,000 (26 U.S.C. § 723).

The contributing partner has no tax consequences upon contribution of the property to the partnership, but will have tax consequences if the partnership interest is transferred or if the partnership terminates and the partner is paid the value of his or her interest. At that time, the partner may have to recognize income.

Sale of Partnership Interests One of the reasons for formation of many real estate partnerships, and in many cases one of the reasons for success of the partnerships, is the ability of the partners to transfer their partnership interests. When a partner transfers a partnership interest, the individual partner will have tax liability.

RELATIONSHIPS

In the absence of an agreement otherwise in the articles of partnership, each partner has an equal say in the management of the partnership and each partner shares in the profits and losses on an equal basis. Many syndicates provide that the profits and losses will be split according to the proportion of the capital investment, but such an agreement must be made to supersede the UPA provisions. The actual capital investment can be cash, property, or even services rendered to the partnership. Regardless of the nature of the contribution, the partner is treated as an equal under the UPA for purposes of management and profit sharing.

Even if a managing partner is used (generally the syndicator fills that role), each partner has a right of access to the books and records of the partnership. Each partner also has the right to an accounting. An **accounting** is an examination of the books and records of the partnership to be certain that each partner has received the appropriate share of profits from the partnership's operation.

Terminating an interest in a partnership or terminating the partnership itself is a difficult process because of liability issues with respect to third parties. Even if a partner transfers his or her interest to another investor, the liability to creditors up to that point continues. In the absence of an agreement, or **novation,** between and among the creditors, the departing partner, remaining partners, and new partner, the existing personal liability of the departing partner does not end with a transfer. Further, the departing partner must give public and private notice of the transfer or departure so that he or she is not personally liable for any future obligations of the partnership.

A new partner cannot be admitted without the unanimous consent of the existing partners. A transfer without approval from the other partner means that the transferee is entitled to the flow-through of the profits and losses, but would not have a say as a partner. A transfer without permission is an assignment of a personal property interest, or the right to income and losses, but it would not be a transfer of partner status.

Syndication Forms—Limited Partnerships

A **limited partnership,** is a form of doing business and syndication governed by the **Uniform Limited Partnership Act (ULPA)** and the **Revised Uniform Limited Partnership Act (RULPA).** These acts, adopted in nearly all the states, have permitted uniformity in standards for the creation of a very popular form of syndication.

NATURE AND CREATION

A limited partnership is a partnership with a slight variation in the liability of those involved. There are two types of partners in a limited partnership: there must be at least one **general partner,** and one **limited partner.** General partners have the same liability as all partners in a general partnership—full and complete personal liability for all partnership obligations and losses. Limited partners' liability is limited to the amount of their capital contributions. Their personal assets are not placed at the risk of the limited partnership's success. The most they can lose is the amount of their investment.

A limited partnership is a statutory creature. Unlike a general partnership that can be formed with an agreement or articles of partnership, a limited partnership must be created formally with a public filing of the document of creation, often called the articles of limited partnership. The articles must be filed with a public office, generally the secretary of state in the state where the limited partnership is created and will do business. The articles must include, under the RULPA, the following information:

- Name of the limited partnership (which cannot include the names of the limited partners because that would be misleading to third parties about the nature of their financial involvement).
- Address of the limited partnership's principal office
- Name and address of the statutory agent (the person who will accept delivery of notices and legal documents)
- Business address of the general partner(s)
- Latest date for dissolution of the limited partnership

RELATIONSHIPS IN A LIMITED PARTNERSHIP

The principal advantage of a limited partnership is that it places on limited partners only limited liability. For limited liability to work, several requirements must be met. First, as discussed above, a certificate of limited partnership must be filed indicating the limited liability status of the limited partners. Second, there must be at least one general partner. The general partner can be a corporation, but the general partner must also have some personal assets to bear the burden of full liability. Third, the limited partners cannot be involved in the management of the business. Such involvement would give the appearance of general partner status. Finally, a limited partner cannot use his or her name in the name of the partnership, which would give the wrong impression to outside parties and create an estoppel type of relationship.

Under the RULPA, the liability of limited partners for participation in the business has been largely eliminated. A limited partner who participates in the management of the firm in the same way the general partner does is liable only to those persons who are led to believe by the limited partner's conduct that the limited partner is a general partner. The RULPA also provides a list of activities that can be engaged in by limited partners without a resulting loss of limited liability status. Those activities include:

1. Being employed by the general partnership as an employee or contractor
2. Consulting with or advising the general partner
3. Acting as a surety or guarantor for the limited partnership
4. Voting on amendments, dissolution, sale of property, or assumption of debt

In many limited partnerships, the general partner contributes an undeveloped piece of property, and the limited partners furnish the money for its development. In limited partnerships, the limited partners are not permitted to contribute services as capital. Limited partners are silent or unknown partners and must not give the appearance of involvement in firm management.

The following case involves an issue of limited partner participation in the management of a business and resulting liability.

American National Ins. Co. v. Gilroy, Sims & Associates, Ltd.

847 F.Supp. 971 (E.D. Mo. 1995)

Facts

Gilroy, Sims & Associates, Ltd. (Gilroy, Sims), was a limited partnership engaged in real estate development whose original general partners were Richard Gilroy and William Sims. Thomas Green and John Murphy, Jr., were listed as limited partners along with certain other individuals on the certificate of limited partnership. Green and Murphy took an active role in the day-to-day operations of the real estate developed by the limited partnership. Financing was obtained to construct the venture's building in St. Louis in 1968, and a mortgage was payable to American National Insurance Co. over 27 years. In 1976, the partnership executed a Restated Agreement, and Green and Murphy became general partners of Gilroy, Sims, agreeing to "unlimited liability for the debts of the partnership." In the fall of 1990, the partnership stopped making mortgage payments. After foreclosure by American National, a deficiency of $1,437,840 was outstanding. Green and Murphy believed that as limited partners when the debt was incurred in 1968, they were absolved from any personal liability beyond the assets of the firm. American National disagreed.

Judicial Opinion

Gunn, D. J. With respect to defendants Green and Murphy's motion for summary judgment for the remaining deficiency, the Court finds that defendants are liable for the remaining deficiency pursuant to the terms of the Restated Agreement.

Even though the Restated Agreement signed by Green and Murphy provides that "the partners shall have unlimited liability for the debts of the partnership," Green and Murphy contend that as incoming partners they are liable for prior debts only to the extent of partnership property and are absolved of personal liability under § 17 of the Uniform Partnership Act. An incoming partner, however, may by agreement bind himself to personal liability for past debts. See *Resolution Trust Corp. v. Teem Partnership,* 835 F.Supp. 563, 570 (D. Colo. 1993) (some jurisdictions interpreting parallel statutes have held that UPA § 17 does not apply to incoming partner who expressly assumes pre-existing obligation).

The dispositive issue before the Court is whether Green and Murphy assumed personal liability for the pre-existing debts and, if so, to what extent. In executing the restated agreement, defendants failed to limit the debts or time period of the debts for which they assumed unlimited liability, but instead assumed liability as general partners for all of the debts of the partnership in section 10. Defendants expressly adopted the partnership obligation incurred prior to their execution of the Restated Agreement by their words as well as their actions. More-over, section 5 of the Restated Agreement describing the duration of the partnership specifically provides that the partnership commenced on November 1, 1968.

Under Missouri law, limited partners are not liable as general partners if they do not take part in the control of the day-to-day business operations of the partnership. *First Wisconsin Nat'l Bank v. Towboat Partners, Ltd.,* 630 F.Supp. 171, 176 (E.D. Mo. 1986) (limited partners not liable if only possible control was over expenditure of funds from extended line of credit agreed to by limited partners under restructuring agreement to keep partnership afloat). Although Green and Murphy's limited partner status would ordinarily limit their potential liability to creditors, their active roles in taking part in the control of the business subjected them to potential general partner liability.

Judgment against Green and Murphy.

Case Questions

1. Were the incoming general partners, Green and Murphy, personally liable for the preexisting partnership obligations in this case?

2. Under what circumstances may limited partners be subjected to general partner liability?

3. Were Green and Murphy subject to unlimited personal liability as general partners for the indebtedness that arose while they were limited partners?

In a limited partnership, only general partners are permitted to participate in management. A limited partner acting as a manager loses status as a limited partner. Limited partners should check the qualifications of the general partner to be certain that the partnership will be well managed. In **blind pool partnerships** (partnerships in which the general partner is selling units in the partnership to raise money, but no specific real estate is as yet involved), the qualifications of the general partner are even more critical because the general partner will be entrusted with the investment decision.

If the limited partners comply with the rules for limited liability, their liability is limited to the amount of their capital contribution. If they have pledged to pay a certain amount as capital over a period of time, they are liable for the full amount. For example, some real estate syndications that are limited partnerships allow limited partners to make their investments in installment payments over two to four years. Limited partners in these types of arrangements are liable for the full amount pledged whenever an obligation to a creditor is not paid.

The general partner has the absolute authority to decide not only when but if distributions will be made; the general partner might decide not to distribute funds but to put them back into the business.

Profits and losses are allocated on the basis of capital contributions. Under the RULPA, any other agreement for sharing of profits and losses must be in writing.

The authority of the general partner in a limited partnership is the same as the authority of the partners in a general partnership. These powers can be restricted by agreement. There are, however, some general activities the general partner cannot perform without the consent of the limited partners. These include:

1. Admitting a new general partner
2. Admitting a new limited partner unless the partnership agreement so allows
3. Extraordinary transactions, such as selling all the partnership assets

Limited partners can monitor the general partner's activity with the same rights provided to partners in general partnerships: the right to inspect the books and records and the right to an accounting.

TRANSFERABILITY OF INTERESTS

Although the assignment of limited partnership interests is not prohibited by the RULPA, the limited partnership agreement may provide for significant restraints on assignment. There are two reasons for the transfer restrictions on limited partners' interests. First, the limited partnership interests may have been sold without registration as exemptions to the federal securities law. If those exempt interests are readily transferable, the exemption could be lost. Also, for the limited partners to enjoy the tax benefits of limited partner status, the ease of transferability is a critical issue. The more easily an interest can be transferred, the more likely the limited partnership is to be treated (for tax purposes) as a corporation.

The assignment of a partnership interest does not terminate the limited partnership. The assignee is entitled only to receive the distributions and profits to which the partner is entitled. The assignee does not become a partner without the consent of the other partners. Under the RULPA, the limited partnership can agree that the assigning limited partner will have the authority to make the assignee a limited partner. The effect of the RULPA provision is to simplify transfers and allow limited partners to decide whether they want to transfer their interest or their limited partner status.

TAX ISSUES IN LIMITED PARTNERSHIPS

Limited partnerships are taxed the same way as general partnerships. The general and limited partners actually report the income and losses on their individual returns and pay the appropriate taxes. The limited partnership files an information return but does not itself pay any taxes. The Tax Reform Act of 1986 has made significant changes in the tax shelter benefits of limited partnerships; for example, passive losses (from interest and income) are limited.

One benefit of limited partnership status is the combination of limited liability with direct tax benefits. In this sense, a limited partnership is the best of both worlds. Because of this ideal situation, limited partnership interests are closely scrutinized by the Internal Revenue Service to determine whether they are, in reality, corporations as opposed to true limited partnerships. Some of the factors examined in determining in which category an organization falls are (1) the transferability of the interests, (2) the assets of the general partner, and (3) the net worth of the general partner. From the perspective of the IRS, organization as a limited partnership is no assurance of treatment as such for tax purposes.

Syndication Forms—Corporations

NATURE AND CREATION

The corporation form of syndication has the advantages of limited liability and unlimited duration. Partnerships are subject to dissolution when a partner withdraws, goes bankrupt, or dies. Limited partnerships have the same problems with regard to their general partners, but corporations can go on in perpetuity regardless of the investors' status. However, as noted below, the corporation does have a different tax status.

State laws on corporation are not as uniform as those on partnerships and limited partnerships. However, the **Model Business Corporation Act (MBCA)** and **Revised Model Business Corporation Act (RMBCA)** are adopted in about one-third of the states, with many other states having portions of these model acts as law or using them as content models for their own laws.

A corporation is also a statutory creature and must be created formally by public filing of a document known as the **articles of incorporation.** The minimum requirements under the RMBCA for these articles are:

1. *The name of the corporation:* Many states require the corporate name to include "Inc." or "Corp." after the name to indicate corporate status.
2. *The proposed business of the corporation:* In real estate corporations, this statement of purpose has usually already been formulated, since the syndicate is set up for the purpose of accomplishing a project or development. A general business purpose can also be stated.
3. *The capital structure of the corporation:* The number of shares, their par value, their voting rights, and so on are all covered. Dividend rights are also covered. (The RMBCA has greatly modified this area.)
4. *The structure of the corporate management:* The setup of the board. Initial members of the board of directors and initial officers may be named.
5. *Administrative information about the corporation:* The address of the principal place of business and the name and address of a statutory agent are examples of details required.

States vary in their requirements for articles of incorporation, but the articles of incorporation are filed with a state agency, and all states require a filing fee.

Most states require that new corporations publish their articles of incorporation in a newspaper of general circulation. The purpose of publication is to provide notice that a corporation exists and that liability of those involved will be limited.

SHAREHOLDER RELATIONSHIPS

Once a corporation is properly formed, the state issues a certificate of incorporation. The corporation may now act as a legal entity, entering into contracts and holding title to property. However, to ensure continued treatment as a corporation, the corporate management must be certain to comply with corporate formalities. Such formalities include holding meetings of the board of directors and annual meetings of shareholders and keeping corporate accounts and business separate from personal accounts and business. If a corporation is used as a mere conduit for an individual's business, it is possible that corporate status will be set aside and individual liability imposed. With regard to smaller real estate corporations formed for tax purposes, it is possible for incorporators to have formed many corporations and to become somewhat casual in operating them. Such casualness may result in the loss of the corporate veil of liability protection, and the incorporators and shareholders may be held individually liable for the corporate debts.

TAX ISSUES OF CORPORATIONS

The contribution of property to a corporation by a shareholder is not a taxable event to either the corporation or the shareholder so long as the shareholder receives only stock in exchange for the property contributed (Internal Revenue Code; 26 U.S.C. § 351).

The corporate basis in property contributed to the corporation in exchange for shares is the basis of the contributing shareholder. For the shareholder, the basis of the stock received is the stock's fair market value.

If a corporation is organized by an individual to shield the individual's income from tax, the organized corporation may be subject to a **personal holding company tax** (26 U.S.C. § 541). The personal holding company tax was created to prevent corporations organized as "incorporated pocketbooks" for those attempting to shield personal income. A personal holding company tax is imposed on corporations meeting the following Section 541 criteria:

1. At least 60 percent of the corporate income is "personal holding company income," which is defined as some passive type of income such as rent, interest, royalties, or dividends. Generally, real estate corporations qualify for this passive type of income production.
2. More than 50 percent of the corporate stock is owned by five or fewer individuals.

In forming a corporation, the issue of whether the personal holding company tax will be imposed is critical because of the additional cost and the loss of the corporate tax benefits.

One benefit of partnership structure that is usually lost in incorporation is the ability of the investors to directly deduct losses from their income. However, the Internal Revenue Code does provide for a form of corporate organization that restores this benefit: the **Subchapter S** or **S corporation.** With a Subchapter S structure, the shareholders have the protection of limited liability and the benefit of direct deduction of losses. This direct deduction of losses is critical in real estate corporations because of the depreciation deductions for real property.

Subchapter S structure is limited to certain types of corporations, and the decision to be treated as Subchapter S must be made before the taxable year ends and requires an election to be filed with the Internal Revenue Service. In order to qualify for Subchapter S treatment, a corporation must meet certain criteria on shareholder number limitations, one class of stock, and income sources.

A corporation that qualifies for Subchapter S treatment does not pay tax, but the profits and losses of the corporation are recognized by the shareholders on their individual returns. The one difficulty for real estate corporations in qualifying for Subchapter S status is meeting the passive income requirement (see Chapter 21).

Syndication Forms: Limited Liability Companies (LLC)

NATURE AND CREATION

The newest trend in business structure that has carried over into real estate syndication is the **limited liability company,** or **LLC.** Now permitted in all states and the District of Columbia, this form of business organization is a business entity that offers the limited liability of a corporation but permits the tax advantages of a partnership. The IRS has issued a favorable ruling that permits the handling of LLC income and losses in the same manner as those of a partnership with the flow-through characteristics.

An LLC must be created according to the filing requirements by state law and most states require that the name of the entity reflect its status by use of the words "limited liability company" or by using the letters "LLC" or "LC" following the company's name.

Generally, the documents for establishing an LLC are filed with a state agency such as the secretary of state. The articles for creation of an LLC must include the LLC's name, purpose, duration, statutory or registered agent, and the location of its principal business offices. Once an LLC is created according to statutory specifications, it can conduct business in its own name. For example, an LLC can be a party to a contract or hold title to land in its name.

RELATIONSHIPS IN LLC

The members manage their LLC through an operating agreement. An operating agreement would be equivalent to the bylaws of a corporation or a partnership agreement. The members can specify that they will manage the LLC together, or they can delegate that responsibility to a managing member, called a manager. In addition, most states permit members to delegate the management of the LLC to someone who is not a member. For example, a real estate LLC may want to delegate its management to a professional property manager. If the members agree to manage the LLC themselves, decisions are made by a majority vote of all the members. If management is delegated to a single member or manager, then the members have no say in day-to-day matters and would have input only in amending the bylaws or in extraordinary activities such as mergers. Managers of LLCs have the same fiduciary responsibilities as corporate officers.

The owners of an LLC are called members, and the members or owners then report their portion of the income or losses on their individual tax returns. However, the LLC members enjoy the limited liability of a corporate structure. The owners, managers, and members of an LLC do not have personal liability for the debts of the LLC itself. There are, however, in some states, LLC statutory provisions for setting aside the limited liability protection for the members in the event the LLC members have engaged in fraudulent or deceptive conduct that misleads creditors or customers.

Members share profits and losses according to the terms of their operating agreement. Interests in an LLC are personal property and freely assignable. However, any management participation rights cannot be delegated without consent of the other LLC members.

There are several important distinctions that contribute to the popularity of the LLC. While other forms of business structure offer limited liability, their restrictions make the LLC more attractive. For example, an S corporation can have the flow-through benefit and limited liability, but, under IRS guidelines, it can have only a maximum of 175 shareholders who must be U.S. citizens or residents. Partnerships and corporations cannot be S corporation shareholders under IRS guidelines, but they can be LLC members. Limited partnerships enjoy flow-through benefit and limited liability, but limited partners cannot participate in management or they lose their limited liability. LLC members can participate in their business and still enjoy limited liability.

LLCs offer the best features of all business forms when the owners wish to enjoy the tax benefits of flow-through income and losses. In real estate investments, the flow-through aspect is often a critical feature for investors provided their liability exposure is limited to their investment. With an LLC, real estate investors can enjoy flow-through benefits, limited liability, and a voice in management without losing that protection.

TAXATION ISSUES IN LLC

An LLC pays no federal taxes on its entity income. All income and losses flow through to the owners of the LLC.

Drawbacks to the LLC include its definitional ambiguity. Because it is neither a corporation nor a limited partnership, it is unclear whether the sale of memberships in an LLC would constitute the sale of securities. This ambiguity has created many widespread sales of interests in real estate and other commodities through the use of an LLC. Another issue is whether differences in state laws on LLC operations and liability affect the limited liability afforded the members in multistate operations.

Syndication Forms—Investment Trusts

NATURE AND CREATION

Real estate investment trusts (REITs) and **mortgage investment trusts (MITs)** are tax-legislation creatures. The purpose of these trusts is to permit the small investor to invest in a diversified portfolio of real estate. Instead of being a limited partner or a shareholder, the investor owns a beneficial interest in a trust. The idea for this form of real estate syndication originated in Massachusetts more than a century ago, and investment trusts still exist because of the tax benefits afforded this form of investment.

The **Massachusetts business trust** originated because of Massachusetts laws that prohibited the ownership of any real estate necessary for corporate operations. The Massachusetts trust allowed a trustee to hold title to property and then issue interests in the trust to investors. This form of syndication became very popular with large public sales of trust interests. But the popularity of the trusts declined when court decisions taxed them as corporations.

In 1960, Congress passed provisions that allowed certain tax benefits for real estate trusts (Internal Revenue Code; 26 U.S.C. §§ 856–858), and REITs and MITs have since increased in popularity as a form of syndication. In 1997, there were $150 billion invested in publicly traded REITs, up from $30 billion in 1993. These vehicles, however, are used now for the income-reporting mechanisms because the passive-loss rules limit their use as tax shelters (see Chapter 21).

A REIT is set up in the same manner as any other trust. A trust agreement or declaration of trust is drawn up, and the properties involved are transferred to the trustee who will hold title and be responsible for the management of the properties or the portfolio of real estate investments. The following list is typical of the format and topics for a declaration of trust:

1. Name of the trust
2. Purpose of the trust
3. Description of beneficiary interests: their transferability, their sale, and the right of the trustee to buy shares

4. Voting rights of beneficiaries, meetings, and distributions to beneficiaries
5. Number of trustees, terms of office, compensation, and powers
6. Duration of trust and termination

Each investor is given a **trust certificate,** which evidences ownership of a portion of the trust and the amount of that ownership. Investors are beneficiaries of the trust arrangement and are not involved in the management of the properties or the portfolio; they allow the trustee to handle the real estate investments.

The portfolio of trusts can vary significantly. **Equity trusts** own real estate and have rental income as their primary source of income. The depreciation benefits for investors (discussed in the tax section following) are greatest with the equity trust. **Mortgage trusts** are trusts with investments in mortgages or other types of liens on real property. Many commercial banks and insurance companies have created mortgage trusts. The primary source of income in mortgage trusts is the interest earned on the owned mortgages. Some trusts are **mixed trusts;** they own both property and mortgages and have rental and interest income. In recent years, trusts have been used as methods for financing individual projects, as when a corporation creates a **specialty trust** for the purpose of expanding its operations. For example, a national restaurant chain could create a trust for the purpose of constructing new restaurants.

RELATIONSHIPS AND OPERATION OF INVESTMENT TRUSTS

The beneficiaries are not personally liable for the obligations of the trust; their liability is limited to the trust assets. The beneficiaries in most trusts have a vote for the management of the trust in that they elect the trustees. In this aspect, the REIT is similar to the corporate syndicate.

The trustee owes a fiduciary duty to the beneficiaries and the trust, and must act with the best interests of the trust and its beneficiaries as a priority. Dealing with the trust without authority or beneficiary approval would be a breach of this fiduciary duty.

TAX ASPECTS OF INVESTMENT TRUSTS

If a trust qualifies for REIT treatment, then certain tax benefits are applicable to the trust and the beneficiaries. The REIT is taxed only on undistributed income and gains. If the income or gains are distributed to the beneficiaries, there are no taxes to the trust. A REIT thus avoids the double taxation of corporations. The beneficiaries are taxed as individuals on the current or accumulated income; however, they are not entitled to the benefit of individual deduction of trust losses.

To qualify as a REIT for purposes of these tax benefits, the REIT must have predominantly passive income from real property. REITs also have size and holding-period restrictions.

If all these qualifications are met, the trust qualifies for REIT treatment under the Internal Revenue Code. If any of the requirements are not met within a given tax year, the trust is taxed as a corporation. Again, the passive-loss restrictions have made these vehicles less attractive (see Chapter 21).

Figure 22.2 is a summary of the various forms of syndication and their characteristics.

FIGURE 22.1   *Forms of Real Estate Syndication*

Type	Management	Creation	Liability	Taxes	Transferability
General Partners	Decentralized	Formal or informal	Full personal liability	Partners pay	Approval of the partners required
Limited Partnership	General partner	Formal/ statutory requirements	General has full liability; limited have liability only to the extent of contribution	Partners pay	RULPA allows transfer without consent if agreed to
Corporation	Centralized board; officers	Formal/ statutory requirements	Shareholders have liability only to the extent of contribution	Corporation pays on income; shareholders pay on dividends	Complete unrestricted transfer
S Corporation	Centralized board; officers	Formal/ statutory requirements	Shareholders have liability only to the extent of contribution	Shareholders pay based on ownership percentage	S Corp. restricts transfers
(LLC) Limited Liability Company	All members/ owners control with delegation possible	Formal/ statutory requirements	Members have liability only to the extent of contribution	Members pay based on ownership percentage and losses or income	Freely transferable; majority of members/ owners must approve management assignment
REIT	Centralized trustee and board for public REITs	Formal/ statutory requirements	Owners have liability only to the extent of contribution	Owners pay based on income	Trust shares easily transferred, public shares are totally unrestricted

Securities Issues in Finance and Syndication

While general partnerships do not involve any sales of securities because the general partners all have debt, work, and contribution responsibilities, limited partnership interests, interests in REITs, share ownership in corporations, and possibly interests in LLCs have been included as a form of securities for the purposes of the application of federal securities laws. Unless exempted, all sales of securities must be registered with both state and federal governments. When registration is required for the sale of interests in whatever form of syndication is chosen, syndication becomes more expensive because of the complicated paperwork involved in the registration process.

LAW GOVERNING: SECURITIES ACT OF 1933

The federal statute that governs the registration of the initial sale of securities is the **Securities Act of 1933** (15 U. S. C. §§ 77 *et seq.*). The 1933 act makes it unlawful to offer or to sell any security by use of the mails or other interstate commerce unless the security has been registered with the act's enforcement agency, the **Securities and Exchange Commission (SEC),** or unless an application for exemption has been filed with the SEC. Because of the time and expense involved in obtaining registration, most real estate partnerships are structured to avoid having to register.

If registration is required, the securities seller must file a registration statement with the SEC. The registration statement includes financial information, background information on the principals in the organization, information on the assets of the firm, and a history of the firm's operations. The seller must also be required to develop and submit for SEC approval a prospectus, which is a pamphlet to be given to investors. Included in the prospectus is much of the same information as in the registration statement but presented in a more attractive and readable fashion. Once all the documents and the filing fee have been submitted, the SEC reviews the registration for completeness. (The SEC makes no findings on the accuracy of the information or the merits of the securities being offered.) The time it takes to obtain SEC approval on first-time securities offerings is an average of six months. Once approved, the seller must still carry the burden of more paperwork by making sure all investors are given a copy of the prospectus. To avoid this complicated, costly, and time-consuming process, many firms structure their offering to fit the exemptions under the Securities Act of 1933.

EXEMPTIONS FROM REGISTRATION UNDER SECURITIES ACT OF 1933

Intrastate Offering Exemption The **intrastate offering exemption** exists because the Commerce Clause prohibits the federal government from regulating purely intrastate matters. To qualify for the intrastate exemption, the investors (offerees) and issuer must all be residents of the same state. (If there is one out-of-state offeree, the exemption will not apply.) Further, the issuer must meet the following requirements:

1. Eighty percent of its assets must be located in the state.
2. Eighty percent of its income must be earned from operations within the state.
3. Eighty percent of the proceeds from the sale must be used on operations within the state.

Small Offering Exemption—Regulation A Although the **small offering exemption (Regulation A)** is not a true exemption, it is a shortcut method of registration. The lengthy, complicated processes of full registration are simplified in that only a short-form registration statement is filed. Regulation A applies to issues of $5 million or less during any 12-month period.

Small Offering Exemption—Regulation D **Regulation D** is the product of the SEC's evaluation of the impact of its rules on the ability of small businesses to raise capital. It was designed to simplify and clarify existing exemptions, expand the availability of exemptions, and achieve uniformity between state and federal exemptions.

Regulation D creates a three-tiered exemption structure that permits sales without registration. Sellers are, however, required to file a Form D informational statement about the sale. Rule 501 of Regulation D lists the definitions of various terms used in the three exemptions. For example, the term **accredited investor** includes any investor who at the time of the sale falls into any of the following categories:

1. Any bank
2. Any private business development company
3. Any director, executive officer, or general partner of the issuer
4. Any person who purchases at least $150,000 of the securities being offered
5. Natural persons whose net worth is greater than $1 million
6. Any person whose individual income exceeded $200,000 in the last two years and who expects income greater than $200,000 in the current year

Rule 502 places a number of limitations on the means an issuer can use in offering securities. Some exempt securities cannot be sold through general advertising or through seminars initiated through advertising. Further, all the securities sold must be subject to restrictions to prevent the immediate rollover of the securities involved in these exempt transactions.

The three tiers of Regulation D exemptions are as follows:

- The **Rule 504 exemption** applies to offerings of up to $1 million (within any 12-month period). This type of issue is used by sellers of securities who are raising a small amount of money and wish to sell shares or interest to small investors. Sales of stock to directors, officers, and employees are not counted in the total aggregate offering limitation of $1 million.
- The **Rule 505 exemption** covers sales of up to $5 million, provided there are no more than 35 nonaccredited investors. If the issue is sold to both accredited and nonaccredited investors, the issuer must give all buyers a prospectus.
- The **Rule 506 exemption** has no dollar limitation, but the number and type of investors is limited. There can be any number of accredited investors, but the number of nonaccredited investors is limited to 35. There must be restrictions on the resale of the shares.

Problems with Integration Although many real estate syndications qualify for one or more of these exemptions, the exemption issue can become a problem when two or more types of offerings occur simultaneously. In other words, there is the possibility that two or more separate and exempt offerings may be considered part of one offering. This combining of separate, exempt offerings is called **integration.**

For example, two limited partnerships may be organized for the purpose of developing two different projects. One may be an intrastate exemption, and one may be a private offering exemption. If the limited partnerships and their projects are deemed to be integrated, one or both exemptions may be lost because the private offering could be sold out of state and the intrastate offering could be sold to an unknowledgeable investor.

For those forming two or more syndicates within relatively short periods of time, the projects undertaken should be geographically separate or of a different nature, and the offerings should be made in different ways or should be structured differently. For example, four different limited partnership offerings in each of four buildings in a complex are likely to be integrated as one offering. Four different limited partnership offerings in four geographically separate buildings would be considered separate offerings.

Figure 22.3 is a summary of the complex security issues in real estate syndication.

FIGURE 22.3   *Security Exemption Issues in Real Estate Syndication*

Name	Size Limitation	Offeree/Buyer Limitation	Resale Limitation	Public Offering
Intrastate exemption, 15 U.C.C. § 77(c)(a)(11)	No	Buyers must be residents of state of incorporation; triple 80 percent requirements	Yes, stock transfer restrictions	Yes, in state
Regulation A Small Offering exemption, 15 U.C.C. § 77D	$5,000,000	Short-form registration required	No	Yes
Regulation D Rule 504	$1,000,000 or less (in 12-month period)	None, unlimited accredited and nonaccredited alike	Some	Yes
Rule 505	Up to $5,000,000	No more than 35 excluding accredited investors	Some	No
Rule 506	No	Unlimited accredited and 35 nonaccredited investors	Yes, stock restrictions	No

STATE LAWS ON SECURITIES

All states have some form of law governing the sale of securities. The types of registrations required and the available exemptions vary from state to state. In some states, copies of the federal registration information may be filed with the state for purposes of state registration; when SEC approval is obtained, the state will give its approval. In merit-review states, the securities and the partnership are actually reviewed to determine the quality of the offering. For partnership interests to be offered in more than one state, a uniform state registration application (developed by the National Association of Securities Dealers) may be filed in all states to ensure compliance with the information requirements of each state.

Consider 22.3

A, a promoter, has put together a real estate limited partnership for the purpose of constructing a shopping center. A has a great deal of experience in commercial development but no financing for the project. His plan is to raise money by selling $10 million of limited partnership interests at a cost of $10,000 each. A does not want to be limited to in-state investors for the sale of the interests. Will A have to register the sale with the SEC?

Ethical Issue

Why do you think issuers and syndicates want to avoid securities registration? Is it ethical to structure a syndication so that securities laws are avoided?

LAND IMPROVEMENT AND CONSTRUCTION

The development, once financed, can now go forward with the physical work of construction. At this point, the developer is not only working to improve the land

and to begin construction, but is working to be sure the property, once operational, retains its status and quality.

Over the past decade, the assurance of a community atmosphere has become important in developments. For example, the Lincoln Institute of Land Policy estimates that there are 4,000,000 residents in 30,000 gated communities. These communities have the appeal not just of safety, but of uniformity and thoughtful planning in the design of the community.

Legal Paperwork for Development and Construction

The developer must provide a subdivision or plat map with easements, roads, and lots clearly indicated and must record the map in the land records. The plat map will be used as a reference point for descriptions of all lots to be sold in the subdivision. (See Chapter 6 for more detail on plat maps and their importance in legal descriptions.)

In addition to the plat map, the developer will have drafted and recorded the **deed restrictions** or **protective covenants** for the subdivision. The purpose of these covenants is to control the type of structures and the conduct of persons residing in the subdivision. Typical provisions included in deed restrictions are:

1. Minimum square footage requirements for all dwelling units constructed within the subdivision
2. Restrictions on in-home business operations
3. Restrictions on the types of animals that may be kept on the lots
4. Restrictions on dividing lots and selling smaller portions of them
5. Restrictions on the types of structures that may be erected in addition to the dwelling units
6. Prohibitions on nuisances

The validity of the deed restrictions is based on the common law concept of covenants. At common law, covenants were restrictions placed in the deed from the grantor to the grantee. In addition to the requirement that the covenant be in the deed, the following elements were required for a covenant to be enforceable:

1. The covenant had to *touch and concern* the land.
2. The grantor and grantee had to intend the covenant to operate as a permanent restriction on the land.
3. The covenant could be enforceable only as against those parties in privity of contract; that is, the grantor and the grantee.

The problem with the common law requirements is that privity exists in the initial sale between the developer and the first buyer but is absent once the first buyer transfers the property. To alleviate this problem, most deed restrictions contain a clause specifying the time period for which they are valid, and the deeds transferring title to the subdivision lots contain clauses that provide the title is subject to all the restrictions that have been recorded for the subdivision.

Additionally, once a pattern of development is established, the covenants that created them are manifest in a view of the subdivision. Those who purchase property in the subdivision are deemed to understand and then comply with the scheme of development that the covenants have created.

The following case deals with an issue of the enforceability of covenants.

Cappello v. Ciresi

691 A.2d 42 (Conn. Supre. 1996)

Facts

Vincent and Irene Cappello (plaintiffs) own property in a subdivision in Fairfield, Connecticut, known as Lakeview Acres. All the lots are subject to a restriction created in 1943 that prohibits the use of the lots for anything other than single-family dwellings. The lots are all delineated on a map recorded in the land records of the town of Fairfield on September 16, 1943. The language in the recorded documents provides: "Such restrictions constitute negative easements which may be enforced by any grantee against any other grantee, each parcel becoming both a dominant and servient parcel."

The Cappellos' property consists of lots one and two and the southern portions of lots five and six as delineated on map number 1251. The parcels are contiguous and, together, constitute a rectangular-shaped parcel with 275 feet of frontage on the Boston Post Road and 111 feet of frontage on Hulls Highway, which intersects with the Boston Post Road. Lot one is a corner lot fronting on both the Boston Post Road and Hulls Highway and is improved with a single-family house. Lot two fronts on Hulls Highway and is improved with a single-family house that has been damaged by fire and is now unoccupied. The southern portions of lots five and six front on the Boston Post Road and contain no improvements. Vincent R. Cappello purchased lot one in 1971, the southern half of lot five in 1972, the southern half of lot six in 1980, and lot two in 1985. The property is now owned by Vincent R. Cappello and Irene M. Cappello.

Anthony Ciresi and others (defendants) are the owners of the other property within the subdivision. Their lots front on Arbor Drive, Arbor Terrace, and Hulls Highway. Three of the defendants testified: Charles McDonald, Ernest Sapp, and Edward Byrne. McDonald relied on the long-term protection provided by the covenants when he purchased his home 41 years ago. Sapp believed the covenants would protect the neighborhood when he purchased his home six years ago. Byrne was aware of the covenants when he purchased his home in 1986 and believed that they would keep the area as a single-family neighborhood.

Lakeview Acres is a mature development consisting of single-family residences that have been improved over the years. No lots are being used for anything other than residential purposes. The rear lot lines of eight of the original lots abut the Boston Post Road. The Cappellos own one of the abutting lots (lot one) and the abutting portion of two other lots (lots five and six). Since 1943, the Boston Post Road has undergone a dramatic change.

Today, the property along the Boston Post Road from the Fairfield-Bridgeport border to the Fairfield-Westport border is used mostly for commercial purposes and is in a designed commercial district zone. Clearly, the best and highest use of the plaintiffs' property would be commercial development. This use would be consistent with the uses along the Boston Post Road but inconsistent with the present use of the lots within Lakeview Acres.

The Cappellos filed suit seeking relief from the restrictions on the use of their land.

Judicial Opinion

Thim, Judge. The first issue involves an inquiry into the manner in which the restrictions can be released and an inquiry into the effect of three quitclaim deeds signed by the present or former owners of some of the lots. A lot owner may extinguish his or her right to enforce the benefit of restrictive covenants by means of a written and recorded release. Generally, "all of the benefited property owners must join in a release in order to completely extinguish the obligation." In the present case, all of the benefited owners have not joined in a release. The plaintiffs do not, however, contend each owner has released his or her interest in the restrictions. Instead, they claim paragraph eleven of the document that created the restrictions in 1945 gave the owners of a majority of the lots the power to extinguish the interests of all. Paragraph eleven of the 1943 document provides that the restrictive covenants may be terminated, in whole or part, at the end of certain periods by an agreement executed by at least fifty-one percent of the then owners of the parcels of land, provided the agreement is recorded in the land records. The plaintiffs further claim a majority has extinguished the interests to all by executing three quitclaim deeds.

The first quitclaim deed was executed between May 20, 1966 and December 31, 1968, by the owners of thirty-four of the lots. The deed was recorded on December 31, 1968. The lot owners released their interest in lots one, two and part of lot five. Since thirty-eight lot owners were needed to meet the fifty-one percent requirement, this deed did not extinguish the interests of all the lot owners. The restrictions automatically continued on January 1, 1969, for a ten year period.

The second quitclaim deed was signed between August 9, 1974 and September 21, 1977, by the owners of thirty-six lots and was recorded on December 6, 1977. The owners released their interests to the southern half of lot six. Because this deed was not signed by the owners of thirty-eight lots, it did not extinguish the interests of the lot owners who did not join as signatories.

The third quitclaim deed was signed on May 7, 1988, by seven lot owners and was recorded on June 9, 1988. Some of the signers of the deed had previously released their interests in part of the plaintiffs' property when they signed the second quitclaim deed. After taking account of the duplications, the effect of the third deed was that four more released their interests in lots one, two and part of lot five, and three more released their interests in the southern half of lot six. The three deeds show the plaintiffs have received releases from thirty-eight owners with respect to the restrictions on lots one, two and part of lot five, and thirty-nine lot owners with respect to the southern half of lot six. The plaintiffs claim that their receipt of the third deed fulfilled the fifty-one percent requirement of paragraph eleven and that the restrictions on their property thereafter terminated at the expiration of the ten year period ending January 1, 1989. The defendants have two responses to this claim.

The defendants first contend that the quitclaim deeds were merely revocable offers to terminate the restrictions and that the offers have been revoked. The defendants cite the case for the proposition that the releases were revocable offers to take part in a termination agreement. Under their theory, a person's offer lapsed when that person died or transferred his or her property. The plaintiffs cite the case for the proposition that a defendant could not revoke a release unless he or she recorded the revocation on the land records before the plaintiffs obtained the last release.

When the owner of a dominant estate releases his or her interest in a servient estate, the releaser does more than merely grant a license to erect a structure. The giving of a license for a specific act, such as erecting a structure, is temporary in nature. If the structure erected in pursuance of the license is removed, the owner of the servient tenement cannot erect another structure without a new license. *Stueck v. G.C. Murphy Co.*, 107 Conn. 656, 666, 142 A. 301 (1928). The giving of a release, on the other hand, extinguishes the releaser's interest in the restrictions. In the present case, the releases were given by quitclaim deeds under seal with a statement that they were given "for the consideration of One Dollar and other valuable considerations received to our full satisfaction . . . " The deeds also express an intention to bind the releasers, heirs, successors, and assigns. The releases are not revocable.

The defendants next claim that the quitclaim deeds did not meet the time requirements of paragraph eleven. Each side interprets paragraph eleven differently. The plaintiffs contend the paragraph authorizes the owners of fifty-one percent of the lots to terminate the interests of all the owners. The defendants contend paragraph eleven requires as a condition for termination that the owners of fifty-one percent of the lots agree contemporaneously that the restrictions be released.

In ascertaining the temporal limitations of paragraph eleven of the 1943 agreement, this court must follow certain well known rules of construction. First, "[t]he words as written . . . must be accorded a fair and reasonable construction and their common, natural, and ordinary meaning and usage where it can sensibly be applied." Second, "[p]arties do not ordinarily insert meaningless provisions in their agreements and, therefore, if it is reasonably possible to do so, every provision must be given effect." Paragraph eleven provides that after January 1, 1969, the restrictions are to continue automatically for ten year periods unless prior to January 1, 1969, or the expiration of the ten year period then in operation "said covenants are terminated . . . by an agreement executed by the then owners of at least fifty-one percent of all of the said parcels. . . . " The use of the phrases "an agreement" and "by the then owners" cannot be disregarded. The word "agreement" is a singular noun which means "the act of agreeing or coming to a mutual arrangement." The word "an" is used as a function word to suggest a limitation in number, i.e, one. The word "then" means "belonging to the time mentioned . . . at that time: at the time mentioned or specified." As used in paragraph eleven, these words express an intent that there be one agreement or mutual arrangement and that the parties to the agreement be lot owners at the time the agreement is formed. In effect, paragraph eleven gives the power of termination to those who are presently benefiting from the restrictions.

The three quitclaim deeds, which were signed over a twenty-two year period, do not constitute "an agreement" executed "by the then owners." By the time the last person signed the third quitclaim deed, the previous signers may no longer have been owners within the subdivision. The evidence does not show otherwise. The persons who signed the deeds did not extinguish the rights of the owners of the other lots to enforce the restrictive covenants.

The second ground on which the plaintiffs seek relief requires this court to determine whether there has been such a change in the area as to defeat the objects and purposes of the restrictive covenants so that they are no longer effective. The plaintiffs claim that the commercial development along the Boston Post Road since 1943 is a sufficient change to warrant the removal of the restrictions. The defendants, on the other hand, contend that the change is not sufficient because Lakeview Acres is still a residential area. The plaintiffs focus on the changes outside the subdivision. The defendants focus on the subdivision.

"In the majority of states, changes outside the limits of the tract, even though they do impinge on the border lots, do not justify any relaxation of enforcement of the

payment of the parties is a major issue in the construction contract and in construction litigation. Indeed, the payment problem is the basis for the mechanic's lien system (see Chapter 5).

There are several problem areas that arise and should be covered in the payment portion of all contracts existing between the parties. The first is when payment is to be made. In most cases, payments are made periodically after the architect or project manager has had an opportunity to inspect the work. After inspection, an architect's certificate is issued, and the certificate authorizes the release of a certain portion of the funds.

The next problem area is that of who is to receive the payment once it is authorized. Too many times, the general contractor is paid but the subcontractors are not, with the result that the owner may face liens for nonpayment.

The following case deals with the problem of nonpayment of subcontractors.

Sasser & Company v. Griffin

210 S.E.2d 34 (Ga. 1974)

Facts

Griffin (defendant/appellant/owner) contracted with Sanford and Space (general/prime contractor) for the construction of a high-rise apartment building. Sasser and Company (plaintiff/appellee/subcontractor) contracted with Sanford and Space to do the plumbing, heating, and air-conditioning work in the building. The project was to be completed by April 1, 1971, but Sasser did not complete its work until August 1971.

The subcontract provided that Sanford and Space were to pay Sasser "as the work progresses, based on estimates and certificates of the Architects or Contractor and payments will be made from money received from the owner only and divided Pro Rate amount [*sic*] all approved accounts of subcontractors and material." These words were struck from the heating and plumbing contract, and there was substituted after the word *made* "by 20th of each month following, less 10% retained until completion of job. Subcontractor will be paid by Contractor for approved work in place even though payment by the Owner has been withheld from Contractor for reasons not the fault of the subcontractor." The air-conditioning contract did not contain the above change but had added to it, "Payment within 10 days of receiving money from owner—approximately 20th of the month."

In July 1971, the designing architect certified the project as complete and ordered the release of all retained funds to Sanford and Space. Griffin denied approval of the project but claimed full payment of Sanford and Space. When Sasser was not paid, he recorded mechanics' liens on the property and filed suit.

From a trial court judgment for Sasser, Griffin appealed.

Judicial Opinion

Eberhardt, Presiding Judge. None of the owners has a contractual liability, jointly or otherwise, to plaintiff since they were not parties to the subcontracts between plaintiff and Sanford and Space, but this does not prevent the establishment of a lien by a subcontractor under Georgia law.

Sanford and Space . . . have defended against plaintiff's action on the contract on two grounds: (a) payment by owners to Sanford and Space was a condition precedent to latter's liability to plaintiff under the terms of both subcontracts, and owners had not paid all sums due under the prime contract; and, (b) plaintiff had breached the subcontract by not completing performance by the time required in the prime contract.

The language in the amendment of the plumbing and heating subcontract clearly shows that the parties intended for plaintiff to be paid independently of payments received from the owners by Sanford and Space. While the owners deny approval of the entire project, they do not dispute the plaintiff has completed his performance under the subcontract. That contract is to be enforced as written. It is the duty of the courts to construe and enforce contracts as made and not to make them for the parties. We are not at liberty to revise a contract while professing to construe it.

There is, however, no such amendment to the air conditioning subcontract, and it provides "payments will be made from money received from the owner only" and "payment within 10 days of receiving money from owner—approximately 20th of the month."

A provision in a contract may make payment by the owner a condition precedent to a subcontractor's right to payment if "the contract between the general contractor and the subcontractor should contain an express condition clearly showing that to be the intention of the parties." . . . The condition is clearly expressed in this subcontract.

Sanford and Space cannot successfully defend their nonpayment of plaintiff on the ground that plaintiff breached the contract by not completing his work in time. Late performance may constitute a breach of contract by the plaintiff, but the remedy is not nonpayment; it is recoupment or what is now a counterclaim. And while it is true that, on acceptance of the work by the owner after the building contractor has rendered the entire service for which he has contracted, the contractor is authorized to proceed to collect the balance due him by the terms of the contract, any damage to the owner resulting through the negligent performance of the contract by the contractor is a matter for recoupment. This same rule applies to actions *ex contractu,* between contractor and subcontractor, and for damages alleged to have been caused by delay in completion of construction.

Therefore, the plaintiff is entitled to summary judgment against Griffin as to the establishment of the lien, in the amount claimed, and against Sanford and Space as to payment due under the plumbing and heating contract.

Affirmed.

Case Questions

1. Diagram the relationships of the parties in the case, following Figure 22.4 as an example.
2. What work is at issue?
3. What changes were made in the subcontracts?
4. When did Sasser complete the work?
5. Does late performance have any effect on Sasser's claim?
6. Is the lien filed by Sasser against Griffin's property proper?
7. Do Sanford and Space's problems with Griffin excuse its nonpayment of Sasser?

To avoid some of the problems occurring in the *Sasser* case, the parties can take protective measures to assure their payment and the performance by other parties to the contract. General contractors are entitled to payment as their work is completed and may stop performance if payment is not made, so that work stoppage is a means of security for them. To further ensure payment, general contractors usually have the benefit of a three-party arrangement, whereby the funds are held by a third party (examples of third parties used are lenders, architects, escrow companies, attorneys, trustees, and banks) and released upon the architect's certification of adequate completion. With the three-party system, the general contractors know the funds exist—it is simply a matter of performance to have them released.

Owners can also use the three-party system to ensure performance by the general contractor. Most standard contracts with such an arrangement permit the withholding of a certain amount of the payment due to cover defective work, late performance, or the general contractor's failure to pay subcontractors and suppliers. The withheld amount is typically 10 percent of the contract price and also 10 percent of each installment made during the construction period.

As noted in the *Sasser* case, general contractors can protect themselves against the subcontractors for the owner's nonpayment through the use of a **flow-down clause.** Under a flow-down clause, the general contractor is not required to pay the subcontractors until the owner has paid the general contractor.

In most projects, the parties do not limit themselves to these internal protections but rather seek and require some outside guarantee or assurance that payment and performance will occur. This outside assurance comes in the form of bonds issued by sureties for a premium (see page 586).

CONTRACT PRICE
Usually, the price in a construction contract is fixed and covers the entire project. Other forms of pricing include **unit pricing,** in which the contract is broken down into units. For example, excavation could be one unit in a project. Framing could be another unit. The overhead costs for the project would be divided

among the units according to the amount of time or cost involved in each unit. The unit system makes the payment division easier. Another form of pricing that leaves many variables and can create problems is the **cost-plus formula,** in which the general contractor recovers whatever the cost of construction is along with a predetermined percentage or amount for profit. The difficulty with the cost-plus system is determining which costs are reimbursable as project costs and which are the general contractor's cost of doing business: personnel salaries, equipment, and other overhead items.

After the price or price formula is determined and construction begins, two possible problem areas may affect the price paid for the project by the owner: changed circumstances and work-order changes.

Changed Circumstances. The general contractor's bid on a project is based on assumptions about the project location, soil content, weather analysis, and other variable factors. If significant, unanticipated changes occur in those assumptions, the general contractor's costs will increase. With these cost increases, the issue arises of whether the price of completion will also increase. A clause in standard form contracts provides for price increases when: (1) there are concealed conditions below the surface of the ground or concealed conditions in any existing structure at variance with those conditions indicated by contract; and (2) there are unknown physical conditions of an unusual nature at the site, differing materially from those ordinarily encountered and generally recognized as part of the work provided for in the contract. Other conditions that are considered unusual and unknown are unseasonal or unusually bad weather conditions, labor problems, and material shortages. Even without a changed-circumstances provision in the contract, the contractor is entitled to obtain an increased price if costs are greater because of misrepresentation of conditions by the owner in the bid information, the negotiations, or the contract.

Change Orders. The second type of situation in which a contractor may increase the project price is through a **change order.** Because of circumstances or preferences, the owner may wish to change plans and specifications that represent additional costs to the contractor.

A change order may be necessary for several reasons. The change may be needed simply because the owner or developer sees the project as it progresses and perceives that it does not look the same as it did in conception or on paper. Zoning changes may have been approved after the time the contract is negotiated but before construction begins or before a building permit has been issued for the plans that now violate the zoning laws. In the case of shopping centers, a change may be necessary to keep an anchor tenant or attract another tenant. There may be facilities missing. For example, with the passage of the Americans with Disabilities Act in 1990, many businesses now must comply by providing access for handicapped employees, changes that are more easily made during construction than after construction is complete. The lender may also require a change in the construction for better utilization of the project. Also, the contractor may discover during the course of construction that additional work is necessary and will want authorization for the work so that additional compensation can be paid. A typical change-order clause will provide as follows:

Practical Tip

Change-order procedures should be placed in the construction contract and followed. Variation from the process will result in the adoption of that process as the parties' agreed-upon means of procedure. Further, confusion and error result when others believe the change-order process remains the same as in the written agreement. Often the time saved by not following the process results in great expense and litigation later.

A change order is a written order to the contractor that is signed by the owner and the architect, issued after execution of the contract, authorizing a change in the contract sum or contract time. The contract sum and contract time may be altered by change order only.

The owner, without invalidating the contract, may order changes in the work within the general scope of the contract, the contract sum and the contract time being adjusted accordingly.

The contractor, provided he receives a written order signed by the owner, shall promptly proceed with the work involved.

The following case deals with the issue of oral change orders.

Hoth v. White

799 P.2d 213 (Utah 1990)

Facts

Amy and Karl White (defendants) contacted Polar Bear Homes to inquire about having it build the Whites' new custom house. Charles R. Team (d/b/a Team Realty) was involved in these discussions. On August 26, 1986, the Whites met with Dean R. Morgan (d/b/a Polar Bear Homes) and Charles Team (appellants) and contracted to have Polar Bear build a custom, energy-efficient house according to plans drafted by Amy White and given to Morgan. Construction was to be completed by December 10, 1986, and the Whites were to supply construction financing of $40,000.

Morgan subcontracted with Michael and Jeffrey Hoth (d/b/a Hoth Brothers/plaintiffs) to frame the house for $6,000. Morgan provided the Hoths with the plans but not the specifications (they were listed on a separate sheet).

The Hoths began framing the house during the first week in October 1986 but did not complete their work until February 12, 1987, two months after the entire house was to have been completed. Many problems arose during construction that required changes to be made in the framing. Some of the required changes resulted from the improper pouring of the foundation, some from the Hoths' ignorance of some of the specifications, some because the plans were incomplete or unclear, and some because Amy White changed her mind as to what she wanted. Amy White was present on the job site nearly every day and interacted frequently with the Hoths. Although the Hoths substantially completed framing the house, they did not completely finish the job, making it necessary for the Whites to hire other subcontractors to come in and complete the work.

During the months of October and November 1986, the Whites made progress payments on the construction but were not provided with any accounting of the funds

spent. By January 1987, the Whites had already provided appellants with $43,000. Soon after January 3, 1987, Morgan acknowledged at least a $10,000 overrun on the contract price and asked the Whites to pay half of that. The Whites deferred making a decision on this request until the house was completed.

The Whites refused to give Morgan any more money and began paying the construction bills directly as well as directly hiring subcontractors to complete the building, thus bypassing Morgan. Morgan testified that he felt he had lost all control of the project and had been taken off the job. The Whites, however, stated that they consistently requested him to return to the job and assume his responsibilities, especially with the numerous structural problems present. They concluded that they had to take over because the construction was substantially behind schedule, and Morgan was not paying the bills or otherwise doing his job.

On March 16, 1987, at Morgan's suggestion, the Hoths filed a mechanic's lien on the house, claiming the unpaid balance of $2,500 plus an additional $1,410 for extra work and material supplied by them beyond the scope of the initial subcontract. Their total claim was $3,910.

In September 1987, the Hoths filed this action to foreclose on their mechanic's lien. On September 25, 1987, the Whites answered and counterclaimed for substandard work, disputing the amount and character of the "extra" items that the Hoths had determined were not within the scope of the original subcontract.

The trial court found that the Whites were liable to pay the Hoths the remaining $2,500 balance on the original contract plus $1,009 of the "extras," less an offset of $516 for the costs the Whites had been required to pay to other subcontractors to finish the framing. It also ordered the Whites to pay the Hoths $1,000 in attorney fees, plus court costs to be determined from the record, for a net judgment of $3,993 plus costs. It then ordered the Hoths to indemnify the Whites in the amount of $2,993 and costs, plus pay $1,000 to the Whites for attorney fees.

On May 12, 1988, the Hoths brought this appeal.

Judicial Opinion

Garff, Judge. The trial court found that either the Whites or appellants ordered certain extras, that some of the "extras" came about as a result of lack of detail in the plans, and that the Hoths were entitled to compensation for them in the amount of $1,009. It also found that, although the Hoths had substantially completed the contract, they had failed to complete a portion of it, requiring the Whites to obtain labor from other sources at a cost of $516, which the court offset against the Hoths' compensation.

As the trial court found, the record indicates that a substantial number of the extras came about as a result of requests by Amy White, although several were requested by Morgan. Viewing the evidence in the light most favorable to the findings, the record suggests that many of the changes requested by the Whites were made to bring the residence into conformance with the specifications, which the Whites gave to Morgan but were not transmitted by Morgan to the Hoths, and because mistakes were made in pouring the foundation which resulted in problems which the extras were designed to correct.

Relevant contract terms provide that "[t]he amount of the purchase price may be increased if additional costs are incurred for extras as described hereafter. Buyer agrees to pay for the cost of all such extras as agreed to in a written change order as part of the purchasing price of the property," and "[n]o changes shall be made to the Plans and Specifications or the purchase price except as agreed to in a written change order signed by Buyer and Contractor which sets forth the change to be made and the amount of adjustment in the purchase price required by said change." The contract thus clearly provides that unless there is a written change order signed by the parties for each extra, the purchase price is not to be increased and the buyer, therefore, is not responsible for paying for the extra. It is undisputed that the parties signed no such written change orders.

We find that the trial court did not err in requiring appellants to pay that portion of the extras not paid for by the Whites.

Affirmed.

Case Questions

1. Diagram the relationship of the parties.
2. Why were there so many changes for the Hoths?
3. Did the contract address change orders?
4. Was anything in writing with respect to the change orders?
5. Who is liable to the Hoths?
6. Who is ultimately liable for the changes?

The United States government's change order clause provides as follows:

[I]f the change causes an increase or decrease in the cost of, or the time required for, performance of any part of the work under this contract, whether changed or not changed by such order, an equitable adjustment shall be made in the contract price or delivery schedule or both.

In some cases, the parties fail to comply with change-order procedures in spite of contract provisions and change forms. The issue that arises is whether the contractor is still entitled to be compensated for the additional work performed.

Substantial Performance by Contractor

Construction contracts present the unique problem of how to determine when the contractor has performed well enough to satisfy the terms of the contract. Because of the nature of construction, certain variations may occur between the plans or specifications and what is actually built. Change orders at the time of the slight modifications can alleviate the problems, but in the event such orders are not obtained, the issue of substantial performance exists. The doctrine of

substantial performance provides that a contractor may recover for completed projects in spite of variations between the plans and the actual finished product.

The following questions must all be answered affirmatively in order to establish substantial performance.

1. Is the construction for practical purposes just as good?
2. Was the minor breach by the contractor nonmalicious?
3. Can the owner be compensated for the substitution or error made by the contractor?

An example of circumstances in which substantial performance is appropriate is when the wrong color scheme or cabinet work is installed in a home or office. The owner may not be as happy, but the error meets the three criteria, and the contractor will be paid the contract price less an adjustment for the owner to be compensated or have the work redone.

Even when the contractor completes the work according to plans and specifications, the liability does not stop with payment by the owner. The contractor is liable for errors in construction and poor workmanship; and in spite of attempts to disclaim such liability in contract exculpatory clauses, public policy will not permit contractors to excuse themselves from injuries and damages resulting from their negligence.

In home construction, the contractor is required for one year (in most states) to repair or replace faulty construction problems under the implied warranty (see Chapter 14).

Compliance with Building Codes

http://
A sampling of city building codes can be seen at: **http://www.topeka.org**.

One of the critical requirements for adequate performance by a contractor is that the structure comply, in all respects, with state and local building codes. Building codes may restrict building height, ceiling height, window placement, fire sprinkler systems, exits, lighting, and materials. Contractors are presumed to be familiar with building codes and will be liable for cutting costs by not complying with the minimum requirements.

Compliance with the Americans with Disabilities Act

http://
For the ADA Accessibility Guidelines for buildings and facilities, visit: **http://www.access-board.gov/adaag/html/adaag.htm**.

Both in the new construction of buildings and under the retrofit requirements of the Fair Housing Act (see Chapter 19), the issue of access and usability for those with disabilities is now a critical part of construction. Buildings constructed after 1988 must have access and accommodations for those with disabilities. The Americans with Disabilities Act (ADA) required all existing buildings to be accessible and that facilities accommodate those with disabilities. There was an 18-month grace period given when the ADA was passed for modification of premises for access and accommodation.

The following case deals with the construction requirements imposed on businesses under the ADA.

Pinnock
v. International House of Pancakes Franchisee

844 F. Supp. 574 (S.D. Cal. 1993)

Facts

Theodore A. Pinnock, an attorney, is unable to walk and uses a wheelchair. Pinnock dined at Majid Zahedi's (defendant) restaurant, a franchise of the International House of Pancakes, on June 21, 1992. When Pinnock went to use the restroom in the restaurant, he discovered the door to the men's room was too narrow to allow his wheelchair to pass through. Pinnock was forced to remove himself from his wheelchair and crawl into the restroom. Pinnock filed suit for violation of ADA, the California Unruh Civil Rights Act, and intentional infliction of emotional distress. Zahedi filed a motion for summary judgment.

Judicial Opinion

Rhoades, District Judge. Zahedi argues that Congress does not have constitutional authority to regulate his facility, asserting that title III of the ADA exceeds the powers granted Congress by the U.S. Constitution. Congress enacted title III pursuant to Article I, Section 8, of the United States Constitution, which grants Congress the power to "regulate Commerce . . . among the several States" and to enact all laws necessary and proper to this end.

As the Supreme Court recognized in the context of racial discrimination, the restaurant industry unquestionably affects interstate commerce in a substantial way.

Even aside from its membership in an interstate industry, Zahedi's restaurant demonstrates characteristics which place it squarely in the category of interstate commerce. It is a franchise of a large, international, publicly traded corporation ("IHOP Corp."), organized under Delaware law. IHOP Corp. had total retail sales of $479 million in 1992, operates 547 franchises in thirty-five states, Canada, and Japan, and employs 16,000 persons. Furthermore, Zahedi's restaurant is located directly across the street from State Highway 163, and within two miles of two interstate highways. There are three hotels within walking distance, and three motels within one and one-half miles of the restaurant. The courts have found these facts to be indicia of a business operating in interstate commerce.

Congressional enactment of title III of the ADA was well within Congress' power to regulate interstate commerce under the Commerce Clause.

Zahedi argues that many of the terms used in section 12182(b)(2) of title III are unconstitutionally vague and

are therefore in violation of the Due Process Clause of the Fifth Amendment. Statutes which fail to adequately specify the actions or conduct necessary to conform with the law pose problems for which the Supreme Court has expressed serious concern.

Title III of the ADA is a civil statute regulating commercial conduct. As such, Zahedi can successfully sustain its challenge only if he can prove that the enactment specifies "no standard of conduct . . . at all."

Title III requires existing places of public accommodation to remove architectural barriers to access, where such removal is "readily achievable." The term is defined in the statute as "easily accomplishable and able to be carried out without much difficulty or expense." The statute enumerates four factors to consider when determining whether a modification is readily achievable, and the legislative history lists examples of the types of changes Congress believes are readily achievable. These include specific examples for small stores and restaurants such as rearranging tables and chairs and installing small ramps and grab bars in restrooms.

In addition, the federal regulation further elucidates the term "readily achievable" by adding other factors. These include the overall financial resources of the parent corporation and safety requirements. The regulation lists 21 examples of barrier removal likely to be "readily achievable" in many circumstances, such as installing ramps and repositioning shelves and telephones.

Finally, the preamble to the regulation provides further explanation and notes that use of a more specific standard would contravene the goals of the ADA:

> the Department has declined to establish in the final rule any kind of numerical formula for determining whether an action is readily achievable. It would be difficult to devise a specific ceiling on compliance costs that would take into account the vast diversity of enterprises covered by the ADA's public accommodation requirements and the economic situation that any particular entity would find itself in at any moment.

Title III provides that where barrier removal is not readily achievable, a covered entity must make its goods or services available through "alternative methods if such methods are readily achievable." The legislative history, the regulation itself, and the preamble all provide specific examples of appropriate alternatives to barrier removal. These include providing curb service or home delivery, coming to the door of the facility to handle transactions, serving beverages at a table for persons with disabilities where a bar is inaccessible, providing assistance to retrieve items from inaccessible shelves, and relocating services and activities to accessible locations.

Illustrations of the term "reasonable modifications" are provided in the title III regulation and its preamble. For example, stores in which all of the checkout aisles are not accessible are required to ensure that an adequate number of accessible checkout aisles are left open at all times. Likewise, facilities that do not permit entry to animals would be required to modify such policies as they apply to service animals accompanying disabled individuals.

The terms "reasonable modifications" and "fundamental alteration" are therefore not unconstitutionally vague.

Title III requires covered entities to afford their goods and services to an individual with a disability "in the most integrated setting appropriate to the needs of the individual." One example provides that

> it would be a violation of this provision to require persons with mental disabilities to eat in the back room of a restaurant or to refuse to allow a person with a disability to full use of a health spa because of stereotypes about the person's ability to participate.

Zahedi challenges the ADA on the grounds that it is retroactive legislation and therefore violates the Due Process Clause of the Fifth Amendment.

The relevant inquiry is whether the legislation imposes liability or penalty for conduct occurring prior to the effective date of the statute. The ADA provided an 18 month notice period in which businesses could comply with the Act's requirements, and no liability was imposed prior to the end of that period. Small businesses were given an even lengthier notice period. Pinnock's complaint was not filed until September 9, 1992, nearly two years after the ADA was passed on July 26, 1990. The requirements of the title III do not subject Zahedi to retroactive legislation.

Zahedi contends that the expenditure of funds necessary to make the restrooms in his facility accessible to individuals in wheelchairs, if required under the ADA, would constitute a taking of private property "for public use, without just compensation" in violation of the Fifth Amendment's Due Process Clause. In *Lucas v. South Carolina Coastal Council*, 505 U.S. 1003, 112 S.Ct. 2886, 120 L.Ed.2d 798 (1992), the Supreme Court delineated three situations in which a governmental restraint is considered a taking, therefore requiring compensation. These three situations are: 1) When the regulation compels a permanent physical invasion of the property; 2) When the regulation

denies an owner all economically beneficial or productive use of its land; 3) When the regulation in question does not substantially advance a legitimate governmental objective. If either of the first two situations occur, the regulation will be considered a taking regardless of whether the action achieves an important public benefit or has only minimal impact on the owner. The expenditure of funds required by title III does not constitute a taking under the Fifth Amendment as defined in Lucas.

A cornerstone of the law of takings is that if a regulation has the effect of establishing a permanent physical occupation, it will be a taking. *Loretto v. Teleprompter Manhattan CATV*, 458 U.S. 419, 430, 102 S.Ct. 3164, 3173, 73 L.Ed.2d 868 (1982).

Zahedi argues that the remodeling required under the ADA may result in the loss of as many as 20 seating places in his restaurant. Zahedi cites *Loretto* in support of his argument that a regulation which requires a restaurant to widen restrooms and thereby restricts the use of part of his property, violates the Fifth Amendment. Zahedi, however, provides an inaccurate recitation of *Loretto*. The Supreme Court's analysis in *Loretto* rests on the finding that a regulation which gives an outside entity the right to physically intrude upon the property is actually the granting of an easement without compensation, which can constitute a taking. This case, however, does not involve the granting of Zahedi's property to another party for its own exclusive use and profit. Rather, the ADA merely proscribes Zahedi's use of part of his own property and it therefore could be likened to a zoning regulation. Since the ADA merely regulates the use of property and does not give anyone physical occupation of Zahedi's property, it is not within the Supreme Court's first category of takings.

The remodeling which Zahedi claims is required under the ADA regulations could result in the loss of approximately 20 seating places in his restaurant. The mere loss of approximately 20 seating places surely will not deny Zahedi all economically viable use of his property.

The Court must also consider whether the requirements of the statute frustrate the property owner's reasonable investment-backed expectations. As discussed above, the ADA was specifically drafted to avoid the imposition of economic hardship upon the operators of public accommodations, particularly those running smaller operations. A showing of frustration of investment-backed expectation is a very difficult one to make, and the impact of the ADA's barrier removal requirements pales in comparison to many of the regulations which the Supreme Court has upheld.

Regulations have been upheld even where they resulted in a complete restriction upon a specific individual's future exploitation of the property for profit.

Zahedi argues that the ADA constitutes a "national building code" which trespasses the regulatory area reserved to the states by the Tenth Amendment.

Title III's statutory scheme does not displace local building codes. It is a federal civil rights act that sets forth accessibility standards that places of public accommodation and commercial facilities must follow. Departures from the ADA Standards are expressly permitted where "alternative designs and technologies used will provide substantially equivalent or greater access to and usability of the facility." State and local building codes remain in effect to be enforced by state officials. State officials are not required to adopt or enforce the ADA Standards for Accessible Design.

Having carefully considered each of Zahedi's constitutional challenges, it is clear that none of these challenges can prevail. Zahedi's motion for summary judgment is denied.

Case Questions

1. What violation of ADA does Pinnock allege occurred?
2. List the constitutional arguments Zahedi made in challenging the application of the ADA to his property.
3. Is Zahedi's restaurant involved in interstate commerce? Why?
4. Does the ADA constitute a taking of property that must be compensated?
5. Is the ADA unconstitutionally vague?
6. Is the ADA retroactive?

Sale of Sites

The final step for the developer is the sale of the lots of housing units in the development or operation of the property. In the case of contracts for sale, the developer should follow the law and tips in Chapter 14.

CAUTIONS AND CONCLUSIONS

Real estate development is a complex process that involves all areas of real estate law. The three steps in development are land acquisition, land finance, and land improvement and construction. In all three steps there are individual rights and governmental regulations. In land acquisition, developers must consider the zoning laws, the planning components of local governments, impact fees, and the rights and interests of those affected by the proposed development. In land finance, the developer must consider the sources of funds available and how best to structure the financing in terms of tax, liability, and management issues. At times, a developer's choice for financing may also involve the sale of securities and require compliance with federal and state laws on the sale of securities. In land improvement and construction, the developer must be aware of private land-use restrictions such as covenants and create a plan consistent with those restrictions. In addition, the entire body of construction law with its protections for payment and performance come into play as buildings are constructed.

Developers must work their ways through a complex process for the creation of a successful project. One key to success is to carefully review and follow all the laws affecting everything from securities sales to construction bonds. Good developers work with policy setters, law makers, neighbors, contractors, and regulators to be certain that their project is not just successful but in compliance with the law and well received by members of the community.

Key Terms

annexation, 560
impact fees, 561
master-planned community, 566
planned unit development (PUD), 566
real estate syndication, 566
general partnership, 567
Uniform Partnership Act (UPA), 567
articles of partnership, 567
accounting, 568
novation, 569
limited partnership, 569
Uniform Limited Partnership Act (ULPA), 569
Revised Uniform Limited Partnership Act (RULPA), 569
general partner, 569
limited partner, 569
blind pool partnerships, 571
Model Business Corporation Act (MBCA), 573
Revised Model Business Corporation Act (RMBCA), 573
articles of incorporation, 573
personal holding company tax, 574
Subchapter S or S corporation, 574

limited liability company (LLC), 574
real estate investment trusts (REITs), 576
mortgage investment trusts (MITs), 576
Massachusetts business trust, 576
trust certificate, 577
equity trusts, 577
mortgage trusts, 577
mixed trusts, 577
specialty trust, 577
Securities Act of 1933, 579
Securities and Exchange Commission (SEC), 579
intrastate offering exemption, 579
small offering exemption (Regulation A), 579
Regulation D, 579
accredited investor, 580
Rule 504 exemption, 580
Rule 505 exemption, 580
Rule 506 exemption, 580
integration, 580
deed restrictions, 582
protective covenants, 582

equitable servitudes, 585
owner, 586
construction lender, 586
permanent lender, 586
lender, 586
general contractor, 586
prime contractor, 586
builder, 586
architect, 586
subcontractors, 586
suppliers, 586
surety, 586
guarantors, 586
insurer, 586
governmental supervisor, 586
bid bond, 586
performance bond, 587
penal sum, 587
payment bond, 587
bid notice, 587
flow-down clause, 590
unit pricing, 590
cost-plus formula, 591
change order, 591
substantial performance, 594

Chapter Problems

1. A wishes to put together a syndicate for the purpose of purchasing and operating two apartment complexes. A feels she can best sell the syndicate interests if the investors are able to directly deduct the depreciation losses that will result from the first three years of operation. What form of syndication will allow A's investors to take such deductions?

2. Burr, a general contractor, was bidding on a plant project for General Motors. Burr had two bids from electrical subcontractors. One was from Corbin-Dykes, and the other from White Sands. White Sands agreed to do the project for $4,000 less than Corbin-Dykes's bid if it could do the work in conjunction with another project it had in the area. Burr used Corbin-Dykes's bid and was awarded the project. However, Burr contracted with White Sands because it could do the work in the same amount of time at $4,000 less. Corbin-Dykes brought suit on the grounds of promissory estoppel and sought to force Burr to pay them. What was the result? *Corbin-Dykes Electric Co. v. Burr,* 500 P.2d 632 (Ariz. App. 1972)

3. Gough agreed to put up the trusses on a Kinney Shoe Store that Chuckrow was building as general contractor. Gough put up the trusses, but later that day, 30 of the 32 erected trusses fell down. Gough put them back up and demanded additional compensation. Chuckrow refused, saying that the trusses fell down because of Gough's poor workmanship. Gough maintained that they fell down because of faulty plans and specifications. What was the result? *Robert Chuckrow Construction Co. v. Gough,* 159 S.E.2d 469 (Ga. App. 1968)

4. Robert and Mary Ann Ederer owned a home in the Davidson Hills Subdivision of Ocean Springs, Mississippi, for over 30 years. A deed restriction in the subdivision provided that no building other than a single-family dwelling and a private car garage could be built on any of the lots.

Frederic Gast purchased a lot in the subdivision and began construction of a boathouse on the front of his lot. He did not construct a home, and the Ederers and others brought suit for violation of the restriction.

Gast says he did not know about the restriction and that he will build a home eventually on the lot as well. Can the neighbors enforce the deed restriction and require the removal of the boathouse? *Gast v. Ederer,* 600 So.2d 204 (Miss. 1992)

5.   Shalimar, Inc., purchased a large tract of land for purposes of constructing a "five-star resort community." The deed from the grantor restricted the use of the land to a resort community. The land tract, however, is not large enough for the construction of a golf course, which would be a necessary component of a five-star resort community. No five-star resort in the United States is without a golf course. The effect of the restriction is to render the land undevelopable. Shalimar would like to use the property to construct single-family homes. Could a court reform the deed and ease the restriction?

6.   Century Homes has been involved in a subdivision development of luxury homes for three years. The market for these large, expensive homes is no longer active, and Century is selling the remaining lots to builders who will be building small, inexpensive homes. Prior to Century's sales of the lots, the smallest home in the subdivision was 2,500 square feet. One builder is planning a 1,500-square-foot home. The existing home owners wish to know if they have any protections. What is the result?

7.   George D. Warner and other property owners in Terry Cove Subdivision, Unit One, a subdivision in Orange Beach, Alabama, filed suit against Orange Beach Marina, Inc., seeking an interpretation of restrictive covenants applicable to the Terry Cove Subdivision, Unit One. A proposed use involved the further subdivision of the lots for the development of a high-quality condominium project that would include 40 single-family residential units arranged in a circular fashion around a private yacht basin or marina with a yacht club, health club, tennis courts, and guardhouse.

The restrictive covenant read as follows:

1. Nothing but a single [family] private dwelling or residence of not less than 900 sq. ft. living area designed for occupancy of families shall be erected on any lot in these units of said subdivision with the exception of those lots or tracts that shall be designated by the said Dot-Dot Corporation [the developer of the subdivision and original fee owner of the subdivision property] shall be the sole authority to designate any area for commercial venture.

2. No residence of any kind of what is commonly known as "boxed," "pilings," or "sheet metal" construction shall be built on said tract unless the same shall be covered over upon all the outside walls with lumber, weatherboard, brick, stone or other materials with the exception of wet or dry marinas on locations as designated by the said Dot-Dot Corporation.

The Trial Court found that the proposed development by Orange Beach violated the restrictive covenants, and that the restrictive covenants could not be amended without the consent of the Terry Cove property owners. Can the restrictive covenants be ignored? *Orange Beach Marina, Inc. v. Warner, 500 So.2d 1068 (Ala. 1986)*

8.   Culver City required Robert Ehrlich, a developer, to pay $280,000 in land-use change impact fees and $33,220 in lieu of meeting the art requirement of all new developments in exchange for approval of Ehrlich's proposed 30-unit town-home development. Ehrlich says the fees do not advance a legitimate public purpose. Can Culver City extract the fees? *Ehrlich v. City of Culver City,* 19 Cal. Rptr. 2d 468 (1993).

9.   James Broward was developing a project in Palm Beach County, Florida. The project was one for 65 luxury condominiums. When the construction contract was awarded to Warren Construction, Inc., each condominium was to have a balcony. When construction was nearly 50 percent completed, the planning commission withdrew its approval for the balconies on the condominium and ruled that the building must have a flat face. The planning commission found that balconies tend to become storage places for occupants and take on a look that is not pleasing aesthetically. Broward wishes to know his rights and whether the timing of the withdrawal of approval is legal. Offer Mr. Broward some advice.

10.   With respect to question 9 above, suppose Mr. Broward decides to go ahead and remove the balcony from the construction plans. He calls to notify the foremen at Warren Construction. Is this oral notification sufficient? What if there are additional costs in changing the building from having balconies to being flat-faced? Can Warren demand more money for the changes?

Internet Activities

1.   For a website "prospectus" on a real estate investment trust (REIT), go to: **http://www.greatlakesreit.com/**.

2.   To see the SEC filing of a REIT, go to: **http://edgar.stern.nyu.edu/EDGAR/SC13d.html** and enter the name of a REIT of your choice.

3.   Search for tax laws concerning tax treatment of income from REITs and MITs at **http://www.irs.ustreas.gov/**.

4.   For a look at the extent of employee pension plan investments in real estate investment vehicles go to: **http://www.gao.gov/AIndexFY98/abstracts/he98028.htm**.

5.   For an explanation of a state county ordinance (Rockingham County Virginia) on subdividing agricultural land, go to: **http://www.co.rockingham.va.us/subagland.htm**.

6.   Georgia State Supreme Court ruled in favor of Georgia State Assembly's power to allow a municipality's annexation of a noncontiguous area of land. To review the summary of the court's decision, go to: **http://www.bbrc.com/lib00033.htm**.

7.   For an overview of construction financing from a commercial lender from the contractor and homebuyers' perspectives, go to: **http://www.1st-ap-mortgage.com/webconst.htm**.

Adverse possession Method of acquiring title to land by openly taking possession of and using another's property for a certain period of time.

Advertisement Under Regulation Z, public disclosure of credit terms.

Aesthetic zoning Zoning that regulates the appearance of property and exists for beautification purposes or architectural uniformity.

Affirmative easement An easement that involves the use of another's property; e.g., a right of access.

After-acquired property clause Mortgage, note, or security interest provision that provides that the security for the loan includes the existing property and any property added after the note; mortgage security interest is attached to newly acquired property.

Agent One who acts on another's behalf. In real estate, the agent is the party who works to bring the buyers and sellers of real estate together in exchange for payment (generally a commission).

Air lot That portion of the airspace from 23 feet above the earth's surface to the heavens.

Air Pollution Control Act The original federal act relating to air pollution; provided for studies but did little to control air pollution (1955).

Air Quality Act 1967 federal act that provided HEW with the authority to oversee state air pollution control plans and implementation.

Air rights Property ownership rights in the air above the surface.

All-adult covenant Deed restriction that limits residency in a particular area to certain ages and prohibits residency of children less than a certain age.

Americans with Disabilities Act (ADA) 1990 federal law prohibiting discrimination on the basis of disability and requiring reasonable accommodation by employers and landowners.

Anaconda mortgage Mortgage covering all debt owed by the mortgagor to the mortgagee.

Anchor tenant The tenant in a shopping center that has the largest store and will draw the greatest amount of traffic; e.g., grocery store in a plaza or a major department store in a mall.

Annexation Taking in an area of land as part of a governmental unit (city, town, or county). Many subdivisions are annexed before they are developed.

Antenuptial agreements Premarital contracts in which the spouses-to-be waive their interests in each other's properties that will be accumulated during the course of the marriage.

Architect Participant in the construction process; may oversee quality of subcontractors' work and issue lien waivers.

Article 9 Section of the Uniform Commercial Code that governs the taking of security interests in personal property and fixtures.

Articles of incorporation Document used to create a corporation.

Articles of partnership Document used to create a partnership.

Articles of limited partnership The limited partnership agreement.

As is Clause in contract that waives any warranty protection.

Asbestos Hazard Emergency Response Act (AHERA) Federal law that mandates inspection of facilities receiving federal funds to determine presence of asbestos and asbestos fibers.

Assessment Process whereby a tax amount is assigned to a parcel of real estate on the basis of the value of the parcel.

Assessor Public official responsible for the valuation and assessment of real property and the subsequent collection of taxes.

Asset Conservation, Lender Liability and Deposit Insurance Protection Act Federal law that clarifies the liability of lenders on real property pledged as security for a loan.

Assignment Process of transferring contract rights to another; e.g., assignment of a mortgage or lease.

Assumption Process whereby a buyer of real property agrees to assume responsibility for payments on an existing mortgage on the property.

At-risk rules Under the Internal Revenue Code, a restriction on taking losses that requires those taking the loss to have funds at the risk of the operation of the business.

Attached home A form of multiunit housing; it generally has common walls with other homes.

B

Balloon payment clause Clause in mortgage that requires a large payment at one time to satisfy the debt obligation.

Balloon payment Provision in a mortgage or mortgage note that calls for the payment of a large lump sum at the end of the mortgage period.

Baselines In the United States Government Survey, the major east-west guide lines.

Basis Property owner's cost of property; used for computing gain or loss on the sale of property.

Bequest A gift of personal property by will.

Best available treatment (BAT) The highest standard the EPA can impose for the control of water pollution.

Best conventional treatment (BCT) A standard for water pollution control that requires a firm to follow the best commonly used treatment methods; a standard that is lower than best available treatment.

Bid bond Guarantor of bid submitted on construction project that guarantees bidder will do work at price bid.

Glossary

A

Abstract of title A concise statement of the substance of documents or facts appearing on the public land records that affect the title to a particular tract.

Abstractor's certificate A summary by the abstractors of what was and was not examined in the title review.

Acceleration clause Provision in note, mortgage, or deed of trust that provides for the acceleration of the due date of the loan; generally results in the full amount of the loan being due for default such as nonpayment.

Acceptance Action of offeree in agreeing to terms of an offer that results in a binding contract.

Accounting In probate, process of providing a report on the collection and distribution of the estate; in partnerships, an equitable proceeding in which the use and distribution of partnership funds are examined to determine whether each partner has received his or her appropriate share.

Accredited investor Under federal securities law, an investor who meets certain financial standards and can qualify for purchases of certain types of securities exempt from registration.

Acid rain An environmental hazard that results from sulfur dioxide pollution from factories and coal-fired utility plants; the pollution is carried long distances and appears in rain and snow in areas far removed from the pollution sources.

Acknowledgment Notary signature and seal; a[...] on deeds and some contracts as well as on w[...]

Acquisition indebtedness For tax purposes, de[...] nation of qualified residential interest; the a[...] of debt entered into for purchase of a prin[...] secondary residence.

Act Statute enacted by a legislative body.

Action for dispossession Court proceeding b[...] lord to have tenant removed from property[...] ally brought for nonpayment of rent or dest[...] of landlord's premises.

Active income For income tax purposes, [...] earned as wages or other forms of comp[...] for work/services performed.

Ad valorem tax Tax based on value that incr[...] value increases. Property taxes are *ad valor*[...]

Ademption In testate distribution, the failure [...] if the property is no longer owned by the t[...] the time of death.

Adjustable rate mortgage (ARM) A type of [...] with a rate that changes according to some [...] rate index.

Administrator Male party responsible for th[...] of an intestate estate.

Administratrix Female party responsible for [...] bate of an intestate estate.

Advancement Common law doctrine that [...] amounts of *inter vivos* gifts from an heir [...] decedent's estate (still followed in some [...]

Bid notice Call for bids on a project by a contractor.

Blind pool partnership A partnership in which the general partner is selling units in the partnership to raise money, but no specific real estate is as yet involved.

Blockbusting Illegal racial discrimination practice wherein real estate brokers attempt (by encouraging listings and sales in a neighborhood) to change the racial composition of a neighborhood.

Board of adjustment Governmental entity (usually at city or county level) that is responsible for approving variances and adjustments.

Bona fide purchaser (BFP) Good faith purchaser.

Bounds See **Metes and bounds**.

Broker Party who is licensed to handle property listings.

Brundage clause Provision in a mortgage that calls for the mortgagor to pay all taxes on the property.

Bubble concept EPA concept of examining all air pollutants in an area as if they came from a single source; this concept is used in making a decision regarding the possibility of a new plant in the area.

Builder See General contractor.

Business judgement rule Standard for imposing liability on directors of corporation; must give time and thought to decisions.

Bylaws In multiunit housing, the document governing the details of operation; voting rights of members, meetings, notices, etc.

C

Capital gains The amount of a net gain made on the sale of property; carries a special lower tax rate.

Caption The legal description in an abstract.

Case precedent Doctrine of stare decisis; examining prior decisions to reach decisions in present cases.

Cash-to-mortgage sale Sale of real property in which the buyer pays the difference between the sales price and the mortgage balance and then takes over the mortgage (assumption).

Centerline rule Rule that provides landowners adjoining streams and rivers ownership of the land beneath these waters to the centerline of the river or stream.

Change order In construction contracts, a change in work, design, or materials.

Citation Legal shorthand referring to cases, statutes, regulations, and ordinances.

Cite See Citation.

Clean Air Act One of the original air pollution statutes that gave HEW authority to monitor interstate pollution problems.

Clean Air Act Amendments of 1990 First major revisions to Clean Air Act with coverage of acid rain and vehicle emissions and provision of new deadlines for SIPs.

Clean Water Act Major federal statute on water pollution that gave the federal government authority and control.

Cleaning deposit The amount set forth in a lease required of the tenant to be paid prior to commencement of the lease to cover the cleaning of the premises when the tenant has gone; under URLTA, the lease must state if it is nonrefundable.

Code of Federal Regulations (CFR) Compilation of regulations of federal agencies.

Codicil An addendum to a will.

Column lots Portion of air rights from the surface of the Earth to 23 feet above the surface.

Commercial mortgage Mortgage on non-residential property.

Common area maintenance (CAM) Fee charged in commercial leases for tenant to pay costs of maintenance of sidewalks in shopping and other commercial centers; fee is often a pro rata share of expenses based on that paid in other commercial projects.

Common law Uncodified law found in cases or in the history of real property.

Community property Method of married persons' co-ownership of property; limited to certain states.

Community Reinvestment Act (CRA) Federal law establishing record-keeping requirements for lenders' investments in inner-city area.

Community-Right-to-Know substance Federal disclosure law requiring notification of presence of toxic substance on property, including items such as asbestos.

Comprehensive Environmental Response, Compensation and Liability Act (CERCLA) The Superfund; program for private payment by polluting industries for clean-up of toxic waste.

Condition precedent In a contract, a requirement before the contract can be performed; e.g., delivering marketable title or qualifying for financing.

Condominium Form of multiunit housing in which the owner owns the area between the walls and ceiling.

Consent statutes Statutes that permit the attachment of a lien if the property owner consented to the work done by the lienor even though there was no direct contract with the owner.

Conservation easement A negative easement given by a property owner that provides that the property will not be used in such a way as to destroy a historical site on the property.

Consideration The detriment given by each party to the contract; e.g., the land by the seller and the money by the buyer.

Construction lender Party serving as financier for a project during construction.

Constructive delivery Delivery other than direct delivery to the person; delivering by precluding access by all others.

Constructive eviction Process whereby a tenant is forced to leave leased premises because the premises are in a state of disrepair and uninhabitable.

Consumer Price Index (CPI) adjustment clause Consumer Price Index adjustment clause that allows for rent increases when the CPI changes.

Contingent remainder Future interest that follows a life estate and that is not certain to follow or has unknown takers.

Contract for deed Another name for an installment contract; financing transaction in which seller carries the buyer and holds onto title until the buyer has paid in full.

Contract statutes With references to liens, statutes that require lienors to have a direct contractual agreement with property owners to be able to place lien on property on which work was performed.

Contractual lien Liens that arise because of a contractual agreement between the lienor and the owner of the liened property.

Conventional mortgage Mortgage not insured by a government agency.

Conventional pollutant One of the categories of water pollutants of the EPA; subject to the least amount of restriction and regulation.

Conversion restrictions Laws that regulate the conversion of leased premises into multiunit houses to afford protection for the existing tenants.

Cooperative Form of multiunit housing in which a corporation owns the property and owners of the shares in the corporation live in each of the units.

Co-ownership Label given to ownership of property by more than one person.

Cost approach Tax appraisal method that bases value of the property on its original cost plus costs of improvement.

Cost-plus formula In construction, a method of pricing in which the contractor charges all costs plus a profit margin.

Council on Environmental Quality (CEQ) Established in 1966 by the National Environment Protection Act as part of the executive branch of government and given the responsibility of formulating national policies on the quality of the environment and making recommendations to lawmakers based on its policies.

Counteroffer Offer made in response to offeror by the offeree; can occur by a change in the offeror's terms.

Covenant Promise in a deed that affects or limits the use of the conveyed property.

Cumulative classification Zoning system that permits higher uses in lower-use areas; e.g., residential uses in commercially zoned areas.

Curtesy rights Right of husband to a life estate in all real property owned by his wife during their marriage provided they had children.

D

Declaration of condominium Master deed for condominium project; the document recorded to reflect the units involved on the real property. See also **Declaration of horizontal property regime and covenants**.

Declaration of covenants, conditions, and restrictions (CCRs) The restrictions and limitations on the use and construction of land.

Declaration of horizontal property regime and covenants Another name for the declaration of condominium; multiunit housing is often referred to as horizontal housing regimes; the master deed recorded to reflect the existence of the multiunit housing and the location and number of units on the property.

Deed in lieu of foreclosure Process of borrower/property owner/mortgagor surrendering title to property to prevent lender's foreclosure.

Deed of bargain and sale A deed with warranty protection limited to the time of the grantor's ownership.

Deed of trust Security interest in real property in which title is held by a trustee until the borrower and occupant of the land repays the beneficiary (lender) the amount of the loan.

Deed restrictions Provisions usually recorded for subdivisions; the CCRs; restrictions of the use, development, and construction of the premises.

Deed Instrument used to convey title to real property.

Default Failure to comply with mortgage or promissory note requirements; generally a failure to pay or obtain insurance.

Deficiency judgment Judgment against the mortgagor or borrower after foreclosure sale, requiring payment of the amount due on the loan that was not obtained through sale of the mortgaged property.

Delivery Requirement for gifts and transfers of property by deed that mandates some form of actual or constructive possession by the grantee.

Department of Housing and Urban Development (HUD) Federal agency responsible for regulation of interstate land sales and other federal acts affecting real property.

Depreciation Wear and tear on property; can be deducted each year and used to offset income earned on income-producing property; greatly limited under TRA.

Designated agency Agency relationship in which seller names agent to act on his/her behalf in closing transaction.

Devise Gift of real property by will.

Devisee Recipient of real property gift by will.

Disinheritance Process of leaving an heir out of a will; not giving anything to someone who would ordinarily receive a share of the estate if there were an intestate distribution.

Doctrine of Ancient Lights Theory that originated in England that provides right to light if so used for 20 years or more; this prescriptive form of rights is no longer followed in the United States.

Doctrine of Correlative Rights Term in oil and gas law that limits recovery of oil and gas in situations where others' rights or deposits would be destroyed.

Doctrine of Emblements In landlord/tenant relationship, the right of the tenant to remove crops from the leased premises even after the lease expires if the tenant is responsible for their production.

Doctrine of Worthier Title Theory that gives a grantee the full fee simple title when the grant is made "to grantee with remainder to the heirs of the grantee"; the two estates are merged into a fee simple estate for the grantee.

Dominant estate A property owner who holds an appurtenant easement in another's property; the land enjoying the benefit of an easement through another's property.

Dominant tenement See **Dominant estate**.

Donee Recipient of a gift.

Donor One who makes a gift.

Dower rights Rights of widow in husband's estate; not applicable in all states.

Dual agency Agency relationship in which broker represents both the buyer and the seller.

Due-on-sale clause Clause in mortgage or mortgage note that requires full payment of the loan when the property is sold; in effect, a prohibition on assumptions.

E

Earnest money Deposit given by buyer on signing a contract for the purchase of property.

Easement Right to use another's property for access, light, and so on.

Easement appurtenant Easement that benefits a particular tract of land; generally an access easement or right of way.

Easement by express grant Easement given in a deed by the original landowner to provide a means of access for the purchaser of one part of the land.

Easement by express reservation Easement reserved in a deed by the original landowner to provide a means of access across a purchaser's land.

Easement by implication Easement that arises based on need because of previous use of the property in the same manner when the property was owned in a single tract.

Easement by necessity Easement given by circumstances that require it; the property is inaccessible or unusable without it.

Easement in gross An easement that does not benefit a particular tract of land; e.g., utility easements that run through all parcels of land in an area.

Effluent guidelines EPA standards for release of materials into waterways.

Emblements With regard to leases, the right of the tenant to harvest growing crops even after the lease has terminated if the tenant was responsible for growing the crops.

Eminent domain Process of governmental entity taking title to private property for public purposes.

Emissions Offset Policy EPA policy of requiring a reduction of other pollution sources in the area to allow the operation of a new plant and source of emissions.

Endangered Species Act (ESA) Federal law that affords protection for habitats of species designated as endangered; requires biological evaluation of impact of development and projects on species population.

Environmental contingency clause Provision in contract that provides buyer with the right to rescind the contract if environmental hazards that cannot be cleared arise during the course of a due diligence search.

Environmental impact statement (EIS) Report required to be filed when a governmental agency is taking action that will have an effect on the environment; e.g., construction of a dam, by the Army Corps of Engineers.

Environmental Protection Agency (EPA) Governmental agency responsible for the enforcement of environmental laws.

Equal Credit Opportunity Act (ECOA) Federal law prohibiting discrimination in credit decisions.

Equal Protection clause Part of the Fifth and Fourteenth Amendments to the Constitution; requires that laws apply equally to all.

Equitable liens Liens created as a result of a mortgage arrangement; also referred to as contractual liens.

Equitable relief Court remedies that require parties to perform certain acts or specifically perform a contract.

Equitable servitude Restriction on land use arising because an area has a common scheme or development that puts buyers on notice that particular uses and construction are required or prohibited.

Equity trust Method of syndication in which investors have an interest in the equity in real estate and will earn an investment through equity appreciation.

Equity participation financing Creative financing technique in which the lender will share in the appreciation of the property and will be entitled to a portion of the equity on sale of the mortgaged property.

Errors and omissions insurance Professional liability insurance for brokers and agents.

Escalation clause Clause generally in a lease, providing for increasing rent.

Escheat Process whereby property of a decedent is given to the state because of no available heirs.

Escrow Process whereby details of property transfer, payments, and deed conveyance are handled by a third party.

Escrow instructions Contract between buyer, seller, and escrow agent for the closing of escrow on a property transfer.

Exclusionary zoning Zoning that prohibits certain types of businesses, activities, or housing in certain areas.

Exclusive agency listing Listing agreement that requires the seller to pay the commission to the broker only if the listing broker sells the property; the seller may sell the property independently and not be required to pay a commission.

Exclusive right (or listing) to sell Listing that requires the seller to pay the broker-agent a commission regardless of who obtains a buyer for the property.

Executor Male party responsible for the probate of a decedent's estate pursuant to the decedent's will.

Executory interest Future interest that is not a remainder and not an interest in the grantor.

Executrix Female party responsible for the probate of a decedent's estate pursuant to the decedent's will.

F

Federal Consumer Credit Protection Act Federal law requiring disclosures, billing practices, rights in consumer credit transactions.

Federal Deposit Insurance Corporation (FDIC) Federal agency that regulates savings and loan institutions.

Federal Environmental Pesticide Control Act Federal law regulating the manufacture, containment, labeling, transportation, and use of pesticides.

Federal Home Loan Bank Board (FHLBB) Federal agency that regulates VA/FHA loans and lending practices.

Federal implementation plan (FIP) Part of the 1990 amendments to the Clean Air Act that requires the imposition of federal standards in the event states fail to meet deadlines and requirements for their SIPs.

Federal Water Pollution Control Act of 1972 Federal law that was the first anti-water pollution law with enforcement and details.

Federal National Mortgage Association (FNMA) or Fannie Mae Government corporation that purchases mortgages on the market.

Federal Water Pollution Control Administration (FWPCA) Originally the agency responsible for developing and enforcing water pollution control; merged into EPA in 1975.

Fee An inheritable interest in land.

Fee interest In oil and gas ownership, owner owns both the surface and subsurface rights.

Fee simple Highest land interest; full title; right to convey or transfer by will or mortgage without restriction.

Fee simple absolute Another term for a fee simple.

Fee simple defeasible A fee simple estate that can be lost by violation of a condition or use restriction placed in the transfer by the grantor.

Fee simple determinable Full title to land so long as certain conduct is avoided; e.g., "To A so long as the premises are never used for a bar."

Fee simple subject to a condition subsequent Full title provided that there is compliance with a condition; e.g., "To A upon the condition that the property is used for school purposes."

Fee tail Full title restricted in its passage to direct descendants of the owner.

Fifth Amendment Provision in United States Constitution that provides guarantee of due process.

Financial Institutions Reform Recovery and Enforcement Act (FIRREA) Federal law that followed the savings and loan debacle that implements controls on banking lending practices on real estate, including appraisals.

Financing statement Document filed to protect a security interest; must contain information about the parties and a description of the collateral.

Fixed rent In shopping center and commercial leases, rental standard of paying net rent (after utility costs or other fees specific in lease).

Fixtures Personal property that becomes attached to and is so closely associated with real property that it becomes a part of the real property.

Flow-down clause Clause in a construction contract that does not require the general contractor to pay subcontractors and suppliers until the owner has paid the general contractor.

Forcible detainer Action by landlord for rent; requires tenant to pay or be evicted by court order.

Foreclosure Process of selling mortgaged property to satisfy the debt owed by the defaulting mortgagor.

Foreclosure by advertisement (notice of sale) Creditor's remedy of sale by providing public notice; used in deeds of trust.

Forfeiture Loss of rights; in a contract for deed, the loss of all interest in the property for nonpayment.

Fourteenth Amendment Application of due process rights to the states (also known as the Equal Protection Clause), which requires uniform application of laws and nondiscrimination; applied in cases in which land conveyances attempt to include racial restrictions.

Fructus industriales Vegetation that grows on property as result of work of owner or tenant; i.e., crops.

Fructus naturales Vegetation that grows naturally on property; not the result of efforts of the owner or tenant.

FWPCA See **Federal Water Pollution Control Administration (FWPCA)**.

G

Garden homes Form of multiunit housing; usually a townhome that includes a small enclosed yard or patio.

General contractor In a construction project, the party responsible for the construction; can hire subcontractors and suppliers but bears ultimate responsibility; has direct contractual relationship with owner, construction lender, or both.

General partner Investor with full personal liability for partnership debt.

General partnership Voluntary association of two or more persons as co-owners in a business for profit.

General plan Development plan and zoning areas as developed by city or county; provides zoning designations for all areas within the municipality or county.

Geothermal energy Form of energy that is the result of naturally formed pockets of hot steam; can be a mineral right.

Good faith purchaser Buyer who buys property with no knowledge (constructive or actual) of any title defects, liens or other problems other than those specifically disclosed by the seller; also called bfp or bona fide purchaser.

Government National Mortgage Association (GNMA) or Ginnie Mae Government agency that insures loans sold on the market.

Grantor/grantee index system Method of record-keeping for land transactions; all transactions are recorded under the name of both the grantor and grantee to permit title to be traced according to the transfers among parties.

Grid The 24-mile square created between each guide meridian and parallel in the United States Government survey.

Gross rent Flat rent in commercial lease; no percentage of profits.

Guarantors Parties who agree to stand liable if a debtor defaults.

Guide meridians Vertical lines placed every 24 miles on the United States Government Survey; intersect with parallels to create 24-miles squares used for describing land parcels.

H

Habendum clause Clause in deed indicating the type of land interest being conveyed; in mineral lease, a clause that establishes the length of the lease, the grounds for termination, and drilling delay penalties.

Hazardous Substance Response Trust Fund Fund created under federal environmental laws; known as the Superfund for use in cleanup of toxic waste.

Hold zoning Interim zoning adopted prior to the time of the finalized general plan.

Holographic will Will entirely in the handwriting of the testator and signed by the testator (valid in some states).

Home equity indebtedness Consumer debt secured by residence of debtor; includes mortgage, other loans, and lines of credit.

Home Mortgage Disclosure Act Federal law mandating disclosure on consumer loans for second mortgages on residential property.

Homestead exemption Debtor protection that entitles the debtor to a certain amount in real property that is exempt from attachment by creditors.

Horizontal property acts or regimes Multiunit housing such as condominiums, cooperatives, and townhouses.

I

Impact fees Fees paid by developers for schools and other public facilities needed because of additional population developer brings in with project.

Implied warranty of habitability One-year implied warranty given by contractors of new homes to buyers; between landlord and tenant, the landlord's guaranty that the premises are fit for habitation and, if not, will be put into that condition.

Incentives for Self-Policing, Disclosure, Correction, and Prevention of Violations EPA guidelines for company's voluntary audit for and disclosure of environmental violations.

Income approach Tax appraisal method that bases value of the property on the income generated by the property.

Installment land contract A contract for deed; method of selling property in which the seller serves as the financier for the buyer and the purchase; seller holds onto title until there has been payment in full under an installment payment plan.

Insurer Party who indemnifies for loss.

Integration SEC practice of combining back-to-back offerings with resulting non-compliance with restrictions for exemption.

Inter vivos During the life of; while alive; e.g., an *inter vivos* gift.

Inter vivos **gift** Gift made while grantor is alive.

Interest Acceleration clause Clause in note that increases interest in the event of a default.

Interim zoning Hold zoning; temporary zoning before general plan is developed.

Internal Revenue Code (IRC) Federal law governing income taxation.

Interstate Land Sales Full Disclosure Act (ILSFDA) Federal law regulating the sale of property across state lines; requires advance filing of sales materials, mandatory disclosure of certain information, and prohibitions on promises about the land's future development.

Interval-ownership grant Form of time-sharing interest ownership.

Intestate Death without a will.

Intestate succession Statutory method for distributing the property of those who die without a will (intestate).

Intrastate offering exemption Under the 1933 Securities Act, an exemption from SEC registration requirements for certain securities offered in one state by a corporation primarily operating in that state.

Invitee Party who has a specific invitation to enter another's property or is a member of the public in a public place.

Involuntary lien Lien that does not result from a contractual arrangement; e.g., a tax lien or a judicial lien.

J

Joint tenancy Method of co-ownership that gives title to the property to the last survivor.

Joint will Will made in conjunction with another's will; requires distribution of property in a certain way regardless of who dies first.

Judicial deed Deed given by court after litigation of rights in the subject property.

Judicial foreclosure Foreclosure accomplished by filing a petition with the proper court; not a power of sale.

Judicial lien Lien on property that is the result of a judgment; lien to collect a court judgment.

Just compensation In eminent domain, the requirement that landowners whose property is taken for public purposes be adequately paid for the loss of that property.

L

Lapse In probate of a will, what happens when beneficiary dies prior to testator; the gift ends.

Laughing heir statute Statute that limits the degree of relationship of relatives who can inherit property from an intestate; causes property to escheat to the state before a remote relative would inherit an intestate's estate.

Lease-purchase Financing method that permits potential buyers to lease property for a period with an option to buy.

Legacy Gift of money by will.

Lender liability Doctrine that makes lenders liable for the lack of timely approval or withdrawal of an approval for financing already issued.

Lender See **Permanent lender**.

Legatee Beneficiary/donee of gift of money by will.

License Revocable right to enter another's property.

Licensee Party who enters another's land with express or implied permission; i.e., a social guest.

Lien theory One theory of mortgages that gives the mortgagor title to the property and the mortgagee a lien on the property as security for debt repayment.

Lien Interest in real property that serves as security for repayment of a debt.

Lienee Person whose property is subject to a lien.

Lienor Party who places a lien on real property.

Life estate Interest in land that lasts for the life of the grantee.

Life estate *pur autre vie* Life estate that lasts for the length of some measuring life other than that of the grantee.

Life tenants Those who hold a life estate in property.

Limited agent Agent whose authority is limited in time or scope.

Limited Liability Company (LLC) Business entity that is a cross between a corporation and a partnership.

Limited partner Investor in limited partnership whose maximum liability is his capital investment.

Limited partnership A partnership with at least one general partner in which limited partners can purchase interest and be liable only to the extent of their interests and not risk personal liability.

Liquidated damages Damages that are specified in formula or in amount in the written and signed agreement of the parties; must be reasonable.

Lis pendens "Suit or action pending"; document recorded with the land records to indicate a suit involving the land is pending; filed in mortgage foreclosures and quiet title actions.

Listing agreement Contract between a broker and landowner for the broker's services in helping to sell the owner's property.

Livery of seisin English ceremony for passage of title; involved a physical transfer of a clod of earth between grantor and grantee.

Living trust Trust created by settlor who is alive.

Living will Term for authorization to take testator off life-support equipment; authorized in many states but must use appropriate or required language and be formally executed.

Long-term land contract See Contract for deed.

Low income housing Under Tax Reform Act of 1986, special housing category affording investors special tax treatment.

M

Market approach Tax appraisal method that bases value of the property on prices of similar properties.

Marketable title Form of title generally required to be delivered in the sale of property; property is free from liens and no defects in title other than those noted or agreed to.

Massachusetts business trust A trust originated by Massachusetts as a business form for dealing in real estate because state statutes prohibited corporations from doing so; the initial form of real estate syndication.

Master deed In a condominium development, the document recorded to reflect the location of the project and the individual units.

Master mortgage Single mortgage document recorded for all loans and referenced to save recording fees.

Master plan General plan for zoning.

Master-planned community Large development project that involves construction of all facilities as well as housing.

Materials lien Lien on property for the amount due for materials furnished to the owner or to others performing work on the land.

Maximum Accelerated Cost Recovery System (MACRS) Under federal tax law, a method of depreciation.

Maximum Achievable Control Technology (MACT) Term under Clean Air Act Amendments of 1990; establishes standards for pollution control on utilities and other targeted industries for scrubbers and other antipollution devices.

Mechanic's liens Liens placed on real property to secure amount due to those who performed work or supplied materials for improvements or other projects on the land.

Metes and bounds Method of land description that begins with a permanent object and then through distances and directions describes the parcel of land.

Metes See **Metes and bounds**.

Mineral interest Ownership right to minerals on property; could also be a lease.

Mineral rights Subsurface rights in property; the rights to mine minerals; also known as mineral interest.

Mineral servitude Easement across the surface of the land for access to the land.

Misrepresentation Giving incorrect or misleading information to a party in contract negotiations or failing to disclose relevant information; inaccurate information that would affect the buying or selling decision.

Mixed trust Real estate investment trust that owns both property and mortgages.

Model Business Corporation Act (MBCA) Uniform law on corporations adopted in approximately one-third of the state.

Model Real Estate Cooperative Act Model act on co–ops.

Model Real Estate Time-Share Act Model act on time-share real property interests.

Monetary relief Form of remedy for contract or trespass which awards money damages for breach.

Mortgage Lien on real property used to secure a debt.

Mortgagee Lender or party who holds the mortgage lien.

Mortgage broker Agent who matches borrowers with mortgage companies.

Mortgage investment trusts (MITs) Real estate syndication method that provides investment opportunity in pool of mortgages.

Mortgage trust Real estate syndication trust that invests in real estate mortgages.

Mortgagor Borrower or party occupying land that is mortgaged.

Multiple listing A listing that appears on more than one broker's inventory of homes.

Multiple listing service (MLS) A specific multiple listing service that is nationwide and to which most brokers subscribe.

Mutual will Wills of parties that are reciprocal in their distribution; usually based on a contract to make a will; generally enforceable.

N

National Association of Realtors (NAR) Professional organization of brokers and agents; has standards for admission and maintenance of membership.

National Environmental Policy Act (NEPA) of 1969 Act that requires federal agencies to do an EIS before they approve a project.

National Pollution Discharge Elimination System (NPDES) Permit system that requires EPA approval for water discharges.

Negative easement An easement that prohibits a property owner from doing something that affects the property of another; e.g., a solar easement is a negative easement.

Net listing Type of listing that allows the broker to collect as a commission any amount received that is above the figure set as the seller's net take on the sale of the property.

Net-net-net See **Triple net**.

No deal, no commission clause Provision in listing agreement that requires a sale of property to close before any commission is due and owing to the broker.

Noise Control Act of 1972 Environmental statute regulating noise levels, disclosure requirements, and precautions.

Nonagent broker Broker who sells property via multi-listing but is not the listing broker.

Nonattainment area In environmental regulation, those areas that have not reached acceptable levels of pollution; highly regulated.

Nonconforming use In zoned areas, a use that does not comply with the area's zoning but that existed prior to the time the zoning was effective.

Nonconventional pollutant Second in line in terms of water pollution dangers; EPA can require higher pretreatment standards for nonconventional pollutants.

Noncumulative classification Method of zoning in which use in a particular area is limited to the zoned use; e.g., industrial zones cannot include residential buildings and apartment areas cannot include single-family dwellings.

Nonownership states Method for oil and gas ownership that disallows ownership of oil and gas until they have been captured through drilling.

Notice statute Form of recording statute that gives later bona fide purchasers priority in the case of multiple purchases for the previous purchasers' failures to give notice by recording their transactions.

Novation Original parties to a contract and a new third party agree to substitute the third party for the performance of the agreement.

Nuisance Use of property in such a way so as to interfere with another's use and enjoyment of property; e.g., bad smells and loud noises.

Nuncupative will Oral will; not valid in all states.

O

Occupational Safety and Health Administration (OSHA) Federal agency responsible for assuring safety in the workplace.

Offer Initial communication in contract formation that, if accepted, results in the formation of a contract.

Oil and gas interest Form of ownership in which a portion of a mineral interest is assigned.

Open listing Listing that pays a commission to whichever broker or salesperson sells the property; permits the owner to list with more than one broker and be liable for only one commission.

Operating expenses In commercial leases, the costs of running the property; varies and defined by lease.

Option Right (which has been paid for) to purchase property during a certain period of time.

Ordinances Laws passed on a local level of country, state, or city governments.

Ownership states Method for oil and gas ownership right determination that states mineral rights can only be lost if someone first captures the oil and gas by drilling.

P

Paid outside closing (POC) Costs not paid through escrow or closing.

Parallels Horizontal guidelines in the United States Government Survey.

Passive income Income from investments for income tax purposes.

Passive loss Loss resulting from passive activity; under the TRA, there are limitations on taking passive losses, i.e., passive losses can only be taken from passive income and not from wages and other income as many taxpayers had done in the past to maximize the benefits of real estate ownership.

Patio home Form of multiunit housing that generally includes a closed-in yard or patio area.

Payment bond In construction, a bond on the general contractor to ensure payment to subcontractors and suppliers; i.e., if the general contractor does not pay, the surety will pay.

Penal sum Sum bonding company must pay to have project completed if contractor fails to perform.

Per capita Method of allocation of intestate property among heirs; basic principle is that each heir gets an equal share.

Per Stirpes Method of distributing property to heirs whereby those closer in relation to the decedent get greater shares.

Percentage rent Rent for commercial properties expressed as a percentage of net or gross income.

Perfection Process of gaining priority on an Article 9 security interest; requires a filing of a financing statement to give public notice of the creditor's interest.

Performance bond Bond on general contractor that guarantees performance; if the general contractor does not perform, the surety will provide performance or payment for damages resulting from noncompletion of the work.

Periodic tenancy Temporary possessory interest in land that runs on a period-to-period basis such as a month-to-month lease.

Permanent lender Once construction is complete, the lender who will carry the permanent financing on the project; pays the construction lender and assumes priority.

Personal holding company tax Under the IRC, a doctrine that permits taxation of certain corporations as through they were not formed and the individuals are personally liable for the tax.

Personal representative Party responsible for the probate of a will under the Uniform Probate Code; formerly referred to as an executor.

Planned unit development (PUD) Subdivision that includes a development of a full community.

Plat map Method of land description that relies on a recorded map of a subdivision, with each deed making reference to the map and the particular lot being transferred.

Point source Discharge point where water leaves land and runs into streams, rivers, and so on.

Possibility of reverter Future interest in the grantor that follows a fee simple determinable.

Posthumous heirs Heirs born after the death of the decedent.

Power of sale In a deed-of-trust financing arrangement, the right of the trustee to sell the property on default by the trustor-borrower.

Power of termination Future interest in the grantor that follows a fee simple subject to a condition subsequent.

Premarital agreements Contracts that serve to waive marital property rights of the spouses; must be voluntary and carefully drafted.

Premises The words of conveyance in a deed; e.g., "do hereby grant and convey."

Prenuptial agreements Agreements in advance of marriage that alter statutory marital property rights.

Prepayment penalty clause Clause in mortgage or promissory note that requires the mortgagor to pay an additional charge for paying off the loan early.

Prescription Process of acquiring an easement through adverse use of the easement over a required period of time.

Pretermitted A testator's child conceived prior to testator's death but born after testator dies.

Prevention of significant deterioration (PSD) areas Part of 1977 Clean Air Act amendments establishing emission standards for clean areas to prevent pollution.

Prime contractor General contractor on a project.

Prime meridians The key vertical lines in the United States Government Survey.

Principal meridians See **Prime meridians**.

Prior Appropriation Doctrine Water allocation policy of first to use the water gets the rights to that water.

Private law Laws between individual parties; e.g., landlord's rules and regulations or the terms of a contract.

Probate Process of collecting the assets of a decedent; paying the decedent's debts, determining the decedent's heirs, and distributing property to the heirs.

Procuring cause of the sale standard Standard of determining commission among brokers under an open listing agreement.

Profit a prendre Right to enter another's land for the purpose of removing soil, water, minerals, or another resource.

Profit Rights of removal in another's property; shorthand for *profit a prendre.*

Promissory note Two-party debt instrument that, in real estate, is generally secured by a mortgage or deed of trust or some other interest in real estate.

Property report Summary of facts about undeveloped land required to be given to purchasers (part of ILSFDA).

Property tax role Assessor's formal records of parcels of land; the valuation and assessment.

Proprietary lease Interest of cooperative owner in a dwelling unit.

Prorated Allocation of prepaid insurance, taxes, and rent; generally done at close of escrow between buyer and seller.

Prorationing rules Rules that limit oil and gas production at the well site.

Protective covenants In development, covenants regarding nature and/or use of structures.

Purchase money mortgage A mortgage used to secure a debt for the funds used to buy the mortgaged property.

Purchase money security interest (PMSI) Under Article 9 of the UCC, a security interest given to a lender who financed the purchase of the property that is the collateral.

Pure race statute Recording priority statute that awards title (in the event of multiple conveyances) to the first purchaser to record.

Q

Qualified residential interest Under the Tax Reform Act of 1986, the interest that qualifies as a deduction on individual tax returns as home interest paid.

Quasi-easement A right-of-way as it existed when there was unity of ownership in a parcel of land.

Quiet title action Court action brought to determine the true owner of a piece of land.

Quitclaim deed Deed that serves to transfer title if the grantor has any such title; there are no guarantees that the grantor has any title or good title.

R

Race/notice system State recording statutes that award title to the first bona fide purchaser to record his or her title when there are conflicting claims of ownership in the property.

Range In the United States Government Survey, the lines placed vertically every six miles between the guide meridians.

Real estate investment trust (REIT) Form of real estate syndication in which investors hold trust interests and enjoy profits of trust's real estate holdings.

Real Estate Settlement Procedures Act (RESPA) Federal statute regulating disclosure of closing costs in advance and prohibiting kickbacks for referring customers to title companies.

Real estate syndication Group investment in real estate in the forms of trusts, partnerships, and corporations.

Realtor Trademark/name used by the National Association of Realtors (NAR) to refer to one of its members.

Recording Process of placing a deed or other document on the public records to give notice of a transaction or interest in the land.

Recreational lease In multiunit housing, a lease that runs for a short period of time during each year; sometimes called time sharing.

Redlining Practice of targeting certain areas or neighborhood as high-risk areas for loans or insurance or requiring lower valuation.

Refinancing Negotiating a new loan for real estate; generally done to obtain a lower rate or in the case of a sale, to allow a buyer to be able to purchase a property.

Regulation D Under the 1933 Securities Act, an SEC regulation that provides three different small offering exemptions from registration according to limitations on size of the offering or the number of investors.

Regulation Z (Truth-in-Lending Act) The Federal Reserve Board's regulations on disclosures in all types of credit transactions.

Remainder Future interest in someone other than the grantor; a remainder follows a life estate.

Rent controls Statutory maximums for rents on residential property.

Repair and deduct A tenant's right to repair leased premises when the landlord fails to do so and to deduct the cost of the repairs from his or her rent.

Rescission Right to treat a contract as if it never existed; rescind contract rights; generally appropriate in cases of fraud and misrepresentation.

Residential mortgage transactions Mortgages for the purchase of property to be used primarily as a residence for the buyer.

Resolution Trust Corporation (RTC) Defunct federal agency that handled saving and load clean-up.

Resource Conservation and Recovery Act of 1976 (RCRA) Federal law regulating hazardous waste and garbage that requires record keeping and controls amounts of garbage.

Reverse mortgage A form of mortgage that enables retired individuals to draw the equity from their homes in the form of a monthly payment. No payments or finance charges are due on the loan underlying the mortgage until the owner dies.

Reversion Future interest in grantor that results after life estate terminates and no remainder interest was given.

Revised Model Business Corporation Act (RMBCA) Model act on corporations; adopted in about one-third of states.

Revised Uniform Limited Partnership Act (RULPA) New statute updating ULPA.

Right of entry Future interest in grantor that results when the grantee fails to honor the condition placed on the grant of a fee simple subject to a condition subsequent.

Riparian Doctrine In water rights, the landowner who adjoins water; a theory that entitles all riparians to use of their water; does not allow one riparian to use all of the water.

Rivers and Harbors Act of 1899 A federal statute that attempted to regulate dumping in rivers and harbors; a predecessor to today's environmental statutes.

Royalty interest Interest landowner retains upon leasing of oil well.

Rules 504-506 exemptions Regulation D; the rules of the SEC on small-offering exemptions in securities sales.

Rule Against Perpetuities Rule that prohibits the control of estates from the grave; provides a duration cap on contingent remainders and executory interests.

Rule in Dumpor's Case English rule that provides that if a landlord consents to one assignment of the lease by the tenant, the landlord consents to all subsequent assignments; most statutes have abolished by statute the effects of this rule.

Rule in Shelley's Case Common law rule that merges future and present and present interests in A when grant is "To A for life, remainder to A's heirs"; has been abolished in many states.

Rule of Capture In mineral rights, a first-in-time-is-first-in-right philosophy in which the first to take subsurface minerals has title regardless of property boundary lines.

Rule of reason In easements, the standard followed in making decisions regarding the expansion of easement use; in antitrust, a standard for determining non per se violations.

S

Safe Drinking Water Act 1986 amendment to Clean Water Act that establishes minimum standards for drinking water purity; states must adopt federal minimums or their own higher standards.

Satisfaction of mortgage Payment of full loan amount by mortgagor.

Saving clause Provision for alternative distribution of property being purchased; can be a defense to liability.

Section In the U.S. Government Survey, one-mile squares in townships.

Securities Act of 1933 Federal law governing the initial sale of securities on the public markets.

Securities and Exchange Commission (SEC) The federal agency responsible for overseeing and policing the sales of securities on the primary and secondary markets.

Security agreement Under Article 9, the contract that gives the creditor a lien in the personal property or fixture; makes it the collateral for the loan.

Security deposit In the lease, the amount of money prepaid by the tenant to secure performance of the lease and often provide the amount of liquidated damages if the tenant does not perform.

Security interest Creditor's right in collateral under Article 9; the lien on the personal property or fixture.

Self-help Remedy for tenants with premises in disrepair; the right to repair defects on the property and then seek reimbursement.

Self-proving will A will that is acknowledged or notarized and thereby enjoys presumption of validity.

Servient estate Land through which an easement runs or that is subject to the easement.

Servient tenement Land through which an easement runs or that is subject to the easement.

Shared-appreciation mortgages Method of creative financing in which the lender charges a lower interest rate in exchange for the right to a return of a portion of the equity, including the increased value, of the home.

Sheriff's deed Form of title given to a buyer at a mortgage foreclosure sale; carries no warranties.

Small offering exemption Exception to SEC registration requirements based on limited amount of the offering or limited numbers of purchasers.

Social issue zoning Use of zoning to control influences in the community; e.g., the prohibition of adult theaters near residential districts.

Solar easement law A negative easement that prevents the servient estate from doing anything that would block the sunlight access of the dominant estate.

Soldiers and Sailors Relief Act Federal law that provides time limitations on foreclosures involving those in active military service.

Solid Waste Disposal Act Initial federal act on waste disposal that provided states with money for research on solid-waste disposal.

Special permit Exception to zoning uses provided by a board of adjustment.

Special warranty deed Deed that provides warranty of title only for the period during which the grantor owned the property.

Specialty trust A trust created for a specific purpose; e.g., a corporate trust created to expand the firm's real estate holdings.

Specific happenings increase provisions In commercial leases; provisions that result in increase in rental fees.

Specific performance Equitable remedy that requires a party to a contract to perform the contract promise or promises.

Squatters's rights A lay term for adverse possession or prescription.

Standard State Zoning Enabling Act Standard act adopted by most jurisdictions to govern the development and enforcement of a zoning plan.

State implementation plans (SIP) All state and local laws and ordinances that make up the state's air pollution control plan.

Statement of record Under ILSFDA, the disclosure document filed with HUD before any sales of underdeveloped land can occur.

Statute of Frauds Statute dictating what types of contracts must be in writing to be enforceable.

Statutory lien Right in land created by statute as a means of ensuring payment for work, materials, or other obligations.

Statutory right of redemption Specified period of time after foreclosure sale for buyer to redeem property by paying full amount of debt, interest, and costs associated with foreclosure.

Steering Form of racial discrimination in which brokers or salespersons direct interested purchasers away from and toward certain neighborhoods to control racial composition.

Straight term mortgage Mortgage with fixed interest rate for a set number of years.

Strawman transaction Transaction that is artificial and nonpermanent; generally used to satisfy the unities required for creating a joint tenancy.

Subchapter S corporation A special form of corporation under the IRC that allows the protection of limited liability but direct flow-through of profits and losses.

Subcontractor A worker hired by the general contractor on a project to complete certain portions of the project.

Subdivision trust Form of financing in which seller and buyer are trust beneficiaries, and a third party acts as trustee. Seller and buyer will share in the profits of land development after the seller has paid for the property.

Subject to sale A transfer of real property in which the buyer takes the property subject to an existing mortgage but does not agree to assume responsibility for the mortgage payments.

Sublease Arrangement in which a tenant leases rental property to another, and the tenant becomes landlord to the subtenant.

Subordinate mortgage Mortgage with a lesser priority than a preexisting mortgage.

Substantial performance Construction doctrine that requires good faith completion of a project but not necessarily perfection.

Superfund The fund created by the federal government to sponsor cleanup of toxic waste disposal sites.

Superfund Amendment and Reauthorization Act Federal law establishing clean-up funding, policies, and liability for toxic wastes.

Surety One who stands as a guarantor for an obligation, as in a payment or performance bond.

Surface Mining and Reclamation Act of 1977 Federal law that regulates surface mining and the required clean-up afterwards.

Suspended losses For tax purposes, losses that exceed passive income and are carried forward to future years' passive income.

T

Taking Term used to describe the government action of using private property for public purposes.

Taking Issues Under Fifth Amendment, constitutional protections in eminent domain.

Tax deed Form of title given in the event property is sold to satisfy taxes; carries no warranties.

Tax lien Lien placed on property for amount of unpaid taxes.

Tax sale Foreclosure sale on property for nonpayment of taxes.

Tenancy at sufferance Tenancy wherein the tenant is on the property of the landlord but has no right to be and may be evicted at any time.

Tenancy at will Tenancy wherein the tenant remains as long as both parties agree; either party may terminate at any time and without notice.

Tenancy by the entirety Method of co-ownership that is a joint tenancy between husband and wife.

Tenancy for years Tenancy for a stated period of time.

Tenancy in common Simplest form of co-ownership; unless otherwise stated, the presumed method of ownership for multiple landowners.

Tenancy in partnership Form of co-ownership in which the parties are partners; similar to joint tenancy in that the partners have a right of survivorship.

Testamentary Disposition by will.

Testamentary capacity The requisite mental capacity needed to make a valid will; a person's need to understand who his or her relatives are and how the property will be distributed by his or her will.

Time-sharing Form of multiunit housing in which owners own the unit for a limited period of time during each year.

Title insurance Insurance that pays the buyer of property in the event certain title defects arise.

Title theory Theory of mortgage law that puts title in the mortgagee and possession in the mortgagor.

Torrens system System for recording land titles designed to prevent the selling of the same parcel of land to more than one person.

Townhouse Form of multiunit housing in which the owner owns the area in the unit and also owns the land on which the unit is located.

Township Term in the United States Government Survey for the six-mile squares formed between the guide meridians and the parallels.

Toxic pollutant EPA classification for the worst form of water pollutants.

Toxic Substances Control Act (TOSCA) Federal law regulating the manufacture, labeling, and distribution of toxic substances.

Tract index system Form of land record that keeps history of title through identification of transactions with the particular tract.

Trade fixture Personal property that is attached to real property but is used in the operation of a business; remains the tenant's property.

Transaction broker Broker used for a sale but not listing broker.

Transfer disclosure statement (TDS) In some states a form that provides information about the residential property being transferred: length of ownership; date of construction; construction and improvements; etc.

Trespass Invasion of the property of another by a person or object.

Trespassers One who is on the property of another without permission.

Triggering language In credit advertisements, language describing credit terms that will require full and complete disclosure of all credit terms under Regulation Z.

Triple net Form of commercial lease rental formula; tenant pays taxes, insurance, and maintenance and fixed rent above these amounts.

Trust certificate In a real estate trust, the evidence of ownership given to each trust holder.

Truth-in-Lending Act Name given to federal statutes and regulations concerning credit terms and their disclosure.

U

Undue influence The use of a confidential relationship to gain benefits under a will or contract.

Uniform Commercial Code (UCC) Uniform statute adopted in most states that governs commercial transactions; Article IX deals with security interests in fixtures.

Uniform Common Interest Ownership Act Uniform law on multiple ownership issues.

Uniform Condominium Act (UCA) Uniform law adopted in some states governing ownership, rights, and obligations in condominium interests.

Uniform Land Transactions Act (ULTA) Uniform act with provisions governing land contracts.

Uniform Limited Partnership Act (ULPA) Uniform act governing formation, operation, and dissolution of limited partnerships.

Uniform Marital Property Act Uniform law that provides for ownership of property by married persons and means of division of property in the event of divorce or death.

Uniform Marketable Title Act Uniform law on what is required to deliver marketable title in sale.

Uniform Partnership Act (UPA) Uniform statute adopted in most states governing the creation, operation, and dissolution of partnerships.

Uniform Premarital Agreement Act Uniform law adopted in some states that governs the drafting and execution of premarital agreements.

Uniform Probate Code (UPC) Uniform law adopted in about one-third of the states governing the distribution of intestate property, the making of wills and probate, and administration of estates.

Uniform Residential Landlord Tenant Act (URLTA) Uniform law governing residential leases.

Uniform Rights of the Terminally Ill Act Proposed uniform law on the rights of the terminally Ill to refuse treatment; would establish rules for electing refusal of treatment.

Uniform Settlement Statement (USS) Under RESPA, the required form for showing how money was paid and distributed at close of escrow.

Uniform Simultaneous Death Act (USDA) Uniform law designed to allow direct distribution to heirs next in line when husband and wife die simultaneously (or within five days of each other).

Unit pricing Means of costing in construction that divides contract into units for prices and payment.

United States Code (U.S.C.) Compilation of all federal laws.

United States Constitution Framework for federal government.

United States government survey National survey of land.

Unities In co-ownership, the presence of requirements on creation; i.e., whether the interests must have been created at the same time as in a joint tenancy.

Usury Charging interest rates in excess of the statutorily allowed maximums.

V

VA Veteran's Administration.

Vacation license Form of time-sharing interest ownership.

Variances Approved uses of land outside the scope of an area's zoning.

Vested remainder A remainder that will automatically take effect when the life estate ends.

Vested remainder subject to complete divestment A remainder that can be completely lost if the terms of vesting are not met; not automatic on termination of the life estate.

Vested remainder subject to partial divestment A remainder that can be partially lost as other remaindermen develop, i.e., more children are born during the life estate.

Voluntary lien A lien created because of a contract as opposed to a tax lien, which is involuntary.

W

Waiver agreement In liens, a document that waives the right of a supplier or laborer to lien the property; generally given in exchange for payment.

Warranty deed Deed that conveys title and carries warranties that the title is good, the transfer is proper, and there are no liens and encumbrances other than the ones noted.

Water Quality Act One of the predecessors to today's federal water pollution control statutory scheme.

Water rights System of priority for water use.

Wetlands Protected areas near water; formerly known as swamps.

Will Legal document that transfers property rights from testator to named beneficiaries.

Workout In commercial real estate loans, the process of adjusting loan repayment because of borrower's financial difficulties.

Z

Zoning Process of regulating land use by designating areas of a community for certain uses.

Zoning commission Governmental agency responsible for developing the zoning plan.

Appendix A

The United States Constitution (Excerpts)

AMENDMENT V [1791]

No person shall be held to answer for a capital, or otherwise infamous crime, unless on a presentment or indictment of a Grand Jury, except in cases arising in the land or naval forces, or in the Militia, when in actual service in time of War or public danger; nor shall any person be subject for the same offence to be twice put in jeopardy of life or limb; nor shall be compelled in any criminal case to be a witness against himself, nor be deprived of life, liberty, or property, without due process of law; nor shall private property be taken for public use, without just compensation.

AMENDMENT XIV [1868]

Section 1

All persons born or naturalized in the United States and subject to the jurisdiction thereof, are citizens of the United States and of the State wherein they reside. No State shall make or enforce any law which shall abridge the privileges or immunities of citizens of the United States; nor shall any State deprive any person of life, liberty, or property, without due process of law; nor deny to any person within its jurisdiction the equal protection of the laws.

Appendix B

Uniform Commercial Code, Article 9* (Excerpts)

ARTICLE 9
SECURED TRANSACTIONS

. . .

§ 9–103. Purchase-Money Security Interest; Application of Payments; Burden of Establishing.

(a) In this section:

    (1) "purchase-money collateral" means goods or software that secures a purchase-money obligation incurred with respect to that collateral; and

    (2) "purchase-money obligation" means an obligation of an obligor incurred as all or part of the price of the collateral or for value given to enable the debtor to acquire rights in or the use of the collateral if the value is in fact so used.

(b) A security interest in goods is a purchase-money security interest:

    (1) to the extent that the goods are purchase-money collateral with respect to that security interest;

    (2) if the security interest is in inventory that is or was purchase-money collateral, also to the extent that the security interest secures a purchase-money obligation incurred with respect to other inventory in which the secured party holds or held a purchase-money security interest; and

*The 1999 version of UCC Article 9 (as changed through 2000) has been adopted in 36 states as of May 1, 2001.

    (3) also to the extent that the security interest secures a purchase-money obligation incurred with respect to software in which the secured party holds or held a purchase-money security interest.

(c) A security interest in software is a purchase-money security interest to the extent that the security interest also secures a purchase-money obligation incurred with respect to goods in which the secured party holds or held a purchase-money security interest if:

    (1) the debtor acquired its interest in the software in an integrated transaction in which it acquired an interest in the goods; and

    (2) the debtor acquired its interest in the software for the principal purpose of using the software in the goods.

(d) The security interest of a consignor in goods that are the subject of a consignment is a purchase-money security interest in inventory.

(e) In a transaction other than a consumer-goods transaction, if the extent to which a security interest is a purchase-money security interest depends on the application of a payment to a particular obligation, the payment must be applied:

    (1) in accordance with any reasonable method of application to which the parties agree;

    (2) in the absence of the parties' agreement to a reasonable method, in accordance with any intention of the obligor manifested at or before the time of payment; or

    (3) in the absence of an agreement to a reasonable method and a timely manifestation of the obligor's intention, in the following order:

        (A) to obligations that are not secured; and

        (B) if more than one obligation is secured, to obligations secured by purchase-money security interests in the order in which those obligations were incurred.

(f) In a transaction other than a consumer-goods transaction, a purchase-money security interest does not lose its status as such, even if:

    (1) The purchase-money collateral also secures an obligation that is not a purchase-money obligation;

    (2) collateral that is not purchase-money collateral also secures the purchase-money obligation; or

    (3) the purchase-money obligation has been renewed, refinanced, consolidated, or restructured.

(g) In a transaction other than a consumer-goods transaction, a secured party claiming a purchase-money security interest has the burden of establishing the extent to which the security interest is a purchase-money security interest.

(h) The limitation of the rules in subsections (e), (f), and (g) to transactions other than consumer-goods transactions is intended to leave to the court the determination of the proper rules in consumer-goods transactions. The court may not infer from that limitation the nature of the proper rule in consumer-goods transactions and may continue to apply established approaches.

. . .

PART 2 *EFFECTIVENESS OF SECURITY AGREEMENT; ATTACHMENT OF SECURITY INTEREST; RIGHTS OF PARTIES TO SECURITY AGREEMENT*

§ 9–201. *General Effectiveness of Security Agreement.*

(a) Except as otherwise provided in [the Uniform Commercial Code], a security agreement is effective according to its terms between the parties, against purchasers of the collateral, and against creditors.

(b) A transaction subject to this article is subject to any applicable rule of law which establishes a different rule for consumers and [insert reference to (i) any other statute or regulation that regulates the rates, charges, agreements, and practices for loans, credit sales, or other extensions of credit and (ii) any consumer-protection statute or regulation].

(c) In case of conflict between this article and a rule of law, statute, or regulation described in subsection (b), the rule of law, statute, or regulation controls. Failure to comply with a statute or regulation described in subsection (b) has only the effect the statute or regulation specifies.

(d) This article does not:

   (1) validate any rate, charge, agreement, or practice that violates a rule of law, statute, or regulation described in subsection (b); or

   (2) extend the application of the rule of law, statute, or regulation to a transaction not otherwise subject to it.

§ 9–202. *Title to Collateral Immaterial.*

Except as otherwise provided with respect to consignments or sales of accounts, chattel paper, payment intangibles, or promissory notes, the provisions of this article with regard to rights and obligations apply whether title to collateral is in the secured party or the debtor.

§ 9–203. *Attachment and Enforceability of Security Interest; Proceeds; Supporting Obligations; Formal Requisites.*

(a) A security interest attaches to collateral when it becomes enforceable against the debtor with respect to the collateral, unless an agreement expressly postpones the time of attachment.

(b) Except as otherwise provided in subsections (c) through (i), a security interest is enforceable against the debtor and third parties with respect to the collateral only if:

   (1) value has been given;

   (2) the debtor has rights in the collateral or the power to transfer rights in the collateral to a secured party; and

   (3) one of the following conditions is met:

      (A) the debtor has authenticated a security agreement that provides a description of the collateral and, if the security interest covers timber to be cut, a description of the land concerned;

      (B) the collateral is not a certificated security and is in the possession of the secured party under Section 9–313 pursuant to the debtor's security agreement;

      (C) the collateral is a certificated security in registered form and the security certificate has been delivered to the secured party under Section 8– 301 pursuant to the debtor's security agreement; or

      (D) the collateral is deposit accounts, electronic chattel paper, investment property, or letter-of-credit rights, and the secured party has control under Section 9–104, 9–105, 9–106, or 9–107 pursuant to the debtor's security agreement.

(c) Subsection (b) is subject to Section 4–210 on the security interest of a collecting bank, Section 5–118 on the security interest of a letter-of-credit issuer or nominated person, Section 9–110 on a security interest arising under Article 2 or 2A, and Section 9–206 on security interests in investment property.

(d) A person becomes bound as debtor by a security agreement entered into by another person if, by operation of law other than this article or by contract:

    (1) the security agreement becomes effective to create a security interest in the person's property; or

    (2) the person becomes generally obligated for the obligations of the other person, including the obligation secured under the security agreement, and acquires or succeeds to all or substantially all of the assets of the other person.

(e) If a new debtor becomes bound as debtor by a security agreement entered into by another person:

    (1) the agreement satisfies subsection (b)(3) with respect to existing or after-acquired property of the new debtor to the extent the property is described in the agreement; and

    (2) another agreement is not necessary to make a security interest in the property enforceable.

(f) The attachment of a security interest in collateral gives the secured party the rights to proceeds provided by Section 9–315 and is also attachment of a security interest in a supporting obligation for the collateral.

(g) The attachment of a security interest in a right to payment or performance secured by a security interest or other lien on personal or real property is also attachment of a security interest in the security interest, mortgage, or other lien.

(h) The attachment of a security interest in a securities account is also attachment of a security interest in the security entitlements carried in the securities account.

(i) The attachment of a security interest in a commodity account is also attachment of a security interest in the commodity contracts carried in the commodity account.

. . .

PART 3 *PERFECTION AND PRIORITY*

§ 9–301. Law Governing Perfection and Priority of Security Interests.

Except as otherwise provided in Sections 9–303 through 9–306, the following rules determine the law governing perfection, the effect of perfection or nonperfection, and the priority of a security interest in collateral:

(1) Except as otherwise provided in this section, while a debtor is located in a jurisdiction, the local law of that jurisdiction governs perfection, the effect of perfection or nonperfection, and the priority of a security interest in collateral.

(2) While collateral is located in a jurisdiction, the local law of that jurisdiction governs perfection, the effect of perfection or nonperfection, and the priority of a possessory security interest in that collateral.

(3) Except as otherwise provided in paragraph (4), while negotiable documents, goods, instruments, money, or tangible chattel paper is located in a jurisdiction, the local law of that jurisdiction governs:

   (A) perfection of a security interest in the goods by filing a fixture filing;

   (B) perfection of a security interest in timber to be cut; and

   (C) the effect of perfection or nonperfection and the priority of a nonpossessory security interest in the collateral.

(4) The local law of the jurisdiction in which the well-head or minehead is located governs perfection, the effect of perfection or nonperfection, and the priority of a security interest in as-extracted collateral.

§ 9–302. Law Governing Perfection and Priority of Agricultural Liens.

While farm products are located in a jurisdiction, the local law of that jurisdiction governs perfection, the effect of perfection or nonperfection, and the priority of an agricultural lien on the farm products.

§ 9–303. Law Governing Perfection and Priority of Security Interests in Goods Covered by a Certificate of Title.

(a) This section applies to goods covered by a certificate of title, even if there is no other relationship between the jurisdiction under whose certificate of title the goods are covered and the goods or the debtor.

(b) Goods become covered by a certificate of title when a valid application for the certificate of title and the applicable fee are delivered to the appropriate authority. Goods cease to be covered by a certificate of title at the earlier of the time the certificate of title ceases to be effective under the law of the issuing jurisdiction or the time the goods become covered subsequently by a certificate of title issued by another jurisdiction.

(c) The local law of the jurisdiction under whose certificate of title the goods are covered governs perfection, the effect of perfection or nonperfection, and the priority of a security interest in goods covered by a certificate of title from the time the goods become covered by the certificate of title until the goods cease to be covered by the certificate of title.

. . .

§ 9–305. Law Governing Perfection and Priority of Security Interests in Investment Property.

(a) Except as otherwise provided in subsection (c), the following rules apply:

    (1) While a security certificate is located in a jurisdiction, the local law of that jurisdiction governs perfection, the effect of perfection or nonperfection, and the priority of a security interest in the certificated security represented thereby.

    (2) The local law of the issuer's jurisdiction as specified in Section 8–110(d) governs perfection, the effect of perfection or nonperfection, and the priority of a security interest in an uncertificated security.

    (3) The local law of the securities intermediary's jurisdiction as specified in Section 8–110(e) governs perfection, the effect of perfection or nonperfection, and the priority of a security interest in a security entitlement or securities account.

    (4) The local law of the commodity intermediary's jurisdiction governs perfection, the effect of perfection or nonperfection, and the priority of a security interest in a commodity contract or commodity account.

(b) The following rules determine a commodity intermediary's jurisdiction for purposes of this part:

    (1) If an agreement between the commodity intermediary and commodity customer governing the commodity account expressly provides that a particular jurisdiction is the commodity intermediary's jurisdiction for purposes of this part, this article, or [the Uniform Commercial Code], that jurisdiction is the commodity intermediary's jurisdiction.

    (2) If paragraph (1) does not apply and an agreement between the commodity intermediary and commodity customer governing the commodity account expressly provides that the agreement is governed by the law of a particular jurisdiction, that jurisdiction is the commodity intermediary's jurisdiction.

    (3) If neither paragraph (1) nor paragraph (2) applies and an agreement between the commodity intermediary and commodity customer governing the commodity account expressly provides that the commodity account is maintained at an office in a particular jurisdiction, that jurisdiction is the commodity intermediary's jurisdiction.

    (4) If none of the preceding paragraphs applies, the commodity intermediary's jurisdiction is the jurisdiction in which the office identified in an account statement as the office serving the commodity customer's account is located.

    (5) If none of the preceding paragraphs applies, the commodity intermediary's jurisdiction is the jurisdiction in which the chief executive office of the commodity intermediary is located.

(c) The local law of the jurisdiction in which the debtor is located governs:

    (1) perfection of a security interest in investment property by filing;

    (2) automatic perfection of a security interest in investment property created by a broker or securities intermediary; and

    (3) automatic perfection of a security interest in a commodity contract or commodity account created by a commodity intermediary.

· · ·

§ 9–308. When Security Interest or Agricultural Lien Is Perfected; Continuity of Perfection.

(a) Except as otherwise provided in this section and Section 9–309, a security interest is perfected if it has attached and all of the applicable requirements for perfection in Sections 9–310 through 9–316 have been satisfied. A security interest is perfected when it attaches if the applicable requirements are satisfied before the security interest attaches.

(b) An agricultural lien is perfected if it has become effective and all of the applicable requirements for perfection in Section 9–310 have been satisfied. An agricultural lien is perfected when it becomes effective if the applicable requirements are satisfied before the agricultural lien becomes effective.

(c) A security interest or agricultural lien is perfected continuously if it is originally perfected by one method under this article and is later perfected by another method under this article, without an intermediate period when it was unperfected.

(d) Perfection of a security interest in collateral also perfects a security interest in a supporting obligation for the collateral.

(e) Perfection of a security interest in a right to payment or performance also perfects a security interest in a security interest, mortgage, or other lien on personal or real property securing the right.

(f) Perfection of a security interest in a securities account also perfects a security interest in the security entitlements carried in the securities account.

(g) Perfection of a security interest in a commodity account also perfects a security interest in the commodity contracts carried in the commodity account.

§ 9–309. Security Interest Perfected upon Attachment.

The following security interests are perfected when they attach:

(1) a purchase-money security interest in consumer goods, except as otherwise provided in Section 9– 311(b) with respect to consumer goods that are subject to a statute or treaty described in Section 9–311(a);

(2) an assignment of accounts or payment intangibles which does not by itself or in conjunction with other assignments to the same assignee transfer a significant part of the assignor's outstanding accounts or payment intangibles;

(3) a sale of a payment intangible;

(4) a sale of a promissory note;

(5) a security interest created by the assignment of a health-care-insurance receivable to the provider of the health-care goods or services;

(6) a security interest arising under Section 2–401, 2–505, 2–711(3), or 2A–508(5), until the debtor obtains possession of the collateral;

(7) a security interest of a collecting bank arising under Section 4–210;

(8) a security interest of an issuer or nominated person arising under Section 5–118;

(9) a security interest arising in the delivery of a financial asset under Section 9–206(c);

(10) a security interest in investment property created by a broker or securities intermediary;

(11) a security interest in a commodity contract or a commodity account created by a commodity intermediary;

(12) an assignment for the benefit of all creditors of the transferor and subsequent transfers by the assignee thereunder; and

(13) a security interest created by an assignment of a beneficial interest in a decedent's estate.

§ 9–310. When Filing Required to Perfect Security Interest or Agricultural Lien; Security Interests and Agricultural Liens to Which Filing Provisions Do Not Apply.

(a) Except as otherwise provided in subsection (b) and Section 9–312(b), a financing statement must be filed to perfect all security interests and agricultural liens.

(b) The filing of a financing statement is not necessary to perfect a security interest:

(1) that is perfected under Section 9–308(d), (e), (f), or (g);

(2) that is perfected under Section 9–309 when it attaches;

(3) in property subject to a statute, regulation, or treaty described in Section 9–311(a);

(4) in goods in possession of a bailee which is perfected under Section 9–312(d)(1) or (2);

(5) in certificated securities, documents, goods, or instruments which is perfected without filing or possession under Section 9–312(e), (f), or (g);

(6) in collateral in the secured party's possession under Section 9–313;

(7) in a certificated security which is perfected by delivery of the security certificate to the secured party under Section 9–313;

(8) in deposit accounts, electronic chattel paper, investment property, or letter-of-credit rights which is perfected by control under Section 9–314;

(9) in proceeds which is perfected under Section 9– 315; or

(10) that is perfected under Section 9–316.

(c) If a secured party assigns a perfected security interest or agricultural lien, a filing under this article is not required to continue the perfected status of the security interest against creditors of and transferees from the original debtor.

. . .

§ 9–333. Priority of Certain Liens Arising by Operation of Law.

(a) In this section, "possessory lien" means an interest, other than a security interest or an agricultural lien:

(1) which secures payment or performance of an obligation for services or materials furnished with respect to goods by a person in the ordinary course of the person's business;

(2) which is created by statute or rule of law in favor of the person; and

(3) whose effectiveness depends on the person's possession of the goods.

(b) A possessory lien on goods has priority over a security interest in the goods unless the lien is created by a statute that expressly provides otherwise.

§ 9–334. Priority of Security Interests in Fixtures and Crops.

(a) A security interest under this article may be created in goods that are fixtures or may continue in goods that become fixtures. A security interest does not exist under this article in ordinary building materials incorporated into an improvement on land.

(b) This article does not prevent creation of an encumbrance upon fixtures under real property law.

(c) In cases not governed by subsections (d) through (h), a security interest in fixtures is subordinate to a conflicting interest of an encumbrancer or owner of the related real property other than the debtor.

(d) Except as otherwise provided in subsection (h), a perfected security interest in fixtures has priority over a conflicting interest of an encumbrancer or owner of the real property if the debtor has an interest of record in or is in possession of the real property and:

(1) the security interest is a purchase-money security interest;

(2) the interest of the encumbrancer or owner arises before the goods become fixtures; and

(3) the security interest is perfected by a fixture filing before the goods become fixtures or within 20 days thereafter.

(e) A perfected security interest in fixtures has priority over a conflicting interest of an encumbrancer or owner of the real property if:

(1) the debtor has an interest of record in the real property or is in possession of the real property and the security interest:

(A) is perfected by a fixture filing before the interest of the encumbrancer or owner is of record; and

(B) has priority over any conflicting interest of a predecessor in title of the encumbrancer or owner;

(2) before the goods become fixtures, the security interest is perfected by any method permitted by this article and the fixtures are readily removable:

(A) factory or office machines;

(B) equipment that is not primarily used or leased for use in the operation of the real property; or

(C) replacements of domestic appliances that are consumer goods;

(3) the conflicting interest is a lien on the real property obtained by legal or equitable proceedings after the security interest was perfected by any method permitted by this article; or

(4) the security interest is:

(A) created in a manufactured home in a manufactured-home transaction; and

(B) perfected pursuant to a statute described in Section 9–311(a)(2).

(f) A security interest in fixtures, whether or not perfected, has priority over a conflicting interest of an encumbrancer or owner of the real property if:

    (1) the encumbrancer or owner has, in an authenticated record, consented to the security interest or disclaimed an interest in the goods as fixtures; or

    (2) the debtor has a right to remove the goods as against the encumbrancer or owner.

(g) The priority of the security interest under paragraph (f)(2) continues for a reasonable time if the debtor's right to remove the goods as against the encumbrancer or owner terminates.

(h) A mortgage is a construction mortgage to the extent that it secures an obligation incurred for the construction of an improvement on land, including the acquisition cost of the land, if a recorded record of the mortgage so indicates. Except as otherwise provided in subsections (e) and (f), a security interest in fixtures is subordinate to a construction mortgage if a record of the mortgage is recorded before the goods become fixtures and the goods become fixtures before the completion of the construction. A mortgage has this priority to the same extent as a construction mortgage to the extent that it is given to refinance a construction mortgage.

(i) A perfected security interest in crops growing on real property has priority over a conflicting interest of an encumbrancer or owner of the real property if the debtor has an interest of record in or is in possession of the real property.

(j) Subsection (i) prevails over any inconsistent provisions of the following statutes: [List here any statutes containing provisions inconsistent with subsection (i).]

PART 5 *FILING*

§ 9–501. *Filing Office.*

(a) Except as otherwise provided in subsection (b), if the local law of this State governs perfection of a security interest or agricultural lien, the office in which to file a financing statement to perfect the security interest or agricultural lien is:

    (1) the office designated for the filing or recording of a record of a mortgage on the related real property, if:

        (A) the collateral is as-extracted collateral or timber to be cut; or

        (B) the financing statement is filed as a fixture filing and the collateral is goods that are or are to become fixtures; or

    (2) the office of [ ] [or any office duly authorized by [ ]], in all other cases, including a case in which the collateral is goods that are or are to become fixtures and the financing statement is not filed as a fixture filing.

(b) The office in which to file a financing statement to perfect a security interest in collateral, including fixtures, of a transmitting utility is the office of [ ]. The financing statement also constitutes a fixture filing as to the collateral indicated in the financing statement which is or is to become fixtures.

§ 9–502 Contents of Financing Statement; Record of Mortgage as Financing Statement; Time of Filing Financing Statement.

(a) Subject to subsection (b), a financing statement is sufficient only if it:

    (1) provides the name of the debtor;

    (2) provides the name of the secured party or a representative of the secured party; and

    (3) indicates the collateral covered by the financing statement.

(b) Except as otherwise provided in Section 9–501(b), to be sufficient, a financing statement that covers as-extracted collateral or timber to be cut, or which is filed as a fixture filing and covers goods that are or are to become fixtures, must satisfy subsection (a) and also:

    (1) indicate that it covers this type of collateral;

    (2) indicate that it is to be filed [for record] in the real property records;

    (3) provide a description of the real property to which the collateral is related [sufficient to give constructive notice of a mortgage under the law of this State if the description were contained in a record of the mortgage of the real property]; and

    (4) if the debtor does not have an interest of record in the real property, provide the name of a record owner.

(c) A record of a mortgage is effective, from the date of recording, as a financing statement filed as a fixture filing or as a financing statement covering as-extracted collateral or timber to be cut only if:

    (1) the record indicates the goods or accounts that it covers;

    (2) the goods are or are to become fixtures related to the real property described in the record or the collateral is related to the real property described in the record and is as-extracted collateral or timber to be cut;

    (3) the record satisfies the requirements for a financing statement in this section other than an indication that it is to be filed in the real property records; and

    (4) the record is [duly] recorded.

(d) A financing statement may be filed before a security agreement is made or a security interest otherwise attaches.

§ 9–503. Name of Debtor and Secured Party.

(a) A financing statement sufficiently provides the name of the debtor:

    (1) if the debtor is a registered organization, only if the financing statement provides the name of the debtor indicated of the public record of the debtor's jurisdiction of organization which shows the debtor to have been organized.

    (2) if the debtor is a decedent's estate, only if the financing statement provides the name of the decedent and indicates that the debtor is an estate;

    (3) if the debtor is a trust or a trustee acting with respect to property held in trust, only if the financing statement:

   (A) provides the name specified for the trust in its organic documents or, if no name is specified, provides the name of the settlor and additional information sufficient to distinguish the debtor from other trusts having one or more of the same settlors; and

   (B) indicates, in the debtor's name or otherwise, that the debtor is a trust or is a trustee acting with respect to property held in trust; and

  (4) in other cases:

   (A) if the debtor has a name, only if it provides the individual or organizational name of the debtor; and

   (B) if the debtor does not have a name, only if it provides the names of the partners, members, associates, or other persons comprising the debtor.

(b) A financing statement that provides the name of the debtor in accordance with subsection (a) is not rendered ineffective by the absence of:

  (1) a trade name or other name of the debtor; or

  (2) unless required under subsection (a)(4)(B), names of partners, members, associates, or other persons comprising the debtor.

(c) A financing statement that provides only the debtor's trade name does not sufficiently provide the name of the debtor.

(d) Failure to indicate the representative capacity of a secured party or representative of a secured party does not affect the sufficiency of a financing statement.

(e) A financing statement may provide the name of more than one debtor and the name of more than one secured party.

§ 9–504. Indication of Collateral.

A financing statement sufficiently indicates the collateral that it covers if the financing statement provides:

(1) a description of the collateral pursuant to Section 9–108; or

(2) an indication that the financing statement covers all assets or all personal property.

§ 9–505. Filing and Compliance with Other Statutes and Treaties for Consignments, Leases, Other Bailments, and Other Transactions.

(a) A consignor, lessor, or other bailor of goods, a licensor, or a buyer of a payment intangible or promissory note may file a financing statement, or may comply with a statute or treaty described in Section 9–311(a), using the terms "consignor", "consignee", "lessor", "lessee", "bailor", "bailee", "licensor", "licensee", "owner", "registered owner", "buyer", "seller", or words of similar import, instead terms "secured party" and "debtor".

(b) This part applies to the filing of a financing statement under subsection (a) and, as appropriate, to compliance that is equivalent to filing a financing statement under Section 9–311(b), but the filing or compliance is not of itself a factor in determining whether the collateral secures an obligation. If it is determined for another reason that the collateral secures an obligation, a security interest held by the consignor, lessor, bailor, licensor, owner, or buyer which attaches to the collateral is perfected by the filing or compliance.

§ 9–506. Effect of Errors or Omissions.

(a) A financing statement substantially satisfying the requirements of this part is effective, even if it has minor errors or omissions, unless the errors or omissions make the financing statement seriously misleading.

(b) Except as otherwise provided in subsection (c), a financing statement that fails sufficiently to provide the name of the debtor in accordance with Section 9–503(a) is seriously misleading.

(c) If a search of the records of the filing office under the debtor's correct name, using the filing office's standard search logic, if any, would disclose a financing statement that fails sufficiently to provide the name of the debtor in accordance with Section 9–503(a), the name provided does not make the financing statement seriously misleading.

(d) For purposes of Section 9–508(b), the "debtor's correct name" in subsection (c) means the correct name of the new debtor.

. . .

§ 9–509. Persons Entitled to File a Record.

(a) A person may file an initial financing statement, amendment that adds collateral covered by a financing statement, or amendment that adds a debtor to a financing statement only if:

(1) the debtor authorizes the filing in an authenticated record or pursuant to subsection (b) or (c); or

(2) the person holds an agricultural lien that has become effective at the time of filing and the financing statement covers only collateral in which the person holds an agricultural lien.

(b) By authenticating or becoming bound as debtor by a security agreement, a debtor or new debtor authorizes the filing of an initial financing statement, and an amendment, covering:

(1) the collateral described in the security agreement; and

(2) property that becomes collateral under Section 9–315(a)(2), whether or not the security agreement expressly covers proceeds.

(c) By acquiring collateral in which a security interest or agricultural lien continues under Section 9–315(a)(1), a debtor authorizes the filing of an initial financing statement, and an amendment, covering the collateral and property that becomes collateral under Section 9–315(a)(2).

(d) A person may file an amendment other than an amendment that adds collateral covered by a financing statement or an amendment that adds a debtor to a financing statement only if:

(1) the secured party of record authorizes the filing; or

(2) the amendment is a termination statement for a financing statement as to which the secured party of record has failed to file or send a

termination statement as required by Section 9–513(a) or (c), the debtor authorizes the filing, and the termination statement indicates that the debtor authorized it to be filed.

(e) If there is more than one secured party of record for a financing statement, each secured party of record may authorize the filing of an amendment under subsection (d).

§ 9–510. Effectiveness of Filed Record.

(a) A filed record is effective only to the extent that it was filed by a person that may file it under Section 9–509.

(b) A record authorized by one secured party of record does not affect the financing statement with respect to another secured party of record.

(c) A continuation statement that is not filed within the six-month period prescribed by Section 9–515(d) is ineffective.

§ 9–511. Secured Party of Record.

(a) A secured party of record with respect to a financing statement is a person whose name is provided as the name of the secured party or a representative of the secured party in an initial financing statement that has been filed. If an initial financing statement is filed under Section 9–514(a), the assignee named in the initial financing statement is the secured party of record with respect to the financing statement.

(b) If an amendment of a financing statement which provides the name of a person as a secured party or a representative of a secured party is filed, the person named in the amendment is a secured party of record. If an amendment is filed under Section 9–514(b), the assignee named in the amendment is a secured party of record.

(c) A person remains a secured party of record until the filing of an amendment of the financing statement which deletes the person.

§ 9–512. Amendment of Financing Statement.

[Alternative A]

(a) Subject to Section 9–509, a person may add or delete collateral covered by, continue or terminate the effectiveness of, or, subject to subsection (e), otherwise amend the information provided in, a financing statement by filing an amendment that:

(1) identifies, by its file number, the initial financing statement to which the amendment relates; and

(2) if the amendment relates to an initial financing statement filed [or recorded] in a filing office described in Section 9–501(a)(1), provides the information specified in Section 9–502(b).

[Alternative B]

(a) Subject to Section 9–509, a person may add or delete collateral covered by, continue or terminate the effectiveness of, or, subject to subsection (e), otherwise amend the information provided in, a financing statement by filing an amendment that:

(1) identifies, by its file number, the initial financing statement to which the amendment relates; and

(2) if the amendment relates to an initial financing statement filed [or recorded] in a filing office described in Section 9–501(a)(1), provides the date [and time] that the initial financing statement was filed [or recorded] and the information specified in Section 9–502(b).

[End of Alternatives]

(b) Except as otherwise provided in Section 9–515, the filing of an amendment does not extend the period of effectiveness of the financing statement.

(c) A financing statement that is amended by an amendment that adds collateral is effective as to the added collateral only from the date of the filing of the amendment.

(d) A financing statement that is amended by an amendment that adds a debtor is effective as to the added debtor only from the date of the filing of the amendment.

(e) An amendment is ineffective to the extent it:

(1) purports to delete all debtors and fails to provide the name of a debtor to be covered by the financing statement; or

(2) purports to delete all secured parties of record and fails to provide the name of a new secured party of record.

§ 9–513. Termination Statement.

(a) A secured party shall cause the secured party of record for a financing statement to file a termination statement for the financing statement if the financing statement covers consumer goods and:

(1) there is no obligation secured by the collateral covered by the financing statement and no commitment to make an advance, incur an obligation, or otherwise give value; or

(2) the debtor did not authorize the filing of the initial financing statement.

(b) To comply with subsection (a), a secured party shall cause the secured party of record to file the termination statement:

(1) within one month after there is no obligation secured by the collateral covered by the financing statement and no commitment to make an advance, incur an obligation, or otherwise give value; or

(2) if earlier, within 20 days after the secured party receives an authenticated demand from a debtor.

(c) In cases not governed by subsection (a), within 20 days after a secured party receives an authenticated demand from a debtor, the secured party shall cause the secured party of record for a financing statement to send to the debtor a termination statement for the financing statement or file the termination statement in the filing office if:

(1) except in the case of a financing statement covering accounts or chattel paper that has been sold or goods that are the subject of a consignment, there is no obligation secured by the collateral covered by the financing statement and no commitment to make an advance, incur an obligation, or otherwise give value;

(2) the financing statement covers accounts or chattel paper that has been sold but as to which the account debtor or other person obligated has discharged its obligation;

(3) the financing statement covers goods that were the subject of a consignment to the debtor but are not in the debtor's possession; or

(4) the debtor did not authorize the filing of the initial financing statement.

(d) Except as otherwise provided in Section 9–510, upon the filing of a termination statement with the filing office, the financing statement to which the termination statement relates ceases to be effective. Except as otherwise provided in Section 9–510, for purposes of Sections 9–519(g), 9–522(a), and 9–523(c), the filing with the filing office of a termination statement relating to a financing statement that indicates that the debtor is a transmitting utility also causes the effectiveness of the financing statement to lapse.

. . .

§ 9–515. Duration and Effectiveness of Financing Statement; Effect of Lapsed Financing Statement.

(a) Except as otherwise provided in subsections (b), (e), (f), and (g), a filed financing statement is effective for a period of five years after the date of filing.

(b) Except as otherwise provided in subsections (e), (f), and (g), an initial financing statement filed in connection with a public-finance transaction or manufactured-home transaction is effective for a period of 30 years after the date of filing if it indicates that it is filed in connection with a public-finance transaction or manufactured-home transaction.

(c) The effectiveness of a filed financing statement lapses on the expiration of the period of its effectiveness unless before the lapse a continuation statement is filed pursuant to subsection (d). Upon lapse, a financing statement ceases to be effective and any security interest or agricultural lien that was perfected by the financing statement becomes unperfected, unless the security interest is perfected otherwise. If the security interest or agricultural lien becomes unperfected upon lapse, it is deemed never to have been perfected as against a purchaser of the collateral for value.

(d) A continuation statement may be filed only within six months before the expiration of the five-year period specified in subsection (a) or the 30-year period specified in sub-section (b), whichever is applicable.

(e) Except as otherwise provided in Section 9–510, upon timely filing of a continuation statement, the effectiveness of the initial financing statement continues for a period of five years commencing on the day on which the financing statement would have become ineffective in the absence of the filing. Upon the expiration of the five-year period, the financing statement lapses in the same manner as provided in subsection (c), unless, before the lapse, another continuation statement is filed pursuant to subsection (d). Succeeding continuation statements may be filed in the same manner to continue the effectiveness of the initial financing statement.

(f) If a debtor is a transmitting utility and a filed financing statement so indicates, the financing statement is effective until a termination statement is filed.

(g) A record of a mortgage that is effective as a financing statement filed as a fixture filing under Section 9–502(c) remains effective as a financing statement filed as a fixture filing until the mortgage is released or satisfied of record or its effectiveness otherwise terminates as to the real property.

§ 9–516. *What Constitutes Filing; Effectiveness of Filing.*

(a) Except as otherwise provided in subsection (b), communication of a record to a filing office and tender of the filing fee or acceptance of the record by the filing office constitutes filing.

(b) Filing does not occur with respect to a record that a filing office refuses to accept because:

(1) the record is not communicated by a method or medium of communication authorized by the filing office;

(2) an amount equal to or greater than the applicable filing fee is not tendered;

(3) the filing office is unable to index the record because:

(A) in the case of an initial financing statement, the record does not provide a name for the debtor;

(B) in the case of an amendment or correction statement, the record:

(i) does not identify the initial financing statement as required by Section 9–512 or 9–518, as applicable; or

(ii) identifies an initial financing statement whose effectiveness has lapsed under Section 9–515;

(C) in the case of an initial financing statement that provides the name of a debtor identified as an individual or an amendment that provides a name of a debtor identified as an individual which was not previously provided in the financing statement to which the record relates, the record does not identify the debtor's last name; or

(D) in the case of a record filed [or recorded] in the filing office described in Section 9–501(a)(1), the record does not provide a sufficient description of the real property to which it relates;

(4) in the case of an initial financing statement or an amendment that adds a secured party of record, the record does not provide a name and mailing address for the secured party of record;

(5) in the case of an initial financing statement or an amendment that provides a name of a debtor which was not previously provided in the financing statement to which the amendment relates, the record does not:

(A) provide a mailing address for the debtor;

(B) indicate whether the debtor is an individual or an organization; or

(C) if the financing statement indicates that the debtor is an organization, provide:

(i) a type of organization for the debtor;

(ii) a jurisdiction of organization for the debtor; or

(iii) an organizational identification number for the debtor or indicate that the debtor has none;

(6) in the case of an assignment reflected in an initial financing statement under Section 9–514(a) or an amendment filed under Section 9–514(b), the record does not provide a name and mailing address for the assignee; or

(7) in the case of a continuation statement, the record is not filed within the six-month period prescribed by Section 9–515(d).

(c) For purposes of subsection (b):

(1) a record does not provide information if the filing office is unable to read or decipher the information; and

(2) a record that does not indicate that it is an amendment or identify an initial financing statement to which it relates, as required by Section 9–512, 9–514, or 9–518, is an initial financing statement.

(d) A record that is communicated to the filing office with tender of the filing fee, but which the filing office refuses to accept for a reason other than one set forth in subsection (b), is effective as a filed record except as against a purchaser of the collateral which gives value in reasonable reliance upon the absence of the record from the files.

§ 9–517. Effect of Indexing Errors.

The failure of the filing office to index a record correctly does not affect the effectiveness of the filed record.

§ 9–518. Claim Concerning Inaccurate or Wrongfully Filed Record.

(a) A person may file in the filing office a correction statement with respect to a record indexed there under the person's name if the person believes that the record is inaccurate or was wrongfully filed.

[Alternative A]

(b) A correction statement must:

(1) identify the record to which it relates by the file number assigned to the initial financing statement to which the record relates;

(2) indicate that it is a correction statement; and

(3) provide the basis for the person's belief that the record is inaccurate and indicate the manner in which the person believes the record should be amended to cure any inaccuracy or provide the basis for the person's belief that the record was wrongfully filed.

[Alternative B]

(b) A correction statement must:

(1) identify the record to which it relates by:

(A) the file number assigned to the initial financing statement to which the record relates; and

(B) if the correction statement relates to a record filed [or recorded] in a filing office described in Section 9–501(a)(1), the date [and time] that the initial financing statement was filed [or recorded] and the information specified in Section 9–502(b);

(2) indicate that it is a correction statement; and

(3) provide the basis for the person's belief that the record is inaccurate and indicate the manner in which the person believes the record should be amended to cure any inaccuracy or provide the basis for the person's belief that the record was wrongfully filed.

[End of Alternatives]

(c) The filing of a correction statement does not affect the effectiveness of an initial financing statement or other filed record.

. . .

§ 9–521. *Uniform Form of Written Financing Statement and Amendment.*

(a) A filing office that accepts written records may not refuse to accept a written initial financing statement in the following form and format except for a reason set forth in Section 9–516(b): [NATIONAL UCC FINANCING STATEMENT (FORM UCC)(REV. 7/29/98)]

[NATIONAL UCC FINANCING STATEMENT ADDENDUM (FORM UCC 1Ad)(REV. 07/29/98)]

(b) A filing office that accepts written records may not refuse to accept a written record in the following form and format except for a reason set forth in Section 9–516(b):

[NATIONAL UCC FINANCING STATEMENT AMENDMENT (FORM UCC)(REV. 07/29/98)]

[NATIONAL UCC FINANCING STATEMENT AMENDMENT ADDENDUM (FORM UCC3Ad)(REV. 07/29/98)]

Appendix C

The Sherman Act
15 U.S.C. § 1 et seq. (Excerpts)

§ 1. TRUSTS, ETC., IN RESTRAINT OF TRADE ILLEGAL; PENALTY

Every contract, combination in the form of trust or otherwise, or conspiracy, in restraint of trade or commerce among the several States, or with foreign nations, is hereby declared to be illegal. Every person who shall make any contract or engage in any combination or conspiracy hereby declared to be illegal shall be deemed guilty of a felony, and, on conviction thereof, shall be punished by fine not exceeding $10,000,000 if a corporation, or, if any other person, $350,000, or by imprisonment not exceeding three years, or by both said punishments, in the discretion of the court.

§ 2. MONOPOLIZATION; PENALTY

Every person who shall monopolize, or attempt to monopolize, or combine or conspire with any other person or persons, to monopolize any part of the trade or commerce among the several States, or with foreign nations, shall be deemed guilty of a felony, and, on conviction thereof, shall be punished by fine not exceeding $10,000,000 if a corporation, or, if any other person, $350,000, or by imprisonment not exceeding three years, or by both said punishments, in the discretion of the court.

Appendix D

The Fair Housing Act
42 U.S.C. § 3601 et seq.
(Excerpts)

§ 3601. DECLARATION OF POLICY

It is the policy of the United States to provide, within constitutional limitations, for fair housing throughout the United States.

§ 3602. DEFINITIONS

As used in this title—

(a) Secretary" means the Secretary of Housing and Urban Development.

(b) "Dwelling" means any building, structure, or portion thereof which is occupied as, or designed or intended for occupancy as, a residence by one or more families, and any vacant land which is offered for sale or lease for the construction or location thereon of any such building, structure, or portion thereof.

(c) "Family" includes a single individual.

(d) "Person" includes one or more individuals, corporations, partnerships, associations, labor organizations, legal representatives, mutual companies, joint-stock companies, trusts, unincorporated organizations, trustees, trustees in cases under Title 11, receivers, and fiduciaries.

(e) "To rent" includes to lease, to sublease, to let and otherwise to grant for a consideration the right to occupy premises not owned by the occupant.

(f) "Discrimatory housing practice" means an act that is unlawful under section 3604, 3605, 3606, or 3617.

(h) "Handicap" means, with respect to a person—

   (1) a physical or mental impairment which substantially limits one or more of such person's major life activities,

   (2) a record of having such an impairment, or

   (3) being regarded as having such an impairment, but such term does not include current, illegal use of or addiction to a controlled substance (as defined in section 802 (of Title 21).

(i) "Aggrieved person" includes any person who—

   (1) claims to have been injured by a discriminatory housing practice or

   (2) believes that such a person will be injured by a discriminatory housing practice that is about to occur.

(j) "Complainant" means the person (including the Secretary) who files a complaint under section 3610 of this title.

(k) "Familial status" means one or more individuals (who have not attained the age of 18 years) being domiciled with—

   (1) a parent or another person having legal custody of such individual or individuals; or

   (2) the designee of such parent or other person having such custody, with the written permission of such parent or other person.

The protections afforded against discrimination on the basis of familial status shall apply to any person who is pregnant or is in the process of securing legal custody of any individual who has not attained the age of 18 years.

(l) "Conciliation" means the attempted resolution of issues raised by a complaint, or by the investigation of such complaint, through informal negotiations involving the aggrieved person, the respondent, and the Secretary.

(m) "Conciliation agreement" means a written agreement setting forth the resolution of the issues in conciliation.

(n) "Respondent" means—

   (1) the person or other entity accused in a complaint of an unfair housing practice; and

   (2) any other person or entity identified in the course of investigation and notified as required with respect to respondents so identified under section 3610(a) of this title.

(o) "Prevailing party" has the same meaning as such term has in section 1988 of this title.

§ 3603. EFFECTIVE DATES OF CERTAIN PROHIBITIONS

(a) Application to certain described dwellings. Subject to the provisions of subsection (b) and section § 3607 of this title, the prohibitions against discrimination in the sale or rental of housing set forth in section 3604 shall apply:

   (1) Upon enactment of this subchapter to—

       (A) dwellings owned or operated by the Federal Government;

(B) dwellings provided in whole or in part with the aid of loans, advances, grants, or contributions made by the Federal Government, under agreements entered into after November 20, 1962, unless payment due thereon has been made in full prior to April 11, 1968;

(C) dwellings provided in whole or in part by loans insured, guaranteed, or otherwise secured by the credit of the Federal Government, under agreements entered into after November 20, 1962, unless payment thereon has been made in full prior to April 11, 1968: *Provided,* That nothing contained in subparagraphs (B) and (C) of this subsection shall be applicable to dwellings solely by virtue of the fact that they are subject to mortgages held by an FDIC or FSLIC institution; and

(D) dwellings provided by the development or the redevelopment of real property purchased, rented, or otherwise obtained from a State or local public agency receiving Federal financial assistance for slum clearance or urban renewal with respect to such real property under loan or grant contracts entered into after November 20, 1962.

(2) After December 31, 1968, to all dwellings covered by paragraph (1) and to all other dwellings except as exempted by subsection (b) of this section.

(b) **Exemptions. Nothing in section 3604 (other than subsection (c)) shall apply to—**

(1) any single-family house sold or rented by an owner: *Provided,* That such private individual owner does not own more than three such single-family houses at any one time: *Provided further,* That in the case of the sale of any such single-family house by a private individual owner not residing in such house at the time of such sale or who was not the most recent resident of such house prior to such sale, the exemption granted by this subsection shall apply only with respect to one such sale within any twenty-four month period; *Provided further,* That such bona fide private individual owner does not own any interest in, nor is there owned or reserved in his behalf, under any express or voluntary agreement, title to or any right to all or a portion of the proceeds from the sale or rental of, more than three such single-family houses at any one time: *Provided further,* That after December 31, 1969, the sale or rental of any such single-family house shall be excepted from the application of this title only if such house is sold or rented (A) without the use in any manner of the sales or rental facilities or the sales or rental services of any real estate broker, agent, or salesman, or of such facilities or services of any person in the business of selling or renting dwellings, or of any employee or agent **of** any such broker, agent, salesman, or person and (B) without the publication, posting or mailing, after notice, of any advertisement or written notice in violation of section §3604(c) of this title; but nothing in this proviso shall prohibit the use of attorneys, escrow agents, abstractors, title companies, and other such professional assistance as necessary to perfect or transfer the title, or

(2) rooms or units in dwellings containing living quarters occupied or intended to be occupied by no more than four families living independently of each other, if the owner actually maintains and occupies one of such living quarters as his residence.

(c) **Business of selling or renting dwellings defined.** For the purposes of subsection (b) of this section, a person shall be deemed to be in the business of selling or renting dwellings if—

    (1) he has, within the preceding twelve months, participated as principal in three or more transactions involving the sale or rental of any dwelling or any interest therein, or

    (2) he has, within the preceding twelve months, participated as agent, other than in the sale of his own personal residence in providing sales or rental facilities or sales or rental services in two or more transactions involving the sale or rental of any dwelling or any interest therein, or

    (3) he is the owner of any dwelling designed or intended for occupancy by, or occupied by, five or more families.

§ 3604. DISCRIMINATION IN THE SALE OR RENTAL OF HOUSING AND OTHER PROHIBITED PRACTICES

[It shall be unlawful]:

(a) To refuse to sell or rent after the making of a bona fide offer, or to refuse to negotiate for the sale or rental of, or otherwise make unavailable or deny, a dwelling to any person because of race, color, religion, sex, familial status, or national origin.

(b) To discriminate against any person in the terms, conditioning, or privileges of sale or rental of a dwelling, or in the provision of services or facilities in connection therewith, because of race, color, religion, sex, familial status, or national origin.

(c) To make, print, or publish, or cause to be made, printed, or published any notice, statement, or advertisement, with respect to the sale or rental of a dwelling that indicates any preference, limitation, or discrimination based on race, color, religion, sex, handicap, familial status, or national origin, or an intention to make any such preference, limitation, or discrimination.

(d) To represent to any person because of race, color, religion, sex, handicap, familial status, or national origin that any dwelling is not available for inspection, sale, or rental when such dwelling is in fact so available.

(e) For profit, to induce or attempt to induce any person to sell or rent any dwelling by representations regarding the entry or prospective entry into the neighborhood of a person or persons of a particular race, color, religion, sex, handicap, familial status, or national origin.

(f) (1) To discriminate in the sale or rental, or to otherwise make unavailable or deny, a dwelling to any buyer or renter because of a handicap of—

        (A) that buyer or renter,

        (B) a person residing in or intending to reside in that dwelling after it is so sold, rented, or made available; or

        (C) any person associated with that buyer or renter.

    (2) To discriminate against any person in the terms, conditions, or privileges of sale or rental of a dwelling, or in the provision of services or facilities in connection with such dwelling, because of a handicap of—

(A) that person; or

(B) a person residing in or intending to reside in that dwelling after it is so sold, rented, or made available; or

(C) any person associated with that person.

(3) For purposes of this subsection, discrimination includes—

(A) a refusal to permit, at the expense of the handicapped person, reasonable modifications of existing premises occupied or to be occupied by such person if such modifications may be necessary to afford such person full enjoyment of the premises except that, in the case of a rental, the landlord may where it is reasonable to do so condition permission for a modification on the renter agreeing to restore the interior of the premises to the condition that existed before the modification, reasonable wear and tear excepted;

(B) a refusal to make reasonable accommodations in rules, policies, practices, or services, when such accommodations may be necessary to afford such person equal opportunity to use and enjoy a dwelling; or

(C) in connection with the design and construction of covered multifamily dwellings for first occupancy after the date that is 30 months after Sept. 13, 1988, a failure to design and construct those dwellings in such a manner that—

(i) the public use and common use portions of such dwellings are readily accessible to and usable by handicapped persons;

(ii) all the doors designed to allow passage into and within all premises within such dwellings are sufficiently wide to allow passage by handicapped persons in wheelchairs; and

(iii) all premises within such dwellings contain the following features of adaptive design:

(I) an accessible route into and through the dwelling;

(II) light switches, electrical outlets, thermostats, and other environmental controls in accessible locations;

(III) reinforcements in bathroom walls to allow later installation of grab bars; and

(IV) usable kitchens and bathrooms such that an individual in a wheelchair can maneuver about the space.

(4) Compliance with the appropriate requirements of the American National Standard for buildings and facilities providing accessibility and usability for physically handicapped people (commonly cited as "ANSI A117.1") suffices to satisfy the requirements of paragraph (3)(C)(iii).

(5) (A) If a State or unit of general local government has incorporated into its laws the requirements set forth in paragraph (3)(C), compliance with such laws shall be deemed to satisfy the requirements of that paragraph.

§ 3605. DISCRIMINATION IN RESIDENTIAL REAL ESTATE RELATED TRANSACTIONS

(a) **In general.** It shall be unlawful for any person or other entity whose business includes engaging in residential real estate-related transactions to discriminate against any person in making available such a transaction, or in the terms or conditions of such a transaction, because of race, color, religion, sex, handicap, familial status, or national origin.

(b) **Definition.** As used in this section, the term "residential real estate-related transaction" means any of the following:

    (1) The making or purchasing of loans or providing other financial assistance—

        (A) for purchasing, constructing, improving, repairing, or maintaining a dwelling; or

        (B) secured by residential real estate.

    (2) The selling, brokering, or appraising of residential real property.

(c) **Appraisal exemption.** Nothing in this title prohibits a person engaged in the business of furnishing appraisals of real property to take into consideration factors other than race, color, religion, national origin, sex, handicap, or familial status.

§ 3606. DISCRIMINATION IN THE PROVISION OF BROKERAGE SERVICES

After December 31, 1968, it shall be unlawful to deny any person access to or membership or participation in any multiple-listing service, real estate brokers' organization or other service, organization, or facility relating to the business of selling or renting dwellings, or to discriminate against him in the terms or conditions of such access, membership, or participation, on account of race, color, religion, sex, handicap, familial status, or national origin.

§ 3607. EXEMPTION

(a) Religious organizations and private clubs   Nothing in this subchapter shall prohibit a religious organization, association, or society, or any nonprofit institution or organization operated, supervised or controlled by or in conjunction with a religious organization, association, or society, from limiting the sale, rental or occupancy of dwellings which it owns or operates for other than a commercial purpose to persons of the same religion, or from giving preference to such persons, unless membership in such religion is restricted on account of race, color, or national origin. Nor shall anything in this title prohibit a private club not in fact open to the public, which as an incident to its primary purpose or purposes provides lodgings which it owns or operates for other than a commercial purpose, from limiting the rental or occupancy of such lodgings to its members or from giving preference to its members.

(b) Numbers of occupants; housing for older persons; persons convicted of making or distributing controlled substances

    (1) Nothing in this subchapter limits the applicability of any reasonable local, State, or Federal restrictions regarding the maximum number of occupants permitted to occupy a dwelling. Nor does any provision in this title regarding familial status apply with respect to housing for older persons.

(ii) the housing facility or community publishes and adheres to policies and procedures that demonstrate the intent required under this subparagraph; and

(iii) the housing facility or community complies with rules issued by the Secretary for verification of occupancy, which shall—

(I) provide for verification by reliable surveys and affidavits; and

(II) include examples of the types of policies and procedures relevant to a determination of compliance with the requirement of clause (ii). Such surveys and affidavits shall be admissible in administrative and judicial proceedings for the purposes of such verification.

(2) As used in this section, "housing for older persons" means housing—

(A) provided under any State or Federal program that the Secretary determines is specifically designed and operated to assist elderly persons (as defined in the State or Federal program); or

(B) intended for, and solely occupied by, persons 62 years of age or older; or

(C) intended and operated for occupancy by persons 55 years of age or older, and

(i) at least 80 percent of the occupied units are occupied by at least one person 55 years of age or older; and

(iii) the publication of, and adherence to, policies and procedures which demonstrate an intent by the owner or manager to provide housing for persons 55 years of age or older.

(3) Housing shall not fail to meet the requirements for housing for older persons by reason of:

(A) persons residing in such housing as of the date of enactment of this Act who do not meet the age requirements of subsections (2)(B) or (C): *Provided,* That new occupants of such housing meet the age requirements of subsections (2)(B) or (C); or

(B) unoccupied units: *Provided,* That such units are reserved for occupancy by persons who meet the age requirements of subsections (2)(B) or (C).

(4) Nothing in this title prohibits conduct against a person because such person has been convicted by any court of competent jurisdiction of the illegal manufacture or distribution of a controlled substance as defined in section 102 of the Controlled Substances Act (21 U.S.C. 802).

(5) (A) A person shall not be held personally liable for monetary damages for a violation of this chapter if such person reasonably relied, in good faith, on the application of the exemption under this subsection relating to housing for older persons.

(B) For the purposes of this paragraph, a person may only show good faith reliance on the application of the exemption by showing that—

(i) such person has no actual knowledge that the facility or community is not, or will not be, eligible for such exemption; and

(ii) the facility or community has stated formally in writing, that the facility or community complies with the requirements for such exemption.

§ 3613. ENFORCEMENT BY PRIVATE PERSONS

(a) **Civil action.**

   (1) (A) An aggrieved person may commence a civil action in an appropriate United States district court or State court not later than 2 years after the occurrence or the termination of an alleged discrimatory housing practice, or the breach of a conciliation agreement entered into under this title, whichever occurs last, to obtain appropriate relief with respect to such discriminatory housing practice or breach.

      (B) The computation of such 2-year period shall not include any time during which an administrative proceeding under this title was pending with respect to a complaint or charge under this title based upon such discriminatory housing practice. This subparagraph does not apply to actions arising from a breach of a conciliation agreement.

   (2) An aggrieved person may commence a civil action under this subsection whether or not a complaint has been filed under section 3610(a) of this title and without regard to the status of any such complaint, but if the Secretary or a State or local agency has obtained a conciliation agreement with the consent of an aggrieved person, no action may be filed under this subsection by such aggrieved person with respect to the alleged discriminatory housing practice which forms the basis for such complaint except for the purpose of enforcing the terms of such an agreement.

   (3) An aggrieved person may not commence a civil action under this subsection with respect to an alleged discriminatory housing practice which forms the basis of a charge issued by the Secretary if an administrative law judge has commenced a hearing on the record under this title with respect to such charge.

(b) **Appointment of attorney by court.** Upon application by a person alleging a discrimatory housing practice or a person against whom such a practice is alleged, the court may—

   (1) appoint an attorney for such person; or

   (2) Authorize the commencement or continuation of a civil action under subsection (a) without the payment of fees, costs, or security, if in the opinion of the court such person is financially unable to bear the costs of such action.

(c) **Relief which may be granted.**

   (1) In a civil action under subsection (a) if the court finds that a discriminatory housing practice has occurred or is about to occur, the court may award to the plaintiff actual and punitive damages, and subject to subsection (d), may grant as relief, as the court deems appropriate, any permanent or temporary injunction, temporary restraining order, or other order (including an order enjoining the defendant from engaging in such practice or ordering such affirmative action as may be appropriate).

   (2) In a civil action under subsection (a), the court, in its discretion, may allow the prevailing party, other than the United States, a reasonable attorney's fee and costs. The United States shall be liable for such fees and costs to the same extent as a private person.

(d) **Effect on certain sales, encumbrances, and rentals.**

Relief granted under this section shall not affect any contract, sale, encumbrance, or lease consummated before the granting of such relief and involving a bona fide purchaser, encumbrancer, or tenant, without actual notice of the filing of a complaint with the Secretary or civil action under this title.

(e) **Intervention by Attorney General.**

Upon timely application, the Attorney General may intervene in such civil action, if the Attorney General certifies that the case is of general public importance. Upon such intervention the Attorney General may obtain such relief as would be available to the Attorney General under section 3614(e) of this title in a civil action to which such section applies.

Appendix E

Interstate Land Sales Full Disclosure Act (ILSFDA)
15 U.S.C. § 1701 et seq.
(Excerpts)

§ 1701. DEFINITIONS

For the purposes of this chapter, the term—

(3) "subdivision" means any land which is located in any State or in a foreign country and is divided or is proposed to be divided into lots, whether contiguous or not, for the purpose of sale or lease as part of a common promotional plan;

(4) "common promotion plan" means a plan, undertaken by a single developer or a group of developers acting in concert, to offer lots for sale or lease, where such land is offered for sale by such a developer or group of developers acting in concert, and such land is contiguous or is known, designated, or advertised as a common unit or by a common name, such land shall be presumed, without regard to the number of lots covered by each individual offering, as being offered for sale or lease as part of a common promotional plan;

(5) "developer" means any person who, directly or indirectly, sells or leases, or offers to sell or lease, or advertises for sale or lease any lots in a subdivision;

(6) "agent" means any person who represents, or acts for or on behalf of, a developer in selling or leasing, or offering to sell or lease, any lot or lots in a subdivision; but shall not include an attorney at law whose representation of another person consists solely of rendering legal services;

(10) "purchaser" means an actual or prospective purchaser or lessee of any lot in a subdivision; and

(11) "offer" includes any inducement, solicitation, or attempt to encourage a person to acquire a lot in a subdivision.

§ 1702. EXEMPTIONS

(a) **Sale or lease of lots generally.** Unless the method of disposition is adopted for the purpose of evasion of this chapter, the provisions of this chapter shall not apply to—

(1) the sale or lease of lots in a subdivision containing less than twenty-five lots;

(2) the sale or lease of any improved land on which there is a residential, commercial, condominium, or industrial building, or the sale or lease of land under a contract obligating the seller or lessor to erect such a building thereon within a period of two years;

(3) the sale of evidences of indebtedness secured by a mortgage or deed of trust on real estate;

(4) the sale of securities issued by a real estate investment trust;

(5) the sale or lease of real estate by any government or government agency;

(6) the sale or lease of cemetery lots;

(7) the sale or lease of lots to any person who acquires such lots for the purpose of engaging in the business of constructing residential, commercial, or industrial buildings or for the purpose of resale or lease of such lots to persons engaged in such business; or

(8) the sale or lease of real estate which is zoned by the appropriate governmental authority for industrial or commercial development or which is restricted to such use by a declaration or covenants, conditions, and restrictions which has been recorded in the official records of the city or county in which such real estate is located, when—

(A) local authorities have approved access from such real estate to a public street or highway;

(B) the purchaser or lessee of such real estate is a duly organized corporation, partnership, trust, or business entity engaged in commercial or industrial business;

(C) the purchaser or lessee of such real estate is represented in the transaction of sale or lease by a representative of its own selection;

(D) the purchaser or lessee of such real estate affirms in writing to the seller or lessor that it either (i) is purchasing or leasing such real estate substantially for its own use, or (ii) has a binding commitment to sell, lease, or sublease such real estate to an entity which meets the requirements of subparagraph (B), is engaged in commercial or industrial business, and is not affiliated with the seller, lessor, or agent thereof; and

(E) a policy of title insurance or a title opinion is issued in connection with the transaction showing that title to the real estate purchased or leased is vested in the seller or lessor, subject only to such exceptions as may be approved in writing by such purchaser or the lessee prior to recordation of the instrument of conveyance or execution of the lease, but (i) nothing herein shall be construed as requiring the recordation of a lease, and (ii) any purchaser or lessee may waive, in writing in a separate document, the requirement of this subparagraph that a policy of title insurance or title opinion be issued in connection with the transaction.

§ 1703. REQUIREMENTS RESPECTING SALE OR LEASE OF LOTS

(a) **Prohibited activities.** It shall be unlawful for any developer or agent, directly or indirectly, to make use of any means or instruments of transportation or communication in interstate commerce, or of the mails—

(1) with respect to the sale or lease of any lot not exempt under section 1702 of this title—

(A) to sell or lease any lot unless a statement of record with respect to such lot is in effect in accordance with section 1706 of this title;

(B) to sell or lease any lot unless a printed property report, meeting the requirements of section 1707 of this title, has been furnished to the purchaser or lessee in advance of the signing of any contract or agreement by such purchaser or lessee;

(C) to sell or lease any lot where any part of the statement of record or the property report contained an untrue statement of a material fact or omitted to state a material fact required to be stated therein pursuant to sections 1704 through 1707 of this title or any regulations thereunder; or

(D) to display or deliver to prospective purchasers or lessees advertising and promotional material which is inconsistent with information required to be disclosed in the property report; or

(2) with respect to the sale or lease, or offer to sell or lease, any lot not exempt under section 1702(a) of this title—

(A) to employ any device, scheme, or artifice to defraud;

(B) to obtain money or property by means or any untrue statement of a material fact, or any omission to state a material fact necessary in order to make the statements made (in light of the circumstances in which they were made and within the context of the overall offer and sale or lease) not misleading, with respect to any information pertinent to the lot or subdivision;

(C) to engage in any transaction, practice, or course of business which operates or would operate as a fraud or deceit upon a purchaser; or

(D) to represent that roads, sewers, water, gas, or electric service, or recreational amenities will be provided or completed by the developer without stipulating in the contract of sale or lease that such services or amenities will be provided or completed.

(b) **Revocation of nonexempt contract or agreement at option of purchaser or lessee; time limit.** Any contract or agreement for the sale or lease of a lot not exempt under section 1702 of this title may be revoked at the option of the purchaser or lessee until midnight of the seventh day following the signing of such contract or agreement or until such later time as may be required pursuant to applicable State laws, and such contract or agreement shall clearly provide this right.

(c) **Revocation of contract or agreement at option of purchaser or lessee where required property report not supplied.** In the case of any contract or agreement for the sale or lease of a lot for which a property report is required by this chapter and the property report has not been given to the purchaser or lessee in advance of his or her signing such contract or agreement, such contract or agreement may be revoked at the option of the purchaser or lessee within two years from the date of such signing, and such contract or agreement shall clearly provide this right.

(e) **Repayment of purchaser or lessee upon revocation of all money paid under contract or agreement to seller or lessor.** If a contract or agreement is revoked pursuant to subsection (b), (c), or (d), if the purchaser or lessee tenders to the seller or lessor (or successor thereof) an instrument conveying his or her rights and interests in the lot, and if the rights and interests and the lot are in a condition which is substantially similar to the condition in which they were conveyed or purported to be conveyed to the purchaser or lessee, such purchaser or lessee shall be entitled to all money paid by him or her under such contract or agreement.

§ 1704. REGISTRATION OF SUBDIVISIONS

(a) **Filing of statement of record.** A subdivision may be registered by filing with the Secretary a statement of record, meeting the requirements of this chapter and such rules and regulations as may be prescribed by the Secretary in furtherance of the provisions of this chapter. A statement of record shall be deemed effective only as to the lots specified therein.

(b) **Payment of fees; use by Secretary.** At the time of filing a statement of record, or any amendment thereto, the developer shall pay to the Secretary a fee, not in excess of $1,000, in accordance with a schedule to be fixed by the regulations of the Secretary.

(c) **Filing deemed to have taken place upon receipt of statement of record accompanied by fee.** The filing with the Secretary of a statement of record, or of an amendment thereto, shall be deemed to have taken place upon the receipt thereof, accompanied by payment of the fee required by subsection (b) of this section.

(d) **Availability of information to public.** The information contained in or filed with any statement of record shall be made available to the public under such regulations as the Secretary may prescribe and copies thereof shall be furnished to every applicant at such reasonable charge as the Secretary may prescribe.

§ 1705. INFORMATION REQUIRED IN STATEMENT OF RECORD

The statement of record shall contain the information and be accompanied by the documents specified hereinafter in this section—

(1) the name and address of each person having an interest in the lots in the subdivision to be covered by the statement of record and the extent of such interest;

(2) a legal description of, and a statement of the total area included in, the subdivision and a statement of the topography thereof, together with a map showing the division proposed and the dimensions of the lots to be covered by the statement of record and their relation to existing streets and roads;

(3) a statement of the condition of the title to the land comprising the subdivision, including all encumbrances and deed restrictions and covenants applicable thereto;

(4) a statement of the general terms and conditions, including the range of selling prices or rents at which it is proposed to dispose of the lots in the subdivision;

(5) a statement of the present condition of access to the subdivision, the existence of any unusual conditions relating to noise or safety which affect the subdivision and are known to the developer, the availability of sewage disposal facilities and other public utilities (including water, electricity, gas, and telephone facilities) in the subdivision, the proximity in miles of the subdivision to nearby municipalities, and the nature of any improvements to be installed by the developer and his estimated schedule for completion;

(6) in the case of any subdivision or portion thereof against which there exists a blanket encumbrance, a statement of the consequences for an individual purchaser of a failure, by the person or persons bound, to fulfill obligations under the instrument or instruments creating such encumbrance and the steps, if any, taken to protect the purchaser in such eventuality;

(7) (A) copy of its articles of incorporation, with all amendments thereto, if the developer is a corporation; (B) copies of all instruments by which the trust is created or declared, if the developer is a trust; (C) copies of its articles of partnership or association and all other papers pertaining to its organization, if the developer is a partnership, unincorporated association, joint stock company, or any other form of organization; and (D) if the purported holder of legal title is a person other than developer, copies of the above documents for such person;

(8) copies of the deed or other instrument establishing title to the subdivision in the developer or other person and copies of any instrument creating a lien or encumbrance upon the title of developer or other person or copies of the opinion or opinions of counsel in respect to the title to the subdivision in the developer or other person or copies of the title insurance policy guaranteeing such title;

(9) copies of all forms of conveyance to be used in selling or leasing lots to purchasers;

(10) copies of instruments creating easements or other restrictions;

(11) such certified and uncertified financial statements of the developer as the Secretary may require; and

(12) such other information and such other documents and certifications as the Secretary may require as being reasonably necessary or appropriate for the protection of purchasers.

§ 1707. INFORMATION REQUIRED IN PROPERTY REPORT; USE FOR PROMOTIONAL PURPOSES

(a) **Contents of report** A property report relating to the lots in a subdivision shall contain such of the information contained in the statement of record, and any amendments thereto, as the Secretary may deem necessary, but need not include the documents referred to in paragraphs (7) to (11), inclusive, of section 1705 of this title. A property report shall also contain such other information as the Secretary may by rules or regulations require as being necessary or appropriate in the public interest or for the protection of purchasers.

(b) **Promotional use** The property report shall not be used for any promotional purposes before the statement of record becomes effective and then only if it is used in its entirety. No person may advertise or represent that the Secretary approves or recommends the subdivision or the sale or lease of lots therein. No portion of the property report shall be underscored, italicized, or printed in larger or bolder type than the balance of the statement unless the Secretary requires or permits it.

§ 1709. CIVIL LIABILITIES

(a) **Violations; relief recoverable** A purchaser or lessee may bring an action at law or in equity against a developer or agent if the sale or lease was made in violation of section 1703 of this title. In a suit authorized by this subsection, the court may order damages, specific performance, or such other relief as the court deems fair, just, and equitable. In determining such relief the court may take into account, but not be limited to, the following factors: the contract price of the lot or leasehold; the amount the purchaser or lessee actually paid; the cost of any improvements to the lot; the fair market value of the lot or leasehold at the time relief is determined; and the fair market value of the lot or leasehold at the time such lot was purchased or leased.

(b) **Enforcement of rights by purchaser or lessee** A purchaser or lessee may bring an action at law or in equity against the seller or lessor (or successor thereof) to enforce any right under subsection (b), (c), (d), or (e) of section 1703 of this title.

(c) **Amounts recoverable** The amount recoverable in a suit authorized by this section may include, in addition to matters specified in subsections (a) and (b), interest, court costs, and reasonable amounts for attorneys' fees, independent appraisers' fees, and travel to and from the lot.

(d) **Contributions** Every person who becomes liable to make any payment under this section may recover contribution as in cases of contract from any person who, if sued separately, would have been liable to make the same payment.

§1717A. CIVIL MONEY PENALTIES

(a) **In general**

    (1) Authority Whenever any person knowingly and materially violates any of the provisions of this chapter or any rule, regulation, or order issued under this chapter, the Secretary may impose a civil money penalty on such person in accordance with the provisions of this section. The penalty shall be in addition to any other available civil remedy or any available criminal penalty, and may be imposed whether or not the Secretary imposes other administrative sanctions.

    (2) Amount of penalty The amount of the penalty, as determined by the Secretary, may not exceed $1,000 for each violation, except that the maximum penalty for all violations by a particular person during any 1-year period shall not exceed $1,000,000. Each violation of this chapter, or any rule, regulation, or order issued under this chapter, shall constitute a separate violation with respect to each sale or lease or offer to sell or lease. In the case of a continuing violation, as determined by the Secretary, each day shall constitute a separate violation.

(b) **Agency procedures**

    (1) Establishment The Secretary shall establish standards and procedures governing the imposition of civil money penalties under subsection (a) of this section. The standards and procedures—

        (A) shall provide for the imposition of a penalty only after a person has been given an opportunity for a hearing on the record; and

        (B) may provide for review by the Secretary of any determination or order, or interlocutory ruling, arising from a hearing.

    (2) Final orders If no hearing is requested within 15 days of receipt of the notice of opportunity for hearing, the imposition of the penalty shall constitute a final and unappealable determination. If the Secretary reviews the determination or order, the Secretary may affirm, modify, or reverse that determination or order. If the Secretary does not review the determination or order within 90 days of the issuance of the determination or order, the determination or order shall be final.

    (3) Factors in determining amount of penalty In determining the amount of a penalty under subsection (a), consideration shall be given to such factors as the gravity of the offense, any history of prior offenses (including offenses occurring before enactment of this section, ability to pay the penalty, injury to the public, benefits received, deterrence of future violations, and such other factors as the Secretary may determine in regulations to be appropriate.

    (4) Reviewability of imposition of penalty The Secretary's determination or order imposing a penalty under subsection (a) of this section shall not be subject to review, except as provided in subsection (c) of this section.

(c) **Judicial review of agency determination**

    (1) In general After exhausting all administrative remedies established by the Secretary under subsection (b)(1), a person aggrieved by a final order of the Secretary assessing a penalty under this section may seek judicial review pursuant to section 1710 of this title.

    (2) Order to pay penalty Notwithstanding any other provision of law, in any such review, the court shall have the power to order payment of the penalty imposed by the Secretary.

(d) **Action to collect penalty** If any person fails to comply with the determination or order of the Secretary imposing a civil money penalty under subsection (a), after the determination or order is no longer subject to review as provided by subsections (b) and (c), the Secretary may request the Attorney General of the United States to bring an action in any appropriate United States district court to obtain a monetary judgment against the person and such other relief as may be available. The monetary judgment may, in the discretion of the court, include any attorneys fees and other expenses incurred by the United States in connection with the action. In an action under this subsection, the validity and appropriateness of the Secretary's determination or order imposing the penalty shall not be subject to review.

(e) **Settlement by Secretary** The Secretary may compromise, modify, or remit any civil money penalty which may be, or has been, imposed under this section.

(f) **Definition of knowingly** The term "knowingly" means having actual knowledge of or acting with deliberate ignorance of or reckless disregard for the prohibitions under this section.

(g) **Regulations** The Secretary shall issue such regulations as the Secretary deems appropriate to implement this section.

(h) **Use of penalties for administration** Civil money penalties collected under this section shall be paid to the Secretary and, upon approval in an appropriation Act, may be used by the Secretary to cover all or part of the cost of rendering services under this chapter.

Appendix F

Truth-in-Lending Act
15 U.S.C. § 1601 et seq.
(Excerpts)

§1637A. DISCLOSURE REQUIREMENTS FOR OPEN END CONSUMER CREDIT PLANS SECURED BY THE CONSUMER'S PRINCIPAL DWELLING

(a) **Application disclosures.** In the case of any open end consumer credit plan which provides for any extension of credit which is secured by the consumer's principal dwelling, the creditor shall make the following disclosures in accordance with subsection (b):

    (1) Fixed annual percentage rate. Each annual percentage rate imposed in connection with extensions of credit under the plan and a statement that such rate does not include costs other than interest.

    (2) Variable percentage rate. In the case of a plan which provides for variable rates of interest on credit extended under the plan—

        (A) a description of the manner in which such rate will be computed and a statement that such rate does not include costs other than interest;

        (B) a description of the manner in which any changes in the annual percentage rate will be made, including—

            (i)   any negative amortization and interest rate carryover;

            (ii) the timing of any such changes;

(iii) any index or margin to which such changes in the rate are related; and

(iv) a source of information about any such index;

(C) if an initial annual percentage rate is offered which is not based on an index—

(i)   a statement of such rate and the period of time such initial rate will be in effect; and

(ii) a statement that such rate does not include costs other than interest;

(D) a statement that the consumer should ask about the current index value and interest rate.

(E) a statement of the maximum amount by which the annual percentage rate may change in any 1-year period or a statement that no such limit exists;

(F) a statement of the maximum annual percentage rate that may be imposed at any time under the plan;

(G) subject to subsection (b)(3), a table, based on a $10,000 extension of credit, showing how the annual percentage rate and the minimum periodic payment amount under each repayment option of the plan would have been affected during the preceding 15-year period by changes in any index used to compute such rate;

(H) a statement of—

(i)   the maximum annual percentage rate which may be imposed under each repayment option of the plan;

(ii) the minimum amount of any periodic payment which may be required, based on a $10,000 outstanding balance, under each such option when such maximum annual percentage rate is in effect; and

(iii) the earliest date by which such maximum annual interest rate may be imposed; and (I) a statement that interest rate information will be provided on or with each periodic statement.

(3) Other fees imposed by the creditor. An itemization of any fees imposed by the creditor in connection with the availability or use of credit under such plan, including annual fees, application fees, transactions fees, and closing costs (including costs commonly described "points"), and the time when such fees are payable.

(4) Estimates of fees which may be imposed by third parties.

(A) Aggregate amount. An estimate, based on the creditor's experience with such plans and stated as a single amount or as a reasonable range, of the aggregate amount of additional fees that may be imposed by third parties (such as governmental authorities, appraisers, and attorneys) in connection with opening an account under the plan.

(B) Statement of availability. A statement that the consumer may ask the creditor for a good faith estimate by the creditor of the fees that may be imposed by third parties.

(5) Statement of risk of loss of dwelling. A statement that—

   (A) any extension of credit under the plan is secured by the consumer's dwelling; and

   (B) in the event of any default, the consumer risks the loss of the dwelling.

(6) Conditions to which disclosed terms are subject.

   (A) Period during which such terms are available. A clear and conspicuous statement—

      (i) of the time by which an application must be submitted to obtain the terms disclosed; or

      (ii) if applicable, that the terms are subject to change.

   (B) Right of refusal if certain terms change. A statement that—

      (i) the consumer may elect not to enter into an agreement to open an account under the plan if any term changes (other than a change contemplated by a variable feature of the plan) before any such agreement is final; and

      (ii) if the consumer makes an election described in clause (i), the consumer is entitled to a refund of all fees paid in connection with the application.

   (C) Retention of information. A statement that the consumer should make or otherwise retain a copy of information disclosed under this subparagraph.

(7) Rights of creditor with respect to extensions of credit. A statement that—

   (A) Under certain conditions, the creditor may terminate any account under the plan and require immediate repayment of any outstanding balance, prohibit any additional extension of credit to the account, or reduce the credit limit applicable to the account; and

   (B) the consumer may receive, upon request, more specific information about the conditions under which the creditor may take any action described in subparagraph (A).

(8) Repayment options and minimum periodic payments. The repayment options under the plan, including—

   (A) if applicable, any differences in repayment options with regard to—

      (i) any period during which additional extensions of credit may be obtained; and

      (ii) any period during which repayment is required to be made and no additional extensions of credit may be obtained;

   (B) the length of any repayment period, including any differences in the length of any repayment period with regard to the periods described in clauses (i) and (ii) of subparagraph (A); and

   (C) an explanation of how the amount of any minimum monthly or periodic payment will be determined under each such option, including any differences in the determination of any such amount with regard to the periods described in clauses (i) and (ii) of subparagraph (A).

(9) Example of minimum payments and maximum repayment period. An example, based on a $10,000 outstanding balance and the interest rate (other than a rate not based on the index under the plan) which is, or was recently, in effect under such plan, showing the minimum monthly or periodic payment, and the time it would take to repay the entire $10,000 if the consumer paid only the minimum periodic payments and obtained no additional extensions of credit.

(10) Statement concerning balloon payments. If, under any repayment option of the plan, the payment of not more than the minimum periodic payments required under such option over the length of the repayment period—

    (A) would not repay any of the principal balance; or

    (B) would repay less than the outstanding balance by the end of such period, as the case may be, a statement of fact, including an explicit statement that at the end of such repayment period a balloon payment (as defined in section 147(f) [15 USCS §1665b(f)] would result which would be required to be paid in full at that time.

(11) Negative amortization. If applicable, a statement that—

    (A) any limitation in the plan on the amount of any increase in the minimum payments may result in negative amortization;

    (B) negative amortization increases the outstanding principal balance of the account; and

    (C) negative amortization reduces the consumer's equity in the consumer's dwelling.

(12) Limitations and minimum amount requirements on extensions of credit.

    (A) Number and dollar amount limitations. Any limitation contained in the plan on the number of extensions of credit and the amount of credit which may be obtained during any month or other defined time period.

    (B) Minimum balance and other transaction amount requirements. Any requirement which establishes a minimum amount for—

        (i)   the initial extension of credit to an account under the plan;

        (ii) any subsequent extension of credit to an account under the plan; or

        (iii) any outstanding balance of an account under the plan.

(13) Statement regarding consultation of tax advisor. A statement that the consumer should consult a tax advisor regarding the deductibility of interest and charges under the plan.

(14) Disclosure requirements established by board. Any other term which the Board requires, in regulations, to be disclosed.

(b) **Time and form of disclosures.**

    (1) Time of disclosure

        (A) In general. The disclosures required under subsection (a) with respect to any open end consumer credit plan which provides for any extension of credit which is secured by the consumer's principal dwelling and the pamphlet required under subsection

      (e) shall be provided to any consumer at the time the creditor distributes an application to establish an account under such plan to such consumer.

    (B) Telephone, publications, and 3rd party applications. In the case of telephone applications, applications contained in magazines or other publications, or applications provided by a third party, the disclosures required under subsection (a) and the pamphlet required under subsection (e) shall be provided by the creditor before the end of the 3-day period beginning on the date the creditor receives a completed application from a consumer.

(2) Form.

    (A) In general. Except as provided in paragraph (1)(B), the disclosures required under subsection (a) shall be provided on or with any application to establish an account under an open end consumer credit plan which provides for any extension of credit which is secured by the consumer's principal dwelling.

    (B) Segregation of required disclosures from other information. The disclosures required under subsection (a) shall be conspicuously segregated from all other terms, data, or additional information provided in connection with the application, either by grouping the disclosures separately on the application form or by providing the disclosures on a separate form, in accordance with regulations of the Board.

    (C) Precedence of certain information. The disclosures required by paragraphs (5), (6), and (7) of subsection (a) shall precede all of the other required disclosures.

    (D) Special provision relating to variable interest rate information. Whether or not the disclosures required under subsection (a) are provided on the application form, the variable rate information described in subsection (a)(2) may be provided separately from the other information required to be disclosed.

(3) Requirement for historical table. In preparing the table required under subsection (a)(2)(G), the creditor shall consistently select one rate of interest for each year and the manner of selecting the rate from year to year shall be consistent with the plan.

(c) **3rd party applications.** In the case of an application to open an account under any open end consumer credit plan described in subsection (a) which is provided to a consumer by any person other than the creditor—

(1) such person shall provide such consumer with—

    (A) the disclosures required under subsection (a) with respect to such plan, in accordance with subsection (b); and

    (B) the pamphlet required under subsection (e); or

(2) if such person cannot provide specific terms about the plan because specific information about the plan terms is not available, no non-refundable fee may be imposed in connection with such application before the end of the 3-day period beginning on the date the consumer receives the disclosures required under subsection (a) with respect to the application.

(d) **Principal dwelling defined.** For purposes of this section and sections 137 and 147 [15 USCS §§1647, 1665b], the term "principal dwelling" includes any second or vacation home of the consumer.

(e) **Pamphlet.** In addition to the disclosures required under subsection (a) with respect to an application to open an account under any open end consumer credit plan described in such subsection, the creditor or other person providing such disclosures to the consumer shall provide—

    (1) a pamphlet published by the Board pursuant to section 4 of the Home Equity Consumer Protection Act of 1988 [note to this section]; or

    (2) any pamphlet which provides substantially similar information to the information described in such section, as determined by the Board.

§ 1647. HOME EQUITY PLANS

(a) **Index requirement.** In the case of extensions of credit under an open end consumer credit plan which are subject to a variable rate and are secured by a consumer's principal dwelling, the index or other rate of interest to which changes in the annual percentage rate are related shall be based on an index or rate of interest which is publicly available and is not under the control of the creditor.

(b) **Grounds for acceleration of outstanding balance.** A creditor may not unilaterally terminate any account under an open end consumer credit plan under which extensions of credit are secured by a consumer's principal dwelling and require the immediate repayment of any outstanding balance at such time, except in the case of—

    (1) fraud or material misrepresentation on the part of the consumer in connection with the account;

    (2) failure by the consumer to meet the repayment terms of the agreement for any outstanding balance; or

    (3) any other action or failure to act by the consumer which adversely affects the creditor's security for the account or any right of the creditor in such security.

(c) **Change in terms.** (1) In general. No open end consumer credit plan under which extensions of credit are secured by a consumer's principal dwelling may contain a provision which permits a creditor to change unilaterally any term required to be disclosed under section 127A(a) [15 USCS §1637a(a)] or any other term, except a change in insignificant terms such as the address of the creditor for billing purposes.

    (2) Certain changes not precluded. Notwithstanding the provisions of subsection (1), a creditor may make any of the following changes:

        (A) Change the index and margin applicable to extensions of credit under such plan if the index used by the creditor is no longer available and the substitute index and margin would result in a substantially similar interest rate.

        (B) Prohibit additional extensions of credit or reduce the credit limit applicable to an account under the plan during any period in which the value of the consumer's principal dwelling which secures any outstanding balance is significantly less than the original appraisal value of the dwelling.

(C) Prohibit additional extensions of credit or reduce the credit limit applicable to the account during any period in which the creditor has reason to believe that the consumer will be unable to comply with the repayment requirements of the account due to a material change in the consumer's financial circumstances.

(D) Prohibit additional extensions of credit or reduce the credit limit applicable to the account during any period in which the consumer is in default with respect to any material obligation of the consumer under the agreement.

(E) Prohibit additional extensions of credit or reduce the credit limit applicable to the account during any period in which—

(i) the creditor is precluded by government action from imposing the annual percentage rate provided for in the account agreement; or

(ii) any government action is in effect which adversely affects the priority of the creditor's security interest in the account to the extent that the value of the creditor's secured interest in the property is less than 120 percent of the amount of the credit limit applicable to the account.

(F) Any change that will benefit the consumer.

(3) Material obligations. Upon the request of the consumer and at the time an agreement is entered into by a consumer to open an account under an open end consumer credit plan under which extensions of credit are secured by the consumer's principal dwelling, the consumer shall be given a list of the categories of contract obligations which are deemed by the creditor to be material obligations of the consumer under the agreement for purposes of paragraph (2)(D).

Appendix G

Real Estate Settlement Procedures Act
12 U.S.C. § 2601 et seq.
(Excerpts)

§ 2601. CONGRESSIONAL FINDINGS AND PURPOSE

(a) The Congress finds that significant reforms in the real estate settlement process are needed to insure that consumers throughout the Nation are provided with greater and more timely information on the nature and costs of the settlement process and are protected from unnecessarily high settlement charges caused by certain abusive practices that have developed in some areas of the country. The Congress also finds that it has been over two years since the Secretary of Housing and Urban Development and the Administrator of Veterans' Affairs submitted their joint report to the Congress on "Mortgage Settlement Costs" and that the time has come for the recommendations for Federal legislative action made in that report to be implemented.

(b) It is the purpose of this Chapter to effect certain changes in the settlement process for residential real estate that will result—

(1) in more effective advance disclosure to home buyers and sellers of settlement costs;

(2) in the elimination of kickbacks or referral fees that tend to increase unnecessarily the costs of certain settlement services;

(3) in a reduction in the amounts home buyers are required to place in escrow accounts established insure the payment of real estate taxes and insurance; and

(4) in significant reform and modernization of local recordkeeping of land title information.

§ 2602. DEFINITIONS

For purposes of this Act—

(1) the term "federally related mortgage loan" includes any loan (other than temporary financing such as a construction loan) which—

    (A) is secured by a first or subordinate lien on residential real property (including units of condominiums and cooperatives) designed principally for the occupancy of from one to four families, including any such secured loan, the proceeds of which are used to prepay or pay off an existing loan secured by the same property;

    (B) (i) is made in whole or in part by anylender the deposits or accounts of which are insured by any agency of the Federal Government, or is made in whole or in part by any lender which is regulated by any agency of the Federal Government; or

        (ii) is made in whole or in part, or insured, guaranteed, supplemented, or assisted in any way, by the the Secretary or any other officer or agency of the Federal Government or under or in connection with a housing or urban development program administered by the Secretary or a housing or related program administered by any other such officer or agency; or

        (iii) is intended to be sold by the originating lender to the Federal National Mortgage Association, the Government National Mortgage Association, the Federal Home Loan Mortgage Corporation, or a financial institution from which it is to be purchased by the Federal Home Loan Mortgage Corporation; or

        (iv) is made in whole or in part by any "creditor", as defined in section 1602(f) of Title 15, who makes or invests in residential real estate loans aggregating more than $1,000,000 per year, except that for the purpose of this chapter, the term "creditor" does not include any agency or instrumentality of any State;

(2) the term "thing of value" includes any payment, advance, funds, loan, service, or other consideration;

(3) the term "settlement services" includes any service provided in connection with a real estate settlement including, but not limited to, the following: title searches, title examinations, the provision of title certificates, title insurance, services rendered by an attorney, the preparation of documents, property surveys, the rendering of credit reports or appraisals, pest and fungus inspections, services rendered by a real estate agent or broker, the origination of a federally related mortgage loan (including, but not limited to, the taking of loan applications, loan processing, and the underwriting and funding of loans), and the handling of the processing, and closing of settlement;

(4) the term "title company" means any institution which is qualified to issue title insurance, directly or through its agents, and also refers to any duly authorized agent of a title company;

(5) the term "person" includes individuals, corporations, associations, partnerships, and trusts;

(6) the term "Secretary" means the Secretary of Housing and Urban Development;

(7) the term "controlled business arrangement" means an arrangement in which (A) a person who is in a position to refer business incident to or a part of a real estate settlement service involving a federally related mortgage loan, or an associate of such person, has either an affiliate relationship with or a direct or beneficial ownership interest of more than 1 percent in a provider of settlement services; and (B) either of such persons directly or indirectly refers such business to that provider or affirmatively influences the selection of that provider; and

(8) the term "associate" means one who has one or more of the following relationships with a person in a position to refer settlement business: (A) a spouse, parent, or child of such person; (B) a corporation or business entity that controls, is controlled by, or is under common control with such person; (C) an employer, officer, director, partner, franchisor, or franchisee of such person; or (D) anyone who has an agreement, arrangement, or understanding, with such person, the purpose or substantial effect of which is to enable the person in a position to refer settlement business to benefit financially from the referrals of such business.

§ 2603. UNIFORM SETTLEMENT STATEMENT

(a) The Secretary, in consultation with the Administrator of Veterans' Affairs, the Federal Deposit Insurance Corporation, and the Federal Home Loan Bank Board, shall develop and prescribe a standard form for the statement of settlement costs which shall be used (with such variations as may be necessary to reflect differences in legal and administrative requirements or practices in different areas of the country) as the standard real estate settlement form in all transactions in the United States which involve federally related mortgage loans. Such form shall conspicuously and clearly itemize all charges imposed upon the borrower and all charges imposed upon the seller in connection with the settlement and shall indicate whether any title insurance premium included in such charges covers or insures the lender's interest in the property, the borrower's interest, or both. The Secretary may, by regulation, permit the deletion from the form prescribed under this section of items which are not, under local laws or customs, applicable in any locality, except that such regulation shall require that the numerical code prescribed by the Secretary be retained in forms to be used in all localities. Nothing in this section may be construed to require that that part of the standard form which relates to the borrower's transaction be furnished to the seller, or to require that that part of the standard form which relates to the seller be furnished to the borrower.

(b) The form prescribed under this section shall be completed and made available for inspection by the borrower at or before settlement by the person conducting the settlement, except that (1) the Secretary may exempt from the requirements of this section settlements occurring in localities where the final settlement statement is not customarily provided at or before the date of settlement, or settlements where such requirements are impractical and (2) the borrower may, in accordance with regulations of the Secretary, waive his right to have the form made available at such time. Upon the request of the borrower to inspect the form prescribed under this section during the business day immediately preceding the day of settlement, the person who will conduct the settlement shall permit the borrower to inspect those items which are known to such person during such preceding day.

§ 2604. SPECIAL INFORMATION BOOKLETS

(a) **Distribution by Secretary to lenders to help borrowers**

The Secretary shall prepare and distribute booklets to help persons borrowing money to finance the purchase of residential real estate better to understand the nature and costs of real estate settlement services. The Secretary shall distribute such booklets to all lenders which make federally related mortgage loans.

(b) **Form and detail; cost elements, standard settlement form, escrow accounts, selection of persons for settlement services; consideration of differences in settlement procedures**

Each booklet shall be in such form and detail as the Secretary shall prescribe and, in addition to such other information as the Secretary may provide, shall include in clear and concise language—

(1) a description and explanation of the nature and purpose of each cost incident to a real estate settlement;

(2) an explanation and sample of the standard real estate settlement form developed and prescribed under section 2603 of this title;

(3) a description and explanation of the nature and purpose of escrow accounts when used in connection with loans secured by residential real estate;

(4) an explanation of the choices available to buyers of residential real estate in selecting persons to provide necessary services incident to a real estate settlement; and

(5) an explanation of the unfair practices and unreasonable or unnecessary charges to be avoided by the prospective buyer with respect to a real estate settlement.

Such booklets shall take into consideration differences in real estate settlement procedures which may exist among the several States and territories of the United States and among separate political subdivisions within the same State and territory.

(c) **Estimate of charges**

Each lender shall include with the booklet a good faith estimate of the range of charges for specific settlement services the borrower is likely to incur in connection with the settlement as prescribed by the Secretary.

(d) **Distribution by lenders to loan applicants at time of receipt or preparation of applications**

Each lender referred to in subsection (a) of this section shall provide the booklet described in such subsection to each person from whom it receives or for whom it prepares a written application to borrow money to finance the purchase of residential real estate. Such booklet shall be provided by delivering it or placing it in the mail not later than 3 business days after the lender receives the application, but no booklet need be provided if the lender denies the application for credit before the end of the 3-day period.

(e) **Printing and distribution by lenders of booklets approved by Secretary** Booklets may be printed and distributed by lenders if their form and content are approved by the Secretary as meeting the requirements of subsection (b) of this section.

§ 2607. PROHIBITION AGAINST KICKBACKS AND UNEARNED FEES

(a) **Business referrals**

No person shall give and no person shall accept any fee, kickback, or thing of value pursuant to any agreement or understanding, oral or otherwise, that business incident to or a part of a real estate settlement service involving a federally related mortgage loan shall be referred to any person.

(b) **Splitting charges**

No person shall give and no person shall accept any portion, split, or percentage of any charge made or received for the rendering of a real estate settlement service in connection with a transaction involving a federally related mortgage loan other than for services actually performed.

(c) **Fees, salaries, compensation, or other payments**

Nothing in this section shall be construed as prohibiting (1) the payment of a fee (A) to attorneys at law for services actually rendered or (B) by a title company to its duly appointed agent for services actually performed in the issuance of a policy of title insurance or, (C) by a lender to its duly appointed agent for services actually performed in the making of a loan, (2) the payment to any person of a bona fide salary or compensation or other payment for goods or facilities actually furnished or for services actually performed, or (3) payments pursuant to cooperative brokerage and referral arrangements between real estate agents and brokers, (4) controlled business arrangements so long as (A) at or prior to the time of the referral a disclosure is made of the existence of such an arrangement to the person being referred and, in connection with the referral, such person is provided a written estimate of the charge or range of charges generally made by the provider to which the person is referred, except that where a lender makes the referral, this requirement may be satisfied as part of and at the time that the estimates of settlement charges required under section 5(c) are provided, (B) such person is not required to use any particular provider of settlement services, and (C) the only thing of value that is received from the arrangement, other than the payments permitted under this subsection, is a return on the ownership interest or franchise relationship, or (5) such other payments or classes of payments or other transfers as are specified in regulations prescribed by the Secretary, after consultation with the Attorney General, the Secretary of Veterans Affairs, the Federal Home Loan Bank Board, the Federal Deposit Insurance Corporation, the Board of Governors of the Federal Reserve System, and the Secretary of Agriculture. For purposes of the proceeding sentence, the following shall not be considered an violation of clause (4)(B): (i) any arrangement that requires a buyer, borrower, or seller to pay for the services of an attorney, credit reporting agency, or real estate appraiser chosen by the lender to represent the lender's interest in a real estate transaction. or (ii) any arrangement where an attorney or law firm represents a client in a real estate transaction and issues or arranges for the issuance of a policy of title insurance in the transaction directly as agent or through a separate corporate title insurance agency that may be established by that attorney or law firm and operated as an adjunct to his or its law practice.

(d) **Penalties for violations; joint and several liability; treble damages; court costs; attorney fees.**

   (2) Any person or persons who violate the prohibitions or limitations of this section shall be jointly and severally liable to the person or persons charged for the settlement service involved in the violation in an amount equal to three times the amount of any charge paid for such settlement service.

   (3) No person or persons shall be liable for a violation of the provisions of section 8(c)(4)(A) [subsec. (c)(4)(A) of this section] if such person or persons proves by a preponderance of the evidence that such violation was not intentional and resulted from a bona fide error notwithstanding maintenance of procedures that are reasonably adapted to avoid such error.

   (4) The Secretary, the Attorney General of any State, or the insurance commissioner of any State may bring an action to enjoin violations of this section.

   (5) In any private action brought pursuant to this subsection, the court may award to the prevailing party the court costs of the action together with reasonable attorneys fees.

   (6) No provision of State law or regulation that imposes more stringent limitations on affiliated business arrangements shall be construed as being inconsistent with this section.

§ 2608. TITLE COMPANIES; LIABILITY OF SELLER

(a) No seller of property that will be purchased with the assistance of a federally related mortgage loan shall require directly or indirectly, as a condition to selling the property, that title insurance covering the property be purchased by the buyer from any particular title company.

(b) Any seller who violates the provisions of subsection (a) shall be liable to the buyer in an amount equal to three times all charges made for such title insurance.

§2609. LIMITATION ON REQUIREMENT OF ADVANCE DEPOSITS IN ESCROW ACCOUNTS

(a) **In general**

A lender, in connection with a federally related mortgage loan, may not require the borrower or prospective borrower—

(1) to deposit in any escrow account which may be established in connection with such loan for the purpose of assuring payment of taxes, insurance premiums, or other charges with respect to the property, in connection with the settlement, an aggregate sum (for such purpose) in excess of a sum that will be sufficient to pay such taxes, insurance premiums and other charges attributable to the period beginning on the last date on which each such charge would have been paid under the normal lending practice of the lender and local custom, provided that the selection of each such date constitutes prudent lending practice, and ending on the due date of its first full installment payment under the mortgage, plus one-sixth of the estimated total amount of such taxes, insurance premiums and other charges to be paid on dates, as provided above, during the ensuing twelve-month period; or

(2) to deposit in any such escrow account in any month beginning with the first full installment payment under the mortgage a sum (for the purpose of assuring payment of taxes, insurance premiums and other charges with respect to the property) in excess of the sum of (A) one-twelfth of the total amount of the estimated taxes, insurance premiums and other charges which are reasonably anticipated to be paid on dates during the ensuing twelve months which dates are in accordance with the normal lending practice of the lender and local custom, provided that the selection of each such date constitutes prudent lending practice, plus (B) such amount as is necessary to maintain an additional balance in such escrow account not to exceed one-sixth of the estimated total amount of such taxes, insurance premiums and other charges to be paid on dates, as provided above, during the ensuing twelve-month period: *Provided, however,* That in the event the lender determines there will be or is a deficiency he shall not be prohibited from requiring additional monthly deposits in such escrow account to avoid or eliminate such deficiency.

(b) **Notification of shortage in escrow account.**

If the terms of any federally related mortgage loan require the borrower to make payments to the servicer (as the term is defined in section 6(i) [12 USCS § 2605(i)]) of the loan for deposit into an escrow account for the purpose of assuring payment of taxes, insurance premiums, and other charges with respect to the property, the servicer shall notify the borrower not less than annually of any shortage of funds in the escrow account.

(c) **Escrow account statements.**

(1) Initial statement.

(A) In general.

Any servicer that has established an escrow account in connection with a federally related mortgage loan shall submit to the borrower for which the escrow account has been established a statement clearly itemizing the estimated taxes, insurance premiums, and other charges that are reasonably anticipated to be paid from the escrow account during the first 12 months after the establishment of the account and the anticipated dates of such payments.

(B) Time of submission

The statement required under subparagraph (A) shall be submitted to the borrower at closing with respect to the property for which the mortgage loan is made or not later than the expiration of the 45-day period beginning on the date of the establishment of the escrow account.

(C) Initial statement at closing

Any servicer may submit the statement required under subparagraph (A) to the borrower at closing and may incorporate such statement in the uniform settlement statement required under section 2603 of this title. The secretary shall issue regulations prescribing any changes necessary to the uniform settlement statement under section 2603 of this section that specify how the statement required under subparagraph (A) of this section shall be incorporated in the uniform settlement statement.

(2) Annual statement.

(A) In general.

Any servicer that has established or continued an escrow account in connection with a federally related mortgage loan shall submit to the borrower for which the escrow account has been established or continued a statement clearly itemizing, for each period described in subparagraph (B) (during which the servicer services the escrow account), the amount of the borrower's current monthly payment, the portion of the monthly payment being placed in the escrow account, the total amount paid into the escrow account during the period, the total amount paid out of the escrow account during the period for taxes, insurance premiums, and other charges (as separately identified), and the balance in the escrow account at the conclusion of the period.

(B) Time of submission.

The statement required under subparagraph (A) shall be submitted to the borrower not less than once for each 12-month period, the first such period beginning on the first January 1st that occurs after the date of the enactment of the Cranston-Gonzalez National Affordable Housing Act [enacted Nov. 28, 1990], and shall be submitted not more than 30 days after the conclusion of each such 1-year period.

(d) **Penalties.**

(1) In general.

In the case of each failure to submit a statement to a borrower as required under subsection (c), the Secretary shall assess to the lender or escrow servicer failing to submit the statement a civil penalty of $50 for each such failure, but the total amount imposed on such lender or escrow servicer for all such failures during any 12-month period referred to in subsection (b) may not exceed $100,000.

(2) Intentional violations.

If any failure to which paragraph (1) applies is due to intentional disregard of the requirement to submit the statement, then, with respect to such failure—

(A) the penalty imposed under paragraph (1) shall be $100; and

(B) in the case of any penalty determined under subparagraph (A), the $100,000 limitation under paragraph (1) shall not apply.

§2610. PROHIBITION OF FEES FOR PREPARATION OF TRUTH-IN-LENDING, UNIFORM SETTLEMENT, AND ESCROW ACCOUNT STATEMENTS

No fee shall be imposed or charge made upon any other person (as a part of settlement costs or otherwise) by a lender in connection with a federally related mortgage loan made by it (or a loan for the purchase of a mobile home), or by a servicer (as the term is defined under section 2605 of this title, for or on account of the preparation and submission by such lender or servicer of the statement or statements required (in connection with such loan) by sections 2603 and 2609 of this title or by the Truth in Lending Act [15 USCS §§ 1601 et seq.].

Index of Statutes, Regulations, and Other Laws

Page references followed by "*" indicate case study. Page references followed by "n" indicate footnote.

Case Index

Subject Index

Page references in bold italic indicate tables and figures. Page references followed by "n" indicate footnote.